D0081554

THE
MISHNAH

THE
MISHNAH

TRANSLATED FROM THE
HEBREW WITH INTRODUCTION
AND BRIEF EXPLANATORY
NOTES

By

HERBERT DANBY, D.D.

OXFORD UNIVERSITY PRESS

Oxford University Press, Walton Street, Oxford OX2 6DP

Oxford New York Toronto
Delhi Bombay Calcutta Madras Karachi
Petaling Jaya Singapore Hong Kong Tokyo
Nairobi Dar es Salaam Cape Town
Melbourne Auckland

and associated companies in
Berlin Ibadan

Oxford is a trade mark of Oxford University Press

Published in the United States
by Oxford University Press, New York

ISBN 0-19-815402-x

First published 1933
Seventeenth impression 1989

Printed in Great Britain
at the University Printing House, Oxford
by David Stanford
Printer to the University

PREFACE

THE object of this translation is to render the contents of the Mishnah easily accessible in their entirety.

The Mishnah has considerable value, whether for the study of comparative religion, or for the study of the civilization of the Near East during the first and second centuries of our era, or for the study of Christian origins, or for the study of the development of Judaism and the conditions of Jewish life during the final stages of its association with the soil of Palestine. It is comparable[1] in its importance with the Apocryphal and Pseudepigraphical literature, as well as with the works of Josephus; but while these have become a familiar subject of study and an easily available quarry of information, most of the Mishnah has been available (to other than rabbinical students and Jews educated according to older orthodox methods) only in the Latin version of Surenhusius (1698–1703)[2] and the German version of Rabe (1760–3).[3]

Certain of the easier portions ('tractates') of the Mishnah have been published from time to time in Latin, German, English, French, and Italian, some of them more than once, and one of them (Aboth, 'The Sayings of the Fathers') many times.[4] Such fragmentary presentation of

---

[1] Sometimes to its advantage. See G. F. Moore, *Judaism*, i. 125–32.

[2] *Mischna sive totius hebraeorum juris, rituum, antiquitatum, ac legum oralium systema, cum clarissimorum rabbinorum Maimonidis et Bartenorae commentariis integris . . . Latinitate donavit ac notis illustravit Guilielmus Surenhusius*, Amsterdam, 1698–1703, 6 vols., fol. For a good account of this and its sources see Erich Bischoff, *Kritische Geschichte der Thalmud-Übersetzungen*, Frankfurt a. M., 1899, pp. 20–3. A Latin version of the complete Mishnah (with annotations to the First Division) was prepared for the University of Cambridge between 1663 and 1675 by a Jewish scholar, Isaac Abendana, but it was never published. It is described by Israel Abrahams in *Transactions of the Jewish Historical Society of England*, viii. 98–116.

[3] Johann Jacob Rabe, *Mischnah oder der Text des Talmuds . . . übersetzt und erläutert*, Onolzbach, 1760–3, 6 vols, 4to. The German Itzkowski–Kanel Edition, 1887–1933 (by Asher Sammter, David Hoffmann, Eduard Baneth, M. Petuchowski, S. Schlesinger, J. Cohn, and Moses Auerbach, containing Hebrew text, translation, and commentary), is now the best European edition; its usefulness is somewhat diminished by the varying standards of treatment adopted by successive editors.

Recent editions in Italian (by Vittoria Castiglione, 1904 ff.), and in German (the 'Giessen Edition', 1912 ff., edited by G. Beer, O. Holtzmann and, since 1928, S. Krauss) are still incomplete. The translations of the Mishnah embedded in the German version of the Babylonian Talmud by Lazarus Goldschmidt (1897 ff.) and in the French version of the Palestinian Talmud by Moïse Schwab (1878–89) scarcely come within the term 'easily accessible'; and 'Rodkinson's so-called English translation [of the Babylonian Talmud, New York, 1896–1902; new edition 1918] is in every respect impossible' (Moore, op. cit., i. 173 n.); apart from its free manner of translation and its arbitrary omissions, it covers only the second and fourth of the six Divisions of the Talmud.

[4] Bischoff, op. cit., pp. 45–53, enumerates seventy-eight translations of Aboth before 1899; it has been frequently translated since.

Of English translations of parts of the Mishnah the following may be noted:
Eighteen Treatises from the Mishna. Translated by the Rev. D. A. de Sola and the Rev. M. J. Raphall, London, 1843 (2nd ed., 1845). This translation contains the tractates Berakoth, Kilaim, Shabbath, Erubin, Pesahim, Yoma, Sukkah, Yom Tob (Betzah), Rosh ha-Shanah, Taanith, Megillah, Moed Katan, Yebamoth, Ketuboth, Gittin, Kiddushin, Hullin, and Yadaim. It was intended for Jewish readers, the selection being confined to

the contents of the Mishnah fails to give a true idea of its nature and may easily give a wrong idea. The Mishnah as we now have it was planned and systematically compiled as a single whole; and it is only by studying it as a single whole and understanding somewhat of the system governing its compilation that we can hope to estimate aright the value of the traditions which it has preserved.

The annotations to the present translation aim only at explaining allusions and removing surface difficulties: they do not pretend to be an adequate commentary. Thus no account is taken of the wealth of illustrative material contained in the literature, history, religion, jurisprudence, handicrafts, beliefs, superstitions, and folklore contemporary with the Mishnah; and in certain cases (particularly some of those treating of levirate marriage and the laws of cleanness and uncleanness) the notes do not trace the logical processes which underlie many of the recorded opinions. An adequate modern commentary on the Mishnah must deal with all these points. But to provide a commentary attempting such detail is probably a task beyond the powers of any single scholar, and certainly beyond the capacity of a single volume of moderate cost. Even with their very limited purpose the present annotations have been kept as few and brief as possible.

Throughout, both in translation and notes, traditional Jewish interpretation has been followed. Considering the centuries of intensive study devoted to the Mishnah and its associated literature by Jewish commentators from the time of the Talmuds to the present day, to neglect or ignore their results is as presumptuous as it is precarious. Novelties of interpretation, however tempting, have been purposely avoided: if

those portions of the Mishnah having significance in modern Jewish life. The translators permitted themselves considerable freedom, and there are many omissions.

The Talmud. By Joseph Barclay. London, 1878. Its title is misleading. It contains seventeen out of the sixty-three tractates of the Mishnah: Berakoth, Shebiith, Shabbath, Erubin, Pesahim, Yoma, Sukkah, Rosh ha-Shanah, Taanith, Hagigah, Sanhedrin, Abodah Zarah, Aboth, Tamid, Middoth, Negaim, Parah, and Yadaim. It was intended for Christian readers and it is not free from an anti-Jewish animus. The translation is at times crudely literal, often obscure, and frequently wrong. At the end of the eighth chapter of Shabbath is the note: 'The remaining two-thirds of this treatise are not translated as they are devoid of interest, and in parts unfit for publication.' The translator (the third Anglican Bishop in Jerusalem, 1879–81) was not a converted Jew as Bischoff (op. cit., p. 85) supposes.

Sayings of the Jewish Fathers: comprising Pirqe Aboth in Hebrew and English. By Charles Taylor. Cambridge University Press, 2nd ed., 1897.

The Mishna on Idolatry: Aboda Zara. By W. A. L. Elmslie. (Hebrew text and English translation.) Cambridge University Press, 1911.

Mishnah Baba Meziah. A Digest of the Basic Principles of the early Jewish Jurisprudence. Translated and annotated by Hyman E. Goldin. New York, 1913. (Noteworthy as an attempt to deal with traditional Jewish law along the lines of the general science of jurisprudence.)

Mishnah Megillah. By Joseph Rabbinowitz. Oxford, 1932.

The Society for the Promotion of Christian Knowledge, London, has published, under the editorship of W. O. E. Oesterley and G. H. Box, *The Sayings of the Jewish Fathers,* (*Pirke Aboth*), 1919; *Tractate Sanhedrin, Mishna and Tosefta,* 1919; *Tractate Berakoth, Mishna and Tosephta,* 1921; *Sukkah, Mishna and Tosefta,* 1925; and *Tractate Shabbath, Mishnah,* 1927.

A bibliography of translations is given in H. L. Strack, *Einleitung in Talmud und Midrash,* 5. Aufl., Munich, 1921, pp. 163 ff. (Engl. tr., pp. 154 ff.); and in Bischoff, op. cit., pp. 15–56.

any have crept in it is through oversight. Where there are differences of opinion among the standard Hebrew commentators attention is drawn to these in the notes, or, more frequently, the interpretation of *Tifereth Yisrael* has been followed. Such differences are comparatively infrequent and seldom affect major issues. For plant nomenclature advantage has been taken of the work of Dr. Immanuel Löw,[1] and in certain archaeological details and in problems arising out of Greek and Latin loan-words (points usually inadequately treated in older works) many of the conclusions of Dr. Samuel Krauss[2] have been adopted.

The text used is that of the ordinary printed editions of the *Mishnayoth* (as published by the Widow Romm and Brothers, Wilna). Some of the more important variant readings are indicated in the notes. There is no such thing as a 'critical text' of the Mishnah, nor has the study of the surviving manuscripts, earliest printed editions, and other textual authorities yet reached the stage which makes it possible to point with confidence to any one text as superior to all others. In the meantime the printed *Mishnayoth* editions have the obvious advantage of being the text which is customarily used and quoted.

With some exceptions the simplified method of transliteration and spelling adopted in the *Jewish Encyclopedia* (New York, 1901–6) has been followed, partly because it is least troublesome to English readers and partly to facilitate reference to that work in matters not fully treated in the present volume (e.g. biographies of rabbinical authorities quoted in the Mishnah). Where transliteration of Hebrew technical terms has been unavoidable simplicity has been preferred even, in a few cases, at the expense of consistency.[3]

The translation aims at being as literal as English idiom will tolerate. Words and passages not represented in the Hebrew text (other than words required to make a sentence grammatically complete in English) are enclosed in square brackets.

Scriptural quotations are given according to the Revised Version, except where the context assumes a different rendering. Where the Hebrew and English versions differ in their enumeration of chapter and verse, the reference is always to the English enumeration.

A very full index has been added. Reference to it will be of use for the understanding of recurrent technical terms which it has not been possible to explain afresh each time they appear in the text. For the same reason Appendixes have been provided, giving a Glossary of the Hebrew *termini technici* retained in the translation, a Table of Money, Weights and Measures, and the Gaon of Wilna's summary of the rules of uncleanness. A chronological list of all the rabbinical authorities quoted or referred to in the Mishnah is given as Appendix III; constant reference to this is essential.

[1] *Die Flora der Juden*, 3 vols., Vienna, 1924–6.
[2] *Griechische und lateinische Lehnwörter in Talmud, Midrasch und Targum*, 2 vols., Berlin, 1898–9; *Talmudische Archäologie*, 3 vols., Leipzig, 1909–12.
[3] The use of the conventional transliterations ḥ, ṭ, ḳ, and ṣ has also been avoided as unnecessary for the Hebraist and meaningless to the non-Hebraist.

I take this opportunity of expressing my deep gratitude to the Rev. Dr. G. A. Cooke, Regius Professor of Hebrew, Oxford, for the interest which he has shown in this English version of the Mishnah; and to the Trustees of the Kennicott Fund for a generous subsidy towards the cost of publication. Also I am greatly indebted to the Rev. M. H. Segal, of the Hebrew University, Jerusalem, who has devoted much time to reading through the proof-sheets of the entire work and whose suggestions and criticisms have been of great help. In conclusion the writer expresses his thanks to the Readers of the Oxford University Press for their helpful and skilful co-operation.

H. D.

St. George's Cathedral
    Jerusalem.

October 1933.

CONTENTS

THE MISHNAH

LIST OF ABBREVIATIONS

(For an alphabetical list of the abbreviations of the titles of the tractates of the Mishnah see p. 806.)

b. = ben, 'the son of'.

Bert. = The commentary on the Mishnah by Obadiah of Bertinoro (d. 1510).

Dor Dor = *Dor Dor w' Dor'shaw* (A history of the Growth of the Oral Law), by Isaac Hirsch Weiss, ed. 1924 (Berlin and New York).

Eliyahu Rabba = The commentary on the Sixth Division of the Mishnah (*Tohoroth*) by Elijah, the Gaon of Wilna (1720–97), compiled by his disciple Meir of Wilna (Brünn, 1802).

J.E. = *The Jewish Encyclopedia*. 12 vols. New York, 1901–6.

J.Q.R. = *The Jewish Quarterly Review*.

Maim. = The commentary on the Mishnah by Moses Maimonides (1135–1204).

Moore = *Judaism in the First Centuries of the Christian Era: the Age of the Tannaim*. By George Foot Moore. 3 vols. Cambridge (U.S.A.), 1927–30.

Neub. = *La Géographie du Talmud*, par Adolphe Neubauer. Paris, 1868.

p. Prefixed to the title of a tractate when the reference is to the Gemara of the Palestinian Talmud.

R. = Rabbi.

Rashi = The commentary on the Babylonian Talmud by 'Rashi' (Rabbi Shelomo Yitzhaki, 1040–1105).

Singer = *The Authorised Daily Prayer Book of the United Hebrew Congregation of the British Empire*. Ed. S. Singer. 8th ed. London, 1908.

S.S. = *Service of the Synagogue: a new edition of the Festival Prayers*. 6th ed. London, 1917–18.

Strack = *Einleitung in Talmud und Midrash*. 5th ed. Munich, 1921. (English translation, Philadelphia, 1931).

t. Prefixed to the title of a tractate when the reference is to the Tosefta.

Tif. Yis. = The commentary on the Mishnah entitled *Tifereth Yisrael*, by Israel Lipschütz (1782–1860).

INTRODUCTION

I. PURPOSE AND CHARACTER OF THE MISHNAH

THE MISHNAH[1] may be defined as a deposit of four centuries of Jewish religious and cultural activity in Palestine, beginning at some uncertain date (possibly during the earlier half of the second century B.C.) and ending with the close of the second century A.D. The object of this activity was the preservation, cultivation, and application to life of 'the Law' (*Torah*), in the form in which many generations of like-minded Jewish religious leaders had learnt to understand this Law. These leaders were known in turn by the names *Soferim* ('Scribes') and *Tannaim* (lit. 'repeaters', teachers of the Oral Law). The latter taught the religious system of the Pharisees as opposed to that of the Sadducees. Until the destruction of the Second Temple in A.D. 70 they had counted as one only among the schools of thought which played a part in Jewish national and religious life; after the Destruction they took the position, naturally and almost immediately, of sole and undisputed leaders of such Jewish life as survived. Judaism as it has continued since is, if not their creation, at least a faith and a religious institution largely of their fashioning; and the Mishnah is the authoritative record of their labour. Thus it comes about that while Judaism and Christianity alike venerate the Old Testament as canonical Scripture, the Mishnah marks the passage to Judaism as definitely as the New Testament marks the passage to Christianity.

From the time of its compilation by Rabbi Judah the Patriarch, the Mishnah has, in Jewish eyes, ranked second only to the Hebrew Scriptures as a national-religious creation and possession. It provided a link between Palestinian and non-Palestinian Judaism strong enough and authoritative enough to endure and to bind together the Jewish people despite their geographical disintegration; it serves as the core of the Babylonian and Palestinian Talmuds, and for orthodox Jewry it is still, what it has been for sixteen centuries, an essential ingredient in the education of youth and an object of devotional study through life.

'The Law' (*Torah*), which it was the Mishnah's purpose to cherish and develop, is a complex conception. It includes the Written Law, the laws explicitly recorded in the Five Books of Moses; it includes also 'the traditions of the elders'[2] or the Oral Law, namely, such beliefs and religious

---

[1] The word is from a root *shanah* meaning 'repeat' and so 'to teach by means of repetition'. From the corresponding Aramaic root *t'na* comes the term *tanna* (pl. *tannaim*), a name applied to the teachers of the Mishnah. 'Mishnah' means both teaching and the substance of the teaching passed on from teacher to pupil by word of mouth. It is used of the teaching of a single teacher or *tanna*, either in the sense of a single tenet held by him, or as a collection of oral laws taught by him. 'The Mishnah', as used without qualification, signifies the collection of oral laws made by Rabbi Judah the Patriarch. The term 'Mishnah' is used also to define the body of law which was transmitted orally as distinct: (i) from *Miqra*, the Law transmitted by written documents and learnt by 'reading'; and (ii) from Midrash ('exposition'), the transmission of the Oral Law in terms of its Scriptural basis. See also App. I. 27, 28.   [2] Josephus, *Ant.* XIII. x. 6; Mark 7[3-13].

practices as piety and custom had in the course of centuries, consciously or unconsciously, grafted on to or developed out of the Written Law; and it includes yet a third, less tangible element, a spirit of development, whereby Written Law and Oral Law, in spite of seeming differences, are brought into a unity and interpreted and reinterpreted to meet the needs of changed conditions.

The Mishnah in its six main Divisions covers the whole range of Pentateuchal legislation: (i) laws dealing with agricultural produce, and the portions of the harvest which fall to the priests and levites and to the poor; (ii) the set feasts; (iii) laws affecting womankind; (iv) property rights and legal proceedings; (v) the holy things of the Temple; and (vi) the laws of uncleanness. The letter of the Written Law is throughout assumed, attention being given almost exclusively to rules of Jewish usage which sometimes seem to be no more than logical restatement or extension or practical application of the Written Law, while sometimes they seem to be independent of it. It is these rules of usage, 'the traditions of the elders', which form the essential and characteristic element in the Mishnah. There is yet another element, sometimes taking the form of logical argument and sometimes the form of Scriptural exegesis, which seeks to derive authority for actual usage from Biblical laws when, superficially, it might have been supposed that the usage lacked Biblical sanction. But whether the Oral Law was deducible from the Written Law or not, the accepted hypothesis was that it was delivered from Mount Sinai at the same time as the Written Law, and preserved by word of mouth, generation after generation, until it found permanent expression in the Mishnah. Between the Written Law and the Oral Law there could be no contradiction: both claimed the same divine origin and both possessed the same authority and binding force.

Although the Mishnah was compiled in its present form at the end of the second century, it deals fully with phases of legislation and religious practice which for more than a hundred years had ceased to have any practical bearing on Jewish life. The destruction of Jerusalem in A.D. 70 made an end of the last vestiges of national self-government, and it marked also the extinction of the priesthood and the Temple worship which until then had been the centre o᷑ Jewish national and religious life. The Mishnah's minute treatment of the Temple cultus and its portrayal of Jewish religious and secular life (with few exceptions) as though the nation still enjoyed privileges lost to it generations earlier, constitute the Mishnah's chief value as well as the chief problem in its study.

It is a matter of extreme difficulty to decide what historical value we should attach to any tradition recorded in the Mishnah. The lapse of time which may have served to obscure or distort memories of times so different; the political upheavals, changes, and confusions brought about by two rebellions and two Roman conquests; the standards esteemed by the Pharisean party (whose opinions the Mishnah records) which were not those of the Sadducean party (whose standards chiefly prevailed during the century before the destruction of Jerusalem)[1]—these are factors which need to be given due weight in estimating the character of the Mishnah's statements. Moreover there is much in the contents of the Mishnah that moves in an atmosphere of academic discussion pursued for its own sake, with (so it would appear) little pretence at recording historical usage: what was ideally true had a higher value in the eyes of the disputants than what once may have been actual but mistaken usage.

On the other hand, this academic tendency sometimes shown by the Mishnah and its purely Pharisean outlook are not necessarily such as wholly to discredit its picture of the fuller Jewish life of pre-Destruction times. The Pharisean standards were, from the time of John Hyrcanus (135–104 B.C.),[2] as conspicuous in national affairs as those of the dominant Sadducean party (according to Josephus[3] they were more generally acceptable to the common people), and Pharisean principles certainly proved strong enough to survive national convulsions which dried up other streams of Jewish life. Again, although the peculiar literary methods of the Mishnah sometimes give an impression of deducing an ideal and theoretical practice out of academic interpretation and application of Scripture, it may often be that the reverse is the truth: what was sought was Scriptural grounds on which to justify long-established usage not expressly ordained or permitted by Scripture.

Yet again, the Mishnah bears no trace of a tendency to effect reforms in the Jewish religious and ceremonial usage or to evolve a new scheme in closer accord with later conceptions of what the Law required: on the contrary, it manifests a veneration for the letter of tradition remarkable for pedantic insistence on verbal exactitude; and there was a purposefulness about the work of the post-Destruction rabbinical schools marking a determination to preserve as exact a knowledge as possible of those aspects of life under the Law which were become the more precious by reason of their present impossibility of realization.[4]

When we turn to the Mishnah's religious importance we are on surer ground: within a generation of its compilation we find it described as 'the iron pillar of the Law',[5] and according to a later teacher[6] the study of it was as meritorious as offering sacrifice. The Mishnah is not a finally

---

[1] In the Mishnah the Sadducees figure only as an insignificant, discredited, and heretical sect.   [2] Cf. *Ant.* XIII. xvi. 2.   [3] Ibid. x. 5.

[4] There still persisted a hope of national restoration (a hope which culminated in the violence of the Bar Cocheba revolt against Rome in the reign of Hadrian), when Jerusalem and the Temple should again become the centre of Jewish national and religious life, and the Law be again applied in its fullness. Hence a knowledge of customs dealing solely with Jerusalem and the Temple (such as Temple and priestly dues, sacrificial ritual, the slighter grades of uncleanness which excluded persons from the Temple Court, the Temple ritual at the greater Festivals) was preserved and handed down, often in the words of men who had themselves experienced the fuller life under the Law in pre-Destruction days. Certain of these traditions (see especially the tractates Yoma, Middoth, Tamid, and parts of Bikkurim and Shekalim), since they no longer applied to Jewish everyday life, have been less overlaid with comment and argument by later generations of teachers, and less exposed to the possibility of revision under the influence of later fashions of interpretation.

[5] Leviticus Rabba, 21[4], reporting Joshua ben Levi, early third century.   [6] Ibid. 7[3].

authoritative corpus of the beliefs and practices of Judaism: it is of the nature of Judaism that it can have no such thing. 'The Law', which alone is Jewish doctrine, has in it an inherent principle of development which, while holding fast to the foundations laid down in the Mosaic legislation, makes it intolerant of dogmatic definition or set credal forms. Yet, even so, the Mishnah is, after Sinai, the greatest landmark in the history of Judaism: it is Judaism's most authoritative formulation of its religious system[1] at a time when the people of Israel, the faith of Israel, and the Land of Israel were thought of as one and inseparable. In the most exact sense the Mishnah is the final expression of the Jewish nation's unimpaired religious life: whatever modifications may have since arisen in the observances of Judaism have arisen out of conditions of exile, conditions in which the religion indeed persisted, but persisted as a thing incomplete, as a maimed survival.

Approximately the half of the Mishnah has no longer any practical bearing on the present religious practice of Judaism, nor had it any practical bearing even when it was compiled. This, however, has never detracted from its worth in Jewish eyes: this unattainable half of Judaism has been as much the object of diligent and devotional study in exile as the dietary laws or the observance of the Sabbath and the Festivals.[2]

The contents of the Mishnah may strike the modern reader as strange. Much of it does not conform with his preconceptions of what constitutes a 'sacred book'. For the most part it is given up to a wide range of topics— agricultural, legal, domestic, commercial, and physiological—which seldom coincide with 'religious subjects' as the present-day mind conceives them; and a quarter of the book is devoted to the subject of 'uncleanness', which is studied and defined with elaboration of detail and classification, and its principles worked out and applied, in a fashion befitting the exposition of an exact natural science.

But in all this the Mishnah does no more than supplement with practical

---

[1] i.e. in the sphere of ceremonial observance. Except in the tractate Aboth and a few incidental passages (see General Index, s.v. 'Ethical principles'), the Mishnah is not concerned with the devotional, ethical, messianic, and eschatological ideas peculiar to Judaism. Though prominent and popular topics in contemporary and later *Haggadah* (see App. I. 10), they were never the subject of juristic argument or of that precise definition which is characteristic of *Halakah*. So long as there was no infringement of the plain and established sense of Scripture, and so long as it made for popular edification, the imagination was allowed free play.

[2] Cf. Samuel Krauss, *Die Mischna* (*Volksschriften über die jüdische Religion*, Frankfurt, 1914), p. 49 f.: 'Die damalige Judenheit lebte tatsächlich mehr in der Vergangenheit, und die Mischna ist die untrügliche Zeugin dieses seltsamen Lebens. Ein starker nationaler Zug durchströmt die Mischna, der mit zu ihrer Bedeutung gehört. Diese trockenen Paragraphen schwelgen in der Erinnerung an die Vergangenheit und weckten dadurch überall die stärkste Zuversicht in die nahe Wiederherstellung der alten Herrlichkeit, eine über den Jammer der Gegenwart siegreich dahinschreitende messianische Hoffnung. Und wer könnte es leugnen, dass das Gefühle sind, deren das Judentum auf seinem langen Leidenswege nur allzusehr bedurfte? Die Mischna schuf dem heimatlos in der Welt umherirrenden und blutig verfolgten Volke die ideale Heimat, ein Vaterland und dadurch einen mächtigen Halt und unendlichen Trost. Das war die letzte grosse Tat Palästinas im Dienste des Judentums; die alte Mutter liess ihre gehetzten und gejagten Kinder nicht ohne innere Stärkung, sie liess sie nicht ohne Hoffnung, den Weg zu ihr doch wieder zu finden.'

detail or give coherence to a range of topics found already in the Written Law, in the Pentateuch, where, as subjects of legislation, they are dealt with either in general terms only, or unsystematically or fragmentarily. These topics are all included within the single divine revelation; all are part of the inspired Word of God; the scrupulous fulfilment of the laws about Fringes and Phylacteries is as much a fulfilling of God's purpose as abstention from idolatry and murder. Granted the acceptance of the Written Law as God's will for Israel, Israel's teachers had not the right to determine the relative importance of this or that injunction. Therefore the Oral Law preserves with equal piety customs and decisions arising out of the 'lightest' as out of the 'weightiest' precepts of the Law revealed to Israel at Sinai.[1]

II. ORIGIN AND DEVELOPMENT

The Mishnah's own account of the origin and history of the Oral Law is given in the tractate Aboth, 1[ff]. At the same time that the Written Law was given from Sinai, the Oral Law, too, was delivered to Moses, and handed down (orally) in turn to the leaders of successive generations—to Joshua, to the Elders (Josh. 24[31]), to the Prophets, to the 'Men of the Great Synagogue' (the body of teachers who administered and taught the Law after the time of Ezra), to Simeon the Just (c. 280 or 200 B.C., one of 'the remnants of the men of the Great Synagogue'), to Antigonus of Soko; then, in turn, to the five 'Pairs' of leaders—Jose ben Joezer and Jose ben Johanan (c. 165 B.C.), Joshua ben Perahyah and Nittai the Arbelite, Judah ben Tabbai and Simeon ben Shetach, Shemaiah and Abtalion, and Hillel and Shammai. Thus the chain of tradition was brought to the threshold of the Christian era.

The Mishnah, in other words, maintains that the authority of those rules, customs, and interpretations which had accumulated around the Jewish system of life and religion was equal to the authority of the Written Law itself, even though they found no place in the Written Law. This, again, is but an assertion (known also in other religious and legal systems) that side by side with a written code there exists a living tradition with power to interpret the written code, to add to it, and even at times to modify it or ignore it as might be needful in changed circumstances, and to do this authoritatively.[2] Inevitably the inference follows that the living tradition (the Oral Law) is more important than the Written Law,[3] since the 'tradition of the elders', besides claiming an authority and continuity equal to that of the Written Law, claims also to be its authentic and living interpretation and its essential complement.

When we attempt to trace the growth, namely the conscious and deliberate amassing of this body of oral tradition, sanctified usage and precedent, we are in the region of guesswork. Since written laws cannot

---

[1] See Aboth 2[1].   [2] See p. 10, n. 12.

[3] See Sanh. 11[3]: 'Greater stringency applies to the observance of the words of the Scribes [namely, the authorized exponents of the law] than to the observance of the [Written] Law.' Cf. Hor. 1[3].

anticipate all possible contingencies, or embrace every detail, or deal in advance with each possible case, it can be assumed that, in applying the Mosaic code to daily life and to the Temple worship, to domestic relations and trade and to the administration of justice, a multitude of usages arising out of practical necessity or convenience or experience became part of the routine of observance of the code, and, in the course of time, shared the sanctity and authority which were inherent in the divinely inspired code itself. Such accretion was, in the nature of things, susceptible to growth and modification according to gradual or sudden change of social and political conditions. We may assume the growth and establishment of such a traditional element before the Babylonian exile; but we cannot know to what extent continuity with pre-exilic unwritten tradition was preserved after the Return. During the centuries which elapsed from the coming of Ezra to the destruction of the Second Temple by the Romans, we may reasonably assume the growth of traditions arising out of the changing social and religious conditions experienced by the Jewish race—Persian suzerainty, the religious and national revival under Ezra and Nehemiah, the system of high-priestly rule, the pressure of Hellenistic civilization, the Maccabean revolt and the subsequent increase of lay influence in the control of Jewish affairs, and finally the intervention of Rome and the rise of the Herodian dynasty. We cannot, however, be certain when these traditions began to be considered as in themselves final and authoritative and part of the divine revelation, and, therefore, an object of zealous preservation and diligent instruction; we cannot, in other words, say certainly what was the beginning of the process of which the Mishnah marks a conclusion.

In religious systems which combine a written code with a body of traditional usage, there comes from time to time a stage when tradition is scrutinized and challenged. The reformer may either condemn all unwritten tradition as superfluous and false; or he may treat it as unimportant and subject to change, and revise it or substitute a rival usage in accordance with his own preferences. The traditionalist, on the other hand, will adhere loyally and unquestioningly to every detail of traditional usage, and venerate it the more by reason of the attacks on its authority and sanctity; and he may also, for purposes of controversy, set himself to find in the written code itself explicit or implicit sanction for traditional usage.

Such a challenge to traditionalism we find in the Judaism of the second century B.C. Josephus, dealing with the controversy between Sadducees and Pharisees in the time of John Hyrcanus (135–104 B.C.), writes: 'The Pharisees have delivered to the people a great many observances by succession from their fathers which are not written in the law of Moses; and for that reason it is that the Sadducees reject them, and say that we are to esteem those observances to be obligatory which are in the Written Word, but are not to observe what are derived from the tradition of our forefathers.'[1] It is a reasonable hypothesis that a result of this controversy

---

[1] *Ant.* XIII. x. 6.

—a controversy which continued for two centuries—was a deliberate compilation and justification of the unwritten tradition by the Pharisean party,
perhaps unsystematic and on a small scale in the earlier stages, but stimu-
lated and fostered from time to time both by opposition from the Sadducees
and by internal controversy (such as, e.g., the disputes between the Schools
of Hillel and Shammai) within the ranks of the Pharisees, culminating in
the collections of traditional laws (*Halakoth*) from which the present
Mishnah drew its material.

According to Jewish tradition[1] the earliest manner of transmitting the
substance of the Oral Law was by means of *Midrash*; that is to say, the
Oral Law was taught in the form of an exposition or running commentary
on the text of Scripture.[2] This was an effective controversial device against
the attacks of the Sadducees; but it was a complicated and cumbersome
means of presenting the Oral Law as a whole; also, in effect, it conceded
the Sadducean thesis that the Written Law alone was authoritative and
that the traditional law was not binding. At some stage a more direct
manner came into use, and the traditional laws, *Halakoth*, were taught and
repeated independently of the Scriptural basis which was claimed for them
(i.e. in specifically *Mishnah* form), and arranged in whatever manner of
grouping was found most convenient. The present Mishnah preserves
traces of various systems of grouping[3] which preceded the ultimately
favoured system of six main Divisions according to topics, with further
subdivisions into tractates.[4]

At the time of the destruction of Jerusalem and the Temple, Johanan
ben Zakkai, who (Aboth 2[8]) 'received the Law from Hillel and Shammai',
established himself at Jabneh.[5] He had been a prominent leader in Jerusalem and a noted opponent of the Sadducees, and, after the extinction of
Jerusalem as the great centre of Jewish life, there gathered around him a
body of students of the Law who, partly by their own moral influence and

---

[1] Reported by Sherira Gaon (head of the Babylonian Jewish academy at Pumbeditha,
c. 980) in his *responsum* to the Kairouan community (published by A. Neubauer, *Mediaeval
Jewish Chronicles*, Oxford, 1887). See also p. M. Kat. iii. 7: 'Who is deemed a disciple of
the Sages? Hezekiah says: Whosoever has studied *Halakoth* together with [Written] Law.
R. Jose said to him: What thou sayest was so beforetime, but now [he is deemed a disciple
of the Sages who has studied] *Halakoth* only.'

[2] This type of *Midrash Halakah* is preserved in the rabbinical commentaries on portions
of the Pentateuch, known as Mekilta, Sifre, and Sifra.   [3] See below, p. xxiv f.

[4] On the problems arising out of this change from *Midrash* to *Mishnah*, see J. Z. Lauterbach, 'Midrash and Mishnah, a study in the early history of the Halakah', *J.Q.R.* (1915), v.
503–27, vi. 23–95, 303–23. He argues that the *Mishnah* form adopted in teaching *Halakoth*
can be traced back to the time of Jose ben Joezer (*c.* 165 B.C.), and that 'the *Mishnah* form was
first used to teach those customs and practices which originated during the time when there
was no official activity of the teachers' (i.e. during the century which followed the death of
Simeon the Just (see Ab. 1[2]), when, it is assumed, the guiding activities of the *Soferim*, the
priestly interpreters of the Written Law, the successors of Ezra the Scribe (*Sofer*), came to
an end, and a large body of traditional usages came into being and established themselves
independently of Scriptural sanction, direct or indirect). 'Having no Scriptural basis, they
could not be taught in connexion with the Scripture, i.e. in the *Midrash* form.' The
Mishnah form was also found preferable when, even if a Midrashic basis existed, the proof
was considered unsound, or when a rival proof was current.

[5] Known in the Greek sources as Jamnia. It lies not far from the coast, a few miles
south of Jaffa.

their reputation for knowledge of the Law and partly by the failure of any other organized body to survive the national catastrophe, came to be regarded by their fellow Jews as the successors of the Jerusalem Sanhedrin. The Roman authorities appear to have acquiesced to this court's exercise of some measure of control and supervision over its co-religionists, and its *Nasi* ('President' or 'Patriarch') became the nation's accredited representative.[1] Upon this Council or 'Sanhedrin' of Jabneh fell the duty of administering and interpreting the religious law and, most important of all, the urgent task of conserving the body of traditional laws and solving the new and confusing problems which arose in the numerous observances dependent on the Temple and the priesthood.

The sixty years of peace (A.D. 70–130) which the country enjoyed before the outbreak of the Bar Cocheba revolt witnessed the activities of those scholars (see Appendix III, the Second and Third Generation) to whom is due the formulation and definition of the Oral Law as we now have it (so far as concerns its essentials) in the Mishnah. The chief of these were Eliezer ben Hyrcanus, Eliezer ben Jacob, Joshua ben Hananiah, and Eleazar ben Azariah among the older contemporaries of the Patriarch Gamaliel II; and, among his younger contemporaries, Akiba, Ishmael ben Elisha, Tarfon, and Johanan ben Nuri. But by far the most outstanding figure during this period is Akiba (c. A.D. 50–135). To him is due the present system of grouping the *Halakoth*, their more exact definition and, still more, their closer approximation to the Written Law. He was put to death during the Bar Cocheba revolt, either because of his enthusiastic support of it or because of his refusal to submit to the emperor Hadrian's edicts against the practice and teaching of the Jewish religion. Behind him he left an illustrious group of disciples who preserved his teachings and continued his methods, and their opinions and arguments are a constant feature in the Mishnah. To this group belong Judah ben Ilai, Jose ben Halafta, Simeon ben Yohai and, chief among them, Rabbi Meir, whose work furnished the link between his master Akiba's teaching and the Oral Law as defined in the Mishnah of Rabbi Judah the Patriarch.

The Mishnah nowhere states that its editor was Rabbi Judah the Patriarch, but in both of the Talmuds the fact is recognized and never disputed.

According to an early tradition,[2] 'Rabbi' (as he is invariably styled in

---

[1] This system of a Patriarchate of Palestinian Jewry was destined to continue for some 350 years. After the retirement of Johanan ben Zakkai the office became hereditary in the Hillel family. Tradition makes Hillel the Elder himself *Nasi* of the Jerusalem Sanhedrin, as also his son (Simeon I, c. A.D. 15), grandson (Gamaliel I, c. A.D. 35, the Gamaliel mentioned in the Acts of the Apostles), and great-grandson (Simeon II, ben Gamaliel, c. A.D. 60, one of the leaders in the revolt against the Romans). Gamaliel II (c. A.D. 90–130) son of Simeon II, succeeded Johanan ben Zakkai as Patriarch of the Court of Jabneh. He, we are told, went with three of his colleagues, c. A.D. 95, as a deputation to Rome on behalf of the Jews of Palestine on a mission whose purpose and result are not recorded. His son and successor, Simeon ben Gamaliel II, survived the massacre of Bether which marked the end of the Bar Cocheba revolt, 132–5, and when the 'Sanhedrin' was re-established at Usha in Galilee he was chosen Patriarch. His son was the Patriarch Judah I, 'the Holy', the compiler of the present Mishnah. After the middle of the third century Palestine gave place to Babylon as the main centre of Jewish learning, and the importance of the Palestinian Patriarchate gradually declined. [2] Genesis Rabba 58[2].

the Mishnah) was born in A.D. 135 on the day that Akiba was put to death. He belonged to the sixth generation in direct descent from Hillel the Elder, and he succeeded his father, Simeon ben Gamaliel II, as Patriarch about the year 165. His early life had been spent at the patriarchal court at Usha, in Galilee, where he had as his teacher R. Judah ben Ilai, whose opinions are cited in the Mishnah more frequently than those of any other authority. Other teachers of Rabbi were Simeon ben Yohai, Eleazar ben Shammua, Nathan the Babylonian, and Jacob ben Korshai. We are told that the language always spoken in his home was not the Aramaic dialect then current in Palestine, but Hebrew, the Holy Language: even the maidservants of this household spoke a pure Hebrew. He was also, we learn, an apt student of Greek. As Patriarch he resided first at Beth Shearim in Galilee, and during the last seventeen years of his life he lived at Sepphoris, also in Galilee. Here he compiled his Mishnah and here he died at a great age.[1] He is said to have lived on amicable terms with the local Roman representative and to have enjoyed the friendship of an emperor named Antoninus.[2] Tradition surrounds the figure of Rabbi with unusual glamour: the luxury of his household was compared with that of emperors, and all nature's gifts were his: he and his sons were alike endowed with beauty, power, wealth, wisdom, old age, honour, and the blessings of children. His exceptional piety earned for him the title of 'Judah the Holy'.

According to a late source[3] Rabbi, in drawing up his Mishnah, made use of thirteen separate collections of *Halakoth*; that is to say, he had a knowledge of that number of varying systems by which the bulk or selections of the *Halakoth* had been transmitted in the names of the earlier authorities and by which they were taught in the schools of the disciples of these authorities. A young contemporary of Rabbi, Johanan ben Nappaha (d. 279), reports[4] that 'anonymous rulings in the Mishnah are those of Rabbi Meir (*c.* 160) . . . and all are according to the teaching of Rabbi Akiba'. The Mishnah itself refers to the Mishnah of Rabbi Akiba and to a 'First Mishnah' of still earlier date.[5] It may be assumed, therefore, that the principal source used by Rabbi was the *Halakah* collection of Rabbi Meir, who had himself made use of the collection of his teacher, Rabbi Akiba.

Traces of other, and probably still earlier, collections are to be seen in the Mishnah's frequent use of the formula 'Beforetime they used to say . . . but afterward . . .'[6] Much of Rabbi's material may go back to a time before or not long after the destruction of the Temple. Thus the tractates

---

[1] About the year 220. But this date is purely conjectural.

[2] Marcus Aurelius visited Palestine in 175 and Septimius Severus in 200. See S. Krauss, *Antoninus und Rabbi*, Vienna, 1910. According to Krauss, Rabbi spent his last years interned at Sepphoris by order of the Roman authorities.

[3] Ned. 41 a.   [4] Sanh. 86 a.

[5] Sanh. 3[4]: 'Such was the Mishnah of R. Akiba; but the First Mishnah . . .' See also Ket. 5[3]; Gitt. 5[6]; Naz. 6[1]; Eduy. 7[2]. In the Gemara we find mention of a Mishnah of R. Eliezer b. Hyrcanus (Men. 18 a) and a Mishnah of R. Eliezer b. Jacob (Yeb. 49 b), both of whom belonged to the generation which preceded R. Akiba. In t. Zab. 1[5] occurs the passage: 'When R. Akiba set in order *Halakoth* for the disciples . . .', which is taken to mean that Akiba was responsible for the present arrangement by topical division.

[6] See especially Ned. 9[6]. Cf. Ned. 11[12]; Gitt. 6[5]; Nidd. 10[6]; Teb. Y. 4[5].

Middoth and Yoma which deal with the structure and the cultus of the Temple are, according to a reliable source,[1] derived (so far as their anonymous contents are concerned) respectively from Eliezer ben Jacob and Simeon of Mizpah, both of whom lived at a time when the Temple was still standing. Another tractate, Tamid ('The Daily Whole-offering'), seems to have been drawn upon by Simeon of Mizpah or to have been derived from him; and portions of the tractate Shekalim[2] also bear indications of a pre-Destruction origin. Again, there is a vivid section in Bikkurim (3[2–6]) which, in addition to its comparatively archaic Hebrew style, points directly, by its natural reference to king Agrippa, to a contemporary narrative: if the account had been purely traditional or an artificial reconstruction of life in the days of the Temple, the probability is that a king of Biblical times would have been mentioned instead.

It was Rabbi's task to bring together this mass of *Halakoth*, the work of many generations, handed down in the form of miscellaneous collections of oral teachings, stored in many memories, and growing ever more complicated and unwieldy by reason of controversy between rival teachers and contradictory traditions; to reassemble this material and to present it as a single coherent whole, arranging it systematically, abbreviating arguments, summarizing discussions, rejecting what seemed superfluous, sometimes in disputed cases giving his own ruling,[3] or adding arguments if these seemed called for.

He did not reproduce his material in a rigidly uniform pattern, reducing it to a single standard of literary style: so far as possible he adhered to the principle of repeating a tradition in the very words in which it had been handed down.[4] Nor did he omit a tradition because it had later been held to be wrong, or suppress the ruling of an individual Sage because it had been repudiated by the Sages as a whole.[5] Thus Rabbi did not aim at promulgating the Mishnah as an authoritative, definitive legal code, a final summary of Jewish law, like the *Shulhan Arukh* of later times. It was, simply, a compilation of the Oral Law as it was taught in the many rabbinical schools of his time; it sought to contain all that was worthy of preservation in older or more recent collections, preserving even divergences of opinion, both such as had originated among earlier generations, as in the Schools of Hillel and Shammai, and such as were due to more recent disputes among the contemporaries and disciples of Rabbi Akiba. Many of these opposing views he leaves without any attempt to decide between them.

Judah the Patriarch's prominence in the community, his reputation in the field of the traditional law, and the skill and modesty with which he fulfilled his task of bringing together into one carefully planned structure all the essential elements of the miscellaneous *Halakah*-collections of his

---

[1] Yom. 16 a. Cf. 14 b. [2] Cf. especially Shek. 5[1].

[3] His name is attached some thirty times (probably by later hands) to rulings in the Mishnah. Sources outside the Mishnah show that he sometimes gives his own opinion as authoritative.

[4] See Eduy. 1[3]; Par. 1[1]. [5] See Eduy. 1[4–6]

predecessors, served almost immediately to win universal recognition for his Mishnah as the only complete and balanced statement of the Oral Law. It displaced all others and became the final authority for legal decisions.[1]

Whether or not Rabbi himself reduced the Mishnah to writing is a problem that has remained in dispute for the last thousand years, the greatest authorities, ancient and modern, being ranged on either side in almost equal numbers.[2] The conclusion that Rabbi could not have left it in written form (and that it was not, indeed, written down until the sixth century) is mainly based on sayings like that of the third-century Palestinian teacher, Johanan ben Nappaha:[3] 'Whosoever writes out the *Halakoth* is as one that burns up the Law'. But it is not intrinsically probable that so voluminous a work should have been transmitted orally through so many generations and yet show such slight traces of later influences. The manner in which it is quoted and referred to in its earliest commentaries, the two Talmuds, strongly suggests that they already had it before them in written form; and this impression is reinforced by the fact that they occasionally point out lacunae in the Mishnah text, and at least some of these belong to the common type of omission due to homoioteleuton,[4] an accident to which written records are peculiarly susceptible.

III. ARRANGEMENT, METHOD, AND LANGUAGE

The Mishnah presents the substance of the Oral Law divided into six main sections (*Sedarim*, lit. 'orders'), which are further divided into sixty-three subsections (*Massektoth*,[5] lit. 'texts') or tractates. This arrangement is probably as early as the Mishnah of Rabbi Akiba.[6] Each main division contains a group of tractates dealing with closely related topics. Sometimes the presence of a certain tractate in a particular Division is at first sight strange (e.g. Berakoth, 'Benedictions', in the First Division which treats of agricultural produce; Nedarim, 'Vows', and Nazir, 'The Nazirite-vow', in the Third Division which treats of laws affecting womankind; and Eduyoth, 'Testimonies', and Aboth, 'The Fathers'—a collection of moral

---

[1] That we have not the text of the Mishnah entirely as Rabbi left it is obvious from the mention of his death (Sota, end) and the citation, though rarely, of teachers belonging to a later generation; e.g. R. Gamaliel and R. Simeon, sons of Rabbi (Ab. 2[2]; Makk. 3[5]), and R. Joshua b. Levi (Uktz. end), and R. Yannai (Ab. 4[5]). See also above, p. xxii, n. 3; and *J.E.* viii. 613 f.

[2] See Strack, pp. 15, 16 (Engl. tr., pp. 18–19). [3] Gitt. 60 a; Tem. 14 b.

[4] See Ch. Albeck, *Untersuchungen über die Redaktion der Mischna*, Berlin, 1923, pp. 151 ff.

[5] Pl. of *masseketh*. This word has an etymological history similar to that of the Latin *textus*.

[6] Cf. above, p. xxi, n. 5. A reference to such a number of tractates (using, however, the favourite round number 'seventy') is possibly contained in the Ezra Apocalypse (c. A.D. 100), 14[44–6]: 'And in forty days were written ninety and four books. And . . . the Most High spake with me [Ezra] and said to me: The twenty and four books [the books of the Bible] that ye have written first, make public, that those who are worthy and those who are not worthy may read therein; but the seventy thou shalt keep and deliver them to the wise of thy people.'

Originally the number of tractates was sixty (*Midrash Rabba* to Song of Songs, 6[9]: 'Sixty queens: these are the sixty tractates of *Halakoth*'); the three tractates Baba Kamma, Baba Metzia, and Baba Bathra were once a single tractate, while Makkoth was originally combined with the preceding Sanhedrin.

maxims—in the Fourth Division which treats of legal matters); but some reason for their inclusion may usually be found.[1] As for the sequence of the tractates within each Division, the only underlying principle seems to have been the mechanical one of arranging them in order of length, with the longest first.[2]

What has already been said of the antecedents of the present Mishnah explains some peculiarities in its method. That the Mishnah consciously aimed at the systematic presentation of its contents is everywhere apparent: its occasional failures are due not to its editor's lack of purpose but to the nature of his material. Perhaps, to the modern mind, the most suitable method of presenting the Oral Law would have been, after propounding the Scriptural basis (if any), to give the general principles which the practice of ages had gradually worked out in applying the Biblical (or non-Biblical) law to daily life, and then to give particular cases falling under the general principles, and cases concerning which there was doubt whether these general principles were applicable. What we actually find is that the Mishnah devotes most of its space to problems arising out of special cases, while general principles are either tacitly assumed[3] or set forth incidentally and unsystematically, often with greater regard to secondary than to primary principles. As for Scriptural basis, it is characteristic of the *Mishnah* method of teaching *Halakoth* that these should be repeated independently of such Scriptural sanction as may be claimed for them; and this rule prevails in the present Mishnah.

Yet the Mishnah has preserved abundant traces of *Midrash*, that earlier method of teaching the traditional laws by means of a running commentary on the Biblical text. Outstanding examples are found, e.g., in Maaser Sheni, 5^{10-14} (commenting clause by clause on Deut. 26^{13-15}); Yebamoth, 12^6 (commenting on Deut. 25^{7-10}); Sota, 8^{1-6} (on Deut. 20^{2-9}); Sotah, 9^{1-6} (on Deut. 21^{1ff}); Sanhedrin, 2^{4-5} (on Deut. 17^{15-19}); Negaim, 12^{5-7} (on Lev. 14^{35ff}).[4] There are two types of *Midrash*, the one simple and unstrained,

---

[1] Thus the tractates in the First Division give the laws governing the dues of the priests and levites, which a man must separate from his crop before it is free for common use; but these tractates are preceded by Berakoth, which deals (*a*) with the prayers which are man's due to God and which must be paid before a man is free to go about his common task, and (*b*) with the Benedictions over food which a man must pronounce before such food is permitted to him. The tractates on Vows and the Nazirite-vow, though not in the main concerned with women, yet treat specifically of women in certain chapters (Ned. 10-11, Naz. 9). Eduyoth and Aboth may owe their present position to their having been originally an appendix to the tractate Sanhedrin, recording judgements and maxims emanating from leading judges in the Sanhedrin.

[2] This principle is not really neglected in the Fourth Division, since its first three tractates were originally one, and Makkoth was once part of Sanhedrin. Though the principle is not observed in the First Division as a whole, it is applied to the concluding tractates. According to the Letter of Sherira Gaon, Rabbi himself adopted no set sequence; and early MSS. are not unanimous in the order they reproduce.

[3] See the introductory notes to the tractates Demai and Hullin.

[4] No less that 217 cases have been counted in the Mishnah of this *Midrash Halakah* (19 in Zeraim, 21 in Moed, 35 in Nashim, 60 in Nezikin, 61 in Kodashin, and 21 in Tohoroth). In addition there are 65 cases of *Midrash Haggadah* (i.e. moral maxims, or teachings of a homiletic character, based on Biblical passages; cf. in Zeraim, Ber. 9^5; Peah 1^1; 8^9; M. Sh. 5^{13}.

as in the cases here quoted, some of which belong to the earliest stage of *Halakah* history, and the other more forced and artificial,[1] derived for the most part from the school of Rabbi Akiba, who, in his attempt to provide *Halakoth* with Scriptural support, sought to lay bare hidden senses in every peculiarity of the Hebrew text, however seemingly insignificant. Yet another type of *Midrash*, more characteristic of the post-Mishnaic period, is that found, for example, in Shabbath, 8[7] to 9[4] (cf. Sanh. 8[2]), where a Biblical text is quoted not as 'proof' for a traditional law but as providing an 'indication' or indirect support for it.[2]

Rabbi's Mishnah also retains numerous traces of those earlier devices for grouping *Halakoth*, devices which were adopted after the *Midrash* method was abandoned. These aimed at assisting the memory by linking together rules (no matter how different in subject) which had some element in common, e.g., rules emanating from the same authority,[3] rules having some numerical feature in common,[4] or rules couched according to a similar formula of words or having a single turn of phrase in common.[5] These groups of heterogeneous rules, sometimes strung together by the slenderest thread of association of ideas, occur so constantly as to become one of the Mishnah's characteristic features. If one rule included in such a group finds natural place in a tractate dealing with the main subject of that rule, then all the rules included in that group are forthwith introduced with it, regardless of their complete inappropriateness in the new context.

Again some lack of uniformity is due to the fact that Rabbi absorbed into his Mishnah certain tractates which had already been shaped, almost in their entirety, by earlier teachers. Thus there is some evidence to show that Kelim[6] and Uktzin[7] existed nearly in their present form a generation earlier, and that the bulk of the tractates Yoma, Tamid,[8] Middoth,[9] and Kinnim[10] date back nearly a century earlier.

Such irregularities, however, scarcely interfere with the Mishnah's unity of plan, and with rare exceptions they leave unaffected its primary purpose, which was to make an end of the confusion which was growing around the subject of the Law owing to the multiplicity of schools and teachers and systems. According to Rabbi's system all rules enunciated in the Mishnah with no record of the Sage or teacher through whom they had

---

[1] Cf. Ber, 1[5]; Pes. 9[2]; Yom. 1[1], 8[9]; Sota 5[1-4]; Sanh. 1[6].

[2] This *Midrash* period in the history of *Halakoth* collections is also responsible for the inclusion of certain subjects in tractates devoted to some quite other subject. Thus Makkoth 2 deals with accidental homicide and the cities of refuge, because these subjects belong to the same chapter of Scripture (Deut. 19) from which the main subject of the tractate ('Stripes') is drawn. Similarly Arakhin, whose subject is the 'commuted vows' of Lev. 27[2 ff], treats also of objects devoted to the Temple (Lev. 27[28 f]), the year of Jubilee (Lev. 25[8-28]), and unwalled cities (Lev. 25[29 ff]), subjects drawn from Biblical passages more or less in juxtaposition.

[3] M. Sh. 5[15]; Shek. 7[6-7]; Ket. 13[1-9]; Sot. 5[2-5]. See also generally the tractates Eduyoth and Aboth.   [4] Shab. 2[6-7]; B.M. 4[7-8].

[5] Bikk. 2[5-8]; Meg. 1[5-11]; Gitt. 4[5-9]; 5[8-9]; Men. 3[5-7]; 4[1-4]; Hull. 1[6-7]; Bekh. 4[5-6]; Arak. 2[1-6]; 3[2-5]; Nidd. 6[2-10].   [6] See Kel. 30[4] (end).   [7] Hor. 13 b.

[8] Yom. 14 b.   [9] Yom. 16 a.   [10] Zeb. 67 b; 68 a.

been handed down, are deemed undisputed and authoritative. Usually such a rule is in accordance with the teachings of the Sages as a whole, though Rabbi sometimes gives as an anonymous and therefore authoritative ruling what was only his personal opinion. If a rule had been disputed Rabbi gives also the name of the disputing Sage or Sages. Thus record is kept of the constant discussions and divergences between the Schools of Hillel and Shammai, c. A.D. 50; between R. Eliezer b. Hyrcanus and R. Joshua b. Hananiah, c. A.D. 90; between R. Akiba and his contemporaries R. Jose the Galilean, R. Johanan b. Nuri, and R. Tarfon, c. A.D. 130, and between R. Judah and R. Nehemiah, c. A.D. 170. Sometimes such opposing views are left without further comment; but more frequently a decisive ruling is given in such terms as 'But the Sages say . . .', or, 'According to the Sages', meaning the consensus of opinion among past and present teachers of the traditional law, or the opinion of Rabbi's court of Sages, or even the opinion of a single Sage, if, as it seemed to Rabbi, that opinion was correct.[1]

In its literary style the Mishnah affects, for the most part, the dryness and preciseness suited to a catalogue of laws. Constant variety, however, is afforded by the interpolation of a contrary ruling by this or that Sage, sometimes supported by appeal to Scripture or by logical argument (at times extremely elaborate), sometimes by reference to some episode or some ruling by an earlier authority adduced as a valid precedent. At times dry brevity gives place to more spacious narrative, and, very rarely, to picturesque description. At the other extreme we find rules phrased so compactly as to be reduced to a few catchwords, meaningless formulae serving no purpose beyond aiding the memory, and incomprehensible without a previous knowledge of the subject.[2] Such variety in style is a natural result of the variety of sources utilized by Rabbi.

The language of the Mishnah is pure Hebrew,[3] but a Hebrew which, in vocabulary, in syntax, and (to a markedly less degree) in morphology, differs from the literary language as it is found in even the latest portions of the Hebrew Bible.[4] Greek, Latin, and Aramaic elements in its vocabulary

---

[1] Hull. 85 a. A few inconsistencies occur, such as quoting an opinion in one place as disputed and elsewhere as authoritative. These may be accounted for by the divergences existing in the sources which Rabbi included unchanged within his own work. See *J.E.* viii. 612 a.

[2] Cf. Yeb. 5¹; 10⁴ (end); Eduy. 1¹. Such passages, of course, cannot be translated literally without conveying a ludicrousness which is not present in the original. Cf. the opening sentence of Arakhin, 4¹, where seventy-seven words in English are needed to convey the meaning of ten Hebrew words.

[3] Brief passages in Aramaic occur only in Ket. 4⁷⁻¹²; Sot. 9¹⁵; Gitt. 9³; B.M. 9³; B.B. 10²; Eduy. 8⁴; Aboth 1¹³; 2⁶; 5²², ²³.

[4] See M. H. Segal, *A Grammar of Mishnaic Hebrew*, Oxford, 1927. He makes an elaborate examination of the relation of Mishnaic Hebrew to Biblical Hebrew and Aramaic, and, as against the opinion occasionally put forward that the Hebrew of the Mishnah was 'merely a Hebraized Aramaic, artificially created by the Schoolmen, like the Latin of the Middle Ages, and that it never had an independent existence as a natural medium of ordinary speech in the daily life of the Jews', he concludes that Mishnaic Hebrew is 'the direct lineal descendant of the spoken Hebrew of the Biblical period, as distinguished from the literary Hebrew of the Biblical period preserved in the Hebrew Scriptures' (p. 11); 'so long as the Jewish people retained some sort of national existence in Palestine Mishnaic Hebrew

are a consequence of the cultural influences with which the Jews had come into contact. Aramaic had entirely, or almost entirely, displaced Hebrew as the language of the Palestinian Jews, and a great number of Greek words, and a few Latin words, were absorbed into the language to denote foreign materials, implements, and institutions introduced into Jewish life during Hellenistic and Roman domination. In its syntax and forms of expression the Hebrew of the Mishnah has been reduced to a bald simplicity, due partly to the influence of Aramaic, but perhaps chiefly to the efforts of the teachers of the Oral Law themselves, who, taking the colloquial Hebrew as their foundation, fashioned the style best fitted to serve as a medium for compact and exact technical definition and instruction.[1]

IV. HISTORY OF INTERPRETATION

The Mishnah of Rabbi Judah the Patriarch was at once conceded authoritative status in the rabbinical schools of Palestine and Babylon. But though the material which Rabbi had included was accepted without challenge, other teachers were not convinced of the lack of value in what he had excluded. Such excluded or 'external' material (*Baraita*), all of it contemporary with Rabbi's material, was brought together and out of it were fashioned other collections compiled in Mishnah fashion. Such collections were known as *Mishnayoth Gedoloth* ('greater' or 'fuller' Mishnahs). This 'external' material was of two kinds: *Halakoth* which Rabbi had discarded as unnecessary or unimportant or not in keeping with his general scheme or even perhaps unauthenticated; and halakic material which was of the nature of explanation, illustration, Scriptural interpretation, or discussion bearing on rules which, in the Mishnah, were recorded without comment.

A collection mainly of this second type of *Baraita* has been preserved in what is known as the *Tosefta* ('Supplement'). In its arrangement it resembles the Mishnah, having the same six main divisions and the same subdivisions into tractates.[2] Whether its compiler intended it, from the first, to be a self-sufficing compendium of traditional law, or whether he intended it to be only a supplement to the present Mishnah (or to the Mishnah collection of Rabbi Meir),[3] the Tosefta is nevertheless an authority of great value for the interpretation of the Mishnah, providing a background of discussion, Scriptural hermeneutics, and illustrative narrative belonging to that same world of ideas from which Rabbi drew.[4]

continued to be the language of at least a section of the Jewish people living in Palestine. As Jewish life in Palestine gradually decayed, and eventually suffered total extinction, so Mishnaic Hebrew was banished step by step from everyday life, and eventually, towards the end of the Mishnaic period, became confined to the learned in the schools and academies' (p. 10).

[1] Cf. J. Klausner, *Ha-Baith ha-Sheni bi-G'dullatho*, Tel-Aviv, 1930, pp. 148–59. He puts forward a theory that this compact legalistic Hebrew style arose early in the Hasmonean age, when the Jews in their newly won freedom found it convenient to revive Hebrew as an official symbol of their independence and as a medium for promulgating their national laws.

[2] It lacks only the tractates Aboth, Tamid, Middoth, and Kinnim.

[3] See J. Z. Lauterbach in *J.E.* xii. 208.

[4] Its relation to the present Mishnah is difficult to determine exactly. Verbal similarity

But the interpretation *par excellence* of the Mishnah is that given in the two Talmuds: the *Talmud Yerushalmi* or Palestinian Talmud, and the *Talmud Babli* or Babylonian Talmud. These works contain the fruit of the labours of several generations of students (*Amoraim*) who set themselves to expound the Law as compiled by Rabbi. So long as centres of Jewish learning continued in Palestine, Rabbi's Mishnah was the principal object of study. It was discussed sentence by sentence, its meaning debated, obscurities explained, authority for each rule was looked for in Scripture, parallels from the *Baraita* were quoted and where they seemed to differ from the Mishnah an attempt was made to harmonize them. In the course of discussion and argument all the knowledge and acumen of the *Amoraim* was poured out, often in a fashion baffling to a modern reader by reason of its inconsequence and profusion. During the same time Rabbi's Mishnah was receiving the same attention in the rabbinical schools of Babylon. There this study persisted for several generations after it had ceased in Palestine,[1] and its results are more elaborate and better preserved. The Palestinian Talmud reached its final shape about the end of the fourth or the beginning of the fifth century, and the Babylonian Talmud about a century later.[2]

For several centuries after the Moslem conquest Babylon continued to be the chief centre of rabbinical learning, its importance ceasing only with the death of Hai ben Sherira Gaon, in 1038. Contact with Arab scholars served in some measure as a renewed stimulus,[3] and the ninth and tenth centuries saw the beginning of the philological and grammatical study of the Hebrew literature; and it is Hai Gaon who is responsible for the earliest extant commentary (in the ordinary sense) on the Mishnah. Only the last part, that on Tohoroth, the Sixth Division, has survived,[4] but scattered quotations in later lexicographical works prove that he commented on the

sometimes extends over complete paragraphs; generally where the one gives scanty details the other is diffuse; the Tosefta does not cover the ground as systematically as the Mishnah, and if we lacked the Mishnah the Tosefta's treatment would often be obscure. Haggadic elements, scarce in the Mishnah, are comparatively abundant in the Tosefta. For specimens of the Tosefta in English, see the translations of Berakoth, Sukkah, and Sanhedrin (ed. S.P.C.K.) mentioned above, p. vi n.

[1] Probably with the extinction of the Patriarchal office, *c.* A.D. 425.

[2] Three tractates from the Babylonian Talmud are accessible to English readers: Berakoth, translated by A. Cohen (Cambridge University Press, 1921), Taanith, translated by Henry Malter (Philadelphia, 1928), and Hagigah, translated by A. W. Streane (Cambridge University Press, 1892).

The Gemara (lit. completion, i.e. commentary of the *Amoraim*) of the Palestinian Talmud covers the first three Divisions of the Mishnah in their entirety (with the exception only of the last four chapters of Shabbath); in the Fourth Division it is lacking for the two tractates Eduyoth and Aboth, and for the third chapter of Makkoth; of the Fifth and Sixth Divisions nothing has survived except the Gemara on a portion of the tractate Niddah.

The Gemara of the Babylonian Talmud covers, in the First Division, only the tractate Berakoth; it covers the whole of the Second, Third, Fourth, and Fifth Divisions (excepting Shekalim in the Second Division, Eduyoth and Aboth in the Fourth Division, and Middoth and Kinnim in the Fifth Division; for Shekalim editions of the Babylonian Talmud give the Palestinian Gemara); in the Sixth Division only the tractate Niddah is provided with Gemara.

[3] See Hartwig Hirschfeld, *Hebrew Grammarians and Lexicographers*, Oxford, 1926, p. 7.

[4] See J. N. Epstein, *Der gaonäische Kommentar zur Ordnung Tohoroth*, Berlin, 1915.

whole of the Mishnah.[1] He deals almost entirely with linguistic problems, and in his search for derivation of obscure words he makes much use of Arabic.

But the real father of Mishnah commentators is Rashi (so called from the initials of his name, Rabbi Shelomo Yitzhaki), a French Jew, 1040–1105, whose reputation is equally great in the fields of Biblical and rabbinical interpretation. His commentary on the Mishnah is but part of his famous commentary on the Babylonian Talmud, and it is therefore not available for those tractates which have no Gemara. Where it deals with the Mishnah text it is a self-contained commentary, with Rashi's characteristic brevity and lucidity and his astonishing skill in unravelling a complication or illuminating an obscurity by a single word or phrase.[2]

Maimonides[3] (1135–1204), one of the great figures of the Middle Ages, wrote in early manhood an introduction and commentary to the entire Mishnah. It was composed in Arabic under the title *Kitab es-Siraj*, 'The Book of the Lamp'. He worked on a larger scale than Rashi: not content with explaining details he endeavours also to keep before his reader the general principles governing the subject of study, so removing one of the chief difficulties in the way of understanding the Mishnah. Also, with a view to the use of the Mishnah as a practical guide to Jewish religious law, he determines what is to be accepted as *Halakah* in the numerous cases not explicitly decided in the Mishnah.[4]

Other of the earlier commentators were Isaac ben Melchizedek of Siponto, *c.* 1110–70, an Italian rabbi of whose Mishnah commentary only the First Division, Zeraim, is extant;[5] Samson ben Abraham of Sens, *c.* 1150–1231, a French Talmudist, who migrated to Palestine *c.* 1211, where he wrote a commentary on those tractates of the Mishnah to which the Babylonian Talmud provides no Gemara;[6] and Asher ben Jehiel (a German Talmudist who migrated to Spain and died at Toledo in 1238), who commented on the tractates of the First Division (excepting Berakoth) and the Sixth Division and on Nedarim.[7]

The commentary which, owing to its adequacy and simplicity, has achieved highest favour, is that by Obadiah ben Abraham of Bertinoro

[1] See *Dor Dor*, iv. 185 f.
[2] The commentary is an indispensable aid to the understanding of the Talmud and, since the first collected edition of 1520, has always been printed side by side with the text. (The edition of the Babylonian Talmud by Lazarus Goldschmidt, 1897 ff., with a German translation, is an exception.)
[3] In Jewish writings generally styled 'Rambam', from the initials of his name, Rabbi Mosheh ben Maimon.
[4] His commentary was translated into Hebrew by various hands, and the Hebrew translation was included in the first edition of the Mishnah (Naples, 1492) and in other early editions, and it has been included in most of the collected editions of the Babylonian Talmud. A Latin translation of the Hebrew version is given in Surenhusius's edition of the Mishnah.   [5] Printed in the 1899 Wilna edition of the Talmud.
[6] First published in the 1523 Bomberg edition of the Talmud, and since then printed in most of the collected editions. More recent Talmud Babli editions print also a commentary on these tractates of the First and Sixth Divisions by Meir b. Baruch of Rothenburg, d. 1293.
[7] He is more famous as the author of a compendium of Talmudic Laws, included in most Talmud editions.

(*c.* 1510), an Italian Jew who in middle life migrated to Palestine (in 1488), and became spiritual head of the Jewish community in Jerusalem. His commentary, covering the whole Mishnah, is based on the work of Rashi, Samson of Sens, and Maimonides; it usually gives also the Gemara's explanation of the Mishnah text. Since its first publication in 1548 very few editions of the Mishnah have been printed without it.[1] A far more elaborate and erudite work is that of Yom-Tob Lipmann Heller (1579–1654), rabbi successively of Vienna, Prague, and Cracow. His commentary, *Tosefoth* (lit. additions, glosses) *Yom-Tob*, was published first in 1614 together with that of Bertinoro, to which it is a learned and critical supplement. Equally critical and penetrating is *Meleketh Shelomoh*, the commentary by Solomon ben Joshua Adeni, a Yemenite Jew, who after migrating to Palestine finished his commentary in Hebron (1622 or 1624).[2]

Of more recent commentaries mention should be made of *Tifereth Yisrael*, by Israel Lipschütz (1782–1860), a diligent scholar and ascetic, successively rabbi of Dessau and Danzig. His work[3] is of great practical value to the student, combining many of the best features of its predecessors, keeping apart simple explanations from elaborate discussion, and prefacing each of the six Divisions with lengthy but lucid expositions of general principles.[4]

V. TEXT AND EDITIONS

The periodical persecutions of Jews during the Middle Ages were usually accompanied by systematic attempts to destroy Hebrew writings, and especially manuscripts of the Talmud. The result is that very few complete manuscripts of the Mishnah have survived and only one of the Babylonian Talmud.[5]

The most important manuscripts of the complete Mishnah[6] are:

The Cambridge Manuscript. It has been published in a reliable transcription by W. H. Lowe, *The Mishnah on which the Palestinian Talmud rests: from the unique manuscript preserved in the University Library of Cambridge. Add. 470. 1.* Cambridge University Press, 1883.

The Kaufmann Manuscript. Now in the possession of the Königliche Ungarische Akademie der Wissenschaften. A facsimile is published by G. Beer (Haag, 1930). The text has been wholly pointed by a second hand.

---

[1] A Latin translation is given in the Surenhusius edition.

[2] Published in the Romm quarto Mishnah (Wilna, 1908–9).

[3] Published, at intervals, between 1830 and 1850; it is included in the Romm quarto Mishnah and (together with Bertinoro) in the Romm octavo *Mishnayoth*.

[4] An exhaustive list of Mishnah commentaries is not here in place. Additional titles will be found in Strack, p. 158 f. (Engl. tr., pp. 145 ff.). Almost all the extant commentaries, in whole or in part, are included in the great Wilna edition (First and Sixth Divisions, 1887; Second to Fifth Divisions, 1908–9) in seven quarto volumes. Z. Frankel's *Dar'ke ha-Mishnah* ('Hodegetica in Mischnam'), Leipzig, 1859, is still the standard work on those subjects which come under the head of ' introduction to the Mishnah'.

[5] Now in the Munich Staatsbibliothek (Kod. Hebr. 95). A photographic facsimile has been published by H. L. Strack (Leiden, 1912).

[6] For a list of MSS. of portions of the Mishnah, see Strack, pp. 80 f. (Engl. tr., p. 79 f.).

The Parma Manuscript (De Rossi, no. 138). See J. B. Rossi, *MSS. Codices Hebraice Biblioth*. i. 99 (Parma, 1803). Nearly a half of the text is pointed.

The Mishnah, together with the commentary of Maimonides, was printed first at Naples, 1492, in folio, by the Soncino press. It was followed by the Venice Justiniani edition, 1546 f., in folio; a quarto edition printed in Venice, 1548 f., with the commentary of Obadiah of Bertinoro; the folio edition of Riva di Trento, 1559, the quarto edition of Sabbioneta and Mantua, 1559–63, and the folio edition of Venice, 1606, containing the commentaries of Maimonides and Bertinoro. The Mishnah with the commentaries of Bertinoro and Yom-Tob Lipmann Heller (*Tosefoth Yom-Tob*) was first published at Prague (1614–17; second edition, revised by Heller, Cracow, 1642–4), and it is this same version, equipped with these same two commentaries, which has since been reproduced in the common six-volume *Mishnayoth* editions.

Two types of Mishnah text have existed from a very early date: the Palestinian type (that embedded within the Gemara of the *Talmud Yerushalmi*), and the Babylonian type (that embedded within the Gemara of the *Talmud Babli*). The texts of the Mishnah which are now printed in the Babylonian Talmud at the beginning of each paragraph, and in the Palestinian Talmud at the head of each chapter, are not pure representatives respectively of the Babylonian and Palestinian types.[1] Originally the Mishnah was not prefixed to paragraphs or chapters of the Talmuds, but was reproduced sentence by sentence (as it also is still) within the Gemara itself. It was the work of copyists of a later time to prefix a continuous text of the Mishnah in the manner now common; and the text they so prefixed was not always one which, in order and text, corresponded with the Mishnah text embedded in or assumed by the Gemara. Thus it comes about that in the Munich MS. of the *Babylonian* Talmud (particularly in Zeraim and Tohoroth) and in the still earlier Florentine MS.,[2] the Mishnah is of the distinctively *Palestinian* type.[3]

The features of the Palestinian type of text are peculiar spellings of some of the commonest words and proper names and variations in syntax best accounted for as colloquialisms arising in a region where the language was not yet wholly dead. In the Babylonian type these irregularities are smoothed out and made to conform to the more literary usage of the language. Variant readings preserved in the two types can be surely identified as Palestinian or as Babylonian only in so far as they are

---

[1] On the present state of the study of the text of the Mishnah, see J. N. Epstein in *Ha-Tekufah*, xiii. 505 ff., Warsaw, 1922, and *Yedi'oth ha-Makon l'Madda'e ha-Yahaduth* (Kitbhe ha-Universita ha-Ivrith b'Yerushalaim), pp. 5–8, Jerusalem, 1925.

[2] Dated 1177. See Strack, p. 83, par. 8.

[3] A curious illustration of the resulting confusion appears in the first paragraph of the Mishnah (Ber. 1¹). The Babylonian Gemara (9 a) comments on the omission by the Mishnah of 'the eating of the Passover-offering'; but this reading is none the less given in the Mishnah text contained in the Munich codex of the Babylonian Talmud. On the other hand the Gemara of the Palestinian Talmud includes the reading, yet it is not included in the prefixed Mishnah text.

assumed in the interpretations given by the respective Gemaras of the two Talmuds.

Although the Cambridge, Kaufmann, and Parma MSS. belong to the Palestinian type of text they all bear marks of revision under the influence of the Babylonian type; and the same applies to the Mishnah printed in the first (Venice, 1523) edition of the *Talmud Yerushalmi* and the subsequent Cracow (1609) and Krotoschin (1866) editions.

The present *textus receptus* of the Mishnah, the text of the printed *Mishnayoth* editions, represents a fusion of the two types. The first printed edition (Naples, 1492) contains readings characteristic of both types but its tendency is in the direction of the Palestinian type. Owing to the dominating position always held by the *Talmud Babli*, later editions of the Mishnah came increasingly under the influence of the Babylonian type. A reverse influence was also at work, readings of the 1492 Mishnah finding their way into the prefixed Mishnah text in the subsequent editions of the *Talmud Babli*, which began to be printed in complete form only in 1520.[1]

---

[1] The first complete edition was published by Daniel Bomberg at Venice in 1520, but several tractates of the Talmud were published separately by the Soncino family between 1484 and 1519.

FIRST DIVISION
ZERAIM[*]
('SEEDS')

BERAKOTH
PEAH
DEMAI
KILAIM
SHEBIITH
TERUMOTH
MAASEROTH
MAASER SHENI
HALLAH
ORLAH
BIKKURIM

BERAKOTH [1] ('BENEDICTIONS')

1. 1. From what time in the evening may the *Shemaʿ* [2] be recited? From the time when the priests[3] enter [the Temple] to eat of their Heave-offering[4] until the end of the first watch.[5] So R. Eliezer. But the Sages say: Until midnight. Rabban Gamaliel says: Until the rise of dawn. His sons once returned [after midnight] from a wedding feast. They said to him, 'We have not recited the *Shemaʿ* '. He said to them, 'If the dawn has not risen ye are [still] bound to recite it. Moreover, wheresoever the Sages prescribe "Until midnight"[6] the duty of fulfilment lasts until the rise of dawn'. The duty of burning the fat pieces and the members [of the animal offerings][7] lasts until the rise of dawn; and for all [offerings] that must be consumed 'the same day',[8] the duty lasts until the rise of dawn. Why then have the Sages said: Until midnight? To keep a man far from transgression.

2. From what time in the morning may the *Shemaʿ* be recited? So soon as one can distinguish between blue and white. R. Eliezer says: Between blue and green. And it should be finished before sunrise. R. Joshua says: Before the third hour: for so is it the way of kings, to rise up at the third hour. He that recites it from that time onward suffers no loss and is like to one that reads in the Law.

3. The School of Shammai say: In the evening all should recline when they recite [the *Shemaʿ*], but in the morning they should stand up, for it is written, *And when thou liest down and when thou risest up.*[9] But the School of Hillel say: They may recite it every one in his own way, for it is written, *And when thou walkest by the way.*[10] Why then is it written, *And when thou liest down and when thou risest up?* [It means] the time when men usually lie down and the time when men usually rise up. R. Tarfon said: I was once on a journey and I reclined to recite [the *Shemaʿ*] in accordance with the words of the School of Shammai, and so put myself in jeopardy by reason of robbers. They said to him: Thou hadst deserved aught that befell thee in that thou didst transgress the words of the School of Hillel.

4. In the morning two Benedictions[11] are said before [the *Shemaʿ*] and one after;[12] and in the evening two Benedictions are said before[13] and two after,[14] the one long and the other short. Where the long is prescribed the short is not permissible; where the short is prescribed the long is not permissible. [Where it is prescribed] to seal[15] [a Benediction] it is not

[1] See Introd. p. xxiv, n. 1. The term includes not only blessing and thanksgiving but also prayer and intercession. The tractate gives rules concerning the times and manner of saying the *Shemaʿ* ('Hear, O Israel!' App. I. 38) and the *Tefillah* (the 'Eighteen Benedictions', App. I. 46), the main constituents of the regular Jewish order of prayer, as well as the forms of prayer or 'grace' to be said over food of various kinds, and the 'ejaculatory prayers' called forth on sundry occasions.　　[2] See Tam. 5[1].
[3] Who have suffered uncleanness (Lev. 22[4-7]). They must immerse themselves and await sunset before they are fit to eat of the Hallowed Things or Heave-offering. After immersion and until sunset they still suffer a lesser degree of uncleanness. See p. 773, n. 6. 773, n. 6.
[4] Num. 18[8-20]. See App. I. 48 (i).
[5] The third or the fourth hour of the night, according to whether the night was divided into four or three watches.　　[6] See Zeb. 5[3, 5, 6, 8]; 6[1].
[7] See Lev. 6[12]; 7[3, 31, 33]. Cf. Meg. 2[6]. Some texts add: And the eating of the Passover offerings. Ex. 12[10]. Cf. Zeb. 5[8].　　[8] Lev. 7[15ff].　　[9] Deut. 6[7].　　[10] Ibid.
[11] See Singer, p. 37 ('Blessed art thou . . . who formest light') and p. 39 ('With abounding love . . .'). Cf. Meg. 4[3, 5].　　[12] Singer, p. 42 ('True and firm . . .').
[13] Singer, p. 96 ('Who bringest twilight', and 'With everlasting love').
[14] Singer, p. 98 ('True and trustworthy . . .') and p. 99 ('Make us lie down . . .').
[15] To end the Benediction with the appropriate formula 'Blessed art thou, O Lord, . . .'

permissible not to seal; and [where it is prescribed] not to seal, it is not permissible to seal.

5. The going forth from Egypt[1] is rehearsed [also] at night. R. Eleazar b. Azariah said: Lo, I am like to one that is seventy years old yet failed to prove[2] why the going forth from Egypt should be rehearsed at night until Ben Zoma thus expounded it: It is written, *That thou mayest remember the day when thou camest forth out of the land of Egypt all the days of thy life*.[3] 'The days of thy life' [would mean] the days only; but *all the days of thy life* [means] the nights also. The Sages say: 'The days of thy life' [means] this world only, but *all the days of thy life* is to include the Days of the Messiah.

2. 1. If a man was reading [the verses of the *Shemaʿ*] in the Law and the time came to recite the *Shemaʿ*, if he directed his heart[4] he has fulfilled his obligation; otherwise he has not fulfilled his obligation. Between the sections[5] he may salute a man out of respect and return a greeting; but in the middle [of a section] he may salute a man [only] out of fear of him, and return a greeting. So R. Meir. R. Judah says: In the middle he may salute a man out of fear of him and return a greeting out of respect; between the sections he may salute a man out of respect and return the greeting of any man.

2. By 'between the sections' is meant: between the first Benediction and the second;[6] between the second Benediction and *Hear, O Israel . . .*;[7] between *Hear, O Israel . . .* and *It shall come to pass if ye shall hearken*;[8] between *It shall come to pass if ye shall hearken* and *And the Lord spake unto Moses*;[9] between *And the Lord spake unto Moses* and 'True and firm . . .'[10] R. Judah says: There may be no break between *And the Lord spake unto Moses* and 'True and firm . . .' R. Joshua b. Karha said: Why does the section *Hear, O Israel* precede *And it shall come to pass if ye shall hearken?*— so that a man may first take upon him the yoke of the kingdom of heaven and afterward take upon him the yoke of the commandments. [And why does the section] *And it shall come to pass if ye shall hearken* precede *And the Lord spake unto Moses?* Because *And it shall come to pass if ye shall hearken* applies both by day and by night, but *And the Lord spake unto Moses* applies by day only.

3. If a man recited the *Shemaʿ* but not loudly enough for himself to hear, he has fulfilled his obligation.[11] R. Jose says: He has not fulfilled it. If he recited it without clearly pronouncing the letters, R. Jose says: He has fulfilled his obligation. R. Judah says: He has not fulfilled it. If a man recited [the sections] in wrong order, he has not fulfilled his obligation. If he recited it and fell into error he should go back to where he fell into error.

4. Craftsmen may recite the *Shemaʿ* on the top of a tree or on top of a course of stones, which they may not do when they say the *Tefillah*.[12]

5. A bridegroom is exempt from reciting the *Shemaʿ* on the first night, or until the close of the [next] Sabbath if he has not consummated the marriage. Once when Rabban Gamaliel married he recited the *Shemaʿ*

---

[1] Referring to the third section of the *Shemaʿ*, Num. 15[37–41], which mentions the exodus in the last verse; but the rest deals only with the law of fringes which does not apply at night time.   [2] Or, 'was not worthy (to understand)'.   [3] Deut. 16[3].
[4] Intentionally read the passage as a fulfilment of his duty. Cf. R. Sh. 3[7i].
[5] The breaks between each Benediction and portion of Scripture constituting the *Shemaʿ*.
[6] See above, 1[4].   [7] Deut. 6[4ff].   [8] Deut. 11[13f].   [9] Num. 15[37f].
[10] Singer, p. 42.   [11] Some texts add: So R. Judah.   [12] See below, 4[1ff], and App. I. 46.

on the first night. His disciples said to him, 'Master, didst thou not teach us that a bridegroom is exempt from reciting the *Shema'* on the first night?' He said to them, 'I will not hearken to you to cast off from myself the yoke of the kingdom of heaven even for a moment'.

6. He washed himself the first night of his wife's death. His disciples said to him, 'Master, didst thou not teach us that a mourner is forbidden to wash himself?' He replied, 'I am not like other men: I am infirm'.

7. And when his slave Tabi died he accepted condolence because of him. They said to him, 'Master, didst thou not teach us that men may not accept condolence because of slaves?' He replied, 'My slave Tabi was not like other slaves: he was a worthy man'.

8. If a bridegroom is minded to recite the *Shema'* on the first night he may recite it. Rabban Simeon b. Gamaliel says: Not every one that is minded to assume the name[1] may assume it.

3. 1. He whose dead lies unburied before him is exempt from reciting the *Shema'*, from saying the *Tefillah* and from wearing phylacteries.[2] They that bear the bier and they that relieve them, and they that relieve these, they that go before and they that follow after the bier—they that are needful for the bier are exempt, but they that are not needful are not exempt [from reciting the *Shema'*]. Both alike are exempt from saying the *Tefillah*.

2. When they have buried the dead and returned, if they can begin [the *Shema'*] and finish it before reaching the Row[3] they begin it; but if they can not, they do not begin it. Of them that stand in the Row, they of the inner line are exempt [from reciting the *Shema'*] but they of the outer line are not exempt.

3. Women and slaves and minors are exempt from reciting the *Shema'* and from wearing phylacteries, but they are not exempt from saying the *Tefillah*, from the law of the *Mezuzah*[4] or from saying the Benediction after meals.

4. He that has suffered a pollution[5] should ponder [over the *Shema'*] in his heart but he may say no Benediction before it or after it. Over a meal he should say the Benediction which follows after but not that which goes before. R. Judah says: He should say both the Benediction which goes before and the Benediction which follows after.

5. If he was standing during the *Tefillah* and then remembered that he had suffered a pollution he should not break off [his prayer] but he must shorten it. If he went down to immerse himself and, before sunrise, had time to come up, clothe himself and recite [the *Shema'*], he may come up, clothe himself and recite it; but if not, he must remain covered with water and recite it. But he must not remain covered with foul water[6] or water used for soaking [flax], unless he had poured [clean] water therein. And [when a man recites the *Shema'*] how far should he go apart from it[7] and from excrement? Four cubits.

6. If a man with flux[8] suffered a pollution, or if a menstruant[9] discharged

---

[1] A reputation for piety which he has not otherwise earned.
[2] See p. 104, n. 16. Some texts add, 'and from all the duties enjoined in the Law'.
[3] After the burial, friends of the mourners form themselves into rows between which the mourners pass and receive condolence. The Mishnah here speaks of a double row. Cf. Meg. 4[3].   [4] App. I. 25.   [5] Lev. 15[16].
[6] Evil-smelling liquid or urine.   [7] Urine.   [8] Lev. 15[2ff].   [9] Lev. 15[19ff].

semen, or if a woman suffered a flow during intercourse, they must immerse themselves.[1] R. Judah pronounces them exempt.

4. 1. The morning *Tefillah*[2] [may be said any time] until midday. R. Judah says: Until the fourth hour. The afternoon *Tefillah* [may be said any time] until sunset. R. Judah says: Until midway through the afternoon. The evening *Tefillah* has no set time; and the Additional *Tefillah* [may be said] any time during the day. R. Judah says: Until the seventh hour.

2. R. Nehunya b. ha-Kanah used to pray a short prayer when he entered the House of Study and when he came forth. They said to him, 'What is the nature of this prayer?' He replied, 'When I enter I pray that no offence shall happen through me, and when I come forth I give thanks for my lot'.

3. Rabban Gamaliel says: A man should pray the Eighteen [Benedictions][3] every day. R. Joshua says: The substance[4] of the Eighteen. R. Akiba says: If his prayer is fluent in his mouth he should pray the Eighteen, but if not, the substance of the Eighteen.

4. R. Eliezer says: He that makes his prayer a fixed task, his prayer is no supplication. R. Joshua says: He that journeys in a place of danger should pray a short prayer,[5] saying, 'Save, O Lord, the remnant of Israel; at their every cross-road[6] let their needs come before thee. Blessed art thou, O Lord, that hearest prayer!'

5. If he was riding on an ass he should dismount [to say the *Tefillah*]. If he cannot dismount he should turn his face [toward Jerusalem]; and if he cannot turn his face, he should direct his heart toward the Holy of Holies.

6. If he was journeying on a ship[7] or a raft he should direct his heart toward the Holy of Holies.

7. R. Eleazar b. Azariah says: The additional *Tefillah* may be said only with the local congregation. But the Sages say: Either with the local congregation or without them. R. Judah says in his[8] name: Wheresoever there is a local congregation the individual is exempt from saying the Additional *Tefillah*.

5. 1. None may stand up to say the *Tefillah* save in sober mood. The pious men of old used to wait an hour before they said the *Tefillah*, that they might direct their heart toward God. Even if the king salutes a man he may not return the greeting; and even if a snake was twisted around his heel he may not interrupt his prayer.

2. We make mention of 'the Power of Rain'[9] in [the Benediction] 'the Resurrection of the Dead',[10] and we pray for rain in the Benediction 'The Years',[11] and [we make mention of] *Habdalah*[12] in [the Benediction] 'Thou

---

[1] Before they may say the *Tefillah*. This is in addition to the immersion prescribed for their particular major uncleanness.
[2] The 'Eighteen Benedictions'. See App. I. 46. Cf. Taan. 2[2].
[3] Now nineteen. One was later added denouncing the 'slanderers' (Singer, p. 48) who brought evil on the congregation. It is now the twelfth in order.
[4] Or 'abstract'. The Gemara (29a) here gives a shortened form, reproduced in the present-day Jewish Prayer-book (Singer, p. 55, *Habinenu*).
[5] Some texts add, 'the substance of the Eighteen'.
[6] In the metaphorical sense. Bert. and Tif. Yis. render: Whensoever they go apart in transgression.   [7] Some texts add, 'wagon'.   [8] R. Eleazar b. Azariah's.
[9] See Taan. 1[1].   [10] The second of the Eighteen Benedictions. Singer, p. 44 (bottom).
[11] The ninth Benediction. Singer, p. 47 (bottom).   [12] See App. I. 9.

favourest man with knowledge'.[1] R. Akiba says: This [last] should be said as a fourth Benediction by itself. R. Eliezer says: Together with the 'Thanksgiving'.[2]

3. If a man said [in his prayer], 'To a bird's nest do thy mercies extend',[3] or 'May thy name be remembered for the good [which thou hast wrought]',[4] or 'We give thanks, we give thanks',[5] they put him to silence.[6] If a man went before the Ark[7] and fell into error, another must take his place: none may decline at such a time. Where does he begin? At the beginning of the Benediction in which the other fell into error.

4. He that goes before the Ark should not answer 'Amen' after [the Benediction of] the Priests[8] for fear of confusion. Even if there is no priest there save himself he should not lift up his hands [in the Benediction of the Priests]; yet if he is assured that he can lift up his hands and return to the *Tefillah*,[9] he may do so.

5. If he that says the *Tefillah* falls into error it is a bad omen for him; and if he was the agent of the congregation[10] it is a bad omen for them that appointed him, because a man's agent is like to himself. They tell of R. Hanina b. Dosa[11] that he used to pray over the sick and say, 'This one will live', or 'This one will die'. They said to him, 'How knowest thou?' He replied, 'If my prayer is fluent in my mouth I know that it is accepted; and if it is not I know that it is rejected'.

6. 1. What Benediction do they say over fruits? Over the fruit of trees a man says, '[Blessed art thou . . .] who createst the fruit of the tree', except over wine, for over wine a man says ' . . . who createst the fruit of the vine'. Over the fruits of the earth a man says, ' . . . who createst the fruit of the ground', except over bread, for over bread a man says ' . . . who bringest forth bread from the earth'. And over vegetables a man says, ' . . . who createst the fruit of the ground'; but R. Judah says, ' . . . who createst divers kinds of herbs'.

2. If over the fruits of trees he said the Benediction '[Blessed art thou . . .] who createst the fruit of the ground, he has fulfilled his obligation; but if over the fruits of the earth he said, ' . . . who createst the fruit of the tree', he has not fulfilled his obligation. If over them all he said, '[Blessed art thou . . .] by whose word all things exist', he has fulfilled his obligation.

3. Over aught that does not grow from the earth he should say, '[Blessed art thou . . .] by whose word all things exist'. Over soured wine or unripe fallen fruits or over locusts he should say, ' . . . by whose word all things exist'.[12] R. Judah says: Over aught that is of the nature of a curse[13] no Benediction should be said.

4. When a man has before him many kinds [of food], R. Judah says: If there is among them one of the seven kinds,[14] he must say the Benediction

---

[1] The fourth Benediction. Singer, p. 46.   [2] The eighteenth Benediction. Singer, p. 51.
[3] See Meg. 4⁹. Cf. Deut. 22⁷. Gem. 33 b: He is silenced 'because he makes the ordinances of God to be simply acts of mercy, whereas they are injunctions'.
[4] Cf. below, 9⁵.   [5] Implying the heresy of dualism.
[6] Some texts add: If a man says, 'The good bless thee', this is the way of the heretics.
[7] Containing the scrolls of the Law, before which congregational prayers were recited.
[8] Num. 6²⁴⁻⁶. See *J. E.* s.v. 'Blessing, Priestly'. Cf. R. Sh. 4⁵; Meg. 4⁵, ⁷.
[9] Without getting confused in his reading. The Priestly Blessing was given between the eighteenth and nineteenth Benedictions.   [10] The 'precentor'. Cf. R. Sh. 4⁹.   [11] Cf. Sot. 9¹⁵.
[12] Some texts add: Over milk, cheese, or eggs he should say, '. . . . by whose word all things exist'.   [13] Like the three things mentioned.
[14] Enumerated in Deut. 8⁸: wheat, barley, grapes, figs, pomegranates, olive oil and (date) honey (cf. Bikk. 1³).

over that one. But the Sages say: He may say the Benediction over which of them he will.

5. If he said the Benediction over the wine before the meal he need not say it over the wine after the meal. If he said the Benediction over the savoury before the meal he need not say it over the savoury after the meal.[1] If he said it over the bread he need not say it over the savoury; but if he said it over the savoury he is not exempt from saying it over the bread. The School of Shammai say: Or over aught that was cooked in the pot.

6. If men sit [apart] to eat, each should say the Benediction for himself; if they reclined [around the table together] one should say the Benediction for all. If wine is brought to them during the meal each should say the Benediction for himself; but if after the meal, one should say the Benediction for all, and he, too, should say the Benediction over the burning spices even though they are brought in only after the meal is over.

7. If salted relish was first brought before him together with bread he should say the Benediction over the salted relish and he need not say it over the bread, since the bread is but an accompaniment. This is the general rule: where there is a main food and aught that is but an accompaniment to it, the Benediction should be said over the main food and it need not be said over the accompaniment.

8. If a man ate figs, grapes or pomegranates, he should say the three Benedictions[2] after them. So Rabban Gamaliel. But the sages say: One Benediction, the substance of the three. R. Akiba says: Even if he ate but boiled vegetables for his meal he must say the three Benedictions after them. If he drank water to quench his thirst he should say, '[Blessed art thou . . .] by whose word all things exist'. R. Tarfon says: [He should say,] ' . . . who createst many living beings'.[3]

7. 1. If three ate together they must say the Common Grace.[4] If one of them ate *demai*-produce,[5] or First Tithe[6] from which Heave-offering[7] had been taken, or Second Tithe[8] or dedicated produce that had been redeemed;[9] if an attendant ate an olive's bulk of food, or [if one that ate was] a Samaritan,[10] they may be included [to make up the number needed] for the Common Grace. But if one of them ate produce that was certainly untithed, or First Tithe from which Heave-offering had not been taken, or Second Tithe or dedicated produce that had not been redeemed, or if a servant ate less than an olive's bulk of food, or [if one that ate was] a gentile, they may not be included [to make up the number needed] for the Common Grace.

2. Women or slaves or minors may not be included [to make up the number needed] for the Common Grace. How much [should one eat] to

---

[1] Corresponding to the *gustus* and the dessert. Cf. Shab. 23[2]; Ab. 3[19].
[2] See *J. E.* vi. 61b.   [3] Some texts add: and their wants.
[4] Lit. summon (the others to say grace jointly).   [5] See App. I. 6.
[6] Which must be given to the levites before the food may be eaten (Num. 18[21]).
[7] The tithe of the First Tithe which the levite must give to the priests (Num. 18[26]).
[8] A further tithe set apart after the levite had received his tithe. This Second Tithe must either be taken to Jerusalem and eaten there by the owner, or he may 'redeem' it with money (adding a fifth of its value) and spend that money on food in Jerusalem. See p. 73, n. 6.
[9] When Second Tithe and dedicated produce (e.g. from a field dedicated to the Temple) are redeemed, to render them permissible for common use not only their value but an 'Added Fifth' (see B. M. 4[8]) must be paid. In the present case it is assumed that the Added Fifth has not been paid; yet even so the Common Grace is permitted.
[10] Lit. Cuthite (cf. 2 Kings, 17[24ff]). And so throughout the Mishnah.

be included [to make up the number needed] for the Common Grace?
An olive's bulk. R. Judah says: An egg's bulk.

3. How do they say the Common Grace? If three are present, one says,
'We will bless [him of whose bounty we have partaken]'; if three besides
himself, he says, 'Bless ye [him of whose bounty . . .]'; if ten[1] are present,
one says, 'We will bless our God [of whose bounty . . .]'; if ten besides
himself, he says, 'Bless ye [our God of whose bounty . . .]'. It is all one
whether there are ten or ten myriads.[2] If a hundred are present, one says,
'We will bless the Lord our God . . .'; if a hundred besides himself, he says,
'Bless ye [the Lord our God . . .]'; if a thousand are present, one says, 'We
will bless the Lord our God, the God of Israel . . .'; if a thousand besides
himself, he says, 'Bless ye [the Lord our God, the God of Israel . . .]';
if ten thousand are present, one says, 'We will bless the Lord our God,
the God of Israel, the God of hosts, who sitteth between the Cherubim, for
the food which we have eaten'; if ten thousand besides himself, he says,
'Bless ye the Lord our God, the God of Israel, the God of hosts . . .'
After the fashion of his Benediction so do the others answer after him,
'Blessed be the Lord our God, the God of Israel, the God of hosts, who
sitteth between the Cherubim, for the food which we have eaten'. R. Jose
the Galilean says: According to the multitude of the congregation do they
frame the Benediction, as it is written, *By congregations bless ye the Lord,
ye that are from the fountain of Israel.*[3] R. Akiba said: What do we find in
the synagogue?[4]—it is all one whether they are many or few: they say,
'Bless ye the Lord'. R. Ishmael says: [They say], 'Bless ye the Lord who
is to be blessed'.

4. If three ate together they may not separate [without saying together
the Common Grace]; so, too, if they are four or five. Six may separate
[into groups of three to say the Common Grace], and so up to ten. But
ten may not separate, and so up to twenty.

5. If two groups ate in the one house and some of the one group were
visible to some of the other group, they may be included together for the
saying of the Common Grace;[5] but if not, each group must say the Common
Grace by itself. They do not say the Benediction over the wine until water
has been added to it. So R. Eliezer. But the Sages say: They may say the
Benediction [even over wine without water].

8. 1. These are the things wherein the School of Shammai and the School
of Hillel differ in what concerns a meal. The School of Shammai say:
[On a Sabbath or a Festival-day] they say the Benediction first over the
day and then over the wine. And the School of Hillel say: They say the
Benediction first over the wine and then over the day.[6]

2. The School of Shammai say: They wash the hands and then mix the
cup. And the School of Hillel say: They mix the cup and then wash the
hands.

3. The School of Shammai say: A man wipes his hands with a napkin

¹ See Meg. 4³.
² Gem. 50a explains this as the ruling of R. Akiba (cf. end of paragraph). The following
differing opinion is that of R. Jose.   ³ Ps. 68²⁶.
⁴ In the Benediction at the reading of the Law (Singer, p. 68) which does not change
according to the number of those present. The name of God is used in the Benediction
which needs the presence of no more than ten.
⁵ To make up the number ten which renders it permissible to use the name of God.
⁶ See Pes. 10².

and lays it on the table. And the School of Hillel say: [He lays it] on the cushion.

4. The School of Shammai say: They sweep up the room and then wash the hands. And the School of Hillel say: They wash the hands and then sweep up the room.

5. The School of Shammai say: [The order of saying the Benedictions at the outgoing of the Sabbath is] the lamp, the food, the spices and the *Habdalah*.[1] And the School of Hillel say: The lamp, the spices, the food and the *Habdalah*. The School of Shammai say: [The Benediction over the lamp is, 'Blessed art thou] who didst create the light of fire'. And the School of Hillel say: ' . . . who createst the lights of fire'.

6. No Benediction may be said over the lamp or the spices of gentiles, or over a lamp or spices used for the dead, or over a lamp or spices used for idolatry. No Benediction may be said over a lamp until one can enjoy its light.

7. If a man ate and forgot to say the Benediction, the School of Shammai say: He must return to his place and say it. And the School of Hillel say: He may say it in the place where he remembers [his error]. Until what time may he say the Benediction? Until the food in his bowels is digested.

8. If wine is brought after the food and there is but that one cup, the School of Shammai say: The Benediction is said over the wine and then over the food. And the School of Hillel say: The Benediction is said over the food and then over the wine. They may answer 'Amen' after an Israelite who says a Benediction, but not after a Samaritan until they have heard the whole Benediction.

9. 1. If a man saw a place where miracles had been wrought for Israel he should say, 'Blessed is he that wrought miracles for our fathers in this place'. [If he saw] a place from which idolatry had been rooted out he should say, 'Blessed is he that rooted out idolatry from our land'.

2. [If he saw] shooting stars, earthquakes, lightnings, thunders and storms he should say, 'Blessed is he whose power and might fill the world'. [If he saw] mountains, hills, seas, rivers and deserts he should say, 'Blessed is the author of creation'. R. Judah says: If a man saw the Great Sea[2] he should say, 'Blessed is he that made the Great Sea', but only if he sees it at intervals of time. For rain and good tidings he should say, 'Blessed is he, the good and the doer of good'. For bad tidings he should say, 'Blessed is he, the true Judge'.

3. If a man built a house or bought new vessels he should say, 'Blessed is he that hath given us life'.[3] A man should say the Benediction for misfortune regardless of [any consequent] good, and for good fortune regardless of [any consequent] evil. If a man cries out [to God] over what is past, his prayer is vain. Thus if his wife was with child and he said, 'May it be thy will that my wife shall bear a male', this prayer is vain. If he was returning from a journey and heard a sound of lamentation in the city and said, 'May it be thy will that they [which make lamentation] be not of my house', this prayer is vain.

4. He that enters into a town should pray twice: once on his coming in and once on his going forth. Ben Azzai says: Four times: twice on his

---

[1] See App. I. 9.   [2] The Mediterranean.
[3] Some texts add: And hath preserved us and suffered us to come to this time.

coming in and twice on his going forth, offering thanks for what is past and making supplication for what is still to come.

5. Man is bound to bless [God] for the evil even as he blesses [God] for the good,[1] for it is written, *And thou shalt love the Lord thy God with all thy heart and with all thy soul and with all thy might.*[2] *With all thy heart* (*lebab*)—with both[3] thine impulses, thy good impulse and thine evil impulse; *and with all thy soul*—even if he take away thy soul; *and with all thy might*—with all thy wealth. Another explanation[4] is: *With all thy might* (*měodeka*)—for whichever measure (*middah o middah*) he measures out to thee, do thou give him thanks (*modeh*) exceedingly (*biměod měod*).

A man should not behave himself unseemly while opposite the Eastern Gate[5] [of the Temple] since it faces toward the Holy of Holies. He may not enter into the Temple Mount with his staff or his sandal or his wallet, or with the dust upon his feet, nor may he make of it a short by-path; still less may he spit there.[6]

At the close of every Benediction in the Temple they used to say, 'For everlasting'; but after the heretics[7] had taught corruptly and said that there is but one world,[8] it was ordained that they should say, 'From everlasting to everlasting'. And it was ordained that a man should salute his fellow with [the use of] the Name [of God]; for it is written, *And, behold, Boaz came from Bethlehem, and said unto the reapers, The Lord be with you. And they answered him, The Lord bless thee.*[9] And it is written, *The Lord is with thee, thou mighty man of valour.*[10] And it is written, *And despise not thy mother when she is old.*[11] And it is written, *It is time to work for the Lord: they have made void thy Law.*[12] R. Nathan says: They have made void thy Law because it was a time to work for the Lord.[13]

PEAH[14] ('GLEANINGS')

1. 1. These are things for which no measure is prescribed:[15] *Peah*,[16] First-fruits,[17] the Festal Offering,[18] deeds of loving-kindness and the study of the Law. These are things whose fruits a man enjoys in this world while the capital is laid up for him in the world to come: honouring father and

---

[1] Cf. above, 5[3]. [2] Deut. 6[5].

[3] Because 'heart' is here written in Hebrew with two *beths* (*lebab*) instead of but one (*leb*).

[4] An example of word-play characteristic of the rabbinical method of Midrash Haggadah (see App. I. 10). See Moore, ii. 253.

[5] See Midd. 2[4]. The Holy of Holies was visible from high ground on the slope of the Mount of Olives.

[6] The Cambridge manuscript adds: If it is forbidden to enter with shodden feet which implies lack of respect, how much more is spitting forbidden which implies contempt.

[7] A variant reading is 'Sadducees'. See *J.Q.R.* vi (1915), p. 314.

[8] The Heb. *ōlām* means both 'world' and 'eternity'.   [9] Ruth 2[4].   [10] Judg. 6[12].

[11] Prov. 23[22]. An ancient custom (like using God's name in greeting) may not lightly be set aside.   [12] Ps. 119[126].

[13] See Moore, i. 259. In times of emergency it may be right to set aside or amend the commandments of God enjoined in his Law: the Law may best be served by breaking it.

[14] The tractate deals with the biblical laws (Lev. 19[9f]; 23[22]; Deut. 24[19–21]) permitting the poor to glean in the fields and vineyards and from the olive trees; and also with 'Poorman's Tithe' (Deut. 14[28f]) which takes the place of Second Tithe (see p. 73, n. 6) in the third and sixth years of the seven-year cycle.   [15] In the written Law.

[16] Lit. 'corner', *sc.* of the field, where the owner is required by Lev. 19[9] and Lev. 23[22] to leave part of his crop unreaped for the benefit of the poor. Though the Law has pre-scribed no limit, the Scribes have fixed a minimum. See 1[2].   [17] Deut. 26[1–11].

[18] Heb. *Reayon*. Deut. 16[16] provides that all male Israelites shall appear thrice a year in the Temple (see App. I. 37) and that they 'shall not appear . . . empty', i.e. without an offering for the Temple; but the nature and value of the offering is not prescribed. See Hag. 1[1–2]. *Reayon* may equally well mean 'appearing', *sc.* in the Temple; i.e. the Israelite may enter the Temple as often as he pleases at the three Feasts.

mother, deeds of loving-kindness, making peace between a man and his fellow; and the study of the Law is equal to them all.

2. *Peah* should be not less than one-sixtieth part [of the harvest]. And although they have said that no measure is prescribed for *Peah*, it should ever accord with the size of the field and the number of the poor and the yield [of the harvest].[1]

3. *Peah* may be left at the beginning of the field or at the middle thereof. R. Simeon says: Provided that the prescribed measure is left at the end. R. Judah says: If a man left behind [at the last] but a single stalk he can rely on that as fulfilling the law of *Peah*, and if he did not [leave aught at the end] what he leaves [at the beginning or the middle of the field] counts only as ownerless property.[2]

4. A general rule have they enjoined concerning *Peah*: whatsoever is used for food and is kept watch over[3] and grows from the soil and is all reaped together and is brought in for storage is liable to the law of *Peah*. Grain and pulse come within this general rule.

5. Among trees, sumach, carob, walnut trees, almond trees, vines, pomegranate trees, olive trees, and palm trees are subject to the law of *Peah*.

6. A man may continue to grant *Peah* [even after the crop has been reaped] and be exempt from giving tithe from it until it is finally stacked. He may grant [part of his crop] as ownerless property and be exempt from giving tithe from it until it is finally stacked. He may feed cattle, wild animals or birds with it and be exempt from giving tithe from it until it is finally stacked. He may take it from the threshing-floor and use it for seed and be exempt from giving tithe from it until it is finally stacked. So R. Akiba. If a priest or a levite bought [the grain while it lay on] a threshing-floor they may keep the Tithe, unless it had been finally stacked. If a man dedicated [his harvest to the Temple] and redeemed it, he is still liable to give Tithe from it, unless the [Temple] treasurer had finally stacked it.

2. 1. These serve as bounds[4] in what concerns *Peah*: a river-bed or pond, a private or a public road, a public path or a private path that is in regular use during both the summer and the rainy season, fallow land and land newly broken up, and a different kind of crop. If a man cut young corn for fodder, [the part so reaped] acts as a bound. So R. Meir. But the Sages say: It does not act as a bound unless he ploughed it up [afresh].

2. If a water-channel [is so wide that the corn on either side] cannot be cut together, R. Judah says: It acts as a bound. If any hill top can be hoed with a mattock, even though the oxen cannot pass over with the plough, a single *Peah* is granted for the whole [field on both sides of the hill].

3. [These] all serve as bounds for sown crops, but a fence alone serves as a bound for [the *Peah* that is granted from] trees. If the branches of the trees [on either side of the fence] were intertwined, the fence does not serve as a bound, and a single *Peah* is granted for all [the trees on either side].

4. For all carob trees that are within sight of each other [a single *Peah* is granted even if fences intervene]. Rabban Gamaliel said: In my father's house they used to grant *Peah* separately for their olive trees in each quarter

---

[1] Or 'according to the poverty (of the people)'; i.e. where poverty is severe *Peah* should be abundant.

[2] It does not fulfil the law of *Peah*, but is available for the rich as well as the poor.

[3] Private property as distinct from ownerless produce. Cf. Maas. 1[1].

[4] i.e. mark out certain areas as units, from each of which *Peah* must be given.

[of the city], and for all carob trees that were within sight of each other.
R. Eliezer the son of R. Zadok says in his name: [A single *Peah*] was granted
for their carob trees also throughout the whole city.

5. If a man sowed his field in one kind, even if he made up two threshing-
floors he need grant but one *Peah*; if he had sown it in two kinds, even if
he made up but one threshing-floor he must grant two *Peahs*. If he sowed
his field in two kinds of wheat and made up one threshing-floor, he grants
one *Peah*; but if two threshing-floors, he must grant two *Peahs*.

6. It once happened that R. Simeon of Mizpah [thus] sowed [his field
and came] before Rabban Gamaliel; and they went up to the Chamber of
Hewn Stone[1] to inquire. Nahum the Scrivener said: I have received a
tradition from R. Measha, who received it from his father,[2] who received
it from the *Zugoth*,[3] who received it from the Prophets as a *Halakah* given
to Moses from Sinai,[4] that if a man sowed his field in two kinds of wheat
and made them up into one threshing-floor, he grants one *Peah*; but if
two threshing-floors, he must grant two *Peahs*.

7. If a field was reaped by gentiles or by robbers, or if ants nibbled the
crop, or if wind or cattle broke it down, it is exempt from *Peah*. If the
owner reaped half and thieves reaped [the remaining] half, it is exempt,
since his liability to *Peah* applied [only] to [the half of the crop that he had
left as] standing corn.

8. If thieves reaped half and the owner reaped [the remaining] half, he
must grant *Peah* from what he has reaped. If he reaped half and sold [the
remaining] half, the buyer must grant *Peah* for the whole. If he reaped
half and dedicated [the remaining] half, he that redeems it from the
[Temple] treasurer must grant *Peah* for the whole.

3. 1. If between olive trees there were plots sown with grain, the School
of Shammai say: *Peah* must be granted from every plot. And the School
of Hillel say: From one for all. But they agree that if the ends of the rows
[of corn] were confused, *Peah* is granted from one [plot] for all.

2. If a man reaped his field in patches, leaving [unreaped] the unripe
stems, R. Akiba says: He must grant *Peah* from every patch. But the Sages
say: From one [patch] for all. The Sages agree with R. Akiba that if a man
sowed dill or mustard seed in three separate places he must grant *Peah*
from each.

3. If he uprooted fresh onions for the market and suffered others to
remain and dry for the store-chamber, he must grant *Peah* from these by
themselves and *Peah* from these by themselves; so, too, with peas and so,
too, with a vineyard. If he thinned them out he need grant [*Peah*] from
what is left [only] according to the quantity that he has suffered to remain;
but if he uprooted them from one place only[5] he must grant *Peah* from what
is left for the whole.

4. Seed-onions are liable to *Peah*. But R. Jose declares them exempt.

---

[1] Cf. Sanh. 11[2]; Eduy. 7[4]; Tam. 2[5]; 4[3]; Midd. 5[4].

[2] Heb. *Abba*. This may be a proper name.

[3] Cf. Ab. 1[4ff]. Lit. 'pairs' of leaders ('President' and 'Father of the Court') from the time
of Jose b. Joezer, *c.* 160 B.C., to the time of Hillel and Shammai. See Hag. 2[2].

[4] A formula (occurring again in Eduy. 8[7]; Yad. 4[3]) denoting an established, ageless tradition not derived or derivable from the Written Law. Compare the formula used in the same
sense, 'Rightly have they said' (Kil. 2[2]; Ter. 2[1]; Shab. 1[3]; 10[4]; Naz. 7[3]).

[5] So Maim. But Bert. renders: If he uprooted some for the selfsame purpose (for which
he leaves the rest).

If plots of onions grew among vegetables, R. Jose says: *Peah* is granted from each. But the Sages say: From one for all.

5. If [two] brothers [who were jointholders] separate, they must grant two *Peahs*; but if they become again jointholders they need grant but one *Peah*. If two persons bought a tree they need grant but one *Peah*; but if one bought the northern half and the other the southern half, each must grant *Peah* separately. If a man sold only the stems of the plants in his field [and not their soil], the buyer must grant *Peah* from each plant. R. Judah said: This applies if the owner of the field had kept back naught for himself; but if the owner of the field had kept back aught for himself he must grant *Peah* for the whole.

6. R. Eliezer says: A quarter-*kab's* space[1] of ground is subject to the law of *Peah*. R. Joshua says : [Ground] that will produce two *seahs*.[2] R. Tarfon says: [Ground measuring] six handbreadths by six. R. Judah b. Bathyra says: [Ground large enough] to need two strokes of the sickle. And the *Halakah* is according to him. R. Akiba says: Any ground soever is subject to the laws of *Peah* and First-fruits; a *prozbol*[3] can be written on its security, and in conjunction with it movable property[4] can be acquired by money, by writ or by usucaption.[5]

7. If one that lay sick[6] assigned his goods to others [as a gift] and kept back any land soever,[7] [if he recovered] his gift remains valid; but if he had kept back no land soever[8] his gift does not remain valid. If he assigned his goods to his children and assigned to his wife any land soever, she forfeits her *Ketubah*.[9] R. Jose says: If she accepted [such an assignment] even though he did not indeed assign it to her,[10] she forfeits her *Ketubah*.

8. If a man assigned his goods to his slave,[11] he becomes a freedman. If he kept back any land soever,[12] he does not become a freedman. R. Simeon says: In either case he becomes a freedman unless the master says, 'Let all my goods be given to such-a-one, my slave, excepting one ten-thousandth part of them'.[13]

4. 1. *Peah* is granted from what is still joined to the ground. From trellised vines and date palms the householder fetches down [the fruit] and distributes it to the poor. R. Simeon says: So, too, with walnut trees. If even ninety-nine were in favour of *Peah* being distributed and but one was in favour of helping themselves, they must listen to him since he has spoken according to *Halakah*.

2. But it is not so with trellised vines and date palms. If even ninety-nine were in favour of helping themselves and but one was in favour of *Peah* being distributed, they must listen to him since he has spoken according to *Halakah*.

---

[1] See App. II, E.   [2] See App. II, D.   [3] See App. I. 34.
[4] Cf. Kidd. 1[5]. Movable property by itself can only be acquired by the purchaser's 'drawing' it towards himself. See B.M. 4[2]; B.B. 5[7].   [5] See B.B. 3[ff].
[6] Likely to die. See B.B. 9[6].
[7] Showing that he had not assigned the rest in anticipation of death.
[8] Showing that he assigned the land only on the assumption that he was about to die.
[9] See App. I. 16. The presumption is that she accepted the assignment in lieu of her *Ketubah*.
[10] It is still to be presumed that she was willing to share with the sons in the inheritance and to forego her claim to her *Ketubah*.
[11] The slave is himself 'goods' and he thus becomes his own possessor.
[12] The slave is still in part enslaved to the owner who has still kept back for himself part of his 'goods'—including the slave.
[13] By which he may have intended to leave the slave himself out of the assignment.

3. If one [of the poor] took part of the *Peah* and threw it over the rest,[1] naught of it belongs to him. If he fell down upon it or spread his cloak over it,[1] it must be taken away. And the same applies to Gleanings[2] and the Forgotten Sheaf.[3]

4. They may not cut the *Peah* with sickles or uproot it with spades, lest they strike one another.

5. [The poor may make] three searches during the day: in the morning, at midday, and at sunset. Rabban Gamaliel says: This is enjoined only lest they search less often. R. Akiba says: This is enjoined only lest they search more often. [The men] of Beth Namer[4] used to reap their crops by the measuring-line and leave *Peah* from every furrow.

6. If a gentile reaped his field and afterward became a proselyte he is exempt from [the law of] Gleanings, the Forgotten Sheaf and *Peah*. R. Judah declares him liable to the law of the Forgotten Sheaf, since that applies at the time of sheaf-binding.

7. If a man dedicated his standing corn and redeemed it while [it was yet] standing corn, he is subject [to the law of the Forgotten Sheaf]. [If he dedicated it while it was] bound up in sheaves and redeemed it while [it was yet] bound up in sheaves, he is still subject [to the law of the Forgotten Sheaf]. [But if he dedicated it while it was yet] standing corn and redeemed it after it was bound up in sheaves, his crop is exempt, since at the time when it would have been liable it was exempt.[5]

8. In like manner if a man dedicated his produce before it had become liable to Tithes[6] and then redeemed it, it is still liable [to Tithes]; if he dedicated it after it had become liable to Tithes and then redeemed it, it is still liable. But if he had dedicated it before it was ripe and it ripened in the charge of the [Temple] treasurer, and he afterward redeemed it, it is exempt [from Tithes], since at the time when it would have been liable it was exempt.

9. If a man gathered up *Peah* and said, 'This is for the poor man such-a-one', R. Eliezer says: It belongs rightfully to such-a-one. But the Sages say: He must give it to the poor man that is found first. The Gleanings, Forgotten Sheaf and *Peah* [that have been taken by the poor from the field] of a gentile are liable to Tithes, unless he had declared them ownerless property.

10. What counts as 'Gleanings'? Whatsoever drops down at the moment of reaping. If a reaper reaped an armful or plucked a handful, and a thorn pricked him and [what he held] fell from his hand to the ground, this belongs to the householder. [What falls from] within the hand or the sickle [belongs] to the poor; [what falls from] the back of the hand or the sickle [belongs] to the householder. [What falls from] the top of the hand or the sickle, R. Ishmael says: [It belongs] to the poor. R. Akiba says: To the householder.

11. [What is found in] ant-holes while the corn is still standing, belongs to the householder; after the reapers [have passed over them], what lies

---

[1] As an assertion that he claimed it.   [2] See below, 4[10].   [3] Deut. 24[19-21]. See below, 5[8].
[4] See Num. 32[36]. Perhaps the modern Nimrin in Transjordan. Also explained as a family name. Modern commentators explain Beth Namer as a field cultivated in irregular strips and patches (see 3[2], where a verbal form of *namer*, 'leopard', is used).
[5] Since the poor have no claims on what is dedicated to the Temple.
[6] Namely when it ripens. See Maas. 1[2ff]. Under 'Tithes' is understood Heave-offering, First (or Levitic) Tithe and Second Tithe or (in the 3rd and 6th years) Poorman's Tithe.

uppermost [in the ant-holes] belongs to the poor, and what is beneath belongs to the householder. R. Meir says: It belongs to the poor in either case, since Gleanings that are in doubt are deemed to be Gleanings.

5. 1. If Gleanings have not been taken from beneath [a place where stands] a heap of corn, whatsoever touches the ground belongs to the poor. If the wind scattered the sheaves [over ground from which Gleanings have not been taken] they estimate what Gleanings the field was like to have yielded, and this they give to the poor. Rabban Simeon b. Gamaliel says: They give to the poor as much as the field would require for seed.[1]

2. If[2] the tip of an ear of corn left standing after the reaping touches the standing corn, and it can be reaped together with the standing corn, it belongs to the householder; otherwise it belongs to the poor. If an ear of corn belonging to the Gleanings was confused with corn that was stacked, the householder must tithe[3] an ear of corn and give it to him. R. Eliezer said: But how can this poor man be given aught in exchange for what he has never possessed?[4]—but, rather, the poor man is granted ownership in the whole heap, and then an ear of corn is tithed and given to him.

3. They may not water the field with a pitcher[5] [before Gleanings have been taken]. So R. Meir. But the Sages permit it because it is [still] possible [for the poor to receive their dues].

4. If a householder was travelling from one place to another and it became needful for him to take Gleanings, the Forgotten Sheaf or *Peah*, or Poorman's Tithe,[6] he may take them, and when he returns to his house he should make restitution. So R. Eliezer. But the Sages say: [He need make no restitution because] at that time he was a poor man.

5. If a man gave the poor aught in exchange [for their Gleanings] what [they give] in exchange for his is exempt [from Tithes], but what [he gives] in exchange for theirs is liable [to Tithes]. If two [poor] men had leased a field on sharing terms,[7] each may give the other his portion of Poorman's Tithe. If a [poor] man undertook to reap a field he is forbidden to take Gleanings, the Forgotten Sheaf, *Peah*, or Poorman's Tithe. R. Judah said: This applies if he received it from the owner on condition of paying a half, third, or quarter [of the harvest]; but if the owner had said to him, 'The third of what thou reapest shall be thine', he is permitted to take Gleanings, the Forgotten Sheaf, and *Peah*, but he is forbidden Poorman's Tithe.

6. If a man sold his field he that sells it is permitted [to benefit from what falls to the poor], but the buyer is forbidden. A man may not hire labourers on the condition that a labourer's son shall glean behind him. If a man will not suffer the poor to glean or suffers one and not another,

---

1 So Maim. See B.M. 9[5]. Bert. and Tif. Yis. would render, 'according to the proportion that usually falls (at the time of reaping)', namely one forty-fifth part.
2 Eduy. 2[4].
3 He must give the poor something that is already certainly tithe-free, since the ear of corn, which was the poor man's due, is tithe-free.
4 According to 4[9] the owner cannot grant *Peah* to any poor man in particular.
5 Because this makes it harder for the poor to glean. Maim. and Bert. render, 'They may not (in sowing) mix vetchlings (with the rest of the grain, since this would be to the detriment of the poor).
6 In the 3rd and 6th years of the Sabbatic cycle, what in other years would be set apart as Second Tithe (see p. 73, n. 6) is given to the poor (Deut. 14[29]).
7 Heb. *arisuth*; they agree to pay the owner a fixed proportion of the crop as rent; or the owner agrees to pay the cultivator a fixed proportion as his hire.

or aids one of them, he is a robber of the poor. Of such a one it is written, *Remove not the landmark of them that come up.*[1]

7. If the labourers forgot a sheaf but the householder had not forgotten it; or if the householder forgot it but the labourers had not forgotten it; or if the poor stood in front of it or covered it with stubble, this is not [rightfully] a Forgotten Sheaf.

8. If he was removing the sheaves elsewhere to bind them into cap-shaped covers or bottom-pieces [for stacks] or cake-shaped [stacks] or [to refashion them] into [larger] sheaves, the law of the Forgotten Sheaf does not apply; if they were taken thence to the threshing-floor the law of the Forgotten Sheaf applies. If he removed the sheaves to the stack, the law of the Forgotten Sheaf applies; but from thence to the threshing-floor the law of the Forgotten Sheaf does not apply. This is the general rule: while the sheaves are taken to the place that marks the end of their preparation, the law of the Forgotten Sheaf applies; but from thence to the threshing-floor the law of the Forgotten Sheaf does not apply; while they are taken to a place that does not mark the end of their preparation the law of the Forgotten Sheaf does not apply; but from thence to the threshing-floor the law of the Forgotten Sheaf applies.

6. 1. The School of Shammai say:[2] [If produce is proclaimed] 'ownerless' for the benefit of the poor it is deemed ownerless [and Tithe-free]. And the School of Hillel say: It can only be deemed ownerless [and Tithe-free] if it is proclaimed ownerless [equally] for the benefit of the rich, as in the Year of Release.[3] If the sheaves in a field were each of one *kab's*[4] bulk and one was of four *kabs*, if this was forgotten the School of Shammai say: It may not be deemed a Forgotten Sheaf. And the School of Hillel say: It may be deemed a Forgotten Sheaf.

2. If a sheaf lay near to a wall or to a stack or to the oxen or to the implements, and it was forgotten, the School of Shammai say: It may not be deemed a Forgotten Sheaf.[5] And the School of Hillel say: It may be deemed a Forgotten Sheaf.

3. [Whether any sheaf at] the ends of rows [may or may not be deemed a Forgotten Sheaf] is proved by a sheaf lying over against it. If the householder laid hold of a sheaf to take it to the city and forgot it, they agree that this may not be deemed a Forgotten Sheaf.

4. These conditions apply to ends of rows: If two began [to gather the sheaves] in the middle of the row, the one facing north and the other facing south,[6] and they forgot [sheaves that had been] in front of them and behind them, what was in front of them may be deemed a Forgotten Sheaf, but what had been behind them [from the beginning] may not be deemed a Forgotten Sheaf; if one alone began from the end of the row and forgot [sheaves] in front of him and behind him, what was in front of him may not be deemed a Forgotten Sheaf, but what was behind may be deemed a Forgotten Sheaf; for here applies the rule, *Thou shalt not go again.*[7] This is the general rule: where the law *Thou shalt not go again* applies, the law of the Forgotten Sheaf applies, but where the law *Thou shalt not go again* does not apply, the law of the Forgotten Sheaf does not apply.

[1] Prov. 22[28]. For *olam*, 'of old', the Mishnah reads *olim*, 'they that come up', meaning either Israelites generally who 'came up' from Egypt, or, euphemistically, those who 'have come down', i.e. become poor. So also in Peah 7[3].   [2] Eduy. 4[3].   [3] Deut. 15[1ff].
[4] See App. II, D.   [5] One may assume that it was deposited there of set purpose.
[6] They are turned back to back with some sheaves between them.   [7] Deut. 24[19].

5. Two sheaves together may be deemed Forgotten Sheaves; three together may not be deemed Forgotten Sheaves. Two heaps of olives or carobs may be deemed 'Forgotten Sheaves'; three may not. Two stalks of flax may be deemed 'Forgotten Sheaves'; three may not. Two grapes may count as grape-gleanings; three may not. Two ears of corn may count as Gleanings;[1] three may not. These [rulings] are according to the School of Hillel. Of them all the School of Shammai say: Where there are three they belong to the poor; where there are four they belong to the householder.

6. If a sheaf containing two *seahs* was forgotten it may not be deemed a Forgotten Sheaf. If there were two sheaves containing two *seahs* between them [and they were forgotten], Rabban Gamaliel says: They belong to the householder. But the Sages say: To the poor. Rabban Gamaliel said: Is the householder's claim strengthened or weakened according to the greater number of the sheaves? They replied: It is strengthened. He said to them: If, therefore, one sheaf containing two *seahs*, when it is forgotten, may not be deemed a Forgotten Sheaf, is not the inference that two sheaves, also containing two *seahs*, shall not be deemed a Forgotten sheaf! They replied: No! as thou arguest of one sheaf, which is as large as a stack, wouldst thou argue also of two sheaves, which are as small as bundles![2]

7. If standing corn containing two *seahs* was forgotten it may not be deemed a Forgotten Sheaf. If it did not contain two *seahs* but was fit to produce two *seahs*, even if it was but a crop of vetchlings, it must be regarded as though it was a yield of barley.

8. Standing corn [that has not been forgotten] saves a sheaf and [other] standing corn [from being deemed forgotten]. A sheaf saves neither [another] sheaf nor standing corn. What standing corn saves the sheaf? Aught soever that has not been forgotten, even though it was but a single stalk.

9. A *seah* of plucked corn and a *seah* of unplucked corn (and the same applies to fruit-trees, garlic and onions) may not be included together to make up two *seahs*, but must be left for the poor. R. Jose says: If aught that rightly falls to the poor separates them they may not be included together; otherwise they may be included together.

10. Corn that is used for green-fodder or for binding up sheaves (and the same applies to binding-stalks of garlic and bunches of garlic and onions) may not be deemed a Forgotten Sheaf. And whatsoever is stored away in the ground, like arum, garlic and onions, R. Judah says: They may not be deemed a Forgotten Sheaf. But the Sages say: They may be deemed a Forgotten Sheaf.

11. If a man reaped by night and tied up sheaves, or if the reaper was blind, the law of the Forgotten Sheaf [still] applies. If he purposed to take away the larger sheaves only, the law of the Forgotten Sheaf does not apply. If he said, 'I am reaping on the condition that what I forget I will take away [afterward]', the law of the Forgotten Sheaf [still] applies.

7. 1. If an olive tree in a field has its special fame, such as an olive tree yielding much oil[3] in its season, and it is forgotten, the law of the Forgotten Sheaf does not apply to it. This applies only to [a tree having] its [special]

---

[1] Lev. 19[10].
[2] For other examples of similar argumentation, cf. Pes. 6[5]; Ned. 10[6]; Shebu. 3[6]; Zeb. 7[4]; Men. 12[5]; Hull. 4[4]; Ker. 3[9,10].   [3] Or, 'as a Netophah olive tree'. For Netophah see Ezr. 2[22].

name, or its [special] works, or its [special] place; its name—that it was a 'Shifkoni' or 'Beshani' tree;[1] its works—that it yielded much; and its place—that it stood beside the winepress or the gap in the wall. But as for other olive trees, if two of them were forgotten the law of the Forgotten Sheaf applies; but if three, it does not apply. R. Jose says: The law of the Forgotten Sheaf does not apply to olive trees.

2. If an olive tree stood among three rows [of other olive trees] bordering two plots [of sown ground], and was forgotten, the law of the Forgotten Sheaf does not apply. If an olive tree which bears two *seahs* was forgotten, the law of the Forgotten Sheaf does not apply. This is so only if they had not begun to pick the tree; but if they had already begun (even if [it is known] as an olive tree yielding much oil[2] in its season), and had then forgotten it, the law of the Forgotten Sheaf applies. So long as aught remains [ungathered on the ground] below [the tree], what is left above still belongs to the householder. R. Meir says: Only after the beater [that knocks off hidden olives] has gone by [does the law of the Forgotten Sheaf apply to what is left].

3. What counts as 'grape-gleanings'?[3] [Single grapes] that fall to the ground during the vintage. If during the vintage the gatherer cut off a cluster which became entangled in the leaves and fell from his hand to the ground, and berries fell off, they still belong to the householder. If a man put a basket beneath the vine while he was gathering the grapes, such a one is a robber of the poor. Of him it is written, *Remove not the landmark of them that come up.*[4]

4. What counts as 'a defective grape-cluster'?[5] Any cluster that lacks both shoulder and pendant. If it has still either shoulder or pendant it belongs to the householder; if it is in doubt, it belongs to the poor. If a defective cluster on the crutch of a branch was cut off together with a cluster [that was not defective], it belongs to the householder; otherwise it belongs to the poor. If a grape grew singly, R. Judah says: It counts as a cluster. But the Sages say: As a defective cluster.

5. If a man thinned out his vines, he may thin out what belongs to the poor like as he thins out what belongs to himself.[6] So R. Judah. R. Meir says: He has rights over what is his but not over what belongs to the poor.

6. The School of Shammai say: The rules of the [Added] Fifth[7] and of Removal[8] do not apply to [the grapes of] a Fourth Year Vineyard.[9] And the School of Hillel say: They do apply. The School of Shammai say: The laws of grape-gleanings and of the defective cluster apply, and the poor redeem the grapes for themselves.[10] And the School of Hillel say: The whole yield goes to the winepress.[11]

7. If a vineyard has in it naught save defective clusters, R. Eliezer says: They belong to the householder. R. Akiba says: To the poor. R. Eliezer

---

[1] i.e. from Beisan (Beth Shean). These two names may be taken as adjectives, meaning 'profusely yielding' and 'ill-yielding'. The latter is also interpreted 'putting (other trees) to shame (by its heavy yield)'.   [2] See p. 17, n. 3.   [3] Heb. *peret*. Lev. 19[10].   [4] See p. 16, n. 1.
[5] Heb. *oleleth*; used (in the plural) in Is. 17[6]; 24[13] in the general sense of grape-gleanings.
[6] i.e. he may thin out the single grapes and the defective clusters.   [7] See B.M. 4[8].
[8] See M. Sh. 5[6]. 'Removal' and the Added Fifth (when the fruit is substituted by its money value) apply to Second Tithe.
[9] After the first three years of 'the fruit of its uncircumcision' (Lev. 19[23-5]) the fruit of any tree (not of vines only) that grows in the fourth year (or the money with which it has been redeemed) must be taken up to Jerusalem and there consumed in conditions similar to those prescribed for Second Tithe (p. 73, n. 6). See M. Sh. 5[4ff].
[10] And take them to Jerusalem.   [11] Of the householder.

said: [It is written], *When thou gatherest the grapes of thy vineyard thou shalt not take the defective clusters.*[1] Since there can be no grape-gathering how can there be defective clusters [for the gleaners]? R. Akiba replied: [It is written], *And from thy vineyard thou shalt not take the defective clusters;*[2]—even though all the grapes are defective clusters. Why, then, is it written, *When thou gatherest the grapes of thy vineyard thou shalt not take the defective clusters?* [To teach that] the poor have no claim to the defective clusters before the vintage.

8. If a man dedicated his vineyard before it can be known which are the defective clusters, the poor have no claim to them; but if he dedicated it after it was known which were the defective clusters, they belong to the poor. R. Jose says: They must reward the Temple for their increase. To what does the law of the Forgotten Sheaf apply in a trellised vine? To whatsoever is beyond a man's reach. And in a ground-trained vine? [To whatsoever is left] after the grape-gatherer has passed by it.

8. 1. From what time are all men permitted to glean from the field? After the last of the poor have gone. And to take grape-gleanings and defective clusters? After the poor have gone into the vineyard and returned. And to glean from the olive trees? After the second rainfall.[3] R. Judah said: But are there not some that do not pick their olives until after the second rainfall?—but, rather, [others may not glean from the olive trees] until such time that when a poor man goes forth he cannot bring back more than four *issars'*[4] worth.

2. [The poor] may be believed[5] about Gleanings, the Forgotten Sheaf, and *Peah* in their season, and Poorman's Tithe in the year thereof.[6] The levite may be believed[7] at all times. But they may be believed only about produce that men are accustomed to give them.

3. [The poor] may be believed about [unground] wheat, but not meal or bread. They may be believed about rice in the husk, but not [husked rice] whether uncooked or cooked. They may be believed about beans, but not crushed beans, whether uncooked or cooked. They may be believed about oil if they say, 'It is Poorman's Tithe', but not if they say, 'It is from olive gleanings'.

4. They may be believed about vegetables that are raw but not if they are cooked, unless the quantity is small; for such is the custom of a householder to take out of his stewpot [and give to the poor].

5. They may not give to the poor from the threshing-floor [as Poorman's Tithe] less than a half-*kab* of wheat or a *kab* of barley (R. Meir says: A half-*kab* of barley) or a *kab* and a half of spelt or a *kab* of dried figs or a *mina* of fig-cake (R. Akiba says: Half a *mina*), a half-*log* of wine (R. Akiba says: A quarter), or a quarter-*log* of oil (R. Akiba says: An eighth). Of any other produce, Abba Saul says: [They should be given] so much that, if they sell it, they can buy therewith food for two meals.

6. This measure is prescribed for priests, for levites, and for Israelites alike. If a man would keep aught back [for his own poor kinsfolk] he should take away half and give half [to the poor that come to him]. If he has but

---

[1] Deut. 24²¹.   [2] Lev. 19¹⁰.   [3] See Shebi. 9⁷. It was about November.   [4] See App. II, A.
[5] When he so describes what he sells to an 'Associate' (see p. 20, n. 9). As such they are tithe-free and the 'Associate' need not assume that they are *Demai*, not certainly tithed.
[6] Namely the 3rd and 6th years of the sabbatic cycle.
[7] If he says that produce, which he is selling, is First Tithe from which Heave-offering of Tithe has been duly separated.

little [and cannot give each of the poor the prescribed measure], he should set it before them while they divide it among themselves.

7. A poor man that is journeying from place to place should be given not less than one loaf worth a *pondion* [from wheat costing] one *sela* for four *seahs*.[1] If he spends the night [in such a place] he should be given what is needful to support him for the night. If he stays over the Sabbath he should be given food enough for three meals. If a man has food enough for two meals he may not take aught from the [Paupers'] Dish,[2] and if enough for fourteen meals he may not take aught from the [Poor]-Fund. The [Poor-]Fund is collected by two and distributed by three.

8. If a man had two hundred *zuz* he may not take Gleanings, the Forgotten Sheaf, *Peah* or Poorman's Tithe; if he had two hundred less one *denar*,[3] and even a thousand [householders] together gave him each [one *denar*], he may take [Gleanings, the Forgotten Sheaf, *Peah* or Poorman's Tithe]. If his goods were pledged to his creditor or were security for his wife's *Ketubah*, he may take [Gleanings, the Forgotten Sheaf, *Peah*, or Poorman's Tithe]. They may not compel a man to sell his house or his articles of service.

9. If a man had fifty *zuz* and he traded with them, he may not take [Gleanings, the Forgotten Sheaf, *Peah* or Poorman's Tithe]. He that does not need to take them yet takes them shall not depart from this world before he falls in need of his fellow men; but he that needs to take them yet does not take them shall not die in old age before he has come to support others out of his own goods. Of such a one it is written, *Blessed is the man that trusteth in the Lord, and whose hope the Lord is.*[4] And if a man is not lame or dumb or blind or halting, yet makes himself like to one of them, he shall not die in old age before he becomes like to one of them, as it is written, *But he that searcheth after mischief it shall come unto him.*[5] And again it is written, *That which is altogether just shalt thou follow.*[6] So, too, is it with a judge that judges a judgement of truth according to its truth. And[7] any judge that takes a bribe and perverts judgement shall not die in old age before his eyes wax dim, as it is written, *And thou shalt take no gift, for a gift blindeth them that have sight.*[8]

DEMAI[9] ('PRODUCE NOT CERTAINLY TITHED')

1. 1. The rules about *demai*-produce do not apply rigidly to wild figs, jujube fruit, hawthorn berries, white figs, sycamore figs, fruit fallen off the

---

[1] Cf. Erub. 8[2].   [2] Cf. Pes. 10[1].   [3] Or *zuz*.   [4] Jer. 17[7].   [5] Prov. 11[27].
[6] Deut. 16[20].   [7] Some texts omit the rest of the paragraph.   [8] Ex. 23[8].
[9] The uninstructed 'People of the land', the *Amme-haaretz*, are under suspicion of not giving Tithes from their produce. They are not, however, suspected of not giving Heave-offering, because this has a higher degree of sanctity and is only a light exaction—it may be fulfilled by giving the priest a single grain of wheat. Their produce is styled *Demai*, doubtful, i.e. it is in doubt whether it has been tithed. Therefore a scrupulous observer of the Law, an 'Associate' (see below, 2[3]), who buys produce from an *Am-haaretz*, must still separate from it (*a*) the portion that is due to the priest out of the First Tithe, namely 'the Heave-offering of Tithe', which is one-hundredth part of the *demai*-produce; and (*b*) Second Tithe in the years when that applies (the 1st, 2nd, 4th, and 5th years of the sabbatic cycle). The former must be set aside and given to a priest, because the penalty of death (at the hands of Heaven) is incurred by the non-priest who eats of it; and Second Tithe may not be eaten in uncleanness and outside of Jerusalem. He need not, however, do more than 'designate' a portion as First Tithe or (in its prescribed years, the 3rd and 6th) Poorman's Tithe, since the onus rests in such cases on the levite or poor man to prove that the produce has not already paid First Tithe and Poorman's Tithe. These rules about *demai*-produce were laid down (Sot. 48a) by Johanan the High Priest (Sot. 9[10]; M. Sh. 5[15]). Characteristically the Mishnah does not state them but takes them for granted.

date palm, late ripening grapes and thorny-capers; or, in Judea, to sumach, Judean[1] vinegar, and coriander. R. Judah says: All wild figs are exempt excepting those bearing twice a year;[2] all jujube fruits are exempt excepting those of Shikmonah; all sycamore figs are exempt excepting those that [ripen on the tree until they] break open.

2. The rules of the [Added] Fifth[3] and of Removal[4] do not apply to [Second Tithe from] *demai*-produce; it may be eaten by a mourner;[5] it may be brought into Jerusalem and taken out;[6] if small in quantity it may be lost by the way;[7] it may be given to an *Am-haaretz*[8] and the like quantity [of other produce] eaten [in Jerusalem];[9] [its redemption price][10] may be converted to common use, silver [coins] being exchanged for [other] silver [coins], or copper for copper, or silver for copper; and copper [coin that is Second Tithe redemption money may be exchanged] for produce,[11] provided that one again redeems[12] the produce [by money]. So R. Meir. But the Sages say: The produce [itself] is brought up and consumed in Jerusalem.

3. If a man bought it for sowing or for [feeding] cattle, or if it was meal for [preparing] hides, or oil for the lamp, or oil for greasing utensils, it is exempt from the rules of *demai*-produce. [Produce from] the country beyond Chezib[13] is exempt from the rules of *demai*-produce. The Dough-offering[14] of an *Am-haaretz*, produce mixed with Heave-offering,[15] produce bought with Second Tithe money, and the residues of the Meal-offerings are exempt from the rules of *demai*-produce.[16] Sweet oil, the School of Shammai declare liable, but the School of Hillel declare it exempt.

4. *Demai*-produce may be used for an *Erub* or for *Shittuf*;[17] the Benediction over food and the Common Grace[18] may be said over it; [Tithes] may be set apart from it [even] if the man be naked,[19] or at twilight [on the eve of Sabbath].[20] If the Second Tithe is taken from it before the First Tithe it matters naught.[21] The oil with which the weaver greases his fingers is subject to the rules of *demai*-produce, but the oil which the woolcomber puts on the wool is exempt.

2. 1. Tithe must everywhere[22] be given from these things as being *demai*-produce: fig-cake, dates, carobs, rice, and cummin; but whosoever uses rice from outside the Land [of Israel] is exempt.

2. He that undertakes to be trustworthy[23] must give tithe from what he eats and from what he sells and from what he buys [to sell again]; and he may not be the guest of an *Am-haaretz*. R. Judah says: Even he that is the guest of an *Am-haaretz* may still be reckoned trustworthy. They

---

[1] Some texts omit.   [2] Or, 'those of Dufra'. See also Shebi. 9[4].
[3] When it is redeemed (Lev. 27[31]). Cf. B.M. 4[8].
[4] See Deut. 14[28]; 26[13]. Cf. M. Sh. 5[6ff, 10].   [5] Deut. 26[14].
[6] Contrary to the regular use (M. Sh. 3[5]).   [7] If it is burdensome.
[8] Even though he will eat it in uncleanness.   [9] In cleanness.
[10] To which the sanctity of the Second Tithe is transferred.
[11] All of which are contrary to the regular use. M. Sh. 2[5-8].
[12] Variant: And he may again redeem.
[13] The biblical Achzib, Judg. 1[31]. It was the northernmost town within the borders of Palestine, 9 miles N. of Acre.   [14] Num. 15[21]. See p. 83, n. 1.
[15] If the Heave-offering is a hundredth part, or more, of the mixture it must, usually, be sold to a priest because of the Heave-offering in it.
[16] The *Am-haaretz* can be presumed to have duly tithed them all owing to the exceptional sanctity attaching to them.   [17] See App. I. 8 and 39. See Erub. 3[1, 2].   [18] Ber. 7[1].
[19] See Ter. 1[6].   [20] Shab. 2[7].   [21] See M. Sh. 5[11]; Ter. 3[6].
[22] Even beyond Chezib.   [23] i.e. scrupulous in giving Tithes.

replied: He would not be trustworthy in what concerns himself; how then could he be trustworthy in what concerns others?[1]

3. He that undertakes to be an Associate[2] may not sell to an *Am-haaretz* [foodstuff that is] wet[3] or dry, or buy from him [foodstuff that is] wet; and he may not be the guest of an *Am-haaretz* nor may he receive him as a guest in his own raiment.[4] R. Judah says: Nor may he rear small cattle[5] or be profuse in vows or levity or contract uncleanness because of the dead, but he should minister in the House of Study. They said to him: These things come not within the scope of the subject [of the Associate].

4. If [they that undertake to be Associates are] bakers, the Sages lay upon them only the duty of setting apart [from *demai*-produce] enough for Heave-offering of Tithe and Dough-offering. If [they are] shop-keepers, they may not sell *demai*-produce. All that deal in large quantities may sell *demai*-produce. Who are they that deal in large quantities? The like of wholesale merchants and dealers in grain.

5. R. Meir says: If what is usually measured out in large quantities is measured out in small quantities, the small quantity falls under the rule governing large quantities; if what is usually measured out in small quantities is measured out in large quantities, the large quantity falls under the rule governing small quantities. What is accounted a large quantity? Three *kabs* dry measure or a *denar's* worth of liquid. R. Jose says: If baskets of figs or baskets of grapes or hampers of vegetables are sold by estimation, they are exempt [from the rules of *demai*-produce].

3. 1. *Demai*-produce may be given to the poor and to billeted troops[6] to eat. Rabban Gamaliel used to give *demai*-produce to his labourers to eat. The School of Shammai say: Almoners should give what has been tithed to them that do not give tithe and what is untithed to them that do give tithe; thus all will eat of what is duly tithed. But the Sages say: Almoners may collect food and distribute it regardless [of the rules of *demai*-produce], and let him that is minded to tithe it [according to the rules of *demai*-produce] tithe it.

2. If a man would lop off the leaves of vegetables to lighten his load, he should not throw them away until he has given tithe of them.[7] If he bought vegetables in the market and then[8] determined to give them back, he may not give them back until he has given tithe, since naught was lacking[9] save the numbering. If he was about to buy them but saw a better load, he may retract [and need not give tithe], since he had not drawn [them into his possession].

3. If he found produce by the way and took it in order to eat it and then determined to put it aside, he may not do so until he has given tithe; but if in the beginning he took it only lest it be lost, he is exempt. Whatsoever a man may not sell if it is *demai*-produce, he may not send [as a gift] to

---

[1] For the rule see Bekh. 5[4].

[2] One who undertook to observe the Law to the full, in particular the rules of tithing and of cleanness and uncleanness. On the relation of the Associates to the Pharisees, see Moore, iii. 26.   [3] Whereby it becomes 'susceptible to uncleanness'. See p. 758, n. 1.

[4] See Hag. 2[7].

[5] B.K. 7[7]. Because their habit is to stray into others' premises and to cause damage.

[6] Or, 'passing guests'.   [7] Lest an *Am-haaretz* pick them up and eat them untithed.

[8] Before paying for them.

[9] He had already made them his own possession by the act of 'drawing' them to himself. See Kidd. 1[5]; B.M. 4[2]; B.B. 9[7].

his fellow if it is *demai*-produce. R. Jose permits [him to send] what is certainly untithed, provided that he makes the matter known.

4. If a man brought his wheat[1] to a miller that was a Samaritan or to a miller that was an *Am-haaretz*, its condition [after grinding] remains as before in what concerns Tithes and Seventh Year produce;[2] but if he brought it to a miller that was a gentile, [after it has been ground] it is accounted *demai*-produce.[3] If he gave his produce into the keeping of a Samaritan or an *Am-haaretz*, its condition remains as before in what concerns Tithes and Seventh Year produce; but if into the keeping of a gentile, it is accounted like to the gentile's own produce.[4] R. Simeon says: It is accounted *demai*-produce.

5. If a man gave [food to be cooked] to the mistress of the inn he must tithe what he gives her[5] and also what he receives back from her, since she must be suspected of changing it. R. Jose said: We are not answerable for deceivers: he need tithe only what he receives back from her.

6. If a man gave [food to be cooked] to his mother-in-law he must tithe what he gives her and also what he receives back from her, since she must be suspected of changing what is spoilt. R. Judah said: She has a mind to the well-being of her daughter and feels shame for her son-in-law. R. Judah agrees that if a man gave to his mother-in-law [food that it is lawful to eat] in the Seventh Year, she need not be suspected of changing it and giving her daughter [forbidden] Seventh Year produce to eat.

4. 1. If a man bought produce from one that was not deemed trustworthy in the matter of Tithes, and he forgot to tithe it [on the eve of Sabbath],[6] and he inquired on the Sabbath of him that sold it, he may eat at his word; but if it was already nightfall at the close of the Sabbath he may not eat until he has given tithe. If he could not find him, but another that was not deemed trustworthy in the matter of Tithes said to him, 'It is already tithed', he may eat at his word; but if it was already nightfall at the close of the Sabbath he may not eat until he has given tithe. If Heave-offering of Tithe from *demai*-produce fell back to where it was, R. Simeon of Shezur says: Even on a weekday a man need but inquire of the seller and eat at his word.[7]

2. If a man compels his fellow by a vow to eat with him, and his fellow does not deem him trustworthy in the matter of Tithes, he may eat with him during the first week although he does not deem him trustworthy in the matter of Tithes, provided that the other shall say to him, 'The food is tithed'; but on the second Sabbath, even if the other vowed to derive no benefit from him [if he ate not with him], he may not eat until he has given tithe.

3. R. Eliezer says: They need not [even] designate part of *demai*-produce as Poorman's Tithe. But the Sages say: They should designate it, but they need not set it apart.

4. If a man had designated part of *demai*-produce as Heave-offering of

---

1 That was duly tithed.
2 See p. 39, n. 4. The miller is not presumed to have exchanged it for untithed produce or Seventh Year produce that had been bought.
3 He may have exchanged it for produce brought by an *Am-haaretz*.
4 Which is not subject to tithes.
5 Since an Associate may not give any food not duly tithed, so that others shall be saved from doing wrong.   6 It is forbidden to tithe on the Sabbath (Shab. 2[7]).
7 That it was, indeed, duly tithed from the first.

Tithe, or part of certainly untithed produce as Poorman's Tithe, [the priest or the poor man] may not take them on the Sabbath; but if a priest or a poor man was accustomed to eat with him they may come and eat [of them on the Sabbath] provided that he tells them [that what they eat is Heave-offering of Tithe or Poorman's Tithe].

5. If a man said to one that was not deemed trustworthy in the matter of Tithes, 'Buy food for me from some one that is trustworthy', or 'from one that pays Tithes', [the agent] may not be trusted; [but if he said, 'Buy it] from such-a-one', he may be trusted. If he went to buy it from such-a-one but [returned and] said, 'I did not find him and I bought it for thee from another that is trustworthy', he may not be deemed trustworthy.

6. If a man entered a city where he knew no one, and said, 'Who is there here that is trustworthy? Who is there here that pays Tithes?' and one said to him, 'I', he may not be believed; but if he said, 'Such-a-one is trustworthy', he may be believed. If he went to buy from him and said to him, 'Who is there here that sells old produce?'[1] and he answered, 'He that sent thee to me', although they seem like them that requite one another, they may be believed.

7. If ass-drivers entered a city and the one said, 'My produce is new and that of my fellow is old', or 'My produce is not duly tithed but that of my fellow is duly tithed', they may not be believed. R. Judah says: They may be believed.

5. 1. If a man bought bread from the baker[2] how should he apportion the Tithe? He should take[3] sufficient for Heave-offering of Tithe and for Dough-offering,[4] and say: The hundredth part of what is here, to this side, shall be [Heave-offering of] Tithe, with the rest of the [First] Tithe adjoining it; that which I first made Tithe shall be Heave-offering of Tithe for the rest; and the rest [which I set apart] shall be Dough-offering; let what is to the north or south of it be Second Tithe and rendered free for common use by [the setting aside of its redemption] money.

2. If a man was minded to set apart Heave-offering and Heave-offering of Tithe together [from certainly untithed produce],[5] he should take one part in thirty-three and a third, and say: Let one hundredth part of what is here, to this side, be common food, and the rest[6] Heave-offering for the whole; and let the one hundredth part of common food that is here, at this side, be Tithe with the rest of the [First] Tithe adjoining it; and let that part which I made Tithe be Heave-offering of Tithe for the rest of the [First] Tithe; and the rest [which I set apart] shall be Dough-offering; let what is to the north or south of it be Second Tithe and rendered free for common use by [the setting aside of its redemption] money.

3. If a man bought from the baker he may give Tithe from what is freshly baked instead of from stale bread, or from stale bread instead of from what is freshly baked, even though they are of many [diverse] moulds. So R. Meir. R. Judah forbids it since one may suppose that wheat of yesterday came from one man [and was untithed] while that of to-day came from another [and was tithed]. R. Simeon forbids it with Heave-offering of Tithe but permits it with Dough-offering.

---

[1] Last year's harvest. Produce of the current year is forbidden unless the Omer has first been reaped and offered. See Men. 10[5]; App. I. 31.

[2] Whose bread must be deemed *demai*-produce.   [3] Designate but not separate.

[4] See p. 83, n. 1.   [5] This Mishnah is not concerned with *demai*-produce.

[6] i.e. the remaining two hundredths of the whole.

4. If a man bought from a bread shop he should give Tithe from each separate kind. So R. Meir. R. Judah says: [He may give tithe] from one for them all. R. Judah agrees that if a man bought from a dealer[1] that buys from many bakers, he must give Tithe from every kind.[2]

5. If a man bought from the poor (so, too, if a poor man is given pieces of bread or fragments of fig-cake) he must give Tithe from every kind; but if [he bought] dates and dried figs he may mix them together and [then] give Tithe. R. Judah said: This applies when the gift is large; but when the gift is small he must give Tithe from every kind.

6. If a man bought from a provision-dealer and bought from him again a second time, he may not give Tithe from the one purchase for the other, although they are from the same store-basket or of the same kind. But the provision-dealer may be believed if he says, 'They are from the same stock'.

7. If a man bought from a householder and bought from him again a second time, he may give Tithe from the one purchase for the other, even though they are from two hampers or from two towns. If a householder sold vegetables in the market and they were brought to him from his own gardens, [he that buys] may give Tithe from one kind for all; but if from other gardens, he must give Tithe from each kind.

8. If a man bought untithed produce from two places he may give Tithe from the one for the other. Yet although they have said this, none may sell untithed produce except of necessity.

9. Tithe may be given from what is bought from an Israelite for what is bought from a gentile, or from what is bought from a gentile for what is bought from an Israelite; or from what is bought from an Israelite for what is bought from Samaritans, or from what is bought from Samaritans for what is bought from [other] Samaritans. R. Eliezer forbids the tithing of what is bought from [certain] Samaritans for what is bought from [other] Samaritans.

10. A holed plant-pot is reckoned like to the ground itself.[3] If a man gave Heave-offering from what grows from the earth for what grows in a holed plant-pot, his Heave-offering is valid; if from what grows in an unholed plant-pot for what grows in a holed plant-pot, the Heave-offering is accounted valid, yet he must give Heave-offering afresh; if from what grows in a holed plant-pot for what grows in an unholed plant-pot, the Heave-offering is accounted valid, yet[4] it may not be consumed until Heave-offering and Tithes have been taken from it.

11. If a man gave Heave-offering from *demai*-produce for [other] *demai*-produce, or from *demai*-produce for produce certainly untithed, the Heave-offering is accounted valid, but he must give Heave-offering afresh; but if from produce certainly untithed for *demai*-produce, the Heave-offering is accounted valid, yet it may not be consumed until Heave-offering and Tithes have been taken from it.

6. 1. If a man leased[5] a field from an Israelite, a gentile, or a Samaritan, he must divide [the produce] in their presence.[6] If he hired[7] a field from

---

1 Heb. *monopol*, one having the sole right of selling bread.
2 In this and the two following paragraphs the principle observed is to avoid giving tithe from what may be already tithed for what has not been tithed; or from what is exempt from tithes for what is not exempt.
3 What grows from it is subject to Heave-offering and Tithes, but what grows from an unholed plant-pot is exempt.
4 Produce of the holed plant-pot is still unpermitted until it is duly tithed for its own sake.
5 See p. 15, n. 7.   6 He is not responsible for tithing what belongs to them.
7 For a prescribed quantity of produce, irrespective of the total yield.

an Israelite he must first separate Heave-offering and [then] give [the owner the produce prescribed as rent]. R. Judah said: This applies when he pays him from the same field or from the same kind of produce; but when he pays him from another field or from another kind of produce, he must separate Tithes as well[1] and then make payment.

2. If he hired a field from a gentile he must set aside Tithes [as well as Heave-offering] and then make payment. R. Judah says: Also if he leased from a gentile the field of his fathers he must set aside Tithes as well and then make payment.

3. If a priest or levite leased a field from an Israelite, they [and the owner] share in the Heave-offering as well as in the common produce. R. Eliezer says: The Tithes belong to them, for on this condition would they have come [to cultivate the field].

4. If an Israelite leased a field from a priest or levite, the Tithes belong to the owner. R. Ishmael says: If a man from the provinces leased a field from a man of Jerusalem, the Second Tithe belongs to the man of Jerusalem. But the Sages say: The man from the provinces is able himself to go up and consume it in Jerusalem.[2]

5. If a man[3] leased olive trees for to gather the oil, he and the owner share in the Heave-offering as well as in the common produce. R. Judah says: If an Israelite leased olive trees from a priest or levite for to gather the oil, on condition of receiving half of the profit, the Tithes belong to the owner.

6. The School of Shammai say: A man may sell his olives only to an Associate. The School of Hillel say: Even to one that [only] pays Tithes.[4] Yet the more scrupulous of the School of Hillel used to observe the words of the School of Shammai.

7. If two men gathered their grapes and brought them to the winepress, and one of them pays Tithes and the other does not, he that pays Tithes may pay what is incumbent on him, and his portion may be wheresoever he will.

8. If two men leased a field, or inherited it, or became jointholders, [and the one was an Associate and the other an *Am-haaretz*], the one may say: 'Do thou take the wheat from this place and I will take it from that', or 'Do thou take wine from this place and I will take it from that'; but he may not say, 'Do thou take wheat and I will take barley', or 'Do thou take wine and I will take oil'.[5]

9. If an Associate and an *Am-haaretz* inherited jointly from their father who was an *Am-haaretz*, the Associate may say to the other, 'Do thou take the wheat that is in this place and I will take the wheat that is in that place', or 'Do thou take the wine that is in this place and I will take the wine that is in that place'; but he may not say to the other, 'Do thou take the wheat and I will take the barley', or 'Do thou take the wet produce and I will take the dry'.

10. If a proselyte and a gentile inherited jointly from their father who was a gentile, the proselyte may say to the other, 'Do thou take what pertains to idolatry and I will take the money', or 'Do thou take the wine and

---

[1] It is as though he paid him from his own wares, and an Associate may not part with his produce unless it is duly tithed.　　　　[2] See p. 73, n. 6.
[3] An Israelite from a levite or priest.
[4] And is not scrupulous in observing the laws of cleanness.
[5] For then he would be as one that exchanged or sold produce that was not duly tithed.

I will take the produce'; but after the property has come into the possession of the proselyte it is forbidden to him.[1]

11. If a man sold produce in Syria[2] and said, 'It is from the Land of Israel', Tithes must be paid from it. [If he said,] 'It is already tithed', he may be believed, since the mouth that forbids is the mouth that permits.[3] [If he said,] 'It is of my own [growing]',[4] it must be tithed; [but if he said,] 'It is already tithed', he may be believed, since the mouth that forbids is the mouth that permits; and if it was known that he had another field in Syria, the produce must be tithed.

12. If an *Am-haaretz* said to an Associate, 'Buy me a bunch of vegetables', or 'Buy me a loaf of bread', he may buy it [as well as what he buys for himself] without regard to which is for himself and which is for his fellow and be exempt [from tithing that of his fellow]; but if he had said, 'This I buy for myself and this for my fellow', and then they were confused together, he must tithe [them both], even if [what belongs to his fellow is] a hundred times [more than his own].

7. 1. If a man invited his fellow to eat with him [on the Sabbath] and his fellow does not deem him trustworthy in the matter of Tithes, on the eve of the Sabbath[5] he may say: Of what I shall set apart to-morrow let part be Tithe[6] with the rest of the [First] Tithe adjoining it; let what I have made Tithe be Heave-offering of Tithe for the whole, and let the Second Tithe be to the north or south of it and rendered fit for common use by [the setting aside of its redemption] money.

2. When they have mixed him the cup [on the Sabbath], he may say, 'Let what I am about to leave at the bottom of the cup be Tithe with the rest of the [First] Tithe adjoining it; let what I have made Tithe be Heave-offering of Tithe for the whole, and let the Second Tithe be at the mouth of the cup and rendered free for common use by [the setting aside of its redemption] money'.

3. If a labourer does not deem the householder trustworthy he may take one dried fig and say, 'Let this and the nine which follow after it be Tithe for the ninety that I shall eat; let this one be Heave-offering of Tithe for all of them; and let the Second Tithe be in the last fig and rendered free for common use by [the setting aside of its redemption] money'; and he should reserve one dried fig. Rabban Simeon b. Gamaliel says: He should not reserve it, for he thus lessens the work that he does for the householder. R. Jose says: He should not reserve it, because this[7] is a condition enjoined by the Court.

4. If a man buys wine among Samaritans he may say, 'Let two *logs*[8] which I shall set apart be Heave-offering, and ten [others] [First] Tithe and nine Second Tithe'; then, after he has set apart the redemption money, he may drink.

5. If a man had in his house untithed figs and [he remembered them] while he was in the House of Study or in the field [before sunset on the eve of Sabbath], he may say, 'Let two figs[9] which I shall set apart be

---

[1] To make any such proposal.   [2] North of Chezib. See p. 21, n. 13.
[3] For the application of the same formula, see Ket. 2[2, 5]; Eduy. 3[6].
[4] From my own field in Syria.
[5] It was forbidden to separate tithe on the Sabbath (Shab. 2[7]).
[6] i.e. Heave-offering of Tithe which the levite, had he received First Tithe, should have given to a priest.
[7] That the householder is responsible for tithing his produce before his labourers eat of it.   [8] Out of every hundred which he buys.   [9] Out of every hundred.

Heave-offering, and ten First Tithe and nine Second Tithe'. If they were *demai*-produce let him say, 'Let what I shall separate to-morrow be Tithe with the rest of the [First] Tithe adjoining it; let what I have made Tithe be Heave-offering of Tithe for the whole of it; and let the Second Tithe be to the north or south of it and rendered fit for common use by [the setting aside of its redemption] money'.

6. If he had before him two baskets full of untithed produce and said, 'Let the Tithes of that basket be in this', the first basket is thereby tithed; [if he said], 'Let the Tithes of that basket be in this, and let the Tithes of this basket be in that', the first basket [only] is thereby tithed; [if he said], 'Let the Tithes from either basket be within the other', he has thereby designated as Tithe [produce within them both].

7. If a hundred parts of untithed produce [were mixed with] a hundred parts of produce already tithed, a hundred and one parts must be taken out [as untithed produce]. If a hundred parts of untithed produce [were mixed with] a hundred parts of Tithe, a hundred and one parts must be taken out [as Tithe]. If a hundred parts of duly tithed produce [were mixed with] a hundred parts of Tithe, a hundred and ten parts must be taken out [as Tithe]. If a hundred parts of untithed produce [were mixed with] ninety parts of Tithe, or ninety parts of untithed produce with eighty parts of Tithe, naught is lost. This is the general rule: when the greater part is untithed produce naught is lost.

8. If a man had ten rows each containing ten jars of wine and he had said, 'In the outer row let one be Tithe', and it is not known which row it was, he must take two jars from diagonally opposite corners. [If he had said,] 'In the half of the outer row let one be Tithe', and it is not known which half row it was, he must take four jars from the four corners. [If he had said,] 'In one row let one jar be Tithe', and it is not known which row it was, he must take [ten jars, one from] every row diagonally. [If he had said], 'In one half row let one jar be Tithe', and it is not known which half row it was, he must take [twenty jars from] two diagonal rows. [If he had said,] 'Let one jar be Tithe', and it is not known which jar, he must take Tithe from every jar.

KILAIM[1] ('DIVERSE KINDS')

1. 1. Wheat and tares[2] are not accounted Diverse Kinds. Barley and goat-grass, spelt and oats, the common bean and the kidney bean, the everlasting-pea and the vetchling, the white bean and haricot bean are not accounted Diverse Kinds.

2. The cucumber and the musk-melon are not accounted Diverse Kinds. R. Judah says: They are accounted Diverse Kinds. Lettuce and willow-lettuce, chicory and wild chicory, the leek and the wild leek, coriander and wild coriander, mustard and Egyptian mustard, the Egyptian gourd and the bitter gourd, the Egyptian bean and the carob are not accounted Diverse Kinds.

3. The turnip and the radish, the cabbage and the cauliflower, beet and orach are not accounted Diverse Kinds. R. Akiba added: Garlic and wild

---

[1] Lit. 'two kinds'. Lev. 19[19] and Deut. 22[9-11] forbid four types of 'Diverse Kinds': sowing a vineyard with Diverse Kinds, sowing a field or garden with Diverse Kinds of seed, allowing cattle to gender with a Diverse Kind, and wearing a garment of Diverse Kinds of stuff (woollen and linen) mingled together. Diverse Kinds of seeds are only forbidden in the case of plants which differ in name, taste, and appearance.   [2] Bearded darnel.

garlic, onions and wild onions, lupine and wild lupine are not accounted Diverse Kinds.

4. Among trees the pear and the pippin,[1] the quince and the hawthorn are not accounted Diverse Kinds. Although the apple and the medlar, the peach and the almond, the jujube and the Zizyphus are like to each other, they are accounted Diverse Kinds.[2]

5. Although the long radish and the round radish, mustard and wild mustard, the Greek gourd and the Egyptian or bitter gourd are like to each other, they are accounted Diverse Kinds.

6. The wolf and the dog, the wild-dog and the jackal, goats and gazelles, wild goats and sheep, the horse and the mule, the mule and the ass, the ass and the wild ass, although like to each other are accounted Diverse Kinds.

7. One kind of tree may not be grafted on to another kind, nor one kind of vegetable on to another kind, nor a tree on to a vegetable, nor a vegetable on to a tree. R. Judah permits [the grafting of] a vegetable on to a tree.

8. Vegetables may not be planted in the stump of a sycamore tree, nor may rue be grafted on to white cassia, since that is [to graft] a vegetable on to a tree. A fig-tree shoot may not be planted in scutchgrass that this may shade it, nor may a vine-shoot be trained into a water-melon that this may pour its juice into it, since that is [to graft] a tree on to a vegetable. A gourd seed may not be put into bugloss to protect it, since that is [to graft] one kind of vegetable on to another.

9. If a man buried turnips and radishes under a vine, and some of the leaves were left uncovered, he need not fear lest he transgress thereby [the law of] Diverse Kinds or [the laws of] the Seventh Year[3] or of Tithes;[4] and they may be removed on the Sabbath.[5] If a man sowed wheat and barley together, they are accounted Diverse Kinds. R. Judah says: They are not accounted Diverse Kinds unless there are two [kinds] of wheat and one of barley, or one of wheat and two of barley, or one of wheat, one of barley, and one of spelt.[6]

2. 1. If in a *seah*[7] [of seed] there is a quarter-[*kab*][8] of another kind, this must be lessened. R. Jose says: It must be wholly removed whether it is of one kind or of two kinds. R. Simeon says: They have spoken of but one kind. But the Sages say: Any Diverse Kinds soever [that are found] in a *seah* of seed are included together to make up the [forbidden] quarter-*kab*.

2. This applies when one kind of grain is mixed with another kind, or one kind of pulse with another kind, or when grain is mixed with pulse or pulse with grain. Rightly have they said:[9] The seeds of garden produce which are not used as food, are included together to make up [the proportion that renders them forbidden as Diverse Kinds] if they are one twenty-fourth part of what is sown in a *seah's* space. R. Simeon says: Like as they have spoken in such wise that the rule bears with stringency so have they spoken in such wise that it bears with leniency: thus if flax seed was mixed

---

[1] Heb. *krustomel*. Maas. 1³; Uktz. 1⁶. Cf. χρυσόμηλον, quince.
[2] Because they differ in taste.   [3] When it is forbidden to sow anything (see p. 39, n. 4.).
[4] Which are not due from what has not been sown but only buried.
[5] As being plucked already, therefore he is not transgressing the law against reaping on the Sabbath (Shab. 7²).
[6] R. Judah interprets Lev. 19¹⁹ and Deut. 22⁹ as meaning that Diverse Kinds may not be sown in a field where something else is growing already; thus you may not sow Diverse Kinds in a vineyard (Deut. 22⁹). Therefore three species are required for the transgression of the Law.   [7] See App. II, D.   [8] i.e. one twenty-fourth of the *seah*.   [9] See p. 12, n. 4.

with grain it is included together to make up [the proportion that renders it forbidden as Diverse Kinds] only if it is one twenty-fourth part of what is sown in a *seah's* space.[1]

3. If a man's field was sown with wheat and he then determined to sow it with barley, he must wait until the seed begins to send out wormlike shoots and turn up the soil and then sow it [with barley]. If it had already sprouted he may not say, 'I will sow first and then turn up the soil', but he must first turn up the soil and then sow. How deep should he plough? As deep as the furrows made after a rainfall. Abba Saul says: So that he does not leave [unturned] a quarter-*kab's* space within a *seah's* space.

4. If his field was sown and he then determined to plant it, he may not say, 'I will plant it first and then turn up the soil', but he must first turn up the soil and then plant it. If it was planted and he then determined to sow it, he may not say, 'I will sow it first and then uproot [what was planted]', but he must first uproot and then sow. If he would do so he may cut down the plants to less than a handbreadth and sow and then uproot the plants.

5. If his field was sown with caraway[2] or arum he may not sow over them because they ripen only after three years. If in a crop of grain there sprang up aftergrowths of woad (so, too, in the place of threshing-floors if many kinds sprang up; so, too, if fenugreek made weeds to spring up), he is not bound to weed them out. But if he has weeded them or cropped them, they say to him, 'Uproot them all save one kind only'.

6. If he would lay out his field in plots each bearing a different kind [of crop], the School of Shammai say: [Between each he must leave a space equal to] three furrows of ploughed land. And the School of Hillel say: The width of a Sharon yoke. And the opinion of the one is not far from the opinion of the other.

7. If the point of the angle of a field of wheat entered into a field of barley, this is permitted, since it is manifestly the limit of the field. If one man's field was sown with wheat and that of his fellow with some other kind, he may flank his own with that other kind; if his was sown with wheat and that of his fellow with wheat, he may flank it with a furrow of flax, but not with a furrow of another kind. R. Simeon says: It is all one whether it is [a furrow of] flax or of some other kind. R. Jose says: Even in the middle of a field it is permitted to test [the field] with a furrow of flax.

8. They may not flank a field of grain with mustard or seed of safflower, but they may flank a field of vegetables with mustard or seed of safflower. They may flank [with a Diverse Kind] a plot of untilled or newly broken land, or a loose stone wall, or a pathway or a fence ten handbreadths high or a ditch ten handbreadths deep and four wide, or a tree that overshadows the ground, or a rock ten handbreadths high and four wide.

9. If a man would lay out his field in patches each bearing a different kind [of crop], he may lay out twenty-four patches within a *seah's* space, one patch to every quarter-*kab's* space, and sow therein what kind of seed he will; if [in a field of grain] there was but one patch or two [each of a quarter-*kab's* space], he may sow them with mustard-seed; but if three,

---

[1] Because while one *seah* of grain or pulse is sown over a *'seah's* space' (2,500 sq. cubits), only a quarter-*seah* of seeds of garden produce are sown over one *seah's* space, while three *seahs* of flax-seed are sown over the like area. Therefore if garden-seed is one ninety-sixth of the mixed seed the mixture is forbidden, whereas flax-seed must be one-eighth of the mixture to render it forbidden.

[2] Most texts read 'hemp' (*kannabos* for *karbos*); but that ripens yearly.

he may not sow them with mustard-seed, since it might appear like to a field of mustard. So R. Meir. But the Sages say: [Only] nine patches [of a quarter-*kab's* space] may be sown [with different kinds of seed in the *seah's* space], and ten are forbidden. R. Eliezer b. Jacob says: Even if his entire field measured a *kor's* space, he may not make therein more than one patch.

10. Anything within the patch of a quarter-*kab's* space [that intervenes between one crop and another] must be counted within the measure of the quarter-*kab's* space. The ground required for a vine or a grave or a rock must be counted within the measure of the quarter-*kab's* space. Grain may be sown alongside [another kind of] grain only if a quarter-*kab's* space [intervenes]; vegetables may be planted alongside [other] vegetables only if six handbreadths [intervene]; grain may be sown alongside vegetables, or vegetables alongside grain only if a quarter-*kab's* space [intervenes]. R. Eliezer says: Vegetables may be sown alongside grain only if six hand-breadths [intervene].

11. If grain [grows in a place where it] leans over another kind of grain, of if vegetables lean over other vegetables, or if grain leans over vegetables or vegetables over grain, all are permitted save only in the case of a Greek gourd. R. Meir says: A cucumber or Egyptian bean also;—yet[1] I approve their words rather than mine.

3. 1. A garden-bed six handbreadths by six, may be sown with five kinds of seeds—four kinds in its four corners[2] and one in the middle. If it has a border one handbreadth high, it may be sown with thirteen kinds—three[3] along each border [on the four sides] and one in the centre. Turnip-tops should not be planted in the border since they might fill it. R. Judah says: Six kinds may be sown in the middle.[4]

2. Not every kind of seed may be sown in a garden-bed, but any kind of vegetable may be sown therein. Mustard and small beans are deemed a kind of seed and large beans a kind of vegetable. If a border that was one handbreadth high was made lower it continues valid since it was valid in the beginning. In a furrow or [dried up] water channel one handbreadth deep, three kinds of seed may be sown; one at either end and one in the middle.

3. If the point of the angle of a field of vegetables entered into a field of other vegetables, this is permitted since it is manifestly the limit of the field. If a man's field was sown with vegetables and he sought to plant therein a row of another kind of vegetable, R. Ishmael says: [He may not do so] unless the furrow extends unstopped from one end of the field to the other. R. Akiba says: It need be but six handbreadths in length and fully as wide. R. Judah says: As wide as the width of the sole of a foot.

4. If a man planted two rows of cucumbers, two rows of gourds, then two rows of Egyptian beans, this is permitted; but if one row of cucumbers, one row of gourds, then one row of Egyptian beans, this is forbidden. R. Eliezer allows one row of cucumbers, one row of gourds, one row of Egyptian beans, then one row of cucumbers; but the Sages forbid it.

---

1 'In spite of this tradition which I have received and which I now report, I approve . . .'
2 Or, 'along its four sides'.
3 Each one handbreath square and separated one handbreadth from the next.
4 Sketches showing the possible dispositions of Diverse Kinds of seeds are given in the ordinary Mishnayoth editions.

5. A man may plant a cucumber and a gourd in the same hollow provided that the one grows out in one direction and the other in the other,[1]
the foliage of the one stretching in one direction and the foliage of the other
in the other; for whatsoever the Sages have forbidden they have so decreed
only for appearance's sake.

6. If a man's field was sown with onions and he sought to plant therein
rows of gourds, R. Ishmael says: He should uproot two rows [of onions]
and plant one row [of gourds] and leave the standing crop of onions over
a space of two rows, then again uproot two rows [of onions] and plant one
row [of gourds]. R. Akiba says: He may uproot two rows [of onions] and
plant two rows [of gourds] and leave the standing crop of onions over
a space of two rows, then again uproot two rows and plant two rows. But
the Sages say: Unless there is a space of twelve cubits between one row
[of gourds] and the next, what is sown between them may not be suffered
to remain.

7. If gourds are planted beside vegetables they are given the same space
as vegetables,[2] but if beside grain they must be given a quarter-*kab's* space.
If a man's field was sown with grain and he sought to plant therein a row
of gourds, it must be allowed six handbreadths [on either side] for its
tillage, and if its growth exceeds this the grain must be uprooted before it.
R. Jose says: It should be allowed four cubits for its tillage. They said
to him: Dost thou require here greater stringency than for the vine? He
replied: We find that here greater stringency applies than for the vine,
since for a single vine six handbreadths are allowed for its tillage, while for
a single gourd a quarter-*kab's* space is allowed. R. Meir says in the name
of R. Ishmael: Where there are three gourds within a *seah's* space other
seed may not be sown within the *seah's* space. R. Jose b. ha-Hotef
Ephrathi said in the name of R. Ishmael: Where there are three gourds
within a *kor's* space other seed may not be sown within the *kor's* space.

4. 1. The School of Shammai say: A vineyard patch[3] must be [at least]
twenty-four cubits [square]. The School of Hillel say: Sixteen cubits. The
School of Shammai say: The outer space of a vineyard must be [at least]
sixteen cubits. The School of Hillel say: Twelve cubits. What is a 'vineyard patch'? [The part of] a vineyard that is bare of vines in its midst. If
this is less than sixteen cubits [square], seed may not be sown there; but
if it is [at least] sixteen cubits [square] they must allow the vines enough
space for their tillage,[4] and they may sow in what is left.

2. What is the 'outer space'[5] of a vineyard? The space between the
vines and the boundary-fence. If this is less than twelve cubits, seed may
not be sown there; but if it is [at least] twelve cubits they must allow the
vines enough space for their tillage, and they may sow in what is left.

3. R. Judah says: Such is but the vineyard's boundary-fence.[6] What,
then, is the 'outer space' of a vineyard?[7] [The space] between two vineyards. And what counts as a 'fence'?[8] Such that is ten handbreadths high.
And a 'ditch'? Such that is ten handbreadths deep and four wide.

---

[1] Some texts omit the rest of the paragraph. Cf. 9[2] below.   [2] Six handbreadths.
[3] Lit. 'bald spot'; i.e. a space empty of vines in which it is desired to raise other crops
without transgressing the law of Diverse Kinds in the vineyard.
[4] Four cubits all round.   [5] About which the Schools of Shammai and Hillel disputed.
[6] And so long as there is four cubits for the tillage of the vines you may sow over what
remains between the vines and the fence.   [7] That needs to be at least twelve cubits.
[8] That can be flanked with vines on the one side and sown crops on the other.

4. If the space between the reeds of a reed-partition was less than three handbreadths which would suffice for a kid to enter, it is deemed a valid partition. If a fence was breached for a space of ten cubits, such may be deemed an entrance; if more than this, it is forbidden [to sow] opposite the breach. If many breaches were made in the fence yet what remains standing exceeds what is broken down, it is permitted [to sow] opposite the breach; and if what is broken down exceeds what remains standing, it is forbidden.

5. If a man planted a row of five vines, the School of Shammai say: This counts as a vineyard. But the School of Hillel say: It does not count as a vineyard unless there are there two rows. Wherefore if he sows within the four cubits of the vineyard the School of Shammai say: He renders forfeit[1] one row; and the School of Hillel say: He renders forfeit two rows.[2]

6. If a man planted two vines opposite two others, with another projecting like a tail, this counts as a vineyard; but if two opposite two others and one between them, or two opposite two others and one in the midst— this does not count as a vineyard—but only if there are two opposite two others with another projecting like a tail.

7. If a man planted a row of vines on his own land and there was a row on that of his fellow, although there was between them a private path or a public path or a fence less than ten handbreadths high, both rows are included together [so that they count as a vineyard]. But if the fence was higher than ten handbreadths they are not included together. R. Judah says: If he trained them together above, they must be included together.

8. If a man planted two rows [of vines] he may not sow seed there unless there was a space of eight cubits between them.[3] If there were three rows he may not sow seed there unless there was a space of sixteen cubits between one row and the next. R. Eliezer b. Jacob says in the name of Hananiah b. Hakinai: Even if the middle [row of vines] was left waste and there was not sixteen cubits between one row and the next, seed may not be sown there; though if in the beginning he had planted them [in two rows] it would have been permitted [to sow seed there] if there were but eight cubits between.

9. If a man planted his vineyard [in rows] sixteen cubits apart, it is permitted to sow seed there. R. Judah said: It once happened in Zalmon that a man planted his vineyard in rows sixteen cubits [apart], and trained the foliage of every two rows to one side and sowed over the cleared land; and on another year he trained the foliage towards the place that had been sown and sowed over the fallow land; the case came before the Sages and they pronounced it permissible. R. Meir and R. Simeon say: Even if a man planted his vineyard in rows of eight cubits apart, it is permitted [to sow there].

5. 1. If a vineyard lay waste yet grapes could still be gathered off ten vines within a *seah's* space,[4] and they were planted according to *Halakah*,[5] it may be called a 'poor vineyard'. If a vineyard[6] was planted out in irregular fashion yet there could still be found two vines aligned parallel to three others, it counts as a vineyard; otherwise it does not count as a vineyard.

---

[1] Deut. 22⁹.   [2] Since it requires at least two rows to count as a vineyard.
[3] In addition to the four cubits allowed for the tillage of the vines of each row.
[4] 2,500 sq. cubits. See App. II, E.
[5] App. I, 11. i.e. according to 4⁵ above.   [6] Variant: poor vineyard.

R. Meir says: Since it appears like in form to [other] vineyards, it may be deemed a vineyard.

2. If a vineyard was planted in rows less than four cubits apart, R. Simeon says: It is not deemed a vineyard. But the Sages say: It counts as a vineyard, and the middle rows are regarded as though they were not.

3. If a ditch that passes through a vineyard is ten [handbreadths] deep and four wide, R. Eliezer b. Jacob says: If it extends from the one end of the vineyard to the other it is regarded as lying between two vineyards, and seed may be sown therein; but if not, it is reckoned as like to a wine-press. If a winepress in a vineyard is ten [handbreadths] deep and four wide, R. Eliezer says: They may sow seed therein. But the Sages forbid it. If the watchman's booth in a vineyard is ten [handbreadths] high and four wide, they may sow seed therein; but if it is overhung by interlaced foliage it is forbidden.

4. If a vine was planted in a winepress or rift, they must allow it enough space for its tillage and they may sow in what is left. R. Jose says: Unless there is there [at least] four cubits' space seed may not be sown there. If there is a house in the vineyard seed may be sown therein.

5. If a man planted vegetables in a vineyard or allowed them to grow there he may render forfeit forty-five vines. This applies if [the vines] were planted in rows four or five cubits apart. If they were planted in rows six or seven cubits apart, he renders forfeit [the vines] within a radius of sixteen cubits in every direction—reckoning in circles and not in squares.[1]

6. If a man saw vegetables growing in the vineyard and said, 'When I reach them I will pluck them', they are not forbidden [under the law of Diverse Kinds]; [but if he said,] 'When I come again I will pluck them', they are forbidden even if they have grown only another two-hundredth part.

7. If he was passing through the vineyard and seeds fell from him, or if they came in with the manure or with the water, or if he was sowing and the wind blew seed behind him, it is not unlawful;[2] but if the wind blew it before him [into the vineyard], R. Akiba says: [If it grows into] the blade it must be hoed up; if into the ear it must be broken off; if into the full corn it must be burnt.

8. If a man suffered thorns to grow up in the vineyard, R. Eliezer says: [They count as Diverse Kinds and] this renders forfeit [the adjacent vines]. But the Sages say: That alone is rendered forfeit the like of which is [ordinarily] suffered to grow. Iris, ivy, and fritillary and all kinds of seeds are not accounted Diverse Kinds in the vineyard. Hemp, according to R. Tarfon, does not come under the law of Diverse Kinds; but the Sages say: It does so. The artichoke comes under the law of Diverse Kinds in the vineyard.

6. 1. What was the 'trellised vine' [about which the School of Shammai and the School of Hillel disputed]? If a row of five vines was planted beside a fence ten handbreadths high or beside a ditch ten handbreadths deep and four wide, four cubits are allotted for its tillage. The School of Shammai say: The four cubits need be measured only from the root of the vines toward the field [beyond the wall]. And the School of Hillel say: From the wall

---

[1] The vines are forfeit that lie within a circle of sixteen cubits radius, not within the square that contains the circle.   [2] Since it was not sown either consciously or intentionally.

[itself] toward the field. R. Johanan b. Nuri said: All err that say so; but [the School of Hillel said that] if there was a space of four cubits from the root of the vines to the wall, space enough is allotted for its tillage, and seed may be sown over what is left. And how much is the space needful for the tillage of the vine? Six handbreadths in every direction. R. Akiba says: Three.

2. If trellised vines projected from a terrace [of a hillside], R. Eliezer b. Jacob says: If a man standing on the ground can gather all the grapes, the trellised vines render four cubits of the field forbidden; otherwise they render forbidden only what is directly beneath them. R. Eliezer says: If a man planted one [of the two rows] on the ground and the other on the terrace, and it is ten handbreadths higher than the ground, it is not included together with the other row [to make up a vineyard]; if it is not so high it is included together with it.

3. If a man trained a vine over part of the trellis-frame he may not sow seed beneath the rest of it; yet if he has done so he does not render [the vine] forfeit. But if tendrils spread along [the rest of the frame, what is sown] is forbidden. So, too, if a man trained [a vine] over part of a *serak* tree.[1]

4. If he trained the vine over part of a fruit tree he may sow seed beneath the rest, and if new tendrils spread along [the rest of the tree] they must be turned back. Once R. Joshua went to R. Ishmael at Kefar Aziz[2] and he showed him a vine that was trained over part of a fig tree. He said to him, 'May I sow seed beneath the rest [of the tree]?' He answered, 'It is permitted'. And he brought him up from thence to Beth Hamaginyah and showed him a vine trained over part of a beam[3] and the stump of a sycamore tree, whereon were many beams.[3] He said to him, 'Under this beam it is forbidden [to sow], but under the others it is permitted'.

5. What is a *serak* tree? Any that does not bear fruit. R. Meir says: All trees are *serak* trees excepting the olive tree and the fig tree. R. Jose says: Any tree with the like of which whole fields are not planted is a *serak* tree.

6. Gaps in trellised vines may measure eight cubits and a little more. Among all the measurements concerning a vineyard that are spoken of by the Sages, there is no 'and a little more' save only in the case of the gaps in trellised vines. These count as 'gaps in trellised vines': if trellised vines lie waste at their centre and five vines are left on either side and the gap is [no more than] eight cubits, seed may not be sown there; if it is eight cubits and a little more, space enough is allotted for their tillage, and seed may be sown over what is left.

7. If trellised vines [in the angle of two walls] project along the wall beyond the angle and [then] stop, space enough is allotted for their tillage and seed may be sown over the space that is left. R. Jose says: If the space was less than four cubits seed may not be sown there.

8. If the canes [of the framework] project beyond the trellised vines and they had refrained from cutting them short, it is permitted to sow seed directly beneath them; but if they were prepared for the young tendrils to spread along them, it is forbidden [to sow seed beneath them].

9. If blossom projected beyond the trellised vines it is reckoned as if a plummet was suspended from it: it is forbidden [to sow seed] directly

---

[1] See below, par. 5.   [2] In the land of Edom. See Ket. 5[8].
[3] Or: severed branches.

beneath it. So, too, with a dangling branch. If a vine-shoot stretched from tree to tree, it is forbidden [to sow] beneath it. If it was made fast with a ligature of rope or reed-grass, it is permitted [to sow seed] beneath the ligature; but if the ligature was prepared for the young tendrils to spread along it, it is forbidden [to sow seed beneath it].

7. 1. If a vine-shoot was sunk into the ground and there was not three handbreadths of soil above it, seed may not be sown over it even though it was sunk through a gourd-shell or pipe. If it was sunk into stony ground and there was but three fingerbreadths of soil above it, seed may be sown over it. [In measuring the six handbreadths prescribed for the tillage of a single vine] measurement need be taken only from the second root of the sunken vine-shoot.

2. If three vines are sunk into the ground and their roots become visible, R. Eliezer b. R. Zadok says: If the space between them is from four to eight cubits, they must be included together [with the parent vines]; otherwise they are not included together. If a vine is withered it is forbidden [to sow near it], but this does not render [the vine] forfeit. R. Meir says: Moreover it is forbidden to plant the cotton-tree, but it does not render [the adjacent vines] forfeit. R. Eliezer b. R. Zadok says in his name: Moreover it is forbidden to sow over [the sunken shoots of] the vine, but it does not render [the vine] forfeit.

3. Over these [places] it is forbidden [to sow] but it does not render [the vines] forfeit; the surplus ground[1] in a vineyard patch; the surplus ground in the vineyard's outer space; the surplus ground beneath the gaps of trellised vines; and the surplus ground beneath the trellis-frames. But the space beneath the vine and the space needful for tending the vine, and the four cubits in the vineyard, these render forfeit [the adjacent vines].

4. If a man suffered his vine to overshadow his fellow's growing corn he renders it forfeit and he is answerable therefor. R. Jose and R. Simeon say: None can render forfeit what does not belong to him.

5. R. Jose said: It once happened that a man sowed his vineyard in the Seventh Year,[2] and the case came before R. Akiba, who said: None can render forfeit what does not belong to him.

6. If a usurping occupant[3] sowed a vineyard and it was recovered from him, the [forbidden] crop may be cut[4] even on the middle-days of a Feast. How much more need the owner pay the labourers? As much as one-third more. [If they exact] more than this, he may continue to cut the crop in his own fashion even if it be after the Feast. After what time is the vineyard called by the name of the usurping occupant? After [the name of its first owner] is forgotten.[5]

7. If the wind hurled vines over a grain crop [and they took root] they must be cut away at once; but if hindrance befell [the owner] the vines and crop are not forbidden [under the law of Diverse Kinds]. If growing corn swayed under a vine (and the same applies with vegetables) it must be bent back, but [even if it is not bent back] it does not render [the vine]

---

[1] An empty patch less than the prescribed (see above 4[1]) sixteen cubits.
[2] See p. 39, n. 4.   [3] See p. 313, n. 6.
[4] Forthwith by its rightful owner, to clear himself of the charge of sowing Diverse Kinds in his vineyard, even though it means performing work forbidden during mid-festival (p. 207, n. 19; M. Kat. 2[3]) when produce may only be gathered from fear of its being lost.
[5] Then the Diverse Kinds serve to render forfeit the produce sown and the fruit of the vineyard (Deut. 22[9]).

forfeit. After what time is a grain crop [sown near a vine] rendered forfeit? After it has struck root. And grapes? After they have grown to the size of a white bean. If the grain had become fully dried or the grapes fully ripe they cannot be rendered forfeit.

8. [Seed sown in] a holed plant-pot in the vineyard may render [vines] forfeit, but in an unholed plant-pot it does not render them forfeit. But R. Simeon says: Neither is permitted yet neither renders [the vines] forfeit. If a man carried a holed plant-pot through a vineyard, and [while he carried it past the vines what was in it] increased by a two-hundredth part, it becomes forbidden.[1]

8. 1. It is forbidden to sow Diverse Kinds in a vineyard or to suffer them to grow, and it is forbidden to make any use of them. It is forbidden to sow Diverse Kinds of seeds or to suffer them to grow, but they are permitted as food.[2] Diverse Kinds in stuff are permitted in all things, and it is only forbidden to wear them. Diverse Kinds among cattle are permitted to be reared and maintained, and it is only forbidden to breed them. It is forbidden to mate Diverse Kinds of cattle one with another.

2. One kind of cattle with another, one kind of wild animal with another, cattle with wild animals, wild animals with cattle, one kind of unclean beast with another, one kind of clean beast with another, an unclean beast with a clean, a clean beast with an unclean—it is forbidden to plough with them, draw with them, or drive them.

3. If a man drove them he incurs the Forty Stripes;[3] if he sat in a wagon [drawn by them] he incurs the Forty Stripes, but R. Meir declares him exempt. Also if a third beast [of a Diverse Kind from the other two] was bound to the harness, it is forbidden.

4. A horse may not be tied to the sides of a wagon or behind a wagon [that is drawn by oxen], nor may they harness Libyan asses with camels. R. Judah says: All offspring of a horse though sired by an ass are permitted [to be yoked] together; and all offspring of an ass though sired by a horse are permitted [to be yoked] together. But it is forbidden [to yoke together] the offspring of a horse with the offspring of an ass.

5. It is forbidden to mate mules if it is unknown whether their dam was a horse or an ass; but a mule foaled by a horse is permitted [to be yoked] with a horse]. Wild men[4] are [classed with] wild animals. R. Jose says: [When dead] they convey uncleanness by overshadowing[5] as does [the corpse of] a man. The hedgehog and weasel are [classed with] wild animals. As for the weasel, R. Jose says that the School of Shammai say: An olive's bulk conveys uncleanness by carrying, and a lentil's bulk by contact.[6]

6. Wild oxen are deemed a kind of cattle. But R. Jose says: A kind of wild animal. The dog is reckoned a kind of wild animal. R. Meir says: A kind of cattle. The swine is reckoned a kind of cattle, the wild ass a kind

---

[1] But not the vines, since the plant-pot was not set on the ground.
[2] Some texts add: Still more for use.
[3] The punishment for the transgression of a negative command. See Makk. 3[1ff].
[4] The meaning is doubtful. Perhaps the chimpanzee or gorilla is meant.
[5] Lit. 'tent-uncleanness', Num. 19[14]. 'Tent' is used to indicate any confined space or any space that is roofed wherein a corpse, or part of a corpse, conveys uncleanness to whatsoever is under the same roof. See p. 649, n. 3.
[6] According to the School of Shammai it is in doubt whether the weasel is to be classed as a wild animal (an olive's bulk of whose flesh conveys uncleanness), or as a creeping thing (a lentil's bulk of which conveys uncleanness by contact but not by carrying). See App. IV. 8.

of wild animal, and the elephant and ape a kind of wild animal; and with any of them a man may draw or plough or drive.

9. 1. Wool and linen alone are forbidden under the law of Diverse Kinds; wool and linen alone become unclean by leprosy-signs;[1] and when the priests minister in the Temple they wear wool and linen alone. If camel's hair and sheep's wool have been hackled together and the greater part is camel's hair, this is permitted [to be mixed with linen]; but if the greater part is sheep's wool it is forbidden. If they are in equal parts it is forbidden. So, too, if hemp and flax have been hackled together.

2. Silk[2] and bast-silk[3] do not come under the law of Diverse Kinds, but they are forbidden for appearance's sake. Mattresses and cushions do not come under the law of Diverse Kinds provided that a man's naked flesh does not touch them. Diverse Kinds may not be worn even momentarily, and Diverse Kinds may not be worn even over ten [other garments], even[4] to escape customs dues.

3. Handkerchiefs, wrappers for scrolls [of the Law], and bath-towels do not come under the law of Diverse Kinds. But R. Eliezer forbids them [if they have in them wool and linen). Barbers' towels are forbidden [if made from wool and linen] under the law of Diverse Kinds.

4. The wrappings of a corpse and asses' pack-saddles do not come under the law of Diverse Kinds. A man may not put the pack-saddle on his shoulder even to carry forth dung thereon.

5. Clothes dealers may sell [garments made from Diverse Kinds and display them] in usual fashion, provided that they do not use them of set purpose in the sun as protection from the sun or in the rain as protection from the rain. Howbeit the more scrupulous wrap them around a staff behind them.

6. Tailors may sew [garments made from Diverse Kinds and hold them] in usual fashion, provided that they do not use them of set purpose in the sun as protection from the sun or in the rain as protection from the rain. Howbeit the more scrupulous sew them [while setting them] on the ground.

7. The [woollen] rugs from Bera and Bered,[5] or Dalmatian hosen, or slippers of felt may not be worn until they have been examined. R. Jose says: Stuff brought from the sea coast or from beyond the sea need not be examined since the presumption is that it is made out of hemp. Woollen-lined shoes do not come under the law of Diverse Kinds.

8. Spun and woven work alone are forbidden under the law of Diverse Kinds, as it is written, *Thou shalt not wear* Sha'atnez[6]—that which is *shu'a* (hackled), *tawui* (spun), and *nuz* (woven). R. Simeon b. Eleazar says: [It means that he that wears it] is 'estranged' (*naloz*) and 'estranges' (*meliz*) his Father in heaven against him.

9. Felted stuff [of Diverse Kinds] is forbidden because it is hackled. An edging of wool on a linen garment is forbidden since it interlaces the web [of the garment]. R. Jose says: Girdles of purple-dyed wool are forbidden because a man stitches them [to his shirt] before he ties it.

---

[1] Lev. 13[47ff]. See Neg. 11[2].   [2] A kind of silk resembling flax.
[3] Silk resembling wool.   [4] Some texts omit the last clause.
[5] The meaning of both terms is doubtful. Heb. *birsin, bardasin*. They are explained as woollen bed-covers, the one kind thick and the other thin.
[6] Deut. 22[11]. R.V. 'mingled stuff'. What follows is an example of Midrash Haggadah, making play with the consonants of the unusual word *sha'atnez*.

A cord of wool may not be tied on to one made of linen to bind up the loins, even if there is a [leathern] strap between them.

10. The marks of weavers and washermen are forbidden under the law of Diverse Kinds. If [two pieces of stuff, one of linen and the other of wool], are fastened with a single stitch, this does not form a connective [for purposes of cleanness and uncleanness][1] nor does the law of Diverse Kinds apply, and if a man undoes it on the Sabbath he is not culpable.[2] But if he brings both ends [of the thread] to the same side, this forms a connective, the law of Diverse Kinds applies, and if a man undoes it on the Sabbath he is culpable. R. Judah says: Only if a man makes three stitches. A sack and a basket [that are bound together and patched the one with wool and the other with linen] are included together so that they come under the law of Diverse Kinds.[3]

SHEBIITH[4] ('THE SEVENTH YEAR')

1. 1. Until what time may a tree-planted field be ploughed in the year before the Seventh Year? The School of Shammai say: So long as this benefits the produce [of the sixth year]. The School of Hillel say: Until Pentecost. And the opinion of the one is not far from the opinion of the other.

2. What counts as 'a tree-planted field?' Any in which three trees grow within a *seah's* space.[5] If they are [each] fitted to produce a cake of dried figs weighing sixty *minas*,[6] Italian measure, the whole *seah's* space may be ploughed for their sake; but if less than this, only such space may be ploughed which is occupied by the fruit-picker and his basket, [when his basket lies] behind him.

3. It is all one whether they are *serak*[7] trees or fruit trees: they are reckoned as though they were fig trees; if they are [of a size] fitted to produce a cake[8] of dried figs, weighing sixty *minas*, Italian measure, the whole *seah's* space may be ploughed for their sake; but if less than this, only such space may be ploughed as is needful for them.

4. If one tree can produce [such] a cake[8] of dried figs but [the other] two cannot, or if two can do so but one cannot, only such space may be ploughed as is needful for [each of] them. This applies when there are from three to nine trees [in the *seah's* space]; if there are ten or more than ten, whether or not they can produce [the prescribed measure] the whole *seah's* space may be ploughed for their sake. For it is written, *In plowing time and in*

---

[1] So that if one piece contracts uncleanness this is not transmitted to the other piece, and if one piece is rendered clean again (by being sprinkled with the Sin-offering water—see Num. 19[18f]) the other piece remains unclean.

[2] See Shab. 7[2].

[3] A slight variant in the parallel text in Sifre (a Midrash, containing material much of which is contemporary with that in the Mishnah) gives the easier sense: 'A sack or basket (in which are wool and linen) causes (its contents) to be included together so that they come under the law of Diverse Kinds'—therefore it is forbidden to carry such a sack or basket on the shoulder (ed. Friedmann, p. 117 b).

[4] Lit. 'seventh' (year). The subject of the tractate is the law (Ex. 23[10f]; Lev. 25[2-7, 20-2]; Deut. 15[1-3]) forbidding the cultivation of the land in the seventh year. The land must lie fallow. What grows in that year is 'ownerless property', and the public has equal rights with the owner to the produce. None may trade with Seventh Year produce. Also all debts are remitted in the Seventh Year.

[5] See App. II, E. It is a space fifty cubits square. Such a space normally contains ten trees, each tree being supposed to stand within a square with sides of 16 cubits.

[6] Or: a talent of figs which is sixty *minas* (so, too, in par. 3).

[7] See Kil. 6[5].   [8] See above, n. 6.

harvest thou shalt rest.[1] There was no need to speak of the *plowing time* and *harvest* of the Seventh Year; but it refers to the *plowing time* in the sixth year which enters into the Seventh Year, and to the *harvest* of the Seventh Year which extends into the year after the Seventh Year. R. Ishmael says:[2] As the time of ploughing is of free choice, so is the time of harvest of free choice, save only the time of harvesting the Omer.[3]

5. If the three trees belong to three persons, they are included together and the whole *seah's* space may be ploughed for their sake. How much space should there be between them? Rabban Simeon b. Gamaliel says: Enough for oxen and yoke to pass through.

6. If ten saplings are spread out over a *seah's* space, the whole *seah's* space may be ploughed for their sake, until the New Year, but if they are set out in a row or surrounded by a fence, only such space may be ploughed as is needful for them.

7. Saplings and gourds may be included together [to make the total of ten] within a *seah's* space. Rabban Simeon b. Gamaliel says: Wheresoever there are ten gourds within a *seah's* space, the whole *seah's* space may be ploughed for their sake until the New Year.

8. Until when can they be called 'saplings'? R. Eleazar b. Azariah says: until [the fourth year when] they become free for common use.[4] R. Joshua says: Until they are seven years old. R. Akiba says: 'Sapling' [must be understood] according to its [accepted] sense—[newly planted]. If a tree was cut down and [its stump] put forth fresh shoots, if they are one handbreadth or less high it is accounted a sapling; but if they are more than a handbreadth high it is accounted a tree. So R. Simeon.

2. 1. Until when may a white field[5] be ploughed in the year before the Seventh Year? Until the ground has dried,[6] [or] such time as the ground is still ploughed for planting out beds of cucumbers and gourds. R. Simeon said: Thou puttest the law for each man into his own hand!—but, rather, a white field may be ploughed until Passover and a tree-planted field until Pentecost.

2. Beds of cucumbers or gourds may be dunged and hoed until the New Year; so, too, irrigated fields. Until the New Year they may cut off flaws, strip off leaves, cover up roots or fumigate plants. R. Simeon says: A man may even remove a [withered] leaf from a grape cluster in the Seventh Year itself.

3. Until the New Year they may clear away the stones. Until the New Year they may trim trees, prune them, or lop off dead branches. R. Joshua says: What applies to pruning and lopping off in the fifth year applies also in the sixth year. R. Simeon says: So long as it is still permitted me to tend a tree it is permitted me also to lop off its dead branches.

4. Until the New Year they may besmear saplings, wrap them round, protect them with ashes,[7] make shelters for them or water them. R. Eliezer b. Zadok says: A man may even water the foliage in the Seventh Year itself, but not the roots.

[1] Ex. 34[21]. The quotation refers to the beginning of the chapter and answers the question, Why is ploughing forbidden during the 6th year? The quotation is concerned with the Sabbath; but since, according to rabbinical interpretation, it is superfluous so far as the Sabbath is concerned (work having already been forbidden on the Sabbath) it must be applied to the sabbatic year.   [2] This *Halakah* deals with the Sabbath.
[3] See App. I. 31.   The reaping of it is a religious duty and overrides the Sabbath (Men. 10[9]).   [4] After they cease to be *Orlah*-fruit. See Lev. 19[23ff] and App. I. 32.
[5] A sown field, i.e. not planted with trees which cast a dark shadow.
[6] After the rainy season, i.e. about the middle or end of April.   [7] Or, 'clip them'.

5. Until the New Year they may oil unripe figs or pierce them; but unripe figs of the sixth year which remain on the tree until the Seventh Year, or unripe figs of the Seventh Year which remain on the tree until the eighth year, these they may not oil or pierce. R. Judah says: Where the custom is to oil the figs they may not do so, since that would rank as work; but where it is not the custom to oil the figs they may do so. R. Simeon permits work to be done to the tree [itself], since it is permitted to tend a tree [but not the fruit].

6. In the sixth year, within thirty days of the New Year, they may not plant trees or sink vine-shoots or graft trees; if a man planted or sank or grafted, he must uproot what he has done. R. Judah says: If within three days an engrafting has not struck root it will never do so. R. Jose and R. Simeon say: Within two weeks.

7. Rice, durra, panic and sesame that have taken root before a New Year are[1] tithed after the manner of the past year[2] and they are permitted in the Seventh Year; otherwise they are forbidden in the Seventh Year and are[1] to be tithed after the manner of the coming year.

8. R. Simeon of Shezur says: Egyptian beans, if from the outset they were sown only for seed, are treated in like manner. R. Simeon says: Large beans are treated in like manner. R. Eleazar says: Large beans are treated in like manner only if they have formed pods before the New Year.

9. Shallots and Egyptian beans that have not been watered within thirty days of the New Year are tithed after the manner of the past year and are permitted in the Seventh Year; otherwise they are forbidden in the Seventh Year and are tithed after the manner of the coming year. So, too, is it with [the produce of] a naturally watered field[3] that has not been watered for two spells.[4] So R. Meir. But the Sages say: Three.

10. Gourds that have been left growing for seed only may be left growing during the Seventh Year if they have hardened before the New Year and become unfit for human food; otherwise they may not be left growing during the Seventh Year. Their buds are forbidden during the Seventh Year. They may water[5] the soil of a white field. So R. Simeon. But R. Eliezer b. Jacob forbids it. They may flood a rice field in the Seventh Year. R. Simeon says: But they may not cut [the rice plant].

3. 1. From what time [in the Seventh Year] may dung be brought out to the dung-heaps [in the field]? After transgressors[6] have ceased [to tend their fields]. So R. Meir. R. Judah says: After the moisture [of the dung][7] is dried up. R. Jose says: After it turns solid.

2. How much dung may they lay down? Three dung-heaps in every *seah's* space, ten skep-loads[8] of dung to every heap, one *lethek*[9] to every skep-load. They may increase the number of skep-loads but not the number of heaps. R. Simeon says: Also the number of heaps.

[1] In an ordinary year.
[2] If the past year was the 1st, 2nd, 4th or 5th of the Sabbatic cycle they grant First Tithe and Second Tithe; if it was the 3rd or 6th year they grant First Tithe and Poorman's Tithe.
[3] Wholly dependent on the winter rainfall. Lit. '(fields) of Baal'. The term is still in use among the Arab peasants of Palestine. Cf. Ter. 10[11]; B.B. 3[1].
[4] i.e. two times when rain might normally have been expected.
[5] In the 6th and 7th years so that plants may survive for the 8th year.
[6] Those who tend their land and harvest their crops contrary to the law of the Seventh Year.
[7] So Bert.; Tif. Yis.: 'the (ground) moisture'. See below, 9[6], where the same expression, translated 'moisture' (lit. sweetness), is used.
[8] Lit. 'refuse baskets'. See Kel. 19[10]; 24[9]; Ohol. 8[4].   [9] App. II, D.

3. A man may set out in his field three dung-heaps to every *seah's* space; if more, they must be set out circlewise.[1] So R. Simeon. But the Sages forbid it unless they are heaped [in special places] three handbreadths above or below [ground level].[2] A man may pile up all his dung together. R. Meir forbids this unless it is heaped [on a special place] three handbreadths above or below [ground level]. If he had but little [he may pile it on the field and] he may go on adding to it. R. Eleazer b. Azariah forbids this unless it is heaped [in a special place] three handbreadths above or below [ground level], or laid on rocky ground.

4. If a man used his field for a cattle-fold he should make a pen covering two *seahs'* space, and [when that has been filled with dung] uproot three sides of the pen [and set them up around the adjoining two *seahs'* space] leaving the middle wall standing as before; thus four *seahs'* space will have been used for a cattle-fold. Rabban Simeon b. Gamaliel says: Eight *seahs'* space [may be used after that same fashion for a cattle-fold].[3] It the whole field covered but four *seahs'* space he must leave a part of it [unused by the cattle-fold] for appearance's sake. He may shift the dung from the cattle-fold and set it out on his field [in heaps] after the [prescribed] manner of them that bring out dung.

5. A man may not open up a stone-quarry within his field for the first time [in the Seventh Year] unless there is [visible] there [sufficient stone to provide] courses each three cubits long, three wide and three high, making twenty-seven stones in all.[4]

6. If a wall [that stood in his field] had in it ten stones each a two-men's load, these may be removed. Such a wall must be [not less than] ten handbreadths high; if it is less than this it is accounted a quarry for stone and may be levelled until it is no more than one handbreadth[5] from the ground. This applies to a man's own field; but from his fellow's he may remove what stones he will. Moreover it applies if a man had not begun [to remove the stones] in the sixth year; but if he had begun in the sixth year he may remove what stones he will.

7. Stones that the plough has turned up, or that were covered and are now laid bare, may be removed if there are two among them each a two-men's load. If a man would clear away [loose] stones from his field, he may remove the top layers but must let alone those touching the soil. So, too, with a heap of pebbles or a pile of stones—he may remove the top layers but must let alone those touching the soil; but if beneath these there is stony ground or straw, they may be removed.

8. In the sixth year, after the rains have ceased, steps may not be built up the sides of ravines,[6] since this would be to make them ready for the Seventh Year; but they may be built in the Seventh Year after the rains have ceased, since this is to make them ready for the eighth year. They[7] may not be blocked in with earth, but made only into a rough stone bank; any stone [lying in the field] which a man [building the bank] need but stretch out his hand to take, may be removed.

---

[1] Variant: if more, it is permitted.
[2] To make it plain that they are not actually manuring the ground.
[3] Without incurring suspicion of deliberately manuring the ground in the Seventh Year.
[4] He must not appear to be clearing stones off the field for the sake of sowing; for that is forbidden (2^3) after the beginning of the Seventh Year.
[5] This must be left, to avoid the appearance of clearing away stones for the sake of sowing.
[6] From which water can be drawn for the field during the rainy season.
[7] The steps, or a dam to stop the water from flowing away.

9. 'Shoulder stones' may be brought from anywhere, and a builder[1] may bring stones from anywhere. These are 'shoulder-stones': any that cannot be taken away in one hand. So R. Meir. R. Jose says: 'Shoulder stones' are what their name implies: such as are carried away, two or three together, on a man's shoulder.

10. If a man would build a wall between his own and the public domain, he may dig down to rock level.[2] What must he do with the earth? He may heap it up in the public domain and afterward restore it to order. So R. Joshua. R. Akiba says: As a man may not cause disorder in the public domain neither may he afterward restore it to order; what, then, must he do with the earth? He may heap it up in his own field after the [prescribed] manner of them that bring out dung. So, too, if a man would dig a cistern, a trench, or a cavern.

4. 1. Beforetime they used to say: A man may gather pieces of wood and stones[3] from off his own field when they are big, like as he may gather them from his fellow's field [whether they are big or little];[4] but when transgressors grew many[5] it was ordained that a man might only gather them from another's field, and another gather them from his field, but not as a [mutual] favour, nor, needless to say, to exact maintenance in return.

2. A field that has been cleared of thorns [in the Seventh Year] may be sown in the eighth year; but one that has been prepared,[6] or [wholly] used by cattle, may not be sown in the eighth year. The School of Shammai say that the produce of a prepared field may not be consumed in the Seventh Year; but the School of Hillel say that it may. The School of Shammai say: They may not eat produce of the Seventh Year if it is by favour[7] [of the owner]. The School of Hillel say: They may eat it whether it is by favour or not. R. Judah says: The rule is to the contrary, for here the School of Shammai adopt a more lenient and the School of Hillel a more stringent ruling.

3. Newly ploughed land may be hired in the Seventh Year from a gentile but not from an Israelite; and gentiles may be helped [when labouring in the fields] in the Seventh Year, but not Israelites. Moreover, greetings may be offered to gentiles in the interests of peace.

4. If a man would thin out olive trees [in the Seventh Year], the School of Shammai say: He may only raze them to the roots. The School of Hillel say: He may uproot them. But they agree that if a man would level his field he may only raze [the trees to the roots]. Who is he that 'thins out'? [He that removes but] one or two. And he that 'levels'? [He that removes at least] three growing side by side. This applies to what grows within a man's own domain; but within the domain of his fellow he that levels may also uproot.

5. If a man would split wood off an olive tree [in the Seventh Year] he may not cover up the rent with earth, but he may cover it with stones or straw. If he would cut down the trunk of a sycamore tree he may not cover up the rent with earth, but he may cover it with stones or straw. A virgin sycamore[8] may not be cut down in the Seventh Year since that counts as cultivation.[9] R. Judah says: If after the usual manner, it is forbidden; but

---

[1] Heb. *kablan*, contractor. It may also mean one who leases a field.
[2] And not be suspected of tending his land in the Seventh Year.
[3] Some texts read 'herbs'. [4] See above, 3[6].
[5] Who removed everything. [6] i.e. ploughed and sown.
[7] Eduy. 5[1]. [8] One whose boughs had not before been cut. [9] It is to the tree's benefit.

ten handbreadths or more may be left standing, or it may be razed to ground level.

6. If a man would clip vines or cut reeds [in the Seventh Year], R. Jose the Galilean says: He should leave them [uncut at least] one handbreadth [from the ground]. R. Akiba says: He may cut them in his usual manner with axe, sickle or saw, or with whatsoever he will. If a tree is split it may be tied up in the Seventh Year that the split may grow no greater, but not so as to repair it.[1]

7. After what time may the fruit of trees be eaten in the Seventh Year? After young figs have begun to mature[2] a man may eat his bread with them in the field. After they have ripened he may bring them into his house. And similarly with fruits of like kind [he may bring them in when they are so ripe that] in the other years of the week [of years] he would be liable to Tithes.[3]

8. After unripe grapes have begun to produce juice, a man may eat his bread with them in the field. After they have ripened he may bring them into his house. And similarly with fruits of like kind [he may bring them in when they are so ripe that] in the other years of the week [of years] he would be liable to Tithes.

9. If a *seah* of olives can yield a quarter-*log* [of oil], a man may crush them and eat them in the field; if they can yield a half-*log* he may press them in the field and use their oil; if they can yield a third [of their full possible yield], he may press them in the field and bring them into his house. And similarly with fruits of like kind [he may bring them in when they are so ripe that] in the other years of the week [of years] he would be liable to Tithes. With all other fruit of trees their season for Tithes is their season when they are permitted in the Seventh Year.

10. After what time is it forbidden to cut down trees in the Seventh Year? The School of Shammai say: No tree [may be cut down] after it puts forth [leaves]. The School of Hillel say: Carob trees—after their branches begin to droop; vines—after they produce berries; olive trees—after they blossom; and any other tree—after it puts forth [leaves]. Any tree that has reached the season when it is liable to Tithes may be cut down. How much should an olive tree produce so that it may not be cut down?[4] A quarter-*kab*. R. Simeon b. Gamaliel says: All depends on the kind of olive tree.

5. 1. The Seventh Year [law] may apply to white figs in the second year [of the week of years] since they ripen but once in three years. R. Judah says: The Seventh Year [law] may apply to Persian figs in the year after the Seventh Year since they ripen but once in two years. It was replied: They have spoken only of white figs.

2. If arum is covered up with earth in the Seventh Year, R. Meir says: It must be not less than two *seahs* in quantity, three handbreadths high, and covered with earth one handbreadth deep.[5] But the Sages say: It must be not less than four *kabs* in quantity, one handbreadth high and covered

---

[1] Cf. Shab. 23⁵.   [2] Lit. 'glisten'.   [3] See Maas. 1²ᶠᶠ.
[4] According to the Gemara of the Babylonian Talmud (B.K. 91b) this refers not to the Seventh Year law but to Deut. 20¹⁹, forbidding the destruction of trees belonging to a besieged city. But according to the Jerusalem Talmud it refers to the Seventh Year, the argument being that a tree should not be cut down if it involved loss.
[5] To avoid the appearance of sowing.

with earth one handbreadth deep: moreover it must be covered up with earth in ground over which men walk.[1]

3. When arum has remained after the passing of the Seventh Year, R. Eliezer says: If the poor have gathered the leaves thereof, it is well; if not, an allotment[2] must be made to the poor. R. Joshua says: If the poor have gathered the leaves thereof, it is well; if not, no allotment need be made to the poor.

4. When arum remains from the sixth year until the Seventh Year (so, too, with summer-onions and madder from good soil) the School of Shammai say: They may only be dug up with wooden rakes.[3] The School of Hillel say: With metal spades. But they agree that madder from stony[4] soil may be dug up with metal spades.

5. When may arum be gathered after the close of the Seventh Year? R. Judah says: Forthwith. But the Sages say: After the new crop is come up.

6. These are implements which the craftsman may not sell in the Seventh Year: a plough and whatsoever pertains thereto, a yoke, winnowing fan or mattock. But he may sell a sickle or a scythe or a wagon and whatsoever pertains thereto. This is the general rule: any implement is forbidden whose sole use is one that transgresses [the Seventh Year law], but it is allowed if its use may be either one forbidden or one permissible.

7. The potter may sell [to one person] five oil-jars and fifteen wine-jars, since a man is accustomed to get so much from the ownerless produce [of the Seventh Year]; and if he gets more it is permitted [to sell to him more jars]. The potter may sell [more than this number] to gentiles within the Land [of Israel] and to Israelites outside the Land.

8. The School of Shammai say: A ploughing heifer may not be sold to a man in the Seventh Year. But the School of Hillel permit it since he may perchance slaughter it. One may sell him produce even in time of sowing; even if it is known that he has a threshing-floor one may lend him a *seah*-measure; and one may give him small money in change even if it is known that he employs labourers. But if [it is known that these things are required] expressly [to transgress the Seventh Year law] they are forbidden.

9. A woman may lend a sifter, sieve, hand-mill or oven to her neighbour that is suspected of transgressing the Seventh Year law, but she may not winnow or grind corn with her. The wife of an Associate[5] may lend a sifter or sieve to the wife of an *Am-haaretz* and may winnow, grind or sift corn with her; but when she pours water over the flour she may not draw near to her, since help may not be given to them that commit transgression. All these have been enjoined in the interests of peace. Gentiles may be helped [when labouring in the fields] in the Seventh Year, but not Israelites. Moreover, greetings may be offered to gentiles in the interests of peace.

6. 1. Three countries[6] are to be distinguished in what concerns the Seventh Year: throughout that part of the Land of Israel which they occupied

---

[1] To prevent its sprouting.
[2] The poor must be given as much as is estimated to have grown in the Seventh Year.
[3] The produce is permitted to its owner in the Seventh Year since it grew in the sixth year, but he must not appear to be cultivating his field.
[4] Variant: from the sides of the field.
[5] This Halakah is concerned not with the Seventh Year but with the laws of uncleanness. Once water is poured over the flour it is rendered 'susceptible to uncleanness' (Lev. 11[34]). See p. 758, n. 1.   The paragraph is repeated in Gitt. 5[9].   On Associate see p. 22, n. 2.
[6] See below, 9[2]; Hall. 4[8]. Neub. p. 5ff. Cf. Yad. 4[3].

that came up from Babylon, as far as Chezib,[1] [Seventh Year produce] may not be eaten[2] nor [may the soil be] cultivated; throughout that part which they occupied that came up from Egypt,[3] from Chezib to the River[4] and Amanah, [Seventh Year produce] may be eaten but [the soil] may not be cultivated; while in the country from the River and Amanah and inwards, [Seventh Year produce] may be eaten and [the soil] cultivated.

2. In Syria they may continue work with grain already gathered but not with what is still unreaped: they may thresh, winnow, and trample the corn and bind it into sheaves; but they may not reap the crops or gather the grapes or olives. R. Akiba laid down a general rule: the like of whatsoever is permitted to be done in the Land of Israel may be done also in Syria.

3. Onions [remaining in the field until the Seventh Year] on which rain has fallen and which have sprouted, are forbidden if their leaves are dark coloured, but if they are green they are permitted. R. Hananiah b. Antigonus says: If they can be pulled up by their leaves they are forbidden, whereas in the year following the Seventh Year the like of these[5] are permitted.

4. When may a man buy vegetables after the close of the Seventh Year? When that same crop [again] ripens. Where the first ripening crop is ready the later ripening crops are permissible. Rabbi permitted the buying of vegetables immediately after the close of the Seventh Year.

5. [Heave-offering][6] oil that [has become unclean and] must be burnt and Seventh Year produce may not be taken out of the Land to another country. R. Simeon said: I have heard an express tradition that they may be taken to Syria but not outside the Land [of Israel].

6. Heave-offering may not be brought to the Land [of Israel] from outside the Land. R. Simeon said: I have heard an express tradition that it may be brought from Syria but not from outside the Land [of Israel].

7. 1. An important general rule have they laid down concerning Seventh Year produce: whatsoever is food for man or for cattle or that is a species of dyeing matter, if it is not left growing in the ground, the Seventh Year law applies both to it[7] and to its money substitute.[8] The law of Removal[9] applies both to it and to its money substitute. Which [plants] are these [that are food for man]? The leaf of arum, the leaf of miltwaste, chicory, leeks, purslane, and asphodel. And food for cattle? Thorns and thistles. And dyeing matter? Aftergrowths of woad and seed of safflower. The Seventh Year law applies both to them and to their money substitute, and the law of Removal also applies both to them and to their money substitute.

2. Another general rule have they laid down: whatsoever is not food for man or for cattle nor a species of dyeing matter, and is left growing in the ground, the Seventh Year law applies both to it and to its money substitute; but the law of Removal does not apply to it or to its money substitute. Which [plants] are these? The root of arum and the root of miltwaste, hart's-tongue, Bethlehem-star and hazelwort; and dyeing matter—madder and round-leaved cyclamen. The Seventh Year law applies both to them and to their money substitute, but the law of Removal does not apply to

---

[1] The biblical Achzib, between Acre and Tyre. Judg. 1[31], Josh. 19[29].
[2] If unlawfully cultivated.
[3] And not by them that returned from Babylon.   [4] Euphrates.
[5] That remained over from the sixth year, through the Seventh Year, until the eighth year.   [6] See App. I. 48 (1).   [7] i.e. that it must be eaten free and not sold.
[8] If it is sold in the manner permitted in par. 3.   [9] Deut. 26[13]. See below, 9[2].

them or to their money substitute. R. Meir says: The law of Removal applies to their money substitute until the New Year. The Sages answered: The law of Removal does not apply to the plants themselves; still less can it apply to their money substitute.

3. The Seventh Year law applies to the husks and blossoms of pomegranates and the shells and kernels of walnuts, and also to their money substitute. The dyer may dye [with Seventh Year produce] for his own benefit but not for hire, since none may traffick with Seventh Year produce, or with Firstlings,[1] or with Heave-offering, or with carrion, or with what is *terefah*,[2] or with forbidden beasts[3] or creeping things.[4] [In the Seventh Year] a man may not gather wild vegetables and sell them in the market; yet he may collect them and his son sell them for him in the market. If he had gathered them for his own use and aught remains over, this he may sell.

4. If a man bought a Firstling[5] for his son's wedding feast or for a Feast [at Jerusalem], and he does not need it, he may sell it. If hunters of wild animals, birds and fishes chanced upon species that are unclean, they may sell them. R. Judah says: Also if a man came upon such by accident he may buy or sell them provided that this is not his trade. But the Sages forbid it.

5. The Seventh Year law applies to branches of the sorb tree and the carob tree, as well as to their money substitute; the law of Removal also applies to them and to their money substitute. The Seventh Year law applies to branches of the terebinth, the pistachio, and the white-thorn, as well as to their money substitute; but the law of Removal does not apply to them or to their money substitute. Yet the law of Removal applies to the leaves since these fall off from their stem.

6. The Seventh Year law applies to the rose, henna, balsam, and the lotus, as well as to their money substitute. R. Simeon says: It does not apply to balsam since this is not a fruit.

7. If a fresh rose [of Seventh Year produce] was preserved in old[6] oil, the rose may be taken away; but if an old rose [of Seventh Year produce] was preserved in fresh oil[7] [the whole] is subject to the law of Removal. If fresh carobs [of Seventh Year produce] were preserved in old wine, or old carobs [of Seventh Year produce] in new wine,[7] both are subject to the law of Removal. This is the general rule:[8] if one kind is mixed with a different kind, and it is enough to give its flavour, [the whole] is subject to the law of Removal; if it is mixed with a like kind, in no matter what quantity,[9] [the whole is subject to the law of Removal]. If Seventh Year produce is mixed with a like kind it renders [the rest] forbidden in no matter what quantity, and if with a different kind [it renders the rest forbidden] only if it is enough to give its flavour.

8. 1. An important general rule have they laid down concerning Seventh Year produce: whatsoever is gathered solely as food for man may not be used as an emollient for man, or, needless to say, for cattle; whatsoever is not gathered solely as food for man may be used as an emollient for man but not for cattle; and whatsoever is not [customarily] gathered solely as food for man or as food for cattle, yet was intended as food both for man

[1] See p. 529, n. 8; 533, n. 9.　　[2] See App. I. 47.　　[3] Lev. 11 4ff.
[4] Lev. 11 29ff.　　[5] Blemished, and so permitted to non-priests.
[6] Of the previous year.　　[7] Of the eighth year.
[8] Applying to all kinds of produce that are subject to restrictions enjoined in the Law.
[9] Even if not enough to give its flavour.

and for cattle, the more stringent rules affecting both man and cattle apply to it. If [when it was gathered] it was intended for use [only] as wood, it is so accounted; like, for example, savory, marjoram, and calamint.

2. Seventh Year produce is intended for use as food, drink or unguent: that is to be used as food which is customarily eaten, and that used as drink which is customarily drunken, and that used as unguent which is customarily used for anointing. A man may not use wine or vinegar for anointing, but must anoint with oil. The same[1] applies to Heave-offering and Second Tithe; but greater leniency applies to [oil from] Seventh Year produce in that it can be used for kindling a lamp.

3. Seventh Year produce may not be sold, whether by bulk, weight or number: even figs [may not be sold] by number nor vegetables by weight. The School of Shammai say: Nor even in bundles. And the School of Hillel say: What is usually tied up in bundles in the house may be tied up in bundles in the market; like, for example, leeks and asphodel.

4. If a man said to a labourer [in the Seventh Year], 'Here is an *issar*[2] for thee: gather me vegetables to-day', his payment is permitted; but if he said, 'In return [for the *issar*] gather me vegetables to-day', his payment is forbidden. If a man bought from the baker a loaf worth a *pondion*[3] [and said,] 'When I have collected vegetables from the field I will bring them to thee', this is permitted; but if he bought it from him with no conditions, he may not pay him with the price of Seventh Year produce, since a debt may not be defrayed with the price of Seventh Year produce.

5. One may not pay therewith a well-digger, a bath-house keeper, a barber or a sailor, but it may be given to a well-digger [to buy wine] to drink; and it may be given to any of them as a free gift.

6. Seventh Year figs may not be cut off with the fig-knife, but they may be cut off by a [different] knife; grapes may not be trodden out in a wine-press, but they may be trodden out in a vat; and olives may not be prepared in an olive-press or with an olive-crusher, but they may be crushed and brought into a small press. R. Simeon says: They may even be ground in the [proper] olive-press and then brought into a small press.

7. Seventh Year vegetables may not be cooked in Heave-offering oil, lest they make it invalid.[4] R. Simeon permits it. [If Seventh Year produce is exchanged for aught else and this again exchanged] the last thing [got in exchange] is subject to the Seventh Year law, and the [Seventh Year] produce itself remains forbidden.

8. Slaves or lands or unclean beasts may not be bought with the price of Seventh Year produce; but if a man has done so he must [buy and] consume [produce of] equal value.[5] It is forbidden to bring as the offerings of a man or woman that suffered a flux[6] or of a woman after childbirth[7] birds that have been bought with the price of Seventh Year produce; if one has done so he must [buy and] consume [produce of] equal value. Vessels may not be anointed with oil from Seventh Year produce, and if one has done so he must [buy and] consume [produce of] equal value.

9. If a hide has been smeared with Seventh Year oil, R. Eliezer says: It must be burnt. But the Sages say: A man must [buy and] consume [produce of] equal value. They declared before R. Akiba that R. Eliezer

---

[1] That it can be used only for food, drink, or unguent.
[2] See App. II, A.　　　　　[3] Ibid.　　　　　[4] See p. 714, n. 3.
[5] The price of Seventh Year produce must itself be used only for purchasing other food.
[6] Lev. $15^{14-15, \ 29-30}$.　　　　　[7] Lev. $12^{6, \ 8}$.

used to say: A hide that has been smeared with Seventh Year oil is to be burnt. He replied: Hold your peace; I will not say to you what R. Eliezer has taught concerning this.[1]

10. Moreover they declared before him that R. Eliezer used to say: He that eats the bread of the Samaritans is like to one that eats the flesh of swine. He replied: Hold your peace; I will not say to you what R. Eliezer has taught concerning this.

11. If a bath was heated with Seventh Year straw or stubble, it is permitted to wash therein. But a man that is held in honour will not wash therein.

9. 1. Rue, goosefoot, purslane, hill-coriander, celery, and meadow-eruca are exempt from Tithes and may be bought from any one in the Seventh Year, since no watch is kept over the like of these.[2] R. Judah says: Aftergrowths of mustard are permitted since transgressors are not under suspicion concerning them. R. Simeon says: All aftergrowths are permitted excepting the aftergrowths of cabbage, since the like of these do not come within the class of wild vegetables. But the Sages say: All aftergrowths are forbidden.

2. Three countries[3] are to be distinguished in what concerns the law of Removal:[4] Judea, beyond Jordan and Galilee; and each of these is divided into three lands. [Galilee is divided into] upper Galilee, lower Galilee, and the valley: from Kefar Hanania upwards, wheresoever sycamores do not grow, is upper Galilee; from Kefar Hanania downwards, wheresoever sycamores grow, is lower Galilee; the region of Tiberias is the valley. And in Judea are the hill-country, the plain[5] and the valley.[6] The plain of Lydda is deemed to pertain to the plain of the south, and the hill-country near by is like to the king's hill-country.[7] From Beth-horon to the sea is reckoned a single district.

3. Why have they spoken of three countries? That they may eat [of Seventh Year produce] in each country only until the last [of the Seventh Year produce] in that country is ended. R. Simeon says: They have spoken of three countries only in what concerns Judea; the rest of the countries are as the king's hill-country.[8] All these countries are alike in what concerns olives and dates.

4. They may eat [Seventh Year produce which they have collected into their houses] only so long as like produce is still found free in the fields, but not so long as it is still found watched over [in private ownership]. R. Jose

---

[1] R. Eliezer (b. Hyrcanus) was at one time under a ban because of his heretical views (cf. p. 783, n. 5).

[2] They are ownerless property and the sanctity of the Seventh Year does not apply to them.

[3] See Neub. 59f.

[4] If Seventh Year produce was gathered by any person he is permitted to eat it so long as like produce is still growing in the country where he lives. Once this produce has begun to wither in the fields, the gathered produce of that same species must be 'removed', i.e. be eaten forthwith, or burnt or thrown into the sea. Cf. M. Sh. 5⁶.

[5] Shephelah.

[6] t. Shebi. 7⁸: from Engedi to Jericho. For the threefold division cf. Josh. 10⁴⁰; Judg. 1⁹. Beyond Jordan is divided in like manner into hill-country, plain, and valley (see p. Shebi. 9²: the hill-country is Machwar, Gadar, and the rest; the plain is Heshbon with all the towns on the plain, such as Dibhon, Bamoth Baal, Beth Baal Meon, and the rest; the valley is Beth Haran, Beth Nimrah, and the rest).

[7] i.e. like the hill country of Judea; and they may eat the Seventh Year produce there until the like kind disappears in the fields of the king's hill-country.

[8] In Galilee and beyond Jordan they may continue eating Seventh Year produce until the like produce comes to an end in the Judean hill-country (i.e. where, owing to its altitude, the time of ripening is late).

allows it also when it is still found watched over [in private ownership]. They may [continue to] eat [Seventh Year produce] by virtue of [the continuance in the open field of] late-ripening grain, or of trees that bear twice in the year, but not by virtue of winter grapes. R. Judah allows this if they began to ripen before the summer [of the Seventh Year] was over.

5. If three kinds of vegetables [of Seventh Year produce] were preserved in a single jar, R. Eliezer says: They may be eaten only such time as the first [of the three kinds to ripen] remains in the field. R. Joshua says: Even until the last [of the three to ripen] still remains. Rabban Gamaliel says: When the like kind comes to an end in the field the law of Removal applies to that same kind that is in the jar. And the *Halakah* is according to him. R. Simeon says: All vegetables are alike in what concerns the law of Removal: one may continue eating [Seventh Year] purslane until vetches come to an end in the valley of Beth Netopha.[1]

6. If a man gathered fresh vegetables [of Seventh Year produce, he may continue to eat of them] until the [ground] moisture is dried up. If he gathered dried vegetables [he may continue to eat of them] until the second rainfall[2] [of the next year]. Leaves of reeds or of vines [may continue to be used] until they [that are still left in the field] fall from their stem; or if they were gathered dry, until the second rainfall. R. Akiba says: In every case [they may continue to be used] until the second rainfall.

7. In like manner if a man hired a house to his fellow 'until the rains', [this signifies] 'until the second rainfall'. If a man was under a vow[3] to derive no benefit from his fellow 'until the rains', [this signifies] 'until the second rainfall'. Until when may the poor enter the gardens[4] [to glean]? Until the second rainfall. After what time may the straw and stubble[5] of the Seventh Year be made use of or burnt? After the second rainfall.

8. If a man still had Seventh Year produce and the time came for Removal, he must allot food for three meals to every person [in his household]. The poor may eat [of such produce] after the time of Removal, but not the rich. So R. Judah. R. Jose says: Poor and rich alike may eat after the time of Removal.

9. If a man had Seventh Year produce that had fallen to him by inheritance or gift, R. Eliezer says: It must be given [free] to them that would eat of it. But the Sages say: The sinner[6] may not be benefited!—but, rather, the produce should be sold to them that would eat of it, and its price divided among them all. If a man ate of dough made from Seventh Year produce before Dough-offering was taken from it, he is guilty of death.[7]

10. 1. The Seventh Year cancels[8] any loan whether it is secured by bond or not. It does not cancel debts due to a shopkeeper,[9] but if they were turned into a loan it cancels them. R. Judah says: If a later debt is incurred the former [is deemed to be a loan and] is cancelled. The hire of an hireling is not cancelled, but if it was turned into a loan it is cancelled. R. Jose says: If the work must stop in the Seventh Year the hire is cancelled, but if it need not stop in the Seventh Year the hire is not cancelled.

---

[1] Neub. p. 128. Purslane is given here as lasting longest after being plucked; and Netopha as a place where, owing to its plentiful supply of water, the crops remain longest in the field.   [2] Usually falls during November.   [3] Ned. 8[5].   [4] Peah 8[1].
[5] Which the Law enjoins (Ex. 23[11]; Lev. 25[7]) shall, in the Seventh Year, be food for the cattle and not be for man's profit.   [6] He had received a forbidden gift.
[7] Although Seventh Year produce is tithe-free it is liable to the Dough-offering (p. 83, n. 1).
[8] Deut. 15[1ff].   [9] For goods given on trust.

2. If a man slaughtered a heifer and divided it [among purchasers] on the first day of the [eighth] year, and the month was intercalated,[1] the debt [incurred by them that buy the flesh] is cancelled; but if not, it is not cancelled. [The fines incurred by] the violator,[2] the seducer[3] and him that *hath brought up an evil name*,[4] and all payments enjoined by the court are not cancelled. A loan secured by a pledge and one of which the bonds are delivered to the court, these are not cancelled.

3. [A loan secured by] a *prozbul*[5] is not cancelled [by the Seventh Year]. This is one of the things that Hillel the Elder ordained. When he saw that the people refrained from giving loans one to another and transgressed what is written in the Law, *Beware that there be not a base thought in thine heart* . . .,[6] Hillel ordained the *prozbul*.

4. This is the formula of the *prozbul*: 'I affirm to you, such-a-one and such-a-one, the judges in such-a-place, that, touching any debt due to me, I will collect it whensoever I will.' And the judges sign below, or the witnesses.

5. An ante-dated *prozbul* is valid, but if it is post-dated it is not valid. Ante-dated bonds are not valid, but if post-dated they are valid. If one borrows from five persons, a *prozbul* is drawn up for each [creditor]; if five borrow from one person, only one *prozbul* is drawn up for them all.

6. A *prozbul* may only be written for [a loan secured by] immovable property. If the debtor has none, the creditor gives him title to part, however small, of his own land. If the debtor has land held in pledge in the city, a *prozbul* may be written on its security. R. Huspith says: They may write a *prozbul* for a man on the security of his wife's property, or for an orphan on the security of his guardians' property.

7. A[7] bee-hive, R. Eliezer says, counts as immovable property, a *prozbul* may be written on its security, it is not susceptible to uncleanness while it remains in its own place,[8] and if a man scraped honey from it on the Sabbath he is culpable.[9] But the Sages say: It does not count as immovable property, a *prozbul* may not be written on its security, it contracts uncleanness while remaining in its own place, and if a man scraped honey from it on the Sabbath he is not culpable.

8. If a man would repay a debt in the Seventh Year the creditor must say to him, 'I cancel it'. If he replied, 'None the less [I will repay it]', the creditor may take it from him; for it is written, *And this is the* word *of the release*.[10] In like manner[11] if a manslayer went into exile to a city of refuge and the men of the city were minded to do him honour, he must say to them, 'I am a manslayer'. If they replied, 'None the less [we would do thee honour]', he may accept [the honour] from them; for it is written, *This is the* word *of the manslayer*.[12]

9. If a man repays a debt in the Seventh Year the Sages are well pleased with him. If a man borrows from a proselyte whose sons have become proselytes with him, he need not repay the debt to the sons;[13] but if he

---

[1] If the last month of the Seventh Year was given 30 instead of 29 days, so that the day when he divided the beast was thus the last day of the Seventh Year.
[2] Deut. 22[29].   [3] Ex. 22[16-17].   [4] Deut. 22[13ff].
[5] See App. I. 34.   [6] Deut. 15[9].   [7] Uktz. 3[10].
[8] It is deemed like the ground, and not a 'vessel', and so it is not susceptible to uncleanness.
[9] It would be the equivalent of plucking something from the ground, offending against the law against 'reaping' on the Sabbath (Shab. 7[2]).
[10] Deut. 15[2]. The 'word', i.e. simple admission of the obligation, satisfies the law.
[11] Makk. 2[8].   [12] Deut. 19[4].
[13] Since the sons of a proselyte do not inherit from their father.

repays it to them the Sages are well pleased with him. All movable goods are [legally] acquired [only] by the act of drawing [them into the purchaser's possession];[1] but whosoever fulfils his [bare] word, the Sages are well pleased with him.

TERUMOTH ('HEAVE-OFFERINGS')

1. 1. There are five that may not give Heave-offering,[2] and if they do so their Heave-offering is not valid: a deaf-mute (*ḥērēsh*), an imbecile, a minor, he that gives Heave-offering from what is not his own; and a gentile who gives Heave-offering from what belongs to an Israelite—even if it was with his consent his Heave-offering is not valid.

2. He that is not dumb but [only] deaf may not give Heave-offering, but if he does so his Heave-offering is valid. The *ḥērēsh* of which the Sages have spoken is always one that is both deaf and dumb.

3. If a minor has not produced two hairs,[3] R. Judah says: His Heave-offering is valid. R. Jose says: If [he gave Heave-offering] before he reached an age when his vows are valid[4] his Heave-offering is not valid; but if after he reached an age when his vows are valid his Heave-offering is valid.

4. Heave-offering may not be given from olives instead of from oil, or from grapes instead of from wine. If this is done, the School of Shammai say: It may still be deemed Heave-offering of the olives or of the grapes themselves. And the School of Hillel say: Their Heave-offering is not valid.

5. Heave-offering is not given from Gleanings, or from the Forgotten Sheaf, or from *Peah*,[5] or from ownerless produce, or from First Tithe from which Heave-offering[6] has been[7] taken, or from Second Tithe[8] or dedicated produce that have been[7] redeemed. [Heave-offering may not be given] from what is liable [to Tithes] instead of from what is exempt, or from what is exempt instead of from what is liable, or from what is plucked instead of from what is unplucked, or from what is unplucked instead of from what is plucked, or from this year's produce instead of from last year's produce, or from last year's produce instead of from this year's produce, or from produce of the Land [of Israel] instead of from produce from outside the Land, or from produce from outside the Land instead of from produce of the Land. And if this is done the Heave-offering is not valid.

6. There are five that may not give Heave-offering, yet if they do so their Heave-offering is valid: he that is dumb, or drunken, or naked, or blind, or that has suffered a pollution;[9] these may not give Heave-offering, yet if they do so their Heave-offering is valid.

7. Heave-offering may not be given by measure, by weight or by number, but it may be given from what has been measured, or weighed, or numbered. Heave-offering may not be given in a basket or in a hamper that holds a [known] measure, but it may be given therein if it is a half or a third part filled. It may not be given in a *seah*[-measure] half filled since the half thereof is a [known] measure.

---

[1] See Kidd. 1[4,5]; B.M. 4[2]; B.B. 5[7]; 9[7].

[2] Heb. *terumah*. See App. I. 48. It is the portion (from a sixtieth to a fortieth) that must be given to the priests from the produce of the harvest, and the produce is forbidden to be eaten by non-priests until such Heave-offering has been set aside.

[3] The token of puberty. Cf. San. 8[1]; Nidd. 6[11].

[4] For a boy it is thirteen years and a day; for a girl twelve years and a day. See Nidd. 5[6].

[5] For these three see Peah 4[10, 11]; 5[7ff]; 1[1ff].   [6] See App. I. 48 (2).

[7] Variant: 'not been'.   [8] See p. 73, n. 6.   [9] Lev. 15[16].

8. Heave-offering may not be given from oil instead of from olives that are to be pressed, or from wine instead of from grapes that are to be trodden; yet if this is done the Heave-offering is valid, but Heave-offering must again be given. [And of these two Heave-offerings] the first renders [other produce into which it may fall] subject to the law of Heave-offering, and [if it is eaten in error by a non-priest] it is subject to the law of the [Added] Fifth;[1] but it is not so with the second.[2]

9. Heave-offering may be given from oil instead of from olives that are to be preserved, or from wine instead of from grapes that are to be made into raisins. If a man gave Heave-offering from oil instead of from olives intended for eating, or from [other] olives instead of from olives intended for eating, or from wine instead of from grapes intended for eating, or from [other] grapes instead of from grapes intended for eating, and he afterward determined to press them, he need not give Heave-offering afresh.

10. Heave-offering may not be given from produce whose preparation is finished instead of from produce whose preparation is unfinished, or from produce whose preparation is unfinished instead of from produce whose preparation is finished, or from produce whose preparation is unfinished instead of from [other] produce whose preparation is unfinished. But if this is done the Heave-offering is valid.

2. 1. Heave-offering may not be given from what is clean instead of from what is unclean; yet if this is done the Heave-offering is valid. Rightly have they said:[3] If part of a cake of pressed figs was unclean, Heave-offering may be given from the part that is clean instead of from the part that is unclean. So, too, with a bundle of vegetables or a heap of grain. If there were two cakes, two bundles, or two heaps, and one of them was unclean and the other clean, Heave-offering may not be given from the one instead of from the other. R. Eliezer says: Heave-offering may be given from the clean instead of from the unclean.

2. Heave-offering may not be given from what is unclean instead of from what is clean; if this was done in error the Heave-offering is valid, and if wantonly the act is void. So, too, if a levite had [unclean] Tithe from which Heave-offering [of Tithe] had not been given, and he gave Heave-offering from this instead of from other produce, if this was done in error his Heave-offering is valid, and if wantonly his act is void. R. Judah says: If he knew before [that it was unclean], even if he acted in error his act is void.

3. If a man immersed [unclean] vessels on the Sabbath[4] and he acted in error, he may use them, and if wantonly he may not use them. If he set apart tithe or cooked aught on the Sabbath and he acted in error, he may eat of it, and if wantonly he may not eat of it. If a man planted aught on the Sabbath and he acted in error, he may let it remain, and if wantonly he must uproot it; but in the Seventh Year, whether he acted in error or wantonly, he must uproot it.

4. Heave-offering may not be given from one kind instead of from another kind, and if this is done the Heave-offering is not valid. All kinds of wheat count as one and all kinds of figs, dried figs and fig-cakes count as one, and Heave-offering can be given from one kind instead of from

---

[1] Lev. 5[16].

[2] Since this is not enjoined in the Law but is only a 'hedge around the Law' ordained as a precaution by the Scribes.   [3] See p. 12, n. 4.

[4] Forbidden as an act of work, since it is the equivalent of repairing a utensil.

another. Where there is a priest Heave-offering must be given from the choicest kind; but where there is no priest [it should be given] from the kind that best endures. R. Judah says: Heave-offering should ever be given from the choicest kind.

5. They should give as Heave-offering a whole small onion and not half a large onion. R. Judah says: Not so; but [they should give] half a large onion. So, too, R. Judah used to say: Heave-offering may be given from town onions instead of from village onions but not from village onions instead of from town onions, since these are the food of the better folk.

6. Heave-offering may be given from oil-olives instead of from pickling-olives but not from pickling-olives instead of from oil-olives; [it may be given] from unboiled wine instead of from boiled wine but not from boiled wine instead of from unboiled wine. This is the general rule: if the two kinds of produce are Diverse Kinds, Heave-offering may not be given from one instead of from the other, even from the better instead of from the worse; if they are not Diverse Kinds, Heave-offering may be given from the better instead of from the worse, but not from the worse instead of from the better; yet if Heave-offering is given from the worse instead of from the better the Heave-offering is valid, save only when tares[1] are given instead of wheat, since they are not food. Cucumbers and musk-melons count as a single kind. R. Judah says: Two kinds.[2]

3. 1. If a man gave a cucumber as Heave-offering and it was found to be bitter, or a water-melon and it was found to be rotten, it is valid, but he must again give Heave-offering. If he gave a jar of wine as Heave-offering and it was found turned to vinegar, the Heave-offering is invalid if it was known that it had turned to vinegar before it was given as Heave-offering; but if it had turned to vinegar after it was given as Heave-offering, the Heave-offering is valid; if it was in doubt, the Heave-offering is deemed valid but he must again give Heave-offering. [And of these two Heave-offerings] the first does not of itself render [other produce into which it may fall] subject to the law of Heave-offering, and [if it is eaten in error by a non-priest] it is not subject to the law of the [Added] Fifth; and so, too, is it with the second.

2. If one of them fell into common produce[3] it does not render it subject to the law of Heave-offering; if the other fell elsewhere [in the same produce] it does not render it subject to the law of Heave-offering; but if both fell into the same place they render it subject to the law of Heave-offering according to [the bulk of] the smaller of the two [Heave-offerings].[4]

3. If jointholders gave Heave-offering the one after the other, R. Akiba says: The Heave-offering of them both is valid. But the Sages say: The Heave-offering of the first [alone] is accounted Heave-offering. R. Jose says: If the first gave Heave-offering in full measure the Heave-offering of the second is not accounted Heave-offering; but if the first did not give Heave-offering in full measure the Heave-offering of the second is accounted Heave-offering.

4. This[5] applies if the one had not bidden [the other give Heave-offering]. But if a man empowered one of his household or his bondman or his bond-

---

[1] See Kil. 1[1].   [2] Kil. 1[2].

[3] Heb. *hullin*, lit. 'profane'; it here means produce from which Heave-offering has already been taken and which is therefore free for unrestricted consumption.

[4] i.e. it renders the rest subject to the law of Heave-offering only if it is at least one-hundredth of the whole mixture.   [5] The opinion of R. Akiba.

woman to give Heave-offering, such Heave-offering is valid. If he annulled his word the Heave-offering is invalid if he annulled it before the Heave-offering was given, but if he annulled it after the Heave-offering was given, the Heave-offering remains valid. Labourers[1] have no right to give Heave-offering, excepting the treaders of grapes, since they[2] would straightway render the winepress unclean.

5. If a man said, 'Let the Heave-offering of this heap be within it', or 'Let the Tithes thereof be within it', or 'Let the Heave-offering of Tithe be within it', R. Simeon says: He has validly designated it.[3] But the Sages say: Not until he says, 'Let it be to the north of it' or 'to the south of it'. R. Eleazar Hisma says: If he said, 'Let Heave-offering be given from this heap for this heap', he has validly designated it.[3] R. Eliezer b. Jacob says: If he said, 'May the tenth part of this Tithe be Heave-offering of Tithe', he has validly designated it.[3]

6. If a man gave Heave-offering before First-fruits, or First Tithe before Heave-offering, or Second Tithe before First Tithe, his act is valid, although he transgresses a negative command, for it is written, *Thou shalt not delay to offer of the abundance of thy fruits and of thy liquors.*[4]

7. And whence [do we learn] that First-fruits come before Heave-offering [even though] the one is called [by the Scripture] 'Heave-offering' and 'the first', and the other is called 'Heave-offering' and 'the first'?[5] First-fruits come first because they are, of all produce, the 'First-fruits'. And Heave-offering comes before First Tithe since it is called 'the first'. And First Tithe comes before Second Tithe because it includes [the Heave-offering of Tithe which is called] 'the first'.

8. If a man intended to say 'Heave-offering' and he said 'Tithe', or 'Tithe' and he said 'Heave-offering'; or if he intended to say 'Whole-offering' and he said 'Peace-offering', or 'Peace-offering' and he said 'Whole-offering'; or if he intended to say [in his vow], 'I will not enter this house', and he said 'that house', or 'I will derive no benefit from this', and he said 'that', his word remains void until mouth and heart agree.

9. Heave-offering or Tithes or Hallowed Things[6] that are given by a gentile or a Samaritan are valid. R. Judah says: The law of the Fourth Year Vineyard[7] does not apply to gentiles.[8] But the Sages say: It does apply. The Heave-offering of gentiles renders [other produce with which it is mixed] subject to the law of Heave-offering, and [if it is eaten in error by a non-priest] it is subject to the law of the [Added] Fifth. But R. Simeon declares it exempt [from the law of the Added Fifth].

4. 1. If a man set aside [from a heap] only part of the Heave-offering and Tithes [to which it was liable], he may still take [the remaining] Heave-offering [or Tithes] for that [heap] from that [heap], but he may not take

---

1 Who are 'Associates' working for one who is an *Am-haaretz* (see App. I. 3).

2 Householders who are *Amme-haaretz*.

3 So that the Heave-offering, &c., may be taken from that heap only.   4 Ex. 22[29].

5 Deut. 12[6, 17] speaks of 'the heave-offering of your hand', and Deut. 26[4], speaking of first-fruits, says 'the priest shall take the basket out *of thine hand*'; there, first-fruits are called 'heave-offering'. Ex. 23[19] says, 'the first, the first-fruits of thy ground'; Num. 18[8] says of Aaron, 'Behold I have given thee the charge of mine heave-offerings'; and Deut. 18[4] says, 'The *first* of thy corn, of thy wine . . . thou shalt give him (the priest)'.

6 The term includes anything dedicated to the Temple or set aside to be offered in the Temple, or which, according to the Law, should belong to the Temple.

7 Lev. 19[23-5]. See Peah 7[6]; M. Sh. 5[1-4].

8 i.e. Jews may eat from gentiles' vineyards in the fourth year.

aught from that heap [as Heave-offering or Tithes] for produce elsewhere. R. Meir says: He may take Heave-offering and Tithes from that heap for produce elsewhere.

2. If his produce was in the store-chamber and he gave one *seah* to a levite and one *seah* to a poor man,[1] he may thereupon set aside as much as eight *seahs* and consume them. So R. Meir. But the Sages say: He may set aside produce in accordance with the exact quantity [that still remains with the levite and the poor man].

3. The proper measure of Heave-offering, if a man is liberal, is one-fortieth part (the School of Shammai say: One-thirtieth); if he is liberal in medium degree, one-fiftieth part; if he is mean, one-sixtieth part. If a man gave Heave-offering and found that it was only one-sixtieth, it is valid and he need not again give Heave-offering. If he added more, this is subject to Tithes.[2] If he found that it was only one sixty-first, the Heave-offering is valid but he must give Heave-offering again as much as his custom is, [and this may be given] according to measure, weight, or number. R. Judah says: It can be taken even from produce not lying near by.

4. If a householder said to his agent, 'Go and give Heave-offering', the agent should give Heave-offering according to the householder's mind. If he does not know the householder's mind he should give Heave-offering according to medium measure, one-fiftieth part. If he gave ten parts less or more [in error] the Heave-offering is valid, but if of set purpose he added even one part more, the Heave-offering is not valid.[3]

5. If a man would give more Heave-offering, R. Eliezer says: He may give up to one-tenth, as with Heave-offering of Tithe; if more than this, let him make the surplus Heave-offering of Tithe[4] for produce elsewhere. R. Ishmael says: [He need keep but] half as common produce and [he may give] half as Heave-offering. R. Tarfon and R. Akiba say: [He may give as much Heave-offering as he will] so long as he keeps back somewhat[5] as common produce.

6. At three times do they take the measure of the basket [in which to give First Tithe and Heave-offering of Tithe]: at the time of the first ripe fruits and of the late summer fruits and in the middle of the summer. To count the fruits is praiseworthy, to measure them is more praiseworthy, but to weigh them is the most praiseworthy of the three.[6]

7. R. Eliezer says: Heave-offering becomes neutralized in a hundred and one parts.[7] R. Joshua says: In somewhat more than a hundred; and this 'somewhat more' has no prescribed measure. R. Jose b. Meshullam says: This 'somewhat more' must be [at least] one *kab*[8] to a hundred *seahs*,[8] namely a sixth of that [*seah* of Heave-offering] which would render [the ninety-nine and 'somewhat more' *seahs*] subject to the law of Heave-offering.

8. R. Joshua says: Black figs serve to neutralize in conjunction with white, and white figs serve to neutralize in conjunction with black; large

[1] As First Tithe and Poorman's Tithe (see p. 15, n. 6). These, according to R. Meir, serve to render another eight *seahs* duly tithed. With this obscure Mishnah cf. Gitt. 3[8].
[2] Since it is not validly Heave-offering but part of the tithable residue.
[3] Since he has wilfully not fulfilled his trust he has invalidated his agency. Cf. Meil. 6[4].
[4] Cambridge text adds: 'but not' for produce, &c.
[5] Cf. Hall. 1[9].   [6] Cf. Ab. 1[16].
[7] If one *seah* of Heave-offering fell into 100 *seahs* of ordinary produce, making 101 in all, any one *seah* may be taken out and given to the priest, and the rest is free for common use.
[8] App. II, D.

cakes of figs serve to neutralize in conjunction with small cakes, and small in conjunction with large; round cakes serve to neutralize in conjunction with square cakes, and square in conjunction with round. But R. Eliezer does not permit this. R. Akiba says: If it was known which kind fell [among the common produce] differing kinds do not serve to neutralize in conjunction with each other; but if it was not known which kind fell, differing kinds serve to neutralize in conjunction with each other.

9. Thus if there were fifty black figs and fifty white figs [of common produce] and one black [Heave-offering] fig fell among them, the black figs are forbidden but the white are permitted; if a white fig fell among them the white figs are forbidden but the black are permitted; but if it was not known which kind fell among them the two kinds serve to neutralize in conjunction with each other. Here R. Eliezer adopts the more stringent and R. Joshua the more lenient ruling.

10. But in this [that follows] R. Eliezer adopts the more lenient and R. Joshua the more stringent ruling. If a *litra* of dried [Heave-offering] figs were stuffed into the mouth of a jar [which was one among many jars of figs each holding a hundred *litras*], but it is not known into which, R. Eliezer says: The Heave-offering figs are deemed [not a single mass but] separated figs [dispersed among the figs that are common produce], and those below serve to neutralize in conjunction with those above. R. Joshua says: They do so only if there are a hundred jars.

11. If a *seah* of Heave-offering fell into the mouth of a store-jar and the top layer was skimmed off, R. Eliezer says: If in the layer removed there was a hundred *seahs*, [the *seah* of Heave-offering] becomes neutralized [as being but one] in a hundred and one. R. Joshua says: It is not neutralized. If a *seah* of Heave-offering fell into the mouth of a store-jar, the top layer must be skimmed off. If so, why have they said: Heave-offering becomes neutralized in a hundred and one parts? [That applies only] if it is not known whether it has become mixed up, or where it had fallen.

12. If there were two baskets, or two store-jars, and a *seah* of Heave-offering fell into one of them and it is not known into which of them it fell, each serves to neutralize in conjunction with the other. R. Simeon says: Even if they are found in two separate towns they serve to neutralize in conjunction with each other.

13. R. Jose said: A case once came before R. Akiba about fifty bundles of vegetables among which a like bundle was fallen of which the half was Heave-offering; and I decided before him, 'It is neutralized'—not that Heave-offering can be neutralized in fifty and one, but because there were there a hundred and two halves.

5. 1. If one *seah* of unclean Heave-offering fell into less than a hundred *seahs* of common produce, First Tithe, Second Tithe, or dedicated produce, whether they were clean or unclean, they must be left to rot; if that *seah* was clean, they must be sold to priests at the price of Heave-offering,[1] excepting the price of that one *seah*.[2] If it fell into First Tithe the whole must be designated Heave-offering of Tithe, and if it fell into Second Tithe or into dedicated produce, these must be redeemed. If the common produce was unclean it may be eaten dried or roast or kneaded with fruit

---

[1] Which is naturally much less than that of common food since it is only consumable by priests.   [2] Which must be given free.

juice[1] or divided among lumps of dough so that in no single place is there an egg's bulk.[2]

2. If one *seah* of unclean Heave-offering fell into a hundred *seahs* of common produce, they remain clean. R. Eliezer says: [One *seah*] can be taken up and burnt, since I should assume that the *seah* which fell in is the *seah* which comes up. But the Sages say: It is neutralized and it may be eaten dried or roast or kneaded with fruit juice or divided among lumps of dough so that in no single place is there an egg's bulk.

3. If one *seah* of clean Heave-offering fell into a hundred *seahs* of unclean common produce it is neutralized and may be eaten dry or roast or kneaded with fruit juice or divided among lumps of dough so that in no single place is there an egg's bulk.

4. If one *seah* of unclean Heave-offering fell into a hundred *seahs* of clean Heave-offering, the School of Shammai forbid the whole, but the School of Hillel permit it. The School of Hillel said to the School of Shammai: Since clean [Heave-offering] is forbidden to non-priests and unclean is forbidden to priests, if the clean can be neutralized cannot the unclean be neutralized also? The School of Shammai answered: No! if common produce (to which leniency applies and which is permitted to non-priests) neutralizes what is clean, should Heave-offering (to which stringency applies and which is forbidden to non-priests) neutralize what is unclean! After they had agreed,[3] R. Eliezer said: It should be taken up and burnt. But the Sages say: It is lost through its scantness.

5. If one *seah* of Heave-offering fell into a hundred [*seahs* of common produce] and was lifted out and again fell [into common produce] elsewhere, R. Eliezer says: It renders it subject to the law of Heave-offering as though it was undoubted Heave-offering. But the Sages say: It may render it subject to the law of Heave-offering only if it is in the prescribed proportion.

6. If one *seah* of Heave-offering fell into less than a hundred [*seahs* of common produce] and these were [thereby] rendered subject to the law of Heave-offering, and some of this produce mixed with Heave-offering fell [into common produce] elsewhere, R. Eliezer says: It renders it subject to the law of Heave-offering as though it was undoubted Heave-offering. But the Sages say:[4] What contains Heave-offering renders [other produce] subject to the law of Heave-offering only if it is in the prescribed proportion. What is leavened [with Heave-offering] renders [other dough] leavened [as with Heave-offering] only if it is in the prescribed proportion. Drawn water renders the Immersion-pool[5] invalid only if it is in the prescribed proportion.

7. If one *seah* of Heave-offering fell into a hundred [*seahs* of common produce] and was lifted out and another *seah* fell in and was lifted out [and so on], the common produce is not forbidden until the Heave-offering exceeds the common produce.

8. If one *seah* of Heave-offering fell into a hundred [*seahs* of common produce] and before it was lifted out another *seah* fell in, such common produce is forbidden [to non-priests]. R. Simeon declares it permitted.

[1] Such as the juice of olives or pomegranates which do not, like certain liquids (cf. Maksh. 6[4]) render food susceptible to uncleanness (Lev. 11[34]).

[2] The minimum quantity susceptible to food uncleanness (see Toh. 3[4]).

[3] The School of Shammai admitted the truth of the opinion of the School of Hillel, 'and nowhere else have we found that the School of Shammai admitted the truth of the opinion of the School of Hillel' (Tif. Yis.).

[4] Tem. 1[4].   [5] See Mikw. 2[4].

9. If one *seah* of Heave-offering fell into a hundred [*seahs* of common produce] and they were ground [together] and reduced in bulk, as the common produce becomes less so the Heave-offering becomes less, and [the whole] is [still] permitted. If one *seah* of Heave-offering fell into less than a hundred [*seahs* of common produce] and they were ground together and increased in bulk, as the common produce increases so the Heave-offering increases, and [the whole] is [still] forbidden. If it was known that the wheat that was common produce was of better quality than the wheat that was Heave-offering, it is permitted. If one *seah* of Heave-offering fell into less than a hundred [*seahs* of common produce] and [other] common produce afterward fell therein, if it was in error the whole is permitted, but if wantonly it is forbidden.

6. 1. If a man ate Heave-offering in error he must repay its value and the [Added] Fifth.[1] It is all one whether he ate or drank or anointed himself, or whether the Heave-offering was clean or unclean: he must repay the [Added] Fifth and [even] the fifth of the [Added] Fifth.[2] He may not repay in Heave-offering but in duly tithed common produce. This [too] becomes Heave-offering, and what may be repaid in its stead[3] also becomes Heave-offering; [therefore] even if the priest would remit he may not.

2. If the daughter of an Israelite[4] ate Heave-offering and was afterward married to a priest,[5] if she had eaten Heave-offering not yet acquired by a priest she may pay its value and the [Added] Fifth to herself; but if she had eaten Heave-offering already acquired by a priest she should pay its value to the owner and the [Added] Fifth to herself; for they have taught: If a man ate Heave-offering in error he must repay the value to the owner but [he may pay] the [Added] Fifth to whomsoever he will.

3. If a man gave his labourers or guests Heave-offering to eat, he himself must repay the value while they pay the [Added] Fifth. So R. Meir. But the Sages say: They must pay both the value and the [Added] Fifth, while he repays to them the price of their meal.

4. If a man stole Heave-offering but did not eat it, he must make twofold restitution[6] at the price of Heave-offering; but if he ate it he must repay twice the value and the [Added] Fifth—the value and the [Added] Fifth in common produce together with the value at the price of Heave-offering. If he stole dedicated Heave-offering[7] and ate it, he must pay two [Added] Fifths[8] together with the value [only], for twofold restitution does not apply in [the theft of] dedicated produce.

5. Restitution may not be made from Gleanings, the Forgotten Sheaf, *Peah* or ownerless produce, nor yet from First Tithe from which Heave-offering has not[9] been taken or Second Tithe or dedicated produce which have not[9] been redeemed; for what is dedicated cannot redeem aught else that is dedicated. So R. Meir. But the Sages permit it.[10]

6. R. Eliezer says: Restitution may be made from one kind instead of

---

[1] Lev. 5[16], 22[14].
[2] If he ate the Added Fifth (to which attaches Heave-offering sanctity) he must repay it together with yet another Added Fifth.   [3] If he ate this also.
[4] As very frequently in the Mishnah (see General Index, Israelites, II), Israelite is here used in the restricted sense of one who is not a priest or levite.
[5] When it is her right to eat of Heave-offering (Lev. 22[11]).   [6] Ex. 22[4].
[7] Which a priest had dedicated to the Temple.
[8] One each for 'acting amiss' (Lev. 5[16]) with Heave-offering and with 'dedicated produce'.
[9] So Cambridge text; Mishnah editions omit.
[10] With Tithes and dedicated produce.

from another kind provided that it is from a better instead of from a worse kind. But R. Akiba says: Restitution may be made only from the like kind. Therefore if a man ate [Heave-offering] cucumbers grown in the year before the Seventh Year he must wait for the cucumbers of the year after the Seventh Year and repay from them.[1] From the same Scripture[2] whence R. Eliezer derives the more lenient ruling R. Akiba derives the more stringent ruling; for it is written, *And he shall give unto the priest the holy thing*—[namely] whatsoever is fit to be holy. So R. Eliezer. But R. Akiba says: *And he shall give unto the priest the holy thing*—[namely] the [same kind of] hallowed thing that he had eaten.

7. 1. If a man ate Heave-offering wantonly, he must repay its value, but he need not pay the [Added] Fifth. The produce with which he repays remains common produce; [therefore] if the priest would remit he may remit.

2. If a priest's daughter was married to an Israelite[3] and afterward ate Heave-offering, she must repay its value but she need not pay the [Added] Fifth; and [if she committed adultery] her death is by burning. If she was married to any of them that are not eligible [for marriage into the priestly stock][4] she must repay the value of Heave-offering and also the [Added] Fifth; and [if she committed adultery] her death is by strangling. So R. Meir. But the Sages say: In either case they repay the value but not the [Added] Fifth; and [if they committed adultery] their death is by burning.

3. If a man gave Heave-offering to eat to his children that are minors, or to his slaves whether minors or of age, or if he ate Heave-offering that came from another country, or if he ate less than an olive's bulk of Heave-offering, he must repay the value but not the [Added] Fifth; and what is given in repayment remains common produce; [therefore] if the priest would remit he may remit.

4. This is the general rule: whensoever a man repays the value and the [Added] Fifth, what is given in repayment is Heave-offering, [therefore] if the priest would remit, he may not remit; and whensoever a man repays the value but not the [Added] Fifth, what is given in repayment remains common produce, therefore if the priest would remit, he may remit.

5. If there were two baskets, one of Heave-offering and one of common produce, and a *seah* of Heave-offering fell into one of them but it is not known into which of them it fell, I may assume that it fell into the basket of Heave-offering. But if it is not known which is the basket of Heave-offering and which the basket of common produce, and a man ate from one of them, he is not culpable, and the other basket is deemed to be Heave-offering. According to R. Meir, Dough-offering[5] must be given from it; but R. Jose exempts it. If another man ate from the other basket, he is not

---

[1] Since the sixth year cucumbers would have hardened, and the Seventh Year cucumbers are forbidden in any case. [2] Lev. 22[14].

[3] Thereby losing her right to eat of Heave-offering (Lev. 22[12]). She need not pay the Added Fifth since she may become a widow and return to her father's house (Lev. 22[13]) and recover the right to eat of Heave-offering. The sanctity of the priestly stock still attaches to her (hence if she commits adultery she is to be burnt: Sanh. 9[1]; cf. 11[1]). See Lev. 21[9]. She must repay the value, however, in that she ate what was not hers.

[4] See Kidd. 4[1ff]. She falls out of the priestly stock, and, according to R. Meir, the previous conditions no longer apply; but according to the Sages she continues to be reckoned of priestly stock.

[5] Since its condition is in doubt it rests under the obligations that fall upon common produce. See Hall. 1[3].

culpable; but if one man ate from both of them he must repay according to the value of the smaller of the two.

6. If one of these baskets fell into common produce it does not render it subject to the law of Heave-offering, and the other basket is deemed to be Heave-offering. According to R. Meir, Dough-offering must be given from it, but R. Jose exempts it. If the other basket fell elsewhere [into common produce] it does not render it subject to the law of Heave-offering; but if they both fell into the same place they render it subject to the law of Heave-offering if what is in the smaller of the two is of the prescribed proportion.

7. If a man used one as seed he is not culpable, and the other is deemed to be Heave-offering. According to R. Meir, Dough-offering must be given from it, but R. Jose exempts it. If another man used the other as seed he is not culpable. But if one man used both as seed and it is of a kind whose seed perishes [in the ground] it is permitted [to be eaten by non-priests], but if it is not of a kind whose seed perishes, it is forbidden.

8. 1. If a [priest's] wife[1] was eating Heave-offering and they came and said to her, 'Thy husband is dead', or 'He has divorced thee'; and so, too, with a [priest's] slave,[2] if he was eating Heave-offering and they came and said to him, 'Thy master is dead', or 'He has sold thee to an Israelite', or 'He has given thee away', or 'He has freed thee'; and so, too, with a priest, if he was eating Heave-offering and it became known that he was the son of a divorced woman or of a woman that had performed *halitzah*;[3]—R. Eliezer declares them liable to the repayment of the value and the [Added] Fifth, but R. Joshua declares them exempt. If a priest was standing and sacrificing at the Altar and it became known that he was the son of a divorced woman or of a woman that had performed *halitzah*, R. Eliezer says: All the offerings that he offered on the Altar are invalid. But R. Joshua declares them valid. If it became known that he had a blemish[4] his ministration is invalid.

2. Of them all, if there was Heave-offering in their mouths, R. Eliezer says: They may swallow it. But R. Joshua says: They should spit it out. If they said to him [that was eating Heave-offering], 'Thou hast become unclean', or 'The Heave-offering has become unclean', R. Eliezer says: He may swallow it. But R. Joshua says: He should spit it out. [But if they said to him], 'Thou wast unclean', or 'The Heave-offering was unclean', or if it became known that it was untithed produce, or First Tithe from which Heave-offering had not been taken, or Second Tithe or dedicated produce that had not been redeemed, or if he tasted the flavour of a bed-bug in his mouth, then he should spit it out.

3. If a man was eating[5] a cluster of grapes, and from the garden he entered into the courtyard, R. Eliezer says: He may finish [eating it]. But R. Joshua says: He may not finish. If it was growing dusk before the Sabbath[6] R. Eliezer says: He may finish [eating the cluster of grapes]. But R. Joshua says: He may not finish.

---

[1] Who was the daughter of an Israelite, i.e. a non-priest. Her right to eat of Heave-offering continues only so long as she is married to a priest (or is the mother of a priest's son). Cf. above, 7[2].   [2] Lev. 22[11].

[3] Making him ineligible to serve as a priest. For *halitzah* see App. I. 12. The law that a priest may not marry a divorced woman (Lev. 21[7]) was, by rabbinical interpretation, made to include also the woman who had performed *halitzah*.   [4] Lev. 21[18]. See Bekh. 7[1ff].

[5] A casual meal. The fruit is tithe-free until it is brought within the owner's domain, when it is forbidden to eat of it until it has been duly tithed. See Maas. 1[5].

[6] When it is forbidden to tithe (Shab. 2[7]).

4. If Heave-offering wine has stood uncovered it must be poured away;[1] still less need this be said of what is not Heave-offering wine. Three liquids become forbidden through being uncovered: water, wine and milk; while all other liquids are permitted[2] [for use although they have remained uncovered]. How long must they have remained [uncovered] to become forbidden? Such time as it would take a serpent to come forth from a place near by and drink.

5. The quantity of water that may remain uncovered must be such that the poison [of a serpent] would be lost in it. R. Jose says: Water in vessels, whatsoever its quantity, [is forbidden if it has remained uncovered], and water on the ground [is forbidden] if it is forty *seahs* [or less].

6. Figs, grapes, cucumbers, gourds, water-melons or musk-melons that have been gnawed, even if there is as much as a talent[3] [of fruit on the tree], whether [the fruit is] large or small, plucked or unplucked, are forbidden so long as there is juice in them. [A beast] that is bitten by a serpent is forbidden because of the danger to life.[4]

7. A wine-strainer is forbidden as a cover;[5] but R. Nehemiah permits it.

8. If the uncleanness of a jar of Heave-offering is in doubt, R. Eliezer says: If it lay in an exposed place it should be put in a hidden place, and if it was uncovered it should be covered. But R. Joshua says: If it was lying in a hidden place it should be put in an exposed place, and if it was covered it should be uncovered.[6] Rabban Gamaliel says: Naught new should be done to it.

9. If a jar [of clean Heave-offering] in the upper part of the winepress was broken, and the lower part was unclean, R. Eliezer and R. Joshua agree that if a man could save a quarter-*log* of the Heave-offering wine in cleanness he should save it; but if not, R. Eliezer says: Let it all flow away and become unclean and let him not render it unclean with his hands.[7]

10. So, too, if a jar of oil was upset, R. Eliezer and R. Joshua agree that if a man could save a quarter-*log* of it in cleanness, he should save it; but if not, R. Eliezer says: Let it flow away and be absorbed [into the ground] and let him not render it unclean[8] with his hands.

11. Of both these cases[9] R. Joshua said: Such Heave-offering is not such whereof I must take heed lest I render it unclean, but lest I eat of it; but what Heave-offering is it which one may not render unclean? If a man was passing from one place to another with Heave-offering loaves in his hand and a gentile said to him, 'Give me one of them and I will defile it, and if not I will defile them all', R. Eliezer says: Let him defile them all but do not give him one in order that he may defile it. R. Joshua says: He should leave one of them on a stone before him.

12. So, too, if gentiles said to many women, 'Give us one from among you that we may defile her, and if not we will defile you all', let them defile them all, but let them not betray to them one soul from Israel.[10]

---

[1] A serpent may have drunk of it.   [2] Since a serpent does not drink them.
[3] App. II, B. Even though the fruit is so abundant that a serpent could not be supposed to have gnawed all of it (Tif. Yis.).   [4] Hull. 3[5].
[5] It cannot protect from the snake's poison.   [6] To make its doubt a certainty.
[7] See p. 778, n. 8.   [8] Some texts read: 'Let him not gather it up'.
[9] Namely Heave-offering whose uncleanness is in doubt, and Heave-offering which is in danger of being lost.
[10] 'No person may be sacrificed to save others; if, however, one of them in particular had been specified she may be delivered up. But if they had demanded one in particular of a number of men to kill him, the others may not deliver him up unless he had been legally

9. 1. If a man sowed Heave-offering in error it is permitted to plough it up, but if wantonly it must be left to grow. If it had reached a third of its growth, whether sown in error or wantonly, it must be left to grow. Flax, even if sown wantonly, must be ploughed up.

2. [What grows therefrom] is subject to the laws of Gleanings, the Forgotten Sheaf and *Peah*; poor Israelites and poor priests may glean therefrom, and poor Israelites must sell their portions to priests at the price of Heave-offering; but its price shall belong to them. R. Tarfon said: Only poor priests may glean, lest [others] forget and put it into their mouths. R. Akiba replied: If so, then none may glean save [priests that are] clean.

3. It is subject to Tithes and Poorman's Tithe; poor Israelites and poor priests may take thereof and poor Israelites must sell their portions to priests at the price of Heave-offering, but its price shall belong to them. He that threshes it with the flail is praiseworthy. How should they act when it is trodden out [by cattle]?[1] A nosebag is hung about the cattle's necks and a like kind of produce is put therein; thus one neither muzzles the cattle nor gives them Heave-offering to eat.

4. What grows from Heave-offering is Heave-offering, and what grows in the next stage is common produce; but what grows from untithed produce, First Tithe, aftergrowths of Seventh Year produce, Heave-offering of produce grown outside the Land [of Israel], common produce mixed with Heave-offering, and First-fruits, is common produce. What grows from dedicated produce and Second Tithe is common produce, but it must be redeemed [at its worth] at the time when it was sown.

5. If a hundred beds of soil were sown with Heave-offering and one with common seed [and it is not known which], they are all permitted if the produce is of a kind whose seed perishes [in the ground]; but produce whose seed does not perish, even though there were a hundred beds of common produce and one of Heave-offering, they are all forbidden.

6. What grows from untithed produce is permitted if the produce is of a kind whose seed perishes, but produce whose seed does not perish, even what grows from it in the next stage is forbidden. What produce is there whose seed does not perish? The like of arum, garlic and onions. R. Judah says: Onions are to be reckoned [in this respect] like barley.

7. If a man was weeding plants of the like of onions in a gentile's field he may make a chance meal of them although the produce is untithed. If Heave-offering seedlings that had become unclean were transplanted, they become clean, in that they do not convey uncleanness; but none may eat of them until the edible part has been cut away. R. Judah says: Until what grows again is itself again cut away.

10. 1. If an onion [that was Heave-offering] was put into [cooked] lentils [that were common produce] and the onion was entire, the lentils are permitted [to non-priests], but if the onion was cut up [the matter is determined] by the principle of 'that which gives a flavour'.[2] And with other cooked dishes, whether [the onion was] entire or cut up, [the matter is determined] by the principle of 'that which gives a flavour'. R. Judah permits pickled-fish [in which a Heave-offering onion has been cooked] since it is used only to take away the stench.

condemned to death, though some are of the opinion that if any one was particularly specified it is permitted to deliver him up to save the rest' (Tif. Yis.).   [1] Deut. 25⁴.

[2] If the lentils have been flavoured by the onion, they are forbidden.

2. If an apple [that was Heave-offering] was chopped up and put into dough so that this was leavened, the dough is forbidden. If barley [that was Heave-offering] fell into a cistern of water, the water is permitted even though the barley tainted it.

3. If a man took off hot bread[1] from the side of the oven and put it over the mouth of a jar of Heave-offering wine, R. Meir permits [the bread as food for non-priests], but R. Judah forbids it. R. Jose permits it if it is wheaten bread but forbids it if it is barley bread, since barley absorbs [the wine fumes].

4. If an oven was heated with cummin that was Heave-offering, and bread was baked therein, the bread is permitted since it is only the smell and not the flavour of cummin [that is conveyed to it].

5. If fenugreek fell into the wine vat, and it was Heave-offering or Second Tithe, [it is forbidden] only if the seed without the stalk was enough to give a flavour; but if it was Seventh Year produce or Diverse Kinds from the vineyard[2] or dedicated produce [it is forbidden] even when seed and stalk together [are needed to] give a flavour.

6. If a man had bunches of fenugreek that were Diverse Kinds from the vineyard, they must be burnt. If he had bunches of fenugreek from which Heave-offering had not been given, he must beat out the seed and reckon how much seed there is in them and set apart [Heave-offering] from the seed; but he need not do so from the stalks. But if he set apart [Heave-offering from the stalks also] he may not say, 'I will beat out the seeds and keep the stalks and give the seed', but he must give the stalks together with the seed.

7. If olives that were common produce were pickled together with Heave-offering olives, whether crushed [olives] that were not Heave-offering [were pickled] with crushed Heave-offering olives, or with uncrushed Heave-offering olives, or [if they were pickled] in juice that was Heave-offering, they are forbidden; but if uncrushed [olives] that were not Heave-offering [were pickled] with crushed Heave-offering olives, they are permitted.

8. If unclean fish was pickled together with clean fish the brine thereof is forbidden if in a jar holding two *seahs* the unclean fish weighs ten *zuz*[3] Judean measure (which is five *selas* Galilean measure).[4] R. Judah says: [It is forbidden if there is] a quarter-*log*[5] in two *seahs*. And R. Jose says: Only if [the unclean is] one-sixteenth part.

9. If unclean locusts were pickled together with clean locusts they do not render the brine forbidden. R. Zadok testified[6] that the brine made from unclean locusts is clean.

10. Whatsoever vegetables are pickled together,[7] they are permitted, excepting only leeks. If leeks that were not Heave-offering were pickled with Heave-offering leeks, or other vegetables that were not Heave-offering with Heave-offering leeks, this is forbidden; but if Heave-offering leeks were pickled with other Heave-offering vegetables, this is permitted.

11. R. Jose says: Whatsoever is stewed[7] with beet is forbidden since this imparts a flavour. R. Simeon says: If a cabbage from irrigated soil [was

---

[1] Cf. Maksh. 3[3].   [2] See p. 28, n. 1; Kil. 4[1ff].
[3] i.e. one nine-hundred-and-sixtieth of the contents (1 *seah*—24 *logs*; 1 *log*—2 *litras*; 8 *litras*—100 *zuz*; thus two *seahs* equals 9,600 *zuz*; therefore 10 *zuz* is one part in 960 of two *seahs*).   [4] Cf. Ket. 5[9].   [5] One part in 192 of the contents. See App. II, D.
[6] Eduy. 7[2].   [7] Heave-offering with common produce.

stewed] with one from rain-watered soil, it is forbidden, since one absorbs [the moisture from the other]. R. Akiba[1] says: Whatsoever the things are that are cooked together, they are permitted, excepting flesh [cooked with flesh]. R. Johanan b. Nuri says: Liver [which is forbidden] renders [other kinds of flesh] forbidden, but is not itself rendered forbidden [by another kind of flesh that is forbidden], since it exudes [its own juices] and does not absorb [the juices of other flesh].

12. If an egg is cooked with forbidden[2] spices even its yolk is forbidden, since it absorbs [other flavours]. Liquid in which Heave-offering has been stewed or pickled is forbidden to non-priests.

11. 1. Fig-cake or dried figs [that are Heave-offering] may not be put into fish-brine[3] since this spoils them; but [Heave-offering] wine may be put into fish-brine. [Heave-offering] oil may not be made into perfumed oil, but [Heave-offering] wine may be made into honied-wine. [Heave-offering] wine may not be boiled since this lessens its quantity; but R. Judah permits it since it improves it.

2. [If a non-priest drank in error] date-honey, cider, vinegar from winter-grapes, or any other juices [excepting wine and oil] from Heave-offering fruits, R. Eliezer declares him liable to the payment of the value and the [Added] Fifth, but R. Joshua declares him exempt [from the Added Fifth]. R. Eliezer declares [these liquids] susceptible to uncleanness under the law concerning liquids;[4] but R. Joshua said: The Sages have not made count of seven liquids in the manner of them that count up spices,[5] but they have said: Seven liquids[6] are susceptible[7] to uncleanness: all other liquids are not susceptible.

3. Dates may not be made into honey nor apples into cider nor winter-grapes into vinegar, nor may other fruits be changed from their natural state if they are Heave-offering or Second Tithe, excepting only olives and grapes. The penalty of the Forty Stripes[8] incurred through transgression of the law of *Orlah*-fruit[9] applies only by reason of the product of olives and grapes; no liquids are brought as First-fruits[10] excepting the product of olives and grapes; no fruit juice is susceptible to uncleanness under the law concerning liquids[4] excepting the product of olives and grapes; and no fruit juice is offered on the Altar excepting the product of olives and grapes.

4. The stalks of fresh figs, dried figs, acorns[11] or carobs that are Heave-offering are forbidden to non-priests.

5. Kernels of Heave-offering fruits are forbidden while the priest has them in keeping, but if he has thrown them away they are permitted. So, too, the bones of animal-offerings are forbidden while the priest has them in keeping, but if he has thrown them away they are permitted. Coarse bran [that comes from Heave-offering] is permitted, but fine bran is

---

[1] Some texts read: R. Judah.
[2] Such as *Orlah*-fruit, Heave-offering and the like.
[3] Salt water in which chopped fish or locusts have been pickled. According to A. Zar. 2[4] wine was sometimes added.
[4] Lev. 11[34, 38].   [5] Giving a rough calculation.   [6] Maksh. 6[4].
[7] Can contract and convey uncleanness, and, in contact with dry foodstuffs, render them susceptible to uncleanness. See p. 758, n. 1.
[8] Which is the punishment incurred for transgressing a negative command. Cf. Kil. 8[3]. See Makk. 3[1ff].   [9] App. I. 32.   [10] See Bikk. 1[3].
[11] The meaning of the word is uncertain. Maim. explains it as a kind of fig; Rashi as a kind of pea or bean; others suppose it to be the fruit of the Judas-tree.

forbidden if it comes from fresh wheat;[1] if it comes from old wheat it is permitted, and the Heave-offering may then be treated as common produce is treated.[2] When a man prepares fine flour, one or two *kabs* to the *seah*, he should not destroy the residue but put it in some hidden place.[3]

6. If a man emptied out Heave-offering wheat from a store-chamber he is not bound to sit down and gather it all grain by grain, but he may sweep it out in his usual fashion, and put common produce therein.

7. So, too, if a jar of Heave-offering oil was upset, he is not bound to sit down and scoop it up with his fingers, but he may deal with it as he would with common oil.

8. If a man poured out [Heave-offering liquid] from one jar into another and [at the end] allowed three drops to drip, he may then put common liquid into the emptied jar; but if he turned the jar on its side to drain it, whatsoever more comes out is Heave-offering. What quantity of Heave-offering of Tithe from *demai*-produce[4] need there be for it to be taken to a priest? An eighth part of the eighth [of a *log*].

9. Heave-offering vetches may be given [by a priest] as fodder to cattle, wild animals or fowls. If an Israelite hired a cow from a priest he may give it Heave-offering vetches to eat; but if a priest hired a cow from an Israelite, although he is responsible for its food he may not feed it with Heave-offering vetches. If an Israelite undertook to tend the cow of a priest and share in its increased value,[5] he may not feed it with Heave-offering vetches, but if a priest undertook to tend the cow of an Israelite in like manner, he may feed it with Heave-offering vetches.

10. Heave-offering oil that [has become unclean and] must be burnt, may be kindled in synagogues, in houses of study, in dark alley-ways and over sick people, in that it is a place where a priest may enter in. If an Israelite's daughter married to a priest is accustomed to resort to her father, her father may kindle [such oil in his house] in that it is a place where she may enter in. It may be kindled in a house where is a wedding feast,[6] but not in a house of mourning. So R. Judah. But R. Jose says: It may be kindled in a house of mourning[7] but not in a house where is a wedding feast. R. Meir forbids it in either place.[8] R. Simeon permits it in either place.

MAASEROTH[9] ('TITHES')

1. 1. A general rule have they laid down about Tithes: whatsoever is used for food and is kept watch over and grows from the soil[10] is liable to Tithes.

---

[1] Since being moist much of the grain adheres after being ground, while it is not so with old, dried wheat.   [2] The non-edible parts may be thrown away without scruple.
[3] Since it is still to some extent edible.
[4] See App. I. 6 and p. 20, n. 9. Such Heave-offering is accounted unclean from the *Am-haaretz's* contact.   [5] Cf. B.M. 5[1, 5].
[6] Since a priest may enter there; whereas he may not enter a place of mourning for fear of contracting corpse uncleanness.
[7] Since they sit there quietly and do not move the lamps from place to place, and there is no fear that they will spill the oil on their clothes, as they may do at a wedding feast.
[8] Applying the arguments of both R. Judah and R. Jose and adopting the more stringent ruling. R. Simeon adopts the more lenient ruling, and the *Halakah* is according to him.
[9] The term here includes Heave-offering also. There were three 'Tithes' (excluding Heave-offering): (a) First or Levitic Tithe (Num. 18[21]) which must be given to a levite, who, in his turn, must give a tenth of it ('Heave-offering of Tithe') to a priest (Lev. 18[26]); (b) Second Tithe which the owner himself must consume in Jerusalem (Deut. 14[22ff]); the actual Second Tithe produce need not itself be conveyed to Jerusalem but could be 'redeemed', i.e. converted into money (plus a fifth of its value) and reconverted into food in Jerusalem (Deut. 22[26]); and (c) Poorman's Tithe (Deut. 14[28ff]; 26[12]) which takes the place of Second Tithe in the third and sixth years of the seven-year cycle.   [10] Cf. Peah 1[4].

Yet another general rule have they laid down: whatsoever is used for food either in its earlier or in its later condition [of ripeness], though it is suffered to remain ungathered to provide the more food, is liable [to Tithes] whether [gathered] in its earlier or its later condition [of ripeness]; but whatsoever is not used for food in its earlier condition but only in its later condition, is not liable to Tithes until it is become fit for food.

2. When do fruits become liable to Tithes? Figs—after their earliest ripening;[1] grapes and wild grapes—after their stones become visible; sumach and mulberries—after they become red (and all red fruits [are liable] after they become red); pomegranates—after they soften; dates—after they begin to swell; peaches—after they begin to show red veins; walnuts—after their cells take shape. R. Judah says: Walnuts and almonds —after their kernel-skins take shape.

3. Carobs—after they form dark spots (and all black fruits [are liable] after they form dark spots); pears, pippins,[2] quinces and medlars[3]—after their surface becomes smooth (and all white fruits [are liable] after their surface becomes smooth); fenugreek—when its seeds are fit to be sown; grain and olives—after they have reached a third of their growth.

4. Among vegetables, cucumbers, gourds, water-melons, musk-melons, apples, and citrons are liable whether gathered in their earlier or later condition [of ripeness]. R. Simeon declares citrons exempt in their earlier condition. When a man[4] is liable to give Tithes from bitter almonds[5] he is exempt from giving Tithes from sweet almonds, and when he is liable to give Tithes from sweet almonds he is exempt from giving Tithes from bitter almonds.

5. When is their tithing season? Cucumbers and gourds—after their fringe is lost, or, if they have not lost their fringe, after they have been stacked; water-melons—after they have become smooth, or, if they have not become smooth, when they are stored away to dry; vegetables that are [usually] tied in bundles [become liable] after they have been tied in bundles, or, if they are not tied up in bundles, after a vessel has been filled with them, or, if a vessel is not to be filled with them, after they have been collected in the manner needful. [Produce that is packed up in] a basket [is liable to Tithes] after it has been covered, or, if it is not to be covered, after a vessel is filled with it, or, if a vessel is not to be filled with it, after it has been collected in the manner needful. This applies when a man brings the produce to market; but if he brings it to his own house he may make a chance meal from the produce [without tithing it] until he reaches his house.

6. Dried split-pomegranates, raisins, and carobs [are liable to Tithes] after they are stacked; and onions—after they are stript, or, if they are not stript, after they are stacked; grain [is liable] after the pile is smoothed off, or, if the pile is not smoothed off, after it has been stacked; pulse [is liable] after it has been sifted, or, if it is not sifted, after the pile has been smoothed off. Even after the pile has been smoothed off one may remove unground fragments or what is fallen by the sides, or what remains unhusked,[6] and eat thereof [without tithing].

7. Wine [is liable to Tithes] after it has been skimmed; but even after

---

[1] So soon as their tips become white.   [2] See Kil. 1[4].
[3] Variant: hawthorn-berries.   [4] Hull. 1[6].
[5] Which are gathered at an earlier stage, while sweet almonds are left to a later stage.
[6] See Maas. 5[4].

it has been skimmed one may still collect some from the upper wine-press or the duct and drink thereof [without tithing]. Oil [is liable] after it has dripped down into the trough; but even after it has dripped down one may still take of the oil from the olive-truss[1] or from between the pressing-stone and the boards of the olive-press [without tithing] and put it on a cake or dish, but not in a pot or kettle while the contents are boiling.[2] R. Judah says: He may put it in aught save that which contains vinegar or fish-brine.[3]

8. A cake of figs [is liable to Tithes] after its surface has been smoothed off. It may be smoothed off with [the juice of] untithed figs or grapes. R. Judah forbids this. If it is smoothed off with grape juice it is not rendered susceptible to uncleanness;[4] but R. Judah declares it susceptible. Dried figs [are liable] after they have been stamped down; and [if they are to be put into] a store-jar [they are liable] after they have been pressed together. If, after they have been stamped down into a jar or pressed into a store-jar, the jar is broken or the store-jar breached, none may make a chance meal from them [without tithing]. R. Jose permits it.

2. 1. If a man[5] was passing through the street and said, 'Take ye of my figs', people may eat them and be exempt from Tithes;[6] therefore if they bring them into their houses they must tithe them as if they were certainly untithed. [If he said], 'Take ye of my figs and take them into your houses', they may not make a chance meal from them; therefore if they bring them into their houses they need only tithe them as if they were *demai*-produce.[7]

2. If men were sitting in a doorway or shop and he said to them, 'Take ye of my figs', they may eat them and be exempt from Tithes, but the owner of the doorway or shop is liable [to Tithes]. R. Judah declares him exempt unless he turns away his face or changes his position.[8]

3. If a man brought up produce from Galilee to Judea or if he went up to Jerusalem, he may eat of it [without tithing] until he reaches his journey's end; and so, too, if he went back again. R. Meir says: [Only] until he reaches the place where he will spend the Sabbath. Pedlars that go around from town to town may make a [chance] meal [of untithed produce that they have received] until they come to the place where they will spend the night. R. Judah says: The first house [that he reaches in the town] is reckoned to be his house [in what concerns Tithes].

4. If Heave-offering had been given from produce before the work of storing it was finished, R. Eliezer forbids making a chance meal from it [without tithing]; but the Sages permit it save when it is a basket of figs. If Heave-offering had been given from a basket of figs [before the work of storing it was finished], R. Simeon permits [making a chance meal from it without tithing], but the Sages forbid it.

---

[1] Uncertain. The same word occurs in Toh. 10[8]; Maksh. 5[7] (a ship's bilge); Zab. 4[7]. It is variously explained as a rope basket in which the olives are contained during the pressing process (Bert.), or the basket into which the pressed-out olives are thrown (Maim. and Tif. Yis.).

[2] This would be to use the oil in cooking, breaking the rule that only a 'chance meal' (1[5]) may be made of it.

[3] Their tartness effects a change in the oil equivalent to cooking.

[4] See Lev. 11[34, 38]. Maksh. 6[4].

[5] An *Am-haaretz*, who is under suspicion of not giving tithes.

[6] On the assumption that they have not yet been taken into the man's house.

[7] See p. 20, n. 9. They need only give the Heave-offering of Tithe to the priest and they may keep the First and Second Tithe.

[8] So, as it were, seeking a place where he is not ashamed to eat. Cf. the rule of R. Nehemiah below, 3[5].

5. If a man said to his fellow, 'Here is an *issar*[1] for thee: give me five figs for it', he may not eat of them until he has tithed them.[2] So R. Meir. But R. Judah says: If he [took and] ate them one by one he is exempt; but if he took several at a time he is liable to Tithes. R. Judah said: It once happened in a rose garden in Jerusalem that figs were sold three or four for an *issar*, and neither Heave-offering nor Tithe was ever given.

6. If a man said to his fellow, 'Here is an *issar* for thee in exchange for ten figs which I shall choose', he may choose them and eat them singly [without tithing]; [or if he said,] 'for a cluster of grapes which I shall choose', he may pick them grape by grape and eat [without tithing]; [or if he said,] 'for a pomegranate which I shall choose', he may pick it seed by seed and eat [without tithing]; [or if he said,] 'for a water-melon which I shall choose', he may cut it and eat it slice by slice [without tithing]. But if he said, 'for these twenty figs', or 'for these two clusters', or 'for these two pomegranates', or 'for these two water-melons', he may eat them after his usual fashion and be exempt from Tithes, since he bought them in an unplucked condition.

7. If a man hired a labourer to help him harvest figs and he answered, 'On condition that I may eat of the figs', he may eat them [without tithing]; but if [he said,] 'On condition that I and my family may eat of them', or 'that my son may eat of them instead of my receiving a wage', he himself may eat and be exempt [from Tithes], but when his son eats he is liable to Tithes. [If he said,] 'On condition that I may eat of them during the fig-harvest and after the fig-harvest', during the fig-harvest he may eat of them and be exempt, but after the fig-harvest if he ate of them he is liable to Tithes since he did not eat of them after the fashion permitted by the Law.[3] This is the general rule: if a man eats after the fashion permitted by the Law he is exempt from Tithes; but if not after the fashion permitted by the Law he is liable to Tithes.

8. If a man was harvesting poor figs he may not eat of the good kind, and if he was harvesting the good kind he may not eat of the poor figs; but he may restrain himself until he comes to the place where are the good kind, and then eat. If a man agreed to exchange his fresh figs for his fellow's fresh figs, or his dried figs for the other's dried figs, or his dried figs for the other's fresh figs, he thereby becomes liable to Tithes. R. Judah says: If he agreed to exchange [his figs] for the other's fresh figs he becomes liable, but if for the other's dried figs he is exempt.

3. 1. If a man was taking figs through his courtyard to a place where they were to be dried his children and the members of his household may eat of them and be exempt [from Tithes]. Labourers that work with him may eat them free of Tithes if he is not answerable for their maintenance; but if he is answerable for their maintenance they may not eat thereof.

2. If a man sent out his labourers into the field and he was not answerable for their maintenance they may eat [of the figs] and be exempt [from Tithes]; but if he was answerable for their maintenance they may eat of the figs one at a time but not from what is collected in a basket or hamper or drying-place.

---

[1] See App. II, A. If the *denar* or *zuz* is taken to be roughly equal to a shilling, the *issar* is worth a halfpenny.
[2] The act of purchasing what is plucked determines its liability to tithes.
[3] Deut. 23[25].

3. If a man hired a labourer to tend his olives, and he answered, 'On condition that I may eat of the olives', and he [took and] ate of them one at a time, he is exempt [from Tithes], but if he took several together he is liable to Tithes. [If he was hired] to weed out onions, and he answered, 'On condition that I may eat of the vegetables', he may pluck them a blade at a time and eat them, but if he took many together, he is liable to Tithes.

4. If a man found harvested figs[1] on the road or even beside a field in which harvested figs [were spread out to be dried] (so, too, if a fig-tree overhangs the road and figs were found below it), they are permitted [as not coming] within the category of theft[2] and they are exempt from Tithes; but olives and carobs [found in like condition] are liable [to Tithes]. If a man found dried figs at a time when men had already pressed their figs, he is liable to Tithes; but if they had not, he is not liable. If he found pieces of fig-cake he is liable [to Tithes], for it is manifest that they come from produce [whose harvesting is] complete. If carobs have not yet been stored on the roof he may take some down for the cattle and be exempt from Tithes, since he can put back what is left over.

5. What kind of courtyard renders [produce brought thither] liable to Tithes?[3] R. Ishmael says: A courtyard in the Tyrian style in which watch is kept over the goods therein. R. Akiba says: Any courtyard which one [occupant] may open and another may shut [as they please] does not render [produce brought thither] liable to Tithes. R. Nehemiah says: Any courtyard in which a man is not ashamed to eat renders [produce brought thither] liable to Tithes. R. Jose says: Any courtyard into which any may enter and not be asked, 'Whom seekest thou?' does not render [produce] liable to Tithes. R. Judah says: If there were two courtyards one within the other, the inner one renders [produce brought thither] liable to Tithes, but the outer one does not render it liable.

6. Roofs do not render [produce brought thither] liable to Tithes even though they pertain to a courtyard which itself renders it liable. A doorway, portico, or balcony is reckoned as like to the courtyard: if this renders produce liable to Tithes, they also render it liable; if it does not, they do not.

7. Cone-shaped huts, watch-booths, and summer huts do not render [produce brought thither] liable [to Tithes]. A Genesareth hut,[4] even though it has in it a handmill and poultry, does not render produce liable. A potter's [double] hut—the inner part renders [produce brought thither] liable to Tithes but not the outer part. R. Jose says: Whatsoever does not serve both as a summer and a winter dwelling, [produce brought thither] is exempt from Tithes. The *Sukkah*[5] used at the Feast renders [produce brought therein] liable to Tithes during the Feast according to R. Judah; but the Sages declare [produce brought thither] exempt.

8. If a fig-tree stood in the courtyard a man may eat figs from it one at a time and be exempt from Tithes; but if he took several together he is liable. R. Simeon says: [A man may have at the same time] one in his left hand, one in his right, and one in his mouth [and be exempt from Tithes]. If he climbed to the top of the tree he may fill his bosom and eat.

9. If a vine was planted in the courtyard a man may take a whole cluster

---

[1] Partly dried.   [2] They do not count as private property.
[3] What kind can be counted as coming within the category of a private house? See above, 1[5] (end).
[4] The more substantially built and more permanently occupied hut in which watch was kept over fruit around the Sea of Galilee.   [5] App. I. 42.

and eat [without tithing]; so, too, with a pomegranate or a water-melon. So R. Tarfon. R. Akiba says: He should take the grapes one at a time from the cluster, or the seeds one at a time from the pomegranate, or consume the water-melon slice by slice. If coriander was sown in the courtyard it may be plucked a leaf at a time and eaten [without tithing]; but if more is consumed together, it is liable to Tithes. Savory, marjoram, and calamint, if grown in the courtyard and kept watch over, are liable to Tithes.

10. If a fig-tree stood in the courtyard and overhung a garden, a man [in the garden] may eat of it after his usual fashion and be exempt from Tithes; but if it stood in the garden and overhung the courtyard, a man [in the courtyard] may eat of it one fig at a time and be exempt, but if he ate more than one at a time, he is liable [to Tithes]. If it stood within the Land [of Israel] and overhung the country outside, or [if it stood] in the country outside and overhung the Land [of Israel], the matter[1] is determined according to the position of the root. And in what concerns houses in a walled city[2] the matter is determined by the position of the root; but [in what concerns] cities of refuge,[3] by the lie of the branches;[4] and in what concerns Jerusalem,[5] by the lie of the branches.

4. 1. If a man pickled, stewed, or salted [produce while he was yet] in the field,[6] he is liable to Tithes; if he stored it in the ground he is exempt; if he seasoned it [and ate it while he was yet] in the field, he is exempt; if he bruised olives to rid them of their sour sap, he is exempt; if he squeezed them against his skin he is exempt; but if he squeezed them and dropped the oil into his hand he is liable. If he skimmed [wine] to put into a cooked dish he is exempt, but if to put it into a pot he is liable [to Tithes] since it may be deemed a small vat.

2. If children hid figs [in the field] for the Sabbath and forgot to tithe them [before the Sabbath], they may not be eaten after the Sabbath until they have been tithed.[7] A basket of fruit intended for the Sabbath, the School of Shammai declare exempt [from Tithes], but the School of Hillel declare it liable.[8] R. Judah says: Also if a man gathered a basketful to send to his fellow he may not eat therefrom until he has given tithe.

3. If a man took olives out of the vat he may dip them in salt and eat them one at a time, but if he salted them and set them down in front of himself he is liable[9] to Tithes. R. Eliezer says: [If an unclean person took them] from a clean vat he is liable, but if from an unclean vat he is exempt, since he can put back what is left over.

4. Men may drink wine out of the winepress,[10] whether mixed with hot water or cold, and be exempt from Tithes. So R. Meir. R. Eliezer b.

---

[1] Its liability to Heave-offering and Tithes.

[2] Lev. 25[29f]. See Arak. 9[3ff]. Whether the tree is included in the terms of the law depends on whether the root of the tree is within the specified bounds.

[3] Deut. 19[2ff]. See Makk. 2[7].

[4] If the tree was within the boundary and the foliage stretched outside, the fugitive is safe so soon as he reaches ground beneath the foliage.

[5] In what concerns Second Tithe produce, which, once it enters Jerusalem, may not go out again (M. Sh. 3[5, 7]); or in what concerns the 'Lesser Holy Things' which may be consumed only within the walls of Jerusalem (Kel. 1[8]). See also Pes. 7[12].

[6] Some texts omit 'in the field'. This and the following paragraphs give cases turning on the principle of 1[5], that produce is liable to Tithes once it can be reckoned completely harvested; otherwise only a 'casual meal' may be taken from it on the principle of Deut. 23[25].

[7] The fact of their being set aside to be eaten on the Sabbath marks the end of their ingathering; therefore they are liable to Tithes.

[8] They differ as to its liability if consumed before the Sabbath.

[9] Since they cannot be put back.   [10] See Erub. 10[6].

R. Zadok declares them liable. But the Sages say: If mixed with hot water he [that drinks thereof] is liable,[1] but if with cold he is exempt.

5. If a man husked barley he may do so and eat thereof grain by grain; but if he husked [several grains] and put them in his hand he is liable to Tithes. If a man rubbed ripe ears of wheat he may sift them from one hand to the other and eat them [without tithing], but if he sifted them and collected the grains into his bosom, he is liable. If coriander was sown for the sake of the seed, the plant is exempt; but if it was sown for the sake of the plant, both seed and plant must be tithed. R. Eliezer says: From dill the seeds, plant, and pods must be tithed. But the Sages say: Both seeds and plant are tithed only in the case of pepperwort and eruca.

6. Rabban Gamaliel says: The stalks of fenugreek, of mustard, and of white beans are liable to Tithes.[2] R. Eliezer says: From the caper, Tithes are taken from stalks, caperberries, and caper-flowers. R. Akiba says: Only the caperberries are tithed, because they [alone] count as fruit.

5. 1. If a man uprooted seedlings [already fit for food] from within his own domain and planted them [elsewhere] within his own domain, he is exempt;[3] if he bought seedlings in their unplucked state he is exempt; if he picked them to send to his fellow he is exempt.[4] R. Eleazar b. Azariah says: If their like were then being sold in the market they would be liable to Tithes.[5]

2. If a man uprooted turnips and radishes from within his own domain and planted them [elsewhere] within his own domain to serve as seed, he is liable to Tithes, since this would count as harvesting them. If onions [stored] in an upper room have put forth roots they become free from uncleanness that they may have contracted.[6] If rubbish fell on them and they remained uncovered,[7] it is as though they were planted in the field.

3. After produce has reached its tithing season none may sell it to one that is not trustworthy in what concerns Tithes,[8] nor, in the Seventh Year, [may he give it] to one that is suspect in what concerns Seventh Year produce. If some [only] of the produce was already ripe [and liable to Tithes] he may remove what is ripe and sell the residue.

4. A man may not sell his straw or olive-peat or grape-residue[9] to one that is not trustworthy in what concerns Tithes, for him to extract the juices therefrom. And if he extracted them he is liable to Tithes but exempt from Heave-offering, since when a man sets aside Heave-offering he has in mind 'the unground fragments, what falls to the sides and what remains in the husk'.[10]

5. If a man bought a field of vegetables in Syria before the tithing season, he is liable to Tithes, but if after the tithing season, he is exempt and may continue to gather the crop himself after his usual fashion. R. Judah says: He may also hire labourers to help gather the crop. R. Simeon b. Gamaliel said: This[11] applies if he had bought the land; but

---

[1] He may not put it back after it has been heated since this would spoil the rest.
[2] As being fit for food.
[3] If he ate of them or even brought them into his house, since their growth is not complete.
[4] It is as though he made a gift of unplucked produce.
[5] On the principle laid down in 1[1], of produce that is used as food in its earlier stage of ripeness.
[6] According to the rule of Lev. 11[34, 33].   [7] As to their leaves.
[8] In fulfilment of the principle of Lev. 19[14], not to put a stumbling-block before the 'blind'.
[9] The squeezed-out olives and grapes, from which it is still possible to squeeze out inferior oil or wine.   [10] Cf. Maas. 1[6].
[11] That he is liable if he acquired the field before the time for Tithes.

if he had not bought the land, although it was before the tithing season, he is exempt. Rabbi says: Howbeit he should give tithe according to the proportion [which the crop had grown after he acquired it].

6. If a man made grape-skin wine[1] putting in a certain measure of water, and he [afterward] found the like measure,[2] he is exempt [from tithing it] (R. Judah declares him liable); but if he found more than the like measure he must give tithe therefor from other wine according to the proportion [of the increase in measure].

7. If ant-holes have been present throughout a night near a heap of corn that was liable to Tithe, what is found in them is also liable, since it is manifest that the ants dragged away [the corn] throughout the night from produce completely harvested.

8. Baalbek-garlic,[3] Rikhpa onions, Cilician beans, and Egyptian lentils (R. Meir adds colocasia, and R. Jose wild lentils) are exempt from Tithes[4] and may be bought from any one in the Seventh Year. The higher seed-pods of the arum, the seed of leeks, the seed of onions, and the seed of turnips and radishes and other seeds of garden produce which are not used as food, are exempt from Tithes and may be bought from any one in the Seventh Year; and even if the stock from which they were grown was Heave-offering, they may still be eaten [by non-priests].[5]

MAASER SHENI[6] ('SECOND TITHE')

1. 1. Second Tithe may not be sold, pledged, or bartered, nor may it be used to weigh [other produce] therewith; nor may a man say to his fellow [even] in Jerusalem, 'Here is wine: give me oil'; so, too, with any other produce. But they may give it one to another as a gift.

2. Tithe of Cattle,[7] when unblemished, may not be sold alive; if blemished it may not be sold alive or slaughtered, and none may betroth a woman therewith;[8] a Firstling,[9] when unblemished, may be sold alive; if blemished it may be sold alive or slaughtered, and a woman may be betrothed therewith. Second Tithe may not be exchanged for unminted metal,[10] or for coin that is not current, or for money that is not at command.

3. If a man bought[11] cattle for a Peace-offering or a wild animal for use as food, sanctity [of Second Tithe] does not apply to the hide even though its value was more than that of the flesh. [If he bought] sealed jars of wine where it was usual to sell them sealed, sanctity [of Second Tithe] does not apply to the empty jar; nor does it apply to the shells of walnuts and

---

1 Poured water over untithed grape-skins or wine dregs.
2 Of liquid; less than a third more (Bert.), or a sixth more (Tif. Yis.).
3 Or 'weeping-garlic', i.e. so strong that it makes the eyes water.
4 Since they grow wild.   5 In spite of the rule of Ter. 9⁴.
6 Deut. 14²²ᶠᶠ. In the first, second, fourth, and fifth years of the seven-year cycle after the harvested produce has paid Heave-offering to the priest (from a sixtieth to a fortieth part) and (First) Tithe to the levite, it is still liable to 'Second Tithe'. This the owner must take to Jerusalem and there consume it, or else he must 'redeem' it, i.e. put aside coins of the value (plus one-fifth) of this Second Tithe of his produce, and then that produce which was Second Tithe becomes free for use as ordinary food. The coins themselves then count as 'Second Tithe money' and the sanctity of Second Tithe is transferred to them or to other coins for which they, in turn, may be exchanged. They must be taken up to Jerusalem and with them food (or Peace-offerings) must be bought and consumed 'in cleanness' in Jerusalem. In the third and sixth years what would have been Second Tithe must be given to the poor as 'Poorman's Tithe' (Deut. 14²⁸ᶠᶠ; 26¹²).
7 Lev. 27³²; Bekh. 9¹ᶠᶠ.   8 Cf. Kidd. 2⁸,⁹.   9 See p. 529, n. 8; p. 533, n. 9.
10 Eduy. 3². It must, according to Deut. 14²⁵, be actual money, current coin.
11 With Second Tithe money in Jerusalem.

almonds. Grape-skin wine[1] may not be bought with [Second] Tithe money before it has fermented,[2] but it may be bought after it has fermented.

4. If a man bought a wild animal for a Peace-offering or cattle for use as food, sanctity [of Second Tithe] applies to the hide. [If he bought] jars of wine, open or sealed, where it was usual to sell them open, sanctity [of Second Tithe] applies to the empty jar. [If he bought] baskets of olives or grapes together with the basket, sanctity [of Second Tithe] applies to the value of the basket.

5. If a man bought water or salt or unplucked produce, or produce that cannot be taken up to Jerusalem, he has not acquired a [valid] substitute for Second Tithe. If he bought produce in error[3] the money must be restored; if wantonly, the produce must be taken up to the Place[4] and there consumed; and if it cannot be taken to the Holy City[5] it must be allowed to rot.

6. If a man bought cattle in error the money must be restored; if wantonly, it must be taken up to Jerusalem and there consumed; and if it cannot be taken to the Holy City it must be buried with its hide.

7. Bondmen or bondwomen, immovable property or unclean cattle may not be bought with Second Tithe money, and if a man bought the like he must still consume the like value [as Second Tithe in Jerusalem]. Bird-offerings of a man or a woman that suffered a flux, or of a woman after child-birth,[6] or Sin-offerings or Guilt-offerings, may not be offered if bought with Second Tithe money; and if a man had so bought them he must still consume the like value [as Second Tithe in Jerusalem]. This is the general rule: if with Second Tithe money a man bought other than food, drink, or unguent, he must still consume the like value [as Second Tithe in Jerusalem].

2. 1. Second Tithe is appointed for use as food, drink, or unguent: that is to be eaten which it is usual to eat, and that is to be drunken which it is usual to drink, and that is to be used for anointing which it is usual to use for anointing. A man may not anoint himself with wine or vinegar, but only with oil. He may not make perfumed oil from Second Tithe or buy perfumed oil with Second Tithe money; but he may spice the wine. If honey or spices fell into the wine[7] and increased its value, the increased value [is assessed] according to the quantity [of what is added].[8] If fish were cooked with Second Tithe leeks and so improved, the increased value [is assessed] according to the quantity [of what is added]. If Second Tithe dough was baked and [so] improved [in value], the increased value is [wholly] reckoned[9] to the Second [Tithe]. This is the general rule: when the improvement is recognized [as due to aught that is added] the increased value [is assessed] according to the quantity [of what is added]; but if the improvement is not recognized [as due to aught that is added] the increased value is [wholly] reckoned to the Second [Tithe].

2. R. Simeon says: A man may not anoint himself with Second Tithe

---

[1] See Maas. 5[6]; Hull. 1[7].　　　　[2] Since it counts as water only. See below, par. 5.
[3] Outside Jerusalem, and he did not known that he was using Second Tithe money.
[4] Jerusalem; for what has been bought with Second Tithe money cannot be redeemed.
[5] Heb. *Mikdash*, lit. 'Temple'; but here used in the wider sense. So also in Pes. 10[3].
[6] For these see p. 598, n 3.
[7] Outside Jerusalem and before its money-substitute had been set aside.
[8] Even if the improvement of the Second Tithe was worth more than the value of the added matter.
[9] Its value is that of baked bread and not of dough only plus the cost of the fire.

oil[1] in Jerusalem. But the Sages permit it. They said to R. Simeon: Since the more lenient ruling applies to the graver matter of Heave-offering,[2] should we not apply the more lenient ruling to the less grave matter of Second Tithe? He answered: No! even if the more lenient ruling applies to the graver matter of Heave-offering (whereto applies a more lenient ruling in what concerns vetches and fenugreek),[3] should we apply a more lenient ruling to the less grave matter of Second Tithe (whereto a more lenient ruling does not apply in what concerns vetches and fenugreek)?

3. Second Tithe fenugreek may be consumed only in its green condition; but as for Heave-offering fenugreek, the School of Shammai say: Whatsoever concerns it must be done in cleanness save combing the head therewith. And the School of Hillel say: Whatsoever concerns it may be done in uncleanness save the soaking of it.

4. Second Tithe vetches may be consumed only in their green condition, and may be brought up to Jerusalem and taken out again. If they have contracted uncleanness, R. Tarfon says: They should be divided among lumps of dough. But the Sages say: They should be redeemed. Of Heave-offering vetches the School of Shammai say:[4] They must be soaked and rubbed in cleanness but they may be given as food in uncleanness. And the School of Hillel say: They should be soaked in cleanness but they may be rubbed and given as food in uncleanness. Shammai says: They may only be eaten dry. R. Akiba says: Whatsoever concerns them may be done in uncleanness.

5. If common money and Second Tithe money were scattered[5] [and confused], whatsoever coins are [first] picked up are deemed Second Tithe until its tally is complete; and the residue is deemed common money. But if the two were mingled together and could be taken up by handfuls, they are allotted according to their original proportion. This is the general rule: What must be picked up coin by coin [is first allotted] to the Second Tithe money; but what is only mingled together is allotted according to the original proportion.

6. If a *sela*[6] of Second Tithe was confused with a *sela* of common money,[7] he should bring a *sela's* worth of [copper] coins and say, 'Let the *sela* of Second Tithe, wherever it may be, be exchanged for these coins'. He should then choose out the finer of the two *selas* and exchange it [again] for the [copper] coins; for they have said: At need silver may be substituted by copper, not that it should remain thus, but that the copper coins should again be substituted by silver.

7. The School of Shammai say: A man may not change his *selas*[8] for golden *denars*.[9] But the School of Hillel permit it. R. Akiba said: I changed silver for golden *denars* for Rabban Gamaliel and R. Joshua.

8. If[10] a man would change a *sela's* worth of Second Tithe money [outside of Jerusalem][11] the School of Shammai say: He may change it for

---

[1] He holds that it may be used only as food.   [2] As taught in Shebi. 8[2].
[3] See Ter. 11[9].   [4] See Eduy. 1[8].
[5] So that they must be picked up one by one.
[6] For the coins mentioned in this and the following paragraphs see App. II, A.
[7] And its owner wished to spend the common money outside of Jerusalem.
[8] Of Second Tithe money.
[9] Lest the difficulty of changing them back into smaller money should hinder his going up to Jerusalem.
[10] Eduy. 1[9].   [11] In order to lighten his burden on the way to Jerusalem.

a whole *sela*. And the School of Hillel say: A shekel's worth of silver and a shekel's worth in copper coin.[1] R. Meir says: They may not change silver and produce [together][2] into [other] silver. But the Sages permit it.

9. If[3] a man would change a *sela* of Second Tithe money in Jerusalem, the School of Shammai say: He must change the whole *sela* into copper coin. And the School of Hillel say: He may take one shekel's worth of silver and one shekel's worth in copper coin. They that made argument before the Sages[4] say: Three *denars'* worth of silver and one of copper. R. Akiba says: Three *denars'* worth of silver and from the fourth [*denar*] a quarter in copper coin. R. Tarfon says: Four *aspers* in silver. Shammai says: Let him deposit it in a shop and [gradually] consume its value.

10. If of a man's sons some were clean and some unclean, he should lay down the *sela* and say, 'For what they that are clean shall drink, let this *sela* [of Second Tithe] be given in exchange'. Thus clean and unclean may drink from the same jar.

3. 1. A man may not say to his fellow, 'Take up this produce to Jerusalem in return for a share therein'; but he may say to him, 'Take it up and we will eat and drink thereof in Jerusalem'. Moreover they may make a present thereof one to another.

2. They may not buy Heave-offering with Second Tithe money, since this renders fewer[5] them that may eat of it. But R. Simeon permits it. R. Simeon said to the Sages: What! if the more lenient ruling applies to Peace-offerings[6] (which are subject to the laws of Refuse,[7] Remnant,[8] and uncleanness)[9] should we not also apply the more lenient ruling to Heave-offering? They answered: What! if the more lenient ruling applies to Peace-offerings (which are permitted to non-priests) should we therefore apply the more lenient ruling to Heave-offering which is forbidden to non-priests?

3. If a man in Jerusalem had [Second Tithe] money and it was needful [for other than food, drink, or unguent] and his fellow had produce [that was unconsecrated], he may say to his fellow, 'Let this money be rendered free for common use by [exchange with] thy produce'. Then the one shall eat his produce in cleanness [as Second Tithe] and the other may do what he will with his money. But he may not say so to an *Am-haaretz*[10] unless the money was [Second Tithe money set aside] for *demai*-produce.[11]

4. If a man had [unconsecrated] produce in Jerusalem and [Second Tithe] money in the provinces, he may say, 'Let that money be rendered free for common use by [exchange with] this produce'. [If he had Second Tithe] money in Jerusalem and [unconsecrated] produce in the provinces, he may say, 'Let this money be rendered free for common use by [exchange

---

[1] Because if all go up with silver it will raise the price of copper coin in Jerusalem.
[2] E.g. a half-*denar's* worth of produce and a half-*denar* together for a whole *denar*.
[3] Eduy. 1[10].
[4] The pupils of R. Akiba: Simeon b. Azzai, Simeon b. Zoma, Hanan the Egyptian (not the Hanan of Ket. 13[1ff]), Simeon b. Nanos, and Hananiah b. Hakinai.
[5] It may not be eaten by non-priests or even by priests unless they are wholly free from uncleanness.   [6] In that they can be bought with Second Tithe money.
[7] Lev. 7[18] ('Abomination'), Zeb. 2[2ff]. An offering eaten after its prescribed time or outside its prescribed place.
[8] Ex. 29[34], Lev. 7[17]. An offering that remains after the time appointed for eating it, and that must be burnt.
[9] See Lev. 7[20].
[10] Who could not be trusted to eat his produce in 'cleanness, as Second Tithe'.
[11] See p. 20, n. 9.

with] that produce', provided that the produce is brought up and consumed in Jerusalem.

5. [Second Tithe] money that is brought into Jerusalem may be taken out again, but [Second Tithe] produce that is brought in may not be taken out again. Rabban Simeon b. Gamaliel says: Even produce may be brought in and taken out again.[1]

6. If produce that was fully harvested passed through Jerusalem,[2] the Second Tithe thereof must be brought back again to Jerusalem and there consumed. If it was not yet fully harvested (the like of grapes [that are borne] in baskets to the winepress or figs in baskets to the drying-place), the School of Shammai say: The Second Tithe thereof must be brought back to Jerusalem and there consumed. And the School of Hillel say: It may be redeemed and eaten anywhere. R. Simeon b. Judah in the name of R. Jose says: The School of Shammai and the School of Hillel did not dispute about produce that was not fully harvested, whose Second Tithe can be redeemed and eaten anywhere. But about what did they dispute? About produce that was fully harvested, whose Second Tithe, according to the School of Shammai, should be brought back and consumed in Jerusalem, and, according to the School of Hillel, could be redeemed and eaten anywhere. Demai-produce may be brought in and taken out again and may be redeemed.

7. If a tree stood within the wall [of Jerusalem] and [its boughs] stretched outside, or stood outside and [its boughs] stretched inwards, the part of the foliage directly above the wall and inwards is deemed within [Jerusalem] and the part directly above the wall and outwards is deemed outside. If the entrance to olive-presses [in the city wall] was within [Jerusalem] and their contained space outside, or their entrance outside and their contained space within [Jerusalem], the School of Shammai say: The whole is deemed within [Jerusalem]. And the School of Hillel say: The part directly above the wall and inwards is deemed within and the part directly above the wall and outwards is deemed outside.

8. In the chambers[3] built in the Temple [Court] and opening into ground that was not holy, no sanctity attaches to the space within them, but their roofs are deemed to be within holy ground; in those built in ground that was not holy and opening into the Temple [Court], the space within them is holy but no sanctity attaches to their roofs; in those built both within the Temple [Court] and on ground that was not holy and opening both into the Temple [Court] and into ground that was not holy, [then in what concerns] the space within them and their roofs, directly above the Temple [Court] and inwards toward the Temple [Court] is holy, and directly above the Temple [Court] and outward toward ground that is not holy, is not holy.

9. If Second Tithe was brought into Jerusalem and contracted uncleanness, whether from a Father of Uncleanness or from an Offspring of Uncleanness,[4] whether within or without [the walls of Jerusalem], the School of Shammai say: It should be redeemed and it may be consumed within [the walls] excepting only what was rendered unclean by a Father of Uncleanness outside [the walls]. And the School of Hillel say: It should be redeemed and it must be consumed outside [the walls] excepting only

---

[1] To grind or bake it cheaply and then bring it back to Jerusalem.
[2] Before Heave-offering and First Tithe had been taken from it.
[3] See Midd. 1[8]; 4[5].   [4] App. IV. 3, 4. See p. 604, n. 2; cf. Pes. 1[6].

what was rendered unclean by an Offspring of Uncleanness within [the walls].

10. If what was bought with Second Tithe money contracted uncleanness it may be redeemed. R. Judah says: It must be buried. They said to R. Judah: If Second Tithe itself, that is rendered unclean, may be redeemed, must we not infer that what was bought with Second Tithe money and contracted uncleanness may also be redeemed? He replied: No! as ye argue of Second Tithe itself (that can be redeemed in clean condition far away from the Temple), would ye likewise argue of what is bought with Second Tithe money (that cannot be redeemed in clean condition far away from the Temple)?

11. If a gazelle bought with Second Tithe money died, it must be buried with its hide. R. Simeon says: It may be redeemed. If it was bought alive and slaughtered and then contracted uncleanness, it may be redeemed. R. Jose says: It must be buried. If it was bought ready slaughtered and then contracted uncleanness, it is treated in like fashion as produce.[1]

12. If a man lent empty jars for [wine already designated] Second Tithe, even though he sealed them up, they do not count as [Second] Tithe. If he poured therein wine that was still undesignated [and the wine was designated Second Tithe] before the jars were sealed up, they do not count as [Second] Tithe; but if [it was designated] after they were sealed up, they count as [Second] Tithe.[2] [So, too, if wine was designated Heave-offering] before the jars were sealed up [and they are confused with others], they are neutralized in a hundred and one; but if after they were sealed up, they render holy [others with which they are confused] in any quantity soever. Until he has sealed them up he may give Heave-offering from one on behalf of all; but after he has sealed them up, he must give Heave-offering from each singly.

13. The School of Shammai say: [If he would give Heave-offering from one on behalf of all after he has sealed them up], he must open [the jars] and empty them into the winepress. But the School of Hillel say: He must open them but he need not empty them. This applies to places where their custom is to sell [the jars] sealed; but where their custom is to sell them open the sanctity [of Heave-offering] applies to the jar. And if the seller restricts himself to selling by measure, sanctity does not apply to the jar. R. Simeon says: Moreover if a man said to his fellow, 'I sell thee this jarful, not including the empty jar', sanctity does not apply to the jar.

4. 1. If a man took Second Tithe produce from a place where prices were high to a place where prices were low, or from a place where prices were low to a place where prices were high, he must redeem it at the price that prevails in the place where he is. If a man brought produce from the threshing-floor to the town, or jars of wine from the winepress to the town, the increase in value falls to the Second [Tithe] and the outlay [for removal] falls on his household.

2. Second Tithe is redeemed at the cheaper rate—the rate at which the shopkeeper buys and not at the rate at which he sells; [and Second Tithe money is exchanged at] the rate at which the money-changer takes in exchange and not at the rate at which he gives. Second Tithe may not be

---

[1] And the principles of par. 10 apply.
[2] The sanctity of Second Tithe attaches to them, and their value must be included when the wine is 'redeemed'.

redeemed by guesswork; if it has a known price it may be redeemed according to the estimate of but one,[1] and if its price is not known (like as when wine is turned sour or produce has gone bad or coins have rusted) it should be redeemed according to the estimate of three.[2]

3. If a householder bid a *sela* and another bid a *sela*, the householder's claim comes first, since he must add the Fifth.[3] If the householder bid a *sela* and another bid a *sela* and an *issar*, his claim comes first, since he adds to the value. When a man redeems his Second Tithe he must add one-fifth more, whether it was his own or whether it was given to him.

4. Men may act with cunning in what concerns Second Tithe.[4] Thus a man may say to his son or daughter that are of age, or to his Hebrew bondman or bondwoman,[5] 'Here is money: do thou redeem this Second Tithe'. But he cannot speak thus to his son or daughter that are minors or to his Canaanite bondman or bondwoman,[6] since their hand is as his hand.

5. [Or] if he was standing on his threshing-floor and had no money in his hand he may say to his fellow, 'This produce is given thee as a gift', and say moreover, 'Let this be substituted by money that is in the house'.

6. If a man drew into his possession [Second] Tithe from another at the price of one *sela*, but before he could redeem it its value stood at two *selas*, he pays but one *sela* and makes one *sela* profit and the Second Tithe remains his. If he drew into his possession [Second] Tithe from another at the price of two *selas* but before he could redeem it its value stood at one *sela*, he may pay him the one *sela* in common money and the second *sela* from Second Tithe money that belongs to him. If he was an *Am-haaretz* he may pay him [the second *sela*] from *demai*-produce.

7. If a man redeemed Second Tithe yet had not designated it Second Tithe, R. Jose says: It suffices. But R. Judah says: He must designate it expressly. If a man was speaking to a woman about her divorce or her betrothal and gave her her bill of divorce or her betrothal gift but did not expressly designate it such, R. Jose says: It suffices. But R. Judah says: He must designate it expressly.

8. If a man set aside one *issar* [as Second Tithe redemption money] and in virtue of this consumed half its value and then went elsewhere where it was worth a *pondion*, he can still consume another *issar's* worth. If he set aside one *pondion* and in virtue of this consumed half its value and then went elsewhere where it was worth [only] one *issar*, he may consume only another half-*issar's* worth. If he set aside one *issar* as Second Tithe redemption money, he may in virtue of this consume up to[7] one-eleventh of an *issar's* worth [if it was *demai*-produce] and one-hundredth of an *issar's* worth [if it was produce certainly untithed]. The School of Shammai say: In either case one-tenth; and the School of Hillel say: One-eleventh if it was produce certainly untithed, and one-tenth if it was *demai*-produce.

9. Any coins that are found are deemed unconsecrated, even if it was a golden *denar* found with silver and copper coins.[8] If a potsherd was found with them and on it was written 'Tithe', they must be deemed [Second] Tithe [redemption money].

---

[1] Some texts add 'witness'.   [2] Sanh. 1³.   [3] Lev. 27³¹. See Arak. 8¹ᶠᶠ.
[4] To evade the payment of the Added Fifth.   [5] See Kidd. 1².   [6] See Kidd. 1³.
[7] i.e. 'so as to leave ...' The precise interpretation of the rest of this paragraph is doubtful.
[8] Since it is not usual to mix them together; therefore the natural inference would be that they were specially set aside as Second Tithe redemption money.

10. If a man found a vessel and on it was written '*Korban*',[1] R. Judah says: If it was of earthenware the vessel is to be deemed unconsecrated but its contents *Korban*; and if it was of metal it is to be deemed *Korban* but its contents unconsecrated. They said to him: It is not the way of men to put what is unconsecrated into what is *Korban*.

11. If a man found a vessel and on it was inscribed a *Kof*, this is *Korban*; if a *Mem* it is *Maaser* (Tithe); if a *Daleth* it is *demai*-produce (produce not certainly tithed); if a *Tet* it is *Tebel* (produce certainly untithed); and if a *Tau* it is *Terumah* (Heave-offering); for in the times of danger[2] they used to write *Tau* for *Terumah*. R. Jose says: They may all be [the initials of] men's names. R. Jose said: Even if a man found a jar full of produce with '*Terumah*' written on it it should be deemed unconsecrated, since I may assume that it was filled with Heave-offering a year ago and afterward emptied.

12. If a man said to his son, 'There is Second Tithe [redemption money] in this corner', and he found money in another corner, it counts as unconsecrated. If there had been there a hundred *denars* [of Second Tithe redemption money] and he found there two hundred, the surplus counts as unconsecrated. [If there had been there] two hundred *denars* and he found but one hundred, this all counts as [Second] Tithe.

5. 1. A Fourth Year Vineyard[3] must be marked by clods of earth, and trees of *Orlah*-fruit[4] by potsherds, and a grave[5] by whiting mingled with water and poured over the grave. Rabban Simeon b. Gamaliel said: This applies only in the Seventh Year.[6] The truly pious used to lay down money and say: Whatsoever fruit is picked from here may it be redeemed by this money.

2. Fruit of a Fourth Year Vineyard was taken up to Jerusalem [from any place] one day's journey in any direction. And what was the [farthest] limit? Elath[7] to the south, Akrabah[8] to the north, Lydda to the west, and the Jordan to the east. When the fruits became too many it was ordained that they might be redeemed even though [the vineyard was] near to the [city] wall. And this was with the understanding that when they wished, the matter might be restored as beforetime. R. Jose says: This was the understanding after the Temple was destroyed, and the understanding was that when the Temple should be rebuilt the matter would be restored as beforetime.

3. The School of Shammai say:[9] The rules of the [Added] Fifth and of Removal do not apply to [the grapes of] a Fourth Year Vineyard. And the School of Hillel say: They do apply. The School of Shammai say: The laws of grape-gleanings and of the defective cluster apply, and the poor redeem the grapes for themselves. And the School of Hillel say: The whole yield goes to the winepress.

---

[1] 'An offering' dedicated to the Temple, either for use as an offering if it is fitted for such use, or as a Temple utensil. See Shek. 4[6ff]; 5[6].

[2] When in time of persecution, such as followed the Bar Cocheba revolt in the reign of Hadrian, it was forbidden to observe the Jewish religious practices. Cf. Ket. 9[9].

[3] Cf. Lev. 19[24].   [4] Cf. App. I. 32.

[5] To give warning of uncleanness. Cf. Shek. 1[1]; M. Kat. 1[2]; cf. Par. 3[2].

[6] When all produce is ownerless property.

[7] Neub. p. 119f. No place of such a name within one day's journey from Jerusalem has yet been plausibly identified.

[8] Neub. p. 159. Perhaps the modern Akrabah, twenty-five miles north of Jerusalem.

[9] See Peah 7[6]; Eduy. 4[5].

4. How are the fruits of Fourth-year plantings redeemed? The owner lays down a basket before three [that are skilled][1] and says, 'How many [such baskets full] can a man redeem for a *sela*, and yet defray the costs[2] incurred by his household?' And he lays down the money and says, 'Whatsoever is henceforth gathered let it be redeemed by this money at the rate of so many baskets for a *sela*'.

5. But in the Seventh Year it must be redeemed at its [full] value.[3] And if it was all ownerless property, only the cost of gathering is taken into account. If a man redeemed the fruit of his own Fourth-year plantings he must add the fifth of the value, whether it was his own or whether it was given him.

6. On the eve of the first[4] Festival-day[5] of Passover in the fourth[6] and seventh years the duty of Removal[7] was fulfilled. Thus Heave-offering and Heave-offering of Tithe were given to whom they were due, and the First Tithe was given to whom it was due, and Poorman's Tithe was given to whom it was due, and the Second Tithe and the First-fruits everywhere were removed. R. Simeon says: The First-fruits like the Heave-offering were given to the priests. Cooked food[8] should be removed, according to the School of Shammai; but the School of Hillel say: It is accounted a thing removed [already].

7. If a man had produce[9] at this time[10] and the season came for Removal, the School of Shammai say: He must redeem it with money.[11] And the School of Hillel say: It is all one whether it is in the form of produce or of money.

8. R. Judah said: Beforetime they used to send to householders in the provinces [saying], 'Hasten and duly tithe your produce before the time of Removal shall come', until R. Akiba came and taught that all produce was exempt from Removal if its tithing season[12] was not yet come.

9. He whose produce is far removed from him must say expressly to whom the Tithes thereof are due. Once[13] when Rabban Gamaliel and the elders were sailing in a ship Rabban Gamaliel said, 'The Tithe which I should have measured [as First Tithe] is given to Joshua,[14] and the land whereon it grows is rented to him; the other Tithe which I should have measured [as Poorman's Tithe] is given to Akiba b. Joseph that he may possess it on behalf of the poor, and the land whereon it grows is rented to him.' R. Joshua said, 'The Tithe which I should have measured [as Heave-offering of Tithe] is given to Eleazar b. Azariah,[15] and the land on which it grows is rented to him'. And they each received rent from the other.

10. At the time of the Afternoon Offering on the last Festival-day they used to make the Avowal.[16] How used a man to make the Avowal? [He said], *I have removed the Hallowed Things out of mine house*—that is Second

---

[1] Cf. Sanh. 1³.   [2] Of guarding, hoeing, and the like.
[3] Not deducting the cost of labour, since in the Seventh Year it is forbidden to tend it.
[4] Some texts read 'last'.
[5] The first and seventh days of Passover are 'Festival Days' (Heb. *yamim tobim*, good—i.e. holy days); the intervening days, the 'middle days' are called *Hol ha-Moed* (lit. non-holy days of the Feast). See p. 181, n. 11; p. 207, n. 19.   [6] In fulfilment of Deut. 14²⁸.
[7] Cf. Shebi. 9².   [8] That contained any produce subject to Removal.
[9] Second Tithe and Fourth-year fruit which should be consumed in Jerusalem.
[10] When the Temple has ceased to exist.   [11] And throw this into the sea.
[12] Maas. 1²ᶠᶠ. See Deut. 26¹².
[13] On the eve of Passover when the time for Removal was come.
[14] Who was a levite.   [15] Who was a priest.   [16] Deut. 26¹³ᶠᶠ.

Tithe and the fruits of Fourth-year plantings; *I have given them to the Levite*—that is the Tithe of the levites; *and also*[1] [*I have given them*]—that is the Heave-offering and the Heave-offering of Tithe; *to the stranger and the fatherless and the widow*—that is the Poorman's Tithe, Gleanings, the Forgotten Sheaf, and *Peah* (although these do not render the Avowal invalid); *from the house*—that is Dough-offering.

11. *According to all thy commandment which thou hast commanded me*— thus if he granted Second Tithe before First Tithe he may not make the Avowal; *I have not transgressed any of thy commandments*—I have not given from one kind instead of from some other kind or from what has been plucked instead of from what is unplucked or from what is unplucked instead of from what is plucked, or from new produce instead of from old, or from old produce instead of from new; *neither have I forgotten*—I have not forgotten to bless thee or to make mention of thy name over it.

12. *I have not eaten thereof in my mourning*—thus if he had eaten during mourning he may not make the Avowal; *nor have I removed ought thereof being unclean*—thus if he had set it apart in uncleanness he may not make the Avowal; *nor given thereof for the dead*—I have not used aught thereof for a coffin or wrappings for a corpse nor have I given it to other mourners; *I have hearkened to the voice of the Lord my God*—I have brought it to his chosen Temple; *I have done according to all that thou hast commanded me*— I have rejoiced and made others to rejoice therewith.

13. *Look down from thy holy habitation from heaven*—we have done what thou hast decreed concerning us: do thou also what thou hast promised to us; *Look down from thy holy habitation from heaven and bless thy people Israel*—with sons and daughters; *and the ground which thou hast given us*— with dew and wine and with the young of cattle; *as thou swarest unto our fathers, a land flowing with milk and honey*—that thou mayest give flavour to the fruits.

14. From this they have inferred that Israelites and bastards may make the Avowal but not proselytes and freed slaves, who have no share in the Land. R. Meir says: And not priests and levites, because they have not received a share from the Land. R. Jose says: They have the cities of the outskirts.[2]

15. Johanan the High Priest[3] did away with the Avowal concerning the Tithe.[4] He too made an end also of the 'Awakeners'[5] and the 'Stunners'.[6] Until his days the hammer used to smite[7] in Jerusalem. And in his days none needed to inquire concerning *demai*-produce.[8]

---

[1] This is an example of the rule of *Ribbui* and *Mi'ut* ('extension' and 'limitation') taught by R. Nahum of Gimzo, according to which certain particles (as here) 'extend' or else 'limit' the provision enjoined in the law there enjoined. Cf. Shebu. 3[5].

[2] See Num. 35[2ff].   [3] John Hyrcanus, 135–105 B.C. Cf. Sot. 9[10]; Par. 3[5]; Yad. 4[6].

[4] So that a man need not say, 'I have given it to the levite', for Ezra had enacted that, as a punishment to the levites who did not go up with him to Jerusalem, the First Tithe should be given to the priests.

[5] He abolished the daily singing by the levites of the verse (Ps. 44[23]) 'Awake, why sleepest thou, O Lord?' because of its unseemliness.

[6] Who used to stupify the animals in the Temple before slaughtering them. This was abolished as likely to cause a forbidden blemish in the beast. (Lev. 22[19ff]).

[7] In the 'middle days' of the Feasts; i.e. he forbade even necessary work on such days. See p. 207, n. 19.   It is doubtful whether the above rendering of these two clauses (which is that of the Gemara, Sot. 48a) represents the original sense of this early tradition.

[8] Beforetime it was needful to inquire whether a dealer was 'trustworthy' in the matter of tithes or not; and it was necessary to set apart all the dues and tithes in cases of doubt. But Johanan the High Priest issued the ruling that (Sot. 48a) only Heave-offering of Tithe and Second Tithe need be taken account of in *demai*-produce. See p. 20, n. 9.

HALLAH[1] ('DOUGH-OFFERING')

1. 1. Five kinds are liable to Dough-offering: wheat, barley, spelt, goat-grass, and oats. These are liable to Dough-offering and may be included together [to make up the quantity that is liable to Dough-offering];[2] and they are forbidden,[3] such time as they are new produce,[4] [to be made use of] before Passover or to be reaped before the *Omer*.[5] If they have taken root before the *Omer*, the [reaping of the] *Omer* renders them permissible; otherwise they are forbidden until the *Omer* of the next year.

2. He that eats an olive's bulk of them as unleavened bread at Passover has fulfilled his obligation,[6] and if [he ate] an olive's bulk of them leavened he is punishable by Extirpation.[7] If one of them was mixed with some other kind, this transgresses the Passover law.[8] If a man vowed to abstain[9] from bread and grain he is forbidden these [five kinds]. So R. Meir. But the Sages say: If a man vowed to abstain from corn he is forbidden these only. And these [five kinds] are liable to Dough-offering and to Tithes.

3. These are liable to Dough-offering but exempt from Tithes: Gleanings, the Forgotten Sheaf, *Peah*,[10] ownerless crops, First Tithe from which Heave-offering has been taken, Second Tithe and dedicated produce that have been redeemed,[11] the residue of the *Omer*,[12] and grain that has not reached a third of its growth.[13] R. Eliezer says: Grain that has not reached a third of its growth is [also] exempt from Dough-offering.

4. These are liable to Tithes but exempt from Dough-offering: rice, durra, panic, sesame and pulse, and less than five quarter-[*kabs*][14] of [the five kinds of] grain. Spongy-cakes, honey-cakes, paste-balls, pancakes, and [produce that is] mixed with Heave-offering are exempt from Dough-offering.

5. Dough which at its beginning was intended for spongy-cakes and in the end was used for spongy-cakes is exempt from Dough-offering. If at its beginning it was ordinary dough and in the end was used for spongy-cakes, or if at its beginning it was intended for spongy-cakes and in the end was used as ordinary dough, it is liable to Dough-offering. So, too, Kenubka[15] cakes are liable.

6. Flour-paste[16] is exempt according to the School of Shammai; according to the School of Hillel it is liable. Dumplings[17] are liable according to the School of Shammai; according to the School of Hillel they are exempt. The cakes of the Thank-offering[18] and the wafers of the Nazirite[19] are exempt if a man made them for his own use[20] but if to sell in the market they are liable.

7. If a baker made leaven to distribute [to buyers] it is liable to Dough-offering. If women gave [dough] to the baker from which to make leaven for them, and none [of the portions of dough] was of the prescribed measure,[21] it is exempt from Dough-offering.

---

[1] Lit. 'cake'; Num. 15[18-21] (cf. Ezek. 44[30], Neh. 10[37]) requires that 'when ye eat of the bread of the Land, ye shall offer up an heave offering unto the Lord. Of the first of your dough ye shall offer up a cake . . .'   [2] i.e. five quarter-*kabs*. See 1[4]; 2[6].

[3] Lev. 23[14].   [4] Grown in the current year (reckoning from Passover to Passover).

[5] The sheaf of barley, Lev. 23[9ff]. See also Men. 10[1ff]. App. I. 31.   [6] Ex. 12[18]; Pes. 2[5].

[7] See p. 562, n. 16.   [8] May also be rendered (cf. Pes. 3[1]) 'This must be removed at Passover'.

[9] See Ned. 7[2].   [10] On these see Peah 1[1ff]; 4[10, 11]; 5[7ff].

[11] For these see p. 7, nn. 6-9.   [12] Men. 10[4].   [13] See Maas. 1[3].   [14] Eduy. 1[2].

[15] Unknown meaning. Commentators explain it as dough made by reducing baked bread to crumbs and wetting them as food for young children.

[16] Dough made by pouring flour over boiling water.

[17] Dough made by pouring boiling water over flour.   [18] Lev. 7[12ff].

[19] Num. 6[15].   [20] Sanctity already rests on them.   [21] Five quarter-*kabs*.

8. Dog's-dough,[1] if herdsmen can eat of it, is liable to Dough-offering, and it may be used for *Erub* and *Shittuf*,[2] and Benedictions[3] and the Common Grace[4] must be said over it; it may be made on a Festival-day,[5] and by [eating unleavened an olive's bulk of] it a man can fulfil his obligation at Passover. But if herdsmen cannot eat of it it is not liable to Dough-offering; nor may it be used for *Erub* and *Shittuf*, and Benedictions and Common Grace need not be said over it; it may not be made on a Festival-day, and by [eating unleavened an olive's bulk of] it a man does not fulfil his obligation at Passover. In either case it is susceptible to food-uncleanness.[6]

9. Through Dough-offering and Heave-offering penalty of death may be incurred;[7] they are subject to the law of the [Added] Fifth;[8] they are forbidden to non-priests; they are the property of the priest; they are neutralized in a hundred and one;[9] they require washing of hands[10] and the awaiting of sunset;[11] they may not be taken from what is clean instead of from what is unclean,[12] and they must be taken [only] from what lies near by and from produce whose harvesting is completed. If a man said, 'Let all [the grain in] my threshing-floor be Heave-offering', or 'Let all my dough be Dough-offering', his word is void unless he keeps back a part[13] [as common produce].

2. 1. Produce from outside the Land [of Israel] that enters the Land is liable to Dough-offering; if it was taken out thither from here [in the Land of Israel] R. Eliezer declares it [still] liable, but R. Akiba declares it exempt.

2. [Whatsoever grows in] soil from outside the Land that comes to the Land in a ship is liable to Tithes and subject to the Seventh Year law. R. Judah said: This applies only when the ship touches the land. Dough that has been kneaded with fruit juice is liable to Dough-offering, and it may be eaten with unwashed hands.[14]

3. A woman may cut off her Dough-offering while sitting and in nakedness, because she is able to cover herself; but not so a man. If a man cannot prepare his dough in cleanness let him prepare it in portions of one *kab* each,[15] but let him not prepare it in uncleanness. But R. Akiba says: Let him prepare it in uncleanness, but let him not prepare it in portions of one *kab* each: for like as he must designate what is clean [as Dough-offering] so should he designate what is unclean; he must designate the one Dough-offering and he must designate the other Dough-offering, whereas portions of but one *kab* each have no share in what is designated [Dough-offering].[16]

4. If a man prepared his dough in portions each of one *kab* and they touched one another, they continue exempt from Dough-offering unless they wholly adhere. R. Eliezer says: Howbeit if they are taken off from the side of the oven and put together in a basket, the basket causes them to be

---

[1] Which has a large proportion of bran.
[2] App. I. 8, 39.   [3] See Ber. 6[1].   [4] Ber. 7[1-5].
[5] See Ex. 12[16]. The rule is that only necessary food may be prepared on a Festival-day. See p. 181, n. 11.   [6] See p. 714, n. 3; Toh. 8[6].   [7] Lev. 22[9].   [8] Lev. 22[14]. Cf. B.M. 4[8].
[9] See Ter. 4[7].
[10] i.e they are susceptible to 'Third-grade uncleanness'; see p. 714, n. 3; p. 778, n. 8.
[11] Before they can be eaten by a priest who had contracted uncleanness and had already immersed himself. Lev. 22[6-7]; see p. 773, n. 6.   [12] See Ter. 2[1].   [13] Cf. Ter. 4[5].
[14] Because it has not been rendered susceptible to uncleanness through being made wet by one of the seven liquids (Maksh. 6[4]). See Lev. 11[34ff].
[15] Less than the quantity liable to Dough-offering.
[16] Better to offer from what is unclean than to evade the obligation of Dough-offering altogether.

included together [and, if they together make up five quarter-*kabs*, liable] to Dough-offering.

5. If a man set aside his Dough-offering while it was yet flour, it is not deemed [valid] Dough-offering; in the hand of a priest it would count as property wrongly acquired; the dough itself would still be liable to Dough-offering, and the flour also [which the priest received] would be liable to Dough-offering if it was of the prescribed quantity, and it would be forbidden to non-priests. So R. Joshua. They said to him: It once happened that an elder, who was not a priest, seized [the like of this and ate] it. He answered: Nevertheless he rendered himself liable to punishment and gave occasion to others [to act amiss and yet rely upon him].

6. Five quarter-*kabs* [or more] of meal are liable to Dough-offering:[1] if in the meal, including the yeast and fine bran and coarse bran, there is in all five quarter-*kabs*, it is liable. If the coarse bran was taken out and it afterward fell in again, it is exempt.

7. The measure prescribed for the Dough-offering is one twenty-fourth part. Whether a man prepared the dough for himself or for his son's wedding-feast, [the Dough-offering must be] one twenty-fourth part. If a baker prepared it to sell in the market—so, too, if a woman prepared it to sell in the market—[the Dough-offering may be] one forty-eighth part. If [a woman's] dough was rendered unclean by error or constraint [the Dough-offering may be] one forty-eighth part; but if wantonly [the Dough-offering must be] one twenty-fourth part, so that any that sins shall gain no advantage.

8. R. Eliezer says: Dough-offering may be taken from what is clean instead of from what is unclean. Thus if a man had clean dough and unclean dough, he may take sufficient for the Dough-offering [for both] from [clean] dough from which Dough-offering has not been given; but he must put less than an egg's bulk [of the unclean dough] between [the two] so that he [thus] takes [the Dough-offering] from what lies near at hand. But this the Sages forbid.

3. 1. They may eat of the dough haphazard until it has been rolled out if it is from wheaten flour, or until it has been kneaded into a lump if it is from barley. If the wheaten dough has been rolled out and the barley-dough kneaded into a lump, he that eats thereof is punishable with death. So soon as a woman puts in water she must take up the Dough-offering, provided that there were[2] five quarter-*kabs* of flour.

2. If before she rolled it out her dough was mixed with Heave-offering, it is exempt, since what is subject to the law of Heave-offering is exempt [from Dough-offering]; but if it was mixed after it was rolled out it remains liable. If before she rolled it out there befell her a condition of uncleanness that was in doubt, it may be prepared in uncleanness;[3] but if after she rolled it out, it must be prepared in cleanness.[4]

3. If before she rolled it out she dedicated it [to the Temple] and redeemed it, it is [still] liable [to Dough-offering]; if [she dedicated it] after she rolled it out and then redeemed it, it is still liable; if she dedicated

---

[1] See Eduy. 1[2].
[2] Some texts read 'were not'. This is interpreted: provided that there no longer remained five quarter-*kabs* of flour in the baking-trough still unkneaded, for this flour would not be exempt from Dough-offering.
[3] Since it had not yet become subject to the Dough-offering obligation.
[4] Since it contained the Dough-offering within it which must be kept clean for the priest.

it before she rolled it out and the [Temple] treasurer rolled it out, and afterward she redeemed it, it is exempt, since at the moment when it would have been liable[1] it was exempt.

4. In like manner if a man dedicated his produce before its time for tithing was come, and he redeemed it, it is still liable [to Tithes]; if [he dedicated it] after its time for tithing and he then redeemed it, it is still liable; but if he dedicated it before it was fully harvested and the [Temple] treasurer completed its harvesting, and afterward the owner redeemed it, it is exempt [from Tithes], since at the moment when it would have been liable[2] it was exempt.

5. If a gentile gave dough to an Israelite to prepare for him it is exempt from Dough-offering. If he gave it him as a gift and [it was given] before it was rolled out, it is liable; if after it was rolled out, it is exempt. If a man prepared his dough together with [dough belonging to] a gentile, and the portion belonging to the Israelite was less than the measure liable to Dough-offering, it is exempt from Dough-offering.

6. If a man became a proselyte and he had dough that was already rolled out before he became a proselyte, he is exempt from Dough-offering; but if [it was rolled out] after he became a proselyte he is liable. If it is in doubt, he is liable; but because of it none[3] can become liable to the [Added] Fifth.[4] R. Akiba says: All is determined according to the moment when the dough forms a crust in the oven.[5]

7. If a man prepared dough from wheat and rice and it has the taste of corn, it is liable to Dough-offering, and by [eating unleavened an olive's bulk of] it a man fulfils his obligation at Passover. But if it has not the taste of corn it is not liable to Dough-offering and by [eating of] it none can fulfil his obligation at Passover.

8. If a man took leaven from dough from which Dough-offering had not been taken and put it into dough from which Dough-offering had been taken, if he had provision elsewhere [of dough that was liable to Dough-offering] he should take [Dough-offering] from it in the quantity required; but if he had not, he should take [from the mixed dough] one Dough-offering for the whole.

9. In like manner if harvested olives were mixed up with olives belonging to the gleaners,[6] or if harvested grapes were mixed up with grapes belonging to the gleaners, and he had provision [of untithed olives or grapes] elsewhere, he should take [Tithes] from them in the quantity required; but if he had not, he should take Heave-offering and the Heave-offering of Tithe [from the mixed produce] for the whole;[7] and the rest is allotted as Tithe and Second Tithe [only] in the quantity required [at the outset].

10. If a man took leaven from dough of wheaten flour and put it in dough of rice-flour and the dough had the taste of corn, it is liable to Dough-offering; if it had not, it is exempt. Why, then, have they said: Any untithed produce soever renders [other produce] forbidden? [That applies only when] one kind [is mixed] with like kind; [but when one kind is] not [mixed] with like kind, [then applies the principle of] 'that which gives a flavour'.[8]

[1] At the moment of being rolled out.   [2] At the moment its harvesting was complete.
[3] A non-priest who consumes it in error.   [4] See 1[9].
[5] And not according to the time when the dough was rolled out.   [6] And so tithe-free.
[7] As though the whole was liable to Tithes.   [8] Cf. Shebi. 7[7]; Ter. 10[1, 11].

4. 1. If two women rolled out two [pieces of dough] each of one *kab*, and these touched one another, they are exempt [from Dough-offering] even if they are of the same kind [of grain]; if they belonged to the same woman they are liable [to Dough-offering] if like kind touched like, but they are exempt if the one touched [a *kab* of dough of] another kind.

2. What is implied by 'if like kind touched like'? Wheat may be included together[1] with naught save only spelt; barley may be included together with aught save only wheat. R. Johanan b. Nuri says: The rest [of the five kinds] can be included together one with the other.

3. If there were two [pieces of dough] of one *kab* each [of one kind of grain], with one *kab* of rice or one *kab* of Heave-offering between them, [if they touch] they cannot be included together to make up [the quantity that is liable to] Dough-offering. But if between them [there lies] dough from which Dough-offering has been taken they are included together, since it [is dough that] is already made liable to Dough-offering.

4. If a *kab* [of dough from] this year's flour wholly adheres to a *kab* from last year's flour,[2] R. Ishmael says: One may take [Dough-offering] from the middle. But this the Sages forbid. If a man took Dough-offering from a single *kab*, R. Akiba says: It is valid Dough-offering. But the Sages say: It is not valid Dough-offering.

5. If Dough-offering was taken from two [pieces of dough] each of one *kab*, from each one by itself, and they are then made into a single piece of dough, R. Akiba declares it exempt [from Dough-offering], but the Sages declare it liable. Thus the more stringent ruling [in the one case][3] becomes the more lenient [in the other].

6. [If a man had pieces of dough of *demai*-produce that was unclean] he may take sufficient Dough-offering for them from [clean] dough from which Dough-offering had not been taken but which had been prepared in cleanness, and he may go on separating Dough-offering [from the clean dough] instead of from the *demai*-produce until it rots; because Dough-offering for *demai*-produce may be taken from what is clean instead of from what is unclean, and from what does not lie near by.

7. If Israelites leased a field from gentiles in Syria, R. Eliezer declares their produce liable to Tithes and subject to the Seventh Year law; but Rabban Gamaliel declares it exempt. Rabban Gamaliel says: Two[4] Dough-offerings [are given] in Syria. But R. Eliezer says: One Dough-offering. [Beforetime] they accepted the more lenient ruling of Rabban Gamaliel and the more lenient ruling of R. Eliezer, but afterward they followed the rulings of Rabban Gamaliel in both things.

8. Rabban Gamaliel says: Three regions are distinguished in what concerns Dough-offering. In the Land of Israel as far as Chezib one Dough-offering [is given]; from Chezib to the River[5] and to Amanah,[6] two Dough-offerings, one for the fire and one for the priest; that for the fire has the prescribed measure, but that for the priest has no prescribed measure. From the River and from Amanah, inwards,[7] two Dough-offerings

---

[1] To make up the total of five quarter-*kabs* that renders the dough liable to Dough-offering.

[2] And it is forbidden to take Dough-offering from the one instead of from the other.

[3] R. Akiba's decision in the foregoing paragraph.

[4] One for the fire and one for the priest. One is burnt, since it is unclean like the country of gentiles; and one is given to the priest so that the obligation shall not be forgotten.

[5] Eastward; to the Euphrates.

[6] Northward, to the river Amanah (2 Kings 5¹²), which rises in the Antilebanon and flows through Damascus.   [7] Between the River and Amanah.

[are given], one for the fire and one for the priest; that for the fire has no prescribed measure; and one that had immersed himself the selfsame day [because of uncleanness][1] may eat of it.[2] R. Jose says: He does not [even] need immersion. But it is forbidden to a man or a woman that suffers a flux, a menstruant, or a woman after childbirth.[3] It may be eaten in the company of a non-priest at the same table, and it may be given to any priest.[4]

9. These things may be given to any priest: devoted things,[5] Firstlings,[6] the redemption price of a [first-born] son,[7] the redemption price of the first-born of an ass,[8] and the shoulder and the two cheeks and the maw,[9] the first of the fleece,[10] the [Heave-offering] oil that [is become unclean and] must be burnt,[11] the Hallowed Things of the Temple,[12] and First-fruits.[13] R. Judah forbids First-fruits. R. Akiba permits Heave-offering vetches[14] but the Sages forbid them.

10. Nittai of Tekoa brought Dough-offerings from Be-ittur[15] and they would not accept them. The men of Alexandria brought their Dough-offerings from Alexandria and they would not accept them. The men of mount Zeboim[16] brought their First-fruits before the Feast of Pentecost, and they would not accept them because of what is written in the Law, *And the feast of harvest,*[17] *the first-fruits of thy labours which thou sowest in the field.*[18]

11. Ben Antigonus[19] brought up Firstlings from Babylon and they would not accept them. Joseph the Priest[20] brought his First-fruits of wine and oil, and they would not accept them.[21] He also brought his sons and the men of his household to keep the Lesser Passover[22] in Jerusalem, but they turned him back lest it should be established as an obligation. Ariston brought his First-fruits from Apamia[23] and they accepted them from him, for they said: He that owns [land] in Syria is as one that owns [land] in the outskirts of Jerusalem.[24]

[1] Who still awaits sundown to become wholly clean and fit to eat of Heave-offering. See p. 773, n. 6.   [2] The portion for the fire.   [3] On these see App. IV. 2.
[4] Even to one that is an *Am-haaretz* (so Maim.), or one that does not eat his food in the prescribed conditions of cleanness.   [5] Lev. 27[28]; Num. 18[14].
[6] Unfit for the Altar by reason of a blemish. Bekh. 5[1]; Num. 18[15-18]; Deut. 15[21-3].
[7] Bekh. 8[7]; Num. 18[16].   [8] Ex. 13[13]; Bekh. 1[ff].   [9] Deut. 18[3]; Hull. 10[1]; 11[1].
[10] Deut. 18[4]; Hull. 11[1f].   [11] Cf. Ter. 11[10].
[12] Offerings which may be consumed only within the Temple. See below, n. 24.
[13] Ex. 23[19]. See tractate 'Bikkurim'.
[14] To be given to any priest. See Ter. 11[9]; M. Sh. 2[4].
[15] Or Beth Tor or Bittur. Outside the Land of Israel (Neub., p. 110). See Taan. 4[6], where the Bether spoken of is the site south of Jerusalem where was the last stand of the Bar Cocheba revolt.   [16] Neh. 11[34]. See Bikk. 1[3].   [17] Which is the Feast of Pentecost.
[18] Ex. 23[16].   [19] Some texts read Antinos.   [20] See Mikw. 10[1].
[21] Since liquids could only be brought as First-fruits if they had not been harvested in the beginning as First-fruits.
[22] Or 'Second' Passover. Num. 9[10ff]. Pes. 9[1ff].   [23] Neub., pp. 28, 304.
[24] The Munich codex adds: Twenty and four dues were given to the priests: ten in the Temple and four in Jerusalem and ten within the borders (of the Land of Israel). These are the ten that were given to them in the Temple: Sin-offerings, Sin-offerings of birds, the Unconditional and the Suspensive Guilt-offerings, the public Peace-offerings, the Leper's *Log* of Oil, the residue of the *Omer*, the Two Loaves, the Shewbread, and the residue of Meal-offerings. And these are the four that were given them in Jerusalem: the Firstlings, the First-fruits, the Heave-offering from the Thank-offering and the ram of the Nazirite, and the Bird-offerings from among the Hallowed Things. And these are the ten that were given them within the borders (of the Land of Israel): Heave-offering, Heave-offering of Tithe, Dough-offering, the First of the Shearing, the Priests' Dues (of every beast that was slaughtered for food), the redemption price of the first-born son, and the redemption price of the firstling of an ass, the field of possession, and a field that was devoted, and what was wrongly gotten of a proselyte. No priest that is not skilled in these things may receive them as dues.
The passage is a gloss on 4[9].

ORLAH[1] ('THE FRUIT OF YOUNG TREES')

1. 1. If a man planted [a fruit-tree] as a fence or [only] for timber, he is exempt from the law of *Orlah*. R. Jose says: Even if he said, 'Let the inner side serve for food and let the outer side serve for a fence', the inner side [alone] is liable and the outer side is exempt.

2. When our fathers came to the Land [of Israel], if they found [a fruit-tree] already planted, it was exempt, but if they themselves planted aught it became liable, even though they had not subdued [the Land]. If a man planted [a tree] for the use of the many it is liable. R. Judah declares it exempt. If he planted it in the public domain, or if a gentile planted it, or if a robber[2] planted it, or if it was planted in a ship, or if it grew of itself, it is subject to the law of *Orlah*.

3. If a tree was uprooted together with its clod of earth, or if a river swept it away together with its clod of earth, and it was able to live [from that clod alone], it is exempt; but if not,[3] it is liable. If its clod of earth was torn away from it, or if the plough broke it up, or if it was broken up and dealt with like the earth [around it],[4] if it was still able to live it is exempt, but if not, it is subject [to the law of *Orlah*].

4. If a tree was uprooted but one root still remained [firm in the ground], it is exempt. How thick need the root be? Rabban Simeon b. Gamaliel in the name of R. Eleazar b. Judah of Bartotha says: As thick as a weaver's stretching-pin.

5. If a tree was uprooted but had still a sunken shoot by which the tree could live, the old tree becomes now like the sunken shoot [in what concerns the law of *Orlah*].[5] If fresh shoots were sunk year after year and then broken off [from the parent tree, the space of three years during which it is subject to the law of *Orlah*] is reckoned from the time when it was broken off. Grafting on vines and regrafting on a grafted part, even though they sink this into the ground, does not render [the added shoots] subject to the law of *Orlah*. R. Meir says: If [the grafting was] upon a part where the tree's growth was healthy it is not subject to the law of *Orlah*, but if upon a part where it was weak, it is subject [to the law of *Orlah*]. So, too, if a sunken shoot laden with fruit was broken off and it increased by one two-hundredth part, it is subject to the law of *Orlah*.

6. If a sapling that was subject to the law of *Orlah*, or to the law of Diverse Kinds in the Vineyard,[6] was confused[7] with other saplings, none may pick [any fruit from any of them]; if a man did so it may be neutralized in two hundred and one, provided that he did not pick with this in mind. R. Jose says: He may pick with this in mind and it may still be neutralized in two hundred and one.

7. The leaves and the shoots and the sap of vines and newly fashioned grape-berries are not forbidden under the laws of *Orlah*, of Fourth Year [fruit], or of the Nazirite-vow;[8] but they are forbidden if they come from an *Asherah*.[9] R. Jose says: Newly fashioned berries are forbidden since

---

[1] Lit. 'uncircumcision'. The law is that given in Lev. 19²³⁻⁴, which forbids the use of the fruit of young trees. The fruit is wholly forbidden during the first three years. In the fourth year the fruit is still holy, but it may be redeemed (the fifth of its value being added—see Peah 7⁶) and so rendered free for common use (cf. M. Sh. 5⁴). In the fifth year it is wholly permitted.

[2] Or: 'usurping occupant'; see Gitt. 5⁶.   [3] Then it counts as a newly-planted tree.

[4] And the tree was again planted in the earth.

[5] Its age is deemed to be that of the sunken shoot.

[6] See Kil. 4¹ff.   [7] And indistinguishable.   [8] Num. 6¹⁻⁴; Naz. 6¹ᶠ.

[9] Any tree worshipped by heathen. See A. Zar. 3⁷.

they count as fruit. R. Eliezer says: If milk was curdled with the sap of *Orlah*-fruit it is forbidden. R. Joshua said: I have heard an explicit tradition that if milk was curdled with the sap of the leaves or with the sap of the roots it is permitted; but if with the sap of unripe figs it is forbidden, since they count as fruit.

8. Defective grapes, grape-pips, grape-skins, or grape-skin wine made from them, the rind of a pomegranate or its sprout, walnut-shells and fruit-stones are forbidden under the law of *Orlah* or if they come from an *Asherah*, and [they are forbidden] under the law of the Nazirite-vow; but they are not forbidden under the law of Fourth-year [fruit].[1] Fallen fruit is forbidden in all [four] cases.

9. R. Jose says: A slip from an *Orlah*-tree may be planted, but not a walnut from an *Orlah*-tree, since this counts as a fruit; nor may [a slip with] early date-berries from an *Orlah*-tree be used for grafting.

2. 1. Heave-offering, the Heave-offering of Tithe from *demai*-produce, Dough-offering, and First-fruits are neutralized in a hundred and one,[2] and they can be included together,[3] and [a like quantity] must be taken out.[4] *Orlah*-fruit and Diverse Kinds of the Vineyard are neutralized in two hundred and one, and they can be included together, but [a like quantity] need not be taken out. R. Simeon says: They cannot be included together. R. Eliezer says: They can be included together in [cases determined by the principle of] 'that which gives a flavour',[5] but not [in the case of dry produce] in such wise as to render [the rest] forbidden.

2. Heave-offering may serve to neutralize[6] *Orlah*-fruit, and *Orlah*-fruit Heave-offering. Thus if one *seah* of Heave-offering fell among [common produce, making in all] a hundred [*seahs*], and afterward there fell in three *kabs* of *Orlah*-fruit, or three *kabs* of Diverse Kinds of the Vineyard, such is a case where Heave-offering would serve to neutralize the *Orlah*-fruit, or *Orlah*-fruit the Heave-offering.[7]

3. *Orlah*-fruit may neutralize the Diverse Kinds, and Diverse Kinds the *Orlah*-fruit, or *Orlah*-fruit other *Orlah*-fruit. Thus if one *seah* of *Orlah*-fruit fell into [common produce, making in all] two hundred [*seahs*], and afterward there fell in one *seah* or more of [other] *Orlah*-fruit, or one *seah* or more of Diverse Kinds of the Vineyard, such is a case where *Orlah*-fruit would serve to neutralize the Diverse Kinds, or Diverse Kinds the *Orlah*-fruit, or *Orlah*-fruit other *Orlah*-fruit.

4. Whatsoever is leavened, flavoured, or mingled[8] with Heave-offering, *Orlah*-fruit, or Diverse Kinds of the Vineyard, is forbidden. The School of Shammai say: It[9] can also convey uncleanness. And the School of Hillel say: It can never convey uncleanness unless it is an egg's bulk in quantity.

---

[1] That they may not be eaten outside Jerusalem unless they have been redeemed.
[2] When they are confused with non-hallowed produce.
[3] e.g. if a quarter-*seah* of each of these four together fell into less than a hundred *seahs* of common produce, they render it holy; so, too, if a non-priest ate an olive's bulk of any of them in combination he incurs the penalty of the Forty Stripes.
[4] From the produce in which any of these has fallen (and been neutralized); and the part taken out must be given to a priest.   [5] As with cooked and liquid produce.
[6] To make up in combination with common produce a quantity sufficient to neutralize the other.   [7] See Ter. 4⁷.
[8] The verb applies specifically to liquid produce. The three processes here have in mind produce that conveys marked flavour; therefore the principle of being neutralized in a hundred and one, or two hundred and one, cannot apply.
[9] If it is unclean, even though it is less than an egg's bulk (which is the quantity necessary to convey food-uncleanness; see Toh. 1¹; 2¹).

5. Dositheus of Kefar Yatmah was one of the disciples of the School of Shammai, and he said: I have heard a tradition from Shammai the Elder who said: It can never convey uncleanness unless it is an egg's bulk in quantity.

6. Why have they said, 'Whatsoever is leavened, flavoured, or mingled...', applying a stringent ruling? [So is it] where like is mixed with like; but it applies both with leniency and with stringency where like is mixed with unlike. Thus if wheaten leaven[1] fell into wheaten dough[2] and there was enough to leaven it, it is forbidden whether or not there was little enough for it to be neutralized in a hundred and one; if there was not little enough for it to be neutralized in a hundred and one, it is forbidden whether or not there was enough to leaven it.

7. 'But it applies both with leniency and with stringency where like is mixed with unlike'—thus if crushed beans[1] were cooked with lentils[2] and there was enough of them to give a flavour, they are forbidden whether or not there was little enough for them to be neutralized in a hundred and one; if there was not enough of them to give a flavour, they are permitted, whether or not there was little enough for them to be neutralized in a hundred and one.

8. If common leaven fell into dough and there was enough of it to leaven the dough, and afterward[3] there fell into the dough Heave-offering leaven or leaven made from Diverse Kinds of the Vineyard, and there was enough of it to leaven the dough, it is forbidden.

9. If common leaven fell into dough and leavened it, and afterward there fell into it Heave-offering leaven or leaven made from Diverse Kinds of the Vineyard, and it was enough to have leavened the dough, it is forbidden. But R. Simeon permits it.

10. Condiments of two or three different categories[4] and of one kind,[5] or of three [kinds of a like category], are forbidden[6] and can be included together.[7] R. Simeon says: Two categories of a like kind, or two kinds of a like category may not be included together.

11. If common leaven and Heave-offering leaven fell into dough and neither of them sufficed to leaven the dough, but included together they leavened it, R. Eliezer says: I should decide by which of them fell in last. But the Sages say: Whether the forbidden substance[8] fell in first or last it can never render the dough forbidden unless it sufficed of itself to leaven the dough.

12. Joezer of the Birah[9] was one of the disciples of the School of Shammai, and he said: I asked of Rabban Gamaliel the Elder when he was standing in the Eastern Gate,[10] and he said: It can never render the dough forbidden unless it sufficed of itself to leaven the dough.

13. If utensils were greased with unclean oil and then again with clean oil, or if they were greased with clean oil and then again with unclean oil, R. Eliezer says: I should decide[11] by which of them came first. But the Sages say: By which came last.

---

1 That was Heave-offering, *Orlah*, or Diverse Kinds of the Vineyard.
2 That was common food.   3 But before the first leaven had acted.
4 Lit. 'names'; meaning the like of Heave-offering, *Orlah*, &c., which are forbidden for common consumption.
5 Different varieties of seasoning-matter, such as onions, pepper, and the like.
6 By conveying a flavour they render forbidden common food in whch they are mixed.
7 To make up in combination a quantity too great to be neutralized.
8 Variant: (Heave-offering) leaven.   9 See Pes. 3[8].   10 Cf. Ber. 9[5]; Yom. 1[3].
11 Whether the utensil was clean or unclean.

14. If Heave-offering leaven and leaven made from Diverse Kinds of the Vineyard both fell into dough, and neither of them sufficed to leaven the dough, but included together they leavened it, it is forbidden to non-priests and permitted to priests. R. Simeon permits it both to non-priests and to priests.

15. If Heave-offering condiments and condiments made from Diverse Kinds of the Vineyard both fell into a pot and neither of them sufficed to flavour [the food in the pot], but included together they flavoured it, it is forbidden to non-priests and permitted to priests. R. Simeon permits it both to non-priests and to priests.

16. If a piece of [flesh from] the Most Holy Things[1] and a piece of [flesh that was] Refuse or Remnant[2] were cooked together with other pieces of flesh,[3] it is forbidden to non-priests and permitted to priests. R. Simeon permits it both to non-priests and to priests.

17. If flesh from the Most Holy Things and flesh from the Lesser Holy Things[4] were cooked together with ordinary flesh, it is forbidden to them that are unclean and permitted to them that are clean.

3. 1. If a garment was dyed with [dye made from] shells of *Orlah*-fruit, it must be burnt. If it was confused with others, all must be burnt. So R. Meir. But the Sages say: It is neutralized in two hundred and one.

2. If a man dyed so much as one *sit's* length[5] [of thread] in [dye made from] shells of *Orlah*-fruit, and he wove it into a garment and it is not known which [thread] it was, R. Meir says: The garment must be burnt. But the Sages say: It is neutralized in two hundred and one.

3. If a man wove into a garment one *sit's* length of wool from a Firstling, the garment must be burnt. If [he wove] into a sack a Nazirite's hair or hair from the first-born of an ass,[6] the sack must be burnt. And in the case of [other] Hallowed Things,[7] they render [the rest] hallowed in any quantity soever.

4. Food cooked with shells from *Orlah*-fruit must be burnt. If it was confused with other foodstuffs, it is neutralized in two hundred and one.

5. If an oven was heated with shells from *Orlah*-fruit and bread was baked in it, the bread must be burnt. If it was confused with other [bread] it is neutralized in two hundred and one.

6. If a man had bunches of fenugreek[8] that were Diverse Kinds of the Vineyard, they must be burnt; if they were confused with others, all must be burnt. So R. Meir. But the Sages say: They are neutralized in two hundred and one.

7. For R. Meir used to say: Whatsoever a man is wont to count [when he sells them] can [when it is forbidden produce] render forbidden [other produce with which they are mixed, so that they all must be burnt]. But the Sages say: Only six [such] things render forbidden [that with which they are confused] (R. Akiba says: Seven), and these are they: Nuts from Perekh, pomegranates from Baddan,[9] sealed jars, beetroot-tops, cabbage-

---

[1] These were Whole-offerings, Sin-offerings, Guilt-offerings, and the Peace-offerings of the Congregation at Pentecost. See Zeb. 5[1-5].   [2] See p. 76, nn. 7–8. See Meil. 1[3].
[3] Which were common and permitted food, and which were just enough to neutralize either of the others.
[4] All offerings other than those included under the Most Holy Things. See Zeb. 5[6-8].
[5] App. II, C. The distance between the tips of the outstretched thumb and fore-finger.
[6] On the ground of Deut. 15[19].   [7] See p. 55, n. 6.   [8] Ter. 10[6].
[9] Kel. 17[5]. A place in Samaria, north-east of Shechem.

stalks, and Greek gourds; and R. Akiba says: Also the loaves of a householder [which he bakes himself]. To such among these as may come from
Orlah-fruit the law of *Orlah* applies; and to such among these as may come
from Diverse Kinds of the Vineyard the law of Diverse Kinds of the
Vineyard applies.

8. If[1] the nuts were split, the pomegranates cut open, the jars opened,
the gourds cut into, or the loaves broken into, they are neutralized in two
hundred and one.

9. *Orlah*-fruit that is in doubt[2] is forbidden in the Land of Israel[3] but
in Syria it is permitted. Outside the Land a man may go down [to the
garden] and buy such fruit, provided that he does not see it gathered.
If a vineyard was planted with vegetables[4] and vegetables [of like kind]
were sold outside it, they are forbidden in the Land of Israel but in Syria
they are permitted; and outside the Land he may go down[5] and gather
them, provided that he[6] does not gather them with [his own] hand. New
produce[7] is forbidden by the Law everywhere;[8] the Law of *Orlah* is
Halakah,[9] and the law of Diverse Kinds[10] is from the words of the Scribes.[11]

BIKKURIM[12] ('FIRST-FRUITS')

1. 1. Some there are that may bring the First-fruits and make the Avowal;[13]
others that may bring them but not make the Avowal; and some there are
that may not [even] bring them. These may not bring them: he that plants
a tree in his own domain but sinks a shoot of it [so that it grows] in another's
domain or in the public domain; so, too, he that sinks a shoot from [a tree
planted in] another's domain or the public domain [so that it grows] in his
own domain; or he that plants a tree in his own domain and sinks it [so
that it still grows] in his own domain but with a private or public road
between. Such a one may not bring the First-fruits. R. Judah says: Such
a one may bring them.

2. For what reason may he not bring them? Because it is written, *The
first-fruits of thy land*[14]—[thou mayest not bring them] unless their growth
is wholly from thy land. They that lease the land or that hire it,[15] a usurping
occupant[16] or a robber may not bring them for the like reason, because it is
written, *The first-fruits of thy land*.

3. First-fruits may be brought only from the seven kinds,[17] and not from
dates from the hill-country nor from produce from the valleys, nor from
any oil-olives that are not of the choicest kind. Firstfruits may not be
brought before Pentecost.[18] The men of mount Zeboim[19] brought their

---

[1] Some texts prefix 'How?' But what follows does not explain the preceding rule.
[2] e.g. if a gentile had fruit to sell, and it was known that he had *Orlah*-trees but it was in
doubt whether this fruit was from those particular trees.
[3] On the principle that stringency applies in cases of doubt touching a prohibition enjoined in the Law.   [4] Which thus constitute 'Diverse Kinds of the Vineyard'.
[5] The gentile who sells them.
[6] The Israelite who buys them.   [7] See Hall. 1[1]; Men. 10[5ff].
[8] Even outside the Land of Israel. See Lev. 23[14], 'In *all* your dwellings'.
[9] The accepted Law. Here in the sense of an unwritten law given to Moses at Sinai. Cf. p. 12,
n. 4; p. 446, n. 2.   [10] i.e. of the Vineyard. Deut. 22[9] applies only to the Land of Israel.
[11] See Kel. 13[7]; Sanh. 11[3]. Cf. Yeb. 2[3, 4]; 3[2].
[12] See Deut. 26[1ff].   [13] See Deut. 26[5ff].   [14] Ex. 23[19].
[15] The former pay the owner a prescribed proportion of the crop, the latter a fixed
quantity of produce.   [16] See Gitt. 5[6].
[17] For which the land was famed: wheat, barley, grapes, figs, pomegranates, olive-oil,
and (date-)honey. See Deut. 8[8], Ber. 6[4].
[18] Lit. 'solemn assembly' (Deut. 16[8], Is. 1[13]); a usual title of the Feast of Weeks, or Pentecost.   [19] See Hall. 4[10].

First-fruits before Pentecost but they were not accepted because of what is written in the Law, *The feast of harvest, the first-fruits of thy labours which thou sowest in the field.*[1]

4. These may bring the First-fruits but they may not make the Avowal: the proselyte may bring them but he may not make the Avowal since he cannot say, *Which the Lord sware unto our Fathers for to give us.*[2] But if his mother was an Israelite he may bring them and make the Avowal. And when he prays in private he should say, 'O God of the fathers of Israel'; and when he is in the synagogue he should say, 'O God of your fathers'. But if his mother was an Israelite he may say, 'O God of our fathers'.

5. R. Eliezer b. Jacob says: A woman that is the offspring of proselytes may not marry into the priestly stock unless her mother was an Israelite; it is all one whether [she is the offspring of] proselytes or freed slaves, even to the tenth generation: [her like may not marry into the priestly stock] unless their mother was an Israelite.[3] A guardian, an agent, a bondman, a woman, one of doubtful sex, or an *androgynos*[4] may bring the First-fruits, but they may not make the Avowal since they cannot say, *Which thou, O God, hast given me.*

6. If a man bought two trees in his fellow's domain he may bring the First-fruits but he may not make the Avowal. R. Meir says: He may do both. If the well was dried up or the trees cut down he may bring the First-fruits but he may not make the Avowal. R. Judah says: He may do both. A man may bring the First-fruits and make the Avowal [at any time] from Pentecost until the Feast [of Tabernacles];[5] while from the Feast [of Tabernacles] until [the Feast of] the Dedication[6] he may bring them but he may not make the Avowal. R. Judah b. Bathyra says: He may do both.

7. If a man set apart his First-fruits and then sold his field, he may bring them but he may not make the Avowal. The other [that bought the field] may bring not that kind but another kind of produce as Firstfruits, and he may make the Avowal. R. Judah says: He may bring Firstfruits of that kind and yet make the Avowal.

8. If a man set apart his First-fruits and they were plundered or went bad or were stolen or were lost or contracted uncleanness, he may bring others in their stead, but he may not make the Avowal; and these others are not subject to the law of the [Added] Fifth.[7] If they contracted uncleanness while in the Temple Court, he must scatter them and he may not make the Avowal.

9. Whence do we learn that a man is answerable for them until they are brought to the Temple Mount? Because it is written, *The first of the first-fruits of thy land thou shalt bring into the house of the Lord thy God,*[8] which teaches that a man is answerable for them until they are brought to the Temple Mount. If he brought produce of one kind and made the Avowal and then brought produce of another kind, he may not make the Avowal [a second time].

10. These may bring the First-fruits and make the Avowal: [They that bring them] from Pentecost until the Feast of [Tabernacles]; [they that

---

[1] Ex. 23[16].   [2] Deut. 26[3].   [3] Cf. Kidd. 4[7].
[4] A being of double sex. See below, ch. 4.   [5] Roughly from May to October.
[6] Chislev 25, which falls in the first half of December. The Feast of the Dedication (*sc.* of the Altar) commemorates the victory of the Maccabees (1 Maccabees 4[48ff]).
[7] If a non-priest consumed them in error. Lev. 22[14]; see B.M. 4[8]. Cf. Ter. 6[1]; Bikk. 2[1].
[8] Ex. 23[19].

bring any] from the seven kinds, from the produce of the hill-country and from the dates that are from the valleys, and from the oil-olives from beyond Jordan. R. Jose the Galilean says: They may not bring First-fruits from beyond Jordan since that is not a land flowing with milk and honey.

11. If a man bought three trees in his fellow's domain, he may bring First-fruits and make the Avowal. R. Meir says: Even [if he bought but] two. If he bought one tree together with the ground whereon it stands he may bring First-fruits and make the Avowal. R. Judah says: Even they that lease the land or they that hire it[1] may bring First-fruits and make the Avowal.

2. 1. Through Heave-offering and First-fruits penalty of death may be incurred;[2] they are subject to the law of the [Added] Fifth;[3] they are forbidden to non-priests; they are the property of the priest;[4] they are neutralized in one hundred and one;[5] they require the washing of hands[6] and the awaiting of sunset.[7] These rules apply to Heave-offering and First-fruits, but not to [Second] Tithe.

2. There are rules that apply to [Second] Tithe and to First-fruits but not to Heave-offering: for [Second] Tithe and First-fruits require to be brought to the Place[8] and the [reciting of the] Avowal, and they are forbidden to a mourner[9] (but R. Simeon permits First-fruits) and they are subject to the law of Removal[10] (but R. Simeon declares First-fruits exempt); and in any quantity soever [if they are mixed with common produce of like kind] they are forbidden to be consumed [as common food] in Jerusalem; and what grows from them [when they are used for seed] is forbidden to be consumed in Jerusalem by non-priests or by cattle; but R. Simeon permits this. These rules apply to [Second] Tithe and to First-fruits but not to Heave-offering.

3. There are rules that apply to Heave-offering and to [Second] Tithe but not to First-fruits: for Heave-offering and [Second] Tithe [before they have been set apart] render forbidden what is on the threshing-floor; and they have a prescribed quantity;[11] and they must be set apart from all produce whether or not the Temple still stands, and by them that lease the land or hire it, and by a usurping occupant or a robber.[12] These rules apply to Heave-offering and to [Second] Tithe but not to First-fruits.

4. And there are rules that apply to First-fruits but not to Heave-offering or [Second] Tithe: for First-fruits can be acquired[13] while they are still unplucked,[14] and a man may grant his whole field as First-fruits, and he is answerable for them [until they are brought to the Temple Mount], and they require a Peace-offering,[15] singing,[16] waving,[17] and spending the night[18] [in Jerusalem].

5. Heave-offering of Tithe in two things is like to First-fruits and in two things like to Heave-offering. It may be taken from what is clean instead of from what is unclean and from what does not lie near by,[19] like First-fruits. [Before it has been set apart] it renders forbidden what is on the threshing-floor and it has a prescribed quantity, like Heave-offering.

[1] See above, 1[2].   [2] By the non-priest who consumes them of set purpose. Cf. Hall, 1[9].
[3] When a non-priest who consumes them in error makes restitution.
[4] Cf. below, 3[12].   [5] See Ter. 4[7].   [6] Cf. Hag. 2[5]; see p. 714, n. 3; p. 778, n. 8.
[7] Before they can be consumed by a priest who had immersed himself because of uncleanness that day. Lev. 22[6f]; p. 773, n.6.   [8] Jerusalem.
[9] During the day of the death of one near of kin. See Deut. 26[14].
[10] Cf. Deut. 26[12f]; M. Sh. 5[6].   [11] See Peah 1[1]; Ter. 4[3].   [12] Cf. Ter. 1[1,] M. Sh. 5[14]; Bikk. 1[2].
[13] Become the property of the priests.   [14] See below, 3[1].   [15] Cf. below, 3[3].   [16] Cf. below, 3[4].
[17] Cf. below, 3[6].   [18] Deduced from Deut. 16[7].   [19] See Ter. 2[1]; Hall. 1[9].

6. The citron-tree is in three things like to a tree and in one thing like to a vegetable. It is like to a tree in what concerns the laws of *Orlah*, of Fourth-year plantings and of the Seventh Year; and like to a vegetable in one thing, in that the season of its gathering is the season for its tithing.[1] So Rabban Gamaliel. R. Eliezer says: It is like to a tree in all things.

7. The blood of two-legged creatures is like to the blood of cattle in that it renders seeds susceptible[2] [to uncleanness], and [like to] the blood of creeping things [in that] none can become culpable by reason of it.[3]

8. The *koy*[4] is in some things like to wild animals and in some things like to cattle; and in some things it is like to cattle and to wild animals; and in some things it is like neither to cattle nor to wild animals.

9. Wherein is it like to a wild animal? Its blood requires to be covered up[5] like the blood of a wild animal; it may not be slaughtered on a Festival-day but if it was slaughtered its blood may not be covered up; its fat conveys carrion uncleanness[6] like a wild animal, but its own uncleanness is in doubt; and [if it is a Firstling] it is not redeemed under the law of the first-born of an ass.[7]

10. Wherein is it like to cattle? Its fat is forbidden like the fat of cattle, and by reason of it a man is not punishable by Extirpation;[8] it may not be bought with [Second] Tithe money to be consumed in Jerusalem; and it is subject to the [priests' dues of the] shoulder, and the two cheeks, and the maw.[9] But R. Eliezer exempts it since on him that would exact aught from his fellow lies the burden of proof.[10]

11. Wherein is it like neither to cattle nor to wild animals? By virtue of the law of Diverse Kinds it is forbidden [to yoke it][11] with a wild animal or with cattle; and if a man assigned to his son his 'wild animals' and his 'cattle', he has not [thereby] assigned to him the *koy*. If a man said, 'May I be a Nazirite[12] if this is neither wild animal nor cattle!' he must become a Nazirite. In all else it is like both to wild animals and to cattle: it requires slaughtering[13] like them both, and like them both it can convey uncleanness by virtue of the rules applying to carrion[14] and to a member of a living being.[15]

3. 1. How do they set apart the First-fruits? When a man goes down to his field and sees [for the first time] a ripe fig or a ripe cluster of grapes or a ripe pomegranate, he binds it round with reed-grass and says, 'Lo, these are First-fruits'. R. Simeon says: Even so, he should again designate them as First-fruits after they are plucked from the soil.

2. How do they take up the First-fruits [to Jerusalem]? [The men of] all the smaller towns that belonged to the *Maamad*[16] gathered together in the town of the *Maamad* and spent the night in the open place of the town and came not into the houses; and early in the morning the officer [of the *Maamad*] said, *Arise ye and let us go up to Zion unto*[17] *the Lord our God.*[18]

3. They that were near [to Jerusalem] brought fresh figs and grapes, and they that were far off brought dried figs and raisins. Before them went

---

[1] Cf. Shebi. 4[7ff].   [2] Lev. 11[34]; Maksh. 6[4].
[3] The blood of animals is expressly forbidden (Lev. 7[26]), but the reptile is forbidden as a reptile (Lev. 11[29ff]), and the prohibition does not apply specifically to its blood.
[4] In Hull. 79b defined as a cross between a goat and a gazelle. See also Naz. 5[7]; Hull. 6[1]; Bekh. 1[5].   [5] Lev. 17[13]. Cf. Betz. 1[2]; Hull. 6[1ff].   [6] Lev. 7[24].
[7] Ex. 32[19-20].   [8] See p. 562, n. 16.   [9] Deut. 18[3].
[10] For the same principle see B.K. 3[11]; B.B. 9[6]; Hull. 10[4]; Bekh. 2[6, 7, 8]; Toh. 4[12].
[11] See Kil., 1[6], 8[4].   [12] See Naz. 5[7].   [13] Before it can be used for food.
[14] Lev. 11[8].   [15] See Ohol. 2[1].   [16] See Taan. 4[2]; App. I. 21.
[17] Some texts insert 'the house of'; cf. Is. 2[3].   [18] Jer. 31[6].

the ox,[1] having its horns overlaid with gold and a wreath of olive-leaves on its head. The flute was played before them until they drew nigh to Jerusalem. When they had drawn nigh to Jerusalem they sent messengers before them and bedecked their First-fruits. The rulers and the prefects[2] and the treasurers of the Temple went forth to meet them. According to the honour due to them that came in used they to go forth. And all the craftsmen in Jerusalem used to rise up before them and greet them, saying, 'Brethren, men of such-and-such a place, ye are welcome!'

4. The flute was played before them until they reached the Temple Mount. When they reached the Temple Mount even Agrippa the king would take his basket on his shoulder and enter in as far as the Temple Court. When they reached the Temple Court, the levites sang the song, *I will exalt thee, O Lord, for thou hast set me up and not made mine enemies to triumph over me.*[3]

5. The pigeons that were hung upon the baskets were sacrificed as Whole-offerings, and what the people bore in their hands they delivered to the priests.

6. While the basket was yet on his shoulder a man would recite the passage[4] from *I profess this day unto the Lord thy God*, until he reached the end of the passage. R. Judah says: Until he reached the words *An Aramean ready to perish was my father*. When he reached the words *An Aramean* . . . he took down the basket from his shoulder and held it by the rim. And the priest put his hand beneath it and waved it; and the man then recited the words from *An Aramean ready to perish* . . . until he finished the passage. Then he left the basket by the side of the Altar and bowed himself down and went his way.

7. Beforetime all that could recite [the prescribed words] recited them, and all that could not recite them rehearsed the words [after the priest]; but when these refrained[5] from bringing [their First-fruits] it was ordained that both they that could recite them and they that could not should rehearse the words [after the priest].

8. The rich brought their First-fruits in baskets overlaid with silver and gold, while the poor brought them in wicker baskets of peeled willow-branches, and baskets and First-fruits were given to the priests.

9. R. Simeon b. Nanos says: They used to bedeck the First-fruits with produce other than the seven kinds.[6] R. Akiba says: They bedecked the First-fruits only with produce of the seven kinds.

10. R. Simeon says: There are three degrees among the First-fruits: the [veritable] First-fruits, the additions to the First-fruits, and what bedecks the First-fruits. The additions to the First-fruits may be of like kind, but what bedecks the First-fruits may be of some other kind. The additions to the First-fruits must be eaten in cleanness, and they are not subject to the rules of *demai*-produce,[7] but the rules of *demai*-produce apply to what bedecks the First-fruits.

11. In what case have they said that additions to the First-fruits are like to the First-fruits [themselves]? When they come from the Land [of Israel]; but when they do not come from the Land of [Israel] they are not like to the First-fruits [themselves].

12. Why have they said that the First-fruits are like to the goods of the

---

[1] Intended as a Peace-offering.
[2] Explained as the chiefs of the priests and the chiefs of the levites (cf. Luke 22[52], 'The chief priests and captains of the temple'). Cf. Shek. 5[1].   [3] Ps. 30.
[4] Deut. 26[3ff].   [5] Out of shame.   [6] See 1[3].   [7] See p. 20, n. 9.

priest? Because with them he may buy bondmen, immovable property, and unclean cattle, and a creditor can take them in payment of his debt, or a woman in payment of her *Ketubah*,[1] as [they may also do with] a scroll of the Law. But R. Judah says: They may give the First-fruits only to [a priest that is] an Associate[2] and as a favour.[3] And the Sages say: They give them to any [priests] that are on duty in the Temple, and these may share among themselves as [they do] with the Hallowed Things[4] of the Temple.

4[5] 1. The *androgynos* is in some things like to men and in some things like to women, and in some things like both to men and to women, and in some things like neither to men nor to women.

2. How is he like to men? He conveys uncleanness with 'the white'[6] like men; he is subject to the law of levirate marriage like men;[7] he dresses and trims his hair like men; like men he can take a wife but cannot be taken to wife; like as at the birth of men his mother continues unclean because of him in the blood of purification;[8] like men he may not remain alone with women;[9] like men he does not receive maintenance with the daughters;[10] like men he may not transgress the laws *Ye shall not round the corners of your head, neither shalt thou mar the corners of thy beard*,[11] and *Thou shalt not defile thyself for the dead*;[12] and like men he is bound by all the commandments enjoined in the Law.

3. How is he like to women? He conveys uncleanness with 'the red'[13] like women; like women he may not remain alone with men; like women he is not subject to the law of levirate marriage; like women he does not share in the inheritance with the sons; like women he may not eat of the Hallowed Things in the Temple; like women he does not bestow the right to eat of Heave-offering;[14] like as at the birth of women his mother continues unclean because of him in the blood of uncleanness; like women he is not eligible to give any testimony enjoined in the Law; and like women if he has suffered unlawful connexion he is ineligible to eat of Heave-offering.

4. How is he like both to men and to women? For smiting him or cursing him[15] guilt is incurred as for smiting or cursing men and women; if a man slew him[16] in error he is liable to exile, and if wantonly he is put to death like as for other men and women; his mother must bring an offering because of him like as at the birth of both men and women; and he may inherit any inheritance like both men and women.

5. How is he like neither to men nor to women? Heave-offering need not be burnt because of uncleanness of his issue nor is penalty incurred through his entering the Temple while he is unclean, unlike both men and women; he cannot be sold[17] as a Hebrew bondservant, unlike both men and women; and his Valuation[18] cannot be vowed, unlike both men and women. And if a man said, 'May I be a Nazirite if this is neither a man nor a woman!' he must be a Nazirite. R. Jose says: An *androgynos* is a creature by itself, and the Sages could not decide about it whether it was man or woman. But it is not so with one of doubtful sex, since such a one is at times a man and at times a woman.

---

1 App. I. 16.   2 See App. I. 3, 6.   3 Cf. Shebi. 4[1, 2].   4 See p. 55, n. 6.
5 This chapter is included in all printed editions but it is no part of the Mishnah. It is derived (and expanded variously in different editions) from the Tosefta of Bikkurim (2[3]). It develops the subject of the *androgynos* (referred to in the Mishnah, 1[5]) in the style of the teachings in 2[5ff]. The text is in great confusion, both as to order and contents. The version here given shows the text in its more expanded form.
6 Seminal discharge or flux. Lev. 15[2, 16]; Zab. 2[1].   7 See p. 218, n. 1.   8 Lev. 12[1ff].
9 See Kidd. 4[12].   10 See Ket. 4[6]; B.B. 9[2].   11 Lev. 19[27].   12 Cf. Lev. 21[1].
13 Menstrual flow. Lev. 15[19ff].   14 Cf. p. 651, nn. 4, 5.   15 Ex. 21[15, 17].
16 See Ex. 21[12–14].   17 Ex. 21[2, 7].   18 See Lev. 27[2ff]; Cf. p. 544, n. 1.

SECOND DIVISION
MOED
('SET FEASTS')

SHABBATH
ERUBIN
PESAHIM
SHEKALIM
YOMA
SUKKAH
BETZAH (YOM TOB)
ROSH HA-SHANAH
TAANITH
MEGILLAH
MOED KATAN
HAGIGAH

SHABBATH ('THE SABBATH')

1. 1. There are two (which are, indeed, four)[1] kinds of 'going out'[2] on the Sabbath for him that is inside, and two (which are, indeed, four) for him that is outside. Thus if a poor man stood outside and the householder inside, and the poor man stretched his hand inside and put aught into the householder's hand, or took aught from it and brought it out, the poor man is culpable and the householder is not culpable; if the householder stretched his hand outside and put aught into the poor man's hand, or took aught from it and brought it in, the householder is culpable and the poor man is not culpable. But if the poor man stretched his hand inside and the householder took aught from it, or put aught into it and [the poor man] brought it out, neither is culpable; and if the householder stretched his hand outside and the poor man took aught from it, or put aught into it and [the householder] brought it in, neither is culpable.

2. A man should not sit down before the barber near to the time of the afternoon *Tefillah*[3] unless he has already prayed it; a man should not enter a bath-house or a tannery, nor should he [begin to] eat a meal or decide a suit, though if any have begun [a like deed] they need not interrupt it. They must interrupt [their doings] to recite the *Shema'*,[4] but they need not interrupt them for the *Tefillah*.

3. A tailor should not go out with his needle [on Friday] near to nightfall lest he forget and 'go out';[5] nor should a scrivener [go out then] with his pen; nor should a man search his clothes [for fleas] or read by lamplight.[6] Rightly have they said:[7] A school-master may look where the children are reading but he himself may not read.[8] In like manner a man that has a flux may not eat with a woman that has a flux, since it lends occasion to transgression.[9]

4. These[10] are among the rulings[11] which the Sages enjoined while in the upper room of Hananiah b. Hezekiah b. Gorion.[12] When they went up to visit him they voted, and they of the School of Shammai outnumbered them of the School of Hillel; and eighteen things did they decree on that day.

5. The School of Shammai say: Ink, dyestuffs, or vetches may not be

---

[1] For form of phrase cf. Shebu. 1[1]. Two are derivable from the Written Law (performing the complete act of removing a burden from one domain to another), and two more are 'from the words of the Scribes' (in which the forbidden act is not completed by the one person). A man is culpable in the first two cases but not in the second two. See below, 10[2, 5].

[2] Based on Ex. 16[29], 'Let no man go out of his place on the seventh day'. 'To go out' is taken to imply also 'carrying a burden' (Jer. 17[22]) from one domain (e.g. a private house) into another (e.g. a public thoroughfare or another private house).

[3] On Friday afternoon. See Ber. 4[1]; App. I. 46. It could be said until sunset.

[4] App. I. 38; Ber. 1–2.   [5] See n. 2 above.

[6] He may, forgetful of the Sabbath, tilt the lamp to make the oil flow into the wick more abundantly to give a brighter light.   [7] See p. 12, n. 4.

[8] Since it may lend occasion for transgression of the Sabbath law. See n. 6.

[9] Lev. 15[24].   [10] That they should not search clothes or read.

[11] Heb. *Halakoth*. See App. I. 11. What the other decrees were is not certainly known. Some have tried to count eighteen teachings in the preceding three paragraphs, and others explain 'these' as referring to the decisions in par. 5. See *Dor Dor*, I. 186. Eighteen rulings of extreme stringency, reflecting the standpoint of the School of Shammai, are given by the Gemara at this point (13b, 14a); they include the two on searching the clothes and reading (the fifteenth and sixteenth of the eighteen). Only one other ruling (the fourteenth) deals with the Sabbath, namely that which requires a Jew travelling with a gentile on the eve of Sabbath to give his purse into the gentile's keeping. See Shab. 24[1].

[12] Variant: Garon. He was the head of the School of Shammai in the generation before the destruction of Jerusalem. It is he who succeeded in restoring the book of Ezekiel to its place in the Canon. See Moore, I. 246.

soaked [on a Friday] unless there is time for them to be [wholly] soaked the same day. And the School of Hillel permit it.

6. The School of Shammai say: Bundles of flax may not be put in an oven unless there is time for them to steam off the same day; nor may wool be put into a [dyer's] cauldron unless there is time for it to absorb the colour the same day. And the School of Hillel permit it. The School of Shammai say: Nets may not be spread for wild animals, birds, or fishes unless there is time for them to be caught the same day. And the School of Hillel permit it.

7. The School of Shammai say: They may not sell aught to a gentile or help him to load his beast or raise [a burden] on his shoulders unless there is time for him to reach a place near by [the same day]. And the School of Hillel permit it.

8. The School of Shammai say: Hides may not be given to a [gentile] tanner nor clothes to a gentile washerman unless there is time for the work to be done the same day. And all these the School of Hillel permit such time as the sun is up.

9. Rabban Simeon b. Gamaliel said: In my father's house they used to give white clothes to a gentile washerman three days before Sabbath. Both [the School of Shammai and the School of Hillel] agree that men may lay down the olive-press beams or the winepress rollers.

10. Flesh and onions and eggs may not be roasted unless there is time for them to be roasted the same day; nor may bread be put into the oven when darkness is falling, nor may cakes be put upon the coals unless there is time for their top surface to form into crust. R. Eliezer says: Time for their bottom surface [only] to form into crust.

11. The Passover-offering may be let down[1] into the oven when darkness is falling; and fire may be kindled in the fireplace of the Chamber of the Hearth,[2] but elsewhere only if there is time [before the Sabbath] for the fire to take hold on the greater part [of the wood]. R. Judah says: With charcoal [it is permitted if there is time for the fire to take hold on] any quantity soever.

2. 1. With what may they light [the Sabbath lamp] and with what may they not light it? They may not use cedar-fibre or uncarded flax or raw silk or a wick of bast or a wick of the desert[3] or duck-weed; or pitch or wax or castor-oil or [Heave-offering] oil that [is become unclean and] must be burnt, or [grease from] the fatty tail or tallow. Nahum the Mede says: They may use melted tallow. But the Sages say: It is all one whether it is melted or not melted: they may not light therewith.

2. [Heave-offering] oil that [is become unclean and] must be burnt may not be used for lighting on a Festival-day.[4] R. Ishmael says: Tar may not be used out of respect for the Sabbath. But the Sages permit all kinds of oils: sesame-oil, nut-oil, fish-oil, colocynth-oil, tar, and naphtha. R. Tarfon says: They may use only olive-oil.

3. Naught that comes from a tree[5] may be used for lighting [the Sabbath lamp] excepting flax; and naught that comes from a tree can contract uncleanness by overshadowing[6] excepting flax. If a wick made from [a

---

[1] At the Samaritan Passover at the present time the ovens are pits in the ground.
[2] See Tam. 1¹; Midd. 1¹.   [3] The fibre out of the 'apples of Sodom' or 'Dead-Sea fruit'.
[4] See p. 181, n. 11.   [5] i.e. no wick of vegetable origin.
[6] From Num. 19¹⁴ᶠ is derived the rule that whatever is overshadowed by the same roof or object that overshadows a corpse, and whatever (not being a permanently fixed roofing) overshadows a corpse, becomes unclean. See p. 649, n. 3.

piece of] cloth was twisted but not singed, R. Eliezer declares it susceptible to uncleanness[1] and not to be used for lighting [the Sabbath lamp]; but R. Akiba says: It is not susceptible to uncleanness[2] and it may be used for lighting [the Sabbath lamp].

4. A man may not pierce an egg-shell and fill it with oil and put it on the opening of the lamp[3] so that the oil will drip from it;[4] [it is forbidden] even if it was made of earthenware (but R. Judah permits it); but if the potter had joined it [with the lamp] from the first, it is permitted in that it is a single vessel. A man may not fill a dish with oil and put it beside a lamp and put the end of the wick in it so that it will absorb [the oil]. But R. Judah permits it.

5. If a man put out the lamp [on the night of Sabbath] from fear of the gentiles or of thieves or of an evil spirit, or to suffer one that was sick to sleep, he is not culpable; [but if he did it with a mind] to spare the lamp or to spare the oil or to spare the wick, he is culpable. But R. Jose declares him exempt in every case excepting that of the wick, since he thereby forms charcoal.[5]

6. For three transgressions do women die in childbirth: for heedlessness of the laws of the menstruant,[6] the Dough-offering,[7] and the lighting of the [Sabbath] lamp.

7. Three things must a man say within his house when darkness is falling on the eve of Sabbath: Have ye tithed?[8] Have ye prepared the *Erub*?[9] and, Light the lamp. If it is in doubt whether darkness has already fallen or not, they may not set apart Tithes from what is known to be untithed, or immerse utensils or light the lamps; but they may set apart Tithes from *demai*-produce[10] and prepare the *Erub* and cover up what is to be kept hot.

3. 1. If a double-stove[11] had[12] been heated with stubble or straw, cooked food may[13] be set on it; but if with peat or wood, cooked food may not be set on it until it has been swept out or covered with ashes. The School of Shammai say: Hot water but not cooked food may be set thereon. And the School of Hillel say: Both hot water and cooked food. The School of Shammai say: They may be removed [on the Sabbath] but not put back. And the School of Hillel say: They may also be put back.

2. If an oven had been heated with stubble or straw naught may be put within it or upon it. If a single-stove had been heated with stubble or straw, it is regarded in like manner as the double-stove; and if [it had been heated] with peat or wood, it is regarded in like manner as an oven.

3. An egg may not be put beside a kettle [on the Sabbath] so that it shall get cooked, nor may it be cracked within [hot] wrappings; but R. Jose

---

[1] Kel. 27 [1, 2]. It is susceptible to corpse-uncleanness if, before it was twisted up, it measured three fingerbreadths square, since what is of such a size is 'usable' (and whatever still remains as, of itself, a usable article is susceptible to uncleanness).

[2] Being twisted up it ceases to count as usable cloth having a measure of three fingerbreadths square, and so ceases to count as, of itself, a usable article. See Kel. 27[12].

[3] For the shape of this lamp see p. 581, n. 6.

[4] So artificially replenishing the contents of the lamp during the Sabbath. The Palestinian lamp of the time hardly held more oil than would burn for an hour. Shab. 7[2] includes both kindling and extinguishing fire among the thirty-nine main classes of forbidden work.

[5] Thereby performing 'work' in that he achieves a desirable end, since the singed end is easier to light the next time.   [6] Lev. 15[19ff].   [7] Num. 15[20]. See p. 83, n. 1.

[8] It was forbidden to tithe on the Sabbath the food eaten on the Sabbath. Cf. Dem. 7[1, 5].

[9] App. I. 8. See *J.E.* v. 204a; Erub. 3[1ff].   [10] App. I. 6. See Dem. 1[4].   [11] Kel. 5[2].

[12] Before the onset of Sabbath.   [13] On the Sabbath.

permits this. Nor may it be buried in [hot] sand or in the dust of the road so that it shall get roasted.

4. The men of Tiberias once passed a tube of cold water through a spring of hot water. The Sages said to them: If this is done on the Sabbath it is like water heated on the Sabbath and is forbidden both for washing and drinking; and if it is done on a Festival-day it is like water heated on a Festival-day and is forbidden for washing, but permitted for drinking.[1] If a *miliarum*[2] was cleared of its ashes[3] one may drink from it on the Sabbath, but one may not drink from an *antikhi*[2] even though it was cleared of its ashes.

5. If a kettle [holding hot water] was taken off [from a stove], cold water may not be put in it to be made hot; but enough may be put therein or into [hot water in] a cup to make [the hot water] lukewarm. Spices may not be put into a pan or pot that was taken off [from a stove] while boiling, but they may be put into [hot food in] a plate or a dish. R. Judah says: They may be put into aught excepting what has in it vinegar or fish-brine.[4]

6. A vessel may not be put under the lamp [on the Sabbath] to collect the [dripping] oil; but if it was put there before nightfall it is permitted. But no use may be made of that oil [on the Sabbath] since it is not a thing already prepared [for the Sabbath]. A new lamp may be moved from one place to another, but not an old lamp. R. Simeon says: Any lamp may be moved from one place to another excepting a lamp already alight[5] on the Sabbath. A man may put a vessel under the lamp to catch the sparks but he may not put water therein, since he would thereby quench [the sparks].

4. 1. With what may they cover up hot food and with what may they not cover it up? They may not cover it up with peat or dung or salt or lime or wet sand or dry, or straw or grape-skins or flocking, or herbs that are still wet[6] (but they may do so if they are dried). They may cover up hot food with clothes or produce[7] or feathers or sawdust or hackled flax. R. Judah forbids fine hackled flax but permits the coarse.

2. They may cover up hot food with hides and may move them about; and with wool-shearings, but these they may not move about. How should a man act?[8] He should take off the lid [of the pot] while the wool-shearings fall away [of themselves]. R. Eleazar b. Azariah says: The basket should be turned over on its side and the food thus removed, lest perchance the pot is removed in such wise that it cannot be replaced. But the Sages say: It may be removed and replaced. If it was not covered up while it was yet day, it may not be covered up after nightfall; but if it was covered up and became uncovered, it may be covered up afresh. A jug may be filled [on the Sabbath with cold food or liquid] and put under a cushion or under a bolster.

5. 1. With what [burdens] may cattle[9] go out[10] [on the Sabbath] and with what may they not go out? The camel may go out with its curb, the female

---

[1] It is permitted (on the ground of Ex. 12[16]) to cook necessary food on a Festival-day. See Betz. 2[5].

[2] Water-heating vessels with fuel-compartments. The *antikhi* is said to retain its heat more effectively than the *miliarum*, therefore what derives heat from it on the Sabbath is under suspicion of being deliberately heated on the Sabbath.

[3] Before the onset of Sabbath.

[4] Since these through their tartness have the effect of 'cooking' the spices. Cf. Maas. 1[7].

[5] There is danger of extinguishing it.   [6] All these were likely to generate fresh heat.

[7] Such as corn.   [8] When he wishes to take out the hot food.

[9] To which also the Sabbath law applies (Ex. 20[10]; Deut. 5[14]).

[10] See above, p. 100, n. 2. In this and the following chapter discrimination is attempted between permissible ornaments or appurtenances and forbidden burdens.

camel with its nose-ring, the Libyan ass with its bridle, the horse with its chain, and all beasts which wear a chain may go out with a chain and be led by the chain; and these things may be sprinkled and immersed[1] without being removed.

2. The ass may go out with its saddle-cloth if this was fastened on [before the Sabbath]; rams may go out strapped up,[2] and the ewes may go out wearing the strap over or under their tails or wearing the protective cloth; and goats may go out [with their udders] bound up. All these things R. Jose forbids excepting ewes wearing the protective cloth. R. Judah says: Goats may go out [with their udders] bound up if this is to keep them dry, but not if it serves to collect the milk.

3. And with what may they not go out? A camel may not go out with a rag[3] hung to its tail or with fore and hind legs bound together, or with hoof tied to thigh. So, too, is it with all other cattle. Camels may not be led along tied together, but a man may hold their ropes in his hand provided that he does not twist them together.[4]

4. The ass may not go out with its saddle-cloth if this was not fastened on [before the Sabbath], or with a bell even though it is plugged, or with the ladder-yoke[5] round its neck, or with its leg-strap. Fowls may not go out with their bands or their straps on their legs.[6] Rams may not go out with their wagon[7] under their fat tail, nor may ewes go out with the wood-chip[8] in their nose; nor may the calf go out with its rush-yoke,[9] nor the cow with the hedgehog-skin[10] [tied round its udder] or with the strap between its horns. R. Eleazar b. Azariah's cow[11] used to go out with the strap between its horns, which was not with the consent of the Sages.

6. 1. With what may a woman go out and with what may she not go out? A woman may not go out with bands of wool or bands of flax or with her head-straps (nor should she immerse herself with them unless she has loosened them);[12] nor [may she go out] with forehead-band or head-bangles if they are not sewn [on the head-dress], or with a hair-net [when she goes] to a public place. Nor [may she go out] with a 'golden city'[13] or a necklace or nose-rings or with a ring that bears no seal or with a needle that has no eye. Yet if she went out [wearing the like of these] she is not liable to a Sin-offering.[14]

2. A man may not go out with sandals shod with nails or with a single sandal if he has no wound in his foot,[15] or with phylacteries,[16] or with an

---

[1] See Num. 19[19] and the tractate Parah, pp. 697 ff.   [2] With male organ confined.
[3] Identification mark or ornament or amulet. The word (*metoteleth*) is used in Kel. 12[8] in the sense of plummet, and in Tam. 5[4] in an obscure sense, perhaps 'covering'. Modern commentators explain the word as meaning 'pad'.
[4] Lest they constitute 'Diverse Kinds' through being made of wood and flax. Kil. 9[1]; Deut. 22[1].
[5] A device to prevent it from twisting its neck round to bite at its saddle-sores.
[6] Identification signs.
[7] A small cart supporting the heavy tail (a prized part of the sheep) and saving it from harm through contact with stones and rocks.
[8] Explained as a device to incite the ewes to sneeze and so free their heads from worms.
[9] A light imitation yoke to break in the calf.
[10] To prevent creeping beasts from sucking out its milk.
[11] Betz. 2[8]; Eduy. 3[11]. The strap was either for ornament or protection. According to a Baraita (Shab. 54b) it was not Eleazar's own cow but that of a female neighbour; but since he had not protested against it he was associated with the illegality.
[12] This rule is not concerned with Sabbath observance. See Mikw. 9[1].
[13] Eduy. 2[7]; Kel. 11. A tiara shaped like Jerusalem.   [14] Lev. 4[27ff].
[15] Otherwise he incurs suspicion of carrying the other under his cloak.
[16] The small leather boxes containing, written on parchment, in one sheet or in four

amulet that has not been prepared by one that was skilled,[1] or with a breast-plate or helmet or greaves. But if he went out [wearing the like of these] he is not liable to a Sin-offering.

3. A woman may not go out with a needle that has an eye, or with a ring that bears a seal, or with a cochlea brooch, or with a spice-box, or with a perfume-flask; and if she went out [bearing the like of these] she is liable to a Sin-offering. So R. Meir. But the Sages permit a spice-box or a perfume-flask.

4. A man may not go out with a sword or a bow or a shield or a club or a spear; and if he went out [with the like of these] he is liable to a Sin-offering. R. Eliezer says: They are his adornments. But the Sages say: They are naught save a reproach, for it is written, *And they shall beat their swords into plowshares, and their spears into pruning-hooks: nation shall not lift up sword against nation, neither shall they learn war any more.*[2] A garter is not susceptible to uncleanness[3] and they may go out therewith on the Sabbath; but ankle-chains are susceptible to uncleanness and they may not go out therewith on the Sabbath.

5. A woman may go out with bands of hair, whether it is her own or another's, or from cattle, or with a forehead-band or head-bangles sewn [on the head-dress] or with a hair-net or with false locks [if she remains] in [her own] courtyard; or with wool in her ear, or with wool in her sandals, or with the wool that she has arranged for her menstruous flow, or with a peppercorn or piece of salt or aught that she puts in her mouth, if only she does not first put it there on the Sabbath; but if it falls out she may not put it back. Rabbi permits a false tooth or a gilded tooth; but the Sages forbid it.

6. They may go out with the *sela*[4] that is put on a bunion; small girls may go out with threads or even chips in their ears;[5] women of Arabia may go out veiled and women of Media with their cloaks looped up over their shoulders; and so may any one, but the Sages spoke only of actual custom.

7. A woman may loop up[6] her cloak with a stone or nut or coin, provided that she does not loop it up first[7] on the Sabbath.

8. A cripple[8] may go out with his wooden stump. So R. Meir. But R. Jose forbids it. If it has a cavity[9] for pads[10] it is susceptible to uncleanness. His knee-pads[11] are susceptible to *midras*-uncleanness;[12] yet he may go out with them on the Sabbath or enter with them into the Temple Court.[13] His stool and its pads are susceptible to *midras*-uncleanness; and he may not go out with them on the Sabbath or enter with them into the

compartments, the passages Ex. 13[1-10], 13[11-16], Deut. 6[4-9]; 11[13-21]. They are now worn (at the daily week-day morning services) in fulfilment of Deut. 6[8], one on the forehead and one on the left arm (on the inner side immediately above the elbow).

[1] Who has not yet proved the curative power of his amulets.   [2] Is. 2[4].
[3] It is only an adjunct to a piece of wearing-apparel. See Kel. 12[1ff].
[4] A silver coin. App. II. A. This is a cure for bunions.
[5] To keep open a hole pierced for ear-rings. Though they cannot be reckoned ornaments they are permissible.
[6] One corner of the garment is wrapped around some object to form a sort of button, and this is fastened to a loop or hole in another corner.
[7] According to Maim. this limitation applies only to the use of the coin.
[8] Whose leg is cut off.
[9] See Kel. 2[1]; 15[1ff]. The rest of this paragraph deals with the subject of ch. 15 of the tractate Kelim.
[10] Padding put in the concave top of the wooden leg to protect the end of the cripple's limb.   [11] Leather pads that protect his extremities while shuffling on the ground.
[12] App. I. 26. See Zab. 2[4], and General Index, s.v. *Midras*.   [13] Cf. Ber. 9[6]; Kel. 1[8].

Temple Court. Clogs[1] are not susceptible to uncleanness; and none may go out with them [on the Sabbath].

9. Sons may go out with bindings[2] and the sons of kings with little bells; and so may any one, but the Sages spoke only of actual custom.

10. Men may go out with a locust's egg[3] or a jackal's tooth[4] or with a nail of [the gallows of] one that was crucified,[5] as a means of healing. So R. Meir.[6] But the Sages say: Even on ordinary days this is forbidden as following in the ways of the Amorite.[7]

7. 1. A great general rule have they laid down concerning the Sabbath: whosoever, forgetful of the principle of the Sabbath,[8] committed many acts of work on many Sabbaths, is liable only to one Sin-offering; but if, mindful of the principle of the Sabbath, he yet[9] committed many acts of work on many Sabbaths, he is liable for every Sabbath [which he profaned]. If he knew that it was the Sabbath and he yet[10] committed many acts of work on many Sabbaths, he is liable for every main class of work [which he performed]; if he committed many acts of work of one main class, he is liable only to one Sin-offering.

2. The main classes of work are forty save one: sowing, ploughing, reaping, binding sheaves, threshing, winnowing, cleansing crops, grinding, sifting, kneading, baking, shearing wool, washing or beating or dyeing it, spinning, weaving, making two loops, weaving two threads, separating two threads, tying [a knot], loosening [a knot], sewing two stitches, tearing in order to sew two stitches, hunting a gazelle, slaughtering or flaying or salting it or curing its skin, scraping it or cutting it up, writing two letters, erasing in order to write two letters, building, pulling down, putting out a fire, lighting a fire, striking with a hammer and taking out aught from one domain into another.[11] These are the main classes of work: forty save one.

3. Another general rule have they laid down: whatsoever it is proper to keep stored and is in such quantity as it is usual to keep stored, and a man takes it out on the Sabbath, he is liable thereby to a Sin-offering. But whatsoever it is not proper to keep stored or that is not in such quantity as it is usual to keep stored, and a man takes it out on the Sabbath, he only is culpable that [usually] keeps [the like of] it stored.[12]

4. [He is culpable] that takes out straw equal to a cow's mouthful, or pea-stalks equal to a camel's mouthful, or ears of grain equal to a lamb's mouthful, or grass equal to a kid's mouthful, or a dried fig's bulk of fresh garlic or onion-leaves, or, if dry, a kid's mouthful [thereof]; and these may not be included together [to make up the forbidden quantity] since their prescribed measures are not equal. But if a man takes out even a dried fig's bulk of foodstuff[13] he is culpable, and they[14] can be included

---

[1] The meaning is quite uncertain. Other renderings proposed are 'mask' or a wooden donkey's head worn by mummers. See also Kel. 15[6], where the word occurs closely associated with 'lute' and 'drum'.

[2] The Gemara here explains that if a son longs after his father, to cure him the father ties the string of his right sandal to his son's left sandal, and the string of his left sandal to his son's right sandal.   [3] Cures ear-ache.

[4] If from a live jackal it cures sleepiness; if from a dead one it cures sleeplessness.

[5] Cures festering in a wound. According to Maim, it was used to cure tertian fever.

[6] Variant: So R. Jose. But R. Meir says.

[7] Heathenish superstition. See Hull. 4[7].   [8] Or ignorant of the Sabbath law.

[9] Forgetful that it was the Sabbath.   [10] Not knowing them to be forbidden.

[11] These thirty-nine acts of work are treated in various degrees of detail in chh. 11ff.

[12] Cf. 10[1].   [13] Meant for human consumption.   [14] Human foodstuffs.

together [to make up the forbidden quantity] since their prescribed measures are equal, excepting[1] their husks, kernels, and stalks, and coarse or fine bran. R. Judah says: Excepting the husks of lentils which are cooked together with them.[2]

8. 1. [He is culpable] that takes out wine enough to mix the cup,[3] or milk enough for a gulp, or honey enough to put on a sore, or oil enough to anoint the smallest member,[4] or water enough to rub off eye-plaster, or a quarter-*log* of any other liquid or a quarter-*log* of liquid refuse. R. Simeon says: The prescribed measure is a quarter-*log* in every case; and they have enjoined these [several] measures only on them that keep the like of these things stored.

2. [He is culpable] that takes out rope enough to make a handle for a basket, or reed-grass enough to make a hanger for a sifter or sieve (R. Judah says: Enough to take from it the measure of a child's shoe), or paper enough to write thereon a taxgatherer's label (he, also, that takes out a taxgatherer's label is culpable), or used paper enough to wrap up the mouth of a small perfume-flask.

3. [He is culpable] that takes out leather enough to make an amulet,[5] or vellum enough to write on it the shortest passage in the phylacteries, namely, *Hear, O Israel . . .;*[6] or ink enough to write two letters, or eye-paint enough to paint one eye.

4. [He is culpable that takes out] lime enough to put on the tip of the lime-twig; or pitch or sulphur enough for a small hole to be made [in it], or wax enough to stop up a small hole, or clay enough to fashion the [bellows]-hole of a goldsmith's crucible (R. Judah says: Enough to make one of the props[7] [of the crucible]); or bran enough to put over the mouthpiece[8] of a goldsmith's crucible; or quicklime enough to smear the little finger of girls.[9] R. Judah says: Enough to take off the hair on the temples. R. Nehemiah says: Enough to take off the hair on the forehead.

5. [He is culpable that takes out] red clay enough for the seal[10] of a large sack (so R. Akiba; but the Sages say: For the seal of letters); or manure or fine sand enough to manure a cabbage-stalk (so R. Akiba; but the Sages say: Enough to manure a leek); or coarse sand enough to cover a plasterer's trowel; or reed enough to make a pen, or, if it is thick or broken, enough to cook the smallest egg mixed [with oil] and put in a pan.

6. [He is culpable that takes out] bone enough to make a spoon (R. Judah says: Enough to make a tooth of a key); or glass enough to scrape the end of the shuttle; or a pebble or a stone big enough to throw at a bird (R. Eliezer b. Jacob says: Big enough to throw at cattle).

7. [He is culpable that takes out] a potsherd big enough to place between one board and another.[11] So R. Judah. But R. Meir says: Big enough to scoop up fire. And R. Jose says: Big enough to hold a quarter-*log* [of liquid]. R. Meir says: Although there is no proof of the matter there is

---

[1] These are not taken into account towards making up the forbidden dried fig's bulk.
[2] Therefore these *are* taken into account.
[3] Explained as the quarter of a quarter-*log* (i.e. three-eighths of an egg's bulk).
[4] The little toe of a one-day old child.
[5] Some texts add: parchment enough to write a *Mezuzah* thereon.   [6] See p. 104, n. 16.
[7] So Maim. and Bert. Tif. Yis. explains it as 'to plaster the bottom of the crucible'. See Kel. 5[11]; 6[1].   [8] To conserve the heat.
[9] Or, 'the smallest of girls'. The reference is to depilatory use.   [10] Ohol. 17[5].
[11] To fill in a gap (Maim.) or to keep piled boards rigid and so avoid warping (Bert. and Tif. Yis.).

an indication in that it is written, *And there shall not be found among the pieces thereof a sherd to take fire from the hearth.*[1] R. Jose replied: There is proof from the selfsame verse: *Or to scoop up water withal out of the cistern.*

9. 1. R. Akiba said: Whence do we learn of an idol that like a menstruant[2] it conveys uncleanness by carrying?[3] Because it is written, *Thou shalt cast them away like a menstruous thing; thou shalt say unto it, Get thee hence.*[4] Like as a menstruant conveys uncleanness by carrying, so does an idol convey uncleanness by carrying.

2. Whence do we learn of a ship that it is not susceptible to uncleanness? Because it is written, *The way of a ship in the midst of the sea.*[5] Whence do we learn of a garden-bed, six handbreadths square, that five kinds of seed may be sown therein, four on the sides and one in the middle?[6] Because it is written, *For as the earth bringeth forth her bud and as the garden causeth the seeds sown in it to spring forth.*[7] It is not written *Its seed*, but the *seeds sown in it.*[8]

3. Whence do we learn of a woman who emits semen on the third day[9] that she is unclean? Because it is written, *And be ready against the third day*, [*come not near a woman*].[10] Whence do we learn that they may bathe[11] a circumcised child on the third day even if this falls on a Sabbath? Because it is written, *And it came to pass on the third day when they were sore.*[12] Whence do we learn that they tie a strip of crimson on the head of the scapegoat?[13] Because it is written, *Though your sins be as scarlet they shall be as white as snow.*[14]

4. Whence do we learn that on the Day of Atonement anointing is equal to drinking?[15] Although there is no proof of the matter there is an indication in that it is written, *And it came into his inward parts like water and like oil into his bones.*[16]

5. [He is culpable] that takes out [on the Sabbath] wood enough to cook the smallest egg, or spices enough to flavour a light egg (and [various spices] can be included together [to make up the forbidden quantity]); or shells of walnuts or skins of pomegranates or woad or madder enough to dye a garment small as a hair-net; or urine, soda, soap, cimolian earth, or lion's-leaf[17] enough to cleanse a garment small as a hair-net. R. Judah says: Enough to spread over a stain.[18]

6. [He is culpable that takes out] any quantity soever of sweet pepper, or of tar; or any quantity soever of any kind of spices or of any kind of metals; or any quantity soever of altar-stones or of altar-earth or of worn-out sacred books or their worn-out covers that have been stored away in

---

[1] Is. 30[14].   [2] Lev. 15[19ff], Kel. 1[3].   [3] Cf. A. Zar. 3[6].   [4] Is. 30[22].
  [5] Prov. 30[19]; here the last few words, being self-evident, might be deemed superfluous; but since no words in Scripture are superfluous the addition must be intended to mean that, in regard to the laws of cleanness and uncleannness, a ship is accounted like the sea itself, incapable of contracting uncleannness.   [6] See Kil. 3[1].   [7] Is. 61[11].
  [8] The Gemara here adds: R. Judah said: 'The earth bringeth forth her bud'; 'bringeth forth'—one; 'her bud'—one; making two. 'Seeds sown' means (at least) two more; making four; 'causeth to spring forth'—one; making five in all.
  [9] The semen being still potent. But see Mikw. 8[3].
  [10] Ex. 19[15].   [11] And even heat water.
  [12] Gen. 34[25]. The effects of the circumcision, and therefore its power to override the Sabbath, endure to the third day. Cf. below, 19[1, 3].
  [13] Yom. 4[2].   [14] Is. 1[18]. See Yom. 6[8].   [15] See Yom. 8[1].   [16] Ps. 109[18].
  [17] Heb. *Ashlag*. Bert.: 'I cannot explain what it is.' The word is now used to translate potash. .   [18] Cf. Nidd. 9[6].

order to hide them.[1] R. Judah says: Or any that takes out aught soever pertaining to idols, for it is written, *And there shall cleave nought of the devoted thing to thine hand*.[2]

7. If a man took out a pedlar's basket, although there are in it many different kinds, he is liable only to one Sin-offering. [So, too, if he took out] garden-seeds little less than a dried fig's bulk (R. Judah b. Bathyra says: Five [garden-seeds]); or two cucumber-seeds, two gourd-seeds, two seeds of Egyptian beans; or a live locust, however small, or a dried fig's bulk if it is dead; or 'birds of the vineyard',[3] alive or dead, however small, since such are kept as a means of healing. R. Judah says: Even if a man took out a living, unclean locust, however small, [he is culpable] since it is kept as a child's plaything.

10. 1. If a man stored up aught[4] as seed, or as a sample, or as a means of healing, and he took it out on the Sabbath, he is culpable, however little the quantity; but any other becomes culpable thereby only if [he took out] the [forbidden][5] quantity thereof. If any brought it in again, he becomes culpable thereby only if it is as much as the [forbidden] quantity.

2. If a man took out[6] foodstuff and put it on the threshold, he does not become culpable if he afterward took it out altogether, or if another took it out, since he did not perform his [whole] act of work at the one time. If he put a basket full of produce on the outer threshold, even if the greater part of the produce was outside, he is not culpable, but only if he took out the whole basket.[7]

3. If a man took out aught in his right hand or in his left hand, in his bosom or on his shoulder, he is culpable; for this last was the manner of carrying of the sons of Kohath.[8] If [he took it out] on the back of his hand, or with his foot or with his mouth or with his elbow, or in his ear or in his hair or in his wallet [carried] mouth downwards, or between his wallet and his shirt, or in the hem[9] of his shirt, or in his shoe or in his sandal, he is not culpable since he has not taken it out after the fashion of them that take out [a burden].

4. If a man intended to take out a thing in front of him and it slipped behind him, he is not culpable; but if [he intended to take it out] behind him and it slipped in front of him, he is culpable. Rightly have they said:[10] If a woman wore drawers [and took aught out therein] either in front of her or behind her, she is culpable, since it is likely to move round. R. Judah says: So, too, with letter-carriers.[11]

5. If a man took out a loaf into the public domain he is culpable; if two men took it out they are not culpable. But if one could not take it out and [so] two men took it out, they are culpable; but R. Simeon declares them not culpable. If a man took out in a vessel foodstuff less than the forbidden quantity, he is not culpable by reason of the vessel, since the vessel is secondary. [If he took out] a living man on a couch he is not culpable by reason of the couch,[12] since the couch is secondary; but if [he took out]

---

[1] The verb is from the same root as 'Genizah', the chamber or cellar in which old sacred writings were stored away. Though unusable they retain their sanctity.
[2] Deut. 13[17].   [3] A species of locust.   [4] Cf. 7[3].   [5] As prescribed, e.g., in 9[6, 7]
[6] The Mishnah here resumes the topic of 1[1].
[7] At the one time.   [8] Num. 7[9].
[9] Perhaps 'sleeve'. Cf. Shek. 3[2].   [10] See p. 12, n. 4.
[11] Royal messengers, who bore letters contained in tube-shaped devices which tended to swing behind them.
[12] Nor by reason of the living man since a living man could walk by himself.

a dead man on a couch, he is culpable.[1] So, too, [if he took out] as much as an olive's bulk[2] of a corpse or an olive's bulk of carrion, or a lentil's bulk of a creeping thing,[3] he is culpable. But R. Simeon declares him not culpable.[4]

6. If a man removed his finger-nails by means of his nails or his teeth, and so, too, if [he pulled out] the hair of his head, or his moustache or his beard; and so, too, if a woman dressed her hair or painted her eyelids or reddened[5] [her face]—such a one R. Eliezer declares liable [to a Sin-offering];[6] but the Sages forbid [acts the like of these only] by virtue of the [rabbinically ordained] Sabbath rest.[7] If a man plucked aught from a holed plant-pot he is culpable; but if from an unholed plant-pot he is not culpable. R. Simeon declares him not culpable in either case.

11. 1. If a man threw aught from a private domain to the public domain, or from the public domain to a private domain, he is culpable; but if from a private domain to another private domain with the public domain between, R. Akiba declares him culpable, but the Sages not culpable.

2. Thus if there were two balconies opposite one another [extending] into the public domain and a man stretched out or threw aught from the one to the other, he is not culpable. If they were [different private domains but on the same side of the street and] in the same story,[8] and a man stretched aught out [from one to the other], he is culpable; but if he threw it he is not culpable. Such was the service of the levites:[9] there were two wagons the one behind the other in the public domain, and they used to stretch out the beams from the one to the other but did not throw them. If a man took aught from the bank around a cistern[10] or from a rock that was ten handbreadths high and four wide, or put aught upon them, he is culpable; but if they were less than this he is not culpable.

3. If a man threw [aught from a distance of] four cubits [so that it remained] on a wall, and it was higher than ten handbreadths, it is as though he threw it into the air;[11] but if less than ten handbreadths it is as though he threw it on to the ground.[12] If a man threw [aught to a distance of] four cubits on the ground he is culpable; but if he threw it less than four cubits and it rolled beyond the four cubits, he is not culpable. But if he threw it beyond four cubits and it rolled back within the four cubits he is culpable.

4. If a man threw [aught to a distance of] four cubits into the sea[13] he is not culpable; if it was a piece of shallow water through which passed a public path, and a man threw aught therein [to a distance of] four cubits, he is culpable.[14] What depth counts as shallow water? Less than ten hand-breadths. If into shallow water, through which passed a public path, a man threw aught [to a distance of] four cubits, he is culpable.

5. If a man threw aught from the sea to the dry land,[15] or from the dry

---

[1] For it was an act with a purpose (which constitutes an act of work), in order to remove uncleanness.   [2] See Ohol. 2¹.   [3] App. IV. 8.

[4] Holding that this is not an act necessary in itself.

[5] Doubtful. Also explained as 'parted the hair' (Tif. Yis.).

[6] Her acts can be deemed 'building' or 'dyeing' (see above, 7²).

[7] See Erub. 10³, ¹⁵.   [8] See Erub. 8¹¹.

[9] So that they could continue the work of building the Tabernacle without profaning the Sabbath.   [10] See Erub. 8³.

[11] Which is accounted public domain, where he is not culpable.

[12] And he is culpable as though he had thrown from a public to a private domain.

[13] Which counts as neither public nor private domain (such is termed *karmelith*).

[14] Since it counts as public domain.   [15] From *karmelith* to public domain.

land to the sea, or from the sea to a ship,[1] or from a ship to the sea, or from one ship to another, he is not culpable. If the ships were tied together [goods] may be moved from one to the other; if they were not tied together, even though they lay closely together, naught may be moved from the one to the other.

6. If a man threw aught and he remembered [that it was the Sabbath] after it left his hand,[2] or if another intercepted it, or if a dog intercepted it, or if it was burnt, he is not culpable. If he threw it in order to wound either a man or a beast, and before the wound was inflicted he remembered [that it was the Sabbath], he is not culpable. This is the general rule: they that may be liable to a Sin-offering[3] are not liable unless the beginning and the end of their act were done in error. If they began the act in error and ended it wittingly, or if they began it wittingly and ended it in error, they are not liable: [they are not liable] unless both the beginning and the end of their act were done in error.

12. 1. If a man built aught [on the Sabbath] how much must he build to become culpable? He is culpable that builds aught soever, or that at all hews stone, or wields a hammer, or chisels or bores a hole. This is the general rule: if a man performs work on the Sabbath and his work is enduring he is culpable. Rabban Simeon b. Gamaliel says: Even if a man but struck a hammer on the anvil during work he is [thereby] culpable, since he is as one that sets [other] work aright.[4]

2. He is culpable that ploughs aught soever, or that at all weeds or cuts off dead leaves or prunes. [He is culpable] that gathers any wood soever if it is to set [the ground] in order; and if it is to burn, [he is culpable that gathers] enough to cook the smallest egg. [He is culpable] that gathers any herbs soever if it is to set [the field] in order; and if it is for the cattle, [he is culpable that gathers] enough to fill a kid's mouth.

3. He is culpable that writes two letters, whether with his right hand or with his left, whether the same or different letters, whether in different inks[5] or in any language. R. Jose said: They have declared culpable the writing of two letters only by reason of their use as a mark;[6] for so used they to write on the boards of the Tabernacle that they might know which adjoined which. Rabbi said: We find a short name[7] formed from a longer name: Shem from Shimeon or Shemuel, Noah from Nahor, Dan from Daniel, Gad from Gadiel.

4. If during one act of forgetfulness [that it was the Sabbath] a man wrote two letters, he is culpable. Whether he wrote in ink or caustic or red dye or gum or copperas[8] or aught that leaves a lasting mark, or on two walls forming an angle or on two tablets of an account-book so that [the two letters] could be read together, he is culpable. If a man wrote on his skin he is culpable. If he scratched [letters] on his skin, R. Eliezer declares him liable to a Sin-offering, but R. Joshua declares him not culpable.

5. If a man wrote with liquids or with fruit-juice or with dust from the roads or with writer's sand or with aught that leaves no lasting mark, he

---

1 Private domain.   2 The act began in error but its end was not in error.
3 See Lev. 4[27f]; the beginning and end of the act must both come within the scope of 'un-witting sin'. If he profaned the Sabbath wittingly he is liable to Extirpation (p. 562, n. 16).
4 He smooths the surface of the anvil (or of the hammer-face).
5 Variant: signs.   6 Purposeful act from which advantage is derived, i.e. work.
7 Thus constituting a completed act of work.   8 See p. 203, n. 15.

is not culpable. [If he wrote] with the back of his hand or with his foot or with his mouth or with his elbow, or if he wrote one letter at the side of a letter already written, or if he wrote over what was already written, or if he intended to write a *heth* (ח) and wrote two *zains* (זז), or [if he wrote] one letter on the ground and another on the roof, or if he wrote [the two letters] on two walls of a house or on two pages of an account-book so that [the two letters] could not be read together, he is not culpable. If he wrote one letter as an abbreviation, R. Joshua b. Bathyra declares him culpable, but the Sages declare him not culpable.

6. If a man wrote two letters during two acts of forgetfulness, once in the morning and again towards evening, Rabban Gamaliel declares him culpable, but the Sages declare him not culpable.

13. 1. R. Eliezer says: He is culpable that weaves three threads [on the Sabbath] at the beginning [of the web], or a single thread on to a piece already woven. But the Sages say: Whether at the beginning or end [of the web] the forbidden quantity is two threads.

2. He is culpable that makes two loops to the heddles or the sley [of a loom],[1] or [two warps] in a sifter or sieve or basket, or that sews two stitches or that tears aught in order to sew two stitches.

3. If he tore [his raiment] in his anger or because of his dead, or if any one acted destructively, he is not culpable. But if he destroyed with the intention to set in order, for him the [forbidden] measure is the same as for him that sets aught in order.

4. The [forbidden] measure is a double *sit*[2] for bleachers, hacklers, dyers, and spinners; or the breadth of one *sit* for him that weaves two threads.

5. R. Judah says: If a man hunted a bird [and drove it] into a tower-trap, or [if he drove] a gazelle into a house, he is culpable. But the Sages say: A bird [may be driven] into a tower-trap or a gazelle into a house or a courtyard or an animal-pen[3] [on the Sabbath]. Rabban Simeon b. Gamaliel says: Not all animal-pens are alike. This is the general rule: if it must still be hunted he [that pens it in on the Sabbath] is not culpable; but if it no longer needs to be hunted he is culpable.[4]

6. If [on the Sabbath] a gazelle entered into a house and a man shut it in, he is culpable; but if two shut it in they are not culpable.[5] If one alone was not able to shut it in and [therefore] two shut it in, they both are culpable; but R. Simeon declares them not culpable.

7. If one sat in the doorway but could not block it and [therefore] another sat there and blocked it, the second is culpable. If the first sat in the doorway and blocked it, and then the second came and sat beside him, the first is culpable and the second not culpable, even if the first rose up and went away. For to what is such a one like? He is like to one that shut up his house to guard it and a gazelle was found shut up therein already.

14. 1. If [on the Sabbath] a man hunted or wounded any of the eight creeping things spoken of in the Law,[6] he is culpable;[7] but if he wounded any other forbidden beast or creeping thing, he is not culpable.[8] If he

---

1 Kel. 21[1].   2 Orl. 3[2].   App. II, C.   3 Heb. *bibarin*, vivarium.
4 Cf. Betz. 3[1].   5 See above, 10[5].   6 Lev. 11[29-30].
7 Since they have skins (but cf. Hull. 9[2]) he is guilty in breaking the skin by wounding them, an act falling within the forbidden main category of 'threshing' (7[2]); or if he bruised them and the skin was suffused with blood, it is an act falling within the category of 'dyeing'.
8 Such as worms, snails, or scorpions which are supposed not to have skins.

hunted them to make use of them he is culpable, and if not to make use of them he is not culpable.[1] If he hunted wild animals or birds in his private domain[2] he is not culpable, but if he wounded them he is culpable.

2. Pickling-brine may not be prepared on the Sabbath, but a man may prepare salt water and dip his bread therein or put it into cooked food.[3] R. Jose said: But would not such count as pickling-brine[4] whether it is much or little?—this, rather, is the salt water that is permissible: such that oil[5] is first put into the water or into the salt.

3. Greek hyssop[6] may not be eaten on the Sabbath since it is not the food of them that are in health, but a man may eat pennyroyal[7] or drink knotgrass-water.[8] He may eat any foodstuffs that serve for healing or drink any liquids except purgative water or a cup of root-water, since these serve to cure jaundice; but he may drink purgative water to quench his thirst, and he may anoint himself with root-oil if it is not used for healing.

4. If his teeth pain him he may not suck vinegar through them but he may take vinegar after his usual fashion,[9] and if he is healed he is healed. If his loins pain him he may not rub thereon wine or vinegar, yet he may anoint them with oil but not with rose-oil. Kings' children may anoint their wounds with rose-oil since it is their custom so to do on ordinary days. R. Simeon says: All Israelites are kings' children!

15. 1. These are knots for which they [that tie them on the Sabbath] are accounted culpable: camel-drivers' knots and sailors' knots; and as a man is culpable through the tying of them so is he culpable through the untying of them. R. Meir says: None is accounted culpable because of any knot which can be untied with one hand.

2. Some knots there are for which they are not accounted culpable as they are for camel-drivers' knots and sailors' knots. A woman may tie up the slit of her shift, or the strings of a hair-net or belt, or the straps of a shoe or sandal, or [leather] bottles of wine or oil, or [a cover over] a pot of flesh. R. Eliezer b. Jacob says: A rope may be tied up before cattle lest they stray forth. A bucket may be tied[10] to a belt but not to a rope; but R. Judah permits this. R. Judah laid down a general rule: none is accounted culpable for any knot that is not lasting.

3. A man may fold up his garments [that he wears on the Sabbath] as many as four or five times. Beds may be spread on the night of Sabbath for the Sabbath day, but not on the Sabbath for the night following the Sabbath. R. Ishmael says: Garments may be folded up and beds spread on the Day of Atonement[11] for the Sabbath; and the fat pieces of the Sabbath offering[12] may be brought[13] on the Day of Atonement.[14] R. Akiba says: They may bring neither those for the Sabbath on the Day of Atonement nor those for the Day of Atonement on the Sabbath.

---

[1] Cf. Eduy. 2⁵ on a serpent hunted in self-defence or for profit.
[2] 'The act of hunting has been in part achieved already.   [3] i.e. in small quantity.
[4] And forbidden by 7² under 'salting'.   [5] Which impairs the salt's action.
[6] A remedy for worms in the stomach (Gem. 109b).
[7] A remedy for worms in the liver.
[8] An antidote to harmful liquids. The two latter were both taken by those in health.
[9] At a meal.   [10] In lowering it down a well.
[11] That falls on the eve of Sabbath.   [12] Num. 28 ⁹ᶠ.
[13] The Sabbath exceeds the Day of Atonement in importance, since profaning the Sabbath is punishable by stoning, but profaning the Day of Atonement is punishable only by Extirpation (Tif. Yis.).
[14] Some texts add: but not those for the Day of Atonement on the Sabbath.

16. 1. Any of the Holy Scriptures[1] may be saved from burning [by bearing them from one domain to another on the Sabbath], whether they are such that are read[2] [on the Sabbath] or not.[3] In no matter what language they are written [if they become unfit for use] they require to be hidden away.[4] And why are certain among the Scriptures not read? Lest they make the House of Study of none effect.[5] The case of a scroll may be saved together with the scroll and the case of phylacteries[6] together with the phylacteries, even though there is money in them. Whither should they be taken for safety? To an alley-way that is no thoroughfare. Ben Bathyra says: Even to one that serves as a thoroughfare.

2. [If fire broke out on the Sabbath] they may save food enough for three meals—for men food that is suited to men and for cattle food that is suited to cattle. Thus if fire broke out in the night of the Sabbath they may save food enough for three meals; if in the morning, they may save enough for two meals; if in the afternoon, enough for one meal. R. Jose says: They may always save food enough for three meals.

3. They may save a basketful of loaves even though it is enough for a hundred meals; or a cake of figs or a jar of wine. One man may say to others, 'Come and save [food] for yourselves', and if they were prudent minded they made their reckoning[7] with him after the Sabbath was over. Whither should they take the food for safety? To a courtyard that is included within the *Erub*.[8] Ben Bathyra says: Even to one that is not included within the *Erub*.

4. Thither a man may take out all his utensils, and he may put on him all the clothes that he can put on and wrap himself with whatsoever he can wrap himself. R. Jose says: [He may put on only] eighteen things,[9] but he may return and put on others and take them out, and he may say to others, 'Come and help me to save them'.

5. R. Simeon b. Nanos says: They may spread the hide of a kid over a chest, a box, or a cupboard that have caught fire, since it will [only] scorch;[10] and they may make a partition wall of all the vessels, whether filled [with water] or empty, so that the fire shall not spread. R. Jose forbids new earthenware vessels filled with water since these cannot withstand the fire but burst and put out[11] the fire.

6. If a gentile came to put out the fire they may not say to him, 'Put it out', or 'Do not put it out', since they are not answerable for his keeping Sabbath. But if it was a minor[12] that came to put it out they may not permit him, since they are answerable for his keeping Sabbath.

7. They may cover a lamp with a dish so that it shall not scorch a rafter, and [cover] animal droppings to protect a child,[13] or a scorpion so that it

---

[1] Even the Prophets and the Hagiographa; but only if they are written in Hebrew.
[2] The Prophets that are read as the Sabbath proper lessons or *Haftaroth*.
[3] The Hagiographa.
[4] In the Genizah; see 9[6]. But these may not be saved on the Sabbath (Tif. Yis.).
[5] The Hagiographa, owing to their seductive attractiveness, tend to distract the mind from the graver subject of Sabbath instruction in matters relating to the Law.   [6] See p. 104, n. 16.
[7] Too honest to profit by keeping his goods which they rescued, they can at least bargain for some return for their labour.   [8] App. I. 8.
[9] Gem. 120a : overmantle, smock, hollow belt, linen vest, shirt, felt cap, cloak, two leggings, two shoes, two socks, a pair of drawers, a girdle around his loins, a hat on his head, and a wrap around his neck.   [10] And not kindle another fire. See 7[2]; Ex. 35[3].
[11] Likewise forbidden under 7[2].   [12] Under thirteen years of age, and a Jew.
[13] The passage is, literally, 'and (cover) the excrement of a child'. But Gem. 121b, followed by Maim. and others, explains it as not human excrement which it would be permissible to shift, but as the droppings of fowls, &c., lest a child should dirty itself by playing with them.

shall not bite. R. Judah said: Such a case once came before R. Johanan b. Zakkai in Arab,[1] and he said: I doubt whether he is not liable[2] to a Sin-offering.

8. If a gentile lighted a lamp an Israelite may make use of the light, but if he lighted it for the sake of the Israelite it is forbidden. If he filled [a trough] with water to give his cattle to drink, an Israelite may give his own cattle to drink after him, but if the gentile did it for the Israelite, it is forbidden. If he made a gangway by which to come down [from a ship] an Israelite may come down after him, but if he did it for the Israelite, it is forbidden. Rabban Gamaliel and the elders were once travelling in a ship,[3] and a gentile made a gangway by which to come down, and Rabban Gamaliel and the elders came down by it.

17. 1. Any [household] objects[4] may be moved about on the Sabbath together with their [detached] doors even though they were detached on the Sabbath;[5] for they are not as house-doors, in that these are not such that are fashioned [to be moved about].

2. A man may take up a hammer to crush walnuts, or a hatchet to split a fig-cake, or a saw to cut through cheese, or a shovel to scoop up dried figs, or a winnowing-shovel or fork to give aught thereon to a child,[6] or a spindle or a shuttle-staff to thrust into something, or a sewing-needle to take out a thorn, or a sackmaker's needle to open a door.

3. A reed for olives[7] is susceptible to uncleanness if it has a knot at the end;[8] otherwise it is not susceptible. In either case it may be removed on the Sabbath.

4. R. Jose says: Any utensil may be removed excepting a large saw or plowshare. Any utensil may be removed in case of need or not in case of need. R. Nehemiah says: They may be removed only in case of need.

5. Whatsoever utensils may be removed on the Sabbath, fragments thereof may likewise be removed provided that they can perform aught in the nature of work: to wit, fragments of a kneading-trough that can cover the mouth of a jar, or fragments of a glass vessel that can cover the mouth of a cruse. R. Judah says: Provided that they can perform aught in the nature of their former work: to wit, fragments of a kneading-trough that can have porridge poured therein, or fragments of a glass vessel that can have oil poured therein.

6. If a stone that is put in a gourd-shell [to weight it] does not fall out when water is drawn up therein, the gourd-shell may be used for drawing up water; but if the stone falls out, the gourd-shell may not be used.[9] If a branch is tied to a pitcher, water may be drawn up therewith on the Sabbath.

7. R. Eliezer says: They may shut up a window [on the Sabbath] with the window-shutter if it is fastened or hung [on the window-frame], but if not it may not be so used.[10] But the Sages say: In either case it may be used to shut up the window.

---

[1] Near Sepphoris in Galilee.   [2] As having hunted a beast.   [3] Cf. M. Sh. 5[9].
[4] That have doors or lids to them, like cupboards or boxes.
[5] Some texts omit: 'on the Sabbath'. Gem. 122b explains: Even though they were detached on a weekday they may be moved about on the Sabbath.
[6] Standing on the other side of a rift.
[7] With which to probe maturing olives to see whether they are ready for pressing.
[8] Closing one end and making the reed into a receptacle. Cf. Kel. 17 [15-17].
[9] If it is tightly fastened it counts as a true part of the vessel; otherwise it is as though a stone was being carried in the gourd-shell.
[10] Since it would count as adding to the building of a house.

8. Whatsoever lids of vessels have handles may be removed on the Sabbath. R. Jose says: This applies to lids over openings in the ground; but lids of vessels may be removed on the Sabbath whether they have handles or not.

18. 1. They may clear away [on the Sabbath] as much as four or five baskets of straw or grain to make room for guests or [to avoid] hindrance in the House of Study, but they may not do the like to the store-chamber. They may clear away clean Heave-offering,[1] *demai*-produce,[2] First Tithe from which Heave-offering has been given, Second Tithe[3] and dedicated produce which have been redeemed,[4] or dried lupine, since this is food for the poor;[5] but not untithed produce, or First Tithe from which Heave-offering has not been given, or Second Tithe and dedicated produce which have not been redeemed, or arum or mustard. Rabban Simeon b. Gamaliel permits [the clearing away of] arum, since it is food for the ravens [in the house].

2. Bundles of straw, bundles of branches, and bundles of young shoots may be removed from their place if they were put in readiness[6] as cattle fodder; but if not, they may not be removed. A basket may be upturned before chickens so that they may run up and down it; if a hen has escaped it may be driven along until it comes in again. Calves or young asses may be pulled along in the public road. A woman may pull her child along. R. Judah said: When? When the child can lift up one leg and put down the other; but if it is only dragged along this is forbidden.

3. They may not deliver the young of cattle on a Festival-day, but they may give help to the dam. They may deliver a woman on the Sabbath and summon a midwife for her from anywhere, and they may profane the Sabbath for the mother's sake and tie up the navel-string. R. Jose says: They may also cut it. And they may perform on the Sabbath all things that are needful for circumcision.[7]

19. 1. R. Eliezer says: If they had not brought the implement[8] on the eve of Sabbath it may be brought openly on the Sabbath; and in time of danger[9] a man may cover it up in the presence of witnesses. R. Eliezer said moreover: They may cut wood [on the Sabbath] to make charcoal in order to forge an iron implement. R. Akiba laid down a general rule:[10] Any act of work that can be done on the eve of Sabbath does not override the Sabbath, but what[11] cannot be done on the eve of Sabbath overrides the Sabbath.

2. They may perform on the Sabbath all things that are needful for circumcision: excision, tearing, sucking [the wound], and putting thereon a bandage and cummin.[12] If this had not been pounded up on the eve of the Sabbath a man may chew it with his teeth and then apply it. If the wine and oil had not been mixed on the eve of the Sabbath each may be applied by itself. They may not newly make the special bandage [on the Sabbath] but a rag may be wrapped around the member. If this had not been prepared on the eve of the Sabbath one may bring it wrapped around his finger even from another courtyard.

1 App. I. 48.   2 App. I. 6.   3 See p. 73, n. 6.   4 See p. 7, nn. 6–9.
5 Variant: goats.   6 Before the Sabbath.   7 Cf. Ned. 3[11] (R. Jose).
8 Circumcision knife.   9 When it was forbidden to observe the Jewish rites.
10 Again in Pes. 6[2]; Men. 11[3].
11 Variant: but circumcision which . . .   12 See *J. E.* iv. 92ff.

3. They may wash the child either before or after the circumcision and sprinkle it by means of the hand, but not by means of a vessel. R. Eleazar b. Azariah says: They may wash the child[1] on the third day if this falls on a Sabbath, for it is written, *And it came to pass on the third day when they were sore.*[2] They may not profane the Sabbath for the sake of a child about which there is doubt[3] or that is androgynous;[4] but R. Judah permits it for one that is androgynous.

4. If a man had two children one of which was to be circumcised on the day after the Sabbath[5] and the other was to be circumcised on the Sabbath, and he forgot and circumcised on the Sabbath the one that was to be circumcised after the Sabbath, he is culpable; if one was to be circumcised on the eve of Sabbath and the other on the Sabbath, and he forgot and circumcised on the Sabbath the one that was to be circumcised on the eve of Sabbath, R. Eliezer declares him liable to a Sin-offering, but R. Joshua declares him exempt.

5. A child can be circumcised on the eighth, ninth, tenth, eleventh, or twelfth day, but never earlier and never later. How is this?[6] The rule is that it shall be done on the eighth day; but if the child was born at twilight the child is circumcised on the ninth day; and if at twilight on the eve of Sabbath, the child is circumcised on the tenth day; if a Festival-day falls after the Sabbath the child is circumcised on the eleventh day; and if the two Festival-days of the New Year fall after the Sabbath the child is circumcised on the twelfth day. If a child is sick it is not circumcised until it becomes well.

6. These shreds [of the foreskin, if they remain,] render the circumcision invalid: flesh that covers the greater part of the corona (such a one [if a priest] may not eat of Heave-offering);[7] if he waxes fat [and the corona is covered anew] this must be set aright for appearance's sake. If one is circumcised without having the inner lining torn, it is as though he had not been circumcised.

20. 1. R. Eliezer says: On a Festival-day they may stretch out a filter[8] [over a vessel's mouth] and, on the Sabbath, pour [wine] through it while it is yet stretched out. But the Sages say: They may not stretch out a filter on a Festival-day or pour [wine] through it on the Sabbath[9] while it is yet stretched out; but on a Festival-day they may pour [wine] through it[10] when it is already stretched out.

2. They may pour water over wine-dregs to dilute them, and strain wine through a napkin or Egyptian basket;[11] they may put an egg in a mustard-strainer and prepare honied wine on the Sabbath. R. Judah says: They may prepare it on the Sabbath in a cup, on a Festival-day in a flagon,[12] and during mid-festival[13] in a jar.[14] All depends on the number of the guests.

3. They may not soak asafoetida in warm water but they may put it

---

[1] See Shab. 9³.   [2] Gen. 34²⁵.

[3] Whether it is an eight- or a nine-months child, and it is in doubt whether it can live.

[4] Of double sex. See Bikk. 1⁵; 4¹ᶠᶠ.   [5] The eighth day (Lev. 12³).

[6] The principle is, that if the ceremony is not done on the eighth day itself it does not override a Sabbath or Festival-day.

[7] He is not qualified to serve as a priest. Cf. Bekh. 7⁵.

[8] Though this constitutes 'building' something like a tent.

[9] It is work of the nature of sifting (see 7²).

[10] It is permitted on a Festival-day to prepare necessary food (Ex. 12¹⁶; cf., p. 181, n. 11).

[11] Or 'basket of rushes'. Cf. Sot. 2¹; 3¹.

[12] Heb. *lagin*, a jug (of metal or glass) used at a meal (cf. A. Zar. 5⁵).

[13] See p. 207, n. 19.   [14] Heb. *habith*. Such as is used for storage.

into vinegar. And they may not soak vetches or rub them; but they may put them into a sieve or basket. They may not sift chopped straw through a sieve or set it on a high place so that the chaff will fall away, but it may be taken up in a sieve and poured into the feeding-trough.

4. They may clean out [the crib] before a fatted ox and sweep aside [spilt fodder] to protect it from excrement. So R. Dosa. But the Sages forbid it. They may remove fodder from before one beast and put it before another on the Sabbath.

5. A man may not shift about the straw on the bed with his hand but he may shift it about with his body. If it was meant to be cattle fodder or if there was a cushion or sheet over it he may shift it about with his hand. A householder's clothes-press may be loosened [on the Sabbath] but not tightened; and that of washermen may not be touched. R. Judah says: If it was [partly] loosened on the eve of the Sabbath it may be wholly loosened [on the Sabbath] and [garments] extracted from it.[1]

21. 1. A man may lift up[2] his child even though it has a stone in its hand, or a basket even though it contains a stone;[3] and he may move from place to place unclean Heave-offering together with clean [Heave-offering] or common produce. R. Judah says: They may also take out the one part of Heave-offering[4] that is fallen into another hundred parts of common produce.

2. If a stone lay on the mouth of a jar, the jar may be turned on its side so that the stone falls off. If the jar was among other jars[5] it may be lifted up and then turned on its side so that the stone falls off. If there were coins on a cushion the cushion may be shaken so that the coins fall off. If there was filth on it, this may be wiped off with a rag.[6] If the cushion was made of hide,[7] water may be poured over it until the filth disappears.

3. The School of Shammai say: Bones and shells may be taken up from the table [on the Sabbath]. And the School of Hillel say: The entire table must be taken and shaken.[8] Less than an olive's bulk of crumbs, or of pods of chick-peas and lentils, may be removed from the table, since they are cattle fodder. If a sponge has a leather hand-piece they may use it to wipe with [on the Sabbath], but if it has not they may not use it to wipe with. And the Sages say:[9] In either case it can be taken from its place on the Sabbath; and it is not susceptible to uncleanness.[10]

22. 1. If a jar was broken [on the Sabbath] enough [wine] from it may be saved for three meals, and a man may say to others, 'Come and save [wine] for yourselves', provided that they do not soak it up with a sponge.[11] They may not squeeze fruits to press out the juice, and [even] if the juice comes out of itself it is forbidden. R. Judah says: If they were intended to be eaten the juice that comes from them is permitted, but if [they were kept only] for the sake of their juice, the juice that comes from them is forbidden.

---

1 On the principle illustrated in 10[2, 5].
2 In a courtyard validly included within the *Erub* (App. I. 8).
3 But only if the basket is full of fruit, the stone not being the sole contents.
4 See Ter. 4[7].
5 And there was danger of the falling stone breaking other jars.
6 But not with water, which would be the forbidden act of washing (7[2]).
7 Which is not such as is washed with water.
8 Gem. 143a remarks that the teaching of the two Schools was the reverse.
9 The Munich codex omits the concluding sentence.   10 See Kel. 17[13].
11 This would lead to squeezing, which is forbidden under the general head (7[2]) of threshing.

If honeycombs were broken on the eve of the Sabbath and the honey came out of itself [on the Sabbath] it is forbidden. But R. Eliezer permits it.

2. Whatsoever was put into hot water on the eve of the Sabbath may be [again] soaked in hot water on the Sabbath, but what was not put into hot water on the eve of the Sabbath may only be rinsed in hot water on the Sabbath, excepting only old salted fish[1] and Spanish tunny-fish, for which rinsing is the completion of their preparation.

3. A man may broach a jar to eat dried figs therefrom provided that he does not intend to make a utensil of it.[2] They may not pierce the plug of a jar [on the Sabbath]. So R. Judah. But the Sages[3] permit it. They may not pierce it at the side; and if it was pierced already a man may not put wax on it [on the Sabbath] since he would [need to] smooth it over.[4] R. Judah said: Such a case once came before Rabban Johanan b. Zakkai in Arab,[5] and he said: I doubt whether he is not liable to a Sin-offering.

4. They may put a cooked dish in the cistern to preserve it,[6] or put [a vessel containing] fresh water into foul to keep it cool, or cold water into hot to warm it. If a man's clothes dropped into the water while he was on the way, he may go on walking in them without scruple;[7] when he has reached the outermost courtyard [of the town] he may spread them out in the sun, but not in the sight of the people.[8]

5. If a man bathed in the water of a cave or in the water of Tiberias and dried himself, even though it was with ten towels, he may not bring them away in his hand;[9] but if ten men dried themselves with one towel, [wiping] their faces, their hands, and their feet, they may bring the towel away in their hands.[10]

6. They may anoint or rub their stomach[11] but not have themselves kneaded or scraped. They may not go down to Kordima,[12] and they may not use artificial emetics;[13] they may not straighten a [deformed] child's body or set a broken limb. If a man's hand or foot is dislocated he may not pour cold water over it, but he may wash it after his usual fashion, and if he is healed, he is healed.

23. 1. [On the Sabbath] a man may borrow of his fellow jars of wine or jars of oil, provided that he does not say to him, 'Lend[14] me them'; so, too, a woman [may borrow] of her neighbour loaves of bread; and if one does not trust the other, the other may leave his cloak with the lender and make a reckoning with him after the Sabbath. So, too, in Jerusalem on the eve of Passover when it falls on a Sabbath, a man may leave his cloak and take

[1] Variant: 'small salted fish'.
[2] By repairing the broken jar (offending against the principle, 7[2], 'tearing in order to sew'); or to make of the breach a serviceable opening for future use.
[3] Variant: R. Jose.   [4] Offending against the principle of scraping.
[5] See 16[7].   [6] Keep it cool.   [7] That he will be suspected of having washed them.
[8] So exposing himself to suspicion.
[9] From fear of offending against the principle of squeezing out, however little the moisture in them.
[10] So many would keep each other warned of the danger of squeezing (Tif. Yis.).
[11] Some texts omit 'their stomach'.
[12] Text doubtful. Tif. Yis. explains it as the name of a river, with a slippery clay bottom. Bert. reads *Peloma*, πήλωμα, clay. In either case it is forbidden because of the danger of persons falling into the water and afterwards squeezing out their clothes.
[13] According to Gem. 147b 'in the name of R. Johanan', it is forbidden to use a drug (because of the need to crush spices on the Sabbath—Tif. Yis.), but permitted to thrust the finger down the throat to induce vomiting. But according to R. Nehemiah this is forbidden even on a weekday because of its wastefulness.
[14] Implies an agreed transaction valid for a specified time; and there would be a danger lest the transaction should involve writing.

his Passover-lamb and make his reckoning with the seller after the close of the Festival-day.

2. A man may reckon up the number of his guests and his savoury portions[1] by word of mouth but not from what is written down. And he may cast lots with his children and with his household at a meal [for the several portions] provided that he does not intend thereby to allot a large as against a small portion, [which is forbidden] on the grounds of playing dice. They[2] may cast lots on a Festival-day for the Hallowed Things[3] but not for the portions.[4]

3. A man may not hire labourers on the Sabbath or say to his fellow that he should hire labourers for him. They may not go to await nightfall at the Sabbath limit[5] [to be in readiness] to hire labourers or to bring in produce, but a man may do so in order to safeguard produce and [then after nightfall] he may bring back the produce in his hand. Abba Saul laid down a general rule: Whatsoever I may rightly enjoin [as a religious duty], for that I may await nightfall [at the Sabbath limit].

4. They may await nightfall at the Sabbath limit to see to the business of [the reception of] a bride or of [the burial of] a corpse, to fetch its coffin and wrappings. If a gentile brought the flutes on the Sabbath an Israelite may not play dirges on them unless they had been brought from near by. If a coffin had been made [on the Sabbath for a gentile] and a grave dug for him, an Israelite may be buried therein; but if it had been prepared for an Israelite no Israelite may ever be buried therein.

5. They may make ready [on the Sabbath] all that is needful for the dead, and anoint it and wash it, provided that they do not move any member of it. They may draw the mattress away from beneath it and let it lie on sand that it may be the longer preserved; they may bind up the chin, not in order to raise it but that it may not sink lower. So, too, if a rafter is broken they may support it with a bench or with the side-pieces of a bed that the break may grow no greater, but not in order to prop it up.[6] They may not close a corpse's eyes on the Sabbath; nor may they do so on a weekday at the moment when the soul is departing; and he that closes the eyes [of the dying man] at the moment when the soul is departing, such a one is a shedder of blood.

24. 1. If [on the eve of the Sabbath] darkness overtook a man while he was on the way, he must give his purse to a gentile,[7] and if there was no gentile with him he must put it on the ass. When he has reached the outermost courtyard [of the town] he may take off [from the ass] such baggage as can be taken off on the Sabbath, and for what cannot be taken off on the Sabbath he may loosen the cords so that the sacks fall down of themselves.

2. They may loosen bundles of hay in front of cattle and shake loose stalks of fresh rice, but [they may] not [loosen] triply-bound bundles of straw. They may not chop up unripe stalks of corn or carobs in front of small or large cattle. R. Judah permits it with carobs for small cattle.

3. They may not stuff a camel [with food] or cram food into its mouth,

---

[1] Choice viands eaten at the close of a meal. See Ber. 6[5]; (Pes. 10[3]); Ab. 3[19].
[2] Priests in the Temple.   [3] Offered on the Festival-day.   [4] See Betz. 5[7]; Gen. 43[34].
[5] 2,000 cubits from the place where a man lives, beyond which it was forbidden to go on the Sabbath. See Erub. 4[3]; 5[7].   [6] Cf. Shebi. 4[6].
[7] See p. 100, n. 11. A Jew is answerable for his beast's keeping Sabbath (Ex. 20[10]), but not for the gentile's keeping it. Only where there is no gentile should he put it on his own ass.

but they may put food into its mouth [after the usual fashion]; they may not stuff calves [with food against their will], but they may put food into their mouths [after the usual fashion], and they may strew food for the fowls. They may put water into the bran but not knead it; and they may not set water before bees or before doves that are in the dovecots;[1] but they may set it before geese and fowls[2] or Herodian doves.[3]

4. They may chop up gourds for the cattle or a carcase for the dogs. R. Judah says: It is forbidden if it was not already dead on the eve of the Sabbath, since it would not then belong to what was set in readiness [for the Sabbath].

5. They may annul vows[4] on the Sabbath and seek exemption[5] from vows which concern what is needful for the Sabbath. They may stop up a light-hole[6] or measure a piece of stuff[7] or an Immersion-pool.[8] It once happened in the days of the father of R. Zadok and in the days of Abba Saul b. Batnit that [on the Sabbath] they stopped up the light-hole with a pitcher and tied a pot[9] with reed-grass [to a stick] in order to find out if there was in the roofing an opening of one square handbreadth or not.[10] And from their words we learn that on the Sabbath men may shut up, and measure and tie up.

ERUBIN[11] ('THE FUSION OF SABBATH LIMITS')

1. 1. If [the cross-beam above] the alley-entry[12] is higher than twenty cubits it must be made lower. R. Judah says: This is not necessary. If the entry is wider than ten cubits it must be made narrower; yet if it has the shape of a doorway, even though it is wider than ten cubits, it need not be made narrower.

2. To render such an alley-entry valid, the School of Shammai say: [It must have] both side-post and cross-beam. And the School of Hillel say: Either side-post or cross-beam. R. Eliezer says: There should be two side-posts. In the name of R. Ishmael a disciple stated before R. Akiba: The School of Shammai and the School of Hillel did not dispute about an entry less than four cubits [wide], which is valid if it has either side-post or cross-beam;

---

[1] These can find water for themselves.   [2] Which are kept indoors.
[3] Domesticated, indoor doves. Herod is supposed to have bred them. Cf. Hull. 12[1].
[4] A husband or father may annul the vows of a wife or daughter (Num. 30[5, 8,13]; see Ned. 10[1, 8]).   [5] From a Sage. See Ned. 9[1ff].   [6] Cf. 17[7].
[7] To see if it is large enough (three fingerbreadths square) to contract or convey uncleanness. See Kel. 27[1ff].
[8] To see if it measures three cubic cubits, and so will contain forty *seahs*. See Mikw. 1[7] and *passim*.   [9] Measuring a handbreadth.
[10] The commentators explain that there were two houses separated by a passage. The passage was surmounted by a barrel-shaped roof in which was a crack. Windows in each house overlooked the passage. A person in one of the houses was at the point of death. If he died, corpse-uncleanness would pass through the window of that house and it would be conveyed (by means of the common roof over the passage) to the opposite house and enter into it by the window. Therefore they stopped up the window of the second house, and tied a certain-sized pot to a stick and applied it to the breach in the roof, for (see Ohol. 3[6]) if there was a hole a handbreadth square in the roof it would suffice to give egress to the uncleanness and prevent it spreading (cf. p. 649, n. 3).
[11] See App. I. 8. This tractate is a supplement to Shabbath. Its purpose is to define the rules which permit a wider interpretation of the term 'domains' within which it is lawful to move a burden, and to deal with cases when the rule of the 2,000 cubits of a 'Sabbath day's journey' is capable of less rigid application.
[12] What is here dealt with is a rectangular space (alley) having courtyards opening into it on three of its sides, and the fourth side opening into the public road. By constructing at this fourth side an 'alley-entry', in the semblance of a doorway, the alley and the courts opening into it become a single private domain, throughout the whole of which all the occupants have complete freedom of movement on the Sabbath.

but about what did they dispute?—about one whose width was from four to ten cubits, which, according to the School of Shammai, must have both side-post and cross-beam, and, according to the School of Hillel, either side-post or cross-beam. R. Akiba said: They disputed about both cases.

3. The cross-beam of which they spoke must be wide enough to hold a half-brick. Such a half-brick is the half of a brick three handbreadths [square]. It is enough if the cross-beam is one handbreadth wide, such as will hold a half-brick lengthwise.[1]

4. [It must be] wide enough to hold a half-brick and strong enough to hold a half-brick. R. Judah says: Wide enough even if not strong enough.

5. If [the cross-beam] is made of straw or reed it is reckoned as though it was made of metal; if curved it is reckoned as though it was straight; if round it is reckoned as though it was square. Whatsoever is three handbreadths in circumference is one handbreadth in width.[2]

6. The side-posts of which they have spoken must be [at least] ten handbreadths high and their width and thickness aught soever. R. Jose says: They should be three handbreadths wide.

7. They may make the side-posts out of anything, even out of a thing that has life. But R. Jose forbids this. It[3] can convey uncleanness [if it is used] as the stone that seals a tomb.[4] But R. Meir declares it not susceptible to uncleanness. They may write thereon a woman's bill of divorce.[5] But for this R. Jose the Galilean declares it invalid.

8. If a caravan encamped in a valley and was surrounded by [a fence made from] the trappings of the cattle, they may move aught about therein, provided that the fence is ten handbreadths high and that the gaps therein are not more than the built-up parts. Any gap [not more than] ten cubits wide is permitted, since it serves as a doorway; but if wider than this it is forbidden.

9. They may surround [the camp] with three [circles of] ropes, the one above the other, provided that between each rope the space is less than three handbreadths. The size of the ropes, their [total] thickness, must be more than one handbreadth, so that the whole [barrier] shall be ten handbreadths [high].

10. They may surround [the camp] with reeds provided that the space between them is less than three handbreadths.[6] [In all this] they have spoken [only] of a caravan. So R. Judah. But the Sages say: They have spoken of a caravan [only] as of an actual case. Any partition that has not both warp and woof[7] is not accounted a partition. So R. Jose b. R. Judah. But the Sages say: One alone of the two [suffices]. Four things have they permitted to men that are in a camp: they may fetch wood from any place, they are exempt from the washing of hands,[8] from the laws of *demai*-produce,[9] and from preparing *Erub*.[10]

2. 1. Around wells[11] [upright] boards must be set up: four corner-pieces having the appearance of eight [single boards]. So R. Judah. R. Meir

---

[1] The length of the half-brick running the length of the cross-beam. A variant reading is 'such as will contain (i.e. support) the breadth of the half-brick'. The meaning is the same.
[2] Approximately.
[3] If a living animal (which is not susceptible to uncleanness) should be used to cover up the entrance to a tomb.   [4] See Ohol. 2⁴; 15⁹.   [5] See Gitt. 2³.
[6] Cf. Kil. 4⁴.   [7] i.e. it must be made both with upright and with horizontal reeds.
[8] Before eating.   [9] App. I. 6.
[10] They may shift goods from tent to tent without making *Erub* to combine them into a single domain for the Sabbath.
[11] Which are in the public domain. By being enclosed by a square, however slightly defined, a certain area around them is given the semblance and status of a private domain, so enabling their use by cattle on the Sabbath.

says: Eight boards having the appearance of twelve, four being corner-pieces and four single. They must be ten handbreadths high, six wide, and their thickness may be aught soever, while between them there must be space enough for two teams of three oxen each (so R. Meir; R. Judah says: Four oxen each) brought closely together and not widely apart, so that one team can enter in while the other goes out.

2. The boards may be brought close to the well provided that the head and the greater part of a cow shall be within [the enclosure] when it drinks. They may be shifted back any distance [from the well] provided that the number of the boards is increased.

3. R. Judah says: [They may be removed] only so far as to leave two *seahs'* space.[1] They replied: The measure of two *seahs'* space has been prescribed only in what concerns a garden or an outer area;[2] but in what concerns a cattle-pen or fold or store-yard[3] or courtyard, five or even ten *kors'* space[4] is permitted; [therefore here, too, the boards] may be shifted back any distance provided that the number of the boards is increased.

4. R. Judah says: If a public path passed through them it should be diverted. But the Sages say: This is not necessary. It is all one whether it is a public cistern or a public well or a private well: they may be encompassed by the like boards; but a private cistern must be surrounded by a partition-wall ten handbreadths high. So R. Akiba. But R. Judah b. Baba says: Boards are set up around a public well only, while around all the others a girdle is set up ten handbreadths high.

5. R. Judah b. Baba moreover said: Within a garden or outer area [not more than] seventy cubits and two-thirds square,[5] surrounded by a wall ten handbreadths high, aught may be carried about[6] provided that there is in it a watchman's hut or a dwelling-place or that it is close to the town. R. Judah says: Even if there is naught save a cistern or pit or cavern they may carry aught about therein. R. Akiba says: Even if there is none of these they may carry aught about therein provided that it is seventy cubits and two-thirds square. R. Eliezer says: If its length is more than its breadth even by a single cubit they may not carry aught about therein. R. Jose says: Even if its length is twice its breadth they may carry aught about therein.

6. R. Ilai said: I heard from R. Eliezer: Even if it contains as much as one *kor's* space.[7] I also heard from him that if one of the occupants of the courtyard forgot to prepare *Erub*[8] it is forbidden to him to take aught in or out of his house, but permitted to the others. I also heard from him that men can fulfil their obligation[9] at Passover by [eating] even hart's-tongue; and I went around among all his disciples and sought a fellow-[disciple][10] and found none.

---

[1] App. II, E. See Lev. 27[16]; 1 Kings 18[32]. It is an area equal to the forecourt of the Tabernacle (Ex. 27[18]), 100 cubits by 50, and such as can be sown over with two *seahs* of seed.

[2] Heb. *karpaf*. An enclosure outside a settlement and enclosed for storing wood or the like, but not made to be inhabited.   [3] Or rearcourt.

[4] From 375,000 to 750,000 sq. cubits. One *kor* equals 30 *seahs*.

[5] Given as the approximate square root of 5,000 sq. cubits, or 'two *seahs'* space'. The error is slight. See also 5[2, 3].

[6] i.e. it is deemed 'private domain' as distinct from *karmelith*, which is neither public domain nor private domain.   [7] 75,000 sq. cubits.

[8] See below, 6[3].   [9] To eat bitter herbs. Ex. 12[8].

[10] One who could support the testimony. Cf. Ab. 1[6]; Yeb. 16[7].

3. 1. *Erub*[1] and *Shittuf*[2] may be made from any food[3] save water or salt. Any food may be bought with [Second] Tithe money[4] save water or salt. If a man vowed to abstain[5] from food he is still allowed water or salt. They may prepare *Erub* for a Nazirite with wine, and for a non-priest with Heave-offering[6] (Symmachos says: With common produce [alone]). [They may prepare it] for a priest in a Grave-area.[7] R. Judah says: Even in a grave-yard, since he can go and make himself a partition[8] and so eat [in cleanness].

2. They may prepare *Erub* with *demai*-produce,[9] with First Tithe from which Heave-offering has been given,[10] with Second Tithe or dedicated produce which have been redeemed (and priests [may prepare *Erub*] with Dough-offering[11] or Heave-offering);[12] but not with untithed produce or First Tithe from which Heave-offering has not been given, or Second Tithe or dedicated produce which have not been redeemed. If a man sent his *Erub* by the hand of a deaf-mute, an imbecile, or a minor, or by the hand of one that does not admit the lawfulness of *Erub*,[13] the *Erub* is not valid; but if he had told another to receive it from him, then the *Erub* is valid.

3. If he put it on a tree higher then ten handbreadths, his *Erub* is not valid, but if lower than ten handbreadths, it is valid. If he put it in a cistern, even a hundred cubits deep, his *Erub* is valid. If he put it on the end of a reed or on the end of a stick that had been uprooted and thrust in [the ground], even though it is a hundred cubits high, the *Erub* is valid. If he put it in a cupboard and shut it up and the key was lost, the *Erub* is valid. R. Eliezer says: Unless he knows that the key is in its place the *Erub* is not valid.

4. If while it was yet day[14] it rolled beyond the Sabbath limit, or if a heap [of stones] fell on it, or if it was burnt, or if, being Heave-offering, it contracted uncleanness,[15] the *Erub* is not valid; but if the like mishap befell it after nightfall the *Erub* is valid; and if it is in doubt, R. Meir and R. Judah say: It is like the ass-driver and camel-driver.[16] R. Jose and R. Simeon say: Where there is doubt concerning *Erub* it is deemed valid. R. Jose said: Abtolemos in the name of five elders testified of an *Erub* about which there was doubt, that it is deemed valid.

5. A man may make conditions[17] about his *Erub* and say, 'If gentiles[18] come from the east let my *Erub* be to the west; if from the west, let my *Erub* be to the east; if from both sides let me go to which side I will; if they come from neither side, let me be as the people of my town';[19] [or]

---

[1] App. I. 8. Here, and in the following two chapters, the *Erub* (commingling, fusing) of Sabbath limits is intended. See below, 8[1, 2]. '*Erub* of courtyards' is effected with a loaf only; see 7[10].

[2] App. I. 39. The 'association of alley-ways'—creating a right of unrestricted access in the associated courtyards and alley-ways.　　　　　[3] See below, 7[10].

[4] Deut. 14[22ff]. See M.Sh. 1[5].　　　　　[5] Cf. Ned. 6[1ff].; 7[1ff].

[6] Though not fit for him it is fit for others. For the Nazirite see Num. 6[2], and for Heave-offering see App. I. 48, *Terumah*.

[7] See Ohol. 17[1ff].　　　　[8] See Ohol. 8[1ff].　　　　[9] App. I. 6.

[10] The levite must give to the priest as Heave-offering a tithe from the tithe ('First Tithe') which he, the levite, has received.　　　[11] Num. 15[20]; p. 83, n. 1.

[12] Some texts omit the bracketed sentence.　　　[13] A Samaritan or a Sadducee.

[14] Before sunset on Friday evening.

[15] Therefore unfit for food for any one, even a priest.

[16] He is unable to decide whether he has acquired right to move 2,000 cubits in any direction from the point where the Erub was laid down, or whether he has only right to move within 2,000 cubits of his home; just so a man who leads a camel and an ass cannot progress, since the ass will only move if urged from behind, and a camel if led from before.

[17] He lays down two *Erubs*, one at the Sabbath limit to the east and one at the Sabbath limit to the west, leaving it conditional which he shall abide by.

[18] Taxgatherers (Tif. Yis.).　　　[19] With the right to go 2,000 cubits in any direction.

'If a Sage comes from the east let my *Erub* be to the east; if from the west let my *Erub* be to the west; if one comes from both sides let me go to which side I will; if none comes from either side let me be as the people of my town'. R. Judah says: If one of them was his teacher, he should go to his teacher; if both were his teachers, he may go to which side he will.

6. R. Eliezer says: On a Festival-day next to a Sabbath, whether before it or after it, a man may prepare two *Erubs* and say, 'Let my *Erub* for the first day be to the east and that for the second to the west', [or] 'Let my first be to the west and the second to the east', [or] 'Let my *Erub* [be valid] for the first day, and for the second [let me be] as the people of my town', [or] 'Let my *Erub* [be valid] for the second day, and for the first [let me be] as the people of my town'. But the Sages say: He prepares *Erub* for one direction or it is no *Erub* at all;[1] he prepares *Erub* for both days or it is no *Erub* at all. What must he do [that the *Erub* shall be valid for two days]? On the first day he that brings [the food] waits over it until nightfall[2] when he takes it and goes his way;[3] on the second day he [takes it to the Sabbath limit and] waits over it until nightfall and then eats it; thus he secures the benefit both of his journeying and of his *Erub*.[4] If [the food] is eaten on the first day it serves as *Erub* for the first day but not for the second. R. Eliezer said: Ye agree with me that they are accounted two [distinct] times of holiness.

7. R. Judah says: If at the New Year a man feared that [the month] might be intercalated,[5] he may prepare two *Erubs* and say, 'Let my *Erub* for the first day be to the east and that for the second day to the west', [or] 'Let that for the first day be to the west and that for the second to the east', [or] 'Let my *Erub* [be valid] for the first day, and for the second let me be as the people of my town', [or] 'Let my *Erub* [be valid] for the second day, and for the first let me be as the people of my town'. But the Sages did not agree with him.[6]

8. Moreover R. Judah said: A man may make conditions about a basket [of fruit][7] on a first Festival-day and eat it on the second. So, too, an egg[8] laid on the first day may be eaten on the second. But the Sages did not agree with him.

9. R. Dosa b. Harkinas says: He that goes before the Ark[9] on the first Festival-day of the New Year says: 'Give us strength, O Lord our God, this first day of the month, whether it be to-day or to-morrow'; and on the morrow he says, ' . . . whether it be to-day or yesterday'. But the Sages did not agree with him.

---

[1] In opposition to R. Eliezer the Sages regard the two days as a single unit; just as for the Sabbath one *Erub* cannot be valid for the first half of the day and another for the second half, so, too, when the holy period extends over two days.

[2] After which (see 3[4]) it is effective for the whole of the day which then begins.

[3] Back to his home, and preserves it for the following evening.

[4] For if the *Erub* had been lost the first day he would, for the second day, have lacked both the *Erub* and the right of journeying beyond the Sabbath limit.

[5] See R.Sh. 3[1]. In cases of such delay of evidence of the appearance of the new moon, the Court added another day to Elul, the last month of the year. The New Year feast was then observed both on the 30th of Elul and the 1st of Tishri.

[6] They ruled that the two days counted as a single continuous sacred period.

[7] Of untithed produce. Gem. 39b explains: On the first day he says, If to-day is not holy let this produce be Heave-offering for the rest; and if to-day is holy let my words be void, since Tithe and Heave-offering may not be set apart on a holy day. The next day he says, If yesterday was holy and to-day not holy, let what I yesterday designated Heave-offering be Heave-offering for the rest, and if to-day is holy and yesterday was not holy, it is in anywise Heave-offering. And he may then eat of the tithed produce and leave aside the Heave-offering.   [8] See Betz. 1[1].   [9] Cf. Ber. 5[3].

4. 1. If a man was taken out [beyond the Sabbath limit] by gentiles or an evil spirit, he may only move within four cubits. If they brought him back again it is as though he had never gone out. If they brought him to another town, or set him in a cattle-pen or a cattle-fold, Rabban Gamaliel and R. Eleazar b. Azariah say: He may traverse their whole [area]; but R. Joshua and R. Akiba say: He may only move within four cubits. It happened when they came from Brundisium[1] and when their ship was sailing in the sea, that Rabban Gamaliel and R. Eleazar b. Azariah walked the whole length of the ship, but R. Joshua and R. Akiba did not stir beyond four cubits, since they were minded to apply to themselves the more stringent ruling.

2. Once they did not enter into the harbour until nightfall [on Friday]. They said to Rabban Gamaliel, 'Is it permissible for us to land?' He answered, 'It is permitted; for I have already made observation,[2] and we were within the Sabbath limit before nightfall'.

3. If a man went out [beyond the Sabbath limit] on a permissible errand[3] and it was then told him that the [needful] act had been done already, he has the right to move within two thousand cubits in any direction; if he was within the Sabbath limit it is as though he had not gone forth; for whosoever goes out to deliver [one that is in danger] may return to his place [of starting].

4. If a man sat down while on a journey [on the eve of the Sabbath] and rose up [after nightfall] and saw that he was near to a town,[4] since it had not been his intention[5] he may not enter the town. So R. Meir. But R. Judah says: He may enter. R. Judah said: It once happened that R. Tarfon entered [a town in like case] although it had not been his intention [to pass the Sabbath there].

5. If a man fell asleep while on a journey and knew not that night had fallen, he may move within two thousand cubits in any direction. So R. Johanan b. Nuri. But the Sages say: He may only move within four cubits. R. Eliezer says: Himself being in the middle of them. R. Judah says: He may walk in any direction he will. And R. Judah agrees that when once he has chosen [his direction] he may not go back on it.

6. If there were two persons whose [limits of four] cubits in part overlapped one another, they may bring [their food] and eat it in the middle, provided that the one does not put forth what belongs to him into the space pertaining [only] to his fellow. If there were three persons and [the limit of] the middle person was wholly overlapped by [the limit of] the two others, he is permitted [to eat] with them or they with him, but not the two outer persons with each other. R. Simeon said: To what can it be likened? It is like to three courtyards opening the one into the other, and also opening into the public domain. If the two [outer] courtyards made *Erub* with that in the middle, it is permitted access to them and they to it; but the two outer courtyards are forbidden access the one to the other.

7. If a man was on a journey and darkness overtook him,[6] and he recognized a tree or a fence[7] and said, 'Let my Sabbath resting-place be

---

[1] Brindisi. See *J. E.* v. 560 on the journey of these four on a mission to Rome. Cf. M.Sh. 5[9]; Shab. 16[8].
[2] With some simple telescopic device (Gem. 43b) for the calculation of distances. On Rabban Gamaliel's astronomical knowledge cf. R.Sh. 2[8].
[3] e.g. to bear witness of the appearance of the new moon, or to save life. Cf. below, 8[1].
[4] Within the Sabbath limit.   [5] Of spending Sabbath in that town.
[6] Variant: And he feared lest darkness should overtake him.
[7] Which he could reach before nightfall, but he was weary and wished to rest where he was (Bert.).

under it', he has said nothing;[1] [but if he said], 'Let my Sabbath resting-place be at its root', he may walk from where he stands to its root [up to a distance of] two thousand cubits, and from its root to his house [up to a distance of] two thousand cubits. Thus he can travel four thousand cubits after it has become dark.

8. If he does not recognize [any like landmark] or is not skilled in *Halakah*,[2] and he says, 'Let my Sabbath resting-place be where I stand', his position gives him right to travel within two thousand cubits in any direction as [though he was within] a circle. So R. Hananiah b. Antigonus. But the Sages say: As [though he was within] a square, like a square tablet, so that he wins the benefit of the corners.

9. This it is of which they have said, 'The poor man makes *Erub* with his feet'.[3] R. Meir said: We are concerned with the poor man only. R. Judah says: It is all one whether it is a poor man or a rich man, for they have only enjoined that *Erub* is made with bread so that it shall be easier for the rich man and that he need not himself go out and make *Erub* with his feet.

10. If a man went out [with the *Erub* food] to go to another town[4] with which [the people of his town] were making *Erub*, and his fellow induced him to return, he himself is permitted to go [to the other town on the Sabbath] but all the [other] people of his town are forbidden. So R. Judah. R. Meir says: Whosoever could have made *Erub* and did not do so, it is like the ass-driver and the camel-driver.[5]

11. If a man went out beyond the Sabbath limit, even a single cubit, he may not enter again. R. Eliezer says: If [he went out a distance of] two cubits he may enter again, but if three he may not. If darkness overtook a man when only one cubit outside the Sabbath limit he may not enter within it. R. Simeon says: Even if [he was] fifteen cubits [outside] he may enter in, since the surveyors do not measure exactly,[6] for the sake of them that act in error.

5. 1. How can the confines of a town be extended? If [among the outermost houses] one house recedes and another projects, if part of the town wall recedes and part projects, or if there are ruins ten handbreadths high or bridges or tomb-monuments[7] in which is a dwelling-chamber, the limits of the town are extended so that it shall contain them, and [the area of the town is] shaped like to a square tablet, so that it wins the benefit of the corners.

2. An outer area[8] is added to the town. So R. Meir. But the Sages say: They have prescribed an outer area only as between two towns: if to the one [was added a further space of] seventy cubits and two-thirds [and these would then adjoin one another], they may add an outer area for each town, so that they become as one.

[1] He must specify a spot confined within four cubits.   [2] App. I. 11.

[3] Since he cannot send another to set down bread at the Sabbath limit.

[4] 4,000 cubits away. The two towns would then by means of *Erub* be within Sabbath range of one another.

[5] It is in doubt. See 3[4]. He may have right to profit like the poor man, from having specified the place which he intended to use as his Sabbath base, or he may be restricted like his fellow-townsmen to 2,000 cubits from his home.

[6] They mark out the Sabbath limit within the 2,000 cubits for safety's sake, 'to keep a man far from transgression'.

[7] Shek. 2[5]; Ohol. 7[1]. Such as the structure east of Jerusalem known as the Tomb of Absalom, which contains such a chamber as is here mentioned.

[8] See 2[3]. The 2,000 cubits, according to R. Meir, begin from the bounds of this outer area. But according to the Sages it begins immediately at the actual confines of the town.

3. So, too, if three villages were arranged trianglewise, and between the two outermost[1] there was a distance of one hundred and forty-one cubits and a third, the middle village causes the three of them to be reckoned as one.[2]

4. They may measure only with a rope fifty cubits long, neither less nor more; and a man may only measure [while holding the end of the rope] over against his heart. If in his measuring he reached a rift or a wall he must take count only of the horizontal span and continue measuring. If he reached a hill he must take the horizontal span [only], and continue measuring, provided that he does not go outside the Sabbath limit.[3] If he cannot span it [with the rope]—in this case R. Dositheus b. R. Yannai said in the name of R. Meir: I have heard that they bore through[4] hills.

5. They may only measure at the hand of one that is skilled. If his measure in one place exceeded his measure in another, the greater measure is observed. If one measured a greater distance and another measured a lesser distance, the greater distance is observed. Even a bondman and even a bondwoman may be believed when they say,[5] 'Thus far is the Sabbath limit', since the Sages have not enjoined the rule of the Sabbath limit for the sake of stringency but for the sake of leniency.

6. If a town[6] having a single owner was made into a town having many owners it can all be included in a single *Erub*; but if a town having many owners was made into a town having a single owner it may not be included in a single *Erub* unless there was a residue outside it,[7] like the town of Hadashah in Judea, wherein are fifty inhabitants. So R. Judah. R. Simeon says: Three courtyards having each two houses.

7. If [on the Sabbath] a man was in the east and he had said to his son [on the eve of the Sabbath], 'Make me *Erub* to the west', or if he was in the west and he had said to his son, 'Make me *Erub* to the east', and the distance between him and his house was two thousand cubits, and between him and his *Erub* more than this, [the road] to his house is permitted, but that to his *Erub* is forbidden. If the distance to his *Erub* was two thousand cubits, and that to his house more than this, [the way] to his house is forbidden and that to his *Erub* permitted. If a man put his *Erub* within the confines[8] of the city, he has done nothing. If he put it even a cubit beyond the limit [of the city's confines] he loses [in one direction] what he gains [in another].

8. The people of a large town may traverse the whole of a small town;[9] but the people of a small town may not[10] traverse the whole of a large town.[11]

---

[1] Those at the ends of the longest side of the triangle.

[2] e.g. the village *A* forming the triangle's apex (if less than 2,000 cubits from either of the others) is to be regarded as placed between the two, *B* and *C*, at the base. If then between *A* and *B* and between *A* and *C* the distance (disregarding the contained area of the villages) is not more than 141⅓ cubits in either case, the three can be considered one (Tif. Yis.).

[3] Lest they that see him suppose the limit to extend thus far.

[4] Metaphorical for taking the net horizontal distance. Gem. 58b explains how in measuring over a steep incline they used a short rope, one man holding one end to his heart and another, higher up, holding it horizontally at foot-level; the process is then continued through the entire incline. [5] Cf. Ket. 2[10].

[6] The subject is suddenly changed from the *Erub* of Sabbath limits to the *Erub* of courtyards and streets within a town.

[7] So that it shall not be forgotten that only by means of *Erub* is it permissible to move burdens from house to house or from courtyard to courtyard.

[8] Within the seventy cubits and two-thirds of the 'outer area'.

[9] All of which falls within the large town's Sabbath limit.

[10] Omitted in some texts.

[11] But only (unless they have made *Erub*) to the limit of their 2,000 cubits.

Thus[1] if a man was in a large town and he put his *Erub* in a small town, or if he was in a small town and he put his *Erub* in a large town, he may walk through the whole of it and two thousand cubits beyond. R. Akiba says: He may walk only within two thousand cubits from the place of his *Erub*.

9. R. Akiba said to them: Do ye not agree with me that if a man put his *Erub* in a cave he can only walk within two thousand cubits from his *Erub*? They replied: This applies if none dwelt therein; but if any dwelt therein he may walk through the whole of it and two thousand cubits beyond. Thus it is less stringent for him within the cave than [if he had put his *Erub*] above it. As to the measurer of whom they have spoken, he is allowed only two thousand cubits, even if the end of his allotted measure expires in a cave.

6. 1. If a man lived in the same courtyard with a gentile or with one that does not admit [the lawfulness of] *Erub*,[2] this restricts him [from the use of the courtyard].[3] R. Eliezer b. Jacob says: He can never suffer restriction unless it is two Israelites that restrict each other.

2. Rabban Gamaliel said: A Sadducee once lived with us in the same alley in Jerusalem and my father[4] said to us, 'Hasten and put out all the [needful] vessels in the alley before he brings out[5] [his vessels] and so restricts you'. R. Judah recounts [the tradition] in other fashion: 'Hasten and do what is needful[6] in the alley, before [the eve of Sabbath] is ended and he so restricts you'.

3. If one of them that lived in the courtyard forgot to take part in the *Erub*, his house is forbidden both to him and to them for taking [a burden] in or out; but their houses are permitted both to him and to them. If they had given him right of access to their houses he is permitted [to take aught in and out of his house and the courtyard] but they are forbidden. If there were two [that forgot], each restricts the other, since one person can give and one person can take the right of access; whereas two can give the right but not take the right.

4. When can they give right of access? The School of Shammai say: While it is yet day. And the School of Hillel say: After it has become dark. If a man had granted the right of access and then took aught out, whether by error or wantonly, this restricts [the other]. So R. Meir. R. Judah says: If wantonly, it restricts; but if in error, it does not restrict.

5. If a householder was a jointholder with his neighbours,[7] with the one in wine and with the other in wine, they need not make *Erub*; but if he was a jointholder with one in wine and with the other in oil, they must make *Erub*. R. Simeon says: In neither case need they make *Erub*.

---

[1] But it does not proceed to an explanation of what goes before. Gem. 61a points out that there is a lacuna here, and that (keeping the 'not' of the previous sentence, and omitting 'thus') we should read: 'This applies only to him who measures the Sabbath limit, but if a man...'. This accounts for the reference to the 'measurer' in the next paragraph.
[2] See above, 3².
[3] Some texts add: 'So R. Meir'. The courtyard space is held in common by the surrounding householders. Unless by means of *Erub* they all combine to form a single 'family', making the whole, houses and courtyard, into a single domain, the householders are 'restricted' in that they cannot move anything from the house into the courtyard, or from the courtyard into the house. If one of the householders is a gentile the others must, for the Sabbath, rent from him his right in the courtyard.   [4] Rabban Simeon b. Gamaliel.
[5] Thereby asserting his own right. The Sadducee is to be reckoned with as a dissentient Jew.   [6] Pay him rent for his right in the courtyard. He is to be regarded as a gentile.
[7] e.g. if they all possessed a stock of wine in common.

6. If five companies kept the Sabbath in the same eating-hall,[1] the School of Shammai say: *Erub* is needful for each company.[2] And the School of Hillel say: One *Erub* suffices for all. But they agree that if some of them occupied rooms or upper chambers,[3] an *Erub* is needful for each company.

7. If brothers[4] ate at their father's table but slept in their own houses,[5] *Erub* is needful for each. Therefore if one of them forgot to take part in the *Erub* he must forego his right. This applies when their *Erub* is taken to some other place; but if the *Erub* is brought to them, or if they alone occupy the courtyard, they need not make *Erub*.

8. If there were five courtyards opening into each other and also opening into the alley,[6] and they made *Erub* in the courtyards[7] but did not make *Shittuf* in the alley, they are unrestricted in the courtyards but restricted in the alley; but if they made *Shittuf* in the alley they are unrestricted in both. If they made *Erub* in the courtyards and *Shittuf* in the alley, but one of the occupants of a courtyard forgot to take part in the *Erub*, they are [still] unrestricted[8] in both. If one of the occupants of the alley forgot to take part in the *Shittuf*, they are unrestricted in the courtyards but restricted in the alley, since the alley to the courtyards is as the courtyard to the houses.

9. If there were two courtyards one within the other[9] and [the occupants of] the inner one made *Erub* but not [they of] the outer one, the inner one is unrestricted but the outer one is restricted. If the outer one made *Erub* but not the inner one, both are restricted. If they each made *Erub* for themselves, each is unrestricted as regards themselves. R. Akiba restricts the outer courtyard since the right of thoroughfare restricts it. But the Sages say: The right of thoroughfare does not restrict it.

10. If an occupant of the outer courtyard forgot to take part in the *Erub*, the inner courtyard is unrestricted but the outer one is restricted. If an occupant of the inner courtyard forgot to take part in the *Erub* they are both restricted. If they made their *Erub* in the same place, and an occupant of either the inner or the outer courtyard forgot to take part in the *Erub*, they are both restricted. But if each courtyard has but a single owner they do not need to make *Erub* [with one another].

7. 1. If there was a window [in the dividing wall] between two courtyards four handbreadths square and within ten handbreadths [from the ground], they may make *Erub* singly or, if they wish, they may make *Erub* jointly. If the window was less than four handbreadths square, or higher than ten handbreadths, they must make *Erub* singly and may not make *Erub* jointly.

2. If there was a wall between two courtyards, ten handbreadths high and four thick, they must make *Erub* singly and may not make *Erub* jointly. If produce was found thereon, they may climb up on either side and eat thereof provided that they do not bring it down. If there was a gap in the wall less than ten cubits, they may make *Erub* singly or if they will

---

[1] *Triclinium*. See B.B. 6[4]. Explained as a large room subdivided into cubicles, one to each company, each cubicle having separate access to the courtyard.

[2] i.e. each company must contribute towards providing the loaf for the *Erub*.

[3] Wholly isolated.   [4] Some texts add: 'that were jointholders'.

[5] Within the same courtyard,   [6] See p. 121, n. 12.   [7] Rendering all five a unity.

[8] He has still a share in the *Shittuf*. The *Erub* in the courtyards is not essential when *Shittuf* of the alleys has been prepared. See 7[9].

[9] The outer one opening into the public domain and the inner one having right of way through the outer one.

they may make *Erub* jointly, since it is, as it were, a doorway. If the gap was greater they may make *Erub* jointly and need not make *Erub* singly.

3. If there was a trench between two courtyards, ten handbreadths deep and four wide, they must make *Erub* singly and may not make *Erub* jointly, even though it was filled up with straw or chopped hay. If it was filled up with earth or small stones they may make *Erub* jointly and need not make *Erub* singly.

4. If a board was set across it, four handbreadths wide (so, too, if there were two balconies opposite one another[1]), they may make *Erub* singly or if they will they may make *Erub* jointly. But if the board was narrower they must make *Erub* singly and may not make *Erub* jointly.

5. If a heap of straw, ten handbreadths high, separated the two court-yards they must make *Erub* singly and may not make *Erub* jointly. These may feed their cattle from the one side and the others from the other side. If the [heap of] straw was reduced to less than ten handbreadths, they may make *Erub* jointly and need not make *Erub* singly.

6. How do they prepare *Shittuf* in the alley?[2] One sets down a jar[3] and says, 'This belongs to all the occupants of the alley', and he may thus grant possession to them through a man's son or daughter that are of age, or through his Hebrew bondman or bondwoman, or his wife; but he may not thus grant possession through a man's son or daughter that are minors or through his Canaanite bondman or bondmaid, since their hand is as his hand.

7. If the food [in the jar] has grown less than the prescribed quantity he must add to it and grant possession [to the others of this also]; but he need not repeat the declaration; but if the occupants of the alley become more in number, he must add more to the food and grant them possession and repeat the declaration.

8. What is the prescribed quantity? When the people are many, there should be enough for two meals for each one;[4] When they are few, a dried fig's bulk (such as it is lawful to carry out on the Sabbath) for each one.

9. R. Jose says: This applies only when the *Erub* is first prepared; but for what is afterward added to the *Erub* the quantity may be aught soever, since they have only spoken of making *Erub* in the courtyards so that the children should not be suffered to forget.

10. *Erub* or *Shittuf* may be made from any food save water or salt. So R. Eliezer. R. Joshua says: A [whole] loaf is the [proper] *Erub*;[5] a baking of one *seah*[6] of flour, if but part of a loaf, may not be used for *Erub*. A loaf costing one *issar*,[7] if it is a whole loaf, may be used for *Erub*.

11. A man may give a *maah*[8] to a wine-seller or a baker to secure for him a share in an *Erub*. So R. Eliezer. But the Sages say: His money [alone] cannot secure for him a share.[9] But they agree that with any others[10] his money can secure for him a share. Moreover none may make *Erub* for another save only with his consent. R. Judah said: This applies only to *Erub* of Sabbath limits; but for the *Erub* of courtyards they may make *Erub* with or without his consent, since they may act to another's advantage in his absence, but not to his disadvantage in his absence.[11]

---

[1] And a board connected them.

[2] To form, for purposes of the Sabbath, a single domain of the street and courtyards opening into it.   [3] Containing any food, excepting water or salt (see above, 3[1]).

[4] Defined as eighteen times the bulk of a dried fig.   [5] Of courtyards.

[6] App. II, D.   [7] App. II, A.   [8] App. II, A.

[9] Payment of money is not enough to secure title to property. See p. 353, n. 1.

[10] If he had so spoken to any excepting bakers.   [11] Cf. Gitt. 1[6].

8. 1. How do they prepare *Shittuf* at the Sabbath limits? They set down a jar and say, 'Let this be for all the people of my town, for any that would go to a house of mourning or to a house of feasting'.[1] All that accept it while it is yet day, to them it is permitted; but if [they accept it only] after nightfall, to them it is forbidden, since none may make *Erub* after nightfall.

2. What is its prescribed quantity? Food for two meals for each one: fare such as he would eat on weekdays and not on the Sabbath.[2] So R. Meir. But R. Judah says: Such as he would eat on a Sabbath and not on weekdays. And they were each minded to give the more lenient ruling. R. Johanan b. Beroka says: [Not less than] one loaf worth a *pondion*[3] from wheat costing one *sela*[3] for four *seahs*.[4] R. Simeon says: Two-thirds of a loaf of [a size] three to the *kab*.[5] The half of it [is the quantity prescribed] in what concerns a house afflicted with leprosy,[6] and the half of its half [is the quantity which, if unclean,] renders the body unfit [to consume Heave-offering].[7]

3. If they that dwell in a courtyard and they that dwell in the gallery [above the courtyard] forgot to make *Erub*, then what is higher than ten handbreadths pertains to the gallery, and what is lower than this to the courtyard. A bank around a cistern, or a stone, if higher than ten handbreadths,[8] pertains to the gallery; but if lower than this, to the courtyard. This applies only to what adjoins [the gallery]; if it is separate, even if higher than ten handbreadths, it pertains to the courtyard. And what is that which 'adjoins'? Aught that is not farther than four handbreadths.

4. If a man put his *Erub*[9] in a gate-house, portico, or gallery, it is not a [valid] *Erub*; and none that dwells therein can restrict him. [If he put it] in a straw-shed or cattle-shed or wood-shed or store-house, it is a [valid] *Erub*, and one that dwells therein can restrict him. R. Judah says: If the householder has there a right of storage, the other cannot restrict him.

5. If a man left his house and went to keep Sabbath in another town, whether he was a gentile or an Israelite, [his house] restricts [the other occupants of the courtyard].[10] So R. Meir. R. Judah says: It does not restrict.[11] R. Jose says: [The empty house of] a gentile restricts, but [that of] an Israelite does not restrict, since it is not the custom of an Israelite to return on the Sabbath. R. Simeon says: Even if he left his house and went to keep the Sabbath with his daughter in the same town, it does not restrict, since he has already banished from his mind [the intention of returning].

6. If there was a cistern between two courtyards [which had not made *Erub*], they may not draw water therefrom[12] on the Sabbath unless they had made for it a partition[13] ten handbreadths high, either above or[14] below[15] or [only] within its rim.[16] Rabban Simeon b. Gamaliel says: The School of Shammai say, Below, and the School of Hillel say, Above. R. Judah said: The partition should not be higher than the wall that is between the courtyards.

---

[1] Usually has the sense of wedding feast.   [2] Cf. Kel. 17[11]   [3] App. II, A.
[4] Cf. Peah 8[7].   [5] App. II, D.   [6] See Neg. 13[9]. Cf. Ker. 3[3].
[7] This was one of the eighteen stringent decrees mentioned in Shab. 1[4] as enjoined through the influence of the School of Shammai.   [8] Cf. Shab. 11[2].   [9] Of courtyards.
[10] Since they have not made *Erub* jointly with him. Though empty, his house must still be taken account of, since he may return on the Sabbath to occupy it.
[11] No account need be taken of an empty house.
[12] Since each would be taking water out of the other's domain, since half the well counts as outside each courtyard.   [13] Marking the line of division between the courtyards.
[14] Some texts omit 'above or'.   [15] Reaching one handbreadth below surface level.
[16] And not touching the water. The reading 'above' is thus superfluous.

7. If a water-channel[1] passed through the courtyard they may not draw therefrom on the Sabbath unless they had made for it a partition ten handbreadths high at its coming in and at its going out. R. Judah says: The wall above it is deemed the partition. R. Judah said: It happened with a water-channel in Abel that they used to draw from it on the Sabbath by the consent of the Elders. But the Sages replied: That was because it was not of the prescribed size.[2]

8. If there was a balcony[3] above the water, they may not draw from it on the Sabbath unless they had made for it a partition[4] ten handbreadths high either above or below. So, too, if there were two balconies one above the other: if they had made [a partition] for the upper one but not for the lower one,[5] both are forbidden [to draw water] until they have made *Erub*.

9. They may not pour out water on the Sabbath into a courtyard whose area is less than four cubits[6] unless they had made a cavity holding two *seahs*,[7] from the opening downwards,[8] whether it was outside or inside [the courtyard]; save only that if it was outside it must be covered over, but if inside it need not be covered over.

10. R. Eliezer b. Jacob says: Water may be poured into a [roof-]drain[9] on the Sabbath if four cubits [of the drain] were covered over in the public domain. But the Sages say: Even if a roof or a courtyard is a hundred cubits in area, water may not be poured over the mouth of the drain, but it may be poured from roof to roof, so that the water flows down into the drain. The courtyard and the portico are included together in making up the prescribed four cubits.

11. So, too, if there were two habitations over against one another, and [the occupants of] the one made a cavity but not [the occupants of] the other, they that made the cavity are permitted [to throw out water] but they that had not done so are forbidden.

9. 1. All the roofs of a town count as a single domain provided that no roof is ten handbreadths higher or ten handbreadths lower than its neighbour. So R. Meir. But the Sages say: Every roof is a domain in itself. R. Simeon says: It is all one with roofs or courtyards or outer areas:[10] they count as a single domain in what concerns vessels contained therein on the Sabbath, but not in what concerns vessels contained within the house on the Sabbath.

2. If a large roof adjoined a small roof, [to take up aught to] the larger roof is permitted, but [to take aught from the larger to] the smaller is forbidden. If there was a breach between a large courtyard and a small, [access to] the larger courtyard is permitted but [access to] the smaller is forbidden, since it is reckoned a doorway to the larger courtyard. If there was

[1] If ten handbreadths or more wide and four deep it counts as *karmelith*, a separate and neutral domain, neither public nor private.
[2] Which was necessary to constitute it *karmelith*.
[3] Having a hole in its floor through which the water-jar could be drawn up from water that was in public or neutral domain.
[4] Perpendicularly from the balcony limits, built either downwards from the balcony or upwards from the water's edge.
[5] Some texts add: 'or for the lower one but not for the upper one'.
[6] Since such an area is too small to absorb the water that may be thrown out, the water will flow away into the public domain, which offends against the rule about throwing a thing from one domain into another; Shab. 11[1]. Cf. Erub. 10[5].
[7] The average quantity of water needing to be thrown away on the Sabbath.
[8] i.e. the cavity must be on a lower level than the exit from the courtyard.
[9] Whose mouth is in a courtyard measuring only four cubits square.
[10] Cf. 2[5]; 5[2]. See Betz. 4[2]. The sense here is 'a rearcourt to a house'.

a breach[1] between a courtyard and the public domain, and a man brought in aught therefrom into a private domain, or into it from a private domain, he is culpable.[2] So R. Eliezer. But the Sages say: [Whether he brought in aught] from within it into the public domain, or from the public domain into the courtyard, he is not culpable, since it is deemed neutral domain.[3]

3. If a breach was made on both sides[4] of a courtyard towards the public domain (so, too, if a breach was made in a house on two sides, or if an alley-entry lost its cross-beam or side-posts)[5] they are permitted for that Sabbath,[6] but forbidden on future Sabbaths. So R. Judah. R. Jose says: If they are permitted for that Sabbath they are permitted for future Sabbaths; and if they are forbidden for future Sabbaths they are forbidden for that Sabbath.

4. If a man built an upper room above two houses [that are on opposite sides of an alley] (and so, too, with viaducts) they may move aught beneath them from place to place on the Sabbath. So R. Judah. But the Sages forbid it. Moreover R. Judah said: They may make *Erub* in an alley that is a thoroughfare. But this the Sages forbid.

10. 1. If a man found phylacteries[7] [in the open field] he should bring them in, one pair at a time.[8] Rabban Gamaliel says: Two pairs[9] at a time. This applies only if they were old;[10] but [even] if they were new [and he brought them in] he is not culpable. If he found them bound up in sets or bundles, he should wait by them until nightfall and then bring them in. If it was in time of danger[11] he may cover them up and go his way.

2. R. Simeon says: He may give them to his fellow and his fellow [may pass them] to his fellow [and so on] until they reach the outermost court-yard [of the town]. So, too, with his child [born in the open field]: he may give him to his fellow and his fellow [may pass him] to his fellow [and so on], even though they are a hundred. R. Judah says: A man may give a jar to his fellow and his fellow [may pass it] to his fellow even beyond the Sabbath limit. But the Sages replied: It cannot go farther than the feet of its owner.

3. If a man was reading in a scroll [of Scripture] on the threshold and the scroll rolled out of his hand, he may roll it back to himself. If he was reading on the edge of the roof and the scroll rolled out of his hand, if it does not reach ten handbreadths [from the ground] he may roll it back to himself; but after it has reached [lower than] ten hand-breadths, he must turn it over on to the written side.[12] R. Judah says: If it is distant only a needle's thickness from the ground he may roll it back to himself. R. Simeon says: Even if it touches the very ground he may roll it back to himself, since there is naught that concerns the Sabbath rest[13] that can withstand [the honour due to] the Holy Scriptures.

---

[1] Ten handbreadths or more, which destroys its status of 'private domain'.
[2] Since it counts then as public domain.   [3] Heb. *karmelith*. Cf. 8[7].
[4] At a corner.   [5] See 1[2-7].   [6] On which the mishap befell.   [7] See p. 104, n. 16.
[8] One on the head and one on the arm, in the manner in which they were worn on week-days.
[9] According to him they were not worn on the Sabbath for the synagogue service. Therefore they can be worn two at a time and regarded as ornaments.
[10] Recognizable by their worn straps as proper phylacteries. If the straps show no signs of use they may be merely amulets.
[11] When it was forbidden to practice the rites of Judaism.
[12] He may not draw it back, since it has reached into the public domain. The best he can do is to turn its writing downwards to protect the writing from dust or rain.
[13] The elaborations of the biblical law of doing no work on the Sabbath as they were devised and multiplied by rabbinical interpretation. See below, 10[15] (end).

4. If there was a projection[1] in front of the window, they may put aught upon it or take aught from off it[2] on the Sabbath. A man may stand within a private domain and move aught about in the public domain; or stand within the public domain and move aught about in a private domain, provided that he does not extend them beyond four cubits.

5. A man may not stand within a private domain and make water in the public domain; nor may he stand within the public domain and make water in a private domain; nor may he spit in like manner. R. Judah says: Even he whose spittle is loose in his mouth must spit before he has walked four cubits.

6. A man may not stand within a private domain and drink in the public domain, nor may he stand within the public domain and drink within a private domain unless he has inserted his head and the greater part of his body into the place where he drinks. So, too, with a winepress.[3] A man may catch up water out of a gutter[4] if it is less than ten handbreadths[5] from the ground, and he may drink from [the mouth of] a water-spout[6] after any fashion.[7]

7. If a cistern was in the public domain, with a surrounding bank ten handbreadths high, a man may draw water out of it on the Sabbath from a window above it. If a dungheap was in the public domain, ten handbreadths high, they may throw water thereon on the Sabbath from a window above it.

8. If the boughs of a tree overshadowing the ground were less than three handbreadths from the ground they may carry aught about under it. If its roots were three handbreadths [or more] above the ground a man may not sit thereon.[8] They may not stop up gaps in a rearcourt with a door, or a breach with briers or with matting, unless they hang higher than the ground.[9]

9. A man may not stand within a private domain and open [a door] in the public domain, [or stand] within the public domain and open [a door] in a private domain, unless he had made a partition ten handbreadths high.[10] So R. Meir. The Sages said to him: It happened in the poulterers'[11] market in Jerusalem that they used to shut their shops and leave the key in a window above the door. R. Jose says: It was the wool-dealers' market.

10. R. Eliezer forbids a bolt with a knob on its end,[12] but R. Jose permits it. R. Eliezer said: It happened in the synagogue in Tiberias that they deemed it permitted until Rabban Gamaliel and the Elders came and forbade them. R. Jose says: They deemed it forbidden, but Rabban Gamaliel and the elders came and gave them permission.

11. They may shut up [the gates] in the Temple with a bolt that is dragged [on the ground],[13] but not in the provinces; but one that can be

---

[1] See Ohol. 14 [1, 2]. At least ten handbreadths from the ground.
[2] From within the house. The projection counts as the same private domain.
[3] See Maas. 4[4]. The present passage is not concerned with the Sabbath. A man may take a haphazard drink from the winepress and be exempt from Tithes, provided that the greater part of his person is within the domain of the winepress.
[4] That drains off the water from a roof.
[5] This is reckoned public domain, and he too is standing in the public domain.
[6] Its outlet projects some distance from the roof; it is in all respects in the public domain.
[7] He can even collect it in a vessel, and drink.
[8] See Betz. 5[2]. Above three handbreadths comes under the prohibition against climbing a tree on the Sabbath; less than this is regarded as no more than ground level.
[9] Thus avoiding the appearance of 'building' (Shab. 7[2]).
[10] In the public domain enclosing the doorway.   [11] Or: butchers'.
[12] To be used to shut up a door on the Sabbath, unless it is hung or fastened to the door.
[13] i.e. it was fastened to the gate by a long rope and not merely suspended.

laid apart[1] is forbidden in either place. R. Judah says: One that could be laid apart was permitted in the Temple, and one that was dragged [on the ground was permitted] in the provinces.

12. They may thrust back [to its socket] the lower pivot [of a door] in the Temple, but not in the provinces; and [to thrust back] the upper one is forbidden in either place.[2] R. Judah says: The upper [was forbidden] in the Temple, and the lower one in the provinces.

13. They may replace a plaster [on a wound] in the Temple, but not in the provinces; and in either place it is forbidden to put it on for a first time. They may tie up a string[3] in the Temple, but not in the provinces, and in either place it is forbidden to tie it up for a first time. They may cut off a wen in the Temple but not in the provinces; and if it is done with an implement it is forbidden in either place.

14. If a priest was wounded in the finger he may wrap reed-grass around it in the Temple but not in the provinces. If it was done to force out blood it is forbidden in either place. They may scatter salt on the [Altar-]Ramp[4] that [the priests] shall not slip; and they may draw water with a wheel on the Sabbath from the Golah-cistern and from the Great Cistern,[5] and from the Haker Well[6] on a Festival-day.

15. If a creeping thing[7] was found in the Temple a priest may remove it with his girdle that he suffer not the uncleanness to remain. So R. Johanan b. Baroka. R. Judah says: He should remove it with wooden tongs that he suffer not the uncleanness to increase.[8] From what places must it be removed? From the Sanctuary and from the Porch and from between the Porch and the Altar. So R. Simeon b. Nanos. R. Akiba says: It must be removed from any place where a man [if he entered being unclean] would be liable to Extirpation if he acted wantonly, or to a Sin-offering if he acted in error. Elsewhere they put a psykter[9] over it. R. Simeon says: Wheresoever the Sages have permitted aught to thee they have but given thee what is already thine, for what they have permitted thee is only that which they had withheld by virtue of the Sabbath rest.[10]

PESAHIM ('FEAST OF PASSOVER')

1. 1. On the night of[11] the 14th [of Nisan] the *hametz*[12] must be searched for by the light of a lamp. Any place into which *hametz* is never brought needs no searching. Then why have they said: [They must search] two rows in a wine-vault? They are a place into which *hametz* might be brought. The School of Shammai say: [They must examine] the two rows on the whole surface[13] of [the stack of jars in] the wine-vault. And the School of Hillel say: Only the two outermost rows that are uppermost.[14]

---

[1] Not fastened at all.   [2] It demands greater exertion.
[3] Of a musical instrument.   [4] Midd. 3[3]. Cf. Yom. 2 [1f]. See Ex. 20[26].
[5] Names of two cisterns in the Temple Court. See Midd. 5[4]. 'Golah' means exiled Israel, and the Golah-cistern is explained as a cistern dug by the returned exiles.
[6] A well in the provinces on the road of the pilgrims to Jerusalem. To draw water from it with a wheel was permitted by the Prophets even on Festival-days.
[7] Dead. Lev. 11[29-31].   [8] It would have rendered the girdle unclean too.
[9] ψυκτήρ=wine-cooler. A large brass vessel. See Tam. 5[5].   [10] See above, 10[3].
[11] i.e. the night preceding the day which, in modern usage, would be called the 14th of the month.
[12] Anything, food or not food (Pes. 3[1]), made from or containing what is made from grain, flour or bran of wheat, barley, spelt, goat-grass, or oats (Hall. 1[1, 2]), which, from contact with water or liquid containing water, has fermented or is in process of fermenting. Ex. 12[19] forbids *hametz* throughout the seven days (15th–21st Nisan) of Passover.
[13] Front or top.   [14] The top two rows facing you as you enter.

2. They need not fear that a weasel may have dragged [*hametz*] from house to house, or from place to place; for if so [it may likewise have dragged it] from courtyard to courtyard, or from town to town: there is no end to the matter.

3. R. Judah says: They may search out [the *hametz*] on the night of[1] the 14th or on the morning of the 14th or at the very time for its removal.[2] But the Sages say: If a man has not searched on the night of the 14th let him search on the 14th; if he has not searched on the 14th let him search during the Feast; if he has not searched during the Feast let him search after the Feast. And what he would leave over,[3] let him put in safe keeping that he shall not afterward need to search for it.

4. R. Meir says: They may eat [*hametz*] throughout the fifth [hour[4] on the 14th], but at the beginning of the sixth hour they must burn it. R. Judah says: They may eat it throughout the fourth hour, hold it in suspense[5] throughout the fifth hour, and burn it at the beginning of the sixth hour.

5. Moreover R. Judah said: Two cakes of the Thank-offering[6] that had become unfit[7] were laid on the roof of the portico;[8] so long as they were laid there all the people could eat [*hametz*]; when one was taken away they remained in suspense, neither eating nor burning [the *hametz*]; when both were taken away all the people began to burn [the *hametz*]. Rabban Gamaliel says: [*Hametz*] that was common food could be eaten only throughout the fourth hour, but Heave-offering[9] [could be eaten] throughout the fifth hour; and [both] were burnt at the beginning of the sixth hour.

6. R. Hanina the Prefect of the Priests says:[10] The priests never refrained from burning flesh that had become unclean from a derived uncleanness[11] together with flesh that had become unclean from a primary unclean-ness,[12] although they thereby added uncleanness to its uncleanness. More-over R. Akiba said: The priests never refrained from burning in a lamp rendered unclean by one that had contracted corpse-uncleanness,[13] [Heave-offering] oil that was rendered unfit by one that had immersed himself the selfsame day [because of uncleanness],[14] although they thereby added uncleanness to its uncleanness.

7. R. Meir said: From their words we learn that at Passover men may burn clean Heave-offering [that is *hametz*] together with unclean. R. Jose answered: That is not the inference. And R. Eliezer and R. Joshua agree that each should be burnt by itself. About what did they dispute? About what was doubtfully unclean and what was unclean, of which R. Eliezer says: Let each be burnt by itself. And R. Joshua says: Both of them together.

[1] See p. 136, n. 11. [2] See below, 2[1]. [3] For food until the time prescribed for burning *hametz*.
[4] Until 11 a.m.   [5] Neither eating nor burning it.
[6] Lev. 7[13].   [7] Left over after the time appointed for eating it. Lev. 22[30].
[8] See Shek. 8[4]; Sukk. 4[4].   [9] See *Terumah*, App. I. 48.   [10] Eduy. 2[1].
[11] Lit. 'offspring of uncleanness'; i.e. the flesh had contracted uncleanness from some other thing which had contracted uncleanness from a primary (or 'father of') uncleanness. See Kel. 1[ff].; App. IV.
[12] Lit. 'father (i.e. primary source) of uncleanness'. The first flesh suffered 'second-grade' uncleanness and the other 'first-grade' uncleanness. By burning them together the first flesh also contracts the graver 'first-grade' uncleanness. See p. 714, n. 3; Toh. 1[5].
[13] A corpse is a 'father of fathers of uncleanness'. What a corpse renders unclean is also a 'father of uncleanness'; the lamp that touches it becomes (exceptionally: see p. 649, n. 3, (c); App. IV. 7) also a 'father of uncleanness'.
[14] Heb. *tebul yom*. Lit. 'immersed the same day'. He is a priest who although he had already immersed himself because of an uncleanness (see Tam. 1[1]) still needs to await sunset (Lev. 15[5, 16]) before he is clean and qualified to eat of Heave-offering (see Ber. 1[1]). He still counts as suffering 'second-grade' uncleanness, and the Heave-offering oil which he has touched suffers 'third-grade' uncleanness. This oil, being put in a lamp which has become a 'father of uncleanness', is raised from third- to first-grade uncleanness owing to contact with a 'father of uncleanness'. See p. 773, n. 6.

2. **1**. So long as it is permitted to eat of the *hametz* a man may give it as fodder to cattle, wild animals, and birds, or sell it to a gentile; and [after any fashion] it is permitted to derive benefit from it. But when the time is past it is forbidden to derive benefit from it, nor may one light an oven or stove with it. R. Judah says: Removal[1] of the *hametz* may only be by burning. But the Sages say: It may be crumbled up and scattered to the wind or thrown into the sea.

2. [An Israelite] may derive benefit from *hametz* belonging to a gentile which has remained over Passover; but it is forbidden to derive benefit from that belonging to an Israelite, for it is written, *Let it not be seen of thee*.[2]

3. If a gentile lent aught to an Israelite on security of his *hametz*, it is allowed to derive benefit from it after Passover.[3] But if an Israelite lent aught to a gentile on security of his *hametz*, it is forbidden to derive benefit from it after Passover.[4] If a falling building fell upon *hametz* it is deemed 'removed'. Rabban Simeon b. Gamaliel says: Whatsoever a dog is unable to search out [is deemed 'removed'].

4. If during Passover a man consumed Heave-offering that was *hametz*, if in error he must pay its value and the [Added] Fifth;[5] but if wantonly he is exempt from making restitution[6] and [even] from [paying] its worth as wood[-fuel].

5. These are the things by [eating] which [unleavened] at Passover a man fulfils his obligation:[7] wheat, barley, spelt, goat-grass, and oats. The obligation is fulfilled if they are *demai*-produce,[8] First Tithe from which Heave-offering has been taken, Second Tithe or dedicated produce which have been redeemed;[9] and the priest [fulfils his obligation if they are] Dough-offering[10] or Heave-offering. [But the obligation is] not [fulfilled] if they are untithed produce, or First Tithe from which Heave-offering has not been taken, or Second Tithe or dedicated produce which have not been redeemed. A man cannot fulfil his obligation [by eating] the cakes for the Thank-offerings[11] or the wafers of a Nazirite[12] if he made them for himself; but if he made them to sell in the market he can fulfil his obligation therewith.

6. And these are the herbs by [eating] which at Passover a man fulfils his obligation:[13] lettuce, chicory, pepperwort, snakeroot, and dandelion. He fulfils it whether they are fresh or dried, but not if they are pickled, stewed, or cooked. And these may be included together to make up [the prescribed quantity of] an olive's bulk. He can fulfil his obligation if he eats but their stalks, or if they are *demai*-produce, or First Tithe from which Heave-offering has been taken, or Second Tithe or dedicated produce which have been redeemed.

7. They may not soak bran for fowls, but must scald it.[14] A woman may not soak the bran which she takes with her to the bath-house, but must rub it on her skin dry. At Passover a man may not chew grains of wheat to put on his wound, since they will ferment.

8. They may not put meal in the *haroseth*[15] or in the mustard;[16] and if they do so they must consume it at once. R. Meir forbids it. The Passover-

---

[1] Ex. 12[15].   [2] Ex. 13[7].   [3] During Passover it was in gentile possession.
[4] During Passover it was in an Israelite's possession.   [5] Lev. 5[16]; see B.M. 4[8].
[6] It is worthless at Passover even as fuel (par. 1 above). See Ter. 7[1].   [7] Ex. 12[8].
[8] App. I. 6.   [9] For these terms see p. 7, nn. 6–9.   [10] Num. 15[18ff]. See p. 83, n. 1.
[11] Lev. 7[12].   [12] Num. 6[15].   [13] Of eating bitter herbs, Ex. 12[8].
[14] During Passover. Hot water does not cause fermentation.   [15] See 10[3].
[16] Since these have water mixed with them.

lamb may not be cooked in liquids[1] or fruit-juice,[2] but it may be basted therewith or dipped therein. Water that has been used by a baker must be poured away, since it ferments.

3. 1. These must be removed at Passover: Babylonian porridge, Median beer, Edomite vinegar, and Egyptian barley-beer; also dyers' pulp, cooks' starch-flour, and writers' paste. R. Eliezer says: Also women's cosmetics. This is the general rule: whatsoever is made from any kind of grain must be removed at Passover. These are included in the prohibition, yet punishment by Extirpation is not thereby incurred.[3]

2. If dough remained in the cracks of a kneading-trough and there was an olive's bulk in any one place, it must be removed. If there was less than this it is negligible in its scantness. So, too, in a matter of uncleanness:[4] he that is scrupulous about it must make a partition;[5] if he wishes it to remain it can be reckoned as [one with] the kneading-trough. Dough that is still 'dumb'[6] is forbidden if other dough like to it has already fermented.

3. How is the Dough-offering set apart on a Festival-day if the dough is unclean?[7] R. Eliezer says: She should not designate it [Dough-offering] until it is baked. R. Judah b. Bathyra says: She should throw it into cold water. R. Joshua said: Such *hametz* is not included in the prohibitions *Let it not be seen*,[8] and *Let it not be found*;[9] but, rather, she should set it apart and leave it until evening, and if it becomes *hametz* it becomes *hametz*.

4. Rabban Gamaliel says: Three women may knead dough at the same time and bake it in the same oven one after the other.[10] But the Sages say: Three women may occupy themselves [at the same time] with the dough, one kneading, one rolling it out, and one baking. R. Akiba says: All women and all kinds of wood and all ovens are not equal.[11] This is the general rule: if the dough swells let her slap it with cold water.

5. Dough beginning to ferment (*si'ur*) must be burnt; but he that eats it is not culpable. Dough wholly fermented [*sidduk*) must be burnt and he that eats it is liable to punishment by Extirpation. What is *si'ur*? [Dough on which streaks appear] like the horns of a locust. And *sidduk*? [Dough] on which the cracks are all entangled together. So R. Judah. But the Sages say: If a man ate either [of these] he is liable to punishment by Extirpation. But what is *si'ur*? [Dough] whose surface turns pallid like a man's face when his hair stands on end.

6. If the 14th falls on a Sabbath all[12] *hametz* must be removed before the Sabbath. So R. Meir. But the Sages say: [Not until] its appointed time.[13] R. Eliezer b. R. Zadok says: Heave-offering [must be removed] before the Sabbath, but common food [not until] its appointed time.

7. If a man was on the way to slaughter his Passover-offering or to circumcise his son or to eat the betrothal meal at his father-in-law's

---

[1] Meaning the six specified in Maksh. 6[4].
[2] See Ex. 12[9], 'nor sodden at all with water'.
[3] See p. 562, n. 16.   [4] If a dead creeping thing touched an olive's bulk of the dough.
[5] Cf. Ohol., chh. 8, 9.   [6] Signs of fermentation not yet apparent.
[7] Since it is forbidden to burn it (as in Pes. 2[4]) on a Festival-day, and it may not be left until the next day lest it ferment. The Festival-day spoken of is the 15th of Nisan.
[8] Ex. 13[7].   [9] Ex. 12[19].
[10] He means that the delay will not suffice to make the dough ferment.
[11] Some women are idle, some wood is damp, and some ovens heat slowly, so even so there is danger that delay will give time for fermentation.
[12] Heave-offering or common food.
[13] Pes. 1[4]. The burning of the *hametz* overrides the Sabbath. Heave-offering *hametz* should be burnt before, since it affects but the few; but to burn ordinary food would deprive most men of food on the Sabbath.

house and he remembered that he had left *hametz* in his house, if he has yet time to go back and remove it and return to fulfil his religious duty, let him go back and remove it; but if not, he may annul it in his heart. [If he was on the way] to render help against ravaging soldiery or a flood or a fire or a falling building, he may annul the *hametz* in his heart; but if it was but to keep the Feast at a place of his own choice he must return at once.

8. So, too, if a man had gone forth from Jerusalem and remembered that he still had with him flesh that was hallowed,[1] if he had already passed Zofim[2] he may burn it there and then; but if not, he must return and burn it before the Birah[3] with wood for the Altar-hearth.[4] By reason of how much [flesh or *hametz*] must they return? R. Meir says: In either case an egg's bulk. R. Judah says: In either case an olive's bulk. But the Sages say: An olive's bulk of hallowed flesh or an egg's bulk of *hametz*.

4. 1. Where the custom is to do work until midday on the day before Passover they may do so; where the custom is not to do work, they may not work. If a man went from a place where they do so to a place where they do not, or from a place where they do not to a place where they do, to him is applied the more stringent use of the place which he has left[5] and the more stringent use of the place to which he has gone; but let no man behave differently [from local use] lest it lead to conflict.

2. In like manner if a man brought Seventh Year produce from a place where it is come to an end to a place where it is not come to an end, or from a place where it has not come to an end to a place where it has come to an end, he is under obligation to 'remove' it.[6] R. Judah says: They say to him,[7] 'Do thou thyself also go and fetch it'.[8]

3. Where[9] the custom is to sell small cattle to gentiles they may sell them; where the custom is not to sell them, they may not sell them. And nowhere may they sell them large cattle, calves, or foals, whole or maimed. R. Judah permits a maimed beast [to be sold] and Ben Bathyra permits a horse.

4. Where the custom is to eat flesh roast on the nights of Passover they may eat it so; where the custom is not to eat it roast, they may not eat it so. Where the custom is to kindle the lamp on the nights of the Day of Atonement, they may do so; where the custom is not to kindle it, they may not do so. But they may kindle it in synagogues, houses of study, dark alleys, and over sick persons.

5. Where the custom is to do work on the Ninth of Ab, they may do so; where the custom is not to do work, they may not work. But everywhere the disciples of the Sages cease from work. Rabban Simeon b. Gamaliel says: A man should always behave as a disciple of the Sages. Moreover the Sages say: In Judea they used to do work until midday on the eves of Passover, but in Galilee they used to do nothing at all. In what concerns the night [between the 13th and 14th of Nisan], the School of Shammai forbid [any work], but the School of Hillel permit it until sunrise.

---

[1] That had formed part of an offering. Even the Lesser Holy Things become invalid if taken out of Jerusalem. See Zeb. 14[8].

[2] Mount Scopus, the hill north-east of Jerusalem, on the northern road, from which the city first becomes visible.

[3] Cf. Orl. 2[12]; Pes. 7[8]; Zeb. 12[5]; p. 582, n. 8; Midd. 1[9]; Par. 3[1]. The actual Temple structure. In the Talmud it is variously explained as a place in the Temple Mount, the whole of the Temple Mount, and a tower in the Temple Mount.

[4] And not wood of his own.   [5] In case he should return.

[6] Cf. Shebi. 9[5].   [7] Some texts omit 'They say to him'.

[8] Ironical. Such produce is no more found locally in the fields.   [9] A. Zar. 1[6].

6. R. Meir says: Whatsoever work a man has begun before the 14th he may finish on the 14th; but he may not begin it from the beginning on the 14th even though he was able to finish it. But the Sages say: Three crafts-men may do work until mid-day on the eve of Passover and these are they: tailors, barbers, and washermen. R. Jose b. R. Judah says: Shoemakers also.

7. They may set up hen-coops on the 14th and if a [brooding] hen escaped it may be restored to its place, and if it died another may be made to sit in its stead. They may clear away [refuse] beneath the feet of cattle on the 14th, and during the Feast[1] they may clear it away to the sides [of the stall]. They may take utensils to the house of a craftsman and bring them away even though they are not needful for the Feast.

8. The men of Jericho did six things:[2] for three they reproved them and for three they did not reprove them. And these are the things for which they did not reprove them: they grafted palms [on the 14th of Nisan] the whole day, they did not make the prescribed divisions in the *Shema'*,[3] they reaped and stacked before the *Omer*;[4] and they did not reprove them. And these are the things for which they reproved them: they permitted the use of Egyptian figs [from stems that had been] dedicated to the Temple, they ate on the Sabbath fruit that lay fallen under the tree,[5] and they gave *Peah*[6] from vegetables; and the Sages reproved them.[7]

5. 1. The Daily Whole-offering[8] was slaughtered at a half after the eighth hour, and offered up at a half after the ninth hour; [but] on the eve of Passover it was slaughtered at a half after the seventh hour and offered up at a half after the eighth hour, whether it was a weekday or the Sabbath. If the eve of Passover fell on the eve of a Sabbath, it was slaughtered at a half after the sixth hour and offered up at a half after the seventh hour. And, after this, the Passover-offering [was slaughtered].

2. If a Passover-offering was slaughtered but under some other name,[9] or if its blood was received, conveyed, and tossed, but under some other name, or under its own name and [then] under some other name, or under some other name and [then] under its own name, it becomes invalid. How [can it be treated] 'under its own name and [then] under some other name'? [If, to wit, it was treated first] under the name of a Passover-offering and [then] under the name of a Peace-offering. [And how can it be treated first] 'under some other name and [then] under its own name'? [If, to wit, it was treated first] under the name of a Peace-offering and [then] under the name of a Passover-offering.

3. If it was slaughtered for such as cannot eat of it,[10] or for such as were not numbered[11] among them that should eat of it, or for the uncircumcised,[12]

---

[1] i.e. during the mid-festival days. See p. 207, n. 19.
[2] That were unlawful.   [3] See Ber. 2[2].   [4] Men. 10[7, 8]. App. I. 31.
[5] It may have fallen on the Sabbath itself and so be forbidden.
[6] Lev. 19[9-10]; See Peah 1[4ff].
[7] Many texts add the following Baraita (i.e. teaching not included in the Mishnah, but related to and contemporary with the teachings of the Mishnah, and recorded in the Gemara; the present Baraita is taken from Pes. 56a):
'Six things did king Hezekiah: with three they consented and with three they did not consent. He dragged the bones of his father on a bed of ropes—and they consented He ground small the bronze serpent—and they consented. He hid away the scroll of healings—and they consented. With three things they did not consent. He cut in pieces the doors of the Sanctuary and sent them to the king of Assyria—and they did not consent. He stopped up the water of the upper Gihon—and they did not consent. He intercalated Nisan with Nisan—and they did not consent.'
[8] Of the evening. See Num. 28[1-8] and tractate Tamid. Cf. below, 10[1].
[9] See Zeb. 1[1,4].   [10] See Pes. 8[7].   [11] See Pes. 8[3].   [12] Ex. 12[48].

or the unclean,[1] it is not valid; but if both for such as can and for such as cannot eat of it, or both for such as have and for such as have not been numbered among them that should eat of it, or both for the uncircumcised and for the circumcised, or both for the unclean and for the clean, it is valid. If it was slaughtered before midday it is invalid, for it is written, *Between the evenings*.[2] If it was slaughtered before the Daily Whole-offering it is valid, provided that some one stir up its blood until the blood of the Daily Whole-offering has been tossed;[3] but if it was tossed before, it is valid.

4. If a man slaughters the Passover-offering with *hametz* [in his possession], he transgresses a negative command.[4] R. Judah says: Also [if he so slaughters] the Daily Whole-offering [after midday on the 14th]. R. Simeon says: [If a man slaughters] the Passover-offering on the 14th under its own name [while he was near to *hametz*], he is culpable; but if under some other name he is not culpable; and for all other offerings, whether slaughtered under their own name or not, a man does not become culpable. During the Feast itself if [he slaughtered it] under its own name, he is not culpable; but if under some other name, he is culpable; while for all other offerings, whether slaughtered under their own name or not, he is culpable, except for a Sin-offering[5] which has been slaughtered under some other name.

5. The Passover-offering was slaughtered [by the people] in three groups, for it is written, *And the whole assembly of the congregation of Israel shall slaughter it*[6]—'assembly', 'congregation', and 'Israel'. When the first group entered in and the Temple Court[7] was filled, the gates of the Temple Court were closed. [On the *shofar*] a sustained, a quavering, and again a sustained blast[8] were blown. The priests stood in rows and in their hands were basons of silver and basons of gold. In one row all the basons were of silver and in another row all the basons were of gold. They were not mixed up together. Nor had the basons bases, lest the priests should set them down and the blood congeal.

6. An Israelite slaughtered his [own] offering and the priest caught the blood. The priest passed the bason to his fellow, and he to his fellow, each receiving a full bason and giving back an empty one. The priest nearest to the Altar tossed the blood in one action against the base [of the Altar].

7. When the first group went out the second group came in; and when the second group went out the third group came in. As the rite was performed with the first group so was it performed with the second and the third. [In the meantime the levites] sang the *Hallel*.[9] If they finished it they sang it anew, and if they finished it a second time they sang it a third time, although it never happened that they thrice completed it. R. Judah says: Never during the turn of the third group did they reach so far as *I love the Lord because he hath heard* [*my voice*],[10] since the folk in that group were but few.

8. As the rite was performed on a weekday so was it performed on a Sabbath, save that the priests swilled the Temple Court, which was not with the consent of the Sages. R. Judah says: They used to fill a cup with the mingled blood [that was spilt] and toss it in one action against the Altar.[11] But the Sages did not agree with him.

---

[1] Num. 9[6f].   [2] Ex. 12[6].   [3] See below, 5[6]; p. 468, n. 15.   [4] Ex. 34[25].
[5] Zeb. 1[1].   [6] Ex. 12[6].   [7] See p. 589, n. 11.
[8] Cf. Sukk. 5[4]; R.Sh. 4[9]   [9] Pss. 113–18.   [10] Ps. 116[1].
[11] After all had slaughtered their offerings. This made valid any of the offerings whose blood had not been rightly treated.

9. How did they hang up the carcases and flay them? There were iron hooks fixed in the walls and pillars,[1] and on these they used to hang the carcases and flay them. And if any had no place where to hang and flay, there were thin smooth staves which a man could put on his own and his fellow's shoulder and so hang and flay [his offering]. R. Eliezer says: If the 14th fell on a Sabbath a man would rest his hand on his fellow's shoulder, while the hand of his fellow rested on his shoulder, and so would they hang and flay [their offerings].[2]

10. When he had slit the carcase and removed the sacrificial portions,[3] he put them on a tray and [the priest] burned them on the Altar. When the first group went out they remained within the Temple Mount [if the 14th fell on a Sabbath], and the second group in the Rampart,[4] and the third group remained where they were [within the Temple Court]. After nightfall they went out and roasted their Passover-offerings.

6. 1. These acts pertaining to the Passover-offering override the Sabbath: slaughtering it, tossing its blood, scraping its entrails, and burning its fat pieces. But the roasting of it and rinsing its entrails do not override the Sabbath. Carrying it [to the Temple] and bringing it from outside to within the Sabbath limit, and cutting off a wen [from the carcase] do not override the Sabbath. R. Eliezer says: They do override it.

2. R. Eliezer said: Is not that the inference?—if slaughtering, which comes within the category of work,[5] overrides the Sabbath, may not those things override the Sabbath which come [only] within the category of Sabbath rest?[6] R. Joshua said to him: A Festival-day affords proof,[7] for on it they have permitted acts which come within the category of work and have forbidden acts which come within the category of Sabbath rest.[8] R. Eliezer said to him: What is this, Joshua! How can a voluntary act be any proof concerning an obligatory act?[9] R. Akiba answered and said: Sprinkling [with the Sin-offering water][10] affords proof, for it is obligatory, it comes within the category of Sabbath rest, yet it cannot override the Sabbath. Wonder not that these [other acts] also, although they are obligatory and come within the category of Sabbath rest, do not override the Sabbath. R. Eliezer said to him: Thereon, too, do I base my inference; if slaughtering, which comes within the category of work, overrides the Sabbath, should not sprinkling [the Sin-offering water] override the Sabbath in that it [only] comes within the category of Sabbath rest? R. Akiba said to him: Nay, on the contrary!—if sprinkling [the Sin-offering water] which [only] comes within the category of Sabbath rest does not override the Sabbath, does it not follow that slaughtering, which comes under the category of work, cannot override the Sabbath? R. Eliezer said to him:

---

[1] See Midd. 3[5].

[2] But the *Halakah* is not according to him; it was permitted to move the staves about on the Sabbath, since the rabbinical rules of the Sabbath rest (as distinct from work which is forbidden by Scripture) did not apply in the Temple. Cf. Erub. 10[3, 15]. Also the slaughtering of the Passover-offering overrides the Sabbath.   [3] The parts specified in Lev. 3[3-4].

[4] See Midd. 2[3].   [5] Such as Scripture forbids. See Shab. 7[2].

[6] Extra restrictions imposed by rabbinical authority only. See Erub. 10[3, 15].

[7] By Ex. 12[16] the preparing of necessary food is permissible on a Festival-day.

[8] See Betz. 5[2].

[9] On a Festival-day slaughtering is voluntary, but at Passover it is compulsory.

[10] See Num. 19[1ff]., especially v. 19. Cf. p. 697, n. 3. If the third or seventh day falls on a Sabbath, by rabbinical ruling the sprinkling is forbidden. It is obligatory in that unless the unclean person has received the prescribed sprinklings he cannot slaughter the Passover lambs.

Akiba, wouldest thou uproot[1] what is written in the Law, *Between the evenings in its appointed time*,[2]—whether this be a weekday or a Sabbath? He answered: Rabbi, bring me an 'appointed time' [enjoined in the Scriptures] for these acts equal [in its explicitness] to the 'appointed time' [enjoined] for slaughtering [the Passover-offering]! R. Akiba laid down a general rule:[3] Whatsoever work[4] can be done on the day before the Sabbath cannot override the Sabbath. Slaughtering which cannot be done on the day before the Sabbath overrides the Sabbath.

3. When may a man bring also a [freewill] festal-offering?[5] When the Passover-offering is offered on a weekday, and in cleanness, and is insufficient. But when it is offered on a Sabbath, or is sufficient, or [is offered] in uncleanness, none may bring a [freewill] festal-offering.

4. The [freewill] festal-offering may be taken from the sheep or from the oxen, from the lambs or from the goats, from the males or from the females, and consumed during two days and one night.[6]

5. If on the Sabbath a man slaughtered a Passover-offering under some other name, he is thereby liable to a Sin-offering;[7] with any other animal-offering, if it was slaughtered as a Passover-offering and was not fitted [for the Passover-offering], he is culpable;[8] and if it was fitted, R. Eliezer declares him liable to a Sin-offering, but R. Joshua declares him exempt. R. Eliezer said: What! if the Passover-offering is permitted [to be slaughtered on the Sabbath] when [it is slaughtered] under its own name, though a man is culpable if [he slaughtered it] under some other name, is not the inference that, with other animal-offerings, which [in any wise] are forbidden[9] [to be slaughtered on the Sabbath] even when [slaughtered] under their own name, a man is culpable if [he slaughtered them] under some other name? R. Joshua answered: No! as thou arguest of the Passover-offering that was slaughtered under some other and forbidden name, wouldest thou argue of [other] animal-offerings that were slaughtered under some other but permitted name? R. Eliezer said to him: The public offerings[10] afford proof, since they are permitted when slaughtered [on the Sabbath] under their own name, yet he that slaughters [other offerings] under that name [on the Sabbath] is culpable. R. Joshua answered: No! as thou arguest concerning public offerings, whose number has a limit, wouldest thou argue concerning the Passover-offerings whose number has no limit? R. Meir says: Howbeit he that slaughters [other animal-offerings on the Sabbath] under the name of the public offerings is not culpable.

6. If a man slaughtered [the Passover-offering on the Sabbath] for such as could not eat of it, or for such as were not numbered among them that should eat of it, or for the uncircumcised or the unclean, he is culpable; but if both for such as could and for such as could not eat of it, or both for

---

[1] Cf. Hor. 1³.   [2] Num. 9³.   [3] Shab. 19¹, Men. 11³.
[4] Arising from the Passover-offering.
[5] Heb. *hagigah*; but it is not identical with the compulsory offering, *Re'iyyah*, dealt with in the tractate Hagigah. The offering here spoken of was intended to supplement if need be the meal on the night of Passover. Unlike the Passover-offering itself, the slaughtering of it does not override the Sabbath or the laws of cleanness (see below, 7⁴).
[6] i.e. on the 14th and 15th, and the night between them, whereas the Passover lamb must be a male from the sheep or the goats, and eaten during the night of the 15th.
[7] Lev. 4²⁷ff. It does not, like the Passover-offering, override the Sabbath.
[8] Liable to a Sin-offering.
[9] i.e. in a category of offering forbidden to be slaughtered on the Sabbath.
[10] Such as the Daily Whole-offering.

such as were and for such as were not numbered among them that should eat of it, or both for the circumcised and for the uncircumcised, or both for the clean and for the unclean, he is not culpable. If he slaughtered it and it was found to have a blemish, he is culpable. If he slaughtered it and it was found to be *terefah*[1] within, he is not culpable. If he slaughtered it and it then became known that the owners had withdrawn from sharing in the eating of it or had died or had contracted uncleanness, he is not culpable, since he had slaughtered it permissibly.

7. 1. How do they roast[2] the Passover-offering? They bring a skewer of pomegranate-wood and thrust it through from its mouth to its buttocks, laying its legs and its entrails inside it. So R. Jose the Galilean. R. Akiba says: That would be of the nature of cooking:[3] but, rather, they hang them outside it.

2. The Passover-offering is roasted neither on a [metal] spit nor on a grill. R. Zadok said: Rabban Gamaliel once said to his slave Tabi, 'Go and roast the Passover-offering for us on the grill'. If it touched the earthenware of the oven, that part must be pared away.[4] If some of its juice dripped on to the earthenware and dripped again on part of the carcase, that part must be taken away. If some of its juice dripped on to the flour, he must take a handful away from that place [and burn it].

3. If it had been basted with Heave-offering oil, they may eat it if they are a company of priests; but if they were Israelites,[5] it must be rinsed if it was raw, and if roasted the surface must be pared off. If a man basted it with Second Tithe oil its value may not be charged to the members of the company, since Second Tithe may not be sold in Jerusalem.[6]

4. Five things may be offered in uncleanness but they may not be eaten in uncleanness: the *Omer*,[7] the Two Loaves [of Pentecost],[8] the Shewbread,[9] the Peace-offerings of the congregation,[10] and the goats offered at the New Moon.[11] If the Passover-offering is offered in uncleanness it may also be eaten in uncleanness, since from the beginning it was offered only to be eaten.

5. If the flesh contracted uncleanness but the fat continued [clean], the blood is not tossed [against the base of the Altar]; if the fat contracted uncleanness but the flesh continued [clean], the blood is tossed. But it is not so with the other offerings, for even if the flesh contracted uncleanness and only the fat continued [clean], the blood may be tossed.

6. If the congregation or the greater part thereof contracted uncleanness, or if the priests were unclean but the congregation clean, the Passover may be kept in uncleanness. If the lesser part of the congregation contracted uncleanness they that are clean keep the first Passover and they that are unclean the second.[12]

7. If the blood of a Passover-offering had been tossed [against the base of the Altar] and it was afterward known that it was unclean, the [High Priest's] frontlet effects acceptance,[13] but if the person [of any of the partakers] was unclean the frontlet does not effect acceptance; because they

---

[1] App. I. 47.   [2] In fulfilment of the terms of Ex. 12[8–9].
[3] Since its entrails and legs were, as it were, laid in a pot.
[4] Because it was not directly 'roast with fire' but by the heat of the oven-side. So, too, with the juice that had touched the side.   [5] i.e. non-priests.
[6] See M.Sh. 1[1].   [7] App. I. 31.   [8] Lev. 23[17].   [9] Ex. 25[30], Lev. 24[5–9]; Men. 11[5].
[10] Lev. 23[19–20].   [11] Num. 28[15].   [12] Num. 9 [6–11]; Pes. 9[1ff].
[13] Cf. Zeb. 8[12]. See Ex. 28[36–8].

have said: For the Nazirite[1] and for him that keeps the Passover the frontlet effects acceptance where there is uncleanness of the blood, but the frontlet does not effect acceptance where there is uncleanness of the [partaker's] person. If a man contracted uncleanness by uncleanness from the deep,[2] the frontlet effects acceptance.

8. If the whole or the greater part [of the Passover-offering] contracted uncleanness it must be burnt before the Birah[3] with wood for the Altar-hearth. If the lesser part, or what remained over,[4] contracted uncleanness they may burn it in their own courtyards or on their own roofs with their own wood. The niggardly burn it before the Birah to enjoy the use of the wood for the Altar-hearth.

9. If the Passover-offering was taken out [of Jerusalem] or contracted uncleanness, it must be burnt at once. If its owners contracted uncleanness or died, its appearance must be spoilt[5] and it must be burnt on the 16th [of Nisan]. R. Johanan b. Baroka says: This, too, should be burnt at once, since there is none to eat thereof.

10. The bones and sinews and what remains over must be burnt on the 16th. If the 16th falls on a Sabbath they must be burnt on the 17th, since they override neither the Sabbath nor a Festival-day.

11. All that can be eaten of a full-grown ox can be eaten of a small kid, even the ends of the shoulder-blades and the gristly parts. If a man breaks a bone[6] of a clean Passover-offering he incurs the Forty Stripes.[7] But if he suffers aught to remain from a clean [Passover-offering] or breaks a bone of one that is unclean, he does not incur the Forty Stripes.

12. If the limb [of a Passover-offering] projected outside[8] [the wall of Jerusalem] it must be cut away until the bone is reached, and the flesh then pared off until the joint is reached, and then it may be cut off. With other offerings it may be chopped off with a chopper, since they do not come under the rule of 'the breaking of a bone'. From the jamb of the door inwards counts as inside, and from the jamb of the door outwards counts as outside; the windows and the thickness of the wall count as inside.

13. If two companies ate [the Passover-offering] in the one room these should eat with their faces turned in one direction and the others should eat with their faces turned in the other direction, with the kettle[9] between them; and when the servant[10] stands up to mix the cups [of the other company] he should close his mouth and turn his face the other way until he [again] reaches his own company and goes on eating. And a bride should turn her face aside while she eats.

8. 1. If a woman was living in her husband's house and her husband slaughtered [the Passover-offering] for her, and her father slaughtered for her, she shall eat from that of her husband. If she went to keep the first Feast[11] in her father's house, and her father slaughtered for her and her husband slaughtered for her, she shall eat it in which place she will. An orphan for whom [many] guardians have slaughtered may eat it in which

---

[1] Num. 6[1ff.]. [2] From a hidden or unsuspected grave. Cf. Naz. 9[2]; Par. 3[2, 6].
[3] See p. 140, n. 3. [4] Ex. 12[10]. [5] Cf. Pes. 9[7]; Shek. 7[3]; Zeb. 8[4].
[6] Ex. 12[46], Num. 9[12]. [7] See Makk. 3[3].
[8] On the 14th; or on the night of the 15th; outside the house where it is being eaten. It offends against Ex. 12[46].
[9] In which the water is warmed for mixing with the wine.
[10] Who shares with one company and serves both. [11] After her marriage.

place he will. A slave belonging to jointholders may not eat from the Passover-offering of both. He that is half-slave and half-free[1] may not eat from that of his master.

2. If a man said to his slave, 'Go and slaughter the Passover-offering for me', and he slaughtered a kid, the master may eat of it; and if he slaughtered a lamb he may eat of it. If he slaughtered both a kid and a lamb he should eat of the first [that was slaughtered]. If he forgot what his master told him, [whether it should be a kid or a lamb,] what should he do? Let him slaughter a lamb and a kid and say, 'If my master told me to slaughter a kid, let the kid be his and let the lamb be mine; and if he told me to slaughter a lamb let the lamb be his and let the kid be mine'. If his master forgot what he told him, they must both go forth to the place of burning, but they are exempt from keeping the Second Passover.

3. If a man said to his sons, 'I will slaughter the Passover-offering for whichsoever of you shall first come up to Jerusalem', so soon as one has put his head and the greater part of his body inside [Jerusalem] he has gained his portion; and he must grant portions to his brothers also. Others may always be received within the number so long as there remains an olive's bulk of the Passover-offering for each one. They may be received within the number and withdraw from it until such time as it is slaughtered. R. Simeon says: Until the blood is about to be tossed on his behalf.

4. If a man invited others [to share] with him in his portion, the other members of the company have the right to give him [only] what belongs to him, and he [with them that he has invited] eats of what belongs to him while the others eat of what belongs to them.

5. If a man that had a flux[2] suffered two issues, they may slaughter for him on his seventh day;[3] if he suffered three, they may slaughter for him on his eighth day. A woman that awaits day against day,[4] for her they may slaughter on her second day. If she suffered flows for two days, for her they may slaughter on the third day. A woman that had a flux,[5] for her they may slaughter on her eighth day.

6. They may slaughter for one that mourns his near kindred,[6] or for one that clears away a ruin[7]; so, too, for one whom they have promised to bring out of prison, for a sick man, or for an aged man that is able to eat an olive's bulk. For none of these in particular may they slaughter, lest they cause the Passover-offering to become invalid.[8] Therefore if aught befell any of them to make them ineligible, they are exempt from keeping the Second Passover,[9] excepting him that clears away a ruin, since he was [liable to become] unclean from the first.

7. They may not slaughter the Passover-offering for one person. So R. Judah. But R. Jose permits it. They may not slaughter it even for

---

[1] See Gitt. 4[5].   [2] Lev. 15[1-15].   [3] Lev. 15[13].

[4] Meg. 2[4]; Hor. 1[3]; Nidd. 4[7]; Zab. 1[1]. A menstruant who suffered an issue during the eleven days between one fixed period and the next, and having immersed herself on the next day, awaits a complete day free of a flow, after which she is deemed clean; thus on her second day, if this begins on Passover night, she may eat of the Passover-offering.   [5] Lev. 15[25ff].

[6] He is forbidden to eat of Hallowed Things (cf. Deut. 26[14]) throughout the day in which his father, mother, brother, sister, son, daughter, or wife have died; also, by rabbinical authority only, throughout the following night (and the following day also if the burial is delayed until then).

[7] To rescue one who may be found dead, so rendering the rescuer unclean. Cf. Yom. 8[7].

[8] The Munich codex adds: 'but they may slaughter for them together with others'. See 5[3].   [9] Because the offering was valid when its blood was tossed.

a company of a hundred that are not able to eat an olive's bulk, nor may a company be made up of women, slaves, and minors.

8. He that mourns his near kindred may, after he has immersed himself, eat the Passover-offering in the evening, but he may not eat of [other] Hallowed Things.[1] If a man heard of the death of one of his near kindred or caused the bones of his dead to be gathered together,[2] he may, after he has immersed himself, eat of Hallowed Things. The School of Shammai say:[3] If a man became a proselyte on the day before Passover he may immerse himself and consume his Passover-offering in the evening. And the School of Hillel say: He that separates himself from his uncircumcision is as one that separates himself from a grave.[4]

9. 1. *If any man . . . shall be unclean . . . or be in a journey afar off*[5] and he has not kept the First [Passover], let him keep the Second. If through error or constraint he did not keep the First, let him keep the Second. If so, why is it said, [*If any man . . .*] *shall be unclean . . . or in a journey afar off*? Because these are not punishable by Extirpation, but others are punishable by Extirpation.

2. What counts as *a journey afar off*? Beyond Modiith,[6] or a like distance in any direction. So R. Akiba. R. Eliezer says: Beyond the threshold of the Temple Court. R. Jose said: Therefore there is a point over the *He*,[7] as if to say, Not because it is indeed afar off, but [only as far off as] beyond the threshold of the Temple Court.

3. Wherein does the First Passover differ from the Second? To the first apply the prohibitions *It shall not be seen* and *It shall not be found*,[8] whereas at the Second a man may have both unleavened bread and *hametz* with him in the house. At the eating of the First, the *Hallel*[9] must be sung, but at the eating of the Second, the *Hallel* need not be sung. Both require the *Hallel* to be sung while they are preparing, and both are eaten roast with unleavened bread and bitter herbs, and both override the Sabbath.

4. If the Passover-offering was offered in uncleanness,[10] men or women that a suffer a flux or menstruants[11] or women after childbirth[12] may not eat thereof, yet if they ate thereof they are not punishable by Extirpation.[13] R. Eliezer declares them exempt even if [in like case][14] they enter the Temple.

5. Wherein does the Passover of Egypt[15] differ from the Passover of the generations[16] [that followed after]? At the Passover of Egypt the lamb was got on the 10th [of Nisan], sprinkling [of the blood] with a bunch of hyssop was required on the lintel and on the two side-posts, and it was eaten in

---

[1] See p. 55, n. 16.

[2] About a year after burial in a rock-sepulchre the bones were gathered together out of the tomb-niche (see M.Kat. 1[5, 6]) and deposited in an ossuary, a small stone or earthenware casket.　　　　　　　　　　　　　　　[3] Eduy. 5[2].

[4] And needs to be sprinkled (see above, p. 143, n. 10) on the third and seventh days following, before he becomes clean.　　　　　　　　[5] See Num. 9[9f].

[6] Also Modaith, Modiin. See 1 Maccabees 2[1]. Perhaps the modern Mediyeh, seventeen miles north-west of Jerusalem (the Talmud describes it as fifteen miles—each of 2,000 cubits—from Jerusalem).

[7] The last letter in the Hebrew word rendered 'afar off'. The point is reproduced in the present Massoretic text. See C. D. Ginsberg, *Introduction to the Massoretico-Critical Edition of the Hebrew Bible*, London, 1897, pp. 318 ff.　　　　　　[8] Ex. 12[19]; 13[7].

[9] See above, 5[7].　　[10] See above, 7[6].　　[11] Lev. 15[19ff].　　[12] Lev. 12[1-8].

[13] Lev. 7[20f].　　　[14] When the Passover is offered in uncleanness. See Num. 19[20].

[15] As ordained in Ex. 12[1-13].　　　　　　　[16] As ordained in Ex. 12[14-20].

haste and during one night;[1] whereas the Passover of the generations [that followed after] continued throughout seven days.

6. R. Joshua said: I have heard a tradition that a substitute[2] for the Passover-offering can be offered, and, also, that a substitute for the Passover-offering cannot be offered; and I cannot explain it. R. Akiba said: I will explain it: if a Passover-offering [that had been lost] was found before the slaughtering of the [substituted] Passover-offering, it must be left to pasture until it suffers a blemish, when it must be sold and a Peace-offering offered with the price thereof; and so, too, with its substitute; but if it was found after the slaughtering of the [substituted] Passover-offering, it can itself be offered as a Peace-offering; and so, too, with its substitute.

7. If a man set aside a female as his Passover-offering, or a male two years old, it must be left to pasture until it suffers a blemish, when it must be sold and a Peace-offering offered with the price thereof. If a man set aside his Passover-offering and then died, his son after him may not offer it as a Passover-offering but as a Peace-offering.

8. If a Passover-offering was confused with [other] animal-offerings,[3] they must all be left to pasture until they suffer a blemish, when they must be sold and an offering of the one kind offered with the price of the best among them, and an offering of the other kind offered with the price of the best among them; and the added cost let him lose from his own substance.[4] If it was confused with Firstlings, R. Simeon says: If [they belonged to] a company of priests they must all be consumed [during the night of Passover].

9. If a company lost their Passover-offering and said to one of their number, 'Go and seek out and slaughter us another', and he went and sought out and slaughtered one, while they also took and slaughtered another, if it was his that was first slaughtered, he eats of his, and they eat of his with him; and if it was theirs that was first slaughtered, they eat of theirs and he eats of his. But if it is not known which of them was first slaughtered, or if they were slaughtered both at the same time, then he eats of his, and they do not eat with him; and theirs goes forth to the place of burning, but they are exempt from keeping the Second Passover. If he said to them, 'If I delay, go ye and slaughter for me', and then he went and sought out and slaughtered one, while they also took and slaughtered another, if it was theirs that was first slaughtered, they eat of theirs and he eats with them, and if it was his that was first slaughtered, he eats of his and they eat of theirs. But if it is not known which of them was first slaughtered, or if they were slaughtered both at the same time, then they eat of theirs and he does not eat with them; and his goes forth to the place of burning, but he is exempt from keeping the Second Passover. If he said to them and they said to him that all would eat of the first [that should be slaughtered] and it is not known which of them was first slaughtered, they both go forth to the place of burning. If he said naught to them and they said naught to him, they need have no regard the one to the other.

10. If the Passover-offerings of two companies were confused, these draw one of them and the others draw one of them. Then a member of

---

[1] The Gemara (96b) points out that there is here a lacuna in the Mishnah which should state that the prohibition of leavened bread lasted in the Passover of Egypt but one day, whereas, &c. . . .

[2] See Lev. 27[10]. See tractate Temurah.   [3] Guilt-offerings or Whole-offerings.

[4] Cf. Zeb. 8[2].

this company comes to the other company, and a member of the other company comes to this company, and they speak thus: 'If this Passover-offering is ours do thou withdraw thyself from thine own and be counted in with ours, and if this Passover-offering is thine, we withdraw ourselves from our own and are counted in with thine'. So also is it with [even] five companies of five or ten members each: one [of the confused Passover-offerings] is drawn by each company, and they speak in like fashion.

11. If the Passover-offerings of two persons were confused, they each draw one of them and each appoints a partner from the street and each comes to the other, and they speak thus: 'If this Passover-offering belongs to me do thou withdraw thyself from thine and be counted in with mine; and if this Passover-offering is thine, I will withdraw myself from mine and be counted in with thine'.

10. 1. On the eve of Passover, from about the time of the Evening Offering,[1] a man must eat naught until nightfall. Even the poorest in Israel must not eat unless he sits down to table, and they must not give them less than four cups of wine to drink, even if it is from the [Paupers'] Dish.[2]

2. After they have mixed him his first cup, the School of Shammai say: He says the Benediction first over the day and then the Benediction over the wine. And the School of Hillel say: He says the Benediction first over the wine and then the Benediction over the day.[3]

3. When [food][4] is brought before him he eats it seasoned with lettuce, until he is come to the breaking of bread;[5] they bring before him unleavened bread and lettuce and the *haroseth*,[6] although *haroseth* is not a religious obligation. R. Eliezer b. R. Zadok says: It is a religious obligation.[7] And in the Holy City[8] they used to bring before him the body of the Passover-offering.

4. They then mix him the second cup. And here the son asks his father (and if the son has not enough understanding his father instructs him [how to ask]), 'Why is this night different from other nights? For on other nights we eat seasoned food once, but this night twice; on other nights we eat leavened or unleavened bread, but this night all is unleavened;[9] on other nights we eat flesh roast, stewed, or cooked, but this night all is roast'.[10] And according to the understanding of the son his father instructs him. He begins with the disgrace and ends with the glory; and he expounds from *A wandering Aramean was my father* . . . until he finishes the whole section.[11]

5. Rabban Gamaliel used to say: Whosoever has not said [the verses[12] concerning] these three things at Passover has not fulfilled his obligation. And these are they: Passover, unleavened bread, and bitter herbs: 'Passover'—because God passed over the houses of our fathers in Egypt;

---

[1] See Num. 28[8]. See above 5[1].   [2] Cf. Peah 8[7].   [3] See Ber. 8[1].
[4] Some texts add: 'vegetables and lettuce'.
[5] So Bert. Variant: 'the bread condiment' (*parpereth*, as in Ber. 6[5], Ab. 3[19]), i.e. the bitter herbs.
[6] Made of nuts and fruit pounded together and mixed with vinegar. The bitter herbs were dipped into this to mitigate their bitterness. Some texts add: 'and two cooked dishes'.
[7] To recall, by its appearance, the mortar out of which the Israelites made bricks in Egypt.   [8] Lit. Temple. See M.Sh. 1[5].
[9] Some texts add: 'on other nights we eat all other manner of vegetables, but this night bitter herbs'.
[10] Some texts add: 'on other nights we dip but once, but this night twice'.
[11] Deut. 26[5ff].   [12] Ex. 12[27,39], 1[4].

'unleavened bread'—because our fathers were redeemed from Egypt; 'bitter herbs'—because the Egyptians embittered the lives of our fathers in Egypt. In every generation a man must so regard himself as if he came forth himself out of Egypt, for it is written, *And thou shalt tell thy son in that day saying, It is because of that which the Lord did for me when I came forth out of Egypt.*[1] Therefore are we bound to give thanks, to praise, to glorify, to honour, to exalt, to extol, and to bless him who wrought all these wonders for our fathers and for us. He brought us out from bondage to freedom, from sorrow to gladness, and from mourning to a Festival-day, and from darkness to great light, and from servitude to redemption; so let us say before him the *Hallelujah.*[2]

6. How far do they recite [the *Hallel*]? The School of Shammai say: To *A joyful mother of children.*[3] And the School of Hillel say: To *A flint-stone into a springing well.*[4] And this is concluded[5] with the *Ge'ullah.*[6] R. Tarfon says: 'He that redeemed us and redeemed our fathers from Egypt and brought us to this night to eat therein unleavened bread and bitter herbs'. But there is no concluding Benediction.[7] R. Akiba adds: 'Therefore, O Lord our God and the God of our fathers, bring us in peace to the other set feasts and festivals which are coming to meet us, while we rejoice in the building-up of thy city and are joyful in thy worship; and may we eat there of the sacrifices and of the Passover-offerings whose blood has reached with acceptance the wall of thy Altar, and let us praise thee[8] for our redemption and for the ransoming of our soul. Blessed art thou, O Lord, who hast redeemed Israel!'

7. After they have mixed for him the third cup he says the Benediction over his meal. [Over] a fourth [cup] he completes the *Hallel* and says after it the Benediction over song. If he is minded to drink [more] between these cups he may drink; only between the third and the fourth cups he may not drink.

8. After the Passover meal they should not disperse to join in revelry.[9] If some fell asleep [during the meal] they may eat [again]; but if all fell asleep they may not eat [again]. R. Jose says: If they but dozed they may eat [again]; but if they fell into deep sleep they may not eat [again].

9. After midnight the Passover-offering renders the hands unclean.[10] The Refuse[11] and Remnant[12] make the hands unclean. If a man has said the Benediction over the Passover-offering it renders needless a Benediction over [any other] animal-offering[13] [that he eats]; but if he said the Benediction over [any other] animal-offering it does not render needless the Benediction over the Passover-offering. So R. Ishmael. R. Akiba says: Neither of them renders the other needless.

---

[1] Ex. 13[8]. This whole sentence is omitted by older sources.
[2] Usually referred to as the *Hallel*, i.e. Pss. 113–18. See above, 5[7].   [3] End of Ps. 113.
[4] End of Ps. 114, 'When Israel came out of Egypt. . .'
[5] Lit. 'sealed'. Cf. Ber. 1[4].
[6] Lit. 'redemption', i.e. a Benediction recounting God's redemption of his people out of the hands of the Egyptians.
[7] As in the following version by R. Akiba.
[8] Some texts add: 'with a new song'.
[9] Heb. *Epikoman*, ἐπὶ κῶμον. Cf. Is. 30[29]. The joy of the Passover meal with its solemn symbolism must not degenerate into an ordinary convivial gathering. The traditional interpretation, however, is: 'they may not finish with "desert" '.
[10] It could be eaten only until midnight; see Zeb. 5[8]. Ex. 12[10] only forbids it to remain 'until the morning'. Cf. Ber. 1[1].
[11] Lit. 'abomination'. Lev. 7[18]; 19[7]. Cf. Zeb. 2[2-3]; 3[4]; Men. 1[3].
[12] Lev. 7[15], 19[6].   [13] The freewill festal-offering spoken of above, 6[3-4].

SHEKALIM ('THE SHEKEL DUES')

1. 1. On the first day of Adar[1] they give warning of the Shekel dues[2] and against [the sowing of] Diverse Kinds.[3] On the 15th thereof they read the *Megillah*[4] in walled cities and repair the paths and roads[5] and pools of water[6] and perform all public needs and mark the graves;[7] and they also go forth [to give warning] against Diverse Kinds.

2. R. Judah said: At first they used to root them out and cast them down before the owner, but when transgressors grew many they used to root them out and cast them down by the waysides; [later] they ordained that [where Diverse Kinds grew] the whole field should be accounted ownerless property.

3. On the 15th thereof the tables [of the money-changers] were set up in the provinces; and on the 25th thereof they were set up in the Temple. After they were set up in the Temple they began to exact pledges.[8] From whom did they exact pledges? From levites, Israelites, proselytes, and freed slaves, but not from women, slaves, or minors. If the father had begun to pay the Shekel on behalf of [his son that was] a minor, he may never again cease to pay it. They did not exact pledges from the priests, in the interests of peace.[9]

4. R. Judah said: Ben Bukri testified at Jabneh that if a priest paid the Shekel he committed no sin. Rabban Johanan b. Zakkai answered: Not so! but, rather, if a priest did not pay the Shekel he committed sin; but the priests used to expound this scripture to their advantage, *And every meal offering of the priest shall be wholly burnt: it shall not be eaten:*[10] since the *Omer* and the Two Loaves and the Shewbread are ours, how can they be eaten?[11]

5. Although they have said, 'They do not exact pledges from women, slaves, or minors', if they have paid the Shekel it is accepted of them; but if a gentile or a Samaritan paid the Shekel it is not accepted of them. Nor do they accept of them the Bird-offerings of a man or woman that has a flux[12] or of a woman after childbirth,[13] or Sin-offerings or Guilt-offerings; but they may accept of them vow-offerings or freewill-offerings. This is the general rule: What is vowed or freely offered is accepted of them, but what is not vowed or freely offered is not accepted of them; and so is it expressly enjoined by Ezra, for it is written, *Ye have nothing to do with us to build a house unto our God.*[14]

---

1 App. I. 2.
2 i.e. the half-shekel (see Ex. 30[13ff].) due to the Temple from every Israelite 'twenty years old and upward' before the 1st of Nisan each year; on and after the 1st of Nisan the public offerings may be brought only from the newly paid shekel dues.
3 See p. 28, n. 1.   4 Book of Esther. See Meg. 1[1ff].
5 After the winter rains, in readiness for the Passover pilgrimage.
6 To equip them as valid 'immersion-pools'. See tractate Mikwaoth.
7 With lime (see M.Sh. 5[1]), lest any become unclean by coming near them (cf. Num. 6[6]; 19[16]).
8 From such as had not paid.
9 Cf. Gitt. 5[8, 9]. The Jerusalem Talmud here reads: 'by reason of respect'.
10 Lev. 6[23].
11 Meaning that since these three Meal-offerings are brought as public offerings at the charges of the Temple fund (which is maintained by the Shekel contributions), the priests may not contribute to the Temple fund: if they contributed to the cost of these Meal-offerings they would need to be burnt; and this would be contrary to Scripture.
12 Lev. 15[14-15, 29-30].   13 Lev. 12[8].   14 Ezra 4[3].

6. And these are they that are liable to surcharge:[1] levites and Israelites[2] and proselytes and freed slaves; but not priests, women, slaves, or minors. If a man paid the Shekel on behalf of a priest or a woman or a slave or a minor, he is exempt. If he paid for himself and for his fellow he is liable to but a single surcharge. R. Meir says: A double surcharge. If a man gave a *sela*[3] and took back a shekel he is liable to a double surcharge.

7. If a man paid the Shekel on behalf of a poor man or on behalf of his fellow or on behalf of a fellow-townsman, he is exempt; but if he had lent it to them he is liable. If brothers[4] that were jointholders are liable to surcharge[5] they are exempt from Tithe of Cattle;[6] and if they are liable to Tithe of Cattle[7] they are exempt from surcharge. And how much is the surcharge? A silver *maah*.[8] So R. Meir. But the Sages say: Half a *maah*.

2. 1. Shekels may be changed into darics[9] because of [lightening] a journey's load. Like as there were Shofar-chests[10] in the Temple so were there Shofar-chests in the provinces. If the people of a town sent their Shekels [to the Temple] and they were stolen or lost, if *Terumah*[11] had already been taken [the messengers] swear an oath[12] before the treasurers; otherwise they swear an oath before the people of the town, and the people of the town must pay the Shekel dues anew; if the dues [that were lost] were found again or if the thieves restored them, these, too, are taken as Shekel dues[13] and they do not count in fulfilment of their obligation for the coming year.

2. If a man gave his Shekel to his fellow to pay on his behalf and he paid it on his own behalf, if *Terumah* had already been taken, he has committed Sacrilege.[14] If a man paid his Shekel from money that belonged to the Temple, if *Terumah* had already been taken and a sacrifice[15] offered, he has committed Sacrilege. If it was from Second Tithe money or the price of Seventh Year produce, he must [still] consume [produce of] the like value.[16]

3. If a man brought together coins and said, 'Lo, these are for my Shekel,' the School of Shammai say: The surplus falls also to the Temple fund.[17] And the School of Hillel say: The surplus is free for common use. [But if he said,] 'These are for my Sin-offering', they agree that the surplus falls to the Temple fund; [but if he said,] 'I will offer my Sin-offering from them', they agree that the surplus is free for common use.

4. R. Simeon said: Wherein do Shekel dues differ from a Sin-offering? The Shekel dues have a prescribed limit but the Sin-offering has no

---

1 Compensation to the Temple's Shekel-collectors to reimburse them for any loss incurred in changing the shekels or half-shekels into or out of other money.
2 Neither priests nor levites. This is a frequent sense of 'Israelite' throughout the Mishnah.
3 App. II, A.   4 Hull. 1⁷; Bekh. 9³.   5 If they had divided their goods.
6 That were born when their goods were still undivided.
7 If they had not divided their goods.   8 App. II, A.
9 A Persian gold coin worth about sixteen shekels.
10 To receive the Shekel dues. 'Shofar' possibly refers to the tapering shape of these money-chests.
11 See 3¹, and App. I. 48 (3). This taking of a *Terumah* imposes on the money so drawn upon the sanctity of Temple property.
12 So becoming exempt from making restitution. See B.M. 3¹.
13 Valid for the current year.
14 Misappropriation of Temple property, Lev. 5¹⁵ᶠ. See p. 573, n. 2.
15 Bought from the money taken in the *Terumah*.
16 In the conditions prescribed for Second Tithe (M.Sh. 2¹⁻⁴) or Seventh Year produce (Shebi. 9⁴ᶠ.)   17 Lit. 'for a freewill offering'.

prescribed limit. R. Judah says: Shekel dues have also no prescribed limit, for when Israel returned from exile they used to pay the Shekel in darics,[1] then they changed and paid the Shekel in double-shekels,[2] then they changed and paid the Shekel in shekel-pieces, and then they sought to pay the Shekel in *denars*.[3] R. Simeon said: Nevertheless the charge for all was equal; whereas for a Sin-offering one man offers the value of one *sela*, another two *selas*, and another three.

5. The surplus of [money that had been assigned to] Shekel dues is free for common use, but the surplus of [the price of] the Tenth of the Ephah,[4] or of the Bird-offerings[5] of a man or woman that have a flux, or of a woman after childbirth, or of Sin-offerings or Guilt-offerings—their surplus falls to the Temple fund. This is the general rule: the surplus of what had been assigned [as the price of] a Sin-offering or a Guilt-offering falls to the Temple fund. The surplus of [money assigned to] a Whole-offering [must be used] for a Whole-offering; the surplus of [money assigned to] a Meal-offering [must be used] for a Meal-offering; the surplus of [money assigned to] a Peace-offering [must be used] for a Peace-offering; the surplus of [money assigned to] a Passover-offering [must be used] for a Peace-offering; the surplus of [money assigned to] Nazirites' offerings [must be used] for [other] Nazirites' offerings; the surplus of [money assigned to] one Nazirite's offerings falls to the Temple fund; the surplus of [money collected for] the poor [must be used] for the poor; the surplus of [money collected for] one poor man [must be given] to that poor man; the surplus of [money collected to ransom] captives [must be used] for [other] captives; the surplus of [money collected to ransom] one captive [must also be used] for that captive; the surplus of [money collected to pay for the burial of] the dead [must be used] for [other] dead; the surplus of [money collected to pay for the burial of] one dead person [must be used] for his heirs. R. Meir says: The surplus of [money collected to pay for the burial of] one dead person must be left until Elijah comes. R. Nathan says: It is used to build a monument over his grave.

3. 1. Three times in the year did they take up *Terumah*[6] out of the Shekel-chamber: a half month before Passover, a half month before Pentecost, and a half month before the Feast [of Tabernacles]; and these same are the appointed seasons for the Tithe of Cattle.[7] So R. Akiba. Ben Azzai says: On the 29th of Adar, and on the 1st of Siwan, and on the 29th of Ab. R. Eliezer and R. Simeon say: On the 1st of Nisan, on the 1st of Siwan, and on the 29th of Elul. Why did they say, 'On the 29th of Elul' and not 'On the 1st of Tishri'? Because that is a Festival-day[8] and it is not possible to tithe on a Festival-day; therefore they made it earlier, on the 29th of Elul.

2. In three baskets, each holding three *seahs*,[9] did they take up *Terumah* out of the Shekel-chamber, and on them was inscribed [the letters] *Aleph*, *Beth*, and *Gimel*. R. Ishmael says: On them was inscribed in Greek [the

---

[1] Not the same as in 2[1]. Perhaps a Persian silver coin of that name is intended.
[2] Lit. *selas*.
[3] Equal in value to half a shekel. Some texts add: 'but these were not accepted of them'.
[4] Lev. 5 [11-13].   [5] See p. 152, nn. 12,13.
[6] The word is that which is generally translated 'Heave-offering'. Here it has no longer the restricted sense of the portions of harvested produce due to the priest (cf. Ned. 2[4]). See App. I. 48, and cf. above 2[1]. In modern Hebrew the word does duty for 'subscription', 'contribution'.   [7] Lev. 27[32]. See Bekh. 9[5].   [8] See p. 181, n. 11.   [9] App. II, D.

letters] *Alpha, Beta,* and *Gamma.* He that went in to take up *Terumah* did not wear a sleeved cloak or shoes or sandals or phylacteries or an amulet, lest if he became poor men should say that he became poor through a sin against the Shekel-chamber, or if he became rich they should say that he became rich from the *Terumah* taken up out of the Shekel-chamber; for a man must satisfy mankind even as he must satisfy God, for it is written, *And be guiltless towards the Lord and towards Israel,*[1] and again it says, *So shalt thou find favour and good understanding in the sight of God and man.*[2]

3. They of the house of Rabban Gamaliel[3] used to go in with their Shekel between their fingers and throw it in front of him that took up *Terumah,* and he that took up *Terumah* was at pains to thrust it into the basket. He that took up *Terumah* never took it up without saying, 'Shall I take up *Terumah?*' and they thrice made answer, 'Take up *Terumah!* Take up *Terumah!* Take up *Terumah!*'

4. After taking up the first [*Terumah*] he put a covering over [the residue]; and after the second he again put a cover over [the residue] (but after the third he put no covering over [the residue]), lest he should forget and again take up *Terumah* [from those Shekels] from which *Terumah* had already been taken. He took up the first [*Terumah*] on behalf of the Land of Israel, and the second on behalf of the cities near by, and the third on behalf of Babylon, Media, and the regions afar off.

4. 1. What did they do with the *Terumah?* They bought therewith the Daily Whole-offerings[4] and the Additional Whole-offerings[5] and their drink-offerings,[6] the *Omer*[7] and the Two Loaves[8] and the Shewbread,[9] and all [else needful for] the offerings of the congregation. The guardians of the Seventh Year[10] aftergrowths[11] received their hire from the *Terumah* of the Shekel-chamber. R. Jose says: He that was so minded could offer himself as guardian without hire. They answered: Thou, too, sayest that these are offered only from public means.

2. The [Red] Heifer[12] and the scapegoat[13] and the crimson thread[14] were bought with the *Terumah* from the Shekel-chamber. The causeway for the [Red] Heifer[15] and the causeway for the scapegoat[16] and the thread between its horns,[17] the [upkeep of the] water-channel,[18] the city wall and the towers thereof and all the city's needs were provided from the residue[19] of the Shekel-chamber. Abba Saul says: The causeway for the [Red] Heifer was built by the High Priests at their own charges.

3. What did they do with the surplus of the residue of the Shekel-chamber? Wine, oil, and flour were bought therewith,[20] and the profit fell to the Temple. So R. Ishmael. But R. Akiba says: They may not traffick with what belongs to the Temple, nor with what belongs to the poor.

---

[1] Num. 32²².   [2] Prov. 3⁴.
[3] To ensure that their Shekel dues should be used directly for the Temple offerings, and not be left as the residue. See below, 4⁴.   [4] Num. 28¹⁻⁸.
[5] The special offerings for Sabbaths, New Moons, and Festival-days; Num. 28⁹⁻³¹; 29¹⁻⁴⁰.   [6] And Meal-offerings.   [7] Lev. 23⁹ᶠᶠ. App. I. 31.   [8] Lev. 23¹⁶⁻¹⁷.
[9] Ex. 25³⁰; Lev. 24⁵ᶠᶠ.   [10] Lev. 25²⁻⁷.   [11] Required for the *Omer.*
[12] Num. 19¹ᶠᶠ. See tractate Parah.   [13] Lev. 16¹⁰, ²¹ᶠᶠ.
[14] To distinguish between the two goats; Lev. 16⁵ᶠᶠ. See Yom. 4².
[15] Par. 3⁶.   [16] Yom. 6⁴.   [17] Yom. 6⁶.
[18] That flowed through the Temple Court. Yom. 5⁶; Zeb. 87ᶠᶠ.; Tem. 7⁶; Tam. 5⁵; Midd. 3².   [19] What was left after the *Terumah* had been taken.
[20] To be sold to those bringing private offerings.

4. What did they do with the surplus of the *Terumah*?[1] Golden plating for bedecking the Holy of Holies. R. Ishmael says: The surplus of the profits[2] was devoted to [offerings for] the Altar such time as it lay idle, and the surplus of the *Terumah* was devoted to vessels of ministry. R. Akiba says: The surplus of the *Terumah* was devoted to [offerings for] the Altar such time as it lay idle, and the surplus from the drink-offerings[3] was devoted to vessels of ministry. R. Hanina the Prefect of the Priests says: The surplus from the drink-offerings was devoted to [offerings for] the Altar such time as it lay idle, and the surplus of the *Terumah* was devoted to vessels of ministry. Of these two neither admitted that profits were permissible.

5. What did they do with the surplus of the incense?[4] They set apart therefrom the hire of the craftsmen,[5] and, after they had redeemed it with the money due to the craftsmen, they gave it to the craftsmen as their hire and bought it back from them again [with money] from the new *Terumah*. If the new *Terumah* came in due time they bought it back with new *Terumah*; but if not, with old.

6. If a man dedicated his goods to the Temple, even if there were among them things fit for the offerings of the congregation they should be given to the craftsmen as their hire. So R. Akiba. Ben Azzai said to him: That is not the manner prescribed:[6] but, rather, they used to set apart therefrom the hire of the craftsmen, and, after they had redeemed them with the money due to the craftsmen, they gave them to the craftsmen as their hire and bought them back again [with money] from the new *Terumah*.

7. If a man dedicated his goods to the Temple, even if there were among them cattle, male and female, fit for the Altar, R. Eliezer says: The males should be sold to them that need Whole-offerings and the females[7] to them that need Peace-offerings; and their price and the rest of the goods fall to the Temple fund. R. Joshua says: The males themselves should be [forthwith] offered as Whole-offerings, and the females should be sold to them that need Peace-offerings, and with their price Whole-offerings should be offered, and the rest of the goods falls to the Temple fund. R. Akiba says: I prefer the opinion of R. Eliezer to that of R. Joshua, for R. Eliezer applied his rule equally while R. Joshua made distinction. R. Papias said: I have heard a tradition that accords with both their opinions: that if a man dedicates his goods on explicit terms it is according to R. Eliezer's opinion; but if without terms, it is according to R. Joshua's opinion.

8. If a man dedicated his goods to the Temple, even if there were among them things fit for the Altar—wine, oil, flour, or birds—R. Eleazar says:

---

[1] What was left after the purchase of the things specified in par. 1 and the beginning of par. 2.

[2] On the wine, oil, and flour sold to those bringing private offerings.   [3] See 5[4].

[4] An ordinary lunar year had 354 days and a leap-year 384. Every year they prepared 368 minas of incense (a tradition handed down by Moses from Sinai), hence some years had a surplus (the consumption of incense was half a mina each morning and afternoon, and three minas more on the Day of Atonement); whereas there was a deficit for leap-years. The problem was how to carry over one year's surplus without offending against the rule that, beginning with each 1st of Nisan, what was offered should be only from the newly-taken *Terumah*.

[5] Who compounded the incense, baked the Shewbread, and guarded the Seventh Year aftergrowths.   [6] According to the principle in the foregoing paragraph.

[7] Since these could not be Whole-offerings (Lev. 1[3]).

They should be sold to them that need that kind of offering, and with their price Whole-offerings should be offered; and the rest of the goods falls to the Temple fund.

9. Once in thirty days prices were assessed [anew] with the Shekel-chamber. If any had undertaken to provide flour at four [*seahs* a *sela*], and the price stood [that month] at three [*seahs* a *sela*], he must still provide it at four; if [he had undertaken to provide it] at three, and the price stood [that month] at four [*seahs* a *sela*], he must provide it at four, since the Temple has the upper hand. If the flour turned maggoty he must bear the loss; if the wine turned sour he must bear the loss. He cannot receive payment until after the Altar has effected acceptance.[1]

5. 1. These are the officers which served in the Temple: Johanan b. Phineas was over the seals,[2] Ahijah was over the drink-offerings, Mattithiah b. Samuel[3] was over the lots,[4] Petahiah was over the Bird-offerings[5] (this same Petahiah was Mordecai; why was his name called Petahiah?— because he was able to 'open'[6] matters and to expound them,[7] and he knew seventy languages); Ben Ahijah was over the bowel sickness,[8] Nehunyah was the trench-digger,[9] Gabini was the herald,[10] Ben Geber was over the shutting of the gates, Ben Bebai was over the knout,[11] Ben Arza was over the cymbal,[12] Hygros b. Levi was over the singing,[13] the House of Garmu[14] was over the preparation of the Shewbread, the House of Abtinas[15] was over the preparation of the incense, Eleazar was over the hangings, and Phineas was over the vestments.

2. There were never less than three treasurers and seven supervisors; nor were less than two persons suffered to hold office over the public in aught concerning property, save only Ben Ahijah who was over the bowel sickness and Eleazar who was over the hangings, whom the congregation[16] agreed to accept.

3. There were four seals in the Temple and on them was inscribed 'Calf', 'Ram', 'Kid', 'Sinner'. Ben Azzai says: There were five and on them was inscribed in Aramaic, 'Calf', 'Ram', 'Kid', 'Poor sinner', and 'Rich sinner'. 'Calf' signified drink-offerings[17] for [offerings from the] herds, whether large or small, male or female; 'Kid' signified drink-offerings for [offerings from the] flock, large or small, male or female, excepting rams; 'Ram' signified the drink-offerings for rams alone; 'Sinner' signified the drink-offerings for the three beasts offered by lepers.[18]

4. If any wished for drink-offerings he would go to Johanan who was over the seals and give him money and receive from him a seal; he would then go to Ahijah who was over the drink-offerings and give him the seal and from him

---

[1] Cf. Pes. 7[7]; Zeb. 8[12]. Then only does the merchant cease to be answerable for the quality of his wares.   [2] See below, 5[3–4].   [3] Mentioned in Yom. 3[1]; Tam. 3[2].
[4] Yom. 2[1–4].   [5] See p. 598, n. 3.
[6] The literal meaning of 'Petahiah' is 'The Lord has opened'.
[7] A probable reference to the complicated problems arising out of these offerings. See tractate Kinnim, chh. 2 and 3. Cf. Ab. 3[19].
[8] To which the priests were liable owing to going about barefooted and their abundant flesh diet (Bert.).
[9] He used to dig the wells and cisterns needed to supply the pilgrims to Jerusalem with water.   [10] His voice could be heard in Jericho; Tam. 3[8].
[11] To scourge priests or levites found sleeping while on guard (Midd. 1[2]). The word rendered 'knout' is also explained (in the Jerusalem Talmud) in the sense of 'wick'; i.e. Ben Bebai was in charge of the lamps of the Seven-branched Candlestick.
[12] See Tam. 7[3].   [13] See Yom. 3[11].   [14] See Yom. 3[11].   [15] See Yom. 3[11].
[16] Some texts read: 'most of the congregation'.   [17] And Meal-offerings.
[18] Lev. 14[10].

receive drink-offerings. And in the evening the two came together and Ahijah brought out the seals and took their corresponding value in money; and if there was any surplus the surplus fell to the Temple,[1] and if there was any lack Johanan paid it from his own means, since the Temple has the upper hand.

5. If a man lost his seal they made him wait until evening; if they found [money left over] enough for his seal, they gave him a seal, but if they did not find enough he received none. And the name of the day was inscribed thereon because of defrauders.

6. There were two chambers in the Temple: one the Chamber of Secrets and the other the Chamber of Utensils.[2] Into the Chamber of Secrets the devout used to put their gifts in secret and the poor of good family received support therefrom in secret. The Chamber of Utensils—whosoever made a gift of any article used to cast it therein, and every thirty days the treasurers opened it; and any article which they found of use for the Temple fund they left there; and the rest were sold and their price fell to the Chamber of the Temple fund.

6. 1. There were thirteen Shofar-chests, thirteen tables, and thirteen prostrations in the Temple. They of the House of Gamaliel and of the House of R. Hanina the Prefect of the Priests used to make fourteen prostrations. And where was the added one? Opposite the wood-store, for thus was the tradition among them from their forefathers, that there the Ark lay hidden.

2. Once when a priest was occupied [therein] he saw a block of pavement that was different from the rest. He went and told it to his fellow, but before he could make an end of the matter his life departed. So they knew assuredly that there the Ark lay hidden.

3. Where[3] did they make the prostrations? Four times in the north, four times in the south, thrice in the east and twice in the west, opposite the thirteen gates. The southern gates, counting from the west, were: the Upper Gate, the Kindling Gate, the Gate of the Firstlings, and the Water Gate. And why was it called the Water Gate? Because through it they brought in the flagon of water for the libation at the Feast [of Tabernacles].[4] R. Eliezer b. Jacob says: Through it *the waters trickle forth* and hereafter they will *issue out from under the threshold of the House*.[5] And opposite them, on the north, counting from the west: the Gate of Jeconiah, the Gate of the Offering, the Gate of the Women, and the Gate of Singing. And why was it called the Gate of Jeconiah? Because through it Jeconiah went forth when he went into exile. To the east was the Gate of Nicanor, and it had two wickets, one to the right and one to the left. And there were two [gates] to the west which had no name.

4. There were thirteen tables[6] in the Temple: eight of marble in the shambles on which they rinsed the inwards, and two to the west of the [Altar-]Ramp, one of marble and one of silver; on that of marble they laid the parts of the offering, and on that of silver the vessels of ministry; and there were two in the Porch within, at the entering in of the House,[7] the one of marble and the other of gold. On the table of marble they laid the Shewbread when it was brought in, and on that of gold [they laid it]

---

[1] And was used (see 4[4]) to provide vessels of ministry.   [2] Tam. 3[4].
[3] Cf. Midd. 2[6].   [4] See Sukk. 4[9].   [5] Cf. Ezek. 47[1–5].   [6] See Tam. 3[5]; Midd. 3[5].
[7] Here meaning the *Hekal* or Sanctuary; see Midd. 4[1]. The present passage is repeated in Men. 11[7].

when it was brought out, since what is holy must be raised [in honour] and not brought down. And within was a table of gold whereon the Shewbread lay continually.[1]

5. There were thirteen Shofar-chests[2] in the Temple, whereon was inscribed: 'New Shekel dues', 'Old Shekel dues', 'Bird-offerings', 'Young birds for the Whole-offering', 'Wood', 'Frankincense', 'Gold for the Mercy-seat',[3] and, on six of them, 'Freewill-offerings'. 'New Shekel dues' —those for each [present] year; 'Old [Shekel dues]'—if any had not paid his Shekel in the last year he must pay it in the next year. 'Bird-offerings' —these are the turtle-doves; and 'Young birds for the Whole-offering'— they are the young pigeons; and both of these are for Whole-offerings. So R. Judah. But the Sages say: Of the Bird-offerings one is a Sin-offering and the other a Whole-offering, but the 'Young birds for the Whole-offering' are all of them for Whole-offerings.[4]

6. If a man said: 'I pledge myself to offer [pieces of] wood',[5] he must bring not less than two faggots; if 'frankincense', he must bring not less than a handful; if 'gold', he must give not less than a golden denar.[6] 'And, on six of them, [was inscribed] "Freewill-offerings" '—what did they do with the Freewill-offerings? They bought Whole-offerings with them, the flesh for God and the hides for the priests. Jehoida the High Priest gave the following exposition: *It is a guilt offering: he is certainly guilty before the Lord*[7]—this is the general rule: all that comes [from the residue of money assigned to an offering incurred] by an act of Sin or guilt, Whole-offerings must be bought therewith—the flesh for God and the hide for the priests. Thus both scriptures are fulfilled: [*He shall bring*] *his guilt offering to the Lord*,[8] and *For a guilt offering unto the priest*.[9] It says also, *The money for the guilt offerings and the money for the sin offerings was not brought into the house of the Lord: it was the priests'*.[10]

7. 1. If money was found between the chest for 'Shekels' and the chest for 'Freewill-offerings' and it lay nearer to the chest for 'Shekels', it falls to the chest for 'Shekels', if nearer to the chest for 'Freewill-offerings' it falls to the chest for 'Freewill-offerings', if midway, it falls to the chest for 'Freewill-offerings'; if it was found between the chest for 'Wood', and the chest for 'Frankincense' and it lay nearer to the chest for 'Wood' it falls to the chest for 'Wood', if nearer to the chest for 'Frankincense' it falls to the chest for 'Frankincense', if midway, it falls to the chest for 'Frankincense'; if it was found between the chest for 'Bird-offerings' and the chest for 'Young birds for Whole-offerings' and it lay nearer the chest for 'Bird-offerings' it falls to the chest for 'Bird-offerings', if nearer to the chest for 'Young birds for Whole-offerings' it falls to the chest for 'Young birds for Whole-offerings', if midway, it falls to the chest for 'Young birds for Whole-offerings'. If [the money was found] between common money and Second Tithe [money][11] and it lay nearer to the common money, it falls to the common money, if nearer to the Second Tithe [money] it falls to the Second Tithe [money], if midway, it falls to the Second Tithe [money]. This is the general rule: they shall decide in accordance with which is the

---

[1] Ex. 25 [23-30].   [2] See above, 2[1].
[3] Ex. 25[17-21]. But there was no Ark in the Second Temple. Bert. explains the word (*kapporeth*) as 'vessels of ministry'.   [4] See Kinn. 1[1].   [5] Men. 13[3].
[6] Twenty-five silver denars. App. II, A.   [7] Lev. 5[19].   [8] Lev. 5[15].   [9] Lev. 5[18].
[10] 2 Kings 12[16].   [11] Deut. 14[22-5]. See p. 73, n. 6.

nearer, even if leniency ensues; but where it lies midway they shall decide according to the more stringent ruling.[1]

2. If money was found before cattle-dealers, it must be deemed to be [Second] Tithe [money];[2] if [it was found] in the Temple Mount it may be deemed to be common money; if in Jerusalem, during a Feast it must be deemed [Second] Tithe [money], and at all other times of the year common money.

3. If flesh was found in the Temple Court and it was [in the form of] entire members,[3] it must be deemed to belong to a Whole-offering; if in cut-up pieces, to a Sin-offering.[4] If it was found in Jerusalem,[5] it must be deemed to belong to a Peace-offering.[6] But in every like case its appearance must be spoilt and it must be taken away to the place of burning. If it was found elsewhere within the borders [of the Land of Israel] and it was in the form of entire members, it must be deemed to be carrion,[7] but if in cut-up pieces it is permitted [for use]; and at the time of a Feast, when there is much flesh, even [if it was found in the form of] entire members, it is permitted.[8]

4. If cattle are found between Jerusalem and as far as Migdal Eder,[9] or within the like distance in any direction, males must be deemed to be Whole-offerings and females Peace-offerings.[10] R. Judah says: If fitted to be Passover-offerings,[11] they must be deemed to be Passover-offerings [if they are found during] thirty days before the Feast.

5. Beforetime they used to exact pledges from any that found [a straying beast] until he should offer its drink-offerings; but when they began to let them alone and flee from them, the Court ordained that the drink-offerings thereof should be offered at the charges of the congregation.

6. R. Simeon said: The Court ordained seven things and this was one of them. [Moreover they ordained that] if a gentile sent his Whole-offering from a region beyond the sea and sent the drink-offerings also, these are offered; but if he did not, they are to be offered at the charges of the congregation. So, too, if a proselyte died and left animal-offerings, and there were drink-offerings also, these are offered out of his goods, but if not, they are to be offered at the charges of the congregation. It was also a condition enjoined by the Court, that if a High Priest died, his Meal-offering[12] should be offered at the charges of the congregation. R. Judah says: From the property of his heirs. It was offered undivided.[13]

7. [Moreover they ordained] concerning the salt and the wood that the priests should have free use of them, and concerning the [Red] Heifer[14] that the law of Sacrilege[15] did not apply to its ashes, and concerning Bird-offerings that were invalid, that [others in their place] should be offered at the charges of the congregation. R. Jose says: He that provides the Bird-offerings must provide others in place of them that are invalid.

---

[1] i.e. in favour of a Whole-offering, of which the priests receive no share.
[2] Since most cattle sold in Jerusalem were bought with Second Tithe money.
[3] As described in Tam. 4[2-3].
[4] Since such was cut up and divided among the priests.
[5] Not in the Temple Court.
[6] Only such could be eaten outside the Temple Court.
[7] Deut. 14[21].
[8] Provided that the majority of the population are Israelites.
[9] Gen. 35[21]. Near Bethlehem.
[10] Since (Lev. 1[3]) they were not valid as Whole-offerings.
[11] Males from the sheep or the goats, less than one year old.
[12] Lev. 6[14-16].
[13] See Men. 4[5].   [14] Num. 19[1ff.].   [15] See p. 573, n. 2.

8. 1. Any spittle found in Jerusalem may be deemed[1] free from unclean-ness,[2] excepting what is found in the Upper Market.[3] So R. Meir. R. Jose says: Other times of the year they [that walk] in the middle [of a street] must be deemed unclean, and they [that walk] at the sides may be deemed clean; but during a Feast they [that walk] in the middle [may be deemed] clean and they [that walk] at the sides [must be deemed] unclean; because when they are but few they withdraw to the sides [of a street].

2. All utensils found in Jerusalem on the path down to the place of immersion must be deemed unclean; but [if they are found] on the path back they may be deemed clean; for the path by which they are taken down is not the same as that by which they are brought back. So R. Meir. R. Jose says: All may be deemed clean excepting the basket, shovel, or pick especially used in digging graves.

3. If a knife was found on the 14th [of Nisan] a man may slaughter therewith at once[4] [without immersion]; but if on the 13th, it must be immersed again; but a chopper[5] in either case must be immersed again. If the 14th fell on the Sabbath a man may slaughter therewith at once; if [it was found] on the 15th a man may slaughter therewith at once. If it was found fastened to the knife, it may be treated in like fashion as the knife.

4. If the veil [of the Temple] contracted uncleanness from a derived uncleanness,[6] it may be immersed within [the Temple Court] and forth-with brought in again; but if from a primary uncleanness,[7] it must be immersed outside and spread out on the Rampart,[8] since it must await sunset [to be wholly clean]. If it is new it should be spread out on the roof of the portico[9] that the people may see how fine is the craftsmanship thereof.

5. Rabban Simeon b. Gamaliel says in the name of R. Simeon son of the Prefect: The veil was one handbreadth thick and was woven on [a loom having] seventy-two rods,[10] and over each rod were twenty-four threads.[11] Its length was forty cubits and its breadth twenty cubits; it was made by eighty-two young girls,[12] and they used to make two in every year; and three hundred priests immersed it.

6. If flesh of the Most Holy Things[13] contracted uncleanness, whether from a primary uncleanness or from a derived uncleanness, whether inside [the Temple Court] or outside it, the School of Shammai say: It must ever be burnt within, save when it has contracted uncleanness outside from a primary uncleanness. And the School of Hillel say: It must ever be burnt outside, save when it has contracted uncleanness inside from a derived uncleanness.[14]

---

[1] By him that is scrupulous, an 'associate' (Dem. 2³) or a Pharisee (cf. Hag. 2⁷).
[2] As not issuing from one that had a flux; see Kel. 1⁵.
[3] Since this was largely frequented by gentiles.
[4] It can be assumed to have been immersed in readiness for slaughtering the Passover-offering that day.
[5] Which serves to break bones (cf. Pes. 7¹²), therefore it is not fitting for use at Passover, and so may not have been specially immersed.
[6] See p. 137, n. 11.   [7] See p. 137, n. 12.
[8] The *Khel*. See Midd. 2³. It marked the boundary of the outermost court. Cf. Kel. 1⁸. It must remain there until sunset. See Lev. 11³².
[9] See Pes. 1⁵, Sukk. 4⁴.   [10] Variant: 'woven on seventy-two strands'.
[11] Or 'each strand was of twenty-four threads'.
[12] Variant: 'at a cost of 82 myriad (*denars*)'.
[13] See Zeb. 5¹⁻⁵: Whole-offerings, Sin-offerings, Guilt-offerings, and the Peace-offerings of the congregation. They could only be consumed, some entirely on the Altar and some by the priests, within the Temple Court.   [14] Cf. M.Sh. 3⁹.

7. R. Eliezer says: What has contracted uncleanness from a primary uncleanness, whether inside [the Temple Court] or outside it, must be burnt outside, and what has contracted uncleanness from a derived uncleanness, whether inside [the Temple Court] or outside it, must be burnt inside. R. Akiba says: Where it contracted uncleanness there should it be burnt.

8. The members of the Daily Whole-offering[1] were set down on the [Altar-]Ramp on the lower half, on the west[2] side of it; those of the Additional-offerings[3] on the lower half of the [Altar-]Ramp[4] on the east[5] side of it; those of the New Moon offerings[6] were set down on the rim of the Altar above.[7] [The laws concerning] the Shekel dues and First-fruits[8] apply only such time as the Temple stands; but [the laws concerning] the Tithe of Corn[9] and the Tithe of Cattle[10] and Firstlings[11] apply such time as the Temple stands and such time also as it does not stand. If a man dedicates[12] the Shekel dues or First-fruits, they become Hallowed Things. R. Simeon says: If he declares his First-fruits hallowed, they do not [thereby] become Hallowed Things.

YOMA ('THE DAY OF ATONEMENT')

1. 1. Seven days before the Day of Atonement[13] the High Priest was taken apart from his own house unto the Counsellors' Chamber[14] and another priest was made ready in his stead lest aught should befall him to render him ineligible.[15] R. Judah says: Also another wife was made ready for him lest his own wife should die, for it is written, *He shall make atonement for himself and for his house*;[16] 'his house'—that is his wife. They said to him: If so there would be no end to the matter.

2. Throughout the seven days he must toss the blood[17] and burn the incense[18] and trim the lamps[19] and offer the head and the hind leg;[20] but on other days he offers [only] if he is minded to offer;[21] for the High Priest has first place in offering a portion [of the animal-offerings] and has first place in taking a portion.

3. They delivered unto him elders from among the elders of the Court, and they read before him out of the [prescribed] rite for the day; and they said to him, 'My lord High Priest, do thou thyself recite with thine own mouth, lest thou hast forgotten or lest thou hast never learnt'. On the eve of the Day of Atonement in the morning they make him to stand at

---

1 See above, 4[1]. Cf. Tam. 4[2-3]; Yom. 2[3].   2 See Tam. 4[3]. Variant: 'east'.
3 See above, 4[1].
4 The inclined plane, south of the Altar, used instead of steps. See Midd. 3[3].
5 Variant: 'west'.   6 Num. 28[11].
7 This would be the top surface of the Altar outside the 24 sq. cubits of the Altar fire (see Midd. 3[1]). A variant reading is: 'beneath the rim of the Altar below'; this would correspond to 'the place on which the feet of the priests trod' (Midd. 3[1]).
8 Deut. 26[1-11].
9 General term to include the dues (Heave-offering, First Tithe, Heave-offering of Tithe, Second Tithe, and Poorman's Tithe) exacted from corn, wine, and oil.
10 Lev. 27[32].   11 Ex. 13[11-13], Num. 18[15-18].   12 At a time when there is no Temple.
13 Which falls on the 10th of Tishri. See Lev. 16[1-34], Num. 29 [7-11].
14 Heb. *lishkath palhedrin* (πάρεδροι). Cf. Midd. 5[4] (where the High Priest's room is called 'the wood-chamber') and Par. 3[1] ('the house of stone'). The Gemara (8b) explains that the name 'counsellors' was applied to the High Priests because they had become little more than royal officials who were changed year by year.
15 By becoming unclean or by suffering certain bodily defects. Cf. Ab. 5[5].
16 Lev. 16[6].   17 Of the Daily Whole-offerings; Ex. 29[38ff].   18 Ex. 30[1-8].
19 Ex. 27[20-1]; 30[7-8].   20 See Tam. 4[3], 'The first bore the head and a hind leg'.
21 See Tam. 7[3].

the Eastern Gate and pass before him oxen, rams, and sheep, that he may gain knowledge and become versed in the [Temple-]Service.

4. Throughout the seven days they did not withhold food and drink from him; but on the eve of the Day of Atonement toward nightfall they did not suffer him to eat much, since food induces sleep.

5. The elders of the Court delivered him to the elders of the priesthood and they brought him up to the upper chamber of the House of Abtinas.[1] They adjured him and took their leave and went away having said to him, 'My lord High Priest, we are delegates of the Court, and thou art our delegate and the delegate of the Court. We adjure thee by him that made his name to dwell in this house that thou change naught of what we have said unto thee'. He turned aside and wept and they turned aside and wept.

6. If he was a Sage he used to expound [the Scriptures], and if not the disciples of the Sages used to expound before him. If he was versed in reading [the Scriptures] he read, and if not they read before him. And from what did they read before him? Out of Job and Ezra and Chronicles.[2] Zechariah b. Kabutal says: Many times I read before him out of Daniel.

7. If he sought to slumber, young members of the priesthood[3] would snap their middle finger before him and say to him, 'My lord High Priest, get up and drive away [sleep] this once [by walking] on the[cold] pavement'. And they used to divert him until the time of slaughtering drew near.

8. Every day they used to remove the ashes from off the Altar at cockcrow, or near to it, either before it or after it; but on the Day of Atonement [they did so] at midnight, and on the Feast[4] at the first watch. And before the [time of] cock-crow drew near the Temple Court[5] was filled with Israelites.

2. 1. Beforetime whosoever was minded to clear the Altar of ashes did so. If they were many they used to run and mount the [Altar-]Ramp[6] and he that came first within four cubits secured the task. If two were equal the officer[7] said to them, 'Raise the finger'. And how many did they stretch out? One or two, but they did not stretch out the thumb in the Temple.

2. It once happened that two were equal and they ran and mounted the [Altar-]Ramp; and one of them pushed his fellow so that he fell and his leg was broken; and when the Court saw that they incurred danger they ordained that they should not clear the Altar save by lot. There were four lots: and this was the first lot.

3. The second lot [was to determine] who should slaughter, who should toss the blood, who should take away the ashes from the Inner Altar, and who should take away the ashes from the Candlestick and who should take up to the [Altar-]Ramp the members[8] [of the Whole-offering]—the head and [right] hind leg, the two fore-legs, the rump and the [left] hind leg, the breast and the neck, and the two flanks, and the inwards; also [who should take up] the fine flour[9] and the Baken Cakes[10] and the wine.[11] Thus thirteen

---

[1] Tam. 1[1]; Midd. 1[1].
[2] For they are books that divert the mind and drive away sleep (Bert.).
[3] Some texts read 'levites'.   [4] Passover, Pentecost and Tabernacles.
[5] See p. 589, n. 11.   [6] Midd. 3[3].
[7] Who was 'over the lots'; see Shek. 5[1], 'Mattithiah b. Samuel'.   [8] See Tem. 4[3].
[9] Num. 28[5].   [10] Lev. 6[21f]. Cf. Men. 4[5].   [11] Num. 28[7]; Ex. 29[40].

priests secured a task. Ben Azzai said before R. Akiba in the name of R. Joshua: It was offered in the order in which it had walked.

4. [At] the third lot [the officer used to say], 'Fresh priests come and draw lots for the incense!' And at the fourth lot, 'Fresh priests and old, who will take up the members from the [Altar-]Ramp to the Altar!'

5. The Daily Whole-offering was offered by nine, ten, eleven, or twelve [priests], never more and never less. Thus it was itself offered by nine; at the Feast [of Tabernacles] one held in his hand the flagon of water[1]— and so they were ten; in the afternoon [it was offered] by eleven, [the Daily Whole-offering] itself by nine, while two held in their hands the two faggots of wood;[2] on the Sabbath [it was offered] by eleven, itself by nine while two held in their hands the two dishes of frankincense for the Shewbread,[3] and on a Sabbath that fell during the Feast [of Tabernacles] another held in his hand the flagon of water.

6. A ram was offered by eleven: the flesh by five, and the inwards, the fine flour, and the wine by two each.[4]

7. A bullock was offered by twenty-four: the head and the [right] hind leg—the head by one and the hind leg by two; the rump and the [left] hind leg—the rump by two and the hind leg by two; the breast and the neck —the breast by one and the neck by three; the two forelegs by two; the two flanks by two; the inwards, the fine flour, and the wine by three each. This applies to offerings of the congregation; but in private offerings [one priest] that is minded to offer may offer [all]. For the flaying and the dis-membering of both [the offerings of the congregation and private offerings] like rules apply.

3. 1. The officer said to them, 'Go and see if the time is come for slaughter-ing'. If it was come, he that perceived it said, 'It is daylight!' Mattithiah b. Samuel[5] used to say: [He that perceived it said,] 'The whole east is alight'. 'As far as Hebron?' and he answered, 'Yea!'

2. And why was this required of them? Because once when the light of the moon arose they thought that it was the dawn and slaughtered the Daily Whole-offering, and they had to take it away to the place of burning.[6] They led the High Priest down to the place of immersion.[7] This was the rule in the Temple: whosoever covered his feet must immerse himself, and whosoever made water must sanctify his hands and his feet.

3. None may enter the Temple Court for [an act of the Temple-] Service, even though he is clean, until he has immersed himself. On this day the High Priest five times immerses himself and ten times he sanctifies [his hands and his feet], each time, excepting this alone, in the Temple by the Parwah Chamber.[8]

4. They spread a linen sheet between him and the people. He stripped off his clothes, went down and immersed himself, came up and dried himself. They brought him raiments of gold and he put them on and sancti-fied his hands and his feet. They brought to him the Daily Whole-offering. He made the incision[9] and another completed the slaughtering on his behalf; and he received the blood and tossed it.[10] He went inside to burn the morning incense and to trim the lamps; and [he then went] to offer the

---

[1] Sukk. 4[9].   [2] To replenish the Altar-fire   [3] Lev. 24[7-8].   [4] Num. 15[6f].
[5] Shek. 5[1]; Tam. 3[2].   [6] Cf. Pes. 8[2]; 9[9].   [7] Cf. Tam. 1[1].
[8] Midd. 5[3]. See below, 3[6].   [9] Slit the wind-pipe and gullet. See Hull. 1[3].
[10] Cf. Pes. 5[6].

head and the members [of the Daily Whole-offering] and the Baken Cakes and the wine.

5. The morning incense was offered between [the tossing of] the blood and [the burning of] the members; the afternoon incense between [the burning of] the members and the Drink-offerings.[1] If the High Priest was aged or infirm they prepared for him hot water which they poured into the cold to abate its coldness.

6. They brought him to the Parwah Chamber which stood in holy ground.[2] They spread a linen sheet between him and the people. He sanctified his hands and his feet and stripped off his clothes. R. Meir says: He [first] stripped off his clothes and afterward sanctified his hands and his feet. He went down and immersed himself, came up and dried himself. They brought him white garments; he put them on and sanctified his hands and his feet.

7. In the morning he was clothed in Pelusium linen worth twelve *minas*,[3] and in the afternoon in Indian linen worth eight hundred *zuz*.[4] So R. Meir. But the Sages say: In the morning he wore [vestments] worth eighteen *minas* and in the afternoon [vestments] worth twelve *minas*, thirty *minas* in all. These were at the charges of the congregation,[5] and if he was minded to spend more he could do so at his own charges.

8. He came to his[6] bullock and his bullock was standing between the Porch and the Altar, its head to the south and its face to the west;[7] and he set both his hands upon it and made confession. And thus used he to say: 'O God, I have committed iniquity, transgressed, and sinned before thee, I and my house. O God, forgive the iniquities and transgressions and sins which I have committed and transgressed and sinned before thee, I and my house, as it is written in the Law of thy servant Moses, *For on this day shall atonement be made for you to cleanse you; from all your sins shall ye be clean before the Lord.*'[8] And they answered after him,[9] 'Blessed be the name of the glory of his kingdom for ever and ever!'

9. He came to the east, to the north of the Altar, with the Prefect[10] on his right and the chief of the father's house[11] on his left. And two he-goats[12] were there and there also was a casket in which were two lots. They were of box-wood, but Ben Gamla made some of gold, and his memory was kept in honour.

10. Ben Katin made twelve stop-cocks for the laver[13] which before had but two; and he also made a device[14] for the laver that its water should not be rendered unfit by remaining overnight.[15] King Monobaz[16] made of gold

---

[1] Ex. 30[8].   [2] i.e. within the Temple Court. It lay south of the Court of the Priests.
[3] App. II, A.   [4] App. II, A.
[5] Variant: 'So much he used to receive from the Temple fund'.
[6] See Lev. 16[3, 6]. The second bullock (see below, 7[3]) was one of the 'Additional offerings' (Num. 29[8]).
[7] It stood north to south, with its head twisted to the west to face the Sanctuary.
[8] Lev. 16[30]. The final word 'Lord' was pronounced by the High Priest as it was written and not, as usually, by a reverential pseudonym or alternative divine name such as Adonai.
[9] On hearing God's name expressly pronounced. See below, 6[2]. Cf. Tam. 2[8].
[10] The second in rank to the High Priest and the chief officer of the Temple.
[11] The priests were divided into twenty-four 'courses' (1 Chron. 24[1–19]), each course coming up to the Temple for one week's service. Each 'course' was sub-divided into 'fathers' houses', each serving one day out of the seven. Cf. Taan. 2[6].
[12] Lev. 16[5, 7].   [13] Ex. 30[18ff].   [14] Tam. 1[4]; 3[8].
[15] What stands in a sacred vessel itself becomes holy (Zeb. 9[7]), and any holy thing that remains overnight becomes 'invalid', unusable (cf. Men. 7[4]).
[16] King of Adiabene shortly before the fall of Jerusalem. Cf. Josephus, *Ant.* xx. iv. 1ff.

all the handles for the vessels used on the Day of Atonement. His mother Helena[1] set a golden candlestick over the door of the Sanctuary. She also made a golden tablet on which was written the paragraph of the Suspected Adulteress.[2] Miracles had befallen the gates of Nicanor[3] and his memory was kept in honour.

11. But [the memory of] these [was kept] in dishonour: They of the House of Garmu[4] would not teach [any other] how to prepare the Shewbread. They of the House of Abtinas[5] would not teach [any other] how to prepare the incense. Hygros b. Levi[6] had a special art in singing but he would not teach it [to any other]. Ben Kamtzar[7] would not teach [any other] in [his special] craft of writing. Of the first it is written, *The memory of the just is blessed;*[8] and of these [others] it is written, *But the name of the wicked shall rot.*[9]

4. 1. He shook the casket and took up the two lots. On one was written 'For the Lord', and on the other was written 'For Azazel'.[10] The Prefect was on his right and the chief of the father's house on his left. If the lot bearing the Name came up in his right hand the Prefect would say to him, 'My lord High Priest, raise thy right hand'; and if it came up in his left hand the chief of the father's house would say to him, 'My lord High Priest, raise thy left hand'. He put them on the two he-goats and said, 'A Sin-offering to the Lord!'[11] R. Ishmael says: He needed not to say 'A Sin-offering', but only 'To the Lord'. And they answered[12] after him, 'Blessed be the name of the glory of his kingdom for ever and ever!'

2. He bound a thread of crimson wool on the head of the scapegoat and he turned it towards the way by which it was to be sent out; and on the he-goat that was to be slaughtered [he bound a thread] about its throat. He came to his bullock the second time,[13] laid his two hands upon it, and made confession. And thus used he to say: 'O God, I have committed iniquity and transgressed and sinned before thee, I and my house and the children of Aaron, thy holy people. O God, forgive, I pray, the iniquities and transgressions and sins which I have committed and transgressed and sinned before thee, I and my house and the children of Aaron, thy holy people, as it is written in the law of thy servant Moses, *For on this day shall atonement be made for you to cleanse you: from all your sins shall ye be clean before the Lord.*[14] And they answered after him, 'Blessed be the name of the glory of his kingdom for ever and ever!'

3. He slaughtered [the bullock] and received its blood in a bason; and he gave it to the one that should stir it up on the fourth terrace[15] of the Sanctuary so that it should not congeal. He took the fire-pan and went up to the top of the Altar; and he cleared the coals to this side and to that, and scooped out glowing cinders from below, and came down and set the fire-pan on the fourth terrace in the Temple Court.

---

[1] Cf. Naz. 3[6].   [2] Num. 5[11-31].
[3] Shek. 6[2]; Sot. 1[5]; Midd. 1[4]; 2[3, 6]; Neg. 14[8]. According to the Tosefta (2[4]) when the gates were being brought by sea from Alexandria the ship was caught by a storm, and to lighten the ship they threw one of the gates overboard, and when they were about to throw the second he said to them, 'Throw me after it'. The storm at once ceased, and when they landed at Jaffa the other gate was found beneath the ship's keel.
[4] Shek. 5[1].   [5] Shek. 5[1].   [6] Shek. 5[1].
[7] With four feathers between his five fingers he could write a name of four different letters at the same time.   [8] Prov. 10[7].   [9] Ibid.
[10] Lev. 16[10].   [11] Pronouncing the divine name.   [12] See above, p. 165, n. 9.
[13] See above, 3[8].   [14] Lev. 16[30]. See above, p. 165, n. 8.   [15] Or 'pavement'. See Midd. 3[6].

4. Other days he used to scoop out [the cinders] with a [fire-pan] of silver[1] and empty it into one of gold, but this day he scoops them out with the one of gold in which also he brings in [the cinders]. Other days he used to scoop them out with one holding four *kabs*[2] and empty it into one holding three *kabs*; but this day he scoops them out with one holding three *kabs* in which also he brings in [the cinders]. R. Jose says: Other days he used to scoop them out with one holding a *seah* and empty it into one holding three *kabs*; but this day he scoops them out with one holding three *kabs* in which also he brings in [the cinders]. Other days it was a heavy one, but this day a light one. Other days its handle was short, but this day long. Other days it was of yellow gold, but this day of red gold. So R. Menahem. Other days he used to offer half a *mina* [of incense][3] in the morning and half a *mina* in the afternoon; but this day he adds also his two hands full. Other days it was of fine quality, but this day it is the finest of the fine.

5. Other days the priests went up on the east side of the [Altar-]Ramp[4] and came down on the west side, but this day the High Priest goes up in the middle and comes down in the middle. R. Judah says: The High Priest always goes up in the middle and comes down in the middle. Other days the High Priest sanctified his hands and his feet [in water] from the laver; but this day from a golden jug. R. Judah says: The High Priest always sanctified his hands and his feet from a golden jug.

6. Other days there were four wood-stacks there,[5] but this day five. So R. Meir. R. Jose says: Other days three, but this day four. R. Judah says: Other days two, but this day three.

5. 1. They brought out to him the ladle and the fire-pan and he took his two hands full [of incense] and put it in the ladle, which was large according to his largeness [of hand], or small according to his smallness [of hand]; and such [alone] was the prescribed measure of the ladle. He took the fire-pan in his right hand and the ladle in his left. He went through the Sanctuary until he came to the space between the two curtains separating the Sanctuary from the Holy of Holies. And there was a cubit's space between them. R. Jose says: Only one curtain was there, for it is written, *And the veil shall divide for you between the holy place and the most holy.*[6] The outer curtain was looped up on the south side and the inner one on the north side.[7] He went along between them until he reached the north side; when he reached the north he turned round to the south and went on with the curtain on his left hand until he reached the Ark. When he reached the Ark he put the fire-pan between the two bars.[8] He heaped up the incense on the coals and the whole place became filled with smoke. He came out by the way he went in, and in the outer space[9] he prayed a short prayer. But he did not prolong his prayer lest he put Israel in terror.

2. After the Ark was taken away[10] a stone remained there from the time of the early Prophets,[11] and it was called 'Shetiyah'.[12] It was higher than the ground by three fingerbreadths. On this he used to put [the fire-pan].

3. He took the blood from him that was stirring it and entered [again] into the place where he had entered and stood [again] on the place whereon

---

[1] Cf. Tam. 1[4].   [2] Six *kabs* make one *seah* (App. II, D).   [3] App. II, B.
[4] See above, 2[1].   [5] On the Altar.   [6] Ex. 26[33].
[7] The two curtains formed a corridor one cubit wide. Access from the Sanctuary to the corridor was on the left side, and from the corridor to the Holy of Holies on the right (north) side.   [8] Ex. 25[13f].   [9] The Sanctuary.
[10] See Shek. 6[1, 2].   [11] i.e. the time of David and Solomon.   [12] Lit. 'Foundation'.

he had stood, and sprinkled [the blood] once upwards and seven times downwards, not as though he had intended to sprinkle upwards or downwards but as though he were wielding a whip. And thus used he to count: One, one and one, one and two, one and three, one and four, one and five, one and six, one and seven. He came out and put it on the golden stand in the Sanctuary.

4. They brought him the he-goat. He slaughtered it and received its blood in a bason. He then entered [again] into the place wherein he had entered and stood [again] on the place whereon he had stood, and sprinkled [the blood] once upwards and seven times downwards, not as though he had intended to sprinkle upwards or downwards, but as though he were wielding a whip. And thus used he to count: One, one and one, one and two, one and three, one and four, one and five, one and six, one and seven. He came out and put it on the second stand in the Sanctuary. R. Judah says: Only one stand was there. He took the blood of the bullock and set down [in its place] the blood of the he-goat, and [then] sprinkled [the blood of the bullock] on the curtain outside, opposite the Ark, once upwards and seven times downwards, not as though he had intended to sprinkle upwards or downwards, but as though he were wielding a whip. And thus used he to count: One, one and one, one and two, one and three, one and four, one and five, one and six, one and seven. Then he took the blood of the he-goat and set down [in its place] the blood of the bullock, and [then] sprinkled [the blood of the he-goat] on the curtain outside, opposite the Ark, once upwards and seven times downwards, not as though he had intended to sprinkle upwards or downwards, but as though he were wielding a whip; and thus used he to count: One, one and one, one and two, one and three, one and four, one and five, one and six, one and seven. He emptied out the blood of the bullock into the blood of the he-goat and poured [the contents of] the full [vessel] into the empty one.

5. Then he went to the Altar which is before the Lord[1]—that is the golden Altar.[2] When he begins to sprinkle[3] downwards, where does he begin? From the north-east horn, then the north-west, then the south-west, then the north-east. Where he begins the sprinkling of the outer Altar,[4] there he completes the sprinkling of the inner Altar. R. Eliezer says: He used to stand in the one place and sprinkle, and he sprinkled every horn from below upwards, excepting the horn before which he was standing, which he used to sprinkle from above downwards.

6. He then sprinkled the cleansed surface[5] of the Altar seven times and poured out the residue of the blood at the western base of the outer Altar; and [the residue] of [the blood sprinkled on] the outer Altar he poured out at the southern base.[6] Both mingled together in the channel[7] and flowed away into the brook Kidron. And it was sold to gardeners as manure, and the law of Sacrilege[8] applied to it.

7. Every act [of the High Priest] on the Day of Atonement here enumerated according to the prescribed order—if one act was done [out of order]

---

[1] Lev. 16[18].   [2] Ex. 30[1ff].

[3] Or: 'purge from sin'. The expression is taken from Ex. 29[36] (see R.V. mg.).

[4] Zeb. 5[3].

[5] Lev. 16[19]. So Bert. and Tif. Yis. Others propose 'the back', i.e. the top, of the Altar.

[6] Lev. 4[7].   [7] Cf. Shek. 4[2].

[8] Lev. 5[15]. Cf. Meil. 3[3]. The mixed blood and water was sold for the benefit of the Temple; hence it might not be used without payment.

before another act, it is as if it was not done at all. If he [sprinkled] the blood of the he-goat before the blood of the bullock, he must start anew and sprinkle the blood of the he-goat after the blood of the bullock. And if the blood was poured away before [the High Priest] had finished the sprinklings within [the Holy of Holies], he must bring other blood and start anew and sprinkle afresh within [the Holy of Holies]. So, too, in what concerns the Sanctuary and the Golden Altar, since they are each a separate act of atonement. R. Eleazar and R. Simeon say: At the place where he broke off there he begins again.

6. **1.** The two he-goats of the Day of Atonement should be alike in appearance, in size, and in value, and have been bought at the same time.[1] Yet even if they are not alike they are valid, and if one was bought one day and the other on the morrow they are valid. If one of them died before the lot was cast, a fellow may be bought for the other; but if after the lot was cast, another pair must be brought and the lots cast over them anew. And if that cast for the Lord died, he[2] should say, 'Let this on which the lot "For the Lord" has fallen stand in its stead'; and if that cast for Azazel died, he should say, 'Let this on which the lot "For Azazel" has fallen stand in its stead'. The other is left to pasture until it suffers a blemish,[3] when it must be sold and its value falls to the Temple fund; for the Sin-offering of the congregation may not be left to die.[4] R. Judah says: It is left to die. Moreover R. Judah said: If the blood was poured away the scapegoat is left to die; if the scapegoat died the blood is poured away.

2. He then came to the scapegoat and laid his two hands upon it and made confession. And thus used he to say: 'O God, thy people, the House of Israel, have committed iniquity, transgressed, and sinned before thee. O God, forgive, I pray, the iniquities and transgressions and sins which thy people, the House of Israel, have committed and transgressed and sinned before thee; as it is written in the law of thy servant Moses, *For on this day shall atonement be made for you to cleanse you: from all your sins shall ye be clean before the Lord.*[5] And when the priests and the people which stood in the Temple Court heard the Expressed Name[6] come forth from the mouth of the High Priest, they used to kneel and bow themselves and fall down on their faces and say, 'Blessed be the name of the glory of his kingdom for ever and ever!'

3. They delivered it to him that should lead it away. All were eligible to lead it away, but the priests[7] had established the custom not to suffer an Israelite[8] to lead it away. R. Jose said: It once happened that Arsela of Sepphoris led it away and he was an Israelite.

4. And they made a causeway[9] for it because of the Babylonians[10] who used to pull its hair, crying to it, 'Bear [our sins] and be gone! Bear [our sins] and be gone!' Certain of the eminent folk of Jerusalem used to go with him to the first booth. There were ten booths from Jerusalem to the ravine[11] [which was at a distance of] ninety *ris* (which measure seven and a half to the mile).

5. At every booth they used to say to him, 'Here is food, here is water', and they went with him from that booth to the next booth, but not from

---

[1] Cf. Neg. 14⁵.   [2] The High Priest.   [3] Lev. 22¹⁹.   [4] See Tem. 4³ (end).
[5] Lev. 16³⁰.   [6] See above, 3⁸. Cf. Sot. 7⁶.   [7] Variant: 'High Priests'.
[8] i.e. a non-priest.   [9] See Shek. 4²; Par. 3⁶.   [10] See p. 509, n. 2
[11] According to Maim., 'Tzok', a place-name. But see below, par. 6 (end).

the last booth; for none used to go with him to the ravine; but they stood at a distance and beheld what he did.

6. What did he do? He divided the thread of crimson wool and tied one half to the rock and the other half between its horns, and he pushed it from behind; and it went rolling down, and before it had reached half the way down the hill it was broken in pieces. He returned and sat down beneath the last booth until nightfall. And from what time does it render his garments unclean?[1] After he has gone outside the wall of Jerusalem. R. Simeon says: From the moment that he pushes it into the ravine.

7. [The High Priest] came to the bullock and the he-goat which were to be burnt.[2] He cut them open and took away the sacrificial portions[3] and put them on a dish and burnt them upon the Altar. He twisted [the limbs of the beasts] around carrying-poles,[4] and brought them out to the place of burning. And from what time do they render garments unclean?[5] After they have gone outside the wall of the Temple Court. R. Simeon says: When the fire has caught a hold on the greater part of them.

8. They said to the High Priest, 'The he-goat has reached the wilderness'. And whence did they know that the he-goat had reached the wilderness? They used to set up sentinel-posts and [from these] towels were waved and [so] they would know that the he-goat had reached the wilderness. R. Judah said: And had they not a most manifest sign? From Jerusalem to Beth Haroro[6] was three miles; they could walk a mile, return a mile, wait time enough to go a mile, and then they would know that the he-goat had reached the wilderness. R. Ishmael says: Had they not another sign also?—a thread of crimson wool was tied to the door of the Sanctuary and when the he-goat reached the wilderness the thread turned white; for it is written, *Though your sins be as scarlet they shall be as white as snow.*[7]

7. 1. Then the High Priest came[8] to read. If he was minded to read in the linen garments he could do so; otherwise he would read in his own white vestment. The[9] minister of the synagogue used to take a scroll of the Law and give it to the chief of the synagogue, and the chief of the synagogue gave it to the Prefect, and the Prefect gave it to the High Priest, and the High Priest received it standing and read it standing. And he read *After the death . . .*[10] and *Howbeit on the tenth day . . .*[11] Then he used to roll up the scroll of the Law and put it in his bosom[12] and say, 'More is written here than I have read out before you'. *And on the tenth . . .*[13] which is in the Book of Numbers, he recited by heart. Thereupon he pronounced eight Benedictions: for the Law, for the Temple-Service, for the Thanksgiving, for the Forgiveness of Sin, and for the Temple separately, and for the Israelites separately, and for the priests separately; and for the rest a [general] prayer.[14]

2. He that can see the High Priest when he reads cannot see the bullock and the he-goat that are being burnt; and he that can see the bullock and the he-goat that are being burnt cannot see the High Priest when he

---

[1] Lev. 16[26].   [2] Lev. 16[27].   [3] Lev. 4[8–10].   [4] Cf. Zeb. 12[6].   [5] Lev. 16[28].
[6] Variants: Hiddudo, Horon. Cf. Neub., p. 45. Perhaps Wadi el-Hod, near Bethany.
[7] Is. 1[18].   [8] To the Court of the Women (see p. 589, n. 11).
[9] Repeated in Sot. 7[7].   [10] Lev. 16.   [11] Lev. 23[26–32].
[12] Under his arm (Tif. Yis.); in its case (*J.Q.R.* vi (1915), p. 214).   [13] Num. 29[7–11].
[14] Of these eight, the second, third, and fourth correspond with the seventeenth, eighteenth, and sixth in the modern form of the 'Eighteen Benedictions'. See *J.E.* xi. 271.

reads: not that it was not permitted, but because the distance apart was great and both acts were performed at the same time.

3. If he read in the linen vestments, he [afterward] sanctified his hands and his feet, stripped off his clothes, went down and immersed himself, and came up and dried himself. They brought to him the vestments of gold, and he put them on and sanctified his hands and his feet and went out and offered his ram[1] and the ram of the people and the seven unblemished lambs of a year old.[2] So R. Eliezer. R. Akiba says: They offered these with the morning Daily Whole-offering, and the bullock for the Whole-offering and the he-goat that is offered outside[3] were offered with the afternoon Daily Whole-offering.

4. He then sanctified his hands and his feet, stripped off his clothes, went down and immersed himself, and came up and dried himself. They brought to him the white vestments, and he put them on and sanctified his hands and his feet. He then went in to bring out the ladle and the fire-pan. He sanctified his hands and his feet, stripped off his clothes, went down and immersed himself, came up and dried himself; and they brought to him the golden vestments; and he put them on and sanctified his hands and his feet, and went in to burn the afternoon incense[4] and trim the lamps.[5] He sanctified his hands and his feet and stripped off his clothes. Then they brought him his own raiment and he put it on. And they went with him to his house. And he made a feast for his friends for that he was come forth safely from the Sanctuary.[6]

5. The High Priest ministers in eight pieces of raiment, and a common priest in four—in tunic, drawers, turban, and girdle. To these the High Priest adds the breastplate, the apron, the upper garment, and the frontlet. In these were the Urim and Thummim[7] inquired of; and they were not inquired of for a common person,[8] but only for the king, for the Court, or for one of whom the congregation had need.[9]

8.

1. On the Day of Atonement, eating, drinking, washing, anointing, putting on sandals, and marital intercourse are forbidden. A king or a bride may wash their faces and a woman after childbirth may put on sandals. So R. Eliezer. But the Sages forbid it.

2. If a man ate a large date's bulk,[10] the like of it together with its stone, or if he drank a mouthful, he is culpable.[11] Any foods may be included together to make up the date's bulk, and any liquids may be included together to make up the mouthful. What a man eats and what he drinks may not be included together.

3. If he both ate and drank in a single act of forgetfulness[12] he is liable to one Sin-offering only. If he ate and also performed an act of work, he is liable to two Sin-offerings. If he ate foods which are not fit for eating or drank liquids which are not fit for drinking, or even if he drank brine or fish-brine,[13] he is not culpable.

---

[1] Lev. 16[3]. [2] Num. 29[8].

[3] Num. 29[11]. Its blood was sprinkled only on the *outer* Altar, as opposed to that of the he-goat mentioned in 5[4]. [4] Ex. 30[8]. [5] Ex. 27[21].

[6] Some texts omit 'from the Sanctuary'. [7] Ex. 28[30].

[8] Some texts omit 'for a common person'. [9] Cf. Makk. 2[7].

[10] Cf. Kel. 17[12]. A quantity equal to a large date from which the stone has not been taken.

[11] He is punishable by Extirpation (Lev. 23[29]) if he transgressed wantonly, and if in error he is liable to a Sin-offering (Lev. 4[27-35]).

[12] That it was the Day of Atonement. Cf. Shab. 7[1].

[13] Both were liquids in which fish were pickled. Cf. Ter. 11[1]; Ned. 6[4]; A. Zar. 2[4]; Mikw. 7[2].

4. They do not cause children to fast on the Day of Atonement, but they should exercise them therein one year or two years before [they are of age],[1] that they may become versed in the commandments.

5. If a pregnant woman smelled [food and craved after it], they may give her food until she recovers herself. He that is sick may be given food at the word of skilled persons; and if no skilled persons are there, he may be given food at his own wish, until he says, 'Enough!'

6. If ravenous hunger[2] seized a man he may be given even unclean things to eat until his eyes are enlightened.[3] If a mad dog bit him he may not be given the lobe of its liver to eat; but R. Mattithiah b. Heresh permits it. Moreover R. Mattithiah b. Heresh said: If a man has a pain in his throat they may drop medicine into his mouth on the Sabbath, since there is doubt whether life is in danger, and whenever there is doubt whether life is in danger this overrides the Sabbath.

7. If a building fell down upon a man and there is doubt whether he is there or not, or whether he is alive or dead, or whether he is a gentile or an Israelite, they may clear away the ruin from above him. If they find him alive they may clear it away [still more] from above him; but if dead, they leave him.

8. The Sin-offering[4] and the unconditional Guilt-offering[5] effect atonement; death and the Day of Atonement effect atonement if there is repentance. Repentance effects atonement for lesser transgressions against both positive and negative commands in the Law; while for graver transgressions it suspends punishment until the Day of Atonement comes and effects atonement.

9. If a man said, 'I will sin and repent, and sin again and repent', he will be given no chance to repent. [If he said,] 'I will sin and the Day of Atonement will effect atonement', then the Day of Atonement effects no atonement. For transgressions that are between man and God the Day of Atonement effects atonement, but for transgressions that are between a man and his fellow the Day of Atonement effects atonement only if he has appeased his fellow. This did R. Eleazar b. Azariah expound: *From all your sins shall ye be clean before the Lord*[6]—for transgressions that are between man and God the Day of Atonement effects atonement; but for transgressions that are between a man and his fellow the Day of Atonement effects atonement only if he has appeased his fellow. R. Akiba said: Blessed are ye, O Israel. Before whom are ye made clean and who makes you clean? Your Father in heaven; as it is written, *And I will sprinkle clean water upon you and ye shall be clean.*[7] And again it says, *O Lord the hope* (mikweh)[8] *of Israel*;[9]—as the *Mikweh* cleanses the unclean so does the Holy One, blessed be he, cleanse Israel.

SUKKAH[10] ('THE FEAST OF TABERNACLES')

1. 1. If a *Sukkah* is more than twenty cubits high it is not valid (R. Judah declares it valid), and if it is not ten handbreadths high or has not three

---

[1] Thirteen years for a boy, twelve for a girl.   [2] βούλιμος, bulimy, 'ox-hunger'.
[3] 1 Sam. 14[27].   [4] Lev. 4[27-35].
[5] Prescribed in Lev. 5[15]; 6[6], as opposed to the 'suspensive' or 'conditional' Guilt-offering (Lev. 5[17ff]).   [6] Lev. 16[30].   [7] Ezek. 36[25].
[8] A play upon words. *Mikweh* means also the 'Immersion-pool' (see tractate Mikwaoth) prescribed for the cleansing of those who contract uncleanness.   [9] Jer. 17[13].
[10] The booth set up at the Feast of Tabernacles in fulfilment of Lev. 23[42], 'Ye shall dwell

sides or if what is unshaded is more than what is shaded, it is not valid. The School of Shammai declare an old *Sukkah* invalid, and the School of Hillel declare it valid. And what is deemed an 'old' *Sukkah?* Any that was made thirty days before the Feast. But if it was made for the sake of the Feast, even at the beginning of the year,[1] it is valid.

2. If a man built his *Sukkah* under a tree it is as though he had built it within a house.[2] If one *Sukkah* was built above another, the upper one is valid but the lower invalid. R. Judah says: If there were no occupants in the upper one the lower is valid.

3. If a man spread a sheet over it[3] because of the sun, or beneath it because of the droppings,[4] or if he spread it over the frame of a four-post bed, the *Sukkah* is not valid; but he may spread it over the frame of a two-post bed.[5]

4. If he trained a vine or a gourd or ivy over it and spread [proper] *Sukkah*-roofing over them, it is not valid.[6] But if the [proper] *Sukkah*-roofing exceeded them in quantity, or if he cut them, the *Sukkah* is valid. This is the general rule: What is susceptible to uncleanness[7] or does not grow from the soil[8] may not serve as *Sukkah*-roofing; but what is not susceptible to uncleanness and grows from the soil[9] may serve as *Sukkah*-roofing.

5. Bundles of straw or bundles of wood or bundles of brushwood cannot serve as *Sukkah*-roofing,[10] but if they are untied they are valid. And all these things[11] are valid for the sides of the *Sukkah*.

6. Boards may be used for *Sukkah*-roofing. So R. Judah. But R. Meir forbids them. If a man put a board four handbreadths wide over the *Sukkah* it is valid provided that he does not sleep beneath it.

7. If there was a timber roofing that had no plastering,[12] R. Judah says: The School of Shammai say that it must be loosened and one beam removed between each two; and the School of Hillel say: It may either be loosened or one beam removed between each two. R. Meir says: One beam should be removed between each two, but the roofing need not be loosened.

8. If a man used spits or the side-pieces of a bed for the roof-beams of his *Sukkah*, and the space between them equals their own thickness, the *Sukkah* is valid. If a man hollowed out space in a stack of grain to make a *Sukkah* therein, it is no *Sukkah* at all.

9. If the sides are suspended[13] from above and hang three handbreadths higher than the ground, the *Sukkah* is not valid; but if [the sides are built] from below upwards and measure ten handbreadths,[14] it is valid.

in booths seven days; all that are homeborn in Israel shall dwell in booths'. Cf. Neh. 8[17f.] The Feast began on the 15th of Tishri, and the dwelling in booths was obligatory throughout seven days. The eighth day was also to be observed as a Festival-day (Lev. 23[35], 'Ye shall do no servile work').

[1] The New Year begins only fifteen days earlier, on the 1st of Tishri. The phrase must be intended to mean 'many months before'.
[2] The branches of the tree are not a valid roofing. See below, n. 6.
[3] The roofing.   [4] Such as leaves from the branches that constitute the roofing.
[5] Over the four posts it would form a roof, but not so over two posts only.
[6] Since what is still growing out of the soil is not valid.
[7] Food, utensils, and woven stuff. See tractate Kelim, passim.
[8] Bones, hides, mineral matter.   [9] Straw, brushwood, and the like.
[10] They would not have been set there solely for the sake of the *Sukkah* but only to be left to dry.   [11] Which are forbidden, under the above rules, for the roofing.
[12] And it was proposed to use the space below as a *Sukkah*.
[13] The reference is to the use of some woven material as the sides of the *Sukkah*.
[14] Some texts omit 'from the ground'.

R. Jose says: As from below upwards the height [of the side] need be but ten handbreadths, so from the top downwards there need be but ten handbreadths.[1] If the roofing is three handbreadths distant[2] from the sides, the *Sukkah* is not valid.

10. If *Sukkah*-roofing was put over [the gaps in the roof of] a damaged house[3] and there was a space[4] of four cubits between the wall and the *Sukkah*-roofing, it is not valid. So, too, with a courtyard surrounded by a peristyle.[5] If [the roofing[6] of] a large *Sukkah* was surrounded with material which may not be used for *Sukkah*-roofing, and there was a space of four cubits below it, the *Sukkah* is not valid.

11. If a man made his *Sukkah* like a cone-shaped hut, or propped it up against a wall, R. Eliezer declares it invalid, since it has no roof; but the Sages declare it valid. A large reed-mat[7] that has been made for lying upon is susceptible to uncleanness and may not be used for a *Sukkah* roofing; [if it was made] for *Sukkah*-roofing it may be used for *Sukkah*-roofing and it is not susceptible to uncleanness. R. Eliezer says: It is all one whether [the reed-mat] is large or small: if it was made for lying upon it is susceptible to uncleanness and may not be used for *Sukkah*-roofing, [but if it was made] for *Sukkah*-roofing it may be used for *Sukkah*-roofing and it is not susceptible to uncleanness.

2. 1. If a man slept under a bed in the *Sukkah* he has not fulfilled his obligation.[8] R. Judah said: It was our custom to sleep under the bed in the presence of the Elders, and they said naught to us. R. Simeon said: Tabi, the slave of Rabban Gamaliel, once slept under the bed, and Rabban Gamaliel said to the Elders, 'Ye have seen Tabi, my slave, that he is a learned scholar, and knows that slaves are exempt[9] from [the law of] the *Sukkah*; and so he sleeps under the bed'. So, incidentally, we learn that if a man slept under a bed he has not fulfilled his duty.

2. If a man propped up his *Sukkah* with the legs of a bed, it is valid. R. Judah says: If it cannot stand of itself it is not valid. If [the roofing of] a *Sukkah* is loosely fashioned[10] yet what is shaded is more than what is unshaded, it is valid. If [the roofing] is close knit, like that over a house, it is valid, even though the stars cannot be seen through it.

3. If a man built his *Sukkah* on the top of a wagon or on the deck of a ship, it is valid, and they may go up into it on a Festival-day.[11] [If he built it] on the top of a tree or on the back of a camel, it is valid, but none may go up into it on a Festival-day. If two [sides of the *Sukkah*] were a tree and one was made by men's hands, or if two were made by men's hands and one was a tree, the *Sukkah* is valid, but they may not go up[12] into it on a Festival-day. If three [sides were made] by men's hands and one was a tree, it is valid and they may go up into it on a Festival-day. This is the general rule: If the *Sukkah* could stand of itself if the

---

[1] Even though the lower edge of the wall is more than three handbreadths from the ground. [2] Measuring horizontally.
[3] As often in the Mishnah, 'house' has the sense of a single chamber on the ground floor. [4] Still served by the remains of the original roof.
[5] Thus leaving only the centre of the courtyard open to the sky.
[6] Of valid material and of the prescribed extent, namely, seven handbreadths square.
[7] Cf. Kel. 17[17]; 20[7].
[8] It would be a booth within a booth (Maim.). [9] See below, 2[8].
[10] Or 'ill-arranged'. [1] ¹See Betz. 5[2].
[12] Since the booths were often built on the flat roofs of houses, the term 'go up' is commonly used for 'enter'. Cf. 4[8].

tree was taken away, it is valid, and they may go up into it on a Festival-day.

4. If a man built his *Sukkah* between trees and the trees formed its sides, it is valid. They that are sent forth on a pious duty are exempt from the [law of the] *Sukkah*. The sick and they that attend on them are exempt. Men may eat and drink at haphazard outside the *Sukkah*.

5. Once when they brought cooked food to Rabban Johanan b. Zakkai to taste and two dates and a pail of water to Rabban Gamaliel, they said, 'Bring them up to the *Sukkah*'.[1] And [once] when they gave R. Zadok less than an egg's bulk of food he took it in a towel[2] and ate it outside the *Sukkah* and did not say the Benediction after it.[3]

6. R. Eliezer said: A man is bound to eat fourteen meals in the *Sukkah*, one [each] day and one [each] night. But the Sages say: There is no pre-scribed number save [that he must eat within the *Sukkah*] on the night of the first Festival-day of the Feast. Moreover R. Eliezer said: If a man has not eaten [a meal in the *Sukkah*] on the night of the first Festival-day he must fulfil the lack on the night of the last Festival-day. But the Sages say: The lack cannot be fulfilled, for it is written, *That which is crooked cannot be made straight; and that which is wanting cannot be reckoned.*[4]

7. If a man's head and the greater part of his body are within the *Sukkah*, but his table is within the house, the School of Shammai declare it invalid, and the School of Hillel declare it valid. The School of Hillel said to the School of Shammai: Did not the Elders of the School of Sham-mai and the Elders of the School of Hillel once go to visit R.[5] Johanan b.[5] ha-Horoni, and find him sitting with his head and the greater part of his body within the *Sukkah* while his table was within the house?[6] The School of Shammai answered: Is there proof from that? But they indeed said to him, 'If such has been thy custom thou hast never in thy life fulfilled the law of the *Sukkah*'.

8. Women, slaves, and minors are exempt from [the law of] the *Sukkah*; but a minor that no more needs his mother must fulfil the law of the *Sukkah*. The daughter-in-law of Shammai the Elder once bore a child [during the Feast] and he broke away some of the roof-plaster and made a *Sukkah*-roofing over the bed for the sake of the child.

9. Throughout the seven days [of the Feast] a man must make his *Sukkah* a regular abode and his house a chance abode. If rain fell, when may he empty out [the *Sukkah*]? When the porridge would spoil. They propounded a parable: To what can it be compared?—to a slave who came to fill the cup for his master and he poured the pitcher over his[7] face.

3. 1. If a palm-branch was got by robbery[8] or was withered, it is not valid.

---

[1] They would not eat and drink even haphazard outside the booth.

[2] Because he had not washed his hands, even though this was not necessary for less than an egg's bulk of food.

[3] Implying that the Benediction after food was (on the ground of Deut. 8[10]) called for only if 'thou shalt eat and be full'. Cf. also Ber. 7[2].   [4] Eccles. 1[15].

[5] Some texts omit 'Rabbi' and 'b.' (son of).

[6] Some texts add 'and they said naught to him'.

[7] The slave's. At the Feast of Tabernacles rain is a sign of God's anger (Taan. 1[1]). The slave (Israel) would perform his duties (the observance of the divinely ordained Feasts and living in booths), but his master (God) only shows his displeasure.

[8] Lev. 23[40] is interpreted: 'Ye shall take (only) of what is yours'. The palm-branch, myrtle-branch, and willow-branch discussed in this and the following paragraphs constitute the *Lulab* (see App. I. 20) which, with the citron (see below, 3[5, 6]), must be carried during the Feast.

If [it came] from an *Asherah*[1] or from an apostate city,[2] it is not valid.
If its tip was broken off or if its leaves were split, it is not valid; if its leaves
were spread apart it is valid. R. Judah says: It may be tied up at the end.
The thorn-palms of the Iron Mount[3] are valid. A palm-branch three
handbreadths in length, long enough to shake, is valid.

2. If a myrtle-branch was got by robbery or was withered, it is not valid,
If [it came] from an *Asherah* or from an apostate city, it is not valid. If its
tip was broken off or if its leaves were severed or if its berries were more
numerous than its leaves, it is not valid; if a man lessened the number of
berries it is valid, but he may not lessen them on a Festival-day.

3. If a willow-branch was got by robbery or was withered, it is not valid.
If [it came] from an *Asherah* or from an apostate city, it is not valid. If its
tip was broken off or if its leaves were severed, or if it was a mountain-
willow, it is not valid. If it was shrivelled or had lost some of its leaves
or had grown in a field[4] it is valid.

4. R. Ishmael says: Three myrtle-branches [are needful][5] and two willow-
branches and one palm-branch and one citron;[6] but even if two [of the
myrtle-branches] have their tips broken off while one has not [they are
valid]. R. Tarfon says: Even if all the three have their tips broken off.
R. Akiba says: Like as one palm-branch and one citron [are alone needful],
so also but one myrtle-branch and one willow-branch [are needful].

5. If a citron was got by robbery or was withered, it is not valid. If
[it came] from an *Asherah* or from an apostate city, it is not valid. If it was
Orlah-fruit[7] or unclean Heave-offering,[8] it is not valid. If it was clean
Heave-offering it should not be carried, but if it is carried it is valid. If it
was *demai*-produce[9] the School of Shammai declare it invalid, but the
School of Hillel declare it valid. If it was Second Tithe[10] it should not be
carried [even] in Jerusalem, but if it is carried it is valid.

6. If the larger part of the citron was covered with scars, if its nipple
was gone, if it was peeled, split, or had a hole and lacked aught soever, it
is not valid. If the smaller part of it was covered with scars, if its stalk
was gone, or if it had a hole yet lacked naught soever, it is valid. A dark-
coloured[11] citron is not valid. A citron green like a leek R. Meir declares
valid and R. Judah declares it invalid.

7. The smallest size for the citron, according to R. Meir, is that of a
walnut. R. Judah says: That of an egg. The largest size is such that two
can be held in one hand. So R. Judah. But R. Jose says: Even one [that
can only be held] in the two hands.

8. The *Lulab*[12] may only be bound up with strands of like species.
So R. Judah. But R. Meir says: [It may be bound up] even with a cord.
R. Meir said: The men of Jerusalem used to bind up their *Lulab* with
threads of gold. They answered: But below [these] they bound it up with
strands of like species.

---

[1] A tree worshipped by the heathen (Deut. 12³).   [2] Deut. 13¹⁶.
[3] A hill near Jerusalem.
[4] And not by a brook (Lev. 23⁴⁰). The word rendered 'field' denotes unirrigated land.
See p. 41, n. 3.
[5] To be tied up together to make up the *Lulab* which combines the three species of
branches prescribed in Lev. 23⁴⁰.
[6] This represents 'the fruit of goodly trees' (Lev. 23⁴⁰).   [7] App. I. 32.
[8] See *Terumah*, App. I. 48.   [9] App. I. 6.   [10] See p. 73, n. 6.
[11] Lit. Kushite, Ethiopian.
[12] Lit. palm-branch, but here denoting the bunch of palm-, myrtle-, and willow-branches.

9. And where do they shake the *Lulab*? At the beginning and the end of the Psalm *O give thanks unto the Lord*,[1] and at *Save now, we beseech thee, O Lord*.[2] So the School of Hillel. The School of Shammai say: Also at *O Lord, we beseech thee, send now prosperity*.[3] R. Akiba said: I once watched Rabban Gamaliel and R. Joshua, and while all the people were shaking their *Lulabs*, they shook them only at *Save now, we beseech thee, O Lord*. If a man was on a journey and could not carry the *Lulab*, when he returns home he must carry it even [if he only remembered it] while at table. If he had not carried it in the morning he must carry it in the afternoon, for the whole day[4] is valid for carrying the *Lulab*.

10. If a slave, a woman, or a minor recited [the *Hallel*][5] to him he must repeat after them what they say (and let it be a curse to him!)[6] If one that was of age recited it to him he responds only with 'Hallelujah!'[7]

11. Where the custom is to repeat,[8] they repeat; [where the custom is] to say it once only, they say it once only; [where the custom is] to say the Benediction after it,[9] they say the Benediction after it: all should follow local use. If a man bought a *Lulab* from his fellow during the Seventh Year he must give him a citron as a gift, for he is not permitted to buy it during the Seventh Year.[10]

12. Beforetime the *Lulab* was carried seven days in the Temple, but in the provinces one day only. After[11] the Temple was destroyed, Rabban Johanan b. Zakkai ordained that in the provinces it should be carried seven days in memory of the Temple; also [he ordained] that on the whole of the Day of Waving[12] it should be forbidden [to eat of new produce].[13]

13. If the first Festival-day of the Feast falls on a Sabbath all the people bring their *Lulabs* to the synagogue [on the day before]. The next day they come early and each man discerns his own *Lulab* and carries it; for the Sages have said: None can fulfil his obligation on the first Festival-day of the Feast with his fellow's *Lulab*. But on other days of the Feast a man may fulfil his obligation with his fellow's *Lulab*.

14. R. Jose says: If the first Festival-day of the Feast fell on a Sabbath and a man forgot and brought out the Lulab into the public domain, he is not culpable since he brought it out [with intent] to fulfil a licit act.[14]

15. A woman may take it out of the hand of her son or out of the hand of her husband and put it back in water on the Sabbath. R. Judah says: On a Sabbath it may be put back [in the same water], on a Festival-day [water] may be added, and during mid-festival [the water] may be changed. If a boy that is not of age[15] knows how to shake it he must carry the *Lulab*.[16]

4. 1. [The rites of] the *Lulab* and the Willow-branch[17] [continue] six

---

[1] Ps. 118. See *S. S.*, Tabernacles, p. 98.   [2] Ps. 18²⁵.   [3] Ps. 118²⁵.
[4] But not the night.   [5] Pss. 113–118. See *S. S.*, Tabernacles, p. 96 ff.
[6] That he has not learnt to read.   [7] At the end of every verse. Cf. Sot. 5⁴.
[8] The last nine verses of Ps. 118.
[9] The Benediction before the *Hallel* (see *S. S.*, Tabernacles, p. 96) is obligatory. For the form of the concluding Benediction see op. cit., p. 99 (bottom).
[10] Lev. 25¹⁻⁷; cf. Shebi. 7³.   [11] R.Sh. 4³; Men. 10⁵.
[12] Second day of Passover. Lev. 23¹¹.
[13] Reaped that spring and first permitted for use after 'waving of the sheaf' on the 16th of Nisan; but Rabban Johanan forbade it until the day following.
[14] Or: 'a meritorious act'.   [15] Not yet aged thirteen.   [16] Cf. above, 2⁸.
[17] The priests used to go in procession around the Altar on the days of the Feast bearing willow-branches.

and sometimes seven days; the *Hallel*[1] and the Rejoicing,[2] eight days; the *Sukkah* and the Water-libation,[3] seven days; the Flute-playing,[4] sometimes five and sometimes six days.

2. '[The rites of] the *Lulab* . . . seven days'—thus if the first Festival-day of the Feast fell on a Sabbath the *Lulab* [is carried] seven days; but if it fell on any other day [it is carried] six days only.[5]

3. 'The Willow-branch . . . seven days'—thus if the seventh day of [the rites of] the Willow-branch fell on a Sabbath [the rites of] the Willow-branch continue seven days; but if it fell on any other day, six days only.[6]

4. How was the rite of the *Lulab* fulfilled [on the Sabbath]? If the first Festival-day of the Feast fell on a Sabbath, they brought their Lulabs to the Temple Mount and the ministers took them and set them in order on the roof of the portico,[7] but the elders set theirs in a [special] chamber. The people were taught to say, 'Whosoever gets possession of my *Lulab*, let it be his as a gift'.[8] The next day they came early and the ministers threw the *Lulabs* down before them and the people snatched at them and beat each other. And when the Court saw that they incurred danger, they ordained that every one could carry his *Lulab* in his own home.

5. How was the rite of the Willow-branch fulfilled? There was a place below Jerusalem called Motza.[9] Thither they went and cut themselves young willow-branches. They came and set these up at the sides of the Altar so that their tops were bent over the Altar. They then blew [on the *shofar*] a sustained, a quavering and another sustained blast.[10] Each day[11] they went in procession a single time around the Altar, saying, *Save now, we beseech thee, O Lord! We beseech thee, O Lord, send now prosperity.*[12] R. Judah says:[13] '*Ani waho!* save us we pray! *Ani waho!* save us we pray!' But on that day[14] they went in procession seven times around the Altar. When[15] they departed what did they say? 'Homage[16] to thee, O Altar! Homage to thee, O Altar!' R. Eliezer says: 'To the Lord and to thee, O Altar! To the Lord and to thee, O Altar!'

6. As was the rite on a week-day so was the rite on a Sabbath, save that they gathered [the willow-branches] on the eve of the Sabbath and set them in gilded troughs that they might not wither. R. Johanan b. Baroka says: They used to bring palm tufts and beat them on the ground at the sides of the Altar, and that day was called, 'The day of beating the palm tufts'.

7. Straightway[17] the children used to cast away their *Lulabs* and eat their citrons.

---

[1] See above, 3[9-11].

[2] Deut. 16[14] in the prescriptions for the observance of the Feast of Tabernacles says 'and thou shalt rejoice in thy feast'.

[3] After the morning Daily Whole-offering. See below, 4[9].   [4] See below, 5[1-4].

[5] Since the carrying of the *Lulab* overrides the Sabbath only if the first Festival-day of the Feast falls on a Sabbath.

[6] The willow-branch procession could override the Sabbath only on its most significant, the seventh, day, when (see below, 4[5]) they went seven times around the Altar.

[7] Cf. Shek. 8[4]; Pes. 1[5]. Gem. 45a disputes whether 'above' the portico is meant or only on the seats beneath the portico where they would not be liable to wither.

[8] Cf. above, 3[13]. There, however, it speaks of a synagogue where confusion was less likely. Cf. 3[1f]. 'got by robbery'.   [9] Josh. 18[26].

[10] See R.Sh. 4[9]; cf. Pes. 5[5].   [11] For the first six days.   [12] Ps. 118[25].

[13] Instead of the repeated 'We beseech thee, O Lord' (*ana YHWH*, which involves pronouncing the Sacred Name) they modify the sounds to *ani waho*. Cf. Yom. 6[2].

[14] The seventh.   [15] Some texts omit the rest of the paragraph.   [16] Lit. 'Beauty'.

[17] The Hebrew may be rendered (so Rashi): They took away the *Lulabs* from the children and ate their citrons.

8. 'The *Hallel* and the Rejoicing, eight days'—this is to teach us that a man is bound to recite the *Hallel* and observe the Rejoicing and give the honour [due to the Feast] on the last Festival-day[1] of the Feast as on all other days of the Feast. 'The *Sukkah* . . . seven days'—thus, after a man has finished eating [the last meal of the Feast][2] he should not pull down the *Sukkah*, but he should bring down[3] the contents thereof only in the afternoon and later, because of the honour due to the last Festival-day of the Feast.

9. 'The Water-libation, seven days'[4]—what was the manner of this? They used to fill a golden flagon holding three *logs*[5] with water from Siloam. When they reached the Water Gate they blew [on the *shofar*] a sustained, a quavering and another sustained blast. [The priest whose turn of duty it was] went up the [Altar-]Ramp[6] and turned to the right where were two silver bowls. R. Judah says: They were of plaster, but their appearance was darkened because of the wine. They had each a hole like to a narrow snout, one wide and the other narrow, so that both bowls emptied themselves together.[7] The bowl to the west was for water and that to the east was for wine. But if the flagon of water was emptied into the bowl for wine, or the flagon of wine into the bowl for water, that sufficed. R. Judah says: With one *log* they could perform the libations throughout eight days. To the priest who performed the libation they used to say, 'Lift up thine hand!' for once a certain one poured the libation over his feet, and all the people threw their citrons at him.[8]

10. As was the rite on a weekday so was the rite on a Sabbath save that on the eve of the Sabbath they used to fill with water from Siloam a golden jar that had not been hallowed,[9] and put it in a [special] chamber. If it was upset or uncovered, they refilled it from the laver,[10] for wine or water which has been uncovered is invalid[11] for the Altar.

5. 1. 'The Flute-playing, sometimes five and sometimes six days'—this is the flute-playing at the Beth ha-She'ubah,[12] which overrides neither a Sabbath nor a Festival-day. They have said: He that never has seen the joy of the Beth ha-She'ubah has never in his life seen joy.

2. At the close of the first Festival-day of the Feast they went down[13] to the Court of the Women[14] where they had made a great amendment.[15] There were golden candlesticks there with four golden bowls on the top of them and four ladders[16] to each candlestick, and four youths of the priestly stock and in their hands jars of oil holding a hundred and twenty *logs* which they poured into all the bowls.

3. They made wicks from the worn out drawers and girdles of the priests and with them they set the candlesticks alight, and there was not

---

[1] The eighth day. See Lev. 23[36].   [2] On the morning of the Seventh day.
[3] Cf. p. 174, n. 12.   [4] Some texts omit 'seven days'.
[5] About one and a half pints App. II D.   [6] See Midd. 3[3].
[7] Wine flowing out more slowly than water.
[8] The incident is told by Josephus, *Ant.* XIII. xiii. 5.
[9] If it had been hallowed the water could not remain overnight. See p. 165, n. 16.
Cf. Meil. 3[7].   [10] Ex. 30[18ff].   [11] Cf. Ter. 8[4].
[12] Texts vary as between this reading and Beth ha-Sho'ebah. The precise sense of the expression is uncertain. The root has the meaning 'to draw water'. Cf. Is 12[3], 'Therefore with joy shall ye draw water'. The probable sense is 'The place (or the act) of the Water-drawing'.
[13] From the Court of the Israelites, which was fifteen steps higher.
[14] See Midd. 2[5].   [15] A special women's gallery (Midd. 2[5]).
[16] According to the Talmud the candlesticks were fifty cubits high.

a courtyard in Jerusalem that did not reflect the light of the Beth ha-She'ubah.

4. Men of piety and good works[1] used to dance before them with burning torches in their hands, singing songs and praises. And countless levites [played] on harps, lyres, cymbals and trumpets and instruments of music, on the fifteen steps leading down from the Court of the Israelites to the Court of the Women, corresponding to the Fifteen Songs of Ascents in the Psalms;[2] upon them the levites used to stand with instruments of music and make melody. Two priests stood at the upper gate[3] which leads down from the Court of the Israelites to the Court of the Women, with two trumpets in their hands. At cock-crow they blew a sustained, a quavering and another sustained blast. When they reached the tenth step they again blew a sustained, a quavering and another sustained blast. When they reached the Court [of the Women] they again blew a sustained, a quavering and another sustained blast. They went on until they reached the gate that leads out to the east. When they reached the gate that leads out to the east, they turned their faces to the west[4] and said, 'Our fathers when they were in this place turned *with their backs toward the Temple of the Lord and their faces toward the east, and they worshipped the sun toward the east*;[5] but as for us, our eyes are turned toward the Lord'. R. Judah says: They used to repeat the words 'We are the Lord's, and our eyes are turned to the Lord'.

5. They blew never less than twenty-one blasts[6] in the Temple [in a day] and never more than forty-eight. On all days they blew twenty-one blasts: three at the opening of the gates, nine at the morning Daily Whole-offering, and nine at the evening Daily Whole-offering.[7] At the Additional offerings[8] they blew nine more blasts. On the eve of Sabbath they used to blow six more blasts, three to cause the people to cease from work and three to mark the break between the sacred and the profane.[9] If, [therefore], the eve of Sabbath fell within the [week of the] Feast, they blew forty-eight blasts: three at the opening of the gates, three at the upper gate,[10] three at the lower gate,[11] three at the water-drawing, three at the Altar, nine at the morning Daily Whole-offering, nine at the evening Daily Whole-offering, nine at the Additional-offerings, three to cause the people to cease from work, and three to mark the break between the sacred and the profane.

6. On the first Festival-day of the Feast there were offered thirteen bullocks, two rams and one he-goat.[12] There [still] remained the fourteen he-lambs for the [other] eight Courses[13] of priests. On the first day six offered two each and the remaining two one each. On the second day[14]

---

[1] The sense may be 'workers of miracles'; cf. Sot. 9[15] and Ber. 5[5] concerning R. Hanina b. Dosa.   [2] Pss. 120–34. Cf. Midd. 2[5].
[3] Not that described by this name in Shek. 6[3]; Midd. 2[6], but the Nicanor Gate (see p. 166, n. 3).   [4] Towards the Temple building.   [5] Ezek. 8[16].
[6] i.e. seven times repeating the series 'a sustained, a quavering and another sustained blast'.   [7] See Tam. 7[3].   [8] On Sabbaths, New Moons and Festival-days.
[9] To mark the entering in of the Sabbath.   [10] Nicanor Gate.
[11] 'That leads out to the East'.
[12] Sixteen beasts which together with fourteen he-lambs were prescribed (Num. 29[13, 16]) as Additional-offerings from the 1st to the 7th day of Tabernacles; the number of bullocks was reduced by one each successive day.
[13] At the three Feasts all the twenty-four Courses of priests were present at the Temple and shared equally in the offerings.
[14] There being one less bullock to offer, one of the sixteen Courses occupied the first day will now offer one of the fourteen he-lambs, which, the first day, had been left to the remaining eight Courses; and on the third day there are two less bullocks, and two of the sixteen Courses will offer two of the fourteen lambs; and so on.

five offered two each and the rest one each. On the third day four offered two each and the rest one each. On the fourth day three offered two each and the rest one each. On the sixth day one offered two and the rest one each. On the seventh day[1] all were equal. On the eighth day they once again cast lots as at the other Feasts. It was enjoined that whosoever offered bullocks the one day should not offer them on the morrow, but that they should offer them in turn.

7. Three times[2] in the year all the Courses of priests shared equally in the offerings prescribed for the Feast and in the division of the Shewbread.[3] At Pentecost[4] they used to say to the priest, 'Here is unleavened bread for thee, here is leavened'. The Course of priests whose time of service was determined [for that week][5] offered the Daily Whole-offerings, vow-offerings, freewill-offerings, and all other offerings of the congregation; it offered them all. On a Festival-day which fell next to a Sabbath, either before or after, all the Courses of priests shared equally in the division of the Shewbread.

8. If a day intervened [between a Festival-day and a Sabbath] the Course of priests whose time of service was determined [for that week] used to take ten loaves, but they that delayed[6] [in the Temple] took two. On other days of the year the incoming Course of priests took six, and the outgoing Course took six. R. Judah says: The incoming Course took seven and the outgoing Course took five. The incoming Course divided [the Shewbread] to the north and the outgoing Course divided it to the south. [The Course of] Bilgah[7] always divided it to the south,[8] since their ring[9] was immovable and their wall-niche[10] blocked up.

YOM TOB[11] OR 'BETZAH'[12] ('FESTIVAL-DAYS')

1. 1. If an egg was laid on a Festival-day, the School of Shammai say:[13] It may be eaten.[14] And the School of Hillel say: It may not be eaten.[15] The

[1] There was one offering each (see Num. 29 32–34) for twenty-four Courses.
[2] Passover, Pentecost, and Tabernacles.
[3] Lev. 24 5–9. See Men. 11 5f. The twelve loaves were divided among the priests on the Sabbath.
[4] If it fell on a Sabbath there was due to the priests both the twelve unleavened loaves of the Shewbread and the two leavened loaves ('the bread of the first-fruits') offered at Pentecost (Lev. 23 17).
[5] Whose pre-ordained weekly course fell during the seven days of the Feast. They have the right to all offerings that are not specially prescribed for the Feast.
[6] After their week of service was completed. [7] 1 Chron. 24 14.
[8] They had lost the usual rights belonging to the Courses of priests. The reasons given (t. Sukk. 4 28) are that Miriam, the daughter of one among their number, had married a Greek soldier and had denounced the priesthood; or that they had been so dilatory in their duty that the Course of Jeshebeab replaced them.
[9] At the north side at which they should have slaughtered (Midd. 3 5).
[10] In which the priestly vestments were kept (Tam. 5 3). It was to the north of the Nicanor Gate.
[11] On the 1st and 7th days of Passover, the 1st and 8th days of Tabernacles, the day of Pentecost, and New Year's Day, all work is forbidden. See Lev. 23 7, 8, 21, 25, 35, 36. Whatever is forbidden on the Sabbath (See Shab. 7 2) is forbidden on a Festival-day except the preparation of necessary food (Ex. 12 16), and only such as is necessary for that day; thus slaughtering, flaying, kneading, cooking, or baking are permissible, but what could equally well have been done the day before (reaping, threshing, grinding, sifting, or hunting) are forbidden. But these permissible acts require that preparation be made for them before the Festival-day. Objects needed must be 'set in readiness'. Contrariwise, whatever was laid aside, without previous intention of use, may not be used on a Festival-day. This includes what was not previously in existence (e.g. an egg laid on a Festival-day) or what first became fit for use on the Festival-day, or what serves to the performance of some forbidden act, e.g. a needle or the like.
[12] Lit. 'an egg'. This alternative title is given to the tractate from its opening word.
[13] See Eduy. 4 1.   [14] The same day.   [15] Until the day is over.

School of Shammai say: An olive's bulk of leaven and a date's bulk of what is leavened.[1] And the School of Hillel say: An olive's bulk of either.[2]

2. If[3] a man slaughtered a wild animal or a bird on a Festival-day, the School of Shammai say: He may dig with a mattock and cover up [the blood].[4] And the School of Hillel say: He should not slaughter unless he had earth set in readiness [to cover up the blood] from the day before. But they agree that if he had slaughtered, he may dig with a mattock and cover up [the blood]. [Moreover they agree] that the ashes of a stove may count as set in readiness.

3. The School of Shammai say: They may not remove a ladder from one dovecot to another[5] but only incline it from one opening to another [of the same dovecot]. And the School of Hillel permit it. The School of Shammai say: A man may not take [pigeons for slaughtering on a Festival-day] unless he stirred them up[6] the day before. And the School of Hillel say: He need only go up and say, 'This one and this one shall I take'.

4. If he had bespoken black ones but found white, or white ones but found black; or two but found three, they are forbidden; [but if he had bespoken] three but found two they are permitted. [If he had bespoken birds] within the nest and found them in front of the nest, they are forbidden. But if none save these were there they are permitted.

5. The School of Shammai say: They may not take off cupboard doors[7] on a Festival-day. But the School of Hillel even permit them to be put back. The School of Shammai say: They may not lift up a pestle[8] to hack meat on it. And the School of Hillel permit it. The School of Shammai say: They may not put a hide before the treading-place[9] and they may lift one up only if there is an olive's bulk of flesh on it.[10] And the School of Hillel permit it. The School of Shammai say: They may not carry out a child or a *Lulab*[11] or a scroll of the Law into the public domain. And the School of Hillel permit it.

6. The School of Shammai say: They may not take Dough-offering[12] or [Priests'] Dues[13] to the priest on a Festival-day whether they were set apart on the day before or on the same day. And the School of Hillel permit it. The School of Shammai replied with an analogy: Dough-offering and [Priests'] Dues are a gift to the priest, and the Heave-offering[14] is a gift to the priest; as they may not bring Heave-offering, neither may they bring [Priests'] Dues. The School of Hillel replied: No! as ye argue of Heave-offering (which a man has not the right to set apart[15] [on a Festival-day]) would ye also argue of [Priests'] Dues (which a man has the right to set apart [on a Festival-day])?[16]

7. The School of Shammai say: Spices may be pounded with a wooden

---

[1] May not be suffered to remain at Passover (referring to Ex. 13[7]).
[2] The Cambridge text adds: 'If a beast was born on a Festival-day they agree that it is permitted, but if a chicken was hatched from an egg they agree that it is forbidden.'
[3] Eduy. 4[2].   [4] Lev. 17[13]. See Hull. 6[1ff]. Cf. Bikk. 2[9].
[5] To bring down the birds that are to be slaughtered.
[6] Handled those which he proposed to eat the next day, to see if they were fat enough.
[7] As transgressing the rule forbidding building and pulling down (Shab. 7[2]).
[8] Generally used in pounding grain; the rule against 'grinding' would therefore apply to it.
[9] As a door-mat, since trampling on it constitutes the work necessary for preparing it for use.
[10] Since only what is needful for necessary food may be carried about on a Festival-day.
[11] App. I. 20.   [12] Num. 15[17-21].
[13] Lit. 'gifts'. Deut. 18[3], 'the shoulder, and the two cheeks, and the maw'. See Hull. 10[1ff].
[14] See Num. 18[11f].
[15] Since it is set apart in concluding the storing of the produce and counts as an act of work.
[16] Since slaughtering is permitted.

pestle and salt in a cruse and with a wooden pot-stirrer. And the School of Hillel say: Spices may be pounded after their usual fashion with a stone pestle, and salt with a wooden pestle.

8. If a man picked out pulse on a Festival-day, the School of Shammai say: He must [forthwith] eat the edible parts as he picks them out. And the School of Hillel say: He may pick them out after his usual fashion, into his lap or into a basket or into a dish; but not on to a board or into a sifter or sieve.[1] Rabban Gamaliel says: He may even swill them and separate the husks.

9. The School of Shammai say: They may send only [prepared] portions[2] as gifts on a Festival-day. And the School of Hillel say: They may send cattle, wild animals or birds, whether alive or slaughtered. They may send wine, oil, flour, or pulse, but not grain.[3] But R. Simeon permits grain.[4]

10. They may send articles [of apparel] whether sewn up[5] or not [yet] sewn up,[6] even though there are Diverse Kinds [of stuff][7] in them, if they are to serve [only] the need of the Feast;[8] but not a nailed sandal[9] or an unsewn shoe.[10] R. Judah says: Nor even a white shoe, since it requires a craftsman [to blacken it]. This is the general rule: whatsoever a man can [forthwith] make use of may be sent [as a present] on a Festival-day.

2. 1. If a Festival-day fell on the eve of Sabbath, a man may not cook on the Festival-day food [intended] from the outset for the Sabbath; but he may cook food [intended solely] for the Festival-day, and if any is left over, it is left over for the Sabbath; or he may prepare a dish on the eve of the Festival-day and depend on it for the Sabbath.[11] The School of Shammai say: Two dishes. And the School of Hillel say: One dish. But they agree that a fish covered with an egg counts as two dishes. If the dish [intended for the Sabbath] was eaten or lost, a man may not cook another anew in its stead, but if aught soever of it remained, he may depend on that for the Sabbath.

2. If a Festival-day fell on the day after the Sabbath, the School of Shammai say: All [that need it] must be immersed on the day before the Sabbath. And the School of Hillel say: Vessels [must be immersed] before the Sabbath, but men [may immerse themselves] on the Sabbath.

3. Howbeit they agree that [on a Festival-day] they may render [unclean] water clean by [surface] contact[12] in a stone vessel, but they may not immerse it;[13] and that they may immerse [vessels on a Festival-day] if they are to be changed from one use to another,[14] or [at Passover] from one company to another.

---

[1] Lest he appear to be preparing food for the next day.
[2] That must needs be consumed the same day. [3] Which would need to be ground.
[4] It may be cooked forthwith. [5] Ready as clothing.
[6] They can be used as coverings. [7] Deut. 22[11]. See Kil. 9[1ff].
[8] Not as clothing but, e.g., as a table-cloth. [9] Shab. 6[2].
[10] Which still needs craftsman's labour.
[11] This is the rule known as *Erub tabshilim* ('amalgamation of cooking') by which, by a formal beginning of the cooking for Saturday on Thursday before sunset (the eve of Friday, when this is a Festival-day), the cooking for Saturday may be continued after sunset, i.e. on the Festival-day itself.
[12] See Mikw. 6[8]. Foodstuffs and liquids once unclean can never be rendered clean. The only exception is water. If this becomes unclean it is sufficient to dip a stone vessel containing the unclean water into clean water, and so soon as the two waters make contact, 'even by a hairsbreadth', the unclean becomes clean.
[13] Together with a containing vessel that is unclean.
[14] Cf. Hag. 2[6, 7]. E.g. if he had immersed them for Heave-offering and then determined to

4. The School of Shammai say: They may bring Peace-offerings [on a Festival-day] and not lay their hands thereon;[1] but they may not bring Whole-offerings.[2] And the School of Hillel say: They may bring both a Peace-offering and Whole-offerings and lay their hands thereon.

5. The School of Shammai say: A man may not heat water for his feet unless it is also such as could be drunk. And the School of Hillel permit it. A man may make a fire and warm himself before it.

6. In three things[3] Rabban Gamaliel gives the more stringent ruling following the opinion of the School of Shammai: Hot food may not be covered up on a Festival day for the Sabbath,[4] nor may a candlestick be put together[5] on a Festival-day; nor may bread be baked into large loaves[6] but only into thin cakes. Rabban Gamaliel said: Never did my father's household bake bread into large loaves but only into thin cakes. They said to him: What shall we infer from thy father's household, which applied the stringent ruling to themselves but the lenient ruling to Israel, so that they might bake the bread both in large loaves and thick cakes!

7. Moreover[7] he gave three opinions applying the more lenient ruling: They may sweep up between couches[8] and put the spices[9] on the fire on a Festival-day, and prepare a kid roasted whole on Passover night.[10] But these things the Sages forbid.

8. Three things[11] did R. Eleazar b. Azariah permit and the Sages forbid: A man's cow may go out [on the Sabbath] with the strap that is between its horns, and they may curry cattle on a Festival-day, and grind pepper in its proper mill. R. Judah says: They may not curry cattle on a Festival-day since it may cause a weal, but they may comb them. And the Sages say: They may neither curry them nor comb them.

9. Pepper-mills are susceptible to uncleanness by virtue of [falling within] three categories of utensil: a utensil which has a receptacle,[12] a metal utensil,[13] and a utensil used for sifting.[14]

10. A child's cart is susceptible to *midras*-uncleanness,[15] and it may be carried [by hand] on the Sabbath,[16] but it may not be dragged save over [other] articles.[17] R. Judah says: No articles may be dragged excepting a wagon, since this only presses [the earth without breaking the surface].

3. 1. They may not catch fish from a vivarium on a Festival-day or put food before them; but they may catch wild animals and birds from a vivarium and put food before them. Rabban Simeon b. Gamaliel says:

---

immerse them for something of a higher sanctity, e.g. flesh of animal-offerings, he may do so on a Festival-day. So, too, if he had immersed himself preparatory to joining one company to eat the Passover lamb, and then determined to join himself to another company who required a higher degree of sanctity, he may immerse himself again on the Festival-day itself.

[1] Lev. 3[2]. Laying on of hands was done with the exertion of much pressure, therefore (according to the School of Shammai) it was forbidden in virtue of the rabbinically ordained rules of 'Sabbath rest' (cf. Erub. 10[3, 15]). See Hag. 2[2].

[2] Since these cannot count as 'necessary food' as can Peace-offerings (which, except for their sacrificial portions, are consumed by their owners). Freewill offerings are here meant.

[3] Eduy. 3[10].   [4] It counts as cooking for the Sabbath (see above, 2[1]).

[5] It counts as building (Shab. 7[2]).   [6] It involves burdensome labour.

[7] Eduy. 3[11].   [8] In the eating-hall.   [9] Cf. Ber. 6[6].

[10] The Sages forbid this (namely after the destruction of the Temple) as seeming to eat of the Passover offering outside of Jerusalem (cf. Pes. 7[12]).

[11] Eduy. 3[12]. Cf. Shab. 5[4].   [12] See Kel. 11[1].   [13] See Kel. 11[2].

[14] Cf. Kel. 16[3]; 17[4].   [15] App. I. 26.   [16] As being an article used within a house.

[17] Such as matting. Otherwise it breaks the surface of the ground, transgressing the rule (Shab. 7[2]) against ploughing.

Not all vivaria are alike. This is the general rule:[1] What must still be hunted is forbidden, but what needs not to be hunted is permitted.

2. If traps for wild animals, birds or fish were set on the eve of a Festival-day, what are caught may not be taken out on the Festival-day unless it is known that they were caught during the eve of the Festival-day. A gentile once brought fish to Rabban Gamaliel. He said, 'They are permitted but I have no wish to accept them from him'.

3. A beast at the point of death may be slaughtered only if there is time enough on that day to eat from it an olive's bulk of roast flesh.[2] R. Akiba says: Even an olive's bulk of raw flesh [suffices] from the slaughtering wound.[3] If it was slaughtered in the field, a man may not bring it in on a pole or a barrow, but he may bring it in piece by piece in his hands.

4. If a Firstling[4] fell into a pit, R. Judah says: Let a skilled person go down and look at it; if it has incurred a blemish let him bring it up and slaughter it; otherwise it may not be slaughtered. R. Simeon says: In that its blemish was not perceived on the day before, it cannot count as what is set in readiness.

5. If a beast died it may not be moved. They once asked R. Tarfon touching this matter and Dough-offering[5] that was become unclean. He went into the House of Study and inquired, and they answered: They may not be moved.

6. They may not allot shares[6] in a beast from the outset on a Festival-day, but if they have done so on the eve of a Festival-day they may slaughter it and divide it between them. R. Judah says: They may take the weight of flesh using a vessel or a hatchet for a weight. But the Sages say: They may not use scales at all.

7. They may not whet a knife on a Festival-day, but they may draw it over another knife. A man may not say to the butcher, 'Sell me[7] a *denar's* worth of flesh', but he may slaughter [the beast] and they can share it together.

8. A man may say to a shopkeeper,[8] 'Fill me this vessel', but not 'with the measure'. R. Judah says: If it was a measuring-vessel he may not fill it. It is told how Abba Saul b. Batnith used to fill up his measures on the eve of a Festival-day and give them to his customers on the Festival-day. Abba Saul says: He used also to do so during mid-festival[9] for[10] the sake of clearness of measure. And the Sages say: He used also to do so on an ordinary day for the sake of exactness of measure.[11] A man may go to the shopkeeper with whom he is familiar[12] and say to him, 'Give me eggs and nuts by number', for such is the way of a householder to make his reckoning in his own home.

4. 1. If a man took jars of wine from place to place he should not take them in a basket or hamper[13] but on his shoulder or in front of him. So,

---

[1] Cf. Shab. 13[5].
[2] Otherwise this would be preparing food on a Festival-day for another day.
[3] If there is no time to flay the beast.
[4] Which may be slaughtered outside the Temple only if it has incurred a blemish. Deut. 15[19-22].   [5] Num. 15[17-21]. See Pes. 3[3].
[6] Since, knowing its weight and market-price, they would be transacting business.
[7] Variant: 'weigh me out'.   [8] Variant: 'his fellow'.
[9] The 2nd to the 6th days of Passover, and the 2nd to the 7th days of Tabernacles.
[10] Some texts omit the rest of the sentence.   [11] To avoid measuring in haste.
[12] And the shopkeeper trusts him to settle the reckoning after the Festival-day.
[13] As he would on a week-day.

too, if a man removed chopped straw he should not hang the hamper behind him but bring it in his hand. He may newly break into a stack of chopped straw,[1] but not into wood that is [stored away] in the rear-court.[2]

2. They may not take any of the wood from the [structure of the] *Sukkah*[3] but only what lies against it. They may bring out of the field wood from what has been collected together and, out of an outer-area,[4] even what is scattered about. What counts as an 'outer-area'? Any area adjoining the town. So R. Judah. R. Jose says: Any enclosure that one must enter with a key and that is also within the Sabbath limit.[5]

3. They may not split firewood from beams or from a beam broken on a Festival-day; nor may they split wood with an axe or a saw or a scythe, but only with a chopper.[6] If a house was full of produce and blocked up, but with a breach therein, one may take [produce] from the breach. R. Meir says: One may even breach it[7] from the outset and take therefrom.

4. A man may not make a hole in a lump of clay for a lamp, since he would be making a vessel. They may not make charcoal, or sever a wick into two. R. Judah says: One may sever it with a flame between two lamps.[8]

5. They may not break a potsherd or cut paper to roast salt-fish thereon; nor may they clear out an oven or stove, but they may level down the ashes; nor may they put two jars close together to set the pot thereon, nor may they prop up a pot with a chip, and the same applies to a door. And they may not lead out cattle with a staff on a Festival-day. But R. Eleazar b. R. Simeon permits it.

6. R. Eliezer says: A man may take a wood-splinter to clean his teeth from what lies before him, and heap up what is in the courtyard to make a fire, for whatsoever is in the courtyard counts as set in readiness. But the Sages say: He may heap up only what lies before him to make a fire.

7. They may not produce fire[9] out of wood,[10] stone,[11] earth[12] or water,[13] nor may they heat tiles white hot to roast thereon. Moreover, R. Eliezer said: A man may stand by the rear-court[14] on the eve of a Sabbath[15] in the Seventh Year[16] and say: From this part will I eat to-morrow. But the Sages say: Only if he marks it out and says, 'From here to there'.

5. 1. They may let down fruit[17] through a hatchway[18] on a Festival-day, but not on a Sabbath; and they may cover up fruit with vessels because of dripping rain; so, too, jars of wine and oil. Even on the Sabbath they may set a vessel to catch dripping rain.

2. Any act that is culpable on the Sabbath, whether by virtue of the

---

[1] For cattle-fodder.
[2] Its use is not confined to the cooking of necessary food, but it might be used for building.
[3] App. I. 42.   [4] Cf. Erub. 9[1].   [5] See Erub. 5[2].
[6] A smaller implement used for cutting up flesh is here meant.
[7] If it was built of loose stones.
[8] The two ends of one wick are put into two lamps (the flat saucer-shaped lamps are meant with wick-nozzles on the rims) and a light applied to the middle of the wick between the lamps.
[9] On the Festival-day. This would be to bring into existence what was not already in readiness. He may only use flame or brands kindled the day before.
[10] By rubbing two sticks together.   [11] By friction with metal.
[12] Perhaps sulphur or the like.
[13] 'A glass vessel is filled with water and put in a hot sun; the glass emits flame which will kindle a wick brought near to it' (Bert.).
[14] Where fruit is spread out to dry; and since the fruit's preparation is not complete it is tithe-free.   [15] When it is forbidden to tithe.
[16] Lev. 25[1-7]. In the Seventh Year fruit is tithe-free.
[17] Spread out on the roof to dry.   [18] Opening through the roof. Cf. Ohol. 10[1f].

rules concerning Sabbath rest[1] or concerning acts of choice or concerning pious duties, is culpable also on a Festival-day. And these [acts are culpable] by virtue of the rules concerning Sabbath rest: none may climb a tree or ride a beast or swim on water or clap the hands or slap the thighs[2] or stamp with the feet.[3] And these [acts are culpable] by virtue of the rules concerning acts of choice: none may sit in judgement or conclude a betrothal or perform *halitzah*[4] or contract levirate marriage.[5] And these [acts are culpable] by virtue of the rules concerning pious duties: none may dedicate aught[6] or make a vow of Valuation[7] or devote aught[8] or set apart Heave-offering[9] or Tithes.[10] All these things have they prescribed [as culpable] on a Festival-day: still more so [are they culpable] on the Sabbath. A Festival-day differs from the Sabbath in naught save in the preparing of needful food.

3. A man's cattle and utensils[11] are [restricted to the same limits] as his feet. If a man committed his beast to his son or to his herdsmen, they are [restricted to the same limits] as his feet. If utensils are for the use in particular of one among brethren that are in a house, they are [restricted to the same limits] as his feet; but if they are not for his use in particular, they may go [only] where all [the brethren] may go.[12]

4. If a man borrowed a vessel from his fellow on the eve of a Festival-day it is [restricted to the same limits] as the feet of the borrower; but if on a Festival-day, as the feet of the lender. If a woman borrowed from her fellow spices, water, and salt for her dough, these are [restricted to the same limits] as the feet of them both.[13] R. Judah exempts the water since it has no abiding substance.[14]

5. A burning coal is [restricted to the same limits] as its owner, but the flame [may spread] anywhere.[15] The law of Sacrilege[16] applies to a burning coal belonging to the Temple; no use may be made of its flame, yet none thereby commits Sacrilege. If[17] a man thrust out a burning coal into the public domain [on the Sabbath] he is culpable; but if he took out the flame [alone] he is not culpable. If a cistern belonged to one person [its water is restricted to the same limits] as that person, and if it belonged to the people of that town [its water is restricted to the same limits] as the people of that town;[18] and that of them that returned from Babylon[19] [is restricted to the same limits] as the feet of him that draws water therefrom.

6. If a man's produce was in another town and the men of that town made *Erub*[20] in order to bring to him some of his produce, they may not

---

[1] See Erub. 10[3, 15].   [2] Or: 'make music'.   [3] Or: 'dance'.

[4] The ceremony prescribed (Deut. 25[7ff.].) when a man refuses to contract levirate marriage, i.e. to marry his deceased, childless brother's widow (Deut. 25[5–6]).

[5] All these four acts are forbidden since they may lead to writing out some document.

[6] Such as the produce of his field.

[7] The 'commuted vows' described in Lev. 27[1–7]; see tractate Arakhin.

[8] See Arak. 8[6].   [9] See *Terumah*, App. I. 48.   [10] See Deut. 14[22–9].

[11] On a Sabbath or Festival-day.

[12] e.g. if the various brethren have various Sabbath limits (see p. 120, n. 5), their common property is restricted to the area common to them all.

[13] The limits common to both.   [14] It is unrecognizable in the dough.

[15] e.g. if a lamp is lit from it, the lamp is not restricted to the limits of the owner of the burning coal.   [16] 'Misappropriation' (Lev. 14[–16]; see p. 573, n. 2).

[17] Some texts omit this sentence.

[18] 2,000 cubits in every direction beyond the outer-area of seventy and two-thirds cubits (Erub. 5[1ff.].).

[19] The wells made for the exiles who returned from Babylon. They were ownerless property, and the water from them became the property of him who drew it and lay under the same restrictions as his feet.   [20] App. I 8.

bring it to him;[1] but if he himself made *Erub*, his produce is [free to move within the same limits] as himself.

7. If a man invited guests to his home they may not take away portions with them unless he had granted them possession of their portions on the eve of the Festival-day. They may not give drink to animals of the wilderness or slaughter them, but they may give drink to household animals or slaughter them. Which are deemed household animals? Such that spend the night in a town. And animals of the wilderness? Such that spend the night in [more distant] pasturage.[2]

ROSH HA-SHANAH ('FEAST OF THE NEW YEAR')

1. 1. There are four[3] 'New Year' days: on the 1st of Nisan is the New Year for kings[4] and feasts;[5] on the 1st of Elul is the New Year for the Tithe of Cattle[6] (R. Eleazar and R. Simeon say: The 1st of Tishri); on the 1st of Tishri is the New Year for [the reckoning of] the years[7] [of foreign kings], of the Years of Release and Jubilee years,[8] for the planting [of trees][9] and for vegetables;[10] and the 1st of Shebat is the New Year for [fruit-]trees (so the School of Shammai; and the School of Hillel say: On the 15th thereof).

2. At four times in the year is the world judged:[11] at Passover, through grain; at Pentecost, through the fruits of the tree; on New Year's Day all that come into the world pass before him like legions of soldiers,[12] for it is written, *He that fashioneth the hearts of them all, that considereth all their works*;[13] and at the Feast [of Tabernacles] they are judged through water.[14]

3. Because of six New Moons do messengers go forth [to proclaim the time of their appearing]: because of Nisan, to determine the time of Passover,[15] because of Ab, to determine the time of the Fast;[16] because of Elul, to determine the New Year;[17] because of Tishri, to determine aright the set feasts;[18] because of Chislev, to determine the time of [the feast of] the Dedication;[19] and because of Adar, to determine the time of Purim.[20] And while the Temple still stood they went forth also because of Iyyar, to determine the time of the Lesser Passover.[21]

4. Because of two New Moons may the Sabbath be profaned:[22] [the New Moon] of Nisan and [the New Moon] of Tishri, for on them messengers

---

[1] The produce, being his private property, lay under the same restrictions as his feet.

[2] And so cannot come within the definition of 'what is set in readiness'.

[3] Of these the third, the 1st of Tishri, is alone spoken of throughout the rest of the tractate as 'the New Year'. This 'New Year' is the feast described in Lev. 23[24] as 'a solemn rest unto you, a memorial of blowing of trumpets', and in Num. 29[1] as 'a day of blowing of trumpets'.

[4] From which date was calculated the years of the reign of Israelitish kings; thus if a king was enthroned in the preceding month, Adar, he begins his second year of reign on the following 1st of Nisan.   [5] See Num. 28[16ff].

[6] Lev. 27[32]. What was born before the 1st of Elul may not be given as tithe for cattle born on and after the 1st of Elul. Cf. Bekh. 9[5f].

[7] i.e. foreign eras. Cf. Gitt. 8[5].   [8] Deut. 15[1ff]., Lev. 25[8ff].   [9] Lev. 19[23].

[10] What was gathered before the 1st of Tishri may not be given as tithe for later produce.

[11] God's verdict on the world's worth is shown by the richness or meagreness of the harvest.   [12] Or: 'flocks of sheep'.   [13] Ps. 33[15].   [14] Cf. p. 175, n. 7.

[15] The 15th of Nisan.   [16] The Ninth of Ab. See Taan. 4[6].

[17] Which falls on the 1st of the following month.

[18] The Day of Atonement and the Feast of Tabernacles.

[19] Hanukkah, the 25th of Chislev.   [20] The 14th of Adar.

[21] 14th of Iyyar. See Num. 9[9ff].; Pes. 9[1-3].

[22] Any who have seen the new moon may transgress the Sabbath limits to go and give evidence before the court of the appearance of the new moon.

used to go forth to Syria, and by them the set feasts were determined. And while the Temple still stood the Sabbath might also be profaned because of any of the New Moons, to determine aright the time of the offerings.[1]

5. Whether [the New Moon] was manifestly visible or not, they may profane the Sabbath because of it. R. Jose says: If it was manifestly visible they may not profane the Sabbath because of it.

6. Once more than forty pairs [of witnesses] came forward, but R. Akiba in Lydda restrained them. Rabban Gamaliel sent to him [saying], 'If thou restrainest the multitude thou wilt put a stumbling-block in their way for the future'.

7. If a father and his son saw the new moon they may [both] go [to bear witness]; not that they can be included together [as a valid pair of witnesses], but that if one of them is found ineligible the other may be included to make a pair with some other [witness]. R. Simeon says: A father and his son, and any that are near of kin, are eligible to bear witness about the new moon. R. Jose said: Once Tobiah the Physician saw the new moon in Jerusalem, together with his son and his freed slave; and the priests[2] accepted him and his son but pronounced his freed slave ineligible. And when they came before the court they accepted him and his slave but declared his son ineligible.

8. These are they that are ineligible:[3] a dice-player, a usurer, pigeon-flyers, traffickers in Seventh Year produce,[4] and slaves. This is the general rule: any evidence that a woman is not eligible to bring, these are not eligible to bring.

9. If a man saw the new moon but could not walk, he may be taken on an ass [on the Sabbath] or even on a bed; and if any lie in wait for them[5] they may take staves in their hands. If it was a far journey they may take food in their hands, since for a journey enduring a night and a day they may profane the Sabbath and go forth[6] to bear witness about the new moon, for it is written, *These are the set feasts of the Lord, even holy convocations which ye shall proclaim in their appointed season.*[7]

2. 1. If the witness was not known [to the judges] another was sent with him to testify of him. Beforetime they used to admit evidence about the new moon from any man, but after the evil doings of the heretics[8] they enacted that evidence should be admitted only from them that they knew.

2. Beforetime they used to kindle flares, but after the evil doings of the Samaritans[9] they enacted that messengers should go forth.

3. After what fashion did they kindle the flares? They used to take long cedar-wood sticks and rushes and oleaster-wood and flax-tow; and a man bound these up with a rope and went up to the top of the hill and set light to them; and he waved them to and fro and up and down until he could see his fellow doing the like on the top of the next hill. And so, too, on the top of the third hill.

4. And from what place did they kindle the flares? From the mount of Olives [they signalled] to Sarteba, and from Sarteba to Agrippina, and

---

[1] Num. 28[11-15].   [2] See p. 245, n. 14.   [3] Cf. Sanh. 3[3].   [4] See Shebi. 7[3].
[5] Or: 'if they are in any fear'.   [6] With a burden; see p. 100, n. 2.
[7] Lev. 23[4].
[8] Or 'sectaries', who tried to confuse the Sages by hiring false witnesses.
[9] Who kindled misleading flares.

from Agrippina to Hauran, and from Hauran to Beth Baltin.[1] They did not go beyond Beth Baltin, but there the flare was waved to and fro and up and down until a man could see the whole exile[2] before him like a sea of fire.

5. There was a large courtyard in Jerusalem called Beth Yaazek, where all the witnesses assembled, and there the Court examined them. And they prepared large meals for them so that they might make it their habit to come. Beforetime they might not stir thence the whole day; but Rabban Gamaliel the Elder ordained that they might walk within two thousand cubits in any direction. And not these, only, but a midwife that comes to help a delivery, or any that comes to rescue from a burning house or ravaging troops, or from a river-flood or a fallen house; they, too, are deemed to be people of the city and may move within two thousand cubits in any direction.

6. How do they examine the witnesses? The pair which comes first they examine first. They bring in the elder of the two and say to him, 'Tell us how thou sawest the moon: facing the sun or turned away from it?[3] to the north or to the south? how high was it? to which side was it leaning? and how broad was it?' If he said, 'Facing the sun', he has said naught.[4] Afterward they bring in the second witness and examine him. If their words are found to agree their evidence holds good. The other pairs of witnesses were asked [only] the main points, not because there was need of them, but that they should not go away disappointed and that they might make it their habit to come.

7. The chief of the court says, 'It is hallowed!' and all the people answer after him, 'It is hallowed! it is hallowed!' They acclaim it as hallowed whether it appeared at its proper time or not. R. Eliezer b. Zadok says: If it did not appear at its proper time they need not acclaim it as hallowed, since Heaven has hallowed it already.

8. Rabban Gamaliel[5] had pictures of the shapes of the moon on a tablet and on the wall of his upper chamber. These he used to show to the unskilled and say, 'Didst thou see it on this wise or on that?' It once happened that two came and said, 'We saw it in the east in the morning and in the west in the evening'. R. Johanan b. Nuri said: They are false witnesses. But when they came to Jabneh Rabban Gamaliel accepted their evidence. And two others came and said, 'We saw it at its expected time, yet in the night of the added day[6] it did not appear'; and Rabban Gamaliel accepted their evidence. R. Dosa b. Harkinas said: 'They are false witnesses: how can they say of a woman that she has given birth if the next day her belly is between her teeth!' R. Joshua said to him, 'I approve thy words'.

9. Rabban Gamaliel sent to him [saying], 'I charge thee that thou come to me with thy staff and thy money on the Day of Atonement as it falls according to thy reckoning'.[7] R. Akiba went to R. Joshua and found him sore perplexed. He said to him, 'I can teach thee [from Scripture] that

---

[1] See Neub. 42 f.   [2] In Babylon.   [3] Lit. 'before the sun or after the sun'.
[4] It was either the old moon that he had seen or nothing at all.   [5] Cf. Erub. 4².
[6] A 30th day added to the usual 29 days of the month when the new moon failed to be seen at its expected time. Cf. Arak. 2².
[7] Because Rabban Gamaliel had decided that the Day of Atonement according to R. Joshua's reckoning (reached by ignoring witnesses whom Rabban Gamaliel accepted) was not the Day of Atonement at all, and so it would be permissible to carry a burden.

whatsoever Rabban Gamaliel has done is done [aright], for it is written, *These are the set feasts of the Lord, even holy convocations, which ye shall proclaim.*[1] Whether in their proper season or not in their proper season I know none other "set feasts" save these'.[2] R. Joshua then went to R. Dosa b. Harkinas and said to him, 'If we come to inquire into [the lawfulness of the decisions of] the court of Rabban Gamaliel, we shall need to inquire into [the decisions of] every court which has arisen since the days of Moses until now, for it is written, *Then went up Moses and Aaron, Nadab and Abihu, and seventy of the elders of Israel.*[3] And why are the names of the elders not expressly set forth if not to teach that every three [judges] which have risen up as a court over Israel are like to the court of Moses!' He took his staff and his money in his hand and went to Jabneh to Rabban Gamaliel on the day which fell according to his reckoning on the Day of Atonement. Rabban Gamaliel stood up and kissed him on the head and said to him, 'Come in peace, my master and my disciple!—"my master" in wisdom and "my disciple" in that thou hast accepted my words'.

3. 1. If[4] the court itself and all Israel had seen the new moon and the witnesses had been examined, yet night fell before they could proclaim 'It is hallowed!' then it is an intercalated month.[5] If the court alone saw it, two [of them] should stand up and bear witness before them, and then they may say, 'It is hallowed! it is hallowed!' If it was seen by three who [themselves] make up the court, two [of them] must stand up and set [two] of their fellows beside the single [other judge] and bear witness before them, and then they may say, 'It is hallowed! it is hallowed!' For no single person can be deemed trustworthy in himself.

2. All *shofars* are valid save that of a cow, since it is a 'horn'. R. Jose said: But are not all *shofars* called by the name 'horn'? for it is written, *When they make a long blast with the ram's horn.*[6]

3. The *shofar* [blown in the Temple] at the New Year was [made from the horn] of the wild goat, straight, with its mouthpiece overlaid with gold. And at the sides [of them that blew the *shofar*] were two [that blew upon] trumpets. The *shofar* blew a long note and the trumpets a short note, since the duty of the day fell on the *shofar*.

4. [The *shofars*] on days of fasting were rams' horns, rounded, with their mouthpiece overlaid with silver. And between them were two [that blew upon] trumpets. The *shofar* blew a short note and the trumpets a long note, since the duty of the day fell on the trumpets.

5. The Year of Jubilee is like to the New Year in the blowing of the *shofar* and in the Benedictions.[7] R. Judah says: At the New Year they use rams' horns and at the Years of Jubilee wild goats' horns.

6. A *shofar* that has been split and stuck together again is not valid. If the broken pieces of a *shofar* have been stuck together again it is not valid. If a hole had been made in it and it was stopped up again, if it hinders the blowing it is not valid, but if it does not, it is valid.

---

[1] Lev. 23[4].   [2] Which the court enjoins.   [3] Ex. 24[9].

[4] This paragraph logically follows after 2[7].

[5] That day, although manifestly the first of the new month, is treated as the 30th day of the preceding month.

[6] Josh. 6[5].   [7] See below, 4[5].

7. If the *shofar* was blown in a cistern or in a cellar or in a large jar,[1] and a man heard the sound of the *shofar*, he has fulfilled his obligation; but if he heard only an uncertain noise he has not fulfilled his obligation. So, too, if a man was passing behind a synagogue, or if his house was near to a synagogue, and he heard the sound of the *shofar*, or[2] the reading of the *Megillah*,[3] if he directed his heart he has fulfilled his obligation, but if he did not he has not fulfilled his obligation. Though one may have heard and another may have heard, the one may have directed his heart and the other may not have directed his heart.

8. *And it came to pass when Moses held up his hand that Israel prevailed, and when he let down his hand Amalek prevailed.*[4] But could the hands of Moses promote the battle or hinder the battle!—it is, rather, to teach thee that such time as the Israelites directed their thoughts on high and kept their hearts in subjection to their Father in heaven, they prevailed; otherwise they suffered defeat. After the like manner thou mayest say, *Make thee a fiery serpent and set it upon a standard, and it shall come to pass that every one that is bitten when he seeth it shall live.*[5] But could the serpent slay or the serpent keep alive!—it is, rather, to teach thee that such time as the Israelites directed their thoughts on high and kept their hearts in subjection to their Father in heaven, they were healed; otherwise they pined away. A deaf-mute, an imbecile, or a minor cannot fulfil an obligation[6] on behalf of the many. This is the general rule: any on whom an obligation is not incumbent cannot fulfil that obligation on behalf of the many.

4. 1. If a Festival-day of the New Year fell on a Sabbath they might blow the *shofar* in the Holy City but not in the provinces. After the Temple was destroyed Rabban Johanan b. Zakkai ordained that they might blow it wheresoever there was a court.[7] R. Eliezer said: Rabban Johanan b. Zakkai ordained it so only for Jabneh. They replied: It is all one whether it was Jabneh or any other place wherein was a court.

2. In this also Jerusalem surpassed Jabneh in that they could blow the *shofar* in any city that could see Jerusalem and that could hear [the *shofar* in Jerusalem] and that was near,[8] and that was able to come;[9] but at Jabneh they could blow it only in the court.

3. Beforetime[10] the *Lulab* was carried seven days in the Temple, but in the provinces one day only. After the Temple was destroyed, Rabban Johanan b. Zakkai ordained that in the provinces it should be carried seven days in memory of the Temple; also [he ordained] that on the whole of the Day of Waving it should be forbidden [to eat of new produce].

4. Beforetime they used to admit evidence about the new moon throughout the day.[11] Once the witnesses tarried so long in coming that the levites were disordered in their singing;[12] so it was ordained that evidence could

---

[1] Heb. *pithos*. Cf. B.M. 4[12]; Kel. 3[6].   [2] At Purim.   [3] The Book of Esther.
[4] Ex. 17[11].   [5] Num. 21[8].
[6] i.e. such a one may not blow the *shofar* at the New Year.   [7] See Sanh. 1[6] (end).
[8] Within the Sabbath limit.   [9] To Jerusalem, and not cut off by flood.
[10] Sukk. 3[12]; Men. 10[5].
[11] Of the New Year. After sunset on the night after the 29th of Elul they treated the coming day as a Festival-day in case witnesses arrived the next day to report that the new moon was visible the previous evening. If they did not come that day, the next day was made a Festival-day, and the day before was counted as the 30th of Elul. Cf. 3[1].
[12] Of the psalm at the Daily Whole-offering. See Tam. 7[3-4]. The usual afternoon Daily Whole-offering was slaughtered at 2.30 p.m. But if it was the 1st of the month Additional-

be admitted only until the afternoon offering. And if witnesses came from the time of the afternoon offering onwards, then this day was kept holy and also the morrow was kept holy. After the Temple was destroyed Rabban Johanan b. Zakkai ordained that they might admit evidence about the new moon throughout the day. R. Joshua b. Karha said: Rabban Johanan b. Zakkai ordained this also that wheresoever the chief of the court might be, witnesses should go only to the place of assembly.

5. As for the order of the Benedictions[1] a man recites 'the Fathers', 'Power', and 'the Hallowing of the Name',[2] and combines with them the Sovereignty verses;[3] but he does not then sound the *shofar*; [he then recites] 'the Hallowing of the Day'[4] and sounds the *shofar*; [he then recites] the Remembrance verses[5] and sounds the *shofar*; [he then recites the *Shofar* verses[6] and sounds the *shofar*; then he recites the Benedictions, 'the [Temple-]Service', and the 'Thanksgiving'[7] and the Benediction of the Priests.[8] So R. Johanan b. Nuri. R. Akiba said to him: If he does not sound the *shofar* at the Sovereignty verses why does he make mention of them?[9] but, rather, he recites 'the Fathers', 'Power', and 'the Hallowing of the Name', and combines the Sovereignty verses with the 'Hallowing of the Day', and sounds the *shofar*; [he then recites] the Remembrance verses and sounds the *shofar*; [he then recites] the *Shofar* verses and sounds the *shofar*; and then he recites the Benedictions, 'the [Temple-] Service', and the 'Thanksgiving' and the Benediction of the Priests.

6. They may not recite less than ten Sovereignty verses, ten Remembrance verses, or ten *Shofar* verses. R. Johanan b. Nuri says: If he recites three of each he has fulfilled his obligation. They may not make mention of any Remembrance, Sovereignty, or *Shofar* verses that record divine chastisement. They begin with [verses from] the Law and end with [verses from] the Prophets. R. Jose says: If a man ended with [verses from] the Law he has fulfilled his obligation.

7. When a man passes before the Ark [to lead the prayer] on a Festival-day of the New Year [not he but] the second[10] blows the *shofar*; but at the times when the *Hallel* is recited[11] the first recites the *Hallel*.

8. For the sake of a *shofar* for the New Year none may pass beyond the

---

offerings must be brought (Num. 28[11-15]) besides the Daily Whole-offering. Therefore the offering was delayed as long as possible for the arrival of witnesses to know whether or not Additional Offerings should be brought and whether the levites should sing the psalm for an ordinary day or for a Festival-day. This time the delay was so long that there was not time for the prescribed psalm.

[1] Special to the New Year and introduced into the *Tefillah*. These are the *Malkuyoth* (Sovereignty verses), the *Zikronoth* (Remembrance verses), and the *Shofaroth* (Shofar verses).

[2] The first three Benedictions (Singer, pp. 44–5) of the *Shemoneh Esreh*, the 'Eighteen', contained in the *Tefillah* (see *J. E.* xi. 270 ff.).

[3] The *Malkuyoth*, ten verses of Scripture in which God is described as King. For the modern form of these, see *S. S.*, New Year, p. 135 f.

[4] The special Benediction for all Festival-days—the prayer now beginning 'Thou hast chosen us'.

[5] The *Zikronoth*, ten verses of Scripture recounting God's remembrance of his creatures. For the modern form of these see *S. S.*, New Year, pp. 136–8.

[6] See *S. S.*, New Year, pp. 139–40.

[7] The 17th and 18th of the 'Eighteen Benedictions' (Singer, pp. 50, 51).

[8] Which precedes the nineteenth Benediction in the daily *Tefillah* (Singer, p. 53).

[9] According to R. Akiba the sole object of the interpolations in the *Tefillah* is to provide appropriate introductions to the sounding of the *shofar*.

[10] Who is deputed to lead the 'Additional Prayer' (said on Festival-days and Sabbaths).

[11] On all Festival-days (see p. 181, n. 11) except the New Year. The *Hallel*, Pss. 113–18, is in keeping only with the more joyous festivals.

Sabbath limit, or clear away a heap of stones, or climb a tree or ride on cattle or swim on the water;[1] nor may one cut it,[2] whether in a fashion that transgresses the rules of the Sabbath rest[3] or that transgresses a negative command [in the Law];[4] but if he wished to pour water or wine therein he may pour it. They should not hinder children from blowing the *shofar*, but should engage with them in this until they learn [how to blow]; but he that is engaged in practice has not fulfilled his obligation, nor has he fulfilled his obligation that hears another engaged in practice.

9. The manner of blowing the *shofar* is three blasts[5] thrice repeated. A sustained blast is three times the length of a quavering blast, and a quavering blast is three times the length of an alarm[6] blast. If a man blew the first blast, then prolonged the second blast equal to two, that is reckoned to him only as one blast. If a man had recited the Benedictions and was then assigned a *shofar*, he should blow thrice a sustained, a quavering, and another sustained blast. Like as the agent of the congregation[7] is bound [to say the daily *Tefillah*] so is each person bound. Rabban Gamaliel says: The agent of the congregation fulfils the obligation that rests upon the many.

TAANITH ('DAYS OF FASTING')

1. 1. From what time do they make mention of 'the Power of Rain'?[8] R. Eliezer says: From the first Festival-day of the Feast [of Tabernacles].[9] R. Joshua says: From the last Festival-day[10] of the Feast. R. Joshua said to him: Since rain is but a sign of a curse[11] at the Feast, why should they make mention of it? R. Eliezer answered: I did not, indeed, say 'pray for' but 'make mention of' [the rain]: 'Who maketh the winds to blow and sendeth down the rain'[12]—in its due season. He said to him: If so a man may make mention thereof at all times.[13]

2. They pray for rain only near to the time for rain. R. Judah says: When one passes before the Ark on the last Festival-day of the Feast, the last alone[14] makes mention thereof. On the first Festival-day of Passover, the first alone makes mention thereof; the last makes no mention thereof.[15] Until what time should they pray for rain? R. Judah says: Until Passover is over. R. Meir says: Until the end of Nisan, for it is written, *And he causeth to come down for you the rain, the former rain and the latter rain in the first [month].*[16]

---

1 See Betz. 5[2].   2 From a ram's head; or in order to improve it.
3 See Erub. 10[3, 15].
4 To make a new instrument transgresses the Law; to improve it transgresses the rabbinical rules devised to ensure the Sabbath rest.
5 A sustained, a quavering, and another sustained blast.
6 Heb. *yabbabah*. Onkelos (Lev. 23[24]) gives this as the translation of *teruah* (here rendered 'quavering blast'). The Gemara (33b) renders it 'outcry' or 'moaning'.   7 Cf. Ber. 5[5].
8 In the second of the Eighteen Benedictions (Singer, p. 44). See Ber. 5[2]; R. Sh. 4[5].
9 About this time (latter half of October) the first rain usually falls in Palestine.
10 The eighth.
11 Making impossible the observance of the command to dwell in booths. See p. 175, n. 7; R.Sh. 1[2].
12 Quotation from the Second Benediction.   13 Even in summer.
14 Of those who serve as 'delegates of the congregation' in leading the prayers, the last of all (who reads the Additional-prayer—cf. *S. S.*, Tabernacles, p. 137) should include the mention of rain, since the rain 'is acceptable' only at the latest moment of the Feast.
15 Since by that time (Nisan 21), about the middle of April, no more rain normally falls before the following Feast of Tabernacles.
16 Joel 2[23]. The first month is Nisan. 'In' is assumed to mean 'throughout'.

3. On the 3rd of Marheshwan they pray for rain. Rabban Gamaliel says: On the 7th, fifteen days after the Feast [of Tabernacles], to give time for the last of the Israelites[1] to reach the Euphrates.

4. If the 17th of Marheshwan was come and no rain had fallen, single persons[2] begin to fast [and observe] three days of fasting. They may eat and drink after nightfall,[3] and they are permitted to work, to wash themselves, to anoint themselves, to put on sandals, and to have marital intercourse.

5. If the 1st of Chislev[4] was come and no rain had fallen, the court enjoins on the congregation three days of fasting. They may eat and drink after nightfall, and they are permitted to work, to wash themselves, to anoint themselves, to put on sandals, and to have marital intercourse.

6. If these days passed by and their prayers were not answered, the court enjoins on the congregation three more days of fasting. They may eat and drink [only] while it is yet day,[5] and they are forbidden to work, to wash themselves, to anoint themselves, to put on sandals, or to have marital intercourse; and the bath-houses are shut up. If these days passed by and their prayers were not answered, the court enjoins on the congregation seven more [days of fasting]—thirteen days in all. These days surpass the first days, in that on these days they blow the *shofar* and close the shops. On Mondays[6] they may partially open [the shops] when it grows dark, and on Thursdays they are permitted [to open the shops the whole day] because of the honour due to the Sabbath.

7. If these days passed by and their prayers were not answered, they must give themselves but little to business, building or planting, betrothals or marriages, or greetings one to another, as becomes men that suffer God's displeasure. Single persons continue to fast until the end of Nisan. If Nisan ended and then the rain fell,[7] it is a sign of [God's] curse, for it is written, *Is it not wheat harvest to-day?*[8] *I will call unto the Lord that he send thunder and rain, and ye shall know and see that great is your wickedness which ye have wrought in the sight of God to ask for yourselves a king.*[9]

2. 1. How did they order the matter on the [last seven] days of fasting? They used to bring out the Ark[10] into the open space in the town and put wood-ashes on the Ark and on the heads of the President and the Father of the court; and every one took [of the ashes] and put them on his head. The eldest among them uttered before them words of admonition: Brethren, it is not written of the men of Nineveh that 'God saw their sackcloth and their fasting', but *And God saw their works that they turned from their evil way;*[11] and in [his] protest[12] [the Prophet] says, *Rend your heart and not your garments.*[13]

---

1 Who had come from Babylon to celebrate the Feast in Jerusalem.
2 Of outstanding merit and piety.
3 On the nights which ushered in their days of fasting.   4 Late in November.
5 Their fasting must begin with the onset of the nights which usher in their prescribed days of fasting.
6 The series of three days of fasting fell on successive Mondays, Thursdays, and following Mondays (see below, 2⁹).
7 Variant: 'and no rain had fallen'.   8 Late in May, when rain is a misfortune.
9 1 Sam. 12¹⁷   10 Containing the scrolls of the Law.
11 Jonah 3¹⁰.
12 Heb. *kebalah*. So recent interpreters. Older interpreters read *kabbalah* ('tradition'), with the technical sense of a scriptural passage outside the Pentateuch.
13 Joel 2¹³

2. They stood up in prayer and sent down before the Ark an old man, well versed [in prayer], one that had children and whose house was empty [of sustenance], so that he might be whole-hearted in the prayer. He recited before them twenty-four Benedictions: the 'Eighteen' of daily use, adding to them yet six more.

3. And these are they: the Remembrance and the *Shofar* verses,[1] and *In my distress I cried unto the Lord and he answered me . . .*,[2] and *I will lift up mine eyes unto the hills . . .*,[3] and *Out of the deep have I cried unto thee, O Lord . . .*,[4] and *A prayer of the afflicted when he is overwhelmed. . . .*[5] R. Judah says: He need not recite the Remembrance and *Shofar* verses, but he recites in their stead the passages, *If there be in the land, famine, if there be pestilence . . .*,[6] and *The word of the Lord that came to Jeremiah concerning the drought. . . .*[7] And he seals[8] each of them with its proper ending.

4. [Thus] after the first[9] he says, 'May he that answered Abraham our father in mount Moriah answer you and hearken to the voice of your crying this day. Blessed art thou, O Lord, redeemer of Israel!' After the second he says, 'May he that answered our fathers at the Red Sea answer you and hearken to the voice of your crying this day. Blessed art thou, O Lord, that art mindful of things forgotten!' After the third he says, 'May he that answered Joshua in Gilgal answer you and hearken to the voice of your crying this day. Blessed art thou, O Lord, that hearest the blowing of the *shofar*!' After the fourth he says, 'May he that answered Samuel at Mizpah answer you and hearken to the voice of your crying this day. Blessed art thou, O Lord, that hearest them that cry!' After the fifth he says, 'May he that answered Elijah in Carmel answer you and hearken to the voice of your crying this day. Blessed art thou, O Lord, that hearest prayer!' After the sixth he says, 'May he that answered Jonah in the belly of the fish answer you and hearken to the voice of your crying this day. Blessed art thou that answerest in time of trouble!' After the seventh he says, 'May he that answered David and his son Solomon in Jerusalem answer you and hearken to the voice of your crying this day. Blessed art thou, O Lord, that hast compassion on the land!'

5. It happened in the days of R. Halafta and R. Hananiah b. Teradion[10] that [the reader] used to go before the Ark and finish the whole Benediction[11] without their answering 'Amen' after him. 'Blow[12] the *tekiah*,[13] ye priests, blow the *tekiah*!' 'May he that answered Abraham our father at mount Moriah answer you and hearken to the voice of your crying this day!' 'Blow the *teruah*,[14] ye sons of Aaron, blow the *teruah*!' 'May he that answered our fathers at the Red Sea answer you and hearken to the voice of your crying this day!'[15] And when the matter came before the Sages, they said: Such was our custom only at the Eastern Gate and[16] in the Temple Mount.

---

[1] See p. 193, nn. 5,6.   [2] Ps. 120.   [3] Ps. 121.
[4] Ps. 130.   [5] Ps. 102.   [6] I Kings 8[37ff].   [7] Jer. 14[1ff].   [8] See Ber. 1[4]
[9] Not of the foregoing six only, since the Mishnah here gives seven concluding formulas. This 'first' refers to the Seventh of the Eighteen Benedictions, after which the six additional ones were inserted.
[10] Early in the second century.   [11] The Seventh of the Eighteen.
[12] The order was given by the minister of the synagogue.
[13] The sustained blast described in R.Sh. 4[9].   [14] The quavering blast.
[15] And so on with the other Benedictions.   [16] Some texts omit this clause.

6. On the first three days of fasting, the priests of the Course[1] fasted but not the whole day; and they of the father's house[2] did not fast at all. On the second three days, the priests of the Course fasted throughout the whole day, and they of the father's house fasted but not the whole day. But on the last seven days, both of them fasted throughout the whole day. So R. Joshua. But the Sages say: On the first three days of fasting neither fasted at all. On the second three days the priests of the Course fasted but not the whole day, and they of the father's house did not fast at all. On the last seven days, the priests of the course fasted throughout the whole day, and they of the father's house fasted but not the whole day.

7. The priests of the Course were permitted to drink wine during the night but not during the day, and they of the father's house neither during the night nor during the day. The priests of the Course and the men of the *Maamad*[3] were forbidden to cut their hair or wash their clothes; but on a Thursday it was permitted because of the honour due to the Sabbath.

8. Any day whereof it is written in the Scroll of Fasting[4] that 'None may mourn', it is [also] forbidden to mourn [the day] before; but it is permitted the following day. R. Jose says: It is forbidden both the day before and the following day. [Where it is written,] 'None may fast', it is permitted [to fast] both the day before and the following day. R. Jose says: It is forbidden the day before but permitted the following day.

9. They may not decree a public fast beginning with a Thursday lest they disturb [market] prices, but they appoint the first three days of fasting for a Monday and the following Thursday and Monday; but they may appoint the second three days of fasting for a Thursday and the following Monday and Thursday. R. Jose says: Like as the first [three days of fasting] may not begin on a Thursday so the second [three] and the last [seven] may not begin on a Thursday.

10. They may not decree a public fast on the first day of a month or during [the Feast of] the Dedication[5] or at Purim.[6] But if they had begun they may not interrupt the fast. So Rabban Gamaliel. R. Meir said: Although Rabban Gamaliel has said, 'They may not interrupt the fast', he admitted that they need not fast the whole day. So, too, with the Ninth of Ab[7] if it fell on the eve of a Sabbath.

3. 1. The order on these days of fasting as here prescribed applies if the first rainfall is withheld; but if the crops fail they forthwith sound the *shofar*. So, too, if rain had failed for forty days between rainfall and rainfall, they forthwith sound the *shofar*, since it means the onset of dearth.

2. If rain fell [in fashion good] for the crops but not for the trees, or [good] for the trees but not for the crops, or [good] for them both but not for the cisterns, pits, or caverns, they forthwith sound the *shofar*.

3. So, too, if no rain fell upon a city (as it is written, *And I caused it to rain upon one city and caused it not to rain upon another city: one piece*

[1] Which was on duty in the Temple for that week. There were twenty-four Courses (1 Chron. 24⁴ᶠᶠ) serving in the Temple in rotation each for one week. Cf. Sukk. 5⁶⁻⁸.

[2] Each course was divided into families or 'fathers' houses' (cf. Yom. 3⁹) who served one day each. On their day of duty the rules of fasting on the earlier days were relaxed for their benefit.   [3] App. I. 21. See below, 4².

[4] Referring to a list of notable days. A similar list is still extant, enumerating 35 days arranged in order of the months, telling briefly the event which marked the day and adding after each the words 'It is forbidden to fast', or 'It is forbidden to mourn'.

[5] The 25th of Chislev. It lasts eight days.

[6] 14th and 15th of Adar.   [7] See below, 4⁶.

was rained upon and the piece whereupon it rained not withered)[1] that city fasts and sounds the *shofar*; and all the places around it fast but do not sound the *shofar*. R. Akiba says: They sound the *shofar* but do not fast.

4. So, too, if a city suffered from pestilence or if its houses fell, that city fasts and sounds the *shofar*, and the places around it fast but do not sound the *shofar*. R. Akiba says: They sound the *shofar* but do not fast. What is deemed a pestilence? If, in a city that can count three hundred men of war, three dead go forth in three days, one after the other, this is deemed a pestilence; but if less than this it is not deemed a pestilence.

5. For these things they sound the *shofar* in every place: *blasting or mildew; locust or caterpiller*,[2] wild beasts or the sword. They sound the *shofar* in that they are an overrunning affliction.

6. The Sages once went down from Jerusalem to their own towns and decreed a fast because in Ashkelon there appeared blight the extent of an oven's mouth. Moreover they decreed a fast because wolves devoured two children beyond the Jordan. R. Jose says: Not because they devoured, but because they were seen.

7. For these things they sound the *shofar* even on the Sabbath: for a city that is encompassed by gentiles or by flood; for a ship that is storm-tossed out at sea (R. Jose says: To summon help, not to cry to God). Simeon of Teman says: Also for pestilence. But the Sages did not agree with him.

8. They sound the *shofar* because of any public distress—may it never befall! but not because of too great abundance of rain. Once they said to Onias the Circle-maker, 'Pray that rain may fall'. He answered, 'Go out and bring in the Passover ovens[3] that they be not softened'. He prayed, but the rain did not fall. What did he do? He drew a circle and stood within it and said before God, 'O Lord of the world, thy children have turned their faces to me, for that I am like a son of the house before thee. I swear by thy great name that I will not stir hence until thou have pity on thy children'. Rain began falling drop by drop. He said, 'Not for such rain have I prayed, but for rain that will fill the cisterns, pits, and caverns'. It began to rain with violence. He said, 'Not for such rain have I prayed, but for rain of goodwill, blessing, and graciousness'. Then it rained in moderation [and continued] until the Israelites went up from Jerusalem to the Temple Mount because of the rain. They went to him and said, 'Like as thou didst pray for the rain to come, so pray that it may go away!' He replied, 'Go and see if the Stone of the Strayers[4] has disappeared!' Simeon b. Shetah[5] sent to him [saying], 'Hadst thou not been Onias I had pronounced a ban against thee! But what shall I do to thee?—thou importunest God and he performeth thy will, like a son that importuneth his father and he performeth his will; and of thee Scripture saith, *Let thy father and thy mother be glad, and let her that bare thee rejoice*.'[6]

9. If they fasted and rain fell, [and it fell] before the sun rose, they do not fast the whole day; but if after the sun rose, they fast the whole day. R. Eliezer says: If [it fell] before midday they do not fast the whole day; but if after midday, they fast the whole day. Once they decreed a fast in

---

1 Amos 4[7].   2 1 Kings 8[37].   3 Made of dried clay.
4 Explained as a high stone from which lost articles were proclaimed (cf. B.M. 2[1-6]), the 'Strayers' being those in search of their missing property.
5 Circ. 80 B.C.   6 Prov. 23[25].

Lydda and the rain fell before midday. R. Tarfon said to them, 'Go and eat and drink and keep it as a Festival-day'; and they went and ate and drank and kept it as a Festival-day. And in the afternoon they came and recited the Great *Hallel*.[1]

4. 1. Three times in the year the priests four times lift up their hands during the day (at the Morning Prayer,[2] at the Additional Prayer,[3] at the Afternoon Prayer[4] and at the Closing of the Gates):[5] namely, on the days of fasting, at the *Maamads*[6] and on the Day of Atonement.

2. What are the *Maamads*? In that it is written, *Command the children of Israel and say unto them, My oblation, my food for my offerings made by fire, of a sweet savour unto me, shall ye observe to offer unto me in their due season*[7]—how can a man's offering be offered while he does not stand by it? Therefore the First Prophets[8] ordained twenty-four Courses,[9] and for every Course there was a *Maamad* in Jerusalem, made up of priests, levites and Israelites. When the time was come for a Course to go up, the priests and the levites thereof went up to Jerusalem, and the Israelites that were of the selfsame Course came together unto their own cities to read the story of Creation, and[10] the men of the *Maamad* fasted four days in the week, from the second until the fifth day; and they did not fast on the eve of the Sabbath because of the honour due to the Sabbath, nor on the first day of the week, that they should not go forth from rest and pleasure to weariness and fasting, and so be like to die.

3. On the first day they read from *In the beginning . . .* to *Let there be a firmament*; and on the second day, from *Let there be a firmament . . .* to *Let the waters be gathered together*; and on the third day from *Let the waters be gathered together . . .* to *Let there be lights*; and on the fourth day, from *Let there be lights . . .* to *Let the water bring forth abundantly*; and on the fifth day, from *Let the waters bring forth abundantly . . .* to *Let the earth bring forth*; and on the sixth day, from *Let the earth bring forth . . .* to *And the heaven and the earth were finished*. If it was a long section it was read by two, and if a short section, by one, both at Morning Prayer and at the Additional Prayer; but at the Afternoon Prayer they came together and recited it by heart like as they recite the *Shema*ʿ.[11] At the Afternoon Prayer on the eve of a Sabbath they did not come together, because of the honour due to the Sabbath.[12]

4. On a day when the *Hallel*[13] was appointed,[14] no *Maamad* assembled[15] in the morning;[16] when an Additional Offering would be brought,[17] no *Maamad* assembled at the Closing [of the Gates]; when a Wood-offering[18] would be brought, no *Maamad* assembled in the afternoon. So R. Akiba.

---

1 Ps. 136; so called to distinguish it from the ordinary *Hallel* (Pss. 113–18).
2 *Shaharith*.   3 *Musaf*.   4 *Minhah*.
5 *Neilah*. These names for the Synagogue services are transferred from the Temple usage, the first three corresponding to the morning Daily Whole-offering, the Additional Offerings (on Sabbaths, New Moons, and Festival-days), and the afternoon Daily Whole-offering, respectively. The *Neilah* (now the closing prayer on the Day of Atonement) preserves the name of the closing ceremony in the Temple when the Priests dismissed the people at the end of the day. The paragraph refers to the use of the priestly Benediction (Num. 6[24–6]). 6 See App. I. 21. Cf. Bikk. 3². 7 Num. 28². 8 David and Solomon.
9 See above, 2⁶. 10 The rest of the paragraph is omitted by many texts. 11 App. I. 38.
12 On the eve needed to busy themselves with the preparations for the Sabbath.
13 Pss. 113–18. 14 On the eight days of Hanukkah (the Feast of the Dedication).
15 For the reading of the first chapter of Genesis.
16 The reference is to the use at Jerusalem at the time of the Temple.
17 On the first days of a month.   18 See the following paragraph.

Ben Azzai said to him: R. Joshua taught thus: When an Additional Offering would be brought no *Maamad* assembled in the afternoon; when a Wood-offering would be brought no *Maamad* assembled at the Closing [of the Gates]. R. Akiba retracted and taught according to Ben Azzai.

5. The Wood-offering[1] of the priests and the people was brought nine times [in the year]: on the 1st of Nisan, by the family of Arah of the tribe of Judah;[2] on the 20th of Tammuz by the family of David of the tribe of Judah;[3] on the 5th of Ab, by the family of Parosh of the tribe of Judah;[4] on the 7th of the selfsame month, by the family of Jonadab the son of Rechab;[5] on the 10th, by the family of Senaah of the tribe of Benjamin;[6] on the 15th, by the family of Zattu[7] of the tribe of Judah together with the priests and levites and all whose tribal descent was in doubt,[8] and the family of the Pestle-smugglers and the family of the Fig-pressers.[9] On the 20th of the same month [it was brought] by the family of Pahath Moab of the tribe of Judah;[10] on the 20th of Elul, by the family of Adin of the tribe of Judah;[11] on the 1st of Tebet no *Maamad* assembled at all since on that day there was appointed the *Hallel*,[12] an Additional Offering,[13] and a Wood-offering.[14]

6. Five things befell our fathers on the 17th of Tammuz and five on the 9th of Ab. On the 17th of Tammuz the Tables [of the Ten Commandments] were broken, and the Daily Whole-offering ceased,[15] and the City[16] was breached, and Apostomus[17] burnt the [Scrolls of the] Law, and an idol was set up[18] in the Sanctuary. On the 9th of Ab it was decreed against our fathers that they should not enter into the Land [of Israel],[19] and the Temple was destroyed the first and the second time,[20] and Beth-Tor[21] was captured and the City was ploughed up. When Ab comes in, gladness must be diminished.

7. In the week wherein falls the 9th of Ab it is forbidden to cut the hair or wash the clothes; but it is permitted on the Thursday because of the honour due to the Sabbath. On the eve of the 9th of Ab let none eat of two cooked dishes, let none eat flesh and let none drink wine. Rabban Simeon b. Gamaliel says: A man need but make some difference.[22] R. Judah says: A man must turn up his couch.[23] But the Sages did not agree with him.

8. Rabban Simeon b. Gamaliel said: There were no happier days for Israel than the 15th of Ab and the Day of Atonement, for on them the

---

[1] See Neh. 10[34]; 13[31].   [2] Neh. 7[10].
[3] No such family is mentioned in the seventh chapter of Nehemiah.   [4] Neh. 7[8].
[5] 2 Kings 10[15].   [6] Neh. 7[38].   [7] Neh. 7[13].   [8] Neh. 7[64].
[9] The Tosefta (Taan. 4[7]) explains how once, when the Greek (Syrian) overlords forbade the observance of the Jewish rites the decree was evaded by one who covered up his fresh produce with dried figs, and, equipped with a pestle, contrived to pass the guards and enter into Jerusalem on the pretence of going to a certain person's mortar to stamp his figs into fig-cakes. And so he was able to bring his First-fruits.
[10] Neh. 7[11].   [11] Neh. 7[20].
[12] Since it fell within the eight days of the Feast of Dedication (beginning on the 25th of Chislev).   [13] Since it was the first of the month (Num. 28[11ff]).
[14] By the family of Parosh.
[15] Owing to scarcity during the siege by the Romans (or that in the time of Nebuchadnezzar may be meant).   [16] Jerusalem.
[17] Posthumus. He is said to have been a Syrian general. Nothing is known of him.
[18] Variant: 'He (Apostomus) set up'.
[19] Num. 14[29ff].   [20] By Nebuchadnezzar and by Titus.
[21] Or Bethar; the present Bittir, south of Jerusalem, the scene of Bar Cocheba's final defeat in A.D. 135.   [22] e.g. eat somewhat less than is his custom.
[23] And sleep on the ground. A sign of mourning. Jer. 14[2]. Cf. M. Kat. 3[7].

daughters of Jerusalem used to go forth in white raiments; and these were borrowed, that none should be abashed which had them not; [hence] all the raiments required immersion.[1] And the daughters of Jerusalem went forth to dance in the vineyards. And what did they say? 'Young man, lift up thine eyes and see what thou wouldest choose for thyself: set not thine eyes on beauty, but set thine eyes on family; for *Favour is deceitful and beauty is vain, but a woman that feareth the Lord she shall be praised*;[2] moreover it saith, *Give her of the fruit of her hands and let her works praise her in the gates*.[3] Likewise it saith, *Go forth ye daughters of Sion, and behold king Solomon with the crown wherewith his mother hath crowned him in the day of his espousals and in the day of the gladness of his heart*:[4] In the day of his espousals—this is the giving of the Law; *and in the day of the gladness of his heart*—this is the building of the Temple. May it be built speedily, in our days! Amen.

MEGILLAH[5] ('THE SCROLL OF ESTHER')

1. 1. The Scroll [of Esther] is read on the 11th, 12th, 13th, 14th, or 15th [of Adar],[6] never earlier and never later. Cities encompassed by a wall since the days of Joshua the son of Nun read it on the 15th.[7] Villages and large towns read it on the 14th,[8] save that villages [sometimes] read it earlier on a day of assembly.[9]

2. Thus, if the 14th fell on a Monday villages and large towns read the Scroll on that day, and walled cities on the day after. If it fell on a Tuesday or a Wednesday, villages read it earlier on the day of assembly,[10] and large towns on the day itself, and walled cities on the next day. If it fell on a Thursday, villages and large towns read it on that day, and walled cities on the next day. If it fell on a Friday, villages read it earlier on the day of assembly,[11] large towns and walled cities on the day itself. If it fell on the Sabbath, villages and large towns read it earlier on the day of assembly,[12] and walled cities on the next day. If it fell on the day after the Sabbath, villages read it earlier on the day of assembly,[13] large towns on the day itself, and walled cities the next day.

3. What is deemed a large town? Any in which are ten unoccupied men.[14] If there are fewer than this, it is a village. Of these [times[15]] they have said: They may read it earlier and not later. But [the time of] the priests' Wood-offering,[16] the 9th of Ab,[17] the Festal-offering,[18] and the

---

[1] Before being worn, lest they should have been rendered unclean under the conditions of Lev. 15[25ff]. Variant: the sons of J.   [2] Prov. 31[30].   [3] Prov. 31[31].   [4] Cant. 3[11].

[5] Lit. 'Scroll', a usual designation of the Book of Esther. The tractate deals with the time and manner of the public reading of the Scroll at the Feast of Purim (cf. Esth. 9[28]); and it goes on to treat of the times and manner of public reading of other portions of Scripture.

[6] App. I. 2. If another month is added to the (lunar) year, the Scroll is read on the corresponding day of this intercalated month, which is known as 'Second Adar'.

[7] After the precedent of the first celebration in 'Shushan the fortress', Esth. 9[18].

[8] Esth. 9[17, 19].

[9] A Monday or Thursday. Then the courts of law were in session (cf. Ket. 1[1]) when some learned person could be counted upon to be present to read the Scroll.

[10] i.e. Monday the 13th or 12th.   [11] i.e. Thursday the 13th.

[12] i.e. Thursday the 12th.   [13] i.e. Thursday the 11th.

[14] Heb. *batlanim*; they can be counted upon to form the quorum of ten necessary for the saying of the prescribed congregational prayers. See below, 4[3].

[15] When the 14th or 15th of Adar falls on the Sabbath.

[16] See Taan. 4[5].   [17] Taan. 4[6].   [18] Deut. 16[16-17]. Cf. Hag. 1[1ff].

[Great] Assembling,[1] may be made later but they may not be made earlier.[2] Although they have said, 'They may[3] read it earlier and not later', they may make lamentation or keep a fast[4] or make gifts to the poor.[5] R. Judah said: This applies[6] only to a place where they hold assembly on Mondays and Thursdays; but if they do not hold assembly on Mondays and Thursdays they may read it only at its appointed time.

4. If they had read the Scroll in First Adar, and the year was intercalated,[7] they must read it again in Second Adar. First Adar differs from Second Adar only in the reading of the Scroll and in giving gifts to the poor.[8]

5. A Festival-day differs from the Sabbath only in the preparing of necessary food.[9] The Sabbath differs from the Day of Atonement only in that for the wanton profaning of the one [punishment is] is by man's hand,[10] and for the wanton profaning of the other by Extirpation.[11]

6. A man that is forbidden by vow[12] to have any benefit from his fellow differs from him that is forbidden by vow to take any food from him only in the treading of his foot [in the other's domain] and the use of vessels in which necessary food is not prepared. Vow-offerings differ from Freewill-offerings[13] only in that he is answerable for Vow-offerings [and must replace them if they die or are lost] and he is not answerable for Freewill-offerings [and need not replace them if they die or are lost].

7. He that has a flux and suffers two issues[14] differs from him that suffers three only in the bringing of the offering.[15] The leper[16] that is shut up differs from the leper that is certified unclean only in unkempt hair and rent garments. [The leper that is pronounced] clean after having been shut up differs from the leper that has been certified clean only in the cutting off of the hair and the Bird-offerings.

8. The Books [of Scripture] differ from phylacteries[17] and *Mezuzahs*[18] only in that the Books may be written in any language,[19] while phylacteries and *Mezuzahs* may be written in the Assyrian writing[20] only. Rabban Simeon b. Gamaliel says: The Books, too, they have only permitted to be written in Greek.[21]

9. The [High] Priest anointed with the oil of unction[22] differs from him that is dedicated by the many garments[23] only in the bullock that is offered for [the unwitting transgression of] any of the commandments.[24] The [High]

[1] Deut. 31[10-13]. See Sot. 7[8].   [2] If they chance to fall on the Sabbath.
[3] On the ante-dated Purim observed by villages.
[4] It is not such a Feast when mourning is forbidden. See Taan. 2[8].
[5] See Esth. 9[22]. If they give them on the earlier day they are exempt from giving them on the actual date of Purim.   [6] That the reading may be advanced.
[7] The Jewish lunar year of 354⅓ days needed the intercalation of a complete month in, approximately, every third year to draw level with the solar year. Such intercalation was sometimes enjoined only late in 'First Adar'.
[8] i.e. if a man did these in First and not in Second Adar he has not fulfilled his obligation.
[9] See p. 181, n. 11. The following seven paragraphs illustrate a characteristic mnemonic device in the Mishnah of bringing together topics which, however irrelevant in subject-matter, are linked by a similar formula. Cf. in this tractate 2[4, 5]; 4[3] (end). See Naz. 9[4]; B.M. 4[7, 8]; Men. 3[6-7]; Hull. 1[1ff.]; Arak. 2[1ff.]   [10] Num. 15[35]; Sanh. 7[4].
[11] Lev. 23[30]. See p. 562, n. 16.   [12] Ned. 4[1].   [13] Cf. Kinn. 1[1].
[14] Lev. 15[1-15].   [15] To which the latter alone is liable. Cf. Zab. 1[1ff.].
[16] Lev. 13[1ff.]. See Neg. 8[8].   [17] See p. 104, n. 16.
[18] App. I. 25.   [19] And any script.
[20] In Hebrew and in the 'square' characters. Cf. Meg. 2[1,2]; Yad. 4[5].
[21] Meaning, of course, in addition to Hebrew.
[22] With which High Priests were anointed only until the time of Josiah.
[23] See Yom. 7[5]; Hor. 3[4].
[24] Lev. 4[3] applies this expressly to the 'anointed' (High) Priest.

Priest in office[1] differs from the [High] Priest that is passed [from his high-priesthood][2] only in the bullock[3] that is offered on the Day of Atonement and the Tenth of the Ephah.[4]

10. A great high place[5] differed from a lesser high place[6] only in the Passover-offerings.[7] This is the general rule: what was vowed or freely offered could be offered on a [lesser] high place,[8] but what was not vowed or freely offered could not be offered on a [lesser] high place.

11. Shiloh[9] differed from Jerusalem only in that at Shiloh they could consume the Lesser Holy Things[10] and the Second Tithe[11] anywhere within sight [of Shiloh]; but at Jerusalem only within the city wall. But both here and there the Most Holy Things[12] could be consumed only within the Curtains.[13] After the sanctification of Shiloh it was permissible [to set up high places elswhere]; but after the sanctification of Jerusalem it was not permissible [to set up high places elsewhese].

2. 1. If a man read the Scroll in wrong order, he has not fulfilled his obligation. If he read it by heart, or if he read it in Aramaic or in any other language, he has not fulfilled his obligation. But it may be read in a foreign tongue to them that speak a foreign tongue; and if one that spoke a foreign tongue heard [the Scroll read in Hebrew] in [a roll written in] Assyrian[14] he has fulfilled his obligation.

2. If a man read it piecemeal or drowsily, he has fulfilled his obligation; if he was copying it, expounding it, or correcting a copy of it, and he directed his heart [to the reading of the Scroll], he has fulfilled his obligation; otherwise he has not fulfilled his obligation. If it was written with caustic, red dye, gum, or copperas,[15] or on paper or unprepared leather, he has not fulfilled his obligation; but only if it was written in Assyrian writing, on parchment and with ink.

3. If a dweller in a town went to a city,[16] or a dweller in a city went to a town, and he intended to return to his own place, he should read [the Scroll] as if he was in his own place; but if [he did] not [intend to return] he must read it with them [of the place to which he is come]. And from what words must a man read the Scroll to fulfil his obligation? R. Meir says: The whole of it. R. Judah says: From *There was a certain Jew* . . .[17] R. Jose says: From *After these things* . . .[18]

4. All are eligible to read the Scroll excepting one that is deaf[19] or an imbecile or a minor.[20] R. Judah declares a minor eligible. None may read

---

[1] Hor. 3[4].

[2] i.e. one who had served temporarily as the substitute of the High Priest on the Day of Atonement; see Yom. 1[1].   [3] Lev. 16[6].

[4] Lev. 6[19ff]. Neither may be offered by the substitute.

[5] For the whole congregation (e.g. at Nob and Gibeon) before the building of the Temple in Jerusalem. Cf. Zeb. 14[4ff].

[6] Such as were permitted to individuals before the building of the Temple in Shiloh, and after the destruction of the latter and before the building of the Jerusalem Temple.

[7] Which could only be offered at the great high place.

[8] Permitted to individuals.   [9] Cf. Zeb. 14[6].

[10] See Zeb. 5[6ff].; they were the Passover-offerings, private Thank-offerings and Peace-offerings, Firstlings and Tithe of Cattle.   [11] Deut. 14[22–6]. See p. 73, n. 6.

[12] See Zeb. 5[1–5]; they were the Sin-offerings and Guilt-offerings, Whole-offerings and the Peace-offerings of the congregation at Pentecost.

[13] i.e. the enclosing walls of the Temple Court. The term is derived from the Tabernacle (Ex. 27[9]). See p. 474, n. 6. Cf. Eduy. 8[6]; Zeb. 11[5]; 14[4ff]. See above, 1[8]. See p. 474. n. 6.

[14] See above, 1[8].

[15] Sulphate of iron. Cf. Shab. 12[4]; Sot. 2[4]; Gitt. 2[3]; Par. 9[1]; Yad. 1[3].

[16] i.e. from a place where it is read on the 14th to where it is read on the 15th.

[17] Esth. 2[5].   [18] Esth. 3[1].   [19] The usual meaning of the word is 'deaf-mute'; see Ter. 1[2].

[20] A boy under thirteen.

the Scroll, or circumcise, or immerse himself,[1] or sprinkle [the Sin-offering water][2] (so, too, she that awaits day against day[3] may not immerse herself) until the sun has risen; but if they had so done [already] after dawn appeared, it is valid.

5. The whole day[4] is valid for reading the Scroll, and for reciting the Hallel,[5] and for blowing the shofar,[6] and for carrying the Lulab,[7] and for the Additional Prayer,[8] and for the Additional Offering, and for the Avowal at the offering of the bullocks,[9] and for the Avowal concerning the [Second] Tithe,[10] and for the Confession on the Day of Atonement,[11] for the laying on of hands,[12] for slaughtering,[13] for the Waving,[14] for bringing near [the Meal-offering], taking the Handful and burning it;[15] for wringing the necks of the Bird-offerings,[16] and for receiving the blood,[17] and for sprinkling the blood,[18] and for giving the water to the Suspected Adulteress,[19] for breaking the heifer's neck,[20] and for the purifying of the leper.[21]

6. The whole night[22] is valid for reaping the Omer,[23] for burning the fat-pieces and the members.[24] This is the general rule:[25] any act whose fulfilment is prescribed for the day is valid during the whole of the day; and any act whose fulfilment is prescribed for the night is valid during the whole of the night.

3. 1. If the people of a town sell their open space[26] they must buy a synagogue with the price thereof; if they sell a synagogue they must buy an Ark [with the price thereof]; if an Ark, they must buy [Scroll] wrappings; if wrappings, they must buy Books [of the Scriptures]; if Books, they must buy [a copy of] the Law. But if they sold [a copy of] the Law they may not buy Books [of the Scriptures]; or if Books [of the Scriptures], they may not buy wrappings; or if wrappings, they may not buy an Ark; or if an Ark, they may not buy a synagogue; or if a synagogue, they may not buy an open space. So, too, with the residue [of the price of any of these]. They may not sell to a private person what was a public possession, for thereby they lower its sanctity. So R. Judah. They said to him: If so, [they may] not [sell] aught from a larger town to a smaller.

2. They may not sell a synagogue except it is on the condition that when they will they may take it back again. So R. Meir. But the Sages say: They may sell it for all time except for [use as] four things: a bath-house, a tannery, an immersion-pool, or a urinal.[27] R. Judah says: They may sell it for a courtyard and the buyer may do with it what he will.

---

[1] After having contracted some uncleanness.   [2] Num. 19[17ff.]; see p. 697, n. 3.
[3] See p. 147, n. 4.   [4] Sunrise to sunset.
[5] Pss. 113–18, prescribed for certain Festival-days.
[6] At the New Year (Lev. 23[24]) and on the Day of Atonement (Lev. 25[9]).
[7] App. I. 20.
[8] Supplementary to the usual congregational prayers on Sabbaths, New Moons, and Festival-days, corresponding to the occasions (Num. 28[9] to 29[40]) when Additional Offerings were offered in the Temple.   [9] Lev. 4[4, 15].   [10] Deut. 26[13-15]; M.Sh. 5[10].
[11] Lev. 16[21]; Yom. 3[8]; 4[2]; 6[2].   [12] By one who brings a private offering (Lev. 3[2]).
[13] Of all the offerings excepting those which have a prescribed time (the Daily Whole-offerings and the Passover-offering).   [14] Lev. 7[30]; 23[11, 20]; Num. 5[26]; 6[20].
[15] Lev. 2[2].   [16] Lev. 1[15]; 5[8].   [17] By the priest in a bason.   [18] On the Altar.
[19] Num. 5[24]. Cf. the tractate Sotah.   [20] Deut. 21[4]. See Sot. 9[1ff.].
[21] Lev. 14[1-32].   [22] Cf. Ber. 1[1].   [23] App. I. 31.
[24] Of the offerings brought that day.   [25] Cf. Ber. 1[1]; Zeb. 5[3].
[26] This paragraph illustrates the principle (Shek. 6[4]; Men. 11[7]) 'What is holy must be raised in honour and not brought down'. Some sanctity attaches to the town's open place since here the Ark of the Law was sometimes brought (see Taan. 2[1]).
[27] Or, 'wash-house'.

3. Moreover R. Judah said: [Even] if a synagogue was in ruins lamentation for the dead may not be made therein, nor may they twist ropes therein or stretch out nets therein,[1] or spread out produce [to dry] on its roof, or make of it a short by-path;[2] for it is written, *And I will bring your sanctuaries into desolation*[3]—their sanctity [endures] although they lie desolate. If herbs spring up therein they may not be plucked up[4] because of grief of soul.

4. If the first day of the month Adar falls on the Sabbath, they read the section [in the Law] 'Shekels';[5] if it falls in the middle of the week they read it earlier on the Sabbath that goes before, and on the next Sabbath they break off [from the reading of the four portions prescribed for the month of Adar[6]]. On the second [Sabbath of the month they read the section] *Remember what Amalek did*;[7] on the third, the section of 'The Red Heifer';[8] on the fourth, the section *This month shall be unto you . . .*[9] On the fifth they revert to the set order.[10] At all these times they break off [from the set order in the reading of the Law]: on the first days of the months, at the [Feast of the] Dedication,[11] at Purim, on days of fasting, and at *Maamads*[12] and on the Day of Atonement.

5. At Passover they read the section 'The Set Feasts'[13] in the Law of the Priests;[14] at Pentecost, [the section] 'Seven weeks';[15] at the New Year, *In the seventh month in the first day of the month . . .*,[16] on the Day of Atonement, *After the death . . .*;[17] on the first Festival-day of the Feast [of Tabernacles] they read the section 'The Set Feasts' in the Law of the Priests, and, on all the other days of the Feast, about the offerings at the Feast.[18]

6. At the [Feast of the] Dedication [they read the section] 'The Princes';[19] at Purim, *Then came Amalek . . .*;[20] on the first days of the months, *And on the first days of your months . . .*;[21] at the *Maamads*, from the story of Creation;[22] on the days of fasting, The Blessings and the Cursings.[23] They make no break in the reading of the curses, but the one [reader] reads them all. On Mondays and Thursdays and on Sabbaths at the Afternoon Prayer they read according to the set order;[24] and these are not taken into account.[25] For it is written, *And Moses declared unto the children of Israel the set feasts of the Lord*[26]—the law prescribed for them is that they should be read each one in its set time.

4. 1. He that reads the Scroll[27] may stand or sit.[28] If one reads it, or if two read it, they[29] have fulfilled their obligation. Where the custom is to say a Benediction [after it] they say it; where it is not the custom, they

---

[1] No manner of work is permitted; these two examples are given as work for which a large enclosed space would be sought.   [2] Cf. Ber. 9⁵.   [3] Lev. 26³¹.

[4] And used as cattle-fodder; for this would signify indifference to the place's sanctity.

[5] Ex. 30¹¹⁻¹⁶; cf. Shek. 1¹.

[6] i.e. they do not read on the first Sabbath in the month the portion 'Remember', but leave this for the second Sabbath, and read some other on the first Sabbath.

[7] Deut. 25¹⁷⁻¹⁹.   [8] Num. 19¹⁻²².   [9] Ex. 12¹⁻²⁰.

[10] i.e. to the ordinary cycle of Sabbath readings from the Pentateuch.

[11] Hanukkah (25th of Chislev).

[12] See Taan. 4²ᶠ. App. I. 21. Variant: 'the set feasts'. The following paragraphs suggest that the text should read, 'at the set feasts and at *Maamads*'.

[13] Lev. 23¹ᶠᶠ.   [14] i.e. the Book of Leviticus.   [15] Deut. 16⁹⁻¹².   [16] Lev. 23²³ᶠᶠ.

[17] Lev. 16¹⁻³⁴. Cf. Yom. 7¹.   [18] Num. 29¹⁷ᶠᶠ.   [19] Num. 7¹⁻⁸⁹.

[20] Ex. 17 ⁸⁻¹⁶.   [21] Num. 28¹¹⁻¹⁵.   [22] Gen. 1¹⁻²³. See Taan. 4³.   [23] Lev. 26³⁻⁴⁶.

[24] The Pentateuch was divided into weekly portions, to be read in full at each Sabbath morning service. On Sabbath afternoons, Mondays, and Thursdays part of the portion prescribed for the next Sabbath was read.

[25] What was read at these times was read again on the following Sabbath.

[26] Lev. 23⁴⁴.   [27] Of Esther at Purim.

[28] Whereas he that reads the Law must stand.   [29] That read and that listen.

do not say it. On[1] a Monday and a Thursday and on the afternoon of a Sabbath the Law is read by three: they may not take from them or add to them, and they do not close with a reading from the Prophets.[2] He that begins the reading from the Law and he that completes it say a Benediction the one at the beginning and the other at the end.

2. And in the beginnings of the months and during mid-festival[3] the Law is read by four; they may not take from them or add to them, and they do not close with a reading from the Prophets. He that begins the reading from the Law and he that completes it say a Benediction the one at the beginning and the other at the end. This is the general rule: when the Additional Prayer is appointed[4] and it is not a Festival-day, the Law is read by four. On a Festival-day it is read by five, on the Day of Atonement by six, and on the Sabbath by seven. They may not take from them but they may add to them, and they close with a reading from the Prophets. He that begins the reading from the Law and he that completes it say a Benediction the one at the beginning and the other at the end.

3. If there are less than ten present they may not recite the *Shema*ʿ with its Benedictions,[5] nor may one go before the Ark,[6] nor may they lift up their hands,[7] nor may they read the [prescribed portion of] the Law or the reading from the Prophets, nor may they observe the Stations[8] [when burying the dead] or say the Benediction of the Mourners[9] or the mourners' consolation,[10] or the Benediction over the newly wed,[11] nor may they make mention of the name of God in the Common Grace.[12] Also[13] [the redemption value of dedicated] immovable property[14] [is assessed] by nine and a priest; and similarly [for the Valuation-vow[15] of] men.

4. He that reads in the Law may not read less than three verses; he may not read to the interpreter[16] more than one verse, or, in [a reading from] the Prophets, three verses; but if these three are three separate paragraphs,[17] he must read them out singly. They may leave out verses in the Prophets, but not in the Law. How much may they leave out? Only so much that he leaves no time for the interpreter to make a pause.

5. He that gives the concluding reading from the Prophets recites also the *Shema*ʿ with its Benedictions; and he goes before the Ark, and he lifts up his hands [in the Benediction of the Priests]. If he is a minor, his father or his teacher goes before the Ark on his behalf.

6. A minor may read in the Law and interpret, but he may not recite the *Shema*ʿ with its Benedictions or go before the Ark or raise his hands [in the Benediction of the Priests]. He whose clothes are ragged may recite

---

[1] The reference is no longer to Purim and the reading of the Book of Esther, but to the regular reading of the Law. [2] As on the morning of Sabbaths and Festival-days.
[3] From the second to the sixth days of Passover and the second to the seventh days of Tabernacles. [4] See above, p. 204, n. 8. [5] See Ber. 1⁴; Singer, pp. 37–52.
[6] Containing the Scrolls of the Law, to lead the prescribed congregational prayers.
[7] In pronouncing the Blessing of the Priests, Num. 6²⁴⁻⁶.
[8] Lit. 'the standing and the sitting'. During the funeral procession it was the custom to stop seven times and make lamentation over the dead. Cf. Ket. 2¹⁰; B.B. 6⁷; Ohol. 18⁴.
[9] On returning from the burial they that take part stand together, and one pronounces a Benediction over the mourners (Ket. 100a).
[10] They who visit the mourners stand in lines (Ber. 3²) of not less than ten each, family by family; the mourner passes before them and they utter words of consolation. Cf. Ber. 2⁷; Sanh. 2¹. Some texts omit 'or the mourners' consolation'.
[11] The 'Seven Benedictions'; see Singer, p. 299. [12] See Ber. 7³.
[13] Sanh. 1³. See above, p. 202, n. 9. [14] Lev. 27¹⁴ff. [15] Lev. 27¹ff. See p. 544, n. 1.
[16] From the Hebrew into the Aramaic speech of the unlearned.
[17] As in Is. 52³⁻⁵ in the Hebrew text.

the *Shema'* with its Benedictions and interpret, but he may not read in the Law or go before the Ark or lift up his hands. He that is blind may recite the *Shema'* with its Benedictions and interpret. R. Judah says: He that has never seen the light may not recite the *Shema'* with its Benedictions.

7. If a priest has blemishes in his hands, he may not raise his hands [in the Benediction of the Priests]. R. Judah says: Moreover if a man's hands are dyed with woad or madder he may not lift up his hands, because the people would gaze on him.

8. If a man said, 'I will not go before the Ark in coloured raiment', he may not even go before it in white raiment. [If he said,] 'I will not go before it in sandals', he may not even go before it barefoot. If a man made his phylacteries round,[1] it is a danger and is no fulfilling of the commandment. If he put them on his forehead[2] or on the palm of his hand,[3] this is the way of heresy. If he overlaid them with gold or put them over his sleeve,[4] this is the way of the sectaries.

9. If[5] a man said [in his prayer], 'Good men shall bless thee!' this is the way of heresy; [if he said,] 'Even to a bird's nest do thy mercies extend', or 'May thy name be remembered for the good [which thou hast wrought]!' or 'We give thanks, we give thanks!' they put him to silence. If a man does not read literally the laws about the forbidden degrees,[6] they put him to silence. If a man says *And thou shalt not give any of thy seed to make them pass through [the fire] to Molech*[7] [means] 'and thou shalt not give of thy seed to make it pass to heathendom',[8] they put him to silence with a rebuke.

10. The story of Reuben[9] is read out but not interpreted; the story of Tamar[10] is read out and interpreted. The first story of the calf[11] is read out and interpreted, and the second[12] is read out but not interpreted. The Blessing of the Priests[13] and the story of David[14] and of Amnon[15] are read out but not interpreted.[16] They may not use the chapter of the Chariot[17] as a reading from the Prophets; but R. Judah permits it. R. Eliezer says: They do not use the chapter *Cause Jerusalem to know*[18] as a reading from the Prophets.

MOED KATAN[19] ('MID-FESTIVAL DAYS')

1. 1. During mid-festival and during the Seventh Year[20] an irrigated field[21] may be watered whether from a newly flowing spring[22] or from a spring that is not newly flowing; but it may not be watered from [collected]

---

[1] Instead of cube-shaped. See p. 104, n. 16. The 'danger' of these, according to the older commentators, is that if he knocks against anything a round (nut-shaped) head-phylactery would pierce the forehead.   [2] i.e. wore the head-phylactery too low down.
[3] Instead of above the inside of the elbow.   [4] To make it conspicuous.   [5] Ber. 5³.
[6] Lev. 18⁶⁻¹⁸. e.g. if, from prudery, he read 'shame' for 'nakedness'.   [7] Lev. 18²¹.
[8] i.e. beget children by a gentile mother. The expression 'to make pass' can here also be translated 'render pregnant' (cf. Job 21¹⁰).   [9] Gen. 35²².   [10] Gen. 38¹³ff.   [11] Ex. 32¹⁻²⁰.
[12] Not Deut. 9¹²⁻²¹, but Ex. 32²¹⁻⁵, ³⁵.   [13] Num. 6²⁴⁻⁶.   [14] 2 Sam. 11²⁻¹⁷.
[15] 2 Sam. 13¹ff.   [16] Variant: 'neither read out nor interpreted'.
[17] Ezek. 1⁴ff. Cf. Hag. 2¹.   [18] Ezek. 16¹ff.
[19] This is the name applied to the days between those Festival-days (cf. p. 181, n. 11) which mark the beginning and end of the Feasts of Passover and Tabernacles. *Moed Katan* signifies 'minor feast'; the more usual term applied to these days is *Hol ha-moed*, meaning the 'non-sacred days of the feast'. The rules governing the observance of Festival-days apply with less stringency to mid-festival days; work is permissible that serves the needs of the Feast and that is intended to prevent damage that would ensue by postponing the work until after the Feast; but heavy labour is forbidden. Mourning, though permissible, must be rendered inconspicuous.   [20] Lev. 25⁴ᶠ. See p. 39, n. 4.
[21] That cannot be properly watered by rainfall.
[22] That would require some labour to utilize it by the digging of new channels.

rain-water or from a swape-well; nor may channels be digged around the vines.

2. R. Eleazar b. Azariah says: During mid-festival and during the Seventh year they may not dig a new water-channel. But the Sages say: During the Seventh Year they may dig a new water-channel, and during mid-festival they may repair what has been broken down; they may repair damaged water-ways in the public domain and clean them out; and[1] they may repair roads, open places, and pools of water, and perform all public needs and mark the graves; and they also go forth [to give warning] against Diverse Kinds.

3. R. Eliezer b. Jacob says: They may lead the water from tree to tree provided that they do not water the entire field; seeds that have not been watered before mid-festival may not be watered during mid-festival. But the Sages permit both the one and the other.

4. During mid-festival and during the Seventh Year they may catch moles and mice from tree-planted fields and from sown fields, if this is not[2] done after the usual fashion. But the Sages say: From a tree-planted field after the usual fashion, but from a sown field not after the usual fashion. During mid-festival they may block up a breach[3] and during the Seventh Year they may even build it up after the usual fashion.

5. R. Meir says: During mid-festival they may examine leprosy signs[4] if it will lead to leniency, but not if it will lead to stringency.[5] But the Sages say: They may not examine them whether it will lead to leniency or to stringency. Moreover R. Meir said: A man may gather together the bones of his father or his mother,[6] since this is to him an occasion for rejoicing.[7] But R. Jose says: It is to him an occasion for mourning. A man may not call for mourning over his dead or make lamentation[8] over him for thirty days before a Feast.

6. They may not hew out tomb-niches[9] or tombs during mid-festival, but [old] niches may be refashioned during mid-festival. During mid-festival they may dig a grave,[10] and make a coffin while the corpse lies in the [selfsame] courtyard.[11] R. Judah forbids it unless a man had the boards [sawn in readiness].

7. During mid-festival they may not marry wives, whether virgins or widows, or contract levirate marriage,[12] since this is an occasion for rejoicing;[13] but a man may take back his divorced wife. And a woman may prepare her adornments during mid-festival. R. Judah says: She may not use lime,[14] since this is a disfigurement to her.

8. He that is not skilled may sew after his usual fashion, but the craftsman may make only irregular stitches.[15] They may twist together the ropes for the bed.[16] R. Jose says: They may even[17] tighten them.

9. They may set up an oven or stove or hand-mill[18] during mid-festival.

[1] See Shek. 1[1].   [2] Some texts omit the negative.   [3] In haphazard fashion.
[4] Lev. 13[ff]. Some texts here add 'for a first time'.
[5] So as not to impair the man's joy during the Feast. Cf. Neg. 1[4-6].   [6] Cf. Pes. 8[8].
[7] And so not inconsonant with the special joy proper to the Feast.
[8] By hired mourners. Their cost would deprive him of the means necessary for the proper celebration of the Feast.   [9] B.B. 6[8].   [10] Less laborious than a rock-tomb.
[11] Proving that the work is urgent.   [12] See p. 218, n. 1.
[13] Which may eclipse the joy of the Feast.   [14] As a depilatory.
[15] Lit. 'sew dog-tooth-wise'.
[16] For the under-webbing. For the nature of the bed see Kel. 18[5-7]; 19[1-6].
[17] Variant: 'only'.   [18] These were portable, but in use were fixed to the ground with clay.

R. Judah says: They may not roughen the millstones for the first time.

10. They may make a parapet for a roof or a gallery in unskilled fashion, but not in the fashion of a craftsman. They may plaster up cracks and smooth them down with a roller or with the hand or the foot, but not with a trowel. If a hinge or a socket or a roof-beam or a lock or a key was broken, it may be repaired during mid-festival, provided that a man had not purposed[1] to do his work during mid-festival. And whatsoever pickled foods a man can eat during mid-festival, he may put in pickle.

2. 1. If a man had turned over his olives[2] and then mourning[3] or aught of constraint befell him, or if labourers had played him false,[4] he may apply the pressing beam [to the olives] for a first time and then leave it until after the Feast. So R. Judah. R. Jose says: He may squeeze out the oil completely and seal it up after his usual fashion [in jars].

2. So, too, if his wine was in the cistern and then mourning or aught of constraint befell him, or if labourers had played him false, he may empty out the wine completely and seal it up after his usual fashion [in jars]. So R. Jose. R. Judah says: He may make for it a covering of shingles so that the wine shall not turn sour.

3. A man may bring in his produce for fear of thieves, or take his flax out of soak lest it perish, provided that he had not purposed to do his work during mid-festival. But in every like case if they had purposed to do their work during mid-festival it must be left to perish.

4. They may not buy houses, slaves, or cattle save for the needs of the Feast, or for the needs of the seller if he have naught to eat.[5] Goods may not be emptied out from one house into another,[6] but a man may empty them out into [another house in] his own courtyard. Utensils may not be brought away from the house of a craftsman; but if a man fears for their safety he may remove them into another courtyard.

5. They may cover up fig-cakes with straw. R. Judah says: They may [even] pile them up. Sellers of produce, clothes, and utensils may sell them privately for the needs of the Feast. Hunters, groats-makers, and grist-millers may do their work privately for the needs of the Feast. R. Jose says: They apply the more stringent ruling to themselves.[7]

3. 1. These [alone] may cut their hair during mid-festival: he that comes from beyond the sea, or from captivity, or out of prison; or he that was under a ban[8] and was released[9] by the Sages; and so, too, he that sought of a Sage [release from a vow][10] and was released; and the Nazirite[11] and the leper that is come forth from uncleanness to cleanness.[12]

2. And these [alone] may wash their clothes during mid-festival: he that comes from beyond the sea, or from captivity, or out of prison; or he that was under a ban and was released by the Sages; and so, too, he that

[1] Deliberately postponed it until the leisure of the mid-festival days.
[2] To soften them all over while ripening. In this stage they were ready for immediate pressing and would suffer from delay.
[3] When for three days he is forbidden to work. [4] Cf. B.M. 6[1].
[5] And must sell something to enable him to keep the Feast in seemly fashion.
[6] If he must pass through a public thoroughfare.
[7] And do no work at all during mid-festival.
[8] When it is forbidden to cut the hair or wash the clothes. [9] During mid-festival.
[10] In which he had vowed not to cut his hair for the stated time. Cf. Ned. 9[1ff]. for reasons which enable a Sage to grant release from a vow.
[11] If the end of his period fell within mid-festival. See Num. 6[5]. [12] Lev. 14[8-9].

sought of a Sage [release from a vow] and was released. [Also it is permitted to wash] hand-towels, barber's towels, and bath-towels. Men or women that had a flux,[1] menstruants[2] and women after childbirth,[3] and all that pass from conditions of uncleanness to cleanness are permitted [to wash their clothes]; but for all others it is forbidden.[4]

3. And these may be written out during mid-festival:[5] deeds of betrothal, letters of divorce, and quittances,[6] testaments, deeds of gift, *prozbols*,[7] valuations,[8] deeds of alimony,[9] records of *halitzah*[10] and Refusal,[11] deeds of arbitration, decrees of the court, and official deeds.[12]

4. Bonds of indebtedness may not be written out during mid-festival, but one may be written out if any man was not deemed trustworthy, or if he had naught to eat. They may not write out Books [of Scripture] or phylacteries[13] or *Mezuzahs*[14] during mid-festival, or correct a single letter even in the scroll of the Temple Court.[15] R. Judah says: A man may write out phylacteries and *Mezuzahs* for himself, or spin on his leg the purple thread for his fringe.[16]

5. If a man buried his dead[17] three days before the Feast, the rule of seven [days' mourning] is annulled for him; if eight days before, the rule of the thirty days is annulled for him. For they have said: The Sabbath is included[18] and does not interrupt;[19] but Feasts[20] interrupt and are not included.

6. R. Eliezer says: Since the destruction of the Temple Pentecost is deemed like to the Sabbath.[21] Rabban Gamaliel says: The New Year and the Day of Atonement are deemed like to the Feasts.[22] But the Sages say: It is not according to the opinion of either of them, but Pentecost is [still] deemed like to a Feast, and New Year and the Day of Atonement like to the Sabbath.

7. [During a Feast] none save the near of kin may rend their garments and bare the shoulder and be given the food of the mourners;[23] and food of the mourners must be given with the couches[24] set up [in usual fashion]. They may not take [the food] to a house of mourning on a plate or a salver or a flat basket, but in [common] baskets. And they may not say the Benediction of the Mourners during the Feast, but they stand in the row

---

[1] Lev. 15[1-15, 25-30].   [2] Lev. 15[19-24].   [3] Lev. 12[1-8].
[4] Since they could have done so before the Feast.
[5] Otherwise dispute or loss may ensue.
[6] Usually a woman's receipt for her *Ketubah*, paid to her by her husband when he divorces her. It is here used in a more general sense.   [7] App. I. 34.
[8] By the court of a debtor's goods, the document to be deposited as security with the creditor.
[9] Undertaking the support of orphans, or a wife's children by another husband.
[10] App. I. 12. See p. 218, n. 1.
[11] An orphan who had been betrothed by her mother or brothers may, before the onset of puberty, refuse to consummate the marriage, and so secure her freedom without the need of a bill of divorce. See Yeb. 13[2].   [12] Or: 'letters written of free choice'.
[13] See p. 104, n. 16.   [14] App. I. 25.
[15] See Yom. 7[1]. Variant: 'the Book of Ezra', i.e. the book of the Law as copied by Ezra (the Scribe, Neh. 8[9]), which served as the exemplar for future copies. Cf. p. 626, n. 5.
[16] Num. 15[38].
[17] The rules for mourning were that the first three days should be given to weeping, and the first seven to lamenting the dead; the tokens of mourning were to be worn for thirty days.
[18] In the first seven days.   [19] The seven days' spell entirely.
[20] If part of the time has already been observed.
[21] It does not interrupt the seven days of mourning.
[22] And annul the remainder of the seven days.   [23] 2 Sam. 3[35].
[24] On which they reclined while eating. These must not be 'turned up' in the usual manner at a time of mourning. Cf. Taan. 4[7].

and offer consolation;[1] and they [forthwith] dismiss them that are gathered together.

8. They may not set down the bier in the open street lest they give occasion for lamentation; and the bier of a woman they may never set down, out of respect. The women may sing dirges during the Feast but they may not clap their hands. R. Ishmael says: They that are near to the bier may clap their hands.

9. On the first days of the months and at [the Feast of] the Dedication[2] and at Purim they may sing lamentations and clap their hands; but during none of them may they wail. After the corpse has been buried they may not sing lamentations or clap their hands. What is a lamentation? When all sing together. And a wailing? When one begins by herself and all respond after her; for it is written, *Teach your daughters a lament, and every one her neighbour wailing.*[3] But for a time that is to come, it says, *He hath swallowed up death for ever, and the Lord God will wipe away tears from off all faces; and the reproach of his people shall he take away from off all the whole earth: for the Lord hath spoken it.*[4]

HAGIGAH[5] ('THE FESTAL-OFFERING')

1. 1. All are subject to the command to *appear [before the Lord]*[6] excepting a deaf-mute, an imbecile, a child, one of doubtful sex, one of double sex,[7] women, slaves that have not been freed,[8] a man that is lame or blind or sick or aged, and one that cannot go up [to Jerusalem] on his feet. Who is deemed a child? Any that cannot ride on his father's shoulders and go up from Jerusalem to the Temple Mount. So the School of Shammai. And the School of Hillel say: Any that cannot hold his father's hand and go up [on his feet] from Jerusalem to the Temple Mount, as it is written, *Three regalim.*[9]

2. The School of Shammai say: The *Re'iyyah*-offering[10] [must be not less in value than] two pieces of silver,[11] and the Festal-offering [not less than] one *maah* of silver. And the School of Hillel say: The *Re'iyyah*-offering [must be not less in value than] one *maah* of silver, and the Festal-offering [not less than] two pieces of silver.

3. Whole-offerings during mid-festival[12] are brought from [beasts bought

---

[1] See Meg. 4[3].   [2] Hanukkah, 25th of Chislev. See 1 Maccabees 4[59].
[3] Jer. 9[20].   [4] Is. 25[8].
[5] The principal subject is the manner of fulfilment of Deut. 16[16], 'Three times in a year shall all thy males appear before the Lord thy God in the place which he shall choose; in the feast of unleavened bread, and in the feast of weeks, and in the feast of tabernacles: and they shall not appear before the Lord empty (i.e. without an offering): every man shall give as he is able, according to the blessing of the Lord thy God which he hath given thee'. See also Ex. 23[14], and note 10, below.
[6] In fulfilment of the command of Ex. 23[14]; Deut. 16[16].
[7] 'Androgynos'. See Bikk. 4[1ff].
[8] To exclude those that are 'half free', e.g. if a slave had two owners and only one of them had set him free.
[9] Ex. 23[14]. The expression *regalim* is used in this passage (only again in the Old Testament in Num. 22[28, 32, 33]) in the sense of 'times'; on the basis of Ex. 23[14] it is often used in the Mishnah of the three great Feasts (Passover, Pentecost, and Tabernacles). Its usual meaning is 'feet', so that the quoted passage can convey the sense 'three times on foot'.
[10] Lit. 'appearing' (in the Temple); cf. Peah. 1[1]. On the basis of the combined passages Deut. 16[16] and Ex. 23[14] it is deduced that every male Israelite must bring on the first Festival-day (i) a Whole-offering (here called *Re'iyyah*) to be wholly burnt on the Altar, and (ii) a Peace-offering (here called Festal-offering, from which the tractate takes its name 'Hagigah'), of which only the fat-pieces, the kidneys, and the blood are offered on the Altar (see Lev. 3[15]), and the rest he consumes himself.   [11] i.e. two *maahs*. App. II, A.
[12] As opposed to the Festival-days. See p. 181, n. 11; p. 207, n. 19.

with] unconsecrated money,[1] and Peace-offerings[2] also from [what is bought with Second] Tithe [money];[3] on the first Festival-day of Passover, the School of Shammai say: They are brought from [beasts bought with] unconsecrated money. And the School of Hillel say: Also from [what is bought with Second] Tithe [money].

4. Israelites[4] may fulfil their obligation[5] by bringing vow-offerings and freewill-offerings[6] and Tithe of Cattle;[7] and the priests by bringing Sin-offerings and Guilt-offerings,[8] and Firstlings,[9] and the breast and the shoulder,[10] but not by bringing Bird-offerings[11] or Meal-offerings.[12]

5. He that has many that eat [with him] but few possessions may offer many Peace-offerings and few Whole-offerings; [he that has] many possessions but few that eat [with him] should offer many Whole-offerings and few Peace-offerings; [he that has] few of either, for such a one they have enjoined 'one *maah* of silver' and 'two pieces of silver' [as the value of his offerings]; [he that has] many of both, of such a one it is written, *Every man shall give as he is able, according to the blessing of the Lord thy God which he hath given thee.*[13]

6. He that made no offerings on the first Festival-day of the Feast must offer them [some other time] throughout the course of the Feast, even on the last Festival-day of the Feast. If the time of the Feast went by and he had made no offerings, it is not incumbent on him to make them good. Of such a one it is written, *That which is crooked cannot be made straight; and that which is wanting cannot be reckoned.*[14]

7. R. Simeon b. Menasya says: What is *that which is crooked* and which *cannot be made straight*? He that has connexion with one of the forbidden degrees[15] and by her begets bastard issue. Wouldest thou say that it applies to the thief or the robber?—but he may make restitution and *be made straight*. R. Simeon ben Yohai says: None can be called *crooked* excepting one that was first straight and afterward became crooked; and who is this?—a disciple of the Sages who forsakes the study of the Law.

8. [The rules about] release from vows[16] hover in the air and have naught to support them;[17] the rules about the Sabbath,[18] Festal-offerings, and Sacrilege[19] are as mountains hanging by a hair, for [teaching of] Scripture [thereon] is scanty and the rules many; the [rules about] cases [concerning property] and the [Temple-]Service, and the rules about what is clean and unclean and the forbidden degrees, they have that which supports them, and it is they that are the essentials of the Law.

2. 1. The forbidden degrees[20] may not be expounded before three persons,

---

[1] As opposed to what is already consecrated as Second Tithe money. See p. 73, n. 6. In other words (see Men. 7[6]) the Whole-offering is here deemed an 'offering of obligation'.
[2] Of which the flesh is available for the pilgrim's use to enable him to keep the Feast suitably.
[3] The Gemara points out that there is here a lacuna, and that it should read: 'On the 14th (of Nisan) a Festal-offering (cf. Pes. 6[4]) may be brought from (beasts bought with) Second Tithe money, but on the first Festival-day of Passover . . .'
[4] i.e. those who are not priests.
[5] To bring Peace-offerings and rejoice at the Feast.   [6] See Meg. 1[6].
[7] Lev. 27[32].   [8] Which only the priests may eat (Num. 18[9ff].)
[9] The flesh of which is to be eaten by the priests and their families (Num. 18[17-19]).
[10] See Lev. 7[31-39].   [11] See tractate Kinnim.
[12] Lev. 2[1-10]; what is left, after burning the 'handful', belongs to the priests.
[13] Deut. 16[17].   [14] Eccles. 1[15].   [15] Lev. 18[6-18].
[16] By resort to a Sage. See Ned. 9[1ff], 10[2ff].
[17] They have no basis except Num. 30[3-16].   [18] See tractate Shabbath; cf. Erub. 10[3, 15].
[19] Lev. 5[14-16]. See tractate Meilah.   [20] Lev. 18[6ff].

nor the Story of Creation[1] before two, nor [the chapter of] the Chariot[2] before one alone, unless he is a Sage that understands of his own knowledge. Whosoever gives his mind to four things it were better for him if he had not come into the world—what is above? what is beneath? what was beforetime? and what will be hereafter? And whosoever takes no thought for the honour of his Maker, it were better for him if he had not come into the world.

2. Jose ben Joezer[3] says: [On a Festival-day a man] may not lay [his hands on the offering[4] before it is slaughtered]; Joseph ben Johanan says: He may. Joshua b. Perahyah says: He may not; Nittai the Arbelite says: He may. Judah b. Tabbai says: He may not; Simeon b. Shetah says: He may. Shemaiah says: He may; Abtalion says: He may not. Hillel and Menahem did not differ, but Menahem went forth[5] and Shammai entered in. Shammai says: He may not lay on his hands; Hillel says: He may. The former [of each of these several pairs] were Presidents, and the others were Fathers[6] of the Court.

3. The School of Shammai say:[7] They may bring Peace-offerings [on a Festival-day] and not lay the hands thereon, but they may not bring Whole-offerings. And the School of Hillel say: They may bring both Peace-offerings and Whole-offerings and lay their hands thereon.

4. If the Feast of Pentecost fell on the eve of a Sabbath, the School of Shammai say: The day for slaughtering[8] is after the Sabbath. And the School of Hillel say: It needs no other day for slaughtering.[9] But they agree that if [the Feast] fell on a Sabbath, the day for slaughtering is after the Sabbath.[10] The High Priest may not put on his high-priestly vestments,[11] and mourning and fasting are permitted, to lend no support to the words of them that say, 'Pentecost falls on the day after the Sabbath'.[12]

5. For [the eating of food that is] unconsecrated or [Second] Tithe[13] or Heave-offering,[14] the hands need but to be rinsed;[15] and for Hallowed Things[16] they need to be immersed;[17] and in what concerns the Sin-offering water,[18] if a man's hands are unclean his whole body is deemed unclean.

[1] Gen. 1[1-2, 3].   [2] Ezek. 1[4ff.]; cf. Meg. 4[10].
[3] On him and the other 'Pairs', see Ab. 1[4-10].
[4] Cf. Lev. 1[4]. The controversy turns on whether it is permissible on a Festival-day (to which apply the same rules about work as apply to the Sabbath, except for the preparing of necessary food) to lay the hands on the beast that is to be sacrificed, since this act is performed with a man's whole weight, so that he 'makes use of' an animal in making it bear his burden, so profaning the Sabbath rule.
[5] Into king Herod's service. According to another tradition he became an Essene.
[6] 'Vice-presidents'.   [7] Betz. 2[4].
[8] The Re'iyyah Whole-offering. According to the School of Shammai it could not be offered on the Festival-day itself nor on the following Sabbath. Therefore Pentecost, though lasting but one day, is, for purpose of offerings, to be prolonged.
[9] Since it is permissible to slaughter it on the Festival-day. Some texts add: 'after the Sabbath'.
[10] Since, among private offerings, only the Passover-offering overrides the Sabbath.
[11] The eight mentioned in Yom. 7[5].
[12] i.e. the Sadducees, who maintained that it must always fall on a Sunday, because (Lev. 23[15ff.]) it is said that the Omer is offered on 'the morrow after the Sabbath', after which they were to number fifty days 'unto the morrow of the seventh Sabbath', when they keep the feast of Pentecost. Cf. Men. 10[3]. They took 'Sabbath' literally, and not, as the Pharisees, in the sense of the first Festival-day of Passover.   [13] See p. 73, n. 6.
[14] See App. I. 48, Terumah. Cf. p. 714, n. 3.
[15] Washed in the manner prescribed in Yad. 1[1].
[16] Such that need to be offered in the Temple, and are partly or in their entirety devoted to the Altar, and may only be consumed within the Temple Court.
[17] In a valid Immersion-pool containing forty seahs of undrawn water. See tractate Mikwaoth.
[18] Num. 8[7] (R.V.) 'the water of expiation'. See Num. 19[17-18]; p. 697, n. 3.

6. If a man immersed himself to render himself fit to eat of unconsecrated produce, and his intention was confined to unconsecrated produce, he may not touch [Second] Tithe. If he immersed himself to render himself fit to eat of [Second] Tithe, and his intention was confined to [Second] Tithe, he may not touch Heave-offering. If he immersed himself to render himself fit to eat of Heave-offering, and his intention was confined to Heave-offering, he may not touch Hallowed Things. If he immersed himself to render himself fit to eat of Hallowed Things, and his intention was confined to Hallowed Things, he may not touch Sin-offering water. If he immersed himself for the sake of what has a higher degree of sanctity, he is permitted to touch what is of lower degree. If he immersed himself but without special intention, it is as though he had not immersed himself at all.

7. For Pharisees[1] the clothes of an *Am-haaretz*[2] count as suffering *midras*-uncleanness;[3] for them that eat Heave-offering[4] the clothes of Pharisees count as suffering *midras*-uncleanness; for them that eat of Hallowed Things the clothes of them that eat Heave-offering count as suffering *midras*-uncleanness; for them that occupy themselves with the Sin-offering water the clothes of them that eat of Hallowed Things count as suffering *midras*-uncleanness. Joseph b. Joezer was the most pious in the priesthood, yet for them that ate of Hallowed Things his apron counted as suffering *midras*-uncleanness. Johanan b. Gudgada always ate [his common food] in accordance with [the rules governing] the cleanness of Hallowed Things, yet for them that occupied themselves with the Sin-offering water his apron counted as suffering *midras*-uncleanness.

3. 1. Greater stringency applies[5] to Hallowed Things than to Heave-offering; for vessels within vessels may be immersed together for Heave-offering, but not for Hallowed Things. The outside and inside and handle [of vessels are deemed separate][6] for Heave-offering, but not for Hallowed Things. He that carries aught that has contracted *midras*-uncleanness may carry[7] Heave-offering but not Hallowed Things. For [them that eat of] Hallowed Things the clothes of them that eat Heave-offering count as suffering *midras*-uncleanness. The rule [for the immersion of garments] for [them that would eat of] Heave-offering is not like the rule for [them that would eat of] Hallowed Things, since for Hallowed Things [a knot] must be unloosed and dried and immersed and then re-tied; but for Heave-offering it may be immersed while it is yet untied.

2. Utensils that have been completed and kept free of uncleanness require immersion before their use for Hallowed Things, but not before their use for Heave-offering. With Hallowed Things a vessel unites[8] all that is therein, but it is not so with Heave-offering. Hallowed Things can be rendered invalid [by uncleanness] at a fourth remove,[9] but Heave-

[1] Those who accept the Law according to its strictest interpretation; to their body belong those 'who undertake to be Associates'; cf. Dem. 2³.
[2] Lit. 'people of the land'. See App. I. 3.
[3] App. I. 26. Cf. Dem. 2³.   [4] Priests.   [5] In the eleven cases that follow.
[6] If one of these parts was made unclean by contact with an unclean liquid the others are not accounted unclean. See Kel. 25⁶ᶠᶠ.
[7] At the same time a vessel containing Heave-offering. But he must not touch the Heave-offering.
[8] If one portion is unclean it renders everything in the vessel unclean, even when they are not in contact.
[9] See App. IV. 17; cf. p. 714, n. 3; Toh. 2⁷. If *A* is a 'father of uncleanness' (cf,

offering only at a third remove. With Heave-offering, if one hand of a man contracted uncleanness, the other remains clean; but with Hallowed Things he must immerse them both, for the one hand renders the other unclean for Hallowed Things but not for Heave-offering.

3. Dry foodstuffs that are Heave-offering may be consumed with unwashed hands, but it is not so with Hallowed Things. He that mourns his near of kin[1] [even though he has not contracted corpse uncleanness] and he whose atonement is yet incomplete,[2] needs to immerse himself for Hallowed Things, but not for Heave-offering.

4. Greater stringency may apply to Heave-offering, for in Judea they are deemed trustworthy throughout the year in what concerns the cleanness of wine and oil,[3] but in what concerns Heave-offering [they are deemed trustworthy] only at the seasons of wine-presses and olive-vats.[4] If the season of the wine-presses and olive-vats was passed, and they brought to the priest a jar of Heave-offering wine, he may not accept it; howbeit [the owner] may leave it until the next season. But if he[5] had said to him, 'I have set apart a quarter-*log* as a Hallowed Thing',[6] he is deemed trustworthy.[7] They may be deemed trustworthy concerning jars of wine and jars of oil that are mixed with Heave-offering[8] during the season of wine-presses and olive-vats and seventy days[9] before the season of wine-presses.

5. From Modiith[10] and inwards[11] men may be deemed trustworthy[12] in what concerns earthenware vessels; from Modiith and outwards they may not be deemed trustworthy. Thus, if the potter himself sold the pot and came in hither from Modiith, in what concerns himself the potter, the selfsame pots, and the selfsame buyers,[13] he may be deemed trustworthy. If he went out [beyond Modiith] he may not be deemed trustworthy.

6. If tax-collectors entered a house[14] (so, too, if thieves restored [stolen] vessels), they may be deemed trustworthy if they say, 'We have not touched'. In Jerusalem men may be deemed trustworthy in what concerns Hallowed Things and, at the time of a Feast,[15] in what concerns Heave-offering also.

7. If a man opened his jar [of wine] or broke into his dough [to sell them] for the needs of the Feast,[16] R. Judah says: He may finish [selling them after the Feast]. But the Sages say: He may not finish.[17] When the Feast

---

p. 137, n. 11; App. IV. 3ff.) and touches *B*, and *B* touches *C*, and *C* touches *D*, if *D* is a Hallowed Thing it becomes invalid; and if *C* is Heave-offering it becomes invalid; but if *D* was Heave-offering it would not become invalid.   [1] See p. 147, n. 6.

[2] See Ker 2[1]. They are such who, having passed through the time of uncleanness prescribed in their case, have duly immersed themselves and awaited sunset, but have not yet brought their prescribed offerings.

[3] If an *Am-haaretz* averred that he had prepared them in conditions of cleanness they are reckoned valid for drink-offerings and Meal-offerings.

[4] When it is assumed that all has been done in cleanness, because of the sanctity of the Heave-offering. See Toh. 9[4].   [5] The *Am-haaretz* to the priest.

[6] 'I have put so much wine in this vessel to be used as a drink-offering.'

[7] As to its cleanness.

[8] Which must be sold to a priest at the price of Heave-offering, except for the value of the Heave-offering, which is the priest's by right. See Ter. 5[1ff].

[9] When they begin to clean the vessels for the wine.

[10] Pes. 9[2].   [11] Towards Jerusalem.

[12] The *Am-haaretz* is to be believed if he avers that they have been prepared in cleanness.

[13] Who themselves saw him come in and bought from him.   [14] Cf. Toh. 7[6].

[15] When all are assumed to be in a condition of cleanness.

[16] When men could buy from him (although he was an *Am-haaretz*) without fearing that his wares had been rendered unclean by him or others.

[17] i.e. the scrupulous may not buy from him afterwards, since it can no longer be assumed that the wares remain clean.

was over, they entered upon the cleansing of the Temple Court;[1] but they did not do so if the Feast ended on a Friday because of the honour due to the Sabbath. R. Judah says: Nor yet on a Thursday, for the priests had not [as yet] the leisure.[2]

8. How did they enter upon the cleansing of the Temple Court? They used to immerse the vessels that were in the Temple and say [to the priests],[3] 'Take heed lest ye touch the table[4] and render it unclean'. For all the utensils that were in the Temple they had a second and a third set, that if the first contracted uncleanness they might bring a second in their stead. All the utensils that were in the Temple required immersion, excepting the altar of gold[5] and the altar of bronze,[6] for they were reckoned as like to the ground.[7] So R. Eliezer. But the Sages say: Because they were plated [with metal].[8]

---

[1] Rashi: 'They used to remove the utensils from the Temple Court', to clean them lest they had been touched by any priest who was an *Am-haaretz*.
[2] They must first clear the Altar of ashes.
[3] Who were suspected of not being clean.
[4] The table of the Shewbread is meant. Some texts add: 'And the Candlestick'.
[5] Ex. 30[1ff.]   [6] 1 Kings 8[64].
[7] And as such they were not susceptible to uncleanness. Cf. Shebi. 10[7]; Uktz. 3[10].
[8] Cf. Kel. 11[2, 4, 6].

THIRD DIVISION
NASHIM
('WOMEN')

YEBAMOTH
KETUBOTH
NEDARIM
NAZIR
SOTAH
GITTIN
KIDDUSHIN

YEBAMOTH ('SISTERS-IN-LAW')

1. 1. Fifteen women [being near of kin to their deceased childless husband's brother][1] render their co-wives,[2] and the co-wives of their co-wives (and so on, without end) exempt from *halitzah* and levirate marriage; and these are they: his daughter, his daughter's or son's daughter, his wife's daughter and her son's or daughter's daughter, his mother-in-law and his mother-in-law's mother, his father-in-law's mother, his sister by the same mother and his mother's sister, his wife's sister and the wife of his brother by the same mother, and the wife of his brother who did not live at the same time as he, and his daughter-in-law; these render their co-wives, and the co-wives of their co-wives (and so on, without end) exempt from *halitzah* and levirate marriage. But if any among these died, or exercised right of Refusal,[3] or were divorced, or were found sterile, their co-wives are not exempt. Howbeit, thou canst not say of a man's mother-in-law or mother-in-law's mother or father-in-law's mother that they were found sterile or that they exercised right of Refusal.

2. How comes it that they 'render their co-wives . . . exempt'? If a man's daughter, or any women within the forbidden degrees, was married to his brother, who had yet another wife, and [this brother] died, then as his daughter is exempt so is her co-wife exempt. If his daughter's co-wife went and married a second [surviving] brother, who had yet another wife, and [this brother] died, then as his daughter's co-wife is exempt, so is the co-wife of the co-wife of his daughter exempt [and so on] even if they are a hundred [brothers]. How comes it that 'if they died . . . their co-wives are not exempt'? If a man's daughter, or any woman within the forbidden degrees, was married to his brother who had yet another wife, and his daughter died or was divorced, and afterward his brother died, her co-wife is not exempt [from *halitzah* and levirate marriage]. Any that had power to exercise right of Refusal but did not, [and her husband died], her co-wife must perform *halitzah* and may not contract levirate marriage.

3. To six [other] women within the forbidden degrees greater stringency applies than to these, since they may only be married to others;[4] and their co-wives are permitted [in marriage to the deceased husband's brother]: namely, his mother, his father's wife, his father's sister, his sister by the same father, his father's brother's wife, and the wife of his brother by the same father.

4. The School of Shammai[5] permit [levirate marriage] between the co-wives[6] and the [surviving] brothers; but the School of Hillel forbid it. If

---

[1] This tractate treats of the laws of 'levirate marriage' (*levir*, a brother-in-law) of Deut. 25[5-10], which require a man to take to wife his brother's widow if his brother had died childless. She may not be married to another unless he has refused to marry her. If he refuses he must submit to the ceremony of *halitzah*, 'the drawing-off' of the shoe, in the manner prescribed in Deut. 25[9f]. He must, however, have lived, no matter how short a time, in his deceased brother's lifetime. The widow must not be among those enumerated (Lev. 18[6-17]) among the 'forbidden degrees'. Furthermore if the deceased husband had two or more wives of whom one was within the degrees forbidden to the surviving brother, she renders the other wives exempt from the obligation of levirate marriage, without need of *halitzah*. This limitation is deduced by interpretation of Lev. 18[18]. On the prevalence of the custom of levirate marriage cf. Bekh. 1[7].

[2] See Lev. 18[18]; 1 Sam. 1[6], where the word is rendered 'rival'.

[3] See below, p. 237, n. 5.

[4] They were unlawfully married to the deceased brother (Maim.).

[5] Eduy. 4[8].   [6] Enumerated in par. 1.

they had performed *halitzah* the School of Shammai declare them ineligible to marry a priest,[1] but the School of Hillel declare them eligible. If they had been taken in levirate marriage the School of Shammai declare them eligible,[2] but the School of Hillel ineligible.[3] Notwithstanding that these forbid what the others permit, and these declare ineligible whom the others declare eligible, yet the [men of] the School of Shammai did not refrain from marrying women from [the families of] the School of Hillel, nor the [men of] the School of Hillel from marrying women from [the families of] the School of Shammai. Despite all the disputes about what is clean and unclean wherein these declare clean what the others declare unclean, neither scrupled to use aught that pertained to the others in matters concerned with cleanness.

2. 1. How comes it that 'the wife of his brother who did not live at the same time as he' [exempts the co-wife]? If there were two [married] brothers, and the first one died [childless] and a [third] brother was then born; and afterward the second brother took in levirate marriage his deceased brother's wife and then himself died; the wife of the first brother is exempt [from levirate marriage with the third brother] in that she was 'the wife of his brother who did not live at the same time as he', and the wife of the second brother [is exempt from levirate marriage with the third brother] in that she was her co-wife. If the second brother had only bespoken her[4] for himself and then died, his [first] wife must perform *halitzah* and may not contract levirate marriage [with the third brother].

2. If there were two [married] brothers and the first one died [childless] and the second took in levirate marriage his deceased brother's wife; and afterward a [third] brother was born and then the second brother died; the wife of the first brother is exempt [from levirate marriage with the third brother] in that she was 'the wife of his brother who did not live at the same time as he', and the wife of the second brother is exempt in that she was her co-wife. If the second brother had only bespoken her for himself and then died, his [first] wife must perform *halitzah* and may not contract levirate marriage [with the third brother]. R. Simeon says: He may contract levirate marriage with which of them he will, or submit to *halitzah* from which of them he will.

3. A general rule have they laid down about a childless brother's widow: if she is exempt by virtue of the forbidden degrees, she need neither perform *halitzah* nor contract levirate marriage; if she is exempt by virtue of an ordinance [of the Scribes] or by virtue of the holiness [of the levir] she must perform *halitzah* and may not contract levirate marriage; if her sister is also her sister-in-law[5] she may either perform *halitzah* or contract levirate marriage.

4. 'Exempt by virtue of an ordinance [of the Scribes]'—to wit, the secondary grades [of forbidden degrees] enjoined by the Scribes.[6] 'By

---

[1] Lev. 21[7]. Such count, according to the School of Shammai, as 'put away', divorced.
[2] If widowed.
[3] Since the levirate marriage was invalid they count as harlots (Lev. 21[7]).
[4] i.e. had not consummated the levirate union (as required by Deut. 25[5]) but had formally, before witnesses, accepted her as betrothed to him.   [5] See below, 3[3].
[6] Gem. 21a gives these as: (1) father's mother, (2) mother's mother, (3) father's father's mother, (4) mother's father's mother, (5) father's father's wife, (6) mother's father's wife, (7) mother's father's brother's wife, (8) father or mother's mother's brother's wife, (9) son's daughter's daughter, (10) daughter's daughter's daughter, (11) son's son's daughter,

virtue of the holiness [of the levir]'—to wit, a widow [is forbidden in marriage] to a High Priest,[1] a divorced woman or one that had performed *halitzah* [is forbidden] to a common priest,[2] a woman that is a bastard[3] or a *Nethinah*[4] [is forbidden] to an Israelite,[5] and a daughter of an Israelite [is forbidden] to a *Nathin* or a bastard.

5. If a man has any kind of brother,[6] such a brother imposes on his brother's wife the duty of levirate marriage, and he counts as his brother in every respect[7] unless he was the son of a bondwoman or a gentile woman.[8] If a man has any kind of son, such a son renders the wife of his father exempt from levirate marriage, he is culpable if he strikes or curses his father,[9] and he counts as his son in every respect unless he was the son of a bondwoman or a gentile woman.

6. If a man betrothed one of two sisters and he does not know which of them he betrothed, he must give a bill of divorce to each of them; if he died and had but one brother, such a one must submit to *halitzah* from each of them; if he had two brothers, one of them must submit to *halitzah* [from the one] and the other may [then] contract levirate marriage [with the other]; though if the two brothers had already taken them in marriage none can take them from them.

7. If two men betrothed two sisters and neither of them knows which of the two he betrothed, each of them must give two bills of divorce. If they died, and each had a brother, each of these must submit to *halitzah* from the two sisters. If one had one brother and the other two brothers, the one brother must submit to *halitzah* from both sisters, and of the two brothers one must submit to *halitzah* [from the one] and the other may [then] contract levirate marriage [with the other]; but if the two brothers had already taken them in marriage none may take them from them. If each of the two men [that died] had two brothers, then a brother of the first must submit to *halitzah* from one of the sisters and a brother of the second must submit to *halitzah* from the other of the sisters; and the other brother in each case may then contract levirate marriage with the sister at whose hands his brother submitted to *halitzah*; though if the two brothers of the first man had already submitted to *halitzah* the other two brothers may not then both contract levirate marriage, but the one must submit to *halitzah* and the other may [then] contract levirate marriage; but if they had already taken the two sisters in marriage none can take them from them.

8. The duty of levirate marriage falls on the elder [surviving brother], but if the younger brother forestalls him his marriage is valid. If a man was suspected of intercourse with a slave who afterward was freed, or with a gentile woman who afterward became a proselyte, he may not marry her; but if he married her none can take her from him. If a man was suspected of intercourse with a married woman and [the court] dissolved her marriage with her husband, even though he married her they must take her from him.[10]

---

(12) daughter's son's daughter, (13) wife's daughter's daughter's daughter, (14) wife's son's son's daughter, (15) wife's mother's mother's mother, (16) wife's father's mother's mother, (17) wife's mother's father's mother, (18) wife's father's father's mother, (19) son's daughter-in-law, (20) daughter's daughter-in-law. Some also add: (21) father's mother's father's wife, (22) father's father's brother's wife, (23) father or mother's father's father's sister, and (24) mother's mother's sister.   [1] Lev. 21[19].

[2] Lev. 21[7]; cf. above, p. 219, n. 1.   [3] See Yeb. 4[13].

[4] On the ground of Deut. 7[3]. See App. I. 29.   [5] A non-priest.   [6] Even a bastard.

[7] He can inherit from him and, if he is a priest, can (Lev. 21[2]) contract uncleanness because of him.   [8] In both cases the child has only the mother's status.

[9] Ex. 21[15, 27].   [10] According to Sot. 5[1] she is forbidden also to the paramour.

9. If a man brought a bill of divorce from [a man] beyond the sea,[1] and said: 'It was written in my presence and it was signed in my presence', he may not marry the man's wife. [If he said,] 'He is dead, [or] 'I killed him', [or] 'We killed him', he may not marry the man's wife. R. Judah says: [If he said,] 'I killed him', she may not marry [again], [but if he said,] 'We killed him', she may marry [again].

10. If a Sage pronounced a woman forbidden to her husband because of her vow,[2] the Sage may not marry her. If in her presence she exercised right of Refusal or performed *halitzah*, he may marry her, since he was [but a member of] the court.[3] And in every case, if they had wives and these [afterward] died, the [other] women may be married to them. And in every case if the women were married to others and [afterward] were divorced or became widows, they may be married to them; and in every case they may be married to their sons or brothers.[4]

3. 1. If[5] two of four brothers married two sisters, and the two that married the two sisters died, the sisters must perform *halitzah* and may not contract levirate marriage; and if the brothers had already married them they must put them away. R. Eliezer says: According to the School of Shammai they may continue the marriage, but according to the School of Hillel they must put them away.

2. If one of the sisters was forbidden to one of the brothers by virtue of the forbidden degrees,[6] he may not marry her, but he may marry her sister;[7] the second brother may not marry either. If one of the sisters was forbidden by virtue of an ordinance [of the Scribes] or by virtue of the holiness [of the levir] she must perform *halitzah* and may not contract levirate marriage.

3. If one of the sisters[8] was forbidden to one of the brothers by virtue of the forbidden degrees, and the other sister was forbidden to the other brother by virtue of the forbidden degrees, the sister forbidden to the first brother is permitted to the second, and the sister forbidden to the second is permitted to the first. This is the case whereof they have said: If her sister is also her sister-in-law she may either perform *halitzah* or contract levirate marriage.[9]

4. If two of three brothers married two sisters, or a woman and her daughter, or a woman and her daughter's daughter, or a woman and her son's daughter [and the two brothers died childless], the two widows must perform *halitzah* and may not contract levirate marriage [with the third brother]. R. Simeon declares them exempt [even from *halitzah*]. If one of the sisters was forbidden to him by virtue of the forbidden degrees, he is forbidden to her but he is not forbidden to the other; but if by virtue of an ordinance [of the Scribes] or by virtue of the holiness [of the levir], she must perform *halitzah* and may not contract levirate marriage.

5. If[10] there were three brothers, two married to two sisters and one unmarried, and one of the married brothers died and the unmarried one bespoke[11] the widow, and then his second brother died, the School of

---

1 Includes any place beyond the borders of the land of Israel.
2 She vowed that he should have no benefit from her, and the husband did not annul the vow (Num. 30[8]).   3 Of three; see Sanh. 1[3].
4 Of the messengers, witnesses, or Sages.
5 Eduy. 5[5].   6 If, e.g., she was his mother-in-law.
7 Since she is not a sister to one bound to him by the levirate tie.
8 Mentioned in par. 1.   9 See above, 2[3].   10 Eduy. 4[9].   11 See p. 219, n. 4.

Shammai say: His [bespoken] wife abides with him and the other is free as being the wife's sister. And the School of Hillel say: He must put away his [bespoken] wife both by bill of divorce and by *halitzah*, and his brother's wife by *halitzah*. This is the case whereof they have said, 'Woe to him because of [the loss of] his wife! and woe to him because of [the loss of] his brother's wife.'[1]

6. If there were three brothers, two married to two sisters and the other to a woman not near of kin, and the husband of one of the sisters died and the brother married to the woman not near of kin married the widow and then died, the widow is free [from levirate marriage with the surviving brother] in that she is the sister of his wife, and the woman not near of kin is free in that she was her co-wife. If he had only bespoken her for himself and then died, the woman not near of kin must perform *halitzah* and may not contract levirate marriage [with the surviving brother]. If there were three brothers, two married to two sisters and the other to a woman not near of kin, and the brother married to the woman not near of kin died and the husband of one of the sisters married the widow and then died, the first woman is free [from levirate marriage with the surviving brother] in that she is the sister of his wife, and the other woman in that she was her co-wife. If he had only bespoken her for himself and then died, the woman not near of kin must perform *halitzah* and may not contract levirate marriage [with the surviving brother].

7. If there were three brothers, two married to two sisters and the other to a woman not near of kin, and the husband of one of the sisters died and the husband of the woman not near of kin married the widow and then the wife of the other husband died, and afterward the husband of the woman not near of kin died also, then she[2] is forbidden to him for all time since she was forbidden to him during a certain time. If there were three brothers, two married to two sisters and the other to a woman not near of kin, and the husband of one of the sisters divorced his wife and the brother married to the woman not near of kin died, and then the brother who divorced his wife married the widow and then died; such is a case whereof they have said,[3] 'If any among them died . . . or were divorced . . . their co-wives are not exempt.'

8. And in every case[4] if their betrothal or divorce was in doubt, the co-wives must perform *halitzah* and may not contract levirate marriage. How can the betrothal be in doubt? If when he threw to her the betrothal-gift it was in doubt whether it lay nearer to him or nearer to her, such is a case where the betrothal was in doubt. How can the divorce be in doubt? If a man wrote out [the bill of divorce] in his own handwriting but there were no witnesses, or if there were witnesses but no date was given, or if there was a date given but only one witness was present, such is a case where the divorce was in doubt.

9. If three brothers were married to three women not near of kin and one of the brothers died and the second brother only bespoke the widow for himself and then died, the [two] widows must perform *halitzah* and may not contract levirate marriage [with the third brother], for it is written, [*If brethren dwell together*] *and one of them die . . . her husband's brother shall go in unto her*[5]—thus she is bound only to one brother-in-law and is not

---

[1] Cf. Yeb. 13[7].   [2] The surviving third sister.   [3] Above, 1[1].
[4] Of the fifteen enumerated above, 1[1].   [5] Deut. 25[5].

bound to two brothers-in-law. R. Simeon says: He may contract levirate marriage with which of them he will and submit to *halitzah* from the other. If two brothers were married to two sisters and one of the brothers died and afterward the wife of the other brother died, [the wife of the first brother] is forbidden to him for all time since she was forbidden to him during a certain time.

10. If two men had betrothed two women and when they entered into the bride-chamber the two women were exchanged, then both are culpable by virtue of the law of thy neighbour's wife;[1] and, if they were brothers, by virtue of the law of thy brother's wife;[2] and, if they were sisters, by virtue of the law of a woman and her sister;[3] and, if they were both menstruants, by virtue of the law of the menstruant.[4] They must be kept apart for three months lest they be with child. If they were minors and not like to bear children, they may forthwith be restored [to their proper husbands]. If they were priests' daughters they are rendered ineligible to eat of Heave-offering.[5]

4. 1. If a man submitted to *halitzah* from his deceased brother's wife and she was then found with child and gave birth, if the child was like to live,[6] [the *halitzah* is deemed void]: each is permitted to marry the other's kindred;[7] and he has not rendered her ineligible for marriage with a priest. But if the child was not like to live, neither is permitted to marry the other's kindred, and he has rendered her ineligible for marriage with a priest.

2. If a man consummated marriage with his deceased brother's wife and she was found [already] with child and gave birth, if the child was like to live, he must put her away and they must offer a [Sin-]offering.[8] But if the child was not like to live he may continue the marriage If it is in doubt whether what is born is a nine-months' child of the former [husband] or a seven-months' child of the latter [husband], he must put her away; the child is deemed legitimate; but they must offer a Suspensive Guilt-offering.[9]

3. If[10] a woman awaiting levirate marriage[11] inherited property, the School of Shammai and the School of Hillel agree that she may sell it or give it away and the act will be valid. If she died what should be done with her *Ketubah*[12] and property that comes in and goes out with her?[13] The School of Shammai say: The heirs of her [deceased] husband[14] share with the heirs of her father.[15] And the School of Hillel say: Her [*ṣon barzel*][16] property falls [equally] to them [both]: the *Ketubah* falls to the [deceased] husband's heirs, and the property that comes in and goes out with her falls to her father's heirs.

4. But if[17] the brother-in-law had consummated marriage with her, she counts as his wife in all respects save that her *Ketubah* is a charge on her first husband's goods.

---

[1] Lev. 18[20].   [2] Lev. 18[16].   [3] Lev. 18[18].   [4] Lev. 18[19].
[5] On the ground of Lev. 22[12, 13].   [6] Not a premature birth.
[7] See below, par. 7.   [8] Because of a forbidden connexion in error. Cf. Ker. 1[1-2].
[9] As prescribed in Lev. 5[17ff]. Cf. Ker. 1[2].   [10] Ket. 8[6].
[11] Tied to the surviving brother by the levirate bond, but not yet knowing whether he will take her, or submit to *halitzah*.   [12] See App. I. 16.
[13] *Melog* property. See App. I. 24. Cf. Yeb. 7[1].   [14] On the ground of B.B. 8[1].
[15] According to Gem. 39a the case here is one where the brother-in-law had 'bespoken her' (see p. 219, n. 4), and it is in doubt whether he can be accounted her husband (and heir).   [16] See App. I. 41.   [17] Ket. 8[7].

5. The duty of levirate marriage falls on the eldest [surviving] brother. If he was not willing it passes in turn to each of the other brothers, and if they were not willing they come again to the eldest and say to him, 'The duty falls on thee: submit to *halitzah* or contract levirate marriage'.

6. If he would hold his decision in suspense until a brother that was not of age should have come of age, or until an elder brother should have returned from beyond the sea, or until a brother that was a deaf-mute or an imbecile should recover, they do not listen to him but say, 'The duty falls on thee: submit to *halitzah* or contract levirate marriage'.

7. If a man submitted to *halitzah* from his deceased brother's wife he still counts as one of the brothers in what concerns inheritance;[1] but if the father was living the property falls to him.[2] If he consummated marriage with his deceased brother's wife he thereby acquires title to the property of his brother. R. Judah says: In either case if the father was living the property falls to him. If a man submitted to *halitzah* from his deceased brother's wife neither may marry the kindred of the other: [namely,] he may not marry her mother, her mother's mother, or her father's mother, her daughter, her daughter's daughter or her son's daughter or her sister (such time as the deceased brother's wife is living; but his brothers may marry her); and she may not marry his father, his father's father or his mother's father, his son, or his son's son or his brother or his brother's son. A man may marry one that is near of kin to the co-wife of his deceased brother's wife at whose hands he has submitted to *halitzah*, but not the co-wife of one that is near of kin to his deceased brother's wife at whose hands he has submitted to *halitzah*.

8. If a man submitted to *halitzah* from his deceased brother's wife and his brother married her sister and then died, the sister must perform *halitzah* and may not contract levirate marriage [with the first brother]; but if a man divorced his wife and his brother married her sister and then died, the sister is exempt both from *halitzah* and from levirate marriage.

9. If a woman awaited levirate marriage with a man whose [younger] brother betrothed her sister, the Sages said in the name of R. Judah b. Bathyra: They must say [to the younger brother], 'Wait until thine elder brother shall decide'.[3] If the elder brother submitted to *halitzah* or consummated the marriage the younger brother may consummate the marriage with his [betrothed] wife. And if the sister-in-law died, the younger brother may consummate the marriage with his [betrothed] wife. But if the elder brother died, he must put away his [betrothed] wife by a bill of divorce and submit to *halitzah* from his brother's wife.

10. Three months [of her widowhood] must pass by before the wife of the deceased brother may perform *halitzah* or contract levirate marriage. So, too, other widows may not [again] be betrothed or married before three months have passed, whether they are virgins or not virgins, whether they are divorced or widows, whether they were married or [only] betrothed. R. Judah says: They that had been married may forthwith be betrothed, and they that had been [only] betrothed may forthwith be married, excepting betrothed women in Judea, since [there] the bridegroom is less shamefast[4] before her. R. Jose says: All women may be

---

[1] From his deceased brother.   [2] See B.B. 8[2].

[3] Since the levirate tie applies to every brother, and in the event of the elder brother's failure to contract levirate marriage or to release her by *halitzah* the younger brother will be bound to two sisters.   [4] Cf. Ket. 1[5].

betrothed [again forthwith] excepting the widow, because of her [pre-scribed] time of mourning.[1]

11. If four brothers married four women and then died, and the eldest [of the brothers that remained] was minded to contract levirate marriage with all the widows, it is his right. If a man was married to two women and died, consummation or *halitzah* with the one wife exempts the co-wife. If one of them was eligible [for marriage with a priest] and the other ineligible, if the brother-in-law submitted to *halitzah* it must be from her that was ineligible; and if he contracted levirate marriage it must be with her that was eligible.

12. If a man re-married his divorced wife,[2] or married one at whose hands he had submitted to *halitzah* or one that was near of kin to her, he must put her away, and any child that is born is a bastard. So R. Akiba. But the Sages say: The child is not a bastard. But they agree that if a man married one that was near of kin to his divorced wife, any child [that is born] is a bastard.

13. Who is accounted a bastard?[3] [The offspring from] any [union of] near of kin which is forbidden [in the Law]. So R. Akiba. Simeon of Teman says: [The offspring of any union] for which the partakers are liable to Extirpation[4] at the hands of heaven. And the *Halakah*[5] is accord-ing to his words. R. Joshua says: [The offspring of any union] for which the partakers are liable to death at the hands of the court.[6] R. Simeon b. Azzai said: I found a family register in Jerusalem and in it was written, 'Such-a-one is a bastard through [a transgression of the law of] thy neigh-bour's wife',[7] confirming the words of R. Joshua. If a man's wife died he is permitted to marry her sister. If he divorced her and she afterward died he is permitted to marry her sister. If she was married again to another man and afterward died, he is permitted to marry her sister. If a man's deceased brother's wife died, he is permitted to marry her sister. If he submitted to *halitzah* from her and she afterward died, he is permitted to marry her sister.[8]

5. 1. Rabban Gamaliel said: No bill of divorce has validity after another bill of divorce,[9] and no statement [of betrothal] after another statement [of betrothal],[10] and no act of consummation after another act of consumma-tion, and no act of *halitzah* after another act of *halitzah*.[11] But the Sages say: A bill of divorce has validity after another bill of divorce, and a statement [of betrothal] after another statement [of betrothal]; but naught can validly follow consummation or *halitzah*.[12]

2. Thus if a man bespoke for himself his deceased brother's wife and then gave her a bill of divorce, he must still submit to *halitzah*. If he

---

1 Thirty days.   2 After she had married again. See Deut. 24[4].
3 Deut. 23[2].   4 Lev. 18[29]. See also Kidd. 3[12].   5 App. I. 11.   6 Sanh. 7[4].
7 Lev. 18[20].
8 Some texts add: 'If she afterward married another and then died, he is permitted to marry her sister. And in every case he is forbidden to marry her near of kin.'
9 i.e. if a man left two widows and the levir gave a bill of divorce to the first widow and afterwards another to the second, the second has no power, and the near of kin of the second are not forbidden to him.
10 If he bespoke one of them and then the second, the second needs no bill of divorce to release her; so, too, if two brothers bespoke the same widow one after the other, the word of the second brother has no binding force.
11 The second does not render the widow ineligible for marriage into the priestly stock.
12 The one act is the clinching of the levirate tie, the other is its final severance.

bespoke her and then submitted to *halitzah* she still requires of him a bill of divorce.[1] If he bespoke her and then consummated the marriage, such is her due.

3. If he gave her a bill of divorce and then bespoke her, she must receive of him a bill of divorce and must still perform *halitzah*. If he gave her a bill of divorce and then consummated the marriage, she must receive of him a bill of divorce and she must still perform *halitzah*. If he gave her a bill of divorce and then submitted to *halitzah*, naught can validly follow the *halitzah*. If he submitted to *halitzah* and then bespoke her, or gave her a bill of divorce and then consummated the marriage, or consummated the marriage and then bespoke her, or gave her a bill of divorce and then submitted to *halitzah*, naught can validly follow the *halitzah*, and it is all one whether there was one deceased brother's wife to one brother-in-law, or two deceased brothers' wives to one brother-in-law.

4. Thus if a man bespoke both deceased brothers' wives he must give two bills of divorce and submit to *halitzah* [from one of them]. If he bespoke one and gave a bill of divorce to the other, he must give the one a bill of divorce and submit to *halitzah* from the other. If he bespoke the one and consummated marriage with the other, he must give two bills of divorce and submit to *halitzah* [from one of them]. If he bespoke the one and submitted to *halitzah* from the other, the first must be given a bill of divorce. If he gave a bill of divorce to each, he must submit to *halitzah* from one. If he gave a bill of divorce to one and bespoke the other, he must give a bill of divorce to one and submit to *halitzah* from one. If he gave a bill of divorce to one and submitted to *halitzah* from the other, then after *halitzah* naught can validly follow.

5. If he submitted to *halitzah* from both or submitted to *halitzah* from one and bespoke the other, or gave a bill of divorce to one and consummated marriage with the other, or consummated marriage with both, or consummated marriage with one and bespoke the other, or gave a bill of divorce to one and submitted to *halitzah* from the other, naught can validly follow the *halitzah*, whether there was one brother-in-law to two deceased brothers' wives, or two brothers-in-law to one deceased brother's wife.

6. If he submitted to *halitzah* from her and then bespoke her, or gave her a bill of divorce or consummated marriage with her, or consummated marriage and then bespoke her or gave her a bill of divorce or submitted to *halitzah* from her, then naught can validly follow *halitzah*, whether this came in the beginning or in the middle or at the end. If the consummation came in the beginning, naught can validly follow; but if it came in the middle or at the end, somewhat else can validly follow.[2] R. Nehemiah says: It is the same with consummation as with *halitzah*: whether in the beginning or in the middle or at the end, naught can validly follow.

6. 1. If a man had connexion with his deceased brother's wife, whether in error or wantonness, whether under constraint or willingly, or even if he acted in error and she in wantonness, or he in wantonness and she in error, or he under constraint and she not under constraint, or she under constraint and he not under constraint, whether the act was partial or complete—he has thereby acquired her to wife; and there is no distinction respecting the manner of connexion.

---

[1] To annul the 'bespeaking', which has the force of betrothal (p. 219, n. 4).
[2] If consummation was not valid the levirate tie is still neither severed nor complete.

2. So, too, if a man had connexion with one from among the forbidden degrees spoken of in the Law, or from among them that are ineligible, (to wit,[1] a widow [who is forbidden in marriage] to a High Priest, a divorced woman or one that had performed *halitzah* to a common priest, a woman that is a bastard or a *Nethinah* to an Israelite, and a daughter of an Israelite to a bastard or a *Nathin*), he has thereby rendered her ineligible;[2] and there is no distinction respecting the manner of connexion.

3. If a widow was betrothed to a High Priest, or a divorced woman or one that had performed *halitzah* to a common priest, they[3] may not eat of Heave-offering.[4] R. Eliezer and R. Simeon declare them eligible. If they became widows or were divorced after wedlock, they are ineligible, but if after betrothal [only], they remain eligible.

4. A High Priest may not marry a widow[5] whether she had become a widow after betrothal or after wedlock; and he may not marry one that is past her girlhood.[6] But R. Eliezer and R. Simeon declare one that is past her girlhood eligible. He may not marry one that is not *virgo intacta*. If he had betrothed a widow and was afterward appointed High Priest, he may consummate the union. It once happened that Joshua b. Gamla betrothed Martha the daughter of Boethus, and he consummated the union after that the king appointed him High Priest. If a woman awaited levirate marriage with a common priest and he was appointed High Priest, although he had bespoken her he may not consummate the union. If the brother of the High Priest died, the High Priest must submit to *halitzah* and may not contract levirate marriage.[7]

5. A common priest may not marry a sterile woman unless he already had a wife or children. R. Judah says: Although he already had a wife or children he may not marry a sterile woman, for such is the harlot spoken of in the Law.[8] But the Sages say: The harlot refers only to a female proselyte, or to a freed bondwoman, or to one that suffered connexion of the nature of fornication.

6. No man may abstain from keeping the law *Be fruitful and multiply,*[9] unless he already has children: according to the School of Shammai, two sons; according to the School of Hillel, a son and a daughter, for it is written, *Male and female created he them.*[10] If he married a woman and lived with her ten years and she bare no child, it is not permitted him to abstain. If he divorced her she may be married to another and the second husband may live with her for ten years. If she had a miscarriage the space [of ten years] is reckoned from the time of the miscarriage. The duty to be fruitful and multiply falls on the man but not on the woman. R. Johanan b. Baroka says: Of them both it is written, *And God blessed them and God said unto them, Be fruitful and multiply.*[11]

7. 1. If a widow [was married] to a High Priest, or if a divorced woman or one that had performed *halitzah* [was married] to a common priest,[12] and she brought him in [as her dowry] *melog*[13] slaves and *ṣon barzel*[14] slaves, the *melog* slaves may not eat of Heave-offering,[15] but the *ṣon barzel* slaves may

---

[1] See above, 2[4].   [2] To marry a priest, or to eat of Heave-offering.
[3] Being of priestly stock.
[4] In their father's house, since they had married unlawfully.   [5] Lev. 21[14].
[6] Heb. *bogereth*, ripe for childbearing (see Nidd. 5[6ff.]), i.e. over twelve years and six months.   [7] Cf. Sanh. 2[1].   [8] Lev. 21[7].   [9] Gen. 1[28].
[10] Gen. 5[2].   [11] Gen. 1[28].   [12] See above, 2[4].   [13] App. I. 24.   [14] App. I. 41.
[15] The chapter deals with cases arising out of Lev. 22[10-13]. See also below, 9[c-6].

eat thereof. *Melog* slaves are such that, if they die, the wife suffers the loss, and if their value increases the wife enjoys the increase; though the husband is responsible for their maintenance they may not eat of Heave-offering. *Ṣon barzel* slaves are such that, if they die, the loss is suffered by the husband, and if their value increases the husband enjoys the increase; since his obligation is to restore them in full they may eat of Heave-offering.

2. If the daughter of an Israelite was married to a priest and [as her dowry] she brought him in slaves, be they *melog* or *ṣon barzel* property, they may eat of Heave-offering; but if a priest's daughter was married to an Israelite and brought him in either *melog* slaves or *son barzel* slaves, they may not eat of Heave-offering.[1]

3. If the daughter of an Israelite was married to a priest and he died leaving her with child, her slaves may not eat of Heave-offering by virtue of the portion that falls to the unborn child; for the unborn child can deprive[2] [a woman] of the right to eat [of Heave-offering] but it cannot bestow[3] [on her] the right. So R. Jose. The Sages said to him: After thou hast affirmed this to us of the daughter of an Israelite [married] to a priest, [wouldest thou also affirm] of the daughter of a priest [married] to a priest who died [childless] and left her with child, that her slaves may not eat of Heave-offering by virtue of the portion that falls to the unborn child?[4]

4. An unborn child, a levir, betrothal, a deaf-mute, or a boy nine years old and a day can deprive[5] [a woman] of the right to eat [of Heave-offering], but they cannot bestow [on her] the right, even if it is in doubt whether he is nine years old and a day or not,[6] or whether he has produced two hairs or not.[7] If a house fell upon a man and [his wife who was] his brother's daughter, and it is not known which of them died first, her co-wife must perform *halitzah* and may not contract levirate marriage.

5. The violator[8] and the seducer[9] and he that is an imbecile cannot deprive [the woman with whom they have connexion] of the right to eat [of Heave-offering][10] nor can they bestow [on her] the right;[11] but if they are such that are not fit to enter [into the congregation of] Israel,[12] they can deprive [the woman] of the right to eat.[13] Thus if an Israelite had connexion with the daughter of a priest she may [still] eat of Heave-offering; if she was got with child she may not eat of Heave-offering; if the unborn child in her bowels was cut out she may eat. If a priest had connexion with the daughter of an Israelite, she may not eat of Heave-offering; if she was got with child she may not eat; if she gave birth she may eat. [Thus] the power of the child is greater than that of the father. A slave disqualifies [a woman from eating of Heave-offering] by virtue of congress but not by

---

[1] They count during the marriage as his property. See Lev. 22[11, 12].

[2] If a priest's daughter was with child by an Israelite who died childless, she does not return to her father's house, there to eat of Heave-offering.

[3] If an Israelite's daughter was with child by a priest who died childless, the unborn child does not empower her to eat of Heave-offering; and the restriction applies equally to her slaves.

[4] A *reductio ad absurdum*, if the reason was that an unborn child grants no rights. R. Jose's reason, however, was that what is within the body of one of non-priestly stock counts as non-priestly stock in all respects.

[5] The priest's daughter is tied to the levir (a non-priest) and so cannot eat Heave-offering in her father's house. By betrothal the man acquires her as his property. Marriage to a deaf-mute is reckoned valid. Intercourse with one nine years and a day old renders her ineligible to marry a priest. Cf. Nidd. 5[5].

[6] But cf. Yeb. 10[8].   [7] Cf. Sanh. 8[1]; Nidd. 6[11].   [8] Deut. 22[29].

[9] Ex. 22[16-17].   [10] If she is the daughter of a priest.   [11] If they are priests.

[12] Deut. 23[2-9].   [13] Lev. 22[12].

virtue of offspring. Thus if the daughter of an Israelite was married to a priest, or a priest's daughter to an Israelite, and she bore a son by him, and the son went and had connexion with a bondwoman, and she bore a son by him, such a child is a bondman; and if his father's mother was the daughter of an Israelite married to a priest she may not eat of Heave-offering; but if she was a priest's daughter married to an Israelite she may eat of Heave-offering. A bastard may deprive [a woman] of the right to eat [of Heave-offering] and also bestow the right. Thus if the daughter of an Israelite was married to a priest, or a priest's daughter to an Israelite, and she bore a daughter by him and the daughter went and married a slave or a gentile and bore a son by him, such a child is a bastard; and if his mother's mother was the daughter of an Israelite married to a priest she may eat of Heave-offering, but if she was a priest's daughter married to an Israelite she may not eat of Heave-offering.

6. There are times when a High Priest can deprive [a woman] of the right [to eat of Heave-offering]. Thus if a priest's daughter was married to an Israelite and she bore a daughter by him, and the daughter went and married a priest and bore a son by him, such a child is fit to become a High Priest, to stand and minister at the Altar; he bestows on his mother[1] the right to eat [of Heave-offering], but he deprives his mother's mother of the right; and she may say, 'Let there not be the like of my grandson, the High Priest, who deprives me of the right to eat of Heave-offering'.

8. 1. The uncircumcised[2] and all they that are unclean may not eat of Heave-offering; [but] their wives and their slaves may eat of Heave-offering. *He that is wounded in the stones, or hath his privy member cut off*,[3] they and their slaves may eat of Heave-offering but their wives may not eat; but if such a one did not thereafter have connexion with his wife,[4] she may eat of Heave-offering.

2. Who is deemed *wounded in the stones*? He whose testicles are wounded or one only of them. And [who is he that] *hath his privy member cut off*? He whose member is cut. But if so much as a hair-thread of the crown remains he is eligible [to eat of Heave-offering]. *He that is wounded in the stones or hath his privy member cut off* is permitted to marry a female proselyte or a freed slave, only he may not enter into the assembly, for it is written, *He that is wounded in the stones or hath his privy member cut off shall not enter into the assembly of the Lord*.[5]

3. *An Ammonite or a Moabite*[6] is forbidden and forbidden for all time [to marry an Israelite], but their women are permitted forthwith. An Egyptian or an Edomite[7] whether male or female is forbidden only for three generations. R. Simeon declares their women forthwith permitted. R. Simeon said: It is an inference from the less to the greater: if where the menfolk[8] are for all time forbidden their women are forthwith permitted, how much the more where the menfolk are forbidden for but three generations should their women be forthwith permitted! They answered: If this is *Halakah*[9] [which thou hast received] we receive it; but if it is but an inference [of thine own] a counter-inference may rebut it. He answered:

---

[1] When his father is dead.
[2] Gem. 64b: a priest suffered to remain so, because his two brothers died of the operation.
[3] Deut. 23¹.   [4] But she was married to him prior to his disability.
[5] Deut. 23¹; i.e. may not marry an Israelite.   [6] Deut. 23³. Cf. Yad. 4⁴.
[7] Deut. 23⁷.   [8] And male offspring.   [9] App. I, 11.

Not so, but I declare what is *Halakah*. Bastards[1] and *Nathins*[2] are forbidden and forbidden for all time, whether they are males or females.

4. R. Joshua said: I have heard a tradition that a eunuch submits to *halitzah* and his brothers submit to *halitzah* from his wife; also [I have heard a tradition] that a eunuch does not submit to *halitzah* nor do his brothers submit to *halitzah* from his wife; and I cannot explain it. R. Akiba said: I will explain it. If he was a man-made eunuch he submits to *halitzah* and his brothers submit to *halitzah* from his wife, because there was a time when he was potent; but if he was a eunuch by nature he does not submit to *halitzah* nor do his brothers submit to *halitzah* from his wife, because there never was a time when he was potent. R. Eliezer says: Not so! but a eunuch by nature submits to *halitzah* and his brothers submit to *halitzah* from his wife, since he may be healed; but a man-made eunuch does not submit to *halitzah* nor do his brothers submit to *halitzah* from his wife, since he cannot be healed. R. Joshua b. Bathyra testified of Ben Megusath who lived in Jerusalem [and was] a man-made eunuch, that they contracted levirate marriage with his wife, confirming the words of R. Akiba.

5. A eunuch [by nature] does not submit to *halitzah* or contract levirate marriage; so, too, a woman that is sterile does not perform *halitzah* or contract levirate marriage. If a eunuch submitted to *halitzah* from his deceased brother's wife, he does not disqualify her [for marriage with a priest]; but if he had connexion he disqualifies her, since such connexion is of the nature of fornication. So, too, if brothers submitted to *halitzah* from a woman that is sterile they do not disqualify her, since connexion with her is of the nature of fornication.

6. If a priest that was a eunuch by nature married the daughter of an Israelite, he gives her the right to eat of Heave-offering. R. Jose and R. Simeon say: If a priest that was of double sex married the daughter of an Israelite, he gives her the right to eat of Heave-offering. R. Judah says: If one of doubtful sex was found to be a male when the impediment was removed, he may not submit to *halitzah* since he is accounted a eunuch [by nature]. One that is of double sex may marry [a wife], but none may marry him. R. Eliezer says: [Through connexion with] one that is of double sex the penalty of stoning is incurred as with a male.[3]

9. 1. Some women are permitted in marriage to their husbands and forbidden to their brothers-in-law; some are permitted in marriage to their brothers-in-law and forbidden to their husbands; some are permitted to both, and some are forbidden to both. These [are the cases in which the women] are permitted in marriage to their husbands and forbidden to their brothers-in-law: a common priest who married a widow and has a brother that is a High Priest; a man of impaired priestly stock[4] who married a woman that was eligible [for marriage with a priest] and has a brother of unimpaired priestly stock; an Israelite who married the daughter of an Israelite and has a bastard brother; a bastard who married a woman that is a bastard and has a brother who is an Israelite; these are the cases in which the women are permitted in marriage to their husbands and forbidden to their brothers-in-law.

2. These are the cases in which the women are permitted in marriage to

[1] Yeb. 4[13].   [2] App. I. 29.   [3] Sanh. 7[4].
[4] Lit. 'profaned'; cf. Lev. 21[4, 15]; see Kidd. 4[1, 6]. Such are the offspring of a union that transgresses the laws governing the marriage of the priestly stock. Lev. 21[7, 9, 13, 14].

their brothers-in-law and forbidden to their husbands: a High Priest who betrothed a widow and has a brother who is a common priest; a priest of unimpaired priestly stock who married a woman of impaired priestly stock and has a brother of impaired priestly stock; an Israelite who married a woman that was a bastard and has a brother who is a bastard; a bastard who married the daughter of an Israelite and has a brother who is an Israelite; these are the cases in which the women are permitted in marriage to their brothers-in-law and forbidden to their husbands. These are the cases in which the women are forbidden in marriage both to their husbands and to their brothers-in-law; a High Priest who married a widow and has a brother who is a High Priest or a common priest; a priest of unimpaired priestly stock who married a woman of impaired priestly stock and has a brother of unimpaired priestly stock; an Israelite who married a bastard and has a brother who is an Israelite; a bastard who married the daughter of an Israelite and has a bastard brother; these are the cases in which the women are forbidden in marriage both to their husbands and to their brothers-in-law. All other classes of women are permitted in marriage both to their husbands and to their brothers-in-law.

3. In what concerns the secondary grade [of forbidden degrees] enjoined by the Scribes,[1] if a woman is within the secondary grade of kinship to the husband but not within the secondary grade of kinship to the brother-in-law, she is forbidden in marriage to the husband and permitted to the brother-in-law; if she is within the secondary grade of kinship to the brother-in-law but not within the secondary grade of kinship to the husband, she is forbidden in marriage to the brother-in-law and permitted to the husband. If she is within the secondary grade of kinship to both she is forbidden in marriage to both, and she cannot lay claim to her *Ketubah*,[2] or to the increase [on her *melog* property], or to alimony,[3] or to indemnity [for loss on her *melog* property]; a child that is born is eligible [for the priesthood], but they compel the husband to put her away. If she was[4] a widow [married] to a High Priest, a divorced woman or one that had performed *halitzah* [married] to a common priest, a bastard or a *Nethinah* [married] to an Israelite, or the daughter of an Israelite [married] to a bastard or a *Nathin*, she can lay claim to her *Ketubah*.

4. If the daughter of an Israelite was betrothed to a priest, or was got with child by a priest, or awaited levirate marriage with a priest (and the same applies to a priest's daughter and an Israelite) she may not eat of Heave-offering. If the daughter of an Israelite was betrothed to a levite, or was got with child by a levite, or awaited levirate marriage with a levite (and the same applies to a levite's daughter and an Israelite) she may not eat of Tithe. If a levite's daughter was betrothed to a priest, or was got with child by a priest, or awaited levirate marriage with a priest (and the same applies to a priest's daughter and a levite) she may not eat of Heave-offering or of Tithe.

5. If the daughter of an Israelite was married to a priest she may eat of Heave-offering; if he died and she had a son by him, she may eat of Heave-offering. If she was married to a levite she may eat of Tithe; if he died and she had a son by him, she may eat of Tithe. If she was then married to an Israelite she may not eat of Heave-offering or of Tithe; if he died and

---

she had a son by him, she may not eat of Heave-offering or of Tithe. But
if her son by the Israelite died, she may [again] eat of Tithe; if her son by
the levite died, she may [again] eat of Heave-offering; if her son by the
priest died, she may not eat of Heave-offering or of Tithe.

6. If a priest's daughter was married to an Israelite she may not eat
of Heave-offering; if he died and she had a son by him she may not eat of
Heave-offering. If she was married to a levite she may eat of Tithe; if he
died and she had a son by him, she may eat of Tithe. If she was married
to a priest she may eat of Heave-offering; if he died and she had a son by
him, she may eat of Heave-offering. If her son by the priest died, she may
not eat of Heave-offering; if her son by the levite died, she may not eat of
Tithe; if her son by the Israelite died, she may return to her father's house;
and of her it is written, *If she is returned unto her father's house, as in her
youth, she shall eat of her father's bread.*[1]

10. 1. If a woman's husband had gone beyond the sea and it was told her,
'Thy husband is dead', and she married again and her husband then
returned, her marriage with them both is annulled, and she must receive
a bill of divorce from each of them, and from neither of them can she lay
claim[2] to her *Ketubah*, or to the increase [of her *melog* property], or to
alimony, or to indemnity [for loss on her *melog* property]; if she had taken
aught from either of them she must restore it; a child begotten by either
husband is a bastard; neither of them may contract uncleanness[3] for her
[if she died], and neither has a claim to aught found[4] by her or to the work
of her hands, or the right to set aside her vows.[5] If she was the daughter of
an Israelite she becomes ineligible for marriage with a priest, or, if the
daughter of a levite, to eat of Tithe, or, if the daughter of a priest, to eat of
Heave-offering. The heirs of neither husband may inherit her *Ketubah*.
If the husbands die, their brothers must submit to *halitzah* and may not
contract levirate marriage. R. Jose says: Her *Ketubah* remains a charge on
her first husband's goods. R. Eleazar says: The first husband has a claim
to aught found by her and to the work of her hands, and the right to set
aside her vows. R. Simeon says: If the first husband's brother consummated levirate marriage with her or submitted to *halitzah* from her she
renders her co-wife exempt [from levirate marriage], and a child begotten
by him is not a bastard. But if she had married again without the consent
[of the court being needful][6] she may return to her first husband.

2. If she had married again with the consent of the court [and her first
husband then returned], the [second] marriage is annulled, and she is not
liable to a Sin-offering;[7] but if [she had married again] without the consent
of the court, the marriage is annulled and she is also liable to a Sin-offering.
[Thus] the authority of the court exempts from the Sin-offering. If the
court gave her instruction that she could marry again but she contracted a
forbidden union, she is liable to the Sin-offering,[8] since their permission
was but that she could marry again.

3. If a woman's husband and son had gone beyond the sea and it was
told her, 'Thy husband died and then thy son died also', and she married
again and they then said to her, 'It was otherwise: [thy son died first and

---

[1] Lev. 22[13].   [2] See above, 9[3].   [3] If they were priests. See Lev. 21[1f].
[4] See B.M. 1[5]   [5] Num. 30[7f].   [6] If two had testified to her of her husband's death.
[7] Since it was an unwitting transgression as the result of the court's decision. See Hor.1[1].
[8] For unwitting transgression (Lev. 4[22ff].) of Lev. 18[6].

then thy husband]', the marriage must be annulled and a child born before or after [the second testimony] is a bastard. If they had said to her, 'Thy son died and then thy husband died also', and she thereupon contracted levirate marriage, and they then came and said, 'It was otherwise', the marriage must be annulled, and a child born before or after [the second testimony] is a bastard. If they had said to her, 'Thy husband is dead', and she married again, and they then came and said, 'He was then alive but he has since died', the marriage must be annulled, and if a child was born before [the second testimony] it is a bastard, but if it was born afterward it is not a bastard. If they had said to her, 'Thy husband is dead', and she became betrothed and her husband then returned, she is permitted to return to him. Although her [betrothed] husband gave her a bill of divorce he has not thereby disqualified her [for marriage with a priest]. This did R. Eleazar b. Mattai expound: [It is written,] *Neither shall they take a woman put away from her husband*;[1] and not 'from a man that is not [yet fully] her husband'.

4. If a man's wife had gone beyond the sea and it was told him, 'Thy wife is dead', and he married her sister, and his wife then came back, she is permitted to return to him; and he is permitted to marry the near of kin to the second woman, and the second woman is permitted to marry his near of kin; and if the first died he is permitted to marry the second. If they had said to him, 'Thy wife is dead', and he married her sister, and they then said to him, 'She was then alive but she has since died', if a child was born before [the second testimony] it is a bastard, but if it was born afterward it is not a bastard. R. Jose says: Whosoever disqualifies [his wife] for [marriage with] others, disqualifies her for himself, and whosoever does not disqualify her for [marriage with] others does not disqualify her for himself.

5. If they had said to him, 'Thy wife is dead', and he married her sister by the same father,[2] [and they then said to him], 'She too is dead', and he married her sister by the same mother,[3] [and they then said to him,] 'She too is dead', and he married her sister by the same father,[2] [and they then said to him,] 'She too is dead', and he married her sister by the same mother,[3] and it is then found that they are all alive, he is permitted [to continue] with the first, with the third, and with the fifth;[4] and these render their co-wives exempt [from levirate marriage]; and he is forbidden [to continue] with the second and the fourth, and although he consummated the union with either of them they do not render their co-wives exempt. If he had connexion with the second after the death of the first, he is then permitted to marry the second and the fourth, and these render their co-wives exempt; but he is then forbidden [to continue] with the third and with the fifth, and although he consummated the union with either of them they do not render their co-wives exempt.

6. A boy nine years old and a day can render a deceased brother's wife ineligible for [marriage with] his brothers;[5] and his brothers can render her ineligible for [marriage with] him, save that he can render her ineligible

---

[1] Lev. 21[7].   [2] But another mother.
[3] And another father and so unrelated to the previous wife but one.
[4] Since these are not related to each other. Though the third is sister to the second, the second's marriage is no marriage; and the near kin of a woman who has had extra-marital relations with a man are still permitted to that man. See below, 11[1].
[5] If he had connexion with her or had bespoken her (p. 219, n. 4).

only from the outset, whereas they can render her ineligible whether from the outset or at the end. Thus if a boy nine years old and a day had connexion with his deceased brother's wife, he renders her ineligible for [marriage with] his brothers [although they had bespoken her]; but whether the brothers had connexion with her, or bespoke her, or gave her a bill of divorce, or submitted to *halitzah* from her, they render her ineligible for him.

7. If a boy nine years old and a day had connexion with his deceased brother's wife, and then his brother who was nine years old and a day had connexion with her, he renders her ineligible for the former. R. Simeon says: He does not render her ineligible.

8. If a boy nine years old and a day had connexion with his deceased brother's wife, and he then had connexion with her co-wife, he renders [both] ineligible for [marriage with] himself. R. Simeon says: He does not render them ineligible. If a boy nine years old and a day had connexion with his deceased brother's wife, and he then died, she must perform *halitzah* and may not contract levirate marriage. If he had married [some other] woman and then died, she is exempt [from *halitzah* and levirate marriage].

9. If boy nine years old and a day had connexion with his deceased brother's wife and after he was come of age he married another woman and then died, if he had not known the first one after he has come of age, the first one must perform *halitzah* and may not contract levirate marriage, and the second may either perform *halitzah* or contract levirate marriage. R. Simeon says: He may contract levirate marriage with which of them he will and submit to *halitzah* from the other. It is all one whether he is nine years old and a day or whether he is twenty years old and has not grown two hairs.[1]

11. 1. A man may marry the near of kin of a woman that was violated or seduced [by him]. He that violates or seduces the near of kin of his married wife is culpable.[2] A man may marry a woman that was violated or seduced by his father, or a woman that was violated or seduced by his son. R. Judah forbids a man to marry a woman that was violated or seduced by his father.

2. If the sons of a female proselyte became proselytes with her, they[3] are not subject to the law of *halitzah* or of levirate marriage, even if the one son was born in holiness[4] but not conceived in holiness while the second was both born and conceived in holiness. So, too, if the sons of a bond-woman have been freed with her.

3. If the [newly-born] children of five women were confused together and grew up still confused,[5] and married wives and then died, four [of their other brothers who were not confused] must submit to *halitzah* from one of the wives, and the one [other brother] may then contract levirate marriage with her; then he and three others [of the surviving brothers] must submit to *halitzah* from the next wife and another brother may then contract levirate marriage with her, [and so, too, with the three remaining wives]; thus each wife four times performs *halitzah* and once contracts levirate marriage.

---

[1] If he had not the recognized signs of puberty he still counts as not of age: see Nidd. 5⁹.
[2] Lit. 'liable', namely to death by burning or Extirpation. Lev. 20¹⁴; 18²⁹.
[3] If one of the sons died childless.   [4] i.e. after the mother became a proselyte.
[5] And each had another son not confused.

4. If a woman's newly-born child was confused with the newly-born child of her daughter-in-law, and they grew up still confused, and married wives and then died, the [unconfused] sons of the daughter-in-law must submit to *halitzah* and may not contract levirate marriage, since [for each] it is in doubt whether the widow is the wife of his brother or of his father's brother; but the [unconfused] sons of the grandmother may either submit to *halitzah* or contract levirate marriage, since [for each] it is only in doubt whether the widow is his brother's wife or his brother's son's wife. If the unconfused sons died, the confused sons must submit to *halitzah* from the widows of the sons of the grandmother, and may not contract levirate marriage, since [for each] it is in doubt whether the widow is his brother's wife or his father's brother's wife; and [as touching the widows of] the sons of the daughter-in-law, [of the two confused sons] one submits to *halitzah* and the second may then contract levirate marriage with the other.

5. If the child of a priest's wife was confused with the child of her bondwoman, both may eat of Heave-offering and take their share together at the threshing-floor;[1] they may not contract uncleanness because of the dead;[2] and they may not marry women that are eligible or that are ineligible [for marriage with a priest].[3] If they grew up still confused and then freed one another, they may only marry women eligible for [marriage with] the priestly stock,[4] and they may not contract uncleanness because of the dead; but if they do contract uncleanness they do not incur the Forty Stripes;[5] they may not eat of Heave-offering, but if they have eaten thereof they do not pay the value and the [Added] Fifth;[6] they may not share at the threshing-floor; they may sell the Heave-offering[7] and keep the price; they may take no share in the Hallowed Things[8] of the Temple; none may give them Hallowed Things, but none may take away from them what they have; they are exempt from [giving to the priests] the shoulder, and the two cheeks and the maw;[9] and their Firstlings[10] must be left to pasture until they suffer a blemish; and the more stringent rulings touching priests and touching Israelites apply to them.[11]

6. If a woman had not delayed three months after [separation[12] from] her husband and married again and gave birth, and it is not known whether it was a nine-months' child by the former [husband] or a seven-months' child by the latter [husband], if she has sons both by the earlier and the later husbands these must submit to *halitzah* [from the widow of the son whose father is in doubt] and may not contract levirate marriage; so, too, he [whose father is in doubt] must submit to *halitzah* [from their widows] and may not contract levirate marriage. If he has brothers by both the first husband and the second husband, but not by the same mother, he may either submit to *halitzah* or contract levirate marriage; but as for them, [if he died childless and left a widow] a son [by the first or else by the

---

[1] Where the portion for Heave-offering was allotted. According to Lev. 22[11] a priest's bondman may eat of Heave-offering.   [2] Lev. 21[1]. Since either may be a priest.

[3] Since each might be a priest or might be a slave.   [4] See Kidd. 4[1ff].

[5] See Makk. 3[1f]. Stripes are the punishment incurred for transgression of a negative command where the Law has not specified a particular punishment.

[6] Lev. 22[11]; see B.M. 4[8].   [7] From their own harvest.

[8] Not even the hides of the offerings or what is devoted (Num. 18[14]) to the Temple.

[9] See Deut. 18[3]; Hull. 10[1ff].

[10] Num. 18[18]. They cannot consume them since they may not be priests, and they cannot be forced to give them to priests since they themselves may be priests.

[11] According to Gem. 100a this refers to the Meal-offering, and both Lev. 2[1-3] and 6[14-17] apply.   [12] By divorce or death.

second husband] must submit to *halitzah*, then a son [by the second or else by the first husband] may contract levirate marriage.

7. If one [of these husbands] was an Israelite and the other a priest, he [whose father is in doubt] may marry none save a woman eligible for [marriage with] a priest; and he may not contract uncleanness because of the dead, but if he contracts uncleanness he does not incur the Forty Stripes; he may not eat of Heave-offering, but if he has eaten thereof he does not pay the value and the [Added] Fifth; he may take no share at the threshing-floor; he may sell the Heave-offering and keep the price; he may take no share in the Hallowed Things of the Temple; none may give him Hallowed Things, but none may take away from him what he has; he is exempt from [giving to the priests] the shoulder, and the two cheeks and the maw; and his Firstlings must be left to pasture until they suffer a blemish; and the more stringent rulings touching priests and touching Israelites apply to him. If both [the husbands] were priests, he must perform mourning for them and they must perform mourning for him,[1] but he may not contract uncleanness because of them nor may they contract uncleanness because of him; he may not inherit from them, but they may inherit from him,[2] and he is not culpable if he smites or curses either of them,[3] he may go up [to serve in the Temple] during the [weekly] Course[4] of either of them; he may not share with them [in the offerings]; but if they both serve in the same Course he may take a single portion.

12. 1. The rite of *halitzah* must be performed before three judges,[5] even though the three are laymen. If the woman performed *halitzah* with a shoe it is valid, but if with a felt sock it is not valid; if with a sandal that has a heel-piece it is valid, but if with one that has no heel-piece it is not valid. [If the straps of the sandal were fastened] below the knee, her *halitzah* is valid; but if above the knee, it is not valid.

2. If she performed *halitzah* with a shoe that did not belong to the brother-in-law, or with a wooden sandal, or with a left-foot shoe worn on the right foot, her *halitzah* is valid; if she performed it with a shoe that was too large for him but such that he could walk in it, or with a shoe that was too small for him but such that it covered the greater part of his foot, her *halitzah* is valid. If she performed it by night her *halitzah* is valid. But R. Eliezer declares it invalid. If she performed it with the left foot her *halitzah* is invalid. But R. Eliezer declares it valid.

3. If she drew off the shoe and spat but did not pronounce the prescribed words her *halitzah* is valid. If she pronounced the words and spat but did not draw off the shoe, her *halitzah* is invalid. If she drew off the shoe and pronounced the words but did not spit, according to R. Eliezer her *halitzah* is invalid, but according to R. Akiba it is valid. R. Eliezer said: [It is written,] *So shall it be done . . .*;[6] hence aught that is a 'deed' [if unperformed] impairs [the validity of the rite]. R. Akiba answered: [My] proof is from the same verse: *So shall it be done to the man . . .*; hence [the validity of the rite depends on] any deed that needs to be *done to the man.*

4. If *halitzah* was performed on a deaf-mute or by a woman that was a deaf-mute, or if a woman performed *halitzah* on a minor, her *halitzah* is not valid. If a girl that was still a minor performed *halitzah* she must

---

[1] If they or he died. On the day of the death of his near of kin a priest is forbidden to minister in the Temple or to eat of Hallowed Things.   [2] B.B. 8².
[3] Ex. 21¹⁵, ¹⁷.   [4] Taan. 2⁶.   [5] Sanh. 1³.   [6] Deut. 25⁹.

[again] perform *halitzah* when she is of age, and if she does not do so her [first] *halitzah* becomes invalid.

5. If she performed *halitzah* before two judges only, or before three of whom one was found to be near of kin or ineligible [as a judge], her *halitzah* is invalid. R. Simeon and R. Johanan the Sandal-maker declare it valid. Once a man submitted to *halitzah* when he and she were alone together in prison; the case came before R. Akiba and he declared it valid.

6. This is the prescribed rite[1] of *halitzah*: When the man and his deceased brother's wife are come to the court the judges proffer such advice to the man as befits him, for it is written, *Then the elders of the city shall call him and speak unto him.* And she shall say: *My husband's brother refuseth to raise up unto his brother a name in Israel: he will not perform the duty of a husband's brother to me.* And he shall say, *I like not to take her.* And they used to say this in the Holy Language.[2] *Then shall his brother's wife come unto him in the presence of the elders and loose his shoe from off his foot and spit in his face*—such spittle as can be seen by the judges; *and she shall answer and say, So shall it be done unto the man that doth not build up his brother's house.* Thus far used they to rehearse [the prescribed words]. But when R. Hyrcanus under the terebinth in Kefar Etam[3] rehearsed it and completed it to the end of the section, the rule was established to complete the section.[4] [To say the words] *And his name shall be called in Israel, The house of him that hath his shoe loosed,* was a duty that fell upon the judges and not upon the disciples. But R. Judah says: It was a duty that fell upon all them that stood there to cry out, 'The man that hath his shoe loosed! The man that hath his shoe loosed! The man that hath his shoe loosed!'

13. 1. The School of Shammai say: Only they that are betrothed may exercise right of Refusal.[5] And the School of Hillel say: Both they that are betrothed and they that are married. The School of Shammai say: [They may exercise the right] against a husband [only], and not against a brother-in-law.[6] And the School of Hillel say: Either against a husband or against a brother-in-law. The School of Shammai say: [It must be exercised] in his presence. And the School of Hillel say: Either in his presence or not. The School of Shammai say: It must be before the court. And the School of Hillel say: Either before the court or not. The School of Hillel said to the School of Shammai: While she is yet under age she may exercise right of Refusal four or five times. The School of Shammai answered: The daughters of Israel are not [such] ownerless property! but, rather, she exercises right of Refusal and waits until she is come of age, or she exercises right of Refusal and [forthwith] marries [some other].

2. Who is the minor that must exercise right of Refusal? Any whose mother or brothers have with her consent given her in marriage. If they did so without her consent she need not exercise right of Refusal. R. Hanina b. Antigonus says: Any girl that is unable to keep safe her betrothal-gift[7] does not need to exercise right of Refusal. R. Eliezer says: The act of a minor is in no wise valid: she is but as one that has been

---

[1] Deut. 25[7-10].   [2] Cf. Sot. 7[4].   [3] 2 Chron. 11[6].   [4] To include verse 10.
[5] If a girl that was a minor was, after her father's death, given in marriage by her mother or brothers, she may abjure the contract before two witnesses, and be set free without the need of a bill of divorce.   [6] With whom she is bound by the levirate tie.
[7] See Kidd. 2[1f].

seduced; if she was the daughter of an Israelite and married to a priest she may not eat of Heave-offering; and if she was a priest's daughter married to an Israelite she may eat of Heave-offering.[1]

3. R. Eliezer b. Jacob says: If any hindrance [in the marriage] arose from the husband, it is accounted as though she had been his wife; but if any hindrance arose not from the husband, it is accounted as though she had not been his wife.

4. [Thus] if she exercised right of Refusal against a man, he is permitted to marry her near of kin, and she is permitted to marry his near of kin; and he has not thereby disqualified her for marriage with a priest. If he gave her a bill of divorce, they are forbidden to marry each other's near of kin, and he thereby disqualifies her for marriage with a priest. If he gave her a bill of divorce and afterward remarried her, or if she exercised right of Refusal against him and married another and then became a widow or was divorced, she is permitted to return to him. If she exercised right of Refusal against him and he afterward married her, or if he gave her a bill of divorce and she married another, and she then became a widow or was divorced, she is forbidden to return to him. This is the general rule: if the bill of divorce followed after that she exercised right of Refusal she is forbidden to return to him; if she exercised right of Refusal after the bill of divorce, she is permitted to return to him.

5. If she exercised right of Refusal against a man and married another and he divorced her, and she was [then] given in marriage to another, and she exercised right of Refusal against him, and she then married another and he divorced her, and she was then given in marriage to another and she exercised right of Refusal against him, from whatsoever man she was separated by a bill of divorce to him she is forbidden to return; but if [she was separated] by her exercise of right of Refusal, to him she is permitted to return.

6. If a man divorced his wife and married her again, she is permitted to marry her deceased husband's brother; but R. Eliezer forbids it. So, too, if a man divorced [his wife who was] an orphan and married her again she is permitted to marry her deceased husband's brother; but R. Eliezer forbids it. If a minor was given in marriage by her father and she was divorced, she is deemed 'an orphan in her father's lifetime';[2] if he married her again all agree that she is forbidden to marry her deceased husband's brother.

7. If two brothers were married to two sisters that were minors and orphans, and the husband of one of them died, she is exempt [from levirate marriage] by virtue of being the sister of his wife;[3] so, too, with two sisters that were deaf-mutes. If one was of age and the other a minor and the husband of the minor died, she is exempt [from levirate marriage] by virtue of being the sister of his wife. If the husband of her that was of age died, R. Eliezer says: The minor is instructed to exercise right of Refusal against her husband. Rabban Gamaliel says: If she does so the Refusal is valid; but if she does not, she may wait until she is of age, and then the other is exempt [from levirate marriage] by virtue of being the sister of his wife. R. Joshua says: Woe to him[4] because of [the loss of] his wife and

---

[1] Lev. 22[12]. She still counts as in her father's control.
[2] She does not count as within her father's control and he cannot give her in betrothal. Cf. Ned. 11[10].   [3] Lev. 18[18].   [4] Yeb. 3[5].

woe to him because of [the loss of] his brother's wife! He must put away his wife by a bill of divorce, and from his brother's wife he must submit to *halitzah*.

8. If a man was married to two orphans that were under age and he died, consummation or *halitzah* with the one exempts her co-wife. So, too, with two deceased brothers' widows that were deaf-mutes.[1] But if the one was a minor and the other a deaf-mute, consummation with the one does not exempt her co-wife. But if one was of sound senses and the other a deaf-mute, consummation with the first exempts the second; but consummation with the second does not exempt the first. If one was of age and the other a minor, consummation with the first exempts the second; but consummation with the second does not exempt the first.

9. If a man was married to two orphans that were minors, and he died, if the deceased husband's [eldest surviving] brother had connexion with the first and then again with the second, or if his brother had connexion with the second, this does not render the first ineligible [to continue the levirate marriage]. So, too, with two that were deaf-mutes. If one was a minor and the other a deaf-mute, and the deceased husband's [eldest surviving] brother had connexion with the minor and then again with the deaf-mute, or if his brother had connexion with the deaf-mute, this does not render the minor ineligible [to continue the levirate marriage]. If the deceased husband's brother had connexion with the deaf-mute and then again with the minor, or if his brother had connexion with the minor, this renders the deaf-mute ineligible [to continue the levirate marriage].

10. If one [of the deceased husband's widows] was of sound senses and the other a deaf-mute, and the deceased husband's brother had connexion with her of sound senses and then again with the deaf-mute, or if his brother had connexion with the deaf-mute, this does not render ineligible her of sound senses. But if the deceased husband's brother had connexion with the deaf-mute and then again with her of sound senses, or if his brother had connexion with her of sound senses, this renders the deaf-mute ineligible.

11. If one was of age and the other a minor and the deceased husband's brother had connexion with her that was of age and then again with her that was a minor, or if his brother had connexion with the minor, this does not render her that was of age ineligible. But if the deceased husband's brother had connexion with the minor and then again with her that was of age, or if his brother had connexion with her that was of age, this renders the minor ineligible. R. Eliezer says: The minor is instructed to exercise against him her right of Refusal.

12. If a deceased husband's brother that was a minor had connexion with his deceased brother's wife that was a minor, they must wait together until they are of age; if he had connexion with his deceased brother's wife that was of age, she must wait until he is of age. If during thirty days a deceased brother's wife said [of the deceased husband's brother], 'I have not been granted consummation', they compel him to submit to *halitzah* from her. If she said so after thirty days, they may only ask of him to submit to *halitzah* from her. But if he admitted her charge they compel him to submit to *halitzah* from her, even if it is after twelve months.

13. If in her husband's lifetime a woman vowed to have no benefit from

---

[1] Though *halitzah* cannot be valid with deaf-mutes.

her husband's brother, they compel him to submit to *halitzah* from her. But if she had so vowed with this intent during her husband's lifetime they may only ask of him to submit to *halitzah* from her.

14. 1. If a man that was a deaf-mute married a woman that was of sound senses, or if a man that was of sound senses married a woman that was a deaf-mute, if he will he may put her away, and if he will he may continue the marriage. Like as he married her by signs[1] so he may put her away by signs. If a man of sound senses married a woman of sound senses and she became a deaf-mute, if he will he may put her away, and if he will he may continue the marriage. If she became imbecile he may not put her away. If he became a deaf-mute or imbecile he may never put her away. R. Johanan b. Nuri said: Why should it be that if the woman became a deaf-mute she may be put away, yet if the man became a deaf-mute he cannot put her away? They answered: The man that divorces is not like to the woman that is divorced; for a woman is put away with her consent or without it, but a husband can put away his wife only with his own consent.

2. R. Johanan[2] b. Gudgada testified of a woman that was a deaf-mute and that was given in marriage by her father [while she was yet a minor], that she could be put away by a bill of divorce. The Sages said to him:[3] In such case, too, the same rule applies.

3. If two deaf-mute brothers were married to two deaf-mute sisters, or to two sisters of sound senses, or to two sisters of whom one was a deaf-mute and the other of sound senses; or if two deaf-mute sisters were married to two brothers of sound senses, or to two deaf-mute brothers, or to two brothers of whom one was a deaf-mute and the other of sound senses—such women [if their husbands die childless] are exempt from *halitzah* and levirate marriage. But if [the women] were not near of kin they must be taken in marriage [by their brother-in-law and they may not perform *halitzah*]; and if it is their wish to put them away they may put them away.

4. If two brothers, of whom one was a deaf-mute and the other of sound senses, were married to two sisters of sound senses, and the deaf-mute husband of the wife of sound senses died, what shall the husband of sound senses with the wife of sound senses do? [Nothing, because] the widow is exempt [from levirate marriage] by virtue of being the sister of his wife. If the husband of sound senses with the wife of sound senses died, what shall the deaf-mute husband with the wife of sound senses do? He must put away his wife by a bill of divorce, and his brother's wife is for all time forbidden to him [in marriage].

5. If two brothers of sound senses were married to two sisters of whom one was a deaf-mute and the other of sound senses, and the husband of sound senses with the deaf-mute wife died, what shall the husband of sound senses with the wife of sound senses do? [Nothing, because] the widow is exempt [from levirate marriage] by virtue of being the sister of his wife. If the husband of sound senses with the wife of sound senses died, what shall the husband of sound senses with the deaf-mute wife do? He must put away his wife by a bill of divorce and submit to *halitzah* from his brother's wife.

6. If two brothers of whom one was a deaf-mute and the other of sound

---

1 Cf. Gitt. 5[7].   2 Gitt. 5[5]; Eduy. 7[9] (Nehunya).   3 Johanan b. Nuri.

senses were married to two sisters of whom one was a deaf-mute and the other of sound senses, and the deaf-mute husband with the deaf-mute wife died, what shall the husband of sound senses with the wife of sound senses do? [Nothing, because] the widow is exempt [from levirate marriage] by virtue of being the sister of his wife. If the husband of sound senses with the wife of sound senses died, what shall the deaf-mute husband with the deaf-mute wife do? He must put away his wife by a bill of divorce and his brother's wife is for all time forbidden to him.

7. If two brothers, of whom one was a deaf-mute and the other of sound senses, were married to two women not near of kin, of sound senses, and the deaf-mute husband with the wife of sound senses died, what shall the husband of sound senses with the wife of sound senses do? He may either submit to *halitzah* or contract levirate marriage. If the husband of sound senses with the wife of sound senses died, what shall the deaf-mute husband with the wife of sound senses do? He must take her in marriage and he may never put her away.

8. If two brothers of sound senses were married to two women not near of kin of whom one was of sound senses and the other a deaf-mute, and the husband of sound senses with the deaf-mute wife died, what shall the husband of sound senses with the wife of sound senses do? He must marry her, and if he would put her away he may. If the husband of sound senses with the wife of sound senses died, what shall the husband of sound senses with the deaf-mute wife do? He may either submit to *halitzah* or contract levirate marriage.

9. If two brothers, of whom one was a deaf-mute and the other of sound senses, were married to two women not near of kin of whom one was a deaf-mute and the other of sound senses, and the deaf-mute husband with the deaf-mute wife died, what shall the husband of sound senses with the wife of sound senses do? He must marry the widow and if he would put her away he may. If the husband of sound senses with the wife of sound senses died, what shall the deaf-mute husband with the deaf-mute wife do? He must marry the widow and he may never put her away.

15. 1. If a woman and her husband went beyond the sea and there was peace between him and her and peace in the world, and she came back and said, 'My husband is dead', she may marry again. [If she said,] 'My husband died [childless]', she may contract levirate marriage. If there was peace between him and her but war in the world, or contention between him and her but peace in the world, and she came back and said, 'My husband is dead', she may not be believed. R. Judah says: She may never be believed unless she returns weeping and with garments rent. The Sages answered: It is all one [whether she does so or not]: she may not marry again.

2. The School of Hillel[1] say: We have heard no such tradition save of a woman that returned from the harvest and within the same country, and of a case that happened in fact. The School of Shammai answered: It is all one whether she returned from the harvest or from the olive-picking or from the vintage, or whether she came from one country to another: the Sages spoke of the harvest only as of a thing that happened in fact. The

---

[1] See Eduy. 1[12]

School of Hillel changed their opinion and taught according to the opinion of the School of Shammai.

3. The School of Shammai say: She may marry again and take her *Ketubah*.[1] And the School of Hillel say: She may marry again but she may not take her *Ketubah*. The School of Shammai answered: Since ye have declared permissible the graver matter of forbidden intercourse,[2] should ye not also declare permissible the less important matter of property? The School of Hillel answered: We find that brothers may not enter into an inheritance on her testimony.[3] The School of Shammai answered: Do we not learn from her *Ketubah*-scroll that he thus prescribes for her: 'If thou be married to another thou shalt take what is prescribed for thee'? And the School of Hillel changed their opinion and taught according to the opinion of the School of Shammai.

4. All may be deemed trustworthy when they testify to a woman [that her husband is dead] excepting[4] her mother-in-law, her mother-in-law's daughter, her co-wife, her husband's brother's wife, and her husband's daughter. Wherein[5] does [evidence of] divorce differ from [evidence of] death? The written document [in divorce] affords proof. If one witness said, 'He is dead', and the wife married again and another came and said, 'He is not dead', she need not be put away. If one witness said, 'He is dead', and [afterward] two witnesses said, 'He is not dead', even if she had married again [before the second testimony] she must be put away. If two witnesses said, 'He is dead', and one [afterward] said, 'He is not dead', even if she had not married again she may still do so.

5. If one woman said, 'My husband is dead', and the other [wife] said, 'He is not dead', she that said, 'He is dead', may marry again and take her *Ketubah*; and she that said, 'He is not dead', may not marry again or take her *Ketubah*. If one said, 'He is dead', and the other said, 'He has been killed', R. Meir says: Since they contradict one another neither may marry again. R. Judah and R. Simeon say: Since both admit that he is not alive they may both marry again. If one man testified and said, 'He is dead', and another man testified and said, 'He is not dead', and one woman said, 'He is dead', and another woman said, 'He is not dead', she may not marry again.

6. If a woman and her husband went beyond the sea and she came back and said, 'My husband is dead', she may marry again and take her *Ketubah*, but her co-wife is forbidden [to marry]. If the co-wife was the daughter of an Israelite married to a priest she may eat of Heave-offering. So R. Tarfon. R. Akiba says: This is not the way to put her beyond the reach of transgression: but, rather, she should be forbidden to marry again and forbidden to eat of Heave-offering.

7. If she said, 'My husband died and then my father-in-law died', she may marry again and take her *Ketubah*; but her mother-in-law is forbidden [to marry again]. If she was the daughter of an Israelite married to a priest she may eat of Heave-offering. So R. Tarfon. R. Akiba says: This is not the way to put her beyond the reach of transgression: but, rather, she should be forbidden to marry again and forbidden to eat of Heave-offering. If a man betrothed one of five women and he does not know which of them

---

[1] App. I. 16.   [2] Despite the danger of transgressing Lev. 18[20].
[3] But require two witnesses of the death. The evidence of one witness suffices to permit her to remarry only. See below, 16[7].   [4] Cf. Gitt. 2[7].   [5] Gitt. 2[7].

he betrothed, and each said, 'He betrothed me', he should give a bill of divorce to each one of them and leave the amount of the *Ketubah* among them, and·go away. So R. Tarfon. R. Akiba says: This is not the way to put him beyond the reach of transgression: but, rather, he should give a bill of divorce and the [full] amount of the *Ketubah* to each one of them. If a man robbed one of five people and he does not know which of them he robbed, and each says, 'He robbed me', he must leave the amount of the robbery between them and go away. So R. Tarfon. R. Akiba says: This is not the way to put him beyond the reach of transgression: but, rather, he should pay to each one the [full] amount of the robbery.

8. If a woman and her husband and her son went beyond the sea and she came back and said, 'My husband died and then my son died', she may be believed. [If she said], 'My son died and then my husband died', she may not be believed; yet they have regard to her words, and she must perform *halitzah* and she may not contract levirate marriage.

9. [If she said,] 'A son was born to me while I was beyond the sea', and she then said, 'My son died and then my husband died', she may not be believed, yet they have regard to her words, and she must perform *halitzah* and she may not contract levirate marriage.

10. [If she said,] 'A brother-in-law was born to me while I was beyond the sea', and then said, 'My husband died and then my brother-in-law died', or 'My brother-in-law died and then my husband died', she may be believed. If she and her husband and her brother-in-law went beyond the sea and she said, 'My husband died and then my brother-in-law died', or 'My brother-in-law died and then my husband died', she may not be believed; for a woman may not be believed if she says, 'My brother-in-law is dead'—so that she may marry again; nor [if she says,] 'My sister is dead' —so that she may enter his house; nor may a man be believed when he says, 'My brother is dead', so that he may contract levirate marriage with his wife, nor [when he says,] 'My wife is dead'—so that he may marry her sister.

16. 1. If a woman's husband and her co-wife went beyond the sea and it was told her, 'Thy husband is dead', she may not marry again or contract levirate marriage until she knows whether her co-wife is with child.[1] If she has a mother-in-law she need not have regard to her,[2] but if she went away while with child she must have regard to her. R. Joshua says: She need not have regard to her.

2. If there were two sisters-in-law [wives of two brothers,] and each said, 'My husband is dead', each is forbidden [to remarry] because of the other's husband.[3] If one had witnesses and the other had no witnesses, she that had witnesses is forbidden[4] but she that had no witnesses is permitted [to remarry]. If the one had children but the other had none, she that had children is permitted [to remarry] and she that had none is forbidden [to remarry]. If they had contracted levirate marriage with the brothers-in-law, and these brothers-in-law died, the widows are forbidden to remarry. R. Eliezer says: Since they were permitted to marry their brothers-in-law they are allowed to marry any one.

---

[1] Releasing her from the levirate tie.
[2] i.e. fear lest she bear a male child who would bind her to the levirate obligation.
[3] Who may yet be living and under levirate obligation towards his brother's widow.
[4] Lest the first husbands be yet alive.

3. Evidence may not be given [of the identity of a corpse] save from [proof afforded by] the face together with the nose, even though there were [other] marks [of identity] on its body or its clothing. Evidence [of a man's death] may be given only after his soul is gone forth, even though he was seen mortally wounded or crucified or being devoured by a wild beast. Evidence [of the identity of a corpse] may be given only during the first three days [after death]; but R. Judah b. Baba says: [Decay in corpses is] not alike in all men, in all places, and at all times.

4. If a man had fallen into the water, whether or not within sight of shore, his wife is forbidden [to marry another]. R. Meir said: Once a man fell into a large well and came up again after three days. But R. Jose said: Once a blind man went down into a cave to immerse himself and his guide went down with him; and they waited time enough for life to become extinct and then permitted their wives to marry again. Again it once happened in Asya that a man was let down by a rope into the sea and they drew up again naught save his leg. The Sages said: If [the part of the leg recovered] included the part above the knee his wife may marry again; but if only the part below the knee she may not marry again.

5. Even if a man [only] heard women saying, 'Such-a-one is dead', that suffices.[1] R. Judah says: Even if he [only] heard children saying, 'We are going to bewail and bury such-a-one', that suffices, whether or not he had an intention [to give evidence thereof]. R. Judah b. Baba says: If it was an Israelite, even though he had the intention [to give evidence, his evidence would be valid]; but if it was a gentile and he had the intention [to give evidence], his evidence would not be valid.

6. They may give evidence [of identity, if they have but seen the corpse] by the light of a lamp or by the light of the moon, and they may suffer a woman to marry again [solely on evidence afforded] by an echo. Once a man stood on the top of a hill and called out, 'Such-a-one, the son of such-a-one, from such-a-place is dead'; and although when they went they found no man there, they suffered his wife to marry again. Moreover it once happened at Zalmon that a man called out, 'A serpent has bitten me, such-a-one, the son of such-a-one, and I am dying', and although when they went [to him] they did not recognize him they suffered his wife to marry again.

7. R. Akiba said: When I went down to Nehardea to ordain a leap-year there met me Nehemiah of Beth Deli, and he said to me, 'I have heard that in the Land of Israel the Sages, excepting R. Judah b. Baba,[2] do not suffer a woman to marry again on the evidence of one witness'. I answered, 'It is so'. He said to me, 'Tell them in my name (ye know that this country is in confusion by reason of ravaging troops) I received a tradition from Rabban Gamaliel the Elder that they may suffer a woman to marry again on the evidence of one witness'. And when I came and recounted the matter before Rabban Gamaliel[3] he rejoiced at my words and said, 'We have now found a fellow [disciple][4] for R. Judah b. Baba. Whereupon Rabban Gamaliel remembered that certain men were killed at Tel Arza and Rabban Gamaliel the Elder suffered their wives to marry again on the evidence of one witness.[5] And the rule was established to suffer a woman

---

[1] To justify him in giving evidence of death or in marrying the widow.
[2] Cf. Eduy. 6[1].   [3] Grandson of Gamaliel the Elder.   [4] Cf. Erub. 2[6].
[5] Some texts add: 'And the rule was established to suffer a woman to marry again on the evidence of one witness'.

to marry again on the evidence of one witness [who testifies what he has heard] from [another] witness, or from a slave or from a woman or from a bondwoman. R. Eliezer and R. Joshua say: They may not suffer a woman to marry again on the evidence of one witness. R. Akiba says: Nor on the evidence of a woman[1] or of them that are near of kin. The Sages answered: Once certain levites went to Zoar,[2] the City of Palms, and one of them fell sick by the way, and they brought him to an inn. When they returned thither, they asked the mistress of the inn, 'Where is our companion?' She answered, 'He is dead and I buried him'. And they suffered his wife to marry again. The Sages said to R. Akiba, 'And should not a priest's wife be [deemed as trustworthy] as the mistress of an inn?' He answered, 'Only when the mistress of an inn could be deemed trustworthy! [For in this case] the mistress of the inn brought out to them his staff[3] and his bag and the scroll of the Law that had belonged to him'.

KETUBOTH ('MARRIAGE DEEDS')

1. 1. A virgin should be married on a Wednesday and a widow on a Thursday, for in towns the court sits twice in the week, on Mondays and on Thursdays;[4] so that if the husband would lodge a virginity suit[5] he may forthwith go in the morning to the court.

2. The *Ketubah*[6] of a virgin is 200 [*denars*],[7] and of a widow one *mina*.[8] The *Ketubah* of a virgin who after betrothal [only] became a widow or was divorced or performed *halitzah*[9] is 200 *denars*, and a virginity suit may be lodged against her. The *Ketubah* of a female proselyte, captive, or slave who was redeemed, proselytized, or freed under the age of three years and a day is 200 *denars*, and a virginity suit may be lodged against her.

3. If he that was of age had connexion with her that was a minor,[10] or if he that was a minor[11] had connexion with her that was of age or, through accident,[12] not *virgo intacta*, her *Ketubah* is 200 *denars*. So R. Meir. But the Sages say: The *Ketubah* of her that through accident is not *virgo intacta* is one *mina*.

4. The *Ketubah* of a virgin who after wedlock became a widow or was divorced or performed *halitzah* is one *mina*, and no virginity suit may be lodged against her. The *Ketubah* of a female proselyte, captive, or slave who was redeemed, proselytized, or freed after the age of three years and a day is one *mina*, and no virginity suit may be lodged against her.

5. If in Judea[13] a man ate in the house of his father-in-law and had no witnesses he may not lodge a virginity suit against her, since he had [already] remained alone with her. It is all one whether a woman is the widow of an Israelite or the widow of a priest, her *Ketubah* is one *mina*. The court of the Priests[14] used to levy 400 *zuz*[15] [as *Ketubah*] for a virgin, and the Sages did not reprove them.

---

1 Some texts add: 'or of a bondman or of a bondwoman'.
2 See Neub., p. 256.   3 Some texts add: 'and his shoes'.
4 Cf. Meg. 1¹.   5 Against the alleged virgin. See Deut. 22¹⁴.
6 See App. I. 16.   7 App. II, A.
8 100 *denars*. Also used as a weight; see Ket. 5⁸.   9 App. I. 12.
10 Less than three years and a day.   11 Less than nine years and a day.
12 Lit. 'hurt by a piece of wood'.   13 Cf. Yeb. 4¹⁰.
14 Cf. Ket. 13¹; Ohol. 17⁵, 'Sons of the High Priests'. The reference is probably to a Sanhedrin dominated by Sadducaic or high-priestly influence, as opposed to the Pharisaic school of thought represented by Hillel. Cf. R. Sh. 1⁷.   15 Or *denars*.

6. If a man married a woman and *found not in her the tokens of virginity*,[1] and she said, 'After thou didst betroth me I was forced and thy field was laid waste', and he said, 'Not so, but [it befell] before I betrothed thee, and my bargain was a bargain made in error', Rabban Gamaliel and R. Eliezer say: She may be believed. But R. Joshua says: We may not rely on her word; but she must be presumed to have suffered intercourse before she was betrothed and to have deceived her husband unless she can bring proof for her words.

7. If she said, 'It was through accident', and he said, 'Not so, but thou hast been trampled of man', Rabban Gamaliel and R. Eliezer say: She may be believed. But R. Joshua says: We may not rely on her word, but she must be presumed to have been trampled of man unless she can bring proof for her words.

8. If they saw her speaking with some man in the street and said to her, 'What manner of man is this?' [and she answered], 'His name is NN. and he is a priest', Rabban Gamaliel and R. Eliezer say: She may be believed. But R. Joshua says: We may not rely on her word, but she must be presumed to have suffered intercourse with a *Nathin*[2] or a bastard[3] unless she can bring proof for her words.

9. If she was found with child and they said to her, 'What manner of unborn child is this?' [and she answered,] 'It is by one named NN. and he is a priest', Rabban Gamaliel and R. Eliezer say: She may be believed. But R. Joshua says: We may not rely on her word, but she must be presumed to be with child by a *Nathin* or a bastard unless she can bring proof for her words.

10. R. Jose said: A young maid once went down to draw water from the spring and she was forced. R. Johanan b. Nuri said: If most of the men of the town were eligible to give [their daughters] in marriage to the priestly stock[4] she too may be married into the priestly stock.

2. 1. If a woman was left a widow or was divorced and said [to the heirs or to the husband], 'I was married as a virgin',[5] and [the husband][6] said, 'No, but I married thee when thou wast already a widow', if there are witnesses that she went forth [to the marriage] in a litter[7] and with hair unbound, her *Ketubah* shall be 200 *denars*. R. Johanan b. Baroka says: The sharing out of roast corn likewise affords proof.[8]

2. But R. Joshua agrees[9] that if a man said to his fellow, 'This field belonged to thy father and I bought it from him', he may be believed, since the mouth that forbade is the mouth that permitted;[10] but if there are witnesses [to say] that it belonged to that man's father and he says, 'I bought it from him', he may not be believed.

3. If witnesses said, 'This is indeed our handwriting, but we acted under constraint', or 'we were minors', or 'we were not eligible to bear witness', they may be believed; but if there are witnesses [to say] that it is their

---

[1] Deut. 22[14].   [2] App. I. 29.   [3] Yeb. 4[13].   [4] See Kidd. 4[1].
[5] Claiming 200 *denars* as her *Ketubah*.   [6] Who divorced her.
[7] Or 'a veil'. Heb. *hinuma* may = ὑμέναιος, the 'bridal-song' customary at a virgin's marriage.
[8] That at her marriage she was deemed a virgin.   [9] As against his attitude in 1[6, 7, 8].
[10] Cf. Dem. 6[11]; Eduy. 3[6]. According to Gem. 17b the case here cited is that of one who held land by usucaption (see B.B. 3[1]), and claimed to possess it by purchase; he thus partially and voluntarily admits the counter-claim of the original owner's son, and in this his statement can be accepted; but if that statement is in any event provable by others, his statement affords no proof of his credibility.

handwriting or if it is manifestly their handwriting from [its likeness to their handwriting] elsewhere, they may not be believed.

4. If a man said, 'This is my handwriting and that is my fellow's handwriting', and the other says, 'This is my handwriting and that is my fellow's handwriting', they may be believed. If one said, 'This is my handwriting', and another said, 'This is my handwriting', they must add to themselves another witness. So Rabbi. But the Sages say: They need not add to themselves another witness; but a man may be believed when he says, 'This is my handwriting'.

5. If a woman said,[1] 'I have been married but am now divorced', she may be believed, since the mouth that forbade is the mouth that permitted. But if there are witnesses [to say] that she was married and she says, 'I am divorced', she may not be believed. If she said, 'I was taken captive yet I remain clean', she may be believed, since the mouth that forbade is the mouth that permitted; but if there are witnesses [to say] that she was taken captive and she says, 'Yet I remain clean', she may not be believed. But if [such] witnesses come after that she is married she may not be put away.

6. If two women had been taken captive and one said, 'I was taken captive yet I remain clean', and the other said, 'I was taken captive yet I remain clean', they are not to be believed; but when they testify thus of each other they are to be believed.

7. So, too, if there were two men and one said, 'I am a priest', and the other said, 'I am a priest', they may not be believed; but when they testify thus of each other they may be believed.

8. R. Judah says: They may not admit any to the standing of a priest[2] on the evidence of a single witness. R. Eleazar[3] says: This applies only when there are some that protest; but when none protests they may admit any to the standing of a priest on the evidence of a single witness. Rabban Simeon b. Gamaliel in the name of R. Simeon the son of the Prefect[4] says: They admit any to the standing of a priest on the evidence of a single witness.

9. If a woman was imprisoned by gentiles for an offence concerning property she is still permitted to her husband; but if it was for a capital offence she is forbidden to her husband. If a city was overcome by a besieging troop all women therein of priestly stock[5] become ineligible [for marriage with a priest]; but if they had witnesses, even a bondman or a bondwoman, these may be believed. But none may be believed when he testifies of himself. R. Zechariah b. ha-Kazzab[6] said: 'By this Temple, her hand stirred not out of mine from the time the gentiles entered Jerusalem until they left it!' They said to him: None may testify of himself.

10. These when they come of age may be believed when they testify of what they saw while they were yet minors: A man may be believed when he says, 'This is my father's handwriting', or 'This is my teacher's handwriting', or 'This is my brother's handwriting'; 'I remember that woman NN. that she left [her father's house] in a litter and with hair unbound',[7] or 'Such-a-one went out from the school to immerse himself to eat of Heave-offering', or 'He used to share with us at the threshing-floor',[8] or

---

[1] Eduy. 3[6].   [2] See Kidd. 4[1, 5].   [3] Some texts read 'Eliezer'.
[4] The second to the High Priest in rank. See Sot. 7[7].
[5] Or eligible for marriage with a priest.
[6] 'The Butcher'. See Sot. 5[1]; Eduy. 8[2].   [7] See above, 2[1].
[8] Cf. Yeb. 11[5]. Both statements are offered in evidence that he was of priestly stock.

'This place is a Grave-area',[1] or 'Thus far used we to come on the Sabbath'.[2] But none may be believed when he says, 'Such-a-one had a right of way in this place', or 'In this place such-a-one had the right of halting and holding lamentation'.[3]

3. 1. These are girls[4] through whom[5] a fine[6] is incurred [by their seducer]: If a man has connexion with a girl that is a bastard, a *Nethinah*, or a Samaritan; or with a female proselyte, captive, or bondwoman that was redeemed, proselytized, or freed before the age of three years and a day; or with his sister or his father's sister or his mother's sister or his wife's sister or his brother's wife or his father's brother's wife or a menstruant— through them a fine is incurred. Although they [that so transgress] are liable to punishment by Extirpation[7] they are not subject to any death penalty imposed by the court.

2. These are girls through whom no fine is incurred: If a man has connexion with a female proselyte, captive, or bondwoman that was redeemed, proselytized, or freed after the age of three years and a day (R. Judah says: If a female captive was redeemed she is still accounted virgin[8] even if she was of age); if a man had connexion with his daughter or his daughter's daughter or his son's daughter or his wife's daughter or her son's daughter or her daughter's daughter—through them no fine is incurred, because he [that so transgresses] forfeits his life, for his death is at the hands of the court;[9] and he that forfeits his life pays no money, for it is written, *If no damage befall he shall be surely fined.*[10]

3. If a girl was betrothed and afterward divorced, R. Jose the Galilean says: Through her no fine is incurred. But R. Akiba says: A fine is incurred and the fine falls to her.[11]

4. The seducer must pay on three counts and the violator on four. The seducer must pay [compensation for] indignity and [for] blemish and the [prescribed] fine; the violator adds thereto in that he must pay [compensation for] the pain. Wherein does the violator differ from the seducer? The violator pays [compensation for] the pain and the seducer does not pay [compensation for] the pain; the violator must pay forthwith, but the seducer only if he puts her away; the violator must drink out of his earthen pot, but if the seducer is minded to put her away he may put her away.

5. How does he 'drink out of his earthen pot'? [He must marry her] even if she was lame, even if she was blind, and even if she was afflicted with boils. But if she was found unchaste or was not fit to be taken in marriage by an Israelite he may not continue [his union] with her, for it is written, *And she shall be to him for a wife*[12]—a wife that is fit for him.

6. If an orphan was betrothed and then divorced,[13] R. Eleazar says: He that seduces her is exempt but he that violates her is culpable.

7. How much is the [compensation for] indignity? It is in accordance with [the condition of life of] him that inflicts and her that suffers the

---

[1] See Ohol. 17[1].   [2] Erub. 5[5].   [3] See p. 206, n. 8.
[4] Heb. *naaroth*, such as are between the age of twelve and twelve and a half. After that age a woman counts as *bogereth*—past her girlhood.
[5] Even though they are not eligible for marriage with Israelites (Kidd. 4[1]).
[6] Fifty shekels (Deut. 22[29]).
[7] Lev. 18[29].   [8] Lit. 'continues in her sanctity'.
[9] They are to be burnt (Sanh. 9[1]).   [10] Ex. 21[22].
[11] And not to her father. Her status is that of 'an orphan in her father's lifetime'. Yeb. 13[6]; Ned. 11[10].   [12] Deut. 22[29].   [13] Some texts read, 'was violated or seduced'.

indignity.[1] [And the compensation for] blemish? She is looked upon as if she was a bondwoman that was to be sold: how much was she worth before? and how much is she worth now?[2] The [prescribed] fine[3] remains the same for all. Wherever a fixed sum is enjoined in the Law it remains the same for all.

8. Wherever there is right of sale no fine is incurred, and wherever no fine is incurred there is no right of sale. She that is a minor[4] is subject to right of sale[5] and no fine is incurred through her;[6] but through a girl [that is of age][7] a fine is incurred and she is not subject to right of sale. If she is past her girlhood[8] she is not subject to right of sale nor can a fine be incurred through her.

9. If a man said, 'I have seduced the daughter of such-a-one', he must pay [compensation for] indignity and blemish on his own admission, but he does not pay the [prescribed] fine. If a man said, 'I have stolen',[9] he must repay the value on his own admission, but he does not make double[10] or fourfold or fivefold restitution.[11] [If he said,] 'My ox has killed such-a-one', or 'the ox of such-a-one', he must make restitution on his own admission. [If he said,] 'My ox has killed the bondman[12] of such-a-one', he does not make restitution on his own admission. This is the general rule: whosoever must pay more than the cost of damage done does not pay on his own admission.

4. 1. If a girl[13] was seduced, [compensation for] indignity and blemish and the [prescribed] fine fall to her father; and also [compensation for] pain because of a girl that was violated. If she gained her suit before her father was dead the dues fall to her father; if her father was dead they fall to the brothers; if her father died before she gained her suit they fall to her.[14] If she gained her suit before she passed her girlhood they fall to her father; if her father was dead they fall to the brothers; if she passed her girlhood before she gained her suit, they fall to her. R. Simeon says: If she passed her girlhood[15] before she could collect the dues they fall to her. But the work of her hands or aught found by her,[16] even if she had not collected the dues and her father died, these fall to the brothers.[17]

2. If a man gave his daughter[18] in betrothal and she was divorced, or if he gave her in betrothal and she was left a widow, her *Ketubah* falls to him. If he gave her in marriage and she was divorced, or if he gave her in marriage and she was left a widow, her *Ketubah* falls to her. R. Judah says: In the former case[19] it falls to the father. They said to him: After her father has given her in marriage he has no claim on her.

3. If the daughter of a female proselyte became a proselyte with her and committed fornication,[20] she [is liable to death] by strangling;[21] to her does

---

1 Cf. Arak. 3[4].   2 Cf. B.K. 8[1].   3 The fifty shekels enjoined in Deut. 22[29].
4 Less than twelve years old.
5 Her father may sell her as a slave.   6 By her violator or seducer.
7 Heb. *naarah*, aged twelve to twelve and a half.
8 Heb. *bogereth*, more than twelve and a half.
9 Some texts add: 'and killed or sold'. See B.K. 7[1ff].   10 Ex. 22[4].
11 Ex. 22[1].   12 For which he is liable to a fine of thirty shekels (Ex. 21[32]).
13 Aged twelve to twelve and a half.
14 Variant: 'R. Simeon says, If her father died before she could collect the dues they fall
to her'.   15 Variant: 'If her father died'.   16 Cf. B.M. 1[5].
17 Who must provide her with maintenance.   18 Not yet twelve and a half years old.
19 Divorce after marriage of one under twelve years and a half.
20 While betrothed to another and still a *naarah*.
21 And not (Deut. 22[21]) by stoning, since she was not born 'in Israel'.

not apply *to the door of her father's house*[1] or 'the hundred *selas*'.[2] But if she was conceived while her mother was yet a gentile and born after her mother became a proselyte, she [is liable to death] by stoning; to her does not apply *to the door of her father's house*, or 'the hundred *selas*'. But if she was both conceived and born after her mother became a proselyte, she is regarded as a daughter of Israel in every respect. If she has a 'father' and no 'door of her father's house', or if she has a 'door of her father's house' but no 'father'—in either case she [is yet liable to death] by stoning, [for the law of] *the door of her father's house* is only enjoined as a religious duty [in addition to stoning].

4. The father has control over his daughter[3] as touching her betrothal[4] whether it is effected by money, by writ, or by intercourse [whereby betrothal is effected]; and he has the right to aught found by her and to the work of her hands,[5] and [the right] to set aside her vows,[6] and he receives her bill of divorce; but he has not the use of her property[7] during her lifetime. When she is married the husband exceeds the father in that he has the use of her property during her lifetime; and he is liable for her maintenance and for her ransom[8] and for her burial. R. Judah says: Even the poorest in Israel should hire not less than two flutes and one wailing woman.

5. She continues within the control of the father until she enters into the control of the husband at marriage. If the father delivered her to the agents of the husband, she is deemed within the control of the husband; but if the father went with the agents of the husband or if the agents of the father went with the agents of the husband, she is deemed within the control of the father; but if the agents of the father delivered her to the agents of the husband, she is deemed within the control of the husband.

6. The father is not liable for his daughter's maintenance. R. Eleazar b. Azariah thus expounded it[9] before the Sages in the vineyard at Jabneh: 'The sons inherit and the daughters receive maintenance'—but like as the sons inherit only after the death of their father so the daughters receive maintenance only after the death of their father.

7. If the husband had not written out a *Ketubah* for his wife, she may still claim 200 *denars* if she was a virgin [at marriage] or one *mina* if she was a widow, since that is a condition enjoined by the court. If he assigned her a field worth one *mina* instead of 200 *zuz*, and did not write[10] 'All my goods are surety for thy *Ketubah*', he is still liable [for the payment of the whole 200 *zuz*], since that is a condition enjoined by the court.

8. If he had not written for her, 'If thou art taken captive I will redeem thee and take thee again as my wife', or, if she was the wife of a priest, '[I will redeem thee and] will bring thee back to thine own city',[11] he is still liable [so to do] since that is a condition enjoined by the court.

9. If she was taken captive he must ransom her; and if he said, 'Lo, here is her bill of divorce and her *Ketubah*: let her ransom herself', he has not

---

[1] Deut. 22[21].   [2] If she was wrongfully accused (Deut. 22[19]).
[3] Not yet twelve and a half years old.   [4] See Kidd. 1[1].
[5] As he has the right to sell her so he has the right to her labour.
[6] Num. 30[5, 16].   [7] Which she has inherited from e.g. her mother.
[8] If she was captured.
[9] The quotation, from the *Ketubah*-scroll formula, is expounded as though it was a scriptural passage (cf. Shek. 6[6]). See Ket. 13[3]; B.B. 9[1].
[10] The 'conditions' in the following paragraphs are quoted in Aramaic.
[11] Since, by being taken captive, she becomes unfit to remain his, a priest's, wife; and so must return to her father's house.

the right [so to do]. If she received injury he is liable for her healing; but if he said, 'Lo, here is her bill of divorce and her *Ketubah*: let her heal herself', he has the right [so to do].

10. If he had not written for her, 'Male children which thou shalt have by me shall inherit thy *Ketubah* besides the portion which they receive with their brethren', he is still liable [thereto], since this is a condition enjoined by the court.

11. [If he had not written for her,] 'Female children which thou shalt have by me shall dwell in my house and receive maintenance from my goods until they marry husbands', he is still liable [thereto], since this is a condition enjoined by the court.

12. [If he had not written for her], 'Thou shalt dwell in my house and receive maintenance from my goods so long as thou remainest a widow in my house', he is still liable [thereto], since this is a condition enjoined by the court. Thus used the people of Jerusalem to write; and the people of Galilee used to write after the same fashion as the people of Jerusalem. But the people of Judea used to write, '. . . until such time as the heirs are minded to give thee thy *Ketubah*'; therefore if the heirs were so minded they could pay her her *Ketubah* and let her go.

5. 1. Although they have said:[1] 'The *Ketubah* of a virgin is 200 *denars* and of a widow one *mina*', if a man is minded to add thereto, even a hundred *minas*, he may do so. If she was left a widow or was divorced, whether after betrothal or after wedlock, she may lay claim to the whole. R. Eleazar b. Azariah says: If after wedlock, she may lay claim to the whole; but if after betrothal [only], a virgin may lay claim but to 200 *denars* and a widow to one *mina*, since he assigned her [the whole] only on the condition that he married her. R. Judah says: If he was so minded a man may write out a bond for 200 *denars* for a virgin while she writes, 'I have [already] received from thee one *mina*'; [and he may write out a bond for] one *mina* for a widow, while she writes, 'I have [already] received from thee 50 *zuz*'. R. Meir says: If they assign less than 200 *zuz* for a virgin or less than one *mina* for a widow, such is accounted fornication.

2. After the husband has demanded her, a virgin is granted twelve months wherein to provide for herself; and like as [such time] is granted to the woman so is it granted to the man to provide for himself. And a widow [is granted] thirty days. If after such time they have not married, the woman may eat from his goods, and eat of Heave-offering [if he is a priest]. R. Tarfon says: They may give her all her food of Heave-offering. R. Akiba says: One half common food and one half Heave-offering.

3. The levir[2] [that is a priest] may not give Heave-offering [to his deceased brother's wife] to eat. If she had lived six months with her husband and six months [awaiting marriage] with the levir, or even if she lived the whole [twelve months] with her husband less one day [awaiting marriage] with the levir, or the whole [twelve months] awaiting marriage with the levir less one day lived with her husband, she may not eat of Heave-offering. So[3] was it enjoined in the First Mishnah;[4] but after them

---

[1] Ket. 1[2].   [2] See p. 218, n. 1.
[3] The anonymous ruling in the second sentence of par. 2 above.
[4] See Naz. 6[1]; Gitt. 5[6]; Sanh. 3[4]; Eduy. 7[2]. It may refer either to a complete compilation of tradition, like the extant Mishnah of R. Judah the Patriarch, or it may be rendered 'an earlier Mishnah (or teaching)' and refer to a previously accepted ruling on the present point alone.

the court taught: The woman may not eat of Heave-offering until after she has entered the bride-chamber.

4. If a man dedicated his wife's handiwork[1] to the Temple, [nevertheless] she has the right of maintenance while she labours; [but if he had dedicated] the surplus[2] [only], R. Meir says: It is [validly] dedicated. But R. Johanan the Sandal-maker says: It is not validly dedicated.

5. These are works which the wife must perform for her husband: grinding flour and baking bread and washing clothes and cooking food and giving suck to her child and making ready his bed and working in wool. If she brought him in one bondwoman she need not grind or bake or wash; if two, she need not cook or give her child suck; if three, she need not make ready his bed or work in wool; if four, she may sit [all the day] in a chair. R. Eliezer says: Even if she brought him in a hundred bondwomen he should compel her to work in wool, for idleness leads to unchastity. Rabban Simeon b. Gamaliel says: Moreover if a man put his wife under a vow to do no work he should put her away and give her her *Ketubah*, for idleness leads to lowness of spirit.

6. If a man[3] vowed to have no intercourse with his wife, the School of Shammai say: [She may consent] for two weeks. And the School of Hillel say: For one week [only]. Disciples [of the Sages] may continue absent for thirty days against the will [of their wives] while they occupy themselves in the study of the Law; and labourers for one week. The *duty of marriage* enjoined in the Law[4] is: every day for them that are unoccupied; twice a week for labourers; once a week for ass-drivers; once every thirty days for camel-drivers; and once every six months for sailors. So R. Eliezer.

7. If a woman will not consent[5] to her husband he may reduce her *Ketubah* by seven *denars* for every week. R. Judah says: Seven *tropaics*.[6] For how long[7] may he reduce it? [For a time] corresponding to the sum of her *Ketubah*. R. Jose says: He may go on reducing it continually, that if perchance an inheritance falls to her from elsewhere he may claim it from her. So, too, if a husband will not consent to his wife, her *Ketubah* may be increased by three *denars* a week. R. Judah says: Three *tropaics*.

8. If a husband maintained his wife at the hands of a third person, he may not grant her less than two *kabs*[8] of wheat or four *kabs* of barley [every week]. R. Jose said: Only R. Ishmael provided her with barley [at such an estimation] because he lived near Edom.[9] He must also give her half a *kab* of pulse and half a *log*[10] of oil and a *kab* of dried figs or a *mina*[11] of fig-cake; and if he has none of these he must provide her with other produce in their stead. He must also give her a bed and a bed-cover and if he has no bed-cover he must give her a rush mat. He must also give her a cap for her head and a girdle for her loins, and shoes at each of the [three] Feasts,[12] and clothing to the value of 50 *zuz* every year. They may not give her new clothes for summer or worn-out clothes for winter; but he should

---

[1] See below, par. 9.
[2] Her work that she may do in excess of the equivalent of the cost of her maintenance. According to the Gemara (58b) the Mishnah here treats of dedicating the surplus after her death. It is not a valid dedication since none can dedicate what is not yet in existence.
[3] Eduy. 4[10].   [4] Ex. 21[10].   [5] To marital intercourse.   [6] Half-*denars*.
[7] Some texts read: 'Up to what sum'.   [8] App. II, D.
[9] Where barley was more plentiful than wheat. Cf. Peah 8[5].
[10] App. II, D.   [11] App. II, B.
[12] Passover, Pentecost, and Tabernacles.

give her clothes to the value of 50 *zuz* for winter, and she may clothe her-self with the rags thereof in the summer time; and the discarded garments belong to her.

9. He must give her[1] a silver *maah*[2] for her needs, and she should eat with him on the night of every Sabbath. If he does not give her a silver *maah* for her needs, what she earns by her own work shall belong to herself. And how much work must she do for him? She must spin for him five *selas*'[3] weight of warp in Judea (which is ten *selas* in Galilee)[4] or ten *selas*' weight of woof (which is twenty *selas* in Galilee); but if she was suckling a child they should lessen her handiwork and increase her maintenance. This applies to the poorest in Israel; but with folk of the better sort all should be according to the honour due to him.

6. 1. Aught found by a wife and the work of her hands belong to her husband, and during her lifetime he has the use of her inheritance. [If she received compensation for] indignity and blemish, it falls to her.[5] R. Judah b. Bathyra says: If it was done to a hidden part [in her body] two-thirds [of the compensation] falls to her and one-third to him; if in a manifest part two-thirds falls to him and one-third to her. His share is given him forthwith; but with hers land is bought and he has the use of it.

2. If a man undertook to give money to his son-in-law and his son-in-law died, [and the levir claimed the money],[6] the Sages have said: He may say, 'It was to thy brother that I was minded to give it: I wish not to give it to thee'.

3. If the woman undertook to bring in to her husband one thousand *denars*, over against this he must assign to her [as her *Ketubah*] fifteen *minas*,[7] but over against goods [which she undertakes to bring in], esti-mated to be of a certain value, he rates it at one-fifth less.[8] If [she would have inscribed in her *Ketubah*] 'goods estimated at one *mina*', and they are [in truth found to be] worth one *mina*, he can only claim the one *mina*.[9] [If she would have inscribed in her *Ketubah*] 'goods estimated at one *mina*' she must bring him in [goods worth] thirty-one *selas* and one *denar*;[10] [and if] 'four hundred *denars*' she must bring him in [goods worth] five hundred *denars*. What the bridegroom assigns he, too, rates at one-fifth less [its estimated worth].

4. If she undertook to bring him in ready money,[11] one silver *sela* shall count as six *denars*.[12] The bridegroom undertakes to give her ten *denars* as pin-money[13] for every *mina* [that she brings in]. Rabban Simeon b. Gamaliel says: In all things they should follow local custom.

5. If a man gave his daughter in marriage without prescribed conditions, he may not assign to her less than fifty *zuz*. If he made it a condition that the bridegroom should take her in naked, the bridegroom may not say, 'After I have taken her into my house I will clothe her with clothing of mine', but he must clothe her while she is yet in her father's house. So, too, if an orphan was given in marriage she shall be assigned not less than

---

[1] Weekly.   [2] App. II, A.   [3] App. II, B.
[4] Cf. Hull. 11[2]. The Galilean *selas* was only half the weight of the Judean *selas*.
[5] Cf. Ket. 4[1].   [6] See Yeb. 4[7].
[7] 1,500 *denars*. It is rated 50 per cent. higher, since he has the use of the money for his own profit. This does not count as usury since it is a condition that he inherits it at her death.   [8] Since they may have been over-assessed in her honour.
[9] And not a *mina* and a quarter's worth of goods which he can write down by one-fifth.
[10] One *mina* and a quarter. App. II, A.   [11] Variant: '*selas*'.
[12] Instead of four.   [13] Lit. 'for the basket'.

fifty *zuz*; if there was [more] in the poor-funds they should provide for her according to the honour due to her.

6. If an orphan was given in marriage by her mother or her brothers with her consent, and they assigned to her as her portion a hundred *zuz* or fifty, when she comes of age she may exact from them what should right-fully[1] have been given to her. R. Judah says: If a man had given his first daughter in marriage, the second should be given the like of what he gave to the first. But the Sages say: Sometimes a man is poor and becomes rich, or is rich and becomes poor: so, rather, they should estimate the value of their goods and give accordingly.

7. If a man deposited money for his daughter with a third person[2] but she says, 'I trust my [betrothed] husband',[3] the third person must still perform that with which he was charged. So R. Meir. R. Jose says: If it was but a field [that was already bought for her] and she wished to sell it, it must be deemed sold from such time.[4] This applies to a woman that is of age; but as for her that is still a minor, the act of a minor remains void.

7. 1. If a man vowed that his wife should derive no benefit from him [and the vow was] for thirty days, he must suffer a guardian to be set up; if for longer, he must put her away and giver her her *Ketubah*. R. Judah says: If he was an Israelite[5] [and the vow was for] one month, he may keep her as his wife, but if for two months he must put her away and give her her *Ketubah*. If she was the wife of a priest[6] [and the vow was for] two months, he may keep her as his wife, but if for three he must put her away and give her her *Ketubah*.

2. If a man vowed to abstain from his wife should she taste a certain fruit, he must put her away and give her her *Ketubah*. R. Judah says: If he was an Israelite [and the vow was for] one day, he may keep her as his wife, but if for two days, he must put her away and give her her *Ketubah*; if she was the wife of a priest [and the vow was for] two days, he may keep her as his wife, but if for three days, he must put her away and give her her *Ketubah*.

3. If a man vowed to abstain from his wife should she put on a certain kind of adornment he must put her away and give her her *Ketubah*. R. Jose says: [This applies to] poor women if he enjoined no set time, and to rich women [if the vow was for] thirty days.

4. If a man vowed to abstain from his wife should she go to her father's house, and he lived with her in the same town, [if the vow was for] one month, he may keep her as his wife, but if for two, he must put her away and give her her *Ketubah*; if he lived in another town [and the vow was for] one Feast,[7] he may keep her as his wife, but if for three [Feasts], he he must put her away and give her her *Ketubah*.

5. If a man vowed to abstain from his wife should she go to a house of mourning or a house of feasting,[8] he must put her away and give her her *Ketubah*, because he has closed [all doors] against her. But if he urged [in

---

[1] One-tenth of the estate.
[2] To buy for her a field, or to be given her as dowry after his death.
[3] 'So give him the trust-money.'
[4] Since it was within her control. The money is then at her own disposal.
[5] i.e. not a priest.   [6] And unable to marry him again after divorce (Lev. 21[7]).
[7] i.e. until the next of the three Feasts—Passover, Pentecost, or Tabernacles.
[8] Usually in the sense of 'wedding-feast'.

favour of the vow] 'a certain other matter',[1] this is permitted. If he said to her[2] ' . . . only on condition that thou say to such-a-one what thou hast said to me', or 'what I have said to thee',[3] or 'that thou draw water and empty it on a dungheap', he must put her away and give her her *Ketubah*.

6. These are they that are put away without their *Ketubah*: a wife that transgresses the Law of Moses and Jewish custom. What [conduct is such that transgresses] the Law of Moses? If she gives her husband untithed food,[4] or has connexion with him in her uncleanness,[5] or does not set apart Dough-offering,[6] or utters a vow and does not fulfil it.[7] And what [conduct is such that transgresses] Jewish custom? If she goes out with her hair unbound, or spins in the street, or speaks with any man. Abba Saul says: Also if she curses his parents in his presence. R. Tarfon says: Also [if she is] a scolding woman.[8] And who is deemed a scolding woman? Whosoever speaks inside her house so that her neighbours hear her voice.

7. If[9] a man betrothed a woman on the condition that she was under no vow and she was found to be under a vow, her betrothal is not valid. If he married her making no conditions, and she was found to be under a vow, she may be put away without her *Ketubah*. [If he betrothed her] on the condition that there were no defects in her, and defects were found in her, her betrothal is not valid. If he married her making no conditions and defects were found in her, she may be put away without her *Ketubah*. All defects which disqualify priests[10] disqualify women also.

8. If defects were found in her while she was yet in her father's house, the father must bring proof that these defects arose in her after she was betrothed, and that his field was laid waste.[11] If she had entered into the control of the husband, the husband must bring proof that these defects were in her before she was betrothed, and that his bargain was a bargain made in error. So R. Meir. But the Sages say: This applies only to secret defects; but he may not make complaint of manifest defects. And if there was a bath-house in that town he may not make complaint even of secret defects, since he can inquire about her from her women kinsfolk.

9. If defects arose in the husband they may not compel him to put away his wife. R. Simeon b. Gamaliel said: This applies only to the lesser defects, but for the greater defects they can compel him to put away his wife.

10. And these are they that are compelled to put away their wives: he that is afflicted with boils, or that has a polypus, or that collects [dog's excrements], or that is a coppersmith or a tanner, whether these defects were in them before they married or whether they arose after they married. And of all these R. Meir said: Although the husband made it a condition with her [to marry him despite his defects], she may say, 'I thought that I could endure it, but now I cannot endure it'. But the Sages say: She must endure him in spite of herself, save only him that is afflicted with boils, because she will enervate him. It once happened in Sidon that a tanner died and had a brother who was a tanner. The Sages said: She may say, 'Thy brother I could endure; but thee I cannot endure'.

---

[1] e.g. that lewd folk frequented such a place.
[2] 'Thy vow shall be annulled only on condition . . .'
[3] e.g. certain foolish talk.   [4] Transgressing Num. 18[21f].
[5] Transgressing Lev. 18[19].   [6] Transgressing Num. 15[18ff].
[7] Transgressing Deut. 23[21].   [8] The Cambridge text reads: 'and this is an addition'.
[9] Kidd. 2[5].   [10] Lev. 21[17ff].; cf. Bekh. 7[1ff].   [11] Cf. Ket. 1[6].

8. 1. If a woman inherited goods before she was betrothed, the School of Shammai and the School of Hillel agree that she may sell them or give them away and that her act is valid. If she inherited them after she was betrothed, the School of Shammai say: She may sell them. And the School of Hillel say: She may not sell them. But they agree that if she sold them or gave them away her act is valid. R. Judah said: They inquired before Rabban Gamaliel, 'Since [the betrothed husband] gets possession of the woman, does he not get possession of her goods also?' He answered: 'We are at a loss [to find reason for giving him right] over her new [possessions],[1] and would ye even burden us with the old also!' If she inherited [goods] after she was married, both agree that if she sold them or gave them away the husband may take them out of the hands of the buyers. If [she inherited them] before she married and she then married, Rabban Gamaliel says: If she sold them or gave them away her act is valid. R. Hananiah b. Akabya said: They inquired before Rabban Gamaliel, 'Since he gets possession of the woman, does he not get possession of her goods also?' He answered, 'We are at a loss [to find reason for giving him right] over her new [possessions], and would ye even burden us with the old also!'

2. R. Simeon makes distinction between one kind of goods and another: goods that are known to the husband she may not sell, and if she sold them or gave them away the act is void; and goods that are not known to the husband she may not sell, but if she sold them or gave them away her act is valid.

3. If she inherited money, land should be bought therewith, and the husband has the use of it. [If she inherited] produce that was already reaped, land should be bought therewith, and the husband has the use of it; and if it was still unreaped, R. Meir says: They estimate how much the land is worth with the produce and how much without it; with the difference land is bought and the husband has the use of it. But the Sages say: What is unreaped falls to him and what is reaped falls to the wife, and with it land is bought and the husband has the use of it.

4. Whereinsoever he has advantage at her coming in [to him in marriage], therein he suffers disadvantage at her going forth; and whereinsoever he suffers disadvantage at her coming in, therein he has advantage at her going forth. At her coming in unreaped produce falls to him, and at her going forth it falls to her; and at her coming in reaped produce falls to her, and at her going forth it falls to him.

5. If she inherited old bondmen and bondwomen they should be sold and land bought with their price, and the husband has the use of it. Rabban Simeon b. Gamaliel says: She should not sell them, because they are the pride of her father's house. If she inherited old olive-trees or vines they should be sold as wood and land bought with their price, and the husband has the use of it. R. Judah says: She should not sell them, because they are the pride of her father's house. If a man spent aught on his wife's property,[2] whether he spent much and gained little, or spent little and gained much, what he has spent he has spent, and what he has gained he has gained. But if he spent and gained naught, let him swear how much he has spent and take [compensation from the property].

---

[1] To justify his claim on property which she newly inherits after marriage.
[2] Of which he has the use, namely *melog* property. See App. I. 24; Yeb. 7[1].

6. If[1] a woman awaiting levirate marriage inherited property, the School of Shammai and the School of Hillel agree that she may sell it or give it away and the act will be valid. If she died what should be done with her *Ketubah* and property that comes in and goes out with her? The School of Shammai say: The heirs of her [deceased] husband share with the heirs of her father. But the School of Hillel say: Her [*son barzel*] property falls [equally] to them [both]; the *Ketubah* falls to the [deceased] husband's heirs, and the property that comes in and goes out with her falls into the possession of her father's heirs.

7. If his brother[2] left money, land is bought therewith and he has the use of it. [If he left] produce that was already reaped, land is bought therewith, and he has the use of it; if unreaped produce, R. Meir says: They estimate how much the land is worth with the produce and how much without it, and with the difference land is bought and he has the use of it. But the Sages say: The unreaped produce falls to him, and as for the reaped produce, whosoever comes first gets possession: if he came first he gets possession; if she came first land is bought therewith and he has the use of it. But[3] if he had consummated marriage with her, she counts as his wife in all respects save that her *Ketubah* is a charge on her first husband's goods.

8. He may not say to her, 'Here lies thy *Ketubah* on the table',[4] but all his goods[5] are surety for her *Ketubah*. So, too,[6] a man may not say to his wife, 'Here lies thy *Ketubah* on the table', but all his goods are surety for her *Ketubah*. If he divorced her, she may claim only her *Ketubah*. If he married her again she is like to all other wives;[7] and she may claim naught save only her *Ketubah*.[8]

9. 1. If a man declared to his [betrothed] wife in writing, 'I will have neither right nor claim to thy property',[9] he may yet have the use of it during her lifetime and inherit her property when she dies. If so, to what purpose did he declare to her in writing, 'I will have neither right nor claim to thy property?'—so that if she sold it or gave it away her act should be valid. If he declared to her in writing, 'I will have neither right nor claim to thy property or to the fruits[10] thereof', he may not enjoy the fruits during her lifetime, but he may inherit her property when she dies. R. Judah says: He can in any wise enjoy the fruits of the fruits[11] unless he declared to her in writing, 'I will have neither right nor claim to thy property or to the fruits thereof, or to the fruits of the fruits thereof, and so on without end'. If he declared to her in writing, 'I will have neither right nor claim to thy property or to the fruits thereof, or to the fruits of the fruits thereof during thy lifetime or at thy death', he may not enjoy the fruits during her lifetime and when she dies he may not inherit her property. Rabban Simeon b. Gamaliel says: If she dies he may still inherit her property because he made a condition contrary to what is enjoined in the

---

[1] Yeb. 4[3].
[2] His brother who died childless leaving a widow with whom he contracts levirate marriage.
[3] Yeb. 4[9].   [4] 'And the rest of what I have inherited from my brother I will sell.'
[5] Inherited from the brother.   [6] Many texts omit the following sentence.
[7] All his property remains as surety for her *Ketubah*.
[8] She cannot claim her old one and a new one also. See below, 9[9].
[9] 'When thou art married to me.'   [10] The use and consequent profits.
[11] The use of what he had added to the value of the original property.

Law,[1] and if a man makes a condition contrary to what is enjoined in the Law, his condition is void.[2]

2. If a man died and left a wife, a creditor, and heirs, and had goods on deposit or on loan in the hand of others,[3] R. Tarfon says: The property should be given to the one that is at the [greatest legal] disadvantage. R. Akiba says: They may not show pity in a legal suit: but, rather, it must be given to the heirs; for all the others need to swear to their claim on oath, but not so the heirs.

3. If a man left reaped produce, whosoever comes first gets possession thereof. If the wife gained possession of more than her *Ketubah* assigned to her, or a creditor more than his due, the surplus, R. Tarfon says, should be given to the one that is at the [greatest legal] disadvantage. R. Akiba says: They may not show pity in a legal suit: but, rather, it is given to the heirs; for all the others need to swear to their claim on oath, but not so the heirs.

4. If a man set up his wife as a shopkeeper or appointed her a guardian, he may exact of her an oath whensoever he will.[4] R. Eliezer says: Even[5] concerning her spindle or her dough.

5. If he declared to her in writing, 'I will require of thee neither vow nor oath', he may not exact of her an oath, but he may exact an oath of her heirs and her lawful successors. [If he said,] 'I will require neither vow nor oath of thee, thine heirs, or lawful successors', he may not exact an oath of her, her heirs, or her legal successors, but his heirs may exact an oath of her, her heirs, or her lawful successors. [If he said,] 'Neither I, nor my heirs, nor my lawful successors will require a vow or an oath of thee, thy heirs, or thy lawful successors', he may not exact an oath of her, nor may his heirs or lawful successors, whether of her or her heirs or her lawful successors.

6. If she went from her husband's grave to her father's house, or returned to her father-in-law's house and was not made a guardian, the heirs may not exact an oath of her. But if she was made a guardian the heirs may exact an oath of her concerning [her trust during] the time after [her husband's death], but not the time before.

7. If[6] a woman impaired her *Ketubah*, the rest may not be paid to her unless she swears [to her claim] on oath; if one witness testified against her that it had been paid [in full], she may not receive payment unless she swears [to her claim] on oath; she may not receive payment from the property of orphans or from assigned property or from property of one that is not present, unless she swears [to her claim] on oath.

8. How does it apply 'if a woman impaired her *Ketubah*'? If her *Ketubah* was a thousand *zuz*, and he said to her, 'Thou didst receive thy *Ketubah* [in full]', and she said, 'I received but one *mina*', the rest may not be paid to her unless she swears [to her claim] on oath. How does it apply if one witness testified against her that it had been paid [in full]'? If her *Ketubah* was a thousand *zuz* and he said to her, 'Thou didst receive thy *Ketubah* [in full]', and she said, 'I have not received it', and a witness testified against her that it had been paid, she may not be paid unless she swears

---

[1] Num. 27[11] has a superfluous 'and he shall possess it (f.)', interpreted to mean 'and a man shall inherit from his wife'.   [2] Cf. B.M. 7[11]; B.B. 8[5].
[3] Who lay claim to payment out of a deceased's estate. See Shebu. 7[1ff].
[4] Shebu. 7[8].   [5] Of his wife when she is not a shopkeeper or guardian.
[6] Shebu. 7[7].

[to her claim] on oath. How does it apply with 'assigned property'? If a man had sold his property to others and she seeks to be paid by them that had bought it, she may not be paid unless she swears [to her claim] on oath. How does it apply with 'the property of orphans'? If the husband died and left his property to [his] orphans and she seeks to be paid by the orphans, she may not be paid unless she swears [to her claim] on oath. How does it apply with 'property of one that is not present'? If a man went beyond the sea and she seeks to be paid in his absence, she may not be paid unless she swears [to her claim] on oath. R. Simeon says: If she claims her *Ketubah* the heirs may exact an oath of her, but if she does not claim her *Ketubah* the heirs may not exact an oath of her.

9. If she brought forth a bill of divorce without a *Ketubah* she is entitled to her *Ketubah*; but if [she brought forth] a *Ketubah* without a bill of divorce and said, 'My bill of divorce is lost', but he said, 'My quittance is lost',[1] (so, too, if a creditor produced a bill of indebtedness without a *prozbol*),[2] the like of these may not be paid. Rabban Simeon b. Gamaliel says: Since the time of danger[3] a woman is entitled to her *Ketubah* without a bill of divorce, and a creditor is entitled to his due without a *prozbol*. [If a woman brought forth] two bills of divorce and two *Ketubahs*, she is entitled to two *Ketubahs*. [If she brought forth] two *Ketubahs* and one bill of divorce, or one *Ketubah* and two bills of divorce, or a *Ketubah* and a bill of divorce and a [proof of her husband's] death,[4] she is entitled only to one *Ketubah*; for if a man puts away his wife and then receives her back, he receives her back only on the conditions of her first *Ketubah*. If a father gave his son, that was a minor, in marriage, her *Ketubah*[5] remains valid, since on this condition[6] he took her for his wife. If a man became a proselyte and his wife with him, her *Ketubah* remains valid, since on this condition he has kept her as his wife.

10. 1. If a man was married to two wives and died, the [claim of the] first wife [to payment of her *Ketubah*] comes before [the claim of] the second, and [the claim of] the heirs of the first wife before the [claim of the] heirs of the second. If he married a first wife and she died, and he married a second wife and then himself died, [the claim of] the second wife and her heirs comes before [the claim of] the heirs of the first wife.

2. If a man was married to two wives and they died and he then died, and the orphans claim the *Ketubah* of their mother, and there is but [enough for] the two *Ketubahs*, they share equally. If there was a surplus of one *denar*, each of them takes the *Ketubah* of their mother.[7] If the orphans said, 'We reckon the value of the property of our father at one *denar* more', so that they may take their mother's *Ketubah*, they do not listen to them, but they estimate the value of the property before the court.

3. If there was property destined to accrue[8] [to the heirs] it does not count as property [already] held in possession. R. Simeon says: Even if

---

[1] 'But I have paid her her *Ketubah*.'   [2] App. I. 34.
[3] When oppressive edicts forbade the observance of Jewish rites, including the issue of bills of divorce and *prozbols*. Cf. M.Sh. 4[11].
[4] He had married her, divorced her, married her again, and then died.
[5] Written when she was a virgin, assigning her 200 *zuz*; it is still valid for that amount although when he came of age she was no longer virgin.   [6] The assigning of 200 *zuz*.
[7] And share the remaining *denar* with the other heirs. See Ket. 4[10].
[8] Loans, business profits, and the like. Cf. Bekh. 8[b].

there was also movable property, it is of none account unless there was also there immovable property worth one *denar* more than the charge of the two *Ketubahs*.

4. If a man was married to three wives and he died and the *Ketubah* of one was one *mina*, of another 200 *denars*, and of the other 300 *denars*, and he left property worth only one *mina*, they divide this equally. If he left 200 *denars*, the one whose *Ketubah* was one *mina* takes 50 *denars*, while they whose *Ketubahs* were 200 *denars* and 300 *denars* take each three golden *denars*.[1] If he left 300 *denars*, she whose *Ketubah* was one *mina* takes 50 *denars*, she whose *Ketubah* was 200 *denars* takes one *mina*, and she whose *Ketubah* was 300 *denars* takes six golden *denars*.[2] So, too, if three persons put money into a fund, and make a loss or a profit, they share in the like fashion.

5. If a man was married to four wives and he died, the [claim of the] first wife comes before that of the second, that of the second before that of the third, and that of the third before that of the fourth. The first must swear on oath to the second, and the second to the third, and the third to the fourth [that she has not received her *Ketubah*]; and the fourth may be paid without swearing [to her claim] on oath. Ben Nanos says: And should she have this advantage because she is the last?—she, too, may not be paid unless she has sworn [to her claim] on oath. If they were all put away on the same day, whosoever preceded her fellow even by an hour acquires [first] right. Thus in Jerusalem they used to declare in writing the hour [of the divorce]. If they were all put away in the same hour, and there was property worth only one *mina*, they share equally.

6. If a man was married to two wives and he then sold his field,[3] and the first wife had declared to the buyer in writing, 'I have neither right nor claim against thee,' the second wife may take [her due] from the buyer, and the first wife from the second wife, and the buyer from the first wife, and so they may go on in turn until they make some compromise between them. So, too, with a creditor,[4] or a woman that is a creditor.[5]

11. 1. The widow receives her maintenance from the property of the orphans, and the work of her hands belongs to them; but they are not responsible for her burial. Her heirs that inherit her *Ketubah* are responsible for her burial.

2. A widow, whether she became a widow after betrothal or after wedlock, may sell [property that was security for her *Ketubah*] without the consent of the court. R. Simeon says: [If she became a widow] after wedlock she may sell without the consent of the court; but if after betrothal [only], she may not sell save with the consent of the court, since she has no claim to maintenance, and she that has no claim to maintenance may not sell save with the consent of the court.

3. If a widow sold her *Ketubah* or part of it, of if she pledged her

---

[1] 75 silver *denars*. App. II, A.   [2] 150 silver *denars*.

[3] Which was security for both their *Ketubahs*.

[4] e.g. if a debtor sold his two fields, whose value covered his debt, to two buyers, and the creditor declared to the second buyer that he had no claim against him, the creditor may seize the property of the first buyer, and the first the property of the second, and then the second can recover from the creditor, the creditor from the first, and so forth.

[5] For her *Ketubah*. If the husband sold two fields, worth the value of her *Ketubah*, and she declared to the second buyer that she had no claim against him, she may satisfy her claim from the property of the first, &c.

Ketubah or part of it, or if she gave away her *Ketubah* or part of it, she may not sell what is left save with the consent of the court. But the Sages say: She may sell it [piecemeal] even four or five times, or sell it for the sake of maintenance without the consent of the court and declare in writing, 'I have sold it for the sake of maintenance'. If she was divorced she may only sell with the consent of the court.

4. If a widow whose *Ketubah* was 200 *denars* sold[1] what was worth one mina for 200 *denars*, or what was worth 200 *denars* for one *mina*, she has [thereby] received her *Ketubah*. If her *Ketubah* was one *mina* and she sold what was worth one *mina* and a *denar* for one *mina*, her bargain is void. Even if she said, 'I will repay the *denar* to the heirs', her bargain is void. Rabban Simeon b. Gamaliel says: Her bargain remains valid always so long as there is [property] enough for her to leave from a field an area of nine *kabs*,[2] or from a garden an area of a half-*kab*; or, according to R. Akiba, an area of a quarter-*kab*. If her *Ketubah* was 400 *zuz* and she sold [part][3] to one person for one *mina* and [a second part] to another person for one *mina*,[4] and to another what was worth one *mina* and a *denar* for one *mina*,[5] the bargain with the last person is void, but all the rest remain valid.

5. If the judges' assessment[6] valued the property at one-sixth too little or one-sixth too much, their bargain is void. Rabban Simeon b. Gamaliel says: Their bargain remains valid: otherwise of what worth is the power of a court? But if they drew up a deed-of-inspection,[7] even if they sold for 200 *denars* what was worth one *mina*, or for one *mina* what was worth 200 *denars*, their bargain remains valid.

6. If a woman had exercised right of Refusal,[8] or was within the secondary grade[9] [of kinship to her husband], or was sterile, she may not lay claim to her *Ketubah* or to the increase[10] [on her *melog* property], or to alimony, or to indemnity [for loss on her *melog* property]; but if at the outset he married her with the knowledge that she was sterile she may lay claim to her *Ketubah*. If a widow[11] was married to a High Priest, or a divorced woman or one that had performed *halitzah* was married to a common priest, or a bastard or a *Nethinah* to an Israelite, or the daughter of an Israelite to a *Nathin* or a bastard, these may lay claim to their *Ketubah*.

12. 1. If a man married a woman and she stipulated that he should maintain her daughter for five years, he is bound to maintain her for five years. If he was [afterward] married to another and she stipulated to him also that he should maintain her daughter for five years, he, too, is bound to maintain her for five years. The first husband may not say, 'If she comes to my house I will maintain her', but he must send her her maintenance to the place where her mother is.[12] So, too, the two husbands may not say, 'We will maintain her jointly', but the one must maintain her and the other must give her the cost of her maintenance.

2. When she is married her husband must give her maintenance, while

<hr>

[1] Land from her husband's estate.   [2] App. II, E.
[3] Of the ground that was security for her *Ketubah*.
[4] Add: 'and a third part to another for one *mina*'.
[5] So realizing more than the claim of her *Ketubah*.
[6] When they valued and sold the deceased husband's property to pay his widow's *Ketubah*.
[7] Proclaiming the sale and permitting public scrutiny of the property.
[8] See Yeb. 13[1f].   [9] See Yeb. 2[4].
[10] Profits gained through the use of her property.   [11] See Yeb. 2[4].
[12] Variant: 'where she is (with her mother)'.

they each give her the cost of her maintenance; when they die their [own] daughters receive maintenance from the unassigned property, while she receives maintenance from property [thereto] assigned, since she is, as it were, a creditor. The prudent-minded used to declare in writing, '... on condition that I maintain thy daughter five years, such time [only] as thou continuest with me'.

3. If a widow said, 'I do not wish to leave my husband's house', the heirs cannot say to her, 'Go to thy father's house and we will maintain thee', but they must maintain her in her husband's house and give her a dwelling befitting her condition. If she said, 'I do not wish to leave my father's house', the heirs may say to her, 'If thou continuest with us thou wilt receive maintenance; but if thou continuest not with us thou wilt not receive maintenance'. If she so pleaded because she was but a child and they were but children, they must maintain her even while she is in her father's house.

4. So long as she continues in her father's house she may claim her *Ketubah* at any time; so long as she continues in her husband's house she may claim her *Ketubah* only at the end of twenty-five years, since in twenty-five years she can render a seemly return for her *Ketubah*. So R. Meir, who spoke in the name of Rabban Gamaliel. But the Sages say: So long as she is in her husband's house she may claim her *Ketubah* at any time; so long as she is in her father's house she may claim her *Ketubah* only at the end of twenty-five years. If she died her heirs must lay their claim to her *Ketubah* within twenty-five years.

13. 1. There were two judges of civil law[1] in Jerusalem, Admon and Hanan b. Abishalom. Hanan gave two decisions and Admon seven. If a man went beyond the sea and his wife claimed maintenance, Hanan says: Let her swear [to her claim] at the end [of the time] and let her not swear at the beginning. But the Sons of the High Priests[2] disputed with him and said, 'Let her swear' at the beginning and let her not swear at the end'. R. Dosa b. Harkinas decided according to their opinion. R. Johanan b. Zakkai said: Hanan said well: let her swear only at the the end.[3]

2. If a man went beyond the sea and another rose up and maintained his wife, Hanan said: His money is lost to him. But the Sons of the High Priests disputed with him and said, 'Let him swear on oath how much he has expended and let him recover it'. R. Dosa b. Harkinas decided according to their opinion. R. Johanan b. Zakkai said: Hanan said well: the man laid his money on the horn of the gazelle.

3. Admon gave seven decisions. If[4] a man died and left sons and daughters, and the property was great, the sons inherit and the daughters receive maintenance;[5] but if the property was small the daughters receive maintenance and the sons go a-begging. Admon says: [The son may say] 'Must I suffer loss because I am a male!' Rabban Gamaliel said: I approve the words of Admon.

4. If[6] a man claimed from his fellow jars of oil and the other admitted [his claim] to the [empty] jars, Admon says: Since he admits the claim in part he must take an oath [in denial of the rest]. But the Sages say: This

---

[1] Heb. *gezeroth*, 'decrees'. Variant: *gezeloth*, 'robberies' or 'malpractices'.
[2] See Ohol. 17[5]; cf. Ket. 1[5] 'Court of the Priests'.
[3] That she had not been maintained from her husband's property.
[4] B.B. 9[1].   [5] Cf. Ket. 4[6].   [6] Shebu. 6[3].

is not an admission in like kind to the claim. Rabban Gamaliel said: I approve the words of Admon.

5. If a man undertook to give money to his [prospective] son-in-law and then stretched out the leg,[1] she may sit down [and remain unmarried] until her hair grows grey. Admon says: She can say, 'Had I myself undertaken it I would sit down until my hair grows grey; but since now it is my father that undertook it because of me, what can I do? Either marry me or set me free'. Rabban Gamaliel said: I approve the words of Admon.

6. If a man contested another's ownership of a field,[2] but had himself signed [the deed of sale] as a witness, Admon says: He may say, 'The second was amenable to me and the first was harsher than he'.[3] But the Sages say: He has lost his title. If he[4] made his field a [boundary-]mark for another,[5] he has lost his title.

7. If a man went beyond the sea and the path to his field was lost,[6] Admon says: He may go to it by the shortest way. But the Sages say: He must buy another path even if it costs a hundred *minas*, or fly through the air.

8. If a man brought forth a bond of indebtedness against his fellow and his fellow brought forth [a deed of sale[7] to prove] that the other had sold him a field, Admon says: He can say, 'Had I been thy debtor thou couldst have received thy due when thou soldest me the field'. But the Sages say: The first man was prudent-minded in that he sold him the field, since he can take it in pledge.

9. If two men brought forth bonds of indebtedness the one against the other, Admon says: [The one[8] can say], 'Had I been thy debtor how camest thou to borrow from me?' But the Sages say: Each exacts payment of his bond.

10. Three countries [are to be distinguished] in what concerns marriage: Judea, beyond Jordan and Galilee. None may take forth [his wife against her will] from one town to another or from one city to another [in another country]; but within the same country he may take her forth with him from one town to another or from one city to another [even against her will], but not from a town to a city, and not from a city to a town. He may take her forth from a bad dwelling to a good one, but not from a good dwelling to a bad one. Rabban Simeon b. Gamaliel says: Nor even from a bad dwelling to a good one, since the good one puts her to the proof.[9]

11. All may be compelled to go up to the Land of Israel but none may be compelled to leave it. All may be compelled to go up to Jerusalem but none may be compelled to leave it, whether they be men or women.[10] If a man married a woman in the Land of Israel and divorced her in the Land of Israel, he must pay her [her *Ketubah*] in the coinage of the Land of Israel. If he married a woman in the Land of Israel and divorced her in Cappadocia, he must pay her in the coinage of the Land of Israel. If he married a woman in Cappadocia and divorced her in the Land of Israel, he must pay her in

---

[1] i.e. became bankrupt.
[2] Urging to the new owner that the seller had stolen it from him, the complainant.
[3] 'I signed it on the assumption that it would be easier to recover my property from the new owner than from the fraudulent seller'.
[4] Who reclaims his field from a fraudulent possessor.
[5] i.e. he signed a deed of sale in which the land transferred was defined as bounded by a field described as the property of the fraudulent owner, though it was in reality his own.
[6] And it is not known which of the adjoining owners had annexed it within the area of his own field.   [7] Dated later than the bond.   [8] Whose bond was dated the later.
[9] Rashi: 'Puts the body to the proof, causes illness'.   [10] Variant: 'or slaves'.

the coinage of the Land of Israel. Rabban Simeon b. Gamaliel says: He may pay her in the coinage of Cappadocia. If he married a woman in Cappadocia and divorced her in Cappadocia he must pay her in the coinage of Cappadocia.

NEDARIM[1] ('VOWS')

1. 1. Any substitute for [the form of words used to utter] a vow, ban, oath, or Nazirite-vow is as binding as the vow, ban, oath, or Nazirite-vow itself.[2] If a man said to his fellow, 'Be it forbidden me by vow', [or] 'May I be kept apart from thee', [or] 'May I be removed far from thee if I eat aught of thine',[3] [or] 'if I taste aught of thine!'—then it is forbidden to him. [If he said,] 'May I be to thee as one cast out', R. Akiba was here fain to apply the more stringent ruling.[4] [If he said,] 'As the vows of the ungodly . . .',[5] his vow is binding as touching the Nazirite-vow, the offering, and the oath. [If he said,] 'As the vows of the pious . . .', he has said naught; [but if he said,] 'As their freewill-offerings . . .', his vow is binding as touching the Nazirite-vow and the offering.

2. If a man said to his fellow, *Konam* or *Konah* or *Konas*, these are substitutes for *Korban*, an Offering.[6] [If he said,] *Herek* or *Herekh* or *Heref*, these are substitutes for *Herem*, a devoted thing.[7] [If he said,] *Nazik* or *Naziah* or *Paziah*, these are substitutes for the Nazirite-vow.[8] [If he said,] *Shebutah* or *Shekukah*, or if he vowed with the word *Mota*,[9] these are substitutes for *Shebuah*, an oath.

3. If he said, 'May what I eat of thine be "not *hullin*"[10] [or] "not valid as food", [or] "not clean", [or] "unclean", [or] "Remnant and Refuse",'[11] it is forbidden to him. [If he said, 'May it be to me] "as the lamb",[12] [or] "as the [Temple-]sheds",[13] [or] "as the wood [for burning on the Altar]", [or] "as the Fire-offerings",[14] [or] "as the Altar", [or] "as Jerusalem" '; or if he vowed by any of the utensils[15] of the Altar, although he did not utter [the word] *Korban*, an offering, it is a vow as binding as if he had uttered the word *Korban*. R. Judah says: If he said, ['May it be] Jerusalem!'[16] he has said naught.

4. If a man said, 'May what I eat of thine be a Whole-offering', or

---

[1] The vow is distinct from the oath, in that a vow forbids a certain thing to be used ('Let such-a-thing be forbidden to me, or to you!'), while an oath forbids the swearer to do a certain thing although it is not a thing forbidden in itself ('I swear that I will not eat such-a-thing!'). Vows are of two kinds: vows of dedication, which render a thing forbidden in future for common use; and vows of abstention, which render forbidden things or acts ordinarily permissible.

[2] According to Gem. 2b there should follow here: 'And all "handles" of vows (i.e. abbreviations of vows) are as binding as the vows themselves'. The formulae in the rest of this paragraph are 'handles' and not substituted words.

[3] Variant: 'for I will eat naught of thine'.

[4] He doubted whether it was a binding vow, but was impelled to rule that it deprived a man of the benefit of his fellow.

[5] The vow, of which this is the 'handle', is (according to Gem. 9a) that of a man with a loaf of bread before him and, a Nazirite passing by, he intends to say, 'May it (the loaf) be to me as the vows of the ungodly (i.e. of this Nazirite) if I eat of it!' If then he eats the loaf he must fulfil the thirty days of the Nazirite-vow (see Naz. 1[3]), he is guilty of Sacrilege (Lev. 5[15]) and must make the prescribed offering, and he is also guilty of 'a rash oath' (Shebu. 3[7]) and must offer (Lev. 5[4–13]) a 'rising and falling' offering (i.e. one that varies according to his means).

[6] A thing as forbidden to him for common use as a Temple offering.

[7] 'Most holy to the Lord'; Lev. 27[28]; Arak. 8[6].   [8] See Naz. 1[ff].

[9] For *Momatha*, the Aramaic equivalent of *Shebuah*, an oath.

[10] i.e. not 'free for common use', but 'a Hallowed Thing'.

[11] See Zeb. 2[3]; 3[4].   [12] The Daily Whole-offering, Num. 28[1–8].

[13] Cf. Midd. 2[5].   [14] Lev. 21[6].   [15] Ex. 27[3].   [16] Without the particle of comparison.

'a Meal-offering', or 'a Sin-offering', or 'a Thank-offering', or 'a Peace-offering', it is forbidden to him. But R. Judah permits it. If a man said, 'May what I eat of thine be the *Korban*', or 'as a *Korban*', or 'a *Korban*', it is forbidden to him. [If he said,] 'For[1] *Korban*! I will not eat of thine', R. Meir declares it forbidden. If a man said to his fellow, 'May my mouth that speaks with thee' or 'my hand that works with thee' or 'my foot that walks with thee, be *Konam*', [such an act] is forbidden to him.

2. 1. These [vows] are not binding: 'May what I eat of thine be *hullin*',[2] [or] 'as swine's flesh',[3] [or] 'as an idol',[4] [or] 'as hides pierced at the heart',[5] [or] 'as carrion',[6] [or] 'as flesh torn of beasts',[7] [or] 'as forbidden beasts',[8] [or] 'as creeping things',[9] [or] 'as Aaron's Dough-offering[10] or as his Heave-offering';[11] such a vow is not binding. If he said to his wife, 'Be thou to me as my mother!' they open for him a door [to repentance] from another side,[12] that he behave not lightly in such a matter. [If he said,] '*Konam*! if I sleep!' [or] 'if I speak!' [or] 'if I walk!', or if he said to his wife, '*Konam*! if I have intercourse with thee!' to such applies [the law], *He shall not profane his word.*[13] [But if he said,] 'I swear on oath that I will not sleep!' [or] 'that I will not speak!' [or] 'that I will not walk!' he is thereby bound.[14]

2. [If he said,] '*Korban*! if I eat of thine', or '*Korban*! if I eat not of thine', or 'No *Korban*! if I eat of thine', he is not thereby bound. [But if he said,] 'By my oath! I will not eat of thine', or 'By my oath! if I eat of thine', 'By no oath! I will not eat of thine', he is thereby bound. Herein greater stringency applies to oaths than to vows. But greater stringency may apply to vows to than oaths. Thus if he said, '*Konam* be the *Sukkah*[15] I build!' [or] 'the *Lulab*[16] I carry!' [or] 'the phylacteries[17] I put on!' with vows this is binding, but with oaths it is not binding, since none may swear on oath to transgress religious duties.

3. There may be a vow within a vow but not an oath within an oath. Thus if a man said, 'May I be a Nazirite if I eat! may I be a Nazirite if I eat!' and he ate, he must fulfil each one of the two vows. [But if he had said,] 'By my oath I will not eat! by my oath I will not eat!' and he ate, he is culpable on one count only.

4. To vows not expressly defined the more stringent ruling applies, but to vows expressly defined the more lenient ruling applies. Thus [if a man said,] 'May it be to me as salted flesh!' [or] 'as wine of the Drink-offering!' and his vow was of the things offered to Heaven,[18] it is binding; and if his vow was of the things offered to idols it is not binding; but if neither was expressly defined, it is binding. [If he said,] 'May it be to me as a devoted thing!' and meant 'as a thing devoted to Heaven',[19] it is binding; and if he meant 'as a thing devoted to the priests', it is not binding; but if neither was expressly defined, it is binding. [If he said,] 'May it be to me as Tithe!'

---

[1] Some texts read 'not' instead of 'for'. See below, 2[2].   [2] See above, p. 264, n. 10.
[3] Lev. 11[7].   [4] Deut. 7[25].   [5] See A. Zar. 2[3].   [6] Deut. 14[21].   [7] Ex. 22[31].
[8] Lev. 11[11].   [9] Lev. 11[29].   [10] Num. 15[20].
[11] Num. 18[8]. All these objects are already forbidden by the Law, and it is not within a man's choice to abstain from them or not.
[12] i.e. he may not have his vow revoked because of his regret at making it, but another cause must be forthcoming, justifying its revocation by a Sage; e.g. in this case the honour due to his mother. See below, 9[1].   [13] Num. 30[2]. See Shebu. 3[8].
[14] If the oath was for a defined and possible duration. Otherwise it is a 'vain oath', and Shebu. 3[7] applies.   [15] App. I. 42.   [16] App. I. 20.   [17] See p. 104, n. 16.
[18] i.e. offered in the Temple; Lev. 2[13]; Num. 15[5].   [19] Lev. 27[28].

and meant 'as Tithe of Cattle',[1] the vow is binding, and if he meant 'as Tithe of the threshing-floor',[2] it is not binding; but if neither was expressly defined, it is binding. [If he said,] 'May it be to me as *Terumah*!' and meant 'as the *Terumah* of the Temple-chamber',[3] it is binding; and if he meant 'as that of the threshing-floor', it is not binding; but if neither was expressly defined, it is binding. So R. Meir. But R. Judah says: If the vow was of undefined *Terumah*, in Judea the vow is binding; but in Galilee it is not binding, since the men of Galilee know naught of the *Terumah* of the Temple-chamber. [And if the vow was of] undefined devoted things, in Judea it is not binding, but in Galilee it is binding, since the people of Galilee know naught of things devoted to [the use of] the priests.

5. If a man vowed and used the word *herem*,[4] but said, 'In my vow I meant only a *herem* (net) of the sea', or if he vowed and used the word *Korban*, but said, 'In my vow I meant only the *Korbans* (gifts) of kings'; or if he vowed, 'May my *etzem*[5] be *Korban*!' but said, 'In my vow I meant only the *etzem* (bone) which I laid before me to vow by it'; or '*Konam* be any benefit I have of my wife!' but said, 'I vowed only [to abstain] from my first wife whom I divorced'—touching all such vows they need not seek [release from the Sages]; but if they seek it they should punish them and apply the more stringent ruling. So R. Meir. But the Sages say: They open for them a door [to repentance] from another side, and instruct them so that they shall not behave themselves lightly in what concerns vows.

3. 1. Four kinds of vow the Sages have declared not to be binding: vows of incitement, vows of exaggeration, vows made in error, and vows [that cannot be fulfilled by reason] of constraint. Which are accounted 'vows of incitement'? If, to wit, a man would sell a thing and said, '*Konam*![6] if I take of thee less than a *sela*!'[7] and the other said, '*Konam*! if I give thee more than a shekel!'[7] and both agree on three *denars*.[7] R. Eliezer b. Jacob says: Also [as] when a man would put his fellow under a vow that he will eat with him. A man may say, 'Let no vow that I vow hereafter be binding', provided that he is mindful of this in the moment of his vow.

2. [Which are accounted] 'vows of exaggeration'? If, to wit, a man said, '*Konam*! if I saw not in this road as many as came up out of Egypt!' [or] 'if I saw not a serpent as big as the beam of an olive-press!' [Which are accounted] 'vows made in error'? If, [to wit, a man said, '*Konam*!] if I have eaten or if I have drunken!' and he remembered that he had eaten or drunken; [or if he said, '*Konam*!] if I eat or if I drink!' and he forgot and ate and drank; [or if he said,] '*Konam* be any benefit my wife has of me, for she has stolen my purse!' or, 'for she has beaten my son!' and it became known that she had not beaten him, or that she had not stolen it. If a man saw others eating [his] figs and said, 'May they be *Korban* to you!' and they were found to be his father and brothers and others with them, the School of Shammai say: For them the vow is not binding, but for the others with them it is binding. And the School of Hillel say: The vow is binding for neither of them.[8]

3. [Which are accounted] 'vows [that cannot be fulfilled by reason] of

---

[1] Lev. 27[32].   [2] Variant: 'corn'. See Num. 18[30].
[3] See Shek. 3[1]; App. I. 48.   [4] See above, 2[1].
[5] May have the sense, 'May I *myself* be as forbidden to thee as *Korban*!'
[6] i.e. 'let such or such a thing be *Korban*, if . . .'   [7] App. II, A.
[8] On the principle that a vow which is invalid in part is wholly invalid. See below, 9[6].

constraint'? If, to wit, his fellow made him vow to come and eat with him and he fell sick, or his son fell sick, or a river-flood hindered him, such would be a vow [that cannot be fulfilled by reason] of constraint.

4. Men may vow to murderers, robbers, or tax-gatherers that what they have is Heave-offering even though it is not Heave-offering; or that they belong to the king's household even though they do not belong to the king's household. The School of Shammai say: They may so vow in any form of words save in the form of an oath. And the School of Hillel say: Even in the form of an oath. The School of Shammai say: A man should not be first with a vow [but he should vow only under constraint]. And the School of Hillel say: He may even be first with a vow. The School of Shammai say: Only in a matter over which a vow is imposed. And the School of Hillel say: Even in a matter over which no vow is imposed. Thus, if they had said to him, 'Say, *Konam* be any benefit my wife has of me!' and he said, '*Konam* be any benefit my wife and my children have of me!' the School of Shammai say: His wife is permitted to him and his children are forbidden. And the School of Hillel say: Both are forbidden.

5. [If a man said,] 'Let these plants be *Korban* if they are not broken!' [or] 'Let this cloak be *Korban* if it does not get burnt!' he may redeem them.[1] [But if he said,] 'Let these plants be *Korban* so long as they are not broken!' [or] 'Let this cloak be *Korban* so long as it is not burnt!' he may not redeem them.

6. If a man vowed to have no benefit 'from any sea-farers', he is per-mitted to have benefit from land-dwellers; but if 'from any land-dwellers', he is forbidden to have benefit from sea-farers, since 'sea-farers' are in-cluded in the term 'land-dwellers'. [By 'sea-farers' is meant] not such as go only from Acre to Jaffa, but such as sail afar off.

7. If a man vowed to have no benefit 'from them that see the sun', he is forbidden to have benefit from blind folk, since the words mean only 'any that the sun sees'.

8. If a man vowed to have no benefit from 'the black-haired', he is forbidden to have benefit from the bald and the grey-haired, but not from women and children, since only men are called 'the black-haired'.

9. If a man vowed to have no benefit from 'creatures that are born' (*yillodim*), he is not forbidden to have benefit from 'creatures that may be born' (*noladim*); but if [he vowed to have no benefit] from 'creatures that may be born' (*noladim*), he[2] is forbidden [to have benefit] from 'creatures that are born' (*yillodim*).[3] R. Meir says that he is not forbidden [to have benefit] from 'creatures that are born' (*yillodim*); and the Sages say: This word (*yillodim*) means only creatures that bring forth [living young].

10. If a man vowed [to have no benefit] from 'them that keep Sabbath', he is forbidden to have benefit from Israelites and from Samaritans; if from 'them that eat garlic', he is forbidden to have benefit from Israelites and from Samaritans;[4] but if 'from them that go up to Jerusalem', he is forbidden [to have benefit] from Israelites, but not from Samaritans.

11. [If he said], '*Konam*! if I have any benefit from the children of

---

[1] Lev. 27[15].   [2] Some texts omit 'he is forbidden . . . (*yillodim*)'.
[3] This distinction between *yillodim* and *noladim*, though apparently recognized in the Hebrew of Mishnaic times, is not apparent in biblical Hebrew; thus *yillodim* is used (Josh. 5[5]) of those already born and (Ex. 1[22]) of those not yet born, and *noladim* is used also of those already born (Gen. 48[5]) and of those yet to be born (1 Kings 13[2]).
[4] Some texts read: 'but not Samaritans'.

Noah!' he is permitted [to have benefit] from Israelites, but not from
other nations; [but if he said, '*Konam*!] if I have any benefit from the seed
of Abraham!' he is forbidden to have benefit from Israelites but not from
other nations. [If he said, '*Konam*!] if I have any benefit from Israelites',
he must buy things for more than their worth and sell them for less;
[and if he said, '*Konam*!] if Israelites have any benefit from me', he must
buy things for less than their worth and sell them for more, if others have
regard to his vow. [If he said, '*Konam*!] if I have any benefit from them or
they from me', he may have benefit from other nations. [If he said,]
'*Konam*! if I have any benefit from the uncircumcised', he is permitted to
have benefit from the uncircumcised of Israel, but not from the circumcised of other nations. [If he said,] '*Konam*! If I have any benefit from the
the circumcised!' he is forbidden to have benefit [even] from the uncircumcised in Israel but he is permitted to have benefit from the circumcised
among the nations of the world, since 'uncircumcised' is but used as a
name for the gentiles, as it is written, *For all the [other] nations are uncircumcised, and all the house of Israel are uncircumcised in heart*.[1] Again it
says, *This uncircumcised Philistine*.[2] Again it says, *Lest the daughters of the
Philistines rejoice, lest the daughters of the uncircumcised triumph.* R. Eleazar
b. Azariah says: Hateful is the uncircumcision, whereby the wicked are
held up to shame, as it is written, *For all the nations are uncircumcised.*
R. Ishmael says: Great is circumcision, whereby the covenant was made
thirteen times.[4] R. Jose says: Great is circumcision which overrides even
the rigour of the Sabbath.[5] R. Joshua b. Karha says: Great is circumcision
which even for the sake of Moses, the righteous, was not suspended
so much as an hour.[6] R. Nehemiah says: Great is circumcision which
overrides the laws of leprosy-signs.[7] Rabbi says: Great is circumcision,
for despite all the religious duties which Abraham our father fulfilled, he
was not called 'perfect' until he was circumcised, as it is written, *Walk
before me and be thou perfect*.[8] After another fashion [it is said], Great is
circumcision: but for it the Holy One, blessed is he, had not created his
world, as it is written, *Thus saith the Lord, but for my covenant day and
night, I had not set forth the ordinances of heaven and earth*.[9]

4. 1. He that is forbidden by vow to have any benefit from his fellow differs
from him that is forbidden by vow to take any food from him only in
respect of the treading of his foot [in the other's domain] and the use of
vessels in which necessary food is not prepared.   If a man is forbidden
by vow to take any food from his fellow, the other may not lend him a sifter
or a sieve or a mill-stone or an oven, but he may lend him a shirt or a ring
or a cloak or nose-rings, or aught that is not used to prepare necessary
food; yet where such things can be hired out [in exchange for money or
food] it is forbidden [to lend them].

2. If a man is forbidden by vow to have any benefit from his fellow,
the one may still pay the other's Shekel-dues[11] for him, or pay him his
debt, or restore to him his lost property; but where a reward is taken for it,
the benefit falls to the Temple.

---

[1] Jer. 9[26].   [2] 1 Sam. 17[36].   [3] 2 Sam. 1[20].
[4] 'Covenant' is repeated thirteen times in the seventeenth chapter of Genesis.
[5] See Shab. 19[1].   [6] Cf. Ex. 4[24ff].   [7] Neg. 7[5] (end).   [8] Gen. 17[1].   [9] Jer. 33[25].
[10] Meg. 1[6]. These two points are forbidden to the former and permitted to the latter.
[11] Ex. 30[13ff]. Cf. Shek. 1[6].

3. The other may set apart for him his Heave-offering and Tithes with his consent, he may offer on the other's behalf the Bird-offerings of a man or woman that has a flux[1] or of a woman after childbirth,[2] and Sin-offerings and Guilt-offerings, and he may teach him *Midrash*,[3] *Halakoth*,[4] and *Haggadoth*,[5] but he may not teach him Scripture, though he may teach Scripture to his sons and to his daughters.[6] He may maintain the other's wife and children even though the other is answerable for their mainte-nance. But he may not feed the other's cattle, whether the clean or the unclean. R. Eliezer says: He may feed the unclean cattle but not the clean. They said to him: How do the clean differ from the unclean? He answered: The life of the clean cattle belongs to Heaven and only their body belongs to the owner, while both the life and the body of the unclean cattle belong to Heaven. They said to him: The life of the unclean cattle also belongs to God, but the body belongs to the owner, because if he will he may sell it to the gentiles or feed the dogs with it.

4. If a man is forbidden by vow to have any benefit from his fellow and his fellow came in to visit him, he may stand but not sit down.[7] He may heal him, himself, but not what belongs to him;[8] he may bathe with him in a large tub but not in a small one;[9] and he may sleep with him in one bed. R. Judah says: In hot weather, but not in the rainy season, since then he would benefit him.[10] He may sit at meat with him on the same couch and eat at the same table but not out of the same dish, but he may eat from the same dish if this passes around the table.[11] He may not eat with him from the same feeding-bowl that is set before labourers. He may not work with him in the same furrow. So R. Meir. But the Sages say: He may work in the same furrow a far distance from him.

5. If a man is forbidden by vow to have any benefit from his fellow, and it was before the Seventh Year, he may not go down to his fellow's field or eat from the produce that hangs over [from the other's property]; if it was during the Seventh Year[12] he may not go down into his field, but he may eat of what hangs over. If he is forbidden by vow to take any food from him, and it was before the Seventh Year, he may go down into his field but he may not eat of the produce; in the Seventh Year, he may go down and also eat.

6. If a man is forbidden by vow to have any benefit from his fellow, he may not lend to him or borrow from him, or give or take a loan, or sell to him or buy from him. If one said to another, 'Lend me your cow', and the other answered, 'It is not at liberty', and he said, '*Konam*! if I ever again plough my field with it', if he himself was wont to plough, the vow is binding on him but not on others; but if he himself was not wont to plough, the vow is binding on himself and on all others.[13]

7. If a man is forbidden by vow to have any benefit from his fellow, and he had naught to eat, his fellow may go to the shopkeeper and say,

---

1 Lev. 15[14, 29].   2 Lev. 12[6, 8].   3 App. I. 27.   4 App. I. 11.   5 App. I. 10.
6 Some texts omit 'and to his daughters'. Cf. Sot. 3[4].
7 If his fellow visits him in sickness he may not stay long with him. The case dealt with turns on the custom of paying those who remain with the sick. Therefore by his staying with him he relieves him of the expense of hiring watchers.
8 Cf. A. Zar. 2[2].   9 The other would increase the depth of water.
10 Provide warmth in the cold weather.
11 The other might eat but little, thereby affording him an added share.
12 When there is no private ownership of the fruits of the earth. He is still, however, for-bidden to benefit from entry into his fellow's domain.   13 Who plough for him.

'Such-a-one is forbidden by vow to have any benefit from me, and I do not know what I shall do'; then the shopkeeper may give food to the one and take payment from the other. If the first needed to build his house or to put up his wall or to reap his field, the other may go to the labourers and say, 'Such-a-one is forbidden by vow to have any benefit from me, and I do not know what I shall do'; then they may go and work with the one and take their hire from the other.

8. If they were on a journey together and the first man had naught to eat, the other may give the food to a third person as a gift, and the first is permitted to use it. If there was none other with them he may lay the food on a stone or on a wall and say, 'This is ownerless property for all that wish', and the other may take and eat it. But this R. Jose forbids.

5. 1. If two jointholders made a vow to have no benefit the one from the other, neither may enter their [common] courtyard.[1] R. Eliezer b. Jacob says: Each may enter the portion that belongs to him, but each is forbidden to put there a mill-stone or an oven, or to rear fowls. If only one was forbidden by vow to have any benefit from his fellow, he may not enter the courtyard. R. Eliezer b. Jacob says: He may say to the other, 'I will enter my portion but I will not enter thine', and they compel him that vowed to sell his portion.

2. If a man from the street was forbidden by vow to have any benefit from one of the jointholders, he may not enter the courtyard. R. Eliezer b. Jacob says: He may say to him, 'I will enter the portion belonging to thy fellow, but I will not enter thine'.

3. If a man was forbidden by vow to have any benefit from his fellow, and his fellow had a bath-house or an olive-press in the town which were hired [to others], and he still had rights therein, the other is forbidden to use them; but if his fellow no more had rights therein, he is permitted to use them. If a man said to his fellow, 'Konam! if I enter thy house', or 'if I buy thy field', and his fellow died or sold his property to another, his vow is not binding. [But if he said,] 'Konam! if I enter this house', or 'if I buy this field', and his fellow died or sold his property to another, the vow is still binding.

4. [If a man said to his fellow,] 'May I be to thee as a thing that is banned!' he against whom the vow is made is forbidden [to have any benefit from him]; [if he said,] 'Be thou to me as a thing that is banned!' he that makes the vow is forbidden [to have any benefit from the other]; [if he said,] 'May I be to thee and thou to me [as a thing that is banned], then each is forbidden [to have any benefit from the other]; both are permitted the things that belong to them that came up from Babylon,[2] but forbidden the things that belong to the [people of that] town.[3]

5. Which are the things that belong to them that came up from Babylon? The like of the Temple Mount, the courts of the Temple,[4] and the well that is midway on the road.[5] And which are the things that belong to the [people of that] town? The public place, the bath-house, the synagogue, the Ark [of the Law], and the Books [of Scripture]. Yet one may assign his share [in these] to the President [of the court; then his fellow that was for-

---

[1] Which is too small to be divided. See B.B. 1⁶.
[2] Inalienable property which can be deemed ownerless. Cf. Shebi. 6¹.
[3] Of which each citizen is a jointholder.
[4] See p. 589, n. 11.   [5] Made for the pilgrims from Babylon to Jerusalem.

bidden by vow to have any benefit from him may have benefit from them].
R. Judah says: It is all one whether he assigned it to the President or to
a private person. How does he that assigns it to the President differ from
him that assigns it to a private person? If he assigned it to the President
he need not grant him title; but if to a private person he must grant him
title. But the Sages say: It is the same either way: they must grant title;
they spoke of the President only as of a usual matter. R. Judah says: The
people of Galilee need not assign their share, since their fathers have done
so for them already.[1]

6. If a man was forbidden by vow to have any benefit from his fellow,
and he had naught to eat, his fellow may give [the food] to another as a
gift, and the first is permitted to use it. It once happened that a man at
Beth Horon, whose father was forbidden by vow to have any benefit from
him, was giving his son in marriage, and he said to his fellow, 'The courtyard and the banquet are given to thee as a gift, but they are thine only
that my father may come and eat with us at the banquet'. His fellow said,
'If they are mine, they are dedicated to Heaven'.[2] The other answered,
'I did not give thee what is mine that thou shouldest dedicate it to Heaven'.
His fellow said, 'Thou didst give me what is thine only that thou and thy
father might eat and drink and be reconciled one with the other, and that
the sin should rest on his head!' When the case came before the Sages,
they said: Any gift which, if a man would dedicate it, is not accounted dedicated, is not a [valid] gift.

6. 1. If a man vowed to abstain from 'what is cooked' he is permitted
what is roasted or seethed. If he said, '*Konam*! if I taste cooked food',
he is forbidden whatsoever is cooked as a mess in a pot but permitted what
is cooked in solid form, and he is permitted lightly boiled eggs or gourds
prepared in hot ashes.

2. If he vowed to abstain from what is 'prepared in a pot', he is forbidden
only food that needs boiling. If he said, '*Konam*! if I taste aught that enters
the pot', he is forbidden whatsoever is cooked in a pot.

3. [If he vowed to abstain] from 'what is preserved', he is forbidden only
preserved vegetables. [If he said, '*Konam*!] if I taste aught that is preserved', he is forbidden all preserved food. [If he vowed to abstain] from
what is seethed, he is forbidden only seethed flesh; [but if he said, '*Konam*!]
if I taste aught that is seethed', he is forbidden all seethed dishes. [If he
vowed to abstain] from what is roasted, he is forbidden only roasted flesh.
So R. Judah. [If he said, '*Konam*!] if I taste aught that is roasted', he is
forbidden all roasted dishes. [If he vowed to abstain] from what is salted,
he is forbidden only salted fish; [but if he said, '*Konam*!] if I taste aught
that is salted', he is forbidden all salted foods.

4. [If he said, '*Konam*!] if I taste of fish or fishes', he is forbidden them,
large or small, salted or unsalted, raw or cooked, but he is permitted
pickled chopped fish and brine. If he vowed to abstain from 'small-fish',
he is forbidden pickled chopped fish, but he is permitted brine and fish-
brine. If[3] he vowed to abstain from pickled chopped fish he is forbidden[4]
brine and fish-brine.

---

[1] The Galileans were a contentious people, and because of their proneness to vows
depriving their fellow-citizens of the common possessions, these were all vested by a former
generation in the President of the court.   [2] To the Temple. See. Lev. 27[28].
[3] Some texts omit this sentence.   [4] Some texts read 'permitted'.

5. If he vowed to abstain from milk he is permitted whey. R. Jose forbids it. [If he vowed to abstain] from whey he is permitted milk. Abba Saul says: If a man vowed to abstain from cheese, he is forbidden it whether salted or unsalted.

6. If a man vowed to abstain from flesh, he is permitted broth and meat-sediment. R. Judah forbids it. R. Judah said: It once happened that R. Tarfon forbade me[1] eggs which had been cooked therein. They answered R. Judah: It was indeed so, [yet] when? When he said, 'Let this flesh be forbidden me!'—since if a man vows to abstain from aught and it is mixed with aught else and is enough to give its flavour, the other, too, is forbidden.

7. If a man vowed to abstain from wine he is permitted a cooked dish which has in it the taste of wine. If he said, 'Konam! if I taste of this wine', and it fell into a cooked dish, and it was enough to give its flavour, it is forbidden. If a man vowed to abstain from grapes he is permitted wine; if from olives, he is permitted oil of olives, If he said, 'Konam! if I taste of these olives or grapes', he is forbidden both them and what comes from them.

8. If he vowed to abstain from dates he is permitted date-honey; if from winter grapes he is permitted vinegar made from winter grapes. R. Judah b. Bathyra says: If it is called after the name of that from which it is made, and it was from that that a man had vowed to abstain, he is also forbidden what comes from it. But the Sages permit it.

9. If a man vowed to abstain from wine, he is permitted the wine of apples; if from oil, he is permitted sesame-oil; if from honey, he is permitted date-honey; if from vinegar, he is permitted winter-grape vinegar; if from leeks, he is permitted shallots; if from vegetables, he is permitted wild vegetables, since each has its special name.[2]

10. [If a man vowed to abstain] from cabbages he is also forbidden young cabbage-shoots;[3] but if from young cabbage-shoots he is permitted cabbages; if from grits he is also forbidden grits-pottage[4] (but R. Jose permits it); [but if he vowed to abstain] from grits-pottage he is permitted grits; if from grits-pottage he is also forbidden garlic (but R. Jose permits it); [but if he vowed to abstain] from garlic he is permitted grits-pottage; if from lentils, he is also forbidden lentil-cakes (but R. Jose permits them); if from lentil-cakes he is permitted lentils. [If a man said, 'Konam!] if I taste of wheat in any form!' he is forbidden it whether as flour or bread. [If he said, 'Konam!] if I eat grits in any form', he is forbidden them whether raw or cooked. R. Judah says: [If he said], 'Konam! if I taste either grits or wheat', he is permitted to chew them raw.

7. 1. If a man vowed to abstain from vegetables, he is permitted gourds; but R. Akiba forbids them. They said to R. Akiba: If a man said to his agent, 'Bring me vegetables', cannot the agent say, 'I could find only gourds'? He answered: That is so, but could he not also say, 'I could find only pulse'?—yet gourds are included among vegetables, and pulse is not included among vegetables. Moreover he is forbidden fresh Egyptian beans, but he is permitted them when dried.

2. If a man vowed to abstain from corn, he is forbidden dried Egyptian

---

[1] Some texts read 'us'.   [2] Cf. Neg. 14[6]; Par. 11[7].   [3] Heb. asparagus.
[4] A concoction of grits, oil, and garlic.

beans. So R. Meir. But the Sages say: He is forbidden only the Five Kinds.[1] R. Meir says: If a man vowed to abstain from [field-]produce, he is forbidden only the Five Kinds; but if he vowed to abstain from corn he is forbidden all [such like things], and he is permitted only fruits of the tree and vegetables.

3. If a man vowed to abstain from raiment, he is permitted sackcloth,[2] curtains, or hangings. If he said, '*Konam*! if I wear aught of wool', he is permitted to clothe himself with wool-shearings; if he said ['*Konam*!] if I wear aught of flax', he is permitted to clothe himself with stalks of flax. R. Judah says: All depends on him that vows: if he was heavily laden and perspired and breathed heavily and said, '*Konam*! if wool or flax come upon me', he is permitted to wear them, but not to fold them up as a load on his back.

4. If a man vowed not to enter the house, he is permitted to enter the upper room. So R. Meir. But the Sages say: An upper room is included in the term 'house'. But if a man vowed not to enter the upper room he is permitted to enter the house.

5. If a man vowed to abstain from a bed he is permitted a couch. So R. Meir. But the Sages say: A couch is included in the term 'bed'. But if a man vowed to abstain from a couch he is permitted a bed. If a man vowed not to enter a town he is permitted to enter within the town's Sabbath limit,[3] but he is forbidden to enter within the confines[4] of the town. If a man vowed not to enter a house, he is forbidden to enter beyond the jamb of the door inwards.[5]

6. If a man said, '*Konam* be these fruits to me!' or 'May they be *Konam* for my mouth!' or 'May they be *Konam* to my mouth!' he is forbidden aught for which he may exchange them or that may grow from them. [But if he said, *Konam*!] if I eat or if I taste [of them]!' he is permitted aught for which he may exchange them or that may grow from them. [This applies] to produce whose seed perishes, but if its seed does not perish, what grows from it and what grows from this again are forbidden.

7. If a man said to his wife, '*Konam* be the work of thy hands to me! *Konam* be they for my mouth! *Konam* be they to my mouth!' he is forbidden aught for which he may exchange them or that may grow from them. [If he said, '*Konam*!] if I eat or if I taste [of them]!' he is permitted aught for which he may exchange them or that may grow from them. [This applies] to produce whose seed perishes, but if its seed does not perish, what grows from it and what grows from this again are forbidden.

8. [If a man said to his wife, '*Konam*!] if I eat aught that thou makest until Passover!' [or] 'if I wear aught that thou makest until Passover!' and she made [them] before Passover, he is permitted to eat or to wear them after Passover. [But if he said, '*Konam*!] if I eat aught that thou makest before Passover!' [or] 'if I wear aught that thou makest before Passover!' and she made them before Passover, he is forbidden to eat or to wear them after Passover.

9. [If he said, '*Konam* be] any benefit that thou hast from me before Passover if thou goest to thy father's house before the Feast [of Tabernacles]!' and she went before the Feast, she is forbidden to have any benefit from him before Passover; but if [she went] after Passover, to such

---

[1] See Hall. 1[2]; Pes. 2[5]; Men. 10[7]. They are wheat, barley, spelt, goat-grass, and oats.
[2] Goat-hair cloth.   [3] P. 120, n. 5.   [4] See Erub. 5[1].   [5] Cf. Pes. 7[12].

applies [the law], *He shall not profane his word.*[1] [If he said, *Konam* be] any benefit thou hast from me before the Feast if thou goest to thy father's house before Passover!' and she went before Passover, she is forbidden to have any benefit from him before the Feast; but she is permitted to go after Passover.

8. 1. If a man said, 'Konam! if I taste wine to-day', it is forbidden him only until nightfall; [if he said,] 'this week', it is forbidden him throughout the week, and the [next] Sabbath is included in that past week; [if he said], 'this month', it is forbidden him throughout the month, and the first day of the [next] month is included in the following month; [if he said,] 'this year', it is forbidden him throughout the year, and the first day of the [next] year is included in the following year; [if he said,] 'this week-of-years', it is forbidden him throughout the week-of-years, and the Seventh Year is included in that past week-of-years. But if he said, 'One day', 'one week', 'one month', 'one year', or 'one week-of-years', it is forbidden him from [that] day until [the same moment on the next] day [or month or year or week-of-years].

2. [If he said,] '. . . until Passover', it is forbidden him until Passover is come; [if] 'until it is [Passover]', it is forbidden him until Passover is over; [if] 'until before Passover', R. Meir says: It is forbidden him until Passover is come. But R. Jose says: Until it is over.

3. [If he said,] '. . . until harvest', 'until the vintage', 'until the olive-gathering', it is forbidden him only until these times are come. This is the general rule: whatsoever has a set duration,[2] and a man has said 'until it is come', his vow is binding until that time is come. If he said, '. . . until it is [Passover or the Feast of Tabernacles]', it is binding until the season is over. And whatsoever has not a set duration,[3] whether a man has said 'until it is', or 'until it is come', his vow is binding only until the season is come.

4. [If he said,] '. . . until summer' or 'until it is summer' [his vow is binding] until the people bring in [the fruit] in baskets. [If he said,] '. . . until the summer is over', it is binding until the knives are put away.[4] [If he said,] '. . . until harvest', [it is binding] until people begin to gather the wheat harvest, but not the barley harvest. All depends on the place where the man vowed: if in the hill-country, [it is decided] according to [harvest-time in] the hill-country; if in the valley, according to [harvest-time in] the valley.

5. [If he said,] '. . . until the rains' or 'until it is [the time of] rains', [his vow is binding] until the second shower has fallen.[5] Rabban Simeon b. Gamaliel says: Until the time is come for the [second] shower. [If he said,] '. . . until the rains are over', [it is binding] until Nisan is over.[6] So R. Meir. But R. Judah says: Until Passover is over. [If he said,] '*Konam*! if I taste wine this year', and the year was made a leap-year, it is forbidden him during that year and also during the added month. [If he said, '. . . until the beginning of Adar', [it is forbidden him] until the beginning of First Adar. [If he said,] '. . . until the end of Adar', [it is

---

1 Num. 30[2].   2 Passover or Tabernacles.   3 Such as harvest or the vintage.
4 The meaning of the Hebrew is uncertain. Other renderings are: 'until the figs are laid in layers', 'until the matting is folded up'.
5 See Shebi. 9[6]. It usually falls in November.   6 March–April.

forbidden him] until the end of First[1] Adar. R. Judah says: If he said, *Konam*! if I taste wine until it is Passover', it is forbidden him only until Passover-night, since his intention was but [to signify] the time when it is the custom of men to drink wine.

6. If he said, '*Konam*! if I taste flesh until it is the time of the Fast',[2] it is forbidden him only until the night of the Fast, since he only intended [to signify] the time when it is the custom of men to eat flesh. His son, R. Jose, says: If a man said, '*Konam*! if I taste garlic until it is Sabbath', it is forbidden him only until the night of Sabbath, since he only intended [to signify] the time when it is the custom of men to eat garlic.

7. If a man said to his fellow, '*Konam*! if I have any benefit from thee unless thou come and take for thy children a *kor*[3] of wheat and two jars of wine', such a one may break his vow without recourse to a Sage, and [the other] can say to him, 'Didst thou not but speak so in my honour?—but this is my honour'.[4] So, too, if a man said to his fellow, '*Konam* be the benefit thou hast from me if thou come not and give my son a *kor* of wheat and two jars of wine!' R. Meir says: The vow is binding until he gives [him them]. But the Sages say: He, too, may break his vow without recourse to a Sage, and he can say to his fellow, 'Lo, it is as though I had already received them'. If they importune a man to marry his sister's daughter and he says, '*Konam*! if she ever has any benefit from me', (so, too, if a man divorces his wife and says, '*Konam*! if my wife has ever any benefit from me') they are [still] allowed to have benefit from him, since his vow had reference only to marriage with them. If a man importuned his fellow to eat with him, and his fellow said, '*Konam*! if I enter thy house', or 'if I taste a drop of cold water of thine', it is permitted him to enter the other's house or to drink cold water with him, since his vow had reference only to eating and drinking [at that meal in particular].

9. 1. R. Eliezer says: They may open for men the way [to repentance] by reason of the honour due to father and mother.[5] But the Sages forbid it. R. Zadok said: Rather than open the way for a man by reason of the honour due to father and mother, they should open the way for him by reason of the honour due to God;[6] but if[7] so, there could be no vows. But the Sages agree with R. Eliezer that in a matter between a man and his father and mother, the way may be opened to him by reason of the honour due to his father and mother.

2. Moreover R. Eliezer said: The way may be opened by reason of what befalls unexpectedly. But the Sages forbid it. Thus if a man said, '*Konam*! if I have any benefit from such-a-one', and this one became a Scribe or was about to give his son in marriage, and the other said, 'Had I known that he would become a Scribe or was about to give his son in marriage, I had not made my vow'; [or if a man said,] '*Konam*! if I enter this house', and the house was made into a synagogue, and he said, 'Had I known that it would be made into a synagogue I had not made my vow',

---

[1] Variant: 'second'.   [2] Day of Atonement.   [3] App. II, D.

[4] Not to take the present.

[5] e.g. they say to him, 'If thou hadst known that thy parents would be despised for bringing up a son so light-minded in his vows, wouldst thou have made thy vow?'

[6] 'If thou hadst known that he who vows is evil in God's sight, wouldst thou have made thy vow?'

[7] Rashi reads: 'But if thou sayest so there could be no vows'. Other authorities read: 'They (the Sages) said to him: If so, there could be no vows'.

such a vow R. Eliezer declares not to be binding, but the Sages declare it binding.

3. R. Meir says: There are things which seem such as befall unexpectedly, yet are not such as befall unexpectedly; and the Sages agree[1] with him. Thus if a man said, '*Konam*! if I marry such-a-one, for her father is evil', and they told him that he was dead or had repented; [or if he said,] '*Konam*! if I enter this house, for an evil dog is in it', [or] 'for there is a snake in it', and they told him that the dog was dead, or that the snake was killed, these are things which seem such as befell unexpectedly, yet are not such as befall unexpectedly. And the Sages agree[1] with him.

4. Moreover R. Meir said: They may open the way by reason of what is written in the Law, and say to him, 'Hadst thou known that thou wouldst transgress the command *Thou shalt not take vengeance*, or *Thou shalt not bear any grudge*,[2] or *Thou shalt not hate thy brother in thy heart*,[3] or *Thou shalt love thy neighbour as thyself*,[4] or *That thy brother may live with thee*,[5] [wouldst thou then have made thy vow?]—perchance he may grow poor and then thou wilt be unable to succour him'. If he said, 'Had I known that this was so, I had not made my vow', then he may be released from his vow.

5. They may open the way for a man by reason of his wife's *Ketubah*.[6] It once happened that a man vowed to have no benefit from his wife, whose *Ketubah* was 400 *denars*. She came before R. Akiba and he declared him liable to pay her her *Ketubah*. He said, 'Rabbi, my father left but 800 *denars*, and my brother took 400 *denars* and I took 400; is it not enough that she should take 200 *denars* and I 200?' R. Akiba said to him. 'Even if thou must sell the hair of thy head thou shalt pay her her *Ketubah*'. The husband answered, 'Had I known that this was so, I had not made my vow', and R. Akiba released him from his vow.

6. They may open the way for a man by reason of Festival-days and Sabbaths.[7] Beforetime they used to say: On these days a vow is not binding but on all other days it is binding. But later R. Akiba came and taught that if a vow is not held binding[8] in part[9] it is not binding at all.

7. Thus if a man said, '*Konam*! if I have any benefit from any of you', and it was held not binding for one of them, it is not binding for any of them. [If he said, '*Konam*!] if I have any benefit from this and that and that . . .', and the first is declared permitted,[10] they are all permitted; if the last is declared permitted, the last is permitted but all [the rest] are forbidden; if the one midway is declared permitted, from that to the last all are permitted, and from that to the first all are forbidden. [If a man said,] '*Korban* be the benefit I have from this! *Korban* be the benefit I have from that!' they need to open for him the way [to repentance] for each separate vow.

8. [If a man said,] '*Konam*! if I taste of wine, for wine is bad for the stomach', and they said to him, 'But is not old wine good for the stomach?' then old wine is permitted to him, and not only is old wine permitted, but all wine. [If he said,] '*Konam*! if I taste of onions, for onions are bad

---

[1] Variant: 'did not agree'.   [2] Lev. 19[18].   [3] Lev. 19[17].
[4] Lev. 19[18].   [5] Lev. 25[36].   [6] App. I. 16.
[7] If, for example, he had vowed to fast for a period of days, but forgot that the period covered certain Festival-days and Sabbaths, when fasting would be improper.
[8] But may be discontinued on a Sabbath or Festival-day.
[9] Variant: 'in its entirety'.
[10] If his vow touching that thing was declared not binding.

for the heart', and they said to him, 'But is not the Cyprus onion good
for the heart?' then Cyprus onions are permitted to him, and not only
are Cyprus onions permitted, but all onions. Such a case once happened
and R. Meir declared all onions permitted.

9. They may open the way [to repentance] for a man by reason of his
own honour and that of his children. They say to him, 'Hadst thou known
that to-morrow people would say of thee, Such is the character of such-a-
one who divorces his wives! And of thy daughters they will say, They are
daughters of a divorced woman! What befell their mother that she was
divorced? [—wouldst thou then have made thy vow?]' If he said, 'Had
I known that it would be so I had not made my vow', he is released [from
his vow].

10. [If a man said,] '*Konam*! if I marry the ugly woman such-a-one',
though she was indeed beautiful; or 'the black woman such-a-one', though
she was indeed white; or 'the short woman such-a-one', though she was
indeed tall; she is [yet] permitted to him, not because she was ugly and
became beautiful, or black and became white, or short and became tall,
but because it was a vow made in error. It once happened that a man
vowed to have no benefit from his sister's daughter; and they brought
her to the house of R. Ishmael and beautified her. R. Ishmael said to him,
'My son, didst thou vow to abstain from this one?' And he said, 'No!'
And R. Ishmael released him from his vow. In that same hour R. Ishmael
wept and said, 'The daughters of Israel are comely but poverty destroys
their comeliness!' When R. Ishmael died the daughters of Israel raised
a lament, saying, 'Ye daughters of Israel, weep over R. Ishmael!' So,
too, it is said of Saul, *Ye daughters of Israel, weep over Saul [who clothed
you in scarlet delicately, who put ornaments of gold upon your apparel]*.[1]

10. 1. If a girl[2] is betrothed, her father and her [betrothed] husband
together revoke her vows.[3] If the father revoked a vow but not the husband, or if the husband revoked it but not the father, the vow is not
revoked; still less need this be said if one of them confirmed the vow.

2. If the father died the [sole] right does not fall to the [betrothed]
husband, but if the husband died the [sole] right falls to the father.
Herein the power of the father surpasses that of the husband. In another
matter the power of the husband surpasses that of the father, in that a
husband can revoke [her vows] when she is past her girlhood,[4] but the father
cannot revoke [her vows] when she is past her girlhood.

3. If she made a vow while she was still betrothed, and was divorced
the same day and betrothed again the same day [and so forth], even to a
hundred times, her father and her latest husband together revoke her
vows. This is the general rule: if she had not, even for an hour, entered
into a state of independence,[5] her father and her latest husband together
revoke her vows.

4. Among the disciples of the Sages, before the daughter of one of them
left his control, the custom was for him to say to her, 'Let every vow that
thou hast vowed in my house be revoked'. So, too, the husband, before
she entered into his control, used to say to her, 'Let every vow that thou
didst vow before thou camest into my control be revoked'. For after she is

---

[1] 2 Sam. 1[24].   [2] Aged twelve years and a day.   [3] See Num. 30[3-16].
[4] When she is older than twelve years and a half.
[5] Which she enters at marriage or at maturity (the age of twelve and a half).

come into his control he cannot revoke [the vows that she had made before marriage].

5. A woman that was past her girlhood and that had waited the twelve months, or a widow the thirty days,[1] [of them] R. Eliezer says: Since her betrothed husband is responsible for her maintenance he can revoke her vows. But the Sages say: Her husband cannot revoke her vows until she has entered into his control.

6. If a woman was awaiting levirate marriage,[2] whether there was one brother-in-law or two [and one had bespoken her],[3] R. Eliezer says: He may revoke her vows. But R. Joshua says: [He may revoke them] when there is but one [brother-in-law], but not when there are two. R. Akiba says: Neither when there is one nor when there are two. R. Eliezer said: What! if a man can revoke the vows of a woman whom he has acquired for himself, how much the more must he be able to revoke the vows of a woman whom he has been caused to acquire by Heaven![4] R. Akiba answered: No! as thou arguest of a woman whom he has acquired for himself and over whom others have no control, wouldest thou also argue of a woman whom he has been caused to acquire by Heaven and over whom others have still control![5] R. Joshua said to him: Akiba, thy words apply only when there are two brothers-in-law; how answerest thou when there is but one? He said to him: The deceased husband's widow is not so wholly bound to the brother-in-law as the betrothed woman is to her [betrothed] husband.[6]

7. If a man said to his wife, 'Let every vow be established that thou shalt vow from this time forth until I return from such-a-place', he has said nothing at all; but if [he said], 'Let them be void', R. Eliezer says: They are made void. But the Sages say: They are not made void. R. Eliezer said: If he can make void vows which have already had the force of a prohibition,[7] can he not also make void vows which have not yet the force of a prohibition? They answered: It is written, *Her husband may establish it or her husband may make it void*[8]—such a vow as he may establish, such a vow he may make void; but such a vow as he may not establish, such a vow he may not make void.

8. The revoking of vows is valid throughout the [same] day.[9] Herein applies sometimes a more stringent, and sometimes a more lenient ruling.[10] Thus if a woman made a vow on the night of the Sabbath, her husband may revoke it during the night of the Sabbath or on the Sabbath day before nightfall; if she vowed when darkness was falling [at the close of the Sabbath] he must revoke it before nightfall, for if it became dark and he had not revoked it, he can no longer revoke it.

11. 1. These are [a woman's] vows which he may revoke: Vows the like of which *afflict the soul*[11]—[if, to wit, she said, '*Konam* for ever be to me the fruits of the world] if I wash!' or 'if I do not wash!' or 'if I adorn myself!'

---

[1] See Ket. 5[2].   [2] Deut. 25[5-10]. Cf. Yeb. 4[3].   [3] See p. 219, n. 4.
[4] i.e. whom he marries by virtue of the Law and not solely of his free choice.
[5] Namely all the other brothers who, equally with him, are included in the levirate bond.
[6] Since he who has connexion with her before the brother-in-law has taken her to wife transgresses a simple negative command (Deut. 25[5]), whereas he who has connexion with a betrothed woman is put to death by stoning (Deut. 22[24]).
[7] Which she has vowed, and which remained in force for a time before he revoked them.
[8] Num. 30[14].   [9] Num. 30[5, 7, 8].
[10] Sometimes a longer and sometimes a shorter delay can occur.   [11] Num. 30[13].

or 'if I do not adorn myself!' R. Jose said: These are not accounted vows the like of which *afflict the soul.*

2. These are vows the like of which *afflict the soul*: [If she said,] '*Konam* be to me the fruits of the world!'—this vow he may revoke. [If she said, '*Konam*] be to me the fruits of this country!' he may bring her fruits from another country. [If she said, '*Konam*] be to me the fruits of this shop-keeper!' he may not revoke it; but if he was his single source of provision[1] he may revoke the vow. So R. Jose.

3. [If she said,] '*Konam*! if I have any benefit from any creature!' he cannot revoke it, but she can [still] have benefit from Gleanings,[2] the Forgotten Sheaf[3] and *Peah.*[4] [If a man said,] '*Konam* be the benefit priests or levites have from me!' they may take [their dues][5] in spite of him. [If he said, '*Konam*] be the benefit that these priests or these levites have from me!' other priests and levites may take [the dues].

4. [If she said,] '*Konam*! if I work for the benefit of my father or of thy father or of my brother or of thy brother', he cannot revoke it; [but if she said, '*Konam*!] if I work for thy benefit', he does not need to revoke it. R. Akiba says: He should revoke it lest she burden him more than is seemly. R. Johanan b. Nuri says: He should revoke it lest he divorce her and she be forbidden to return to him.

5. If his wife vowed and he thought that it was his daughter that vowed, or if his daughter vowed and he thought that it was his wife that vowed; or if she vowed a Nazirite-vow and he thought that she vowed by *Korban*; or if she vowed by *Korban* and he thought that she vowed a Nazirite-vow; or if she vowed to abstain from figs and he thought that she vowed to abstain from grapes; or if she vowed to abstain from grapes and he thought that she vowed to abstain from figs, he must revoke the vow a second time.

6. If she said, '*Konam*! if I taste of these figs and grapes', and he estab-lished the vow as touching figs, the whole vow remains established; if he revoked it as touching figs, it is not revoked until he revokes it also as touching grapes. If she said, '*Konam*! if I taste of figs and if I taste of grapes', here are two separate vows.

7. [If a man[6] said,] 'I knew that there were vows but I did not know that they could be revoked', he may revoke the vow.[7] [If he said,] 'I knew that vows could be revoked but I did not know that this [utterance] counted as a vow [that needed to be revoked]', R. Meir says: He may not revoke it. But the Sages say: He may revoke it.

8. If a man was forbidden by vow to have any benefit from his father-in-law, and he[8] wished to give money to his daughter, he may say to her, 'This money is given thee as a gift on the condition that thy husband shall have no right over it and that thou dea! with it at thine own pleasure'.

9. [It is written,] *But the vow of a widow or of her that is divorced . . . shall stand against her.*[9] Thus if she said, 'I will be a Nazirite after thirty days', although she married again within the thirty days, he cannot revoke it. If she made a vow while she was in the control of her husband, he may revoke it. Thus if she said, 'I will be a Nazirite after thirty days',

---

[1] If no other would give him credit.
[2] Lev. 19[9f].   [3] Deut. 24[19].   [4] App. I. 33.
[5] i.e. the First Tithe for the levites and the twenty-four dues of the priests (see p. 88, n. 24.   [6] The father or husband.
[7] The same day that he learned that he could revoke it.   [8] The father-in-law.
[9] Num. 30[9].

although she became a widow or was divorced within the thirty days, the vow remains revoked. If she made a vow on one day and was divorced on the same day, and he took her back the same day, he may not revoke the vow. This is the general rule: if she had even for an hour entered into a state of independence[1] he cannot revoke her vow.

10. There are nine women[2] whose vows remain binding: she that was past her girlhood and 'an orphan [in her father's lifetime'[3] when she vowed]; she that was still in her girlhood and 'an orphan [in her father's lifetime' when she vowed], and is now past her girlhood; she that was 'an orphan [in her father's lifetime' when she vowed], and is still in her girlhood; she that was past her girlhood and whose father was dead [when she vowed]; she that was still in her girlhood [when she vowed] and she then grew past her girlhood and her father died; she that was still in her girlhood [when she vowed] and that is still not past her girlhood; she that was still in her girlhood [when she vowed] and whose father was dead, and after her father died she grew past her girlhood; she that was past her girlhood [when she vowed], and her father was still alive; and she that was still in her girlhood [when she vowed] and that has grown past her girlhood and whose father is still alive. R. Judah says: Also if a man had given in marriage his daughter that was yet a minor,[4] and she became a widow or was divorced and returned to him, and that is still in her girlhood.

11. [If she said,] 'Konam be any advantage I have of my father or thy father if I work for thy benefit!' or ['Konam] be any advantage I have of thee if I work for the benefit of my father or of thy father!' such a vow he may revoke.

12. Beforetime they used to say: There are three women that must be put away yet they may take their Ketubah:[5] such that say, 'I am unclean to thee',[6] 'Heaven [knows what befalls] betwixt me and thee!'[7] or 'I will remove me from all Jews!'[8] They afterwards taught otherwise lest a wife gaze upon another and behave unseemly against her husband; but, rather, if she says, 'I am unclean to thee', she should bring proof of her words; [if she said,] 'Heaven [knows what befalls] betwixt me and thee!' they should find a way to placate her; [and if she says,] 'I will remove me from all Jews!' the husband should revoke what concerns him [in her vow], so that she shall again minister to him; but from [all other] Jews she may remove herself.

NAZIR ('THE NAZIRITE-VOW')

1. 1. Any substitute for [the form of words used to utter] a Nazirite-vow[9] is as binding as the Nazirite-vow itself.[10] If a man said, 'I will be [such]', he becomes a Nazirite; [if he said,] 'I will be "comely" ', he becomes a Nazirite. [If he said,] 'I will be a Nazik', or 'a Naziah', or 'a Paziah', he becomes a Nazirite. [If he said,] 'I will be like this one',[11] or 'I will

---

[1] See above, 10[3].
[2] Who were betrothed in their girlhood, i.e. when under twelve years and a half.
[3] See Yeb. 13[6]. She was divorced while still a minor. But though she returns to her father's house he no longer has control over her, since the control passed to the husband and can no more return to the father.   [4] Less than twelve years and a day.   [5] App. I. 16.
[6] If, her husband being a priest, she declares that she had been violated. See Ket. 2[9]; cf. Sot. 1[3].   [7] Alleging his impotence.
[8] She cannot endure intercourse.   [9] See Num. 6[1-21].
[10] See p. 264, n. 2. The following sentence deals with 'handles' of vows.
[11] Seeing a Nazirite before him.

plait [it]', or 'I will tend [it]', or 'I pledge myself to let [it] grow unkempt', he becomes a Nazirite. [If he said,] 'I pledge myself to offer birds',[1] R. Meir says: He becomes a Nazirite. But the Sages say: He does not become a Nazirite.

2. [If a man said,] 'I will be an "abstainer"[2] from grape-stones and from grape-skins,[3] from cutting off the hair and from uncleanness', he becomes a Nazirite, and he is pledged to every rule of the Nazirite-vow. [If he said,] 'I will be like Samson', 'like the son of Manoah', 'like the husband of Delilah', 'like him that tore up the gates of Gaza', or 'like him whose eyes the Philistines put out', he becomes a Nazirite the like of Samson.[4] How does a lifelong Nazirite differ from a Nazirite the like of Samson? If the hair of a lifelong Nazirite becomes too heavy he may lighten it[5] with a razor and he then brings the three [offerings of] cattle,[6] and if he becomes unclean he brings the offering for uncleanness;[7] but a Nazirite the like of Samson, if his hair becomes too heavy he does not lighten it, and if he becomes unclean he does not bring the offering for uncleanness.[8]

3. A Nazirite-vow that is vowed without a fixed duration is binding for thirty days. If he said, 'I will be a Nazirite for one long spell', or 'I will be a Nazirite for one short spell', or even 'from now until the end of the world', he must remain a Nazirite for thirty days. [If he said,] 'I will be a Nazirite and for one day more', or 'I will be a Nazirite and for one hour more', 'I will be a Nazirite for one spell and a half', he must remain a Nazirite for two spells. [If he said,] 'I will be a Nazirite for thirty days and one hour', he must remain a Nazirite for thirty-one days, since they may not take the vow of a Nazirite by the measure of hours.[9]

4. [If he said,] 'I will be a Nazirite like as the hairs of my head', or 'like as the dust of the earth', or 'like as the sand of the sea', he becomes a lifelong Nazirite, and he must cut off his hair every thirty days. Rabbi says: Such a one does not cut off his hair every thirty days; but who is he that cuts off his hair every thirty days?—he that says, 'I pledge myself to as many Nazirite-vows as the hairs of my head', or 'as the dust of the earth', or 'as the sand of the sea'.

5. [If he said,] 'I will be a Nazirite a houseful',[10] or 'a basketful', they inquire of him more closely: if he said, 'I vowed to abstain for one long spell', he becomes a Nazirite for thirty days; but if he said, 'I vowed to abstain, but with no set duration', they look upon the basket as if it was full of mustard-seed, and he must be a lifelong Nazirite.

6. [If he said,] 'I will be a Nazirite from here to such-a-place', they make a reckoning of how many days' journey it is 'from here to such-a-place'; if it is less than thirty days, he becomes a Nazirite for thirty days; otherwise he becomes a Nazirite for as many days as the days of the journey.

7. [If he said,] 'I will be a Nazirite according to the number of the days of the solar year', they count up as many Nazirite-vows as the number of the days of the solar year. R. Judah said: Such a case once happened, and when he had fulfilled [his Nazirite-vow] he died.

2. 1. [If he said,] 'I will be an "abstainer"[2] from dried figs and fig-cake',

---

[1] The Nazirite's offering after he has contracted uncleanness. Num. 6[10f].
[2] Heb. *nazir*.   [3] See below, 6[2].
[4] Judg. 13[5]. The Gemara (4a) would here add: If he said, 'I will be a lifelong Nazirite', he must become one.   [5] Deduced from the case of Absalom, 2 Sam. 14[26].
[6] Num. 6[14].   [7] Num. 6[10f].   [8] Inferred from Judg. 14[19].
[9] Because Num. 6[8] says: 'the *days* of his separation'.   [10] Variant: 'a jarful'.

the School of Shammai say: He becomes a Nazirite. And the School of Hillel say: He does not become a Nazirite. R. Judah said: Howbeit when the School of Shammai said this, they spoke only of one that meant, 'May they be to me as *Korban*!'[1]

2. If a man said, 'This cow thinks it will be a Nazirite if it stands up', or 'This door thinks it will be a Nazirite if it opens!'[2] the School of Shammai say: He becomes a Nazirite. And the School of Hillel say: He does not become a Nazirite. R. Judah said: Howbeit when the School of Shammai said this, they spoke only of one that meant, 'May this cow be *Korban* to me if it stands up!'

3. If they filled a man's cup and he said, 'I will be an "abstainer"[3] from it', he becomes a Nazirite. It once happened that a woman was drunk and they filled her a cup but she said, 'I will be an "abstainer" from it'. The Sages said: She only intended to say, 'May it be to me as *Korban*!'

4. [If a man said,] 'I will be a Nazirite on condition that I may drink wine', or 'that I may contract uncleanness because of the dead', he becomes a Nazirite and is nevertheless forbidden these things. [If a man said,] 'I knew that there were Nazirite-vows but I did not know that the Nazirite was forbidden wine', it is nevertheless forbidden him. But R. Simeon permits it. [If he said,] 'I knew that the Nazirite was forbidden wine', [or 'I knew that the Nazirite was forbidden to contract uncleanness because of the dead'], 'but I thought that the Sages would permit it to me since I cannot live without wine', or 'since I am a grave-digger', then to such it is permitted. But R. Simeon forbids it.

5. [If a man said,] 'I will be a Nazirite and I pledge myself to bring the Hair-offering[4] of [another] Nazirite', and his fellow heard him and said, 'I, too; and I pledge myself to bring the Hair-offering of [another] Nazirite', if they are prudent-minded they each bring the Hair-offering of the other; but if not, they must bring the Hair-offering of other Nazirites.

6. [If a man said,] 'I pledge myself to bring half the Hair-offering of a Nazirite', and his fellow heard him and said, 'I, too, pledge myself to bring half the Hair-offering of a Nazirite', each must bring the whole Hair-offering of a Nazirite. So R. Meir. But the Sages say: Each need bring but half of the Hair-offering of a Nazirite.

7. [If a man said,] 'I will be a Nazirite if a son is born to me', and a son was born to him, he becomes a Nazirite; if a daughter was born to him or one of doubtful sex or one of double sex,[5] he does not become a Nazirite. If he said, 'When I see that I have a child [I will be a Nazirite]', even if a daughter was born to him or one of doubtful sex or one of double sex, he becomes a Nazirite.

8. If his wife miscarried he does not become a Nazirite. R. Simeon says: He should say, 'If it is a child like to live, I will be a Nazirite in duty bound; but if it is not, I will be a Nazirite of free choice'. If she afterward

---

[1] See Ned. 1[4]. He meant an ordinary and not a Nazirite-vow.

[2] Such is the literal rendering of the text, with the implication 'but I will be a Nazirite if it does not stand up (or open)'. So Bert. According to Tif. Yis. the meaning is, 'If this cow thinks I will be its Nazirite (i.e. will refrain entirely from it) if it does not stand up, then I am one!' Still more forced is the interpretation, 'If he said (or) she said, As for this cow (or this door), I will be its Nazirite if it stands up (if it opens)'.

[3] Heb. *nazir*.

[4] This expression is used throughout for the offering of the he-lamb, ewe-lamb, and ram and their associated Meal-offering (Num. 6[14, 15]) which the Nazirite brings on the completion of his vow and when he cuts off and burns the 'hair of his separation' (Num. 6[18]).

[5] Heb. *androgynos*. See Bikk. 4[1ff].

bore a child, he must become a Nazirite. R. Simeon says: He should say, 'If the first is a child like to live, the first time [I will be a Nazirite] in duty bound, and for this [other I will be a Nazirite] of free choice; otherwise, the first time [I will be a Nazirite] of free choice, and for this [other I will be a Nazirite] in duty bound.

9. [If he said,] 'I will be a Nazirite and a Nazirite [yet again] if a son is born to me', and he had begun to count[1] [the thirty days] of his [first vow] and then a son was born to him, he must complete [the thirty days] of his [first vow] and then count [the other thirty days vowed by reason] of his son. [If he said,] 'I will be a Nazirite if a son is born to me and a Nazirite [yet again unconditionally], and he had begun to count [the thirty days] of his [unconditional vow] and then a son was born to him, he should leave off [the thirty days] of his [unconditional vow] and count [the thirty days vowed by reason] of his son, and afterward complete [the thirty days] of his [unconditional vow].

10. [If he said,] 'I will be a Nazirite if a son is born to me and [yet again unconditionally] a Nazirite for a hundred days', and a son was born to him before seventy days, he will have suffered no loss;[2] but if after seventy days, it makes of none effect [the days that he had counted after] the seventy days, since a Nazirite may not cut off his hair within less than thirty days.

3. 1. If a man said, 'I will be a Nazirite', he should cut off his hair on the thirty-first day, but if he cut it off on the thirtieth day he has fulfilled his obligation; [but if he said,] 'I will be a Nazirite for thirty days', and he cut it off on the thirtieth day, he has not fulfilled his obligation.

2. If a man vowed two Nazirite-vows he should cut off his hair after the first spell on the thirty-first day, and after the second on the sixty-first day. If, after the first spell, he cut off his hair on the thirtieth day, he should cut off his hair after the second spell on the sixtieth day; but if he cut off his hair on the fifty-ninth day, he has fulfilled his obligation. And this testimony did R. Papias[3] bear concerning one that vowed two Nazirite-vows: that if after the first spell he cut off his hair on the thirtieth day he should cut off his hair after the second spell on the sixtieth day, but if he cut off his hair on the fifty-ninth day he has fulfilled his obligation, since the thirtieth day can be reckoned to him among the number [of days of the second Nazirite-vow].

3. If a man said, 'I will be a Nazirite', and he contracted uncleanness on the thirtieth day, he makes the whole of none effect. R. Eliezer says: He makes seven days only of none effect.[4] [If he said,] 'I will be a Nazirite for thirty days', and he contracted uncleanness on the thirtieth day, he makes the whole of none effect.

4. [If he said,] 'I will be a Nazirite for a hundred days', and he contracted uncleanness on the hundredth day, he makes the whole of none effect. R. Eliezer says: He makes thirty days only of none effect.[5] If he contracted

---

[1] To put into practice his first, unconditional, Nazirite-vow.

[2] e.g. if the son was born after he had completed 65 days of his 100-days vow, he must break this off and complete the 30 days of the other vow, and then complete the remaining 35 days. But if the son was born, for example, after 75 days, he must break off the first vow and complete the second, and then revert to the remainder of the first; but instead of the remaining 25 days he must observe a minimum of 30. [3] Eduy. 7[5].

[4] According to him the vow was already completed, and he could cut off his hair on the thirtieth day. He need wait only another seven days (Num. 19[12]) and then become clean so that he can bring his 'Hair-offering'.

[5] i.e. he need now only fulfil the minimum spell afresh.

uncleanness on the one hundred and first day, he makes thirty days of none effect. R. Eliezer says: He makes seven days only of none effect.

5. If a man took the Nazirite-vow while he was in a graveyard, even if he remained there thirty days these are not reckoned to him among the number of days, nor may he bring the offering for uncleanness. But if he went out and entered in again, those days are reckoned to him among the number and [after he has entered in the graveyard] he must bring the offering for uncleanness. R. Eliezer says: Not [if he contracted uncleanness] on the same day, for it is written, *But the former days shall be void*;[1] only when former days can be reckoned to him [may he bring the offering for uncleanness].

6. If[2] a man vowed to be a Nazirite for a longer spell and he fulfilled his Nazirite-vow and afterward came to the Land [of Israel], the School of Shammai say: He need continue a Nazirite [only for] thirty days [more].[3] And the School of Hillel say: He must again fulfil his vow as from the beginning. It once happened that the son of queen Helena[4] went to war and she said, 'If my son returns in safety from the war I will be a Nazirite for seven years', and her son returned from the war, and she was a Nazirite for seven years. At the end of the seven years she came up to the Land [of Israel], and the School of Hillel taught her that she must be a Nazirite for yet another seven years; and at the end of this seven years she contracted uncleanness. Thus she continued a Nazirite for twenty-one years. R. Judah said: She needed to remain a Nazirite for fourteen years only.

7. If[5] two pairs of witnesses testified of a man, and the one testified that he had vowed two Nazirite-vows and the other that he had vowed five, the School of Shammai say: Their testimony is at variance,[6] and the Nazirite-vow cannot be held binding. And the School of Hillel say: The two are included within the five, so that he must remain a Nazirite for the two spells.

4. 1. If a man said, 'I will be a Nazirite', and his fellow heard and said, 'I, too', [and another heard and said], 'I, too', they all become Nazirites. If the first was released [from his vow] they are all released; if the last was released, the last is released but the others all remain bound. If a man said, 'I will be a Nazirite', and his fellow heard and said, 'Let my mouth be as his mouth!' or 'Let my hair be as his hair!' he becomes a Nazirite. [If he said,] 'I will be a Nazirite', and his wife heard and said, 'I, too', he may revoke her vow but his own remains binding. [If she said,] 'I will be a Nazirite', and her husband heard her and said, 'I, too', he cannot revoke her vow.

2. [If he said,] 'I will be a Nazirite; and [wilt] thou?' and she said, 'Amen!' he may annul her vow but his own remains binding. [If she said,] 'I will be a Nazirite; and [wilt] thou?' and he said, 'Amen!' he cannot revoke her vow.

3. If a woman vowed to be a Nazirite and then drank wine or contracted uncleanness because of the dead, she incurs the Forty Stripes.[7] If her husband revoked her vow and she did not know that he had revoked it,

---

[1] Num. 6[12].   [2] Eduy. 4[11].
[3] The Nazirite-vow is only valid if observed in the Land of Israel; other lands are 'unclean', and their soil conveys corpse uncleanness. See below, 7[3].
[4] Queen of Adiabene. Cf. Yom. 3[10].   [5] Eduy. 4[11].
[6] Cf. Yeb. 15[5].   [7] For transgressing Num. 6[3, 6] Cf. Makk. 3[7].

and she drank wine and contracted uncleanness because of the dead, she does not incur the Forty Stripes. R. Judah says: If she does not incur the Forty Stripes she must nevertheless suffer punishment for disobedience.

4. If a woman vowed to be a Nazirite and had set apart her cattle[1] [for the offering], and her husband then revoked her vow, if her cattle were his, they may go forth and pasture with the flock; but if they were hers, [the ewe-lamb intended for] the Sin-offering shall be left to die,[2] and [the he-lamb intended for] the Whole-offering shall be offered as a Whole-offering, and [the ram intended for] the Peace-offering shall be offered as a Peace-offering; they must be consumed on the same day,[3] and they do not require the Bread-offering.[4] If she has money set aside yet un-assigned [to each of the three offerings], it falls [to the Temple treasury] as a Freewill-offering; but if the money was assigned, the money intended for the Sin-offering must be thrown into the Dead Sea (none may have benefit from it, but it is not subject to the law of Sacrilege); with that intended for the Whole-offering a Whole-offering shall be offered, and the money is subject to the law of Sacrilege; and with that intended for the Peace-offering a Peace-offering shall be offered; they must be consumed in the same day, and they do not require the Bread-offering.

5. After the blood of one of the offerings has been tossed[6] for her [against the Altar], he may not revoke the vow. R. Akiba says: Even after one of the beasts has been slaughtered for her, he may not revoke it. This applies only after the Hair-offering has been offered [and the vow fulfilled] in cleanness; but if the Hair-offering [was not offered, and the vow fulfilled] not in cleanness [and the vow needed to be fulfilled afresh], he may revoke her vow, since he may say, 'I have no pleasure in a squalid[7] woman'. Rabbi says: It applies even after the Hair-offering has been offered in cleanness, since he may say, 'I have no pleasure in a shorn woman'.

6. A man may impose the Nazirite-vow on his son, but a woman may not impose the Nazirite-vow on her son. How [shall they treat the offerings] if he cut off his hair or his kindred cut it off for him, or if he protested [and would not keep the vow] or his kindred protested for him? If [the father] had cattle already assigned, the Sin-offering shall be left to die, the Whole-offering shall be offered as a Whole-offering, and the Peace-offering shall be offered as a Peace-offering; they must be consumed on the same day and they do not require the Bread-offering. If he had money [set aside for the offerings but] yet unassigned [to each of the three offerings] it falls [to the Temple treasury] as a Freewill-offering; but if the money was assigned, the money intended for the Sin-offering must be thrown into the Dead Sea (none may have benefit from it, but it is not subject to the law of Sacrilege); with that intended for the Whole-offering a Whole-offering shall be offered, and the money is subject to the law of Sacrilege; and with that intended for the Peace-offering a Peace-offering shall be offered; they must be consumed in the same day, and they do not require the Bread-offering.

7. A man may bring the Hair-offering for his father's Nazirite-vow, but a woman may not bring the Hair-offering for her father's Nazirite-vow. Thus if a man's father was a Nazirite and had set aside for his Nazirite-vow money that was yet unassigned [to each of the three offerings], and

---

[1] Num. 6[14].   [2] Cf. Zeb. 8[1]; Tem. 4[1].   [3] Lev. 7[15].   [4] Num. 6[15].
[5] Lev. 5[15].   [6] See p. 468, n. 15.   [7] Through abstention from wine.

he then died, and the son said, 'I will be a Nazirite on the condition that I may bring my Hair-offering from my father's money' [, he may bring it]. R. Jose said: The money falls [to the Temple treasury] as a Freewill-offering: such a one may not bring the Hair-offering for his father's Nazirite-vow. Who may bring the Hair-offering for his father's Nazirite-vow? If both a man and his father were Nazirites, and his father set aside for his Nazirite-vow money that was yet unassigned and he died, the son may bring the Hair-offering for his father's Nazirite-vow.

5. 1. The School of Shammai say: If a thing is dedicated in error its dedication is binding.[1] And the School of Hillel say: It is not binding. Thus if a man said, 'The black ox that first comes out of my house shall be dedicated', and a white one came out,[2] the School of Shammai say: Its dedication is binding. And the School of Hillel say: It is not binding.

2. [If he said,] 'The golden *denar* that first comes to my hand shall be dedicated', and a silver *denar* came to his hand, the School of Shammai say: Its dedication is binding. And the School of Hillel say: It is not binding. [If he said,] 'The jar of wine that first comes to my hand shall be dedicated', and a jar of oil came to his hand, the School of Shammai say: Its dedication is binding. And the School of Hillel say: It is not binding.

3. If a man vowed to be a Nazirite and he inquired of a Sage, and he declared the vow binding, he must count [the thirty days] from the time when he vowed. If he inquired of a Sage, and he declared it not binding, and he had cattle already assigned [for the three offerings], they may go forth and pasture with the flock. The School of Hillel said to the School of Shammai: Do ye not admit that here, although it is a thing dedicated in error, it should go forth and pasture with the flock? The School of Shammai answered: Do ye not admit that if a man erred and called the ninth [of the herd] the tenth, or the tenth the ninth, or the eleventh the tenth, its dedication is binding?[3] The School of Hillel answered: It is not the rod that has dedicated them: what if he erred and laid the rod on the eighth or the twelfth: would he have done aught at all?—but, rather, the Scripture which declared 'the tenth' holy, has declared the ninth and the eleventh holy also.[4]

4. If a man vowed to be a Nazirite, and he went to bring his cattle and found that they had been stolen, and he had made his Nazirite-vow before they were stolen, his vow is binding: but if he had made his Nazirite-vow after they were stolen, his vow is not binding. A like error befell Nahum the Mede when Nazirites came up from the Exile [to Jerusalem] and found the Temple destroyed. Nahum the Mede said to them, Would ye have vowed to be Nazirites had ye known that the Temple was destroyed? They answered, No. And Nahum the Mede released them from their vow. But when the matter came before the Sages they said to him: If any man vowed to be a Nazirite before the Temple was destroyed, his Nazirite-vow remains binding; but if he vowed after the Temple was destroyed, his Nazirite-vow is not binding.

5. If [six] persons were on a journey and another came towards them, and one of them said, 'May I be a Nazirite if this is such-a-one!' and

---

[1] Lev. 27[10].   [2] And he dedicated this.
[3] As the Tithe of Cattle. Lev. 27[32]. See Bekh. 9[7].
[4] If they are, even in error, styled 'the tenth'.

another said, 'May I be a Nazirite if this is not such-a-one!' [and a third said], 'May I be a Nazirite if one of you is a Nazirite!' [and a fourth said,] 'May I be a Nazirite if one of you is not a Nazirite!' [and a fifth said,] '. . . if ye both are Nazirites!' [and a sixth said,] '. . . if ye are all of you Nazirites!' according to the School of Shammai they are all Nazirites; and according to the School of Hillel none of them is a Nazirite excepting him whose words are not[1] confirmed. But R. Tarfon says: None of them is a Nazirite.

6. If he turned away suddenly, none of them is a Nazirite. R. Simeon says: [Each] one [of them] should say, If it was according to my words I will be a Nazirite in duty bound; but if not, I will be a Nazirite of free choice!'

7. If one man saw a *koy*[2] and said, 'May I be a Nazirite if this is a wild animal!' [and another said], 'May I be a Nazirite if this is not a wild animal!' [and a third said], 'May I be a Nazirite if this is a tame beast!' [and a fourth said], 'May I be a Nazirite if this is not a tame beast!' [and a fifth said,] 'May I be a Nazirite if this is both a wild animal and a tame beast!' [and a sixth said,] 'May I be a Nazirite if this is neither a wild animal nor a tame beast!' [and then one of another party said,] 'May I be a Nazirite if one of you is a Nazirite!' [and another said,] 'May I be a Nazirite if none of you is a Nazirite!' [and a third said,] 'May I be a Nazirite if ye are all Nazirites!'—then are they all Nazirites.

6. 1. Three things are forbidden to the Nazirite: uncleanness,[3] cutting off the hair, and aught that comes from the vine. Whatsoever comes from the vine can be included together,[4] and he is not culpable unless he eats an olive's bulk of what comes from the grapes. The First Mishnah[5] [taught]: '. . . unless he drinks a quarter-*log* of wine'. R. Akiba says: Even if he soaks his bread in wine and there is enough to make up together an olive's bulk he is culpable.

2. He may become culpable by reason of wine by itself, or grapes by themselves, or grape-stones (*hartzannim*) by themselves, or grape-skins (*zagim*) by themselves. But R. Eleazar b. Azariah says: He does not become culpable unless he eats two grape-stones together with the skins. What is meant by *hartzannim*, and what is meant by *zagim*? *Hartzannim* are what is outside (*hitzonim*), and *zagim* are what is inside. So R. Judah. But R. Jose says: That thou mayest not err—it is, rather, like the bell (*zug*) of cattle: what is outside is called the *zug* (the hood), and what is inside is called *inbal* (the clapper).

3. A Nazirite-vow that is vowed without a fixed duration is binding for thirty days. If he cut off his hair himself or if robbers cut it off, it makes the thirty days of none effect. If a Nazirite cut off his hair with shears or with a razor or pulled out any hair soever, he is culpable. A Nazirite may rub or scratch his hair but he may not comb it. R. Ishmael says: He may not rub it with earth since it makes the hair fall out.

4. If[6] a Nazirite drank wine throughout the day he is liable only on one count. If they said to him [repeatedly], 'Do not drink! Do not drink!' and he nevertheless drank, he is liable on each count. If he cut off his

---

[1] The course of the Mishnah's discussion is so involved that it is disputed in the Gemara (33a) whether the 'not' is correct or not.   [2] App. I. 19. See Bikk. 2[8].
[3] Contracted from a corpse.
[4] To make up the total quantity of an olive's bulk by eating which the Nazirite becomes liable to punishment by the Forty Stripes.   [5] See p. 251, n. 4.   [6] Makk. 3[7].

hair throughout the day, he is liable only on one count. If they said to him [repeatedly], 'Do not cut it off! Do not cut it off!' and he nevertheless cut it off, he is liable on each count. If he contracted uncleanness because of the dead throughout the day, he is liable only on one count. If they said to him [repeatedly], 'Do not contract uncleanness! Do not contract uncleanness!' and he nevertheless contracted uncleanness, he is liable on each count.

5. Three things are forbidden to the Nazirite: uncleanness, cutting off the hair, and aught that comes from the vine. Greater stringency applies to uncleanness and cutting off the hair than to what comes from the vine, in that uncleanness and cutting off the hair make [the days already fulfilled] of none effect, but what comes from the vine does not make [the days already fulfilled] of none effect. Greater stringency applies to what comes from the vine than to uncleanness and cutting off the hair, in that for what comes from the vine no exception is permitted, but for uncleanness and cutting off the hair exceptions are permitted, as when cutting off the hair[1] or the burying of a corpse are enjoined in the Law.[2] And greater stringency applies to uncleanness than to cutting off the hair, in that uncleanness makes the whole [of the days fulfilled] of none effect, and he is thereby made liable to an offering;[3] whereas cutting off the hair makes only thirty days of none effect and he is not thereby made liable to an offering.

6. What was the rite prescribed for the cutting off of the hair after contracting uncleanness? He was sprinkled on the third and the seventh day,[4] he cut off his hair on the seventh day and brought his offerings[5] on the eighth day; but if he cut off his hair[6] on the eighth day he brought his offerings on the same day. So R. Akiba. R. Tarfon said to him: How does he differ from the leper?[7] He answered: His cleansing is suspended [only] until [the passing of] the days prescribed for him, while the cleansing of the leper is suspended until he cuts off his hair, and he may not bring the offering until he has awaited sunset.[8]

7. What was the rite prescribed for the cutting off of the hair [after the vow was fulfilled] in cleanness? He brought three beasts:[9] a Sin-offering, a Whole-offering, and a Peace-offering; and he slaughtered the Peace-offering and thereupon cut off his hair. So R. Judah. R. Eliezer says: He cut off his hair only at [the time of] the Sin-offering, since the Sin-offering has always priority;[10] but if he cut off his hair at [the time of] any of the three offerings he has fulfilled his obligation.

8. Rabban Simeon b. Gamaliel says: If he brought the three beasts but had not assigned [each to its purpose], what is fit for a Sin-offering is offered as a Sin-offering, and what is fit for a Whole-offering is offered as a Whole-offering, and what is fit for a Peace-offering is offered as a Peace-offering. Then he takes *the hair of the head of his separation*[11] and casts it under the cauldron. But if he cut off his hair [outside the Temple] in the City[12] he

does not[1] cast it under the cauldron. This applies to the cutting off of the hair [after the vow was fulfilled in] cleanness; but at the cutting off of the hair after contracting uncleanness, he does not cast the hair under the cauldron. R. Meir says: All cast their hair under the cauldron excepting him that was unclean [and cut off his hair outside the Temple] in the City.

9. When he had cooked or seethed the Peace-offering, the priest took *the sodden shoulder of the ram and one unleavened cake out of the basket and one unleavened wafer and put them upon the hands of the Nazirite*[2] and waved them. Thenceforth the Nazirite is permitted to drink wine and to contract uncleanness because of the dead. R. Simeon says: When once the blood of one of the offerings has been tossed for him [against the Altar] the Nazirite is permitted to drink wine and to contract uncleanness because of the dead.

10. If he cut off his hair after one of the offerings and this was found invalid, the cutting off of his hair also becomes invalid and his offerings are not reckoned to his credit. If he cut off his hair after a Sin-offering that had not been so assigned, and he then brought the other offerings each properly assigned, the cutting off of his hair is invalid and his offerings are not reckoned to his credit. If he cut off his hair after a Whole-offering or a Peace-offering that had not been so assigned, and he then brought his other offerings each properly assigned, the cutting off of his hair is invalid and his offerings are not reckoned to his credit. R. Simeon says: That single offering is not reckoned to his credit but the other offerings are reckoned to his credit. But if he cut off his hair after all of the three offerings and one [only] of them was found valid, the cutting off of his hair is valid, and he need but bring the other offerings afresh.

11. If the blood of one of the offerings was tossed for him [against the Altar] and he contracted uncleanness, R. Eliezer says: This makes the whole of none effect. But the Sages say: He may bring the rest of the offerings when he is become clean. They said to him: It once happened to Miriam of Palmyra that the blood of one of the offerings was tossed for her [against the Altar], and certain came and told her that her daughter was in danger, and she went and found that she was dead, and the Sages said: Let her bring the rest of the offerings when she is become clean.

7. 1. A High Priest[3] or a Nazirite[4] may not contract uncleanness because of their [dead] kindred, but they may contract uncleanness because of a neglected corpse.[5] If they were on a journey and found a neglected corpse, R. Eliezer says: The High Priest may contract uncleanness but the Nazirite may not contract uncleanness. But the Sages say: The Nazirite may contract uncleanness but the High Priest may not contract uncleanness. R. Eliezer said to them: Rather let the priest contract uncleanness for he needs not to bring an offering because of his uncleanness, and let not the Nazirite contract uncleanness for he must bring an offering because of his uncleanness.[6] They answered: Rather let the Nazirite contract uncleanness, for his sanctity is not a lifelong sanctity, and let not the priest contract uncleanness, for his sanctity is a lifelong sanctity.

2. Because of these[7] uncleannesses must the Nazirite cut off his hair:

---

[1] Some texts omit the negative.   [2] Num. 6[19].   [3] Lev. 21[11].   [4] Num. 6[6].
[5] *Meth mitzwah.* See above, p. 288, n. 2.   [6] Num. 6[9f].   [7] See Ohol. 2[1].
3349

[uncleanness contracted from] a corpse, or an olive's bulk [of the flesh] of a corpse, or an olive's bulk of corpse-dregs, or a ladleful of corpse-mould, or the backbone or the skull or any [severed] member of a corpse, or any [severed] member of a living man that still bears its proper flesh, or a half-*kab*[1] of bones, or a half-*log*[1] of blood, whether [the uncleanness is contracted] from contact with them or carrying them or by over-shadowing;[2] or [uncleanness contracted from] a barleycorn's bulk of bone whether by contact or carrying. Because of these a Nazirite must cut off his hair and be sprinkled on the third and the seventh day;[3] and it makes the preceding days of none effect and he may not begin to count afresh until he is become clean and has brought his offerings.

3. But because of [uncleanness contracted from over-shadowing] inter-laced foliage or projecting stones,[4] or from a Grave-area,[5] a land of the gentiles, a stone that seals a tomb and its buttressing stone,[6] a quarter-*log* of blood, a 'tent'[7] [wherein lies a corpse], a quarter-*kab* of bones, or vessels that have touched a corpse; or because of his days of reckoning[8] [after he has suffered leprosy] and the days during which he is certified unclean[9] [with leprosy]—because of these [conditions of uncleanness] the Nazirite need not cut off his hair, but he is sprinkled on the third and the seventh day and the preceding days are not rendered of none effect; he may begin to count forthwith [the number of days that still remain] and he need not bring the offering.[10] Rightly have they said:[11] the days of [the uncleanness of] a man or woman that have a flux[12] and the days when the leper is shut up,[13] these are reckoned to his credit.[14]

4. R. Eleazar said in the name of R. Joshua: For whatsoever uncleanness from a corpse a Nazirite must cut off his hair,[15] for that, too, is a man culpable if he enters into the Temple; and for whatsoever uncleanness from a corpse a Nazirite need not cut off his hair,[16] for that, too, is a man not culpable if he enters into the Temple. R. Meir said: Would there not thus be less stringency than [when uncleanness is contracted from] a creeping thing![17] R. Akiba said: I argued before R. Eliezer: If because of the contact or carrying of a barleycorn's bulk of bone[18] (which does not render a man unclean by overshadowing)[19] a Nazirite must cut off his hair, how much more, then, aught he to cut off his hair because of the contact or carrying of a quarter-*log* of blood[20] (which renders a man unclean by overshadowing)! He said to me, What is this, Akiba? We cannot here argue from the less to the greater.[21] But when I came and declared these words before R. Joshua, he said to me: Thou hast well spoken; but thus have they enjoined as *Halakah*.[22]

8. 1. If a man said to two Nazirites, 'I saw that one of you contracted uncleanness, but I do not know which of you it was', they must [both] cut off their hair and must bring [together] one offering because of unclean-

---

[1] App. II, D.
[2] Cf. Num. 19[14ff]. Uncleanness is conveyed by (*a*) being under the same roof or 'tent' as the corpse (or portion of corpse), (*b*) being perpendicularly above it, or (*c*) being perpendicularly below it. See p. 649, n. 3; App. IV. 6.   [3] See above, p. 288, n. 4.
[4] See Ohol. 8[2].   [5] Ohol. 17[1].   [6] Ohol. 2[9].   [7] Num. 19[14ff].
[8] The seven days after the leper has been pronounced clean; Lev. 14[8].
[9] See Lev. 13[3, 8, 11].   [10] Num. 6[10].   [11] See p. 12, n. 4.   [12] Lev. 15[2ff, 19ff].
[13] Lev. 13[4, 5].   [14] If they befall within the time of a Nazirite-vow.
[15] Detailed above, par. 2.   [16] Above, par. 3.   [17] See Lev. 5[2]; Num. 19[20].
[18] See above, par. 2.   [19] Ohol. 2[3].   [20] See above, par. 3.
[21] Since it is the accepted ruling.   [22] App. I. 11.

ness[1] and one offering [for a vow fulfilled] in cleanness;[2] and each must say, 'If it is I that became unclean let mine be the offering brought because of uncleanness, and thine the offering brought in cleanness; but if it is I that remained clean let mine be the offering brought in cleanness and thine the offering brought because of uncleanness'. And they must count[3] [another] thirty days and bring one offering [for a vow fulfilled] in cleanness; and [each] must say, 'If it is I that became unclean, the offering brought because of uncleanness was mine and thine the offering brought in cleanness, and this offering brought in cleanness is mine; but if it is I that remained clean, the offering brought in cleanness was mine, and thine the offering brought because of uncleanness, and this offering brought in cleanness is thine'. If one of them died, R. Joshua said: Let him ask one from the street to vow to be a Nazirite in the other's stead and say to him, 'If it was I that became unclean, be thou a Nazirite forthwith; but if it was I that remained clean be thou a Nazirite after thirty days'. They should then count thirty days and bring an offering because of uncleanness and an offering [for a vow fulfilled] in cleanness. Then he shall say, 'If it is I that became unclean this is my offering brought because of uncleanness and thine the offering brought in cleanness; but if it is I that remained clean, the offering brought in cleanness is mine, and the offering brought because of uncleanness is in doubt'. They then count another thirty days and bring an offering [for a vow fulfilled] in cleanness, and he says, 'If it is I that became unclean, the offering brought because of uncleanness was mine and thine the offering brought in cleanness, and this offering brought in cleanness is mine; but if it is I that remained clean, then the offering brought in cleanness was mine and the offering brought because of uncleanness was in doubt, and this offering brought in cleanness is thine.' Ben Zoma said to him: But who will hearken to him to vow to be a Nazirite in the other's stead!—but, rather, he should bring a bird as a Sin-offering and a beast as a Whole-offering and say, 'If it was I that became unclean here is my Sin-offering brought in duty bound, and a Whole-offering brought of free choice; if it was I that remained clean here is my Whole-offering brought in duty bound and the Sin-offering is brought by reason of the doubt'. Then he should count thirty days and bring an offering in cleanness and say, 'If it was I that became unclean the first Whole-offering was brought of free choice and this is brought in duty bound; but if it was I that remained clean the first Whole-offering was brought in duty bound, and this is offered of free choice, and here is the rest of my offering!'[4] R. Joshua said: He would then be bringing his offerings piecemeal. But the Sages agree with Ben Zoma.

2. If it is in doubt whether a Nazirite is unclean and whether signs of leprosy in him are unclean, he may eat of Hallowed Things after sixty days, and after one hundred and twenty days drink wine and contract uncleanness because of the dead, since the cutting off of the hair because of leprosy overrides the cutting off of the hair because of the Nazirite-vow only when it is not in doubt; but when it is in doubt it does not override it.

9. 1. Gentiles may not vow the Nazirite-vow. Women and slaves may vow the Nazirite-vow. Greater stringency applies to women than to slaves, since one may compel his slave [to break the vow], but he cannot compel his

---

[1] As prescribed in Num. 6[10].   [2] As prescribed in Num. 6[14ff].
[3] See above, p. 283, n. 1.   [4] The prescribed Sin-offering and Peace-offering.

wife. Greater stringency applies to slaves than to women, since a man may revoke his wife's vows[1] but he cannot revoke those of his slave.[2] If he revoked his wife's [Nazirite-]vow he has revoked it for all time; but if he revoked that of his slave and the slave was set free, he must complete his Nazirite-vow. If he escaped from his master, R. Meir says: He may not drink [wine]. But R. Jose says: He may drink.

2. If a Nazirite had cut off his hair and [before he brought his offerings] it became known to him that he had become unclean, if it was an uncleanness that was known, it renders void [the whole of the days of his vow], but if it was an uncleanness from the deep,[3] it does not render void [the whole of the days of his vow]; and if [his uncleanness was known to him] before he cut off his hair, in either case it renders them void. Thus if he had gone down to immerse himself in a cavern and a corpse was found floating at the mouth of the cavern, he becomes unclean; but if it was found sunk on the floor of the cavern and he had gone down [only] to cool himself [in the water], he is [still accounted] clean; but if he had gone down to be cleansed from corpse-uncleanness, he remains unclean; for he that was unclean is presumed to be still unclean, and he that was clean is presumed to be still clean, since there is proof whereon to rely.

3. If[4] for a first time a man found a corpse lying in usual fashion he may remove it and the soil about it [for burial elsewhere]; if he found two he may remove them and the soil about them. But if he found three and a space of four to eight cubits between them, then this must be accounted a graveyard, and he must examine the ground over a space of twenty cubits. If he found another corpse twenty cubits away he must examine yet another twenty cubits from that point, since there is proof whereon to rely [that this is indeed a graveyard]; although if for a first time a man found a corpse, he may remove it and the soil about it.

4. Any[5] condition of doubt in the beginning in what concerns leprosy-signs is deemed clean if it has not already come within the bonds of uncleanness; but if it had come within the bonds of uncleanness, its condition of doubt is deemed unclean. Along seven lines[6] do they examine him that has a flux if he has not already come within the bonds of uncleanness as one that has a flux: concerning what he had eaten, what he had drunk, what he had carried, whether he had jumped, whether he had been sick, what he had seen, and whether he had had impure thoughts. After he has come within the bonds of uncleanness as one that has a flux they do not examine him; for any flux that he suffers from inadvertence, or a flux that is in doubt, or a discharge of semen, such are adjudged unclean, since there is proof whereon to rely. If a man struck[7] his fellow and they considered him like to die, and he then grew better and afterward grew worse and died, he [that struck him] is culpable. R. Nehemiah declares him not culpable since there is proof whereon to rely [for belief that there was some other cause of death].

5. According to R. Nehorai, Samuel was a Nazirite, for it is written, *And there shall no razor*[8] *come upon his head.*[9] Since it is said of Samson, *And no razor shall come upon his head,*[10] and it is said also of Samuel, *And no razor . . . ,* as the razor spoken of concerning Samson means that he was to

---

[1] See Ned. 11[1, 2].　　　　　　[2] Though he can compel him not to keep them.
[3] From a hitherto unknown grave. Cf. Par. 3[3, 6].　　　　[4] Ohol. 16[3].
[5] Neg. 5[4].　　　　[6] Zab. 2[2].　　　　[7] Sanh. 9[1].
[8] Heb. *morah*. This word has also the meaning 'lordship'.　　[9] 1 Sam. 1[11].　　[10] Judg. 13[5].

be a Nazirite so the razor spoken of concerning Samuel means that he was to be a Nazirite. R. Jose said: But is not [this word] *morah*[1] meant only of flesh and blood? R. Nehorai said to him: But was it not once said, *And Samuel said, How can I go? If Saul hear it, he will kill me*[2]—thus upon him there came once *morah* (the authority) of flesh and blood![3]

SOTAH[4] ('THE SUSPECTED ADULTERESS')

1. 1. If a man would warn[5] his wife, R. Eliezer says: He must warn her before two witnesses, and he may [then] make her drink[6] on the evidence of one witness or on his own evidence.[7] R. Joshua says: He must warn her before two witnesses, and he may make her drink [only] on the evidence of two witnesses.

2. How does he warn her? If he said to her before two witnesses, 'Speak not with such-a-one', and she spoke with him, she may still consort with her husband and she may eat of Heave-offering.[8] If she went aside with him in secret and remained with him time enough to suffer defilement she may not consort with her husband and she may not eat of Heave-offering. If her husband died[9] she must perform *halitzah*[10] and may not contract levirate marriage.[11]

3. These may not eat of Heave-offering:[12] she that says, 'I am unclean to thee',[13] and she against whom witnesses have testified that she was unclean,[14] and she that says, 'I will not drink', and she whose husband is not minded to make her drink, and she whose husband has connexion with her while on the way.[15] How should he behave towards her? He should bring her to the court that is in that place[16] and they appoint for him two disciples of the Sages[17] lest he have connexion with her while on the way. R. Judah says: Her husband is accounted trustworthy concerning her.

4. They used to bring her up to the great court[18] that was in Jerusalem and admonish her in like manner as they admonished witnesses in capital cases,[19] and say to her, 'My daughter, much [sin] is wrought by wine, much by light conduct, much by childishness, and much by evil neighbours; do thou behave for the sake of his great Name, written in holiness,[20] that it be not blotted out through the water [of bitterness]'. And they speak before her words which neither she nor the family of her father's house are worthy to hear.

5. If she said, 'I am unclean', she takes payment of her *Ketubah*[21] and is put away. But if she said, 'I am clean', they take her up to the Eastern Gate[22] which is over against the entrance of the Nicanor Gate, where they give Suspected Adulteresses to drink [of the water of bitterness], purify women after childbirth,[23] and purify lepers.[24] A priest lays hold on her

---

[1] Giving it the sense of 'lordship' or 'human authority'.   [2] 1 Sam. 16[2].
[3] Therefore *morah* in 1 Sam. 1[11] cannot have been used in the sense of 'fear', but only in the sense of 'razor'.
[4] Num. 5[11–31].   [5] Lit. 'be jealous of'. See Num. 5[14].
[6] 'The water of bitterness that causeth the curse'; Num. 5[18].
[7] That she had gone aside in secret with another.
[8] If her husband was a priest; Lev. 22[11].
[9] Childless. See Deut. 25[5ff].   [10] App. I. 12.   [11] p. 218, n. 1.
[12] If their husbands were priests. Since the test of the water of bitterness is not applied she must be divorced.   [13] See Ned. 11[12].   [14] Had committed adultery.
[15] Up to Jerusalem.   [16] Where they lived.   [17] Cf. Makk. 2[5].
[18] Sanh. 11[2].   [19] See Sanh. 4[5].
[20] See Num. 5[23]. The sacred name was written together with the curse on the scroll whose writing was to be blotted out in the water of bitterness.   [21] App. I. 16.
[22] Midd. 1[3]; 2[6]. Cf. Shek. 6[3].   [23] See Lev. 12[1ff].   [24] See Lev. 14[11].

garments—if they are torn they are torn, if they are utterly rent they are utterly rent[1]—so that he lays bare her bosom. Moreover he loosens her hair.[2] R. Judah says: If her bosom was comely he did not lay it bare; if her hair was comely he did not loosen it.

6. If she was clothed in white garments he clothed her in black. If she bore ornaments of gold and chains and nose-rings and finger-rings, they were taken from her to shame her. He then brought an Egyptian rope[3] and tied it above her breasts. Any that wished to behold came and beheld, excepting her bondmen and bondwomen, since with them she feels no shame.[4] And all women are allowed to behold her, for it is written, *That all women may be taught not to do after your lewdness.*[5]

7. With what measure a man metes it shall be measured to him again: she bedecked herself for transgression—the Almighty[6] brought her to shame; she laid herself bare for transgression—the Almighty likewise laid her bare; she began transgression with the thigh first and afterward with the belly—therefore the thigh shall suffer first and afterward the belly; neither shall aught else of the body go free.

8. Samson went after [the desire of] his eyes—therefore the Philistines put out his eyes, as it is written, *And the Philistines laid hold on him and put out his eyes*;[7] Absalom gloried in his hair—therefore he was hanged by his hair; and inasmuch as he came in upon the ten concubines of his father, therefore they thrust ten spear-heads into his body, as it is written, *And ten young men that bare Joab's armour compassed about and smote Absalom and slew him*;[8] and inasmuch as he stole away three hearts, the heart of his father, the heart of the court, and the heart of Israel (as it is written, *So Absalom stole the hearts of the men of Israel*),[9] therefore three darts were thrust into him, as it is written, *And he took three darts in his hand and thrust them through the heart of Absalom.*[10]

9. So, too, in a goodly matter: Miriam awaited Moses one hour, as it is written, *And his sister stood afar off*,[11] therefore Israel delayed for her seven days, as it is written, *And the people journeyed not till Miriam was brought in again.*[12] Joseph was reckoned worthy to bury his father, and none of his brothers was greater than he, as it is written, *And Joseph went up to bury his father . . . and there went up with him both chariots and horsemen.*[13] Whom have we greater than Joseph, for none other than Moses occupied himself with him. Moses was reckoned worthy to take the bones of Joseph, and none in Israel is greater than he, as it is written, *And Moses took the bones of Joseph with him.*[14] Whom have we greater than Moses, for none other than the Almighty occupied himself with him, as it is written, *And he buried him in the valley.*[15] And not of Moses alone have they spoken thus, but of all the righteous, for it is written, *And thy righteousness shall go before thee; the glory of the Lord shall gather thee [in death].*[16]

2. 1. [The husband] brought her Meal-offering[17] in an Egyptian basket[18] and put it in her hands so as to tire her. All [other] Meal-offerings, at the

---

[1] Cf. Makk. 3[12].   [2] Num. 5[18].   [3] Or 'rope of rushes'.
[4] The same phrase as in Gitt. 7[4, 8][9]; Ab. 4[7]. Rashi, however, interprets it here in the sense, 'She is too proud ever to make confession of her guilt before them'.
[5] Ezek. 23[48].   [6] Lit. 'the Place'.   [7] Judg. 16[21].   [8] 2 Sam. 18[15].
[9] 2 Sam. 15[6]. Some texts omit the bracketed passage.
[10] 2 Sam. 18[14].   [11] Ex. 2.[4]   [12] Num. 12[15].   [13] Gen. 50[7, 9].
[14] Ex. 13[19].   [15] Deut. 34[6].   [16] Is. 58[8].
[17] Num. 5[15].   [18] Or 'basket of rushes'.

outset and at the last,[1] are contained in the vessels of ministry; but this at the outset is contained in an Egyptian basket, and at the last in the vessels of ministry. All [other] Meal-offerings require oil and frankincense,[2] but this requires neither oil nor frankincense. All [other] Meal-offerings are of wheat,[3] but this is of barley. The Meal-offering of the Omer,[4] though offered from barley, is offered in the form of sifted flour, but this is offered in the form of [unsifted] meal. Rabban Gamaliel says: Since her deed was the deed of cattle, her offering is the food of cattle.

2. The priest used to bring a new[5] earthenware bowl and put in it a half-*log*[6] of water from the laver.[7] R. Judah says: A quarter-*log*; as the writing is made less so the water is made less. The priest entered within the Sanctuary[8] and turned to the right where was a place, one cubit long and one cubit wide, having a marble flagstone on which was fixed a ring. This he raised and took dust from beneath it and put in the bowl enough to be visible on the water, as it is written, *And of the dust that is on the floor of the tabernacle the priest shall take and put it into the water.*[9]

3. When he came to write the scroll, from what place used he to write? from *If*[10] *no man have lien with thee . . . but if thou hast gone aside with another instead of thy husband*, and he left out *And the priest shall cause the woman to swear*. He wrote also *The Lord make thee a curse and an oath among thy people . . . and this water that causeth the curse shall go into thy bowels and make thy belly to swell and thy thigh to fall away*. And he left out, *And the woman shall say, Amen, Amen!* R. Jose says: He made no break. R. Judah says: He wrote altogether naught else save *The Lord make thee a curse and an oath . . . and this water that causeth the curse shall go into thy bowels . . .*; and he left out *And the woman shall say, Amen, Amen!*

4. He did not write on a tablet or on papyrus or on unprepared skin, but only on a [parchment] scroll, as it is written, *In a book*.[11] And he may not write with gum or copperas[12] or aught that leaves a lasting trace, but only with ink, for it is written, *And he shall blot them out*; [he must write with] what can be blotted out.

5. To what does she reply, *Amen, Amen!*? [She says] *Amen* to the word curse, and *Amen* to the word oath; '*Amen*, [for that I have not gone aside] because of this man,[13] *Amen*, [for that I have not gone aside] because of any other man; *Amen*, for that I have not gone aside while I was betrothed, or while I was married, or while I was awaiting levirate marriage, or after consummation; *Amen*, for that I have not been defiled; and if I have been defiled may [all these curses] come upon me!' R. Meir says: '*Amen*, for that I have not been defiled; *Amen*, for that I will never become defiled'.

6. All agree that he[14] may not take account of her[15] concerning a time before she was betrothed or a time after she had been divorced.[16] If [after she had been put away] she went aside with another man and became defiled, and he afterward received her back, he[14] may not take account of her concerning this. This is the general rule: If she has intercourse with such as do not render her forbidden [to her husband], he[14] may not take account of her concerning this.

---

1 From the time they are first brought by their owner until they are consumed.
2 Lev. 2[1].   3 Cf. Ex. 29[2].   4 App. I. 31.   5 Some texts omit 'new'.
6 App. II, D.   7 Ex. 30[18ff.]; Midd. 3[6].   8 Midd. 4[1].   9 Num. 5[17].   10 Num. 5[19f].
11 Num. 5[23]. Heb. *sefer*. Its usual sense is a book written in scroll-form, not with bound-up leaves.   12 Cf. Meg. 2[2].   13 About whom I am now accused.
14 The priest.   15 In applying the words of Num. 5[19].
16 And remarried by her present husband before he had 'warned her'.

3. 1. The husband used to take her Meal-offering out of the Egyptian basket[1] and put it into a vessel of ministry, and this he put in her hand; and the priest set his hand beneath hers and [so] waved[2] [the Meal-offering].

2. After he had waved it and brought it [unto the Altar], he took the handful [therefrom] and burnt it, and the residue was consumed by the priests. He first gave her to drink [of the bitter water] and then offered her Meal-offering. R. Simeon says: He offered her Meal-offering and then gave her to drink, for it is written, *And afterward he shall make the woman drink the water*.[3] But if he gave her to drink and afterward offered her Meal-offering, it is valid.

3. If, before the writing on the scroll was blotted out, she said, 'I will not drink', her scroll[4] must be hidden away[5] and her Meal-offering scattered on the ash-heap. Her scroll is not valid for use for any other Suspected Adulteress. If the writing on the scroll was blotted out and she then said, 'I am unclean', the water is poured away and her Meal-offering scattered on the ash-heap. If the writing on the scroll was blotted out and she then said, 'I will not drink', they urge her and give her to drink against her will.

4. Hardly has she finished drinking before her face turns yellow and her eyes bulge and her veins swell, and they say, 'Take her away! take her away! that the Temple Court be not made unclean!' But if she had any merit this holds her punishment in suspense. Certain merits may hold punishment in suspense for one year, others for two years, and others for three years; hence Ben Azzai says: A man ought to give his daughter[6] a knowledge of the Law so that if she must drink [the bitter water] she may know that the merit [that she had acquired] will hold her punishment in suspense. R. Eliezer says: If any man gives his daughter a knowledge of the Law it is as though he taught her lechery. R. Joshua says: A woman has more pleasure in one *kab*[7] with lechery than in nine *kabs* with modesty. He used to say: A foolish saint and a cunning knave and a woman that is a hypocrite and the wounds of the Pharisees, these wear out the world.

5. R. Simeon says: Merit does not hold in suspense the punishment of the bitter water; for if thou sayest, 'Merit holds in suspense the punishment of the curse-giving water', thou wilt make the water of little effect for all the women that drink; and thou wilt bring an evil name against all undefiled women that have drunk, for it will be said, 'They are in truth defiled but merit has held their punishment in suspense'. Rabbi[8] says: Merit holds in suspense the punishment of the curse-giving water; but nevertheless she will not bear children or continue in comeliness, but she will waste away by degrees and in the end will die the selfsame death.

6. If her Meal-offering became unclean before it was sanctified in the vessel of ministry, like all other Meal-offerings it may be redeemed; but if after it was sanctified in the vessel [of ministry], like all other Meal-offerings it must be burnt.[9] The Meal-offerings of these must be burnt: [the Meal-offering of a woman] that says,[10] 'I am unclean to thee', or she against whom witnesses testified that she was unclean, or she that says, 'I will not drink', or she whose husband is not minded to make her drink,

---

[1] Or 'basket of rushes'.   [2] Num. 5[25].   [3] Num. 5[26].
[4] On which the curse was written.
[5] Like all writings of Scripture that have become unusable.   [6] Cf. Ned. 4[3].
[7] App. II, D.   [8] R. Judah the Patriarch. See below, 9[15] (end).   [9] See Men. 12[1].
[10] See 1[3].

or she whose husband has connexion with her while on the way; and the Meal-offerings of all that are married to priests must be burnt.[1]

7. If she was an Israelite's daughter married to a priest, her Meal-offering must be burnt; and if she was a priest's daughter married to an Israelite, her Meal-offering is consumed [by the priests]. Wherein does a priest differ from a woman from the priestly stock? Her Meal-offering is consumed [by the priests]; his may not be consumed; she may impair her priestly rights, but he cannot impair his priestly rights;[2] she may contract uncleanness because of the dead, but he may not contract uncleanness because of the dead;[3] a priest may eat of the Most Holy Things,[4] but she may not eat of the Most Holy Things.

8. How does a man differ from a woman? He may go with hair unbound and with garments rent,[5] but she may not go with hair unbound and with garments rent; he may impose the Nazirite-vow on his son, but she may not impose the Nazirite-vow on her son;[6] a man may bring the Hair-offering for the Nazirite-vow of his father, but a woman may not bring the Hair-offering for the Nazirite-vow of her father;[7] a man may sell his daughter,[8] but a woman may not sell her daughter; a man may give his daughter in betrothal,[9] but a woman may not give her daughter in betrothal; a man is stoned naked, but a woman may not be stoned naked;[10] a man is hanged, but a woman may not be hanged;[11] a man may be sold [to make restitution] for what he has stolen,[12] but a woman cannot be sold [to make restitution] for what she has stolen.

4. 1. A woman that is betrothed or that awaits levirate marriage[13] may not drink [the bitter water] or receive her *Ketubah*; for it is written, *When a wife, being under her husband, goeth aside*,[14] thus excluding her that is betrothed or that awaits levirate marriage. If[15] a widow is married to a High Priest, or a woman that was divorced or that had performed *halitzah* is married to a common priest, or a bastard or *Nethinah* to an Israelite, or the daughter of an Israelite to a bastard or a *Nathin*, they may not drink[16] [the bitter water] or receive their *Ketubah*.

2. These do not drink and do not receive their *Ketubah*: She that says, 'I am unclean [to thee]', and she against whom witnesses have testified that she was unclean, and she that says, 'I will not drink'. But she whose husband is not minded to make her drink, or she whose husband has connexion with her while on the way, she receives her *Ketubah* and does not drink. If their husbands died before their wives drank [the bitter water], the School of Shammai say: They receive their *Ketubah* and do not drink. And the School of Hillel say: They do not drink and they do not receive their *Ketubah*.

3. If a woman was with child by another husband[17] or was giving suck [to a child] by another husband, she does not drink and she does not receive her *Ketubah*. So R. Meir. But the Sages say: He should set her

---

[1] i.e. the residue may not be consumed by the priests, since it is a Meal-offering brought by a priest; and the Meal-offerings of priests must be wholly burnt (Lev. 6[22]).
[2] By marrying one of the impaired priestly stock or a harlot.   [3] Lev. 21[1].
[4] Sin-offerings and Guilt-offerings and the Peace-offerings of the congregation. See Zeb. 5[1–5].   [5] Lev. 13[45].   [6] Naz. 4[6].
[7] Naz. 4[7].   [8] Ex. 21[7]; cf. Ket. 3[8].   [9] Ket. 4[4].   [10] Sanh. 6[3].   [11] Sanh. 6[4].
[12] Ex. 22[3].   [13] See Deut. 25[5]; p. 218, n. 1.   [14] Num. 5[29].   [15] Cf. Yeb. 2[4].
[16] Since they are not women fit to be their wives.
[17] Who had died or divorced her, and she married before the two years prescribed by the Rabbis had elapsed.

apart and take her back after the [prescribed] time. A sterile woman, an aged woman, and one that is not like to bear children do not drink and do not receive their *Ketubah*. R. Eliezer says: He has the right to marry another and to *be fruitful and multiply*[1] by her. All other women either drink or they do not receive their *Ketubah*.

4. A priest's wife may drink [the bitter water] and [if she is found innocent] she is permitted to her husband. The wife of a eunuch must drink. Wives may be warned that are suspected of any incestuous connexion save only with a minor or with aught that is not human.

5. And these are they that are warned by the court: any woman whose husband has become a deaf-mute or an imbecile or that lies bound in prison. They did not say this [to empower the court] to make her drink [the bitter water], but to disqualify her from receiving her *Ketubah*. R. Jose says: Also to make her drink, so that when her husband comes forth from prison he may make her drink.

5. 1. As the water puts her to the proof so does it put the paramour to the proof, for it is written, *And it shall come*, and again, *And it shall come*.[2] As she is forbidden to the husband so is she forbidden to the paramour, for it is written, *And she is become unclean*, and again, *And she is become unclean*.[3] So R. Akiba. R. Joshua said: So used Zechariah b. ha-Kazzab to expound. Rabbi says: Twice in the section of Scripture is it written, *And she is become unclean*, *And she is become unclean*: once for the husband and once for the paramour.

2. That same day R. Akiba expounded, *And every earthen vessel whereinto any of them falleth, whatsoever is in it conveys uncleanness*;[4] it does not say *is unclean* but *shall render unclean*, so that it makes other things unclean. This teaches that a loaf suffering second-grade uncleanness renders another unclean in the third grade.[5] R. Joshua said: Who will take away the dust from off thine eyes, O Rabban Johanan ben Zakkai!—for thou didst say that another generation would declare the third loaf clean, for there is no verse in the Law to prove that it is unclean; and now does not thy pupil Akiba bring a verse from the Law to prove that it is unclean! for it is written, *Whatsoever is in it shall render unclean*.

3. That same day R. Akiba expounded, *And ye shall measure without the city for the east side two thousand cubits . . .*,[6] while another verse[7] says, *From the wall of the city and outward a thousand cubits round about*. It is not possible to say [that the measure is] a thousand cubits, since it is also written *two thousand cubits*; and it is not possible to say two thousand cubits, since it is also written *one thousand cubits*. How can we explain this?—the one thousand cubits are the outskirts,[8] while the two thousand cubits are the Sabbath limit.[9] R. Eleazer b. R. Jose the Galilean says: The one thousand cubits are the outskirts and the two thousand cubits are the [surrounding] fields and vineyards.

4. That same day R. Akiba expounded, *Then sang Moses and the children*

---

[1] Gen. 1[28].   [2] Num. 5[22, 24].   [3] Num. 5[13, 14].

[4] Lev. 11[33], implying a pointing different (*pi'el*) from that (*qal*) in the present Massoretic text, which is rendered 'shall be unclean'.

[5] Cf. Toh. 1[8]; 2[3]. The vessel suffered 'first-grade uncleanness', the loaf in it 'second-grade', and, according to R. Akiba, it conveyed third-grade uncleanness to other food that it touched, contrary to the accepted rule that common food contracted no uncleanness from what suffered only second-grade uncleanness.   [6] Num. 35[5].   [7] Num. 35[4].

[8] Which pertain to the city but may not be built upon.   [9] See App. I. 8, 'Erub'.

of Israel this song unto the Lord and spake saying.[1] There was no need for Scripture to say *saying*; what then does it mean by *saying*? It teaches us that Israel made answer to every thing after Moses, like as when they recite the *Hallel*;[2] therefore it says *saying*. R. Nehemiah says: Like as when they recite the *Shema*'[3] and not like as when they recite the *Hallel*.

5. That same day R. Joshua b. Hyrcanus expounded: Job served the Holy One, blessed is he, only from love, as it is written, *Though he slay me yet will I wait for him.*[4] Thus far the matter rests in doubt [whether it means] 'I will wait for him' or 'I will not wait';[5] but Scripture says, *Till I die I will not put away mine integrity from me,*[6] teaching that he acted from love. R. Joshua said, 'Who will take away the dust from off thine eyes, O Rabban Johanan ben Zakkai!—for all thy days thou didst expound that Job served the Holy One, blessed is he, only from fear, for it is written, *The man was perfect and upright and one that feared God and eschewed evil*;[7] and has not Joshua, thy disciple's disciple, now taught us that he acted from love?

6. 1. If a man had warned his wife and she nevertheless went aside in secret, if he but heard thereof from a flying bird he may put her away and give her her *Ketubah*. So R. Eliezer. R. Joshua says: [He may not do so] until the women that spin their yarn by moonlight gossip about her.

2. If one witness said, 'I saw her that she was defiled', she does not need to drink;[8] and not so only but even if a bondman or bondwoman [bore like witness] they are accounted trustworthy even to disqualify her from receiving her *Ketubah*. Her mother-in-law, her mother-in-law's daughter, her co-wife, her husband's brother's wife, and her husband's daughter— these are accounted trustworthy, not, however, to disqualify her from receiving her *Ketubah*, but [to prove her guilt] so that she has no need to drink [the bitter water].

3. For the inference might be: Since the first testimony[9] (which does not render her forbidden for all time)[10] cannot be sustained by less than two witnesses, should we not, therefore, infer that the last testimony[11] (which renders her forbidden for all time) cannot be sustained by less than two witnesses! But Scripture says, *And there be no witness against her*[12]— [meaning] any manner of evidence against her. From this to the first testimony is an argument from the less to the greater: If the last testimony (which renders her forbidden for all time) can be sustained by one witness, should we not therefore infer that the first testimony (which does not render her forbidden for all time) can also be sustained by one witness! But Scripture says, *Because he hath found some unseemly matter in her,*[13] and elsewhere it says, *At the mouth of two witnesses . . . shall a matter be established.*[14] As the *matter* there spoken of must be at the mouth of two witnesses, so, here, it must be at the mouth of two witnesses.

4. If one witness said, 'She was defiled', and another said, 'She was not defiled'; or if one woman said, 'She was defiled', and another woman said

---

[1] Ex. 15[1].
[2] Pss. 113–18. The congregation responds to each verse with some brief refrain. Cf. Sukk. 3[10]. Some texts here quote: 'I will sing unto the Lord for he hath triumphed gloriously', as the refrain to each verse of the Song of Moses.
[3] App. I. 38. The congregation repeats the whole of it.   [4] Job. 13[15].
[5] The Hebrew homophone *lô* or *lō*' means both 'for him' or 'not'.   [6] Job. 27[5].   [7] Job. 1[1].
[8] But can be divorced, receiving her *Ketubah*.   [9] Concerning her going aside in secret.
[10] But only until she has been tested by the bitter water.
[11] Of her having become defiled.   [12] Num. 5[13].   [13] Deut. 24[1].   [14] Deut. 19[15].

'She was not defiled', she must be made to drink. If one said, 'She was defiled', and two said, 'She was not defiled', she must be made to drink.[1] But if two said, 'She was defiled', and one said, 'She was not defiled', she need not be made to drink.[2]

7. 1. These may be said in any language: the paragraph of the Suspected Adulteress,[3] the Avowal concerning the [Second] Tithe,[4] the recital of the *Shemaʿ*,[5] the *Tefillah*,[6] the Benediction over food,[7] the oath of testimony,[8] and the oath concerning a deposit.[9]

2. These must be said in the Holy Language: the paragraph of the First-fruits,[10] the words of *halitzah*,[11] the Blessings and the Cursings,[12] the Blessings of the Priests,[13] and the blessings of the High Priest,[14] the paragraph of the king,[15] the paragraph of the heifer whose neck is to be broken,[16] and [the words of] the Anointed for Battle[17] when he speaks unto the people.

3. Why does this apply to the paragraph of the First-fruits? [Here it is written,] *And thou shalt answer and say before the Lord thy God*,[18] and there it is written, *And the Levites shall answer and say*;[19] as there the answering must be in the Holy Language, so here the answering must be in the Holy Language.

4. Why does this apply to the words of *halitzah*? [Here it is written,] *And she shall answer and say*,[20] and there it is written, *And the Levites shall answer and say*;[21] as there the answering must be in the Holy Language, so here the answering must be in the Holy Language. R. Judah says: *And she shall answer and say thus*;[22] [therefore it is not valid] unless she speaks according to this very language.

5. Why does this apply to the Blessings and the Cursings? When Israel crossed the Jordan and came unto mount Gerizim and unto mount Ebal in Samaria, near by Shechem, beside the oaks of Moreh, as it is written, *Are not they beyond Jordan . . .*[23] (there it is written, *And Abram passed through the land unto the place of Shechem unto the oak of Moreh*;[24] as there the oak of Moreh that is spoken of is [at] Shechem, so here the oak of Moreh that is spoken of is [at] Shechem), six tribes went up to the top of mount Gerizim and six tribes went up to the top of mount Ebal. And the priests and the levites and the Ark stood below in the midst; and the priests surrounded the Ark and the levites surrounded the priests, and all Israel were on this side and on that, as it is written, *And all Israel and their elders and officers and their judges stood on this side of the ark and on that . . .*[25] They turned their faces towards mount Gerizim and began with the blessing.[26] Blessed be the man that maketh not a graven or molten image. And both these and these answered, 'Amen!' They turned their faces towards mount Ebal and began with the curse, *Cursed be the man that maketh a graven or molten image*.[27] And both these and these answered, 'Amen!'—until they completed the Blessings and the Cursings. And afterward they brought

---

[1] In these three cases her guilt is in doubt and needs to be put to the test.
[2] Since her guilt is no longer in doubt.   [3] Num. 5[19-22].
[4] Deut. 26[13-15]; cf. M.Sh. 5[10ff].   [5] App. I. 38.   [6] App. I. 46.   [7] Cf. Ber. 6-7.
[8] Cf. Shebu. 4[1ff].   [9] Cf. Shebu. 5[1ff].   [10] Deut. 26[3, 5-10].
[11] Deut. 25[7, 9]; cf. Yeb. 12[6].   [12] Deut. 27[15-26] (cf. Deut. 28[2-68], Josh. 8[34]).
[13] Num. 6[24-6].   [14] On the Day of Atonement. See below, 7[7].
[15] Deut. 17[14-20]. See below, 7[8].   [16] Deut. 21[7f].   [17] Deut. 20[2-7]. See below, 8[1ff].
[18] Deut. 26[5].   [19] Deut. 27[14].   [20] Deut. 25[9].   [21] Deut. 27[14].
[22] Separating 'thus' or 'so' from the following clause.   [23] Deut. 11[30].   [24] Gen. 12[6].
[25] Josh. 8[33].   [26] First reciting all the curses in the form of blessings.
[27] Cf. Deut. 27[15].

the stones and built the altar and plastered it with plaster. And they wrote thereon all the words of the Law in seventy languages, as it is written, *Very plainly*.[1] And they took the stones and came and spent the night in their own place.

6. After what manner was the blessing of the priests? In the provinces it was pronounced as three blessings,[2] but in the Temple as a single blessing; in the Temple they pronounced the Name as it was written,[3] but in the provinces by a substituted word; in the provinces the priests raised their hands as high as their shoulders, but in the Temple above their heads, excepting the High Priest who raised his hand only as high as the frontlet.[4] R. Judah says: The High Priest also raised his hand above the frontlet, for it is written, *And Aaron lifted up his hands toward the people and blessed them*.[5]

7. After what manner were the blessings of the High Priest? The minister[6] of the synagogue used to take a scroll of the Law and give it to the chief of the synagogue, and the chief of the synagogue gave it to the Prefect and the Prefect gave it to the High Priest, and the High Priest received it standing and read it standing. And he read, *After the death* . . .[7] and *Howbeit on the tenth day* . . .[8] Then he used to roll up the [scroll of the] Law and put it in his bosom and say, 'More is written here than I have read out before you'. *And on the tenth* . . . which is in the Book of Numbers[9] he recited by heart, thereupon he pronounced eight Benedictions: for the Law, for the Temple-Service, the Thanksgiving, on the Forgiveness of Sin, and for the Temple and for the Israelites, and for the priests and for Jerusalem,[10] and, for the rest, a [general] prayer.

8. After what manner was the paragraph of the king? After the close of the first Festival-day of the Feast [of Tabernacles], in the eighth year, after the going forth of the Seventh Year, they used to prepare for him in the Temple Court a wooden platform on which he sat, for it is written, *At the end of every seven years in the set time*. . . .[11] The minister of the synagogue used to take a scroll of the Law and give it to the chief of the synagogue, and the chief of the synagogue gave it to the Prefect, and the Prefect gave it to the High Priest, and the High Priest gave it to the king, and the king received it standing and read it sitting. King Agrippa received it standing and read it standing, and for this the Sages praised him. And when he reached *Thou mayest not put a foreigner over thee which is not thy brother*,[12] his eyes flowed with tears; but they called to him, 'Our brother art thou! our brother art thou! our brother art thou!' He read from the beginning of Deuteronomy to *Hear*, [*O Israel*];[13] and the paragraphs *Hear*, [*O Israel*] . . . and *And it shall come to pass if ye shall hearken* . . .[14] and *Thou shalt surely tithe* . . .[15] and *When thou hast made an end of tithing* . . .[16] and the paragraph of the king,[17] and the Blessings and the Cursings,[18] until the end. With the same blessings with which the High Priest blesses them the king blesses them, save that he pronounces the blessing for the Feasts instead of the blessing for the forgiveness of sin.

8. 1. When the Anointed for Battle speaks unto the people he speaks in

---

[1] Deut. 27[8].   [2] The people responding 'Amen' to each of the three verses, Num. 6[24-6].
[3] Yom. 6[2].   [4] Ex. 28[36].   [5] Lev. 9[22].   [6] See Yom. 7[1].   [7] Lev. 16[1ff].
[8] Lev. 23[26ff].   [9] Num. 29[7-11].   [10] Some texts omit 'and for Jerusalem'.
[11] Deut. 31[10].   [12] Deut. 17[15]. Agrippa was of Edomite descent.   [13] Deut. 6[4].
[14] Deut. 11[13ff].   [15] Deut. 14[22ff].   [16] Deut. 26[12ff].   [17] Deut. 17[14-20].
[18] Deut. 27[15-26]. Cf. Deut. 28[2-68].

the Holy Language, for it is written,[1] *And it shall be when ye draw nigh unto the battle, that the priest shall approach* (this is the priest anointed for the battle) *and shall speak unto the people* (in the Holy Language), *and shall say unto them, Hear, O Israel, ye draw nigh unto battle this day against your enemies*—and not against your brethren, not Judah against Simeon, and not Simeon against Benjamin, for if ye fall into their hands they will have mercy upon you, for it is written, *And the men which have been expressed by name rose up and took the captives and with the spoil clothed all that were naked among them, and arrayed them and shod them and gave them to eat and to drink and anointed them and carried all the feeble of them upon asses and brought them to Jericho, the city of palm trees, unto their brethren: then they returned to Samaria.*[2] Against your enemies do ye go, therefore if ye fall into their hands they will not have mercy upon you. *Let not your heart be faint, fear not nor tremble, neither be ye affrighted . . . Let not your heart be faint* at the neighing of the horses and the flashing of the swords; *fear not* at the clashing of shields and the rushing of the tramping shoes; *nor tremble* at the sound of the trumpets, *neither be ye affrighted* at the sound of the shouting; *for the Lord your God is he that goeth with you.* They come in the strength of flesh and blood, but ye come in the strength of the Almighty. The Philistines came in the strength of Goliath.[3] What was his end? In the end he fell by the sword and they fell with him. The children of Ammon came in the strength of Shobach.[4] What was his end? In the end he fell by the sword and they fell with him. But not so are ye, *for the Lord your God is he that goeth with you, to fight for you . . .* This is the Camp of the Ark.

2. *And the officers shall speak unto the people, saying, What man is there that hath built a new house and hath not dedicated it, let him go and return to his house . . .* It is all one whether he builds a house for straw, a house for cattle, a house for wood, or a house for stores; it is all one whether he builds or buys or inherits [a house] or whether it is given him as a gift. *And what man is there that hath planted a vineyard and hath not used the fruit thereof. . .* It is all one whether he plants a vineyard or plants five fruit-trees, even if they are of five kinds. It is all one whether he plants vines or sinks them into the ground or grafts them; it is all one whether he buys a vineyard or inherits it or whether it is given him as a gift. *And what man is there that hath betrothed a wife . . .* It is all one whether he betrothes a virgin or a widow, or even one that awaits levirate marriage, or whether he hears that his brother has died in battle—let him return home. These all hearken to the words of the priest concerning the ordinances of battle; and they return home and provide water and food and repair the roads.

3. And these are they that may not return: he that builds a gate-house or portico or gallery, or plants but four fruit-trees, or five trees that do not bear fruit; or he that takes back his divorced wife; or[5] a High Priest that marries a widow, or a common priest that marries a woman that was divorced or that performed *halitzah*,[6] or an Israelite that marries a bastard or a *Nethinah*,[7] or a bastard or a *Nathin*[7] that marries the daughter of an Israelite—these may not return. R. Judah says: He also that rebuilds his

---

[1] Deut. 20[2ff]. The chapter is a *Midrash* (App. I. 27) on these verses of Deuteronomy.
[2] 2 Chron. 28[15].   [3] 1 Sam. 17[4].   [4] 2 Sam. 10[16].
[5] Cf. Yeb. 2[4].   [6] App. I. 12.   [7] App. I. 29.

house as it was before may not return. R. Eliezer says: He also that builds a house of bricks in Sharon[1] may not return.

4. And these are they that stir not from their place: he that built a house and dedicated it, he that planted a vineyard and used the fruits thereof, he that married his betrothed wife, or he that consummated his union with his deceased brother's wife, for it is written, *He shall be free for his house one year: for his house*[2]—this applies to his house; *he shall be*—this is [to include also] his vineyard; *and shall cheer his wife*—this applies to his own wife; *whom he hath taken*—this is to include also his deceased brother's wife. These do not provide water and food and do not repair the roads.

5. *And the officers shall speak further unto the people [and they shall say, What man is there that is fearful and fainthearted?]* R. Akiba says: *Fearful and fainthearted* is meant literally—he cannot endure the armies joined in battle or bear to see a drawn sword. R. Jose the Galilean says: The *fearful and fainthearted* is he that is afraid for the transgressions that he has committed; wherefore the Law has held his punishment in suspense [and included him] together with these others, so that he may return because of his transgressions. R. Jose says: If a widow is married to a High Priest, or a woman that was divorced or that had performed *halitzah* is married to a common priest, or a bastard or a *Nethinah* to an Israelite, or the daughter of an Israelite to a bastard or a *Nathin*—such a one it is that is *fearful and fainthearted*.

6. *And it shall be when the officers have made an end of speaking unto the people that they shall appoint captains of hosts at the head of the people*, and at the rearward of the people; they stationed warriors in front of them and others behind them with axes of iron in their hands, and if any sought to turn back the warrior was empowered to break his legs, for with a beginning in flight comes defeat, as it is written, *Israel is fled before the Philistines, and there hath been also a great slaughter among the people*.[3] And there again it is written, *And the men of Israel fled from before the Philistines and fell down slain . . .*[4]

7. What has been said applies to a battle waged of free choice; but in a battle waged in a religious cause all go forth, even the bridegroom out of his chamber and the bride out of her bridechamber. R. Judah said: What has been said applies to a battle waged in a religious cause; but in a battle waged in duty bound all go forth, even the bridegroom out of his chamber and the bride out of her bridechamber.

9. 1. The rite of the heifer whose neck is to be broken is performed in the Holy Language, as it is written, *If one be found slain in the land [lying in the field] . . . then thy elders and thy judges shall come forth*.[5] Three[6] used to come forth from the great court in Jerusalem.[7] R. Judah says: Five, for it is written, *Thy elders*, [that is, not less than] two; and thy judges [that is, not less than] two; the court must not be divisible equally, so they add to them yet one more.

2. If he is found hidden in a heap or hung on a tree or floating on the water, they do not break the heifer's neck, for it is written *in the land*, and not hidden in a heap; and *lying*, and not hung on a tree; and *in the field*, and not floating on the water. If it is found near to a frontier, or to a city

---

[1] Where the bricks were unsubstantial and not suited for building houses.
[2] Deut. 24[5].   [3] 1 Sam. 4[17].   [4] 1 Sam. 31[1].
[5] Deut. 21[1].   [6] Sanh. 1[3].   [7] Sanh. 11[2].

wherein the greater part are gentiles, or to a city wherein is no court, they do not break the heifer's neck. They make measurement only from a city wherein is a court. If it is found at a like distance from both towns, they each bring a heifer, two in all. So R. Eliezer. Jerusalem does not bring the heifer whose neck is to be broken.[1]

3. If the head of the slain is found in one place and his body in another, they bring the head to the body. So R. Eliezer. R. Akiba says: They bring the body to the head.

4. Whence did they measure? R. Eliezer says: From his navel. R. Akiba says: From his nose. R. Eliezer b. Jacob says: From the place in which he was wounded—from the neck.

5. When the elders of Jerusalem had departed and gone away the elders of that city brought *a heifer from the herd which had not been wrought with and which had not drawn in the yoke*[2] (a blemish does not disqualify it), and they brought it down *unto a rugged* (etan)[3] *valley* (and *etan* is meant literally, 'rough'; but even if it is not 'rough' it is valid). And they brake its neck with a hatchet from behind it. And that place is forbidden for sowing and tillage, but it is permitted to comb out flax there and to quarry stones there.

6. The elders of that city washed their hands in water at the place where the heifer's neck was broken, saying, *Our hands have not shed this blood, neither have our eyes seen it.*[4] But could it have come up into our minds that the elders of the court were shedders of blood?—but [they mean], It is not so that he came into our hands and we sent him away[5] without food,[6] nor did we see him[7] [journeying] and leave him with none to accompany him. And the priests[8] say, *Forgive, O Lord, thy people Israel, whom thou hast redeemed, and suffer not innocent blood in the midst of thy people Israel.* They needed not to say, *And the blood shall be forgiven them.* But the Holy Spirit proclaims to them, 'Whensoever ye do thus *the blood shall be forgiven them.*'

7. If[9] the slayer was found before the heifer's neck was broken, it may go forth and pasture among the flock; but if after the heifer's neck was broken, it must be buried in the selfsame place; for in the beginning it was brought in a matter of doubt, it made atonement for what was in doubt, and so its purpose is fulfilled. If the heifer's neck was broken and the slayer was afterward found, then he shall be slain.

8. If one witness said, 'I saw the slayer', and another said, 'Thou didst not see him'; if a woman said, 'I saw him', and another said, 'Thou didst not see him', they must break the heifer's neck. If one said, 'I saw him', and two said, 'Thou didst not see him', they must break the heifer's neck. But if two said, 'We saw him', and one said to them, 'Ye did not see him', they did not need to break the heifer's neck.[10]

9. When murderers became many the rite of breaking the heifer's neck

[1] Gem. 45b: Because it is written 'Which the Lord thy God giveth thee to possess it'; i.e. it applies only to land divided among the tribes, thereby excluding Jerusalem.
[2] Deut. 21[3].
[3] R.V. 'with running water'; and it is so interpreted by Maim. Gem. 46a (end) supports the meaning 'rugged' from Num. 24[21], where *etan* (R.V. 'strong') has 'rock' in the parallel clause; and from Mic. 6[2] (R.V. 'enduring') where it is parallel to 'mountains'; while from Jer. 5[15] (cf. R.V. mg.) it bears the sense of 'old' or 'continuing'. [4] Deut. 21[7].
[5] And he was reduced to attempt robbery and therefore killed (Rashi).
[6] Some texts omit 'without food'.
[7] Some texts omit the rest of the sentence.
[8] Cf. Deut. 21[5]. [9] Ker. 6[2]. [10] Cf. above, 6[4].

ceased. When Eleazar b. Dinai[1] came (and he was also called Tehinah b. Parishah) they changed his name to Son of the Murderer. When adulterers became many [the rite of] the bitter water ceased; and R. Johanan b. Zakkai brought it to an end, for it is written, *I will not punish your daughters when they commit whoredom nor your daughters-in-law when they commit adultery, for they themselves [go apart with whores . . .]*[2] When Jose b. Joezer of Zeredah and Jose b. Johanan[3] of Jerusalem died, the 'grape-clusters'[4] ceased, as it is written, *There is no cluster to eat, my soul desireth the first-ripe fig.*[5]

10. Johanan[6] the High Priest did away with the Avowal concerning the [Second] Tithe. He made an end also of the 'Awakeners' and the 'Stunners'. Until his days the hammer used to smite in Jerusalem; and in his days none needed to inquire concerning *demai*-produce.

11. When the Sanhedrin ceased, singing ceased at the wedding feasts, as it is written, *They shall not drink wine with a song . . .*[7]

12. When the First Prophets[8] died, Urim and Thummim[9] ceased. When the Temple was destroyed the Shamir-worm[10] ceased and the honey of Zofim;[11] and faithful men came to an end, as it is written, *Help, Lord, for the godly man ceaseth . . .*[12] Rabban Simeon b. Gamaliel says in the name of R. Joshua: Since the day that the Temple was destroyed there has been no day without its curse; and the dew has not fallen in blessing and the fruits have lost their savour. R. Jose says: The fruits have also lost their fatness.

13. R. Simeon b. Eleazar says: [When] purity [ceased in Israel it] took away the flavour and the fragrance; [when] the Tithes [ceased they] took away the fatness of the corn; and, the Sages say,[13] fornication and sorceries have made an end of them altogether.

14. During the war of Vespasian[14] they forbade the crowns of the bridegrooms and the [wedding] drum. During the war of Titus[15] they forbade the crowns of the brides and that a man should teach his son Greek. In the last war[16] they forbade the bride to go forth in a litter inside the city; but our Rabbis permitted the bride to go forth in a litter inside the city.

15. When R. Meir died there were no more makers of parables. When Ben Azzai died there were no more diligent students. When Ben Zoma died there were no more expounders. When R. Joshua died goodness departed from the world. When Rabban Simeon b. Gamaliel died the locust came and troubles grew many. When R. Eleazar b. Azariah died wealth departed from the Sages. When R. Akiba died the glory of the Law

---

[1] See Josephus, *Ant.* xx. vi. 1 ; cf. Kel. 5[10].
[2] Hos. 4[14]; Gem. 47b: 'If ye yourselves are above reproach the water will put your wives to the proof; otherwise it will not put them to the proof'.   [3] Cf. Ab. 1[4].
[4] Metaphor for those of outstanding merit. An early midrashic explanation of the word (*eshkol*) is *ish-she-ha-kol-bo*, 'a man in whom is everything'.   [5] Mic. 7[1].
[6] 'M.Sh. 5[15] repeats the paragraph. See notes there (p. 82).   [7] Is. 24[9].
[8] Cf. Yom. 5[2]; Taan. 4[2]; Yad. 4[3]. Here, according to Gem. 48b, all the Prophets except Haggai, Zechariah, and Malachi are meant.
[9] Ex. 28[30]. They ceased to have power to indicate God's will.
[10] See Ab. 5[6]. It was created at twilight on the last of the six days of creation. It was of great hardness, a barleycorn in size; Solomon used it to cut the stones for the Temple and it was used to engrave the names of the tribes on the two stones for the shoulders of the Ephod (Ex. 28[9ff]).   [11] Cf. p. 765, n. 1; 1 Sam. 1[1].
[12] Ps. 12[1].   [13] Some texts omit 'and, the Sages say'.
[14] Roman Emperor, A.D. 69–79.
[15] Son of Vespasian and the destroyer of Jerusalem. The Cambridge text reads 'Quietus', who was governor of Judea in A.D. 117.
[16] Bar Cocheba's revolt, A.D. 132–5.

ceased. When R. Hanina b. Dosa died the men of good deeds[1] ceased. When R. Jose Katnutha[2] died there were no more saintly ones. And why was his name called Katnutha? Because he was of the 'small' remnants of the saintly ones.[3] When Rabban Johanan b. Zakkai died the splendour of wisdom ceased. When Rabban Gamaliel the Elder died, the glory of the Law ceased and purity and abstinence died. When R. Ishmael b. Piabi[4] died the splendour of the priesthood ceased. When Rabbi died, humility and the shunning of sin ceased.

R. Phineas b. Jair[5] says: When the Temple was destroyed the Associates[6] and the freemen were put to shame and walked with covered head, and the men of good works waxed feeble; and men of violence and men of loud tongue prevailed. And [now] there is none that expoundeth [to Israel] and none that seeketh [compassion for them], and none that inquireth [after his fellow's welfare]. On whom can we stay ourselves?—on our Father in heaven.

R. Eliezer the Great[7] says: Since the day that the Temple was destroyed the Sages[8] began to be like school-teachers, and the school-teachers like synagogue-servants, and the synagogue-servants like the people of the land; and the people of the land waxed feeble, and there was none to seek [compassion for them]. On whom can we stay ourselves?—on our Father in heaven.

With the footprints of the Messiah[9] presumption shall increase and dearth reach its height;[10] the vine shall yield its fruit but the wine shall be costly; and the empire shall fall into heresy and there shall be none to utter reproof. The council-chamber shall be given to fornication. Galilee shall be laid waste and Gablan[11] shall be made desolate; and the people of the frontier[12] shall go about from city to city with none to show pity on them. The wisdom of the Scribes shall become insipid and they that shun sin shall be deemed contemptible, and truth shall nowhere be found. Children shall shame the elders, and the elders shall rise up before the children, *for the son dishonoureth the father, the daughter riseth up against her mother, the daughter-in-law against her mother-in-law: a man's enemies are the men of his own house.*[13] The face of this generation is as the face of a dog, and the son will not be put to shame by his father. On whom can we stay ourselves?—on our Father in heaven.

R. Phineas b. Jair says: Heedfulness leads to cleanliness, and cleanliness leads to purity, and purity leads to abstinence,[14] and abstinence leads to holiness, and holiness leads to humility, and humility leads to the shunning of sin, and the shunning of sin leads to saintliness, and saintliness leads to [the gift of] the Holy Spirit, and the Holy Spirit leads to the resurrection

---

[1] Cf. Sukk. 5[4]. The sense may be 'men of might' or 'workers of miracles'. Cf. Ber. 5[5].

[2] The Tosefta here reads 'of Ketonith', a place-name.

[3] Play on words. The root *katon* means 'small'.

[4] Variant 'Fabi'. He was made High Priest in A.D. 59. Cf. Par. 3[5].

[5] Cambridge text reads 'R. Liezer' (Eliezer). The rest of the chapter does not belong to the Mishnah. Neither Maim. nor Bert. includes it in his commentary. It is included in the Mishnahs prefixed to the two Talmuds, though certain editions omit the final paragraph.

[6] Cf. p. 22, n. 2.

[7] Ben Hyrcanus, usually referred to simply as R. Eliezer. The Cambridge text reads 'R. Joshua'.

[8] The rest of the sentence is given in Aramaic.

[9] The signs which herald the coming of the Messiah at the end of the time of exile.

[10] This sentence is in Aramaic.

[11] Perhaps the province Gabalena, south-east of Palestine. See Neub., p. 65f.

[12] Or, 'the people of Gebul' (Ps. 83[8]).   [13] Mic. 7[6].   [14] Heb. *perishuth*, separatism.

of the dead. And the resurrection of the dead shall come through Elijah of blessed memory. Amen.

GITTIN ('BILLS OF DIVORCE')

1. 1. If a man brought a bill of divorce[1] from beyond the sea[2] he must say, 'It was written in my presence and it was signed in my presence'. Rabban Gamaliel says: Or even if he brought it from Rekem or Hagar.[3] R. Eliezer says: Or even from Kefar Ludim[4] to Lydda.[5] But the Sages say: He need say, 'It was written in my presence and it was signed in my presence', only if he brings it from beyond the sea. If he bore it and brought it [in a country] beyond the sea from one province to another he must say, 'It was written in my presence and it was signed in my presence'. Rabban Simeon b. Gamaliel says: Or even [if he bore it] from one jurisdiction to another [within the same town].

2. R. Judah says: Rekem and the country east of Rekem count as the east [and outside the Land of Israel]; Ashkelon and the country south of Ashkelon count as the south; and Acre and the country north of Acre count as the north. R. Meir says: Acre counts as within the Land of Israel in what concerns bills of divorce.

3. If a man brought a bill of divorce [from one place to another] within the Land of Israel he need not say, 'It was written in my presence and it was signed in my presence'. If any dispute it, let it be confirmed by them that signed it. If a man brought a bill of divorce from beyond the sea and he cannot say, 'It was written in my presence and it was signed in my presence', but there are witnesses to it, let it be confirmed by them that signed it.

4. In what concerns him that bears or brings them, writs of divorce and writs of emancipation are alike.[6] And this is one matter in which writs of divorce and writs of emancipation are alike.

5. No writ is valid which has a Samaritan as witness excepting a writ of divorce or a writ of emancipation. They once brought a bill of divorce before Rabban Gamaliel at Kefar Othnai,[7] and its witnesses were Samaritans; and he pronounced it valid. Any writ is valid that is drawn up in the registries of the gentiles, even if they that signed it were gentiles, excepting a writ of divorce or a writ of emancipation. R. Simeon says: These, too, are valid; they are mentioned [as invalid] only if they were prepared by such as were not [authorized] judges.

6. If a man said, 'Deliver this bill of divorce to my wife', or 'this writ of emancipation to my slave', and he wished in either case to retract, he may retract. So R. Meir. But the Sages say: [He may retract] if it was a bill of divorce but not if it was a writ of emancipation, since they may act to another's advantage in his absence[8] but not to his disadvantage save in his presence; for if a man is minded not to provide for his slave, this is his

---

[1] Heb. *get*, lit. 'writ' (of separation), pl. *gittin*.
[2] Sent by a husband living outside the Land of Israel to be delivered to his wife who is living within the Land of Israel. 'Beyond the sea' denotes all countries outside the Land excepting Babylon.
[3] The Targum of Onkelos (Gen. 16[14]) identifies these two places with Kadesh and Bered. Josephus (*Ant*. IV. vii. 1) identifies 'Arekem' with Petra.
[4] Although three sides of this were in the Land of Israel, and the people of Lydda were constantly found there (Tif. Yis.).   [5] Shebi. 9[2]; M.Sh. 5[2]; R.Sh. 1[6].
[6] Both must declare that they were written and signed in their presence.
[7] On the borders of Galilee and Samaria. Cf. below, 7[7]. But see Neub., p. 56 f.
[8] Cf. Erub. 7[11].

right; but if he is minded not to provide for his wife, this is not his right. R. Meir said to them: Does he not thereby disqualify his slave from eating Heave-offering[1] just as he disqualifies his wife? They answered: [He has the right to do so to his slave] because he is his chattel. If a man said, 'Deliver this bill of divorce to my wife', or 'this writ of emancipation to my slave', and he died, they may not deliver it after his death. [But if he had said,] 'Give a *mina* to such a man', and he died, they must give it even after his death.

2. 1. If a man brought a bill of divorce from beyond the sea and said, 'It was written in my presence but it was not signed in my presence', or 'It was signed in my presence but it was not written in my presence', or 'The whole of it was written in my presence and a half was signed in my presence', or 'A half was written in my presence and the whole was signed in my presence', it is not valid. If one said, 'It was written in my presence', and another said, 'It was signed in my presence', it is not valid. If two said, 'It was written in our presence', and another said, 'It was signed in my presence', it is not valid. But R. Judah pronounces it valid. If one said, 'It was written in my presence', and two said, 'It was signed in our presence', it is valid.

2. If it was written by day and signed by day, [or written] by night and signed by night, [or written] by night and signed by day, it is valid. [If it was written] by day and signed by night it is invalid. R. Simeon pronounces it valid; for R. Simeon used to say: No writ written by day and signed by night is valid excepting a bill of divorce.

3. It may be written with anything—ink, caustic, red dye, gum, copperas,[2] or with whatsoever is lasting; but it may not be written with liquids or fruit-juice or with whatsoever is not lasting. It may be written on anything—on an olive-leaf or on a cow's horn (and he must give her the cow)[3] or on the hand of a slave (and he must give her the slave). R. Jose the Galilean says: It may be written on naught that is living or a food-stuff.

4. It may not be written on what is fixed to the ground; but if a man had written on what is fixed to the ground and he then severed it and signed it and gave it to her, it is valid. R. Judah pronounces it invalid unless it is both written and signed after it has been severed. R. Judah b. Bathyra says: It may not be written on papyrus from which other writing has been erased or on unprepared skin, since such can [easily] be falsified. But the Sages pronounce these valid.

5. All are qualified to write a bill of divorce, even a deaf-mute, an imbecile, or a minor. A woman may write her own bill of divorce and a man may write his own quittance,[4] since the validity of the writ depends on them that sign it. All are qualified to bring a bill of divorce excepting a deaf-mute, an imbecile, a minor, a blind man, or a gentile.

6. If it was received [from the husband] by a minor who became of age [before he delivered it to the wife], or by a deaf-mute whose senses became sound, or by an imbecile who became sane, or by a gentile who became a proselyte, it is still invalid. But if [it was received from the husband by] one of sound senses who then became a deaf-mute and again became of sound senses [before he delivered it to the wife], or by one with sight who

---

[1] If he is a priest. See Lev. 22[11]; App. I. 48.
[2] Cf. Meg. 2[2].
[3] Cf. Erub. 1[7].
[4] Which the woman signs and leaves with him on receipt of her *Ketubah*.

then became blind and again received his sight, or by one who was sane who then became an imbecile and again became sane, it is valid. This is the general rule: If at the beginning and at the end an act is performed knowingly, it is valid.

7. Howbeit women that are not deemed trustworthy if they say, 'Her husband is dead',[1] are deemed trustworthy when they bring her bill of divorce; namely, her mother-in-law, her mother-in-law's daughter, her co-wife, her husband's brother's wife, and her husband's daughter. Wherein[2] does [evidence of] divorce differ from [evidence of] a death? The written document [in divorce] affords proof. The woman herself may bring her own bill of divorce, save only that she must say, 'It was written in my presence and it was signed in my presence'.

3. 1. No bill of divorce is valid that is not written expressly for the woman. Thus if a man was passing through the market and heard the scribes calling out,[3] 'Such a man is divorcing such a woman of such a place', and he said, 'That is my name and that is the name of my wife', it is not a valid document wherewith to divorce his wife. Moreover, if he had drawn up a document wherewith to divorce his wife but he changed his mind, and a man of his city found him and said to him, 'My name is like thy name and my wife's name like thy wife's name', it is not a valid document wherewith to divorce his wife; moreover if he had two wives and their names were alike and he had drawn up a document wherewith to divorce the elder, he may not therewith divorce the younger; moreover if he said to the scrivener, 'Write it so that I may divorce therewith whom I will', it is not a valid document wherewith to divorce any one.

2. He that writes out copies of the formula of a bill of divorce should leave space for the man, for the woman, and for the date; in bonds of indebtedness he should leave space for the lender, for the borrower, for the sum, and for the date; in deeds of sale he should leave space for the buyer, for the seller, for the price, for the field, and for the date—because of the advantage.[4] R. Judah pronounces them all invalid. R. Eliezer pronounces them all valid, excepting the writs of divorce, for it is written, *And he shall write for her*[5]—expressly for her.[6]

3. If a man brought a bill of divorce and lost it but straightway found it again, it remains valid; otherwise it becomes invalid. If he found it in a satchel or a bag, and recognized it, it remains valid. If a man brought a bill of divorce, and he had left the husband aged or sick, he must deliver it to her with the presumption that he is still living. If the daughter of an Israelite was married to a priest and her husband went beyond the sea, she may eat of Heave-offering[7] with the presumption that he is still living. If a man sent his Sin-offering from beyond the sea, it is offered with the presumption that he is still living.

4. Three things did R. Eleazar b. Perata declare before the Sages and they confirmed his words: concerning [them that live in] a town that is besieged, or [that travel in] a ship storm-tossed at sea, or a man that is gone forth to be judged[8]—these must be presumed to be still living; but concerning [them that lived in] a town that was overcome after a siege, or

---

[1] Yeb. 15[4]; cf. Sot. 6[2].   [2] Yeb. 15[4].
[3] Dictating the prescribed formula to their pupils.
[4] That scriveners might have copies available at need.   [5] Deut. 24[1].
[6] Some texts omit 'expressly for her'.   [7] Lev. 22[10f].   [8] On a capital charge.

[them that travelled in] a ship that was lost at sea, or a man that has been condemned to death, the more stringent rulings for the living and the more stringent rulings for the dead apply to them; [thus whether the wife of such-a-one was] the daughter of an Israelite married to a priest, or a priest's daughter married to an Israelite, she may not eat of Heave-offering.[1]

5. If within the Land of Israel a man brought a bill of divorce and fell sick, he may send it by another's hand; but if the husband had said, 'Take from her such a thing for me', he may not send it by another's hand, since it was not the will of the husband that his pledge should fall into another's hand.

6. If a man brought a bill of divorce from beyond the sea and fell sick, the court appoints another and sends him, but the first messenger must say before the court, 'It was written in my presence and it was signed in my presence'; and the other messenger needs not to say, 'It was written in my presence and it was signed in my presence'; but he says, 'I am the messenger of the court'.

7. If a man lent money to a priest or a levite or a poor man, so that in its stead he may set apart what would fall to their lot,[2] he may set it apart with the presumption that they are still living, and he need not fear lest the priest or the levite shall have died or that the poor man shall have become rich. If they died he must get permission from the heirs;[3] but if he had lent the money in the presence of the court he need not get permission from the heirs.

8. If a man put aside produce so that by virtue of it he may set apart Heave-offering or Tithes,[4] or if he put aside money so that by virtue of it he may set apart the Second Tithe,[5] he may, by virtue of them, continue to set apart his dues[6] with the presumption that what he put aside still endures; but if it was lost he must assume [that it had been lost] throughout the past twenty-four hours. So R. Eleazar b. Shammua. R. Judah says: At three times must they examine wine[7] [that has thus been put aside]: during the east wind that follows the Feast [of Tabernacles], when the berries first appear, and when the juice enters into the unripe grapes.

4. 1. If a man sent a bill of divorce to his wife and then overtook the messenger or sent another messenger after him, and said to him, 'The bill of divorce that I gave to thee is void', it thereby becomes void. If he reached his wife first or sent another messenger to her, and said to her, 'The bill of divorce that I have sent to thee is void', it thereby becomes void. But [if he or the messenger reached her] after the bill of divorce came into her hand he can no more render it void.

2. Beforetime a man used to set up a court [of three] elsewhere[8] and

---

[1] The former must presume her husband to be dead, and the latter must presume him to be alive.

[2] As Heave-offering, Tithe, or Poorman's Tithe, respectively, and sell (to another priest) the Heave-offering, and consume the Tithe or Poorman's Tithe, reserving their value towards the repayment of his loan; but he must set aside the 'Heave-offering of Tithe', since this is forbidden to a non-priest.

[3] Lest they prefer to pay off the debt and receive the dues in kind.

[4] And regard that produce as taking the place of the dues for which other produce of his would be liable.

[5] And regard it as redeemed and free for his use (see p. 73, n. 6.)

[6] i.e. regard what he has put aside as representing his dues.   [7] Lest it has gone sour.

[8] Where the husband was; he did not disannul the bill of divorce before the wife or messenger.

disannul it [before them]; but Rabban Gamaliel the Elder ordained that they should not do so, as a precaution for the general good.[1] Beforetime a man used to change his name and her name, and the name of his city and the name of her city.[2] Rabban Gamaliel the Elder ordained that [in the bill of divorce] there should be written, 'Such-a-man' and all other names that he had, and 'Such-a-woman' and all other names that she had, as a precaution for the general good.

3. A widow may not receive payment [of her *Ketubah*] from the property of the orphans unless she swears [to her claim] on oath.[3] But when they refrained from making her swear on oath, Rabban Gamaliel the Elder ordained that she should vow to the orphans whatsoever they would,[4] and receive her *Ketubah*. Witnesses sign the bill of divorce as a precaution for the general good. Hillel ordained the *prozbol*[5] as a precaution for the general good.

4. If a bondman was taken captive and others ransomed him, if he was ransomed as a bondman he must remain a bondman, but if he was ransomed as a free man he may not remain a bondman. Rabban Simeon b. Gamaliel says: In either case he must remain a bondman. If a man pledged his bondman to others as security and then set him free, by right the slave is in no wise bound [to his new master]; but as a precaution for the general good they compel his [new] master and he sets him free, and [the bondman] writes him a bond of indebtedness for his value. Rabban Simeon b. Gamaliel says: He writes nothing, but [his first master] that set him free [is liable for his value].

5. If[6] a man was half bondman and half freedman[7] he should labour one day for his master and one day for himself. So the School of Hillel. The School of Shammai said to them: Ye have ordered it well for his master, but for him ye have not ordered it well: [thus] he cannot marry a bond-woman since he is half freedman, and he cannot marry a freedwoman since he is half bondman. May he never marry? And was not the world only created for fruition and increase, as it is written, *He created it not a waste; he formed it to be inhabited*?[8] But as a precaution for the general good they should compel his master and he sets him free; and the bondman writes him a bond of indebtedness for half his value. The School of Hillel changed their opinion and taught according to the opinion of the School of Shammai.

6. If a man sold his bondman to a gentile or to any one outside the Land [of Israel], he goes forth a freedman. Captives should not be ransomed for more than their value as a precaution for the general good.[9] Captives should not be helped to escape, as a precaution for the general good.[10] Rabban Simeon b. Gamaliel says: As a precaution for the good of the captives. And none should buy scrolls [of the Law], phylacteries,[11] or *Mezuzahs*[12] from gentiles for more than their value, as a precaution for the general good.[13]

---

[1] Lest she remarry on the strength of a cancelled bill of divorce.
[2] He had adopted a changed name and home-town to conceal his identity for certain other reasons, and used this changed name in the bill of divorce.   [3] Cf. Ket. 9⁶.
[4] e.g. '*Korban* be to me the fruits of the earth if I have received my *Ketubah*!'
[5] See App. I. 34.   [6] Eduy. 1¹³.
[7] He had been the property of two jointholders and one of them had set him free.
[8] Is. 45¹⁸.   [9] Lest kidnapping become a lucrative trade.
[10] Lest captives be bound in chains.   [11] p. 114, n. 16.
[12] App. I. 25.   [13] Lest the theft of them be encouraged.

7. If a man put away his wife because of her evil fame, he may not take her back; and if because of a vow, he may not take her back. R. Judah says: If because of a vow that was known to many he may not take her back; but for one that was not known to many he may take her back. R. Meir says: For any vow that needed inquiry of a Sage[1] he may not take her back; but for any that did not need inquiry of a Sage he may take her back. R. Eliezer said: They did not forbid the one[2] except by reason of the other.[3] R. Jose b. R. Judah said:[4] It once happened in Sidon that a man said to his wife, 'Konam! if I do not divorce thee', and he divorced her; but the Sages permitted him to take her back as a precaution for the general good.

8. If a man put away his wife[5] because she was barren, R. Judah says: He may not take her back. But the Sages say: He may take her back. If she then married another and had children by him, and she claimed her Ketubah, R. Judah said: He should say to her, 'Thy silence is fairer than thy speech!'[6]

9. If a man sold himself and his children to a gentile, they may not redeem him, but they may redeem his children after the death of their father. If a man sold his field to a gentile, and an Israelite bought it back again, the buyer should bring the First-fruits[7] from it as a precaution for the general good.

5. 1. Compensation for damage is paid out of the best land,[8] a creditor out of medium land, and a wife's Ketubah out of the poorest land. R. Meir says: A wife's Ketubah also is paid out of medium land.

2. Payment may not be taken from mortgaged property if there is also unmortgaged property at hand, even if this is the poorest land. Payment may not be taken from the property of orphans save only from the poorest land.

3. They may not exact indemnity from mortgaged property for produce consumed during wrongful tenure, or for what has been expended on improvement of land,[9] or for the maintenance of a widow and her daughters,[10] as a precaution for the general good. If a man found lost property he need not take an oath [that he has not impaired it], as a precaution for the general good.[11]

4. If orphans were supported by a householder, or if their father appointed a guardian for them, he must give Tithe[12] from the produce that

[1] i.e. a vow which the husband had not power to revoke. Cf. Ned. 11[1ff].

[2] That needed inquiry.

[3] That did not need inquiry; since in the case of the latter there is no fear of his saying, 'If I had known that a Sage could revoke the vow I should not have divorced her'.

[4] Gem. 46a suggests a lacuna here: 'This applies only when it is the wife that has vowed; but if it was the husband that vowed he may take her back. It once happened, etc.'

[5] Without her Ketubah (Ket. 11[6]).

[6] Since he could say, 'I divorced thee on the ground that thou wast barren, and thou art not barren; therefore the divorce is void, the second marriage invalid, and the children bastards'.

[7] Deut. 26[2ff]. Even though they grew while the field was in gentile possession. Some texts read: 'If a man sold his field to a gentile he must buy the First-fruits from him (every year) and bring them (to the Temple) as a precaution, etc.'—so that Israelites shall not be encouraged to sell their land to gentiles.   [8] Cf. Ex. 22[5].

[9] e.g. if B wrongfully acquired A's field and sold it to C who did not know that it was stolen, and it produced a crop and C spent money in improving the field, A may seize land, crop, and improvements, and if C had already consumed the crop he is liable to A for its value; when C seeks to recover from B he may recover the cost of the field from B's mortgaged property, but the value of crop and improvements only from B's unmortgaged property.   [10] From the husband's estate.

[11] Since their cost could not be ascertainable in advance and due preparation be made to meet it.

[12] The term here includes Heave-offering, First (levitic) Tithe, Second Tithe, and Poorman's Tithe.

belongs to them. If a guardian was appointed by the orphans' father he must take an oath [that he has not impaired their property]; if he was appointed by the court he need not take an oath. Abba Saul says: The rule is to the contrary. If a man rendered another's food unclean, or if he mixed Heave-offering[1] [with another's common produce], or if he mixed another's wine with libation wine,[2] he is not culpable if he did so in error, but if wantonly he is culpable. If priests rendered offerings in the Temple unfit, and did so wantonly, they are culpable.

5. R. Johanan b. Gudgada[3] testified of a woman that was a deaf-mute and that was given in marriage by her father [while yet a minor] that she could be put away by a bill of divorce; and that a minor, that was an Israelite's daughter and married to a priest, could eat of Heave-offering, and that if she died her husband could inherit from her;[4] and that if a man built a stolen beam into a structure he need only repay its value, as a precaution for the benefit of the penitent;[5] and that a Sin-offering that was stolen property, if this was not known to many, could [still] effect atonement—as a precaution for the benefit of the Altar.

6. In Judea until the [days when the Israelitish owners were] slain in battle, the law concerning the usurping occupant[6] was not applied; after the [days when the Israelitish owners were] slain in battle, the law concerning the usurping occupant was applied. Thus if a man bought [a field] from the usurping occupant and then bought it from the owner, the sale is void;[7] but if he had bought it from the owner and then bought it from the usurping occupant the sale remains valid. If he bought [a field][8] from the husband and then bought it from the wife, the sale is void;[9] but if he bought it from the wife and then bought it from the husband, the sale remains valid. This was according to the First Mishnah;[10] but a later court enjoined that if a man bought [a field] from the usurping occupant he must give a quarter to the owner. This applies when the owner himself has not the means to buy it; but if he has the means to buy it he has first right of purchase. Rabbi set up a court and they decided by vote that after the field had been in the usurping occupant's possession for twelve months, whosoever first bought it secured the title, but that he must give a quarter to the owner.

7. A deaf-mute may communicate by signs and be communicated with by signs. Ben Bathyra says: He may communicate by movements of the mouth and be communicated with by movements of the mouth in matters concerned with movable property. In matters concerned with movable property a purchase or sale effected by children[11] is valid.

8. These things have they enjoined in the interests of peace. A priest

---

[1] Cf. Ter. 5[1ff].

[2] Wine belonging to gentiles or used, or intended to be used, as a libation to idols. Cf. A. Zar. 5[2].

[3] Yeb. 14[2]; Eduy. 7[9] (where the reading is Nehunya b. Gudgada).

[4] i.e. in these two cases, though she is still a minor, the status and rights of her husband have priority over those of her father.

[5] He need not pull down his structure to restore the beam.

[6] Cf. Bikk. 1[2]; 2[3]. He was one who had seized the property of those absent or killed or taken captive in war, or who received property confiscated by Romans from its Jewish owner. The reference is probably to the time of the Hadrianic persecutions following the Bar Cocheba revolt.

[7] The owner may have sold only from fear.

[8] Belonging to the wife, or the security for her *Ketubah*.

[9] The wife may have sold only from fear.   [10] p. 251, n. 4.   [11] Above six years of age.

reads first, and after him a levite, and after him an Israelite—in the interests of peace. They put the *Erub*[1] in the wonted house—in the interests of peace. The cistern nearest to a water-channel is filled first—in the interests of peace. The law of theft applies[2] in part to what is caught in traps set for wild animals, birds, or fishes—in the interests of peace. R. Jose says: The law of theft applies in every respect. The law of theft applies in part to what is found by a deaf-mute, an imbecile, or a minor—in the interests of peace. R. Jose says: The law of theft applies in every respect. When a poor man beats the top of an olive-tree,[3] the law of theft applies to what is beneath him[4]—in the interests of peace. R. Jose says: The law of theft applies in every respect. They do not try to prevent the poor among the gentiles from gathering Gleanings,[5] the Forgotten Sheaf[6] and *Peah*[7]— in the interests of peace.

9. A woman[8] may lend a sifter, a sieve, a handmill, or an oven to her neighbour that is suspected of transgressing the Seventh Year law, but she may not winnow or grind corn with her. The wife of an Associate may lend a sifter or a sieve to the wife of an *Am-haaretz* and may winnow, grind, or sift corn with her; but when she pours water over the flour she may not draw near her, since help may not be given to them that commit transgression. All these have they enjoined in the interests of peace. Gentiles may be encouraged [when tending their fields] in the Seventh Year, but not Israelites. Moreover greetings[9] may be offered to gentiles in the interests of peace.

6. 1. If a man said, 'Do thou accept this bill of divorce on behalf of my wife', or 'Take this bill of divorce to my wife', and he wished to retract [before it came into her hands], he may retract. If the woman had said, 'Do thou accept my bill of divorce on my behalf', and he wished to retract, he may not retract;[10] therefore if the husband answered, 'I do not wish thee to accept it for her, but take it [at my bidding] and give it to her', and he wished to retract, he may retract. Rabban Simeon b. Gamaliel says: Even if she said, 'Take my bill of divorce for me', and he wished to retract, he may not retract.

2. If the woman said, 'Do thou accept my bill of divorce on my behalf', she must have two pairs of witnesses: two that say, 'She said so in our presence', and two that say, 'He received it and tore it up[11] in our presence', even though the first witnesses are the same as the latter witnesses, or if there is one from the first pair or one from the latter and a third one associated with them. If a girl was [only] betrothed, she and her father receive her bill of divorce. R. Judah said: Two hands cannot together take possession: but, rather, her father alone receives her bill of divorce. And any that is unable to take care of her bill of divorce cannot be divorced.

3. If a woman that was a minor said, 'Do thou accept my bill of divorce on my behalf', it is not a valid bill of divorce until it reaches her hand; therefore if the husband wished to retract he may retract, since a minor may not appoint an agent. But if her father had said to him, 'Do thou go

---

[1] App. I. 8.   [2] As if to property held in valid ownership.   [3] In taking gleanings.
[4] That has fallen owing to his searching.   [5] Lev. 19[9f].
[6] Deut. 24[19].   [7] App. I. 33.   [8] See Shebi. 5[9].
[9] Bidding them 'Peace' (*Shalom*) even though this is one of the names of God (Judg. 6[24]).
[10] Since she had accepted the bill of divorce and thereby become divorced.
[11] Referring to a time when the observance of Jewish rites was forbidden, and it was necessary to destroy such a document.

and accept my daughter's bill of divorce on her behalf', and he wished to retract, he may not retract. If a man said, 'Give this bill of divorce to my wife in such a place', and they gave it to her in another place, it is not valid. [But if he said,] 'Lo, she is in such a place', and they gave it to her in another place, it is valid. If the woman said, 'accept my bill of divorce on my behalf at such a place', and they accepted it on her behalf at another place, it is not valid. R. Eliezer pronounces it valid. [If she said,] 'Bring me my bill of divorce from such a place', and it was brought to her from another place, it is valid.

4. [If she said,] 'Bring me my bill of divorce', she may[1] eat of Heave-offering until the bill of divorce comes into her hand. [If she said,] 'Do thou accept my bill of divorce on my behalf', she is forthwith forbidden to eat of Heave-offering. [If she said,] 'Do thou accept my bill of divorce on my behalf in such a place', she may eat of Heave-offering until the bill of divorce can reach such a place. But R. Eliezer forbids her forthwith.

5. If a man said, 'Write out a bill of divorce and give it to my wife', [or] 'Divorce her', [or] 'Write a letter and give it to her', then they may write it out and deliver it. [But if he said,] 'Set her free', [or] 'Make provision for her', [or] 'Do for her as is proper', [or] 'Do for her as is seemly', he has said nothing. Beforetime they used to say: If a man was led forth in fetters[2] and said, 'Write out a bill of divorce for my wife', they should write it out and also deliver it. Then they changed this and said: Also if a man went on a voyage or set out with a caravan. R. Simeon of Shezur says: Also if a man was at the point of death.

6. If a man was cast into a pit and said, 'Let him that hears my voice write out a bill of divorce for my wife', they should write it out and [also] deliver it. If a man in sound health said, 'Write out a bill of divorce for my wife', he is minded only to mock her. It once happened that a man in sound health said, 'Write out a bill of divorce for my wife', and he went up to the top of the roof and fell down and died. Rabban Simeon b. Gamaliel said: The Sages said, 'If he fell down of himself the bill of divorce is valid;[3] but if the wind blew him down, it is not valid'.

7. If a man said to two persons, 'Deliver a bill of divorce to my wife', or said to three, 'Write out a bill of divorce and deliver it to my wife', they should write it out and deliver it. If he said to three, 'Deliver a bill of divorce to my wife', they may tell others to write it out, because he has turned them into a court of law. So R. Meir. And this *Halakah* did R. Hananiah of Ono bring up from [R. Akiba in] prison: I have received the tradition that if a man said to three persons, 'Deliver a bill of divorce to my wife', they may tell others to write it out, since he has turned them into a court of law. R. Jose said: We said to the messenger, We too have received the tradition that even if a man said to the great court in Jerusalem,[4] 'Deliver a bill of divorce to my wife', they must learn[5] and write it out and deliver it. If he said to ten persons, 'Write out a bill of divorce for my wife', one should write it out and two should sign it. [But if he had said,] 'All of you write it', one should write it out but all should sign it. Therefore if one of them died, the bill of divorce becomes invalid.

---

[1] If her husband was a priest.   [2] Teb. Y. 4[5].
[3] Since it can be assumed that he meant also to say 'Deliver it'.
[4] Sanh. 11[2].   [5] How to write if they did not know already.

7. 1. If a man was seized with delirium[1] and said, 'Write out a bill of divorce for my wife', he has said nothing. If he said, 'Write out a bill of divorce for my wife', and was then seized with delirium and retracted and said, 'Do not write it', his last words count for nothing. If a man lost his speech and they said to him, 'Shall we write out a bill of divorce for thy wife?' and he bowed his head, they must prove him three times whether for 'no' he said 'no' and for 'yes' he said 'yes'. Then they may write it out and deliver it.

2. If they said to him, 'Shall we write out a bill of divorce for thy wife?' and he said, 'Write'; and they spoke to a scribe and he wrote, and to witnesses and they signed, although they had written it and signed it and delivered it to him and he then delivered it to her, nevertheless the bill of divorce remains void until he himself has said to the scribe, 'Write', and to the witnesses, 'Sign'.

3. [If he said,] 'This is thy bill of divorce if I die', or 'This is thy bill of divorce if I die of this sickness', or 'This is thy bill of divorce after my death', he has said nothing. [But if he said,] ['This is thy bill of divorce] from to-day if I die', or 'from now if I die', the bill of divorce is valid. [But if he said,] 'From to-day and after my death,' it is valid and it is not valid; and if he died she must perform *halitzah*[2] and may not contract levirate marriage.[3] [If he said,] 'This is thy bill of divorce from to-day if I die of this sickness', but he rose up and went into the street and again grew sick, and died, they must find the likely cause of death: if he died of the first sickness, the bill of divorce is valid; otherwise it is not valid.

4. She may not afterward continue together with him unless in the presence of witnesses, if it is but a bondman or but a bondwoman (excluding her own bondwoman, since with her she feels no shame).[4] What is her standing in those days? R. Judah says: She counts as a married woman in all respects. R. Jose says: She counts both as divorced and as not divorced.

5. [If he said,] 'Lo, this is thy bill of divorce on condition that thou give me 200 *zuz*', then she is divorced and gives it to him. [If he said,] 'On condition that thou give it me before thirty days', and she gave it to him within thirty days, she is divorced, otherwise she is not divorced. Rabban Simeon b. Gamaliel said: It once happened in Sidon that a man said to his wife, 'Lo, this is thy bill of divorce on condition that thou give me my cloak', and the cloak was lost. But the Sages said: Let her give him its value.

6. [If he said,] 'Lo, here is thy bill of divorce on condition that thou serve my father', or 'that thou suckle my son' (how long must she suckle him? Two years. R. Judah says: Eighteen months), if the son died or if the father died, the bill of divorce remains valid. [If he said,] 'Lo, here is thy bill of divorce on condition that thou serve my father for two years', or 'that thou suckle my son for two years', and the son died, or the father died or said, 'I do not wish thee to serve me', without provocation from her, the bill of divorce is not valid. Rabban Simeon b. Gamaliel says: Such a bill of divorce remains valid. Rabban Simeon b. Gamaliel laid down a general rule: if no hindrance arose through her, the bill of divorce remains valid.

7. [If he said,] 'Here is thy bill of divorce if I come not back within thirty days', and he was going from Judea to Galilee and went as far as

---

[1] Heb. *kordiakos*. Gem. 67b: 'one bitten by new wine', or 'overcome by an evil spirit called *Kordiakos*'. Maim.: 'a kind of epilepsy'.
[2] App. I. 12.   [3] See p. 218, n. 1.   [4] Cf. Sot. 1⁶.

Antipatris[1] and came back, his condition becomes void. [If he said,] 'Here is thy bill for divorce if I come not back within thirty days', and he was going from Galilee to Judea and he went as far as Kefar Othnai[2] and then returned, his condition becomes void. [If he said,] 'Here is thy bill of divorce if I come not back within thirty days', and he was going beyond the sea, and he went as far as Acre and then returned, his condition becomes void. [If he said,] 'Here is thy bill of divorce if I remain away from thy presence thirty days', and he was all the time coming and going, since he did not continue together with her the bill of divorce is valid.

8. [If he said,] 'Here is thy bill of divorce if I come not back within twelve months', and he died within twelve months, the bill of divorce is not valid. [But if he said,] 'Here is thy bill of divorce from now onward if I come not back within twelve months', and he died within twelve months, the bill of divorce is valid.

9. [If he said,] 'If I have not returned before twelve months, write out and deliver a bill of divorce to my wife', and they wrote out the bill of divorce before the twelve months and delivered it after the twelve months, it is not valid. [If he said,] 'Write out and deliver a bill of divorce to my wife if I have not returned before twelve months', and they wrote it out before the twelve months and delivered it after the twelve months, it is not valid. R. Jose says: Such a bill of divorce is valid. If they wrote it out after the twelve months and delivered it after the twelve months, and the husband died, if the bill of divorce was [delivered] before his death it is valid; but if he died before the bill of divorce was delivered, it is not valid. And if it is not known, this is a case of which they have said: She counts both as divorced and as not divorced.

8. 1. If a man threw a bill of divorce to his wife while she was within her house or her courtyard, she is divorced. If he threw it to her while she was in his house or his courtyard, even though he was with her in bed, she is not divorced; but if [he threw it] into her bosom or into her basket, she is divorced.

2. If he said to her, 'Collect this bond of indebtedness', or if she found it behind him and read it and, lo, it was her bill of divorce, it is not valid unless he shall say to her, 'Here is thy bill of divorce'. If he put it into her hand while she was asleep and she awoke and read it, and, lo, it was her bill of divorce, it is not valid unless he shall say to her, 'Here is thy bill of divorce'. If she was standing in the public domain and he threw it to her and it fell nearer to her, she is divorced, but if nearer to him she is not divorced; if half-way, she counts both as divorced and as not divorced.

3. So, too, in a matter of betrothal and in a matter of a debt: if a man's creditor said to him, 'Throw me my debt', and he threw it to him and it fell nearer the lender, the borrower is no longer liable; if nearer to the borrower, the borrower is still liable; if half-way, they share in the sum. If she was standing on top of the roof and he threw up to her [her bill of divorce] and it reached the level of the roof, she is divorced. If he was above and she below and he threw it down to her, once it had left the region of the roof, even if its writing was blotted out, or if it was burnt, she is divorced.

4. The School of Shammai say:[3] A man may dismiss his wife with an old bill of divorce. And the School of Hillel forbid it. What is an old bill of divorce? If he continued alone with her after he had written it for her [it becomes an 'old' bill of divorce].

---

[1] On the borders of Judea and Galilee.   [2] See above, 1[5].   [3] Eduy. 4[7].

5. If he wrote it [dating it] according to another era,[1] according to the era of the Medes, or the era of Macedon,[2] or 'after the building of the Temple', or 'after the destruction of the Temple'; [or] if he was in the east and he inscribed it 'In the west', or in the west and he inscribed it 'In the east', then she must be divorced by him and by her next husband, and she must receive a bill of divorce both from him and from her next husband; and she cannot lay claim[3] to her *Ketubah* or to the increase [on her *melog* property], or to alimony, or to indemnity [for the loss on her *melog* property], whether against him or against her next husband. If she had taken them from either she must restore them, and the child begotten by either is a bastard; neither of them may contract uncleanness because of her;[4] neither has any right over what she finds or the work of her hands, or any power to annul her vows. If she was an Israelite's daughter she is rendered ineligible for marriage with a priest; if the daughter of a levite—to eat of Tithe; if a priest's daughter—to eat of Heave-offering; and the heirs of neither husband can inherit her *Ketubah*; and if the husbands die their brothers must submit to *halitzah* and may not contract levirate marriage. [In like manner] if he had changed his name or her name, or the name of his city or the name of her city [in the bill of divorce], she is married neither to him nor to her next husband, and all the above conditions apply.

6. Concerning any of the forbidden degrees of whom it is enjoined[5] that their co-wives are exempt [from levirate marriage], if their co-wives went and married while they themselves are found to be barren, such a one is married neither to the first husband nor to the second, and all the above conditions apply.

7. If a man consummated marriage with his deceased brother's wife, and her co-wife went and married another, and she[6] was found to be barren, she[7] is married[8] neither to the first[9] husband nor to the second,[10] and all the above conditions apply.

8. If the scribe wrote a bill of divorce for the husband and a deed of quittance[11] for the wife, and erred and gave the bill of divorce to the wife and the quittance to the husband, and these gave them one to the other, and afterward [when she married again] the bill of divorce was found in the possession of the man and the quittance in the possession of the woman, she is married neither to the first husband nor to the second, and all the above conditions apply. R. Eliezer says: If the error became known immediately it is not a valid bill of divorce, but if afterward, it is valid: because it is not altogether within the power of the first [husband] to render void the right of the second.[12] If a man wrote [a bill of divorce] to divorce his wife and he changed his mind, the School of Shammai say: She is already rendered ineligible for marriage with a priest. And the School of Hillel say: Even if he gave it to her on a condition and the condition was not fulfilled, she is not rendered ineligible for marriage with a priest.

9. If[13] a man divorced his wife and she then lodged with him in an inn,

---

[1] A manner of dating not current in his own country but current elsewhere.
[2] Some texts read 'Greece', and some 'the gentiles'.   [3] Cf. Yeb. 9³; Ket. 11⁶.
[4] If they are priests (Lev. 21^{1f}.).   [5] Yeb. 1¹.
[6] Who married her deceased husband's brother.   [7] The co-wife.
[8] Since the other's levirate marriage was not valid, therefore the co-wife was not free to marry elsewhere.
[9] Her present husband.   [10] The deceased husband's brother.
[11] The receipt which she gives her husband in exchange for her *Ketubah*.
[12] He may have conspired with his wife.   [13] Eduy. 4⁷.

the School of Shammai say: She does not need from him a second bill of divorce. And the School of Hillel say: She needs a second bill of divorce from him. This applies when she was divorced after wedlock; but they agree that if she was divorced after betrothal [only] she does not need a second bill of divorce from him, since he is not yet shameless before her. If a man married a woman having a defectively witnessed[1] bill of divorce, she is married neither to the first husband nor to the second, and all the above conditions apply.[2]

10. As for a defectively witnessed bill of divorce, any person may complete it.[3] So Ben Nanos. R. Akiba says: Only they may complete it who, though near of kin, are in other respects fitted to bear witness. What is accounted a defectively witnessed bill of divorce? One that has more folds than witnesses.[4]

9. 1. If a man divorced his wife and said to her,[5] 'Thou art free to marry any man excepting such-a-one', R. Eliezer permits it, but the Sages forbid it. What should he do? He should take it from her and give it to her again and say, 'Lo, thou art free to marry any man'; but if he had so written therein, even if he erased it, it remains invalid.

2. [If he said,] 'Thou art free to marry any man excepting my father and thy father, my brother and thy brother, a slave or a gentile', or any one with whom she may not contract betrothal, it is valid. [If he said,] 'Thou art free to marry any man excepting[6] a High Priest (if she was a widow), or a common priest (if she was a divorced woman or had performed *halitzah*), or an Israelite (if she was a bastard or a *Nethinah*), or a bastard or a *Nathin* (if she was an Israelite's daughter)', or any one with whom she may, howbeit through transgression, contract betrothal, the bill of divorce is invalid.

3. The essential formula in the bill of divorce is, 'Lo, thou art free to marry any man'. R. Judah says:[7] 'Let this be from me thy writ of divorce and letter of dismissal and deed of liberation, that thou mayest marry whatsoever man thou wilt'. The essential formula in a writ of emancipation is, 'Lo, thou art a freedwoman: lo, thou belongest to thyself'.

4. Three kinds of bills of divorce are invalid, yet if she married again the offspring is legitimate: one that a man wrote with his own hand but there were no witnesses to it; one to which there were witnesses but which bore no date; and one which bore the date but had one witness only. Lo, these three bills of divorce are invalid, yet if she married again the offspring is legitimate. R. Eliezer says: Even though it was not signed by witnesses yet was delivered before witnesses, it is valid, and she may exact her *Ketubah* from mortgaged property; for the witnesses sign only as a precaution for the general good.

5. If two persons sent two bills of divorce with like names, and they became confused, the messenger must give both to each woman. Therefore if one of them was lost, the other becomes void. If five wrote altogether in the [same] bill of divorce, 'Such a man divorces such a woman, and such a man divorces such a woman [and so forth]', and the names of the witnesses were subscribed, they are all valid, and it must be delivered to each woman. If the formula was written [anew in full] for each of them and

---

[1] Lit. 'bald'. See B.B. 10[1].   [2] See above, par. 5.
[3] As signatories, even a bondman or a transgressor.   [4] See p. 380, n. 2.
[5] By word of mouth, but not in the written document.
[6] On these unions see p. 220, nn. 1ff.   [7] His formula is given in Aramaic.

[then] the names of the witnesses were subscribed, that alone is valid to which the names of the witnesses were subscribed.

6. If two bills of divorce were written out together side by side, and there were two names of witnesses written in Hebrew running from under the one to the other, and two names of witnesses written in Greek running from under the one to the other,[1] that bill of divorce together with which the first witnesses' names are read is [alone] valid;[2] but if there was the name of a witness written in Hebrew and then the name of a witness written in Greek, and again the name of a witness written in Hebrew and then the name of a witness written in Greek, running from under the one to the other, both bills of divorce are invalid.[3]

7. If part of the [text of the] bill of divorce remained over and was written in the second column, and the names of the witnesses were subscribed beneath it,[4] it is valid. If the witnesses signed at the top of the column, at the side,[5] or on the back of an unfolded bill of divorce, it is invalid. If the top of one was joined to the top of the other,[6] with the witnesses between, both are invalid.[7] If[8] the bottom of one was joined to the bottom of the other, with the witnesses between, that one together with which the names of the witnesses are read[9] is [alone] valid. If the top of one was joined to the bottom of the other, with the witnesses between, that at the bottom of which the names of the witnesses are read is [alone] valid.

8. If a bill of divorce was written in Hebrew and the names of the witnesses in Greek, or if it was written in Greek and the names of the witnesses in Hebrew, or if one witness signed in Hebrew and the other in Greek, or if it was signed by the scribe and one witness, it is valid. [If it was written,] 'Such-a-one, witness', it is valid; [if] 'Son of such-a-one, witness', it is valid; [if] 'Such-a-one, son of such-a-one', without 'witness' being written, it is valid. And so used the more scrupulous in Jerusalem to write. If a man wrote [only] his family name[10] and her family name, it is valid. A bill of divorce given under compulsion is valid if it is ordered by an Israelitish court, but if by a gentile court it is invalid; but if the gentiles beat a man and say to him, 'Do what the Israelites bid thee', it is valid.

9. If the report goes forth in the city concerning a woman that she is betrothed, she is deemed to be betrothed; if that she is divorced, she is deemed to be divorced, provided that there is not cause enough to gainsay it. What is accounted cause enough to gainsay it? If such a man had divorced his wife subject to some condition, or had thrown to her her betrothal gift and it was in doubt whether it fell nearer to him or nearer to her, such counts as 'cause enough to gainsay it'.

---

[1] In Hebrew the first names of the two signatories, e.g. Reuben and Simon, would come under the formula of the first bill in the right-hand column, and the remainder of each of their names, e.g. (Reuben) 'the son of Isaac', and (Simon) 'the son of Abraham', would come under the formula on the second bill in the left-hand column. The reverse would be the case with the names of the signatories written in Greek.

[2] i.e. the right-hand text will have two first names written immediately below it, and will be valid; the left-hand text will have two first names written in Greek, but not immediately beneath it, so will not be validly signed.

[3] Neither has two first names subscribed immediately below it.
[4] Under the second column.   [5] Right- or left-hand margins.
[6] So that one is upside down.
[7] Because the signatories are signed under neither of them.
[8] Some texts omit the following case.
[9] Without needing to turn the text upside down.
[10] Or a commonly used descriptive name, denoting a person's trade, characteristics, or native town.

10. The School of Shammai say: A man may not divorce his wife unless he has found unchastity in her, for it is written, *Because he hath found in her* indecency *in anything*.[1] And the School of Hillel say: [He may divorce her] even if she spoiled a dish for him, for it is written, *Because he hath found in her indecency in* anything. R. Akiba says: Even if he found another fairer than she, for it is written, *And it shall be if she find no favour in his eyes* . . .[2]

KIDDUSHIN ('BETROTHALS')

1. 1. By three means is the woman acquired[3] and by two means she acquires her freedom.[4] She is acquired by money[5] or by writ[6] or by intercourse.[7] 'By money'—the School of Shammai say: By a *denar*[8] or a *denar's* worth. And the School of Hillel say: By a *perutah*[8] or a *perutah's* worth. And how much is a *perutah*? The eighth part of an Italian *issar*.[8] And she acquires her freedom by a bill of divorce or by the death of her husband. A deceased brother's wife[9] is acquired by intercourse[10] and she acquires her freedom by *halitzah*[11] or by the death of her deceased husband's brother.

2. A Hebrew bondman[12] is acquired by money or by writ;[13] and he acquires his freedom by [service lasting six] years[14] or by [the entering in of] the year of Jubilee[15] or by [redeeming himself at] his outstanding value.[16] The Hebrew bondmaid has the advantage of him in that she acquires her freedom also through [manifesting] the tokens [of puberty].[17] The bondman that has his ear bored through[18] is acquired by the act of boring, and he acquires his freedom by [the entering in of] the year of Jubilee or by the death of his master.

3. A Canaanitish bondman[19] is acquired by money or by writ or by usucaption;[20] and he acquires his freedom by money paid by others or by a writ [of indebtedness] uttered by himself.[21] So R. Meir. But the Sages say: By money paid by himself or by a writ uttered by others, provided that the money is that of others.

4. Large cattle are acquired by the act of delivery[22] and small cattle by the act of lifting up.[23] So R. Meir and R. Eliezer. But the Sages say: Small cattle are acquired by the act of drawing.[24]

---

[1] Deut. 24[1].   [2] Ibid.
[3] By a man, so that he can only put her away by a bill of divorce.
[4] Lit. 'acquires herself'.
[5] On his saying to her, 'Be thou betrothed to me by this money'.
[6] A document stating 'Be thou betrothed to me', delivered to her by him in the presence of witnesses.
[7] Cf. Ket. 4[4]. According to Maim. and Bert. it must be 'in the presence of witnesses', but (Tif. Yis.) 'not literally, but that there must be witnesses to their being alone together, and to his saying, Thou art betrothed to me by this intercourse'.
[8] App. II, A.   [9] See p. 218, n. 1.
[10] With the deceased husband's brother.   [11] App. I. 12.   [12] Ex. 21[2].
[13] The bondman writes, 'Behold, I am sold to thee'. Cf. Lev. 25[39].
[14] Ex. 21[2].   [15] Lev. 15[40].
[16] He is worth proportionately less two years before the Jubilee year (or before the expiry of his six years) than he is five years earlier.
[17] After she has reached the age of twelve years and a day. Cf. Ex. 21[8-11].
[18] Ex. 21[6].
[19] Lev. 25[45]. He is there called a 'possession'; therefore since ground-property is also called a 'possession' (cf. Lev. 27[16]), the same conditions which apply to ground-property (see below, par. 5, 'property for which there is security') apply also to him.
[20] See B.B. 3[1ff].   [21] Cf. Gitt. 4[5].
[22] The buyer taking hold of it by the bit or hair in the presence and at the bidding of the seller.   [23] To a height of not less than three handbreadths.
[24] Shebi. 10[9]; B.M. 4[2]; B.B. 5[7]. The purchaser draws the article towards himself.

5. Property for which there is security[1] can be acquired by money or by writ or by usucaption; and that for which there is no security can be acquired only by the act of drawing. Property for which there is no security in conjunction with property for which there is security[2] can be acquired by money, by writ, or by usucaption, and[3] imposes the need for an oath also on property for which there is security.

6. If one thing was assessed as full value in exchange for another thing, so soon as the one party has acquired the one thing, the other party becomes answerable for what is given in exchange.[4] Thus if a man bartered a bullock for a cow or an ass for a bullock, so soon as the one party has acquired the one thing, the other party is answerable for what is given in exchange. The Temple's right to property is acquired by payment of money[5] [alone, no matter where is the property], but a common person's right to property is acquired only through real possession. Dedication to the Temple by word of mouth is equal to the act of delivery to a common person.

7. All the obligations of a father towards his son[6] enjoined in the Law are incumbent on men but not on women, and all obligations of a son towards his father[7] enjoined in the Law are incumbent both on men and on women. The observance of all the positive ordinances that depend on the time of year[8] is incumbent on men but not on women, and the observance of all the positive ordinances that do not depend on the time of the year[9] is incumbent both on men and on women. The observance of all the negative ordinances, whether they depend on the time of year or not, is incumbent both on men and on women, excepting the ordinances *Thou shalt not mar [the corners of thy beard]* and *Ye shall not round [the corners of your heads,]*[10] and, *Thou shalt not become unclean because of the dead.*[11]

8. The rites of the laying on of hands,[12] waving,[13] bringing-near [the Meal-offering], taking the Handful and burning it,[14] and wringing the necks of the Bird-offerings,[15] sprinkling the blood[16] and receiving the blood[17] are performed by men but not by women, excepting in the Meal-offerings of the Suspected Adulteress[18] and of the female Nazirite,[19] for which they themselves perform the act of waving.

9. Any religious duty that does not depend on the Land [of Israel][20] may be observed whether in the Land or outside of it; and any religious duty that depends on the Land[21] may be observed in the Land [alone]; excepting the laws of *Orlah*-fruit[22] and of Diverse Kinds.[23] E. Eliezer says: Also the law of new produce.[24]

---

[1] Immovable property. See B.B. 9[7].   [2] Peah 3[6]; Shebu. 6[3].
[3] Some texts here repeat 'the property for which there is no security'.
[4] i.e. when one party to an act of barter acquires (by drawing to himself) the object which he is taking in exchange, the other party thereby becomes the responsible owner of the other object, without the formal act of drawing it into his possession.
[5] Contrary to the principle laid down in B.M. 4[1].
[6] Such as circumcision or redeeming the Firstborn.   [7] Honour and fear.
[8] Such as carrying the *Lulab*, living in booths at the Feast of Tabernacles.
[9] Such as putting up the *Mezuzah*, letting the young go free with the mother-bird.
[10] Lev. 19[27].   [11] Lev. 21[1].
[12] On the beast's head before it is slaughtered, by those who bring a private offering; Lev. 1[4]. Cf. Meg. 2[5].   [13] See Men. 5[6].
[14] Lev. 2[2].   [15] Lev. 1[15]; 5[8].   [16] Of the offerings on the Altar.
[17] By the priest in a bason (cf. Pes. 5[6]).   [18] See Sot. 3[1].
[19] Num. 6[2]. That she waves her own Meal-offering is deduced by comparison of Num. 5[18] with 6[19].
[20] Sabbath, circumcision, and all laws affecting personal conduct.
[21] Such as Heave-offering, Tithes, the Seventh Year law, Gleanings.
[22] App. I. 32.   [23] See p. 28, n. 1.   [24] Lev. 23[14]. See App. I. 31, 'Omer'.

10. If a man performs but a single commandment it shall be well with him and he shall have length of days and shall inherit the Land; but if he neglects a single commandment it shall be ill with him and he shall not have length of days and shall not inherit the Land. He that has a knowledge of Scripture and Mishnah and right conduct will not soon fall into sin, for it is written, *And a threefold cord is not quickly broken.*[1] But he that has no knowledge of Scripture and Mishnah and right conduct has no part in the habitable world.

2. 1. A man may betroth a woman either by his own act or by that of his agent; and a woman may become betrothed either by her own act or by that of her agent. A man may give his daughter in betrothal while she is still in her girlhood[2] either by his own act or by that of his agent. If a man said to a woman, 'Be thou betrothed to me with this date, or be thou betrothed to me with this', and one of them was worth a *perutah*, her betrothal is valid; otherwise it is not valid. If [he said, 'Be thou betrothed to me] with this and with this and with this', and they were together worth a *perutah*, her betrothal is valid; otherwise it is not valid. If she was eating them one after the other, her betrothal is not valid unless one of them was worth a *perutah*.

2. [If he said,] 'Be thou betrothed to me with this cup of wine', and it was found to be honey; or 'with this cup of honey', and it was found to be wine; or 'with this silver *denar*', and it was found to be gold; or 'with this golden *denar*', and it was found to be silver; or [if he said, 'Be thou betrothed to me] on the condition that I am rich', and he was found to be poor; or 'that I am poor', and he was found to be rich; her betrothal is not valid. R. Simeon says: If he deceived her to her advantage her betrothal is valid.

3. [If he said, 'Be thou betrothed to me] on the condition that I am a priest', and he was found to be a levite; or 'that I am a levite', and he was found to be a priest; or 'that I am a *Nathin*',[3] and he was found to be a bastard; or 'that I am a bastard', and he was found to be a *Nathin*; or 'that I am from a town', and he was found to be from a city; or 'that I am from a city', and he was found to be from a town; or 'on the condition that my house is near to a bath-house', and it was found to be far off; or 'that it is far off from a bath-house', and it was found to be near; or 'on the condition that I have a daughter or bondwoman that is a hairdresser', and he had them not; or 'on condition that I have them not', and he had them; or 'on condition that I have no children', and he had them; or 'on condition that I have them', and he had them not;—in all such cases even though she said, 'It was in my heart to be betrothed to him', her betrothal is not valid. And so, too, if it was she that deceived him.

4. If he said to his agent, 'Go and betroth to me such a woman at such a place', and he went and betrothed her at another place, her betrothal is not valid; but if he had said, 'Lo, she is at such a place', and he betrothed her at another place, her betrothal is valid.

5. If[4] a man betrothed a woman on the condition that she lay under no vow, and she was found to be under a vow, her betrothal is not valid. If he married her making no conditions, and she was found to be under a vow, she may be put away without her *Ketubah*. If [he betrothed her] on the

---

[1] Eccles. 4[12].
[2] While she is a *naarah*, i.e. during six months after she has become of age, twelve years and a day. Cf. Ket. 3[1].   [3] App. I. 29.   [4] The paragraph is repeated in Ket. 7[7].

condition that there were no defects in her, and defects were found in her, her betrothal is not valid. If he married her making no conditions and defects were found in her, she may be put away without her *Ketubah*. All blemishes which disqualify priests disqualify women also.

6. If a man betrothed two women with what was worth a *perutah*, or one woman with what was worth less than a *perutah*, the betrothal is not valid, even if he afterward sent her presents, since he sent them by reason of the first betrothal. So, too, if a minor betrothed a woman [and sent her presents after he came of age].

7. If a man betrothed a woman and her daughter or a woman and her sister at the same time, their betrothal is not valid.[1] It once happened to five women among which were two sisters, that a man took a basket of figs that belonged to them and that contained Seventh Year produce,[2] and said, 'Lo, ye are all betrothed to me with this basketful'. And one of them accepted it on behalf of them all. And the Sages said: The betrothal of the sisters was not valid.

8. If a man betrothed a woman with his portion[3] of either the Most Holy Things or the Lesser Holy Things,[4] her betrothal is not valid. If [he betrothed her] with Second Tithe,[5] whether in error or wantonly, the betrothal is not valid.[6] So R. Meir. R. Judah says: If he acted in error[7] the betrothal is not valid, but if wantonly[8] the betrothal is valid. If it was with dedicated produce and he acted wantonly the betrothal is valid, and if in error the betrothal is not valid. So R. Meir. R. Judah says: If in error the betrothal is valid,[9] but if wantonly the betrothal is not valid.[10]

9. If a man betrothed a woman with *Orlah*-fruit[11] or Diverse Kinds of the Vineyard,[12] or with an ox condemned to be stoned,[13] or with a heifer whose neck was to be broken,[14] or with the Bird-offerings of a leper,[15] or with the Hair-offering of a Nazirite,[16] or with the firstborn of an ass,[17] or with flesh cooked with milk,[18] or with unconsecrated beasts slaughtered in the Temple Court,[19] the betrothal is not valid. But if he had sold them and betrothed her with their price her betrothal is valid.

10. If a man betrothed a woman with Heave-offering[20] or Tithes or [Priests'] Dues[21] or Sin-offering water or the ashes of the Sin-offering,[22] her betrothal is valid, even if he was an Israelite.[23]

3. 1. If a man said to his fellow, 'Go and betroth to me such-a-woman',

---

[1] Lev. 18[17f].

[2] When it was ownerless property (Lev. 25[6f].). In other years what belonged to them could not have been used by him to betroth them.

[3] Which he had received with his fellow-priests.   [4] See Zeb. 5[1-8].

[5] See p. 73, n. 6.

[6] Since it was not his but the Temple's; it is his only to eat.

[7] i.e. he had intended taking it up to Jerusalem; therefore he did not consider it common produce, free for his ordinary use.

[8] He proved that he had no intention of taking it up to Jerusalem or of redeeming it, thereby rendering it common produce.

[9] He has committed Sacrilege (Lev. 5[15f].) and rendered the Hallowed Thing unfit for its purpose; but he can make restitution.

[10] Since he cannot make restitution; the Hallowed Thing still remains the property of the Temple.   [11] App. I. 32.   [12] See p. 28, n. 1.   [13] Ex. 21[28].   [14] Deut. 21[1ff].

[15] Lev. 14[4].   [16] See p. 282, n. 4.   [17] Ex. 34[20].

[18] Ex. 23[19]; 34[26]; Deut. 14[21].   [19] All of which are forbidden for any kind of use.

[20] App. I. 48.

[21] The shoulder and the two cheeks and the maw, which an Israelite must give to the priest from every beast he slaughters. Deut. 18[3].   [22] Num. 19[9ff].

[23] i.e. a non-priest, who had received these as his rightful property by inheritance, e.g. from his mother's father (who was a priest) or his mother, who had married an Israelite.

and he went and betrothed her to himself, her betrothal is valid. So, too, if a man said to a woman, 'Be thou betrothed to me after thirty days' time', and another came and betrothed her during the thirty days, she is betrothed to the second; and if she was the daughter of an Israelite and he a priest, she may eat of Heave-offering. [If he said, 'Be thou betrothed to me] from now and after thirty days', and another came and betrothed her during the thirty days, she is betrothed and she is not betrothed; and if she was the daughter of an Israelite and he a priest, or if she was the daughter of a priest and he an Israelite, she may not eat of Heave-offering.

2. If a man said to a woman, 'Be thou betrothed to me on the condition that I give thee 200 *zuz*', her betrothal is valid, but he must give it to her; [if] 'on condition that before thirty days I give it thee', and her gave it her within the thirty days, the betrothal is valid; otherwise it is not valid. [If he said, 'Be thou betrothed to me] on the condition that I have 200 *zuz*', the betrothal is valid if he has them; [if he said], 'on the condition that I show thee 200 *zuz*', the betrothal is valid, but he must show her them; and if he showed her them on a [money-changer's] table, her betrothal is not valid.

3. [If he said, 'Be thou betrothed to me] on the condition that I have a *kor's* space[1] of land', her betrothal is valid if he has it; [if he said,] 'on the condition that I have land in such a place', and he has it in such a place, her betrothal is valid; otherwise it is not valid. [If he said, 'Be thou betrothed to me] on the condition that I show thee a *kor's* space of land', the betrothal is valid if he shows it to her; but if he showed her [land] in the valley [which was not his] her betrothal is not valid.

4. R. Meir says: No condition is valid that is not according to the condition of the children of Gad and the children of Reuben,[2] as it is written, *And Moses said unto them, If the children of Gad and the children of Reuben will pass over*, and it is also written, *But if they will not pass over armed*.[3] R. Hanina b. Gamaliel says: It was needful that this should be said, for otherwise the meaning might be that even in the land of Canaan they should inherit naught.

5. If a man betrothed a woman and said, 'I had thought that she was the daughter of a priest and, lo, she is the daughter of a levite', or 'that she was the daughter of a levite and, lo, she is the daughter of a priest', or 'that she was poor and, lo, she is rich', 'that she was rich and, lo, she is poor', her betrothal is valid, since it was not she that deceived him. If a man said to a woman, 'Be thou betrothed to me after that I shall become a proselyte', or 'after that thou shalt become a proselyte', or 'after that I shall have been freed', or 'after that thou shalt have been freed', or 'after that thy husband dies', or 'after that thy sister dies', or 'after that thou hast performed *halitzah* with thy deceased husband's brother', her betrothal is not valid. So, too, if a man said to his fellow, 'If thy wife bears a female child let it be betrothed to me', her betrothal is not valid.[4] But if his fellow's wife was with child and her pregnancy was manifest, his words hold good, and if she bore a female child her betrothal is valid.

6. If a man said to a woman, 'Be thou betrothed to me on the condition that I speak on thy behalf to the governor', or 'that I work with thee as a labourer', and he spoke on her behalf to the governor or worked with her as

---

[1] App. II, E.   [2] Showing the consequence if the conditions are not fulfilled.
[3] Num. 32[29f].
[4] The Cambridge text reads, 'she has said nothing', and omits the rest of the paragraph.

a labourer, her betrothal is valid; otherwise her betrothal is not valid. [If he said, 'Be thou betrothed to me] on the condition that my father consents', and his father consented, her betrothal is valid ; otherwise it is not valid. If the father died her betrothal is valid. But if the son died, they instruct the father to say that he did not consent.[1]

7. [If a man said,] 'I gave my daughter in betrothal but I do not know to whom I gave her', and one came and said, 'I betrothed her', he may be believed. If one said, 'I betrothed her', and another said, 'I betrothed her', they must both give her a bill of divorce; but if they were so minded the one may give her a bill of divorce and the other may marry her.

8. [If a man said,] 'I gave my daughter in betrothal',[2] or 'I gave her in betrothal and accepted her bill of divorce while she was yet a minor', and she is [still] a minor, he may be believed. [If he said,] 'I gave her in betrothal and accepted her bill of divorce while she was yet a minor' and she is now of age, he may not be believed. [If he said,] 'She was taken captive and I ransomed her', whether she was yet a minor or whether she was of age, he may not be believed. If at the hour of his death a man said, 'I have children',[3] he may be believed; [if he said,] 'I have brothers', he may not be believed. If a man gave one of his daughters in betrothal and did not stipulate which, they that were already past their girlhood[4] are not taken into account.

9. If a man had two groups of daughters by two wives, and he said, 'I have given one of my elder daughters in betrothal but I do not know whether it was the eldest of the older group or the eldest of the younger, or the youngest of the older group that is older than the eldest of the younger group', they are all forbidden excepting the youngest in the younger group. So R. Meir. R. Jose says: They are all permitted excepting the eldest of the older group. [If a man said,] 'I gave one of my younger daughters in betrothal but I do not know whether it was the youngest of the younger group or the youngest of the older group, or the eldest of the younger group that is younger than the youngest of the older group', they are all forbidden excepting the eldest of the older group. So R. Meir. R. Jose says: They are all permitted excepting the youngest of the younger group.

10. If a man said to a woman, 'I betrothed thee', and she said, 'Thou didst not betroth me', he is forbidden in marriage to her near of kin, but she is permitted to his near of kin.[5] If she said, 'Thou didst betroth me', and he said, 'I did not betroth thee', he is permitted in marriage to her near of kin, but she is forbidden to his near of kin. [If he said,] 'I betrothed thee', and she said, 'Thou didst betroth none save my daughter', he is forbidden to the near of kin of the older woman but she is permitted to his near of kin; and he is permitted in marriage to the near of kin of the younger woman and she[6] is permitted to his near of kin.

11. [If he said,] 'I betrothed thy daughter', and she said, 'Thou didst betroth none save me', he is forbidden to the near of kin of the younger woman, but the younger woman is permitted in marriage to his near of

---

[1] So that she shall not be bound to contract levirate marriage.
[2] Some texts add: 'while she was a yet a minor'.
[3] He thereby admits that his widow will not be bound to levirate marriage.
[4] Above twelve years and a half.
[5] Since she has not admitted the tie of betrothal.
[6] The daughter, who has not admitted the betrothal tie herself, nor is her mother to be trusted concerning her.

kin; he is permitted in marriage to the near of kin of the older woman, but she is forbidden to his near of kin.

12. If the betrothal was valid and no transgression befell [by reason of the marriage] the standing of the offspring follows that of the male [parent]. Such is the case when a woman that is the daughter of a priest, a levite, or an Israelite is married to a priest, a levite, or an Israelite. If the betrothal was valid but transgression befell [by reason of the marriage] the standing of the offspring follows that of the blemished party. Such is the case when[1] a widow is married to a High Priest, or a divorced woman or one that had performed *halitzah* is married to a common priest, or a bastard or a *Nethinah* to an Israelite, or the daughter of an Israelite to a bastard or a *Nathin*. If her betrothal with this man was not valid, but her betrothal with others would be valid, the offspring is bastard. Such is the case when a man has connexion with any of the forbidden degrees prescribed in the Law. If her betrothal with this man was not valid, and her betrothal with others would also not be valid, the offspring is of her own standing. This is the case when the offspring is by a bondwoman or gentile woman.

13. R. Tarfon says: Bastard stock can be rendered clean.[2] Thus if a bastard married a bondwoman the offspring is a bondman. If he is set free the son thereby becomes a freeman. R. Eliezer says: Such a one is a bastard slave.

4. 1. Ten family stocks came up from Babylon: the priestly, levitic, and Israelitish stocks, the impaired priestly stocks[3], the proselyte, freedman, bastard, and *Nathin*[4] stocks, and the *shetuki*[5] and *asufi*[6] stocks. The priestly, levitic, and Israelitish stocks may intermarry; the levitic, Israelitish, impaired priestly stocks, proselyte, and freedman stocks may intermarry; the proselyte, freedman, bastard, *Nathin*, *shetuki*, and *asufi* stocks may all intermarry.

2. And who is deemed of *shetuki* stock? Any that knows his mother but does not know his father. And *asufi* stock? Any that was picked up from the street and knows neither his father nor his mother. Abba Saul used to call the *shetuki* stock [by the name] *beduki*.[7]

3. All that are forbidden to enter the congregation[8] may intermarry among themselves. But R. Judah forbids it. R. Eliezer says: They that are of assured stock may intermarry with others that are of assured stock, but they that are of assured stock may not intermarry with them that are of doubtful stock, nor they that are of doubtful stock with others that are of doubtful stock. These are of doubtful stock: the *shetuki*, the *asufi*, and the Samaritan.

4. If a man would marry a woman of priestly stock, he must trace her family back through four mothers, which are, indeed, eight: her mother, mother's mother, and mother's father's mother, and this one's mother; also her father's mother and this one's mother, her father's father's mother, and this one's mother. [If he would marry] a woman of levitic or Israelitish stock, he must trace the descent back to one mother more.[9]

---

[1] For these unions see Yeb. 2[4].   [2] i.e. the offspring need not be bastard.
[3] Those born of unions forbidden (Lev. 21[1ff.]) to them of priestly stock.
[4] App. I. 29.
[5] The meaning of the root is 'to be silent'; and he that is of *shetuki* stock is 'silent' when reproached with his origin.
[6] The meaning of the root is 'to gather'. *Asufi* has thus the sense of 'foundling'.
[7] The meaning of the root is 'inquire, seek out''. The Gemara (74a) explains it on the basis of Ket. 1[9], q.v.   [8] Deut. 23[1–3].
[9] In both lines, namely to her mother's mother's mother, and her father's mother's mother's mother.

5. They need not trace descent beyond the Altar[1] or beyond the Platform[2] or beyond the Sanhedrin;[3] and all whose fathers are known to have held office as public officers or almoners may marry into the priestly stock and none need trace their descent. R. Jose says: Also any whose name was signed as a witness in the old archives[4] at Sepphoris. R. Hananiah b. Antigonus says: Also any whose name was recorded in the king's army.[5]

6. The daughter of a male of impaired priestly stock [and so, too, any female descendant] is for ever[6] disqualified for marriage with priestly stock. If an Israelite married a woman of impaired priestly stock, his daughter is qualified for marriage with priestly stock; but if a man of impaired priestly stock married the daughter of an Israelite, his daughter is disqualified for marriage with priestly stock. R. Judah says: The daughter of a male proselyte is regarded as a daughter of a male of impaired priestly stock.

7. R. Eliezer b. Jacob says: If an Israelite married a proselyte, his daughter is qualified for marriage with priestly stock; and if a proselyte married the daughter of an Israelite, his daughter is qualified for marriage with priestly stock; but if a proselyte married a proselyte, his daughter is not so qualified. A proselyte is regarded as of like standing to freed slaves even to ten generations, until such time as his mother is of Israelitish stock. R. Jose says: Even if a proselyte married a proselyte, his daughter is qualified for marriage with priestly stock.

8. If a man says, 'This my son is a bastard', he may not be believed. Even if they both said of the unborn child in her womb, 'It is a bastard', they may not be believed. R. Judah says: They may be believed.

9. If a man empowered his agent to give his daughter in betrothal and he himself went and gave her in betrothal [to another], if the betrothal by him came first, it is valid, and if the betrothal by his agent came first, that is valid; if it is not known, both[7] must give her a bill of divorce; but if they were so minded the one may give her a bill of divorce, and the other may marry her. So, too, if a woman empowered her agent to give her in betrothal and she herself went and betrothed herself [to another], if her own betrothal came first, it is valid; and if the betrothal by her agent came first, that is valid; if it is not known, both must give her a bill of divorce; but if they were so minded the one may give her a bill of divorce and the other may marry her.

10. If a man and his wife went beyond the sea and he and his wife and his children returned and he said, 'Lo, this is the wife that went with me beyond the sea and these are her children', he need not bring proof[8] about either the woman or the children. If he said, 'She died and these are her children', he must bring proof about the children, but he need not bring proof about the woman.

11. [If he said,] 'I married a woman beyond the sea; lo, this is she and

---

[1] If he found that her father ministered as a priest in the Temple he need not trace her descent further.
[2] Where the levites sang in the Temple; Arak. 2[8]; Midd. 2[6]. If he found that her father sang as a levite in the Temple, that suffices.
[3] In Jerusalem, membership of which provides valid proof of unimpaired stock.
[4] Those inscribed in the court's records as eligible to be judges and witnesses. The commentators take 'ha-Yeshanah' (here rendered 'old') as the name of a place near Sepphoris in Galilee.   [5] The reference may be to 1 Chron. 7[40].
[6] In every successive generation.   [7] Of those to whom she was betrothed.
[8] That it is the same wife (of known pedigree), or that the children are her children (and of known pedigree).

these are her children', he must bring proof[1] about the woman but he need not bring proof about the children. [If he said,] 'She died, and these are her children', he must bring proof about the wife and the children.

12. A man may not remain alone with two women, but a woman may remain alone with two men. R. Simeon says: Even one man may remain alone with two women when his wife is with him, and he may sleep with them in an inn, because his wife watches over him. A man may remain alone with his mother or with his daughter; and he may sleep with them with bodies touching. But if they are become of age, she must sleep in her clothes and he in his.

13. An unmarried man may not be a teacher of children, nor may a woman be a teacher of children. R. Eliezer says: Even a man that has no wife [with him] may not be a teacher of children.

14. R. Judah says: An unmarried man may not herd cattle, nor may two unmarried men sleep under the same cloak. But the Sages permit it. Any man whose business is with women may not remain alone with women; and a man should not teach his son a craft that is practised among women. R. Meir says: A man should always teach his son a cleanly[2] craft, and let him pray to him to whom riches and possessions belong, for there is no craft wherein there is not both poverty and wealth; for poverty comes not from a man's craft, nor riches from a man's craft, but all is according to his merit. R. Simeon b. Eleazar says: Hast thou ever seen a wild animal or a bird practising a craft?—yet they have their sustenance without care and were they not created for naught else but to serve me? But I was created to serve my Maker. How much more then ought not I to have my sustenance without care? But I have wrought evil, and [so] forfeited my [right to] sustenance [without care]. Abba Gorion of Zaidan says in the name of Abba Guria:[3] A man should not teach his son to be an ass-driver or a camel-driver, or a barber or a sailor, or a herdsman or a shopkeeper, for their craft is the craft of robbers. R. Judah says in his name: Ass-drivers are most of them wicked, camel-drivers are most of them proper folk, sailors are most of them saintly, the best among physicians is destined for Gehenna, and the most seemly among butchers is a partner of Amalek. R. Nehorai says: I would set aside all the crafts in the world and teach my son naught save the Law, for a man enjoys the reward thereof in this world and its whole worth remains for the world to come. But with all other crafts it is not so; for when a man falls into sickness or old age or troubles and cannot engage in his work, lo, he dies of hunger. But with the Law it is not so; for it guards him from all evil while he is young, and in old age it grants him a future and a hope. Of his youth, what does it say? *They that wait upon the Lord shall renew their strength.*[4] Of his old age what does it say? *They shall still bring forth fruit in old age.*[5] So, too, it says of our father Abraham, *And Abraham was old and well stricken in years, and the Lord had blessed Abraham in all things.*[6] And we find that Abraham our father had performed the whole Law before it was given, for it is written, *Because that Abraham obeyed my voice and kept my charge, my commandments, my statutes, and my laws.*[7]

---

[1] Of her family stock.   [2] Some texts add 'and an easy'.   [3] Variant: 'Saul'.
[4] Is. 40[31].   [5] Ps. 92[14].   [6] Gen. 24[1].   [7] Gen. 26[5].

FOURTH DIVISION
NEZIKIN
('DAMAGES')

BABA KAMMA
BABA METZIA
BABA BATHRA
SANHEDRIN
MAKKOTH
SHEBUOTH
EDUYOTH
ABODAH ZARAH
ABOTH
HORAYOTH

BABA KAMMA[1] ('THE FIRST GATE')

1. 1. The four primary causes of injury[2] are the ox and the pit and the crop-destroying beast and the outbreak of fire. [The distinctive feature of] the ox is not like [that of] the crop-destroying beast, nor is [the distinctive feature of] the crop-destroying beast like [that of] the ox; nor is [the distinctive feature of] either of these, wherein is life, like [that of] fire, wherein is not life; nor is [the distinctive feature of] any of these, whose way it is to go forth and do injury, like [that of] the pit, whose way it is not to go forth and do injury. What they have in common is that it is the way of them to do injury and that the care of them falls on thee; and if one of them did injury whosoever did the injury must make restitution for the injury with the best[3] of his land.

2. If I am answerable for the care of a thing, it is I that render possible the injury that it may do. If I render possible part of that injury I must make restitution for that injury as he that rendered possible the whole of that injury. This applies to all property that is not subject to the law of Sacrilege,[4] and to property that belongs to the Sons of the Covenant,[5] and to property that is held in ownership and is in any place other than the private domain of the injurer and the common domain of the injured and the injurer. And if the injury is done the injurer must make restitution for the injury with the best of his land.

3. Assessment [of injury] in money or money's worth must be made before a court of law and at the mouth of witnesses that are freemen and Sons of the Covenant. Women may be parties in [suits concerning] injury. Moreover the injured and the injurer [in certain cases may share] in the compensation.

4. Five [agents of injury] rank as harmless and five as an attested danger.[6] Cattle do not rank as an attested danger in so far as they butt, push, bite, lie down, or kick. The tooth [of a beast] is an attested danger in that it consumes whatsoever is fit for it to consume; the leg is an attested danger in that it breaks down [what it tramples upon] as it goes along; so also is an ox which has been declared an attested danger [in that it was wont to gore]; and an ox which causes damage in the [private] domain of him that is injured;[7] and human kind. The wolf, the lion, the bear, the leopard, the panther, and the serpent rank as an attested danger. R. Eliezer says: When they become tame they do not rank as an attested danger, but the serpent ranks always as an attested danger. Wherein does what is harmless differ from what is an attested danger? The harmless pays half-damages from its own body; and the attested danger pays full damages from the best property.[8]

---

[1] This and the two following tractates (entitled 'First Gate', 'Middle Gate', and 'Last Gate') are divisions of what was originally one tractate entitled 'Nezikin', 'Damages', dealing with various problems arising out of property. 'The First Gate' treats of injuries by man or beast and the questions of responsibility and restitution; 'The Middle Gate' treats of lost property, guardianship, usury, and the hire of labourers; and 'The Last Gate' treats of ownership of immovable property and problems relating to it.

[2] Lit. 'fathers of injuries', i.e. they characterize the four main classifications within which miscellaneous kinds of injury can be included. They are therefore given by the Law (Ex. 21[28]–22[6]) as representative cases.   [3] Ex. 22[5].

[4] Lev. 5[15ff].   [5] Israelites.

[6] Ex. 21[29]: 'If the ox were wont to gore in time past and it hath been testified to its owner'.

[7] See below, 2[5].   [8] Of its owner or guardian.

2. 1. 'The leg is an attested danger in that it breaks [what it tramples upon] as it goes along'—thus, a beast is an attested danger [only] in so far as it goes along in its usual way and commits breakage; if it kicked, or if small stones were tossed out from beneath its feet and it thus broke any vessel, one pays [only] half-damages; but if it trampled upon a vessel and broke it, and this itself fell upon another vessel and broke it, for the first one pays full damages, and for the other half-damages. Fowls are an attested danger in so far as they go along in their usual way and commit breakage; but if a fowl had its feet entangled or if it was scratching and it thereby broke any vessel one pays [only] half-damages.

2. 'The tooth [of a beast] is an attested danger in that it consumes whatsoever is fit for it to consume'—thus, a beast is an attested danger only in so far as it consumes fruit and vegetables; if it consumed clothing or utensils he pays [only] half-damages. This applies if it was within the private domain of the injured; but if it was within the public domain the owner is not culpable, and if it derived any benefit he need pay for that benefit only. 'He need pay for that benefit only'—thus, if it consumed aught from the midst of the market-place he need pay only for the benefit that it derived, but if from the sides of the market-place[1] he must pay for the damage that it has done; if from the entrance to a shop, he need pay only for the benefit that it derived, but if from the midst of the shop[1] he must pay for the damage that it has done.

3. If a dog or a kid jumped from a roof and broke any vessels, the owner must pay full damages since [through the like acts] they are an attested danger. If a dog took a cake[2] and went to a stack of corn and ate the cake and set the stack on fire, its owner must pay full damages for the cake but only half-damages for the stack.

4. Which [kind of ox] is accounted harmless and which an attested danger? That is accounted an attested danger against which evidence [of damage] has been brought within the past three days; and it is accounted harmless after it has refrained [from damage] for three days. So R. Judah. R. Meir says: That is accounted an attested danger against which evidence [of damage] has been brought three times; and it is accounted harmless if children can touch it and it will not gore them.

5. 'An ox which causes damage in the [private] domain of him that is injured'—thus, if it gored, pushed, bit, lay down, or kicked in the public domain it pays only half-damages; but if in the private domain of him that was injured, R. Tarfon says: It pays full damages. But the Sages say: Half-damages. R. Tarfon said to them: What! if they have dealt leniently with damage caused by tooth or foot in the public domain (when no restitution is imposed) and stringently with like damage in the private domain of him that is injured (when full damages are imposed), then since they have dealt stringently with damage caused by the horn in the public domain (when half-damages are imposed) ought we not therefore to deal the more stringently with damage caused by the horn in the private domain of him that was injured, so that full damages shall be imposed! They answered: It is enough if the inferred law is as strict as that from which it is inferred:[3] if [for damage

---

[1] Since these count as 'the private domain of the injured'.

[2] i.e. stole it while it was still baking, and a red-hot cinder still adhered.

[3] Nidd. 4⁶. This principle is founded on Num. 12¹⁴: 'If Miriam had suffered reproof from her father would she not be ashamed seven days? How much more if she has suffered reproof from God!'—and yet she was 'shut up without the camp' for seven days only.

caused by the horn] in the public domain half-damages [are imposed], so also [for like damage] in the private domain of him that was injured, half-damages [only are imposed]. He said to them: My inference is not from one case of damage caused by the horn to another case of damage caused by the horn, but from what applies in a case of damage caused by the foot to what should apply in the case of damage caused by the horn: If they have dealt leniently with damage caused by the tooth or foot in the public domain and stringently with damage caused by the horn, then since they have dealt stringently with damage caused by the tooth or foot in the private domain of him that was injured, ought we not, therefore, to deal the more stringently with damage caused by the horn [in the private domain]! They answered: It is enough if the inferred law is as strict as that from which it was inferred: [as in the case of damage caused by the horn] in the public domain half-damages [are imposed], so also [for damage caused by the horn] in the private domain of him that was injured, half-damages [only are imposed].

6. Human kind is always an attested danger, whether [the damage is caused] by error or wantonly, whether awake or asleep. If a man blinded his fellow's eye or broke utensils, he must pay full damages.

3. 1. If a man left a jug in the public domain and another came and stumbled over it and broke it, he is not culpable, and if he was injured thereby the owner of the jug is liable for his injury. If a man's jug broke in the public domain, he is culpable if another slipped in the water or was hurt by the potsherds. R. Judah says: If he was still intent [on claiming the water and the potsherds] he is culpable; otherwise he is not culpable.

2. If a man poured out water in the public domain and another was injured thereby, he is liable for his injury. If a man hid thorns or glass [in the public domain], or made his hedge out of thorns, or if his hedge fell into the public domain, and others were injured thereby, he is liable for their injury.

3. If a man put out his chopped straw and stubble into the public domain to make them into manure, and another was injured thereby, he is liable for his injury; and whosoever comes first may take possession of it. Rabban Simeon b. Gamaliel says: Whosoever leaves things that are unseemly in the public domain, and these cause damage, must make restitution; and whosoever comes first may take possession of them. If a man heaped up cattle-dung in the public domain and another was injured thereby, he is liable for his injury.

4. If two pot-sellers were walking one behind the other and the first one stumbled and fell and the second stumbled over the first, the first one is liable for the injury suffered by the second.

5. If one came carrying his jar and another came carrying his beam, and the jar of the one was broken by the beam of the other, the latter is not culpable since each alike has the right of passage. If the man with the beam came first and the man with the jar came after, and the jar broke against the beam, the man with the beam is not culpable. If the man with the beam had [suddenly] stopped he is culpable, but if had said, 'Stop!' to the man with the jar, he is not culpable. If the man with the jar came first and the man with the beam came after, and the jar broke against the beam, the man behind is culpable. If the man with the jar had [suddenly] stopped,

the other is not culpable, but if the first had said, 'Stop!' to the man with the beam, he is culpable. So, too, if one man came with his light and the other came with his flax.

6. If two were going along in the public domain, the one running and the other walking, or both running, and they injured one another, neither is culpable.

7. If a man was splitting wood within a private domain and injured any one in the public domain, or if he was in the public domain and injured any one in a private domain; or if he was in a private domain and injured any one in another private domain, he is culpable.

8. If two oxen which were accounted harmless hurt one another, half-damages are payable for that one which suffered the greater hurt. If both were attested dangers full damages are payable for that one which suffered the greater hurt. If one was accounted harmless and the other was an attested danger, that which was an attested danger as against that which was accounted harmless must pay full damages for the greater hurt that the other has suffered, while that which was accounted harmless, as against that which was an attested danger, pays only half-damages for the greater hurt that the other has suffered. So, too, if two men hurt one another, full damages are payable for that one which suffered the greater hurt. If a man and a beast which was an attested danger hurt one another, full damages are payable for that one which suffered the greater hurt. If a man and a beast which was accounted harmless hurt one another, the man as against the beast accounted harmless must pay full damages for the greater hurt that the other has suffered; while the beast accounted harmless, as against the man, pays only half-damages for the greater hurt that the other has suffered. R. Akiba says: Even if a beast accounted harmless hurt a man, full damages must be paid for that one which suffered the greater hurt.

9. If an ox worth 100 *zuz*[1] gored an ox worth 200 *zuz*, and the carcase was worth nothing, the injured [party] takes the other ox. If an ox worth 200 *zuz* gored another ox worth 200 *zuz* and the carcase was worth nothing, R. Meir said: Of such it is written, *Then they shall sell the live ox and divide the price of it.*[2] R. Judah replied: Such indeed is the *Halakah*;[3] but if thou hast fulfilled [the Scripture], *Then they shall sell the live ox and divide the price of it*, thou hast not yet fulfilled *and the dead also they shall divide.* How shall this be? If an ox worth 200 *zuz* gored another ox worth 200 *zuz* and the carcase was worth 50 *zuz*, then each takes half [the value] of the living and half [the value] of the dead.

10. A man may be culpable by an act of his ox but not culpable by a like act of his own, and he may not be culpable by an act of his ox but culpable by a like act of his own. If his ox inflicted indignity[4] he is not culpable, but if he himself inflicted indignity he is culpable. If his ox blinded the eye of his bondman or knocked out his tooth, the owner is not culpable; but if he himself blinded the eye of his bondman or knocked out his tooth, he is culpable. If his ox hurt his father or his mother, he is culpable; but if he himself hurt his father or his mother, he is not culpable.[5] If his ox set fire to a stack of corn on the Sabbath he is culpable, but if he himself set fire to a stack of corn on the Sabbath he is not culpable [for burning the stack], since he is become liable with his life [for profaning the Sabbath].

---

11. If an ox pursued another ox and this was injured, and the one owner said, 'Thy ox did the injury', and the other said, 'No, but it was injured by a stone', on him that would exact restitution from his fellow lies the burden of proof.[1] If two oxen pursued a third and the owner of the one said, 'Thy ox did the injury', and the owner of the other said, 'Thy ox did the injury', neither is culpable. If the two belonged to the one owner they are both culpable. If one was large and the other small, and the injured [party] said, 'The large one did the injury', and the one [whose oxen] did the injury said, 'No, but the small one did the injury'; or if the one was accounted harmless and the other was an attested danger, and the injured [party] said, 'That which was an attested danger did the injury', but the one [whose oxen] did the injury said, 'No, but the one accounted harmless did the injury', on him that would exact restitution from his fellow lies the burden of proof. If there were two that were injured, the one large and the other small, and there were two that did the injury, the one large and the other small, and the injured [party] said, 'The large one did the injury to the large one, and the small one the injury to the small one', but he [whose oxen] did the injury said, 'No, but the small one injured the large one, and the large one the small', or if one was accounted harmless and the other was an attested danger, and the injured [party] said, 'That which was an attested danger injured the large one, and the one accounted harmless injured the small one', but the one [whose oxen] did the injury said, 'No, but the one accounted harmless injured the large one and that which was an attested danger the small one', on him that would exact restitution from his fellow lies the burden of proof.

4. 1. If an ox gored four or five oxen, one after the other, compensation is [first] paid [from the value of the goring ox][2] for the last to be injured. If there was still value to spare this is transferred to the last but one; if there was still value to spare this is transferred to the one before;[3] but always the last has the advantage. So R. Meir. R. Simeon says: If an ox worth 200 *zuz* gored another ox worth 200 *zuz* and the carcase was worth nothing, each takes 100 *zuz*.[4] If it again gored another ox worth 200 *zuz*, the owner of the last takes 100 *zuz*[5] and the two other owners take each 50 *zuz*. If it again gored another ox worth 200 *zuz*, the owner of the last takes 100 *zuz*, and the owner of the one before takes 50 *zuz*, and the first two owners take each a golden *denar*.[6]

2. If an ox was an attested danger to its own kind but not to any other kind, or an attested danger to men but not to cattle, or to small beasts but not to large, full damages are payable for injuries to that to which it was an attested danger, but half-damages only for injuries to that to which it was not an attested danger. They said before R. Judah: What of the ox that is an attested danger on Sabbaths but not so on weekdays? He replied: On Sabbaths it must pay full damages and on weekdays half-damages. When

---

[1] Cf. B.B. 9[6]; Bekh. 2[7].

[2] Which had not lost its status of 'harmless', and so was liable to half-damages from the value of its own body (1[4]).

[3] If the five injured oxen were each worth 100 *zuz* and the injuring ox was worth 120 *zuz*, the last to be injured receives 50 *zuz*, the last but one 50, and the last but two 20; the first two receive nothing.

[4] They become joint-owners with equal share of responsibility.

[5] The half-damages for his ox, thus becoming half-owner of the other ox, with a half-responsibility for the damage it does; and the others share the rest of its value equally.

[6] Twenty-five *zuz*.

can it be accounted harmless? After it has refrained from doing injury for three Sabbath days.

3. If an ox of an Israelite gored an ox that belonged to the Temple, or an ox that belonged to the Temple gored the ox of an Israelite, the owner is not culpable, for it is written, *The ox of his neighbour*,[1]—not an ox that belongs to the Temple. If the ox of an Israelite gored the ox of a gentile, the owner is not culpable. But if the ox of a gentile gored the ox of an Israelite, whether it was accounted harmless or an attested danger, the owner must pay full damages.

4. If the ox of a man of sound senses gored the ox of a deaf-mute, an imbecile, or a minor, the owner is culpable; but if the ox of a deaf-mute, an imbecile, or a minor gored the ox of a man of sound senses, the owner is not culpable. If the ox of a deaf-mute, an imbecile, or a minor had gored another, the court must appoint a guardian over them and their oxen are testified against in the presence of the guardian. If the deaf-mute became of sound senses, or the imbecile recovered his reason, or the minor became of age, the ox is thereupon deemed harmless once more. So R. Meir. R. Jose says: It remains as it was before. An ox from the stadium[2] is not liable to be put to death [if it causes death], for it is written, *If an ox gore*,[3] and not 'If it be made to gore'.

5. If an ox gored a man and he died, if it was an attested danger its owner must pay the ransom price,[4] but if it was accounted harmless he is exempt from paying the ransom price. But in either case the oxen are guilty of death.[5] So, too, if it killed a man's son or daughter. But if it gored a bondman or a bondwoman, the owner must pay thirty *selas*[6] whether [the slave was] worth a hundred *minas* or only a *denar*.

6. If an ox rubbed itself against a wall and it fell upon a man [and killed him]; or if it intended to kill a beast but killed a man, or a gentile but killed an Israelite, or an untimely birth but killed a child like to live, it is exempt [from death by stoning].[7]

7. The ox of a woman, or the ox of orphans, or the ox of a guardian, or a wild ox, or an ox belonging to the Temple, or an ox belonging to a proselyte who died without heirs[8]—these are all liable to death [if they kill a man]. R. Judah says: A wild ox, or an ox belonging to the Temple, or an ox belonging to a proselyte who died are exempt from death, since they have no owner.

8. If an ox was condemned to be stoned and its owner dedicated it, its dedication is not valid. If he slaughtered it its flesh is forbidden. But if its owner dedicated it before it was condemned its dedication is valid, and if he slaughtered it its flesh is permitted.

9. If he delivered it to an unpaid guardian or to a borrower, or to a paid guardian or to a hirer,[9] they stand in place of the owner and must pay full damages [for injury] if the beast was an attested danger, or half-damages if it was accounted harmless. If its owner had tied it with a halter, or shut it in properly, but it nevertheless came out and caused damage, the owner is culpable whether it was an attested danger or accounted harmless. So R. Meir. R. Judah says: If it was accounted harmless he is liable, but if an

---

[1] Ex. 21[35].   [2] Where it is incited or trained to fight other beasts or men.
[3] Ex. 21[28].   [4] Pay to the heirs the dead man's value.
[5] And must be stoned. Ex. 21[28].   [6] App. II, A. Ex. 21[32]. The ox must be stoned.
[7] There was no intention to kill (Sanh. 9[2]), but the owner must pay the ransom price for the dead.   [8] Cf. 9[11].   [9] See B.M. 7[8].

attested danger he is not culpable, for it is written, [*And it hath been testified to his owner*] *and he hath not kept him in*;[1] but this one was 'kept in'. R. Eleazar says: Its only safe-keeping is the knife.

5. 1. If an ox gored a cow and her newly-born young was found beside her, and it is not known whether she gave birth before the ox gored her or after it gored her, half-damages must be paid for the cow and quarter-damages for the young. So, too, if a cow gored an ox and her newly-born young was found beside her and it is not known whether she gored the ox before she gave birth or after she gave birth, half-damages must be paid from the cow and quarter-damages from the young.

2. If a potter brought his pots into the courtyard of a householder without permission and the householder's cattle broke them, the householder is not culpable; and if the cattle were injured by them the owner of the pots is culpable; but if he brought them in by permission the owner of the courtyard is culpable. If a man brought his produce into the courtyard of a householder without permission and the householder's cattle ate it, the householder is not culpable, and if the cattle suffered injury the owner of the produce is culpable; but if he brought the produce in by permission the owner of the courtyard is culpable.

3. If a man brought his ox into the courtyard of a householder without permission and the householder's ox gored it or the householder's dog bit it, the householder is not culpable. But if it gored the householder's ox the other is culpable. If [the first man's ox] fell into the householder's cistern and befouled its water, he is culpable. If the householder's father or son was therein [and it killed them] the ox's owner must pay the ransom price. But if he had brought his ox in by permission the owner of the courtyard is culpable. Rabbi says: In no case is the householder culpable unless he had undertaken to watch over it.

4. If an ox intended [to gore] another ox and struck a woman and her young came forth, its owner is not liable for the value of the young.[2] But if a man intended to strike his fellow and struck a woman and her young came forth he must pay the value of the young. How does he pay the value of the young? They assess how much the woman was worth before she brought forth and how much after. Rabban Simeon b. Gamaliel said: If so [he pays naught, for] after she brings forth she is the more valuable![3]—but, rather, they assess how much the young would be worth, and he pays it to the husband or, if she has no husband, to his heirs. But if she was a freed bondwoman or a proselyte no penalty is incurred.

5. If a man digged a pit[4] in a private domain and opened it into the public domain, or if he digged it in the public domain and opened it into a private domain, or if he digged it in a private domain and opened it into another private domain, he is culpable [if any is injured thereby]. If he digged a pit in the public domain and an ox or an ass fell into it and died, he is culpable. No matter whether he digs a pit, trench or cavern or ditches or channels, he is culpable. Then why is it written, *a pit* [only]? As a pit which is deep enough to cause death is ten handbreadths deep, so any [cavity] is deep enough to cause death if it is ten handbreadths deep. If they were less than ten handbreadths and an ox or an ass fell therein and

---

[1] Ex. 21[29].   [2] Cf. Ex. 21[22].
[3] i.e. her life was in danger by reason of the imminent birth, but now she is free from danger.   [4] Ex. 21[35].

died, the owner is not culpable; but if it suffered damage thereby he is culpable.

6. If a pit belonged to two jointholders and one went over it and left it uncovered, and the other also went over it and left it uncovered,[1] the second is culpable. If the first covered it and the second came and found it uncovered and did not cover it, the second is culpable. If he had covered it properly and nevertheless an ox or an ass fell into it and died, he is not culpable; but if he had not covered it properly and an ox or an ass fell into it and died, he is culpable. If it fell forward [into the pit, frightened] because of the sound of the digging, the owner of the pit is culpable; but if backward [outside the pit] because of the sound of the digging, he is not culpable. If an ox fell into it with its trappings and these were broken, or if an ass fell into it with its trappings and these were torn, he is culpable in what concerns the beast, but not culpable in what concerns the trappings.[2] If an ox that was deaf, foolish, or young fell therein he is culpable. If a boy or a girl or a bondman or a bondwoman fell therein, he is not culpable.

7. An ox and all other cattle are alike under the laws concerning falling into a pit, keeping apart from the mount Sinai,[3] two-fold restitution,[4] the restoring of lost property,[5] unloading,[6] muzzling,[7] diverse kinds,[8] and the Sabbath.[9] The like applies also to wild animals and birds. If so, why is it written,[10] *an ox or an ass* [only]? Because Scripture speaks only of what happens in fact.[11]

6. 1. If a man brought his flock into a fold and shut it in properly and it nevertheless came out and caused damage, he is not culpable. If he had not shut it in properly and it came out and caused damage, he is culpable. If the fold was broken through in the night, or if robbers broke into it, and the flock came out and caused damage, he is not culpable. If the robbers brought out the flock the robbers are culpable.

2. If he left the flock in the sun, or if he delivered it to the care of a deaf-mute, an imbecile, or a minor, and it came out and caused damage, he is culpable. If he delivered it to the care of a herdsman, the herdsman stands in the place of the owner. If the flock fell into a garden and derived any benefit, the owner must pay for the benefit that they have derived. If the flock went down in its usual way and caused damage, he must pay for the damage that they have caused. How does he pay for the damage that they have caused? They assess what a *seah's* space[12] of ground in that field was worth before and what it is worth now. R. Simeon says: If they consumed fully grown produce he must repay with fully grown produce; if [the flock destroyed] one *seah*[13] he must repay one *seah*; if two *seahs*, two *seahs*.

3. If a man stacked his sheaves in his fellow's field without permission and the cattle of the owner of the field consumed them, the owner of the field is not culpable, and if the cattle suffered injury through them the owner of the sheaves is culpable; but if he stacked his sheaves there by permission, the owner of the field is culpable.

4. If a man caused fire to break out at the hand of a deaf-mute, an imbecile, or a minor, he is not culpable by the laws of man, but he is culpable

---

[1] Some texts omit this last sentence.
[2] Since Ex. 21[33] speaks only of 'an ox or an ass' and not of their trappings.
[3] Cf. Ex. 19[12].   [4] Ex. 22[7].   [5] Deut. 22[3]; Ex. 23[4].   [6] Ex. 23[5].
[7] Deut. 25[4].   [8] Lev. 19[19]; Deut. 22[10].   [9] Ex. 20[10]; Deut. 5[14].
[10] Ex. 21[33].   [11] Cf. Shab. 6[6,9]; Erub. 1[10]; Yeb. 15[2]; Ned. 5[5]; Eduy. 1[12].
[12] App. II, E.   [13] App. II, D.

by the laws of Heaven. If he caused it to break out at the hand of one of sound senses, this one is culpable.[1] If one brought the fire and then another brought the wood, he that brought the wood is culpable. If one brought wood and then another brought the fire, he that brought the fire is culpable. If a third came and set the wood ablaze, he that set it ablaze is culpable. If the wind set it ablaze none of them is culpable. If a man caused fire to break out and it consumed wood or stones or dust, he is culpable, for it is written, *If fire break out and catch in thorns so that the shocks of corn or the standing corn or the field be consumed, he that kindled the fire shall surely make restitution.*[2] If it passed over a fence four cubits high, or over a public way[3] or a river, he that caused it is not culpable. If a man kindled fire within his own domain, how far may it spread?[4] R. Eleazar b. Azariah says: It is looked upon as though it was in the midst of a *kor's* space[5] of land. R. Eliezer says: Sixteen cubits [in every direction], like a public highway. R. Akiba says: Fifty cubits. R. Simeon says: [It is written,] *He that kindled the fire shall surely make restitution*—all is in accordance with the nature of the fire.

5. If a man set fire to a stack and in it there were utensils and these caught fire, R. Judah says: He must make restitution for what was therein. But the Sages say: He need only make restitution for a stack of wheat or barley. If a kid was fastened to it and a bondman stood near by, and they were burnt together, he that kindled the fire is liable [for the kid but not for the bondman]. If the bondman was bound and a kid stood near by and they were burnt together, he that kindled the fire is not liable[6] [for either]. And the Sages agree with R. Judah that if a man set fire to a large building he must make restitution for everything therein; for such is the custom among men to leave [their goods] in their houses.

6. If a spark flew out from under the hammer and caused damage [the striker] is culpable. If a camel laden with flax passed by in the public domain and its load of flax entered into a shop[7] and caught fire from the shopkeeper's light, and so set fire to a large building, the owner of the camel is culpable; but if the shopkeeper left his light outside, the shopkeeper is culpable. R. Judah says: If it was a Hanukkah-light[8] he is not culpable.

7. 1. More common in use is the rule of twofold restitution[9] than the rule of fourfold and fivefold restitution, for the rule of twofold restitution applies both to what has life and to what has not life; while the rule of fourfold and fivefold restitution applies only to an ox or a sheep, for it is written, *If a man shall steal an ox or a sheep and kill it, or sell it, he shall pay five oxen for an ox and four sheep for a sheep.*[10] If a man stole [stolen beasts] from a thief he does not make twofold restitution; nor does he that kills or sells what is stolen make fourfold or fivefold restitution.

2. If a man stole [an ox or a sheep] according to the evidence of two witnesses, and killed or sold it according to their evidence or that of two others, he must make fourfold or fivefold restitution. If a man stole [an ox or a

---

[1] Cf. below, 8[7] (end). [2] Ex. 22[6]. [3] Sixteen cubits; cf. B.B. 6[7].
[4] And he still be accountable for what damage it causes within that area.
[5] App. II, E. [6] To make money restitution. As to the bondman, cf. 3[10] (end), 8[5].
[7] It is a common sight in the East to see a camel bearing a load so bulky as almost to touch both sides of the narrow street. The entire fronts of the shops lie open to the street.
[8] The lights lit at the windows of houses during the eight days of Hanukkah, the Feast of the Dedication, beginning on the 25th of Chislev. [9] Ex. 22[7]. [10] Ex. 22[1].

sheep] and sold it on the Sabbath, or stole it and sold it for idolatrous use, or stole it and killed it on the Day of Atonement; if he stole what was his father's and killed or sold it, and his father afterward died; or if he stole it and killed it and then dedicated it;—in every case he must make fourfold or fivefold restitution. If he stole it and then killed it as a means of healing, or for dogs, or if he slaughtered it and it was found to be *terefah*,[1] or if he slaughtered it in the Temple Court [intending to consume it] as common food,[2] he must make fourfold or fivefold restitution. In these [last] two cases R. Simeon declares him exempt.

3. If a man stole [an ox or a sheep] according to the evidence of two witnesses, and killed or sold it according to their evidence, and they are found to be false witnesses, they must pay the whole penalty.[3] If he stole it according to the evidence of two witnesses, and killed or sold it according to the evidence of two others, and both pairs alike are found to be false witnesses, the first witnesses must make twofold restitution, and the second witnesses threefold restitution. If the second [only] were found to be false witnesses, the thief must make twofold restitution[4] and they three-fold restitution. If one [only] of the second witnesses was found to be a false witness the evidence of the other is made void; if one of the first witnesses was found to be a false witness, the entire evidence is made void, since if there is no [proved case of] theft there is none of killing or selling [what was stolen].

4. If a man stole [an ox or a sheep] according to the evidence of two wit-nesses but killed or sold it according to the evidence of one witness only, or according to his own evidence, he makes twofold restitution, but not fourfold or fivefold restitution. If he stole [an ox or a sheep] and killed it on the Sabbath, or stole it and killed it for idolatrous use, or stole what was his father's and his father died, and he afterward killed or sold it, or if he stole it and then dedicated it, and afterward killed it or sold it, he makes twofold restitution but not fourfold or fivefold restitution. R. Simeon says: If they were Hallowed Things which must be replaced[5] [if damaged or lost], he must make fourfold or fivefold restitution; but if Hallowed Things which need not be replaced,[6] he is exempt.

5. If he sold it all but a hundredth part, or if he had [already] a share in it, or if he slaughtered it and it became unfit under his hand, or if he pierced [its windpipe] or rooted out [its gullet],[7] he makes twofold restitu-tion but not fourfold or fivefold restitution. If he stole it in the owner's domain, but killed or sold it outside the owner's domain; or if he stole it outside the owner's domain and killed or sold it within the owner's domain; or if he stole it and killed or sold it outside the owner's domain, he must make fourfold or fivefold restitution. But if he stole it and killed or sold it within the owner's domain, he is exempt.

6. If while he was dragging it out it died in the owner's domain, he is exempt; but if he had lifted it up[8] or taken it outside the owner's domain and it died, he is liable. If he brought it as the firstborn offering for his son,[9] or gave it to his creditor, or to an unpaid guardian, or to a borrower or to a paid guardian or to an hirer, and one of them was dragging it away

---

[1] App. I. 47.
[2] Thereby rendering it forbidden for food or use.   [3] Deut. 19[19]; cf. Makk. 1[4].
[4] Since his theft, at least, was proved.   [5] Obligatory and vow-offerings.
[6] Freewill-offerings.   [7] See Hull. 2[1].   [8] Cf. Kidd. 1[4].
[9] As redemption for his firstborn son (Ex. 13[13]).

and it died in the owner's domain, he is exempt. But if he had lifted it up or taken it outside the owner's domain, he is liable.

7. They may not rear small cattle[1] in the Land of Israel, but they may rear them in Syria or in the wildernesses that are in the Land of Israel. They may not rear fowls[2] in Jerusalem because of the Hallowed Things nor may priests rear them [anywhere] in the Land of Israel because of [the laws concerning] clean foods. None[3] may rear swine anywhere. A man may not rear a dog unless it is kept bound by a chain. They may not set snares for pigeons unless it be thirty *ris*[4] from an inhabited place.

8. 1. If a man wounded his fellow he thereby becomes liable on five counts: for injury, for pain, for healing, for loss of time, and for indignity inflicted. 'For injury'—thus, if he blinded his fellow's eye, cut off his hand, or broke his foot, [his fellow] is looked upon as if he was a slave to be sold[5] in the market: they assess how much he was worth and how much he is worth now. 'For pain'—thus, if he burnt his fellow with a spit or a nail, even though it was on his finger-nail where it leaves no wound, they estimate how much money such a man would be willing to take to suffer so. 'For healing'—thus, if he struck him he is liable to pay the cost of his healing; if by reason of the blow ulcers arise he is liable [for the cost of their healing], but if they did not arise by reason of the blow, he is not liable. If the wound healed and then opened and healed again and again opened, he continues liable for the cost of his healing; but once it is properly healed he is no longer liable to pay the cost of his healing. 'For loss of time'—thus, he is looked upon as a watchman of a cucumber-field, since he has already been paid the value of his hand or foot.[6] 'For indignity inflicted'—all is in accordance with [the condition of life of] him that inflicts and him that suffers the indignity.[7] If a man inflicted the indignity on a naked man, or a blind man, or a sleeping man, he is [still] liable; but if he that inflicted the indignity was asleep he is not liable. If a man fell from the roof and caused injury and inflicted indignity, he is liable for the injury but not for the indignity, for it is written, *And she putteth forth her hand and taketh him by the secrets*[8]—a man is liable only when he acts with intention [of causing injury].

2. Herein greater stringency applies to a man than to an ox, since the man must pay for injury, pain, healing, loss of time, and indignity, and make restitution for the value of the young;[9] whereas the ox pays only for the injury and is not liable for the value of the young.[10]

3. If a man struck his father or his mother[11] and inflicted no wound, or if he wounded his fellow on the Day of Atonement, he is liable on all the [five] counts; if he wounded a Hebrew bondman[12] he is liable on all the counts, excepting loss of time, if it was his own bondman. If he wounded a Canaanitish bondman[13] belonging to others he is liable on all the counts. R. Judah says: [Damages for] indignity are not paid for bondmen.

4. It is an ill thing to knock against a deaf-mute, an imbecile, or a minor: he that wounds them is culpable, but if they wound others they are not

---

[1] Because they damage the sown fields. Cf. Dem. 2[3].
[2] Which are liable to pick out a lentil's bulk of a dead creeping thing, so conveying uncleanness to houses.   [3] Some texts read 'no Israelite'.
[4] Four miles. App. II, C.   [5] Cf. Ket. 3[7].
[6] And is now only capable of such work.   [7] Cf. Ket. 3[7]; Arak. 3[4].
[8] Deut. 25[11]. This passage is the basis of the imposition of damages for 'indignity'. The penalty 'thou shalt cut off her hand' is interpreted to mean, 'she shall pay a money-fine'.
[9] Ex. 21[22]. See above, 5[4].   [10] Since Ex. 21[22] speaks only of 'men'.   [11] Ex. 21[15].
[12] Lev. 25[39f].   [13] Lev. 25[44f].

culpable. It is an ill thing to knock against a bondman or a woman: he that wounds them is culpable, but if they wound others they are not culpable; yet they may need to make restitution afterward—if the woman was divorced or the bondman freed they are liable to make restitution.

5. If a man struck his father or his mother and left a wound, or if he wounded his fellow on the Sabbath, he is not culpable on any of the [five] counts, in that he is liable with his life. If a man wounded his Canaanitish bondman he is not culpable on any of the [five] counts.[1]

6. If a man cuffed his fellow he must pay him a *sela*.[1] R. Judah says in the name of R. Jose the Galilean: One hundred *zuz*. If he slapped him he must pay him 200 *zuz*. If [he struck him] with the back of his hand he must pay him 400 *zuz*. If he tore his ear, plucked out his hair, spat and his spittle touched him, or pulled his cloak from off him, or loosed a woman's hair in the street, he must pay him 400 *zuz*. This is the general rule: all is in accordance with a person's honour. R. Akiba said: Even the poorest in Israel are looked upon as freemen who have lost their possessions, for they are the sons of Abraham, Isaac, and Jacob. It once happened that a man unloosed a woman's hair in the street and she came before R. Akiba and he condemned him to pay her 400 *zuz*. He replied, 'Rabbi, give me time'. And he gave him time. He perceived her standing at the entry of her courtyard and he broke before her a cruse that held an *issar's* worth of oil. She unloosed her hair and scooped up the oil in her hand and laid her hand on her head. He had set up witnesses in readiness against her and he came before R. Akiba and said to him, 'Rabbi, should I give such a one as this[2] 400 *zuz*?' He answered, 'Thou hast said naught at all, since he that wounds himself, even though he has not the right, is not culpable; but if others have wounded him, they are culpable'. If a man cut down his own plants, even though he has not the right, he is not culpable; but if others cut them down they are culpable.

7. Even though a man pays [him that suffers the indignity], it is not forgiven him until he seeks forgiveness from him, for it is written, *Now, therefore, restore the man's wife . . . [and he shall pray for thee].*[3] And whence do we learn that if he did not forgive him he would be accounted merciless?[4] Because it is written, *And Abraham prayed unto God and God healed Abimelech . . .*[5] If a man said, 'Blind my eye', or 'Cut off my hand', or 'Break my foot', he [that does so] is culpable; [even if he said], 'on the condition that thou shalt not be culpable', he is [still] culpable. [If he said,] 'Tear my garment', or 'Break my jug', he [that does so] is culpable. [But if he said,] 'on the condition that thou shalt not be culpable', he is not culpable. [If he said,] 'Do so to such-a-one, on the condition that thou shalt not be culpable', he is [still] culpable,[6] whether [it was an offence] against his person or his property.

9. 1. If a man stole[7] wood and made it into utensils, or wool and made it into garments, he makes restitution according to [the value of the stolen property at] the moment of the theft. If he stole a cow that was with young, and it then brought forth young, or an ewe ready to be sheared, and he then sheared it, he repays the value of a cow about to bear young, or of an

---

[1] Four *zuz*.   [2] Who is ready to disgrace herself for an *issar's* worth ('a half-penny's worth') of oil. The *issar* is one twenty-fourth part of a *denar* or *zuz*.   [3] Gen. 20[7].
[4] Variant: 'Whence do we learn that he who must forgive should not be merciless?'
[5] Gen. 20[17].   [6] Cf. 6[4].   [7] Heb. *gazal*, take openly, by force. Similarly in the following paragraphs. In 10[8] the verb is *ganab*, take surreptitiously.

ewe ready to be sheared. If he stole a cow, and while it remained with him it was impregnated and bore young, or [if he stole] a ewe, and while it remained with him it grew its wool and he sheared it, he makes restitution according to [the value at] the moment of the theft. This is the general rule: all thieves make restitution according to [the value at] the moment of the theft.

2. If he stole a beast and it grew old [while it remained with him], or bondmen and they grew old, he makes restitution according to [their value at] the time of the theft. R. Meir says: As for bondmen, the thief may say to the owner, 'Here before thee is what is thine'. If he stole a coin and it cracked, or fruit and it rotted, or wine and it turned sour, he must make restitution according to [the value at] the time of the theft. But if he stole a coin and it went out of use,[1] or Heave-offering and it became unclean,[2] or leaven and the season of Passover arrived,[3] or a beast and it was used for transgression[4] or became unfit to be offered on the Altar or was condemned to be stoned,[5] he may say to the other, 'Here before thee is what is thine'.[6]

3. If he gave aught to craftsmen to be mended, and they spoilt it, they must make restitution. If he gave a carpenter a box, chest, or cupboard to be mended, and he spoilt it, he must make restitution. If a builder undertook to pull down a wall and he broke the stones or caused [other] damage, he must make restitution; but if he was pulling down at the one end and it fell down at the other, he is not culpable; but if it fell by reason of a blow, he is culpable.

4. If a man gave wool to a dyer and the cauldron burned it, the dyer must repay him the value of his wool. If he dyed it badly but the improvement was worth more than the [dyer's] outlay, he must repay him his outlay; and if the outlay was more than the value of the improvement, he need pay only the value of the improvement. If he told him to dye it red and he dyed it black, or black and he dyed it red, R. Meir says: The dyer must pay him the value of the wool. R. Judah says: If the improvement was worth more than the [dyer's] outlay he must pay him his outlay; and if the outlay was more than the value of the improvement, he need pay only the value of the improvement.

5. If[7] a man robbed his fellow of the value of a *perutah* and swore [falsely] to him, [if he would make restitution] he must take it and give it to him even [if his fellow had gone] as far as Media.[8] He may not give it to his son or to his agent,[9] but he may give it to the agent of the court. And if his fellow had died he must restore it to his heirs.

6. If he had repaid him the value but had not paid him the [added] fifth,[10] or if he had been forgiven the value but not the [added] fifth, or if he had been forgiven both save less than a *perutah's* worth of the value, he need not go after him. If he had repaid him the [added] fifth but not the value, or if he had been forgiven the [added] fifth but not the value, or if he had been forgiven both save a [whole] *perutah's* worth of the value, he must go after him.

---

[1] In that country yet remained current elsewhere.
[2] And so unfit to be eaten by the priest.   [3] So that it was forbidden to an Israelite.
[4] Unnatural crime or idolatry. Cf. Zeb. 8[1].   [5] Ex. 21[28].
[6] He is not answerable for loss of value which he could not anticipate.
[7] Cf. B.M. 4[7]. See Lev. 6[2ff].
[8] Where (Is. 13[17]) they have no regard for silver and gold.
[9] Lev. 6[5]: 'unto him to whom it appertaineth shall he give it'.   [10] Lev. 6[5].

7. If he had paid him the value and had sworn [falsely] to him concerning the [added] fifth, he must pay moreover a fifth of the [added] fifth [and so on,] until the value [of the added fifth] becomes less than a *perutah's* worth. So, too, with a deposit, for it is written, *In a matter of deposit or of bargain or of robbery, or if he have oppressed his neighbour or have found that which was lost and deal falsely therein and swear to a lie*[1]—such a one must pay the value and the [added] fifth and [offer] a Guilt-offering.

8. [If one man said,] 'Where is my deposit?' and the other said, 'It is lost', [if the one says,] 'I adjure thee', and the other says, 'Amen!' and witnesses testify against him that he consumed it, he need pay [only] the value. But if he confessed it of himself, he must repay the value and the [added] fifth and [offer] a Guilt-offering. [If one man said,] 'Where is my deposit?' and the other said, 'It is stolen', [if the one says,] 'I adjure thee', and the other says, 'Amen!' and witnesses testify against him that he stole it, he must make twofold restitution. If he confessed it of himself, he must repay the value and the [added] fifth and [offer] a Guilt-offering.

9. If a man stole from his father and swore [falsely] to him, and the father died, he must repay the value and the [added] fifth to the father's sons or brothers; if he will not repay[2] or if he has naught [wherewith to repay], he must borrow and the creditors come and exact payment.[3]

10. If a man said to his son, '*Konam* be any benefit thou hast of mine!' and he died, the son may inherit from him; [but if moreover he said] 'both during my life and at my death!' when he dies the son may not inherit from him and he must restore [what he had received from his father at any time] to the father's sons or brothers; and if he has naught [wherewith to repay] he must borrow, and the creditors come and exact payment.[4]

11. If a man stole from a proselyte and swore [falsely] to him, and the proselyte died, he must repay the value and the [added] fifth to the priests, and the Guilt-offering to the Altar, for it is written, *But if the man have no kinsman to whom restitution may be made for the guilt, the restitution for guilt which is made unto the Lord shall be the priest's, besides the ram of the atonement whereby atonement shall be made for him.*[5] If he brought the money and the Guilt-offering [to the Temple] and then died,[6] the money shall be given to his sons, and the Guilt-offering shall be left to pasture until it suffers a blemish, when it shall be sold; and its value falls to the Temple treasury.

12. If he gave the money to the priests serving their [weekly] Course,[7] and then died, the heirs cannot recover it from their hands, for it is written, *Whatsoever any man giveth the priest it shall be his.*[8] If he gave the money to [the Course of] Jehoiarib and the Guilt-offering to [the Course of] Jedaiah,[9] he has fulfilled his obligation; but if he gave the Guilt-offering to [the Course of] Jehoiarib and the money to [the Course of] Jedaiah, if the Guilt-offering still remains the sons of Jedaiah shall offer it; otherwise he must bring another Guilt-offering. For if a man brought what he had stolen before he offered his Guilt-offering, he has fulfilled his obligation; but if he brought his Guilt-offering before he brought what he had stolen, he has not yet fulfilled his obligation. If he gave the value but not the [added]

---

1 Lev. 6²ᶠ.   2 Out of his own property.
3 i.e. recover the loan from the heirs jointly.   4 See preceding note.
5 Num. 5⁸.   6 So expiating his sin.   7 See Taan. 2⁶.   8 Num. 5¹⁰.
9 The first and second of the weekly Courses (1 Chron. 24⁷).

fifth, the [added] fifth does not hinder [him from offering the Guilt-offering].

10. 1. If a man stole aught and gave it to his children to eat or if he left it to them [after his death], they are exempt from making restitution. But if it was mortgaged property they are liable to make restitution. None may take change for money from the counter of excisemen or from the wallet of tax-gatherers, or take any alms from them;[1] but it may be taken from them at their own house or in the market.[2]

2. If tax-gatherers took a man's ass and gave him another, or if robbers robbed a man of his coat and gave him another, they become his own, since the owner cherishes no hope of recovering them. If a man saved aught from a flood or from marauding troops or from robbers, and the owner cherished no hope of recovering it, it becomes the man's own. So, too, with a swarm of bees: if the owner cherished no hope of recovering them, they become the finder's own. R. Johanan b. Baroka said: A woman or a child may be believed if they say, 'The swarm of bees went away from here'. A man may go into his fellow's field to save his swarm and if he causes damage he must pay for the damage that he has caused; but he may not cut off a branch from his fellow's tree even on the condition of repaying the value. R. Ishmael, the son of R. Johanan b. Baroka, says: He may indeed cut it off and repay the value.

3. If a man recognized any of his utensils or books in another's hands and the report had gone forth in the city that such things had been stolen, he that had bought them may swear to him how much he had paid and take [this price from the owner and restore the goods]. But if [such a report had] not [gone forth] his[3] claim avails him naught, since I might say that he had first sold them to another and yet another had bought them from him.

4. If one came with his jar of wine and the other came with his jug of honey and the jug of honey cracked, and the other poured out his wine and saved the honey [by receiving it] into his jar, he can claim no more than his hire. But if he had said, 'I will save what is thine but do thou pay me the value of what is mine', the other must pay it to him. If a flood swept away a man's ass and the ass of his fellow, and his own was worth 100 *zuz* and that of his fellow 200 *zuz*, and he left his own and saved that of his fellow, he can claim no more than his hire. But if he had said, 'I will save thine, but do thou pay me for mine', the other must pay it to him.

5. If a man stole a field from his fellow and tyrants took it from him, if the whole district[4] suffered, he may say to his fellow, 'Here before thee is what is thine'. But if it was through the thief's own fault,[5] he must provide him with another field. If a flood swept it away, he may say to him, 'Here before thee is what is thine'.

6. If a man stole aught from his fellow in an inhabited region, or borrowed it or received it as a deposit, he may not restore it to him in the wilderness; but if [he had borrowed or received it] with the understanding that he was going out to the wilderness, he may restore it to him in the wilderness.

7. If a man said to his fellow, 'I robbed thee [of such a thing]', or,

---

[1] Since such money is deemed got by robbery.
[2] When they are not practising their calling. [3] The original owner.
[4] If many owners in the neighbourhood suffered; e.g. by government confiscation.
[5] If because of his offence against the government his property was confiscated.

'Thou didst lend it to me' or 'Thou didst deposit it with me, but I do not know whether I restored it or not', he is bound to repay it. But if he said, 'I do not know whether I robbed thee of it', or 'whether thou didst lend it to me' or 'whether thou didst deposit it with me', he is not bound to repay it.

8. If a man stole a lamb from the flock and restored it, but it died or was stolen again, he is answerable for it. If the owner knew neither of its theft nor of its return and counted the flock and found it complete, the thief is not culpable.

9. None may buy wool or milk[1] from herdsmen, or wood or fruit from them that watch over fruit-trees; but from women they may buy[2] garments of wool in Judea and garments of flax in Galilee or calves in Sharon. But if they [that sell them] say that these must be kept hidden, it is forbidden. They may buy eggs and fowls anywhere.

10. Shreds of wool which the washerman pulls out belong to him;[3] but those which the woolcomber pulls out belong to the householder. If the washerman pulled out three threads they belong to him, but if more than this they belong to the householder. If there were black [threads] among the white, and he took them all out, they belong to him. If the tailor had left over thread sufficient to sew with or a piece of cloth three fingerbreadths square, these belong to the householder. What a carpenter takes off with the plane belongs to him; but [what he takes off] with a hatchet belongs to the householder. But if he was working in the domain of the householder even the sawdust belongs to the householder.

BABA METZIA[4] ('THE MIDDLE GATE')

1. 1. If two laid hold of a cloak and one said, 'I found it', and the other said, 'I found it', or if one said, 'The whole of it is mine',[5] and the other said, 'The whole of it is mine',[6] each must take an oath that he claims not less than the half of it and they divide it between them. If one said, 'The whole of it is mine', and the other said, 'The half of it is mine', he that said, 'The whole of it is mine', must take an oath that he claims not less than three-quarters, and he that said, 'The half of it is mine', must take an oath that he claims not less than one quarter; and the former takes three-quarters and the latter one-quarter.[7]

2. If two men were riding on a beast, or if one was riding and the other leading it, and one said, 'The whole of it is mine', and the other said, 'The whole of it is mine', each must take an oath that he claims not less than the half of it, and they divide it between them. But when they admit [that they found it together] or have witnesses [to prove it], they may divide it without taking an oath.

3. If a man was riding on a beast and saw lost property and said to his fellow, 'Give it to me', and the other took it and said, 'I have acquired title to it', his claim to it is valid. But if after he had given it to him he said, 'I acquired title to it first', he has said nothing.

4. If a man saw lost property and fell upon it and another came and seized it, he that seized it has acquired title to it. If a man saw people

---

[1] Some texts add 'or kids'.
[2] Some texts omit 'garments of wool in Judea and'.
[3] They are negligible.
[4] See p. 332, n. 1.
[5] 'I bought it'.
[6] 'I bought it first'.
[7] i.e. they share the half which alone is in dispute.

running [in his field] after lost property, after a lame gazelle, or after pigeons that could not fly, and he said, 'My field gives me title [to them]', his claim is valid. But if the gazelle could run after its proper fashion, or if the pigeons could fly, and he said, 'My field gives me title', he has said nothing.

5. What is found by a man's son or daughter that are minors,[1] what is found by his Canaanitish bondman or bondwoman,[2] and what is found by his wife, belong to him; but what is found by his son or daughter that are of age, what is found by his Hebrew bondman or bondwoman,[3] and what is found by his wife whom he has divorced (even though he has not yet paid her her *Ketubah*),[4] belong to them.

6. If a man found bonds of indebtedness he should not restore them [to the creditor] if they record a lien on property, since the court would exact payment from the property; but if they do not record a lien on property he may restore them, since the court would not exact payment from the property. So R. Meir. But the Sages say: In either case he should not restore them, since [in either case] the court would exact payment from the property.[5]

7. If a man found bills of divorce, or writs of emancipation, or wills, or deeds of gift, or quittances, he should not restore them, for I might say that even if they had been written out, the writer may have bethought himself and determined not to deliver them.

8. If a man found letters of valuation[6] or letters of alimony[7] or deeds of *halitzah*[8] or Refusal,[9] or deeds of arbitration, or any document drawn out by the court, he should restore them. If he found documents in a satchel or bag, or a roll of documents or a bundle of documents, he should restore them. How many count as a bundle of documents? Three tied up together. R. Simeon b. Gamaliel says: [If the document that was found concerned] one man that borrowed from three others, it should be restored to the borrower; but if three men that borrowed from one other, it should be restored to the creditor. If a man found a document among his documents and he does not know what is its nature,[10] it must be left until Elijah comes.[11] If there were postscripts belonging to the documents[12] let him act in accordance with the postscripts.

2. 1. What lost goods belong to the finder and what must be proclaimed?[13] These goods belong to the finder: if a man found scattered fruit, scattered money, small sheaves in the public domain, cakes of figs, bakers' loaves, strings of fish, pieces of flesh, wool-shearings [in the condition in which they have been] brought from their country [of origin], stalks of flax, and strips of purple wool;[14] these belong to the finder. So R. Meir.[15] R. Judah

---

[1] While they are dependent on the father. Cf. Nidd. 5[5, 7].   [2] Lev. 25[44f].
[3] Lev. 25[39f].   [4] App. I. 16.
[5] Assuming that it was only through the scribe's error that security for the debt was unrecorded.
[6] Assessments by the court of the value of a debtor's property which stands as security for his debt.
[7] In which a husband undertakes the maintenance of his stepdaughters (cf. Ket. 12[1f]).
[8] See Yeb. 12[1ff].   [9] See Yeb. 13[1].
[10] Whether it was a bond entrusted to him (cf. B.B. 10[5]) by a borrower or a lender, or whether it was repaid in whole or in part.
[11] He may never restore it to either of them.
[12] The documents themselves being torn or illegible.
[13] See below, par. 6. Cf. p. 198, n. 4.   [14] Cf. Kel. 27[12] (end).
[15] Some texts omit.

says: Whatsoever has in it aught unusual must be proclaimed: thus if he found a fig-cake with a potsherd in it or a loaf with coins in it [he must proclaim it]. R. Simeon b. Eleazar says: [New] merchandise[1] need not be proclaimed.

2. And these must be proclaimed: if a man found fruit in a vessel, or an empty vessel, or money in a bag, or an empty bag, heaps of fruit or heaps of money, three coins one upon another, small sheaves in a private domain, home-made loaves, wool-shearings bought from a [wool-]worker's shop, jugs of wine or jugs of oil, these must be proclaimed.

3. If a man found pigeons tied together behind a fence or a hedge or on footpaths in the fields he may not touch them. If he found an object in the dungheap and it was covered up he may not touch it, but if it was exposed he may take it and proclaim it. If he found it in a heap of stones or in an old wall it belongs to him; if he found it in a new wall and it was on the outer side it belongs to him, but if it was on the inner side it belongs to the householder. But if the house had been hired to others, even if a man found aught [abandoned] within the house, it belongs to him.

4. If he found aught [abandoned] in a shop it belongs to him; but if he found it between the counter and the shopkeeper it belongs to the shop-keeper. If he found it in front of a money-changer it belongs to him; but if between the stool [of the money-changer] and the money-changer, it belongs to the money-changer. If a man bought fruit from his fellow or if his fellow sent him fruit and he found coins therein, they belong to him; but if they were tied up he must take them and proclaim them.

5. A garment also was included amongst all these things.[2] Why was it mentioned separately? To compare [other things] to it: to teach thee that as a particular garment has both special marks and them that lay claim to it, so everything must be proclaimed which has both special marks and them that lay claim to it.

6. For how long must a man proclaim [what he has found]? Until all his neighbours know of it. So R. Meir. R. Judah says: At the three Feasts and for seven days after the last Feast, to allow [to him that lost it] three days to go back to his house, three days to return, and one day wherein to proclaim [his loss].

7. If he named what was lost but could not describe its special marks, it may not be given to him; and it may not be given to a [known] deceiver even though he described its special marks, for it is written, *Until thy brother is inquired of concerning it*;[3] [which is to say] until thou shalt inquire of thy brother whether he is a deceiver or not a deceiver. Whatsoever works and eats,[4] let it work and eat [while it is in the finder's care]; but whatsoever does not work but eats may be sold, for it is written, *And thou shalt restore it to him*; [which is to say,] See how thou canst restore it to him[5] What befalls the price? R. Tarfon says: He may make use of it; therefore if it is lost he is answerable for it. R. Akiba says: He may not make use of it; therefore if it is lost he is not answerable for it.

8. If he found scrolls he may read them once every thirty days; and if he cannot read he must [at least] unroll them. But he may not learn aught

---

[1] Heb. *Enporiya*, ἐμπορία. According to Gem. 24a it refers to new purchases which the owner cannot yet certainly identify.   [2] Which must be proclaimed. Deut. 22³.
[3] Deut. 22². Such is the rendering of the Midrash (*Sifre*, ed. Friedmann, 115a).
[4] Its labour repays the cost of its fodder.
[5] It is better to restore its entire value rather than the beast itself less the cost of its keep.

from them for the first time, nor may another read with him. If he found
clothing he must shake it out once every thirty days and spread it out if it
requires it, but not for his own honour. [If he found] silver or copper vessels
he may make use of them for their own good, but not so as to wear them
out; if [he found] vessels of gold or glass he may not touch them until
Elijah comes. If he found a sack or a large basket or aught that he does not
usually carry about, he need not take it.

9. What is accounted lost property? If he found an ass or a cow grazing
by the way, it is not accounted lost property; but if [he found] an ass with
its trappings upset or a cow running among the vineyards, such is accounted
lost property. If he restored it and it escaped again, and he restored it again
and it escaped yet again, even four times or five, he must still restore it, for
it is written, *Thou shalt surely bring them again unto thy brother*.[1] If he
thereby lost time [to the value] of a *sela*,[2] he may not say to the owner,
'Give me a *sela*', but the owner need pay him only his hire as to a labourer
that was not employed. If there was a court of law in that place the finder
may stipulate before them [for damages for time lost]; but if there was no
court of law, before whom should he stipulate? His own advantage comes
first.[3]

10. If he found the beast [loose and unguarded] in a stable he is not
responsible for it, but if in the public domain he is responsible for it. If
it was in a cemetery he need not contract uncleanness because of it.[4]
[Even] if his father said to him, 'Contract uncleanness', or if he said to him,
'Do not restore it', he may not hearken to him. If he unloaded it[5] and loaded
it [afresh] and again unloaded it and loaded it [afresh], even four times or
five, he is still bound [to continue], for it is written, *Thou shalt surely help
with him*.[6] If the owner went and sat him down and said [to his fellow],
'Since a commandment is laid upon thee, if thou desirest to unload,
unload!' he is not bound [to unload it], for it is written, *with him*. But if
the owner was aged or sick, he is bound [to help him]. It is a religious duty
enjoined in the Law to unload—but not to load. R. Simeon says: To load
also. R. Jose the Galilean says: If the beast was bearing more than its
proper load he is not bound [to help to unload it], for it is written, *under its
burden*, [which is to say] a load which it is able to endure.

11. [If a man went to seek] his own lost property and that of his father,
his own has first place; if his own and that of his teacher, his own has first
place; if that of his father and that of his teacher, his teacher's has first
place—for his father did but bring him into this world, but his teacher
that taught him wisdom brings him into the world to come; but if his
father was also a Sage,[7] his father's has first place. If his father and his
teacher each bore a burden, he must first relieve his teacher and afterward
relieve his father. If his father and his teacher were each taken captive,
he must first ransom his teacher and afterward ransom his father; but if his
father was also a Sage he must first ransom his father and afterward ransom
his teacher.

3. 1. If a man left a beast or utensils in his fellow's keeping[8] and they were

---

[1] Deut. 22[1].   [2] App. II, A.   [3] He need not restore the property.
[4] If he was a priest (Lev. 21[1]) or a Nazirite (Num. 6[6]).   [5] An ass fallen under its load.
[6] Ex. 23[5]. The 'surely' here and in the previous quotation represents a duplicated verbal
form in the Hebrew; by rabbinic interpretation this enjoins repeated action, if need be, in
fulfilling the commandment.   [7] Variant: 'Equal (in wisdom) to his teacher'.
[8] As an 'unpaid guardian. See below, 7[8].

stolen or lost, and his fellow himself made restitution and would not take an oath (for they have taught: An unpaid guardian may take an oath and be quit of liability), the thief, if he is found, must make twofold restitution, and if he had killed or sold [the sheep or the ox] he must make fourfold or five-fold restitution. Whom does he repay? He with whom the property was deposited. If his fellow would not make restitution but took an oath, the thief, if he is found, must make twofold restitution, and if he had killed or sold [the sheep or the ox] he must make fourfold or fivefold restitution. Whom does he repay? The owner of the property deposited.

2. If a man hired a cow from his fellow and lent it to another, and it died a natural death, the hirer must swear that it died a natural death, and the borrower must repay [its value] to the hirer. R. Jose said: Why should that other traffick with his fellow's cow!—but, rather, the [value of the] cow is returned to the owner.

3. If a man said to two others, 'I have robbed one of you of 100 *zuz* and I do not know which of you it is', or 'The father of one of you left 100 *zuz* in my keeping, and I do not know whose father it was', he must give each of them 100 *zuz* since he himself admitted liability.

4. If two men deposited money with a third, the one 100 *zuz*, and the other 200 *zuz*, and one afterward said, 'The 200 *zuz* is mine', and the other said, 'The 200 *zuz* is mine', he should give 100 *zuz* to each of them, and the rest must be suffered to remain until Elijah comes. R. Jose said: But if so, what does the deceiver lose?—but, rather, the whole is suffered to remain until Elijah comes.

5. So, too, [if two men deposited] two things, one worth 100 *zuz* and the other 1,000 *zuz*, and one afterward said, 'The better one is mine', and the other said, 'The better one is mine', he should give the thing of lesser worth to the one, and to the other the value of the thing of lesser worth taken from [the value of] the thing of greater worth; and the rest must be suffered to remain until Elijah comes. R. Jose said: But if so, what does the deceiver lose?—but, rather, the whole is suffered to remain until Elijah comes.

6. If a man left produce in his fellow's keeping, his fellow may not touch it even if it perishes. Rabban Simeon b. Gamaliel says: He may sell it before a court of law; since he may be accounted one that restores lost property to its owner.[1]

7. If a man left produce in his fellow's keeping, his fellow[2] may exact of him these reductions: for wheat and rice nine *kabs*[3] and a half to the *kor*;[3] for barley and durra nine *kabs* to the *kor*; for spelt and linseed[4] three *seahs* to the *kor*—in proportion to the quantity and according to the length of time.[5] R. Johanan b. Nuri said: But what concern have the mice [with quantity and time]![6] will they not continue eating whether the quantity is large or small!—but, rather, he may exact him a reduction only from a single *kor*. R. Judah says: If the quantity was great he may not exact of him any reduction, since the produce increases in bulk [such time as it is stored].

---

[1] See above, p. 349, n. 5.
[2] When he restores the produce. It is assumed that he had mixed the deposited wares with his own, and cannot know what proportion of his fellow's wares have perished by mice and other natural causes.
[3] He may reduce it by one-twentieth. App. II, D.   [4] He may reduce it by one-tenth.
[5] Reducing it by the same proportion each year.
[6] i.e. twice the quantity does not mean twice the number of mice.

8. With wine he may exact of him one-sixth. R. Judah says: One-fifth. He may exact of him three *logs* in every hundred *logs* of oil—one *log* and a half for sediment and one *log* and a half for absorption. If the oil was refined, he may not exact of him aught for sediment; if the jars were old he may not exact of him aught for absorption. R. Judah says: Also if a man sells to his fellow refined oil over the period of a year, the buyer must undertake to submit to a reduction of one *log* and a half in every hundred *logs* because of sediment.[1]

9. If a man left a jar in his fellow's keeping and the owner had not assigned it a special place, and it was moved about and broken; if it was broken while he[2] was handling it he is liable if he moved it for his own sake, but he is not liable if he moved it for the jar's sake. But if it was broken after he had put it in its place,[3] whether he removed it for his own sake or for the jar's sake, he is not liable. If the owner had assigned it a special place, and the other moved it about and it was broken, whether it was broken while he was handling it or after he had put it in place, he is liable if he moved it for his own sake, but he is not liable if he moved it for the jar's sake.

10. If a man left money in his fellow's keeping, and his fellow bound it up and hung it over his back, or delivered it to his son or his daughter that were minors, or shut it up, but not properly [and it was lost], he is liable, since he did not guard it after the manner of guardians. But if he guarded it after the manner of guardians [and it was lost] he is not liable.

11. If a man left money in the keeping of a money-changer and it was sealed up, he may not make use of it and, therefore, if it was lost he is not answerable for it; if the money was loose he may make use of it and, therefore, if it was lost he is answerable for it. If it was left in the keeping of a householder, he may not make use of it whether it was sealed up or loose; if, therefore, it was lost he is not answerable for it. A shopkeeper[4] is to be deemed a householder. So R. Meir. R. Judah says: A shopkeeper is to be deemed a money-changer.[5]

12. If a man put to his own use what had been left in his keeping, the School of Shammai say: He is at a disadvantage whether its value rises or falls.[6] And the School of Hillel say: [He must restore the deposit] at the same value as when he put it to his own use. R. Akiba says: At its value when claimed. If a man had expressed his intention of putting the deposit to his own use, the School of Shammai say: He is forthwith liable.[7] And the School of Hillel say: He is not liable until he has put it to his use, for it is written, *If he have not put his hand unto his neighbour's goods*;[8] thus if he tilted the jar and took from it a quarter-*log* [of wine] and the jar was then broken,[9] he need only repay [the value of the] quarter-*log* [of wine]; but if he lifted it up[10] and took from it a quarter-*log*[11] and the jar was then broken, he must repay the value of the whole.

[1] Though the buyer only stipulated for ordinary oil, as the year passes the oil kept by the dealer automatically clears and becomes more refined; the buyer thus receives refined oil and the dealer retains the sediment.   [2] The guardian.

[3] Where the guardian deemed it in reasonable safety.

[4] In what concerns money deposited with him: he may not make use of it.

[5] Cf. Meil. 6⁵.

[6] If it fell he must repay at its original worth; if it rose, he must pay at its increased worth.

[7] If it was lost, even if he had not yet made use of it; because it is written (Ex. 22⁹), 'For any *word* (R.V. 'matter') of trespass': he is liable even if he spoke of using it.

[8] Ex. 22⁸. Some texts omit this proof-text; and some omit the following 'thus'.

[9] Even through no fault of his.

[10] The deliberate act of acquiring for his use.   [11] Or even if he took nothing at all.

4. 1. Gold acquires[1] silver, but silver does not acquire gold;[2] copper acquires silver, but silver does not acquire copper. Disused coins acquire current coins, but current coins do not acquire disused coins. Unminted metal acquires minted metal, but minted metal does not acquire unminted metal. Movable property acquires coined money, but coined money does not acquire movable property.[3] Movable property acquires other movable property.

2. Thus if the buyer had drawn fruit into his possession from the seller but had not [yet] paid him money, neither may retract; but if he had paid him money but had not [yet] drawn the fruit into his possession from the seller, either may retract. Howbeit they have said, 'He that exacted punishment from the generation of the Flood[4] and the generation of the Dispersion[5] will exact punishment from him that does not abide by his spoken word'. R. Simeon says: He that has the money[6] has the upper hand.

3. [An overcharge of] four pieces of silver[7] out of the twenty-four pieces of silver that make up a *sela*, or one-sixth of the purchase-price, counts as defrauding.[8] Until what time may he [that is defrauded] retract? Time enough to show [his purchase] to a merchant or to a kinsman. R. Tarfon taught at Lydda that [nothing less than an overcharge of] eight pieces of silver out of a *sela*, or one-third of the purchase-price, counts as defrauding, and the merchants of Lydda rejoiced. He said to them, 'But he [that is defrauded] may retract any time within a whole day'. They answered, '[Rather] leave us as we were, Rabbi Tarfon!' and they reverted to the ruling of the Sages.

4. The law against defrauding applies to buyer and seller alike; as the private person[9] has the right to retract because of defrauding, so has the merchant the right. R. Judah says: The merchant has not the right. He that has been imposed upon has the upper hand: if he wished he could say, 'Give me back [all] my money', or 'Give me back that of which thou hast defrauded me'.

5. How defective may a *sela* be and not fall within the rule of defrauding? R. Meir says: Four *issars*, one *issar* to every *denar*.[10] R. Judah says: Four

---

[1] The principle here implied is that the essential element constituting valid purchase is not the receipt of payment by the seller from the buyer, but the buyer's 'drawing' into his possession the article to be purchased; therefore as soon as he has 'drawn' the article he is answerable for it, and if it was destroyed the same moment, although he had not paid money for it, he is still liable to the seller for its value. Therefore it is the transfer of the *commodity* to the one party which gives the other party title to the money to be paid, and not the transfer of the money which gives title to the commodity. This the Mishnah succinctly states by the formula 'the commodity acquires, or gives title to, the purchasing medium; and the purchasing medium does not give title to the commodity'. Consequently the problem arises, in an exchange of coins (gold for silver, &c.), which is the commodity whose 'drawing' makes the purchase valid, and which is the medium of payment whose 'drawing', i.e. passing into the other's possession, does not constitute the essential element in the exchange? The answer is: The less current and less convenient medium constitutes the 'commodity' and the more current and the more convenient medium constitutes the purchasing medium. Here the Mishnah lays down that silver coins are more 'current', an easier purchasing medium, than gold or copper coins, and, obviously, minted metal than unminted metal, and current than non-current coinage.
[2] The reading in the Mishnah assumed by the Gemara of the Jerusalem Talmud transposes the positions of gold and silver. Such is stated to have been Rabbi's teaching in his younger days. Cf. p. 442, n. 6. [3] Some texts here add awkwardly: 'This is the general rule.'
[4] Gen. 6[13].   [5] Gen. 11[9].
[6] Whether it is the seller who has received payment or the buyer who has not parted with his money.   [7] Referring to the coin *maah*, the smallest silver coin current. App. II, A.
[8] Which is forbidden in Lev. 25[14]: 'Ye shall not *wrong* one another' in buying and selling.
[9] The ordinary purchaser.
[10] If it lacks one twenty-fourth of its weight. See App. II, A.

pondions,[1] one *pondion* to every *denar*. R. Simeon says: Eight *pondions*,[2] two *pondions* to every *denar*.

6. Until what time may he [that is defrauded] return the coin? In large towns, until he has had time to show it to a money-changer; and in villages, until the eve of the Sabbath. If he [that had given it in exchange] recognizes it again, he ought to accept it back even after twelve months, though the other has no valid claim against him, but only a cause for complaint. It may be given as Second Tithe money[3] without scruple, for he is but an evil-souled person [that would refuse it].

7. Four pieces of silver[4] count as defrauding; two pieces of silver suffice in a claim [for repayment] and one *perutah's* worth in an admission of indebtedness.[5] In five cases is a *perutah* prescribed: in an admission of indebtedness the admission must be to [not less than] a *perutah's* worth; a woman may be betrothed[6] with a *perutah's* worth; he that derives a *perutah's* worth of benefit from what belongs to the Temple is subject to the law of Sacrilege;[7] if a man found lost property[8] of a *perutah's* worth he must proclaim it; if a man robbed[9] his fellow of a *perutah's* worth and swore [falsely] to him [and would make restitution] he must take it and give it to him even [if his fellow had gone] as far as Media.

8. In five cases is the [Added] Fifth[10] prescribed: he[11] that consumes Heave-offering,[12] Heave-offering of Tithe,[13] Heave-offering of Tithe of *demai*-produce,[14] Dough-offering[15] or First-fruits,[16] must add the fifth [when he makes restitution]; he that redeems [the fruit of] a fourth-year planting[17] or his Second Tithe[18] must add the fifth; he that redeems what he has dedicated[19] must add the fifth; he that derives a *perutah's* worth of benefit from what belongs to the Temple[20] must add the fifth; if a man robbed his fellow[21] of a *perutah's* worth and swore [falsely] to him, he must add the fifth.

9. To these the law against defrauding does not apply:[22] [to trafficking with] bondmen, bills of indebtedness, immovable property, and what belongs to the Temple; nor do the rules of twofold restitution and fourfold or fivefold restitution[23] apply to them. An unpaid guardian need not take an oath, and a paid guardian need not make restitution. R. Simeon says: The law against defrauding applies to the Hallowed Things which must be replaced [if damaged or lost], but not to those which need not be replaced.[24] R. Judah says: The law against defrauding does not apply when a man sells a scroll of the Law, or cattle, or pearls. But they said to him: They have excepted naught save these.[25]

10. Like as the law against defrauding applies to buying and selling, so does it apply to spoken words. A man may not say, 'How much is this thing?' if he does not wish to buy it. If a man had repented they may not

[1] If it lacks one-twelfth of its weight.
[2] i.e. it is accepted as valid currency even if it is only five-sixths of its proper weight.
[3] See M.Sh. 1².   [4] As an overcharge for what was bought for a *sela*.   [5] See Shebu. 6¹.
[6] Kidd. 1¹.   [7] See p. 573, n. 2.   [8] See above, 2¹ff.   [9] B.K. 9⁵.
[10] In addition to the actual value.   [11] Not being a priest.   [12] Ter. 6¹.
[13] The tenth of his Tithe which the levite gives to a priest. Num. 18²⁶.
[14] But cf. Dem. 1². The present ruling is that of R. Meir.   [15] Hall. 1⁹.
[16] Bikk. 2¹.   [17] M.Sh. 5³.   [18] M.Sh. 4³.
[19] Lev. 27¹⁹.   [20] Lev. 5¹⁶.   [21] B.K. 9⁷.
[22] Because the law as stated (Lev. 25¹⁴) refers only to goods bought 'of thy neighbour's hand', which excludes land, and slaves (which are sold on the same conditions as land—p. 321, n. 19), and bonds which have no value of themselves; and Temple property is excluded since Lev. 25¹⁴ says, 'Ye shall not wrong any man his brother'.
[23] See B.K. 7¹ff.   [24] See p. 341, n. 5–6.
[25] The four cited at the beginning of the paragraph.

say to him, 'Remember thy former deeds'; if a man was descended from proselytes they may not say to him, 'Remember the deeds of thy fathers'; for it is written, *And a stranger thou shalt not wrong nor shalt thou oppress him.*[1]

11. Produce may not be mixed together with other produce, even fresh produce with fresh, and, needless to say, fresh with old; howbeit they have permitted strong wine to be mixed with weak, since this improves it. Wine lees may not be mixed with wine, but the buyer may be given lees that come from the same wine that he has bought. A man whose wine is mixed with water may not sell it in a shop unless he has told the buyer [that it is mixed]; and he may not sell it to a merchant even if he has told him, since he [would buy it] only to deceive therewith. In any place where they are accustomed to put water into wine, they may do so.

12. A merchant may buy from five threshing-floors and put the produce into a single store-chamber; or from five wine-presses and put the wine into a single store-jar,[2] provided that there was no intention to mix them [for purpose of fraud].[3] R. Judah says: A shopkeeper may not distribute parched corn or nuts to children, for so he accustoms them to come [only] to him. But the Sages permit it. And he may not lower the price. But the Sages say: [If he does,] let him be remembered with gratitude. He may not sift crushed beans. So Abba Saul. But the Sages permit it. But they agree that he should not sift them [only] at the entry of the store-chamber,[4] since so he would be a deceiver of the eye. He should not bedizen that which he sells,[5] whether human-kind, or cattle, or utensils.

5. 1. What is usury (*neshek*) and what is increase (*tarbith*)?[6] It is usury (*neshek*) when a man lends a *sela*[7] for five *denars*, or two *seahs* of wheat for three;[8] because he is a 'usurer' (*noshek*).[9] And what is increase? When a man increases [his gains] in [trafficking with] produce. How? If one man bought wheat [from another] at a golden *denar*[10] the *kor* when such was the market price, and then wheat rose to thirty [silver] *denars* [the *kor*], and he said, 'Deliver me my wheat since I would sell it to buy wine with the price', and the other said, 'Let thy wheat be reckoned to me at thirty *denars*, and thus thou hast now a claim on me for wine [to that value]!'— although he has no wine.

2. The creditor may not dwell without charge in the debtor's courtyard or hire it from him at a reduced rate, since that counts as usury. A man may increase rent-charge but not purchase value. Thus if the owner hired his courtyard to a tenant and said, 'If thou payest me now it is thine for ten *selas* a year, but if [thou payest] month by month it will be one *sela* a month', this is permitted; but if he sold him his field and said, 'If thou payest me now it is thine for 1,000 *zuz*, but if at the time of threshing it will be 1,200 *zuz*', this is forbidden.

3. If a man sold his field and was given a part of the price and said to the buyer, 'Pay me [the rest of] the price when thou wilt, and then take what is thine', this is forbidden. If a man lent another money on the security

1 Ex. 22[21], using the same term as in Lev. 25[14].
2 *Pithos*. Cf. R.Sh. 3[7]; Kel. 3[6].   3 Bad produce with good.
4 Or 'at the mouth of the bin'.   5 But cf. Arak. 6[5].
6 The terms used in Lev. 25[36]. Cf. v. 37, 'nor give him victuals for increase', interpreted as exploiting the changes in price of market produce.   7 Four *denars*.
8 Some texts add: 'this is forbidden'.   9 Lit. 'because he bites'.
10 25 silver *denars*.

of his field and said to him, 'If thou dost not pay me within three years it shall be mine', then it becomes his. Thus used Boethus b. Zunin[1] to do with the consent of the Sages.

4. None may set up a shopkeeper on the condition of receiving half the profit,[2] or give him money to buy produce therewith on the condition of receiving half the profit, unless he is paid his wage as a labourer. None may set [another's] hens [to hatch out his eggs] on the condition of sharing the profit, or give another calves or foals to rear on the condition of sharing half the estimated loss or gain, unless he is paid his wage for his labour and the cost of the food. But a man may undertake[3] the care of calves and foals in return for half the profits, and rear them until they reach the third of their growth; and asses, until they can bear a burden.

5. A cow or an ass, and whatsoever works and eats,[4] may be put out to rear with the condition of sharing in the profits. Where the custom is to share offspring immediately at birth, they do so; and where the custom is [first] to rear them, they do so. Rabban Simeon b. Gamaliel says: A calf may be put out to rear[5] with its dam and a foal with its dam.[6] A tenant may offer increased rent in exchange for a loan to improve his field,[7] without fearing that this is of the nature of usury.

6. A flock may not be accepted from an Israelite on 'iron' terms[8] since that counts as usury, but it may be accepted from a gentile. Money may be borrowed from gentiles on usury and lent to them on usury, and the same applies with a resident alien.[9] An Israelite may lend the money of a gentile[10] with the knowledge of the gentile, but [if it was money which the gentile had borrowed from an Israelite] he may not lend it with the knowledge of the Israelite.

7. No bargain may be made over produce before its market-price is known. After[11] its market-price is known a bargain may be made, for even if one dealer has not the produce another will have it. If he was the first to reap his crop[12] he may make a bargain with his fellow over grain stacked [on the threshing-floor], or over grapes in their harvesting-baskets, or over olives in the vat; or over the clay-balls of the potter, or over lime so soon as the limestone is sunk in the kiln. Moreover a bargain may be made over manure at any time in the year. R. Jose says: No bargain may be made over manure unless the seller has it on the dungheap. But the Sages permit it. A bargain may be made [to pay for wares] at the cheapest rate [that

---

[1] A. Zar. 5[2].
[2] The shopkeeper must repay the cost of the goods plus half his gains.
[3] The contract not implying liability in case of death or loss.
[4] Earns its keep. See above, 2[7]. In this case the contract is permissible since, instead of wage, he that takes charge of them has the benefit of their labour.
[5] On the condition of sharing the estimated loss or gain.
[6] Since the dams can earn their keep.
[7] *A* leases a field to *B* for 10 *kors* of wheat a year; *B* asks then for a loan of 100 *zuz* in order to manure the field and undertakes in return to give 15 *kors* of wheat a year as rental.
[8] This is a contract to tend another's flock and to share equally with the other in the wool, milk, and young; but if any of the flock are lost or die he that tends them is answerable for their full value. Cf. Bekh. 2[4]. See App. I. 41, *Ṣon barzel*.
[9] A gentile allowed to live among Jews on condition that he abstained from idolatry, blasphemy, murder, theft, incest, and from eating flesh with the blood in it, and on condition that he submitted to the jurisdiction of the Jewish courts. He is also defined as one who, in the presence of three Associates (cf. Dem. 2[3]), pledges himself to abstain from idolatry.
[10] Which he has received from him on usury; i.e. he may transfer this usurious loan to another Israelite, or he may be the intermediary in such a loan between the gentile and his fellow-Israelite.   [11] Certain texts omit this sentence.
[12] And so has produce in hand before the market-price is known.

prevails at the time of delivery]. R. Judah says: Even if the bargain was not made [to pay for wares] at the cheapest rate, he may say, 'Give me the wares at such a price, or give me back my money'.

8. The owner may lend his tenants wheat to be repaid in kind, if it is for sowing, but not if it is for food; for Rabban Gamaliel used to lend his tenants wheat to be repaid in kind when it was for sowing; and if he lent it when the price was high and it afterward fell, or when it was low and it afterward rose, he used to take wheat back from them at the lower rate— not because such was the rule,[1] but because he was minded to apply to himself the more stringent ruling.

9. A man may not say to his fellow, "Lend me a *kor* of wheat and I will repay thee at threshing-time',[2] but he may say, 'Lend it to me until my son comes', or 'until I find the key'. But Hillel used to forbid this. Moreover Hillel used to say: A woman may not lend a loaf of bread to her neighbour unless she determines its value in money, lest wheat should rise in price and they be found partakers in usury.

10. A man may say to his fellow, 'Help me to weed and I will help thee to weed', or 'Help me to hoe and I will help thee to hoe'. But he may not say, 'Help me to weed and I will help thee to hoe,' or 'Help me to hoe and I will help thee to weed'. All days of the dry season are accounted alike and all days of the rainy season are accounted alike. A man may not say to another, 'Help me to plough in the dry season and I will help thee to plough in the rainy season'. Rabban Gamaliel says: There is usury that is paid in advance and usury that is paid afterward. Thus if a man purposed to borrow from another and made him a present and said, 'That thou mayest lend me money', this is usury paid in advance. If a man borrowed from another and repaid it to him, and then sent him a present and said, 'This is for thy money of which thou hadst not the use while it was with me', this is usury that is paid afterward. R. Simeon says: There may be usury [paid in] words: a man may not say to his creditor, 'Know thou that such a man has come from such a place'.[3]

11. These transgress a negative command: the lender, the borrower, the guarantor, and the witnesses. And the Sages say: The scribe also. They transgress the command *Thou shalt not give* [*him thy money upon usury*],[4] and *Take thou no usury of him*,[5] and *Thou shalt not be to him as a creditor*, and *Neither shall ye lay upon him usury*,[6] and *Thou shalt not put a stumbling-block before the blind, but thou shalt fear thy God. I am the Lord*.[7]

6. 1. If a man hired craftsmen and they deceived each other, they have no valid claim against each other, but only cause for complaint. If a man hired an ass-driver or a waggon-driver to bring litter-bearers and pipers for a bride or for a corpse, or labourers to take his flax out of steep, or any matter that will not suffer delay, and they retracted, if it was a place where none others [could be hired for a like wage] he may hire others at their charges or he may deceive them.

2. If a man hired craftsmen and they retracted, they are at a disadvantage;[8]

---

[1] *Halakah.* App. I. 11.
[2] When the price may have increased, and he thus pays 'increase'. He must have the prospect of repaying with wheat at the current cost, though it may not, at the moment, be available.
[3] Giving information of value in consideration of receiving a loan.
[4] Lev. 25[37].   [5] Lev. 25[36].   [6] Ex. 22[25].   [7] Lev. 19[14].
[8] If they contracted to do a piece of work for 20 *zuz* and retracted after doing half of it,

if the householder retracted, he is at a disadvantage. Whosoever changes [the conditions[1] of a contract] is at a disadvantage, and whosoever retracts [from an agreement] is at a disadvantage.

3. If a man hired an ass to drive it through hill country and he drove it through the valley, or to drive it through the valley and he drove it through hill country, even though the distance was alike ten miles, if the ass died the hirer is liable. If a man hired an ass and it went blind or was pressed into the king's service, he may say to the owner, 'Here before thee is what is thine'; but if it died or was lamed, he must provide him with another ass. If a man hired an ass to drive it through hill country and he drove it through the valley, if it slipped he is not liable, but if it was overcome by heat he is liable. If he hired it to drive it through the valley and he drove it through hill country, if it slipped he is liable, but if it was overcome by heat he is not liable; though if this was by reason of the ascent he is liable.

4. If a man hired a heifer to plough in hill country and he ploughed in the valley and the ploughshare was broken, he is not liable; but if he hired it to plough in the valley and he ploughed in hill country and the ploughshare was broken, he is liable. [If he hired it] to thresh pulse and he threshed grain [and the heifer slipped and was injured] he is not liable; but if [he hired it] to thresh grain and he threshed pulse, he is liable, since pulse is more slippery.

5. If a man hired an ass to carry wheat and he used it to carry [a like weight of] barley,[2] [if the ass was injured] he is liable; if [he hired it] to carry grain and he used it to carry [a like weight of] chopped straw, he is liable, since the greater bulk is more difficult to carry. If [he hired it] to carry a *lethek*[3] of wheat and it carried a *lethek* of barley, he is not liable; but if he increased the weight he is liable. What increase in weight renders him liable? Symmachos says in the name of R. Meir: One *seah* for a camel and three *kabs*[4] for an ass.

6. All craftsmen[5] are accounted paid guardians;[6] but all that have said, 'Take what is thine and give me money',[7] are accounted unpaid guardians. If one man said to another, 'Keep that for me and I will keep this for thee', he is accounted a paid guardian; but if [he said], 'Keep this for me', and the other said, 'Put it down before me', he is accounted an unpaid guardian.

7. If a man gave a loan and took a pledge he is accounted a paid guardian.[8] R. Judah says: If he lent him money he is accounted an unpaid guardian; if he lent him produce[9] he is accounted a paid guardian. Abba Saul says: A man may hire out a poor man's pledge[10] and so by degrees reduce the debt, for so he is like to one that restores lost property.[11]

---

and for the other half he had to hire other labourers at 12 *zuz*, the first labourers receive not 10 *zuz* but only 8; so, too, if he was able to hire cheaper labourers, costing for the other half only 8 *zuz*, the first labourers receive not 12 *zuz* but only 10, at the rate originally stipulated. 　　　　　　　　　　　　　　　　　[1] Cf. examples in B.K. 9[4].

[2] Which is bulkier. 　　　　[3] 15 *seahs* or half a *kor*. 　　　　[4] Half a *seah*.

[5] Doing work on others' material but in their own premises (cf. B.K. 9[2]).

[6] He must make restitution in case of loss or damage, and he can retain the object as a pledge until he is paid for his labour.

[7] Indicating that the work is finished and that it is the owner's responsibility to remove it; therefore the craftsman is no longer answerable for its loss.

[8] He is responsible for the safekeeping of the pledge.

[9] R. Judah holds that the lender is thus saved the loss from decay which he would otherwise suffer, and that this advantage is equivalent to receiving hire for the pledge's safekeeping.

[10] If the wear and tear of the object pledged is less than the profits accruing.

[11] He is serving the interests of the other.

8. If a man moved a jar from place to place and broke it, whether he is a paid guardian or an unpaid guardian he may take an oath [that it was not through his neglect, and so be quit of liability]. R. Eliezer says: [I, too, have heard that] in either case he may take an oath; but I wonder whether in either case the oath is valid!

7. 1. If a man hired labourers and bade them to work early or to work late, he has no right to compel them to do so where the custom is not to work early or not to work late; where the custom is to give them their food he should give it them, and where the custom is to provide them with sweetstuff he should provide it. Everything should follow local use.[1] It once happened that R. Johanan b. Matthias said to his son, 'Go and hire labourers for us'. He went and undertook to give them their food. When he came to his father, his father said to him, 'My son, even if thou preparest them a banquet like Solomon's in his time thou wilt not have fulfilled thy duty towards them, for they are sons of Abraham, Isaac, and Jacob. But, rather, before they begin the work go and say to them, On condition that I am not bound to give you more than bread and pulse only'. Rabban Simeon b. Gamaliel says: It was not necessary to speak thus, for everything should follow local use.

2. These may eat [of the fruits among which they labour] by virtue of what is enjoined in the Law:[2] he that labours on what is still growing after the work is finished,[3] and he that labours on what is already gathered before the work is finished;[4] [this applies only] to what grows from the soil. These are they that may not eat: he that labours on what is still growing while the work is still unfinished, and he that labours on what is already gathered after the work is finished, and [he may not eat] of what does not grow from the soil.[5]

3. If he laboured with his hands but not with his feet, or with his feet but not with his hands, or even with his shoulders only, he still may eat. R. Jose b. R. Judah says: Only if he labours both with his hands and with his feet.

4. If he worked among figs he may not eat grapes, and if among grapes he may not eat figs; but he may refrain until he reaches the best fruits and then eat. In no case have they said [that he may eat] save during the time of his labour, but, on the principle of restoring lost property to its owner,[6] they have said: Labourers may eat as they go from one furrow to another or as they return from the winepress; and an ass [may eat] while it is unloading.

5. A labourer may eat cucumbers even to a *denar's* worth, and dates even to a *denar's* worth. R. Eleazar b. Hisma says: A labourer may not eat more than the value of his hire. But the Sages permit it, yet they would teach a man not to be so gluttonous as to close the door against himself.

6. A man may exact terms[7] for himself and for his son or daughter that

---

[1] The Gemara (86a, 86b) suggests that there should follow here: 'If, in a place where the custom was to give them their food, he specially undertook to give them food, this implies that he will give them fine food'.   [2] Deut. 23[24, 25].

[3] At the harvesting of the crops.

[4] Since the produce is afterwards liable to Tithes (Cf. Maas. 1[2ff.].)

[5] During work upon flesh, milk, cheese, and the like.

[6] Hunger and weariness in the labourer would spell loss to the householder.

[7] i.e. stipulate for money compensation against an agreement to refrain from exercising the right of eating fruit.

are of age, and for his bondman or bondwoman that are of age, and for his wife, since these have understanding; but he may not exact terms for his son or daughter that are not of age, or for his bondman or bondwoman that are not of age, or for his cattle, since these have no understanding.

7. If a man hired labourers to work among his fourth-year plantings,[1] they may not eat thereof; if he had not told them [that they were fourth-year plantings] he must first redeem the fruit and then suffer them to eat. If his fig-cakes broke up or his jars burst open,[2] they may not consume aught from these. Unless he had told them [that they were still liable to Tithes] he must first set apart Tithes and then suffer them to eat.

8. They that guard [gathered] produce may eat thereof according to the customs of the country, but not by virtue of what is enjoined in the Law. There are four kinds of guardian: an unpaid guardian, a borrower, a paid guardian, and a hirer. An unpaid guardian may take an oath[3] in every case [of loss or damage and be quit of liability]; a borrower must make restitution in every case; a paid guardian or a hirer may take an oath if the beast was lamed or driven away or dead, but he must make restitution if it was lost or stolen.

9. If one wolf [attacked the flock] it does not count as unavoidable accident,[4] but two wolves count as unavoidable accident. R. Judah says: Such time as wolves come in packs even a single wolf counts as unavoidable accident. Two dogs do not count as unavoidable accident. Jaddua the Babylonian says in the name of R. Meir: If [two dogs came] from one direction they do not count as unavoidable accident, but if [they came] from two directions they count as unavoidable accident. A brigand counts as unavoidable accident. A lion or a bear or a leopard or a panther or a serpent counts as unavoidable accident. When? When they come of themselves; but if a man himself took his flock to a place of wild animals or brigands, they do not count as unavoidable accident.

10. If a beast died a natural death this counts as unavoidable accident, but not if it died of cruel treatment. If it was led up to the top of a crag and it fell down and died, this does not count as unavoidable accident. An unpaid guardian may exact as a condition that he shall be exempt from taking an oath, and a borrower from making restitution, and a paid guardian and a hirer from taking an oath or from making restitution.

11. If a man exacts any condition contrary to what is enjoined in the Law,[5] his condition is void. Any condition that is dependent on an antecedent act is void; and any condition that can in the end be fulfilled and was laid down as a condition from the beginning, such a condition is valid.

8. 1. If a man borrowed a cow together with the service of its owner, or hired its owner together with the cow, or if he borrowed the service of the owner or hired him, and afterward borrowed the cow, and the cow died, he is not liable, for it is written, *If the owner thereof be with it he shall not make it good.*[6] But if he first borrowed the cow and afterward borrowed or hired the service of the owner, and the cow died, he is liable, for it is

---

[1] See Lev. 19²⁴. App. II. 32, *Orlah.*
[2] And Tithes had not been given from the figs or the wine, and he needed craftsmen to re-press the figs, or re-seal the jars.
[3] That the mishap was through no neglect of his.
[4] *Force majeure*, for which no blame attaches to the guardian.
[5] Cf. Ket. 9¹; B.B. 8⁵.   [6] Ex. 22¹⁵.

written, *The owner thereof not being with it he shall surely make restitution.*[1]

2. If a man borrowed a cow, and borrowed it for half a day and hired it for half a day, or borrowed it for one day and hired it for the next; or if he borrowed one cow and hired another, and the cow died—if he that lent the cow says, 'It was the borrowed cow that died', [or] 'On the day when it was borrowed it died', [or] 'During the time when it was borrowed it died', and the other says, 'I do not know', he is liable.[2] If the hirer says, 'It is the hired one that died', [or] 'On the day when it was hired it died', [or] 'During the time when it was hired it died', and the other says, 'I do not know', he is not liable.[3] If the one says, 'It was borrowed', and the other says, 'It was hired', the hirer must take an oath that it was the hired one that died. If the one says, 'I do not know', and the other says, 'I do not know', they share in the loss.

3. If a man borrowed a cow and the owner sent it by the hand of his son or his bondman or his agent, or by the hand of the borrower's son or bondman or agent, and it died [on the way], the borrower is not liable. But if the borrower said, 'Send it to me by the hand of my son or my bondman or my agent, or by the hand of thy son or thy bondman or thy agent', or if the lender said, 'I am sending it to thee by the hand of my son or my bondman or my agent', or 'by the hand of thy son or thy bondman or thy agent', and the borrower said, 'Send it so', and he sent it, and it died, the borrower is liable. So, too, when the cow is returned.

4. If a man took a cow in exchange for an ass, and it brought forth young, (so, too, if a man sold his bondwoman and she brought forth a child), and the one said, 'It was born before I sold her', and the other said, 'It was born after I bought her', let them share the value of what was born. If a man had two bondmen, one large and the other small, or two fields, one large and the other small, [and he sold one of them], and the buyer said, 'It was the large one that I bought', and the other said 'I do not know', the buyer can rightly claim the large one. If the seller said, 'I sold thee the small one', and the other said, 'I do not know', he may take only the small one. If the one said, 'It was the large one', and the other said, 'It was the small one', the seller must take an oath that it was the small one that he sold. If the one said, 'I do not know', and the other said, 'I do not know', let them share the difference in value.

5. If a man sold his olive-trees as firewood and [before the other had uprooted them] they bore fruit that gave less than a quarter-*log* of oil to a *seah*,[4] this belongs to the [new] owner of the olive-trees. If they bore fruit that gave a quarter-*log* of oil [or more] to the *seah*, and the one said, 'It was my trees that produced it', and the other said, 'It was my land that produced it', let them share the produce. If a flood washed away a man's olive-trees and set them in the midst of his fellow's field [where they bore fruit], and the one said, 'It was my trees that produced it', and the other said, 'It was my land that produced it', let them share the produce.

6. If a man let a house to his fellow in the rainy season,[5] he cannot make

---

[1] Ex. 22[14]. The owner must be with the beast from the first moment of its use if he is to be responsible for it.
[2] See above, 7[8], 'a borrower must make restitution in every case'.
[3] See above, 7[8]. He is liable only it if is lost or stolen.   [4] App. II. 4.
[5] Without determining the length of tenure.

him leave it [during the time] from the Feast [of Tabernacles] to Passover; and during the summer [he must give him warning[1] before] thirty days; and in large cities, whether it is during the rainy season or the summer [he must give warning before] twelve months; with shops, alike in large cities or small towns [he must give the tenant warning before] twelve months. Rabban Simeon b. Gamaliel says: If it is a shop occupied by bakers or dyers [he must give warning before] three years.[2]

7. If a man let a house to his fellow he must provide it with a door, a bolt, a lock, and whatsoever is the work of a craftsman; but whatsoever is not the work of a craftsman the tenant must make himself. The manure [left by strange cattle in a hired courtyard] belongs to the owner of the house; and the hirer can claim only the refuse of the oven or stove.

8. If a man let a house to his fellow by the year and the year was made a leap-year, the advantage falls to the tenant. If he let it by the month and the year was made a leap-year, the advantage falls to the owner. It once happened in Sepphoris that a person hired a bath-house from his fellow at 'twelve golden *denars* a year, one *denar* a month', and the case came before Rabban Simeon b. Gamaliel and before R. Jose. They said: Let them share the advantage of the added month.[3]

9. If a man let a house to his fellow and it fell down, the owner must build him another house. If it was small he may not make it larger; and if large he may not make it smaller; if it was a single house he may not make it into two, and if two he may not make it into one. He may not take from the number of windows or add to them save by common consent.

9. 1. If a man leased a field[4] from his fellow and the custom of the place was to cut the crops, he must cut them; if the custom was to uproot them he must uproot them; if the custom was to plough after reaping, he must plough. Everything should follow local use. Like as they share in the grain so they share in the chopped straw and the stubble; like as they share in the wine so they share in the [dead] branches and the reed-props; and both parties must [at the outset] provide [their share of] the reed-props.

2. If a man leased a field from his fellow and it was an irrigated field or a tree-plantation, and the spring dried up or the trees were cut down, he may not give less than his agreed rental. But if he had said, 'Lease me this irrigated field, or this tree-plantation', and the spring dried up or the trees were cut down, he may give less than the prescribed rental.

3. If a man leased a field from his fellow and he let it lie fallow, they assess how much it was likely to have yielded and he must pay the owner accordingly, for thus such a lease prescribes: 'If I suffer the land to lie fallow and do not till it I will pay thee at the rate of its highest yield'.

4. If a man leased a field from his fellow and he was not minded to weed it, but said, 'What concern is it of thine, since I pay thee the agreed rental?' they do not listen to him, for the owner can say to him, 'To-morrow thou wilt perchance leave it and it will bring me forth naught save weeds'.

5. If a man leased a field from his fellow and it was not fruitful, and there was only produce enough to make a heap, he must still cultivate it. R.

---

[1] Of expiry of tenure.
[2] Since such tradesmen are accustomed to grant long credit.
[3] The tenant to pay half a golden *denar* for the thirteenth month.
[4] Instead of rental in money the lessee gives the owner a fourth or fifth share of the produce or such share as is agreed upon.

Judah said: What manner of measure is 'a heap'!—but, rather, [he must cultivate it] even if it yields only as much grain as was sown there.[1]

6. If a man leased a field from his fellow and the locusts devoured the crop or it was blasted [by tempest], if it was a mishap widespread in that region he may give less than the agreed rental, but if it was not a mishap widespread in that region he may not give less than the agreed rental. R. Judah says: If he had leased it from him for a return in money, in neither case may he give less than the agreed rental.

7. If a man leased a field from his fellow in return for ten *kors* of wheat a year and it produced bad wheat, he may pay him out of this crop; but if the wheat was good he may not say, 'I will buy other wheat for thee from the market', but he must pay him from the crop of the field.

8. If a man leased a field from his fellow with the condition that he sowed barley, he may not sow wheat, but if with the condition that he sowed wheat he may sow barley. But Rabban b. Gamaliel forbids this. If it was with the condition that he sowed grain he may not sow pulse; but if with the condition that he sowed pulse he may sow grain.[2] But Rabban Simeon b. Gamaliel forbids this.

9. If a man leased a field from his fellow for but a few years he may not sow flax,[3] and he has no right to cut beams from the sycamore-tree. But if he leased it for seven years he may sow flax the first year and he has a right to cut beams from the sycamore-tree.[4]

10. If a man leased a field from his fellow for 'a week of years'[5] for 700 *zuz*, the Seventh Year is included[6] in the number; but if he leased it from him for 'seven years' for 700 *zuz*, the Seventh Year is not included[7] in the number.

11. He that is hired[8] by the day may exact his wages any time during the [ensuing] night. He that is hired by the night may exact his wages any time during the [ensuing] day. He that is hired by the hour may exact his wages any time during that day and the [ensuing] night. If he was hired by the week, or the month, or the year, or the week of years, and his time expired during the day, he may exact his wages any time during the rest of that day, and if it expired during the night he may exact his wages any time during the rest of that night and the [ensuing] day.

12. The laws *In his day thou shalt give him his hire*,[9] and *The wages of a hired servant shall not abide with thee all night until the morning*[10] apply alike to the hire of a man or of a beast or of utensils. When? When he has laid claim to it; but if he had not laid claim to it the hirer does not thereby[11] commit transgression. If he gave him a draft on a shopkeeper or money-changer he does not thereby commit transgression. If a hireling [claimed his wages] within the set time he may take an oath[12] and receive his wages; but if the set time had passed he may not take an oath and receive his wages;

---

[1] Which is reckoned as one forty-fifth of the average yield. Cf. Peah 5[1].
[2] Since this exhausts the soil less than does barley, and grain exhausts it less than pulse (leguminous produce). Some texts here reverse the positions of grain and pulse.
[3] Which adversely affects the soil's fertility for a space of seven years.
[4] Which after cutting down could reach its former growth in seven years.
[5] See Dan. 9[24ff].
[6] And the tenant may claim no reduction although the land may not be sown or reaped by him that year, and what grows is reckoned ownerless produce. See tractate 'Shebiith'.
[7] And his tenure extends to the eighth year.   [8] See Lev. 19[13].
[9] Deut. 24[15].   [10] Lev. 19[13].
[11] By delaying payment until after the following morning.   [12] See Shebu. 7[1].

but if witnesses testify that he had claimed his wages[1] at the set time [and was not paid], he may take an oath and receive his wages. The law *In his day thou shalt give him his hire* applies also to the resident alien,[2] but not the law, *The wages of a hired servant shall not abide with thee all night until the morning*.[3]

13. If a man lent aught to his fellow[4] he may only exact a pledge from him with the consent of the court, and he may not enter his house to take his pledge, for it is written, *Thou shalt stand without*.[5] If the debtor had two utensils[6] the creditor may take one but must leave[7] the other; and he must give back a pillow during the night-time and a plough during the day-time; but if the debtor dies the creditor need not restore [the pledge][8] to his heirs. Rabban Simeon b. Gamaliel says: Even to the debtor himself he need only return the pledge during a space of thirty days; and after thirty days he may sell it with the consent of the court. A pledge may not be exacted from a widow whether she is poor or rich, as it is written, *Thou shalt not take the widow's raiment in pledge*.[9] If a man takes away the mill-stones, he transgresses a negative commandment, and he is also culpable by virtue of taking two utensils together, for it is written, *No man shall take the mill and the upper millstone to pledge*.[10] They spoke not only of the mill and the upper millstone, but of aught wherewith is prepared necessary food, as it is written, *For he taketh a man's life to pledge*.[11]

10. 1. If a house and an upper room belonging to two persons[12] fell down, the two share in the wood and the stones and the earth;[13] and they consider which stones were the more likely to have been broken.[14] If one of them recognizes some of the stones that were his, he may take them and they form part of his share in the reckoning.

2. If there was a house and an upper room belonging to two persons[15] and the [floor of the] upper room was in part broken down, and the owner of the house below was not minded to mend it, he that occupies the upper room may come down and dwell below until the owner shall mend for him the [floor of the] upper room. R. Jose says: He that dwells below should provide the beams and he that dwells above the plastering.

3. If a house and an upper room belonging to two persons[16] fell down, and the owner of the upper room told the owner of the house below to rebuild it, and he was not minded to rebuild it, the owner of the upper room may rebuild the house below and live in it until the other repays him what he has spent. R. Judah says: He would then[17] have been dwelling within his fellow's domain and should pay him rent![18]—but, rather, the owner of the upper room should rebuild both the house below and the upper

---

¹ Some texts omit 'at the set time'.   ² See above, p. 356, n. 9.
³ Since the law in that same verse (Lev. 19¹³) speaks of 'thy neighbour', i.e. a fellow-Israelite.
⁴ For a specified time, and he was not repaid at the end of the time.
⁵ Deut. 24¹¹.
⁶ Which sufficed as security for the debt, but the debtor had need of one of them.
⁷ Variant: 'Give back'.   ⁸ The pillow or plough at the times prescribed.
⁹ Deut. 24¹⁷.   ¹⁰ Deut. 24⁶.   ¹¹ Deut. 24⁶.   ¹² Each owning one.
¹³ i.e. the mortar and mud which filled in the masonry.
¹⁴ As suggested by the ruins and the manner of the collapse. If, e.g., the stones of the lower story were more likely to have suffered breakage the owner of the lower story must include these in his share when making the division.
¹⁵ The upper story being rented from the occupant of the lower story.
¹⁶ Each owning one.   ¹⁷ After being reimbursed.
¹⁸ Since he profited from the lower story, not having his upper story to live in.

room and put a roof on the upper room and live in the house below until
the other repays him what he has spent.[1]

4. So, too, if an olive-press that is built in a rock has a garden [on its
roof] above it, and this was in part broken down, the owner of the garden
may come down and sow below until the other rebuilds the vaulting of his
olive-press. If a wall or a tree fell into the public domain and caused
damage, the owner is not liable to make restitution. But if a set time had
been given him by which to cut down the tree or pull down the wall, and
they fell down within the time, he is not liable; but if after that time, he is
liable.

5. If a man's wall was near his fellow's garden and it fell down and his
fellow said to him, 'Clear away thy stones', and he answered, 'They are
become thine', they do not listen to him. But if after the other had accepted
the offer he said to him, 'Here is what thou hast spent and I will take away
what is mine', they do not listen to him. If a man hired a labourer to help
him in his work with the chopped straw and stubble, and the labourer said
to him, 'Give me my hire', but the other said, 'Take as thy hire that wherewith thou hast laboured', they do not listen to him. But if after the other had
accepted [his hire in kind], he said, 'Here is thy hire, and I will take what
is mine', they do not listen to him. If a man would cast out manure [from
the courtyard] in the public domain, while the one casts it out another
must take it away to manure [his field]. None may soak clay or make bricks
in the public domain, yet clay may be kneaded[2] in the public domain, but
not bricks.[3] If a man builds in the public domain, so soon as the stones are
brought they must be used in the building; and if he causes any damage he
must make restitution for the damage that he has caused. Rabban Simeon
b. Gamaliel says: He may, indeed, make preparation for his work for thirty
days [in the public domain].

6. If there were two gardens [in terraces] one above the other and
vegetables grew between them, R. Meir says: They belong to the upper
garden. R. Judah says: To the lower garden. R. Meir said: If [the owner
of] the upper garden was minded to remove his soil there would be no
vegetables. R. Judah said: If [the owner of] the lower garden was minded
to fill up his garden [with soil] there would be no vegetables. R. Meir
said: Since each is able to thwart the other, we should consider whence
these vegetables derive their life.[4] R. Simeon said: Whatsoever [the owner
of] the upper garden can take by stretching out his hand belongs to him,
and the rest belongs to [the owner of] the lower garden.

BABA BATHRA[5] ('THE LAST GATE')

1. 1. If two jointholders would make a partition in a courtyard they
should build the wall in the middle. Where the custom is to build of
unshaped stones, or of hewn stones, or of half-bricks, or of whole bricks,
so they should build it: everything should follow local use. If the wall is of
unshaped stones each supplies [a thickness of] three handbreadths; if of
hewn stones each supplies two handbreadths and a half; if of half-bricks
each supplies two handbreadths; and if of whole bricks each supplies a

---

[1] The lower occupant could not then claim rent from the other, since the other had now
his upper room at his own disposal.
[2] For immediate use in a building.   [3] Since labour on them is more protracted.
[4] Whether from the one's soil or the other's airspace.
[5] See p. 332, n. 1.

handbreadth and a half. Hence if the wall fell down the place [on which it stood] and the stones belong to them both.

2. So, too, with [jointholders of] a garden: where the custom is to build a fence [between each holding] a man is bound to do so; but in the valley, where it is not the custom to build a fence, none is bound to do so; but if one [of the jointholders] would build [a fence] he must withdraw within his own portion and there build [his fence] and make the boundary mark outside it; hence if the wall fell down both the place and the stones belong to him. If they acted with each other's consent, they should build the wall in the middle and make the boundary mark on either side; hence if the wall fell down the place and the stones belong to them both.

3. If a man's land surrounded his fellow's land on three sides, and he fenced it on the first and the second and the third sides, the other is not bound [to share in building these walls]. R. Jose says: If the other rose up and fenced it on the fourth side he is compelled to bear his share in the cost of all the other walls.[1]

4. If the wall of a courtyard fell down each of the jointholders is bound to help in building it up to a height of four cubits, and each may be presumed to have paid [his share] unless the other brings proof that he has not paid. If [the other built it to a height of] four cubits he is not bound to help in building it, but if he afterward built another wall over against it,[2] even if he did not put a roof thereon, he is compelled to bear his share in the cost of the whole of the other wall; and he cannot be presumed to have paid [his share] unless he brings proof that he has paid it.

5. Every one [that dwells within a courtyard] is compelled to share in building a gate-house and a door for the courtyard. Rabban Simeon b. Gamaliel says: Not all courtyards are such that need a gate-house. Every one [that dwells within a town] is compelled to share in building a wall for the town and double doors and a bolt. Rabban Simeon b. Gamaliel says: Not every town is such that it needs a wall. How long must a man be in a town to count as one of the men of the town? Twelve months. If he has acquired a habitation therein he forthwith counts as one of the men of the town.

6. A courtyard may not be divided unless it will allow four cubits [by four cubits] to each [occupant]; nor [may] a field [be divided] unless there is nine *kabs*' space of ground[3] to each [jointholder] (R. Judah says: Unless there are nine half-*kabs*' space of ground to each); nor a garden unless there is a half-*kabs*' space of ground to each (R. Akiba says: A quarter-*kab's* space); nor an eating-hall,[4] a watch-tower, a dovecot, a cloak, a bath-house, or an olive-press unless there is a portion sufficient for each jointholder. This is the general rule: whatsoever when divided can still be called by the same name, may be divided; otherwise it may not be divided. This applies if either of the jointholders is not willing [to divide their joint property]; but if both are willing they may divide it even if it is yet smaller. But the Sacred Books may not be divided even if both are willing.

2. 1. None may dig a cistern near his fellow's cistern; nor may he dig a trench, vault, water-channel, or washerman's pool unless it is three hand-

---

[1] From which he now profits, since they provide three-quarters of the fencing of his land.
[2] Thus making the courtyard wall one wall of an enclosure of which he has the whole benefit.   [3] App. II, E.   [4] Cf. Erub. 6[8]; B.B. 6[4].

breadths away from his fellow's wall;[1] and he must plaster it with lime. Piles of olives-refuse, manure, salt, lime, or stones may not be kept within three handbreadths of his fellow's wall and[2] he must plaster it with lime. Seeds or a plough or urine may not be kept within three handbreadths of the wall. The hand-mill may not be kept at such a distance that the wall is less than three handbreadths from the lower mill-stone[3] or four from the upper mill-stone; and an oven may not be kept at such a distance that the wall is less than three handbreadths from the belly of the oven or four from the rim.

2. None may set up an oven within a house unless there is a space of four cubits above it.[4] If he sets it up in an upper room the flooring beneath it must be three handbreadths deep or, for a stove,[5] one handbreadth; and if it causes damage [to the floor] he must pay for the damage that is caused. R. Simeon says: They have prescribed these measurements only that, if damage ensues, he shall not be liable to make restitution.

3. None may open a baker's shop or a dyer's shop under his fellow's storehouse, nor [may he keep] a cattle-stall [near by]. They have, indeed, permitted these under a winestore,[6] but [they have] not [permitted] a cattle-stall.[7] A man may protest against [another that opens] a shop within the courtyard and say to him, 'I cannot sleep because of the noise of them that go in and out'. He that makes utensils should go outside and sell them in the market. But none may protest against another and say, 'I cannot sleep because of the noise of the hammer' or 'because of the noise of the mill-stones' or 'because of the noise of the children'.

4. If one man's wall adjoins his fellow's wall[8] he may not build another wall adjoining[9] it unless it is at a distance of four cubits;[10] [and if he builds a wall opposite his fellow's] windows, whether it is higher or lower than them or level with them, it may not be within four cubits.[11]

5. A man's ladder must not be kept within four cubits of [his neighbour's] dovecot, lest the marten should jump in. His wall may not be built within four cubits from [his neighbour's] roof-gutter, so that the other can set up his ladder [to clean it out]. A dovecot may not be kept within fifty cubits of a town, and none may build a dovecot in his own domain unless his ground extends fifty cubits in every direction. R. Judah says: Four *kors*' space of ground, which is the length[12] of a pigeon's flight. But if he had bought it [and it was built already in that place] and there was only a quarter-*kab*'s space[13] of ground, his right to maintain it may not be disputed.

6. If a young pigeon is found within the fifty cubits it belongs to the owner of the dovecot; but if beyond the fifty cubits it belongs to him that finds it. If it is found between two dovecots and is nearer this one, it

---

[1] i.e. the wall of his fellow's cistern, the dividing wall between the two cavities.
[2] Variant: 'or'.
[3] The lower, convex, millstone is broader but fixed to the earth; the upper, concave, stone is smaller but freely movable.   [4] To prevent burning the roof-beams.
[5] Which does not require so hot a fire as the oven.
[6] Since the wine of Palestine is improved by heat.
[7] Whose stench spoils the wine.   [8] At right angles.
[9] So as to make an enclosure, walled in on three sides.
[10] Sufficient for a footway.
[11] If higher, it must be four cubits higher, for privacy's sake; if lower, it must be four cubits lower, so as not to interfere with the other's light; and if opposite (or level), it must be four cubits away so as to ensure light to the other.
[12] Four *kor*'s space is 300,000 sq. cubits (see App. II, E), a square with sides 548 cubits; i.e. the pigeon's flight is estimated at 274 cubits.
[13] Little more than a hundred sq. cubits.

belongs to him [that owns this dovecot], and if nearer to the other, it belongs to him [that owns the other]; and if it is at a like distance from either, they share it.

7. A tree may not be grown within a distance of twenty-five cubits from the town, or fifty cubits if it is a carob or a sycamore-tree. Abba Saul says: Any tree that bears no fruit may not be grown within a distance of fifteen cubits. If the town was there first the tree shall be cut down and no compensation given; if the tree was there first it shall be cut down and compensation given. If it is in doubt which was there first, the tree shall be cut down and no compensation given.

8. A permanent threshing-floor may not be made within fifty cubits from the city. None may make a permanent threshing-floor within his own domain unless his ground extends fifty cubits in every direction; and it must be far enough away from the plantations and ploughed land of his fellow for it to cause no damage.[1]

9. Carcases, graves, and tanneries may not remain within a space of fifty cubits from the town. A tannery may be set up only on the east side of the town.[2] R. Akiba says: It may be set up on any side save the west but[3] it may not be within a distance of fifty cubits.

10. A pool for steeping flax may not be kept near to vegetables, nor leeks near to onions, nor mustard-plant near to bees. R. Jose permits mustard-plant.

11. A tree may not be grown within twenty-five cubits of a cistern, or within fifty cubits if it is a carob or a sycamore-tree, whether it is higher up or on the same level. If the cistern was there first the tree shall be cut down and compensation given; if the tree was there first it shall not be cut down; if it is in doubt which was there first, the tree shall not be cut down. R. Jose says: Even if the cistern was there before the tree it should not be cut down, since the one digged within his own domain and the other planted within his own domain.

12. A man may not plant a tree near another's field unless it is four cubits away, no matter whether it be a vine or any other tree. If there was a wall between, each may plant up to the wall on either side. If its roots entered within the other's domain, the other may cut them away to a depth of three handbreadths so that they shall not hinder the plough. If he digged a cistern, trench, or vault, he may cut them away as far down as he digs, and the wood shall belong to him.

13. If a tree stretches into another's field, he may cut it away as far as is reached by an ox-goad held over the plough, or, if it is a carob or a sycamore-tree, [he may cut it away] according to the plumbline's measure.[4] All trees that stretch over irrigated fields may be cut away according to the plumb-line's measure. Abba Saul says: All trees that bear no fruit may be cut away according to the plumbline's measure.

14. If a tree stretches into the public domain enough must be cut away to allow a camel and its rider to pass by. R. Judah says: A camel laden with flax or bundles of branches.[5] R. Simeon says: Every such tree must be cut away according to the plumbline's measure, because of uncleanness.[6]

---

1 Through the scattered chaff.
2 The prevailing wind in Palestine is from the north-west.
3 Some texts omit the following clause.   4 i.e. whatever overhangs his border.
5 Which may rise four feet above and spread out four feet on either side of the loaded camel.
6 Overhanging branches may serve as 'the roof of a tent' so that if any uncleanness

3. 1. Title by usucaption[1] to houses, cisterns, trenches, vaults, dovecots, bath-houses, olive-presses, irrigated fields, and slaves, and aught that brings constant gain, is secured by occupation during three completed years; title by usucaption to unirrigated fields[2] [is secured by occupation during] three years and they need not be completed. R. Ishmael says: Three months during the first year and three months during the last year and twelve months during the middle year, which makes eighteen months. R. Akiba says: One month during the first year and one month during the last year and twelve months during the middle year, which makes fourteen months. R. Ishmael said: This applies only to a sown field; but with tree-plantations, as soon as a man has brought in his [grape-]crop and garnered his olives and gathered in his [fig-]harvest, this counts as three years.[3]

2. Three countries[4] are to be distinguished in what concerns usucaption: Judea, beyond Jordan, and Galilee. If the owner was in Judea and another took possession [of his property] in Galilee; or if he was in Galilee and another took possession [of his property] in Judea, such usucaption is not valid: he must be with him together[5] in the same country. R. Judah said: They have prescribed a limit of three years only that if the owner was in Spain[6] and another took possession [of his property] during one year, they could make it known to the owner during the next year and he could return in the third year.

3. Usucaption without an alleged right of possession does not count as valid usucaption. Thus if one said, 'What dost thou in my domain?' and the other answered, 'None ever said aught to me', such usucaption is not valid. But if he answered, 'Thou didst sell it to me', or 'Thou didst give it to me as a gift', or 'Thy father sold it to me', or 'Thy father gave it to me as a gift', such usucaption is valid. If a man held possession [during three years] by virtue of inheritance he does not need to allege any right of possession.[7] Craftsmen,[8] jointholders, tenants, and guardians cannot secure title by usucaption. A husband cannot secure title by usucaption to the property of his wife, nor a wife to the property of her husband, nor a father to the property of his son, nor a son to the property of his father. This applies to one that claims the property by usucaption; but when the property was given as a gift, or when brothers shared a property, or when one claimed title by usucaption to the property of a proselyte,[9] then if the claimant has shut in, walled up, or broken down aught soever, the title by usucaption remains valid.

4. If two testify of another that he has had the use [of property] during three years, and they are found to be false witnesses, they must make full restitution to the owner. If two [false witnesses] testify of the first year, two of the second, and two of the third, payment of restitution is divided

---

(Ohol. 2[1]) lies beneath the branches, its uncleanness is conveyed, 'by overshadowing', to whatever else is beneath the branches. See p. 649, n. 3.

[1] If a man has no title-deeds his claim to rightful ownership can be sustained if he can prove three years' undisputed possession.

[2] Whose fertility is dependent solely on the winter rain, and after the spring harvest remains uncultivable until the following October.

[3] Even though the three crops were brought in within the same year; i.e. his having retained undisputed ownership during these three ingatherings suffices to sustain his title.

[4] Cf. Shebi. 9[2].   [5] The former and present occupants.

[6] Heb. *Ispamia*.   [7] i.e. he need not prove what claim his father had.

[8] Some texts omit 'craftsmen'.

[9] Who died without heirs, and whose property is accounted 'ownerless property' and the possession of the first comer.

between them into three parts. If three brothers bear witness and another is included with them, they can offer the three acts of witness,[1] but their words count as but a single act of witness[2] when the evidence is proved false.

5. In what cases does usucaption remain valid, and in what cases does it not remain valid? If a man put cattle or an oven or stoves or mill-stones in a courtyard, or reared fowls there or put his manure in a courtyard, such usucaption is not valid. But if he set up for his cattle a partition ten hand-breadths high (so, too, if it was for an oven or for stoves or for mill-stones), or if he brought fowls inside the house, or prepared for his manure a place three handbreadths deep or three handbreadths high, such usucaption is valid.

6. A gutter-spout[3] cannot give title by usucaption, but title by usucaption can be claimed to the place [on which it discharges]. A gutter can give title by usucaption. An Egyptian ladder cannot secure title by usucaption, but a Tyrian ladder can do so.[4] An Egyptian window cannot secure title by usucaption, but a Tyrian window can do so.[5] What is an 'Egyptian window'? Any through which a man's head cannot enter. R. Judah says: If it has a frame, even though a man's head cannot enter through it, it can secure title by usucaption. A projection, if it extends a handbreadth [or more] can secure title by usucaption, and the other [into whose premises it projects] can protest against it; but if it is less than a handbreadth it cannot secure title by usucaption, and the other cannot protest against it.

7. None may make his windows to open into the jointly held courtyard. If he bought a house in another [and adjoining] courtyard he may not open it into the jointly held courtyard. If he built an upper room over his house he may not make it to open into the jointly held courtyard; but, if he is so minded, he may build another room within his house or build an upper room over his house and make it to open into his own house. In a jointly held courtyard a man may not build a door directly opposite another's door, or a window directly opposite another's window; if the window was small he may not make it larger; if it was a single window he may not make it into two. But in the public domain he may open a door opposite another's door, or a window opposite another's window; if the window was small he may make it larger; if it was a single window he may make it into two.

8. None may hollow out a space underneath the public domain, [such as] cisterns, trenches, or vaults. R. Eliezer permits it if it is such that a wagon loaded with stones can [safely] go over it. Projections and balconies may not be built out into the public domain; but if a man is so minded he may withdraw [his wall] within his own domain and build out from it. If he bought a courtyard in which were already projections and balconies his right to maintain them there may not be disputed.

4. 1. If a man sold a house, he has not thereby sold its side-chambers, even though they open into the house, nor the room that is behind, nor the roof

---

[1] For each of the three years.

[2] If proved false the brothers are included as one, and pay only half of the restitution, the other witness paying the other half. Some texts omit 'when the evidence is proved false'.

[3] Which is movable and can be attached to the main gutter to drain off the water clear of the wall outside the courtyard. It gives him no title to share in the possession of the courtyard wall.

[4] The former is small and the latter large. The placing of them in one place for a space of three years establishes the right to maintain it there only in the case of the latter.

[5] The latter is larger. If it opened out into a neighbouring courtyard the occupant of the courtyard may not block it up if it had remained open without protest for three years.

if it has a parapet ten handbreadths high (R. Judah says: If the roof has aught fashioned like a doorway, even if the parapet is not ten handbreadths high, it is not sold [as part of the house]).

2. Nor [has he thereby sold] the cistern or the walled cellar, even though he had written [in the deed of sale], 'the depth and the height'; but he must buy himself a way thereto.[1] So R. Akiba. But the Sages say: He need not buy himself a way thereto. And R. Akiba agrees that if he had said, 'Excepting these', he need not buy himself a way thereto. If he sold them to another, R. Akiba says: He [that bought them] need not buy himself a way thereto. But the Sages say: He must buy himself a way thereto.

3. If a man sold a house he has sold also the door, but not the key; he has sold a mortar that is a fixture but not one that is movable; he has sold the convex[2] but not the concave mill-stone, nor[3] [has he sold] the oven or the stove. But if he had said, ['I sell thee] the house and all that is in it', all these are sold also.

4. If a man sold a courtyard, he has sold also its houses, cisterns, trenches, and vaults, but not the movable property; but if he had said, 'It and all that is in it', all these are sold also. But in neither case has he sold the bath-house or the olive-press that are therein. R. Eliezer says: If a man sold a courtyard, he has sold only the open space of the courtyard.

5. If a man sold an olive-press he has sold also the vat, the grindstone, and the posts, but he has not sold the pressing-boards, the wheel, or the beam; but if he had said, 'It and all that is in it', all these are sold also. R. Eliezer says: If a man sold an olive-press he has sold the beam also.

6. If a man sold a bath-house he has not sold the planks or the benches or the hangings; but if he had said, 'It and all that is in it', all these are sold also. But in neither case has he sold the water-containers or the stores of wood.

7. If a man sold a town, he has sold also the houses, cisterns, trenches, vaults, bath-houses, dovecots, olive-presses, and irrigated fields, but not the movable property; but if he had said, 'It and all that is in it', even if cattle and slaves were in it, all these are sold also. Rabban Simeon b. Gamaliel says: If a man sold a town he has sold also the town Warden.[4]

8. If a man sold a field he has sold also the stones that are necessary to it, and the canes in a vineyard that are necessary to it, and its unreaped crop, and any reed-thicket that covers less than a quarter-*kab's* space[5] of ground, and the watchman's hut if it was not fastened down with clay, and ungrafted carob trees and young sycamores.

9. But he has not sold the stones that are not necessary to it or the canes in a vineyard that are not necessary to it or the produce that is already gathered. But if he had said, 'It and all that is in it', all these are sold also. But in neither case has he sold any reed-thicket that covers a quarter-*kab's* space of ground, or the watchman's hut if it was not fastened down with clay, or grafted carob trees or cropped sycamores,[6] or any cistern or winepress or dovecot, whether they lie waste or are in use. And he [that

---

[1] From the new owner if he wishes still to use the cellar.
[2] The lower, usually fixed, stone.
[3] Variant: 'but he has sold the oven and he has sold the stove', a reading which assumes that they were fixtures.
[4] The rendering is uncertain. Other renderings proposed are 'the boundary-marker', or 'the surrounding fields'.   [5] See p. 367, n. 13.
[6] Sycamores which have reached full growth and are valuable for their own sake for their plentiful supply of building-timber.

sold them] must buy himself a way thereto. So R. Akiba. But the Sages
say: He need not. And R. Akiba agrees that if he had said, 'Excepting
these', he need not buy himself a way thereto. If he had sold them to
another, R. Akiba says: He [that bought them] need not buy himself a way
thereto. But the Sages say: He must buy himself a way thereto. This
applies to him that sells [his field]. But if he gives it as a gift, he gives
everything that is in it. If brothers who divided [a heritage] came into
possession of a field, they come into possession of everything that is in it.
If a man secured title by usucaption to the property of a proselyte and secured title to a field, he secures title to everything that is in it. If a man
dedicated[1] a field he has dedicated everything that is in it. R. Simeon says:
If a man dedicated a field, [beside the ground] he has dedicated only
grafted carob trees and cropped sycamores.

5. 1. If a man sold a ship, he has sold also the mast, the sail, the anchor,
and all the means for steering it; but he has not sold the slaves, the packing-
bags, or lading. But if he had said, 'It and all that is in it', all these are sold
also. If a man sold a wagon he has not sold the mules; if he sold the
mules he has not sold the wagon. If he sold the yoke he has not sold the
oxen, and if he sold the oxen he has not sold the yoke. R. Judah says: The
price makes it manifest: thus if one said to him, 'Sell me thy yoke for 200
zuz', it is manifest that no 'yoke' costs 200 *zuz*. But the Sages say: The
price is no proof.

2. If a man sold an ass he has not sold its trappings. Nahum the Mede
says: He has sold its trappings also. R. Judah says: Sometimes they are
sold with it and sometimes not; thus, if the ass was before him and it bore
its trappings and he said, 'Sell me this ass of thine', all the trappings are
sold too; [but if he said, 'Sell me] that ass of thine', its trappings are not
sold with it.

3. If a man sold an ass he has sold[2] its foal also; if he sold a cow he has
not sold her calf; if he sold a dungheap he has sold the dung thereon; if he
sold a cistern he has sold the water therein; if he sold a bee-hive he has
sold the bees; if he sold a dovecot he has sold the pigeons. If a man bought
'the fruit of a dovecot' from his fellow he must let go the first pair that are
hatched;[3] if 'the fruit of a bee-hive' he may take only three swarms and
[then the seller can] render [the stock] unfruitful.[4] [If a man bought] the
honeycombs, he must leave behind two honeycombs. [If he bought] olive-
trees to cut them down, he must leave two shoots.

4. If a man bought two trees in his fellow's field he has not bought the
ground [in which they grow]. R. Meir says: He has bought the ground
[also]. When they grow he may not trim them. What comes up from the
stem belongs to him, but what comes up from the roots belongs to the owner
of the ground. And if they die the ground is not his.[5] If he bought three
trees he has bought also the ground [between them]. When they grow
he may trim them, and what comes up whether from the stem or from the
roots belongs to him. And if they die the ground is his.

5. With large cattle, if a man sold the head he has not sold the feet; if he

---

[1] Lev. 27[16ff]. 2 Variant: 'not sold'. 3 To prevent the parent birds from flying away.
[4] Lit. 'castrate'. One explanation is that the bees are given mustard-seed so that they
cease to breed and devote themselves to storing honey; another is that the buyer takes only
alternate swarms, or, after taking three, his bargain ends.
[5] i.e. he may not plant others there.

sold the feet he has not sold the head. If he sold the lungs he has not sold the liver, and if he sold the liver he has not sold the lungs. But with small cattle, if he sold the head he has sold the feet, but if he sold the feet he has not sold the head. If he sold the lungs he has sold the liver, but if he sold the liver he has not sold the lungs.

6. Four rules apply for them that sell. If a man has sold wheat to another as good wheat and it is found to be bad, the buyer can retract. If he sold it as bad and it is found to be good, the seller can retract. But if he sold it as bad and it is found to be bad, or good and it is found to be good, neither may retract. If he sold it as dark-coloured and it is found to be white, or as white and it is found to be dark-coloured, or if he sold wood as olive wood and it is found to be sycamore wood, or as sycamore wood and it is found to be olive wood; or if he sold aught as wine and it is found to be vinegar, or as vinegar and it is found to be wine, either of them may retract.

7. If a man sold produce to his fellow and the buyer drew it[1] towards him, even if the seller had not yet measured it the buyer has acquired possession of it. If the seller measured it but the buyer had not drawn it towards him, he has not acquired possession. If he is prudent-minded[2] the buyer hires the place where the produce lies.[3] If a man bought flax from his fellow he has not acquired possession until he has moved it from one place to another; if it was still ungathered and he plucked ought of it soever, he has acquired possession.

8. If a man sold wine or oil to his fellow and its value rose or fell, if [the price rose or fell] before the measure[4] was filled up it belongs to the seller [and he may refuse to sell except at the higher price]; but if after the measure was filled up, it belongs to the buyer [and he may refuse to buy except at the lower price]. If there was a middleman between them, and the jar was broken, it is broken to [the loss of] the middleman. [After emptying the measure] the seller must let three more drops drip to the advantage of the buyer. If he then turned the measure over and drained it off, what flows out belongs to the seller. The shopkeeper is not bound to let three more drops drip. R. Judah says: [Only] on the eve of Sabbath as it becomes dark is he exempt.

9. If a man sent his child to a shopkeeper with a *pondion*[5] in his hand and he measured him out an *issar's*[6] worth of oil and gave him an *issar* in change and the child broke the flask and lost the *issar*, the shopkeeper is liable.[7] R. Judah declares him exempt, since the father sent the child for this purpose. And the Sages agree with R. Judah that if the flask was in the child's hand[8] and the shopkeeper measured the oil into it, the shopkeeper is exempt.

10. The wholesale dealer must clean out his measures once every thirty days and the householder once every twelve months. Rabban Simeon b.

---

[1] See p. 353, n. 1.
[2] And is afraid that the seller will retract, and the produce is not such that he can 'draw it' into his possession.
[3] Thus the produce is found in his possession and the purchase completed.
[4] This does not apply if it was the seller's measure. According to the Gemara (87a) the Mishnah is dealing with a case where a middleman's measure is being used.
[5] App. II, A. Some texts omit 'with a *pondion* in his hand'.
[6] Half a *pondion*.
[7] For the flask, the oil, and the *issar*, since the child, being under age, was not a responsible agent.
[8] And thus the shopkeeper had never been liable for its safe-keeping.

Gamaliel says: The contrary is the rule. The shopkeeper must clean out his measures twice in the week and polish his weights once a week and clean out his scales after every weighing.

11. Rabban Simeon b. Gamaliel said: This applies only to liquid measures; with dry measures it is not necessary. Moreover he must let the scales sink down a handbreadth [to the buyer's advantage]. If he gave him exact measure he must give him his overweight—a tenth for liquid measures and a twentieth for dry measures. Where the custom is to measure with small measures they should not measure with large, and where [the custom is to measure] with large measures they should not measure with small; [where the custom is] to smooth down [what is in the measure] they should not heap it up, and [where the custom is] to heap it up they should not smooth it down.

6. 1. If a man sold grain[1] to his fellow and [after it was sown] it did not spring up, even if it was flax-seed he is not answerable. Rabban Simeon b. Gamaliel says: If it was garden-seeds, which are not used as food, he is answerable.

2. If a man sold grain to his fellow, the buyer must undertake to receive a quarter-*kab* of refuse with every *seah*; [if he bought] figs he must undertake to receive ten that are maggoty in every hundred; [if he bought] a cellar of wine he must undertake to receive ten jars gone sour in every hundred; [if he bought] jars in Sharon he must undertake to receive ten in every hundred in faulty condition.[2]

3. If a man sold wine to his fellow and it turned sour he is not answerable; but if it was known [to the seller] that his wine would [soon] turn sour, this is accounted a purchase made in error.[3] If he had said to him, 'I am selling thee spiced wine', he is answerable for its remaining [good] until Pentecost.[4] By 'old wine' is meant wine that remains from last year; by 'very old' is meant that which remains from the year before last.

4. If a man sold his fellow a place to build him a house (so, too, if a man received it from his fellow to build him a bridal-house for his son or a dower-house[5] for his daughter), he must build it four cubits by six. So R. Akiba. R. Ishmael says: This is a cattle-shed! He that would build a cattle-shed should build it four cubits by six; a small house—six by eight; a large house—eight by ten; an eating-hall[6]—ten by ten. The height thereof should be [the sum of] half its length and half its breadth. The Sanctuary affords proof[7] for this. Rabban Simeon b. Gamaliel says: Should all [houses] be according to the building of the Sanctuary?

5. If a man has a cistern behind his fellow's house, he may go in and out only at the time when others are accustomed to go in and out. And he may not lead his cattle and let them drink from his cistern, but he must draw water and let them drink outside. He and the owner of the house should each make himself a lock.

6. If a man has a garden behind his fellow's garden, he may go in and out only at the time when others are accustomed to go in and out. And he

---

[1] Without saying whether it was grain fit to sow or only grain for food.
[2] Not fully baked and so easily broken.   [3] Cf. Ket. 1[6]; 7[8].
[4] i.e. from vintage time (July) until the following May, after which he is not answerable if it spoils during the ensuing hot season.   [5] Lit. 'house of widowhood'.
[6] Cf. Erub. 6[6]; B.B. 1[6].
[7] 1 Kings 6[2, 17]. It was 40 cubits long (excluding the length of the porch), 20 wide, and 30 high.

may not bring in merchants, or enter through it into another field. [The owner of] the outer [garden] may sow seed on the pathway. But if with the other's consent he has been given a path at the side [of the other's garden] he may go in when he will and go out when he will; and he may bring in merchants, but he may not enter through it into another field; and neither of them has the right to sow seed on the path.

7. If a public path passed through a man's field and he took it and gave them [another path] by the side of the field, what he has given he has given and what he has taken for himself does not become his. A private path is four cubits, and a public path sixteen cubits wide; the king's highway has no prescribed measure;[1] the path to a grave[2] has no prescribed measure; the halting-places,[3] according to the judges of Sepphoris, should be four *kab's* space[4] of ground.

8. If a man sold to his fellow a place in which to make a tomb (so, too, if a man received from his fellow a place in which to make him a tomb), he must make the inside of the vault four cubits by six, and open up within it eight niches, three on this side, three on that side, and two opposite [the doorway]. The niches must be four cubits long, seven handbreadths high, and six wide. R. Simeon says: He must make the inside of the vault four cubits by eight and open up within it thirteen niches, four on this side, four on that side, three opposite [the doorway] and one to the right of the doorway and one to the left. He must make a courtyard at the opening of the vault, six cubits by six, space enough for the bier and its bearers;[5] and he may open up within it two other vaults, one on either side. R. Simeon says: Four, one on each of its four sides. Rabban Simeon b. Gamaliel says: All depends on the nature of the rock.[6]

7. 1. If a man said to his fellow, 'I will sell thee a *kor's* space[7] of soil', and it contained rifts ten handbreadths deep or rocks ten handbreadths high, these are not included in the measurement; but if they were less than this they are included. If he said to him, 'About a *kor's* space of soil', even if it contained rifts deeper than ten handbreadths or rocks higher than ten handbreadths, they are included in the measure.

2. [If he said, 'I will sell thee] a *kor's* space of soil as measured by the line', and he gave him any less, the buyer may reduce the price; and if he gave him any more the buyer must give this back. But if he said, 'Be it less or more', even if he gave the buyer a quarter-*kab's* space less in every *seah's* space or a quarter-*kab's* space more in every *seah's* space,[8] it becomes his; if [the error] was more than this, a reckoning must be made. What does he[9] give him back? Its value in money; but if the seller so wished it, he must give him back land. And why have they said that he could give back its value in money? To strengthen the seller's hand; for if, in a field [containing a *kor's* space], there would still have remained to him nine *kabs'* space, or, in a garden, a half-*kab's* space (according to R. Akiba a quarter-

---

[1] Sanh. 2[4]; he has indisputable and unlimited rights of expropriation.
[2] i.e. the bearers of the corpse may trample over sown fields and ignore private property rights.
[3] Where the mourners stop in the course of the funeral procession. Cf. Meg. 4[3]; Ket. 2[10].
[4] 50 cubits by 33⅓. App. II, E.   [5] Some texts omit 'and its bearers'.
[6] Whether the stone is easily hewn out, or whether the outcrop of rock is suitable in shape to open up vaults on each side of the fore-court.
[7] App. II, E.   [8] i.e. one twenty-fourth less or more.
[9] The buyer.

kab's space), the buyer must give it back to him in land;[1] and not only must he give back the quarter-*kab's* space[2] but all the surplus.

3. [If he said,] 'I will sell thee [a *kor's* space of soil] as measured by the line, be it less or more', the condition 'be it less or more' makes void the condition 'as measured by the line'; [and if he said,] 'Be it less or more as measured by the line', the condition 'as measured by the line' makes void the condition 'be it less or more'. So Ben Nanos. [If he said, 'I will sell thee a *kor's* space of soil as measured] by its marks and its boundaries', and the difference was less than the sixth part, the sale holds good; if it was as much as[3] a sixth the buyer may reduce the price.

4. If a man said to his fellow, 'I will sell thee a half of the field', it must be divided between them into portions of equal value,[4] and the buyer shall take the half of the field [which the other allots to him]. [If he said, 'I will sell thee] the half of it on the south', it must be divided between them into portions of equal value, and the buyer takes the half of it on the south. He must undertake to provide the space[5] for the [dividing] wall and the large and small ditches.[6] How large is the 'large ditch'? Six handbreadths. And the 'small ditch'? Three handbreadths.

8. 1. Certain [near of kin] both inherit and bequeath property, some inherit but do not bequeath, some bequeath but do not inherit, and some neither inherit nor bequeath. These both inherit and bequeath: a father inherits from his sons, and sons from their father and brothers by the same father, and they can bequeath property to them. A man inherits from his mother, and a husband from his wife and sisters' sons, but they do not bequeath property to them. A woman bequeaths property to her sons, a wife to her husband and maternal uncles, but they do not inherit from them. Brothers by the same mother [but another father] neither inherit [from one another] nor bequeath property [to one another].

2. This is the order of inheritance: *If a man die and have no son, then ye shall cause his inheritance to pass unto his daughter*[7]—the son precedes the daughter, and all the son's offspring precede the daughter; the daughter precedes the brothers[8] and the daughter's offspring precede the brothers; brothers[8] precede the father's brothers and the brothers' offspring precede the father's brothers. This is the general rule: whosoever has precedence in inheritance, his offspring have also precedence. The father has precedence over all his offspring.[9]

3. The daughters of Zelophehad[10] took three portions of the inheritance: the portion of their father who was of them that came out of Egypt, and

---

[1] And not money, because such a parcel of land is still large enough to cultivate. Cf. above, 1[6].

[2] That he has received in excess in every *seah's* space (and which, according to R. Akiba, justified the seller in reclaiming the difference in land); but also the whole thirty quarter-*kabs* which were wrongly included in the *kor's* space.

[3] Variant: 'more than'.

[4] The more fertile portion being proportionately reduced, and the owner taking his first choice. Cf. Bekh. 2[6, 7] where the same expression occurs and where the choice is between two beasts. There the commentators take the expression to mean that the owner has first choice since 'on him who would exact aught from his fellow lies the burden of proof', i.e. the other must (and, in the circumstances, he cannot) prove his right to the better of the two.

[5] On his side of the common boundary.

[6] A smaller one next to the wall and a larger one beyond, in order to prevent wild beasts clambering over the wall.   [7] Num. 27[8].   [8] Of the deceased.

[9] If none of these is the direct offspring of the deceased.

[10] Num. 27[1ff].

his portion among his brethren from the property of Hepher, who also, in that he was the firstborn, received a double portion.

4. The son and the daughter[1] are alike concerning inheritance, save that the [firstborn] son takes a double portion of the father's property, but he does not take a double portion of the mother's property; and the daughters receive maintenance from the father's property but not from the mother's property.

5. If a man says, 'Such-a-one, my firstborn son, shall not receive a double portion', or 'Such-a-one, my son, shall not inherit with his brethren', he has said nothing, for he has laid down a condition contrary to what is written in the Law.[2] If a man apportioned his property to his sons by word of mouth, and gave much to one and little to another, or made them equal with the firstborn, his words remain valid. But if he had said that so it should be 'by inheritance', he has said nothing. If he had written down, whether at the beginning or in the middle or at the end [of his testament], that thus it should be 'as a gift', his words remain valid. If a man said, 'Such a man shall inherit from me', and he has a daughter;[3] or 'My daughter shall inherit from me', and he has a son, he has said nothing, for he has laid down a condition contrary to what is written in the Law. R. Johanan b. Baroka says: If he said this of one that was qualified to inherit from him, his words remain valid, but if of one that was not qualified to inherit from him his words do not remain valid. If a man assigned his goods to others and passed over his sons, what he has done is done, but the Sages have no pleasure in him. Rabban Simeon b. Gamaliel says: Yet if his sons had not behaved aright, it should be accounted to his credit.

6. If a man said, 'This is my son', he may be believed.[4] If [he said], 'This is my brother', he may not be believed;[5] yet the other may join with him in his portion. If he died the property returns to its place;[6] if he inherited property from elsewhere the other's brothers inherit it together with him.[7] If a man died and a testament[8] was found bound to his thigh, this counts as nothing.[9] But if [he had delivered it and] through it granted title to another, whether of his heirs or of such as were not his heirs, his words remain valid.

7. If a man assigned his goods to his sons he must write, 'From to-day and after my death'. So R. Judah. R. Jose says: He need not do so. If a man assigned his goods to his son to be his after his death, the father cannot sell them since they are assigned to his son, and the son cannot sell them since they are in the father's possession. If his father sold them, they are sold [only] until he dies; if the son sold them, the buyer has no claim on them until the father dies. The father may pluck up [the crop of a field which he has so assigned] and give to eat to whom he will, and if he left anything already plucked up, it belongs to [all] his heirs. If he left elder sons and younger sons, the elder sons may not care for themselves [out of the common inheritance] at the cost of the younger sons, nor may the

---

[1] When there is no son.
[2] Deut. 21[17]. Cf. Ket. 9[1]; B.M. 7[11].   [3] And still more if he has a son.
[4] He thereby frees his widow from the levirate bond (p. 218, n. 1).
[5] He thereby binds his widow to levirate marriage. Or, for example, Reuben said to his brother Simon, 'This man Levi is our brother and must share in our inheritance', he is not to be believed to the extent of reducing Simon's inheritance, but Levi can share Reuben's inheritance.   [6] To Reuben.
[7] Simon (and any other brothers) share with Reuben in property left by Levi.
[8] The sense here is a deed of gift.
[9] He may have changed his mind after writing it.

younger sons claim maintenance at the cost of the elder sons, but they all share alike. If the elder sons married [and drew upon the common inheritance] the younger sons may marry [and draw in like manner]. If the younger sons said, 'We will marry [on the like scale] as ye married [when our father was yet alive]', they do not listen to them; for what their father had given to them, he has given.

8. If he left elder daughters and younger daughters, the elder daughters may not care for themselves at the cost of the younger daughters, nor may the younger daughters claim maintenance at the cost of the elder daughters, but they all share alike. If the elder daughters married [and took each her dowry from the common inheritance] the younger daughters may marry [and take each a like dowry]. If the younger daughters said, 'We will marry [and take the like dowry][1] as when ye married [in our father's lifetime]', they do not listen to them. Herein greater stringency applies to daughters than to sons, since daughters can claim maintenance at the cost of the sons, but they cannot claim maintenance at the cost of [other] daughters.

9. 1. If[2] a man died and left sons and daughters, and the property was great, the sons inherit and the daughters receive maintenance; but if the property was small the daughters receive maintenance and the sons go a-begging. Admon says: [The son may say:] 'Must I suffer loss because I am a male?' Rabban Gamaliel said: I approve the words of Admon.

2. If a man left sons and daughters and one that was of doubtful sex, if the property was great the males may thrust such a one among the females; if the property was small the females may thrust such a one among the males. If a man said, 'If my wife shall bear a male he shall be given 100 *zuz*', and she bore a male, he is given the 100 *zuz*. [If he said,] 'If she shall bear a female she shall be given 200 *zuz*', and she bore a female, she is given the 200 *zuz*. [If he said,] 'If a male, 100 *zuz*, and if a female, 200 *zuz*', and she bore both a male and a female, the male takes 100 *zuz* and the female 200 *zuz*. If she bore one that was of doubtful sex it is given nothing. But if he had said, 'Whatsoever my wife shall bear shall be given so much', then it shall be given so much; and if it was the only heir it inherits everything.

3. If a man left elder sons and younger sons, and the elder sons improved the property, they improve it to the common advantage; but if they said, 'See, what our father has left us, lo, [on that] we will labour and [from that] we will eat', they improve it to their own advantage. So, too, if the widow improved the property she improves it to the common advantage, but if she had said, 'See, what my husband left to me, lo, [on that] I will labour and [from that] I will eat', she improves it to her own advantage.

4. If brothers were jointholders and a public office fell to one of them,[3] it falls to the common advantage. If one [of them] fell sick and needed healing, his healing is at his own charges. If certain of the brothers in their father's lifetime had made a present as groomsmen [at their father's charges], and [after his death] the present was restored to them, it is restored to the common advantage, for the groomsmen's gift [counts as a loan and] can be recovered through a court of law. But if [one of the brothers in his father's lifetime] sent his fellow jars of wine or jars of oil, they cannot be

---

[1] Cf. Ket. 6[6].   [2] Ket. 13[3].   [3] As the representative of his family.

recovered through a court of law, since they count [not as a loan but] as a charitable deed.

5. If a man sent espousal-gifts to his [prospective] father-in-law's house, and he sent there ten thousand *denars'* worth and there consumed an espousal-meal of but one *denar's* worth, [and he afterward divorced his wife] they cannot be reclaimed, but if he did not eat the espousal-meal, they can be reclaimed. If he had sent many espousal-gifts to be returned with her to her husband's house, these can be reclaimed; but if the espousal-gifts were few and to be used in her father's house, they cannot be reclaimed.

6. If one that lay sick[1] assigned his goods to others [as a gift] and kept back any land soever, his gift remains valid; but if had kept back no land soever, his gift does not remain valid. If it was not written therein, 'while that he lay sick', but he said that he lay sick, whereas they said that he was in health, he must bring proof that he lay sick. So R. Meir. But the Sages say: On him that would exact aught from his fellow lies the burden of proof.[2]

7. If a man apportioned his goods by word of mouth, R. Eliezer says: Whether he was in health or at the point of death, property for which there is security[3] can be acquired only by money or by writ[4] or by usucaption; that for which there is no security can be acquired only by the act of drawing into possession.[5] They said to him: It once happened that the mother of Rokhel's sons was sick and said, 'Give my veil to my daughter', and it was worth twelve hundred *denars*; and she died and they fulfilled her words. He said to them, 'May their mother bury the sons of Rokhel!'[6] The Sages say: On a Sabbath his words remain valid,[7] since he cannot write;[8] but not on a weekday. R. Joshua says: If they have said [that he can assign property] on a Sabbath, how much more so on a weekday! In like manner they may acquire possession on behalf of a minor but not on behalf of one that is of age. So R. Eliezer.[9] R. Joshua says: If they have said [that it is permitted] on behalf of a minor, how much more so on behalf of one that is of age.

8. If the house fell down on a man and his father, or upon a man and any from whom he inherits, and he was liable for his wife's *Ketubah* or to a creditor, the father's heirs may say, 'The son died first and the father died afterward', and the creditors may say, 'The father died first and the son died afterward'. The School of Shammai say: Let the claimants share. The School of Hillel say: The property falls to the heirs.

9. If the house fell down on a man and his wife, the husband's heirs may say, 'The wife died first and the husband died afterward',[10] and the wife's heirs may say, 'The husband died first and the wife died afterward'. The School of Shammai say: Let the claimants share. The School of Hillel say: The property falls to the heirs—the *Ketubah* to the husband's heirs and the property that comes in and goes out with her to her father's heir's.[11]

10. If the house fell down on a man and his mother, they agree that the claimants must share. R. Akiba said: I agree here[12] that the property falls

[1] Peah 3[7].   [2] Cf. B.K. 3[11].   [3] Cf. Kidd. 1[5].
[4] e.g. a deed of sale or assignment.   [5] See p. 353, n. 1.
[6] i.e. they were sinners, deserving of a curse, and they were punished by the rule being waived to their detriment.   [7] As an act of assignment.   [8] See Shab. 7[2].
[9] Some texts omit 'So R. Eliezer'.
[10] Therefore the husband's heirs inherit the wife's property.   [11] Cf. Yeb. 4[3]; Ket. 8[6].
[12] With what the School of Hillel decided in the preceding cases.

to the heirs. Ben Azzai said to him: We already grieve over those things wherein they differ; but thou art come to bring dissension over that wherein they agree!

10. 1. An unfolded document has the signatures within[1] [the single page]; a folded[2] document has the signatures behind [each fold]. If in an unfolded document its witnesses signed behind, or if in a folded document its witnesses signed within, they are invalid. R. Hanina b. Gamaliel says: If in a folded document its witnesses signed within, it is valid, since it can be made into an unfolded document. Rabban Simeon b. Gamaliel says: Everything should follow local custom.

2. An unfolded document requires two witnesses; a folded one three. If an unfolded document has but one witness or a folded one but two, both are invalid. If there was written in a bond of indebtedness, '100 *zuz* which are 20 *selas*',[3] the creditor can claim only 20 *selas*; and if '100 *zuz* which are 30 *selas*', he can claim only 100 *zuz*. [If there was written therein,] 'Silver *zuzim* which are . . .' and the rest was effaced, [he can claim] not less than two *zuz*; and if 'silver *selas* which are . . .' and the rest was effaced, [he can claim] not less than two *selas*; '*darics*[4] which are . . .' and the rest was effaced, [he can claim] not less than two. If at the top there was written '100 *zuz*' and at the bottom '200 *zuz*', or '200 *zuz*' at the top and '100 *zuz*' at the bottom, everything must follow the bottom figure. Why, then, do they write the upper figure? So that, if a sign of the lower figure was effaced, they can learn from the upper figure.

3. They may write a bill of divorce for the husband even if his wife is not with him, or a quittance[5] for the wife even if her husband is not with her, provided that he[6] knows them; and the husband must pay the fee. They may write a bond for the debtor even if the creditor is not with him, but they may not write a bond for the creditor unless the debtor is with him; and the debtor must pay the fee. They may write a deed of sale for the seller although the buyer is not with him; but they may not write it for the buyer unless the seller is with him; and the buyer must pay the fee.

4. They may not write deeds of betrothal or marriage save with the consent of both the parties; and the bridegroom must pay the fee. They may not write deeds of tenancy[7] save with the consent of both the parties, and he that assumes the tenure must pay the fee. They may not write a deed of arbitration or any document drawn up before the court save with the consent of both the parties, and both must pay the fee. Rabban Simeon b. Gamaliel says: Two documents are written for the two parties, a separate one for each.

5. If a man had paid part of his debt and the bond was placed with a

---

[1] i.e. at the bottom of the single page of writing.

[2] One or two lines are written and then the written part is folded over, and a signature endorsed on the back of the fold; one or two more lines are written, and this written portion is similarly folded over and a second signature endorsed on the back of this second fold, and so on until the document is completed. A document so drawn up can never be so short as to require less than three witnesses. If one of the backs of the folds is unsigned it is described as 'a bald' document. Cf. Gitt. 8[10].　　　　　　　　　　　　[3] Eighty *zuz*.

[4] Ezra 8[27].

[5] The receipt for her *Ketubah* which she delivers to the husband on divorce.

[6] The scribe or the witnesses.

[7] The Hebrew text gives here the technical terms for the two kinds of lease: one according to which the tenant agrees to give the owner a prescribed proportion of the crop, and the other, according to which he agrees to give a fixed quantity regardless of what may be the resulting crop.

third party,[1] and the debtor said to him, 'If I have not paid thee by such a day, then give him his bond', and the time came and he had not paid, R. Jose says: He should give it to him. R. Judah says: He should not give it to him.

6. If a man's bond of indebtedness was effaced he must call the testimony of the witnesses thereto, and come before the court, and they draw up for him this attestation: 'Such-a-one, son of such-a-one, his bond was effaced on such a day, and such-a-one and such-a-one are witnesses to what was contained therein'. If a man has paid part of his debt, R. Judah says: He should change the bond for another. R. Jose says: He should write him out a quittance. R. Judah said: Then he must needs guard his quittance, too, from the mice. R. Jose answered: Thus it is good for him[2] and no ill is done to the rights of the other.[3]

7. If there were two brothers, the one poor and the other rich, and their father left them a bath-house or an olive-press, and he had made them such as to let out for hire, the hire is to their common advantage; but if he had made them for his own use alone, the rich brother may say to the poor brother, 'Buy thee slaves that they may clean out the bath-house', or 'Buy thee olives and prepare them in the olive-press'. If there were two in the same town and the name of the one was Joseph ben Simon and the name of the other was Joseph ben Simon, neither can bring forth a bill of indebtedness against the other, and another person cannot bring forth a bill of indebtedness against them; and if some person finds among his documents [one wherein it is said] 'The bond of Joseph ben Simon is discharged', the bonds of them both are discharged. What should they do? They should write their names [and their fathers' names] to the third generation, and if the names of the three generations were alike, they should give themselves a descriptive name, and if their descriptive names were alike they should write 'Cohen' [or 'Levite']. If a man said to his son, 'One of my bonds is discharged but I do not know which', then all are deemed discharged; or if two bonds were found pertaining to the one debtor, the larger one is deemed discharged[4] and the smaller undischarged. If a man lent his fellow money on a guarantor's security, he may not exact payment from the guarantor; but if he had said, 'On the condition that I may exact payment from whom I will, he may exact payment from the guarantor. Rabban Simeon b. Gamaliel says: If the borrower had property, in neither case could he exact payment from the guarantor. Moreover Rabban Simeon b. Gamaliel used to say: If a man was guarantor for a woman's *Ketubah* and her husband divorced her, the husband must vow to derive no further benefit from her, lest he make a conspiracy[5] against the property of the guarantor and take his wife back again.

8. If a man lent his fellow money on the security of a bond of indebtedness, he may recover the debt from mortgaged property; but if [he had lent it only] before witnesses he may recover the debt only from unmortgaged property. If [the creditor] brought forth another's note-of-hand [as evidence]

---

[1] Cf. p. 348, n. 10.   [2] He will make the more haste to pay his debt.
[3] By reducing the creditor's hold on the security through a new bond being drawn up for a smaller sum.
[4] The debtor had paid part of his debt and a new bond for the smaller sum was drawn out.
[5] Cf. Arak. 6[1]. He has no money, so he divorces his wife and the guarantor must pay her her *Ketubah*; and on remarriage the husband has the use of this money.

that he was indebted to him, the creditor may recover the debt only
from unmortgaged property. If a man signed as guarantor after the signatures to bills of indebtedness, the creditor may recover the debt only from
[the guarantor's] unmortgaged property. Such a case came before R.
Ishmael and he said: He can recover the debt only from [the guarantor's]
unmortgaged property. Ben Nanos answered, He may recover the debt
neither from mortgaged nor from unmortgaged property. He said to him,
Why? He answered, If a man seized a debtor by the throat in the street
and his fellow found him and said to him, 'Let him alone, I will pay thee',[1]
he is not liable, since not through trust in him had the creditor lent the
debtor money. But what manner of guarantor is liable? [If a man said,]
'Lend him money and I will pay thee', he is liable; for he had lent him the
money through his trust in the guarantor. And R. Ishmael said: He that
would become wise let him occupy himself in cases concerning property,
for there is no branch of the Law greater than they; for they are like a
welling fountain; and he that would occupy himself in cases concerning
property, let him serve [as the pupil of] Simeon ben Nanos.

SANHEDRIN[2] ('THE SANHEDRIN')

1. 1. Cases concerning property[3] [are decided] by three [judges]; cases
concerning theft[4] or personal injury, by three; claims for full damages or
half-damages, twofold restitution,[5] or fourfold or fivefold restitution,[6] and
[claims against] the violator,[7] the seducer[8] and him that *hath brought an
evil name*[9] [are decided] by three [judges]. So R. Meir. But the Sages say:
He that *hath brought an evil name* [must be judged] by three and twenty, for
there may arise therefrom a capital case.[10]

2. [Cases concerning offences punishable by]scourging[11] [are decided]by
three. In[12] the name of R. Ishmael they said: By three and twenty.[13] The
intercalating of the month[14] and the intercalating of the year[15] [are decided
upon] by three. So R. Meir. But Rabban Simeon b. Gamaliel says: The
matter is begun by three, discussed by five, and decided upon by seven; but
if it is decided upon by three the intercalation is valid.

3. The laying on of the elders' hands,[16] and the breaking of the heifer's
neck[17] [are decided upon] by three. So R. Simeon. But R. Judah says: By
five. The rites of *halitzah*[18] and Refusal[19] [are performed] before three.
The fruit of fourth-year plantings[20] and Second Tithe[21] whose value is not
known [are redeemed][22] before three, and things dedicated to the Temple[23]
[are redeemed][24] before three. [Property pledged as security[25] for] vows of
valuation,[26] if movable property [must be sold] before three [judges] (R.
Judah says: One must be a priest), and if pieces of land, before nine and a
priest; and similarly [for the valuation vow of] men.[27]

---

[1] Some texts omit 'I will pay thee'.
[2] As its title implies, this tractate deals with the constitution and procedure of courts of
law, and, particularly, with the administering of capital punishment.
[3] Disputes arising out of loans, inheritances, sales, and the like.   [4] Lev. 6[4ff].
[5] Ex. 22[4].   [6] Ex. 22[1].   [7] Deut. 22[29].   [8] Ex. 22[16, 17].   [9] Deut. 22[19].
[10] The woman concerned is liable to be stoned.
[11] Deut. 25[1–3].   [12] Some texts omit the following sentence.
[13] It is a capital charge. This is deduced by the verbal analogy between Deut. 25[1] (*rasha'*,
wicked) and Num. 35[31] ('guilty—Heb. *rasha'*—of death'). Since death applies to the latter
it applies also to the former.   [14] See R. Sh. 3[1].
[15] See Meg. 1[4].   [16] Lev. 4[15].   [17] Deut. 21[1ff]. Cf. Sot. 9[1].   [18] App. I. 12.
[19] See Yeb. 13[1].   [20] Lev. 19[23ff].   [21] Deut. 14[23ff].   [22] See M.Sh. 4[2]; 5[4].
[23] See Arak. 5[1ff].   [24] Lev. 27[14ff].   [25] See Arak. 5[6].   [26] Lev. 27[2ff]. See Arak. 1[ff].
[27] Cf. Meg. 4[3] (end).

4. Cases concerning offences punishable by death [are decided] by three and twenty [judges]. A beast that commits or suffers unnatural crime [is judged] by three and twenty, as it is written, *Thou shalt slay the woman and the beast*;[1] and again it says, *And ye shall slay the beast*.[2] The ox that is to be stoned[3] [is judged] by three and twenty, as it is written, *The ox shall be stoned and its owner also shall be put to death*[4]—in like manner as the owner is put to death so is the ox put to death. The wolf,[5] the lion, the bear, the leopard, the panther, or serpent [that have killed a man], their death [is decided upon] by three and twenty [judges]. R. Eliezer says: If any killed them before [they were brought before the court] he has acquired merit. But R. Akiba says: Their death [is decided upon] by three and twenty [judges].

5. A tribe,[6] a false prophet,[7] or the High Priest may not be tried save by the court of one and seventy; they may not send forth [the people] to a battle waged of free choice[8] save by the decision of the court of one and seventy; they may not add to the City or the Courts of the Temple[9] save by the decision of the court of one and seventy; they may not set up sanhedrins for the several tribes save by the decision of the court of one and seventy, and they may not proclaim [any city to be] an Apostate City[10] save by the decision of the court of one and seventy. No city on the frontier should be proclaimed an Apostate City, nor three together, but only one or two.

6. The greater Sanhedrin was made up of one and seventy [judges] and the lesser [Sanhedrin] of three and twenty. Whence do we learn that the greater Sanhedrin should be made up of one and seventy? It is written, *Gather unto me seventy men of the elders of Israel*;[11] and Moses added to them makes one and seventy. R. Judah says: [The greater Sanhedrin is made up of] seventy [only]. And whence do we learn that the lesser [Sanhedrin] should be made up of three and twenty? It is written, *The congregation shall judge*, also *The congregation shall deliver*[12]—one congregation judges and another congregation delivers; thus we have twenty. And whence do we learn that a congregation is made up of ten? It is written, *How long shall I bear with this evil congregation!*[13] [which was the twelve spies] but Joshua and Caleb were not included. And whence do we learn that we should bring yet three others [to the twenty]? By inference from what is written: *Thou shalt not follow after the many to do evil*[14]—I conclude that I must be with them to do well.[15] Then why is it written, *[To follow] after the many to change judgement?*[16] [It means that] thy verdict of condemnation shall not be like thy verdict of acquittal, for thy verdict of acquittal is reached by the decision of a majority of one, but thy verdict of condemnation must be reached by the decision of a majority of two.[17] The court must not be divisible equally, therefore they add to them yet one more. Thus they are three and twenty. And how many should there be in a city that it may be fit to have a Sanhedrin? A hundred and twenty men. R. Nehemiah says: Two hundred and thirty, so that [the Sanhedrin of three and twenty] shall correspond with them that are chiefs of [at least] groups of ten.[18]

---

[1] Lev. 20[16].   [2] Lev. 20[15].   [3] That killed a man or woman.   [4] Ex. 21[29].
[5] Some texts omit 'The wolf'.   [6] Of which the majority have committed idolatry.
[7] Deut. 18[20].   [8] Cf. Sot. 8[7].   [9] Cf. Shebu. 2[2].
[10] Deut. 13[12ff]. See below, 10[4ff].   [11] Num. 11[16].   [12] Num. 35[24, 25].
[13] Num. 14[27].   [14] Ex. 23[2].   [15] To acquit.   [16] Ex. 23[2].
[17] Twelve at least must condemn. Therefore (since a 'congregation', ten, shall deliver) the total is twenty-two.   [18] Cf. Ex. 18[21].

2. 1. The High Priest can judge and be judged, he can act as a witness and others can bear witness against him; he can submit to *halitzah* and others can submit to *halitzah* at the hands of his widow or contract levirate marriage with his widow,[1] but he cannot contract levirate marriage since he is forbidden to marry a widow.[2] If any of his near of kin die he may not follow after the bier,[3] but he may go forth with the bearers as far as the city gate, if he and they come not within sight of one another. So R. Meir. But R. Judah says: He may not go forth from the Temple, for it is written, *Neither shall he go out of the Sanctuary.*[4] And when he comforts other mourners the custom is for all the people to pass by, the one after the other, while the appointed [priest][5] places him between himself and the people; and when he receives comfort[6] from others, all the people say to him, 'May we make expiation for thee', and he replies, 'Be ye blessed of Heaven'. When they make for him the funeral meal[7] all the people sit around on the ground and he sits on a stool.

2. The king can neither judge nor be judged, he cannot act as a witness and others cannot bear witness against him. He may not submit to *halitzah* nor do others submit to *halitzah* at the hands of his widow; he may not contract levirate marriage nor may his brothers contract levirate marriage with his widow. R. Judah says: If he was minded to submit to *halitzah* or to contract levirate marriage it is reckoned to his credit. They answered: They should not listen to him. None may marry his widow. R. Judah says: The king may marry the widow of a king, for so have we found it with David, who married the widow of Saul, as it is written, *And I gave thee thy master's house and thy master's wives into thy bosom.*[8]

3. If any of his near of kin die he may not go forth from the door of his palace. R. Judah says: If he is minded to follow the bier he may follow it, for so have we found it with David, who followed the bier of Abner, as it is written, *And king David followed the bier.*[9] They answered: That was but to appease the people. When they make for him the funeral meal all the people sit on the ground and he sits on a couch.

4. He may send forth [the people] to a battle waged of free choice by the decision of the court of one and seventy. He may break through [the private domain of any man] to make himself a road and none may protest against him: the king's road has no prescribed measure.[10] Whatsoever the people take by plunder they must lay it before him and he first takes his portion. *Nor shall he multiply wives to himself*[11]—eighteen only.[12] R. Judah says: He may multiply them to himself provided that they do not turn away his heart. R. Simeon says: If there was but one and she would turn away his heart he may not marry her. Why then is it written, *Nor shall he multiply wives to himself?*—even though they be like Abigail.[13] *He shall not multiply horses to himself*—enough for his chariot only. *Neither shall he*

---

[1] See p. 218, n. 1.   [2] Lev. 21[14]; cf. Yeb. 6[4].
[3] Lev. 21[11].   [4] Lev. 21[12].
[5] The same word as in Shek. 5[1] ('officer'). Here he is identical with the 'prefect' (Yom. 7[1]; Sot. 7[7]) or deputy High Priest. Cf. Yom. 3[1]; Tam. 3[2].   [6] Cf. Ber. 2[7].
[7] 2 Sam. 12[17]; cf. M.Kat. 3[7].   [8] 2 Sam. 12[8].
[9] 2 Sam. 3[31].   [10] See p. 375, n. 1.
[11] Deut. 17[17]. The rest of the chapter is an example of a *midrash* on Deut. 17[15-19], a verse by verse commentary, the system of teaching which probably preceded the system of the Mishnah. See Introduction, p. xix; App. I. 27.
[12] 2 Sam. 3[2ff] gives David six wives, and 2 Sam. 12[8] (lit. 'I would have added unto thee the like of these and the like of these') implies that twice as many more was permissible.
[13] 1 Sam. 25[3].

greatly multiply to himself silver and gold—enough to pay [his soldiers'] wages only. He must write out a scroll of the Law for himself; when he goes forth to battle he shall take it forth with him, and when he returns he shall bring it back with him; when he sits in judgement it shall be with him, and when he sits at meat it shall be before him, for it is written, *It shall be with him and he shall read therein all the days of his life.*

5. None may ride on his horse and none may sit on his throne and none may make use of his sceptre. None may see him when his hair is being cut or when he is naked or when he is in the bath-house, for it is written, *Thou shalt in anywise set him king over thee*[1]—one whose awe shall be over thee.

3. 1. Cases concerning property [are decided] by three [judges]. Each suitor chooses one and together they choose yet another. So R. Meir. But the Sages say: The two judges choose yet another. Each may refuse to accept the judge chosen by the other. So R. Meir. But the Sages say: This applies only if they can bring proof against them that they are kinsfolk or otherwise ineligible; but if they are not ineligible or have special skill none may refuse to accept them. Each may refuse to admit the other's witnesses. So R. Meir. But the Sages say: This applies only if they can bring proof against them that they are kinsfolk or otherwise ineligible; but if they are not ineligible none may refuse to admit them.

2. If one suitor said to the other, 'I accept my father as trustworthy', or 'I accept thy father as trustworthy', or 'I accept three herdsmen as trustworthy', R. Meir says: He may retract. But the Sages say: He cannot retract. If a man must take an oath[2] before his fellow, and his fellow said to him, 'Vow to me by the life of thy head', R. Meir says: He may retract. But the Sages say: He cannot retract.

3. And these are they which are not qualified [to be witnesses or judges]: a dice-player, a usurer, pigeon-flyers, or traffickers in Seventh Year produce.[3] R. Simeon said: Beforetime they used to call them 'gatherers[4] of Seventh Year produce', but after oppressors[5] grew many they changed this and called them[6] 'traffickers in Seventh Year produce.[7] R. Judah said: This applies only if they have none other trade, but if they have some other trade than that they are not disqualified.

4. These are the kinsmen [that are not qualified to be witnesses or judges]: a suitor's father, brother, father's brother, mother's brother, sister's husband, father's sister's husband, mother's sister's husband, mother's husband, father-in-law, or wife's sister's husband, together with their sons and their sons-in-law; also the suitor's step-son only [but not the stepsons' offspring]. R. Jose said: Such was the Mishnah of R. Akiba, but the First Mishnah[8] included also a suitor's uncle, first cousin and all that are qualified to be his heirs. Moreover all that were kinsmen at the time [are not qualified]; but kinsmen that have ceased to be kinsmen become qualified. R. Judah says: If a man's daughter died and left children, her husband still counts as a kinsman.

---

[1] Deut. 17[15].
[2] As, for example, when a claim for repayment is made against him. Cf. Shebu. 8[1ff].
[3] When all crops were deemed ownerless property and free to all. Lev. 25[1ff].
[4] i.e. who did not let their fields lie fallow.
[5] Tax-gatherers, who exacted dues even in the Seventh Year.
[6] This category of ineligible witnesses and judges.
[7] And did not penalize those who gathered the produce only for their own use.
[8] i.e. the rule in force before R. Akiba (*c.* A.D. 100–35). Cf. Ket. 5[3]; Gitt. 5[6]; Naz. 6[1]; Eduy. 7[2].

5. A friend or an enemy [is disqualified]. By friend is meant a man's groomsman,[1] and by enemy any that through enmity has not spoken with him for three days. They replied: Israelites should not be suspected for such a cause.

6. How did they prove witnesses? They brought them in and admonished them; then they put them all forth and kept back the chief among them and said to him, 'Say, how dost thou know that he is in debt to the other?' If he said, 'He said to me "I am in debt to him"', or 'Such-a-one said to me that he was in debt to him', he has said nothing: he must be able to say, 'In our presence he acknowledged to the other that he owed him 200 *zuz*'.[2] Afterward they brought in the second witness and proved him. If their words were found to agree together, the judges discussed the matter. If two said, 'He is not guilty', and one said, 'He is guilty', he is not guilty; if two said, 'He is guilty', and one said, 'He is not guilty', he is guilty; if one said, 'He is not guilty', and one said, 'He is guilty', and even if two declared him not guilty or two declared him guilty while one said, 'I do not know', they must add to the judges.

7. When the judges reached their decision they brought in the suitors. The chief among the judges says, 'Thou, such-a-one, art not guilty', or 'Thou, such-a-one, art guilty'. And whence do we know that after one of the judges has gone forth he may not say, 'I declare him not guilty and my fellows declare him guilty; but what may I do, for my fellows outvoted me?' Of such a one it is written, *Thou shalt not go up and down as a talebearer among thy people*;[3] and it also says, *He that goeth about as a talebearer revealeth secrets [but he that is of a faithful spirit concealeth the matter]*.[4]

8. So long as a suitor can produce any proof the court may reverse the verdict. If they had said, 'Bring all the proofs that thou hast within thirty days', and he brought them within the thirty days, the court may reverse the verdict; but [if he brought any proof] after the thirty days, the court cannot reverse the verdict. Rabban Simeon b. Gamaliel said: What should he do that did not find it within thirty days but found it after thirty days? If they had said to him, 'Bring witnesses', and he said, 'I have no witnesses', or [if they said,] 'Bring proof', and he said, 'I have no proof', and he later found proof or found witnesses, then they are in no wise valid. Rabban Simeon b. Gamaliel said: What should he do that did not know that he had witnesses, then found witnesses, or that did not know that he had proof, then found proof? If they had said to him, 'Bring witnesses', and he said, 'I have no witnesses', or, 'Bring proof', and he said, 'I have no proof', but, when he saw that he would be accounted guilty, he said, 'Come near, such-a-one and such-a-one, and bear witness for me!' or if he brought forth some proof from his wallet, then it is in no wise valid.

4. 1. Non-capital[5] and capital cases are alike in examination and inquiry, for it is written, *Ye shall have one manner of law*.[6] In what do non-capital cases differ from capital cases? Non-capital cases [are decided] by three and capital cases by three and twenty [judges]. Non-capital cases may begin either with reasons for acquittal or for conviction, but capital cases must begin with reasons for acquittal and may not begin with reasons for conviction. In non-capital cases they may reach a verdict either of acquittal

---

[1] Cf. B.B. 9[4].   [2] App. II, A.   [3] Lev. 19[16].   [4] Prov. 11[13].
[5] Lit. 'cases concerning property'; it includes all charges not entailing penalty by death.
[6] Lev. 24[22].

or of conviction by the decision of a majority of one; but in capital cases they may reach a verdict of acquittal by the decision of a majority of one, but a verdict of conviction only by the decision of a majority of two. In non-capital cases they may reverse a verdict either [from conviction] to acquittal or [from acquittal] to conviction; but in capital cases they may reverse a verdict [from conviction] to acquittal but not [from acquittal] to conviction. In non-capital cases all[1] may argue either in favour of conviction or of acquittal; but in capital cases all may argue in favour of acquittal but not in favour of conviction. In non-capital cases he that had argued in favour of conviction may afterward argue in favour of acquittal, or he that had argued in favour of acquittal may afterward argue in favour of conviction; in capital cases he that had argued in favour of conviction may afterward argue in favour of acquittal, but he that had argued in favour of acquittal cannot afterward change and argue in favour of conviction. In non-capital cases they hold the trial during the daytime and the verdict may be reached during the night; in capital cases they hold the trial during the daytime and the verdict also must be reached during the daytime. In non-capital cases the verdict, whether of acquittal or of conviction, may be reached the same day; in capital cases a verdict of acquittal may be reached on the same day, but a verdict of conviction not until the following day. Therefore trials may not be held on the eve of a Sabbath or on the eve of a Festival-day.[2]

2. In non-capital[3] cases concerning uncleanness and cleanness [the judges declare their opinion] beginning from the eldest, but in capital cases they begin from [them that sit at] the side. All [of the family stocks][4] are qualified to try non-capital cases; but all are not qualified to try capital cases, but only priests, levites, and Israelites that may give [their daughters] in marriage into the priestly stock.

3. The Sanhedrin was arranged like the half of a round threshing-floor so that they all might see one another. Before them stood the two scribes of the judges, one to the right and one to the left, and they wrote down the words of them that favoured acquittal and the words of them that favoured conviction. R. Judah says: There were three: one wrote down the words of them that favoured acquittal, and one wrote down the words of them that favoured conviction, and the third wrote down the words both of them that favoured acquittal and of them that favoured conviction.

4. Before them sat three rows of disciples of the Sages, and each knew his proper place. If they needed to appoint [another as a judge], they appointed him from the first row, and one from the second row came into the first row, and one from the third row came into the second; and they chose yet another from the congregation and set him in the third row. He did not sit in the place of the former, but he sat in the place that was proper for him.

5. How did they admonish the witnesses in capital cases? They brought them in and admonished them, [saying,] 'Perchance ye will say what is but supposition or hearsay or at secondhand, or [ye may say in yourselves], We heard it from a man that was trustworthy. Or perchance ye do not know that we shall prove you by examination and inquiry? Know ye, moreover, that capital cases are not as non-capital cases: in non-capital

---

[1] Even disciples of the Sages (see 4⁴, 5⁴) who are not among the judges.
[2] Cf. p. 181, n. 11.   [3] Some texts omit 'non-capital'.   [4] See Kidd. 4¹ᶠᶠ.

cases a man may pay money and so make atonement, but in capital cases the witness is answerable for the blood of him [that is wrongfully condemned] and the blood of his posterity [that should have been born to him] to the end of the world. For so have we found it with Cain that slew his brother, for it is written, *The bloods of thy brother cry*.[1] It says not 'The blood of thy brother', but *The bloods of thy brother*—his blood and the blood of his posterity. (Another[2] saying is: *Bloods*[3] *of thy brother*—because his blood was cast over the trees and stones.) Therefore but a single man was created in the world, to teach that if any man has caused a single soul to perish from Israel[4] Scripture imputes it to him as though he had caused a whole world to perish; and if any man saves alive a single soul from Israel[4] Scripture imputes it to him as though he had saved alive a whole world. Again [but a single man was created] for the sake of peace among mankind, that none should say to his fellow, 'My father was greater than thy father'; also that the heretics should not say, 'There are many ruling powers in heaven'. Again [but a single man was created] to proclaim the greatness of the Holy One, blessed is he; for man stamps many coins with the one seal and they are all like one another; but the King of kings, the Holy One, blessed is he, has stamped every man with the seal of the first man, yet not one of them is like his fellow. Therefore every one must say, For my sake was the world created. And if perchance ye would say, Why should we be at these pains?—was it not once written, *He being a witness, whether he hath seen or known,* [*if he do not utter it, then shall he bear his iniquity*]?[5] And if perchance ye would say, Why should we be guilty of the blood of this man?—was it not once written, *When the wicked perish there is rejoicing?*[6]

5. 1. They used to prove witnesses with seven inquiries: In what week of years?[7] In what year? In what month? On what date in the month? On what day? In what hour? In what place? (R. Jose says: [They asked only,] On what day? In what hour? In what place?) [Moreover they asked:] Do ye recognize him? Did ye warn him? If a man had committed idolatry [they asked the witnesses], What did he worship? and, How did he worship it?

2. The more a judge tests the evidence the more is he deserving of praise: Ben Zakkai once tested the evidence even to the inquiring about the stalks of figs. Wherein do the inquiries differ from the cross-examination? If to the inquiries one [of the two witnesses] answered, 'I do not know', their evidence becomes invalid; but if to the cross-examination one answered, 'I do not know', or if they both answered, 'We do not know', their evidence remains valid. Yet if they contradict one another, whether during the inquiries or the cross-examination, their evidence becomes invalid.

3. If one said, 'On the second of the month', and the other said, 'On the third', their evidence remains valid, since one may have known that the month was intercalated[8] and the other did not know that the month was intercalated; but if one said, 'On the third', and the other said, 'On the fifth', their evidence becomes invalid. If one said, 'At the second hour', and the other said, 'At the third', their evidence remains valid; but if one said, 'At the third hour', and the other said, 'At the fifth', their evidence

---

[1] Gen. 4[10]. [2] An interpolated *Haggadah*. Cf. App. I. 10.

[3] Cf. Shab. 9[2]; Ohol. 2[7]. [4] Some texts omit 'from Israel'.

[5] Lev. 5[1]. [6] Prov. 11[10].

[7] B.M. 9[10]. [8] See R.Sh. 3[1].

becomes invalid. R. Judah says: It remains valid; but if one said, 'At the fifth hour', and the other said, 'At the seventh', their evidence becomes invalid since at the fifth hour the sun is in the east and at the seventh it is in the west.

4. They afterward brought in the second witness and proved him. If their words were found to agree together they begin [to examine the evidence] in favour of acquittal. If one of the witnesses said, 'I have somewhat to argue in favour of his acquittal', or if one of the disciples said, 'I have somewhat to argue in favour of his conviction', they silence him. If one of the disciples said, 'I have somewhat to argue in favour of his acquittal', they bring him up and set him among them and he does not come down from thence the whole day. If there is aught of substance in his words they listen to him. Even if the accused said, 'I have somewhat to argue in favour of my acquittal', they listen to him, provided that there is aught of substance in his words.

5. If they found him innocent they set him free; otherwise they leave his sentence over until the morrow. [In the meantime] they went together in pairs, they ate a little (but they used to drink no wine the whole day), and they discussed the matter all night, and early on the morrow they came to the court. He that favoured acquittal says: 'I declared him innocent [yesterday] and I still declare him innocent'; and he that favoured conviction says, 'I declared him guilty [yesterday] and I still declare him guilty'. He that had favoured conviction may now acquit, but he that had favoured acquittal may not retract and favour conviction. If they erred in the matter the scribes of the judges must put them in remembrance. If they [all] found him innocent they set him free; otherwise they decide by vote. If twelve favour acquittal and eleven favour conviction, he is declared innocent; if twelve favour conviction and eleven favour acquittal, or even if eleven favour acquittal and eleven favour conviction and one says, 'I do not know', or even if twenty-two favour acquittal or favour conviction and one says, 'I do not know', they must add to the number of judges. Up to what number may they add to them? By two at a time up to one and seventy. If then thirty-six favour acquittal and thirty-five favour conviction, he is declared innocent; if thirty-six favour conviction and thirty-five favour acquittal, they debate one with another until one of them that favoured conviction approves of the words of them that favour acquittal.

6. 1. When sentence [of stoning] has been passed they take him forth to stone him. The place of stoning was outside [far away from] the court, as it is written, *Bring forth him that hath cursed without the camp*.[1] One man stands at the door of the court with a towel in his hand, and another, mounted on a horse, far away from him [but near enough] to see him. If [in the court] one said, 'I have somewhat to argue in favour of his acquittal', that man waves the towel and the horse runs and stops him [that was going forth to be stoned]. Even if he himself said, 'I have somewhat to argue in favour of my acquittal', they must bring him back, be it four times or five, provided that there is aught of substance in his words. If then they found him innocent they set him free; otherwise he goes forth to be stoned. A herald goes out before him [calling], 'Such-a-one, the son of such-a-one, is going forth to be stoned for that he committed such or such an offence. Such-a-

[1] Lev. 24[14].

one and such-a-one are witnesses against him. If any man knoweth aught in favour of his acquittal let him come and plead it'.

2. When he was about ten cubits from the place of stoning they used to say to him, 'Make thy confession', for such is the way of them that have been condemned to death to make confession, for every one that makes his confession has a share in the world to come. For so have we found it with Achan. Joshua said to him, *My son, give, I pray thee, glory to the Lord, the God of Israel, and make confession unto him, and tell me now what thou hast done; hide it not from me. And Achan answered Joshua and said, Of a truth I have sinned against the Lord, the God of Israel, and thus and thus have I done.*[1] Whence do we learn that his confession made atonement for him? It is written, *And Joshua said, Why hast thou troubled us? the Lord shall trouble thee this day*[2]—*this day* thou shalt be troubled, but in the world to come thou shalt not be troubled. If he knows not how to make his confession they say to him, 'Say, May my death be an atonement for all my sins'. R. Judah says: If he knew that he was condemned because of false testimony he should say, 'Let my death be an atonement for all my sins excepting this sin'. They said to him: If so, every one would speak after this fashion to show his innocence.

3. When he was four cubits from the place of stoning they stripped off his clothes. A man is kept covered in front and a woman both in front and behind. So R. Judah. But the Sages say: A man is stoned naked but a woman is not stoned naked.

4. The place of stoning was twice the height of a man. One of the witnesses knocked him down on his loins; if he turned over on his heart the witness turned him over again on his loins. If he straightway died that sufficed; but if not, the second [witness] took the stone and dropped it on his heart. If he straightway died, that sufficed; but if not, he was stoned by all Israel, for it is written, *The hand of the witnesses shall be first upon him to put him to death and afterward the hand of all the people.*[3] All that have been stoned must be hanged. So R. Eliezer. But the Sages say: None is hanged save the blasphemer and the idolator. A man is hanged with his face to the people and a woman with her face towards the gallows. So R. Eliezer. But the Sages say: A man is hanged but a woman is not hanged. R. Eliezer said to them: Did not Simeon ben Shetah[4] hang women in Ashkelon? They answered: He hanged eighty women, whereas two ought not to be judged in the one day. How did they hang a man? They put a beam into the ground and a piece of wood jutted from it. The two hands [of the body] were brought together and [in this fashion] it was hanged. R. Jose says: The beam was made to lean against a wall and one hanged the corpse thereon as the butchers do. And they let it down at once: if it remained there overnight a negative command is thereby transgressed, for it is written, *His body shall not remain all night upon the tree, but thou shalt surely bury him the same day; for he that is hanged is a curse against*[5] *God;*[6] as if to say: Why was this one hanged? Because be blessed[7] the Name, and the Name of Heaven was found profaned.

5. R. Meir[8] said: When man is sore troubled, what says the Shekinah?[9]

---

[1] Josh. 7[19].   [2] Josh. 7[25].   [3] Deut. 17[7].
[4] Taan. 3[8]; Hag. 2[2]; Ab. 1[9].   [5] Lit. 'a curse of God'.   [6] Deut. 21[23].
[7] Euphemism for 'cursed'. Some texts read 'cursed'.
[8] The passage that follows is an interpolated *Haggadah*.
[9] Some texts here omit 'the Shekinah', the divine presence.

My head[1] is ill at ease, my arm is ill at ease. If God is sore troubled at the blood of the ungodly that is shed, how much more at the blood of the righteous? Furthermore, every one that suffers his dead to remain over-night transgresses a negative command; but if he had suffered it to remain by reason of the honour due to it, to bring for it a coffin and burial clothes, he does not thereby commit transgression. They used not to bury him in the burying-place of his fathers, but two burying-places were kept in readi-ness by the court, one for them that were beheaded or strangled, and one for them that were stoned or burnt.

6. When the flesh had wasted away they gathered together the bones[2] and buried them in their own place.[3] [After he was put to death] the kins-men came and greeted the judges and the witnesses as if to say, 'We have naught against you in our hearts, for ye have judged the judgement of truth'. And they used not to make [open] lamentation[4] but they went mourning, for mourning has place in the heart alone.

7. 1. The court had power to inflict four kinds of death-penalty: stoning, burning, beheading, and strangling. R. Simeon says: [Their order[5] of gravity is] burning, stoning, strangling, and beheading. This is the ordin-ance of them that are to be stoned.

2. The ordinance of them that are to be burnt [is this]: they set him in dung up to his knees and put a towel of coarse stuff within one of soft stuff and wrapt it around his neck; one [witness] pulled one end towards him and the other pulled one end towards him until he opened his mouth; a wick[6] was kindled and thrown into his mouth, and it went down to his stomach and burnt his entrails. R. Judah says: If thus he died at their hands they would not have fulfilled the ordinance of burning; but, rather, they must open his mouth with tongs by force and kindle the wick[6] and throw it into his mouth, and it goes down to his stomach and burns his entrails. R. Eliezer b. Zadok said: It happened once that a priest's daughter[7] com-mitted adultery and they encompassed her with bundles of branches and burnt her. They said to him: Because the court at that time had not right knowledge.[8]

3. The ordinance of them that are to be beheaded [is this]: they used to cut off his head with a sword as the government[9] does. R. Judah says: This is shameful for him; but, rather, they lay his head on a block and cut it off with an axe. They said to him: There is no death more shameful than this. The ordinance of them that are to be strangled [is this]: they set him in dung up to his knees and put a towel of coarse stuff within one of soft stuff and wrapt it around his neck; one [witness] pulled one end towards him and the other pulled one end towards him, until his life departed.

4. These are they that are to be stoned: he that has connexion with his mother, his father's wife, his daughter-in-law, a male, or a beast, and the woman that suffers connexion with a beast, and the blasphemer and the idolator, and he that offers any of his seed to Molech, and he that has a familiar spirit and the soothsayer, and he that profanes the Sabbath, and

[1] Some texts here prefix: 'If it could be said', a formula commonly used to apologize for some anthropomorphism. There are many textual variants at this point.
[2] Cf. Pes. 8[8]; M.Kat. 1[5].   [3] The family burying-place.   [4] Cf. M.Kat. 3[7f].
[5] Descending order of severity. See below, 9[3].
[6] This is the common meaning of the word. According to the Gemara (52a) it was a strip of lead.   [7] Lev. 21[9].   [8] It was (Gem. 52b) a court made up of Sadducees.
[9] The Romans. The victim was beheaded standing.

he that curses his father or his mother, and he that has connexion with a girl that is betrothed, and he that beguiles [others to idolatry], and he that leads [a whole town] astray, and the sorcerer and a stubborn and rebellious son.[1] He that has connexion with his mother is thereby culpable both by virtue of the law of the mother[2] and of the father's wife.[3] R. Judah says: He is culpable by virtue of the law of the mother only. He that has connexion with his father's wife is thereby culpable both by virtue of the law of the father's wife and of another man's wife,[4] whether in his father's lifetime or after his father's death, whether after betrothal [only] or after wedlock. He that has connexion with his daughter-in-law is thereby culpable both by virtue of the law of the daughter-in-law[5] and of another man's wife, whether in his son's lifetime or after his son's death, whether after betrothal [only] or after wedlock. He that has connexion with a male or with a beast, and she that suffers connexion with a beast, [their death is] by stoning.[6] If it is the man that has sinned how has the beast sinned? But inasmuch as an offence has befallen a man by reason of it, therefore Scripture has said that it shall be stoned. Another saying is: Lest the beast should go through the market and they say, This is the beast by reason of which such-a-one was stoned.

5. 'The blasphemer'[7] is not culpable unless he pronounces the Name itself.[8] R. Joshua b. Karha says: On every day [of the trial] they examined the witnesses with a substituted name, [such as] 'May Jose smite Jose'. When sentence was to be given they did not declare him guilty of death [on the grounds of evidence given] with the substituted name, but they sent out all the people and asked the chief among the witnesses and said to him, 'Say expressly what thou heardest', and he says it; and the judges stand up on their feet and rend their garments, and they may not mend them again. And the second witness says, 'I also heard the like', and the third says, 'I also heard the like'.

6. 'The idolator' [is culpable] no matter whether he worships or sacrifices or burns incense or pours out a libation or bows himself down to it or accepts it as his god or says to it, Thou art my god. But he that puts his arms around it or kisses it or sweeps it or besprinkles it or washes it or anoints it or clothes it or shoes it transgresses [only] a negative command.[9] He that makes a vow in its name or takes an oath in its name transgresses a negative command.[10] But if a man excretes to Baal Peor[11] [he is to be stoned, because] this is how it is worshipped. He that throws a stone at a *Merkolis*[12] [is to be stoned, because] this is how it is worshipped.

7. 'He that offers any of his seed to Molech'[13] is not culpable unless he gives up [the child] to Molech and passes him through the fire: if he gave him up to Molech but did not pass him through the fire, or if he passed him through the fire but did not give him up to Molech, he is not culpable; he must both give him up to Molech and pass him through the fire. 'He that

---

[1] Cf. the list in Ker. 1[1], where, for many of these, 'Extirpation', punishment at the hands of Heaven, is prescribed. Stoning was inflicted if the act was done after warning and in the presence of witnesses and deliberately; if it was done unwittingly the penalty is a Sin-offering (Lev. 4[27ff]).

[2] Lev. 18[7].   [3] Lev. 18[8].   [4] Lev. 18[20].   [5] Lev. 18[15].   [6] Lev. 20[15, 16].

[7] Lev. 24[10ff].   [8] Cf. Yom. 3[8], 6[2]; Sot. 7[6].   [9] Ex. 20[5].   [10] Ex. 23[13].

[11] Num. 25[3, 5]; Deut. 4[3]; Hos. 9[10]. The meaning of the root of 'Peor' is 'open wide'.

[12] Mercurius, the Greek Hermes. See A.Zar. 4[1]. The 'Merkolis' was a pillar surmounted by the head of Hermes. In this guise he was the patron deity of wayfarers.

[13] Lev. 18[21]; 20[2]. Cf. Meg. 4[9].

has a familiar spirit'[1] (such is the Python which speaks from his armpits), 'and the soothsayer'[2] (such is he that speaks with his mouth), these are [to be put to death] by stoning, and he that inquires of them transgresses against a warning.[3]

8. 'He that profanes the Sabbath'[4] [is liable, after warning, to death by stoning] if he committed an act which renders him liable to Extirpation[5] if he acted wantonly, or to a Sin-offering[6] if he acted in error. 'He that curses his father or his mother'[7] is not culpable unless he curses them with the Name.[8] If he cursed them with a substituted name R. Meir declares him culpable but the Sages declare him not culpable.

9. 'He that has connexion with a girl that is betrothed'[9] is not culpable unless she is still in her girlhood,[10] and a virgin, and betrothed, and still in her father's house. If two had connexion with her the first is [liable to death] by stoning, but the second [only] by strangling.

10. 'He that beguiles [others to idolatry]'—such is a common man[11] that beguiles another common man.[12] If he said to another, 'There is a god in such a place that eats this, drinks that, does good in this way and does harm in that way'—they may not place witnesses in hiding against any that become liable to the death-penalties enjoined in the Law save in this case alone. If he spoke [after this fashion] to two, and they are such that can bear witness against him,[13] they bring him to the court and stone him. If he spoke so to one only he may reply, 'I have companions that are so minded'; and if the other was crafty and would not speak before them, witnesses may be placed in hiding behind a wall. Then he says to the other, 'Say [again] what thou didst say to me in private', and the other speaks to him [as before] and he replies, 'How shall we leave our God that is in Heaven and go and worship wood and stone?' If he retracted it shall be well with him, but if he said, 'It is our duty and it is seemly so to do', they that are behind the wall bring him to the court and stone him. If a man said, 'I will worship [another god]' or 'I will go and worship it' or 'Let us go and worship it', or 'I will sacrifice to it' or 'I will go and sacrifice to it' or 'Let us go and sacrifice to it', or 'I will burn incense to it' or 'I will go and burn incense to it' or 'Let us go and burn incense to it', or 'I will make a libation to it' or 'I will go and make a libation to it' or 'Let us go and make a libation to it', or 'I will bow myself down before it' or 'I will go and bow myself down before it' or 'Let us go and bow ourselves down before it', [such a one is culpable]. 'He that leads [a whole town] astray'[14] is he that says, 'Let us go and worship idols'.

11. 'The sorcerer'[15]—he that performs some act is culpable, and not he that [only] deceives the eyes. R. Akiba in the name of R. Joshua says: If two were gathering cucumbers [by sorcery] one gatherer may not be culpable and the other gatherer may be culpable: he that [indeed] performed the act is culpable, but he that [only] deceived the eyes is not culpable.

---

1 Lev. 20[27]. It is rendered 'pythonicus' by the Vulgate.
2 Heb. *yidd'oni*. He used to put the bone of the *yaddu'a* (a wild beast or a bird) in his mouth and it spoke of itself (Gem. 65b).   3 Lev. 19[31], or Deut. 18[11].
4 Num. 15[32–6].   5 Cf. p. 562, n. 16.   6 Lev. 4[27ff].   7 Ex. 21[17]; Lev. 20[9].
8 With any of the special names of God. Cf. Shebu. 4[13].
9 Deut. 22[23f].
10 Between the ages of twelve and twelve and a half. Cf. Nidd. 5[6, 7].
11 Deut. 13[6–11], and not a false prophet (Deut. 13[1–5]) who is punishable by strangling. See below, 11[5].   12 And not a whole town.   13 Are not near of kin.
14 Deut. 13[13].   15 Deut. 18[10]. Cf. Ex. 22[18].

8. 1. 'A stubborn and rebellious son'[1]—when can he be condemned as a stubborn and rebellious son? From the time that he can produce two hairs[2] until he grows a beard (the lower one and not the upper one [is meant], howbeit the Sages spoke in modest language), for it is written, *If a man have a son*;—a son and not a daughter, a son and not a man; a minor[3] is exempt since he has not yet come within the scope of the commandments.

2. When is he culpable? After he has eaten a *tritimor*[4] of flesh and drunk a half-*log*[5] of Italian wine. R. Jose says: A *mina*[4] of flesh and a *log* of wine. If he consumed it at a gathering that was a religious duty,[6] or at the intercalation of the month,[7] or if he consumed it as Second Tithe in Jerusalem,[8] or if he ate carrion[9] or flesh that was *terefah*[10] or forbidden beasts[11] or creeping things,[12] if by consuming it he had fulfilled a command or had committed a transgression, if he ate any foodstuff but did not eat flesh, or drank any liquid but did not drink wine, he cannot be condemned as a stubborn and rebellious son; but only if he eats flesh and drinks wine, for it is written, *A glutton and a drunkard*.[13] And though there is no proof for this, there is an indication,[14] for it is written, *Be not among winebibbers; among gluttonous eaters of flesh*.[15]

3. If he stole it from his father and ate it in his father's domain, or from others and ate it in the others' domain, or from others and ate it in his father's domain, he cannot be condemned as a stubborn and rebellious son; but only if he steals from his father and eats it in the others' domain. R. Jose the son of R. Judah says: Only if he steals from his father and from his mother.

4. If his father was willing [to accuse him] but his mother was not willing, or if his father was not willing but his mother was willing, he cannot be condemned as a stubborn and rebellious son; but only if they both were willing. R. Judah says: If his mother was not fit for his father he cannot be condemned as a stubborn and rebellious son. If either of them was maimed in the hand, or lame or dumb or blind or deaf, he cannot be condemned as a stubborn and rebellious son, for it is written, *Then shall his father and his mother lay hold on him*—so they were not maimed in the hand; *and bring him out*—so they were not lame; *and they shall say*—so they were not dumb; *this our son*—so they were not blind; *he will not obey our voice*—so they were not deaf. They must warn him, and scourge him before three [judges]. If he again behaved evilly he must be tried before three and twenty [judges]; and he may only be stoned if the first three are there, for it is written, *This our son*, to wit, this is he that was beaten before you. If he ran away before sentence was passed on him and afterward grew the lower beard, he is exempt; but if he ran away after sentence was passed on him and afterward grew the lower beard, he is still liable.

5. A stubborn and rebellious son is condemned because of [what he may become in] the end: the Law has said,[16] Let him die innocent and let him not die guilty; for the death of the ungodly is a benefit to them and a

---

[1] Deut. 21[18ff].   [2] Cf. Nidd. 6[11].   [3] A boy under thirteen years and a day.
[4] App. II, B.   [5] App. II, D.   [6] e.g. a wedding or a circumcision.
[7] Cf. R.Sh. 3[1]; cf. 2[5].   [8] Deut. 14[26].   [9] Deut. 14[21].
[10] Ex. 22[31]; cf. App. II. 47.   [11] Lev. 11[1ff].
[12] Lev. 11[42f]. Some texts here add: 'or if he consumed untithed produce or First Tithe from which Heave-offering had not been taken, or Second Tithe or dedicated produce that had not been redeemed'. On these see p. 7, nn. 6–9.
[13] Deut. 21[20].   [14] Cf. Shab. 8[7].   [15] Prov. 23[20]
[16] Some texts omit 'The Law has said'.

benefit to the world, but the death of the righteous is a misfortune to them and a misfortune to the world. The wine and sleep of the ungodly are a benefit to them and a benefit to the world, but the wine and sleep of the righteous are a misfortune to them and a misfortune to the world. The dispersion of the ungodly is a benefit to them and a benefit to the world, but the dispersion of the righteous is a misfortune to them and a misfortune to the world. The gathering together of the ungodly is a misfortune to them and a misfortune to the world, but the gathering together of the righteous is a benefit to them and a benefit to the world. Peacefulness for the ungodly is a misfortune to them and a misfortune to the world, but peacefulness for the righteous is a benefit to them and a benefit to the world.[1]

6. The thief that is found breaking through[2] is condemned because of [what he may do in] the end. If in his breaking through he broke a jar and there would be bloodguiltiness [if the householder killed him],[3] he is liable [to make restitution]; if there would be no bloodguiltiness he is exempt.[4]

7. These may be delivered [from transgression] at the cost of their lives: he that pursues after his fellow to kill him, or after a male, or after a girl that is betrothed; but he that pursues after a beast, or that profanes the Sabbath, or that commits idolatry—they may not be delivered [from transgression] at the cost of their lives.

9. 1. And these are they that are to be burnt: he that has connexion with a woman and her daughter,[5] and the daughter of a priest that has committed adultery.[6] Under the law of 'a woman and her daughter' falls also [any case wherein a man has connexion with] his daughter or his daughter's daughter, or his son's daughter or his wife's daughter, or her daughter's daughter, or her son's daughter, or his mother-in-law, his mother-in-law's mother, or his father-in-law's mother. And these are they that are to be beheaded: the murderer[7] and the people of an Apostate City.[8] If a murderer had struck his fellow with a stone or with [an instrument of] iron, or if he had pressed him down into the water or into the fire and he could not arise out of it, and he died, he is culpable. If he pushed him [and he fell] into the water or into the fire and he could arise out of it, and yet he died, he is not culpable. If he had incited a dog against him or had incited a serpent against him, he is not culpable. If he caused the serpent to bite him R. Judah declares him culpable, but the Sages declare him not culpable. If a man struck his fellow, whether with a stone or with the fist, and they considered him like to die, and he then grew better and afterward grew worse and died, he is culpable. R. Nehemiah declares him not culpable, since there is proof whereon to rely [for believing that there was some other cause of death].[9]

2. If he had intended to kill a beast and killed a man, or a gentile and killed an Israelite, or an untimely birth and killed offspring that was like to live, he is not culpable. If he had intended to strike a man on the loins a blow that on the loins was not enough to cause death, but it lighted upon his heart and it was a blow that on the heart was enough to cause death, and he died, he is not culpable. If he intended to strike a man on the heart

---

[1] In his silence the ungodly meditates mischief but the righteous ponders words of the Law.   [2] Ex. 22[2ff].   [3] 'If the sun be risen upon him'.
[4] From making restitution, since he incurred the graver penalty of death. For the principle see Ket. 3[2]; B.K. 3[10] (end).   [5] Lev. 18[17].
[6] Lev. 21[9]; cf. Ter. 7[2].   [7] Num. 35[16ff].   [8] Deut. 13[15].   [9] Naz. 9[4].

a blow that on the heart was enough to cause death, but it lighted upon his loins and it was a blow that on the loins was not enough to cause death, and yet he died, he is not culpable. If he had intended to strike a grown man a blow that was not enough to cause death to a grown man, but it lighted upon a child and it was a blow that was enough to cause death to a child, and it died, he is not culpable. If he had intended to strike a child a blow that was enough to cause death to a child, but it lighted upon a grown man, and it was a blow that was not enough to cause death to a grown man, and yet he died, he is not culpable. But if he had intended to strike a man on the loins a blow that on the loins was enough to cause death, and it lighted upon his heart, and he died, he is culpable. If he intended to strike a grown man a blow that was enough to cause death to a grown man, and it lighted upon a child, and it died, he is culpable. R. Simeon says: Even if he had intended to kill one but killed another he is not culpable.

3. If a murderer was confused among others, none of them is culpable. R. Judah says: They are all brought into prison. If men liable to different kinds of death-penalty were confused together, they are to be punished by the more lenient death-penalty. If they that were to be stoned were confused with them that were to be burnt, R. Simeon says: They must be punished by stoning since burning is the severer death. But the Sages say: They must be punished by burning since stoning is the severer death. R. Simeon said to them: If burning was not the more severe it would not have been prescribed for the daughter of a priest that committed adultery. They said to him: If stoning was not the more severe it would not have been prescribed for the blasphemer and the idolator. If they that were to be beheaded were confused with them that were to be strangled, R. Simeon says: [They must be punished] by the sword. But the Sages say: By strangling.

4. If a man was found liable to two of the death-penalties that can be inflicted by the court, he must be punished by the more severe of them. If he committed a transgression by which he was found liable to two kinds of death-penalty,[1] he must be punished by the more severe of them. R. Jose says: He must be punished by that penalty which first attaches to his transgression.[2]

5. If a man was scourged [and committed again the same transgression] and was scourged a second time, [if he transgressed a third time] the court must put him in a prison-cell and feed him with barley until his belly bursts. If a man committed murder but there were no witnesses, they must put him in prison and feed him with *the bread of adversity and the water of affliction.*[3]

6. If a man stole a sacred vessel or cursed by Kosem[4] or made an Aramean woman his paramour,[5] the zealots[6] may fall upon him. If a priest served [at the Altar] in a state of uncleanness[7] his brethren the priests did

---

[1] e.g. intercourse with a mother-in-law who was married to a husband renders him liable to strangulation for transgressing the law respecting a man's wife, and to burning for transgressing the law respecting a mother and her daughter; therefore he is punished by burning, the severer penalty.

[2] If the mother-in-law was a widow, and afterwards married, he suffers under the law of the mother and her daughter.   [3] Is. 30[20].

[4] Of uncertain meaning. Variously explained as the name of a god, or a disguised divine name (e.g. an abbreviation of some such title as κοσμοπλάστης), or a pseudonym for God.

[5] Cf. Num. 25[6ff].   [6] Like Phineas.

[7] And legally (Makk. 3[2]) was punishable by scourging only.

not bring him to the court, but the young men among the priests took him outside the Temple Court and split open his brain with clubs.[1] If one that was not a priest served in the Temple, R. Akiba says: [He must be put to death] by strangling. But the Sages say: [He shall suffer death] at the hands of Heaven.

10. 1. All Israelites have a share in the world to come, for it is written, *Thy people also shall be all righteous, they shall inherit the land for ever; the branch of my planting, the work of my hands that I may be glorified.*[2] And these are they that have no share in the world to come: he that says that there is no resurrection of the dead prescribed in the Law,[3] and [he that says] that the Law is not from Heaven, and an Epicurean.[4] R. Akiba says: Also he that reads the heretical books,[5] or that utters charms over a wound and says, *I will put none of the diseases upon thee which I have put upon the Egyptians: for I am the Lord that healeth thee.*[6] Abba Saul says: Also he that pronounces the Name with its proper letters.[7]

2. Three kings and four commoners have no share in the world to come. The three kings are Jeroboam and Ahab and Manasseh. R. Judah says: Manasseh has a share in the world to come, for it is written, *And he prayed unto him, and he was intreated of him and heard his supplication and brought him again to Jerusalem into his kingdom.*[8] They said to him: He brought him again to his kingdom, but he did not bring him to the life of the world to come. The four commoners are Balaam and Doeg and Ahitophel and Gehazi.

3. The generation of the Flood have no share in the world to come, nor shall they stand in the judgement, for it is written, *My spirit shall not judge with man for ever;*[9] [thus they have] neither judgement nor spirit. The generation of the Dispersion have no share in the world to come, for it is written, *So the Lord scattered them abroad from thence upon the face of all the earth;*[10] *So the Lord scattered them abroad*—in this world; *and the Lord scattered them from thence*—in the world to come. The men of Sodom have no share in the world to come, for it is written, *Now the men of Sodom were wicked and sinners against the Lord exceedingly;*[11] *wicked* in this world, *and sinners* in the world to come. But they shall stand in the judgement. R. Nehemiah says: Neither of them shall stand in the judgement, for it is written: *Therefore the wicked shall not stand in the judgement nor sinners in the congregation of the righteous.*[12] *Therefore the wicked shall not stand in the judgement*—this is the generation of the Flood; *nor sinners in the congregation of the righteous*—these are the men of Sodom. They said to him: They shall not stand in the congregation of the righteous, but they shall stand in the congregation of the ungodly. The spies have no share in the world to come, for it is written, *Even those men that did bring up an evil report of the land died by the plague before the Lord;*[13] *died*—in this world; *by the plague*—in the world to come. The generation of the wilderness have no share in

---

[1] Or 'faggots' (intended for the altar fire). It is the word used in Tam. 2³.

[2] Is. 60²¹.   [3] Some texts omit 'prescribed in the Law'.

[4] A frequent epithet applied both to gentiles and Jews opposed to the rabbinical teachings. It is in no way associated with teachings supposed by the Jews to emanate from the philosopher Epicurus; to Jewish ears it conveys the sense of the root *pakar*, 'be free from restraint', and so licentious and sceptical.

[5] Lit. 'external books', books excluded from the canon of Hebrew Scriptures.

[6] Ex. 15²⁶.   [7] Cf. above, 7⁵.   [8] 2 Chron. 33¹³.   [9] Gen. 6³.

[10] Gen. 11⁸.   [11] Gen. 13¹³.   [12] Ps. 1⁵.   [13] Num. 14³⁷.

the world to come nor shall they stand in the judgement, for it is written, *In this wilderness they shall be consumed and there they shall die.*[1] So R. Akiba. But R. Eliezer says: It says of them also, *Gather my saints together unto me, those that have made a covenant with me by sacrifice.*[2] The company of Korah shall not rise up again, for it is written, *And the earth closed upon them,*[3] in this world, *and they perished from among the assembly,* in the world to come. So R. Akiba. But R. Eliezer says: It says of them also, *The Lord killeth and maketh alive, he bringeth down to Sheol and bringeth up.*[4] The Ten Tribes shall not return again, for it is written, *And he cast them into another land like this day.*[5] Like as this day goes and returns not, so do they go and return not. So R. Akiba. But R. Eliezer says: Like as the day grows dark and then grows light, so also after darkness is fallen upon the Ten Tribes shall light hereafter shine upon them.

4. 'The people of an Apostate City' have[6] no share in the world to come. For it is written, *Certain base fellows are gone out from the midst of thee and have drawn away the inhabitants of their city*[7]—they may not be put to death unless the beguilers belong to that same city and that same tribe, and unless the greater part of it has been beguiled, and unless they that beguiled them were men; if women or children beguiled the city, or if the lesser part of it was beguiled, or if they that beguiled it came from elsewhere, they count only as single [idolators],[8] and for each of them two witnesses and forewarning are required. Herein greater stringency applies to single [idolators] than to the many, for single [idolators are put to death] by stoning, therefore their property is saved; but the many [are put to death] by the sword, therefore their property perishes.

5. *Thou shalt surely smite the inhabitants of the city with the edge of the sword*[9]—if ass-drivers or camel-drivers were passing through [the city] from place to place, these can deliver it;[10] *destroying it utterly and all that is therein and the cattle thereof, with the edge of the sword*—hence they have said that the property of the righteous therein perishes, but that which is outside is saved, while that of the wicked, whether inside or outside the city, perishes.

6. *And thou shalt gather all the spoil of it into the midst of the wide place*[11] *thereof*—if it has no open space they must make for it an open space; if the open space was outside, they must bring it inside. *And thou shalt burn with fire the city and all the spoil thereof, every whit, unto the Lord thy God*—the spoil thereof, but not the spoil belonging to Heaven; hence they have said that the dedicated things[12] therein must be redeemed, and the Heave-offerings[13] suffered to rot. The Second Tithe[14] and the Sacred Scriptures must be hidden away. *Every whit unto the Lord thy God*—R. Simeon said: The Holy One, blessed is he, said, 'When ye execute judgement against an Apostate City I will reckon it to you as if ye offered up before me a whole burnt offering'. *And it shall be an heap for ever: it shall not be built again*— it may not even be made into gardens or orchards. So R. Jose the Galilean.

---

[1] Num. 14[35].   [2] Ps. 50[5].   [3] Num. 16[33].   [4] 1 Sam. 2[6].   [5] Deut. 29[28].

[6] Some texts omit 'have no share in the world to come', a phrase which wrongly assimilates what follows to the section immediately preceding. The present paragraph resumes the subjects summarized in 9[1], and might be expected to follow after 9[5].

[7] Deut. 13[13]. To the end of the chapter the *midrash* method of treatment is followed. Cf. Sot. 8[1ff]; 9[1ff].   [8] See above, 7[10].   [9] Deut. 13[15].

[10] They may serve to make the unperverted into a majority. A variant reading is: 'These may be delivered'.   [11] Cf. Taan. 2[1]; Meg. 3[1].

[12] Lev. 27[14ff].   [13] App. II. 48.   [14] p. 73, n. 6.

R. Akiba says: *It shall not be built again* means that it may not be built as it was before, but it may be made into gardens and orchards. *And there shall cleave nought of the devoted thing to thine hand; [that the Lord may turn from the fierceness of his anger and show thee mercy and have compassion upon thee and multiply thee]*—for so long as the ungodly are in the world, *the fierceness of his anger* is in the world; after the ungodly are perished from the world, *the fierceness of his anger* will be removed from the world.

11. 1. These are they that are to be strangled: he that strikes his father or his mother,[1] and he that steals a soul from Israel,[2] and the elder that rebels against the decision of the court, and the false prophet, and he that prophesies in the name of a strange god, and he that has connexion with another man's wife, and the false witnesses against the daughter of a priest and her paramour. 'He that strikes his father or his mother'—he is not culpable unless he causes a wound in them. Herein greater stringency applies to him that curses than to him that strikes, for he that curses them after their death is culpable, but he that strikes them after their death is not culpable. 'He that steals a soul from Israel'—he is not culpable unless he brings him into his own domain. R. Judah says: Unless he brings him into his own domain and makes use of him, for it is written, *And if he deal with him as a slave or sell him.*[3] If a man stole his own son, R. Ishmael b.[4] R. Johanan b. Baroka declares him culpable, but the Sages declare him not culpable. If he stole one that was half bondman and half freedman,[5] R. Judah declares him culpable, but the Sages declare him not culpable.

2. 'The elder that rebels against the decision of the court'—as it is written, *If there arise a matter too hard for thee in judgement, between blood and blood, between plea and plea*...[6] Three courts were there [in Jerusalem]: one used to sit at the gate of the Temple Mount,[7] one used to sit at the gate of the Temple Court,[8] and one used to sit in the Chamber of Hewn Stone.[9] They[10] used to come first to the court that was at the gate of the Temple Mount, and the one would say, 'In this way have I expounded[11] and in that way have my fellows expounded; in this way have I taught[12] and in that way have my fellows taught'. If they [of that court] had heard a tradition,[13] they told it to them; otherwise they betook themselves to them of the court that was at the gate of the Temple Court, and the one would say, 'In this way have I expounded and in that way have my fellows expounded; in this way have I taught and in that way have my fellows taught'. If they [of that court] had heard a tradition, they told it to them; otherwise they both came in to the Great Court that was in the Chamber of Hewn Stone, whence the Law goes forth to all Israel, as it is written, *From that place which the Lord shall choose.*[14] If [any one of the elders that went up to Jerusalem to inquire] returned to his own city and again taught as he was wont to teach, he is not yet culpable; but if he gave a decision concerning what

---

[1] Ex. 21[15].   [2] Deut. 24[7].   [3] Deut. 24[7].
[4] Some texts omit 'R. Ishmael b.'
[5] A slave who had been owned by two jointholders of whom one had set him free.
[6] Deut. 17[8-13].   [7] At the east gate in front of the Court of the Women.
[8] i.e. the entrance to the Court of the Israelites.
[9] North of the Court of the Israelites; cf. Midd. 5[4].
[10] The local court which was in search of guidance.
[11] The Scriptural principle on which the judgement turns.
[12] The application of the principle to the case at issue.
[13] A ruling handed down by their teachers deciding or bearing upon the special point.
[14] Deut. 17[10].

should be done, he is culpable, for it is written, *And the man that doeth presumptuously . . .*;[1] he is not culpable unless he gives a decision concerning what should be done. If a disciple gave a decision concerning what should be done he is not culpable, thus the greater stringency[2] that applies to him on the one hand is seen to serve as leniency on the other.

3. Greater stringency applies to [the observance of] the words of the Scribes than to [the observance of] the words of the [written] Law.[3] If a man said, 'There is no obligation to wear phylacteries'[4] so that he transgresses the words of the Law, he is not culpable; [but if he said], 'There should be in them five partitions', so that he adds to the words of the Scribes, he is culpable.

4. He was not condemned to death either by the court that was in his own city or by the court that was in Jabneh,[5] but he was brought up to the Great Court that was in Jerusalem. He was kept in guard until one of the [three] Feasts[6] and he was put to death on one of the [three] Feasts, for it is written, *And all the people shall hear and fear, and do no more presumptuously.*[7] So R. Akiba. But R. Judah says: They should not delay his judgement but put him to death at once, and write out and send messengers to every place, [saying], 'Such-a-one the son of such-a-one has been condemned to death by the court'.

5. 'The false prophet'[8]—he that prophesies what he has not heard and what has not been told him, his death[9] is at the hands of men; but he that suppresses his prophecy[10] or disregards the words of another prophet[11] or the prophet that transgresses his own words,[12] his death is at the hands of Heaven, for it is written, *I will require it of him.*[13]

6. 'He that prophesies in the name of a strange god'[14] and says, 'Thus saith the god', [is culpable] even if he conformed with the *Halakah*[15] so as to declare unclean what is unclean and to declare clean what is clean. 'He that has connexion with another man's wife'[16]—so soon as she has entered into the control of the husband in wedlock even if she has not suffered consummation, he that has connexion with her shall be put to death by strangling. 'The false witnesses against the daughter of a priest and her paramour'[17]—all false witnesses suffer first that same death-penalty [to which the accused had been made liable] save the false witnesses against the daughter of a priest[18] and her paramour.

---

[1] Deut. 17[12]. [2] In that he was not empowered to give legal decisions.
[3] i.e. it is a more serious offence in a judge who gives false direction in what concerns the rulings of the Scribes (cf. Hor. 1[3]). This paragraph is omitted in the first printed edition of the Mishnah (Naples 1492).
[4] See p. 104, n. 16. [5] Which sat there from A.D. 70 to 118.
[6] Passover, Pentecost, or Tabernacles. [7] Deut. 17[13]. [8] Deut. 18[20].
[9] Some texts omit this clause. [10] Jonah 1[3]. [11] 1 Kings 20[35].
[12] 1 Kings 13[26]. [13] Deut. 18[19]. [14] Deut. 18[20]. [15] App. I. 11. [16] Lev. 18[20].
[17] The law of the false witness (treated in detail in the following tractate 'Makkoth') is based on Deut. 19[16-18].
[18] See above, 9[1]. She is to be put to death by burning, and he by strangling. If the witnesses against them are found false it is in doubt which of these two penalties can be applied. According to the *Tosefta* their death is by burning. But cf. above, 9[1].

MAKKOTH[1] ('STRIPES')

1. 1. How are witnesses dealt with under the law against false witness?[2] [If they had said of a priest,] 'We testify that such-a-one[3] is the son of a divorced woman, or the son of a woman that performed *halitzah*',[4] we cannot say, Let him be made in his stead 'the son of a divorced woman' or 'the son of a woman that performed *halitzah*'; but he must suffer the Forty Stripes.[5] [If false witnesses have said,] 'We testify that such-a-one is liable to exile',[6] we cannot say, Let him be exiled in his stead; but he must suffer the Forty Stripes. [If false witnesses have said,] 'We testify that such-a-one divorced his wife and did not pay her her *Ketubah*'[7] (yet may it not befall,[8] to-day or to-morrow, that he will pay her her *Ketubah*?), they estimate how much a man would be willing to pay [now] for her *Ketubah* on the chance that she might be widowed or divorced, whereas, if she died, her husband would inherit it from her. [If false witnesses have said,]' We testify that such-a-one owes his fellow 1,000 *zuz* with a condition that he shall pay him within thirty days', and the other said, 'Within ten years', they estimate how much a man would be willing to pay to have in his hands 1,000 *zuz* which, instead of being repayable within thirty days, shall be repayable within ten years.

2. [If they have said,] 'We testify that such-a-one owes his fellow 200 *zuz*', and they are found false witnesses, they must be scourged and pay also the 200 *zuz*, since the class of transgression[9] which renders a man liable to scourging[10] is other than that which renders him liable to make recompense.[11] So R. Meir. But the Sages say: He that makes recompense does not suffer the Forty Stripes.

3. [If they have said,] 'We testify that such-a-one is liable to suffer the Forty Stripes', and they are found false witnesses, they must suffer eighty stripes by virtue of the law *Thou shalt not bear false witness against thy neighbour*,[12] and also by virtue of the law *Then shall ye do unto him as he had thought to do*.[13] So R. Meir. But the Sages say: They suffer forty stripes only. A penalty in money may be divided among them, but not a penalty of scourging; thus if they have testified that a man owed his fellow 200 *zuz* and they are found false witnesses, the penalty is divided among them; but if they have testified that he was liable to the Forty Stripes, and they are found false witnesses, each of them suffers the Forty [Stripes].

4. Witnesses become subject to the law against false witness only if they bear false witness about themselves. Thus if they said, 'We testify that such-a-one committed murder', and others answered, 'How can ye testify so, for lo, he that was killed, or he that killed him, was with us that same day in such a place', they are not condemned as false witnesses; but if others answered, 'How can ye testify so, for lo, ye were with us that same day in

---

[1] This tractate, originally combined with 'Sanhedrin' into a single tractate, deals with the manner of applying the law against false witnesses (Deut. 19[19]), with the Cities of Refuge, and with the infliction of the punishment of 'Forty stripes save one'.
[2] i.e. what is done in those cases when Deut. 19[19] ('Then shall ye do unto him as he had thought to do to his brother') is impossible of application?
[3] Is of 'impaired priestly stock and ineligible to serve as a priest'; cf. Kidd. 4[1ff].
[4] App. I. 12.
[5] Deut. 25[1ff]., according to the Gemara, 2b, specifically applies to false witnesses.
[6] To one of the Cities of Refuge. See below, 2[1ff].   [7] App. I. 16.
[8] When he dies, or if he in truth divorces her. Therefore the false witnesses would have occasioned him no loss.   [9] Lit. 'name', i.e. category of law.
[10] Ex. 20[16].   [11] As does Deut. 19[19].   [12] Ex. 20[16].   [13] Deut. 19[19].

such a place', they are condemmed as false witnesses and are put to death at the mouth of the others.

5. If yet others came and proved false the evidence of these others, and yet others came and proved their evidence false, even if [there came] a hundred [pairs of witnesses to prove false the evidence of them that went before], they must all be put to death. R. Judah says: This would be a conspiracy: but the first pair alone are put to death.

6. False witnesses are put to death only after judgement has been given. For lo, the Sadducees used to say: Not until he [that was falsely accused] has been put to death, as it is written, *Life for life*.[1] The Sages answered: Is it not also written, *Then shall ye do unto him as he had thought to do unto his brother*?[2]—thus his brother must be still alive. If so, why was it written, *Life for life*? Could it be that they were put to death so soon as their evidence was received [and found false]?—but Scripture says, *Life for life*; thus they are not put to death until judgement [of death] has been given [against him that was falsely accused].

7. *At the mouth of two witnesses, or three witnesses, shall he that is to die be put to death*:[3] if the evidence can be sustained by two witnesses why has Scripture said 'three' in particular? To compare three to two: as three witnesses[4] may prove two witnesses false, so two may prove three false. Whence [do we learn that two witnesses may prove even] a hundred [false]? Scripture says, 'Witnesses'.[5] R. Simeon says: Like as the two cannot be put to death unless they both are proved false witnesses, so three cannot be put to death unless they all three are proved false witnesses. And whence [do we learn that this applies even to] a hundred? Scripture says, 'Witnesses'. R. Akiba says: The third witness is here mentioned only that the same stringency shall apply to him also, and that his condemnation shall be made like to that of the other two; if, then, Scripture has punished him that is joined to them that commit a transgression in like manner as them that themselves commit transgression, how much more will it recompense a like reward to him that is joined to them that fulfil a commandment as to them that themselves fulfil a commandment!

8. As the evidence of two witnesses is void if one of them is found to be a kinsman or ineligible,[6] so the evidence of three is void if one of them is found to be a kinsman or ineligible. Whence [do we learn that this applies even to one out of] a hundred? Scripture says, 'Witnesses'. R. Jose said: This only applies in capital cases;[7] but in non-capital cases the evidence can be sustained by the remaining witnesses [that are not ineligible]. Rabbi says: It applies alike in non-capital cases and capital cases. When [does it apply in capital cases]? When they[8] joined in warning[9] [the transgressor]; but if they had not joined in the warning—what should two brothers[10] do that saw one that committed murder?[11]

9. If two men saw him from one window and two saw him from another

[1] Deut. 19[21].   [2] Deut. 19[19].   [3] Deut. 17[6].   [4] Being a majority.
[5] Even though they are a hundred the force of their testimony is only as that of two. By the form of expression 'two witnesses, or three witnesses' Scripture indicates an infinite numerical series; the essential and constant element is 'witnesses' (i.e. not less than two).
[6] See Sanh. 3[3,4].   [7] When the accused must be granted every assistance.
[8] The ineligible or near of kin.
[9] The witness must have warned the transgressor, otherwise he is not a valid witness (see Sanh. 5[1]).
[10] Who, together with an unrelated third witness, give evidence.
[11] Only if one of the brothers had not warned him can the other brother and the stranger be accounted valid witnesses.

window, and one in the middle warned him, if some among them can see the others, they are accounted a single body of testimony;[1] otherwise they count as two bodies of testimony. If, therefore, [only] one pair of them were found false witnesses, both the accused[2] and they must be put to death, while the second pair are not culpable. R. Jose says: None may ever be put to death unless he has been warned at the mouth of both his witnesses, for it is written, *At the mouth of two witnesses.*[3] Another saying is: *At the mouth of two witnesses*—that the Sanhedrin should not hear [the evidence only] from the mouth of an interpreter.

10. If a man escaped after judgement had been given against him, and he came [again] before the same court, they may not reverse his condemnation. Where two can rise up and say, 'We testify that judgement [of death] against such-a-one was given in such a court, and such-a-one and such-a-one were his witnesses', he must be put to death. The Sanhedrin may conduct its office either within the Land [of Israel] or outside the Land [of Israel]. A Sanhedrin that puts one man to death in a week of years[4] is called 'destructive'. R. Eliezer b. Azariah says: Or one in even seventy years. R. Tarfon and R. Akiba say: Had we been in the Sanhedrin none would ever have been put to death. Rabban Simeon b. Gamaliel says: They would even have multiplied the shedders of blood in Israel.

2. 1. These must escape into exile:[5] If a man killed a soul unwittingly— if he was rolling [the roof] with a roller[6] and it fell on a man and killed him, or if he was letting down a jar [from the roof] and it fell on a man and killed him, or if he was coming down a ladder and he fell on a man and killed him—he must escape into exile; but if he was pulling up a roller and it fell on a man and killed him, or if he was drawing up a jar and the rope broke and it fell on a man and killed him, or if he was going up a ladder and fell down on a man and killed him, he need not escape into exile. This is the general rule: he [that causes death] in the course of his coming down must escape into exile, but if not in the course of his coming down, he need not escape into exile. If the iron [of an axe] slipped from its haft and killed a man, Rabbi says that he need not escape into exile, but the Sages say that he must do so. If a piece of wood that was being chopped [flew up and killed a man], Rabbi says: He must escape into exile. But the Sages say: He need not escape into exile.

2. If a man threw a stone into the public domain and killed [another], he must escape into exile. R. Eliezer b. Jacob says: If after the stone had left his hand the other put out his head and received the stone, he is not culpable. If he threw the stone into his own courtyard and killed another, if he that was injured had the right to enter thither, the other must escape into exile; but if he had not the right, the other need not escape into exile; for it is written, *As when a man goeth into the forest with his neighbour*[7]—since the forest is a place into which the injurer and the injured have the right to enter, this excludes [from the law of unwitting murder] the courtyard of a householder into which the injured had not the right to enter. Abba Saul says: As the chopping of wood is an act of free choice [the law of

---

1 And no one of them all can be condemned as a false witness unless all are condemned.
2 Who is found guilty on the evidence of the pair not proved false witnesses.
3 Deut. 17[6].   4 Dan. 9[24ff].   5 See below, par. 4.
6 To harden the mixture of straw and clay used for the flat roofing of the house.
7 Deut. 19[5].

unwitting murder applies] to every act of free choice; this excludes the father that smites his son, or the teacher that chastises his pupil, or the agent of the court.[1]

3. The father must escape into exile because of his son,[2] and the son because of his father. All[3] must go into exile because of an Israelite, and an Israelite because of all others, excepting a resident alien.[4] A resident alien need not go into exile save only because of [another] resident alien. He that is blind need not go into exile. So R. Judah. R. Meir says: He must go into exile. An enemy[5] may not go into exile. R. Jose b. Judah says: An enemy must be put to death since he is, as it were, 'an attested danger'.[6] R. Simeon says: There is an enemy that may escape into exile and an enemy that may not escape into exile. This is the general rule: if it can be said, 'He killed wittingly', he may not escape into exile; but if, 'He did not kill wittingly', he may escape into exile.

4. Whither may they go into exile? To the cities of refuge: to the three that are beyond Jordan or to the three that are in the land of Canaan, as it is written, *Ye shall give three cities beyond Jordan and three cities shall ye give in the land of Canaan . . .*[7] The three cities beyond Jordan granted no right of asylum until the three were chosen in the land of Israel, for it is written, *They shall be for you six cities of refuge;*[8] they must all six of them together grant right of asylum.

5. And roads were made ready from one to the other, as it is written, *Thou shalt prepare thee the way and divide the borders of thy land . . .*[9] And they used to appoint for him two disciples of the Sages,[10] that if the avenger of blood would slay him by the way they may speak unto him.[11] R. Meir says: Even he himself[12] may speak unto him,[11] for it is written, *This is the word of the manslayer.*[13]

6. R. Jose b. Judah says: Beforetime both he that killed unwittingly and he that killed wantonly fled forthwith to the cities of refuge, and the court used to send and fetch them from thence. He that was condemned to death by the court was beheaded,[14] and he that was not condemned to death was set free; he that was condemned to exile was sent back to his place, as it is written, *And the congregation shall restore him to his city of refuge . . .*[15] [A High Priest that dies] no matter whether he was anointed with the oil of unction or whether he was dedicated by the many garments or whether he had passed from his high-priesthood,[16] suffers the manslayer to return.[17] R. Judah says: Also he that was anointed for battle[18] [when he dies] suffers the manslayer to return. Therefore the mothers of the [High] Priests provided them [that were in exile] with food and raiment that they should not pray for their sons to die. If judgement had been passed against a man [that he must go into exile] and then the High Priest died, he need not go into exile; if judgement against a man [that he must go into exile] had not yet been passed and the High Priest died and another was appointed in his stead, and judgement was afterward passed against him, he may return [only] at the death of the second [High Priest].

---

[1] Who scourges another at the bidding of the court. See Makk. 3[14].
[2] Whom he has accidentally killed.　　　　[3] Even a bondman or a Samaritan.
[4] See p. 356, n. 9.　　　[5] Sanh. 3[5].　　　[6] Cf. B.K. 1[4].　　　[7] Num. 35[14].
[8] Num. 35[13].　　　[9] Deut. 19[3].　　　　[10] Cf. Sot. 1[3].
[11] To the avenger of blood (Deut. 19[6]) to persuade him that the manslayer was not worthy of death.　　　[12] The manslayer.　　　[13] Deut. 19[4]. Cf. Shebi. 10[8].
[14] See Sanh. 9[1].　　　[15] Num. 35[25].　　　[16] On these three see Meg. 1[9].
[17] See Num. 5[25].　　　[18] See Sot. 8[1].

7. If judgement was passed against him when there was no High Priest, or if any one had slain the High Priest, or if the High Priest had slain any one, he may never come forth from thence. He may not come forth to bear testimony that is a religious duty[1] or testimony in a non-capital case or testimony in a capital case; or even if the Israelites had need of him;[2] and even if he was a captain of the host like to Joab the son Zeruiah he may never come forth from thence, for it is written, *Whither he was fled*[3]—there shall be his dwelling-place, there shall be his death, there shall be his burial. As the city grants asylum so does [all the space within] its Sabbath limit[4] grant asylum. If the manslayer went beyond the Sabbath limit and the avenger of blood found him, R. Jose the Galilean says: It is the duty of the avenger of blood and the right of other men [to kill him]. R. Akiba says: The avenger of blood has the right, and the other men are not guilty if they kill him. If a tree stood within the Sabbath limit and its boughs stretched beyond the Sabbath limit, or if it stood beyond the Sabbath limit and its boughs stretched inside the Sabbath limit, everything is decided according to the position of the branches.[5] If a man slew another within the city itself, he must escape into exile from one quarter [of the city] to another; but a levite[6] must escape into exile from that city to another.

8. In like manner[7] if a manslayer escaped into exile to a city of refuge, and the men of the city were minded to do him honour, he must say to them, 'I am a manslayer'. If they answered, 'None the less [we would do thee honour]', he may accept [the honour] from them, for it is written, *This is the word of the manslayer*.[8] They must pay the levites their hire. So R. Judah. R. Meir says: They need not pay them their hire. He may return to the office which he held before. So R. Meir. R. Judah says: He may not return to the office which he held before.

3. 1. These are they[9] that are to be scourged: he that has connexion with his sister, his father's sister, his mother's sister, his wife's sister, his brother's wife, his father's brother's wife, or a menstruant;[10] a High Priest that married a widow,[11] a common priest that married a woman that was divorced or that had performed *halitzah*, an Israelite that married a bastard or a *Nethinah*, or the daughter of an Israelite that married a bastard or a *Nathin*. If a woman was a widow and also divorced, [and a High Priest married her,] he is thereby culpable on two counts. If a woman was divorced and had also performed *halitzah*, [and a common priest married her,] he is culpable only on one count.[12]

2. [These also are to be scourged:] an unclean person that ate Hallowed Things,[13] or that entered the Temple while he was unclean,[14] or that ate the fat or the blood,[15] the Remnant,[16] or the Refuse[17] [of the offerings], or [an offering] that was become unclean;[18] or that slaughtered [an offering] or offered it outside the Temple;[19] or that ate at Passover what was leavened,[20]

[1] To give evidence of the appearance of the new moon; cf. R.Sh. 1[6ff].
[2] Cf. Yom. 7[5].   [3] Num. 35[25].
[4] Two thousand cubits beyond the city's confines.   [5] Maas. 3[10].
[6] Whose home was in any city of refuge (Num. 35[6]).
[7] Some texts omit the meaningless 'in like manner', which is repeated here from the duplicate paragraph in Shebi. 10[8].   [8] Deut. 19[4].
[9] The list is not exhaustive.   [10] For all these see Lev. 20[17–21].
[11] For those that follow see Yeb. 2[4].
[12] Since the prohibition to marry the latter is not explicit in the Law but a rabbinical inference from Lev. 21[7].   [13] Lev. 7[20].   [14] Cf. Num. 5[3].   [15] Lev. 3[17].   [16] Ex. 29[34].
[17] 'An abomination', Lev. 7[18].   [18] Lev. 7[19].   [19] Lev. 17[4, 9].   [20] Deut. 16[3].

or that ate or did any act of work on the Day of Atonement;[1] or that prepared [the like of] the Anointing Oil[2] or the incense;[3] or that anointed himself[4] with the oil of unction; or that ate carrion or flesh that was unfit or forbidden beasts or creeping things; or that ate untithed produce or First Tithe from which Heave-offering had not been taken; or Second Tithe or dedicated produce that had not been redeemed.[5] How much untithed produce must a man eat to become culpable? R. Simeon says: Any quantity soever. But the Sages say: An olive's bulk. R. Simeon replied: Do ye not agree with me that a man is culpable if he eats an ant,[6] however small? They said to him: Because it is in the form in which it was created. He answered: Also a grain of wheat is in the form in which it was created.

3. If a man ate the First-fruits before he had recited [the Avowal] over them,[7] or ate the Most Holy Things[8] outside the Curtains,[9] or the Lesser Holy Things[10] or the Second Tithe outside the Wall,[11] or broke the bone[12] of a clean Passover-offering, he must suffer the Forty Stripes. But if he left aught over from a clean [Passover-offering] or broke the bone of an unclean [Passover-offering] he does not suffer the Forty Stripes.

4. If a man took the dam and her young,[13] R. Judah says: He incurs the [Forty] Stripes, and he need not [then] let the dam go. But the Sages say: He must let the dam go and he does not suffer the stripes. This is the general rule: [by transgression of] any negative command whereunto is joined a further command to rise up and do,[14] a man does not become liable [to the Forty Stripes].

5. If a man made a baldness on his head,[15] or rounded the corners of his head, or marred the corners of his beard,[16] or made any cuttings for the dead,[17] he is liable [to the Forty Stripes]. If he made one cutting for five that were dead, or five cuttings for one that was dead, he is liable on each count. For [cutting off the hair of] the head [he is liable on] two counts, once for either side; and for [cutting off the hair of] the beard [he is liable on] two counts for either side, and once for below. R. Eliezer says: If he took it off all at once, he is liable only on one count. A man is not culpable unless he takes it off with a razor. R. Eliezer says: Even if he pulled it out with pincers or [scraped it off] with an adze, he is culpable.

6. If a man wrote [on his skin] pricked-in writing [he is culpable]. If he wrote but did not prick it in, or pricked it in but did not write it, he is not culpable, but only if he writes it and pricks it in with ink or eye-paint or aught that leaves a lasting mark. R. Simeon b. Judah says in the name of R. Simeon: He is not culpable unless he writes there the name [of a god], for it is written, *Nor print any marks upon you: I am the Lord.*[18]

7. If[19] a Nazirite[20] drank wine throughout the day he is liable only on one count. If they said to him [repeatedly], 'Do not drink! Do not drink!' and he nevertheless drank, he is liable on each count.

8. If[21] he contracted uncleanness because of the dead throughout the day, he is liable only on one count. If they said to him [repeatedly], 'Do

---

[1] Lev. 23[29-31].   [2] Ex. 30[32].   [3] Ex. 30[37].   [4] Ex. 30[32].
[5] For these see p. 394, nn. 9-12; p. 7, nn. 6-9.   [6] See Lev. 11[41f].
[7] Deut. 26[5-10].   [8] See Zeb. 5[1-5].
[9] Referring to the Tabernacle, Ex. 27[9]. The sense is 'outside the Temple Court'.
[10] See Zeb. 5[6-8].   [11] Of Jerusalem. See p. 73, n. 6.
[12] Ex. 12[46].   [13] Deut. 22[6, 7]; see Hull. 12[4].
[14] There is the negative command not to take the dam, and the positive command to let the dam go.   [15] Deut. 14[1].   [16] Lev. 19[27].   [17] Lev. 19[28].
[18] Lev. 19[28]; the stress is on the 'I'.   [19] See Naz. 6[4].   [20] Num. 6[1ff].   [21] Naz. 6[4]

not contract uncleanness! Do not contract uncleanness!' and he neverthe-less contracted uncleanness, he is liable on each count. If he cut off his hair throughout the day he is liable only on one count. If they said to him [repeatedly], 'Do not cut it off! Do not cut it off!' and he nevertheless cut it off, he is liable on each count. If a man put on a garment of Diverse Kinds[1] the whole day, he is liable only on one count. If they said to him [repeatedly], 'Do not wear it! Do not wear it!' and he took it off and put it on again, he is liable on each count.

9. A man can plough a single furrow and thereby become liable by virtue of eight prohibitions:[2] if he ploughed with an ox and an ass[3] which have been dedicated,[4] among Diverse Kinds in the Vineyard[5] in the Seventh Year[6] on a Festival-day,[7] he being a priest and a Nazirite and in a place of uncleanness.[8] Hananiah b. Hakina says: He may, moreover, be wearing a garment of mixed stuff. They said to him: This does not fall within the same class[9] of transgression. He answered: Nor does his being a Nazirite fall within the same class.

10. How many stripes do they inflict on a man? Forty save one, for it is written, *By number forty*;[10] [that is to say,] a number near to forty. R. Judah says: He suffers the forty stripes in full. And where does he suffer the added one? Between the shoulders.[11]

11. When they estimate the number of stripes that he can bear, it must be a number divisible by three. If they had estimated that he could bear forty [save one], and after he had suffered these only in part they said, 'He cannot bear forty [save one]', he is exempt [from the rest]. If they had estimated that he could bear eighteen, and after he had suffered them they said, 'He can bear forty [save one]', he is exempt [from the rest]. If he had committed a transgression whereby he offended against two prohibitions, and they had made for him one estimate [for them both],[12] he suffers them and is exempt [from more stripes]; but if not,[13] he must suffer [the first estimate], be healed again, and then be scourged a second time.

12. How do they scourge him? They bind his two hands to a pillar on either side, and the minister of the synagogue lays hold on his garments—if they are torn they are torn, if they are utterly rent they are utterly rent[14]—so that he bares his chest. A stone is set down behind him on which the minister of the synagogue stands with a strap of calf-hide in his hand, doubled and re-doubled, and two [other] straps[15] that rise and fall [are fastened] thereto.

13. The handpiece of the strap is one handbreadth long and one hand-breadth wide; and its end must reach to his navel.[16] He gives him one-third of the stripes in front[17] and two-thirds behind;[18] and he may not strike him

---

[1] Linen and woollen. See Deut. 22[11].
[2] And incur eight times forty stripes save one.   [3] Deut. 22[10].
[4] The ox was to be an offering on the Altar and the ass given to the Temple to be sold for the benefit of the Temple treasury. These make three transgressions. In both cases the law of Sacrilege (Lev. 5[15f]) is also transgressed.
[5] Ploughing over newly-sown wheat, barley, and grape-seed. This, according to Maimonides, is a transgression of Lev. 19[19].   [6] Lev. 25[4].   [7] p. 181, n. 11.
[8] Transgressing both Lev. 21[1] and Num. 6[6].
[9] i.e. the single act of ploughing. Cf. Ker. 3[4]. For 'mixed stuff' see Kil. 8[1], 9[1ff].
[10] Deut. 25[2-3].   [11] According to the Gemara 22b this is the inference from Zech. 13[6].
[12] At least 39; and a part (at least 3) of the second 39.
[13] If he had been condemned to but one scourging.
[14] Cf. Sot. 1[5].   [15] Of ass-hide.
[16] When he is struck on the shoulder the strap is long enough for the end to reach the navel.
[17] On the chest.   [18] On that part of the shoulder that is bared.

when he is standing or when he is sitting, but only when he is bending low, for it is written, *The judge shall cause him to lie down.*[1] And he that smites, smites with his one hand with all his might.

14. And the reader reads, *If thou wilt not observe to do . . . the Lord will make thy stripes wonderful and the stripes of thy seed . . .*[2] and he returns again to the beginning of the passage.[3] If he dies under his hand, the scourger is not culpable. But if he gave him one stripe too many and he died, he must escape into exile because of him. If he [that was scourged] befouled himself whether with excrement or urine, he is exempt [from the rest of the stripes]. R. Judah says: A man [is exempt only if he befouled himself] with excrement, and a woman [if she befouled herself] with urine.

15. All they that are liable to Extirpation,[4] if they have been scourged are no longer liable to Extirpation, for it is written, *And thy brother seem vile unto thee*[5]—when he is scourged then he is thy brother. So R. Hanina b. Gamaliel. Moreover R. Hanina b. Gamaliel said: If he that commits one transgression thereby forfeits his soul, how much more, if he performs one religious duty, shall his soul be restored to him! R. Simeon says: From the same place[6] we may learn [the like], for it is written, *Even the souls that do them shall be cut off . . .* ; and it says, *Which if a man do he shall live by them*;[7] thus to him that sits and commits no transgression is given a reward as to one that performs a religious duty. R. Simeon the son of Rabbi says: Lo, it says, *Only be sure that thou eat not the blood, for the blood is the life . . .*;[8] if a man keeps himself apart from blood (which man's soul abhors) he receives a reward, how much more, if he keeps himself apart from robbery and incest (which a man's soul longs after and covets), shall he gain merit for himself and his generations and the generations of his generations to the end of all generations!

16. R. Hananiah b. Akashya says: The Holy One, blessed is he, was minded to grant merit to Israel; therefore hath he multiplied for them the Law and commandments, as it is written, *It pleased the Lord for his righteousness' sake to magnify the Law and make it honourable.*[9]

SHEBUOTH ('OATHS')

1. 1. Oaths are of two kinds,[10] which are, indeed, four;[11] knowledge of uncleanness[12] is of two kinds, which are, indeed, four;[13] going out[14] [with a burden] on the Sabbath is of two kinds, which are, indeed, four; the

---

[1] Deut. 25².   [2] Deut. 28⁵⁸ᶠ.

[3] Some texts insert here: *And thou shalt observe the words of this covenant . . .* (Deut. 29⁹), and he finishes with *But he being full of compassion forgave their iniquity . . .* (Ps. 78³⁸), and he returns again to the beginning of the passage.

[4] Punishment at the hand of Heaven for transgressions about which it is written (e.g. Lev. 18²⁹), 'The souls that do them shall be cut off from among their people'. See p. 562, n. 16.

[5] Deut. 25³. There is here a play on words. The first word of the sentence is *v'niklah* ('and is become vile, unworthy'); the subject 'thy brother' is taken as beginning a new clause, thus giving a sense 'having been made vile, he is thy brother in thy sight'. The following 'When he is scourged' (*lakah*) plays on the 'be vile' (*kalah*) of the earlier word.

[6] i.e. Lev. 18, which in verse 29 speaks of the soul that shall be cut off.

[7] Lev. 18⁵.   [8] Deut. 12²³.

[9] Is. 42²¹. Cf. Ab. 6¹¹. The more commandments there are to be observed, the more ample the scope for Israel to acquire merit.   [10] Positive and negative.

[11] To include positive and negative assertions about things past. See below, 3¹, when the actual subject of the tractate is resumed.

[12] Lev. 5³. See below, 2¹. The two are: if a man eats of Hallowed Things or if he enters the Temple in a state of forgetfulness that he is unclean.

[13] To include the two additional states of forgetfulness that he is eating Hallowed Things or that he has entered the Temple.   [14] See Shab. 1¹.

appearances of leprosy signs[1] are of two kinds, which are, indeed, four.

2. Whensoever[2] there was knowledge [of his uncleanness] in the beginning and knowledge in the end, but unconsciousness[3] in the meantime, a man is liable to a Rising and Falling Offering.[4] If there was knowledge in the beginning but no knowledge in the end, the goat whose blood is sprinkled within[5] [the Holy of Holies] and the Day of Atonement suspend judgement, until his trespass is known to him, and then shall he bring a Rising and Falling Offering.

3. If there was no knowledge in the beginning but there was knowledge in the end, atonement is made by the goat whose blood is sprinkled outside [on the Altar in the Temple Court], and by the Day of Atonement, for it is written, *Beside the sin-offering of atonement;*[6] as one makes atonement so does the other make atonement; as the [sprinkling] within makes atonement only for a matter whereof there was knowledge [in the beginning], so the [sprinkling] outside makes atonement only for a matter whereof there was knowledge [in the end].

4. If there was no knowledge either in the beginning or in the end, the he-goats [offered as Sin-offerings] at the [three] Feasts and at the New Moons make atonement.[7] So R. Judah. R. Simeon says: The goats [offered] at the [three] Feasts make atonement, but not those [offered] at the New Moons. For what do the goats [offered] at the New Moons make atonement? For a clean person who ate what was unclean. R. Meir says: All goats [offered as Sin-offerings, whether at the three Feasts or at the New Moons] alike make atonement for uncleanness that befalls the Temple and its Hallowed Things. R. Simeon used to say: The goats [offered] at the New Moons make atonement for the clean that ate what was unclean, and those [offered] at the [three] Feasts make atonement if there was no knowledge either in the beginning or in the end, and that [offered] on the Day of Atonement makes atonement if there was no knowledge in the beginning but knowledge in the end. They said to him: Can it be that one may be offered at a time appointed for the other? He answered: They may be offered so. They said to him: But since their atonement is not every time alike, how may one be offered at a time appointed for the other? He answered: They all are brought to make atonement for uncleanness that befalls the Temple and its Hallowed Things.

5. R. Simeon b. Judah says in his name: The goats [offered] at the New Moons make atonement for the clean that ate what was unclean; those [offered] at the [three] Feasts surpass them in that they make atonement both for the clean that ate what was unclean and for [a transgression] where there was no knowledge either in the beginning or in the end; that [offered] on the Day of Atonement surpasses them in that it makes atonement both for the clean that ate what was unclean, and for [a transgression] where there was no knowledge either in the beginning or in the end; also

---

[1] See Neg. 1[1].

[2] In the act of sin (eating Hallowed Things or entering the Temple) committed while unclean.

[3] Of his uncleanness, or of the sanctity of the Hallowed Things or the Temple.

[4] So called because the value of what is brought in expiation 'rises' or 'falls', from a lamb to a pair of birds, or the tenth of an ephah of fine flour, according to his means. See Lev. 5[6, 7, 11].   [5] Lev. 16[15]. Cf. Yom. 5[9].   [6] Num. 29[11].

[7] For sins known only to God. See Num. 28[14, 22, 30]; 29[11, 18]. The three feasts are Passover, Pentecost, and Tabernacles.

for [a transgression] where there was no knowledge in the beginning but there was knowledge in the end. They said to him:[1] Can it be[2] that one may be offered at a time appointed for the other? He answered: Yea. They said to him: If so, then those of the Day of Atonement could be offered at the New Moons, but how can those of the New Moons be offered on the Day of Atonement to make atonement which does not pertain to it? He answered: They all are brought to make atonement for uncleanness that befalls the Temple and its Hallowed Things.

6. For uncleanness that befalls the Temple and its Hallowed Things through wantonness,[3] atonement is made by the goat whose blood is sprinkled within [the Holy of Holies] and by the Day of Atonement; for all other transgressions spoken of in the Law, venial or grave, wanton or unwitting, conscious or unconscious, sins of omission or of commission, sins punishable by Extirpation or by death at the hands of the court, the scapegoat[4] makes atonement.

7. [It makes atonement] alike whether they are Israelites, priests, or the Anointed Priest.[5] Wherein do Israelites differ from priests and the Anointed Priest? Only in that the blood of the bullock[6] makes atonement for the priests for uncleanness that befalls the Temple and its Hallowed Things. R. Simeon says: As the blood of the goat that is sprinkled within [the Holy of Holies] makes atonement for the Israelites, so does the blood of the bullock make atonement for the priests; and as the confession of sin recited over the scapegoat[7] makes atonement for the Israelites, so does the confession of sin recited over the bullock[8] make atonement for the priests.

2. 1. 'Knowledge of uncleanness is of two kinds, which are, indeed, four.'[9] If a man contracted uncleanness and knew it, and the uncleanness was then forgotten of him though he was mindful of the holiness [of what he ate], or if the holiness [of what he ate] was forgotten of him though he was mindful of his uncleanness; or if both were forgotten of him, and he thereafter ate what was holy and did not know [that he committed transgression], but after he had eaten he knew it, then he is liable to a Rising and Falling Offering. If he contracted uncleanness and knew it, and the uncleanness was then forgotten of him though he was mindful of [the holiness of] the Temple, or if [the holiness of] the Temple was forgotten of him though he was mindful of the uncleanness, or if both were forgotten of him, and he entered the Temple and did not know [that he committed transgression] but after he came out he knew it, then he is liable to a Rising and Falling Offering.

2. It is all one whether a man enters into the Temple Court[10] or into any space that has been added to the Temple Court, since they may not add to the [Holy] City or to the courts of the Temple save by the decision of a king, a prophet, Urim and Thummim and a Sanhedrin of one and seventy [judges][11] and with the bringing of two Thank-offerings and with singing.[12]

---

[1] R. Simeon b. Judah.
[2] Some texts read: 'Did he' or 'Did the Rabbi also say'. 'Rabbi' refers here to R. Simeon (b. Yohai) in whose name R. Simeon b. Judah had spoken.
[3] But without having been warned. After warning scourging (Makk. 3[2]) is incurred.
[4] Lev. 16[22]. Cf. Yom. 6[2ff].   [5] The High Priest.   [6] Lev. 16[6].
[7] Lev. 16[21]. See Yom. 4[2].   [8] See Yom. 3[8].   [9] See above, 1[1].
[10] See Midd. 1[1].   [11] Cf. Sanh. 1[5].
[12] Cf. Neh. 12[31], where the expression 'two great companies that gave thanks' can be rendered 'two great Thank-offerings'.

The court goes along with the two Thank-offerings behind them[1] and all Israel following after. The innermost[2] [Thank-offering] is consumed [by the priests] and the outermost is burnt. If any addition is made not after this fashion, and a man [that was unclean] entered thither, he is not thereby culpable.

3. If a man contracted uncleanness in the Temple Court, and the uncleanness was forgotten of him, though he was mindful that he was in the Temple; or if the Temple was forgotten of him though he was mindful of his uncleanness; or if both were forgotten of him, and he prostrated himself or stayed time enough to prostrate himself, or if he went out by the longer way,[3] he is liable [to a Rising and Falling Offering]; but if by the shorter way, he is exempt. This is the positive command[4] concerning the Temple, through the transgression of which [if a court gave a wrongful decision] the congregation does not become liable [to a Sin-offering].[5]

4. What is the positive command concerning the menstruant, through the transgression of which they become liable?[6] If a man had connexion with her when she was clean, and she [then] said to him, 'I am become unclean', and he forthwith withdrew, he is [still] liable, since he derives benefit as well by his egress as by his ingress.

5. R. Eliezer says: .... *a creeping thing and it be hidden from him*;[7] because the creeping thing is forgotten of him he becomes liable, but he does not become liable because the Temple is forgotten of him. R. Akiba says: *And it be hidden from him and he be unclean*; because the uncleanness is forgotten of him he becomes liable, but he does not become liable because the Temple is forgotten of him. R. Ishmael says: *Shall be hidden ... shall be hidden*: [it is said] twice,[8] to show that he becomes liable both because the uncleanness is forgotten of him and because the Temple is forgotten of him.

3. 1. 'Oaths are of two kinds, which are, indeed, four';[9] [namely,] 'I swear that I will eat', or 'that I will not eat'; or 'that I have eaten', or 'that I have not eaten'. [If a man said,] 'I swear that I will not eat', and he ate aught soever, he is culpable.[10] So R. Akiba. They said to R. Akiba: But where have we found that a man is culpable that eats aught soever [of what is unclean],[11] and that, therefore, this one, too, is culpable?[12] R. Akiba answered: But where [else] have we found that a man must bring an offering if he does but speak, and that, therefore, this man, too, if he does but speak must bring an offering?[13] [If a man said,] 'I swear that I will not eat', and he ate and drank, he is liable only on one count; but if he said, 'I swear that I will not eat and that I will not drink', and he ate and drank, he is liable on two counts.

2. [If he said,] 'I swear that I will not eat', and he then ate wheaten

---

[1] Such is the literal rendering. Gem. 15b on the ground of Neh. 12[32] argues that it means that the court followed after the Thank-offerings.   [2] That nearest the court.
[3] Midd. 2[2].
[4] In that the unclean person is bidden to go out the shortest way. Cf. Num. 5[2].
[5] See Hor. 2[4]. The congregation need not bring the bullock for a Sin-offering as prescribed in Lev. 4[13ff].
[6] If the court gave a wrongful decision.   [7] Lev. 5[2].   [8] Lev. 5[2, 3].
[9] See above, 1[1].
[10] And must bring the offerings prescribed in Lev. 5[6ff].
[11] Where not 'aught soever' but 'an olive's bulk' must be eaten to render him unclean.
[12] They maintain that, by analogy with the other law, he breaks his oath only if he eats an olive's bulk.
[13] i.e. there can be no analogy possible between this and another law.

bread and bread of barley and bread of spelt, he is liable only on one count;
[but if he said,] 'I swear that I will not eat wheaten bread or bread of
barley or bread of spelt', and he ate [them all], he is liable on each count.

3. [If he said,] 'I swear that I will not drink', and he drank many liquids,
he is liable only on one count; [but if he said,] 'I swear that I will not drink
wine or oil or honey', and he drank [them all], he is liable on each count.

4. [If he said,] 'I swear that I will not eat', and he ate foods which are not
fit for eating, or drank liquids which are not fit for drinking, he is not
culpable. [If he said,] 'I swear that I will not eat', and he ate carrion or
terefah, or forbidden beasts or creeping things,[1] he is culpable; but R.
Simeon declares him not culpable. If he said, '*Konam*[2] be the use I have
of my wife if I have eaten to-day!' and he had eaten carrion or *terefah* or
forbidden beasts or creeping things, his wife is forbidden to him.

5. It is all one whether the things [whereof he swears] belong to him or
whether they belong to others, or whether there is in them aught material
or whether there is in them naught material. Thus [it is all one] whether
he said, 'I swear that I will give this to such a man', or 'that I will not give
it', or 'that I have given it', or 'that I have not given it'; or 'that I will
sleep', or 'that I will not sleep', or 'that I have slept', or 'that I have not
slept'; or 'that I will throw a stone into the sea', or 'that I will not throw
it', or 'that I have thrown it', or 'that I have not thrown it'. R. Ishmael
says: He becomes liable only by reason of [an oath that concerns] the
future, for it is written, *To do evil or to do good*.[3] R. Akiba said to him: If
so, I may take oaths that concern only the doing of evil or the doing of
good! but whence [do we learn that we may take oaths that concern] matters
other than the doing of evil or the doing of good? He answered: From the
extension[4] in the Scripture. He said to him: If the Scripture has extended
[the meaning of the law] in this sense, it has extended it also in the other
sense.[5]

6. If a man had sworn to set a commandment at naught but did not set
it at naught, he is not culpable. If [he had sworn] to fulfil a commandment
but did not fulfil it, he is not culpable. According to R. Judah b. Bathyra it
might be inferred that he should be culpable. R. Judah b. Bathyra said: If
a man becomes culpable by reason of oaths that concern a matter of free
choice (whereto he was not adjured from mount Sinai), how much more
does he become culpable by reason of oaths that concern a commandment
(whereto he was adjured from mount Sinai)! They said to him: No! as
thou arguest about an oath that concerns a matter of free choice (in which
Nay or Yea are alike lawful), wouldst thou argue also about an oath that
concerns a commandment (in which Nay or Yea are not alike lawful)?—
so[6] that if a man had sworn to set it at naught and did not set it at naught,
he is not culpable.

---

[1] See p. 394, nn. 9–12.   [2] App. I. 17.   [3] Lev. 5[4].
[4] Referring to an exegetical method introduced by Nahum of Gimzo (latter half of the
first century) by which certain conjunctions and particles had the effect of 'limitation', and
excluded interpretations and applications of some verse in the written Law which were
excluded by the Oral Law; while certain other conjunctions and particles had the effect of
'extension', and admitted additional interpretations and wider applications of the written
Law, such as had become permissible by the Oral Law. In the present case it is said
(Lev. 5[4]) '*Whatsoever* it be that a man shall swear', thus 'extending' the sense of the preceding clause 'to do evil or to do good'. Cf. p. 82, n. 1.
[5] To include the past also, and not (as R. Ishmael held) the future only.
[6] Some texts omit the following sentence.

7. [If he said,] 'I swear that I will not eat this loaf! I swear that I will not eat it! I swear that I will not eat it!'[1] and he ate it, he is liable only on one count. Such is reckoned 'a rash oath',[2] for which a man is liable to Stripes if he uttered it wantonly, but, if unwittingly, to a Rising and Falling Offering. For 'a vain oath', if it is uttered wantonly, a man is liable to Stripes, but if unwittingly, he is not culpable.

8. What is accounted 'a vain oath'? If, to wit, he swore that a thing well known to men was something different: if he said of a pillar of stone that it was of gold, or of a man that he was a woman, or of a woman that she was a man; or if he swore a thing that was not possible, [to wit, 'I swear that] I saw a camel flying in the air', or 'that I saw a serpent as thick as the beam of an olive-press'. If a man said to witnesses, 'Come and bear witness of me', [but they said,] 'We swear that we will not bear witness of thee', or if a man swore to set a commandment at naught, [to wit,] that he would not build a *Sukkah*[3] or carry a *Lulab*[4] or put on phylacteries,[5] this is accounted 'a vain oath', for which, if it is uttered wantonly, a man is liable to Stripes, but if unwittingly, he is not culpable.

9. [If a man said,] 'I swear that I will eat this loaf! I swear that I will not eat it!' the first is 'a rash oath' and the second 'a vain oath'. If he ate it, he has transgressed by reason of 'a vain oath'; if he did not eat it he has transgressed by reason of 'a rash oath'.

10. [The law about] 'a rash oath' applies[6] to men or to women, to them that are not kinsfolk or to them that are kinsfolk,[7] to them that are qualified [to bear witness] or to them that are not qualified,[8] and [whether uttered] before a court or not before a court; but it must be uttered out of a man's own mouth.[9] If [he uttered it] wantonly he is liable to Stripes, and if unwittingly to a Rising and Falling Offering.

11. [The law about] 'a vain oath' applies to men or to women, to them that are not kinsfolk or to them that are kinsfolk, to them that are qualified [to bear witness] or to them that are not qualified, and [whether uttered] before a court or not before a court; but it must be uttered out of a man's own mouth. If [he uttered it] wantonly he is liable to Stripes, and if unwittingly he is exempt. For either kind of oath, if a man was adjured at the mouth of others, he may still be liable; thus if he said, 'I have not eaten to-day', or 'I have not put on phylacteries to-day', [and another said to him,] 'I adjure thee', and he said, 'Amen!' he is liable.

4. 1. [The law about] 'an oath of testimony'[10] applies to men but not to women, to them that are not kinsfolk but not to them that are kinsfolk, to them that are qualified [to bear witness] but not to them that are not qualified, and it applies only to them that are fit[11] to bear witness; and [it applies whether uttered] before a court or not before a court; but it must be uttered out of a man's own mouth. If [he was adjured] at the mouth of others, he is not liable until he has denied his knowledge before a court.

---

[1] Some texts omit the last repetition.   [2] Cf. Lev. 5[4].   [3] App. I. 42.
[4] App. I. 20.   [5] See p. 104, n. 16.
[6] They are liable to penalty for non-fulfilment.
[7] e.g. if he swore to give something to a certain person and he did not fulfil his oath, he is culpable whether the person was near of kin to him or not.   [8] See Sanh. 3[3].
[9] It is not enough if he confirms another's words; yet if he confirms the other's words by replying 'Amen', it is as though the oath was uttered from his own mouth. See the following paragraph.
[10] Lev. 5[1].   [11] This excludes a king (Sanh. 2[2]) and those mentioned in Sanh. 3[3].

So R. Meir. But the Sages say: Whether [he swore] out of his own mouth or [was adjured] at the mouth of others, a man is not liable until he has denied his knowledge before a court.

2. [If they swore falsely] they are liable whether they swore wantonly or in error if they wantonly denied their knowledge, but they are not liable if they denied it in error. And to what are they liable if they had sworn wantonly? To a Rising and Falling Offering.

3. Of what kind is 'an oath of testimony'? If a man said to two others, 'Come and testify of me', [and they said,] 'We swear that we know of no testimony concerning thee'; [or if they said,] 'We know of no testimony concerning thee', [and he said,] 'I adjure you', and they said, 'Amen!' they are liable [if they swore falsely]. If he had adjured them five times outside the court, and they came to the court and confessed [that they knew of testimony concerning him], they incur no penalty; but if they denied it they are liable on each count. If he adjured them five times before the court and they denied [their knowledge], they are liable only on one count. R. Simeon said: What is the reason? Because they cannot again confess [their knowledge].

4. If they both denied at the same time, they are both liable, but if one denied and then the other, the first is liable and the second exempt. If one denied and the other confessed, he that denied is liable. If there were two pairs of witnesses and the first pair denied and then the second, both pairs are liable, since the testimony could be sustained by either of the two pairs.

5. [If a man said,] 'I adjure you that ye come and testify of me that in the hand of such-a-one there is a deposit and a loan and plunder and lost property of mine', [and they said,] 'We swear that we know of no testimony concerning thee', they are liable only on one count. [But if they said,] 'We swear that we do not know that in the hand of such-a-one there is a deposit and a loan and plunder and lost property of thine', they are liable on each count. [If he said,] 'I adjure you that ye come and testify of me that I have, in the hand of such-a-one, a deposit of wheat, barley, and spelt', [and they said,] 'We swear that we know of no testimony concerning thee', they are liable only on one count; [but if they said,] 'We swear that we know of no testimony concerning thee that thou hast, in the hand of such-a-one, a deposit of wheat, barley, and spelt', they are liable on each count.

6. [If a man said,] 'I adjure you that ye come and testify of me that against such-a-one I have a claim for damages, or half-damages, to twofold restitution or fourfold or fivefold restitution',[1] or 'that such-a-one violated my daughter', or 'that such-a-one seduced my daughter', or 'that my son struck me',[2] or 'that my fellow on the Day of Atonement[3] wounded me,' or 'set fire to my heaped corn', these are liable.

7. [If a man said,] 'I adjure you that ye come and testify of me that I, a priest or a levite, am not the son of a divorced woman[4] or the son of a woman that had performed *halitzah*';[5] or 'that such-a-one, a priest, or a levite, is not the son of a divorced woman, or the son of a woman that had performed *halitzah*', or 'that such-a-one violated his daughter' or 'that he seduced his daughter', or 'that my son wounded me'[6] or 'that my fellow

---

[1] See p. 382, nn. 5–6. Cf. B.K. 1[4], 7[1].
[2] Since no death-penalty is involved (Sanh. 11[1]) there can be payment for damage.
[3] Though this is punishable by Extirpation (Ker. 1[1]) damages are still payable. See B.K. 7[7].
[4] See p. 401, n. 3.   [5] App. I. 12.
[6] The penalty is death, hence no evidence as to damage is needed.

on the Sabbath[1] wounded me' or 'set fire to my heaped corn', these are exempt.

8. [If a man said,] 'I adjure you that ye come and testify of me that such-a-one promised to give me 200 *zuz* and he did not give it to me', they are exempt, since they are liable only in what concerns a claim for property that is like to a deposit.[2]

9. [If a man said,] 'I adjure you that, when ye know of testimony concerning me, ye come and testify of me', they are exempt, since the oath preceded the testimony.

10. If a man stood in the synagogue and said, 'I adjure you that, if ye know of testimony concerning me, ye come and testify of me', they are exempt unless[3] he shall direct himself to some among them in particular.

11. If he had said to two others, 'I adjure you, O such-a-one and such-a-one, that, if ye know of testimony concerning me, ye come and testify of me', [and they said,] 'We swear that we know of no testimony concerning thee', and they knew of testimony concerning him but from the mouth of another witness, or if one of them was a kinsman or not qualified [to be a witness], they are exempt.

12. If a man had sent his slave [to adjure the witnesses], or if he that was sued said to them, 'I adjure you that, if ye know of testimony concerning him, ye come and testify of him', they are exempt; [they are not liable] unless they hear [the adjuration] from the mouth of the claimant.

13. [If a man said,] 'I adjure you', or 'I command you', or 'I bind you', they are liable. [But if he said,] 'By heaven and by earth', they are exempt. [If he adjured them] 'by *Alef-Daleth*'[4] or 'by *Yod-He*'[5] or 'by Shaddai' or 'by Sabaoth' or 'by the Merciful and Gracious' or 'by him that is long-suffering and of great kindness',[6] or by any substituted name,[7] they are liable. If a man cursed [God][8] by any of these he is liable. So R. Meir. But the Sages say: He is exempt. If a man cursed his father or his mother[9] by any of these names, he is liable. So R. Meir. But the Sages declare him exempt. If a man cursed himself[10] or his fellow by any of them, he transgresses a negative command.[11] [If he said,] 'God smite thee' or 'Thus may God smite thee',[12] this is the 'adjuration' that is written in the Law.[13] [If a man said,] 'May he not smite thee' or 'May he bless thee' or 'May he do well with thee',[14] R. Meir declares him liable; but the Sages declare him exempt.

5. 1. [The law about] a 'deposit-oath'[15] applies to men or to women, to them that are not kinsfolk and to them that are kinsfolk, to them that are qualified [to bear witness] and to them that are not qualified, and [it applies whether uttered] before a court or not before a court; but it must be uttered out of a man's own mouth; if [he was adjured] at the mouth of others, a man is not liable unless he withholds the truth before a court. So R. Meir. But

---

[1] See p. 414, n. 6.
[2] As in the cases cited in Lev. 6[2].   [3] Some texts omit the following clause.
[4] The first two letters of 'Adonai', the Lord.
[5] The first two letters of the Sacred Name, YHWH, 'Jehovah'.
[6] Cf. Ex. 34[6]; Ps. 103[8].   [7] Or, 'by one of the attributes of God'.
[8] The blasphemer. See Sanh. 7[5].   [9] Sanh. 7[8].
[10] Cf. Deut. 4[9].
[11] Cf. Lev. 19[14]. If it is forbidden to curse the deaf, how much more the hearing!
[12] 'If thou come not to testify of me!'
[13] i.e. the adjuration intended by Lev. 5[1].
[14] 'If thou come to testify of me!'   [15] Lev. 6[2ff].

the Sages say: Whether [he swore] out of his own mouth or [was adjured]
at the mouth of others, so soon as he has denied his knowledge he becomes
liable. He is liable whether he swore wantonly or in error if he had spoken
wantonly concerning the deposit,[1] but not if he had spoken in error concerning it. To what is he liable [if he swore] wantonly? A Guilt-offering
costing [two] shekels in silver.[2]

2. Of what kind is a 'deposit-oath'? If one man said to another, 'Give
me my deposit which thou hast', [and the other said], 'I swear that I have
naught of thine', or if he said, 'I have naught of thine' [and the first said,]
'I adjure thee', and he said, 'Amen!' he is liable. If he adjured him five times
whether before a court or not before a court, and he denied it, he is liable
on each count. R. Simeon said: What is the reason? Because he can [after
each denial] retract and admit [that he has the deposit].

3. If there were five claimants and they said to him, 'Give us our
deposit which thou hast', [and he said,] 'I swear that I have naught of yours',
he is liable only on one count; [but if he said,] 'I swear that I have naught
of thine, or of thine, or of thine, [&c.]', he is liable on each count. R.
Eliezer says: Only if he repeats the oath at the end. R. Simeon says: Only
if he repeats the oath for each one of them. [If a man said,] 'Give me my
deposit and my loan and the stolen goods and the lost property of mine
which thou hast', [and he said,] 'I swear that I have naught of thine', he is
liable only on one count; [but if he said,] 'I swear that I have neither
deposit nor loan nor stolen goods nor lost property of thine', he is liable on
each count. [If a man said,] 'Give me the wheat and the barley and the
spelt of mine which thou hast', [and he said,] 'I swear that I have naught of
thine', he is liable only on one count; [but if he said,] 'I swear that I have
neither wheat nor barley nor spelt of thine', he is liable on each count.
R. Meir says: Even if he said, '. . . a grain of wheat or barley or spelt', he is
liable on each count.

4. [If a man said,] 'Thou didst violate, or seduce, my daughter', and the
other said, 'I did not violate her, or seduce her', and he said, 'I adjure thee',
and the other said, 'Amen!' he is liable. R. Simeon declares him exempt,
since a man pays no fine through his own admission.[3] They said to him:
Although he pays no fine through his own admission, he must still
pay [compensation for] indignity and blemish[4] through his own admission.

5. [If a man said,] 'Thou hast stolen my ox', [and the other said,] 'I have
not stolen it', [and he said,] 'I adjure thee', and the other said, 'Amen!' he is
liable. [If the other said,] 'I stole it but I have not killed or sold it', [and
he said,] 'I adjure thee', and the other said, 'Amen!' he is not liable. [If a man
said,] 'Thy ox killed my ox', and the other said, 'It did not kill it', [and he
said,] 'I adjure thee', and the other said, 'Amen!' he is liable. [If a man said,]
'Thy ox killed my slave', and the other said, 'It did not kill him', [and he
said,] 'I adjure thee,' and the other said, 'Amen!' he is not liable. If one man
said to another, 'Thou hast wounded me and left a bruise on me', and the
other said, 'I have not wounded thee or left a bruise on thee', [and he said,]
'I adjure thee', and the other said, 'Amen!' he is liable. If a man's slave said to
him, 'Thou hast knocked out my tooth, or blinded my eye', and he said, 'I
have not knocked out thy tooth or blinded thine eye', [and the slave said,]

---

[1] Well knowing that the deposit had been left.   [2] Cf. Lev. 5[15].
[3] See Ket. 3[9].   [4] See Ket. 3[4].

'I adjure thee', and he said, 'Amen!' he is not liable. This is the general rule:[1] he that must pay a fine through his own admission is liable; but if he need not pay a fine through his own admission he is not liable.

6. 1. The oath taken before judges [is imposed if] the claim lodged is [at least the worth of] two silver pieces[2] and the claim admitted is [at least] the worth of a *perutah*; but if the claim admitted is not of like kind with the claim lodged, he is exempt [from taking an oath]. Thus [if the claimant said,] 'Thou hast two silver pieces of mine', and the other said, 'I have but a *perutah* of thine', he is exempt;[3] but if he said, 'Thou hast two silver pieces and a *perutah* of mine', and the other said, 'I have but a *perutah* of thine', he is liable. [If he said,] 'Thou hast 100 *denars* of mine', [and the other said,] 'I have but fifty *denars* of thine', he is liable. [If he said,] 'Thou hast 100 *denars* of my father's', [and the other said,] 'I have but 50 *denars* of thine', he is exempt [from taking an oath], since he is as one that restores lost property.[4]

2. [If the claimant said,] 'Thou hast 100 *denars* of mine', and the other said,[5] 'Yea'; and on the morrow the first one said to him, 'Give it to me', [and the other said,] 'I have given it to thee already', he is exempt; but if he said, 'I have naught of thine', he is liable. [If he said,] Thou hast 100 *denars* of mine', and the other said, 'Yea', [and the first said,] 'Do not give it to me save before witnesses', and on the morrow he said to him, 'Give it to me', and the other said, 'I have given it to thee already', he is liable, since it was needful that he should give it before witnesses.

3. [If the claimant said,] 'Thou hast a *litra*[6] of gold of mine', and the other said, 'I have but a *litra* of silver of thine', he is not liable. [If he said,] 'Thou hast a golden *denar* of mine', and the other said, 'I have but a silver *denar*, or a *teresith*, or a *pondion*,[7] or a *perutah*', he is liable, since all are of the like kind of coin.[8] [If he said,] 'Thou hast a *kor*[9] of grain of mine', and the other said, 'I have but a *lethek*[9] of pulse of thine', he is exempt; [but if he said,] 'Thou hast a *kor* of produce of mine', and the other said, 'I have but a *lethek* of pulse of thine', he is liable, since pulse is reckoned within the category of produce. If he had claimed from him wheat, and he admitted a claim for barley, he is exempt; but Rabban Gamaliel declares him liable. If a man claimed from his fellow jars of oil, and the other admitted his claim to the empty jars, Admon says:[10] Since he admits the claim in part, in like kind, he must take an oath [in denial of the rest]. But the Sages say: This is not an admission in like kind to the claim. Rabban Gamaliel said: I approve the words of Admon. If a man claimed from his fellow utensils and land, and the other admitted the claim to utensils but denied the claim to land, or admitted the claim to land but denied the

---

[1] Cf. Ket. 3[9].

[2] Two *maahs*, the smallest of silver coins. The *maah* was worth thirty-two *perutahs* or one-sixth of a *denar*. See App. II, A.

[3] But not because they are of different metals, the one copper and the other silver. But see below, par. 3, n. 8. Here it is explained that by admitting one *perutah's* indebtedness the amount of the claim is reduced to less than two *maahs*; and therefore no oath can be imposed.

[4] According to Gem. 42b the claim was, in this case, lodged more as a suspicion than as a certainty; the missing money fell, therefore, within the category of 'lost property' for which no oath could be imposed. Cf. Gitt. 5[3].   [5] Some texts add, 'before witnesses'.

[6] App. II, D.   [7] App. II, A.

[8] See above, n. 3, where the accepted explanation involves here the less natural rendering 'All kinds of coinage are alike'.   [9] App. II, D.   [10] See Ket. 13[4].

claim to utensils, he is not liable. If he admitted in part the claim to land, he is not liable; but if he admitted in part the claim to utensils he is liable, since the property for which there is no security imposes the need for an oath also on property for which there is security.[1]

4. No oath is imposed in a claim by a deaf-mute, an imbecile, or a minor, and no oath is imposed on a minor; but an oath is imposed when a claim is lodged against the [property of a] minor, or against dedicated property.[2]

5. In a claim that concerns these[3] no oath is imposed: bondmen, written documents, immovable property, and the property of the Temple; nor do the laws of twofold restitution or fourfold or fivefold restitution apply to them. An unpaid guardian need not take an oath and a paid guardian need not make restitution. R. Simeon says: An oath is imposed in a claim that concerns Hallowed Things which must be replaced [if damaged or lost], but if they are not such that must be replaced no oath is imposed.

6. R. Meir says: Some things there are that are fixed to the ground and are not accounted immovable property; but the Sages do not agree with him. Thus [if a man said], 'I delivered unto thee ten fruit-laden vines', and the other said, 'They were but five', R. Meir would make him take an oath. But the Sages say: What is fixed to the ground is accounted immovable property.[4] Oaths may only be taken about what can be defined according to size, weight, or number; thus [if a man said], 'I delivered unto thee a houseful [of produce]' or 'a bagful of money', and the other said, 'I do not know, but what thou didst leave thou mayest take', he is exempt; but if he said, '[I delivered unto thee a heap of produce] as high as the projection [above the window]', and the other said, 'Only as high as the window', he is liable.

7. If a man lent his fellow money on a pledge, and the pledge was lost, and the lender said, 'I lent thee a *sela*[5] and the pledge was worth a shekel, and the other said, 'Not so, but thou didst lend me a *sela* on it and it was worth a *sela*', he is exempt. [If he said,] 'I lent thee a *sela* on it and it was worth a shekel', and the other said, 'Not so, but thou didst lend me a *sela* on it and it was worth three *denars*', he is liable. [If he said,] 'Thou didst lend me a *sela* on it and it was worth two', but the lender said, 'Not so, but I lent thee a *sela* on it and it was worth a *sela*', he is exempt. [If he said,] 'Thou didst lend me a *sela* on it and it was worth two', but the other said, 'Not so, but I lent thee a *sela* on it and it was worth five *denars*', he is liable. Who takes the oath? He with whom is the deposit, lest after the one takes the oath the other brings out the deposit.[6]

7. 1. All they that take the oaths which are enjoined in the Law take oaths that they need not make restitution; but these take an oath that they may recover their due: the hireling,[7] he that has been robbed, he that has been wounded, he whose fellow-suitor is not trusted even if he takes an oath, and a shopkeeper over [what is written in] his account-book. Thus, if a hireling said to a householder, 'Give me my hire which is in thine hand', and he said, 'I have given it', and he said, 'I have not had it', the hireling shall take an oath and satisfy his claim. R. Judah says: Not unless the claim

---

[1] See Kidd. 1[5].
[2] That was security for a debt, then dedicated by the debtor and claimed by the creditor.
[3] See B.M. 4[9].   [4] Therefore no oath can be imposed.
[5] Two shekels or four *denars*.   [6] To prove that the debtor has worn falsely.
[7] Cf. B.M. 9[12].

was admitted in part: if, to wit, the hireling said, 'Give me my hire of fifty *denars* which is in thine hand', and the other said, 'Thou hast already received a golden *denar*'.[1]

2. 'He that has been robbed'; thus, if they testified of a man that he entered into another's house without right to seize a pledge, and he that was robbed said, 'Thou didst take a vessel of mine', and the other said, 'I took naught', the first may take an oath and recover his property. R. Judah says: Not unless the claim was admitted in part: if, to wit, he had said, 'Thou didst take two vessels', and the other said, 'I took but one'.

3. 'He that has been wounded'; thus, if they testified of a man that another went in unto him whole and came forth wounded, and he said to the other, 'Thou didst wound me', and the other said, 'I did not wound thee', he may take an oath and satisfy his claim for damages. R. Judah says: Not unless the claim was admitted in part. How? If, namely, he had said, 'Thou didst inflict on me two wounds', and the other said, 'Only one'.

4. 'He whose fellow-suitor is not trusted even if he takes an oath'; thus, no matter whether it be an oath of testimony or a deposit-oath or even a vain oath, if one of the suitors is a dice-player, usurer, pigeon-flyer, or a trafficker in Seventh Year produce,[2] his fellow-suitor may take an oath and satisfy his claim. If neither of them was trustworthy the oath returns to its own place.[3] So R. Jose. R. Meir says: They share equally.[4]

5. 'A shopkeeper over [what is written in] his account-book'; this does not mean that he may, for example, say to another, 'It is written in my account-book that thou owest me 200 *zuz*', but that if one had said to him, 'Give my son two *seahs* of wheat', or 'Give my labourer change for a *sela*',[5] and he said, 'I gave it', but they[6] said, 'We have not had it',[7] he must take an oath and recover his due and they[6] must take an oath and recover their due.[8] Ben Nanos said: How is this? shall both be made to swear a vain oath!—but, rather, he should recover his due without an oath, and they should recover their due without an oath.

6. If a man said to a shopkeeper, 'Give me a *denar's* worth of produce', and he gave it to him and then said to him, 'Give me the *denar*', and the other said, 'I gave it to thee, and thou didst put it in the till', the householder must take an oath. If he [first] gave him the *denar* and said to him, 'Give me the produce', and he said, 'I gave it to thee and thou didst take it to thy house', the shopkeeper must take an oath. R. Judah says: He that has possession of the produce, his hand is uppermost.[9] If a man said to a money-changer, 'Give me change for a *denar*', and he gave it to him and then said, 'Give me the *denar*', and the other said, 'I gave it to thee and thou didst put it in the till', the householder must take an oath. If he had [first] given him the *denar*, and then said to him, 'Give me the change', and the other answered, 'I gave it to thee and thou didst put it in thy purse', the money-changer must take an oath.[10] R. Judah says: It is not the way of a money-changer to give even an *issar*[11] unless he receives his *denar*!

7. Like as they have enjoined[12] that 'if a woman impaired her *Ketubah* the

---

[1] 25 silver *denars*. [2] Cf. Sanh. 3³.

[3] To him against whom the claim is lodged, since normally the oath is imposed on him.

[4] Half the claim only is paid.

[5] As his wage (cf. B.M. 9¹²) 'and I will pay the *sela* after a month'.

[6] The son or labourer. [7] Some texts here insert, 'they both take an oath'.

[8] Both of them from the householder. [9] Cf. p. 353, n. 1.

[10] Since he who is alleged to have the silver *denar* is the debtor; the copper coin counts as the commodity. See p. 353, n. 1. [11] App. II, A. [12] Ket. 9⁷.

rest may not be paid to her unless she swears [to her claim] on oath; [and that] if one witness testified against her that it had been paid [in full], she may not receive payment unless she swears [to her claim] on oath; [and that] she may not receive payment from assigned property or from orphans' property unless she swears [to her claim] on oath; and [that] if a woman is paid not in the presence of him [that divorced her] she may not receive payment unless she swears [to her claim] on oath', so, too, orphans may not receive payment[1] unless they swear [to their claim on oath, namely], 'We swear that our father did not enjoin [in his testament], nor did our father say to us, nor have we found written in the documents of our father, that this bond of indebtedness has been paid'. R. Johanan b. Baroka says: Even if the son had been born after his father's death he may take this oath and satisfy his claim. Rabban Simeon b. Gamaliel said: If there are witnesses [to prove] that at the time of his death the father said, 'This bond has not been paid', he may satisfy his claim without taking an oath.

8. An oath may be imposed on these, although no claim is lodged[2] against them: jointholders, tenants, trustees, a wife that manages the affairs of the house, and the son of the house.[3] If one of these said to the claimant, 'What dost thou claim of me?' and the other said, 'I desire that thou swear to me [that thou hast not made wrongful use of what is mine]', he must swear. If jointholders or tenants[4] had already taken their portions, an oath cannot be imposed on them, but if by chance an oath imposed on such a one in some other claim by the same parties, the first claim too can be implied. The Seventh Year[5] removes the obligation of the oath.

8. 1. There are[6] four kinds of guardian: an unpaid guardian, a borrower, a paid guardian, and a hirer. An unpaid guardian may take an oath in every case [of loss or damage and be quit of liability]; a borrower must make restitution in every case; a paid guardian or a hirer may take an oath if the beast was lamed or driven away or dead, but he must make restitution if it was lost or stolen.[7]

2. If the owner said to an unpaid guardian, 'Where is my ox?' and he answered, 'It is dead', whereas it was lamed or driven away or stolen or lost; or if he answered, 'It is lamed', whereas it was dead or driven away or stolen or lost; or if he answered, 'It was driven away', whereas it was dead or lamed or stolen or lost; or if he answered, 'It is stolen', whereas it was dead or lamed or driven away or lost; or if he answered, 'It is lost', whereas it was dead or lamed or driven away or stolen; and the owner said, 'I adjure thee', and he said, 'Amen!' he is exempt.

3. [If the owner said,] 'Where is my ox?' and he answered, 'I do not know of what thou speakest', and the ox was dead or lamed or driven away or stolen or lost, and the other said, 'I adjure thee', and he said, 'Amen!' he is exempt. [If the owner said,] 'Where is my ox?' and he answered, 'It is lost', and the owner said, 'I adjure thee', and the other said, 'Amen!' and witnesses testify of him that he had eaten it, he must pay the value. If he admitted it of himself, he must pay the value and the [Added] Fifth[8] and [offer] a

---

[1] Of a debt owed to their father's estate.
[2] i.e. they are required to swear to any other that has an interest in their business that they have not dealt fraudulently with what has been entrusted to them.
[3] Who manages the joint property of several brothers.
[4] Who owe the landlord a prescribed proportion of their crop in lieu of rent.
[5] When (Deut. 15[1]) debts to fellow-Israelites are remitted. Cf. Shebi. 10[1].
[6] B.M. 7[8].   [7] See Ex. 22[10-13].   [8] See B.M. 4[8].

Guilt-offering.[1] [If the owner said,] 'Where is my ox?' and he answered, 'It is stolen', and the other said, 'I adjure thee', and he said, 'Amen!' and witnesses testify of him that he had stolen it, he must make twofold restitution.[2] If he admitted it of himself, he must pay the value and the [Added] Fifth and [offer] a Guilt-offering.

4. If a man said to another in the street, 'Where is my ox which thou hast stolen?' and he answered, 'I did not steal it', and witnesses testify of him that he stole it, he must make twofold restitution. If he had killed it or sold it, he must make fourfold or fivefold restitution.[3] If he saw witnesses coming nearer and nearer and said, 'I stole it, but I did not kill it or sell it', he need pay only the value.[4]

5. If the owner said to a borrower, 'Where is my ox?' and he answered, 'It is dead', whereas it was lamed or driven away or stolen or lost; or if he said, 'It is lamed', whereas it was dead or driven away or stolen or lost; or if he said, 'It was driven away', whereas it was dead or lamed or stolen or lost; or if he said, 'It was stolen', whereas it was dead or lamed or driven away or lost; or if he said, 'It is lost', whereas it was dead or lamed or driven away or stolen; and the owner said, 'I adjure thee', and he said, 'Amen!' he is not liable.

6. [If the owner said,] 'Where is my ox?' and the other answered, 'I do not know of what thou speakest', whereas it was dead or lamed or driven away or stolen or lost; and the owner said, 'I adjure thee', and he said, 'Amen!' he is liable. If he said to a paid guardian or a hirer, 'Where is my ox?' and he answered, 'It is dead', whereas it was lamed or driven away; or if he answered, 'It is lamed', whereas it was dead or driven away; or if he answered 'It was driven away', whereas it was dead or lamed; or if he answered, 'It is stolen', whereas it was lost; or 'It is lost', whereas it was stolen, and the owner said, 'I adjure thee,' and he said, 'Amen!' he is not liable. If he answered, 'It is dead or lamed or driven away' whereas it was stolen or lost, and the owner said, 'I adjure thee', and he said, 'Amen!' he is liable. If he answered, 'It is lost or stolen', whereas it was dead or lamed or driven away, and the owner said 'I adjure thee', and he said, 'Amen!' he is not liable. This is the general rule: he that by lying makes himself liable [to make restitution] and he was already liable [even if he spoke the truth], or makes himself exempt and he was already exempt [even if he spoke the truth], or makes himself liable, though he was in truth exempt, he is exempt [from the Guilt-offering].[5] But if he made himself exempt, though he was in truth liable [to make restitution], he is liable [to the Guilt-offering]. This[6] is the general rule: He that swears and so renders his penalty less rigorous is liable; but if he renders his penalty more rigorous he is not liable.

---

[1] Lev. 6[2ff]. Num. 5[7].   [2] Ex. 22[9].   [3] Ex. 22[1].   [4] Ex. 22[3].
[5] Lev. 6[6].   [6] Certain texts omit this last sentence.

EDUYOTH[1] ('TESTIMONIES')

1. 1. Shammai says:[2] For all women it is enough for them [that they be deemed unclean only from] their time [of suffering a flow]. Hillel says: [A woman is deemed to have been unclean] from [the previous] examination to [the present] examination, even if [the interval is of] many days. And the Sages say: It is not according to the opinion of either: but [she is deemed to have been unclean] during the preceding twenty-four hours, if this is less than [the time] from [the previous] examination to [the present] examination, or else from [the previous] examination to [the present] examination if this is less than twenty-four hours. If a woman has fixed periods it is enough for her [that she be deemed unclean only from] her time [of suffering a flow]. If she had connexion and used the test-rags, this counts as an examination, and may lessen either the interval of twenty-four hours, or the interval from [the previous] examination to [the present] examination.

2. Shammai says: [Dough made] from one *kab*[3] [of meal] is liable to Dough-offering.[4] And Hillel says: Two *kabs*. And the Sages say: It is not according to the opinion of either: but one *kab* and a half is liable to Dough-offering; and when the weights were made greater they said: Five quarters of a *kab* are liable. R. Jose says: Five [quarters only] are exempt, but five and aught over are liable.

3. Hillel says: One *hin*[5] of drawn water renders the Immersion-pool[6] unfit. ([We speak of *hin*][7] only because a man must use the manner of speaking of his teacher.) And Shammai says: Nine *kabs*. And the Sages say: It is not according to the opinion of either: but when two weavers came from the Dung Gate in Jerusalem and testified in the name of She-maiah and Abtalion[8] that three *logs* of drawn water render the Immersion-pool unfit, the Sages confirmed their opinion.[9]

4. And why do they record the opinions of Shammai and Hillel when these do not prevail? To teach the generations that come after that none should persist in his opinion, for lo, 'the fathers of the world' did not persist in their opinion.

5. And why do they record the opinion of the individual against that of the majority, whereas the *Halakah* may be only according to the opinion of the majority? That if a court approves the opinion of the individual it may rely upon him, since a court cannot annul the opinion of another court unless it exceeds it both in wisdom and in number; if it exceeded it in wisdom but not in number, or in number but not in wisdom, it cannot annul its opinion; but only if it exceeds it both in wisdom and in number.

---

[1] Lit. 'testimonies', from the frequency in the tractate of the phrase 'Such-a-one testified' to some traditional rule, or the like. The spelling 'Ediyoth' has been suggested; this would give the meaning 'the choicest' (teachings). The tractate is several times referred to in the Talmud by the name 'Behirta' (or, in the plural, 'Behiratha'), meaning the 'selected trac-tate' or (more probably) 'selected *Halakoth*, or traditional rules'. This latter title best befits the contents, which are, primarily, one hundred selected *Halakoth* on unrelated topics, some-imes linked loosely together under the names of the teachers who transmitted them. Added to these are the thirty cases where the School of Hillel exceptionally adopted a more stringent and the School of Shammai a more lenient attitude in a controverted ruling, and a few other sayings and discussions. Most of the contents of Eduyoth are repeated elsewhere in the Mishnah in their proper context.   [2] Nidd. 1[1].   [3] App. II, D.
[4] Num. 15[20]; cf. Hall. 2[6].   [5] Three *logs*. App. II, D.
[6] See the tractate Mikwaoth.
[7] A gloss by the editor, R. Judah the Patriarch, to explain the unusual '*hin*' here used instead of 'three *logs*'. Cf. Par. 1[1].   [8] Circ. 60 B.C. Cf. Ab. 1[10].   [9] Cf. Mikw. 3[1ff].

6. R. Judah said: If so, why do they record the opinion of the individual against that of the majority when it does not prevail? That if one shall say, 'I have received such a tradition', another may answer, 'Thou didst hear it [only] as the opinion of such-a-one'.

7. The School of Shammai say:[1] A quarter-*kab* of bones, be they any of the bones or from two [corpses] or from three, [suffices to convey uncleanness by overshadowing].[2] And the School of Hillel say: [It must be] a quarter-*kab* of bones from a [single] corpse, and from bones which are the greater part either in bulk[3] or in number. Shammai says: Even [a quarter-*kab*] from one bone.

8. The School of Shammai say[4] of Heave-offering vetches: They must be soaked and rubbed in cleanness, but they may be given as food in uncleanness. And the School of Hillel say: They must be soaked in cleanness but they may be rubbed or given as food in uncleanness. Shammai says: They may only be eaten dry. R. Akiba says: Whatsoever concerns them may be done in uncleanness.

9. If[5] a man would change a *sela's* worth of Second Tithe money [outside of Jerusalem] the School of Shammai say: He may change it for a whole *sela*. And the School of Hillel say: A shekel's worth of silver and a shekel's worth in copper coin. R. Meir says: They may not change silver and produce [together] into [other] silver. But the Sages permit it.

10. If[6] a man would change a *sela* of Second Tithe money in Jerusalem, the School of Shammai say: He must change the whole *sela* into copper coin. And the School of Hillel say: He may take one shekel's worth of silver and one shekel's worth in copper coin. They that made argument before the Sages say: Three *denars'* worth of silver and one of copper. R. Akiba says: Three *denars'* worth of silver and from the fourth [*denar*] a quarter in copper coin. R. Tarfon says: Four *aspers* in silver. Shammai says: Let him deposit it in a shop and [gradually] consume its value.

11. If[7] a bride's stool lost its seat-boards, the School of Shammai declare it [still] susceptible to uncleanness; and the School of Hillel declare it not susceptible. Shammai says: Even the frame of a stool remains susceptible to uncleanness. If a stool is fixed to a baking-trough, the School of Shammai declare it [still] susceptible to uncleanness, but the School of Hillel declare it not susceptible. Shammai says: Even one that was made [to be used] inside it [is susceptible].

12. In these things the School of Hillel changed their opinion and taught according to the opinion of the School of Shammai: If[8] a woman returned from beyond the sea and said, 'My husband is dead', she may marry again; [and if she said,] 'My husband died [childless]', she may contract levirate marriage. So the School of Shammai. And the School of Hillel say: We have heard no such tradition save of a woman that returned from the harvest. The School of Shammai answered: It is all one whether she returned from the harvest or from the olive-picking or from beyond the sea: they spoke of the harvest only as of a thing that happened in fact. The School of Hillel changed their opinion and taught according to the opinion of the School of Shammai. The School of Shammai say: She may marry

---

[1] Cf. Ohol. 2[1].
[2] Men and vessels become unclean if they are beneath the same roof as the bones, or if they are directly above or below them. Cf. p. 649, n. 3.
[3] Lit. 'building'; i.e. those bones which go towards forming the greater part of the stature.   [4] M.Sh. 2[4].   [5] M.Sh. 2[8].   [6] M.Sh. 2[9].   [7] Kel. 22[4].   [8] Cf. Yeb. 15[1–3].

again and take her *Ketubah*. And the School of Hillel say: She may marry again but she may not take her *Ketubah*. The School of Shammai answered: Since ye have declared permissible the graver matter of forbidden intercourse, should ye not also declare permissible the less important matter of property? The School of Hillel said to them: We find that brothers may not enter into an inheritance on her testimony. The School of Shammai answered: Do we not learn from her *Ketubah*-scroll that he thus prescribes for her, 'If thou be married to another thou shalt take what is prescribed for thee'? The School of Hillel changed their opinion and taught according to the opinion of the School of Shammai.

13. If[1] a man was half bondman and half freedman, he should labour one day for his master and one day for himself. So the School of Hillel. The School of Shammai say: Ye have ordered it well for his master, but for him ye have not ordered it well: [thus] he cannot marry a bondwoman nor can he marry a free woman; shall he remain fruitless? And was not the world only created for fruition and increase, as it is written, *He created it not a waste: he formed it to be inhabited*? But as a precaution for the general good they should compel his master and he sets him free, and the bondman writes him a bond of indebtedness for half his value. The School of Hillel changed their opinion and taught according to the opinion of the School of Shammai.

14. An earthenware vessel[2] can protect aught [that is within it from contracting uncleanness from a corpse that is under the same roof]. So the School of Hillel. And the School of Shammai say: It can protect only foodstuffs and liquids and [other] earthenware vessels.[3] The School of Hillel said: Why? The school of Shammai said: Because with an *Amhaaretz*[4] it is susceptible to uncleanness, and a vessel that is susceptible to uncleanness cannot interpose [to protect from uncleanness]. The School of Hillel answered: But have ye not pronounced the foodstuffs and liquids therein clean? The School of Shammai said to them: When we pronounced the foodstuffs and liquids therein clean, we pronounced them clean for himself[5] [alone]; but when thou declarest the vessel clean thou declarest it so for thyself[6] as well as for him. The School of Hillel changed their opinion and taught according to the opinion of the School of Shammai.

2. 1. R. Hanina the Prefect of the Priests testified concerning four things. The priests[7] never refrained from burning flesh that had become unclean from a derived uncleanness[8] together with flesh that had become unclean from a primary uncleanness, although they thereby added uncleanness to its uncleanness. Moreover R. Akiba said: The priests never refrained from burning in a lamp rendered unclean by one that had contracted corpse uncleanness, oil that was rendered unfit by one that had immersed himself

---

[1] Gitt. 4[5].   [2] Cf. Ohol. 5[3].   [3] Cf. Kel. 10[1].   [4] App. I. 3.
[5] i.e. for such a one as an *Am-haaretz*.
[6] i.e. that it is such that even thou, an 'Associate' (Dem. 2[3]), couldst take it and use it.
[7] Pes. 1[6].
[8] The source of uncleanness is called 'Father of uncleanness' (i.e. a primary uncleanness) what is rendered unclean by it is called 'Offspring of uncleanness' (i.e. a derived uncleanness). What is rendered unclean at first hand by a 'Father of uncleanness' suffers 'first-grade uncleanness'; and what is rendered unclean by the latter suffers 'second-grade uncleanness'. Ordinary food is susceptible only to the above degrees of uncleanness. Heave-offering can suffer uncleanness even at one farther remove, 'third-grade uncleanness'; and the Hallowed Things (Temple-offerings) are susceptible at still a farther remove, 'fourth-grade uncleanness'. See p. 137, nn. 10-13. See App. IV.

the selfsame day [because of uncleanness], although they thereby added uncleanness to its uncleanness.

2. R. Hanina the Prefect of the Priests said:[1] Never have I seen a hide taken out to the place of burning. R. Akiba said: We learn from his words that if a man flayed a Firstling and it was found to be *terefah*, the priests may make use of its hide. But the Sages say: 'We have not seen' affords no proof; but, rather, such a hide must be taken out to the place of burning.

3. He testified also of a little village near by Jerusalem wherein lived a certain old man who used to lend money to all the people of the village, and write out [the bond of indebtedness] in his own hand, and the others[2] signed it; and when the matter came before the Sages they declared it permissible. Hence thou mayest conclude that a woman may write out her own bill of divorce and a man his own quittance,[3] for the validity of a document depends only on its signatories. [He testified also] that if a needle was found in the flesh [of an offering in the Temple Court], the knife and the hands [which touched the flesh] remain clean[4] but the flesh itself is unclean; but if it was found in the excrements, everything is accounted clean.[5]

4. Three things did R. Ishmael say before the Sages in the vineyard at Jabneh. If[6] a beaten-up egg was put on the top of vegetables that are Heave-offering, it serves as a connective, but if it becomes like a cap it does not serve as a connective. Also, if[7] the tip of an ear of corn left standing after the reaping touches the standing corn, and it can be reaped together with the standing corn, it belongs to the householder; otherwise it belongs to the poor. Also, if a small garden [encompassed by a wall] is surrounded by trellised vines,[8] and there is room enough on the one side for the grape-gatherer and his basket, and room enough on the other side for the grape-gatherer and his basket,[9] seed may be sown there;[10] otherwise it may not be sown.

5. Three things did they say before R. Ishmael and he did not declare them either forbidden or permissible; but R. Joshua b. Matthias expounded them. If a man cut open an abscess on the Sabbath in order to make an opening[11], he is culpable; but if it was to let out pus[12] he is not culpable. Also, if a man hunted a serpent on the Sabbath and he so busied himself that it might not bite him, he is not culpable; but if that he might get a healing drug, he is culpable. Also, Heronian[13] stew-pots are not susceptible[14] to uncleanness when they are beneath the same roof as a corpse,[15] but they become unclean if they are carried by one that has a flux.[16] Rabbi Eliezer b. Zadok says: Even if they are carried by one that has a flux they remain clean, since their manufacture is not finished.[17]

---

[1] Zeb. 12[4].   [2] The witnesses.

[3] Which is given by the woman to the man when she is paid her *Ketubah* on being divorced.

[4] Since it is in doubt whether they touched the needle, and (according to Toh. 4[5]), 'a condition of doubt that arises in the public domain is deemed clean'; but the flesh has certainly touched the needle.

[5] Since the presumption is that the needle has not been in contact with the flesh.

[6] See Teb.Y. 3[2].   [7] Peah 5[2].

[8] On the subject of this *Halakah* see Kil. 4[1]; 6[1].

[9] Outside the garden, between the wall and the vines, so that the space of the garden is not needed in the labour on the vines.   [10] The law of Deut. 22[9] will not then apply.

[11] It would come within the forbidden category of 'building' (Shab. 7[2]).

[12] Permissible since the purpose was not to make a permanent opening.

[13] The reading is uncertain.

[14] Since they were airtight. They were made in the form of hollow balls and, after baking in the furnace, were split into two bowls. They are here referred to in their undivided state.

[15] See Num. 19[14f].   [16] See Lev. 15[12].   [17] Cf. Kel. 4[4].

6. Of three things did R. Ishmael speak and R. Akiba did not agree with him: If a man was pressing[1] garlic or unripe grapes or ears of green corn while it was yet the eve of Sabbath, R. Ishmael says: He may finish pressing them[2] after nightfall. But R. Akiba says: He may not finish them.

7. Three things did they say before R. Akiba, two in the name of R. Eliezer and one in the name of R. Joshua. 'Two in the name of R. Eliezer': a woman[3] may go out [on the Sabbath] wearing a 'golden city'; and pigeon-flyers[4] are not eligible to bear witness. 'And one in the name of R. Joshua': if a weasel[5] had a [dead] creeping thing in its mouth and it passed over loaves of Heave-offering and it is in doubt whether [the creeping thing] touched them or did not touch them, their condition of doubt is deemed clean.

8. Three things said R. Akiba; with two they agreed and with one they did not agree: that the sandal[6] of lime-burners is susceptible to *midras*-uncleanness;[7] that the broken remains of a baking-oven[8] must be yet four handbreadths high [in order to continue susceptible to uncleanness]—whereas they had [before] said, 'three'—and they agreed with him. 'And with one they did not agree': if a stool[9] had lost two adjacent boards of its seat R. Akiba declared it [still] susceptible to uncleanness, but the Sages declared it not susceptible.

9. He used to say: A father endows his son with [the blessings] of beauty, strength, riches, wisdom, and length of years; and with [the merits of] the number of the generations that have gone before him, and of them he[10] is the end, for it is written, *Calling the generations from the beginning*;[11] even though it is written, *And shall serve them; and they shall afflict them four hundred years*,[12] it is also written, *And in the fourth generation they shall come hither again.*[13]

10. He also used to say: There are five things that endure for twelve months; the judgement of the generation of the Flood[14] endured twelve months; the judgement of Job[15] endured twelve months; the judgement of the Egyptians endured twelve months;[16] the judgement of Gog and Magog[17] which is to come shall endure twelve months; and the judgement of the unrighteous in Gehenna shall endure twelve months, for it is written, *It will be from one month until its [same] month.*[18] R. Johanan b. Nuri says: [Only as long as] from Passover to Pentecost,[19] for it is written, *And from one Sabbath until its [next] Sabbath.*

3. 1. If[20] aught that conveys uncleanness by overshadowing was divided and brought into a house, R. Dosa b. Harkinas declares clean [whatsoever is found in the house], but the Sages declare it unclean. Thus if a man touched or carried two pieces of carrion, each a half-olive's bulk; or if he touched one half-olive's bulk of a corpse while he overshadowed another half-olive's bulk; or if he touched one half-olive's bulk while a half-olive's bulk overshadowed him; or if he overshadowed two [pieces each of a]

---

[1] Cf. Shab. 22[1].
[2] i.e. have the use of what moisture still oozes from them without any fresh effort of his after the entering in of the Sabbath.
[3] Shab. 6[1].   [4] Sanh. 3[3].   [5] Toh. 4[2].   [6] Made from wood or straw.
[7] App. I. 26.   [8] Cf. Kel. 5[1].   [9] Kel. 22[7].   [10] The son.   [11] Is. 41[4].
[12] Gen. 15[13].   [13] Gen. 15[16].   [14] Cf. Gen. 7[11] and 8[14].
[15] By rabbinical exegesis of Job. 7[3].
[16] Allowing a little over a mouth for each plague.   [17] Cf. Ezek. 38[2ff].
[18] Is. 66[23]; i.e. the same month of the following year.
[19] Seven weeks. Sabbath is here given the sense of 'feast' (cf. Lev. 23[11], where by Sabbath the feast of Passover is meant).   [20] Ohol. 3[1].

half-olive's bulk; or if he overshadowed one half-olive's bulk and another half-olive's bulk overshadowed him—R. Dosa b. Harkinas declares him clean, but the Sages declare him unclean. But if he touched one half-olive's bulk and some other thing overshadowed both him and another half-olive's bulk, or if he overshadowed one half-olive's bulk and some other thing overshadowed both him and another half-olive's bulk, he remains clean. R. Meir said: Here, too, R. Dosa declared him clean, and the Sages declared him unclean. All such conditions render a man unclean save where there is both contact and carrying, or both contact and overshadowing. This is the general rule: if the means of conveying the uncleanness fall within a single category, they convey uncleanness; but if within two categories, they do not convey uncleanness.

2. Separated pieces of [unclean] foodstuff are not included together.[1] So R. Dosa b. Harkinas. But the Sages say: They are included together. Second Tithe[2] may be exchanged for unminted metal. So R. Dosa. But the Sages say: It may not be exchanged for unminted metal. They need immerse only the hands before sprinkling the Sin-offering water.[3] So R. Dosa. But the Sages say: If his hands have become unclean his whole body is unclean.

3. R. Dosa permits to non-priests the entrails of melons and the outer leaves of vegetables[4] that are Heave-offering.[5] But the Sages forbid them. [A flock[6] of] five sheep that have fleeces each of a *mina* and a half are subject to the law of *the first of the fleece*. So R. Dosa. But the Sages say: Five sheep, however much may be their fleeces.

4. All rush mats[7] are susceptible to corpse-uncleanness [only]. So R. Dosa. But the Sages say: [Also] to *midras*-uncleanness. No network[8] is susceptible to uncleanness save that which is used for a girdle. So R. Dosa. But the Sages say: Every kind is susceptible save that used by wool-dealers.

5. If the receptacle of a sling is of woven work it is susceptible to uncleanness; if it is of leather[9] R. Dosa b. Harkinas declares it not susceptible, but the Sages declare it susceptible. If its finger-hold is severed it is not susceptible to uncleanness; but if the thong-hold [only] is severed it remains susceptible.

6. A woman[10] that has been taken captive may eat of Heave-offering. So R. Dosa. But the Sages say: There is a captive that may eat and there is a captive that may not eat. Thus if[11] the woman said, 'I was taken captive, yet I remain clean', she may eat, since[12] the mouth that forbade is the mouth that permitted; but if there are witnesses [to say] that she was taken captive, and she says, 'Yet I remain clean', she may not eat.

7. In[13] four conditions of doubt R. Joshua declares a man unclean but the Sages declare him clean. Thus if one that is unclean stands still and one that is clean passes by, or if one that is clean stands still and one that is unclean passes by; or if what is unclean is in a private domain and what is clean is in the public domain, or if what is clean is in a private domain and

---

[1] To make up the egg's bulk that conveys uncleanness. But cf. Meil. 4[5].
[2] M.Sh. 1[2].   [3] See Hag. 2[5].
[4] Which are discarded as uneatable.   [5] Cf. Lev. 22[10ff].   [6] Hull. 11[2].
[7] For the subject here discussed see Kel. 24[10]; 27[2].
[8] As opposed to woven work; cf. Kel. 27[1ff].   [9] Cf. Kel. 26[3].
[10] An Israelite's daughter married to a priest; cf. Lev. 22[12].   [11] Ket. 2[5].
[12] Some texts omit the following sentence.   [13] Toh. 6[2].

what is unclean is in the public domain, and it is in doubt whether one touched the other or not, or whether one overshadowed the other or not, or whether one shifted [what was unclean] or not, R. Joshua declares a man unclean but the Sages declare him clean.

8. Three[1] things R. Zadok declares susceptible to uncleanness and the Sages declare them not susceptible. The nail of the money-changer, a grist-dealer's chest, and the point of a sundial. R. Zadok declares them susceptible and the Sages declare them not susceptible.

9. Four[2] things Rabban Gamaliel declares susceptible to uncleanness and the Sages declare them not susceptible. The metal basket-cover belonging to householders, the hanger of a strigil, unfinished metal vessels, and a plate broken into two [equal parts]. But the Sages agree with Rabban Gamaliel that if the plate was broken into two pieces the one large and the other small, the larger is susceptible to uncleanness but the smaller becomes insusceptible.

10. In[3] three things Rabban Gamaliel gives the more stringent ruling, following the opinion of the School of Shammai. Hot food may not be covered up on a Festival-day for the Sabbath, nor may a candlestick be put together on a Festival-day, nor may bread be baked into large loaves, but only into thin cakes. Rabban Gamaliel said: Never did my father's household bake bread into large loaves but only into thin cakes. They said to him: What shall we infer from thy father's household which applied the stringent ruling to themselves, but the lenient ruling to Israel, so that they might bake the bread both in large loaves and thick cakes!

11. Moreover[4] he gave three opinions applying the more lenient ruling: they may sweep up between couches and put the spices on the fire on a Festival-day, and prepare a kid roasted whole on Passover night. But the Sages forbid these things.

12. Three things[5] did R. Eleazar b. Azariah permit and the Sages forbid. A man's cow may go out [on the Sabbath] with the strap that is between its horns, and they may curry cattle on a Festival-day, and grind pepper in its proper mill. R. Judah says: They may not curry cattle on a Festival-day since it may cause a weal, but they may comb them. And the Sages say: They may neither curry them nor comb them.

4. 1. In these things the School of Shammai adopted the more lenient, and the School of Hillel the more stringent ruling. If[6] an egg was laid on a Festival-day the School of Shammai say: It may be eaten. And the School of Hillel say: It may not be eaten. The School of Shammai say: An olive's bulk of leaven and a date's bulk of what is leavened. And the School of Hillel say: An olive's bulk of either.

2. If a beast was born on a Festival-day they agree that it is permitted, but if a chicken was hatched from an egg they agree that it is forbidden.[7] If[8] a man slaughtered a wild animal or a bird on a Festival-day, the School of Shammai say: He may dig with a mattock and cover up [the blood]. And the School of Hillel say: He should not slaughter unless he had earth set in readiness [to cover up the blood]. But they agree that if he had slaughtered he may dig with a mattock and cover up [the blood]; [moreover they agreed] that ashes of a stove may be regarded as set in readiness.

---

[1] Kel. 12[5].   [2] Kel. 12[6].   [3] Betz. 2[6].   [4] Betz. 2[7].   [5] Betz. 2[8].   [6] Betz. 1[1].
[7] Some texts omit this first sentence of the paragraph.   [8] Betz. 1[2].

3. The School of Shammai say:[1] [If produce is proclaimed] 'ownerless' for the benefit of the poor, it is accounted ownerless [and tithe-free]. And the School of Hillel say: It can only be accounted ownerless [and tithe-free] if [it is proclaimed] ownerless [equally] for the benefit of the rich as in the year of Release. If the sheaves in a field were each of one *kab's* weight but one was of four *kabs*, if this was forgotten the School of Shammai say: It may not be deemed a Forgotten Sheaf. And the School of Hillel say: It may be deemed a Forgotten Sheaf.

4. If[2] a sheaf lies near to a wall or to a stack or to the oxen or to the implements, and is forgotten, the School of Shammai say: It may not be deemed a Forgotten Sheaf. And the School of Hillel say: It may be deemed a Forgotten Sheaf.

5. The School of Shammai say:[3] The rules of the [Added] Fifth and of Removal do not apply to [the grapes of] a Fourth Year Vineyard. And the School of Hillel say: They do apply. The School of Shammai say: The laws of grape-gleanings and of the defective cluster apply, and the poor redeem the grapes for themselves. And the School of Hillel say: The whole yield goes to the winepress.

6. A jar of pickled olives, according to the School of Shammai, need not be broached.[4] And the School of Hillel say: It must be broached. But they agree that if it had been broached and the lees block up the breach, it is not susceptible to uncleanness.[5] If a man anointed himself with clean oil and then became unclean and he went down and immersed himself, the School of Shammai say: Even though he still drips [with oil] it is clean.[6] and the School of Hillel say: [It is unclean so long as there remains] enough to anoint a small member. And if it was unclean oil at the outset, the School of Shammai say: [It remains unclean, even after he has immersed himself, so long as there remains] enough to anoint a small member. And the School of Hillel say: So long as it remains a moist liquid. R. Judah says in the name of the School of Hillel: So long as it is moist enough to moisten aught else.

7. According to the School of Shammai,[7] a woman is betrothed by [the gift of] a *denar* or a *denar's* worth. And the School of Hillel say: By a *perutah* or a *perutah's* worth. And how much is a *perutah*? The eighth part of an Italian *issar*. The School of Shammai say:[8] A man may dismiss his wife with an old bill of divorce. And the School of Hillel forbid it. What is an old bill of divorce? If he continued alone with her after he had written it for her [it becomes an 'old' bill of divorce]. If[9] a man divorced his wife and she then lodged with him in an inn, the School of Shammai say: She does not need another bill of divorce from him. And the School of Hillel say: She needs another bill of divorce from him. This applies when she was divorced after wedlock; but if she had been divorced from him after betrothal [only], she does not need another bill of divorce from him, since he is not yet shameless before her.

8. The School of Shammai permit[10] levirate marriage between the co-

---

[1] Peah. 6[1].   [2] Peah 6[2].   [3] Peah 7[6]; M.Sh. 5[3].

[4] To let out the moisture that exudes from the fruit, lest the liquid 'render it susceptible to uncleanness' (Lev. 11[34, 38]; Maksh. 6[5]); since moisture renders foodstuffs unclean only if it is applied purposely or to some one's advantage (cf. Maksh. 1[1]).

[5] Since the broaching of the jar has itself proved that the sap was not regarded as an advantage.

[6] It was rendered clean as a part of the body.

[7] Kidd. 1[1].   [8] Gitt. 8[4].   [9] Gitt. 8[9].   [10] Yeb. 1[4].

wives and the surviving brothers. And the School of Hillel forbid it. If they performed *halitzah* the School of Shammai declare them ineligible to marry a priest, but the School of Hillel declare them eligible. If they had been taken in levirate marriage, the School of Shammai declare them eligible but the School of Hillel ineligible. Notwithstanding that these declare ineligible whom the others declare eligible, yet [the men of] the School of Shammai did not refrain from marrying women from [the families of] the School of Hillel, nor [the men of] the School of Hillel from marrying women from [the families of] the School of Shammai; and despite all the disputes about what is clean and unclean, wherein these declare clean what the others declare unclean, neither scrupled to use aught that pertained to the others in matters concerned with cleanness.

9. If[1] there were three brothers, two married to two sisters, and one un-married, and one of the married brothers died, and the unmarried brother bespoke the widow, and then his second brother died, the School of Sham-mai say: His [bespoken] wife abides with him and the other is free as being his wife's sister. And the School of Hillel say: He must put away his [bespoken] wife both by bill of divorce and by *halitzah*, and his brother's wife by *haltizah*. This is a case whereof they have said, 'Woe to him because of [the loss of] his wife, and woe to him because of [the loss of] his brother's wife!'

10. If[2] a man vowed to have no intercourse with his wife the School of Shammai say: [She may consent] for two weeks. And the School of Hillel say: For one week [only]. If[3] a woman miscarried on the night of the eighty-first day, the School of Shammai declare her exempt from an offering. And the School of Hillel declare her liable. The School of Sham-mai declare a linen garment exempt from the law of the Fringe;[4] and the School of Hillel declare it subject to the law. A basket[5] of fruit intended for the Sabbath the School of Shammai declare exempt [from Tithes], and the School of Hillel declare it liable.

11. If a man[6] vowed to be a Nazirite for a longer spell and he fulfilled his Nazirite-vow and afterward came to the Land [of Israel], the School of Shammai say: He need continue a Nazirite [only for] thirty days [more]. And the School of Hillel say: He must again fulfil his vow as from the beginning. If[7] two pairs of witnesses testified of a man, and the one testified that he had vowed two Nazirite-vows, and the other that he had vowed five, the School of Shammai say: Their testimony is at variance, and the Nazirite-vow cannot be held binding. And the School of Hillel say: The two are included within the five, so that he must remain a Nazirite for the two spells.

12. If[8] a man was put there below the split,[9] the School of Shammai say: He does not give passage to the uncleanness. And the School of Hillel say: A man is hollow, and his upper side gives passage to the uncleanness.

5. 1. R. Judah reports six opinions in which the School of Shammai follow the more lenient, and the School of Hillel the more stringent ruling. According to the School of Shammai the blood of a carcase is clean,[10] and

---

[1] Yeb. 3[5].   [2] Ket. 5[6].   [3] Ker. 1[6].
[4] The cord of blue (Num. 15[38]; Deut. 22[12]). It was of wool, thereby infringing the law against 'mingled stuff, wool and linen together' (Deut. 22[11]).
[5] Maas. 4[2].   [6] Naz. 3[6].   [7] Naz. 3[7].   [8] Ohol. 11[3].
[9] i.e. across the roof of a portico (see p. 665, n. 3).   [10] Cf. below, 8[1].

the School of Hillel declare it unclean. An egg from a [bird's] carcase is permitted if it is in like condition to them that are sold in the market,[1] otherwise it is forbidden. So the School of Shammai. And the School of Hillel forbid it [in any condition]. But they agree that an egg from a bird that is *terefah* is forbidden, since it was fashioned in what was forbidden. The blood[2] of a gentile woman and the blood of the purifying of a woman that is a leper, the School of Shammai declare clean; and the School of Hillel say: It is like to her spittle or her urine. According to the School of Shammai[3] they may eat Seventh Year produce by favour [of the owner] or without favour. And the School of Hillel say: They may only eat it by favour [of the owner]. The School of Shammai say: A water-skin[4] [can contract *midras*-uncleanness] when it is tied up with a durable knot. And the School of Hillel say: Even when it is not tied up.

2. R. Jose reports six opinions in which the School of Shammai follow the more lenient and the School of Hillel the more stringent ruling. According to the School of Shammai a fowl[5] may be served up on the table together with cheese but it may not be eaten with it. And the School of Hillel say: It may neither be served up with it nor eaten with it. According to the School of Shammai Heave-offering[6] may be set apart from olives instead of from oil, or from grapes instead of from wine; and the School of Hillel forbid it. According to the School of Shammai if a man sowed seed[7] within a space of four cubits [from the vines] of a vineyard, he renders forfeit one row; and the School of Hillel say: He renders forfeit two rows. The School of Shammai declare flour-paste[8] exempt [from Dough-offering], and the School of Hillel declare it liable. According to the School of Shammai they may immerse[9] themselves in a rain-stream, and the School of Hillel say that they may not do so. The School of Shammai say: If a man became a proselyte[10] on the day before Passover, he may immerse himself and consume his Passover-offering in the evening. And the School of Hillel say: He that separates himself from his uncircumcision is as one that separates himself from the grave.

3. R. Simeon[11] reports three opinions in which the School of Shammai follow the more lenient and the School of Hillel the more stringent ruling. According to the School of Shammai the book of Ecclesiastes[12] does not render the hands unclean. And the School of Hillel say: It renders the hands unclean. According to the School of Shammai Sin-offering water[13] which has fulfilled its purpose is clean; and the School of Hillel declare it unclean. The School of Shammai declare black cummin[14] insusceptible to uncleanness; and the School of Hillel declare it susceptible. So, too, [do they differ] concerning [whether it is liable to] Tithes.

4. R. Eliezer reports two opinions in which the School of Shammai follow the more lenient and the School of Hillel the more stringent ruling. According to the School of Shammai the blood[15] of a woman that has not yet immersed herself after childbirth is like to her spittle or her urine. And the School of Hillel say: [It conveys uncleanness] whether it is wet or dried up. But they agree that if a woman gave birth while she had a flux, it renders unclean whether [the blood was] wet or dried up.

---

[1] Fully fashioned with its shell hard.   [2] Nidd. 4[3].   [3] Shebi. 4[2].   [4] Cf. Kel. 26[4].
[5] Hull. 8[1].   [6] Cf. Ter. 1[4].   [7] Kil. 4[5].   [8] Hall. 1[6].   [9] Mikw. 5[6].
[10] Pes. 8[8].   [11] Variant: Ishmael.
[12] Cf. Yad. 3[5]. According to the School of Shammai it is not canonical Scripture.
[13] Cf. Par. 12[4].   [14] Uktz. 3[6].   [15] Nidd. 4[3].

5. If[1] two of four brothers married two sisters, and the two that married the two sisters died, the sisters must perform *halitzah* and may not contract levirate marriage; and if the brothers had already married them they must put them away. R. Eliezer says: According to the School of Shammai they may continue the marriage; but according to the School of Hillel they must put them away.

6. Akabya b. Mahalaleel testified to four opinions. They answered: Akabya, retract these four opinions that thou hast given and we will make thee Father of the Court[2] in Israel. He said to them: Better that I be called a fool all my days than that I be made a godless man before God even for an hour; for they shall not say of me, He retracted for the sake of office. He declared unclean the residuary hair [in a leprosy sign],[3] and also the yellow blood;[4] but the Sages declare them clean. If the hair[5] of a blemished Firstling fell out and one put it in a wall-niche, and afterward slaughtered the beast, he used to permit the hair [to be used]; but the Sages forbid it. He said: They do not give a proselyte or a freed bondwoman to drink of the water of bitterness].[6] And the Sages say: They give her to drink. They said to him: It happened to Karkemith, a freed bondwoman that was in Jerusalem, that Shemaiah and Abtalion[7] gave her to drink. He replied: Only in show did they make her to drink. Whereupon they laid him under a ban; and he died while he was yet under the ban, and the court stoned his coffin. R. Judah said: God forbid that it should be Akabya that was put under the ban!—for the Temple Court was never shut against the face of any man in Israel so wise and sin-fearing as Akabya b. Mahalaleel. But whom did they put under a ban? Eleazar b. Enoch, because he threw doubt on [the teaching of the Sages concerning] the cleansing of hands.[8] And when he died the court sent and laid a stone on his coffin; whence we learn that if any man is put under a ban and dies while yet under the ban, his coffin must be stoned.

7. In the hour that he[9] died he said to his son, 'My son, retract the four opinions which I gave'. He answered, 'Why didst not thou retract?' He said to him, 'I heard them from a majority, and they also heard their opinions from a majority. I continued steadfast to the tradition that I had heard and they continued steadfast to the decision that they had heard. But thou hast heard [a decision] both from the mouth of an individual and [a contrary decision] from the mouth of the majority. It is better to leave the opinion of the individual and to hold to the opinion of the majority'. He answered, 'Father, commend me to thy fellow Sages'. He said to him, 'I commend thee not'. He answered, 'Perchance thou hast found in me some cause for complaint?' He said to him, 'No, but thine own deeds will bring thee near [to them], or thine own deeds will remove thee far [from them]'.

6. 1. R. Judah b. Baba testified of five things: that they may [at times] instruct women married while minors to exercise right of Refusal;[10] that they may suffer a woman to marry again[11] following the testimony of but one witness; that a cock was stoned[12] in Jerusalem because it killed a man;

---

[1] Yeb. 3[1].   [2] Second to the President. See Hag. 2[2].
[3] See Neg. 5[3].   [4] Nidd. 2[6].   [5] Cf. Bekh. 3[4].
[6] See Num. 5[12ff]: 'Speak to the children of *Israel*'.   [7] See above, 1[3].
[8] As taught in Yad. 3[2].   [9] Akabya.   [10] See Yeb. 13[1ff].
[11] See Yeb. 16[7]. See below, 8[5].   [12] Cf. Ex. 21[28].

that wine forty days old could be poured out as a libation on the Altar, and that the morning Daily Whole-offering was offered at the fourth hour.

2. R. Joshua and R. Nehunya b. Elinathan of Kefar ha-Babli testified that [the smallest] member of a corpse is unclean,[1] concerning which R. Eliezer says: They have taught this only of a member of a living being.[2] They said to him: Is it not an inference from the less to the greater?—if a member severed from a living being (who is clean) is unclean, how much more then should a member severed from a corpse (which is unclean) be unclean! He answered: They have taught this only of a member from a living being. Another answer[3] is: The uncleanness of living beings is greater than the uncleanness of corpses, since a living being conveys uncleanness by lying and sitting to whatsoever is beneath him so that these convey uncleanness both to men and to garments,[4] and [he also conveys] *maddaf*-uncleanness[5] to what is above him so that these convey uncleanness to foodstuffs and liquids, uncleanness which a corpse does not convey.

3. If an olive's bulk of flesh was severed from a member of a living being, R. Eliezer declares it unclean, but R. Joshua and R. Nehunya declare it clean. If a barleycorn's bulk of bone was severed from a living being, R. Nehunya declares it unclean, but R. Eliezer and R. Joshua declare it clean. They said to R. Eliezer: What hast thou seen that thou dost declare unclean an olive's bulk of flesh severed from a member of a living being? He said to them: We find that a member from a living being is reckoned as like to a whole corpse;[6] therefore as, with the corpse, an olive's bulk of flesh severed from it is unclean, so, too, with a member of a living being, an olive's bulk of flesh severed from it must be unclean. They said to him: No! as thou declarest unclean an olive's bulk of flesh severed from a corpse (whereof thou declarest unclean a barleycorn's bulk of bone that is severed from it), wouldest thou also declare unclean an olive's bulk of flesh severed from the member of a living being (whereof thou hast declared clean an olive's bulk of bone that is severed from it)? They said to R. Nehunya: What hast thou seen that thou declarest unclean a barleycorn's bulk of bone severed from the member of a living being? He answered: We find that a member from a living being is reckoned as like to a whole corpse; therefore as, with the corpse, a barleycorn's bulk of bone that is severed from it is unclean, so, too, with a member from a living body, a barleycorn's bulk of bone that is severed from it must be unclean. They said to him: No! as thou declarest unclean a barleycorn's bulk of bone severed from the corpse (whereof thou hast declared unclean an olive's bulk of flesh that is severed from it), wouldest thou also declare unclean a barleycorn's bulk of bone severed from the member of a living being (whereof thou hast declared clean an olive's bulk of flesh that is severed from it)? They said to R. Eliezer: What hast thou seen that thou dost follow different rules?—either pronounce both unclean or both clean. He answered: The uncleanness of flesh is greater than the uncleanness of bones, since [the uncleanness of] flesh applies both to carcases and creeping things, which is not so with [the uncleanness of] bones. Another answer is: A member bearing its proper flesh[7] conveys uncleanness by contact, by

---

[1] And conveys uncleanness by 'overshadowing'. See Ohol. 2[1].
[2] Ohol. 1[7].   [3] By R. Eliezer.
[4] See Lev. 15[5ff]. On the subject here treated see Zab. 4[6]; cf. Par. 10[1ff].
[5] App. I. 21.   [6] Ohol. 2[1].   [7] Cf. Kel. 1[5].

carrying and by overshadowing; if aught of the flesh is lacking it is [still] unclean, but if any bone is lacking, it is clean. They said to R. Nehunya: What hast thou seen that thou dost follow different rules?—either declare both unclean or both clean. He answered: The uncleanness of bones is greater than the uncleanness of flesh, since flesh severed from a living being is clean, and a member severed from it, while in its natural state,[1] is unclean. Another saying is: An olive's bulk of flesh renders unclean by contact, carrying, and overshadowing; and the greater part of the bones [of a corpse] conveys uncleanness by contact, carrying, and overshadowing; but if the flesh lacks aught, it is clean, while if the greater part of the bones lacks aught, although it is clean, in that it does not convey uncleanness by overshadowing, it yet conveys uncleanness by contact and carrying. Another saying is: When the entire flesh of a corpse is less than an olive's bulk, it is clean, but the greater part of a corpse's bulk and members, although they are not a quarter-*kab* in all, are unclean. They said to R. Joshua: What hast thou seen that thou dost declare both clean? He answered: No! as thou arguest of a corpse to which there apply the terms 'greater part', 'quarter', and 'corpse-dust',[2] wouldest thou also argue of a living being to which do not apply the terms 'greater part', 'quarter', and 'corpse-dust'?

7. 1. R. Joshua and R. Zadok testified that if the redemption[-lamb] for the firstborn of an ass died,[3] the priest has no more claim therein, whereas R. Eliezer says: The owner is still answerable for it, as [in like case he is answerable for] the five *selas*, [the redemption price] for a [firstborn] son. But the Sages say: He is not answerable for it as [in like case he is not answerable for] the redemption price of Second Tithe.

2. R. Zadok testified that the brine[4] made from unclean locusts is clean; whereas the First Mishnah [taught]: If unclean locusts have been pickled with clean locusts they do not render their brine unfit.

3. R. Zadok testified[5] that if flowing water was more than the dripping water [with which it was mingled], it was still valid [as flowing water]. Such a case happened at Birath-ha-Piliyya, and when the case came before the Sages they declared it valid.

4. R. Zadok testified that if flowing water was led through [a channel made from] foliage of nuts,[6] it remains valid. Such a case happened at Ahaliyya, and when the case came before the Sages in the Chamber of Hewn Stone[7] they pronounced it valid.

5. R. Joshua and R. Yakim of Haddar testified that if[8] the jar containing [the ashes of] the Sin-offering was set on top of a creeping thing, it became unclean, whereas R. Eliezer declared it clean. R. Papias[9] testified that if a man vowed two Nazirite-vows and cut off his hair after the first spell on the thirtieth day, he should cut off his hair after the second spell on the sixtieth day, but if he cut off his hair on the fifty-ninth day he has fulfilled his obligation, since the thirtieth day can be reckoned to him among the number [of days for the second Nazirite-vow].

6. R. Joshua and R. Papias testified[10] that the young of a Peace-offering could be offered as a Peace-offering, whereas R. Eliezer says: The young of

---

[1] With its proper complement of flesh, bones, and sinews.   [2] Ohol. 2¹.
[3] Bekh. 1⁶.   [4] Cf. Ter. 10⁹.   [5] Mikw. 5⁵.   [6] See Par. 6⁴.
[7] Sanh. 11²; Midd. 5⁴.   [8] Cf. Par. 10³.   [9] See Naz. 3².   [10] See Tem. 3¹.

a Peace-offering may not be offered as a Peace-offering. But the Sages say: It may be so offered. R. Papias said: I testify that we had a heifer that was a Peace-offering; we consumed it at Passover and we consumed its young as a Peace-offering at the following feast [of Pentecost].

7. They testified that the baking-boards[1] of bakers are susceptible to uncleanness, whereas R. Eliezer declared them insusceptible. They testified that if a baking-oven[2] was cut up into rings and sand put between each ring, it still remains susceptible to uncleanness, whereas R. Eliezer declared it insusceptible. They testified that the year could be declared a leap-year[3] any time during Adar; whereas it had been taught: Only until Purim. They testified that the year could be declared a leap-year conditionally. Once Rabban Gamaliel went to have authority given him from the governor in Syria, and he was long in returning; so they declared the year a leap-year on the condition that Rabban Gamaliel should approve; and when he returned he said, 'I approve'; and so the year was reckoned a leap-year.

8. Menahem b. Signai testified that the rim around the boiler[4] belonging to olive-seethers is susceptible to uncleanness, but that belonging to dyers is not susceptible; whereas they used to teach to the contrary.

9. R. Nehunya b. Gudgada testified[5] of a woman that was a deaf-mute and that was given in marriage by her father [while yet a minor], that she could be put away by a bill of divorce; and that a minor, an Israelite's daughter that was married to a priest, could eat of Heave-offering; and that if she died her husband could inherit from her; and that if a man built a stolen beam into a structure he need only repay its value; and that a Sin-offering that was stolen property, if this was not known to many, could [still] effect atonement—as a precaution for the benefit of the Altar.

8. 1. R. Joshua b. Bathyra testified that the blood[6] of carcases was clean. R. Simeon b. Bathyra testified that if an unclean person touched but a part of the ashes of the Sin-offering,[7] he renders the whole unclean. R. Akiba added that if one that had immersed himself [because of uncleanness] the self-same day[8] touched but a part of the fine flour, the incense, the frankincense, and the charcoal,[9] he renders the whole unfit.

2. R. Judah b. Baba[10] and R. Judah the Priest testified of the daughter of an Israelite that was a minor and married to a priest, that she could eat of Heave-offering[11] after she had entered the bride-chamber, even though there had not been consummation. R. Jose the Priest and R. Zechariah b. ha-Kazzab testified of a young girl that was left as a pledge is Ashkelon, and the members of her family[12] kept her far from them, although she had witnesses that testified that she had not gone aside in secret [with any man] and been defiled.[13] The Sages said to them: If ye believe that she was left as a pledge believe also that she had not gone aside in secret and been defiled; but if ye do not believe that she had not gone aside in secret and been defiled do not believe that she was left as a pledge.

3. R. Joshua and R. Judah b. Bathyra testified that the widow of one

---

[1] See Kel. 15[2].   [2] See Kel. 5[10].   [3] See Meg. 1[4].   [4] Kel. 5[5].
[5] See Yeb. 14[2]; Gitt. 5[5].   [6] Cf. above, 5[1].   [7] Num. 19[9].
[8] See p. 773, n. 6.   [9] Lev. 16[12].   [10] Some texts read 'Abba'.
[11] Lev. 22[11].   [12] Who were priests.
[13] And so ineligible for marriage with a priest; Lev. 21[7].

which belonged to an Isah[1] family was eligible for marriage with a priest; [and] that the members of an Isah family are qualified to bear testimony as to which [of themselves] is unclean or clean,[2] and which must be put away and which may be brought near.[3] Rabban Simeon b.[4] Gamaliel said: We accept your testimony, but what shall we do, for Rabban Johanan b. Zakkai decreed that courts may not be set up concerning this. The priests would hearken to you in what concerns putting away but not in what concerns bringing near.

4. R.[5] Jose b. Joezer of Zereda testified that the Ayil-locust[6] is clean,[7] and that the liquid [that flows] in the shambles [in the Temple] is not susceptible to uncleanness; and that he that touches[8] a corpse becomes unclean. And they called him 'Jose the Permitter'.

5. R. Akiba testified[9] in the name of Nehemiah of Beth Deli that a woman is permitted to marry again on the evidence of [but] one witness.[10] R. Joshua testified concerning bones that were once found in the woodshed [of the Temple] that they were unclean;[11] the Sages said: They may be collected bone by bone[12] and all[13] continue clean.

6. R. Eliezer said: I have heard a tradition that while they were building the Temple they made curtains for the Temple and curtains for the courtyards, but they built [the walls of] the Temple[14] outside[15] [the curtains], and [the walls of] the courtyards they built within [the curtains]. R. Joshua said: I have heard a tradition that they may offer sacrifices although there is no Temple, and eat the Most Holy Things although there are no curtains, and the Lesser Holy Things and the Second Tithe although there is no wall;[16] since its first dedication[17] availed both for its own time and for the time to come.

7. R. Joshua said: I have received as a tradition from Rabban Johanan b. Zakkai, who heard from his teacher, and his teacher from his teacher, as a *Halakah* given to Moses from Sinai,[18] that Elijah will not come to declare unclean or clean, to remove afar or to bring nigh, but to remove afar those [families] that were brought nigh by violence and to bring nigh those [families] that were removed afar by violence.[19] The family of Beth Zerepha was in the land beyond Jordan and Ben Zion removed it afar by force. And yet another [family] was there, and Ben Zion brought it nigh by force. The like of these Elijah will come to declare unclean or clean, to remove afar or to bring nigh. R. Judah says: To bring nigh but not to remove afar. R. Simeon says: To bring agreement where there is matter for dispute. And the Sages say: Neither to remove afar nor to bring high, but to make

---

[1] A family claiming to be of Israelitish stock but which was suspected of admixture with doubtful stock. Cf. Kidd. 4[1].   [2] Legitimate or bastard.
[3] i.e. whether marriage of any of them with a priest was invalid or valid.
[4] Some texts omit 'Simeon b.'
[5] Some texts omit 'Rabbi'. Cf. Ab. 1[4]. Joezer's testimony is recorded in Aramaic.
[6] Lit. 'ram.'   [7] Eatable.
[8] Only he and not also what he in turn touches; or it may mean that he is unclean only if t is not in doubt that he touched the corpse.   [9] Cf. Yeb. 16[7].
[10] Who reports the husband's death.
[11] Many texts omit this phrase. The meaning can only be: 'they were recognized as human bones.'
[12] i.e. there is no need to anticipate the presence of other graves there. Cf. Ohol. 16[3].
[13] Men and utensils; none needs to undergo immersion.
[14] The structure itself.   [15] To separate the builders from the Sanctuary.
[16] See p. 406, nn. 10, 11.   [17] By Solomon.
[18] See Peah 2[6]; Yad. 4[3]. Cf. Ab. 1[1].
[19] i.e. he will make no change in the Law but only make an end of injustice.

peace in the world, as it is written, *Behold I will send you Elijah the prophet . . . and he shall turn the heart of the fathers to the children and the heart of the children to their fathers.*[1]

ABODAH ZARAH ('IDOLATRY')

1. 1. For three days before the festivals of the gentiles it is forbidden to have business with them—to lend to them or to borrow from them, to lend them money or to borrow money from them, to repay them or to be repaid by them. R. Judah says: One may take repayment from them since this grieves him. They said to him: Although it now grieves him he will afterward rejoice.

2. R. Ishmael says: For three days before their festivals and for three days after them it is forbidden [to have any business with them]. But the Sages say: Before their festivals it is forbidden, but after their festivals it is not forbidden.

3. And these are the festivals of the gentiles: the Calends,[2] the Saturnalia,[3] the commemoration of empire,[4] the anniversaries[5] of kings, and the day of [their] birth and the day of [their] death. So R. Meir. But the Sages say: Where burning has place at the death [rites] there is idolatry; where burning has no place there is no idolatry. But on the day when a man shaves off his beard and his lock of hair,[6] or the day when he returns from a voyage, or the day when he comes out of prison, or when a gentile makes a wedding-feast for his son, [business with them is] forbidden only on that day and with that man.

4. If there was an idol inside a town it is permitted [to have business with them] outside it; if there was an idol outside, it is permitted [to have business with them] inside. Is it permitted to go in that direction [on the festivals of the gentiles]? If the road leads to that place alone it is forbidden, but if one can go by it to another place it is permitted. If there was an idolatrous festival in a city and some shops therein were adorned and others not adorned—such a case happened in Beth Shean, and the Sages said: Those that are adorned are forbidden and those that are not adorned are permitted.

5. These things it is forbidden to sell to the gentiles:[7] fir-cones, white figs with their stalks, frankincense, or a white cock. R. Judah says: One may sell a gentile a white cock among other cocks, or, if it is by itself, cut off its spur and sell it to him, because they do not sacrifice to an idol what is defective. All other things, if [any idolatrous use is] not specified, are permitted to be sold; but if [any idolatrous use is] specified, they are forbidden. R. Meir says: It is forbidden also to sell to gentiles fine dates, or Hazab or Nicolaus dates.

6. Where[8] the custom is to sell small cattle to gentiles, they may sell them; where the custom is not to sell them, they may not sell them.[9] And

---

[1] Mal. 4[5f].

[2] Here is meant not the first day of each month but the first day of the year, 'eight days after the winter solstice' (Gem. 8a).

[3] December 17, 'eight days before the solstice' (Gem. 8a).

[4] Heb. *kratesis*, κράτησις. 'The day on which Rome seized (world-)sovereignty' (Gem. 8b).

[5] Heb. *genusia*, γενέσια. But according to Gem. 10a it is not the birth but the accession of the emperors that is commemorated.

[6] Which marked a youth's coming of age.

[7] During their festivals, since they sacrifice such things to their gods.   [8] Pes. 4[3].

[9] Some texts add: Let none change the customs, for fear of controversy.

nowhere may they sell them large cattle, calves, or foals, whole or maimed. R. Judah permits a maimed beast [to be sold] and Ben Bathyra permits a horse.

7. None may sell them bears or lions or aught that can do harm[1] to the people. None may help them to build a basilica, scaffold, stadium, or judges' tribunal; but one may help them to build public baths[2] or bath-houses; yet when they have reached the vaulting where they set up the idol it is forbidden [to help them] to build.

8. None may make ornaments for an idol: necklaces or ear-rings or finger-rings. R. Eliezer says: If for payment it is permitted.[3] None may sell them what is attached to the soil[4] but it may be sold after it has been severed. R. Judah says: One may sell it to a gentile on condition that it is severed. None may hire houses to them in the Land of Israel or, needless to say, fields; in Syria houses may be hired to them but not fields; while outside the Land houses may be sold and fields hired to them. So R. Meir. R. Jose says: In the Land of Israel houses may be hired to them but not fields; and in Syria houses may be sold and fields hired to them; while outside the Land either may be sold to them.

9. Howbeit, where they have said 'to hire' they spoke not of a dwelling-house, since he might bring in an idol, for it is written, *And thou shalt not bring an abomination into thine house.*[5] And nowhere may a bath-house be hired to a gentile, since it would be called by the [Israelitish] owner's name.[6]

2. 1. Cattle may not be left in the inns of the gentiles since they are suspected of bestiality; nor may a woman remain alone with them since they are suspected of lewdness; nor may a man remain alone with them since they are suspected of shedding blood. The daughter of an Israelite may not assist a gentile woman in childbirth since[7] she would be assisting to bring to birth a child for idolatry, but a gentile woman may assist the daughter of an Israelite. The daughter of an Israelite may not suckle the child of a gentile woman, but a gentile woman may suckle the child of the daughter of an Israelite in this one's domain.

2. [An Israelite] may accept healing from them for his goods but not for his person,[8] and in no place may he have his hair cut by them. So R. Meir. But the Sages say: In the public domain it is permitted, but not if they are alone.

3. These things that belong to gentiles are forbidden, and it is forbidden to have any benefit at all from them: wine, or the vinegar of gentiles that at first was wine, Hadrianic earthenware,[9] and hides pierced at the heart.[10] Rabban Simeon b. Gamaliel says: If the rent was round, the hide is forbidden, but if straight it is permitted. Flesh that is entering in unto an idol is permitted, but what comes forth is forbidden, for it is as *the sacrifices*

---

[1] Weapons and the like.

[2] Reading *demoseoth*. Variant: *bemoseoth*, meaning 'theatres' or places of public amusement.   [3] Some texts omit this first part of the paragraph.

[4] No gentile may be suffered to acquire rights over land in the Land of Israel.

[5] Deut. 7[26].

[6] Therefore when it is heated on the Sabbath the guilt will be ascribed to the Israelite.

[7] Some texts omit this clause.   [8] Cf. Ned. 4[4].

[9] Or 'Adriatic'. Gem. 32a explains that they were so called after the Emperor Hadrian. Wine was put in vessels of unbaked earthenware which thus became heavily impregnated with the wine; the vessels were then broken and the sherds were used to flavour drinking-water.

[10] Cf. Ned. 2[1]. The heart was removed from a living beast and offered to idols.

of the dead.[1] So R. Akiba. It is forbidden to have business with them that are going on an idolatrous pilgrimage,[2] but with them that are returning it is permitted.

4. The skin-bottles of gentiles or their jars that are filled with the wine of an Israelite are forbidden, and it is forbidden to have any benefit at all from them. So R. Meir. But the Sages say: It is not forbidden to have any benefit at all from them.[3] The grape-stones and grape-skins of the gentiles are forbidden and it is forbidden to have any benefit at all from them. So R. Meir. But the Sages say: When moist they are forbidden, but when dried they are permitted. The fish-brine[4] and Bithynian cheese of the gentiles are forbidden, and it is forbidden to have any benefit at all from them. So R. Meir. But the Sages say: It is not forbidden to have any benefit at all from them.

5. R. Judah said: While they were on a journey R. Ishmael asked R. Joshua and said to him, 'Why have they forbidden the cheese of the gentiles?' He answered, 'Because they curdle it with rennet from a carcase'.[5] He said to him, 'But is not the rennet from a Whole-offering forbidden more stringently than rennet from a carcase, and yet they have said, "If a priest is not squeamish[6] he may suck it out raw"'? (and[7] they did not agree with him but said: They may get no benefit therefrom, yet [if they did] the law of Sacrilege[8] would not apply). [R. Joshua] said to him, 'Because they curdle it with rennet from calves sacrificed to idols'. He said to him, 'If so, why have they not also forbidden any benefit at all from it?' He led him to another matter;[9] he said to him: Ishmael, my brother, how readest thou?— *For thy* (masc.) *love is better than wine*, or *Thy* (fem.) *love . . .?*[10] He answered, *Thy* (fem.) *love . . .* He said to him: It is not so, for lo, its fellow [-verse] teaches us concerning it: *Thine* (masc.) *ointments have a goodly fragrance.*

6. These things of the gentiles are forbidden, but it is not forbidden to have any benefit at all from them: milk which a gentile milked when no Israelite watched him; their bread and their oil (Rabbi and his court permitted the oil), stewed or pickled vegetables into which it is their custom to put wine or vinegar; minced fish, or brine containing no fish (with[11] no *kilbith*-fish[12] floating in it); *hilek*-fish;[13] drops of asafoetida or sal-condi-tum. Lo, these are forbidden, but it is not forbidden to have any benefit at all from them.

7. These are [even] permitted as food: milk which a gentile milked when an Israelite watched him; honey or honeycombs (even though they drip

<hr/>

1 Ps. 106[28].
2 So Tif. Yis. The Hebrew term used conveys the sense 'obscenity'.
3 Only if the jars were impregnated with previous wine belonging to gentiles. It is only forbidden to drink the wine.
4 A sauce made by pickling fish; wine was usually mixed with it.
5 A beast not properly slaughtered. Cf. Hull. 2[2ff].   6 Cf. Men. 11[7].
7 The bracketed sentence is an editorial aside. For similar comments see Sanh. 8[1]; Eduy. 1[3].   8 Lev. 5[15].
9 He was unwilling to give the answer because twelve months had not yet passed since the court's decree concerning the cheese of gentiles, and it was forbidden to divulge the reason for decrees before twelve months for fear of provoking public controversy.
10 Song of Songs, 1[2]. The unvowelled Hebrew is ambiguous: *dodeka* (m.) or *dodaik* (f.)?
11 Many texts omit the bracketed clause, which is a gloss from the Gemara (39b).
12 'A small insect like an unclean fish which breeds in brine made from clean fish but not in that made from unclean fish' (Bert. and Tif. Yis.).
13 A species of clean fish which has no fins in its early stage, and there is danger of its being confused with unclean species.

with moisture they do not come within the law of food rendered susceptible to uncleanness by a liquid);[1] pickled vegetables into which it is not their custom to put wine or vinegar; unminced fish, or brine containing fish; a [whole] leaf of asafoetida or pickled olive-cakes. R. Jose says: If the olives are sodden[2] they are forbidden. Locusts that come out of the [shopkeeper's] basket are forbidden;[3] but those from the shop-store are permitted. And the same applies to Heave-offering.[4]

3. 1. All images are forbidden[5] because they are worshipped once a year.[6] So R. Meir. But the Sages say: Only that is forbidden which bears in its hand a staff or a bird or a sphere.[7] Rabban Simeon b. Gamaliel says: That which bears aught in its hand.

2. If a man found fragments of images, these are permitted. If he found [a fragment in] the shape of a hand or the shape of a foot, these are forbidden, since an object the like of these is worshipped.

3. If a man found objects on which is a figure of the sun, a figure of the moon, or a figure of a dragon, he must throw them into the Dead Sea.[8] Rabban Simeon b. Gamaliel says: If [the figures are found] on objects of value these are forbidden, but if on worthless objects they are permitted. R. Jose says: One should break them into pieces and scatter them to the winds, or throw them into the sea. They said to him: Even so they would become manure, and it is written, *And there shall cleave nought of the devoted thing to thine hand*.[9]

4. Proklos the son of Philosophos[10] asked Rabban Gamaliel in Acre while he was bathing in the Bath of Aphrodite, and said to him, 'It is written in your Law, *And there shall cleave nought of the devoted thing to thine hand. Why [then] dost thou bathe in the Bath of Aphrodite?* He answered, 'One may not make answer in the bath'.[11] And when he came out he said, 'I came not within her limits: she came within mine! They do not say, "Let us make a bath for Aphrodite", but "Let us make an Aphrodite as an adornment for the bath". Moreover if they would give thee much money thou wouldest not enter in before thy goddess naked or after suffering pollution, nor wouldest thou make water before her! Yet this goddess stands at the mouth of the gutter and all the people make water before her. It is written, *Their gods*,[12] only; thus what is treated as a god is forbidden, but what is not treated as a god is permitted.'

5. If the gentiles worship mountains or hills, these themselves are permitted but what is on them is forbidden; for it is written, *Thou shalt not covet the silver or the gold that is upon them nor take it unto thee*.[13] R. Jose the Galilean says: [It is written,] *Their gods upon the high mountains*,[14] not 'The mountains [are] their gods'; and *Their gods . . . upon the hills*, and not 'The

---

[1] Lev. 11[34, 38]. See tractate Makshirin.
[2] So disintegrated that their stones fall out; there is ground for suspicion that they had been soaked in wine.   [3] He is suspected of sprinkling them with wine.
[4] If a priest was suspected of sprinkling his wares with Heave-offering wine. It is assumed that he would only do so with what was exposed for immediate sale.
[5] For any benefit at all to be derived from them.
[6] Even those serving only as ornament.
[7] Symbols of lordship: a staff, in that it is master of all; a bird, in that it holds all mankind like a bird in its hand; and a sphere, in that it holds the whole world in its hand (Gem. 41a, which adds also the symbols sword, crown, and ring).   [8] Lit. 'Sea of Salt'.
[9] Deut. 13[17].   [10] Perhaps the text was originally 'Proklos the philosopher'.
[11] It is forbidden to speak words of the Law while naked.
[12] Deut. 12[3].   [13] Deut. 7[25].   [14] Deut. 12[2].

hills [are] their gods'. And why is an *Asherah*[1] forbidden? Because the hands of man have been concerned therewith, and whatsoever the hands of man have been concerned with is forbidden. R. Akiba said: I will explain and expound the matter before thee: Wheresoever thou findest a high mountain or a lofty hill and a green tree, know that an idol is there!

6. If a man's house adjoined an idol's shrine, and it fell down, it is forbidden to build it again. What shall he do? He must withdraw four cubits[2] within his own domain and then build again. If there was a wall common to him and the idol's shrine, it is deemed to belong half to each; its stones, wood, and earth[3] convey uncleanness as though they were a creeping thing; for it is written, *Thou shalt utterly detest it*.[4] R. Akiba says: Like a menstruant, for it is written, *Thou shalt cast them away as a menstruous thing: thou shalt say unto it, Get thee hence*;[5] as a menstruant conveys uncleanness by carrying, so does an idol convey uncleanness by carrying.

7. Three kinds of houses are to be distinguished [in what concerns idolatry]: if a house was built from the first for idolatry it is forbidden; if it was plastered and bedecked for idolatry, or if aught was done to it anew, one only need remove what was done to it anew; but if a gentile did but bring in an idol and take it out again, such a house is permitted. Three kinds of stones are to be distinguished: if a stone was hewn out from the first for a pedestal, it is forbidden; if it was plastered and bedecked for an idol, or if aught was done to it anew, one only need remove what was done to it anew; but if a gentile did but set up an idol on it and take it away again, the stone is permitted. Three kinds of *Asherah* are to be distinguished: if a tree was planted from the first for idolatry, it is forbidden; if it was chopped and trimmed for idolatry and it sprouted afresh, one only need take away what has sprouted afresh; but if a gentile did but set up an idol beneath it and then desecrate it, the tree is permitted. What is an *Asherah*? Any tree under which is an idol. R. Simeon says: Any tree which is worshipped. It once happened in Sidon that they worshipped a tree under which was a heap of stones. R. Simeon said to them, Examine this heap. They examined it and found an image in it. He said to them, Since it is the image that they worshipped, we permit to you the tree.

8. None may sit in its shadow, but if he has sat there[6] he remains clean; and none may pass under it, and if he has done so he becomes unclean. If it encroached on the public way and one passed under it, he remains clean. They may sow vegetables under it in the rainy season but not in the hot season,[7] but [they may sow] lettuces[8] neither in the rainy season nor in the hot season. R. Jose says: [They may] not even [sow] vegetables [under it] in the rainy season, since the tree's foliage drops down upon them and serves them for manure.

9. If a man took wood from an *Asherah* it is forbidden to have any benefit at all from it. If he heated an oven with it and the oven was new,[9] it must be broken up, and if old it must be suffered to cool again. If he baked bread in it it is forbidden to have any benefit at all from it, and if the bread was

---

[1] App. I. 4.   [2] Many texts omit.
[3] The mud and mortar filling in the masonry of the walls.
[4] Deut. 7²⁶. The passage quoted conveys the sense: 'Thou shalt wholly deem it an abominable thing', with the special sense of Lev. 11¹¹ and 11²⁹.
[5] Is. 30²². Cf. Shab. 9¹.   [6] But not directly beneath its boughs.
[7] Since they have the benefit of its shade.   [8] Which need shade in winter as well.
[9] And not thoroughly hardened; it would thus derive permanent benefit.

mixed up with other bread, it is forbidden to have any benefit at all from any of it. R. Eliezer says: A man should throw the benefit he has had from it into the Dead Sea.[1] They said to him: There can be no redemption price[2] in a matter of idolatry. If he took from it [wood for] a shuttle, it is forbidden to have any benefit at all from it. If he wove a garment with it it is forbidden to have any benefit at all from it; and if it was mixed up with other garments, and these again with others, it is forbidden to have any benefit at all from any of them. R. Eliezer says: A man may throw any benefit he has had from them into the Dead Sea. They said to him: There can be no redemption price in a matter of idolatry.

10. How is an *Asherah* desecrated? If it is trimmed or pruned, or if a branch or a twig or even a leaf is taken from it, then it is desecrated; if it was trimmed for the good of the tree it remains forbidden, but if not for the good of the tree, it is permitted.

4. 1. R. Ishmael says: Three stones beside a *Merkolis*,[3] one beside the other [and one above them],[4] are forbidden, but two only are permitted. But the Sages say: Those that manifestly belong to it are forbidden, and those that do not manifestly belong to it are permitted.

2. If coins, clothing, or [other] objects were found on its head, these are permitted; but bunches of grapes, garlands of corn, flasks of wine or oil or fine flour, or the like of whatsoever is offered on the Altar are forbidden.

3. If a garden or a bath-house belonged to an idol, they may be used if there is no need to offer thanks, but not if there is need to offer thanks.[5] If they belonged both to the idol and to others, they may be used whether there is need to offer thanks or no need.

4. The idol of a gentile is straightway forbidden, but that of an Israelite is not forbidden unless it has been worshipped. A gentile can desecrate his own or his fellow's idol,[6] but an Israelite cannot desecrate a gentile's idol. If a man desecrated an idol he has thereby desecrated the things that pertain to it; if he desecrated [only] the things that pertain to it these are permitted, but the idol itself is forbidden.

5. How is an idol desecrated? If a gentile cut off the tip of its ear or the end of its nose or the tip of its finger, or battered it even though naught was broken off, he has desecrated it. If he spat in its face, or made water before it, or dragged it about, or threw filth at it, he has not desecrated it. If he sold it or gave it in pledge, Rabbi says: He has desecrated it. But the Sages say: He has not desecrated it.

6. An idol whose worshippers have abandoned it in time of peace is permitted, but if in time of war it is forbidden. The idol-pedestals set up in honour of kings are permitted since they set up the images on them [only] when the kings pass by.

7. They asked the elders in Rome,[7] 'If God has no pleasure in an idol why does he not make an end of it?' They answered, 'If men worshipped a thing of which the world had no need he would make an end of it; but lo, they worship the sun and moon and the stars and the planets: shall God

---

[1] And so need not waste the bread.
[2] As for Second Tithe, or as for Sacrilege (Lev. 5[15f].)   [3] See p. 392, n. 12.
[4] The dolmen which 'is the essential element of the Merkolis' (Bert.).
[5] In neither case may payment be made.
[6] Variant: Or that of an Israelite. According to the Gemara (52b) this is what Rabbi taught in his younger days. Cf. p. 353, n. 2.   [7] See p. 126, n. 1.

destroy his world because of fools?' They said to them, 'If so, let him destroy that which the world does not need and leave that which the world needs'. They answered, 'We should but confirm them that worship them, for they would say, Know ye that these are [true] gods, for they have not been brought to an end'.

8. One may buy [the contents of] a trodden winepress from a gentile even though [the gentile] took the grapes in his hand and put them on the heap, for the wine cannot become libation-wine[1] until it flows down into the vat. If some had flowed down into the vat, what is in the vat is forbidden, but the rest is permitted.

9. An Israelite may help a gentile to tread a winepress but he may not gather grapes with him. If an Israelite was preparing [his wine] in [conditions of] uncleanness, none may help him to tread the winepress or to gather grapes, but one may help him to take jars to the winepress or bring them away from the winepress. If a baker was preparing [his bread] in [conditions of] uncleanness, none may help him to knead the dough or roll it, but one may help him to take bread to the dealer.

10. If a gentile was found standing by the side of a wine-vat and he had a lien upon the wine, it is forbidden; but if he had not, it is permitted. If a gentile fell into it and came up again, or if he measured it with a reed, or flicked out a hornet with a reed, or if he patted the mouth of a frothing jar—these cases all happened and the Sages said: It must be sold. But R. Simeon permits it. If he took a jar and in his anger[2] threw it into the vat— this once happened and they declared the wine fit [for drinking].

11. If an Israelite prepared the wine of a gentile in [conditions of] cleanness[3] and left it in the gentile's keeping in a house open to the public domain, if there were both gentiles and Israelites in the city the wine is permitted;[4] but if there were only gentiles[5] it is forbidden, unless he left there a guardian; the guardian need not sit still and keep watch, even if he goes in and out the wine is permitted. R. Simeon b. Eleazar says: It is all one, whatsoever kind was the gentile's domain.[6]

12. If an Israelite prepared the wine of a gentile in [conditions of] cleanness and left it in the gentile's keeping, and the gentile wrote for him [a quittance, saying,] 'I have received from thee its price', then it is permitted. But if the Israelite had wished to remove the wine and the other would not suffer him to do so until he paid its price—this once happened at Beth Shean, and the Sages declared the wine forbidden.

5. 1. If a gentile hired a labourer [that was an Israelite] to help him with libation-wine, his wage is forbidden; but if he had hired him to help him with some other work, even if he said to him, 'Remove me this jar of libation-wine from this place to another', his hire is permitted. If a gentile hired the ass [of an Israelite] to bring thereon libation-wine, its hire is forbidden; but if he had hired it to ride upon, even if the gentile rested his flagon [of libation-wine] upon it, the hire is permitted.

---

[1] Primarily wine which a gentile has dedicated to his god to be poured out as a libation. It has generally the wider meaning of any wine prepared by or belonging to a gentile.
[2] Some texts omit 'in his anger'.
[3] So that the gentile might be enabled to sell such wine to Israelites.
[4] Since the gentile owner is always exposed to the observation of Israelites.
[5] Or if the house was not exposed to observation from the public domain.
[6] For the wine to be permissible a guardian is needful whether the gentile's shop was open to the public domain or not, and whether the city was half Israelitish or not.

2. If libation-wine fell upon grapes, one may rinse them and then they are permitted; but if they were burst they are forbidden. If[1] it fell on figs or dates, and it was enough to leave a flavour, they are forbidden. It once happened that Boethus b. Zunin[2] brought dried figs in a ship and a jar of libation-wine was broken and fell upon them; and he asked the Sages and they declared the figs permitted. This is the general rule: whatsoever derives benefit [from the libation-wine] through its leaving a flavour is forbidden; whatsoever does not derive benefit [from the libation-wine] through its leaving a flavour is permitted—as when vinegar [from libation-wine] falls upon crushed beans.

3. If a gentile helped an Israelite to take jars of wine from one place to another, and the presumption is that the wine was watched, it is permitted; but if the Israelite had told the other that he would be gone, [the wine is forbidden] if [he was gone] time enough for the other to bore a hole and stop it up, and for the clay to dry. Rabban Simeon b. Gamaliel says: Time enough for the other to open the jar and close it up, and for the clay to dry.[3]

4. If he left his wine in a wagon or in a boat and went by a short bypath and entered the town and bathed, the wine is permitted. But if he had told the other that he would be gone, [the wine is forbidden] if [he was gone] time enough for the other to bore a hole and stop it up, and for the clay to dry. Rabban Simeon b. Gamaliel says: Time enough for the other to open the jar and close it up, and for the clay to dry. If a man left a gentile in his shop, although he went in and out, the wine is permitted; but if he had told him that he would be gone, [it is forbidden] if [he was gone] time enough for the other to bore a hole and stop it up, and for the clay to dry. Rabban Simeon b. Gamaliel says: Time enough for the other to open the jar and close it up, and for the clay to dry.

5. If an Israelite was eating with a gentile at a table, and he put flagons [of wine] on the table and flagons [of wine] on the side-table,[4] and left the other there and went out, what is on the table is forbidden and what is on the side-table is permitted; and if he had said to him: 'Mix thy cup and drink', that which is on the side-table is forbidden also. Opened jars[5] are forbidden, and sealed jars [are forbidden if the Israelite was gone] time enough for [the gentile] to open [a jar] and close it up, and for the clay to dry.

6. If a foraging band of gentiles[6] entered a city, and it was a time of peace, opened jars are forbidden but sealed jars permitted; if it was a time of war both alike are permitted since there was no leisure for them to make the wine libation-wine.

7. Israelitish craftsmen to whom a gentile sent a jar of libation-wine as their hire[7] are permitted to say to him, 'Give us its value in money'; but after it has come into their possession it is forbidden [to ask for its value].[8] If a man sold his wine to a gentile and fixed its price before he measured it[9] [into the gentile's vessel], its price is permitted; but if he measured it out

---

[1] Some texts omit this sentence.   [2] B.M. 5³.
[3] The jar mouth was blocked up with a cone-shaped earthenware plug, and this was sealed up with clay.
[4] 'Delphica': a three-legged side-table. See Kel. 22¹,², 24⁶; 25¹.
[5] Where the gentile has been left alone and invited to drink.
[6] Some texts omit 'of gentiles'.   [7] Some texts omit 'as their hire'.
[8] That would be tantamount to selling libation-wine.   [9] Cf. B.B. 5⁷.

before he fixed its price,[1] its price is forbidden. If he took the funnel and measured out wine into a gentile's flask and again measured out wine into an Israelite's flask, and there remained [in the funnel] a drop of wine [from what had been poured into the gentile's flask, the wine in the Israelite's flask] is forbidden.[2] If he poured out [wine] from one vessel[3] into another,[4] [the wine remaining in] that from which he pours is permitted,[5] and that into which he empties is forbidden.

8. Libation-wine in any quantity soever is forbidden and renders [other wine] forbidden. If [libation-]wine was mixed with [other] wine, or [libation-]water with [other] water in any quantity soever, it renders [the other] forbidden. But if [libation-]wine was mixed with water, or [libation-]water with wine, it renders the other forbidden only if it is sufficient to leave a flavour. This is the general rule: if mixed with like kind in any quantity soever, it makes the other forbidden; but if with another kind, it renders the other forbidden only if it is sufficient to leave a flavour.

9. These are forbidden and in any quantity soever they make other things[6] forbidden: [a jar of] libation-wine,[7] an idol,[8] hides pierced at the heart,[9] the ox that is condemned to be stoned,[10] the heifer whose neck is to be broken,[11] the Bird-offerings of a leper,[12] the Hair-offering of a Nazirite,[13] the firstborn of an ass,[14] flesh cooked in milk,[15] the scapegoat,[16] unconsecrated beasts that are slaughtered in the Temple Court;[17] they are forbidden and in any quantity soever they make other things forbidden.

10. If libation-wine fell into the vat, it is forbidden to have any benefit at all from any of it. Rabban Simeon b. Gamaliel says: It may all be sold to gentiles excepting the value of the libation-wine that is in it.

11. If a gentile coated a stone winepress with pitch it may be scoured and is then clean; if it was of wood Rabbi says: It may be scoured. But the Sages say: The pitch must be scaled off. If it was of earthenware, even though the pitch is scaled off it is forbidden.

12. If a man bought utensils from a gentile, those[18] which it is the custom[19] to immerse[20] he must immerse, those which it is the custom to scald[21] he must scald; those which it is the custom to make white-hot in the fire he must make white-hot in the fire. A spit or gridiron must be made white-hot in the fire; but a knife needs but to be polished and it is then clean.

[1] It was then in the gentile's possession and to be considered as libation-wine; the Israelite would therefore be receiving payment for libation-wine.
[2] Since a drop of it had touched the gentile's wine and was therefore contaminated by libation-wine, or by the gentile's vessel which had not been properly cleaned after containing libation-wine.   [3] Belonging to himself.
[4] Belonging to a gentile, or containing libation-wine.
[5] Provided that the liquid stream had not been continuous; otherwise this stream would have formed a 'connective' between the vessels.
[6] i.e. of like kind with which they are confused.
[7] Confused with other jars of wine.
[8] 'An idolatrous coin mixed with other coins' (Maim.).
[9] See above, 2[3].   [10] Ex. 21[28].   [11] Deut. 21[4].   [12] Lev. 14[4-7].
[13] Num. 6[14]. See p. 282, n. 4.   [14] Ex. 13[13]; 34[20].
[15] Ex. 23[19]; 34[26]; Deut. 14[21].   [16] Lev. 16[22].   [17] See p. 341, n. 2.
[18] Of metal or glass; and other vessels used for uncooked food.
[19] In order to free them from uncleanness.
[20] Before use.   [21] Cooking-vessels. Cf. Zeb. 11[7].

ABOTH[1] ('THE FATHERS')

1. 1. Moses received the Law[2] from Sinai and committed it to Joshua, and Joshua to the elders,[3] and the elders to the Prophets;[4] and the Prophets committed it to the men of the Great Synagogue.[5] They said three things: Be deliberate in judgement, raise up many disciples, and make a fence around the Law.

2. Simeon the Just[6] was of the remnants of the Great Synagogue. He used to say: By three things is the world sustained: by the Law, by the [Temple-]service, and by deeds of loving-kindness.

3. Antigonus of Soko received [the Law] from Simeon the Just. He used to say: Be not like slaves that minister to the master for the sake of receiving a bounty, but be like slaves that minister to the master not for the sake of receiving a bounty; and let the fear of Heaven be upon you.

4. Jose b. Joezer[7] of Zeredah and Jose b. Johanan of Jerusalem received [the Law] from them. Jose b. Joezer of Zeredah said: Let thy house be a meeting-house for the Sages and sit amid the dust of their feet and drink in their words with thirst.

5. Jose b. Johanan of Jerusalem said: Let thy house be opened wide and let the needy be members of thy household; and talk not much with womankind. They said this of a man's own wife: how much more of his fellow's wife! Hence the Sages have said: He that talks much with womankind brings evil upon himself and neglects the study of the Law and at the last will inherit Gehenna.

6. Joshua b. Perahyah and Nittai the Arbelite[8] received [the Law] from them. Joshua b. Perahyah said: Provide thyself with a teacher and get thee a fellow[-disciple];[9] and when thou judgest any man incline the balance in his favour.[10]

7. Nittai the Arbelite said: Keep thee far from an evil neighbour and consort not with the wicked and lose not belief in retribution.

[1] The bulk of this tractate 'The Fathers' (sometimes called *Pirke Aboth*, 'Chapters of the Fathers') is a selection of maxims on conduct and sayings in praise of the Law handed down in the names of 60 teachers of the Law who lived between 300 B.C. and A.D. 200 from the time of Simeon the Just to Rabbi Judah the Patriarch, the editor of the Mishnah. The fifth chapter differs in form. Excepting the last four paragraphs the sayings are anonymous and classified in groups in which various numbers, such as ten, seven, or four, are used as a linking device. The sixth chapter is no part of the Mishnah. It is, however, included in all modern editions of the Mishnah and in the Jewish Prayer Book.

[2] The 'Oral Law'. The Law (*Torah*) throughout post-biblical Jewish religious literature has the threefold connotation of (*a*) the Pentateuch, the 'Written Law'; (*b*) the 'traditions of the elders'—rules of Jewish life and religion which in the course of centuries had come to possess a validity and sanctity equal to that of the Written Law and which, as the 'Oral Law', were deemed, equally with the Written Law, to be of divine origin and therefore consonant with and, for the most part, deducible from the Written Law; and (*c*) the study of the Law in its twofold aspect, a study which sought to sanction by deeper understanding the seeming variations between the Oral and Written Law, to apply the Law to present-day life, and by successive interpretations to solve new problems by the authority of the Law, written and oral.   [3] Josh. 24[31].   [4] Jer. 7[25].

[5] 'A body of 120 elders, including many prophets, who came up from exile with Ezra; they saw that prophecy had come to an end and that restraint was lacking; therefore they made many new rules and restrictions for the better observance of the Law' (Tif. Yis.).

[6] Simeon, son of Onias, High Priest *c.* 280 B.C. (see *Ant.* XII. ii. 5.) or Simeon II, High Priest *c.* 200 B.C. (cf. Ecclesiasticus, ch. 50).

[7] *c.* 160 B.C. He is said to have been the uncle of Alcimus (1 Maccabees 7[5]). In this and the following paragraphs (4, 6, 8, 10, 12) are given the names of the 'Pairs' (*Zugoth*; cf. Peah 2[6]) who according to tradition were president and vice-president ('Father of the court') of the Sanhedrin (Hag. 2[2]) during the century and a half after Jose b. Joezer.

[8] *c.* 120 B.C., a contemporary of John Hyrcanus.

[9] For the sense of this term cf. Yeb. 16[7]; Erub. 2[6].

[10] Lit. judge all men in the scale of guiltlessness.

8. Judah b. Tabbai and Simeon b. Shetah[1] received [the Law] from them. Judah b. Tabbai said: Make not thyself like them that would influence the judges; and when the suitors stand before thee let them be in thine eyes as wicked men, and when they have departed from before thee let them be in thine eyes as innocent, so soon as they have accepted the judgement.

9. Simeon b. Shetah said: Examine the witnesses diligently and be cautious in thy words lest from them they learn to swear falsely.

10. Shemaiah and Abtalion[2] received [the Law] from them. Shemaiah said: Love labour and hate mastery and seek not acquaintance with the ruling power.

11. Abtalion said: Ye Sages, give heed to your words lest ye incur the penalty of exile and ye be exiled to a place of evil waters, and the disciples that come after you drink [of them] and die, and the name of Heaven be profaned.

12. Hillel and Shammai[3] received [the Law] from them. Hillel said: Be of the disciples of Aaron, loving peace and pursuing peace, loving mankind and bringing them nigh to the Law.

13. He used to say: A name[4] made great is a name destroyed, and he that increases not decreases, and he that learns not is worthy of death, and he that makes worldly use of the crown shall perish.

14. He used to say: If I am not for myself who is for me? and being for mine own self what am I? and if not now, when?

15. Shammai said: Make thy [study of the] Law a fixed habit; say little and do much, and receive all men with a cheerful countenance.

16. Rabban Gamaliel[5] said: Provide thyself with a teacher and remove thyself from doubt, and tithe not overmuch by guesswork.[6]

17. Simeon his son said: All my days have I grown up among the Sages and I have found naught better for a man than silence; and not the expounding [of the Law] is the chief thing but the doing [of it]; and he that multiplies words occasions sin.

18. Rabban Simeon b. Gamaliel said: By three things is the world sustained: by truth, by judgement, and by peace, as it is written, *Execute the judgement of truth and peace.*[7]

2. 1. Rabbi[8] said: Which is the straight way that a man should choose? That which is an honour to him and gets him honour from men. And be heedful of a light precept as of a weighty one, for thou knowest not the recompense of reward of each precept; and reckon the loss through [the fulfilling of] a precept against its reward, and the reward [that comes] from transgression against its loss. Consider three things and thou wilt not fall into the hands of transgression: know what is above thee—a seeing eye and a hearing ear and all thy deeds written in a book.

2. Rabban Gamaliel[9] the son of R. Judah the Patriarch said: Excellent is study of the Law together with worldly occupation, for toil in them both puts sin out of mind. But all study of the Law without [worldly] labour comes to naught at the last and brings sin in its train. And let all them that labour with the congregation labour with them for the sake of Heaven, for the merit of their fathers supports them and their righteousness endures

---

1 *c.* 80 B.C. 2 Cf. 'Pollion the Pharisee and his disciple Sameas', *Ant.* xv. i. 1.
3 *c.* 30 B.C.–A.D. 10. 4 This saying is quoted in Aramaic.
5 Grandson (or possibly son) of Hillel. 6 Cf. Ter. 4[6]. 7 Zech. 8[16].
8 Judah the Patriarch, compiler of the Mishnah. 9 The Third.

for ever. And as for you, [will God say,] I count you worthy of great reward as though ye [yourselves] had wrought.

3. Be heedful of the ruling power for they bring no man nigh to them save for their own need: they seem to be friends such time as it is to their gain, but they stand not with a man in his time of stress.

4. He used to say: Do his will as if it was thy will that he may do thy will as if it was his will. Make thy will of none effect before his will that he may make the will of others of none effect before thy will.

5. Hillel said: Keep not aloof from the congregation and trust not in thyself until the day of thy death, and judge not thy fellow until thou art come to his place, and say not of a thing which cannot be understood that it will be understood in the end; and say not, When I have leisure I will study: perchance thou wilt never have leisure.

6. He used to say: A brutish man dreads not sin, and an ignorant man[1] cannot be saintly, and the shamefast man cannot learn, and the impatient man cannot teach, and he that engages overmuch in trade cannot become wise; and where there are no men strive to be a man.

7. Moreover he saw a skull floating on the face of the water and he said unto it, Because thou drownedst they drowned thee and at the last they that drowned thee shall be drowned. He used to say: The more flesh the more worms; the more possessions the more care; the more women the more witchcrafts; the more bondwomen the more lewdness; the more bondmen the more thieving; the more study of the Law the more life; the more schooling the more wisdom; the more counsel the more understanding; the more righteousness the more peace. If a man has gained a good name he has gained [somewhat] for himself; if he has gained for himself words of the Law he has gained for himself life in the world to come.

8. Rabban Johanan b. Zakkai[2] received [the Law] from Hillel and from Shammai. He used to say: If thou hast wrought much in the Law claim not merit for thyself, for to this end wast thou created. Five disciples had Rabban Johanan b. Zakkai, and these are they: R. Eliezer b. Hyrcanus,[3] and R. Joshua b. Hananiah,[4] and R. Jose the Priest,[5] and R. Simeon b. Nathaniel,[6] and R. Eleazar b. Arak.[7] Thus used he to recount their praise: Eliezer b. Hyrcanus is a plastered cistern which loses not a drop; Joshua b. Hananiah—happy is she that bare him; Jose the Priest is a saintly man; Simeon b. Nathaniel is fearful of sin; Eleazar b. Arak is an ever-flowing spring. He used to say: If all the Sages of Israel were in the one scale of the balance and Eliezer b. Hyrcanus in the other, he would outweigh them all. Abba Saul said in his name:[8] If all the Sages of Israel were in the one scale of the balance and with them Eliezer b. Hyrcanus, and Eleazar b. Arak was in the other, he would outweigh them all.

9. He said to them: Go forth and see which is the good way to which a man should cleave. R. Eliezer said, A good eye. R. Joshua said, A good

---

[1] Heb. *Am-haaretz*. See App. I. 3.

[2] Died *c.* A.D. 80 at, it is suggested (R.Sh. 30b), the age of 120. It was he who reconstituted the Sanhedrin at Jabneh soon after the destruction of the Temple.

[3] He is mentioned (simply as R. Eliezer) some 400 times in the Mishnah. Sot. 9[15] refers to him as 'R. Eliezer the Great'.

[4] He is mentioned (without patronymic) some 80 times in the Mishnah.

[5] See Eduy. 8[2]. Another 'Joseph' the Priest is mentioned, Hall. 4[11]; Mikw. 10[1].

[6] Only referred to in the Mishnah in the present chapter.

[7] Not mentioned in the Mishnah outside this chapter.

[8] Variant (from the parallel work *Aboth d'R. Nathan*): Abba Saul said in the name of R. Akiba who said in the name of R. Johanan b. Zakkai.

companion. R. Jose said, A good neighbour. R. Simeon said, One that sees what will be. R. Eleazar said, A good heart. He said to them: I approve the words of Eleazar b. Arak more than your words, for in his words are your words included. He said to them: Go forth and see which is the evil way which a man should shun. R. Eliezer said, An evil eye. R. Joshua said, An evil companion. R. Jose said, An evil neighbour. R. Simeon said, He that borrows and does not repay. He that borrows from man is as one that borrows from God, for it is written, *The wicked borroweth and payeth not again but the righteous dealeth graciously and giveth.*[1] R. Eleazar said, An evil heart. He said to them: I approve the words of Eleazar b. Arak more than your words for in his words are your words included.

10. They [each] said three things. R. Eliezer said: Let the honour of thy fellow be dear to thee as thine own, and be not easily provoked, and repent one day before thy death; and warm thyself before the fire of the Sages, but be heedful of their glowing coals lest thou be burned, for their bite is the bite of a jackal and their sting the sting of a scorpion and their hiss the hiss of a serpent, and all their words are like coals of fire.

11. R. Joshua said: The evil eye and the evil nature and hatred of mankind put a man out of the world.

12. R. Jose said: Let the property of thy fellow be dear to thee as thine own; and fit thyself for the study of the Law, for [the knowledge of] it is not thine by inheritance; and let all thy deeds be done for the sake of Heaven.

13. R. Simeon said: Be heedful in the reciting of the *Shema'*[2] and in the *Tefillah*;[3] and when thou prayest make not thy prayer a fixed form, but [a plea for] mercies[4] and supplications before God, for it is written, *For he is gracious and full of compassion, slow to anger, and plenteous in mercy, and repenteth him of the evil*;[5] and be not wicked in thine own sight.

14. R. Eleazar said: Be alert to study the Law and know how to make answer to an unbeliever;[6] and know before whom thou toilest and who is thy taskmaster who[7] shall pay thee the reward of thy labour.

15. R. Tarfon[8] said: The day is short and the task is great and the labourers are idle and the wage is abundant and the master of the house is urgent.

16. He used to say: It is not thy part to finish the task, yet thou art not free to desist from it. If thou hast studied much in the Law much reward will be given thee, and faithful is thy taskmaster who shall pay thee the reward of thy labour. And know that the recompense of the reward of the righteous is for the time to come.

3. 1. Akabya b. Mahalaleel[9] said: Consider three things and thou wilt not fall into the hands of transgression. Know whence thou art come and whither thou art going[10] and before whom thou art about to give account and reckoning. 'Whence thou art come'—from a putrid drop; 'and whither thou art going'—to the place of dust, worm, and maggot; 'and before whom thou art about to give account and reckoning'—before the King of kings of kings, the Holy One, blessed is he.

---

¹ Ps. 37²¹.   ² App. I. 38.   ³ App. I. 46.   ⁴ Some texts omit 'mercies and'.
⁵ Joel 2¹³.   ⁶ Lit. 'Epicurean'. See p. 397, n. 4.
⁷ Some texts omit this clause.   ⁸ *c.* A.D. 130.
⁹ *c.* A.D. 60. See on him, Eduy. 5⁶ᶠ.   ¹⁰ But cf. Hag. 2¹.

2. R. Hanina[1] the Prefect[2] of the Priests said: Pray for the peace of the ruling power, since but for fear of it men would have swallowed up each other alive. R. Hananiah b. Teradion[3] said: If two sit together and no words of the Law [are spoken] between them, there is the seat of the scornful, as it is written, *Nor sitteth in the seat of the scornful.*[4] But if two sit together and words of the Law [are spoken] between them, the Divine Presence[5] rests between them, as it is written, *Then they that feared the Lord spake one with another: and the Lord hearkened, and heard, and a book of remembrance was written before him, for them that feared the Lord, and that thought upon his name.*[6] Scripture speaks here of 'two'; whence [do we learn] that if even one sits and occupies himself in the Law, the Holy One, blessed is he, appoints him a reward? Because it is written, *Let him sit alone and keep silence, because he hath laid it upon him.*[7]

3. R. Simeon[8] said: If three have eaten at one table and have not spoken over it words of the Law, it is as though they had eaten of the sacrifices of the dead,[9] for it is written, *For all tables are full of vomit and filthiness without God.*[10] But if three have eaten at one table and have spoken over it words of the Law, it is as if they had eaten from the table of God, for it is written, *And he said unto me, This is the table that is before the Lord.*[11]

4. R. Hananiah b. Hakinai[12] said: He that wakes in the night or that walks alone by the way and turns his heart to vanity, is guilty against his own soul.

5. R. Nehunya b. Ha-Kanah[13] said: He that takes upon himself the yoke of the Law, from him shall be taken away the yoke of the kingdom[14] and the yoke of worldly care; but he that throws off the yoke of the Law, upon him shall be laid the yoke of the kingdom and the yoke of worldly care.

6. R. Halafta b. Dosa[15] of Kefar Hanania said: If ten men sit together and occupy themselves in the Law, the Divine Presence[16] rests among them, for it is written, *God standeth in the congregation of God.*[17] And whence [do we learn this] even of five?[18] Because it is written, *And hath founded his group upon the earth.*[19] And whence even of three? Because it is written, *He judgeth among the judges.*[20] And whence even of two? Because it is written, *Then they that feared the Lord spake one with another: and the Lord hearkened, and heard.*[21] And whence even of one? Because it is written,

---

[1] Cf. Eduy. 2[1]. The correct reading of the name is probably 'Hananiah'. The two names are regularly confused.

[2] Heb. *Segan*. The chief assistant, or deputy, of the High Priest. Cf. Yom. 7[1]; Sot. 7[7, 8].

[3] Cf. Taan. 2[5]. He was the father-in-law of R. Meir and was killed in A.D. 135 at the time of the Bar Cocheba revolt.

[4] Ps. 1[1].　　　　[5] The Shekinah.　　　　[6] Mal. 3[16].　　　　[7] Lam. 3[28].

[8] Ben Yohai, *c.* A.D. 100–170; a teacher of R. Judah the Patriarch.　　　[9] Ps. 106[28].

[10] Is. 28[8]; lit. 'without place'. 'Place' is a frequent designation of God.

[11] Ezek. 41[22].　　　[12] A disciple of R. Akiba and R. Joshua.　　　[13] *c.* A.D. 70–130.

[14] i.e. the troubles suffered at the hands of those in power.

[15] Latter half of the second century; a disciple of R. Meir. Some texts omit 'b. Dosa'.

[16] The Shekinah.

[17] Ps. 82[1]. That a 'congregation' can be but ten in number is shown in Sanh. 1[6].

[18] The text is here in some confusion. Some versions of the text prove the statement by the preceding proof-text, rendered 'in the congregation of judges', i.e. the minimum of three judges together with two suitors (Bert.), or else 'in the *midst* of the congregation of God', i.e. in half a 'congregation'. Why *aguddah* (a group, or bundle) should mean 'five' is not certainly explained: 'a bundle is what is grasped by the five fingers' (Bert.).

[19] Am. 9[6].

[20] Ps. 82[1]. 'Judges' must be a minimum of three. Some texts prove the number 'three' from the Amos proof-text, *aguddah*, a bundle, being used of the 'bundle' or bunch of hyssop which (Par. 11[9]) must be made up of three stalks.

[21] Mal. 3[16].

In every place where I record my name I will come unto thee and I will bless thee.[1]

7. R. Eleazar b. Judah of Bartotha[2] said: Give unto him what is his for thou and what thou hast are his; and it is written in [the Scripture concerning] David, *For all things come of thee, and of thine own have we given thee.*[3]

8. R. Jacob[4] said: If a man was walking by the way and studying and he ceased his study and said, 'How fine is this tree!' or 'How fine is this ploughed field!' the Scripture reckons it to him as though he was guilty against his own soul.

9. R. Dosethai b. Yannai[5] said in the name of R. Meir: He that forgets one word of his study, the Scripture reckons it to him as though he was guilty against his own soul, for it is written, *Only take heed to thyself, and keep thy soul diligently, lest thou forget the words which thine eyes saw.*[6] Could this be even if his study was too hard for him? Scripture says: *And lest they depart from thy heart all the days of thy life*; thus he is not guilty against his own soul unless he sits and puts them away from his heart.

10. R. Hanina b. Dosa[7] said: He whose fear of sin comes before his wisdom, his wisdom endures; but he whose wisdom comes before his fear of sin, his wisdom does not endure. He used to say: He whose works exceed his wisdom, his wisdom endures; but he whose wisdom exceeds his works, his wisdom does not endure.

11. He used to say: He in whom the spirit of mankind finds pleasure, in him the spirit of God finds pleasure; but he in whom the spirit of mankind finds no pleasure, in him the spirit of God finds no pleasure. R. Dosa b. Harkinas[8] said: Morning sleep and midday wine and children's talk and sitting in the meeting-houses of the ignorant people[9] put a man out of the world.

12. R. Eleazar of Modiim[10] said: If a man profanes the Hallowed Things[11] and despises the set feasts and[12] puts his fellow to shame publicly and makes void the covenant[13] of Abraham our father, and discloses meanings in the Law[14] which are not according to the *Halakah*,[15] even though a knowledge of the Law and good works are his, he has no share in the world to come.

13. R. Ishmael[16] says: Be swift [to do service] to a superior, and kindly to the young,[17] and receive all men cheerfully.

14. R. Akiba[18] said: Jesting and levity accustom a man to lewdness.

---

[1] Ex. 20[24]. And 'thee' can mean only one.
[2] Some texts omit 'b. Judah'. He was a contemporary of R. Akiba. He is again mentioned in Teb.Y. 3[4f]. The 'Eleazar b. Judah' mentioned in Ohol. 3[5], Zab. 1[1] may be of an earlier generation.　　　　　　　　　　　　　　[3] 1 Chron. 29[14].
[4] The father of R. Eliezer b. Jacob (see 4[11]; cf. 4[16]), first half of the second century. Some texts here read 'Simeon' (i.e. b. Yohai) and others 'Akiba'.
[5] Latter half of the second century.　　　　[6] Deut. 4[9].　　　　[7] See Ber. 5[5]; Sot. 9[15].
[8] See Eduy. 3[2ff]. A contemporary of R. Joshua, *c.* A.D. 90.　　　[9] Heb. *Amme-haaretz.*
[10] Cf. 1 Maccabees 2[1]; Pes. 9[2]; lived at the time of the Bar Cocheba revolt.
[11] The laws concerning the offerings. Some texts read 'the Sabbaths'.
[12] Some texts omit this clause.
[13] i.e. to render himself, by artificial device, uncircumcised. Cf. 1 Maccabees 1[15].
[14] The sense is, 'those who ignore or dispute the "traditions of the elders"'. The offence is illustrated in Meg. 4[9]. There is a secondary sense, 'behave impudently against the Law'.
[15] See App. I. 11.
[16] A contemporary of R. Akiba. He is mentioned some eighty times in the Mishnah.
[17] Or, 'amenable to forced service'.
[18] Born *c.* A.D. 50 and killed 135. One of the main supporters of Bar Cocheba. His work in systematizing the topics dealt with by the oral tradition served as the foundation of the Mishnah of his pupil R. Meir, and the final compilation of R. Judah the Patriarch. His name occurs nearly 300 times in the present Mishnah.

The tradition is a fence around the Law; Tithes are a fence around riches; vows are a fence around abstinence; a fence around wisdom is silence.

15. He used to say: Beloved is man for he was created in the image [of God]; still[1] greater was the love in that it was made known to him that he was created in the image of God, as it is written, *For in the image of God made he man.*[2] Beloved are Israel for they were called children of God; still greater was the love in that it was made known to them that they were called children of God, as it is written, *Ye are the children of the Lord your God.*[3] Beloved are Israel, for to them was given the precious instrument; still greater was the love, in that it was made known to them that to them was given the precious instrument by which the world was created, as it is written, *For I give you good doctrine; forsake ye not my Law.*[4]

16. All is foreseen, but freedom of choice is given; and the world is judged by grace, yet[5] all is according to the excess of works [that be good or evil].

17. He used to say: All is given against a pledge, and the net is cast over all living; the shop stands open and the shopkeeper gives credit and the account-book lies open and the hand writes and every one that wishes to borrow let him come and borrow; but the collectors go their round continually every day and exact payment of men with their consent or without their consent, for they have that on which[6] they can rely; and the judgement is a judgement of truth; and all is made ready for the banquet.

18. R. Eleazar b. Azariah[7] said: If there is no study of the Law there is no seemly behaviour, if there is no seemly behaviour there is no study of the Law; if there is no wisdom there is no fear [of God], if there is no fear [of God] there is no wisdom; if there is no knowledge there is no discernment, if there is no discernment there is no knowledge; if there is no meal there is no study of the Law, if there is no study of the Law there is no meal. He used to say: He whose wisdom is more abundant than his works, to what is he like? To a tree whose branches are abundant but whose roots are few; and the wind comes and uproots it and overturns it, as it is written, *He shall be like a tamerisk in the desert and shall not see when good cometh; but shall inhabit the parched places in the wilderness.*[8] But he whose works are more abundant than his wisdom, to what is he like? To a tree whose branches are few but whose roots are many; so that even if all the winds in the world come and blow against it, it cannot be stirred from its place, as it is written, *He shall be as a tree planted by the waters, and that spreadeth out his roots by the river, and shall not fear when heat cometh, and his leaf shall be green; and shall not be careful in the year of drought, neither shall cease from yielding fruit.*[9]

19. R. Eleazar Hisma[10] said: [The rules about] Bird-offerings[11] and the onset of menstruation[12]—these are essentials[13] of the *Halakoth*; but the

---

[1] Some texts omit the following sentence.   [2] Gen. 9⁶.   [3] Deut. 14¹.   [4] Prov. 4².
[5] Variant: And not according to works.   [6] God's record of man's debts.
[7] See Yad. 4². He lived *c.* A.D. 50–120. He was made president of the 'Sanhedrin' at Jabneh when Rabban Gamaliel II was temporarily deposed. He was one of the four (the others were Gamaliel II, R. Joshua, and R. Akiba), see M.Sh. 5⁹, Shab. 16⁸, Erub. 4¹, who made a journey to Rome on a mission, of which the purpose and result are unknown.
[8] Jer. 17⁶. Some texts omit this and the following proof-text.
[9] Jer. 17⁸.
[10] Beginning of the second century. The texts frequently style him 'the son of Hisma'.
[11] As detailed in the tractate Kinnim.   [12] See the tractate Niddah. Cf. Arak. 2¹.
[13] Being difficult and complicated they must be accounted the most important subjects of study.

calculations of the equinoxes and gematria[1] are but the savoury dishes[2] of wisdom.

4. 1. Ben Zoma[3] said: Who is wise? He that learns from all men, as it is written, *From all my teachers have I got understanding.*[4] Who is mighty? He that subdues his [evil] nature, as it is written, *He that is slow to anger is better than the mighty, and he that ruleth his spirit than he that taketh a city.*[5] Who is rich? He that rejoices in his portion, as it is written, *When thou eatest the labour of thy hands happy shalt thou be, and it shall be well with thee.*[6] *Happy shalt thou be*—in this world; *and it shall be well with thee*—in the world to come. Who is honoured? He that honours mankind, as it is written, *For them that honour me I will honour, and they that despise me shall be lightly esteemed.*[7]

2. Ben Azzai[8] said: Run to fulfil the lightest duty even as the weightiest,[9] and flee from transgression; for one duty draws another duty in its train, and one transgression draws another transgression in its train; for the reward of a duty [done] is a duty [to be done], and the reward of one transgression is [another] transgression.

3. He used to say: Despise no man and deem nothing impossible, for there is not a man that has not his hour and there is not a thing that has not its place.

4. Levitas of Jabneh[10] said: Be exceeding lowly of spirit, for the hope of man is but the worm.[11] R. Johanan b. Baroka[12] said: He that profanes the name of Heaven in secret shall be requited openly: in profaning the Name it is all one whether it be done unwittingly or wantonly.

5. R. Ishmael his son said: He that learns in order to teach is granted the means to learn and to teach; but he that learns in order to perform is granted the means to learn and to teach, to observe[13] and to perform. R. Zadok[14] says: Keep not aloof[15] from the congregation, and make not thyself like them that seek to influence the judges. Make them[16] not a crown wherewith to magnify thyself or a spade wherewith to dig. And thus used Hillel[17] to say: He that makes wordly use of the crown shall perish. Thus thou mayest learn that he that makes profit out of the words of the Law removes his life from the world.

6. R. Jose[18] said: He that honours the Law is himself honoured by mankind; and he that dishonours the Law shall himself be dishonoured by mankind.

7. R. Ishmael his son[19] said: He that shuns the office of judge rids

---

[1] Astronomy and geometry are meant. Of these Eleazar Hisma is reported to have been a diligent student. 'Gematria' later came to mean the device of finding esoteric meanings in words by means of the numerical values of their constituent letters. See Uktz. 3[12].

[2] The word is that used in Ber. 6[5], Shab. 23[2] of the relish or savoury which begin or end a meal but are not the essential item of the meal.

[3] Simeon b. Zoma. A younger contemporary of R. Akiba. See Sot. 9[15].

[4] Ps. 119[99].   [5] Prov. 16[32].   [6] Ps. 128[2].   [7] 1 Sam. 2[30].

[8] Simeon b. Azzai. A contemporary of Ben Zoma. See Sot. 9[15].

[9] Most old authorities omit 'even as the weightiest'.

[10] Never mentioned elsewhere.   [11] Quoted from Ben Sira 7[17].

[12] A disciple of R. Joshua.   [13] The rules of the Law. Some authorities omit 'to observe'

[14] Eduy. 7[2f]. Belonged to the latter half of the first century.

[15] Some texts omit these two clauses.

[16] The words of the Law.   [17] See above, 1[13].

[18] Ben Halafta. He is referred to, without patronymic, some 350 times in the Mishnah. He belonged to the fourth generation of Tannaim, *c.* A.D. 140–65.

[19] Some texts omit 'his son'; some read 'Bar Kappara' and others 'R. Simeon'.

himself of enmity and theft and false swearing; and he that is forward[1] in giving a decision is foolish, wicked, and arrogant.

8. He used to say: Judge not alone, for none may judge alone save One. And say not, 'Receive ye my opinion', for it is for them to choose and not for thee.

9. R. Jonathan[2] said: He that fulfils the Law in poverty shall in the end fulfil it in wealth; and he that neglects the Law in wealth shall in the end neglect it in poverty.

10. R. Meir[3] said: Engage not overmuch in business but occupy thyself with the Law; and be lowly in spirit before all men. If thou neglectest the Law many things neglected shall rise against thee; but if thou labourest in the Law He has abundant reward to give thee.

11. R. Eliezer b. Jacob[4] says: He that performs one precept gets for himself one advocate; but he that commits one transgression gets for himself one accuser. Repentance and good works are as a shield against retribution. R. Johanan the Sandal-maker[5] said: Any assembling together that is for the sake of Heaven shall in the end be established, but any that is not for the sake of Heaven shall not in the end be established.

12. R. Eleazar b. Shammua[6] said: Let the honour of thy disciple be as dear to thee as thine own and[7] as the honour of thy companion, and the honour of thy companion as the fear of thy teacher, and the fear of thy teacher as the fear of Heaven.

13. R. Judah[8] said: Be heedful in study, for an unwitting error in study is accounted wanton transgression. R. Simeon said: There are three crowns—the crown of the Law, the crown of the priesthood, and the crown of kingship; but the crown of a good name excels them all.

14. R. Nehorai[9] said: Wander afar to a place of the Law; and say not that it will follow after thee or that thy companions will establish it in thy possession; and lean not upon thine own understanding.

15. R. Yannai[10] said: It is not in our power to explain the well-being of the wicked or the sorrows of the righteous. R. Mattithiah b. Heresh[11] said: Be first in greeting every man; and be a tail to lions and be not a head to jackals.

16. R. Jacob[12] said: This world is like a vestibule before the world to come: prepare thyself in the vestibule that thou mayest enter into the banqueting hall.

17. He used to say: Better is one hour of repentance and good works in this world than the whole life of the world to come; and better is one hour of bliss in the world to come than the whole life of this world.

---

[1] Shameless. The Hebrew term is the same as in Sot. 1[6].

[2] Variants are 'Johanan' and 'Nathan'. This Jonathan was probably Jonathan b. Joseph, a disciple of R. Akiba.

[3] Referred to some 350 times in the Mishnah. He was a disciple of R. Akiba and his work in systematizing the *Halakoth* was the basis of the present Mishnah.

[4] A disciple of R. Akiba. Another Eliezer b. Jacob is referred to in the Mishnah (cf. Midd. 1[2]) who survived the fall of the Temple.

[5] Yeb. 12[5]; Kel. 5[5]. A disciple of R. Akiba.

[6] Again, without patronymic, in Tem. 3[3]. Many texts here omit 'b. Shammua'.

[7] Some texts omit 'as thine own and' (cf. 2[10]).

[8] B. Ilai. The most frequently mentioned teacher (some 650 times) in the Mishnah. Like R. Eleazar he was a disciple of R. Meir.

[9] Naz. 9[5]; Kidd. 4[14]. A contemporary of R. Meir.

[10] He belongs to the post-Mishnaic era, and lived *c*. A.D. 250.

[11] Middle of the second century. Another of his sayings is reported in Yom. 8[6].

[12] Perhaps Jacob b. Korshai, the teacher of R. Judah the Patriarch.

18. R. Simeon b. Eleazar[1] said: Appease not thy fellow in the hour of his anger, and comfort him not while his dead lies before him, and question him not in the hour of his vow, and strive not to see him in the hour of his disgrace.

19. Samuel the Younger[2] said: *Rejoice not when thine enemy falleth, and let not thine heart be glad when he is overthrown, lest the Lord see it and it displease him, and he turn away his wrath from him.*[3]

20. Elisha b. Abuyah[4] said: He that learns as a child, to what is he like? To ink written on new paper. He that learns as an old man, to what is he like? To ink written on paper that has been blotted out. R. Jose b. Judah[5] of Kefar ha-Babli[6] said: He that learns from the young, to what is he like? To one that eats unripe grapes and drinks wine from his winepress. And he that learns from the aged, to what is he like? To one that eats ripe grapes and drinks old wine. Rabbi said: Look not on the jar but on what is in it; there may be a new jar that is full of old wine and an old one in which is not even new wine.

21. R. Eleazar ha-Kappar[7] said: Jealousy, lust, and ambition put a man out of the world.

22. He used to say: They that have been born [are destined] to die, and they that are dead [are destined] to be made alive, and they that live [after death are destined] to be judged, that men may know and make known and understand that he is God,[8] he is the Maker, he is the Creator, he is the Discerner, he is the Judge, he is the Witness, he is the Complainant, and it is he that shall judge, blessed is he, in whose presence is neither guile nor forgetfulness nor respect of persons nor taking of bribes; for all is his. And know that everything is according to the reckoning. And let not thy [evil] nature promise thee that the grave will be thy refuge: for despite thyself wast thou fashioned, and despite thyself wast thou born, and despite thyself thou livest, and despite thyself thou diest, and despite thyself shalt thou hereafter give account and reckoning before the King of kings of kings, the Holy One, blessed is he.

5. 1. By ten Sayings[9] was the world created. And what does the Scripture teach thereby? Could it not have been created by one Saying? But this was to requite the ungodly which destroy the world that was created by ten Sayings, and to give a goodly reward to the righteous which sustain the world that was created by ten Sayings.

2. There were ten generations from Adam to Noah, to show how great was his longsuffering, for all the generations provoked him continually until he brought upon them the waters of the Flood. There were ten generations from Noah to Abraham, to show how great was his long-suffering, for all the generations provoked him continually until Abraham our father came and received the reward of them all.

3. With ten temptations was Abraham our father tempted, and he stood steadfast in them all, to show how great was the love of Abraham our father.

4. Ten wonders were wrought for our fathers in Egypt and ten at the

---

[1] End of the second century.   [2] End of the first century.   [3] Prov. 24[17f].
[4] c. A.D. 90–150. He was put under a ban because of his heretical opinions, and in the Talmud is referred to as 'that other one' (see Hag. 15a).
[5] End of the second century.   [6] A village in Galilee. Cf. Eduy. 6[1].
[7] A contemporary of R. Judah the Patriarch.
[8] Some texts omit 'he is God' and the concluding 'blessed is he'.
[9] i.e. the tenfold 'and God said' in Gen. 1[3, 6, 9, 11, 14, 20, 24, 26, 29], and 2[18].

Sea. Ten[1] plagues did the Holy One, blessed is he, bring upon the Egyptians in Egypt and at the Sea. With ten temptations did our fathers tempt the Holy One, blessed is he, in the wilderness, as it is written, *Yet have they tempted me these ten times and have not hearkened to my voice.*[2]

5. Ten wonders were wrought for our fathers in the Temple: no woman miscarried through the smell of the flesh of the Hallowed Things; and no flesh of the Hallowed Things ever turned putrid; and no fly was seen in the shambles; and the High Priest never suffered a pollution on the Day of Atonement;[3] and the rains never quenched the fire of the wood-pile [on the Altar]; and no wind prevailed over the pillar of smoke; and never was a defect found in the *Omer*[4] or in the Two Loaves[5] or in the Shewbread;[6] [and the people] stood pressed together yet bowed themselves at ease; and never did serpent or scorpion do harm in Jerusalem; and no man said to his fellow, *The place is too strait for me*[7] that I should lodge in Jerusalem.

6. Ten things were created on the eve of Sabbath between the suns at nightfall:[8] the mouth of the earth,[9] the mouth of the well,[10] the mouth of the she-ass,[11] the rainbow,[12] and the manna[13] and the rod[14] and the Shamir,[15] the letters and the writing and the Tables [of stone].[16] Some say also: The evil spirits and the sepulchre of Moses[17] and the ram of Abraham our father.[18] Some say also: The tongs made with tongs.[19]

7. There are seven marks of the clod and seven of the wise man. The wise man does not speak before one that is greater than he in wisdom; and he does not break in upon the words of his fellow; and he is not hasty in making answer; he asks what is relevant and makes answer according to the *Halakah*;[20] and he speaks on the first point first and on the last point last; and of what he has heard no tradition he says, 'I have not heard'; and he agrees to what is true. And the opposites of these are the marks of the clod.

8. Seven kinds of retribution come upon the world for seven classes of transgression. If some give tithe and some do not give tithe, there comes famine from drought: some suffer hunger while some have enough. If [all] resolved that they would not give tithe there comes famine from tumult and drought. And if they will not set apart Dough-offering[21] there comes an all-consuming famine. Pestilence comes upon the world because of crimes deserving of the death-penalties enjoined in the Law that are not brought before the court; and because of [the transgressions of the laws of] the Seventh Year produce.[22] The sword comes upon the world because of the delaying of justice and the perverting of justice; and because of them that teach the Law not according to the *Halakah*.[23]

9. Noisome beasts come upon the world because of false swearing and the profaning of the Name. Exile comes upon the world because of idolatry and incest and the shedding of blood; and because of [neglect of

---

[1] Many texts omit the following sentence.   [2] Num. 14[22].   [3] Cf. Yom. 1[1].
[4] App. I. 31.   [5] Lev. 23[17].   [6] Ex. 25[30]; Lev. 24[5–9].   [7] Is. 49[20].
[8] Some texts omit 'on the eve of Sabbath' and 'at nightfall'. The moment is meant between the six days of creation and the nightfall which ushered in the first Sabbath Day.
[9] Cf. Num. 16[32].
[10] Which gave water to the Israelites in the wilderness. Cf. Num. 21[16–18].
[11] Num. 22[28].   [12] Gen. 9[13].   [13] Ex. 16[15].   [14] Ex. 4[17].   [15] See p. 305, n. 10.
[16] Cf. Ex. 32[15f].   [17] Deut. 34[6].   [18] Gen. 22[13].
[19] Solving the problem, Who made the tongs which held the first tongs that were made?
[20] Bert. explains: The disciple keeps to the point in his questions, so that his teacher can keep his answer within the limits of the *Halakah* (App. I. 11) that he is expounding.
[21] Num. 15[20].   [22] Lev. 25[1–7].   [23] Cf. above, p. 451, n. 14.

the year of] the Release[1] of the land. At four periods pestilence increases: in the fourth year and in the seventh year and in the year after the seventh year, and at the end of the Feast [of Tabernacles] every year. 'In the fourth year'—because of [neglect of] Poorman's Tithe[2] in the third year; 'in the seventh year'—because of [neglect of] Poorman's Tithe in the sixth year; 'in the year after the seventh year'—because of [transgressing the laws of] Seventh Year produce; 'and at the end of the Feast of [Tabernacles] every year'—because of wrongfully withholding the dues[3] of the poor.

10. There are four types among men: he that says, 'What is mine is mine and what is thine is thine'—this is the common type, and some say that this is the type of Sodom; [he that says,] 'What is mine is thine and what is thine is mine'—he is an ignorant man;[4] [he that says,] 'What is mine is thine and what is thine is thine own'—he is a saintly man; [and he that says,] 'What is thine is mine, and what is mine is mine own'—he is a wicked man.

11. There are four types of character: easy to provoke and easy to appease—his loss is cancelled by his gain; hard to provoke and hard to appease—his gain is cancelled by his loss; hard to provoke and easy to appease—he is a saintly man; easy to provoke and hard to appease—he is a wicked man.

12. There are four types of disciple: swift to hear and swift to lose—his gain is cancelled by his loss; slow to hear and slow to lose—his loss is cancelled by his gain; swift to hear and slow to lose—this is a happy lot; slow to hear and swift to lose—this is an evil lot.

13. There are four types of almsgivers: he that is minded to give but not that others should give—he begrudges what belongs to others; he that is minded that others should give but not that he should give—he begrudges what belongs to himself; he that is minded to give and also that others should give—he is a saintly man; he that is minded not to give himself and that others should not give—he is a wicked man.

14. There are four types among them that frequent the House of Study: he that goes and does not practise—he has the reward of his going; he that practises but does not go—he has the reward of his practising; he that goes and also practises—he is a saintly man; he that neither goes nor practises—he is a wicked man.

15. There are four types among them that sit in the presence of the Sages: the sponge, the funnel, the strainer, and the sifter. 'The sponge'—which soaks up everything; 'the funnel'—which takes in at this end and lets out at the other; 'the strainer'—which lets out the wine and collects the lees; 'the sifter'—which extracts the coarsely-ground flour and collects the fine flour.

16. If love depends on some [transitory]thing, and the [transitory] thing passes away, the love passes away too; but if it does not depend on some [transitory] thing it will never pass away. Which love depended on some [transitory] thing? This was the love of Amnon and Tamar.[5] And which did not depend on some [transitory] thing? This was the love of David and Jonathan.[6]

17. Any controversy that is for God's sake shall in the end be of lasting

---

[1] Deut. 15[1]. Cf. Lev. 26[34f].   [2] Deut. 14[28f].
[3] The gleanings, prescribed in Lev. 19[9, 10]; 23[22]; Deut. 14[28-29]; 24[19-22].
[4] Heb. *Am-haaretz*. App. I. 3.   [5] 2 Sam. 13[1ff].   [6] 2 Sam. 1[26].

worth, but any that is not for God's sake shall not in the end be of lasting worth. Which controversy was for God's sake? Such was the controversy of Hillel and Shammai. And which was not for God's sake? Such was the controversy of Korah and all his company.[1]

18. He that leads the many to virtue, through him shall no sin befall; but he that leads the many to sin, to him shall be given no means for repentance. Moses was virtuous and he led the many to virtue; the virtue of the many depended on him, as it is written, *He executed the justice of the Lord and his judgements with Israel.*[2] Jeroboam sinned and he led the many to sin; the sin of the many depended on him, as it is written, *For the sins of Jeroboam which he sinned and wherewith he made Israel to sin.*[3]

19. He in whom are these three things is of the disciples of Abraham our father; but [he in whom are] three other things is of the disciples of Balaam the wicked. A good eye and a humble spirit and a lowly soul—[they in whom are these] are of the disciples of Abraham our father. An evil eye, a haughty spirit, and a proud soul—[they in whom are these] are of the disciples of Balaam the wicked. How do the disciples of Abraham our father differ from the disciples of Balaam the wicked? The disciples of Abraham our father enjoy this world and[4] inherit the world to come, as it is written, *That I may cause those that love me to inherit substance and that I may fill their treasuries.*[5] The disciples of Balaam the wicked inherit Gehenna and go down to the pit of destruction, as it is written, *But thou, O God, shalt bring them down into the pit of destruction; bloodthirsty and deceitful men shall not live out half their days.*[6]

20. Judah b. Tema[7] said: Be strong as the leopard and swift as the eagle, fleet as the gazelle and brave as the lion to do the will of thy father which is in heaven. He used to say: The shameless are for Gehenna and the shamefast for the garden of Eden. May it be thy will, O Lord our God and the God of our fathers, that the Temple be built speedily in our days, and grant us our portion in thy Law with them that do thy will.[8]

21. He used to say:[9] At five years old [one is fit] for the Scripture, at ten years for the Mishnah, at thirteen for [the fulfilling of] the commandments, at fifteen for the Talmud, at eighteen for the bride-chamber, at twenty for pursuing [a calling], at thirty for authority, at forty for discernment, at fifty for counsel, at sixty for to be an elder, at seventy for grey hairs, at eighty for special strength,[10] at ninety for bowed back, and at a hundred a man is as one that has [already] died and passed away and ceased from the world.

22. Ben Bag-Bag said[11]: Turn it and turn it again for everything is in it; and contemplate it and grow grey and old over it and stir not from it for than it thou canst have no better rule.

23. Ben He-He said: According to the suffering so is the reward.

6. KINYAN TORAH:[12] [These things] have the Sages taught in the language of the Mishnah. Blessed is he that made choice of them and their Mishnah!

---

[1] Num. 16[1ff]. Some texts omit 'and all his company'.   [2] Deut. 33[21].   [3] 1 Kings 15[30].
[4] Some texts omit 'enjoy this world and'.   [5] Prov. 8[21].   [6] Ps. 55[23].
[7] End of the second century.   [8] Some texts omit 'with them that do thy will'.
[9] Some texts omit this paragraph. It is by some authorities attributed to Samuel the Younger (cf. above, 4[19]).
[10] Ps. 90[10], 'though men be so strong they come to four score years'.
[11] Like Ben He-He he is said to have been a proselyte and a disciple of Hillel. In the parallel work *Aboth d'R. Nathan* both these sayings are attributed to Hillel.
[12] 'The acquisition of the law'. This chapter (sometimes from its first words called 'the

1. Rabbi Meir said: He that occupies himself in the study of the Law for its own sake merits many things, and, still more, he is deserving of the whole world. He is called friend, beloved [of God], lover of God, lover of mankind; and it clothes him with humility and reverence and fits him to become righteous, saintly, upright, and faithful; and it keeps him far from sin and brings him near to virtue, and from him men enjoy counsel and sound knowledge, understanding and might, for it is written, *Counsel is mine and sound knowledge, I am understanding, I have might.*[1] And it gives him kingship and dominion and discernment in judgement; to him are revealed the secrets of the Law, and he is made like to a never-failing spring and like to a river that flows ever more mightily; and he becomes modest, longsuffering, and forgiving of insult; and it magnifies him and exalts him above all things.

2. R. Joshua b. Levi[2] said: Every day a divine voice goes forth from mount Horeb, proclaiming and saying, 'Woe to mankind for their contempt of the Law!' For he that occupies himself not in the study of the Law is called 'reprobate' (*NaZuF*), as it is written, *As a golden ring in the snout (Nezem Zahab b'aF) of a swine, so is a fair woman without discretion.*[3] And it is written, *And the tables were the work of God, and the writing was the writing of God, graven* (haruth) *upon the tables.*[4] Read not *haruth* but *heruth* (freedom), for thou findest no freeman excepting him that occupies himself in the study of the Law; and he that occupies himself in the study of the Law shall be exalted, for it is written, *From Mattanah to Nahaliel, and from Nahaliel to Bamoth.*[5]

3. He that learns from his fellow a single chapter or a single *Halakah* or a single verse or a single expression or even a single letter, must pay him honour, for so we find it with David, king of Israel, who learned only two things[6] from Ahitophel, but called him his teacher, his companion, and his familiar friend; for it is written, *But it was thou, a man mine equal, my companion and my familiar friend.*[7] And is there not here an inference from the less to the greater?—if David king of Israel, who learned but two things from Ahitophel, called him his teacher, his companion, and his familiar friend, how much more then must he that learns from his fellow a single chapter or a single *Halakah* or a single verse or a single expression or even a single letter pay him honour! And 'honour' is naught else than 'the Law', for it is written, *The wise shall inherit honour,*[8] and *The perfect shall inherit good;*[9] and 'good' is naught else than 'the Law', for it is written, *For I give you good doctrine; forsake ye not my Law.*[10]

4. This is the way [to get thee knowledge] of the Law. Thou shalt eat bread with salt *and thou shalt drink water by measure,*[11] and on the ground shalt thou sleep and thou shalt live a life of trouble the while thou toilest in the Law. If thou doest thus, *Happy shalt thou be and it shall be well with thee;*[12] *happy shalt thou be*—in this world; *and it shall be well with thee*—in the world to come.

---

chapter of R. Meir') is a very late gloss to the five chapters of Aboth. It was probably added because of the common liturgical use of Aboth since the eleventh century as a reading on the six Sabbath afternoons between Passover and Pentecost, when a sixth section was called for.

[1] Prov. 8[14].

[2] He belongs to a time after the Mishnah, to the middle of the third century.

[3] Prov. 11[22].   [4] Ex. 32[16].

[5] Num. 21[19]. The three place-names are understood literally: Mattanah, a gift; Nahaliel, God has led me; Bamoth, (to) high places.

[6] 'Not to learn by himself alone, and not to enter the House of Study with a haughty mien' (Tif. Yis.).

[7] Ps. 55[13].   [8] Prov. 3[35].   [9] Prov. 28[10].

[10] Prov. 4[2]. The first two of these three passages equate 'honour' with 'good' because of the word 'inherit' which is common to both; and the third passage equates 'good' with 'the Law' since they are regarded as balanced items in the two clauses; therefore 'honour' is thus equated with 'the Law'.   [11] Ezek. 4[11].   [12] Ps. 128[2].

5. Seek not greatness for thyself and covet not honour. Practise more than thou learnest; and crave not after the tables of kings, for thy table is greater than their table and thy crown than their crown; and faithful is thy task-master who shall pay thee the reward of thy labour.

6. Greater is [learning in] the Law than priesthood or kingship; for kingship is acquired by thirty excellences and the priesthood by twenty-four; but [learning in] the Law by forty-eight. And these are they: by study, by the hearing of the ear, by the ordering of the lips, by the understanding of the heart, by the discernment of the heart, by awe, by reverence, by humility, by cheerfulness; by attendance on the Sages, by consorting with fellow-students, by close argument with disciples; by assiduity, by [know-ledge of] Scripture and Mishnah; by moderation in business, wordly occu-pation, pleasure, sleep, conversation, and jesting; by longsuffering, by a good heart, by faith in the Sages, by submission to sorrows; [by being] one that recognizes his place and that rejoices in his lot and that makes a fence around his words and that claims no merit for himself; [by being one that is] beloved, that loves God, that loves mankind, that loves well-doing, that loves rectitude, that loves reproof, that shuns honour and boasts not of his learning, and delights not in making decisions; that helps his fellow to bear his yoke, and that judges him favourably, and that establishes him in the truth and establishes him in peace; and that occupies himself assiduously in his study; [by being one] that asks and makes answer, that hearkens and adds thereto; that learns in order to teach and that learns in order to practise; that makes his teacher wiser, that retells exactly what he has heard and reports a thing in the name of him that said it. Lo, thou hast learnt that he that tells a thing in the name of him that said it brings deliverance unto the world, for it is written, *And Esther told the king thereof in Mordecai's name.*[1]

7. Great is the Law, for it gives life to them that practice it both in this world and in the world to come, as it is written, *For they are life unto those that find them, and health to all their flesh;* [2] and it says, *It shall be health to thy navel and marrow to thy bones;* [3] and it says, *She is a tree of life to them that lay hold upon her, and happy is everyone that retaineth her;* [4] and it says, *For they shall be a chaplet of grace unto thine head, and chains about thy neck;* [5] and it says, *She shall give to thine head a chaplet of grace, a crown of glory shall she deliver to thee;* [6] and it says, *For by me thy days shall be multiplied and the years of thy life shall be increased;* [7] and it says, *Length of days is in her right hand; in her left hand are riches and honour;* [8] and it says, *For length of days, and years of life, and peace, shall they add to thee.*[9]

8. R. Simeon b. Judah in the name of R. Simeon b. Yohai said: Beauty and strength and riches and honour and wisdom and old age and grey hairs and children are comely to the righteous and comely to the world, for it is written, *The hoary head is a crown of beauty; it shall be found in the way of righteousness;* [10] and it says, *The glory of young men is their strength and the beauty of old men is the hoary head;* [11] and it says, *The crown of the wise is their riches;* [12] and it says, *Children's children are the crown of old men; and the glory of children are their fathers;* [13] and it says, *Then the moon shall be con-founded and the sun ashamed; for the Lord of hosts shall reign in mount Zion and in Jerusalem, and before his elders shall be glory.*[14] R. Simeon b. Menasya [15] said: These seven qualities which the Sages have reckoned as comely to the righteous were all of them fulfilled in Rabbi and in his sons.

9. R. Jose b. Kisma [16] said: I was once walking by the way and a man met me and greeted me and I returned his greeting. He said to me, 'Rabbi, from

---

[1] Esth. 2[22].   [2] Prov. 4[22].   [3] Prov. 3[8].   [4] Prov. 3[18].   [5] Prov. 1[9].
[6] Prov. 4[9].   [7] Prov. 9[11].   [8] Prov. 3[16].   [9] Prov. 3[2].   [10] Prov. 16[31].
[11] Prov. 20[29].   [12] Prov. 14[24].   [13] Prov. 17[6].   [14] Is. 24[23].
[15] See Hag. 1[7]. A contemporary of 'Rabbi', R. Judah the Patriarch.
[16] A contemporary of R. Hananiah b. Teradion.

what place are thou?' I answered, 'I come from a great city of Sages and scribes'.[1] He said to me, 'If thou wilt dwell with us in our place I will give thee a thousand thousand golden *denars* and precious stones and pearls'. I answered, 'If thou gavest me all the silver and gold and precious stones and pearls in the world I would not dwell save in a place of the Law'.[2] And thus it is written in the Book of Psalms by David, king of Israel, *The Law of thy mouth is better unto me than thousands of gold and silver*.[3] Moreover at the time of a man's departure, neither silver nor gold nor precious stones nor pearls go with him, but only [his knowledge of] the Law and good works; for it is written, *When thou walkest, it shall lead thee; when thou sleepest, it shall watch over thee; and when thou awakest it shall talk with thee*.[4] *When thou walkest it shall lead thee*—in this world; *when thou sleepest, it shall watch over thee*—in the grave; *and when thou awakest, it shall talk with thee*—in the world to come. And it says, *The silver is mine, and the gold is mine, saith the Lord of hosts*.[5]

10. Five possessions did the Holy One, blessed is he, take to Himself in his world; and these are they: the Law is one possession, and the heaven and earth are one possession, Abraham is one possession, Israel is one possession, and the Temple is one possession. Whence [do we learn this of] the Law? Because it is written, *The Lord possessed me in the beginning of his way, before his works of old*.[6] Whence [do we learn this of] heaven and earth? Because it is written, *The heaven is my throne, and the earth is my footstool; what manner of house will ye build unto me and what place shall be my rest?* [7] And it says, *O Lord, how manifold are thy works! In wisdom hast thou made them all: the earth is full of thy riches*.[8] Whence [do we learn this of] Abraham? Because it is written, *And he blessed him, and said, Blessed be Abram of God Most High, possessor of heaven and earth*.[9] Whence [do we learn this of] Israel? Because it is written, *Till thy people pass over, O Lord, till the people pass over which thou hast gotten*.[10] And it says, *Unto the saints that are in the earth, and the excellent in whom is all my delight*.[11] Whence [do we learn this of] the Temple? Because it is written, *The place, O Lord, which thou hast made for thee to dwell in; the sanctuary, O Lord, which thy hands have established*.[12] And it says, *And he brought them to the border of his sanctuary, to this mountain, which his right hand had gotten*.[13]

11. Whatsoever the Holy One, blessed is he, created in his world, he created it only for his glory, as it is written, *Everything that is called by my name and that I have created, I have formed it, yea, I have made it*.[14] And it says, *The Lord shall reign for ever and ever*.[15]

R. Hananiah b. Akashya [16] said: The Holy One, blessed is he, was minded to grant merit to Israel; therefore hath he multiplied for them the Law and commandments, as it is written, *It pleased the Lord for his righteousness sake to magnify the Law and make it honourable*.[17]

HORAYOTH[18] ('DECISIONS')

1. 1. If the court gave a decision contrary to any of the commandments enjoined in the Law[19] and some man went and acted at their word [transgressing] unwittingly, whether they acted so and he acted so together with

---

1 'But there is not enough wealth there for me to earn my living' (Tif. Yis.).
2 Somewhere where they study the Law.
3 Ps. 119[72].   4 Prov. 6[22].   5 Haggai 2[8].   6 Prov. 8[22].   7 Is. 66[1].
8 Ps. 104[24].   9 Gen. 14[19].   10 Ex. 15[16].   11 Ps. 16[3].   12 Ex. 15[17].
13 Ps. 78[54].   14 Is. 43[7].   15 Ex. 15[18].
16 This paragraph is found also at the close of the tractate Makkoth.   17 Is. 42[21].
18 Lit. 'instructions', judicial decisions. The tractate is based on Lev. 4[1-21], which, according to Jewish tradition, deals with occasions when individuals or the majority of the people have been led into transgression through a wrongful decision of the Sanhedrin.
19 Such that wanton transgression of them entailed Extirpation (see below, 2[3]).

them, or they acted so and he acted so after them, or whether they did not act so but he acted so, he is not culpable,[1] since he depended on the [decision of the] court. If the court gave a decision [contrary to the Law] and one of them knew that they had erred, or a disciple that was himself fit to give a decision [knew that they had erred], and he went and acted at their word, whether they acted so and he acted so together with them, or they acted so and he acted so after them, or whether they did not act so but he acted so, such a one is culpable, since he did not depend on [the decision of] the court. This is the general rule: he that can depend on himself is culpable, but he that must depend on the court is not culpable.

2. If a court gave a decision[2] and [afterward] they knew that they had erred, and they retracted, whether they brought their [offering of] atonement[3] or whether they did not bring their [offering of] atonement, if any acted at their word[4] R. Simeon declares him not culpable; and R. Eleazar[5] declares his case in doubt. When is it in doubt? If he had remained at home he would be culpable, but if he went beyond the sea he would not be culpable. R. Akiba said: I agree that such a one is more nearly not culpable than culpable. Ben Azzai said to him: How does he differ from him that remained at home? [R. Akiba answered:] He that remained at home could hear [that the court had retracted], but the other could not hear.

3. If the court gave a decision uprooting an entire principle [in the Law]: if they said, 'There is naught in the Law concerning the menstruant',[6] or 'There is naught in the Law concerning the Sabbath', or 'There is naught in the Law concerning idolatry', they[7] are not culpable.[8] If they gave a decision that in part annulled and in part sustained [what the Law enjoins], they are culpable. Thus, if they said, 'The Law treats of the menstruant, but if a man has intercourse with a woman that awaits day against day[9] he is not culpable', or 'The Law treats of the Sabbath, but if a man carries a burden from a private domain to the public domain he is not culpable',[10] or 'The Law treats of idolatry, but if a man bows down [before an idol] he is not culpable',[11] the court is culpable; for it is written, *If something be hid*[12]— something, but not the whole principle.

4. If the court gave a decision and one of them knew that they had erred and said to them, 'Ye do err', or if the chief judge of the court was not there, or if one of them was a proselyte or a bastard or a *Nathin*[13] or too aged [or one][14] that never had children, they are not culpable; for here[15] it is written *Congregation*, and there[16] it is written *Congregation*: as the 'congregation' there implies that they should all be fit to give a decision, so here it is implied that they should all be fit to give a decision. If the court gave a decision [transgressing] unwittingly, and all the congregation [so] acted,

---

[1] If he later came to know of his sin he is not liable to bring the Sin-offering prescribed in Lev. 4[27ff].   [2] And most of the nation acted according to it.
[3] The Sin-offering prescribed, Lev. 4[13ff].
[4] Not knowing that they had later retracted.
[5] Variant: Eliezer.   [6] Lev. 15[19]; 18[19]; 20[18].   [7] Members of the court.
[8] And need not bring the Sin-offering prescribed in Lev. 4[13ff]; but the individuals who act according to their decision are liable to a Sin-offering.
[9] Cf. Pes. 8[5]; Meg. 2[4]; Nidd. 4[7]; Zab. 1[1]. If she suffered any manner of flow during the eleven days that followed her seven prescribed days of uncleanness (Lev. 15[19]) she is only accounted clean after a complete day of cleanness (absence of flow) shall have followed.
[10] See Shab. 7[2] (end).   [11] See Sanh. 7[6].   [12] Cf. Lev. 4[13].
[13] App. I. 29. These three (see Sanh. 4[2]) were ineligible as judges.
[14] So Maim. These two also (Sanh. 36b) were ineligibile.
[15] Lev. 4[13].   [16] Num. 35[24].

[transgressing] unwittingly, they must offer a bullock.[1] If the court gave a decision [transgressing] wantonly and the congregation [so] acted [transgressing] unwittingly, they[2] must offer a sheep and a goat.[3] If the court [transgressed] unwittingly but the congregation wantonly,[4] they[5] are not culpable.

5. If the court gave a decision [transgressing unwittingly] and all the congregation or the greater part of them acted at their word, they must offer a bullock;[6] and if they had permitted idolatry, they must offer a bullock and a he-goat.[7] So R. Meir. R. Judah says: The twelve tribes offer twelve bullocks; and if there befell idolatry, they must offer twelve bullocks and twelve he-goats.[8] R. Simeon says: [In the first case] thirteen bullocks, and if there befell idolatry, thirteen bullocks and thirteen he-goats: a bullock and a he-goat for each tribe and a bullock and a he-goat for the court. If the court gave a decision [transgressing unwittingly], and seven tribes or the greater part of them[9] acted at their word, they must offer a bullock, and if there befell idolatry, they must bring a bullock and a he-goat. So R. Meir. R. Judah says: The seven tribes which sinned must offer seven bullocks and the rest of the tribes which did not sin must offer a bullock on their behalf, for they also which had not sinned must offer on behalf of them that had sinned. R. Simeon says: Eight bullocks; and if there befell idolatry eight bullocks and eight he-goats—a bullock and a he-goat for each tribe and a bullock and a he-goat for the court. If the court of one of the tribes gave a decision [transgressing unwittingly], and that tribe acted at their word, that tribe is culpable, but the rest of the tribes are not culpable. So R. Judah. But the Sages say: They become culpable only through a decision given by the Great Court,[10] for it is written, *And if the whole congregation of Israel shall err*[11]—and not the congregation of that tribe alone.

2. 1. If the anointed [High] Priest[12] made a decision for himself [that transgressed any of the commandments enjoined in the Law], and he made it unwittingly and acted [transgressing] unwittingly, he must offer a bullock; if he made it unwittingly but acted [transgressing] wantonly, or made it wantonly but acted [transgressing] unwittingly,[13] he is exempt; for the decision of an anointed [High] Priest made for himself is like the decision given by the court for the congregation.[14]

2. If he made the decision alone and acted so alone, he makes his atonement alone. If he made the decision together with the congregation and acted so together with the congregation, he must make atonement together with the congregation. The court becomes liable only if it gives a decision which in part annuls and in part sustains [what the Law enjoins]; so, too, is it with the anointed [High Priest]. And if there befell idolatry [they are] not [liable] unless they annul in part and sustain in part [what the Law enjoins].

---

[1] As prescribed by Lev. 4[13ff].   [2] Members of the court singly.
[3] As prescribed (Lev. 14[27-35]) for individual sinners.
[4] Knowing that the court had erred.
[5] Members of the court and the congregation.   [6] Lev. 4[13ff].
[7] Num. 15[24], which is traditionally believed to apply to the case of mistakenly permitted idolatry.
[8] The difference turns on whether 'assembly' (*kahal*) in Lev. 4[14] means the whole nation jointly or the several tribes.   [9] The nation as a whole.
[10] Sanh. 11[2] 'whence the Law goes forth to all Israel'.   [11] Lev. 4[13].
[12] Lev. 4[3].   [13] i.e. if he had forgotten that he had permitted it.
[14] Decision and act must both be done transgressing unwittingly.

3. They are liable only *if something be hid*[1] and thereby an act [of transgression] is performed unwittingly. So, too, is it with the anointed [High Priest]. Also if there befell idolatry they are liable only *if something be hid*, and thereby an act [of transgression] is performed unwittingly. The court is liable only if it gives a decision that leads to a transgression for which if it is done wantonly the penalty is Extirpation and if unwittingly a Sin-offering. So, too, is it with the anointed [High Priest]. Also if there befell idolatry, they are liable only if they give a decision that leads to a transgression for which if it is done wantonly the penalty is Extirpation and if unwittingly a Sin-offering.

4. They do not become liable through [a decision unwittingly transgressing] a negative or a positive command concerning the Temple, nor need they bring a Suspensive Guilt-offering[2] because of a positive[3] or a negative[4] command concerning the Temple. But they become liable through [a decision unwittingly transgressing] a positive or negative command concerning the menstruant, and they must bring a Suspensive Guilt-offering because of a positive or a negative command concerning a menstruant. What is[5] the positive command concerning a menstruant? 'Separate thyself from a menstruant'. And the negative command? 'Thou shalt not come in unto a menstruant'.

5. They do not become liable through [unwitting transgression of the law touching] him that *heareth the voice of adjuration*,[6] or him that *sweareth rashly with his lips*,[7] or uncleanness in what concerns the Temple and its Hallowed Things.[8] So, too, is it with a Ruler.[9] So R. Jose the Galilean. R. Akiba says: The Ruler is liable in each of these cases excepting that of him that *heareth the voice of adjuration*, because[10] the king can neither judge nor be judged; he[11] cannot act as a witness and others cannot bear witness against him.

6. [Through unwitting transgression] of the commandments in the Law for which the penalty for wanton transgression is Extirpation and for unwitting transgression a Sin-offering, the individual must offer a sheep or a goat,[12] and the Ruler a he-goat,[13] and the anointed [High Priest] and the court a bullock;[14] and if there befell idolatry,[15] the individual and the Ruler and the anointed [High Priest] must offer a she-goat,[16] and the court must offer a bullock and a he-goat—the bullock as a Whole-offering, and the he-goat as a Sin-offering.[17]

7. The individual or the Ruler may become liable to a Suspensive Guilt-offering,[18] but not so the anointed [High Priest] or the court. The individual, the Ruler, and the anointed [High Priest] may become liable to an unconditional Guilt-offering,[19] but not so the court. Through [unwitting transgression of the law touching] him that *heareth the voice of adjuration*, or him that *sweareth rashly with his lips*, or uncleanness in what concerns the Temple and its Hallowed Things, the court is not liable but the individual, the Ruler, and the anointed [High Priest] are liable; save

---

[1] Lev. 4[13].   [2] Lev. 5[17].   [3] Shebu. 2[3].
[4] The unclean are forbidden to enter. Cf. Num. 5[2].   [5] See Shebu. 2[4].
[6] Lev. 5[1]. See Shebu. 4[1ff].   [7] Lev. 5[4].   [8] See Shebu. 1[2ff].
[9] Lev. 4[22ff]. He, too, is exempt from the offering in the three cases cited.
[10] Cited from Sanh. 2[2]; since he does not act as a witness the rules of the oath of testimony do not apply to him.   [11] Some texts omit the following sentence.
[12] Lev. 4[27ff].   [13] Lev. 4[22ff].   [14] Lev. 4[3ff, 13ff].
[15] The prescriptions of Num. 15[22ff] will apply.   [16] Num. 15[27].   [17] Num. 15[24].
[18] Lev. 5[17].   [19] Lev. 5[14-16]; 6[1-7]; 19[20-2]; Num. 6[12]; Lev. 14[12]. Cf. Zeb. 5[5].

only that the High Priest is not liable because of uncleanness in what concerns the Temple and its Hallowed Things. So R. Simeon. And what do they offer?[1] A Rising and Falling Offering.[2] R. Eliezer[3] says: The Ruler[4] offers a he-goat.[5]

3. 1. If the anointed [High] Priest sinned and afterward passed from his high-priesthood;[6] so, too, if the Ruler sinned and afterward[7] passed from his greatness; the anointed [High] Priest must [still] offer a bullock and the Ruler a he-goat.

2. If the anointed [High] Priest passed from his high-priesthood and then sinned; so, too, if the Ruler passed from his greatness and then sinned; the anointed [High] Priest must [still] offer a bullock,[8] but the Ruler is accounted one of the common people.[9]

3. If they sinned before they were appointed and were afterward appointed, each is accounted one of the common people. R. Simeon says: If their sin was made known to them before they were appointed, they are liable,[10] but if after they were appointed, they are exempt.[11] And who is the Ruler? This is the king, for it is written, *And doeth any one of all the things which the Lord his God hath commanded* [*not to be done*][12]—a Ruler that has above him none save the Lord his God.

4. And who is the anointed [High Priest]? He that is anointed with the oil of unction,[13] but not he that is dedicated by the many garments.[14] The [High] Priest[15] anointed with the oil of unction differs from him that is dedicated by the many garments only in the bullock offered for [the unwitting transgression of] any of the commandments. A High Priest in office differs from the priest that is passed [from his high-priesthood] only in the bullock that is offered on the Day of Atonement and the Tenth of the Ephah. Both[16] are equal in the [Temple-]service of the Day of Atonement; and both are subject to the commandment to marry only a virgin,[17] and they both are forbidden to marry a widow,[18] and neither may contract uncleanness because of their near of kin[19] [that have died]; neither may unbind their hair or rend their clothes [in token of mourning];[20] and both [when they die] serve to bring back the manslayer [from the cities of refuge].[21]

5. The High Priest rends his garment[22] from below, but an ordinary priest from above. While his dead lies unburied the High Priest may offer sacrifice, but may not consume it;[23] and an ordinary priest may neither offer sacrifice nor consume it.[24]

6. Whatsoever is offered more often than another precedes that other;[2]

---

[1] The High Priest and the Ruler when they are not liable to the prescriptions of Lev. 4[2-12, 22-6].   [2] See p. 409, n. 4.   [3] Variant: Eleazar.
[4] Because of uncleanness respecting the Temple and the Hallowed Things.
[5] Lev. 4[23].
[6] See p. 203, n. 2.   [7] Before he had offered his bullock.
[8] He still retains high-priestly sanctity; cf. Makk. 2[6]; Meg. 1[9].
[9] And he brings a goat or a sheep (Lev. 4[27ff.])
[10] To bring the Sin-offerings of common people.
[11] Even from the High Priest's or the Ruler's special Sin-offering.
[12] Lev. 4[22].
[13] With which the High Priests were anointed only until the time of Josiah.
[14] Cf. Yom. 7[5].   [15] See Meg. 1[9].
[16] Otherwise both are equally valid officiants.
[17] Lev. 21[13].   [18] Lev. 21[14].
[19] Lev. 21[11]. These include father, mother, sister, brother, wife, son, and daughter.
[20] Lev. 21[10].   [21] See Makk. 2[6].
[22] On the death of any of his seven near of kin.
[23] An inference derived from Lev. 10[19].   [24] Cf. Deut. 26[14].   [25] Zeb. 10[1].

and what is more holy than another precedes that other. If the bullock of the anointed [High Priest] and the bullock of the congregation await sacrifice, the bullock of the anointed [High Priest] precedes the bullock of the congregation in its every act of preparation.[1]

7. A man must be saved alive sooner than a woman, and his lost property must be restored sooner than hers. A woman's nakedness must be covered sooner than a man's, and she must be brought out of captivity sooner than he. When both stand in danger of defilement, the man must be freed before the woman.

8. A priest precedes a levite, a levite an Israelite, an Israelite a bastard,[2] a bastard a *Nathin*,[3] a *Nathin* a proselyte, and a proselyte a freed slave. This applies when they all are [otherwise] equal; but if a bastard is learned in the Law and a High Priest is ignorant of the Law,[4] the bastard that is learned in the Law precedes the High Priest that is ignorant of the Law.

---

[1] Cf. Lev. 16[17].   [2] See Yeb. 4[13].   [3] App. I. 29.
[4] Heb. *Am-haaretz*. See App. I. 3.

FIFTH DIVISION

KODASHIM
('HALLOWED THINGS')

ZEBAHIM

MENAHOTH

HULLIN

BEKHOROTH

ARAKHIN

TEMURAH

KERITHOTH

MEILAH

TAMID

MIDDOTH

KINNIM

ZEBAHIM ('ANIMAL OFFERINGS')

1. 1. All animal-offerings that have been slaughtered under the name of some other offering remain valid[1] (but they do not count to their owner in fulfilment of his obligation)[2] excepting a Passover-offering and a Sin-offering. [This rule applies to] a Passover-offering at its appointed time[3] and to a Sin-offering at any time. R. Eliezer says: Excepting also a Guilt-offering:[4] [this rule therefore applies to] a Passover-offering at its appointed time and to a Sin-offering and a Guilt-offering at any time. R. Eliezer said: A Sin-offering is offered because of a sin and a Guilt-offering is offered because of a sin; therefore as a Sin-offering is invalid if slaughtered under some other name so must a Guilt-offering be invalid if slaughtered under some other name.

2. Jose b. Onias says: If [any other offerings][5] were slaughtered under the name of a Passover-offering or of a Sin-offering, they become invalid. Simeon the brother of Azariah says: If they were slaughtered under the name of a higher grade of offering they remain valid, but if under the name of a lower grade they become invalid.[6] Thus if any of the Most Holy Things[7] were slaughtered under the name of any of the Lesser Holy Things they become invalid; but if any of the Lesser Holy Things were slaughtered under the name of any of the Most Holy Things, they remain valid. If a Firstling[8] or Tithe of Cattle[9] was slaughtered under the name of a Peace-offering[10] it remains valid; but if a Peace-offering was slaughtered under the name of a Firstling or Tithe of Cattle it becomes invalid.

3. If a Passover-offering was slaughtered on the morning[11] of the 14th [of Nisan] under some other name, R. Joshua declares it valid, as though it had been slaughtered on the 13th; but Ben Bathyra declares it invalid, as though it had been slaughtered at twilight. Simeon b. Azzai said:[12] I have heard a tradition from the seventy-two elders on that day[13] when they made R. Eleazar b. Azariah head of the College [of Sages], that any animal-offerings which must be consumed remain valid although slaughtered under some other name (but they do not count to their owner in fulfilment of his obligation) excepting a Passover-offering and a Sin-offering. And Ben Azzai added the Whole-offering only; but the Sages did not agree with him.

4. If a Passover-offering[14] or a Sin-offering was slaughtered under some other name, or if [its blood] was received, conveyed, or tossed[15] under some

---

[1] i.e. their blood may still be tossed against the Altar-base and their 'sacrificial portions' burnt on the Altar.

[2] He must bring anew the offering which was due from him.

[3] The afternoon of the 14th of Nisan.   [4] Cf. Lev. 7[7].

[5] Animal-offerings excepting a Passover or Sin-offering.

[6] For the grading of the offerings see 10[1ff].

[7] Whole-offerings, Sin-offerings, Guilt-offerings, and the Pentecost Peace-offerings of the congregation; all the other animal-offerings are classed as Lesser Holy Things. See below, 5[1ff].   [8] Num. 18[17].   [9] Lev. 27[32]. See below, 5[8].

[10] See below, 5[7]. Though all three are Lesser Holy Things the Peace-offering is of a higher degree of sanctity, since its blood requires sprinkling four times and the others but once; nor do the latter require drink-offerings, laying on of hands, or waving the breast and the thigh.   [11] Instead of the afternoon.   [12] Yad. 4[2].

[13] Ber. 28a, 'Wherever we find the phrase "on that day" it refers to this same occasion.' Eduyoth was also said to have been compiled 'on that day'. See also Shab. 1[4], where another 'on that day' is mentioned referring to a different occasion.   [14] See Pes. 5[2].

[15] See Pes. 5[6]. At least three modes of applying the blood to the Altar are distinguished: 'pouring' it out at the base of the Altar, 'tossing' it out of the bowl against the side of the Altar, and 'sprinkling' it (or daubing it) with the fingers.

other name, or under its own and [then] under some other name, or under
another and [then] under its own name, it becomes invalid. How [can it be
treated] 'under its own and [then] under another name'? [If, to wit, it was
treated first] under the name of a Passover-offering and then under the
name of a Peace-offering. How [can it be treated] 'under another name and
[then] under its own name'? [If, to wit, it was treated first] under the name
of a Peace-offering and [then] under the name of a Passover-offering. For
an animal-offering can be rendered invalid by [any one of] four things: by
the slaughtering or by the receiving or the conveying or the tossing of its
blood. R. Simeon declares it valid during the conveying [under whatsoever name it is conveyed]; for R. Simeon said: [An animal-offering] is
impossible without the slaughtering or without the receiving or the tossing
of the blood, but it is possible without the conveying of the blood, since it
can be slaughtered beside the Altar and [the blood] tossed [forthwith].
R. Eliezer says: In the conveying [of the blood], when conveying is needful,
the intention can render [the offering] invalid; when conveying is not needful the intention cannot render it invalid.

2. 1. All animal-offerings become invalid if their blood is received by one
that is not a priest, or by a priest that is mourning his near of kin,[1] or that
had immersed himself [because of uncleanness] the selfsame day,[2] or that
is not clothed [in proper raiment],[3] or whose atonement is yet incomplete,[4]
or that has not washed his hands and his feet,[5] or that is uncircumcised, or
unclean, or that ministers while sitting,[6] or while standing on any article
or on the back of a beast or on his fellow's feet. If he received the blood in
his left hand, the offering is invalid; but R. Simeon declares it valid. If it
was poured out on the pavement and then gathered up again, it is invalid.
If it was sprinkled on the Ramp[7] and not by the [Altar-]base; or if what
should have been sprinkled above was sprinkled below,[8] or if what should
have been sprinkled below was sprinkled above, or if what should have
been sprinkled within was sprinkled outside,[9] or if what should have been
sprinkled outside was sprinkled within, the offering becomes invalid,[10] but
punishment by Extirpation is not incurred [by them that eat thereof].

2. If a man slaughtered the offering purposing to toss its blood or some
of its blood outside [the Temple Court], or to burn its sacrificial portions
or some of its sacrificial portions outside, or to eat its flesh or an olive's
bulk of its flesh outside, or an olive's bulk of the skin of the fat tail[11] outside,
the offering becomes invalid, but punishment by Extirpation is not incurred
[by them that eat thereof]. If he purposed to toss its blood or some of its
blood on the morrow, or to burn its sacrificial portions or some of its
sacrificial portions on the morrow, or to eat its flesh or an olive's bulk of its
flesh on the morrow, or an olive's bulk of the skin of the fat tail on the

---

[1] See p. 465, nn. 19, 24.
[2] He only becomes clean at sunset; Lev. 22[7]. See p. 773, n. 6.
[3] See Yom. 7[5].   [4] See Hag. 3[3]; Ker. 2[1].   [5] Ex. 30[18ff].   [6] Cf. Deut. 18[5].
[7] The inclined plane on the south by which the Altar was mounted.
[8] The red line which went round the Altar in the middle to distinguish the upper and
lower parts of the side. See Midd. 3[1].
[9] Referring to the great Altar which was in the Temple Court outside the Sanctuary, and
to the Golden Altar inside the Sanctuary. See below, 5[2f].
[10] The sacrificial portions may not be burnt on the Altar and the flesh may not be consumed by the priests or owners.
[11] Which must be burnt 'entire' (Lev. 3[9]). Its skin (see Hull. 9[2]) was considered edible.

morrow, the offering becomes Refuse,[1] and punishment by Extirpation is incurred [by them that eat thereof].

3. This is the general rule: if any man slaughtered or received, conveyed or tossed the blood purposing to eat a thing that it is usual to eat or to burn a thing that it is usual to burn outside its proper place, the offering becomes invalid, but punishment by Extirpation is not incurred [by them that eat thereof]; but if [he purposed the like] outside its proper time, the offering becomes Refuse, and punishment by Extirpation is incurred [by them that eat thereof], provided that what renders [the offering] permissible[2] is offered according to its prescribed rite.

4. How is 'what renders [the offering] permissible' offered according to its prescribed rite? If he had slaughtered in silence,[3] but had received, conveyed, and tossed the blood [while purposing an act] outside its proper time; or if he had slaughtered [an offering, while purposing an act] outside its proper time, but had received, conveyed, and tossed the blood in silence; or if he had slaughtered and received, conveyed and tossed the blood [while purposing an act] outside the proper time, such is a case where 'what renders [the offering] permissible' is offered according to its prescribed rite.[4] How is 'what makes [the offering] permissible' not offered according to its prescribed rite? If he had slaughtered [while purposing an act] outside its proper place, and had also received, conveyed, and tossed the blood [while purposing an act] outside its proper time, and had also received, conveyed, and tossed the blood [while purposing an act] outside its proper place, or if he had slaughtered and had also received, conveyed and tossed the blood [while purposing an act] outside its proper place, or if he had slaughtered a Passover-offering or a Sin-offering under another name, and had received, conveyed, and tossed the blood [while purposing an act] outside its proper time, or if he had slaughtered it [while purposing an act] outside its proper time and had also received, conveyed, and tossed the blood under some other name; or if he had slaughtered and also received, conveyed and tossed the blood under another name[5]—such is a case where 'what renders [the offering] permissible' is not offered according to its prescribed rite.

5. [If a man slaughtered an offering, and received, conveyed, and tossed the blood while purposing] to eat an olive's bulk outside, and an olive's bulk on the morrow; or an olive's bulk on the morrow and an olive's bulk outside; or a half-olive's bulk outside and a half-olive's bulk on the morrow, or a half-olive's bulk on the morrow and a half-olive's bulk outside, the offering becomes invalid, but punishment by Extirpation is not incurred [by them that eat thereof]. R. Judah said: This is the general rule: if the intention about the time preceded the intention about the place, the offering becomes Refuse and punishment by Extirpation is incurred [by them that eat thereof]; but if the intention about the place preceded the intention about the time, the offering becomes invalid but punishment by Extirpation is not incurred [by them that eat thereof]. But the Sages say:

---

[1] Lev. 7[18]; 19[7, 8]: 'it is an abomination . . . one that eateth it . . . shall be cut off'.

[2] That permits the sacrificial portions (cf. Lev. 3[9-11], 14[16]) to be burnt on the Altar, and the flesh to be consumed by the priest or owner. What renders these 'permissible' is the proper sprinkling or tossing of the blood. See below, 4[4]; p. 576, n. 3.

[3] i.e. without the invalidating purpose.

[4] The offering in each case becomes 'Refuse', and the second part of the general rule of par. 3 applies.   [5] While purposing an act outside its proper time.

In both cases the offering becomes invalid, but punishment by Extirpation is not incurred [by them that eat thereof]. [If he purposed] to eat a half-olive's bulk and to burn a half-olive's bulk [outside the proper time or place], the offering remains valid, since eating and burning cannot be included together.[1]

3. 1. If any man slaughtered that was ineligible, his slaughtering is none the less valid, since slaughtering is valid if it is done by them that are not priests, or by women or by bondservants or by them that are unclean, even the [slaughtering of the] Most Holy Things,[2] provided that none that is unclean touches the flesh. Therefore also they render [the offering] invalid through [a wrongful] intention, but if any of them received the blood[3] [while purposing an act] outside the proper time or outside the proper place, and its life-blood yet remained,[4] he that is eligible may come and receive it.

2. If he that was eligible received the blood and gave it to one that was not eligible, he must give it back to him that was eligible. If he received it with his right hand and gave it into his left hand, he must return it to his right hand. If he received it in a sacred vessel and put it into an unhallowed vessel, he must put it back into a sacred vessel. If it was poured out from the vessel on to the pavement, and gathered up again, it remains valid.[5] If it was sprinkled on the Ramp and not by the [Altar-]base, or if what should have been sprinkled below was sprinkled above, or if what should have been sprinkled above was sprinkled below, or if what should have been sprinkled within was sprinkled outside, or if what should have been sprinkled outside was sprinkled within, and its life-blood yet remained, he that is eligible may come and receive it.

3. If a man slaughtered the offering purposing to eat a thing that it is not usual to eat, or to burn a thing that it is not usual to burn [outside its proper time or place], the offering remains valid. R. Eliezer declares it invalid. If [he purposed] to eat a thing that it is usual to eat and to burn a thing that it is usual to burn, and it was less than an olive's bulk, the offering remains valid; or if [he purposed] to eat a half-olive's bulk and to burn a half-olive's bulk, it remains valid, since eating and burning cannot be included together.

4. If a man slaughtered the offering purposing to eat an olive's bulk of the hide or grease or sediment or flayed-off flesh[6] or bones or sinews or hoofs or horns outside the proper time or outside the proper place, the offering remains valid, and none becomes liable[7] thereby[8] through [transgression of the laws of] Refuse[9] or Remnant[10] or uncleanness.[11]

5. If a man slaughtered consecrated beasts [purposing] to eat the foetus or the afterbirth outside [the proper place or time], he does not thereby transgress the law concerning Refuse. If he wrung the necks of the turtle-doves [purposing] to eat their eggs outside [the proper time or place], he

---

[1] The forbidden quantity of an olive's bulk is neither eaten nor burnt.
[2] See above, p. 468, n. 7.   [3] Which they were ineligible to do. See 2[1].
[4] See Lev. 17[11], from which it is inferred that that blood which issues at the moment of death (which is what the Mishnah means by 'life-blood') is the blood that makes atonement.
[5] But not if it had not been put in the sacred vessel. See above, 2[1]. Cf. below, 9[7].
[6] Flesh that is torn off with the hide.   [7] To Extirpation.
[8] Through eating such inedible portions.   [9] See above, p. 470, n. 1.
[10] Ex. 29[34]; Lev. 7[17]; an offering that remains after the time prescribed for eating it, and that must be destroyed by burning.
[11] See Lev. 7[20]; 22[3]; uncleanness in him that eats of the offering.

does not thereby transgress the law concerning Refuse. Because of milk from consecrated beasts or eggs from turtle-doves none becomes liable through [transgression of the laws of] Refuse or uncleanness.

6. If a man slaughtered it and intended to leave its blood or its sacrificial portions for the morrow or to take them outside, R. Judah declares the offering invalid, but the Sages declare it valid. If he slaughtered it and intended to sprinkle it on the Ramp and not by the [Altar-]base, or to sprinkle above what should be sprinkled below, or to sprinkle below what should be sprinkled above, or to sprinkle outside what should be sprinkled within, or to sprinkle within what should be sprinkled outside, or [if he intended] that such as were unclean should eat it, or that such as were unclean should offer it, or that such as were uncircumcised should eat it, or that such as were uncircumcised should offer it, or [if he intended] to break the bones of the Passover-offering[1] or to eat of it raw,[2] or to mingle its blood with the blood of invalid [offerings],[3] it still remains valid, since no other intention can render the offering invalid save that which concerns [an act] outside the proper time or place, or, if it is a Passover-offering or Sin-offering, slaughtering it under another name.

4. 1. The School of Shammai say: Any offering whose blood must be sprinkled[4] on the outer Altar makes atonement even if it is sprinkled with but one act of sprinkling, or, if it is a Sin-offering, with two acts of sprinkling. And the School of Hillel say: Even if it is a Sin-offering it makes atonement if it is sprinkled with but one act of sprinkling. Therefore if the first act of sprinkling was done in the manner ordained, but the second outside the proper time, it still makes atonement; but if the first act of sprinkling was done outside its proper time, and the second outside its proper place, the offering is rendered Refuse and punishment by Extirpation is thereby incurred.

2. Any offering whose blood must be sprinkled on the inner Altar, if it lacks but one of the acts of sprinkling, will not make atonement. Therefore if all the acts of sprinkling were done in the manner ordained and one only in a manner not ordained, the offering is invalid, but punishment by Extirpation is not thereby incurred.

3. Because of these things none can become liable[5] through [transgression of the law of] Refuse: [namely], the Handful,[6] the frankincense,[7] the Incense-offering,[8] the Meal-offering of the priests,[9] the Meal-offering of the anointed [High] Priest,[10] and the Meal-offering offered with drink-offer-ings,[11] and the blood, and the drink-offerings offered by themselves. So R. Meir. But the Sages say: Those, too, that are offered together with a beast. Of the leper's *log* of oil[12] R. Simeon says: None becomes thereby liable through [transgression of the law of] Refuse. But R. Meir says: They may become liable through [transgression of the law of] Refuse, since it is offered together with the blood of the Guilt-offering which it is that renders [the offering] permissible;[13] and whatsoever has that which renders [the offering] permissible, whether for the man[14] or for the Altar,[15] they

---

[1] Cf. Ex. 12⁴⁶.   [2] Cf. Ex. 12⁹.   [3] See below, 8⁷.   [4] See below, 5¹ff.
[5] To Extirpation.   [6] Lev. 2².   [7] Ibid.   [8] Ex. 30⁷,⁸.   [9] Lev. 6²³.   [10] Lev. 6²².
[11] Some texts omit this item. Meal-offerings and libations were brought with the Daily Whole-offerings and with the Additional-offerings on New Moons and Festival-days.
[12] Lev. 14¹⁰.   [13] See above, p. 470, n. 2.
[14] The priest or owner by whom portions of the animal-offering are consumed.
[15] On which the prescribed sacrificial portions are burnt.

may become liable thereby through [transgression of the law of] Refuse.

4. Of the Whole-offering,[1] it is the blood thereof that renders permissible the flesh for the Altar and the hide for the priests. Of the Whole-offering of a bird,[2] it is the blood thereof that renders the flesh permissible for the Altar. Of the Sin-offering of a bird[3] it is the blood thereof that renders the flesh thereof permissible for the priests. Of the bullocks which are to be burnt[4] and the he-goats[5] which are to be burnt, it is the blood thereof that renders permissible their sacrificial portions so that they may be offered [on the Altar]. R. Simeon says: Because of any [offering of which the blood] is not [sprinkled] on the outer Altar, as with a Peace-offering, none becomes liable through [transgression of the law of] Refuse.

5. Because of offerings made by the gentiles none can become liable through [transgression of the laws of] Refuse, Remnant, or uncleanness; and he that slaughters them outside [their proper place or outside their proper time] is not culpable. So R. Meir.[6] But R. Jose declares him culpable. Where none may become liable through [transgression of the law of] Refuse, they may still become liable through [transgression of the laws of] Remnant or uncleanness, but not by reason of the blood.[7] R. Simeon says: [This applies only] to aught that it is usual to eat; but because of the like of the wood, the frankincense, or the incense-offering, none can become liable through [transgression of the law of] uncleanness.

6. An offering must be slaughtered while mindful of six things: of the offerings,[8] of the offerer, of God, of the altar-fires, of the odour, and of the sweet savour; and, if it is a Sin-offering or a Guilt-offering, also of the sin. R. Jose said: Even if a man was not mindful in his heart of one of these things, the offering is valid; for it is a condition enjoined by the court that the intention [which invalidates an offering] is dependent on him alone that performs the act.[9]

5. 1. Which was the place appointed for the animal-offerings? The Most Holy Things were slaughtered on the north side [of the Altar]. The bullock and the he-goat offered on the Day of Atonement were slaughtered on the north side, and their blood was received in a vessel of ministry on the north side, and their blood required to be sprinkled[10] over the space between the bars and upon the veil [of the Holy of Holies] and upon the Golden Altar.[11] [Lack of] one of these acts of sprinkling impaired [the atonement]. The residue of the blood was poured over the western base of the outer Altar, but if such was not done it did not impair [the atonement].

2. The bullocks which were to be burnt and the he-goats which were to be burnt[12] were slaughtered on the north side and their blood was received in a vessel of ministry on the north side, and their blood required to be sprinkled on the veil and on the Golden Altar. [Lack of] one of these acts of sprinkling impaired [the atonement]. The residue of the blood was

---

[1] See Lev. 1[5]; 7[8].   [2] Lev. 1[14–17].   [3] Inferred from Num. 18[9].
[4] Lev. 4[1–12, 13–21]; 16[6].   [5] Lev. 16[5]; Num. 15[24].   [6] Some texts read 'Simeon'.
[7] i.e. if a man consumed blood left over after the first day, or if he consumed it while he was unclean, he is not culpable under the laws of Remnant and uncleanness; he is already culpable under the law of Lev. 17[10f].
[8] That it may not be slaughtered under the name of some other category of offering.
[9] And the court has enjoined that that intention be unspoken, to prevent occasion for error. Cf. Hul. 2[7].
[10] Or tossed. Cf. Pes. 5[6] .See above, p. 468, n. 15. The term employed throughout this chapter is, literally, 'be given', 'applied'.   [11] See Yom. 5[4ff].   [12] See above, nn. 4, 5.

poured over the western base of the outer Altar, but if such was not done it did not impair [the atonement]. These all[1] were burnt in the place of ashes.[2]

3. The Sin-offerings of the congregation and of individuals (these are the Sin-offerings of the congregation: the he-goats offered at the new moons[3] and at the set feasts)[4] were slaughtered on the north side and their blood was received in a vessel of ministry on the north side, and their blood required to be sprinkled with four acts of sprinkling on the four horns [of the Altar]. After what manner? The priest went up the Ramp and went around the Circuit[5] and came to the south-eastern horn, then to the north-eastern, to the north-western, and to the south-western horn. The residue of the blood was poured over the southern base; and the offerings were consumed within the Curtains[6] by males of the priestly stock, and cooked for food after any fashion, during that day and night until midnight.[7]

4. The Whole-offering is of the Most Holy Things; it was slaughtered on the north side and its blood was received in a vessel of ministry on the north side, and its blood required to be sprinkled with two acts of sprinkling (which are, indeed, four);[8] and it required to be flayed and to be cut into pieces; and it was burnt whole on the [Altar-]fire.[9]

5. The Peace-offerings of the congregation[10] and the Guilt-offerings (these are the Guilt-offerings: the Guilt-offerings because of false dealing,[11] the Guilt-offerings because of Sacrilege,[12] the Guilt-offerings because of [intercourse with] a betrothed bondwoman,[13] the Guilt-offering of a Nazirite,[14] the Guilt-offering of the leper,[15] and the Suspensive Guilt-offering)[16] were slaughtered on the north side and their blood was received in a vessel of ministry on the north side and their blood required to be sprinkled with two acts of sprinkling (which are, indeed, four); and they were eaten within the curtains by males of the priestly stock,[17] and cooked for food after any fashion, during that day and night until midnight.

6. The Thank-offering[18] and the ram of the Nazirite[19] are of the Lesser Holy Things; they were slaughtered anywhere in the Temple Court and their blood required to be sprinkled with two acts of sprinkling (which are, indeed, four); and they could be eaten anywhere in the City, by any man, and cooked for food after any fashion, on that day and night until midnight. So, too, was it with what was taken from them as heave-offering,[20] save that it could be eaten only by the priests, their wives, their children, and their bondservants.[21]

7. The Peace-offerings[22] are of the Lesser Holy Things; they were slaughtered anywhere in the Temple Court and their blood required to be sprinkled with two acts of sprinkling (which are, indeed, four); and they could be eaten anywhere in the City, by any man, and cooked for food after any fashion, during two days and a night. The same applied to what

---

[1] The rest of the carcase after the sacrificial portions had been burnt on the Altar.
[2] Outside the city; see Lev. 6[11].　　　　[3] Num. 28[15].
[4] Num. 28[16-31]; 29[1-38].　　　　[5] Cf. Tam. 2[1].
[6] Cf. Meg. 1[11]; Eduy. 8[6]; cf. 11[5, 6]. The meaning is 'within the Temple Court'.
[7] Cf. Ber. 1[1].　　　　[8] On the four horns. Inferred from Lev. 1[5].
[9] Lev. 1[9].　　　[10] Lev. 23[19].　　　[11] Lev. 6[6].　　　[12] Lev. 5[15].
[13] Lev. 19[20]; cf. Ker. 2[5].　　　[14] Num. 6[12].　　　[15] Lev. 14[12].
[16] Lev. 5[17-19].　　　[17] Lev. 7[6, 7].　　　[18] Lev. 7[12].　　　[19] Num. 6[14].
[20] See Lev. 7[14, 32]; cf. Ex. 29[27].　　　[21] Lev. 10[14].
[22] Excluding those of the congregation; cf. above, par. 5.

was taken from it as heave-offering, save that it could be eaten only by the priests, their wives, their children, and their bondservants.

8. The Firstling,[1] the Tithe [of Cattle],[2] and the Passover-offering are of the Lesser Holy Things; they were slaughtered anywhere in the Temple Court and their blood required to be sprinkled with but one act of sprinkling, provided that it was sprinkled against the [Altar-]base. There is a difference in their manner of eating: the Firstling was eaten only by the priests,[3] and the Tithe [of Cattle] by any man; they could be eaten anywhere in the City, and cooked for food after any fashion, during two days and a night; but the Passover-offering could be eaten only during that night[4] and only until midnight, and it could be eaten only by the number that were assigned to it,[5] and it could only be eaten roast.[6]

6. 1. If the Most Holy Things were slaughtered above[7] the Altar, R. Jose says: It is as though they were slaughtered on the north side. R. Jose b. R. Judah says: From midway on the Altar northwards counts as the north side; and from midway southwards counts as the south. The Handfuls[8] from the Meal-offerings could be taken anywhere in the Temple Court, and they were eaten within the curtains by males of the priestly stock, and cooked for food after any fashion, on that day and night until midnight.

2. The Sin-offering of a bird was made ready at the south-western corner. It was valid [if it was made ready] in any other place, but this was its proper place. That corner served three purposes below, and three above: below—for the Sin-offering of a bird, for the bringing near[9] [of the Meal-offerings], and [for pouring away] the residue of the blood; above— for the Water Libation,[10] for the Wine-offering, and for the Whole-offerings of a bird, if these were too many for the [south-]eastern [corner].[11]

3. All that went up to the Altar went up on the right side [of the Ramp], and went round the Altar and came down on the left side, excepting him that went up for these three things,[12] when they used to go up and return back in their own track.

4. How was the Sin-offering of a bird made ready? [The priest] used to wring off its head from its neck but he did not divide it asunder, and he sprinkled of the blood thereof upon the side of the Altar, and the residue of the blood was drained out at the [Altar-]base.[13] The Altar received but the blood thereof and the whole of the offering fell to the priests.

5. How was the Whole-offering of a bird made ready? The priest went up the Ramp and went around the Circuit; when he came to the south-eastern corner he used to wring off its head from its neck and divide it asunder and drain out its blood at the side of the Altar. He took the head and pressed the place where it was severed against the Altar and strewed it with salt[14] and threw it on the [Altar-]fire. He came then to the body and removed the crop and the plumage and the entrails that came forth with the crop and cast them on the place of ashes.[15] Then he slit open the body but did not divide it asunder (but if he did do so the offering remained valid) and he strewed it with salt and threw it on the [Altar-]fire.

---

[1] Num. 18[17].   [2] Lev. 27[32].   [3] Num. 18[18].   [4] Ex. 12[8].   [5] Cf. Pes. 5[3].
[6] Ex. 12[9].   [7] And not, as enjoined in 5[1], at the north side.   [8] Lev. 2[2].
[9] To the priest before he took the Handful.   [10] See Sukk. 4[9].
[11] They were then offered at the south-western corner.
[12] Prescribed to be made ready above, at the south-western corner.
[13] Lev. 5[8f].   [14] Lev. 2[13].   [15] Lev. 6[10]. Cf. Tam. 1[4].

6. If he did not remove the crop or the plumage or the entrails that came forth with the crop, or strew it with salt, or if he did aught in different fashion after he had drained out its blood, the offering remains valid. If he divided asunder the head of the Sin-offering but not that of the Whole-offering, it becomes invalid. If he drained out the blood of the head but not that of the body, it becomes invalid. But if he drained out the blood of the body but not that of the head, it remains valid.

7. If he wrung off the head of the Sin-offering of a bird under some other name, or drained out its blood under some other name, or under its own and [then] under some other name; or under some other name and [then] under its own name, it becomes invalid. But if it was the Whole-offering of a bird it remains valid, yet it does not count to its owner [in fulfilment of his obligation]. It is all one whether it is the Sin-offering of a bird or the Whole-offering of a bird: if he wrung off their heads or drained out their blood [purposing] to eat a thing that it is usual to eat, or to burn a thing that it is usual to burn, outside its proper place, it becomes invalid, but punishment by Extirpation is not incurred; but if [he so purposed] outside its proper time, it becomes Refuse,[1] but punishment by Extirpation is thereby incurred, provided that what renders [the offering] permissible[2] is offered according to its prescribed rite. How is 'what renders [the offering] permissible' offered according to its prescribed rite? If he had wrung off its head in silence and drained out its blood [while purposing an act] outside its proper time; or if he had wrung off its head [while purposing an act] outside its proper time, and had drained out the blood in silence; or if he had wrung off its head and drained out its blood [while purposing an act] outside its proper time, such is a case where 'what renders [the offering] permissible' is offered according to its prescribed rite. How is 'what renders [the offering] permissible' not offered according to its prescribed rite? If he had wrung off its head [while purposing an act] outside its proper place, and drained out its blood [while purposing an act] outside its proper time; or if he had wrung off its head [while purposing an act] outside its proper time and had drained out its blood [while purposing an act] outside its proper place; or if he had wrung off its head and drained out its blood [while purposing an act] outside its proper place; or, if it was a Sin-offering, if he had wrung off its head under another name and drained out its blood [while purposing an act] outside its proper time; or if he had wrung off its neck [while purposing an act] outside its proper time; or if he had wrung off its neck [while purposing an act] outside its proper time and had drained out its blood under some other name; or wrung off its head and drained out its blood under another name, such is a case where 'what renders [the offering] permissible' is offered not according to its prescribed rite. [If he intended] to eat an olive's bulk outside and an olive's bulk on the morrow, or an olive's bulk on the morrow and an olive's bulk outside; or a half-olive's bulk outside and a half-olive's bulk on the morrow; or a half-olive's bulk on the morrow and a half-olive's bulk outside; the offering becomes invalid, but punishment by Extirpation is not thereby incurred. R. Judah said: This is the general rule: if the intention about time preceded the intention about place, the offering becomes Refuse, and

---

[1] Cf. above ,p. 470, n. 1.
[2] See above, 2³; 4⁴. It is the draining out of the blood that renders the body fit for burning on the Altar or eating by the priest.

punishment by Extirpation is thereby incurred; but if the intention about place preceded the intention about time, the offering becomes invalid, but punishment by Extirpation is not thereby incurred. But the Sages say: In both cases the offering becomes invalid, but punishment by Extirpation is not thereby incurred. [If he intended] to eat a half-olive's bulk and to burn a half-olive's bulk, the offering remains valid, since eating and burning cannot be included together.

7. 1. The Sin-offering of a bird is valid [only] if it is offered below [the red line][1] after the manner of a Sin-offering and under the name of a Sin-offering. It is invalid if it is offered after the manner of a Sin-offering and under the name of a Whole-offering; or after the manner of a Whole-offering and under the name of a Sin-offering; or after the manner of a Whole-offering and under the name of a Whole-offering. If it was offered above in a manner like to any of them, it is invalid.

2. The Whole-offering of a bird is valid if it is offered above, after the manner of a Whole-offering and under the name of a Whole-offering; and it remains valid even if it is offered after the manner of a Whole-offering and under the name of a Sin-offering, but it does not count to its owner [in fulfilment of his obligation]. But it becomes invalid if it is offered after the manner of a Sin-offering and under the name of a Whole-offering, or after the manner of a Sin-offering and under the name of a Sin-offering. If it was offered below in a manner like to any of them it is invalid.

3. [Even if they become invalid] none of them conveys uncleanness of the gullet,[2] and the law of Sacrilege[3] still applies to them, excepting the Sin-offering of a bird that was offered below after the manner of a Sin-offering and under the name of a Sin-offering.

4. If the Whole-offering of a bird was offered below after the manner of a Sin-offering and under the name of a Sin-offering, R. Eliezer says: The law of Sacrilege still applies[4] to it. R. Joshua says: The law of Sacrilege no longer[5] applies to it. R. Eliezer said: If the Sin-offering (which is not subject to the law of Sacrilege when it is offered under that name) becomes subject to the law of Sacrilege if it is offered under another name, how much more must the Whole-offering (which is subject to the law of Sacrilege when it is offered under that name) be subject to the law of Sacrilege when it is offered under another name! R. Joshua said to him: No! as thou arguest of a Sin-offering (which, when its name is changed to that of a Whole-offering thereby becomes changed to a thing subject to the law of Sacrilege) wouldest thou also argue of a Whole-offering (which when its name is changed to that of a Sin-offering thereby becomes changed to a thing not subject to the law of Sacrilege)? R. Eliezer said to him: Let Most Holy Things which have been slaughtered on the southern side[6] and

---

[1] See above, p. 469, n. 8.

[2] Any clean bird that dies of itself or is improperly slaughtered, although it does not convey uncleanness by contact or carrying like other carrion (Lev. 11[39]), still conveys uncleanness to one that eats an olive's bulk of it, even if he did not touch it; this category of unclean contact is styled 'uncleanness of the gullet'. Wringing off their heads, like the slaughtering of beasts, removes them from the category of 'carcase' or 'carrion'. Cf. Par. 8[4]; Toh. 1[1, 3]; Zab. 5[9].   [3] Lev. 5[15]. Cf. p. 573, n. 2.

[4] On the principle (see Meil. 1[1]) that its dedication as a Whole-offering still held good, and thus no moment had passed over it during which it was permissible to the priests.

[5] It was now a Sin-offering in all respects, and its body was permitted to the priests (see above, 4[4]).   [6] See above, 5[1].

slaughtered under the name of Lesser Holy Things[1] provide proof; for their name is thus changed to that of a thing to which the law of Sacrilege does not apply, and yet they still remain subject[2] to the law of Sacrilege; so do not thou marvel that, as touching the Whole-offering, although its name is changed to that of a thing not subject to the law of Sacrilege, the law of Sacrilege still applies to it. R. Joshua said to him: No! as thou arguest of Most Holy Things, which have been slaughtered on the southern side and slaughtered under the name of Lesser Holy Things and whose name is thereby changed to one in which there is both what is forbidden and what is permitted,[3] wouldest thou also argue of a Whole-offering whose name is changed to one in which the whole is permitted?[4]

5. If he had wrung off its head with his left hand, or at night, or if he had slaughtered unconsecrated [birds] within [the Temple Court], or consecrated [birds] outside, they do not convey uncleanness of the gullet.[5] If he had wrung off their heads with a knife, or wrung off the heads of unconsecrated [birds] within [the Temple Court], or consecrated [birds] outside, or if they were turtle-doves whose time was not yet come,[6] or young pigeons whose time was past, or if a bird's wings were dried up, or if an eye was blinded, or if its foot was cut off, such a bird conveys uncleanness of the gullet. This is the general rule: if it became invalid while in the Temple it does not convey uncleanness of the gullet; if it became invalid while not in the Temple, it conveys uncleanness of the gullet. If they had wrung off the heads of these invalid [birds], their wringing off is invalid, but they do not convey uncleanness of the gullet.

6. If he had wrung off the head and the bird was found to be *terefah*,[7] R. Meir says: It does not convey uncleanness of the gullet. R. Judah says: It conveys uncleanness of the gullet. R. Meir said: If the slaughtering of a beast (which as carrion would convey uncleanness by contact or carrying)[8] renders clean what was *terefah*, how much more must the slaughtering of a bird (which as carrion does not convey uncleanness by contact or carrying) render clean what was *terefah*![9] Like as we find that the slaughtering thereof renders it fit for eating and renders clean what was *terefah*, so too the wringing off of the head thereof, which renders it fit for eating, must render clean what was *terefah*. R. Jose says: It is enough if the comparison is limited[10] to the carcase of a beast: the slaughtering thereof can render clean [what is *terefah*] but not the wringing off of its head.

8. 1. If animal-offerings were confused with Sin-offerings that had been left to die[11] or with an ox that was to be stoned,[12] though it be but one among ten thousand, all must be left to die. If they were confused with an ox

---

[1] After their blood has been poured out. The law of Sacrilege does not apply to their flesh (which is now permitted to the priests) but only to their sacrificial portions.
[2] See Meil. 1¹.
[3] The sacrificial portions of Lesser Holy Things are forbidden under the law of Sacrilege, while their flesh is permitted.
[4] The Sin-offering of a bird has no sacrificial portions; cf. above, 4⁴.
[5] Although it is forbidden to eat them.
[6] See Hull. 1⁵. Only the older of the doves and the younger of the pigeons were valid. The doves became valid only when the plucking of the feathers no longer drew blood.
[7] App. I. 47a.   [8] Lev. 11³⁹, ⁴⁰.
[9] A principle deduced by rabbinical interpretation from the verse Lev. 11³⁹.
[10] Cf. p. 333, n. 3. 'It is enough if the inferred law is as strict as that from which it was inferred.' Cf. Nidd. 4⁶.
[11] Sin-offerings which cannot be offered and yet may not otherwise be made use of, as, e.g., the Sin-offering set apart by a man who died before he could offer it.
[12] Ex. 21²⁸ᶠ.

with which transgression had been committed, or that had killed a man on the evidence of one witness or on the evidence of the owner,[1] or with an ox that had committed or suffered an unnatural crime, or that had been set apart [for idolatry] or that had been worshipped, or that was *the hire* [*of a harlot*] *or the price* [*of a dog*],[2] or that was cross-bred or *terefah*, or born from the side[3] [of the mother-beast], they must be left to pasture until they suffer a blemish, when they must be sold, and with the price of the best among them an offering of that same kind[4] shall be offered. If it was confused with unblemished unconsecrated beasts, the unconsecrated beasts must all be sold to them that need an offering of that same kind.

2. If consecrated beasts were confused with other consecrated beasts belonging to the like kind of offering, each may be offered on behalf of any of the owners. But if consecrated beasts were confused with other consecrated beasts belonging to a different kind of offering,[5] they must be left to pasture until they suffer a blemish, when they must be sold, and with the price of the best among them an offering of each of those two kinds must be offered, and the added cost let him lose from his own substance.[6] If they were confused with a Firstling or with Tithe [of Cattle], they must be left to pasture until they suffer some blemish, when they may be eaten after the manner of the Firstling or of Tithe [of Cattle].[7] All kinds of offering may suffer confusion one with another excepting a Sin-offering with a Guilt-offering.[8]

3. If a Guilt-offering was confused with a Peace-offering they[9] must be left to pasture until they suffer a blemish. R. Simeon says: They should both be slaughtered at the north side and eaten after the manner of that to which the more stringent rules apply. They said to him: They may not suffer consecrated things to become invalid. If pieces of the flesh [of one offering] were confused with pieces of the flesh [of other offerings], the Most Holy Things with Lesser Holy Things, or what must be eaten the same day with what may be eaten during two days, they must be eaten after the manner of that to which the more stringent rules apply.

4. If the members[10] of a Sin-offering[11] were confused with the members of a Whole-offering,[12] R. Eliezer says: Let them [all] be put above [the Altar-fire]; and I may account the flesh of the Sin-offering above to be but wood.[13] But the Sages say: Let its appearance be spoilt and let it go to the place of burning.[14]

5. If the members [of Whole-offerings] were confused with the members of blemished beasts, R. Eliezer says: If the head of one of them had been

---

[1] Though in these two cases the ox may not be stoned, it may not be used as an offering. To these and the following Lev. 22²⁵ is applied.

[2] See Deut. 23¹⁸; Tem. 6¹⁻⁴. Cf. Zeb. 9³; 14²; Par. 2³.

[3] Lev. 22²⁷ is interpreted as including only a natural birth.

[4] Of offering—Whole-offering, Sin-offering, &c.—which was confused with the invalid beasts.

[5] None of them may be offered since it will be unknown in which of the several manners the blood of each must be sprinkled; see above, 5¹ff.

[6] Pes. 9⁸. If he sold one of them for 5 *zuz* and one for 3 *zuz* he must bring the two new offerings each of 5 *zuz* value, since he does not know which of the two he had intended for which offering. [7] See Tem. 3⁵.

[8] There is a possibility of confusion except between a Sin-offering and a Guilt-offering, since the latter are never other than rams or he-lambs, and Sin-offerings are never other than ewe-lambs or he-goats. [9] Some texts omit the following sentence.

[10] Cf. Tam. 4³ for an account of the several members.

[11] To be consumed by the priests. [12] To be burnt on the Altar.

[13] And not as contributing to 'the odour of a sweet smell'.

[14] Where all invalid offerings are destroyed.

offered,[1] the heads of all may be offered; if the legs of one of them had been offered, the legs of all may be offered. But the Sages say: Even if all the members save one had been offered, this must go to the place of burning.

6. If blood was mixed with water, yet had still the appearance of blood, it remains valid;[2] if it was mixed with wine, the wine is deemed to be but water; if it was mixed with the blood of a beast [that was unconsecrated] or of a wild animal, this is deemed to be but water. R. Judah says: Blood cannot render other blood invalid.

7. If it was mixed with the blood of invalid offerings, it must be poured out into the gutter; if with blood that issued after death,[3] it must be poured out into the gutter (R. Eliezer declares it valid); yet if the priest had not bethought himself and had sprinkled it, it is valid.

8. If the blood of unblemished offerings was confused with the blood of blemished offerings, it must be poured out into the gutter. If bowls [containing the one kind of blood were confused] with bowls [containing the other kind], R. Eliezer says: If one was offered all may be offered. But the Sages say: Even if all of them were offered save one, this must be poured out into the gutter.

9. If blood that should be sprinkled below[4] was confused with blood that should be sprinkled above, R. Eliezer says: Let it be sprinkled above, and what should have been sprinkled below but was sprinkled above I may deem to be but water; and it may be sprinkled afresh below. But the Sages say: It must be poured out into the gutter; yet if the priest had not bethought himself and had sprinkled it, it is valid.

10. If blood that should be sprinkled once was confused[5] with other blood that should be sprinkled once, each is sprinkled once. If what should be sprinkled four times was confused[6] with what should be sprinkled four times, each is sprinkled four times. If what should be sprinkled four times was confused with what should be sprinkled once, R. Eliezer says: Let each be sprinkled four times. R. Joshua said: Let each be sprinkled but once. R. Eliezer said to him: Would he not transgress the law *Thou shalt not diminish from it*?[7] R. Joshua answered: Would not the other transgress the law *Thou shalt not add thereto*?[7] R. Eliezer said to him: The law *Thou shalt not add* applies only to the act in itself.[8] R. Joshua said to him: The law *Thou shalt not diminish* applies also only to the act in itself.[9] Moreover R. Joshua said: If thou sprinklest [more often than is prescribed] thou transgressest the law *Thou shalt not add*, and also thou performest an act [of transgression] with thine hand; whereas if thou sprinklest not, thou transgressest the law *Thou shalt not diminish*, but thou performest no act [of transgression] with thine hand.

11. If what should be sprinkled within [the Sanctuary] was confused with what should be sprinkled outside, they should both be poured out

---

[1] Before it was noticed that other members were confused with members of the Whole-offering.
[2] For the prescribed sprinklings.   [3] See above, p. 471, n. 4.
[4] The red line. See above, p. 469, n. 8.
[5] e.g. the blood of a Firstling with the blood of Tithe of Cattle.
[6] e.g. the blood of a Whole-offering with the blood of a Guilt-offering.
[7] Deut. 12[32].
[8] The sprinkling itself suffices; to sprinkle the one blood three times again is no transgression of 'thou shalt not add thereto' since it can be accounted to be but water.
[9] Therefore there is no need to sprinkle more than the once.

into the gutter. If it was sprinkled outside and again sprinkled within, it remains valid. If it was sprinkled within and then again sprinkled outside, R. Akiba declares it invalid, but the Sages valid. R. Akiba says: Any blood [that should have been sprinkled outside] that is brought within the Sanctuary to make atonement is invalid. But the Sages say: Only the Sin-offering. R. Eliezer says: The Guilt-offering also, for it is written, *As is the Sin-offering, so is the guilt offering.*[1]

12. If the blood of a Sin-offering[2] was received in two bowls, and one of them was taken outside [the Temple Court], that which remains inside is still valid. If one of them was taken within [the Sanctuary], R. Jose the Galilean declares that valid which is still outside [in the Temple Court], but the Sages declare it invalid.[3] R. Jose the Galilean said: If, in the case where intention renders invalid ([as when there is intention to sprinkle blood] outside[4] [the Temple Court]), this does not after the like fashion[5] render invalid the blood that remains, must we not infer, in the case where intention does not render invalid[6] ([as when there is intention to sprinkle blood] inside [the Sanctuary]), that we must not treat that which remains[7] in like fashion as that which enters in?[8] If it was taken inside to make atonement, even if it has not made atonement,[9] it becomes invalid. So R. Eliezer. R. Simeon says: [It does not become invalid] until it makes atonement.[10] R. Judah says: If it was taken inside by error, it is invalid. If any blood was invalid and yet was sprinkled on the Altar, the frontlet[11] does not effect acceptance,[12] but only for [an offering that was afterward found to be] unclean; for the frontlet effects acceptance for [an offering that was afterward found to be] unclean, but it does not effect acceptance for aught taken out [from the Temple Court].

9. 1. The Altar makes holy whatsoever is prescribed as its due. R. Joshua says: Whatsoever is prescribed as the due of the [Altar-]fires, and goes up to them, may not come down again, for it is written, *This is the* Olah *on the hearth upon the Altar*:[13] like as the Whole-offering that is prescribed as the due of the [Altar-]fires, if it goes up to them, may not come down again, so whatsoever is prescribed as the due of the [Altar-]fires, and goes up to them, may not come down again. Rabban Gamaliel says: Whatsoever is prescribed as the due of the Altar and goes up to it may not come down again, for it is written, *This is the Whole-offering on the hearth upon the Altar*: like as the Whole-offering that is prescribed as the due of the Altar, if it goes up to it may not come down again, so whatsoever is prescribed as the due of the Altar, and goes up to it, may not come down again. The words of Rabban Gamaliel differ from the words of R. Joshua only in what concerns the blood and the drink-offerings of which Rabban Gamaliel says:

---

[1] Lev. 7[7].   [2] Which was sprinkled on the four horns of the outer Altar.
[3] See R. Akiba and the Sages in the preceding paragraph.   [4] See above, 2[2].
[5] i.e. in the proposition now put forward, when, if one bowl of the blood is taken outside the Temple Court, the blood in the other bowl remains valid.
[6] For, if, while slaughtering, one had intention of sprinkling blood *within* the Sanctuary, this does not render the offering invalid, as does intention to sprinkle it *outside* the Temple Court.   [7] The second bowl of blood.
[8] Which is invalid. See R. Akiba and the Sages, above, par. 11.
[9] i.e. is still unsprinkled.
[10] i.e. only after it is sprinkled within does it become invalid for sprinkling on the outer Altar.   [11] See Ex. 28[36-8].   [12] Pes. 7[7].
[13] Lev. 6[9]. The word *olah*, a Whole-offering, can have the meaning 'that which goes up'.

They may not come down again, but R. Joshua says: They may come down again. R. Simeon says: If the animal-offering was valid and the drink-offerings[1] invalid, or if the drink-offering were valid and the animal offering invalid, or even if both were invalid, the animal-offering may not come down again, but the drink-offerings may come down again.

2. These, if they go up, may not come down again: what had remained overnight, or that had become unclean, or that had been taken out [of its proper place], or that had been slaughtered [by any that purposed an act] outside its proper time or outside its proper place, or whose blood had been received or tossed by any that were ineligible. R. Judah says: What was slaughtered by night, or whose blood was poured away, or whose blood flowed outside the Curtains— if it went up it must come down again. R. Simeon says: It need not come down again. For R. Simeon used to say: If aught [first] became invalid in the Temple, the Temple accepts it; if it did not [first] become invalid in the Temple, the Temple does not accept it.

3. These are they that did not [first] become invalid in the Temple: a beast[3] that committed or suffered an unnatural crime, or that had been set apart [for idolatry], or that had been worshipped, or that was *the hire [of a harlot]* or *the price [of a dog]*, or that was cross-bred, or *terefah*, or born from the side [of the mother-beast], or that had a blemish. R. Akiba declares valid such as have a blemish. R. Hanina the Prefect of the Priests says: My father used to reject from the Altar such as had a blemish.

4. Like as what goes up may not come down again, so what comes down may not go up again. But if aught went up alive to the top of the Altar, it may come down again. A Whole-offering that went up alive to the top of the Altar may come down again. If it was slaughtered on the top of the Altar it should be flayed and cut up where it lies.

5. These are they which, if they have gone up, may come down again: the flesh of the Most Holy Things, the flesh of the Lesser Holy Things, the residue of the *Omer*,[5] the Two Loaves,[6] the Shewbread,[7] the residues of the Meal-offerings, and the Incense-offering.[8] The wool on the heads of the lambs and the hair of the beard of the goats, and the bones and the sinews and the horns and the hoofs, if they were not severed, must also go up, for it is written, *And the priest shall burn the whole on the Altar.*[9] If they were severed they did not go up, for it is written, *And thou shalt offer thy burnt offerings, the flesh and the blood.*[10]

6. If aught burst off from upon the Altar it need not be put back; so, too, if a coal burst off from the Altar. If members of an animal-offering burst off from upon the Altar, and it was not yet midnight, they must be put back, and the law of Sacrilege[11] applies to them; but after midnight they need not be put back, and the law of Sacrilege does not apply to them.

7. As the Altar makes holy what is prescribed as its due, so also does the Ramp. As the Altar and the Ramp make holy what is prescribed as their due, so also do the vessels [belonging to the Temple]. The vessels for liquids make holy the liquids, and the measures for dry wares make holy the dry wares. The vessels for liquids do not make dry wares holy nor do measures for dry wares make liquids holy. If the sacred vessels have holes

---

[1] Pertaining to that offering; see Num. 28[9, 10, 11] &c.　　　[2] See above, p. 474, n. 6.
[3] See above, 8[1].　　　[4] Since they are consumed by the priests or the oven, etc.
[5] Lev. 23[10]. App. I. 31.　　　[6] Lev. 23[17].
[7] Lev. 24[5-9].　　　[8] Which was destined for the Inner Altar only.
[9] Lev. 1[9].　　　[10] Deut. 12[27].　　　[11] Lev. 5[15].

... are still able to do the like of their work that they did while yet unblemished, but not the work [of anointed priests]; otherwise they do not profit. And none of them can make holy [what is contained in] the vessels... they are within the Temple.

10. 1. What is offered more often than another precedes [the other.] The Daily Whole-offerings precede the Additional Offerings; the Additional Offerings of the Sabbaths precede the Additional Offerings of the new moons; the Additional Offerings of the new moons precede the Additional Offerings of the new year; for it is written, *Ye shall offer these beside the ... offering of the morning which is for a continual burnt offering.*

2. If one is more holy than another it precedes that other. The blood of the Sin-offering precedes the blood of the Whole-offering, since it makes atonement; the members of a Whole-offering precede the sacrificial portions of the Sin-offering, since they are given wholly to the [Altar-]fires; the Sin-offering precedes the Guilt-offering, since its blood is sprinkled on the four horns and on the [Altar-]base; the Guilt-offering precedes the Thank-offering and the ram of the Nazirite, since it is of the Most Holy [things]; the Thank-offering and the ram of the Nazirite precede the Peace-offering, since they are eaten the same day and require a Bread-offering; the Peace-offering precedes the Firstling since its blood requires a fourfold sprinkling and the laying on of hands and drink-offerings and the waving of the breast and the thigh.

3. The Firstling precedes the Tithe [of Cattle] since it is holy from the womb and is eaten [only] by the priests; the Tithe [of Cattle] precedes the Bird-offerings, since it is an animal-offering, and its blood and its sacrificial portions are most holy.

4. The Bird-offerings precede the Meal-offerings since they come within the class of blood [offerings]; the sinner's Meal-offering precedes the freewill Meal-offering since it is offered for sin; the Sin-offering of a bird precedes the Whole-offering of a bird, and in like manner [it precedes the Whole-offering] when they set aside [the two birds] for an offering.

5. All Sin-offerings enjoined in the Law precede the Guilt-offerings, excepting only the Guilt-offering of the leper, since this is offered to render him able [to enter the Temple and to eat of Hallowed Things]. All Guilt-offerings enjoined in the Law are offered from among beasts two years old and must be two shekels in value, excepting only the Guilt-offering of the Nazirite and the Guilt-offering of the leper, which are offered from among beasts one year old, and need not be two shekels in value.

6. Like as these are first to be offered so are they first to be eaten. If there is a Peace-offering of the day before and a Peace-offering of the same day, that of the day before is first [to be eaten]. If there is a Peace-offering of the day before and a Sin-offering and a Guilt-offering of the same day, that of the day before is first [to be eaten]. So R. Meir. But the Sages say: The Sin-offering is first [to be eaten] since it is of the Most Holy Things.

7. And all of them the priests may cook for food after any fashion, and eat them roast, or seethed, or cooked, and put therein unconsecrated spices or Heave-offering spices. So R. Simeon. R. Meir says: They may not put therein Heave-offering spices lest they make the Heave-offering invalid.

[1] Num. ...   [2] Offered on Sabbaths, new moons, and Festival-days.
[3] Num. 28...   [4] Lev. 5...   [5] I.e. they are not on the Altar.   [6] Lev. 5...
[7] Cf. Lev. 12..., Num. 6...   [8] See Lev. 14...   [9] Num. 6...   [10] App. I. 48.

8. R. Simeon said: If thou seest oil spread about in the Temple Court thou needest not to ask, What is it? It can be naught save the residue of the Meal-offering wafers of Israelites[1] or the leper's *log* of oil.[2] If thou seest oil put on the [Altar-]fire, thou needest not to ask, What is it? It can be naught save the residue of the Meal-offering wafers of the priests[3] or the Meal-offering of the anointed [High] Priest,[4] since oil is not offered as a Freewill-offering. R. Tarfon says: Oil is offered also as a Freewill-offering.

11. 1. If the blood of a Sin-offering was splashed on to a garment, it requires washing.[5] Although Scripture speaks only of such [Sin-offerings] as are to be eaten[6] (as it is written, *In a holy place shall it be eaten*) yet it is all one whether it is such as is to be eaten or [such that its blood must be] brought into the inner place: the garment requires washing, for it is written, [*This is*] *the law of the Sin-offering*; the one law applies to all Sin-offerings alike.

2. If the blood of an invalid Sin-offering [was splashed on to a garment] it does not require washing, whether there was a time when the offering was valid, or no time when it was valid. What kind of offering had a time when it was valid? Such that had remained overnight, or that had become unclean, or that had been taken outside [the Temple Court]. What kind of offering had not a time when it was valid? Such that was slaughtered [by one that purposed an act] outside its proper time and outside its proper place, or such that the blood thereof was received or sprinkled in a manner that was invalid.

3. If it was splashed on to a garment from the neck [of the beast] it does not require washing; and if [it was splashed on to a garment] from the horn or the base [of the Altar] it does not require washing. If it was poured over the pavement and gathered up again [and splashed on to a garment] it does not require washing. That blood alone requires washing which has been received in a vessel and is suitable for sprinkling. If it was splashed on to the skin [of a beast] that has not yet been flayed, it does not require washing; but if on skin that has been flayed, it requires washing. So R. Judah. R. Eliezer says: Even after it has been flayed it does not require washing. Only that place requires washing that has been splashed with the blood and that is such that it can contract uncleanness and that is fitted for washing.[7]

4. It is all one whether it is cloth or sackcloth or hide: they require washing in a holy place; so, too, the breaking of an earthenware vessel[8] [must be] in a holy place, and the scouring and rinsing of a brazen vessel[8] [must be] in a holy place. Herein greater stringency applies to the Sin-offering than to the [other] Most Holy Things.[9]

5. If the garment was taken outside the Curtains,[10] it must be brought in again and washed in a holy place. If it became unclean outside the Curtains it must be rent[11] and brought in again and washed in a holy place. If any earthenware vessel was taken outside the Curtains it must be brought

---

¹ Lev. 2⁴.   ² Lev. 14¹².   ³ Lev. 6²³.
⁴ Lev. 6²¹.   ⁵ Lev. 6²⁷.   ⁶ Lev. 6²ᵇ.
⁷ And not such that are rendered clean by scouring, like wood.   ⁸ Lev. 6²⁸.
⁹ Since for them such washing or breaking is not prescribed.
¹⁰ See p. 474, n. 6.
¹¹ The rule (see Kel. 2²; 3¹ᶠ; 27¹ᶠ) for utensils or woven stuff which contract uncleanness is that they become clean again if they are broken or rent to such an extent that they become unable to serve their former function.

in again and broken in a holy place. If it contracted uncleanness outside the Curtains a hole must be made in it, and then it must be brought in again and broken in a holy place.

6. If a brazen vessel was taken outside the Curtains, it must be brought in again and scoured and rinsed in a holy place; if it contracted uncleanness outside the Curtains, it must be reduced in size and brought in again and scoured and rinsed in a holy place.

7. It is all one whether a man had cooked therein or poured therein boiling water, or the Most Holy Things or the Lesser Holy Things: it requires scouring and rinsing. R. Simeon says: Because of the Lesser Holy Things a vessel does not require scouring and rinsing. R. Tarfon says: If a man cooked therein at the beginning of the Feast, he may cook therein[1] throughout the Feast. But the Sages say: Only until the time prescribed for the eating [of the offering].[2] [In] scouring and rinsing, the scouring [must be done] after the manner of the scouring of the cup;[3] and the rinsing [must be done] after the manner of the rinsing of the cup;[4] the scouring must be done with hot water, and the rinsing with cold water.[5] The spit and the grill must be scalded[6] with hot water.

8. If a man cooked therein Hallowed Things and unconsecrated things, or Most Holy Things and Lesser Holy Things, and there was [left from the more holy thing] enough to give a flavour, what is less holy must be eaten in the conditions prescribed for the more holy thing; but this does not render [the vessel] subject to scouring and rinsing, nor does it render other things invalid through contact. If one wafer touched another wafer [that was invalid], or if one piece of flesh [from an offering] touched another piece of flesh [that was invalid], the whole wafer or the whole piece of flesh does not become forbidden, but only the part that was overlapped.

12. 1. [A priest] that had immersed himself [because of uncleanness] the selfsame day,[7] or whose atonement was yet incomplete,[8] may have no share[9] in the Hallowed Things to consume them in the evening. [A priest] that is mourning his near of kin may touch but he may not offer them or have any share[10] in them to consume them in the evening. They that have a blemish,[11] whether lasting or passing, may have a share in them[12] and eat of them, but they may not offer them. And any [priest] on whom it did not fall to perform the [Altar-]service may have no share in the flesh; and he that has no share in the flesh has no share in the hides. Even if he was unclean at the moment of sprinkling the blood but clean at the moment of burning the fat pieces, he may have no share in the flesh; for it is written, *He among the sons of Aaron that offereth the blood of the peace offerings, and the fat, shall have the right thigh for a portion.*[13]

2. If the Altar has not acquired the right to the flesh of an offering[14] the

---

[1] Without washing or rinsing; since owing to the abundance of flesh of the Peace-offerings which a man cooks daily in his pot at that time each day's cooking serves to clean away the remnants of the previous day's Peace-offering before it can fall within the category of 'Remnant' (see above, p. 471, n. 10).

[2] i.e. after he had eaten of an offering he must rinse and scour his pots not later than two days and a night after cooking Peace-offerings, or a day and a night after cooking Sin-offerings.

[3] Used in saying the Benediction over food; this needed to be washed and scoured inside and out.   [4] On the outer side.

[5] Some texts read: both scouring and rinsing must be done with cold water.

[6] Cf. A. Zar. 5[12].   [7] See p. 773, n. 6.   [8] Ker. 2[1].   [9] See Lev. 6[26].

[10] See Deut. 26[14]; Hor. 3[5].   [11] Lev. 21[17ff].   [12] See Lev. 6[18], 'every male'.

[13] Lev. 7[33].   [14] i.e. before the sprinkling of the blood.

priests have not acquired the right to its hide, for it is written, *If . . . man's whole offering* —a Whole-offering that has been offered under one man's [name]. Though the Whole-offering was slaughtered under some other name, although it does not count to its owner [in fulfilment of his obligation], its hide belongs to the priests. It is all one whether it was the Whole-offering brought by a man or the Whole-offering brought by a woman, the hide thereof belongs to the priests.

3. The hides of the Lesser Holy Things belong to their owners, and the hides of the Most Holy Things belong to the priests. It is an inference from the less to the greater: if in the Whole-offering (to whose flesh they have no right) they yet have the right to the hide, how much more, therefore, in the Most Holy Things (to whose flesh they have the right) have they the right to their hide! The Altar affords no proof, since the hide never pertains to it.

4. If aught befell any of the Hallowed Things to render them invalid before they were flayed, their hides do not belong to the priests; but if it befell after they were flayed, their hides belong to the priests. R. Hanina the Prefect of the Priests said: Never have I seen a hide taken out to the place of burning. R. Akiba said: We learn from his words that if a man flayed a Firstling and it was found to be *terefah*, the priests may make use of its hide. But the Sages say: 'We have not seen' affords no proof, but, rather, it must be taken out to the place of burning.

5. If the bullocks which are to be burnt and the he-goats which are to be burnt are burnt according to the prescribed rite, they are burnt in the place of ashes, and they convey uncleanness to garments; but if they are not burnt according to the prescribed rite, they are burnt in the Beth ha-Birah, and they do not convey uncleanness to garments.

6. They used to bear them on poles. If the foremost [bearers] had come out of the Temple Court but the hinder [bearers] had not come out, the garments of the foremost are unclean but the garments of the hinder are not unclean until they have come out. When they both have come out, the garments of them both are unclean. R. Simeon says: The garments of neither become unclean until the fire has caught hold in the greater part of the beasts. Once the flesh has been burnt up, the garments of him that burns them are no longer unclean.

13. 1. If a man both slaughtered and offered [an offering outside the Temple Court], he is culpable by reason of the slaughtering and culpable by reason of the offering. R. Jose the Galilean says: If he slaughtered inside and offered it outside, he is culpable; but if he both slaughtered and offered it outside he is not culpable, since he but offered outside what was [already] invalid. They said to him: Even he that slaughters inside and offers it outside, once he has brought it out, has rendered it invalid.

2. If a man that was unclean ate, either an unclean or a clean Hallowed

---

[1] Lev. 7⁸.　　　　[2] The same play of *ma'al* as in 11², above.
[4] By a converse inference.　　[5] See below, 9¹.　　[6] Although the flesh could not be eaten.
[7] See 4³, 6³, m. 4⁵.　　[8] See above, 5².　　[9] Lev. 16²⁷. If they had become unclean.
[11] The Temple precincts.　　[12] See p. 542, n. 5.
[12] When taking them outside the Temple precincts to the place of burning. See Lev. 16²⁸.
[13] Lev. 17³,⁴.
[14] Lev. 17³,⁴. Each offence if committed wantonly is punishable by Extirpation; if committed unwittingly he must offer a Sin-offering on each count.
[15] By reason of the offering, but not by reason of the slaughtering.
[16] And yet is culpable on each count.

Thing he is culpable.[1] R. Jose the Galilean says: If a man that was unclean ate a clean Hallowed Thing he is culpable, but if an unclean Hallowed Thing he is not culpable, since he but ate a thing that was unclean. They said to him: Even if a man that was unclean ate what is clean, once he has touched it he has rendered it unclean. If a man that was clean ate what was unclean he is not culpable, since a man becomes culpable only by reason of the uncleanness of his own person.[2]

3. Greater stringency may apply to slaughtering than to offering, and [greater stringency may apply] to offering than to slaughtering. Greater stringency may apply to slaughtering, since if a man slaughtered [an offering outside the Temple Court] for a common person,[3] he is culpable; but if he offered it for a common person[4] he is not culpable.[5] Greater stringency may apply to offering, since if two seized a knife and slaughtered [an offering outside the Temple Court] they are not culpable,[6] but if two seized a member [of a slaughtered beast] and offered it, they are culpable.[7] If a man offered [a member of the slaughtered beast] and then again [offered another member], and then offered yet a third time, he is culpable on each count. So R. Simeon. R. Jose says: He is culpable only on one count. None is culpable unless he offers it on an altar. R. Simeon says: Even if he offered it on a rock or a stone he is culpable.

4. It is all one whether the Hallowed Things are valid or whether they are invalid (but became invalid while in the Temple): if a man offered them outside he is culpable. If he offered outside an olive's bulk of a Whole-offering and of sacrificial portions,[8] he is culpable. He is culpable if he offered outside an olive's bulk of the Handful,[9] or of the frankincense, or of the Incense-offering, or of the Meal-offering of the Priests, or of the Meal-offering of the anointed [High] Priest, or of the Meal-offering offered with drink-offerings. But R. Eleazar declares him exempt unless he offered the whole thereof. If he offered any among them within, but left over an olive's bulk of them and offered it outside, he is culpable. But if of any of them aught soever was lacking,[10] and he offered this outside, he is not culpable.

5. If he offered outside [the Temple Court] Hallowed Things together with their [unsevered] sacrificial portions, he is culpable. If he offered outside a Meal-offering from which the Handful had not been taken, he is not culpable; but if the Handful had been taken and then put back, and he offered it outside, he is culpable.

6. If he offered either the Handful or the frankincense outside, he is culpable. R. Eleazar declares him not culpable unless he offers the second also. If he offered the one inside and the other outside, he is culpable. If a man offered either of the two dishes[11] of frankincense outside, he is culpable. R. Eleazar declares him not culpable unless he offers the second also. If he offered the one inside and the other outside, he is culpable.

If he sprinkled a part of the blood outside, he is culpable. R. Eleazar says: If he poured out the Water-libation[1] of the Feast [of Tabernacles] outside, during the Feast, he is culpable. R. Nehemiah says: Even if he offered the residue of the blood[2] outside, he is culpable.

7. If a man wrung off the head of a Bird-offering inside and offered it outside, he is culpable; if he wrung off its head outside and offered it outside, he is not culpable. If he slaughtered the Bird-offering inside and offered it outside, he is not culpable; but if he slaughtered it outside and offered it outside he is culpable. Thus what renders the offering valid inside[3] renders a man exempt from penalty outside;[4] and what renders the offering valid outside,[5] renders a man exempt from penalty inside.[6] R. Simeon says: For whatsoever a man becomes culpable if he did it outside, he becomes culpable for the like act if he did it inside and then offered it outside, save only when he slaughters [a Bird-offering] inside and offers it outside.

8. If a man received the blood of a Sin-offering in a single bowl and [first] sprinkled part of it outside and then sprinkled part inside, or first sprinkled part of it inside and then sprinkled part outside, he is culpable, since all of it was prescribed to be sprinkled inside. If he received its blood in two bowls, and sprinkled both inside, he is not culpable; if he sprinkled both outside he is culpable; if he sprinkled one inside and [then] one outside, he is not culpable;[7] but if one outside and [then] one inside, he is culpable by reason of the outer one, but that [sprinkled] within makes atonement. To what is it like? It is as if a man set apart his Sin-offering and it was lost, and he then set apart another in its stead, and then the first was found again, and thus there were two. If he slaughtered them both inside [the Temple Court] he is not culpable. If he slaughtered them both outside he is culpable; if he slaughtered one within and [then] one outside, he is not culpable; if [he slaughtered] one outside and [then] one inside, he is culpable by reason of the one [slaughtered] outside, but the one [slaughtered] within makes atonement. Like as the [sprinkling of the] blood of an offering renders its flesh free [from the law of Sacrilege][8] so it renders free the flesh of the other offering.[9]

14. 1. If a man burnt[10] the Sin-offering of the [Red] Heifer[11] outside its pit—so, too, if he offered the scape-goat[12] outside—he is not culpable, for it is written, *And hath not brought it unto the door of the tent of meeting*:[13] none can become culpable by reason of any offering for which it is not prescribed that it must be brought unto the door of the tent of meeting.

2. If a man offered outside a beast[14] that had committed or suffered an unnatural crime, or that had been set apart [for idolatry], or that had been

---

1 Sukk. 4[9].   2 That had been poured out on the ground.
3 Namely, the wringing off of the neck. If he wrings off its neck inside it is valid as an offering, so that if he offers it outside he is culpable.
4 If he wrings off its neck outside and offers it outside he is not culpable.
5 Namely slaughtering. If he slaughtered it outside it is valid as an offering, so that if he offers it outside he is culpable.
6 If it was slaughtered inside and offered outside he is not culpable.
7 It was destined in any case to be poured out into the Temple gutter, the first bowlful sufficing for the prescribed sprinkling and pouring out by the Altar-base. See above, 5[3].
8 Lev. 5[15]. See Meil. 1[2]. It is then free to be eaten by the priest.
9 That had been set apart in this one's stead.
10 Rashi gives the variant 'slaughtered'. See Par. 3[10]–4[2].   11 Num. 19[2ff].
12 Lev. 16[10].   13 Lev. 17[4].   14 See above, 8[1].

worshipped, or that was cross-bred or *terefah*, or born from the side [of the mother-beast], he is not culpable, for it is written, *Before the tabernacle of the Lord*:[1] none can become culpable by reason of what is not fit to be brought before the tabernacle of the Lord. If he offered outside beasts that had a lasting or a passing blemish, he is not culpable. R. Simeon says: If a lasting blemish, he is not culpable; but if a passing blemish he thereby transgresses a prohibition.[2] If a man offered outside turtle-doves whose time was not yet come or young pigeons whose time was passed,[3] he is not culpable. R. Simeon says: If they were young pigeons whose time was passed, he is not culpable; but if they were turtle-doves whose time was not yet come, [he transgresses] a prohibition. [If he had offered outside] a beast and its young,[4] or a beast whose time had not yet come, he is not culpable. R. Simeon says: In this case he transgresses a prohibition. For R. Simeon used to say: If an offering is fitted to be offered at a later time, the prohibition applies to it, but punishment by Extirpation is not thereby incurred. But the Sages say: Whensoever punishment by Extirpation is not incurred, the prohibition does not apply.

3. An offering whose time was not yet come [may be such] either by virtue of itself or of its owner. Which is an offering whose time is not yet come by virtue of its owner? If the owner was a man or a woman that had a flux or a woman after childbirth or a leper, and they offered their Sin-offering or their Guilt-offering outside [before its appointed time][5] they are not culpable. If they offered their Whole-offerings or their Peace-offerings outside, they are culpable.[6] None is culpable if, outside, he offers aught[7] of the flesh of a Sin-offering or of a Guilt-offering, or of the flesh of the Most Holy Things,[8] or of the flesh of the Lesser Holy Things, or aught of the residue of the *Omer*,[9] or of the Two Loaves,[10] or of the Shewbread,[11] or of the residues of the Meal-offerings,[12] or if [outside] he poured out [oil over the Meal-offering], or mixed [the meal with the oil], or broke it in pieces, or salted,[13] or waved, or brought near,[14] or set in order the table [of the Shewbread], or trimmed the lamps, or took the Handful, or received the blood. Moreover none can become culpable by reason of these things:[15] because of being non-priests and because of uncleanness and because of not wearing the [proper] priestly raiment and because of the washing of the hands and feet.

4. Before the tabernacle[16] was set up, the high places were permitted and the [Altar-]service was fulfilled by the first born.[17] But after the tabernacle was set up, the high places were forbidden,[18] and the [Altar-]service was fulfilled by the priests; the Most Holy Things[19] were consumed within the Curtains,[20] and the lesser Holy Things throughout the camp of Israel.

5. After they came to Gilgal[21] the high places were again permitted; the

---

[1] Lev. 17[4]. [2] Deut. 12[8, 13]. [3] See above, p. 478, n. 6. [4] Lev. 22[28].
[5] See Lev. 15[14, 29]; 12[6]; 14[10].
[6] Since these are, as Freewill-offerings, permissible and valid before the appointed time.
[7] Of things which were not destined for the Altar.
[8] The Peace-offerings of the congregation. See above, 5[5].
[9] Lev. 23[10]. App. I. 31. [10] Lev. 23[17]. [11] Lev. 24[5ff.]. [12] Lev. 2[3]. [13] Lev. 2[13].
[14] Cf. Lev. 2[5-8]. The last items do not render the man culpable who performs them outside, since they are but preparations for an offering.
[15] Which count only as preparations for an offering.
[16] In the wilderness. [17] Cf. Ex. 24[5]. [18] Cf. Lev. 17[8f.]. [19] See above, 5[1ff.].
[20] Of the tabernacle or tent of meeting; cf. Lev. 6[26]. See p. 474, n. 6.
[21] After crossing the Jordan the tabernacle remained fourteen years at Gilgal until the Temple was set up at Shiloh.

Most Holy Things could be eaten only within the Curtains but the Lesser Holy Things in any place.

6. After they came to Shiloh[1] the high places were forbidden. There was no roof-beam there, but below was a house of stone[2] and above were hangings, and this was the 'resting place'.[3] The Most Holy Things were consumed within the Curtains, and the Lesser Holy Things and the Second Tithe[4] in any place within sight [of Shiloh].

7. After they came to Nob[5] and to Gibeon[6] the high places were permitted; the Most Holy Things were consumed within the Curtains and the Lesser Holy Things throughout the cities of Israel.

8. After they came to Jerusalem the high places were forbidden and never again permitted; and this was the 'inheritance'.[7] The Most Holy Things were consumed within the Curtains and the Lesser Holy Things and the Second Tithe within the wall [of Jerusalem].

9. By reason of any of the offerings dedicated[8] in the time when the high places were forbidden, and offered outside in the time when the high places were forbidden, a man transgressed both a positive[9] and a negative[10] command, and thereby incurred punishment by Extirpation.[11] If they were dedicated in the time when the high places were permitted and offered in the time when the high places were forbidden, a man transgressed both a positive and a negative command, but he did not thereby incur punishment by Extirpation. If they were dedicated in the time when the high places were forbidden and offered in the time when the high places were permitted, by reason of them a man transgressed a positive but not a negative command.

10. These Hallowed Things were [always] offered in the tabernacle: Hallowed Things that were dedicated to the tabernacle: [namely] the offerings of the congregation were offered in the tabernacle, but the offerings of individuals on any high place; the offerings of individuals which were dedicated to the tabernacle were offered in the tabernacle, but if a man offered them on a high place he was not culpable. How did a private high place differ from a public high place?[12] In the laying on of hands,[13] slaughtering on the north side,[14] sprinkling the blood around[15] [the Altar], the waving,[16] the bringing near[17] (R. Judah says: There was no Meal-offering on a high place), the priestly service,[18] the garments of ministry,[19] the vessels of ministry,[20] the sweet-smelling savour, the dividing-line for [the sprinkling of] the blood,[21] and the washing of hands and feet.[22] But they were alike in what concerned the time [of consuming the offerings], and the laws of Remnant[23] and of uncleanness.[24]

[1] Josh. 18[1]. Cf. Meg. 1[11].
[2] In 1 Sam. 1[24] the Temple is referred to as a 'house' (i.e. of stonework) as distinct from a tent or tabernacle.   [3] See Deut. 12[9].   [4] Deut. 14[23].
[5] 1 Sam. 21[1].   [6] 1 Kings 3[4].   [7] See Deut. 12[9].
[8] Set apart to be brought to the Temple as an offering.
[9] Deut. 12[11].   [10] Deut. 12[13].   [11] Lev. 17[9].
[12] Such as Gilgal, Nob, and Gibeon.   [13] Cf. Lev. 1[4f].
[14] Cf. Lev. 1[11].   [15] Cf. Lev. 1[5].   [16] Cf. Lev. 14[12].   [17] Cf. Lev. 2[8].
[18] Cf. Lev. 17[6].   [19] Cf. Ex. 28[43].   [20] Cf. Num. 4[12].   [21] Cf. Ex. 27[5].
[22] Cf. Ex. 30[20]; 40[31f].   [23] See above, p. 471, n. 10.   [24] See above, p. 471, n. 11.

MENAHOTH ('MEAL-OFFERINGS')

1. 1. All Meal-offerings from which the Handful[1] was taken under some other name[2] remain valid[3] (but they do not count to their owner in fulfilment of his obligation)[4] excepting the Sinner's Meal-offering[5] and the Suspected Adulteress's Meal-offering.[6] The Sinner's Meal-offering and the Suspected Adulteress's Meal-offering—if the Handful was taken from them under some other name, or if they were put into the vessel, conveyed, and burnt under some other name, or under their own and [then] under another name, or under another and [then] under their own name, they become invalid. How [can they be treated] 'under their own and [then] under another name'? If [they were treated first] under the name of a Sinner's Meal-offering and [then] under the name of a freewill Meal-offering. And how [can they be treated] 'under another name and [then] under their own name'? If [they were treated first] under the name of a freewill Meal-offering and [then] under the name of a Sinner's Meal-offering.

2. It is all one whether it is a Sinner's Meal-offering or any other Meal-offering: they become invalid if the Handful was taken from them by one that is not[7] a priest or by a priest that is mourning his near of kin or that had immersed himself [because of uncleanness] the selfsame day, or that is not clothed [in proper raiment], or whose atonement is yet incomplete, or that has not washed his hands and feet, or that is uncircumcised, or unclean, or that ministers while sitting, or while standing on any article, or on the back of a beast, or on his fellow's feet. If he took the Handful in his left hand it becomes invalid. Ben Bathyra says: He may put it back and take it again with his right hand. It becomes invalid if, on taking the Handful, he took up also a small stone or a piece of salt or a grain of frankincense; for they have said: The Handful that is too much or too little is invalid. When is it too much? If he took an overflowing handful. And too little? If he took the Handful with the tips of his fingers only. How should he take it? He should stretch his fingers over the palm of his hand.

3. If he put in too much oil or if he put in too little oil,[8] or if he put in too little frankincense,[9] it becomes invalid. If he took the Handful from the Meal-offering [purposing] to eat the residue outside[10] [the Temple Court], or [to eat] outside an olive's bulk of the residue, or to burn the Handful thereof outside, or an olive's bulk of the Handful thereof outside, or to burn the frankincense thereof outside, it becomes invalid but punishment by Extirpation is not thereby incurred. [If he intended] to eat the residue on the morrow, or [to eat] an olive's bulk of the residue on the morrow, or to burn the Handful thereof on the morrow, or to burn

---

[1] Lev. 2². From most Meal-offerings the priest took up a handful and burnt it on the Altar; the residue was a perquisite of the priests. The fixed routine in making the Meal-offering was: taking the Handful from the Meal-offering as brought by the giver, putting it into a vessel of ministry, conveying it up to the Altar, and burning it.

[2] For the varieties of Meal-offering from which the Handful was taken see below, 6³. Besides not counting to its giver if, e.g., the Meal-offering of the Baking-pan was offered under some other name, it was also invalid if it was offered on behalf of some other than its actual giver.

[3] So that the Handful may be burnt on the Altar and the residue consumed by the priests.

[4] Cf. p. 468, n. 2.   [5] Lev. 5¹¹⁻¹³.   [6] Num. 5¹⁵; Sot. 2¹.   [7] See Zeb. 2¹.

[8] A log of oil was the prescribed quantity for each Tenth of an Ephah of fine flour. Cf. Lev. 2¹; 5¹¹.

[9] The prescribed quantity was one handful, however much the Meal-offering. below, 13³.   [10] Cf. Zeb. 2².

an olive's bulk of the Handful thereof on the morrow, or to burn the frank-incense thereof on the morrow, it becomes Refuse[1] and punishment by Extirpation is thereby incurred. This the general rule: if he took the Handful or put it into the vessel or conveyed it or burnt it [purposing] to eat a thing that it is usual to eat, or to burn a thing that it is usual to burn, outside its proper place, it becomes invalid, but punishment by Extirpation is not thereby incurred; but if [he purposed the like] outside its proper time, it becomes Refuse and punishment by Extirpation is thereby incurred, provided that what makes [the offering] permissible[2] is offered according to its prescribed rite. How is 'what makes [the offering] permissible' offered according to its prescribed rite? If he took the Handful in silence,[3] and put it into the vessel and conveyed it and burnt it [while purposing an act] outside its proper time; or if he took the Handful [while purposing an act] outside its proper time, but put it into the vessel and conveyed it and burnt it in silence; or if he took the Handful and put it into the vessel and conveyed it and burnt it [while purposing an act] outside its proper time—such is a case where 'what makes [the offering] permissible' is offered according to its prescribed rite.

4. How is 'what makes [the offering] permissible' offered not according to its prescribed rite? If he took the Handful [while purposing an act] outside its proper place, and put it into the vessel and conveyed it and burnt it [while purposing an act] outside its proper time; or if he took the Handful [while purposing an act] outside its proper time, and put it into the vessel and conveyed it and burnt it [while purposing an act] outside its proper place; or if he took the Handful and put it into the vessel and conveyed it and burnt it [while purposing an act] outside its proper place; or if it was a Sinner's Meal-offering or the Suspected Adulteress's Meal-offering and he took the Handful from them under another name and put it into the vessel and conveyed it and burnt it [while purposing an act] outside its proper time; or if he took the Handful from them [while purposing an act] outside its proper time and put it into the vessel and conveyed it and burnt it under another name; or if he took the Handful from them and put it into the vessel and conveyed it and burnt it under another name, such is a case where 'what makes [the offering] permissible' is offered not according to its prescribed rite. [If he purposed] to eat an olive's bulk outside and an olive's bulk on the morrow; or an olive's bulk on the morrow and an olive's bulk outside, or a half-olive's bulk outside and a half-olive's bulk on the morrow; or a half-olive's bulk on the morrow and a half-olive's bulk outside, it becomes invalid but punishment by Extirpation is not thereby incurred. R. Judah says: This is the general rule: if the intention about time preceded the intention about place, the offering becomes Refuse and punishment by Extirpation is thereby incurred; but if the intention about place preceded the intention about time, the offering becomes invalid, but punishment by Extirpation is not thereby incurred. But the Sages say: In both cases the offering becomes invalid and punishment by Extirpation is not thereby incurred. [If he purposed] to eat a half-olive's bulk and to burn a half-olive's bulk [outside the proper time or place], the offering remains valid, since eating and burning cannot be included together.

---

[1] See p. 470, n. 1.   [2] The Handful and the frankincense. Cf. p. 470, n. 2.
[3] See p. 470, n. 3.

2. 1. If he took the Handful from the Meal-offering [purposing] to eat the residue or to burn the Handful on the morrow, R. Jose agrees that the Handful becomes Refuse and that punishment by Extirpation is thereby incurred. [If he purposed] to burn the frankincense thereof on the morrow, R. Jose says: It becomes invalid and punishment by Extirpation is not thereby incurred. But the Sages say: It becomes Refuse and punishment by Extirpation is thereby incurred. They said to him: How does this differ from an animal-offering? He said to them: With an animal-offering the blood, the flesh, and the sacrificial portions are from the one thing; but the frankincense does not come from the Meal-offering.[1]

2. If a man slaughtered the two lambs[2] [and purposed] to eat one of the [two] loaves[3] on the morrow, or if he offered the two dishes[4] [of frankincense, purposing] to eat one of the rows [of Shewbread] on the morrow, R. Jose says: That loaf and that row about which he purposed become Refuse and punishment by Extirpation is thereby incurred, while the other becomes invalid and punishment by Extirpation is not thereby incurred. But the Sages say: Both alike become Refuse and punishment by Extirpation is thereby incurred. If one of the loaves or one of the rows contracted uncleaness, R. Judah says: They must both be taken to the place of burning, since an offering of the congregation may not be divided. But the Sages say: The unclean [must be treated] as unclean, but what is clean may be eaten.

3. The Thank-offering can make the bread[5] to become Refuse but the bread cannot make the Thank-offering to become Refuse. Thus if a man slaughtered the Thank-offering [purposing] to eat of it on the morrow, both it and the bread become Refuse; [but if he purposed] to eat of the bread on the morrow, the bread becomes Refuse but the Thank-offering does not become Refuse. The lambs can make the bread[6] to become Refuse, but the bread cannot make the lambs to become Refuse. Thus if a man slaughtered the lambs [purposing] to eat of them on the morrow, they and the bread become Refuse; [but if he purposed] to eat of the bread on the morrow, the bread becomes Refuse, but the lambs do not become Refuse.

4. An animal-offering can make the drink-offerings[7] to become Refuse after they have been consecrated in the vessel. So R. Meir. But the drink-offerings cannot make an animal-offering to become Refuse. Thus if a man slaughtered the animal-offering [purposing] to eat of it on the morrow, both it and the drink-offerings thereof become Refuse; [but if he purposed] to offer the drink-offerings on the morrow, they become Refuse but the animal-offering does not become Refuse.

5. If he purposed an act such that would make the Handful to become Refuse but not the frankincense, or the frankincense but not the Handful, R. Meir says: The offering becomes Refuse and punishment by Extirpation is thereby incurred. But the Sages say: Punishment by Extirpation is not thereby incurred unless he made all that[8] to become Refuse which

---

[1] And the frankincense, as well as the Handful, is needful to render the offering permissible and valid.
[2] The Peace-offering at Pentecost; Lev. 23[19].
[3] Lev. 23[17].
[4] Lev. 24[7]; one dish to each row of the Shewbread.
[5] Brought as an adjunct to the Thank-offering. See Lev. 7[13].
[6] Lev. 23[19, 20].
[7] Meal-offerings are also to be understood as included within the term.
[8] Both the frankincense and the Handful.

renders [the offering] permissible. But the Sages agree with R. Meïr that if it was a Sinner's Meal-offering or a Suspected Adulteress's Meal-offering, and he purposed an act that would make the Handful to become Refuse, the offering becomes Refuse and punishment by Extirpation is thereby incurred, since it is the Handful [alone] that renders [these] permissible. If a man slaughtered one of the lambs purposing to eat the two loaves[2] on the morrow, or if he offered one of the dishes [of frankincense] purposing to eat the two rows [of Shewbread] on the morrow, R. Meïr says: The offering becomes Refuse, and punishment by Extirpation is thereby incurred. But the Sages say: It does not become Refuse unless a man makes all that to become Refuse which renders [the offering] permissible. If he slaughtered one of the lambs purposing to eat of it on the morrow, it becomes Refuse, but the other remains valid. [If he slaughtered one of the lambs] purposing to eat of the other on the morrow, they both remain valid.

2. 1. If a man took the Handful from the Meal-offering purposing to eat a thing that it is not usual to eat, or to burn a thing that it is not usual to burn, the Handful remains valid. R. Eliezer declares it invalid. [And if he purposed] to eat a thing that it is usual to eat, or to burn a thing that it is usual to burn, and it is less than an olive's bulk, the Handful remains valid. [If he purposed] to eat a half-olive's bulk and to burn a half-olive's bulk, it remains valid, since eating and burning cannot be included together.

2. If he did not pour [the oil over the fine flour], or mingle [the oil with the unleavened cakes], or break up small [the Baking-pan Meal-offering], or salt it, or wave it,[4] or bring it near, or if he broke it up too small, or did not anoint it, the Meal-offering remains valid.[6] If the Handful of one Meal-offering was confused with the Handful of another, or with the Priests' Meal-offering,[7] or with the Meal-offering of the anointed [High] Priest,[8] or with the Meal-offering offered with drink-offerings,[9] it remains valid. R. Judah says: If it is confused with the Meal-offering of the anointed [High] Priest or the Meal-offering offered with drink-offerings, it becomes invalid, since the mixture of the one[10] is thick and the mixture of the other[11] is thin, so that they become swallowed up the one into the other.

3. If two Meal-offerings from which the Handful had not been taken were mixed together, but the Handful can still be taken from each by itself, they remain valid; otherwise they become invalid. If a Handful was mixed with a Meal-offering from which the Handful had not been taken, it may not be burnt, but if it is burnt, the Meal-offering from which the Handful had been taken is reckoned to the credit of its owner,[12] but that from which the Handful had not been taken is not reckoned to the credit of its owner. If the Handful was mixed with the residue of a Meal-offering

---

[1] These two Meal-offerings have no frankincense; Lev. 5[11], Num. 5[15].
[2] Lev. 23[17]. [3] I.e. both lambs or both dishes of incense.
[4] The Omer or the Suspected Adulteress's Meal-offering. [5] See below, 6[3].
[6] In these cases for which these acts are respectively prescribed. [7] Lev. 6[23].
[8] Lev. 6[23]. These two were both to be wholly burnt.
[9] See p. 452, n. 11. Cf. below, 9[3]. This, too, was wholly burnt.
[10] The ordinary Meal-offering; it had one *log* of oil to the Tenth of an Ephah of flour.
[11] The High Priest's had three *logs* of oil to the Tenth of an Ephah of flour, while for the 'Meal-offering offered with drink-offerings' (i.e. the Meal-offering accompanying Daily and Additional Whole-offerings) the mixture was one Tenth of an Ephah and three *logs* of oil for a lamb, two Tenths and four *logs* for a ram, and three Tenths and six *logs* for a bullock. See below, 9[3]. [12] So that he need not bring another.

or with that of another Meal-offering, it should not be burnt; but if it is burnt it is reckoned to the credit of its owner. If the Handful had become unclean and yet was offered, the frontlet[1] effects acceptance,[2] but if it had been taken out [of the Temple Court] and was [afterward] offered, the frontlet does not effect acceptance; for the frontlet effects acceptance for [an offering that was afterward found to be] unclean, but it does not effect acceptance for aught taken out [from the Temple Court].

4. If the residue of a Meal-offering became unclean, or was burnt or lost, according to the rule of R. Eliezer[3] it remains valid, but according to the rule of R. Joshua it becomes invalid. If it[4] had not been put into a vessel of ministry it is invalid, but R. Simeon declares it valid. If its Handful was burnt in two portions, it remains valid.

5. The smaller part[5] of the Handful can impair [the validness] of the greater part; of the Tenth [of the Ephah][6] the smaller part can impair the greater part; of the wine[7] the smaller part can impair the greater part; of the oil, the smaller part can impair the greater part; of the fine flour and the oil, each can impair the other.

6. Of the two he-goats[8] of the Day of Atonement the one can impair the validness of the other; of the two lambs[9] of Pentecost the one can impair the validness of the other; of the two loaves[10] the one can impair the validness of the other; of the two dishes[11] [of frankincense] the one can impair the validness of the other; of the two rows[12] [of the Shewbread] the one can impair the validness of the other; the two rows and the two dishes can each impair the validness of the other; the two kinds [of cakes] in the offering of the Nazirite,[13] the three kinds used for the [Red] Heifer,[14] and the four kinds used for the Thank-offering,[15] the four kinds used for the Lulab,[16] and the four kinds used for the leper,[17] can each impair the validness of the others. The seven sprinklings[18] [of the blood] of the [Red] Heifer can each impair the validness of the others. The seven sprinklings between the bars[19] and those on the veil [of the Holy of Holies] and those on the Golden Altar can each impair the validness of the others.

7. The seven branches of the candlestick[20] can each impair the validness of the others; its seven lamps[21] can each impair the validness of the others. The two portions [of Scripture] in the *Mezuzah*[22] can each impair the validness of the other: even the shape of one letter can impair their validness. The four portions [of Scripture] in the phylacteries[23] can each impair the

[1] Ex. 28[38].   [2] See Zeb. 8[12]; cf. Pes. 7[1].
[3] Who held (Pes. 77a) that if the blood was sprinkled of a beast whose flesh became unclean or which was lost, the offering is still reckoned valid.
[4] The whole of the Meal-offering or the Handful.
[5] i.e. if aught soever was lacking in it.
[6] The quantity of flour prescribed for most Meal-offerings.
[7] Prescribed as an adjunct to most animal-offerings. It could also be offered alone as a freewill-offering.
[8] Lev. 16[5]. If one was lost or died (see Yom. 6[1]) the other by itself cannot avail; and the same principle, with the necessary modifications, applies in the rest of the items detailed in this and the following paragraphs.
[9] Lev. 23[19].   [10] Lev. 23[17].   [11] Lev. 24[5ff].   [12] Lev. 24[7].   [13] See Num. 6[15].
[14] Cedar-wood, hyssop, and scarlet wool. Num. 10[6].
[15] Unleavened cakes, unleavened wafers, cakes of soaked fine flour, and cakes of leavened bread. Lev. 7[12, 13].
[16] App. I. 20: citron with palm-branch, myrtle, and willow. Lev. 23[40].
[17] Cedar-wood, hyssop, and scarlet wool, and the two living birds. Lev. 14[6].
[18] Num. 19[4].   [19] On the Day of Atonement. Lev. 16[14-19]; cf. Yom. 5[3].
[20] Ex. 37[17].   [21] Ex. 37[23].   [22] App. I. 25.
[23] See p. 104, n. 16.

validness of the others: even the shape of one letter can impair their validness. The four Fringes[1] can each impair the validness of the others, since
the four together are one ordinance. R. Ishmael says: The four are four
ordinances.

4. 1. The blue [in the fringes] does not impair the validness of the white,
nor does the white impair the validness of the blue.[2] The phylactery of the
arm cannot impair the validness of the phylactery of the head, nor can the
phylactery of the head impair the validness of the phylactery of the arm.
The fine flour and the oil cannot impair the validness of the wine,[3] nor can
the wine impair their validness. The sprinklings [of the blood] on the outer
Altar cannot impair the validness of each other.

2. The bullocks and the rams and the he-lambs [for the Feast of Pente-
cost][4] do not impair the validness of each other. R. Simeon says: If they
had [means enough] for the many bullocks but had not [means enough]
for the drink-offerings, they should bring one bullock with its drink-
offerings and should not offer them all without drink-offerings.

3. The bullock and the rams and the lambs and the he-goat[5] do not impair the validness of the Bread-offering, nor does the Bread-offering impair
their validness. The Bread-offering can impair the validness of the lambs
but the lambs cannot impair the validness of the Bread-offering. So R.
Akiba. R. Simeon b. Nanos said: Not so, but the lambs can impair the
validness of the Bread-offering while the Bread-offering cannot impair
the validness of the lambs; for like as we find that when Israel was in the
wilderness forty years they offered lambs without the Bread-offering,[6]
so also now they may offer the lambs without the Bread-offering. R.
Simeon said: The *Halakah*[7] is according to the words of Ben Nanos, but
the reason is not according to his words; for whatsoever [offerings] were
enjoined in the Book of Numbers were offered in the wilderness; whereas
whatsoever offerings were enjoined in the Book of Leviticus were not
offered in the wilderness; but when they were come into the Land [of
Israel] they offered both kinds. Why, then, can I say that they may offer
the lambs without the Bread-offering? Because it is the lambs that
render their own offering permissible[8] without the Bread-offering;[9] but
if the Bread-offering is brought without the lambs, there is naught that
renders it permissible.

4. The Daily Whole-offerings[10] cannot impair the validness of the
Additional Offerings,[11] nor can the Additional Offerings impair the validness of the Daily Whole-offerings, nor can the Additional Offerings impair
the validness of each other. If they have not offered a lamb in the morning
they may offer it in the afternoon. R. Simeon said: When? Only when they
had acted under constraint or in error; but if they acted wantonly and
offered no lamb in the morning, they may not offer it in the afternoon. If

---

[1] See Num. 15[38]; Deut. 22[12].
[2] In each fringe there should be three white threads and one blue, or two of each. But
even if a fringe was all white or all blue it remains valid.
[3] Flour, oil, and wine were prescribed for most of the animal-offerings.
[4] Num. 28[27f].
[5] Offered with the Bread-offering at Pentecost. Lev. 23[18f].
[6] They had no flour but only manna.
[7] App. I. 11.   [8] Cf. p. 470, n. 2.
[9] Some texts omit 'without the Bread-offering'.   [10] Num. 28[3].
[11] The special supplementary offerings brought on Sabbaths, new moons, and Festival-
days; see Num. 28[9–29,38].

they have not burnt the incense[1] in the morning they may burn it in the afternoon. R. Simeon said: The whole [Incense-offering] could be offered in the afternoon, since the Golden Altar was dedicated only by the incense of sweet spices that was offered in the afternoon,[2] and the Altar of the Whole-offering only by the Daily Whole-offering of the morning, and the Table only by the Shewbread on the Sabbath, and the Candlestick only by [the kindling of] its seven lamps in the afternoon.

5. The Baken Cakes[3] of the High Priest were not brought a half[-Tenth of an Ephah] at a time; but a whole Tenth was brought; this was divided, and a half was offered in the morning and a half in the afternoon. If the [High] Priest that offered the half in the morning died, and they appointed another priest in his stead, he may not bring a half of the Tenth from his own house or the half of the Tenth of the first priest; but he must bring a whole Tenth, and bring one half, and suffer the other half to perish. Thus two halves are offered and two halves are suffered to perish. If they did not appoint another priest, at whose charges was the offering made? R. Simeon says: At the charges of the congregation. R. Judah says: At the charges of the heirs; and a whole Tenth must be offered.

5. 1. All Meal-offerings were offered unleavened, excepting the leavened [cakes prescribed] for the Thank-offering and the Two Loaves,[4] which were offered leavened. R. Meir says: The leaven for them is set apart from their own [dough] and [with this] they are leavened. R. Judah says: Even that is not the best way, but [old] leaven is brought and put into the measure and the measure is filled up [with meal]. They[5] said to him: Even so [the quantity prescribed for the Meal-offering] may sometimes be too little and sometimes too much.[6]

2. All Meal-offerings were kneaded in lukewarm water, and care was needful lest they became leavened; if they suffered the residue to become leavened they transgress a negative command, for it is written, *No meal offering which ye shall offer unto the Lord shall be made with leaven.*[7] They may become liable as well in the kneading as in the rolling and as in the baking.

3. Some [Meal-offerings] require oil and frankincense; some require oil but not frankincense; some require frankincense but not oil; and some require neither oil nor frankincense. These require both oil and frankincense: the Meal-offering of Fine Flour,[8] of the Baking-Pan,[9] of the Frying-Pan,[10] of the Cakes and of the Wafers,[11] the Meal-offering of the Priests and the Meal-offering of the anointed [High] Priest;[12] the Meal-offering of a gentile[13] and the Meal-offering of women,[14] and the Meal-offering of the *Omer.*[15] The Meal-offering offered with drink-offerings[16] requires oil but not frankincense; the Shewbread[17] requires frankincense but not oil. The Two Loaves[18] and the Sinner's Meal-offering and the Suspected Adulteress's Meal-offering[19] require neither oil nor frankincense.

---

[1] Ex. 30[7, 8]. Cf. Yom. 1[2].
[2] Some texts omit 'that was offered in the afternoon'.
[3] Lev. 6[21]. These were offered daily, and not only 'in the day when he is anointed'. Cf. Tam. 1[3]; Midd. 1[4].
[4] At Pentecost. See Lev. 23[17].   [5] Some texts read 'he', i.e. R. Meir.
[6] In bulk, depending on whether the yeast was thin or thick in consistency.
[7] Lev. 2[11].   [8] Lev. 2[1ff].   [9] Lev. 2[5f].   [10] Lev. 2[7].   [11] Lev. 2[4].   [12] Lev. 6[20ff].
[13] Cf. Shek. 1[5].   [14] As a freewill-offering.   [15] Lev. 23[9-14].
[16] See p. 472, n. 11. Cf. below, 9[6].   [17] Lev. 24[5ff].
[18] See above, n. 4.   [19] See above, p. 491, nn. 5, 6.

4. A man may become culpable both because of the oil in itself and because of the frankincense in itself. If[1] he put oil thereon he makes it invalid, and if frankincense, he must pick it off again. If he put oil on the residue he has not transgressed a negative command.[2] If he but put the one vessel above the other vessel[3] he does not make it invalid.

5. Some [Meal-offerings] require bringing near[4] but not waving;[5] some require waving but not bringing near; some require both bringing near and waving; some require neither bringing near nor waving. These require bringing near but not waving: the Meal-offering of Fine Flour, of the Baking-Pan, of the Frying-Pan, of the Cakes, and of the Wafers, the Meal-offering of the Priests and the Meal-offering of the anointed [High] Priest, the Meal-offering of a gentile, and the Meal-offering of women, and the Sinner's Meal-offering. R. Simeon says: Bringing near does not apply to the Meal-offering of the Priests and the Meal-offering of the anointed [High] Priest, since no Handful is taken from them;[6] and where no Handful is taken no bringing near is needed.

6. These require waving but not bringing near: the leper's *log* of oil and his Guilt-offering[7] (also the First-fruits,[8] according to R. Eliezer b. Jacob) and the sacrificial portions of the Peace-offering of the individual and the breast and the thigh thereof whether [they are the offerings of] men or women,[9] ([and the waving must be fulfilled] by Israelites and not by others);[10] and the Two Loaves and the Lambs of Pentecost. How is the waving fulfilled? The Two Loaves are put beside the two Lambs, and he puts his two hands beneath them and swings them forward and backward and upward and downward, for it is written, *Which is waved and which is heaved up*.[11] The waving was on the east side and the bringing near on the west side, and the acts of waving came before the acts of bringing near. The Meal-offering of the *Omer* and the Suspected Adulteress's Meal-offering require both waving and bringing near. The Shewbread and the Meal-offering offered with drink-offerings require neither waving nor bringing near.

7. R. Simeon says: For three kinds [of offering] there are required three rites, two always for each kind [of offering] but not the third. And these are they: the Peace-offerings of the individual and the Peace-offerings of the congregation, and the leper's Guilt-offering. The Peace-offerings of the individual require laying on of hands for the living beasts and waving after they are slaughtered, but waving is not required for living beasts. The Peace-offerings of the congregation require waving both for the living beasts and also after they are slaughtered, but the laying on of hands is not required. The leper's Guilt-offering requires the laying on of hands and waving for the living beast, but waving is not required after it is slaughtered.

8. If a man said, 'I pledge myself to a Baking-Pan [Meal-offering]', he may not bring a Frying-Pan [Meal-offering]; and if 'to a Frying-Pan [Meal-offering]', he may not bring a Baking-Pan [Meal-offering]. Wherein does

---

[1] When oil or frankincense are not prescribed.   [2] Lev. 5[11].
[3] The one containing oil or frankincense over one containing the Meal-offering.
[4] To the Altar; Lev. 2[8].   [5] See par. 6.
[6] They are burnt in their entirety.   [7] Lev. 14[10, 12].
[8] Deut. 26[4].   [9] Lev. 7[30]; 10[15].
[10] Because of Lev. 7[29], 'Speak unto the sons of Israel', thus excluding women and gentiles.
[11] Ex. 29[27].

a baking-pan differ from a frying-pan? Only in that the frying-pan has a cover and the baking-pan has no cover. So R. Jose[1]. [Others] R. Hanina b. Gamaliel says: A frying-pan is deep and what is cooked therein quivers, while the baking-pan is flat and what is cooked therein [is hard].

9. If a man said, 'I pledge myself to a Meal-offering [baked] in an oven', he may not bring what is baked in a stove or baked on hot tiles or baked in the cauldrons of the Arabs.' R. Judah says, If he wished to bring what is baked in a stove. [If he said] 'I pledge myself to a baked Meal-offering', he may not offer the half in cakes and half [in wafers]. R. Simeon permits it since both are a [kind of] baking.

6.[2] 1. From these Meal-offerings is the Handful taken, and what [residue] falls to the priests: the Meal-offering of fine flour, and that of the Baking-Pan, and of the Frying-Pan, of the Cakes and of the Wafers, the Meal-offering of a Gentile, the Meal-offering of women, the Meal-offering of the Omer, the Sinner's Meal-offering, and the Suspected [Wife's] Meal-offering. R. Simeon says: The Handful is taken from the Meal-offering brought by priests and the Handful and the residue are offered each by itself.[3]

2. The Meal-offering of the Priests, and the Meal-offering of the anointed [High] Priest, and the Meal-offering of the Drink-offerings belong wholly to the Altar and the priests have no share therein; here in the Altar exceeds the right of the priests. The [Two Loaves] and the Shewbread belong to the priests and the Altar has no share in them; here the right of the priests exceeds the right of the Altar.

3. All Meal-offerings that are made ready in a vessel require three [things] in the putting in of the oil—pouring in of oil in the vessel, putting [the meal] in the oil], and [again] putting in oil in the vessel; the cakes must be made ready. The cakes, too, were mingled [with oil]. So R. Judah. But the Sages say: The fine flour [only].[4] The cakes required to be moistened with oil and the wafers to be anointed. How did they anoint them? In the form of [a cross like the Greek letter] Chi.[5] And the residue of the oil was consumed by the priests.

4. All Meal-offerings that are made ready in a vessel require to be broken in pieces. The Meal-offering of an Israelite was folded into two and the two parts into four, and so sundered; and the Meal-offering of the Priests was folded into two and the two parts into four, but it was not sundered. The Meal-offering of the anointed [High] Priest was not folded. R. Simeon says: Neither the Meal-offering of the Priests nor the Meal-offering of the anointed [High] Priest was broken in pieces, since the Handful was not taken from them; and where the Handful is not taken there is no breaking in pieces. And all of them must be broken up into small pieces the size of an olive.

5. All Meal-offerings require to be rubbed three hundred times and beaten five hundred times. The rubbing and the beating apply to the dough of wheat. R. Jose says: To the dough also. All Meal-offerings were offered ten at a time, excepting the Shewbread and the [Two Loaves] of the [Feast]

[1] See Kel. 5[6].
[2] See above, 5[7].
[3] Burnt separately, since they . . .
[4] Judah the Patriarch.
[5] Cf. p. 636, n. 3.

Priest, which were offered twelve at a time. So R. Judah. R. Meir says: All were offered twelve at a time excepting the cakes of the Thank-offering and of the Nazirite's offering, which were offered ten at a time.

6. The [Meal-offering of the] *Omer* was offered of the Tenth [of an Ephah] taken from three *seahs*;[1] the Two Loaves[2] were of two Tenths taken from three *seahs*; the Shewbread[3] was of twenty-four Tenths taken from twenty-four *seahs*.

7. The *Omer* was sifted through thirteen sieves, the Two Loaves through twelve, and the Shewbread through eleven. R. Simeon says: There was no prescribed number, but they used to bring fine flour that was properly sifted, as it is written, *And thou shalt take fine flour and bake it;*[4] [thou shalt not bake it] until it has been properly sifted.

7. 1. The Thank-offering[5] was brought from five *seahs*, Jerusalem measure (which are six *seahs* Wilderness measure), or two Ephahs (and the Ephah is three *seahs*), or twenty Tenths [of an Ephah], ten for what was leavened and ten for what was unleavened. 'Ten for what was leavened'—one Tenth for each cake. 'And ten for what was unleavened': of what was unleavened there were three kinds—cakes, wafers, and soaked cakes; thus there were three and a third Tenths of each kind, three cakes to every Tenth. By Jerusalem measure there were thirty *kabs*,[6] fifteen for what was leavened and fifteen for what was unleavened; 'fifteen for what was leavened'—a *kab* and a half for each cake. 'Fifteen for what was unleavened': of what were unleavened there were three kinds—cakes, wafers, and soaked cakes; thus there were five *kabs* for each kind, two cakes to every *kab*.

2. For the Consecration[-offering][7] they brought what was unleavened in like manner as for the Thank-offering—cakes, wafers, and soaked cakes. For the Nazirite's offering[8] they brought twice as much of what was unleavened as for the Thank-offering—cakes and wafers, but not soaked cakes; thus there were ten *kabs*, Jerusalem measure, which are six Tenths and something over. And from each one[9] they took one part in ten as Heave-offering, as it is written, *And of it he shall offer one out of each oblation for an heave offering unto the Lord;*[10] one—therefore it may not be taken broken; *out of each oblation*—that every kind from the offering should be equal and that Heave-offering should not be taken from the one kind instead of from another; *it shall be the priest's that sprinkleth the blood of the peace offerings*—and the residue was consumed by the owner.

3. If a man slaughtered the Thank-offering within [the Temple Court] and the Bread[-offering] thereof was outside the wall,[11] the bread is not made holy. If he slaughtered it before [the loaves] became crusted in the oven, or even if all save one had crusted, the bread is not made holy. If he slaughtered it [while purposing an act] outside its proper time or outside

<hr />

[1] Of barley, re-ground and re-sifted until the quantity was reduced to one-tenth; i.e. the bulk was reduced from three *seahs* to three-tenths of a *seah* (three *seahs* equals one Ephah).
[2] The flour for these was ground and sifted until it was reduced from three *seahs* to three-fifths of a *seah*.
[3] Its flour was sifted until it was reduced from twenty-four *seahs* to seven and a fifth *seahs*.
[4] Lev. 24[5].   [5] See Lev. 7[12f].   [6] App. II, D.   [7] See Lev. 8[26].
[8] Num. 6[15].
[9] Of the four kinds of bread from the Thank-offering and of the two kinds from the Nazirite's offering.   [10] Lev. 7[14].
[11] It is in doubt whether the wall of the City or the wall of the Temple Court is intended. R. Johanan (Gem. 75b) explains it as 'the wall of Bethphage': Bethphage marked the limit of the confines of Jerusalem. Cf. below, 11[2].

its proper place the bread is none the less made holy. If he slaughtered it and it was found *terefah*,[1] the bread is not made holy. If he slaughtered it and it was found to have a blemish, R. Eliezer says: The bread is none the less made holy. But the Sages say: It is not made holy. If he slaughtered it under another name (so, too, if the ram of the Consecration[-offering] and the two lambs offered at Pentecost were slaughtered under another name), the bread is not made holy.

4. If the drink-offerings[2] were already made holy in the vessel[3] [of ministry] and the animal-offering was found invalid, and there was also there another animal-offering, they may be offered with it; otherwise they are left to become invalid by remaining overnight.[4] Bread is not required with the young[5] of [a mother-beast that was brought as] a Thank-offering, or with its Substitute,[6] or with a beast that was set apart in the place of another that was set apart and was lost; for it is written, *And he shall offer with the sacrifice of thank-offering*;[7] for the Thank-offering [itself alone] is the bread required; the bread is not required for its young or for what is brought in its stead or for its Substitute.

5. If a man said, 'I pledge myself to a Thank-offering', he must bring both it and the bread thereof from what is unconsecrated. [If he pledged himself to offer] the Thank-offering from what is unconsecrated and the bread thereof from Tithe,[8] he must none the less bring both the Thank-offering and the bread thereof from what is unconsecrated. [If he pledged himself to offer] the Thank-offering from Tithe and the bread thereof from what is unconsecrated he may do so. [If he pledged himself to offer] both the Thank-offering and the bread thereof from Tithe, he may do so; but he may not bring it from Second Tithe wheat but only from [what was bought with] Second Tithe redemption money.

6. Whence do we learn that if a man says, 'I pledge myself to a Thank-offering', he may bring it only from what is unconsecrated? Because it is written, *And thou shalt sacrifice the passover unto the Lord thy God of the flock and the herd*.[9] But is not the Passover-offering brought only from the lambs or from the goats? Why then is it written, *of the flock and the herd*? It is but to compare with the Passover-offering whatsoever is brought from the flock and the herd: like as the Passover-offering is offered in duty bound and offered only from what is unconsecrated, so whatsoever is offered in duty bound may be offered only from what is unconsecrated. Hence if a man says, 'I pledge myself to a Thank-offering', or 'I pledge myself to a Peace-offering', since these are offered in duty bound they may be offered only from what is unconsecrated. The drink-offerings in every case may be offered only from what is unconsecrated.

8. 1. All the [Meal-]offerings of the congregation or of the individual may be offered from [what is grown] within the Land [of Israel] or outside the Land, from fresh [produce][10] or from old, save only the *Omer*[11] and the Two Loaves,[12] which must be offered only from fresh produce and from [what

[1] App. I. 47.   [2] Under 'drink-offerings' the Meal-offerings are also included.
[3] Some texts omit 'in the vessel'.   [4] Cf. p. 165, n. 10.
[5] See Tem. 3[2].   [6] See Lev. 27[10].   [7] Lev. 7[12].
[8] Meaning 'Second Tithe', which, in accordance with the Law, he had brought up to Jerusalem to consume either in kind or by spending its money equivalent. See p. 73, n. 6.   [9] Deut. 16[2].
[10] Grown from the present year's harvest, as opposed to produce from the previous year.
[11] Lev. 23[10].   [12] Lev. 23[17].

is grown] within the Land. Moreover they must be offered from the choicest [produce]. Which is the 'choicest [produce]'? Michmas[1] and Zenoha[2] come first in their quality of fine flour; and second to them is Hapharaim[3] in the valley. The produce from any land was valid, but they used to bring it [only] from these places.

2. They may not bring it[4] from a manured field or from an irrigated field or from a tree-plantation. Yet if they did so it was valid. How was it made ready? In the first year a man would break up fresh ground and in the second sow it seventy days before Passover; thus it would bring forth fine flour in abundance. How was it tested? The [Temple-]treasurer used to thrust his hand into it; if dust came up therein it is invalid until it is sifted [afresh]. If it had become maggoty it is invalid.

3. Tekoa[5] comes first in its quality of oil. Abba Saul says: Second to it is Regeb[6] beyond Jordan. Oil from any land was valid, but they used to bring it [only] from these places. They may not bring it from a manured field or from an irrigated field or from a field sown with seed between the olive-trees, yet if they did so it was valid. They may not bring oil made from unripe olives and if they did so it was invalid. They may not bring it from dried olives which had been soaked in water or from preserved or stewed olives, and if they did so it was invalid.

4. There are three [ways of making ready the] olives, and from each of them come three kinds of oil. The first [way of making ready the] olives is this: the olives are gathered from the top of the tree, and pounded and put into the basket (R. Judah says: Around the basket);[7] this [gives] the first [kind of oil]. The olives are then pressed under the beam (R. Judah says: With stones);[8] this [gives] the second [kind]. They are again ground and pressed; this [gives] the third [kind]. The first kind is fit for the Candlestick, and the others for the Meal-offerings. The second [way of making ready the] olives is this: they are gathered [from the tree] at roof-level,[9] and pounded and put into the basket (R. Judah says: Around the basket); this [gives] the first [kind of oil]. The olives are then pressed under the beam (R. Judah says: With stones); this [gives] the second [kind]. They are again ground and pressed; this [gives] the third [kind]. The first kind is fit for the Candlestick, and the others for the Meal-offerings. The third [way of making ready the] olives is this: They are packed in the house until they are fully ripe, and then brought up and dried on the roof; they are then pounded and put into the basket (R. Judah says: Around the basket); this [gives] the first [kind of oil]. They are then pressed under the beam (R. Judah says: With stones); this gives the second [kind]. They are again ground and pressed; this [gives] the third [kind]. The first is [fit] for the Candlestick, and the others for the Meal-offerings.

5. Than the first kind of oil from the first [way of making ready the] olives there is none better; the second kind of oil from the first [way of making ready the] olives, and the first kind of oil from the second [way of making ready the] olives are equal. The third kind of oil from the first

[1] Ezra 2[27], the Michmash of 1 Sam. 13[5].
[2] Variants: Zanoha, Zataha. Cf. Zanoah, Josh. 15[34, 56].
[3] Josh. 19[19].
[4] It is matter for dispute whether the reference is to the flour for the *Omer* and the Two Loaves, or for the Meal-offerings generally.
[5] Amos 1[1].
[6] Cf. *Ant.* XIII. xv. 5.
[5] Not on the bottom, but adhering to the sides so that the oil before collecting would trickle down and not accumulate sediment.
[6] The heavier pressure of the beam would squeeze out solid matter also.
[7] i.e. from the lower branches where the olives ripen later.

[way of making ready the] olives, and the second kind of oil from the second [way of making ready the] olives, and the first kind of oil from the third [way of making ready the] olives—these are equal. The third kind of oil from the second [way of making ready the] olives and the second kind of oil from the third [way of making ready the] olives—these are equal. Than the third kind of oil from the third [way of making ready the] olives there is none worse. Moreover it might be inferred that the Meal-offerings require the purest olive oil: if the Candlestick, which appertains not to eating, needs pure olive oil, how much more then do the Meal-offerings, which appertain to eating, need pure olive oil! But Scripture says, *Pure olive oil beaten for the light*;[1] but not *pure olive oil beaten* for the Meal-offerings.

6. From whence did they bring the wine? Keruthin[2] and Hattulim[3] come first in their quality of wine; second to them are Beth Rimmah and Beth Luban[4] in the hill-country, and Kefar Signah[5] in the valley. The wine from any country was valid, but they used to bring it [only] from these places. They may not bring it from a manured field or from an irrigated field or from vineyards sown with seed between the vines; but if they did so it was valid. They may not bring it from sun-dried grapes, but if they did so it was valid. They may not bring old wine. So Rabbi. But the Sages declared it valid. They may not bring wine that had been sweetened or smoked or cooked, and if they did so it was invalid. They may not bring it [of grapes grown on] trellised vines but only from vines growing from the ground and from tended vineyards.

7. They did not put it in large store-vessels but in small jars, and they did not fill up the jars to the brim, so that its savour might spread. They did not take the wine that was at the mouth of the jar because of the scum or that at the bottom because of the lees; but from the third part that was in the midst thereof. How was it tested? The [Temple-]treasurer used to sit with a reed in his hand; when [all] the froth was poured away he struck with the reed. R. Jose b. R. Judah says: Wine on which scum has formed is invalid, for it is written, *They shall be unto you without blemish, and their Meal-offering*;[6] and *They shall be unto you without blemish, also their drink offerings.*[7]

9. 1. There were two dry-measures in the Temple, the Tenth[8] and the Half-Tenth. R. Meir says: A Tenth-measure, a [second] Tenth-measure, and a Half-tenth. For what purpose served the Tenth-measure? By it they used to measure all the Meal-offerings. They did not use a Three [-Tenths measure] for [the Meal-offering[9] for] a bullock, or a Two[-Tenths measure] for [the Meal-offering for] a ram, but they measured them by Tenths. For what purpose served the Half-Tenth measure? By it they used to measure the Baken Cakes[10] of the High Priest [which were offered] the half in the morning and the half in the afternoon.

2. There were seven liquid-measures in the Temple: the *Hin*, the Half-

---

[1] Ex. 27[20].
[2] Variant: Karuhim. Neub. (p. 83) suggests Coreae (*Ant.* xiv. iii. 4) in the north of Judea.
[3] Variant: Attulim. Perhaps (Neub., p. 83) Kefr Hatla, north of Gilgal.
[4] The present Beit Rima and Lubban, both about 20 miles north-west of Jerusalem.
[5] Neub. (p. 84) suggests Sukneh, near Jaffa.
[6] Num. 28[19f.]   [7] Num. 28[31].
[8] Of an Ephah.   [9] See below par. 3.   [10] Lev. 6[21]. Cf. above, 4[2].

Hin, the Third-of-a-*Hin*, the Quarter-*Hin*, the *Log*, the Half-*Log* and the Quarter-*Log*. R. Eliezer b. R. Zadok says: There were notches on the *Hin* measure [to mark] thus far for [the Meal-offering for] a bullock, thus far for [the Meal-offering for] a ram, and thus far for [the Meal-offering for] a lamb. R. Simeon says: There was no *Hin* measure there at all, for what would be its use? But there was there a further measure of one and a half *logs*, by which they measured the flour for the High Priest's Meal-offering—a *log* and a half in the morning and a *log* and a half in the afternoon.

3. For what purpose served the Quarter-*Log*? [To measure] a quarter-*log* of water for the leper[1] and a quarter-*log* of oil for the Nazirite.[2] For what purpose served the Half-*Log*? [To measure] a half-*log* of water for the Suspected Adulteress[3] and a half-*log* of oil for the Thank-offering.[4] And with the *Log* they used to measure [the oil] for all the Meal-offerings. Even for a Meal-offering of sixty Tenths[5] they measured out sixty *logs*. R. Eliezer b. Jacob says: Even for a Meal-offering of sixty Tenths they used only the One-*Log* measure, for it is written, *For a Meal-offering even a log of oil*.[6] Six [*logs*] were required for a bullock, four for a ram, and three for a lamb; three and a half for the Candlestick, a half-*log* for each lamp.

4. They may mix the drink-offerings[7] of rams with the drink-offerings of bullocks, or the drink-offerings of lambs with the drink-offerings of [other] lambs, or the drink-offerings of the offering of an individual with the drink-offering of the offering of the congregation, or the drink-offering of one day with the drink-offering of the day before; but they may not mix the drink-offerings of lambs with the drink-offerings of bullocks or of rams. If each was mingled by itself and they were then mixed together, they remain valid; but if they were mixed together before each was mingled by itself, they become invalid. Although the Meal-offering of the lamb that was offered with the *Omer* was doubled,[8] the drink-offerings thereof were not doubled.

5. All measures in the Temple were heaped up save only that of the High Priest which in itself contained heaped up measure.[9] Of liquid measures their overflow was holy; but of dry measures their overflow was not holy. R. Akiba says: Liquid measures are holy, therefore their overflow is holy; but dry measures are not holy, therefore their overflow is not holy. R. Jose says: Not because of that, but because that [by adding a surplus, what is in] the liquid measure is stirred up,[10] but [what is in] the dry measure is not stirred up.

6. All the offerings of an individual or of the congregation require drink-offerings[11] save only the Firstling, the Tithe [of Cattle], the Passover-offering, the Sin-offering, and the Guilt-offering;[12] but the Sin-offering and the Guilt-offering of the leper[13] require drink-offerings.

7. None of the offerings of the congregation requires laying on of hands

---

[1] Lev. 14⁵¹.   [2] For his cakes and wafers. Num. 6¹⁵.   [3] Num. 5¹⁷; Sot. 2².
[4] Lev. 7¹²f.   [5] Cf. below, 12⁴.   [6] Lev. 14²¹.
[7] The term here includes Meal-offerings.
[8] Lev. 23¹³. Two Tenths instead of the usual single Tenth.
[9] Its contents with flattened surface equalled that of the contents of the others when heaped up.
[10] The overflow is not of the surplus liquid only but also of liquid already made holy inside the measure.
[11] Num. 15⁴f. Meal-offerings are here also intended.
[12] Which are excluded by the terms of Num. 15³.
[13] Lev. 14¹⁰ explicitly prescribes Meal-offerings.

save only the bullock that is offered for the transgression [of the congregation] against any of the commandments,[1] and the scapegoat.[2] R. Simeon says: Also the goats offered by reason of idolatry.[3] All the offerings of an individual require laying on of hands save only the Firstling, the Tithe [of Cattle], and the Passover-offering. [If a man dies][4] his heir may perform the laying on of hands and bring the drink-offerings; and he may offer another beast in its stead.[5]

8. All may perform the laying on of hands[6] excepting a deaf-mute, an imbecile, a minor, a blind man, a gentile, a slave, an agent, or a woman. The laying on of hands is a residue[7] of the commandment. Both hands must be laid upon the head; and in the place[8] where they lay on the hands there they slaughter the beast and the slaughtering straightway follows the laying on of hands.

9. Greater stringency applies to the laying on of hands than to waving, and [greater stringency applies also] to waving than to the laying on of hands; for the one may perform the waving on behalf of any other fellow-owners, but the one may not perform the laying on of hands on behalf of any other fellow-owners. Greater stringency applies to waving, for waving has place both in the offerings of the congregation and in the offerings of the individual, and for beasts that are alive and after they are slaughtered, and for things that have life and for things that have not life; not so is it with the laying on of hands.

10. 1. R. Ishmael says: If the *Omer*[9] was brought on the Sabbath, it was taken from [only] three *seahs*[10] [of barley]; if on a weekday, from five. But the Sages say: It is all one whether it was a Sabbath or a weekday: it was taken from three *seahs*. R. Hanina the Prefect of the Priests says: On a Sabbath it was reaped by one man and with one sickle and into one basket; and on a weekday it was reaped by three and into three baskets and with three sickles. But the Sages say: It is all one whether it was a Sabbath or a weekday: it was reaped by three and into three baskets and with three sickles.

2. The prescribed rite for the *Omer* is that it should be brought from [barley growing] near by. If [the crop] near Jerusalem was not yet ripe, it could be brought from any place. It once happened that it was brought from Gaggoth[11] Zarifin, and the Two Loaves[12] from the plain of En Soker.[13]

3. How was it made ready? The messengers of the court used to go out on the eve of the Festival-day and tie the corn in bunches while it was yet unreaped to make it the easier to reap; and the towns near by all assembled there together that it might be reaped with much pomp. When it grew dark he called out, 'Is the sun set?' and they answered, 'Yea!' 'Is the sun set?' and they answered, 'Yea!' 'Is this a sickle?' and they answered

---

[1] Lev. 4[13-21].   [2] Lev. 16[21].   [3] Num. 15[24]. Cf. p. 463, n. 7.
[4] Leaving a beast set apart as an offering .
[5] Lev. 27[10]; and both the beasts are holy.   [6] Lev. 1[4].
[7] i.e. an act which may remain over, unperformed, since the efficacy of the atonement lies in the sprinkling of the blood. Cf. Neg. 14[10].   [8] The Temple Court.
[9] The Tenth of an Ephah of flour offered as a Meal-offering from the *Omer*, the sheaf of barley, on the second day of Passover; Lev. 23[10ff].
[10] Enough barley was reaped to make three *seahs* of meal. See above, 6[6].
[11] Variant: Gannoth, 'gardens of'. Neub., p. 81, suggests Sarafand, near Lydda.
[12] Lev. 23[17].
[13] The 'fountain of Sychar' (cf. John 4[5]). Perhaps the modern Askar, one mile east of Nablus.

'Yea!' 'Is this a sickle?' and they answered, 'Yea!' 'Is this a basket?' and they answered 'Yea!' 'Is this a basket?' and they answered, 'Yea!' On the Sabbath he called out, 'On this Sabbath?' and they answered, 'Yea!' 'On this Sabbath?' and they answered, 'Yea!' 'Shall I reap?' and they answered, 'Reap!' 'Shall I reap?' and they answered 'Reap!' He used to call out three times for every matter, and they answered, 'Yea!' 'Yea!' 'Yea!' Wherefore was all this? Because of the Boethuseans who used to say: The *Omer* may not be reaped at the close of a Festival-day.

4. They reaped it, put it into the baskets, and brought it to the Temple Court. They used to parch it with fire to fulfil the ordinance that it should be *parched with fire*.[2] So R. Meir. But the Sages say: They used to beat it with reeds and the stems of plants that the grains should not be crushed; then they put it into a hollow tube[3] wherein were holes so that the fire might prevail over all of it. They spread it out in the Temple Court so that the wind blew over it. They put it in a grist-mill and took therefrom a Tenth [of an Ephah of flour] which was sifted through thirteen sieves. What remained was redeemed and could be consumed by any one; it was liable to Dough-offering[1] but exempt from Tithes. R. Akiba declares it liable both to Dough-offering and to Tithes. Then they came to the Tenth, put in oil[5] and the frankincense thereof, poured in the oil, mingled it, waved it,[6] and brought it near,[7] took from it the Handful and offered it; and the residue was consumed by the priests.

5. After the *Omer* had been offered they used to go out and find the market of Jerusalem full of meal and parched corn, though this was not with the consent of the Sages. So R. Meir. R. Judah says: They used to do so with the consent of the Sages. After the *Omer* was offered the new corn was forthwith permitted; but for them that lived far off it was permitted only after midday. After the Temple was destroyed R. Johanan b. Zakkai ordained that it should be forbidden throughout the day of the waving.[8] R. Judah said: Is it not forbidden in the Law, in that it is written, *Until this selfsame day*?[9] Why was it permitted to them that lived far off [immediately] after midday? Because they knew that the court would not be dilatory therewith.

6. The *Omer* rendered [the fresh produce] permitted throughout the country, and the Two Loaves [rendered it permitted] within the Temple. None could offer Meal-offerings or First-fruits[10] or the Meal-offering pertaining to offerings of beasts before the *Omer*; and if they did so it was invalid. Nor could they offer them before the Two Loaves; but if they did so it was valid.

7. Wheat, barley, spelt, goat-grass, and oats are subject to Dough-offering,[11] and they can be included together;[12] and they are forbidden as

[1] In rabbinical terminology synonymous with Sadducees. They held (cf. p. 213, n. 12) that Lev. 23², 'the morrow after the Sabbath' must be taken in its literal sense, the day following the first Sabbath after Passover. The Pharisees, however, interpreted 'Sabbath' in this case as meaning 'Festival-day', i.e. the first day of Passover.
[2] Lev. 2¹⁴.   [3] See Kel. 2³.   [4] Num. 15²⁰. See Hall. 1⁴.
[5] A part of the *log* of oil before the fine flour was put in. See above, 5³.
[6] See above, 5⁶.   [7] See above, 5⁶.   [8] I.e. the second day of Passover.
[9] Lev. 23¹⁴, i.e. until the day was completed, which, according to R. Judah, overrides the following words, 'until ye have brought your oblation'.
[10] Seven weeks later, at Pentecost.   [11] Bikk. 1.   [12] See Hall. 1³. Cf. Pes. 2⁵.
[13] To make up the amount of dough (five quarter-*kabs*) which becomes liable to the law of Dough-offering. See Hall. 4⁵.

fresh produce before Passover, and they may not be reaped before the
Omer.[1] If they had taken root before the _Omer_ the _Omer_ makes them
permitted; otherwise they are forbidden until the next [year's] _Omer_ is
offered.

8. They may reap [the crop before the _Omer_] in irrigated fields in the
plains, but they may not heap it up. The men of Jericho used to reap it
with the consent of the Sages, but they stacked it against the consent of the
Sages; and the Sages did not reprove them. They may reap unripe corn
and use it as cattle fodder. R. Judah said: When? If a man had begun
[to reap it] before it had reached a third of its growth. R. Simeon says:
He may reap it and use it as fodder even after it has reached a third of its
growth.

9. It may be reaped if the ground is needed for seedlings or as a station
for mourning[2] or that the House of Study be not impeded.[3] It may not
be bound in bundles but must be left in small heaps. The rule of the
Omer is that it shall be brought from standing corn; but if this cannot
be found it may be brought from the sheaves. The rule is that it shall be
brought from fresh grain; but if this cannot be found it may be brought
from dried grain. The rule is that it shall be reaped by night; but if it
is reaped by day it is valid. Moreover the reaping [of the _Omer_] overrides
the Sabbath.

11. 1. The Two Loaves[4] were kneaded separately and baked separately.
The [loaves of the] Shewbread[5] were kneaded separately and baked in pairs.
They were made ready in a mould; and when they were taken from the
oven they were again put in a mould lest they suffer any hurt.

2. The Two Loaves and the Shewbread were alike in that they were
kneaded and rolled outside but baked inside [the Temple Court] and that
making of them did not override the Sabbath. R. Judah says: They were
wholly made ready inside [the Temple Court]. R. Simeon says: It was
always the custom to say, The Two Loaves and the Shewbread were valid
whether made in the Temple Court or in Bethphage.[6]

3. The Baken Cakes[7] of the High Priest were kneaded, rolled, and baked
within [the Temple Court] and the making of them overrode the Sabbath.
R. Akiba laid down a general rule:[8] Any work that can be done on the day
before the Sabbath does not override the Sabbath, but what cannot be
done on the day before the Sabbath overrides the Sabbath.

4. All Meal-offerings [prepared] within [the Temple Court] must be
prepared in a [sacred] vessel, but those [prepared] outside [the Temple
Court] need not be prepared in a [sacred] vessel. Of what manner[9] [were
the two kinds of loaves?]. The Two Loaves were seven [handbreadths] long
and four wide and their horns[10] were four fingerbreadths [high]. The
[loaves of the] Shewbread were ten [handbreadths] long and five wide and
their horns were seven fingerbreadths [high]. R. Judah says: Lest thou
shouldest err [remember but the words] _ZaDaD_, _YaHaZ_.[11] Ben Zoma

[1] Some texts transpose 'Passover' and '_Omer_' in this sentence, giving a clearer sense.
[2] See p. 375, n. 3.
[3] If there was no room in the House of Study a space may be cleared in the field.
[4] Lev. 23[17]. [5] Lev. 24[5]. [6] See p. 500, n. 11. [7] Lev. 6[20]. Cf. above, 4[1].
[8] See Shab. 19[1]; Pes. 6[2]. [9] Many texts omit 'of what manner'.
[10] Small pieces of dough put on the four upper corners after the manner of the horns of
the Altar.
[11] The six consonants of these words have, respectively, the numerical values 7, 4, 4, 10,
5, 7.

says: *And thou shalt set upon the table shewbread in my sight continually:*[1] it shall have [all] its surfaces visible.

5. The table was ten [handbreadths] long and five wide. [The loaves of] the Shewbread were ten [handbreadths] long and five wide; each loaf was set lengthwise across the breadth of the table and two and a half handbreadths were doubled over on either side so that its length filled the entire breadth of the table. So R. Judah. R. Meir says: The table was twelve [handbreadths] long and six wide and the [loaves of the] Shewbread were ten long and five wide; each loaf was set lengthwise across the breadth of the table and two handbreadths were doubled over on either side, and a space of two handbreadths was left in the midst, so that the wind could blow between them. Abba Saul says: There they used to put the two dishes of frankincense pertaining to the Shewbread. They said to him: Is it not written, *And thou shalt put pure frankincense upon* ('al) *each row?*[2] He answered: But is it not written, *And next unto* ('al) *him shall be the tribe of Manasseh?*[3]

6. There were four golden stays[4] there having their upper ends fashioned into branches;[5] two of them supported the one row and two the other. And there were twenty-eight reeds, each [shaped] like the half of a hollowed reed, fourteen for the one row and fourteen for the other row.[6] Neither the ordering of the reeds nor the removal thereof overrode the Sabbath, but they used to enter in on the day before the Sabbath and draw them out and lay them lengthwise on the table. Every object that was in the Temple was laid lengthwise[7] parallel with the length of the House.

7. In the Porch at the entering in of the House[8] were two tables, the one of marble and the other of gold. On the table of marble they laid the Shewbread when it was brought in and on the table of gold they laid the Shewbread when it was brought out, since what is holy must be raised [in honour] and not brought down. And within was a table of gold whereon the Shewbread lay continually. Four priests entered in, two having the two rows [of Shewbread] in their hands and two the two dishes [of frankincense]; and four went before them, two to take away the two rows and two to take away the two dishes. They that brought them in stood at the north side with their faces to the south; and they that took them away stood at the south side with their faces to the north. These drew [the old loaves] away and the others laid [the new loaves] down, and [always] one handbreadth of the one overlay one handbreadth of the other, for it is written, *Before me continually.*[1] R. Jose says: Although these [first] took away [the old loaves] and [then] the others laid [the new loaves] down, even this fulfils the rule of 'continually'. They went out and laid them on the table of gold that was in the Porch. They burnt the dishes [of frankincense] and

---

[1] Ex. 25[30].   [2] Lev. 24[7].
[3] Abba Saul refers the Sages to Num. 2[20] for proof that the preposition 'al has the sense 'by the side of'.
[4] Props, standing on the ground, two on each opposite side (north and south) of the table.
[5] Each prop had five projecting pieces in that part of it that was higher than the level of the table.
[6] The bottom loaves of each row stood on the table; three reeds were stretched across above it, their ends resting on the prop-projections; this relieved the pressure from the upper five loaves. Three reeds were similarly placed above the second, third, and fourth loaves in the row; and two only above the fifth, since it had to bear the pressure of a single loaf only.
[7] i.e. west to east.
[8] Cf. Midd. 3[7]. See Shek. 6[4], where the present passage recurs.

the loaves were shared among the priests. If the Day of Atonement fell on a Sabbath the loaves were shared out at evening. If it fell on a Friday the he-goat[1] of the Day of Atonement was consumed at evening. The Babylonians used to eat it[2] raw since they were not squeamish.[3]

8. If they set the bread in order on the Sabbath and the dishes [of frankincense] after the Sabbath, and burnt the dishes [of frankincense] on the [next] Sabbath, it is not valid, but none thereby becomes liable through [transgression of the laws of] Refuse, Remnant, or uncleanness.[4] If they set in order the bread and the dishes [of frankincense] on the Sabbath and burnt the dishes [of frankincense] after the Sabbath, it is not valid, but none thereby becomes liable through [transgression of the laws of] Refuse, Remnant, or uncleanness. If they set in order the bread and the dishes [of frankincense] after the Sabbath and burnt the dishes [of frankincense] on the [next] Sabbath, it is not valid. What should be done? It should be left until the following Sabbath, for even if it remains on the table many days it matters naught.

9. The Two Loaves were consumed never earlier than the second and never later than the third day. Thus if they were baked on the eve of the Festival-day[5] and consumed on the Festival-day, that would be the second day. If the Festival-day fell on the day after the Sabbath, they must be consumed on the third day. The Shewbread was consumed never earlier than the ninth and never later than the eleventh day. Thus if it was baked on the day before the Sabbath and consumed on the Sabbath [in the following week], that would be the ninth day; if a Festival-day fell on the day before the Sabbath, it is consumed on the tenth day; if the two Festival-days of the New Year [fell before the Sabbath] it is consumed on the eleventh day; and [the baking of] it overrides neither a Sabbath nor a Festival-day. Rabban Simeon b. Gamaliel says in the name of R. Simeon, son of the Prefect [of the Priests]: It overrides a Festival-day but not the Day of Fasting.[6]

12. 1. If Meal-offerings or drink-offerings became unclean before they were made holy in the vessel [of ministry] they may be redeemed; but they may not be redeemed after they have been made holy in the vessel [of ministry]. But Bird-offerings, the wood, the frankincense, and the vessels of ministry may not be redeemed,[7] since the rule applies only to [offerings of] cattle.

2. If a man said, 'I pledge myself to offer a Baking-Pan[8] [Meal-offering]', and he offered one made in a frying-pan;[9] or if [he pledged himself to offer] a Frying-Pan [Meal-offering] and he offered one made in a baking-pan, what he has offered he has offered, but he has not fulfilled his obligation. [But if he said, I pledge myself to offer] this [fine flour] as a Baking-Pan [Meal-offering], and he offered one made in a frying-pan, it is invalid. [If he said,] 'I pledge myself to offer two Tenths in a single vessel', and he offered them in two vessels, or 'in two vessels', and he offered them in one

---

[1] Num. 29[11], which was the only offering brought on the Day of Atonement whose flesh was to be consumed by the priest.

[2] After the day's fast; and it could not, of course, be cooked on the Sabbath. According to the Gemara (100a) they were not, actually, priests from Babylon, but Alexandrians; and the Palestinian Sages called them Babylonians in hatred of them.

[3] Cf. A. Zar. 2[5].   [4] See Zeb. 3[1].   [5] The day of Pentecost.

[6] Day of Atonement.   [7] Some texts add: 'After they have become unclean'.

[8] Lev. 2[5f].   [9] Lev. 2[7].

vessel, what he has offered he has offered, but he has not fulfilled his obligation. [If he said,] 'I pledge myself to offer these in one vessel', and he offered them in two, or [in two vessels], and he offered them in one, they are invalid. [If he said,] 'I pledge myself to offer two Tenths in one vessel', and he offered them in two, and they said to him, 'Thou didst vow to offer them in one vessel', and he [thereupon] offered them in one vessel, they are valid. But if [he still offered them] in two vessels, they are invalid. [If he said,] 'I pledge myself to offer two Tenths in two vessels', and he offered them in one, and they said to him, 'Thou didst vow to offer them in two vessels', and he [thereupon] offered them in two vessels, they are valid; but if he [still] put them into one vessel, they are reckoned as two Meal-offerings which have been mixed.

3. [If he said,] 'I pledge myself to offer a Meal-offering of barley', he must offer one of wheat; [if] 'from meal', he must offer it of fine flour; [if] 'without oil or frankincense', he must nevertheless offer with it oil and frankincense; [if] 'half a Tenth', he must offer a whole Tenth; [if] 'a Tenth and a half', he must offer two. R. Simeon declares him exempt, since he would not then be making a freewill-offering in the manner proper to them that make freewill-offerings.

4. A man may make a freewill-offering of a Meal-offering consisting of sixty Tenths, and offer them in a single vessel. If a man said, 'I pledge myself to offer sixty-one Tenths', he may offer sixty in one vessel and the one in another vessel; for in like manner the congregation, on the first Festival-day of the Feast of [Tabernacles] when it falls on a Sabbath, [bring as a Meal-offering] sixty-one Tenths; so it is enough for an individual that [his Meal-offering] should be less by one Tenth than that of the congregation. R. Simeon said: But are not some of these [sixty-one Tenths] for the bullocks and some for the lambs, and these may not be mixed the one with the other?[3] But up to sixty they may be mixed the one with the other. They said to him: Can sixty be mingled together and not sixty-one? He answered: It is so in all the measures prescribed by the Sages: a man may immerse himself in forty seahs[4] [of water], but he may not immerse himself in forty seahs less one kortab.[5] A man may not make a freewill-offering of one, two, or five logs[6] [of wine], but it must be of three, four, or six, or anything above six.

5. They may make freewill-offerings of wine but not of oil. So R. Akiba. R. Tarfon says: They may make a freewill-offering of oil. R. Tarfon said: As we find that wine which is offered as an obligation can also be offered as a freewill-offering, so oil which is offered as an obligation can also be offered as a freewill-offering. R. Akiba said to him: No! as thou arguest of wine, which can by itself be offered as an obligation, wouldest thou also argue of oil, which cannot by itself be offered as an obligation? Two men

---

[1] Since all freewill Meal-offerings must be brought from wheaten flour.
[2] See Num. 29[13ff]. For the first Festival-day's Additional offering they bring 13 bullocks (each requiring a 3 Tenths Meal-offering), 2 rams (each requiring 2 Tenths), 14 lambs (each requiring 1 Tenth); for the Sabbath Additional offering (Num. 28[9]) they bring 2 lambs (each requiring 1 Tenth); and these, added to the usual Daily Whole-offering of a lamb, morning and evening (each requiring 1 Tenth), give a total of 61 Tenths.
[3] See above, 9[4].
[4] Cf. Mikw. 1[7].
[5] App. II. D.
[6] As a separate freewill-offering, since he may bring only such quantities as conform to what is prescribed for one or for a group of specific animal-offerings; and nowhere is such a quantity as 1, 2, or 5 logs prescribed. The prescribed quantities were 3 for a lamb, 4 for a ram, and 6 for a bullock.

may not together make a freewill-offering of one Tenth; but they may
[share and may] make a freewill-offering of a Whole-offering or a Peace-
offering, or [share in offering] even a single bird of a pair.

13. 1. [If a man said,] 'I pledge myself to offer a Tenth', he must offer a
Tenth. [If] 'Tenths', he must offer two Tenths. [If he said,] 'I expressly
said [a certain number of Tenths] but I do not know what [number] I said
expressly', he must bring sixty Tenths. [If he said,] 'I pledge myself to
offer a Meal-offering', he may bring whichever kind he will. R. Judah
says: He must bring one of fine flour, since that is the special sense of the
term 'Meal-offering'.

2. [If he said, 'I pledge myself to offer] a Meal-offering', [or] 'some kind
of Meal-offering', he may bring one [of any kind]; [if] 'Meal-offerings', [or]
'some kind of Meal-offerings', he must bring two [of any kind]; [if he said]
'I expressly said [which kind] but I do not know which kind I expressly
said', he must bring the five kinds. [If he said,] 'I expressly said a Meal-
offering of [such a number of] Tenths, but I do not know what [number]
I expressly said', he must bring a Meal-offering of sixty Tenths. Rabbi
says: He must bring Meal-offerings [of every number] of Tenths from one
to sixty.

3. [If he said,] 'I pledge myself to offer [pieces of wood]', he must bring
not less than two faggots; [or if] 'frankincense', not less than a handful.
In five matters is [the quantity of] a handful prescribed: if a man said, 'I
pledge myself to offer frankincense', he may not bring less than a handful;
if he made a freewill-offering of a Meal-offering he must offer a handful of
frankincense with it; if a man offered up the Handful outside, he is culpable;
for the two dishes [of frankincense] two handfuls are required.

4. [If he said,] 'I pledge myself to give gold', he must give not less than
a golden *denar*;[1] [and if] 'silver', he must give not less than a silver *denar*;
[and if] 'copper', he must give not less than [the value of] a silver *maah*;
[and if he said,] 'I expressly said [how much I would give] but I do not
know what I expressly said', he must give [and continue to give] until he
says, 'I did not intend to give so much!'

5. [If he said,] 'I pledge myself to give wine', he must give not less than
three *logs*;[5] [and if] 'oil', not less than one *log*. Rabbi says: Three *logs*. [If
he said,] 'I expressly said [how much I would give] but I do not know what
I expressly said, he must offer what is brought on the day when most is
offered.[6]

6. [If he said,] 'I pledge myself to offer a Whole-offering', he must offer
a lamb. R. Eleazar b. Azariah says: Or a turtle-dove or a young pigeon.[7]
[If he said,] 'I expressly said [what I would offer] but I do not know what I
expressly said', he must bring a bullock or a calf. [If he said, 'I expressly
said a certain kind] of cattle, but I do not know what I expressly said', he
must bring a bullock and a young bullock, a ram, a goat, a kid, and a lamb.

[1] Lev. 2[1] is literally 'And when any *soul* will offer a meal-offering'.
[2] Of fine flour ... of a Meal-offering prepared in a baking-pan or a frying-pan, or prepared
in an oven as cakes or as wafers: five kinds in all.
[3] Shek. 6[5]. [4] App. II, A.
[5] The maximum prescribed, a quarter of a *log*, in 'meal-offerings offered with drink-
offerings' (Num. 28[5]).
[6] 365 *logs* were offered on the first day of Tabernacles. Cf. above, 9[3].
[7] As the minimum for fulfilment. See Lev. 1[14].

[If he said,] 'I expressly said [some kind], but I do not know what I expressly said', he must add thereto a turtle-dove and a young pigeon.

7. [If he said,] 'I pledge myself to offer a Thank-offering or a Peace-offering', he must bring a lamb. [If he said,] 'I expressly said [what beast], but I do not know which I expressly said', he must bring a bullock, a heifer, a young bullock, and a young heifer. [If he said, 'I expressly said a certain kind] of cattle but I do not know which I expressly said', he must bring a bullock and a heifer, a young bullock and a young heifer, a ram and a ewe, a he-kid and a she-kid, a he-goat and a she-goat, and a young ram and a ewe-lamb.

8. [If he said,] 'I pledge myself to offer an ox', he must bring one with its drink-offerings[1] to the value of a *mina*;[2] [and if] 'a young bullock', he must bring one with its drink-offerings to the value of five [*selas*]; [and if] 'a ram', he must bring one with its drink-offerings to the value of two [*selas*]; [and if] 'a lamb', he must bring one with its drink-offerings to the value of one *sela*. [If he pledged himself to offer] 'an ox valued at one *mina*', he must bring one worth a *mina*, apart from its drink-offerings; [or if] 'a young bullock valued at five [*selas*]', he must bring one worth five [*selas*], apart from its drink-offerings; [and if] 'a ram worth two', he must bring one worth two, apart from its drink-offerings; [and if] 'a lamb worth one *sela*', he must bring one worth one *sela*, apart from its drink-offerings. [If he pledged himself to offer] 'one ox worth a *mina*', and he brought two together worth a *mina*, he has not fulfilled his obligation, even if each of them was worth a *mina* less one *denar*. [If he pledged himself to offer] a black one and he brought a white one, or a white one and he brought a black one, or a large one and he brought a small one, he has not fulfilled his obligation; [but if he pledged himself to offer] a small one and he brought a large one, he has fulfilled his obligation. But Rabbi says: He has not fulfilled his obligation.

9. [If he said,] 'This ox shall be a Whole-offering', and it suffered a blemish, if he was so minded he may bring two that are of like value to the first. [If he said,] 'These two oxen shall be a Whole-offering', and they suffered a blemish, if he was so minded he may bring one that is of like value to the two. But Rabbi forbids this. [If he said,] 'This ram shall be a Whole-offering', and it suffered a blemish, if he was so minded he may bring a lamb of like value. [If he said,] 'This lamb shall be a Whole-offering' and it suffered a blemish, if he was so minded he may bring a ram of like value. But Rabbi forbids this. If a man said, 'One of my lambs shall be dedicated', or 'One of my oxen shall be dedicated', and he had two of them, the larger one must be dedicated. If he had three, the middle one must be dedicated. [If he said,] 'I expressly said [which should be dedicated] but I do not know which I dedicated', or if he said, 'My father said to me [which it should be] but I do not know which', then the largest among them must be dedicated.

10. [If he said,] 'I pledge myself to offer a Whole-offering', he must offer it in the Temple. And if he offered it in the House of Onias[3] he has not

---

[1] And Meal-offerings.   [2] App. II, A.

[3] Onias IV, *c.* 164 B.C., failing to succeed his father as High Priest in Jerusalem was welcomed in Egypt by Ptolemy VI Philometer and given a ruined temple at Leontopolis. He rebuilt it in the model of the Jerusalem Temple, but on a smaller scale, and established there the regular Jewish system of sacrifices. It continued until suppressed by the Romans at the same time as the destruction of the Jerusalem Temple. See Josephus, *Ant.* XIII. iii. 1ff.;

fulfilled his obligation. [If he said,] 'I will offer it in the House of Onias', he should offer it in the Temple, but if he offered it in the House of Onias he has fulfilled his obligation. R. Simeon says: Such is not accounted a Whole-offering. [If a man said,] 'I will be a Nazirite', he must offer the Hair-offering[1] in the Temple; and if he offered it in the House of Onias he has not fulfilled his obligation. [If he said,] 'I will offer the Hair-offering in the House of Onias', he should offer it in the Temple; but if he offered it in the House of Onias he has fulfilled his obligation. R. Simeon says: Such a one is not accounted a Nazirite. If priests have ministered in the House of Onias they may not minister in the Temple in Jerusalem; still more does this apply to [priests who have ministered in] that other matter;[2] for it is written, *Nevertheless the priests of the high places came not up to the altar of the Lord in Jerusalem, but they did eat unleavened bread among their brethren*;[3] thus they were like them that have a blemish: they may share and they may eat [of the Holy Things] but they may not offer sacrifice.

11. It is said of the Whole-offering of cattle, *a fire offering, an odour of sweet savour*;[4] and of the Bird-offering, *a fire offering, an odour of sweet savour*;[5] and of the Meal-offering, *a fire offering, an odour of sweet savour*:[6] to teach that it is all one whether a man offers much or little, if only he directs his mind towards Heaven.

HULLIN ('ANIMALS KILLED FOR FOOD')

1. 1. All[7] may slaughter and what they slaughter is valid, save only a deaf-mute, an imbecile, and a minor, lest they impair what they slaughter; but if any among these slaughtered while others beheld them,[8] what they slaughter is valid. What is slaughtered by a gentile is deemed carrion,[9] and it conveys uncleanness by carrying.[10] If a man slaughtered by night (so, too, if a blind man slaughtered) what he slaughters is valid. If he slaughtered on the Sabbath or on the Day of Atonement, although he is guilty against his own soul,[11] what he slaughters is valid.

2. If he slaughtered with a hand-sickle or with a flint or with a reed, what he slaughters is valid. All may slaughter and at any time and with any implement excepting a reaping-sickle or a saw or teeth[12] or the finger-nails,

---

Bell. I. i. 1, VII. x. 3f. The Gemara (109b) explains Onias' flight to Egypt as the result of his inciting his brother, Shimei, to serve at the Altar dressed in women's clothes.

[1] See p. 282, n. 4.   [2] Euphemism for idolatry.

[3] 2 Kings 23[9].   [4] Lev. 1[9].   [5] Lev. 1[17].   [6] Lev. 2[9].

[7] Who are skilled in the rules prescribed for slaughtering a beast. This tractate deals with the killing for food of animals not set aside and consecrated as offerings to be brought to the Temple. Deut. 12[21] ('Thou shalt kill of thy herd and of thy flock, which the Lord hath given thee, as I have commanded thee') implies the existence of a divinely ordained method of slaughtering beasts. This is not found in the Written Law, but was included in the tradition passed down through the ages, and it was received as '*Halakah* given to Moses from Mount Sinai'. According to this tradition five things must be avoided in cutting the throat in order that the slaughtering shall be valid: (*a*) there must be no delay, but the knife must be kept continually moving backwards and forwards; (*b*) no pressure may be exerted; (*c*) there may be no thrusting or digging in of the knife under the skin or between the gullet and windpipe; (*d*) the knife may not be allowed to slip beyond a certain area of the throat—from the large ring of the windpipe to the upper lobe of the inflated lungs; and (*e*) the gullet or windpipe must not be torn out of position in the course of slaughtering.

[8] To testify that the manner of slaughtering was according to the rules prescribed.

[9] Like the flesh of a beast that has died of itself.

[10] As well as by being eaten. Lev. 11[40]. See App. IV.

[11] By performing work which is forbidden on such days and which, if done deliberately, is punishable by Extirpation. See Ker. 1[1f].

[12] Fixed in the jawbone of a dead animal.

since these [do not cut but tear the windpipe and] choke [the beast]. If a man slaughtered with a reaping-sickle, drawing the blade backwards,[1] the School of Shammai declare it invalid but the School of Hillel valid; but if its teeth are filed down, then it is like to a knife.

3. If a man slaughtered [cutting] through the [top cartilage] ring [of the windpipe] and left but a thread's breadth of its whole circumference,[2] what he slaughters is valid.[3] R. Jose b. R. Judah says: [Or but] a thread's breadth of the greater part of its circumference.

4. If he slaughtered [by cutting] at the side [of the throat], what he slaughters is valid; but if he wrung off [the head of a bird] from the side, it is invalid. If he slaughtered [by cutting] at the back of the neck, what he slaughters is invalid, but if he wrung off [the head of a bird] from the back of the neck, it is valid. If he slaughtered [by cutting] below the throat, what he slaughters is valid; but if he wrung off [the head of a bird] below the throat, it is invalid; for the whole back of the neck is valid for wringing off [the head of a bird] and the whole region about the throat is valid for slaughtering [a beast]. Thus what is valid in slaughtering [a beast] is invalid in wringing off [the head of a bird], and what is valid in wringing off [the head of a bird] is invalid in slaughtering [a beast].

5. What serves to make turtle-doves valid makes young pigeons invalid, and what serves to make young pigeons valid makes turtle-doves invalid;[4] so soon as the neck-feathers of either of them grow bright they become invalid.

6. What serves to make the [Red] Heifer[5] valid makes invalid the calf [whose neck is to be broken],[6] and what serves to make the calf valid makes the [Red] Heifer invalid.[7] What does not disqualify priests[8] disqualifies levites,[9] and what does not disqualify levites disqualifies priests.[10] What does not render earthenware vessels unclean[11] renders other vessels unclean; and what does not render other vessels unclean renders earthenware vessels unclean.[12] What does not render wooden vessels unclean renders metal vessels unclean,[13] and what does not render metal vessels unclean renders wooden vessels unclean.[14] When a man[15] is liable to give Tithes from bitter almonds he is exempt from giving Tithes from sweet almonds, and when he is liable to give Tithes from sweet almonds he is exempt from giving Tithes from bitter almonds.

---

[1] The teeth of the sickle are so curved that when drawn backwards they only glide over the surface without tearing it.

[2] i.e. he cut so high that, in the direction of the head, there was left nothing but a circular section of the top ring of the windpipe as thin as a thread.

[3] Since he still cut within the prescribed area. See above, p. 513, n. 7 (d).

[4] Doves may be offered only after they have reached a certain stage of growth, and pigeons only before they have reached that stage; doves only when they are so old that when their feathers are plucked no blood is drawn, and pigeons only before their neck-feathers turn bright yellow.

[5] Num. 19[1ff]. 　　　　　　　　　　[6] Deut. 21[1ff].

[7] The Red Heifer is slaughtered, and the other has its neck broken.

[8] Age.

[9] Who became unfit for service at the age of fifty. Num. 4[23]; 8[24].

[10] Bodily blemishes. Lev. 21[16ff].

[11] When only the outside of the vessel contracts uncleanness.

[12] Other vessels become unclean by contact only, but an earthenware vessel by the presence of uncleanness in its contained air-space (see Kel. 1[1]), even without contact.

[13] Wooden utensils, as opposed to metal utensils, do not contract uncleanness unless they contain a cavity. See Kel. 15[1].

[14] Unfinished wooden utensils are susceptible to uncleanness, but not unfinished metal vessels or utensils. 　　　[15] See Maas. 1[4].

7. Unfermented grape-skin wine[1] may not be bought with [Second] Tithe money, and it renders the Immersion-pool invalid;[2] but if fermented it may be bought with [Second] Tithe money and it does not render the Immersion-pool invalid. If brothers that are jointholders are liable to surcharge[3] they are exempt from Tithe of Cattle,[4] and if they are liable to Tithe of Cattle they are exempt from surcharge. Wheresoever there is right of sale[5] no fine is incurred, and wheresoever a fine is incurred there is no right of sale. Wheresoever there is right of Refusal[6] there is no right of *halitzah*,[7] and wheresoever there is right of *halitzah* there is no right of Refusal. Whenever the *shofar* is blown no *Habdalah* prayer[8] is recited; and where the *Habdalah* prayer is recited no *shofar* is blown. Thus[9] if a Festival-day falls on a Friday the *shofar* is blown and the *Habdalah* prayer is recited; but if on the day after the Sabbath, the *Habdalah* prayer is recited and no *shofar* is blown. How do they[10] recite the *Habdalah* prayer? [They say, 'Blessed art thou] that makest distinction between one holy [season] and another holy [season!'[11] R. Dosa says: '. . . between the more holy [season] and the lesser holy [season]!'

2. 1. If a man slaughtered a bird by [cutting through] either [the windpipe or the gullet], or a beast by cutting through both, what he slaughters is valid; so, too, [if he cut through] the greater part of each. R. Judah says: [Not] unless he cut through the veins [of the neck of the bird]. [If he cut through only] the half of either [the windpipe or the gullet] of a bird, or the whole of one and a half of the other [of the windpipe and the gullet] of a beast, what he slaughters is invalid; but if [he cut through] the greater part of the one in a bird, and the greater part of them both in a beast, what he slaughters is valid.

2. If he cut through two heads at once, what he slaughters is valid; if two persons together held the knife and slaughtered, even if one held the upper and the other the lower end,[12] what they slaughter is valid.

3. If he chopped off the head with a single stroke, it is not valid; but if he was slaughtering[13] and [even so] cut off the head with one stroke, it is valid if the knife was as long again as the thickness of the neck. If in slaughtering he severed two heads at once, it is valid if the knife was as long again as the thickness of one neck.[14] This applies only if he made but one forward stroke and no backward stroke, or but one backward stroke and no forward stroke; but if he made both a forward and a backward stroke, however short [the knife], even if [he slaughtered] with a scalpel, it is valid. If the knife fell [of itself] and slaughtered [a beast], even if it

---

[1] See M.Sh. 1³; cf. Maas. 5⁶.   [2] See Mikw. 7².

[3] See Shek. 1⁷.   [4] See Bekh. 9³.   [5] See Ket. 3⁸.   [6] See Yeb. 13¹ff.

[7] See App. I. 12. It is not valid if performed by a minor (Yeb. 12⁴), and the right of Refusal is valid only if exercised by a minor.

[8] See App. I. 9. It is used only if the next day is an ordinary workday. Cf. Sukk. 5⁵. On the eve of the Sabbath they blew the *shofar* but did not say the *Habdalah* prayer.

[9] Some texts omit 'thus'.

[10] On the occasions when a Festival-day follows after the Sabbath. For 'Festival-day' see p. 181, n. 11.

[11] The usual form of the Benediction being (Singer, p. 216), 'Blessed art thou . . . who makest a distinction between holy and profane!'

[12] The knife being held on an incline. The sentence is also explained as referring to two who slaughter with separate knives at two different places, 'higher up and lower down', within the permitted portion of the neck. See above, p. 513, n. 7 (*d*).

[13] i.e. utilizing the knife in a manner which observed the five rules (p. 513, n. 7).

[14] i.e. it was 'three necks long'.

slaughtered it in proper fashion, it is invalid, for it is written, *Then thou shalt kill . . . and thou shalt eat*:[1] that which *thou* slaughterest shalt thou eat. If the knife fell [while a man was slaughtering] and he picked it up, or if his clothes fell down and he pulled them up, or if he had whetted the knife[2] and become weary, [and he broke off during the slaughtering] and his fellow came and slaughtered—if there befell a delay long enough to slaughter [a beast], it is invalid. R. Simeon says: A delay long enough to examine [the knife].

4. If he cut through the gullet but tore open the windpipe, or cut through the windpipe but tore open the gullet, or if he cut through but one of them and waited until the beast died, or if he sank the knife beneath the second [of the tubes] and so severed it, R. Yeshebab declares it carrion, but R. Akiba *terefah*.[3] R. Yeshebab in the name of R. Joshua laid down a general rule: That which becomes invalid through its manner of slaughter is carrion; but if the manner of slaughter was proper and some other matter rendered it invalid, it becomes *terefah*. And R. Akiba agreed with him.

5. If a man slaughtered cattle or a wild animal or a bird, and the blood did not flow forth, they are valid; moreover they may be eaten with unwashed hands since they have not been rendered susceptible to uncleanness through the blood.[4] R. Simeon says: They have been rendered susceptible to uncleanness through slaughtering.

6. If a man slaughtered a beast that was at the point of death, R. Simeon b. Gamaliel says: [It is not valid] unless it can jerk a fore-leg and a hind-leg. R. Eliezer says: It suffices if [when it is slaughtered] the blood spirts forth. R. Simeon said: [Even] if he had slaughtered it by night and came early in the morning and found the walls [of the neck] filled with blood, it is still valid, since its blood had spirted forth, and it has thus fulfilled the condition of R. Eliezer. But the Sages say: [It is not valid] unless it can jerk a fore-leg or a hind-leg or move its tail, no matter whether it is a small beast or a large beast. If a small beast stretched out its fore-leg but did not withdraw it, it is invalid, since this was but [a token of] its expiring. This applies if the beast was presumed to be at the point of death; but if it was presumed to be sound it is valid even if none of these tokens appeared in it.

7. If a man slaughtered for a gentile, what he slaughters is valid, but R. Eliezer declares it invalid. R. Eliezer said: Even if he slaughtered it [with the intention] that the gentile should eat but the midriff, it is invalid, since an unexpressed intention in a gentile is directed to idolatry.[5] R. Jose said: It is an argument from the less to the greater: if, where intention can render a result invalid (as with animal-offerings) it depends on him alone that performs the acts [required in the offering],[6] how much more, therefore, where intention does not render a result invalid (as in the slaughtering of unconsecrated beasts) does it depend only on him that slaughters them!

8. If a man slaughtered in honour of mountains or of hills or of seas or of rivers or of wildernesses, what he slaughters is invalid. If two took hold of the knife and slaughtered, the one in honour of any among these things

---

[1] Deut. 12²¹.   [2] Before the slaughtering.
[3] See App. I. 47. It does not convey uncleanness like carrion.
[4] See Maksh. 6⁴; Lev. 11³⁴.
[5] Even if the gentile had not said so the presumption is that he intended to eat or offer the flesh in honour of his god.
[6] In the course of his slaughtering, receiving the blood, conveying it, and sprinkling it. See Zeb. 4⁶. The intention of the owners has no power to render the offering invalid.

and the other in honour of a thing permitted, what is slaughtered is invalid.

9. None may slaughter [in such wise that the blood falls] into the sea or into rivers[1] or into vessels; but they may slaughter [in such wise that the blood falls] into a hollow filled with water, or over the outside of vessels on a ship [so that the blood flows into the sea].[2] None may slaughter [in such wise that the blood falls] into any manner of [empty] hole, but a man may make a hole in his house for the blood[3] to flow into; he may not, however, do so in the [open] street lest he confirm the heretics[4] in their ways.

10. If a man slaughtered [an unconsecrated beast outside the Temple Court] under the name of a Whole-offering or a Peace-offering or a Suspensive Guilt-offering[5] or a Passover-offering or a Thank-offering, what he slaughters is invalid. But R. Simeon declares it valid. If two took hold of the knife and slaughtered, the one under the name of any of these things, and the other under the name of a thing permitted, what is slaughtered is invalid. If a man slaughtered [an unconsecrated beast outside the Temple] under the name of a Sin-offering or an Unconditional Guilt-offering[6] or as a Firstling[7] or as Tithe [of Cattle][8] or as a Substitute[-offering],[9] what he slaughters is valid. This is the general rule: If it is a beast that can be vowed or offered as a freewill-offering, and a man slaughtered it under that name, it is invalid; but if it is not such that can be vowed or offered as a freewill-offering and a man slaughtered it under that name, it is valid.

3. 1. These[10] are accounted *terefah* among cattle: if the gullet is pierced or the windpipe torn; or if the membrane of the brain is pierced; or if the heart is pierced as far as the cells thereof; or if the spine is broken and the spinal cord severed; or if the liver is gone and naught soever of it remains; or if the lung is pierced or defective (R. Simeon says: [It is not *terefah*] unless its bronchial tubes[11] are pierced); if the maw is pierced, or the gall-bladder, or the intestines; or if the innermost stomach is pierced, or if the greater part of its outer coating is torn (R. Judah says: A handbreadth in large cattle, or the greater part in small cattle); or if the omasum[12] or the second stomach is pierced on its outermost side; or if the beast has fallen from the roof, or has most of its ribs broken, or if it has been mauled by a wolf (R. Judah says: Small cattle—if they have been mauled by a wolf; large cattle—if they have been mauled by a lion; small birds—if they have been mauled by a hawk; and larger birds—if they have been mauled by a vulture). This is the general rule: If it could not continue alive[13] in like state it is *terefah*.

2. And these are accounted [still] valid among cattle: if the windpipe is pierced or slit (How large may be the hole? Rabban Simeon b. Gamaliel says: As large as an Italian *issar*);[14] if the skull is defective but the membrane of the brain unpierced; if the heart is pierced but not so far as the cells thereof; if the spine is broken but the spinal cord is unsevered; if the liver

---

[1] Lest he appear to slaughter in their honour.
[2] So that he will not appear to be collecting the blood to sprinkle idolatrously, but only as saving the ship from becoming dirty.   [3] Of a beast slaughtered in the courtyard.
[4] Whose method of slaughtering this is.   [5] Lev. 5[17-19].
[6] As enjoined in the cases detailed (see Zeb. 5[5]) in Lev. 5[15]; 6[6]; 14[12]; 19[20ff]; Num. 6[12].
[7] Ex. 13[13]; 34[20]; Num. 18[15].   [8] Lev. 27[32].   [9] Lev. 27[10].
[10] Eighteen signs of *terefah*. Maimonides defines seventy signs.
[11] Or main lung arteries.   [12] The third stomach of a ruminant.
[13] For twelve months.   [14] App. II, A.

is gone but an olive's bulk of it remains; if the omasum or the second stomach is pierced [with holes leading] the one into the other; if the spleen is gone or the kidneys or the lower jaw or the womb, or if [a lung] is dried by an act of heaven.[1] If it has lost its hide R. Meir declares it valid, but the Sages invalid.

3. These are accounted *terefah* among birds: if the gullet is pierced or the windpipe severed; or if a weasel has wounded it in the head where it could render it *terefah*;[2] or if the stomach is pierced, or the small intestines. If it fell into the fire and its inward parts were scorched and they have turned green, it is invalid, but if they remained red, it is valid. If a man mauled it or knocked it against a wall, or if cattle trampled over it but it still flutters and continues alive for one day, and it is then slaughtered, it is valid.

4. And these are accounted [still] valid among birds: if the windpipe is pierced or slit; if a weasel has wounded it on the head where it cannot render it *terefah*; or if its craw has been pierced (Rabbi says: Even if it is gone); if its inward parts protrude but are not pierced; if its wings are broken; if its legs are broken, or if its wing-feathers are plucked. R. Judah says: If its down is gone it is invalid.

5. If [a beast] suffers from congestion of the blood, or is overcome by smoke, or is frozen,[3] or if it has eaten oleander or fowl's offal or drunk filthy water, it is still valid; but if it has eaten poison, or if a serpent has bitten it, although it is not forbidden as *terefah* it is forbidden as a danger to life.[4]

6. The tokens[5] in cattle and wild animals are enjoined in the Law, but not those in birds.[6] But the Sages have said: Any bird that seizes food in its claws is unclean; and any that has an extra talon and a craw and the skin of whose stomach can be stripped off, is clean. R. Eliezer b. Zadok says: Any bird that parts its toes evenly is unclean.

7. Among locusts[7] [these are clean]: all that have four legs, four wings, and jointed legs, and whose wings cover the greater part of their bodies. R. Jose says: Or that are called by the name 'locust'.[8] And among fishes: All that have fins and scales. R. Judah says: Two scales and one fin [suffice]. The scales must be such as are immovable, and the fins the means by which it swims.[9]

4. 1. If a beast was in hard travail and the young put forth its fore-leg and then withdrew it,[10] it[11] may be eaten. If it put forth its head yet withdrew it again, it is deemed [fully] born. If aught was cut off from the young while it was yet in the womb,[12] it may be eaten; but if aught was cut from the spleen or the kidneys [of the dam] it may not be eaten. This is the general rule: What is from the dam's body is forbidden; but what is not from her body is permitted.

2. If a beast that had not before borne young was in hard travail, the members [of the young] may be cut off one by one and thrown to the dogs;

---

[1] Shrivelled from fright by thunder and lightning. But if by act of man or by the roaring of a lion, or the like, it is *terefah*.

[2] By piercing the membrane of the brain.

[3] Some texts omit 'frozen'.   [4] Cf. Ter. 8[6].

[5] By which they are recognized as clean or fit for food. See Lev. 11[1-8]; Deut. 14[3-8].

[6] Cf. Lev. 11[13-23]; Deut. 14[11-20].   [7] See Lev. 11[21f].

[8] To include the varieties (Cf. Lev. 11[22]) that come under the general title of 'locust'.

[9] And not limbs by which it can propel itself on dry land.

[10] And the dam was then slaughtered.

[11] The young; it does not count as a born and living beast that must itself be slaughtered before it may be eaten.

[12] And it was left there, and the dam was then slaughtered.

if the greater part of it had come forth it must be buried, and the dam is exempt from the law of the Firstling.[1]

3. If the young of a beast died in the dam's womb and the herdsman put in his hand and touched it he remains clean whether it was a clean or an unclean beast. R. Jose the Galilean says: He is unclean if it was an unclean beast but clean if it was a clean beast. If the young of a woman died in its mother's womb, and the midwife put in her hand and touched it, the midwife contracts seven-day uncleanness,[2] but the mother remains clean until the child comes forth.

4. If a beast was in hard travail and the young put forth its fore-leg and a man cut it off and then slaughtered the dam, the [whole] flesh is clean.[3] But if he slaughtered the dam and afterward cut off the fore-leg, the flesh [is reckoned as flesh that] has suffered contact with carrion.[4] So R. Meir. But the Sages say: [Only as flesh that has suffered] contact with *terefah*[5] that has been slaughtered; for like as we find that slaughtering renders clean what is *terefah*,[6] so the slaughtering of the beast renders clean the [protruding] member. R. Meir answered: Not so! if the slaughtering of *terefah* renders it clean where the beast [alone] is concerned, can it also render clean the limb which does not pertain to the beast? Whence do we learn that slaughtering renders *terefah* clean? An unclean beast is forbidden as food; *terefah* also is forbidden as food; then as slaughtering does not render clean an unclean beast [must we conclude that] slaughtering does not render *terefah* clean? Not as thou arguest of an unclean beast (which has had no time when it was valid) canst thou argue also of *terefah* (which has had a time when it was valid). Take away such ground for inference! Whence do we learn [the like] touching what was born *terefah* from the womb? [From this inference]: Not as thou arguest of an unclean beast (to which kind slaughtering does not apply) canst thou argue also of *terefah* (to which kind slaughtering does apply). Slaughtering does not render clean a live eight months' birth[7] since slaughtering does not apply to such a kind.[8]

5. If a man slaughtered a beast and found therein an eight months' birth, living or dead, or a dead nine months' birth, he need only sever it and let the blood flow away.[9] If he found a living nine months' birth it needs to be slaughtered and he thereby becomes culpable by virtue of [the law of] *It and its young*.[10] So R. Meir. But the Sages say: The slaughtering of the dam renders it clean.[11] R. Simeon of Shezur says: Even if it grew into a five-year-old beast and ploughed the field, the slaughtering of the dam renders it clean. If a man had cut into the beast and found therein a living nine months' birth, it requires slaughtering,[12] since the dam was not slaughtered.

6. If a beast's hind-legs were cut off below the knee, it is valid;[13] but if

---

[1] Num. 18[15]. What it next bears is not deemed a Firstling.
[2] Num. 19[11].
[3] Although it had touched a severed member from a living creature (Ohol. 1[8]).
[4] Lev. 11[39].
[5] The young is deemed not validly slaughtered. Although the young may not, therefore, be eaten, it does not convey uncleanness.
[6] See Zeb. 7[6].   [7] That had been born and slaughtered.
[8] Slaughtering applies only to a living creature, and an eight months' birth is not deemed such.
[9] i.e. it may be eaten without having been slaughtered; but its blood is forbidden equally with that of the dam.   [10] See below, 5[1ff].
[11] i.e. suffices to make it also permissible.
[12] In the prescribed manner by cutting the gullet and windpipe.
[13] It is not *terefah*. This paragraph belongs to the subject of ch. 3.

above the knee it is invalid; so, too, if the juncture of the [thigh-]sinews was removed. If the bone was broken but most of the flesh remained, slaughtering renders it clean; otherwise slaughtering does not render it clean.

7. If a man slaughtered a beast and found therein an afterbirth, he whose appetite is robust[1] may eat it; it is not susceptible to food-uncleanness or to carrion-uncleanness.[2] If he ate it of set purpose, it can contract food-uncleanness but not carrion-uncleanness.[3] If the afterbirth had emerged in part only,[4] it is forbidden as food; it is a token of [the birth of] young in a woman[5] and a token of [the birth of] young in a beast.[6] If a beast that had not before borne young cast an afterbirth, it may be thrown to the dogs[7] but, if the beast had been set aside as an offering, it must be buried.[8] It should not be buried at cross-roads or hung on a tree, for such are the ways of the Amorite.[9]

5. 1. The law of *It and its young*[10] is binding both in the Land [of Israel] and outside the Land, both during the time of the Temple and after the time of the Temple, both for unconsecrated beasts and for animal-offerings. How does it apply? If a man slaughtered a dam and its young and they were unconsecrated beasts and [slaughtered] outside [the Temple Court], they are both valid, but for the second of them he incurs the Forty Stripes.[11] If they were both animal-offerings and [he slaughtered them] outside [the Temple Court], for the first he is liable to punishment by Extirpation,[12] and they are both invalid, and for each he incurs the Forty Stripes. If they were unconsecrated beasts and [he slaughtered them] within [the Temple Court] they are both invalid and for the second he suffers the Forty Stripes. If they were animal-offerings and [he slaughtered them] within [the Temple Court], the first is valid, and by reason of it he is not culpable, but for the second he incurs the Forty Stripes, and it is invalid.

2. If [the one was] an unconsecrated beast and [the second] an animal-offering [and he slaughtered them] outside [the Temple Court], the first is valid and by reason of it he is not culpable, but for the second he incurs the Forty Stripes, and it is invalid. If [the first was] an animal-offering and [the second] an unconsecrated beast [and he slaughtered them] outside [the Temple Court], for the first he is punishable by Extirpation, and it is invalid; and the second is valid, but for each he incurs the Forty Stripes. If [the one was] an unconsecrated beast and [the second] an animal-offering [and he slaughtered them] within [the Temple Court], both are invalid and

---

[1] Cf. Men. 11[7]; A. Zar. 2[5].

[2] It is accounted neither food nor flesh, being only skin. Some texts read only, 'It is not susceptible to carrion uncleanness'.

[3] Though he has given it the status it is still not flesh.

[4] Before the slaughtering of the dam.

[5] Signifying her uncleanness (Lev. 12[2ff]) even if no embryo was found.

[6] And it may imply that the head of the young had already protruded before the slaughtering of the dam, making the slaughter of the young necessary before it could be used as food. Cf. Bekh. 3[1].

[7] Without feeling scruple that the sanctity of the firstborn male attached to it.

[8] Since the offspring, male or female, to which it pertained cannot be used as common food.

[9] A superstition that thus the beast will be prevented from miscarrying again. Cf. Shab. 6[10].

[10] Which must not be killed both on the one day. Lev. 22[28].

[11] For a transgression of the negative command.

[12] Lev. 17[4]. He is not liable to Extirpation for the second beast since this could not have been brought as an offering without a transgression of the Law; and Extirpation cannot apply to misuse of what was an invalid offering.

for the second he incurs the Forty Stripes. If [one was] an animal-offering and [the second] an unconsecrated beast [and he slaughtered them] within [the Temple Court], the first is valid and by reason of it he is not culpable, while for the second he incurs the Forty Stripes, and it is invalid. If they were both unconsecrated beasts [and he slaughtered the one] outside and [the second] inside [the Temple Court], the first is valid and by reason of it he is not culpable, and for the second he incurs the Forty Stripes, and it is invalid. If both were animal-offerings [and he slaughtered the one] outside and [the second] inside [the Temple Court], for the first he is punishable by Extirpation, and both are invalid, and for each he incurs the Forty Stripes. If both were unconsecrated beasts [and he slaughtered the one] within and [the second] outside [the Temple Court], the first is invalid and by reason of it he is not culpable, while for the second he incurs the Forty Stripes, and it is valid. If [both were] animal-offerings [and he slaughtered the one] inside and [the second] outside [the Temple Court], the first is valid and by reason of it he is not culpable, and for the second he incurs the Forty Stripes, and it is invalid.

3. If a man slaughtered a beast and it was found to be *terefah*, or if he slaughtered it in honour of an idol, or if he slaughtered the [Red] Heifer of the Sin-offering,[1] or an ox that was to be stoned,[2] or the heifer that was to have its neck broken,[3] R. Simeon declares him exempt [from the law of *It and its young*], but the Sages declare him liable. If he slaughtered a beast and it became carrion[4] at his hand, or if he pierced or tore out [the windpipe or gullet], he is not culpable by virtue of the law of *It and its young*. If two bought a cow and its offspring, he that bought first should slaughter first; yet if the second did so first his right holds good. If a man slaughtered a cow and then two of its offspring, he incurs eighty stripes; if he first slaughtered the cow, then its offspring, and then its offspring's offspring, he incurs eighty stripes; if he slaughtered the cow, then its offspring's offspring, and then he afterward slaughtered the cow's offspring, he incurs forty stripes. Symmachos says in the name of R. Meir: He incurs eighty stripes. Four times in the year[5] must he that sells a beast to his fellow tell him, 'Its mother have I also sold to be slaughtered', or 'Its daughter have I also sold to be slaughtered', namely, on the eve of the last Festival-day of the Feast [of Tabernacles], on the eve of the first Festival-day of Passover, on the eve of the Feast of Pentecost, and on the eve of the New Year (also, according to R. Jose the Galilean, on the eve of the Day of Atonement in Galilee).[6] R. Judah said: This applies when there was no space of time[7] [between the sales]; if there was a space of time he need not tell him. But R. Judah agrees that if a dealer sold the dam to the bridegroom and the daughter to the bride, it is needful to tell the matter, since it is known that they will both slaughter [their beast] the same day.

4. At these four times they may make the butcher slaughter a beast against his will; even if it was an ox worth a thousand *denars* and the buyer had but one *denar*[8] they may compel the butcher to slaughter it;

---

[1] Num. 19[1ff].   [2] Ex. 21[28].   [3] Deut. 21[4].
[4] If it was not killed in the manner prescribed for slaughtering.
[5] When all Israelites were accustomed to eat flesh the next day, and when the presumption was that they would slaughter the beasts on the day of buying them.
[6] Where the custom was to eat a rich and heavy meal in preparation for the Fast.
[7] i.e. at least one day.
[8] i.e. he only wanted one *denar's* worth of flesh. If the *denar* passed into the butcher's hand he must fulfil the sale.

therefore if it dies the loss falls on the buyer.[1] But on other days in the year it is not so; if, therefore, the beast dies the loss falls on the seller.

5. The *one day* spoken of in the law of *It and its young* means the day together with the night that went before. This was expounded by R. Simeon b. Zoma: In the story of Creation it is written, *one day*;[2] and in the law of *It and its young* it is written, *one day*: as the *one day* spoken of in the story of Creation means the daytime together with the night that went before, so, too, the *one day* spoken of in the law of *It and its young* means the daytime together with the night that went before.

6. 1. [The law of] the covering up of the blood[3] is binding both in the Land [of Israel] and outside the Land, both during the time of the Temple and after the time of the Temple; for unconsecrated beasts but not for animal-offerings; and it applies both to wild animals and to birds,[4] whether captive or not captive. It applies also to the *koy*[5] since it is an animal about which there is doubt; it may not be slaughtered on a Festival-day, and if a man did slaughter it he need not cover up the blood.[6]

2. If a man slaughtered a beast and it was found to be *terefah*, or if he slaughtered it in honour of an idol, or if he slaughtered unconsecrated beasts within [the Temple Court] or animal-offerings outside, or a wild animal or a bird that was condemned to be stoned,[7] R. Meir declares him liable, but the Sages declare him exempt [from the law of covering up the blood]. If a man slaughtered [a wild animal or a bird] and it became carrion at his hand, or if he pierced or tore out [the windpipe or gullet], he is exempt from the law of covering up the blood.

3. If a deaf-mute, an imbecile, or a minor had slaughtered [a wild animal or a bird] and others beheld them, [one of them that beheld] must cover up [the blood]; but if they were alone, it need not be covered up. So, too, with the law of *It and its young*: if they had slaughtered [one of the two] and others beheld them, it is forbidden to slaughter [the other] afterward [on the same day]; but if they were alone, R. Meir declares it permissible to slaughter [the other] afterward; but the Sages forbid it. But they agree that if a man did slaughter [the second beast] he does not incur the Forty Stripes.

4. If a man slaughtered a hundred wild animals in one place, covering up the blood once suffices for all; if [he slaughtered] a hundred birds in one place, covering up [the blood] once suffices for all; if [he slaughtered] a wild animal and a bird in one place, covering up [the blood] once suffices for all. R. Judah says: If a man slaughtered a wild animal he should [first] cover up its blood and then slaughter the bird. If a man slaughtered aught and did not cover up [the blood], and another beheld him, the other must cover it up. If he covered it and it became uncovered, he need not cover it up again; but if the wind covered it up [and it became uncovered], it must be covered up again.

5. If the blood was mixed with water but still had the appearance of

---

1 Who had thus already acquired part ownership in the ox.   2 Gen. 1[5].
3 Lev. 17[13].   4 But not to cattle.
5 App. I. 19. It is in doubt whether it is a wild beast; and an injunction in the Law (in contradistinction to rabbinical rules) is assumed to be applicable in a matter of doubt. Cf. Toh. 4[11].
6 In this matter the stringency of the Festival-day rule (p. 181, n. 11) applies, since it is in doubt whether it is a tame beast (cattle), to which the law of covering up the blood does not apply.   7 Cf. Eduy. 6[1].

blood, it must be covered up; if it was mixed with wine, this is looked upon as though it was water. If it was mixed with the blood of cattle or of an animal that is still living, this is looked upon as though it was water. R. Judah says: Blood cannot make other blood of none effect.

6. Splashings of blood and blood that remains on the knife must be covered up. R. Judah said: This applies only when there is none other blood there than that; but if there is other blood there than that it need not be covered up.

7. With what may they cover and with what may they not cover up [the blood]? They may cover it up with fine dung or with find sand, with lime, or with [pieces of] potsherd or a brick or the plug of a jar[1] that have been crushed; but they may not cover it up with coarse dung or coarse sand, or with a brick or a plug that have not been crushed, nor may they set over it a vessel turned upside down.[2] Rabban Simeon b. Gamaliel laid down a general rule: They may cover it up with aught in which they can grow plants; they may not cover it up with aught in which they cannot grow plants.

7. 1. The law of *The sinew of the hip*[3] is binding both in the Land [of Israel] and outside the Land, both during the time of the Temple and after the time of the Temple; both for unconsecrated beasts and for animal-offerings; moreover it applies to cattle and to wild animals, to the right thigh or to the left. But it does not apply to birds since they have no *hollow [of the thigh]*. It applies also to a foetus. R. Judah says: It does not apply to a foetus. The fat thereof[4] is permitted; and butchers are not accounted trustworthy[5] in what concerns *the sinew of the hip*. So R. Meir. But the Sages say: They are accounted trustworthy in what concerns both the sinew and the fat.

2. One may send to a gentile the thigh wherein is *the sinew of the hip*, since its place is known. If a man removes *the sinew of the hip* he must remove all of it. R. Judah says: [Only enough] to fulfil the command to remove it.

3. If a man ate an olive's bulk of *the sinew of the hip* he incurs the Forty Stripes. If he ate it and it was less than an olive's bulk he is still culpable. If he ate an olive's bulk from the one thigh and an olive's bulk from the other he incurs eighty stripes. R. Judah says: He incurs forty only.

4. If a thigh was cooked together with *the sinew of the hip* and there was enough of it to give its flavour, it is forbidden. How should it be measured As though it was flesh [cooked] with turnips.[6]

5. If *the sinew of the hip* was cooked together with other sinews and it was recognizable [it must be removed and] the rest are forbidden if there was enough of it to give its flavour, but if [*the sinew of the hip* was] not [recognizable] all are forbidden, and the broth [is forbidden only] if [the sinew] leaves its flavour. So, too, with a piece of carrion flesh; so, too, with a piece of unclean fish that is cooked together with other pieces; if it was recognizable [it must be removed and] the rest are forbidden if there was enough of it to give its flavour; but if [it was] not [recognizable] all are forbidden,

---

[1] See p. 444, n. 3. [2] Some texts add: 'or cover it with stones'.
[3] Gen. 32[32]. [4] Of the foetus.
[5] To have removed it, since this adds to their labour.
[6] The sinew renders the rest forbidden if it is of such bulk in proportion to the rest that if it were flesh and the rest turnips the turnips would be flavoured by the flesh. This bulk is estimated at one-sixtieth.

and the broth [is forbidden only] if [the piece of carrion or unclean fish] leaves its flavour.

6. [The law of *the sinew of the hip*] applies to clean beasts and not to unclean. R. Judah says: To unclean also. R. Judah said: Was not *the sinew of the hip* forbidden from the time of the sons of Jacob when unclean beasts were still permitted to them? They answered: It was enjoined from mount Sinai, but written down its its [present] place.

8. 1. No flesh may be cooked in milk[1] excepting the flesh of fish and locusts; and no flesh may be served up on the table together with cheese excepting the flesh of fish and locusts. If a man vowed to abstain from flesh, he is permitted the flesh of fish and locusts. A fowl[2] may be served up on the table together with cheese, but it may not be eaten with it. So the School of Shammai. And the School of Hillel say: It may neither be served up with it nor eaten with it. R. Jose said: This is one of the cases where the School of Shammai followed the more lenient and the School of Hillel the more stringent ruling. Of what manner of table did they speak? Of a table whereat men eat; but on a table whereon the food is arrayed a man may put the one beside the other without scruple.

2. A man may tie up flesh and cheese in the same cloth provided that they do not touch one another. Rabban Simeon b. Gamaliel says: Two passing guests[3] may eat at the same table, the one flesh and the other cheese, without scruple.

3. If a drop of milk fell upon a piece [of flesh that was cooking in a pot] and there was enough to give its flavour to that piece, [that piece] is forbidden. If a man stirred the pot and there was enough to give the flavour [of the milk] to [all that was in] the pot, it is forbidden. A man should cut open the udder and empty out its milk; but if he has not cut it open he has not transgressed the law. He should cut open the heart and empty out its blood; but if he has not cut it open he has not transgressed the law. If a man served up a fowl and cheese on the table together, he does not transgress the negative command.

4. It is forbidden to cook or to benefit at all from the flesh of a clean beast together with the milk of a clean beast; but it is permitted to cook or to benefit from the flesh of a clean beast together with the milk of an unclean beast, or the flesh of an unclean beast together with the milk of a clean beast. R. Akiba says: Wild animals and birds are not [included in the prohibition] according to the Law, for three times[4] it is written, *Thou shalt not seethe a kid in its mother's milk,* thereby excluding, in particular, wild animals and birds and unclean beasts. R. Jose the Galilean says: It is written, *Ye shall not eat of anything that dieth of itself,*[5] and [in the same verse] it is also written, *Thou shalt not seethe a kid in its mother's milk;* [therefore] whatsoever is forbidden under the law of *anything that dieth of itself,* it is forbidden to seethe the same in milk. It might be inferred that a bird, which also is forbidden under the law of carrion, is forbidden to be seethed in milk; but Scripture says, *In its mother's milk;* thus a bird is excluded since it has no *mother's milk.*

5. [The milk in] the stomach of [a beast that was slaughtered by] a gentile

---

[1] To avoid the possibility of transgressing the thrice repeated law (Ex. 23[19]; 34[26]; Deut. 14[21]) against seething a kid in its mother's milk.
[2] Eduy. 5[2].   [3] Strangers to one another.
[4] Ex. 23[19]; 34[26]; Deut. 14[21].   [5] Deut. 14[21].

or [in the stomach of] carrion is forbidden. If a man curdled [milk] with the skin of the stomach of a validly slaughtered beast, and there was enough to give its flavour, it is forbidden. [The milk in] the stomach of a valid beast which it had sucked from a *terefah* beast is forbidden. [The milk in] the stomach of a *terefah* beast which it had sucked from a valid beast is permitted, since it is absorbed in its intestines.

6. Sometimes greater stringency applies to fat than to blood; and sometimes greater stringency applies to blood than to fat. Greater stringency applies to fat since it is subject to the law of Sacrilege,[1] and since by reason of it a man may become culpable through [transgression of the laws of] Refuse, Remnant, and uncleanness;[2] but it is not so with blood. And greater stringency applies to blood, since the [law forbidding] blood[3] applies to cattle, wild animals, and birds, whether unclean or clean; but the [law forbidding] fat[4] applies to clean cattle alone.

9. 1. The hide, grease, sediment, flayed-off flesh, bones and sinews, horns and hoofs[5] are included together [to make up the quantity that suffices] to convey food-uncleanness, but not [to make up the quantity that suffices to convey] carrion-uncleanness. In like manner, if a man slaughtered an unclean beast for a gentile and it still jerks [its limbs], it can convey food-uncleanness[6] but it only conveys carrion-uncleanness after it is dead or has its head chopped off.[7] [Scripture] has prescribed more conditions that convey food-uncleanness than that convey carrion-uncleanness. R. Judah says: If sufficient pieces of flayed-off flesh were collected together to make up an olive's bulk, one may thereby become culpable.[8]

2. With these [that follow], their skin[9] is deemed one with their flesh[10] [in what concerns uncleanness]: the skin of a man, the skin of the domestic pig (R. Jose says: The skin also of a wild pig), the skin of the hump of a young camel, the skin of the head of a young calf, the skin of the hooves,[11] the skin of the genitals, the skin of a foetus, the skin beneath the fat tail, and the skin of the gecko, the chameleon, the lizard, and the land-crocodile. R. Judah says: The lizard is accounted like to the weasel. But when their hides have been treated or trampled upon to render them fit for use they become clean, save only the skin of a man. R. Johanan b. Nuri says: The skin of the eight creeping things[12] is deemed to be skin [and not one with their flesh].

3. Such time as a man flays cattle or wild animals, clean or unclean, small or large, the skin still counts as a connective [with the carcase] in what concerns uncleanness, so that it can contract uncleanness and convey uncleanness; [this applies if the hide was being flayed] for a covering, [so long as there remains still unsevered] enough to preserve a hold [on the carcase]; [and if it was being flayed] for a water-skin, until the breast has been flayed; or, if it was being flayed from the feet upwards, until the whole hide [is

---

[1] Lev. 5[15f].   [2] See Zeb. 3[4].   [3] Lev. 7[26f].   [4] Lev. 7[25].
[5] Zeb. 3[4]; Toh. 1[4]. Flesh and edible portions that adhere to or are contained in any of these can be included with other flesh to make up a total of an egg's bulk which, if the flesh is unclean, can convey uncleanness to the eater, or to make up the total of an olive's bulk which, if the flesh is carrion, conveys uncleanness to him who touches or carries it.
[6] If it was touched by anything unclean.
[7] When it becomes carrion. Lev. 11[39].
[8] If he touched them and they were unclean and he entered the Temple. The Cambridge text reads 'none may thereby become liable'.   [9] Through its being soft and thin.
[10] And the skin is susceptible to uncleanness even after being severed from the flesh.
[11] The skin of the last joint that remains after the beast is flayed.
[12] Lev. 11[29].

severed]. The skin that is on the neck, according to R. Johanan b. Nuri, does not count as a connective [with the hide that is already flayed];[1] but the Sages say: It counts as a connective until the whole hide is flayed.

4. If there remained an olive's bulk of flesh[2] on the hide and a man touched a shred of it[3] that jutted forth, or a hair on the opposite side, he becomes unclean. If there were two [separate] half-olives' bulk of flesh on it, they convey uncleanness by carrying but not by contact.[4] So R. Ishmael. R. Akiba says: Neither by contact nor by carrying. But R. Akiba agrees that if there were two pieces each of a half-olive's bulk, and a man thrust through them both with a chip and shifted them, he becomes unclean. Why does R. Akiba declare him clean who only touches the hide? Because [they are reckoned as part of the hide and] the hide renders them negligible [in their scantness].

5. If a man touched a marrow-bone from a corpse, or a marrow-bone of an animal-offering, whether it was stopped up or hollowed out, he becomes unclean. If he touched a marrow-bone of a carcase or of a creeping thing, if it was stopped up he remains clean; but if it was at all hollowed out it conveys uncleanness by contact. Whence do we learn that [it conveys uncleanness] also by carrying? Scripture says: *He that toucheth*[5] and *He also that beareth*;[6] what comes within the scope of uncleanness by contact comes also within the scope of uncleanness by carrying; and what does not come within the scope of uncleanness by contact does not come within the scope of uncleanness by carrying.

6. The egg of a creeping thing in which the young is already fashioned is clean. If it is at all pierced it is unclean. If a man touched the flesh in a mouse[7] (which is half flesh and half earth) he becomes unclean; but if he touched the earth, he remains clean. R. Judah says: Also if he touched the earth that is over against the flesh he becomes unclean.

7. If on a beast a member[8] or any flesh hangs loose,[9] they are susceptible to food-uncleanness while they continue in their place,[10] but they need[11] to be rendered susceptible to uncleanness by a liquid.[12] If the beast was slaughtered they are rendered susceptible through the blood. So R. Meir. R. Simeon says: They are not rendered susceptible. If the beast died of itself the flesh must [first] be rendered susceptible to uncleanness by a liquid; the member conveys uncleanness by virtue of being a member [severed] from the living creature: it does not convey uncleanness by virtue of being carrion. So R. Meir. But R. Simeon declares it clean [in both respects].

8. If a member or any flesh hangs loose on a man, they are clean. If the man died the flesh is clean; the member conveys uncleanness by virtue of being a member from a living creature: it does not convey uncleanness by virtue of being a member of a corpse.[13] So R. Meir. But R. Simeon declares it clean [in both respects].

---

[1] And to which it is still attached.   [2] Torn off with the hide, and in one place.
[3] The flesh (Rashi, Bert., Tif. Yis); or the hide (Maim.).
[4] Since in carrying, a whole olive's bulk at a time is carried; but in touching, only half an olive's bulk at a time is touched.   [5] Lev. 11[39].   [6] Lev. 11[40].
[7] A kind of mouse that is generated from the earth itself.
[8] With its bone, flesh, and sinews.   [9] Broken or cut but not wholly severed.
[10] Whereas, if wholly severed, they would convey carrion-uncleanness.
[11] Cambridge text: 'they do not need'.
[12] See Maksh. 6[4]; Lev. 11[34].   [13] Cf. Eduy. 6[3].

10. 1. The law of *the shoulder and the two cheeks and the maw*[1] is binding both in the Land [of Israel] and outside the Land, both during the time of the Temple and after the time of the Temple; it applies to unconsecrated beasts but not to animal-offerings. It might have been argued: If unconsecrated beasts (which are not subject to the law of the breast and the thigh)[2] are subject to these [other three] dues, must we not therefore conclude that animal-offerings (which are subject to the law of the breast and the thigh) are subject also to these [other three] dues? But Scripture says, *And I have given them unto Aaron the priest and unto his sons as a due for ever;*[3] only what is there prescribed pertains to him.

2. All animal-offerings[4] which before they were dedicated suffered a lasting blemish and have been redeemed are subject to the law of the Firstling[5] and [Priests'] Dues,[6] and like unconsecrated beasts they can be shorn and used for labour, and their young and their milk are permitted for use after they have been redeemed; and he that slaughters them outside [the Temple Court] is not culpable, and the Law of the Substitute[7] does not apply to them, and if they died of themselves they may be redeemed, save only a Firstling and Tithe [of Cattle].[8] All [animal-offerings] which after they were dedicated suffered a blemish, or which suffered only a passing blemish before they were dedicated, and there afterward arose in them a lasting blemish, and they were redeemed—they are not subject to the law of the Firstling and [Priests'] Dues, and they may not, like unconsecrated beasts, be shorn or used for labour, and their young and their milk are forbidden even after they have been redeemed; and he that slaughters them outside [the Temple Court] is culpable; the law of the Substitute applies to them, and if they die of themselves they must be buried.

3. If a Firstling[9] was confused among a hundred [other beasts] and a hundred [and one] persons slaughtered them all, they are all exempt[10] [from Priests' Dues]; if one person slaughtered them all, he is exempt [from Priests' Dues] for one beast alone. If a man slaughtered a beast for a priest or a gentile, he is exempt from Priests' Dues; and if he was a jointholder with them this must be shown by some token. If he had said,[11] 'Apart from the [Priests'] Dues', he is exempt from giving the Dues.[12] If a man said: 'Sell me the entrails of a cow', and among them were Priests' Dues,[13] he must give them to the priest, and he may take naught off the price. But if he bought them from him by weight, he must give the Priests' Dues to a priest and he[14] must take it off the price.

4. If a proselyte had a cow and it was slaughtered before he became a proselyte, he is exempt; if it was slaughtered afterward, he is liable; if the

---

1 Deut. 18[3]. Whoever slaughters an ox or a sheep must give these portions as the Priests' Dues.

2 Which (Lev. 7[31]) are taken from the Peace-offerings and given to the priests.

3 Lev. 7[34].   4 Bekh. 2[2–3].

5 If they bear a male firstling (Num. 18[15–18]) this belongs to the priest.

6 When, after being redeemed, they are slaughtered as common food, the priest must be given 'the shoulder and the two cheeks and the maw'.

7 Lev. 27[10].   8 Lev. 27[32].

9 Which had, according to the Law, been given to the priest, but, having a blemish, was found unfit to be offered and consumed by the priest, and was therefore sold by him.

10 Since any one of the owners can allege that what he had slaughtered was the Firstling, which was exempt from Priests' Dues.

11 A priest or gentile when he sold the beast to an Israelite.

12 Since they had not become the property of the Israelite who bought the beast.

13 e.g. the maw, and, if, as was customary, the head was included with the entrails, the two cheeks also.   14 The seller.

matter is in doubt, he is exempt, for on him that would exact aught from his fellow lies the burden of proof.[1] What counts as 'the shoulder'? From the bend of the knee to the shoulder-socket of the fore-leg; such, too, is 'the shoulder' that is prescribed for the Nazirite.[2] And the corresponding part of the hind-leg is called 'the thigh'. R. Judah says: By 'the thigh' is meant from the bend of the knee to the fleshy part of the hind-leg. What counts as 'the cheek'? From the bend of the jaw to the knob of the windpipe.[3]

11. 1. [The law of] *the first of the fleece*[4] is binding both in the Land [of Israel] and outside the Land, both during the time of the Temple and after the time of the Temple, for unconsecrated beasts but not for animal-offerings. Greater stringency applies to the law of *the shoulder and the two cheeks and the maw*, than to the law of *the first of the fleece*, since the law of *the shoulder and the two cheeks and the maw* applies to herds and flocks, whether many or few, but the law of *the first of the fleece* applies only to sheep, and only when they are many.

2. And how many [must they be]? The School of Shammai say: Two sheep; for it is written, *A man shall nourish a young cow and two sheep*.[5] And the School of Hillel say: Five; for it is written, *And five sheep ready dressed*.[6] R. Dosa b. Harkinas says:[7] Five sheep that have fleeces each of a *mina*[8] and a half are subject to the law of *the first of the fleece*. But the Sages say: Five sheep, however much may be their fleeces. And how much must a man give him?[9] Five *selas'* weight in Judea (which is ten *selas* in Galilee),[10] bleached and not in dirty state, enough to make therefrom a small garment, as it is written, *Thou shalt give to him*;[11] there shall be in it enough to count as 'a gift'. If a man could not give it before he dyed it, he is exempt from the obligation; if he had bleached it but not dyed it he is liable. If a man bought the fleeces of the sheep of a gentile he is exempt from the law of *the first of the fleece*. If he bought the fleeces of his fellow's sheep and the seller kept back aught of the fleece, the seller is liable; otherwise the buyer is liable. If he had two kinds, dark and white, and he sold him the dark but not the white, or [if he sold him the fleeces] of the males but not of the females, each must give [the first of the fleece] for himself.

12. 1. [The law to] *let [the dam] go* from the nest[12] is binding both in the Land [of Israel] and outside the Land, both during the time of the Temple and after the time of the Temple, for unconsecrated birds but not for Bird-offerings. Greater stringency applies to the law to cover up the blood than to the law to *let [the dam] go* from the nest; for the law to cover up the blood applies both to wild animals and to birds, whether captive or not captive; but the law to *let [the dam] go* from the nest applies only to birds and only to them that are not captive. Which are they that are not captive? The like of geese and fowls that make their nests in a plantation; but if they made their nests within a house (so, too, Herodian doves)[13] the law to *let [the dam] go* does not apply.

2. The law to *let [the dam] go* does not apply to an unclean bird. If an unclean bird sat on the eggs of a clean bird, or a clean bird on the eggs of an

---

[1] Cf. B.K. 3[11]; B.B. 9[6]; Bekh. 2[6ff]; Toh. 4[12].   [2] Num. 6[19].   [3] Cf. Neg. 10[9].
[4] Deut. 18[4].   [5] Is. 7[21].   [6] I Sam. 25[18].   [7] Eduy. 3[3].   [8] App. II, B.
[9] Explained as: How much, when there are many priests, must the owner of the sheep give to each of the priests?
[10] Cf. Ket. 5[9].   [11] Deut. 18[4].   [12] Deut. 22[6, 7].   [13] See Shab. 24[3].

unclean bird, the law to *let [the dam] go* does not apply. With a cock partridge[1] R. Eliezer declares the law binding, but the Sages declare it not binding.

3. If the dam hovered over the nest and her wings touched the nest a man must let her go; if they do not touch the nest he is not bound to let her go. If there was there but one nestling or one egg, one is bound to *let [the dam] go*; for it is written, *a bird's nest*:[2] any manner of bird's nest. If there were nestlings there able to fly, or spoilt eggs, one is not bound to *let [the dam] go*, for it is written, *And the dam sitting upon the young or upon the eggs*; as the nestlings are such that are like to live, so the eggs must be such that are like to live; thus eggs that are spoilt are excluded. And as the eggs are such that need their dam, so the nestlings must be such that need their dam; thus such that can fly are excluded. If a man let the dam go and she returned and he again let her go and she returned, even four or five times, the law is still binding, for it is written, *Thou shalt in any wise*[3] *let the dam go*. If a man had said, 'I will take the dam and let the young go', he must still let [her] go, for it is written, *Thou shalt in anywise let the dam go*. If he took the young and then restored them to the nest, and afterward the dam returned to them, he is exempt from the law to *let [the dam] go*.

4. If[4] a man took the dam and her young, R. Judah says: He incurs the [Forty] Stripes; and he need not [then] *let the dam go*. But the Sages say: He must let the dam go, and he does not incur the [Forty] Stripes. This is the general rule: [By transgression of] any negative command whereunto is joined a further command to rise up and do, a man does not incur the [Forty] Stripes.

5. A man may not take the dam and her young even for the sake of cleansing the leper.[5] If then of so light a precept concerning what is worth but an *issar*[6] the Law has said *that it may be well with thee and that thou mayest prolong thy days*,[7] how much more [shall the like reward be given] for [the fulfilment of] the weightier precepts of the Law!

BEKHOROTH[8] ('FIRSTLINGS')

1. 1. If a man bought of a gentile the unborn young of his ass or sold the like to him (though this is forbidden),[9] or if he was a jointholder with him, or if he had received [asses] from him or delivered [asses] to him [to rear and to share with him in the increase], he is exempt from the law of Firstlings, for it is written, *[All the firstborn] in Israel*;[10] but not the firstborn pertaining to others. Priests and levites are exempt[11] [by reason of the inference] from the less to the greater: If in the wilderness the [firstborn of] Israelites were exempt [by reason of the levites],[12] how much more must their own [firstborn] be exempt!

2. If a cow bore young that was like to an ass, or if an ass bore young that

---

[1] Jer. 17[11] is, literally, 'as the partridge sitteth on an egg which he hath not laid'.
[2] Deut. 22[6].   [3] Cf. p. 350, n. 6.   [4] See Makk. 3[4].
[5] Lev. 14[4ff].   [6] App. II, A.   [7] Deut. 22[7].
[8] See Ex. 13[2], 'Sanctify unto me all the firstborn . . . both of man and beast; it is mine'. See also 13[12], 'All that openeth the womb . . . the males shall be the Lord's'. Cf. Ex. 22[29, 30]; 34[19-29] ('the firstling of an ass thou shalt redeem with a lamb'), Num. 18[15-18]; Deut. 15[19-20].
[9] Pes. 4[3]; A. Zar. 1[6].   [10] Num. 3[13].
[11] From the redemption of firstborn sons. See below, 2[1].
[12] Cf. Num. 3[45].

was like to a horse, it is exempt from the law of Firstlings, for twice is it written, *The firstling of an ass,*[1] *The firstling of an ass,*[2] [therefore the law of the Firstling applies] only if the mother is an ass and if what is born is an ass. How does this apply in what concerns [forbidden] food? If a clean beast bore young that was like to an unclean beast it is permitted for food; but if an unclean beast bore young that was like to a clean beast it is forbidden for food, for what issues from an unclean beast is unclean, and what issues from a clean beast is clean. If an unclean fish swallowed a clean fish[3] this is permitted for food; but if a clean fish swallowed an unclean fish this is forbidden for food, since it was not bred from the other.

3. If an ass that had not before borne young bore two males [and it was not known which was the Firstling], [the owner] need give but one lamb to the priest; if it bore a male and a female, he must set apart a lamb for himself;[4] if two asses that had not before borne young bore two males, [the owner] must give two lambs to the priest; if they bore a male and a female, or two males and a female, he need give but one lamb to the priest; but if two females and a male, or two males and two females, the priest can claim nothing.

4. If there was one which had not and another which had before borne young, and they bore two males,[5] [the owner] must give one lamb to the priest; if they bore a male and a female he must set apart one lamb for himself. For[6] it is written, *And every firstling of an ass thou shalt redeem with a lamb;*[7] [it may be] from the sheep or from the goats, male or female, large or small, unblemished or blemished. With it[8] he may redeem more Firstlings; it may enter into the pen to be tithed;[9] but if it dies[10] [only the priests] may derive benefit therefrom.

5. None may redeem [a Firstling] with a calf or with a wild animal or with what has been slaughtered or with what is *terefah* or with what is cross-bred or with a *koy*.[11] R. Eliezer permits what is cross-bred but forbids a *koy*, since it is in doubt [whether it can be called 'a lamb'].[12] If a man gave [the Firstling] itself to the priest, the priest may not keep it alive unless he had set apart a lamb in its stead.

6. If a man had set apart the redemption [lamb] for the Firstling of an ass, and it died, R. Eliezer says: He is still answerable for it,[13] as [in like case he is answerable for] the five *selas*[14] [the redemption price] for a [firstborn] son. But the Sages say: He is not answerable for it, as [in like case he is not answerable for] the redemption price of Second Tithe. R. Joshua and R. Zadok testified of the redemption [lamb] for the Firstling of an ass that had died, that the priest can claim nothing. If the Firstling of an ass died, R.

---

[1] Ex. 13[13].   [2] Ex. 34[20].
[3] And this was recovered whole.
[4] Thereby 'cancelling' the sanctity of whichever of the beasts is the Firstling; but he need not give it to the priest, on the principle (see 2[6]) 'On him that would exact aught of his fellow lies the burden of proof'.
[5] And it is not known which was born from which.
[6] The quotation refers to the contents of paragraphs 3–4 as a whole.   [7] Ex. 13[13].
[8] If he bought it back from the priest or was not compelled to give it to the priest.
[9] If it was set apart in redemption of a doubtful Firstling and therefore was not given to the priest.
[10] A lamb which was set apart to redeem a firstling ass, but died before it could be given to the priest.   [11] App. I. 19.
[12] A name about which there is doubt whether it can apply to the young of the *koy*.
[13] And must replace it. The passage is repeated in Eduy. 7[1].
[14] Num. 18[16]. Cf. below, 8[7]. The Tyrian *sela* was taken as the equivalent of the 'shekel of the Sanctuary'.

Eliezer says: It must be buried, and the owner may make use of the lamb [which he had set apart to redeem it]. But the Sages say: It need not be buried[1] and the lamb falls to the priest.

7. If a man was not minded to redeem it he must break its neck[2] from behind with a hatchet and bury it. The duty of redeeming it comes before the duty of breaking its neck, since it is written, *And if thou wilt not redeem it then thou shalt break its neck.*[3] [In like manner] the duty of espousing [a Hebrew bondwoman] comes before the duty of redeeming her, since it is written, *So that he hath not espoused her, then shall he let her be redeemed.*[4] Beforetime the duty of levirate marriage came before the duty of *halitzah*[5] when they acted intent on fulfilling a religious duty; but now when they so act, but not intent on fulfilling a religious duty,[6] they have enjoined that the duty of *halitzah* comes before the duty of levirate marriage. The duty of redeeming [an unclean beast that was dedicated to the Temple] falls upon its owner before all other men, since it is written, [*Then shall he ransom it . . .*] *or if it be not redeemed then it shall be sold according to thy estimation.*[7]

2. 1. If[8] a man bought of a gentile the unborn young of his cow or sold the like to him (though this is forbidden), or if he was a jointholder with him, or if he had received [cows] from him or delivered [cows] to him [to rear and to share with him in the increase], he is exempt from the law of Firstlings, for it is written, [*All the firstborn*] *in Israel*; but not the firstborn pertaining to others. Priests and levites are not exempt; they are not exempt from the law of the Firstling of a clean beast, and they are exempt only from the law to redeem the [firstborn] son and the Firstling of an ass.

2. All[9] animal-offerings which before they were dedicated suffered a lasting blemish and have been redeemed, are subject to the law of the First-ling and [Priests'] Dues,[10] and like unconsecrated beasts they can be shorn and used for labour, and their young and their milk are permitted for use after they have been redeemed; and he that slaughters them outside [the Temple Court] is not culpable, and the law of the Substitute[11] does not apply to them, and if they died of themselves they may be redeemed, save only a Firstling and Tithe [of Cattle].[12]

3. All [animal-offerings] which after they were dedicated suffered a blemish or which suffered only a passing blemish before they were dedi-cated, and there afterward arose in them a lasting blemish, and they were redeemed—they are not subject to the law of the Firstling and [Priests'] Dues, and they may not like unconsecrated beasts be shorn or used for labour, and their young and their milk are forbidden even after they have been redeemed; and he that slaughters them outside [the Temple Court] is culpable; the law of the Substitute applies to them and if they die of them-selves they must be buried.

4. If a man received a flock from a gentile on 'iron' terms,[13] their off-spring are exempt [from the law of Firstlings], but the offspring born of their offspring are not exempt.[14] If [he[15] had stipulated] that the offspring

---

1 Since it is accounted redeemed by the act of setting apart the lamb.
2 Ex. 34[20].   3 Ex. 34[20].   4 Ex. 21[8]. R.V. mg.
5 App. I. 12. See p. 218, n. 1. Deut. 25[5–10].
6 But only with a mind to the widow's beauty or property.   7 Lev. 27[27].
8 Cf. above, 1[1].   9 This and the following paragraph are repeated in Hull. 10[2].
10 See Hull. 10[1].   11 See Lev. 27[10].   12 Lev. 27[32].
13 See B.M. 5[6]; App. I. 41.
14 The gentile's claim is only to the first generation of offspring.
15 The Israelite to the gentile.

should stand in the stead of their dams, the offspring of such offspring are exempt, but the offspring of their offspring are liable. Rabban Simeon b. Gamaliel says: [They are exempt] even to the tenth generation since the gentile has a lien thereon.

5. If a sheep bore young that was like to a goat, or if a goat bore young that was like to a sheep, it is exempt from the law of Firstlings, but if [the offspring] bore any marks [peculiar to the mother-beast] it is liable.[1]

6. If a sheep that had not before borne young bore two males and their heads came forth together, R. Jose the Galilean says: Both fall to the priest, for it is written, *The males shall be the Lord's.*[2] But the Sages say: That cannot be:[3] but, rather, one falls to the owner and the other to the priest. R. Tarfon says: The priest chooses the better for himself. R. Akiba says: It is left for decision between them,[4] and the other is left to pasture until it suffers a blemish, and it is subject to [Priests'] Dues.[5] But R. Jose exempts it.[6] If one of them died, R. Tarfon says: They share [its value]. R. Akiba says: On him that would exact aught from his fellow lies the burden of proof. If [the offspring] were a male and a female, the priest can claim nothing.

7. If two sheep that had not before borne young bore two males, both must be given to the priest; if a male and a female, the male falls to the priest; if two males and a female, one male falls to the owner and the other to the priest. R. Tarfon says: The priest chooses the better for himself. R. Akiba says: It is left for decision between them, and the other is left to pasture until it suffers a blemish, and it is subject to [Priests'] Dues. But R. Jose exempts it. If one of them died, R. Tarfon says: They share [its value]. R. Akiba says: On him that would exact aught from his fellow lies the burden of proof. [If they bore] two females and a male, or two males and two females, the priest can claim nothing.

8. If from a sheep that had already borne young and another that had not before borne young two males were born, one falls to the owner and the other to the priest. R. Tarfon says: The priest chooses the better for himself. R. Akiba says: It is left for decision between them, and the other is left to pasture until it suffers a blemish; and it is subject to [Priests'] Dues. But R. Jose exempts it; for R. Jose used to say: If the priest has a beast given in the other's stead it is exempt from [Priests'] Dues. R. Meir declares it liable. If one of them died, R. Tarfon says: They share [its value]. R. Akiba says: On him that would exact aught from his fellow lies the burden of proof. If [they bore] a male and a female the priest can claim nothing.

9. If the firstborn was extracted from the side and another was born after it, R. Tarfon says: Both must be left to pasture until they suffer a blemish, and they may be consumed by their owners after they have suffered a blemish. R. Akiba says: Neither is reckoned a Firstling—the first because it is not such *that openeth the womb,*[7] the second in that another came before it.

---

[1] An inference from Num. 18[17].
[2] Ex. 13[12]; implying that more than one can come under the law of Firstlings.
[3] i.e. it is impossible to decide that they were, in real truth, simultaneous births.
[4] The same obscure Hebrew term is used in B.B. 7[4]. The sense here seems to be that since the priest cannot prove his claim to either, the owner, being in the stronger position, can leave the less desirable of the two beasts to the priest.
[5] It is then deemed unconsecrated in all respects, and comes under the law of 'the shoulder and the two cheeks and the maw'; cf. Hull. 10[1].
[6] See below, par. 8.   [7] Ex. 13[12].

3. 1. If a man bought a beast of a gentile and it was not known whether it had already borne young or had not already borne young, R. Ishmael says: If it was a goat still in its first year [the first male offspring] shall surely fall to the priest; but if it was older than this it remains in doubt.[1] If it was a sheep still in its second year [the first male offspring] shall surely fall to the priest; but if it was older than this it remains in doubt. If it was a cow or an ass still in its third year [the first male offspring] shall surely fall to the priest; but if it was older than this it remains in doubt. R. Akiba said to him: If the beast was exempted by offspring only, it would be as thou hast said; but they have said: The token of offspring[2] in small cattle is womb-discharge, in large cattle the after-birth; and in women the foetus-sack or the afterbirth. This is the general rule: If it is known that the beast had already borne young the priest can claim nothing; if it had not already borne young [the first male offspring] falls to the priest; if it is in doubt the owner may consume the offspring after it has suffered a blemish. R. Eliezer b. Jacob says: If large cattle discharged a clot of blood this must be buried; and they are exempt from the law of the Firstling.

2. Rabban Simeon b. Gamaliel says: If a man bought of a gentile a beast that was giving suck, he need not scruple lest it be the young of another beast. If he entered among his flock and saw beasts that had not before borne young giving suck and beasts that had already borne young giving suck, he need not scruple lest the young of these may have come to the others [for suck], or lest the young of the others may have come to these.

3. R. Jose b. Meshullam says: When a man slaughters a Firstling he may prepare a place for[3] the hatchet on either side and pluck out hair,[4] provided that he does not remove it;[5] so, too, when a man plucks out hair to inspect the place of a blemish.

4. If the hair of a blemished Firstling fell out and one put it in a wall-niche and afterward slaughtered the beast, Akabya b. Mehalaleel says: It is permitted.[6] But the Sages forbid it. So R. Judah. R. Jose said: Akabya did not need to permit it in this case; but if the hair of a blemished Firstling fell out and one put it in a wall-niche and afterward the beast died, in this case Akabya b. Mehalaleel permits it, but the Sages forbid it. If wool hangs loose from a Firstling[7] it is permitted if it manifestly pertains to the shorn wool,[8] but if it does not manifestly pertain to the shorn wool it is forbidden.

4. 1. How long must an Israelite tend the Firstling[9] [before he gives it to a priest]? Thirty days for small cattle and fifty days for large cattle. R. Jose says: Three months for small cattle. If within this time the priest said to

---

[1] Whether it is really a Firstling. Therefore the owner need not give it to the priest, yet he must leave it to pasture until it suffers a blemish.

[2] A proof that there has been some manner of birth and that the beast is exempt from the law of the Firstling. Cf. Hull. 4[7].

[3] Variant: 'with', or 'the size of' the hatchet with which the throat is to be cut.

[4] By hand, to ensure against the danger of improper slaughtering. See p. 513, n. 7.

[5] It must be left on the beast. Cf. Deut. 15[19].

[6] To make use of the hair. Eduy. 5[6].   [7] That has been slaughtered.

[8] i.e. that had been shorn off after the beast was slaughtered.

[9] If the Firstling was free from blemish it must be offered in the Temple, the blood sprinkled, and the sacrificial portions burnt on the Altar; the rest of the flesh belongs to the priest and must be consumed by him in Jerusalem. If it had a blemish it cannot be offered in the Temple and becomes absolutely the priest's property; he may slaughter it or sell it as he pleases. After the time of the Temple (when the Firstling can no longer be offered) it must be kept by the owner long enough for it to appear whether it is blemished; and unless it is blemished it is forbidden to slaughter it; such blemish must be certified by one that is skilled.

him, 'Give it to me',[1] he may not give it to him. If it was blemished and he said to him, 'Give it to me that I may eat it', it is permitted. During the time of the Temple if the Firstling was without blemish and the priest said to him, 'Give it to me that I may offer it [in the Temple]', it is permitted. The Firstling must be consumed within the year, whether it was unblemished or blemished, for it is written, *Thou shalt eat it before the Lord thy God year by year*.[2]

2. If within the year there arose in it a blemish it may be kept alive throughout the twelve months; but if after the year, it may be kept alive only for thirty days.

3. If a man slaughtered a Firstling and [so first] made its blemish manifest R. Judah permits it. R. Meir says: Since it was not slaughtered at the word of one that was skilled it is forbidden.

4. If one that was not skilled beheld the Firstling and it was slaughtered at his word it must be buried, and he must make restitution from his own property. If he judged a matter of law and declared exempt him that was culpable or declared culpable him that was exempt, or declared unclean what was clean or declared clean what was unclean, what he has done cannot be undone, but he must make restitution from his own property. But if he was a skilled person approved by the court, he need not make restitution. It[3] happened once that R. Tarfon fed the dogs with a cow whose womb had been removed;[4] and the matter came before the Sages and they declared it permitted. Todos[5] the Physician said, There is neither cow nor sow that leaves Alexandria but they cut out its womb so that it cannot bear young. R. Tarfon said, There goes thine ass, Tarfon![6] R. Akiba said to him, R. Tarfon, thou art exempt in that thou art a skilled person approved by the court, and he that is a skilled person approved by the court need not make restitution.

5. If a man takes payment for inspecting Firstlings none may slaughter at his word unless he was as skilled as Ila in Jabneh whom the Sages suffered to take four *issars*[7] for small cattle and six for large cattle, whether unblemished or blemished.

6. If a man takes payment for acting as a judge, his judgements are void; if for bearing witness his witness is void; if for sprinkling [Sin-offering water] or for mixing [with water][8] the ashes [of the Red Heifer], his water becomes but the water of a cavern and his ashes but the ashes of a hearth. If he[9] was a priest and he had thereby become unclean so that he could not partake of Heave-offering, he should be given what he needs for eating, drinking, and anointing. If he was an aged man he should be given an ass to ride. Moreover he may be given such payment as [would be given to] a labourer.

7. If a man is suspected of breaking the law of Firstlings,[10] none may buy of him the flesh of gazelles or untanned hides. R. Eliezer says: They may

---

[1] The priest undertakes the burden of rearing it during the specified time, thus placing the Israelite under obligation to him and ensuring that the Israelite will give it to him and not to another priest.   [2] Deut. 15[20].
[3] Some texts omit the rest of the paragraph.   [4] He pronounced it *terefah*.
[5] Theudas. Cambridge text: Todros (Theodorus).
[6] i.e. he must give up his ass to make restitution for the cow which he had wrongly pronounced *terefah*.   [7] App. II, A.   [8] Num. 19[17f].
[9] Who is called upon to examine whether a Firstling is blemished or to act as a judge, etc.
[10] If a priest is suspected of slaughtering unblemished Firstlings which have been given to him.

buy of him the hides of female beasts but they may not buy of him wool that is bleached but still dirty; and they may buy of him what is already spun or [made into] garments.[1]

8. If a man is suspected of breaking the law of Seventh Year produce,[2] none may buy of him flax even though it is combed; but they may buy of him what has been spun or carded.

9. If a man is suspected of selling Heave-offering as unconsecrated produce, none may buy of him even water or salt. So R. Judah. R. Simeon says: None may buy of him aught that in any wise pertains to Heave-offering or Tithes.[3]

10. If a man is suspected in what concerns Seventh Year produce he need not be suspected in what concerns Tithes; if he is suspected in what concerns Tithes he need not be suspected in what concerns Seventh Year produce; if he is suspected in what concerns either the one or the other he is suspected in what concerns the cleanness [of foodstuffs]; yet he may be suspected in what concerns the cleanness [of foodstuffs] and not be suspected in what concerns either the one or the other. This is the general rule: He that is suspected in what concerns any matter may neither judge nor bear witness thereof.

5. 1. All animal-offerings that have become invalid may [after they have been redeemed] be sold in the market and slaughtered in the market and weighed out by measure,[4] save only the Firstling and Tithe [of Cattle],[5] since the advantage[6] would fall to their owners;[7] but with animal-offerings that have been rendered invalid the advantage falls to the Temple. But a portion of the flesh of a Firstling may be weighed against another portion [of its flesh].[8]

2. The School of Shammai say: An Israelite may not be numbered [in the same company] with a priest for [the consumption of] a Firstling. And the School of Hillel permit it even to a gentile. If a Firstling suffered from a congestion of blood, it may not be bled even though it must otherwise die. So R. Judah. But the Sages say: It may be bled provided that it does not thereby suffer a blemish; but if it suffers a blemish it may not be slaughtered by reason of it. R. Simeon says: It may be bled even if it thereby suffers a blemish.

3. If a man slit the ear of a Firstling it may never be slaughtered. So R. Eliezer. But the Sages say: If there arose in it some other blemish it may be slaughtered by reason of it. It once happened that a quaestor saw an old ram with a long, dangling hair and said, 'What manner of thing is this?' They answered, 'It is a Firstling which may be slaughtered only if it suffers

---

1 Some texts read here 'carded', transposing 'made into garments' to the end of the next paragraph.
2 Who cultivates his field and sells its produce in the Seventh Year. See Lev. 25[4].
3 But water and salt are permitted.
4 Sold in small quantities. Lit. 'by the *litra*'.
5 If unblemished it must be offered in the Temple; its flesh belonged to its owner who must, however, consume it within Jerusalem. If it was blemished and unfit to be an offering it may be slaughtered for food; but it may not be sold, whether alive or slaughtered, whole or piecemeal.
6 The greater profit gained by open sale as against the smaller price resulting from private and more seemly disposal.
7 The priests.
8 In order to share it out equally (so Maim.). Rashi, Bert., and Tif. Yis. render: 'A *mina*'s weight of the flesh of a Firstling may be weighed against a *mina*'s weight (of common flesh)'. Cf. M.Sh. 1[1].

a blemish'. He took a dagger and slit its ear. The matter came before the Sages and they declared it permitted. When he saw that they had declared it permitted he went and slit the ears of other Firstlings; and they declared it forbidden. Once children were playing in the field and tied together the tails of the lambs, and the tail of one of them was torn away, and this was a Firstling. The matter came before the Sages and they declared it permitted. When they saw that they had declared it permitted they went and tied together the tails of other Firstlings; and they declared it forbidden. This is the general rule: If it is done of set purpose[1] it is forbidden; if not of set purpose it is permitted.

4. If a Firstling pursued after a man and he kicked it and caused a blemish in it, it may[2] be slaughtered by reason of it. In what concerns any blemishes likely to happen at the hands of man, herdsmen that are Israelites are accounted trustworthy; but herdsmen that are priests are not accounted trustworthy. Rabban Simeon b. Gamaliel says: A man is accounted trustworthy in what concerns another's [Firstling], but he is not accounted trustworthy in what concerns his own. R. Meir says: He that is suspected in what concerns any matter may neither judge nor bear witness thereof.

5. A priest may be believed if he says, 'I have caused this Firstling to be inspected, and it has a blemish'. All are accounted trustworthy in what concerns blemishes in Tithe [of Cattle].[3] If a Firstling was blind in an eye, or had a fore-leg cut off or a hind-leg broken, it may be slaughtered at the word of three members of the Synagogue.[4] R. Jose says: Even if there were three and twenty it may only be slaughtered at the word of one that is skilled.

6. If a man slaughtered a Firstling and sold it and it became known that he had not caused it to be inspected, what they have eaten they have eaten, but he must give them back what they have paid; and the flesh that they have not eaten must be buried, and he must give them back what they have paid. So, too, if a man slaughtered a cow and sold it and it became known that it was *terefah*, what they have eaten they have eaten, but he must give them back what they have paid, and the flesh that they have not eaten they shall give him back, and he must give them back what they have paid. If they had sold it to gentiles or thrown it to the dogs they need only pay him its value as *terefah*.

6. 1. By reason of these blemishes[5] the Firstling may be slaughtered: if the ear is defective in the gristle but not in the skin; if it is slit, though no part is lacking; if it has a hole in it as big as a vetch, or if it is dried up. 'Dried' means a condition such that, if it was pierced, it would not let forth a drop of blood. R. Jose b. Meshullam says: 'Dried up' means such a condition that it will crumble.

2. If its eyelid is pierced, defective, or slit; if its eyes have in them a speck, a commingling, a snail-shaped or snake-shaped or berry-shaped growth. A 'commingling' means such that the white breaks through the ring and enters the black; if the black enters the white this is not deemed a blemish since what is in the white is not deemed a blemish.

3. White flecks or rheum, if they are lasting. 'Lasting' means such that

---

[1] Deliberately by its owner, in order to make the slaughtering of it permissible.
[2] Variant: may not.
[3] If they allege that the blemish arose from the beast itself.
[4] i.e. that are unskilled.   [5] Cf. Lev. 22[19ff]; Deut. 15[21f].

have continued eighty days. R. Hanina b. Antigonus says: They must inspect the eyes three times within the eighty days. What water [in the eyes]
counts as 'lasting'? If it ate fresh or dry [fodder] from rain[-watered fields
and the blemish remained]. If it ate fresh or dry [fodder] from irrigated
fields, or if it ate dry [fodder] and afterward ate fresh [fodder, and the
blemish remained], it is not accounted a blemish; but only if it ate dry
[fodder] after fresh.

4. If its nose is pierced, defective, or slit; if its lip is pierced, defective, or
slit; if its front teeth are defective or worn down, or its back teeth uprooted.
R. Hanina b. Antigonus says: They do not examine from the double teeth
backwards, nor the double teeth themselves.

5. If the sheath of the male organ is defective (or the female organ in
female beasts brought as animal-offerings), or if there is a defect of the tail in
a bone though not in the joints, or if the [root-]end of the tail has the bone
divided,[1] or if there is a finger's breadth of flesh between one link [of the
tail] and the next.

6. If it has no stones or but one. R. Ishmael says: If it has two pouches it
has two stones; if it has but one pouch it has but one stone. R. Akiba says:
It should be set on its buttocks and squeezed: if there is a stone there it will
in the end come forth. It once happened that they squeezed and it did not
come forth, but when the beast was slaughtered it was found cleaving to the
groin; and R. Akiba declared [the beast] permitted, but R. Johanan b. Nuri
declared it forbidden.

7. If it has five legs or only three; or if it has unparted hooves like those of
an ass; or if it has a dislocated or deformed hip. 'Dislocated' means that the
thigh-bone has slipped [from its socket]; 'deformed' means that one thigh
is higher than the other.

8. If a bone of its fore-leg or hind-leg is broken, even if this is not manifest.
These blemishes did Ila[2] recount in Jabneh and the Sages agreed. Moreover
he added three others. They answered: We have heard no tradition about
these, [namely,] if its eye-socket is round like a man's, or if its mouth is like
a pig's, or if the greater part of the fore-tongue is gone. But the court that
came after them declared that these, too, were blemishes.

9. It once happend that the lower jaw stretched beyond the upper, and
Rabban Simeon b. Gamaliel inquired of the Sages and they declared this a
blemish. [It once happened that] the ear of a kid was folded, and the Sages
said: If [it grows from] a single bone it is a blemish, but if [it does] not [grow
from] a single bone, it is not a blemish. R. Hanina b. Gamaliel says: If the
tail of a kid is like that of a pig or has not three links, it is a blemish.

10. R. Hanina b. Antigonus says: If it has a wart on its eye, or if a bone of
its fore-leg or hind-leg is defective, or if it has lost a bone from its mouth, or
if one eye is big and the other little, or one ear big and the other little, so
that it is manifest and needs not to be measured. R. Judah says: If one of
its stones is twice as big as the other. But the Sages did not agree with
him.

11. If a calf's tail does not reach the knee-joint. The Sages said:
Throughout the growth of calves it is so; while they still grow their tails
grow still longer. Of which knee-joint did they speak? R. Hanina b. Antigonus says: The knee-joint in the middle of the thigh.[3] By reason of these

---

[1] So Maim. Rashi and Bert. render: 'If the end of the backbone is bare of skin and flesh.'
[2] See above, 4[5].   [3] i.e. the upper of the two bends in the hind-leg.

blemishes the Firstling may be slaughtered and animal-offerings that have been rendered invalid may be redeemed by reason of these blemishes.

12. By reason of these blemishes they may not be slaughtered either in the Temple or in the provinces:[1] [if it has] white specks or rheum [in the eye] that are not lasting; or back teeth that are defective but not uprooted; if it suffers from scurvy or warts or lichen; or if it is old or sick or evil-smelling; or if it has suffered an unnatural crime, or if it has killed a man according to the testimony of one witness or of its owner; or if it is of doubtful or double sex; [such may not be slaughtered] either in the Temple or in the provinces. R. Ishmael[2] says: No blemish is greater than this.[3] But the Sages say: It does not count as a Firstling but may be shorn and used for labour.

7. 1. These same blemishes, whether lasting or passing, likewise render [priests] unqualified [to serve in the Temple]. Among men are moreover added: he whose head is wedge-shaped or turnip-shaped or hammer-shaped, or whose head is sunk in or is flat at the back. R. Judah declares the humpbacked qualified, but the Sages declare him unqualified.

2. He that is bald-headed is unqualified. 'Bald-headed' means any that has not a strip of hair going round from ear to ear; but if he has that much he is qualified. If he has no eyebrows or but one—such is the *gibben*[4] spoken of in the Law. R. Dosa says: [*Gibben* means] he whose eyebrows hang down. R. Hanina b. Antigonus says: He that has two backs and two backbones.

3. He that is flat-nosed is unqualified. 'Flat-nosed' means one that can paint both his eyes together. If both his eyes are too high or both his eyes too low, or if one eye is too high or one eye too low; if he can see both the [lower] room and the upper chamber together, or cannot bear the sun; or if he has unmatched or watery eyes [he is unqualified]. He whose eyelashes have fallen out is unqualified by reason of his unsightliness.

4. If his eyes are big like those of a calf or little like those of a goose; if his body is too big or too little compared with his other parts; if his nose is too big or too little compared with his other parts; or if he is *tzimmem* or *tzimme'* [he is unqualified]. *Tzimme'* means he whose ears are too little; *tzimmem* means he whose ears are like a sponge.

5. If his upper lip juts out beyond his lower lip, or the lower beyond the upper, this is a blemish. If he has lost his teeth he is unqualified by reason of his unsightliness. If his breasts hang down like a woman's, if his belly is swollen, if his navel protrudes, if he suffers from falling sickness even but rarely, if lockjaw comes upon him, if his stones or his male organ are too big [he is unqualified]. If he has no stones or but one, this is he *that hath his stones broken*,[5] spoken of in the Law. R. Ishmael says: [It means] any whose stones are crushed. R. Akiba says: Any that has wind in his stones. R. Hanina b. Antigonus says: Any whose complexion is very dark.

6. If his ankles or knees knock together; or if he is afflicted with swellings [in the feet] or is bow-legged ('bow-legged' means any whose soles come

---

[1] In the Temple they may not be slaughtered since they are blemished; and in the provinces they may not be slaughtered (as being definitely invalid) for common food until they suffer one of the previously specified blemishes.
[2] Variant: Simeon.   [3] The beast of double sex.
[4] Lev. 21 [20]. In modern translations usually rendered 'crookbackt'.
[5] Lev. 21 [20].

together and whose knees do not touch); if he has a swelling on the big toe;
if his heel juts out backwards, or if his sole is as wide as that of a goose [he
is unqualified]. If his fingers or toes lie one above the other or are webbed
but only to the [middle] joint, he is qualified; and if beyond the joint, but he
has cut the tissue, he is still qualified. If he had an extra finger and he cut
it off, if there was a bone in it, he is unqualified; but if there was not, he is
qualified. If he had extra fingers and toes, six to each limb, twenty-four in
all, R. Judah declares him qualified, but the Sages declare him unqualified.
If he can use both hands alike, Rabbi declares him unqualified, but the
Sages declare him qualified. If he is black-skinned[1] or red-skinned or an
albino, if he is too long or a dwarf, or a deaf-mute, or an imbecile, or
drunken; if any have leprosy-signs that are adjudged clean, among men
such are unqualified, but among beasts such are accounted valid.[2] R.
Simeon b. Gamaliel says: If a beast is an imbecile it does not fulfil the rule
that it shall be of the choicest.[3] R. Eliezer says: Moreover if any have
dangling warts, among men such are unqualified but among beasts such
are accounted valid.

7. These are qualified among men and invalid among beasts: a father and
his son,[4] one that has inner blemishes[5] or that is born from the mother's
side,[6] one that has suffered an unnatural crime or that has killed a man. He
that has married women that are forbidden[7] is unqualified until he vows to
derive no benefit from them. He that suffers uncleanness because of the
dead is unqualified until he pledges himself to suffer uncleanness no more
because of the dead.[8]

8. 1. A Firstborn may sometimes be deemed a firstborn in what concerns
inheritance[9] but not in what concerns [the rights of] the priest;[10] and a Firstborn may sometimes be deemed a Firstborn in what concerns [the rights of]
the priest but not in what concerns inheritance; and a Firstborn may sometimes be deemed a Firstborn in what concerns both inheritance and [the
rights of] the priest, and a Firstborn may sometimes be deemed a Firstborn
neither in what concerns inheritance nor in what concerns [the rights of]
the priest. Who is he that may be deemed a Firstborn in what concerns
inheritance but not in what concerns [the rights of] the priest? He that was
born after another that failed to live, though its head had emerged while it
lived; or after a nine-months' child whose head had emerged [but the child
was] dead; or after an abortion that was like to a beast or a wild animal or a
bird. So R. Meir. But the Sages say: [Such is accounted *that which openeth
the womb*][11] only if there was in it aught of the form of a man. If the abortion
was in the form of a sandal or an afterbirth or a fully fashioned foetus, or if
what was born needed to be cut up [during delivery], what is born after
them is deemed a Firstborn in what concerns inheritance but not in what
concerns [the rights of] the priest. If a man had no children and married a
woman that had already borne young, even if she was a bondwoman and
was then made free, or a gentile and then became a proselyte, and she bore
[male offspring] after she was married to the Israelite, such is deemed a
Firstborn in what concerns inheritance but not in what concerns [the rights

---

[1] Lit. 'a Kushite'. Cf. Sukk. 3[6].   [2] To be brought as offerings.
[3] Cf. Deut. 12[11].   [4] Cf. Hull. 5[1ff].   [5] Heb. *terefah*.   [6] See p. 479, n. 3.
[7] See Lev. 21[7, 14].   [8] Lev. 21[1, 11].
[9] And may claim the double portion. See B.B. 8[4]; Deut. 21[17].
[10] The redemption price of five *selas*.   [11] Ex. 13[12].

of] the priest. R. Jose the Galilean says: Such is deemed a Firstborn in what concerns both inheritance and [the rights of] the priest, for it is written, *Whatsoever openeth the womb among the children of Israel:*[1] even if it was but the first that she has borne by an Israelite. If a man that had children married a woman that had not given birth; or if the woman became a proselyte while she was already with child, or if she was made free while she was already with child, or if she and a wife of priestly stock, or she and a wife of levitic stock, or she and a wife that had before borne young—if they each bore [a child and it was not known which was the firstborn]; so, too, if a woman had not continued with her husband three months and married another and bore a child and it was not known whether it was a nine-months' child of the former or a seven-months' child of the latter husband—such are deemed Firstborn in what concerns [the rights of] the priest but not in what concerns inheritance. Who is he that is a Firstborn in what concerns both inheritance and [the rights of] the priest? If an abortion was a foetus that was filled with blood or filled with water or filled with variegated matter, or that was the like of fish, locusts, insects, or creeping things, or if it was a forty-day's abortion, then what is born after them is deemed a Firstborn in what concerns both inheritance and [the rights of] the priest.

2. Neither what is born from the side [of the mother] nor what is born after it is deemed a Firstborn, whether in what concerns inheritance or in what concerns [the rights of] the priest. R. Simeon says: The first [is deemed a Firstborn] in what concerns inheritance, and the second in what concerns the five *selas* [that fall to the priest as the price of redemption].

3. If a man's wife had not before borne young and she bore two males,[2] he must give five *selas* to the priest. If one of them died within thirty days the father is exempt. If the father died and the sons remained alive, R. Meir says: If they paid before they divided the inheritance, then they have paid; but if not, they are exempt. R. Judah says: The property is liable. If she bore a male and a female the priest can claim nothing.

4. If two women that had not before borne young bore two males,[3] their husband must give ten *selas* to the priest. If one of them died within thirty days and he had paid the money to one priest, the priest must give him back five *selas*; if to two priests, he cannot exact aught from them. [If the two women bore] a male and a female or two males and a female,[3] he must pay five *selas* to the priest; if two females and a male, or two females and two males,[3] the priest can claim nothing. If one of the women had already borne young but the other had not, and they bore two males, he must pay five *selas* to the priest. If one of them died within thirty days, the father is exempt. If the father died and the sons remained alive, R. Meir says: If they paid before they divided the inheritance, then they have paid; but if not, they are exempt. R. Judah says: The property is liable. If they bore a male and a female, the priest can claim nothing.

5. If two men's wives that had not before borne young bore two males,[3] each must pay five *selas* to the priest. If one of them died within thirty days and they had paid the money to one priest, he must give them back five *selas*; but if to two priests, they cannot exact aught from them. If the wives bore a male and a female,[3] the fathers are exempt, and the son must redeem

---

[1] Ex. 13[2]. [2] And it is not known which was born first.
[3] And it is not known which is the child of which.

himself;[1] if two females and a male, or two males and two females, the priest can claim nothing.

6. If the wife of the one man had already borne young, but the wife of the other had not, and they bore two males,[2] he whose wife had not before borne young must pay five *selas* to the priest; but if they bore a male and a female the priest can claim nothing. If the son died within thirty days, although he had paid [the five *selas*] to the priest, the priest must give them back; if the son died after thirty days, even if he had not paid, he must pay the priest. If the son died on the thirtieth day, it is reckoned as if he died the day before. R. Akiba says: If he had paid he cannot exact it [from the priest], and if he had not paid he need not pay. If the father died within thirty days, the presumption is that the son was not redeemed unless proof thereof is produced; if he died after thirty days, the presumption is that the son was redeemed unless they can say[3] to the son that he was not redeemed. If a man must redeem both himself and his son,[4] he comes before his son. R. Judah says: His son comes before him, since the duty of redeeming him rested upon his father, and the duty of redeeming his son rests upon him.

7. The five *selas* due for the [Firstborn] son[5] should be paid in Tyrian coinage; the thirty due for the slave [that was gored by an ox][6] and the fifty due from the violator[7] and the seducer,[8] and the hundred due from him that *hath brought up an evil name*,[9] are all to be paid according to the value of the shekels of the sanctuary, in Tyrian coinage. Aught that is to be redeemed[10] may be redeemed with silver or its value, save only the Shekel-dues.[11]

8. The price of redemption may not be paid in slaves or in bonds or in land; so, too, in [the redemption of] aught that has been dedicated. If a man wrote a bond for a priest [saying] that he owed him five *selas*, [even after redeeming his bond] he is still in debt to him for [the five *selas*], and his son is not accounted redeemed; therefore, if he was minded [not to exact the five *selas* afresh] the priest has the right to give it to him, [but only] as a gift. If a man set apart the redemption price of his son, and it was lost, he is answerable for it and must replace it, for it is written, *It shall be thine*; and *Thou shalt surely redeem it*.[12]

9. The Firstborn takes a double share of his father's goods, but he does not take a double share of his mother's goods, and he does not take a double share of the increased value,[13] or [a double share] of what is expected to accrue[14] to the estate in like manner as [he receives a double share] of what is already held in possession; and the same applies to the wife in what concerns her *Ketubah*,[15] and to the daughters in what concerns their maintenance,[16] and to him that performs the levirate marriage;[17] none of these may

---

[1] Since it cannot be in doubt that he was the firstborn male.
[2] And it is not known which is the child of which.
[3] Variant: unless proof can be brought.
[4] e.g. if, after a man (who was a firstborn son) had a firstborn son, proof was brought that that man's father had not paid the five *selas* for the man himself.
[5] Num. 18[16]. 'Shekels of the sanctuary' are there prescribed; these are assumed to have been pure silver, like the Tyrian shekel, and so twice the value of the ordinary current shekel which was alloyed with copper.
[6] Ex. 21[32].   [7] Deut. 22[29].   [8] Ex. 22[16, 17].   [9] Deut. 22[19].
[10] Like the firstborn son, or dedicated produce. They may be redeemed with copper coin up to the required value.
[11] The half-shekel which every Israelite must pay yearly to the Temple (see p. 152, n. 2). Such may only be paid in silver.   [12] Num. 18[15].
[13] Of the estate after the death of the father and before the division of the property.
[14] Cf. Ket. 10[3].   [15] App. I. 16.   [16] See Ket. 13[3].
[17] See p. 218, n. 1. He inherits his dead brother's property.

take aught of the increased value or of what is expected to accrue to the estate as they may of what is already held in possession.

10. These do not revert [to their first owners] in the year of Jubilee:[1] the Firstborn's portion, what a man inherits from his wife, what he inherits that performs levirate marriage, and what is given as a gift. So R. Meir. But the Sages say: A gift counts as a sale. R. Eliezer says: They all revert [to their first owners] in the year of Jubilee. R. Johanan b. Baroka says: He that inherits from his wife must restore the property to the members of her family, but he may deduct somewhat from its value.

9. 1. The law concerning Tithe of Cattle[2] is binding both in the Land [of Israel] and outside the Land, both during the time of the Temple and after the time of the Temple, for unconsecrated beasts but not for animal-offerings; and it applies both to the herd and to the flocks (though none may give Tithe from the one instead of from the other), both to sheep and to goats (and one may give Tithe from the one instead of from the other), both to the new breed and to the old (though none may give Tithe from the one instead of from the other).[3] It might have been inferred: if from among the new breed and the old breed (which do not count as diverse kinds) Tithe may not be given from the one instead of from the other, how much more, then, from among the sheep and the goats (which count as diverse kinds) may Tithe not be given from the one instead of from the other! But Scripture says, *And of the flock*;[4] thereby classing all 'flocks' as one.

2. For the Tithe those cattle may be included together as one herd that are found within the distance that cattle wander while pasturing. What is the distance that cattle wander while pasturing? Sixteen miles. If there was a distance of thirty-two miles between one herd and another they cannot be included together; but if any cattle were midway between them, all are counted together with them that are midway between them, and so tithed. R. Meir says: The Jordan serves as a boundary [to a herd] for the Tithe of Cattle.

3. What a man has bought or received as a gift is exempt from the Tithe of Cattle. If brothers that are jointholders are liable to surcharge, they are exempt from Tithe of Cattle;[5] if they are liable to Tithe of Cattle they are exempt from surcharge. If they acquired the cattle from the property of the house [of their father],[6] they are liable [to Tithe]; but if they did not,[7] they are exempt. If they first divided the cattle and then again became jointholders, they are liable to the surcharge and exempt from Tithe of Cattle.

4. All are brought into the cattle-pen to be tithed save only beasts that are cross-bred, or *terefah*, or born from the side [of the mother-beast], or too young, or orphans. 'Orphan' means one whose dam is dead or slaughtered. R. Joshua says: Even if the dam was slaughtered but its hide is still whole, the beast does not count as an orphan.[8]

5. There are three seasons[9] for the Tithe of Cattle: a half month before

---

[1] Lev. 25[10ff].   [2] Lev. 27[32].
[3] i.e. from what was born before the 1st of Elul (cf. R.Sh. 1[1]), in the stead of what was born after.   [4] Lev. 27[32].   [5] See Shek. 1[7] and notes.
[6] And had not divided the herd.   [7] If they had bought it.
[8] Since it can be covered up and protected with the hide.
[9] Lit. 'threshing-floors'; here used in the sense of 'Tithing-time', since the threshing-floor is both the place where grain is made fit for food and where it becomes subject to tithes.

Passover, a half month before Pentecost, and a half month before the Feast [of Tabernacles].[1] So R. Akiba. Ben Azzai says: On the 29th of Adar, on the 1st of Siwan, and on the 29th of Ab. R. Eliezer and R. Simeon say: On the 1st of Nisan, on the 1st of Siwan, and on the 29th of Elul. And why did they say the 29th of Elul and not the 1st of Tishri? Because it is a Festival-day, and it is not possible to tithe on a Festival-day; therefore they made it earlier, on the 29th of Elul. R. Meir says: The 1st of Elul is the New Year for the Tithe of Cattle. Ben Azzai says: Cattle born during Elul are tithed by themselves.

6. All born from the 1st of Tishri to the 29th of Elul[2] can be included together [for the Tithe of Cattle]. Those born five days before and those born five days after the New Year cannot be included together; but those born five days before and those born five days after the seasons for the Tithe can be included together. If so, why was it said, 'There are three seasons for the Tithe of Cattle'? Because before the season has arrived it is permitted to sell and to slaughter, but after the season has arrived none may slaughter, but if a man slaughtered he is not culpable.

7. How do they levy the Tithe? They lead the cattle into the pen and make a small outlet for them so that no two can go forth together. And they count with a rod: One, Two, Three, Four, Five, Six, Seven, Eight, Nine, and the one that comes out tenth is marked with a red mark, and it is said, 'This is Tithe'. If it is not marked with the red mark, or if they have not been counted with the rod, or if they have been counted lying down or standing, they are none the less tithed. If a man had a hundred cattle and he took [any] ten from them, or ten and he took [any] one from them, such are not [valid] Tithe. R. Jose b. R. Judah says: Such are [valid] Tithe. If one of them that was already counted jumped in among the others, the others are exempt; if one of them that was marked as Tithe jumped in among the others, they must all be left to pasture until they suffer a blemish, and after they have suffered a blemish they may be consumed by their owners.

8. If [the first] two came out together, they are all counted in pairs; if they were counted as one, they that are counted as the ninth and the tenth both become unfit for use. If the ninth and the tenth came out together, the ninth and the tenth become unfit for use.[3] If the ninth was called the tenth or the tenth the ninth or the eleventh the tenth, all three become holy; the ninth may only be consumed after it has suffered a blemish, the tenth becomes Tithe and the eleventh must be offered as a Peace-offering, and it can transfer its sanctity to its Substitute.[4] So R. Meir. But R. Judah says: Can one Substitute[5] transfer sanctity to another Substitute? They answered in the name of R. Meir: If it had been a Substitute it could not be offered.[6] If the ninth was called the tenth, and the tenth the tenth, and the eleventh the tenth, the eleventh does not become holy. This is the general rule: If the tenth was not deprived of its proper name, the eleventh does not become holy.

---

[1] Cf. Shek. 3[1].

[2] Between the first and last days of the year (the 'natural' year is reckoned as beginning on 1st Tishri, the seventh month).

[3] Neither is certainly tithe, so neither can be offered in the Temple; and neither is certainly not tithe, so, while they remain unblemished, they cannot be free for common use.

[4] Lev. 27[10].

[5] He held that the eleventh was itself substituted for the tenth, when it, instead of the true tenth, was styled 'the tenth'.

[6] Since there can be no substitute for what is a Firstling or Tithe of Cattle. Cf. Tem. 1[1].

ARAKHIN[1] ('VOWS OF VALUATION')

1. 1. All—priests and levites and Israelites, women and slaves—may vow another's Valuation and their Valuation may be vowed by others, and they may vow another's worth and their worth may be vowed by others. They that are of doubtful or of double sex may vow another's worth and their worth may be vowed by others, and they may vow [another's] Valuation, but their Valuation cannot be vowed by others, since only their Valuation may be vowed who are surely male or surely female. A deaf-mute, an imbecile, or a minor may have their worth or their Valuation vowed by others, but they may not vow another's worth or another's Valuation, since they have no understanding. The worth of one that is less than a month old may be vowed but not the Valuation.

2. R. Meir says: The Valuation of a gentile may be vowed, but he cannot vow another's Valuation. R. Judah says: He may vow another's Valuation but his Valuation cannot be vowed by others. But they agree that he may vow another's worth and that his worth may be vowed by others.

3. The worth or the Valuation of him that is at the point of death or condemned to be put to death may not be vowed. R. Hananiah b. Akabya says: His Valuation may be vowed since its price is fixed; but his worth may not be vowed since its price is not fixed. R. Jose says: He[2] may still vow another's worth and another's Valuation, or dedicate aught to the Temple; and if he caused damage he is [still] liable to make restitution.

4. If a woman was condemned to be put to death they may not wait until she has given birth, but if she had already sat on the birth-stool they wait until she has given birth. If a woman was put to death use may be made of her hair;[3] if a beast was put to death any use of it is forbidden.

2. 1. There can be no [valid] Valuation vow less than one *sela*[4] or more than fifty *selas*. Thus if a man had paid one *sela*[5] and he then became rich, he pays nothing [more]; if he had paid less than a *sela* and he then became rich, he must give fifty. If he owned but five *selas*, R. Meir says: He need pay but one. But the Sages say: He must give them all. There can be no [valid] Valuation vow less than one *sela* or more than fifty *selas*. If a woman has strayed in her reckoning[6] she may not reckon afresh before seven days or later than seventeen. No leprosy-signs[7] are shut up less than one week and none more than three weeks.

2. There are never less than four 'full' months in the year, nor do more

---

[1] Persons may vow to give to the Temple either the 'valuation' or the 'worth' of themselves or another. Their 'valuation' is fixed (Lev. 27[1ff]) by the Law at nothing for a male or female child up to thirty days; at five shekels for a male and three for a female from one month to five years old; at twenty shekels for a male and ten for a female from five years old to twenty; at fifty shekels for a male and thirty for a female from twenty years old to sixty; and at fifteen shekels for a male and ten for a female from sixty years old and upwards. On the other hand, if a person's 'worth' is vowed, that person's 'market-value' must be ascertained and such sum given to the Temple.

[2] Who is condemned to be put to death.   [3] False hair.

[4] Lev. 27[8] makes provision in the case of the poor for a reduction of the prescribed tariff; but any such reduced estimate may not fall below one *sela* (App. II, A). The 'shekel' prescribed in Scripture is, in the Mishnah (cf. p. 541, n. 5), valued at a *sela*, twice the value of the later shekel.

[5] Although (being aged between 20 and 60 years) his prescribed valuation was fifty *selas*, he was so poor that the priest (Lev. 27[8]) reduced it to one.

[6] See Pes. 8[5]; Nidd. 6[14]. If she had not fixed periods and was in doubt whether the flow she suffered was during the seven days or the eleven, she cannot achieve certainty in less than seven days, and she cannot help achieving certainty within seventeen days. Cf. Ab. 3[19].

[7] See Neg. 3[3–8].

than eight months require to be taken into account.[1] The Two Loaves [of Pentecost][2] were consumed never earlier than the second day and never later than the third day.[3] The Shewbread[4] was consumed never earlier than the ninth day and never later than the eleventh day. A child may never be circumcised[5] before the eighth day and never later than the twelfth day.

3. They blew never less than twenty-one blasts in the Temple[6] and never more than forty-eight [in a day]. They played on never less than two harps or more than six, and on never less than two flutes or more than twelve. On twelve days in the year was the flute played before the Altar: at the slaughtering of the First Passover-offering, at the slaughtering of the Second Passover[5]-offering, on the first Festival-day of Passover, and on the Festival-day of Pentecost and on the eight days of the Feast [of Tabernacles].[8] And they did not play on a pipe[9] of bronze but on a reed-pipe, since its sound was the sweeter, and they closed the playing with one pipe only since this made the better close.

4. [They that played the instruments of music] were the slaves of the priests. So R. Meir. R. Jose says: They were from the families of Beth ha-Pegarim and Beth Zipporya and from Emmaus, and they were eligible to give [their daughters] in marriage to the priestly stock.[10] R. Hanina b. Antigonus says: They were levites.

5. There were never less than six inspected lambs in the Chamber of Lambs,[11] sufficient for a Sabbath and the two Festival-days of the New Year;[12] and their number could be increased without end. There were never less than two trumpets, and their number could be increased without end; there were never less than nine lyres, and their number could be increased without end; but of cymbals there was but one.

6. There were never less than twelve levites standing on the Platform,[13] and their number could be increased without end. None that was not of age could enter the Temple Court to take part in the [Temple-]service save only when the levites stood up to sing; and they[14] did not join in the singing with harp and lyre, but with the mouth alone to add spice to the music. R. Eliezer b. Jacob says: They did not help to make up the required number, nor did they stand on the Platform; but they used to stand on the ground so that their heads were between the feet of the levites; and they used to be called the levites' tormentors.[15]

3. 1. The law of the vow of Valuation may sometimes bear leniently and sometimes stringently; the law of the Field of Possession[16] may sometimes bear leniently and sometimes stringently; the law of the ox that is an attested danger[17] and that has killed a bondservant may sometimes bear leniently and sometimes stringently; the law of the violator[18] and the seducer[19] and him that *hath brought up an evil name*[20] may sometimes bear

---

[1] i.e. the year (according to the Jewish reckoning by lunar months) has never less than four months of 30 days (called 'full' or 'pregnant' or 'intercalated' months) and never more than a total of eight had ever been taken into account by the Sages as needing to be made 30 days long. The lunar month is approximately 29 days, 12⅔ hours. Thus, while the months may be given alternately 30 and 29 days, the resultant error involved variations in the time of the Mishnah, when the time of each new moon was determined by ocular proof only.

[2] Lev. 23[17].   [3] See Men. 11[9].   [4] See Men. 11[9].   [5] See Shab. 19[5].
[6] See Sukk. 5[5].   [7] See Pes. 9[1ff].   [8] Sukk. 5[1].   [9] Maim. 'mouthpiece'.
[10] They were Israelites of irreproachable lineage. Cf. Kidd. 4[1ff].
[11] Cf. Tam. 3[3].   [12] When the three fell on consecutive days.   [13] Midd. 2[6].
[14] The children.   [15] So Rashi, Bert. Variant: the little ones of the levites.
[16] Lev. 27[16ff].   [17] Ex. 21[29ff].   [18] Deut. 22[28f].   [19] Ex. 22[16f].   [20] Deut. 22[19].

leniently and sometimes stringently. 'The law of the vow of Valuation may sometimes bear leniently and sometimes stringently'—thus it is all one whether a man vowed the Valuation of the fairest in Israel or of the most unseemly in Israel: he must pay fifty *selas*;[1] but if he said, 'I vow his worth', then he must pay what he is worth.

2. 'The law of the Field of Possession[2] may sometimes bear leniently and sometimes stringently'—thus it is all one whether a man dedicated [a field] in the desert of Machuz[3] or in the gardens of Sebaste:[4] [if he would redeem it] he pays the *fifty shekels of silver* [for every part of a field that suffices for] *the sowing of a homer of barley*;[5] but if it was *a field which he hath bought*,[6] he pays what it is worth. R. Eliezer says: It is all one whether it is a Field of Possession or *a field which he hath bought*:[7] they differ only in that for a Field of Possession he must give the [Added] Fifth[8] and for *a field which he hath bought* he need not give the [Added] Fifth.

3. 'The law of the ox that is an attested danger and that has killed a bondservant may sometimes bear leniently and sometimes stringently'—thus it is all one whether it killed the finest bondservant or the most unseemly bondservant: he[9] pays thirty *selas*;[10] but if it killed a freeman he pays what he is worth. If it wounded him, whether it was a bondservant or a freeman, in either case he must make restitution for the damage in full.

4. 'The law of the violator and the seducer . . . may sometimes bear leniently and sometimes stringently'—thus it is all one whether a man violated or seduced a woman from among the greatest of the priestly stock or the least in Israel: he must pay fifty *selas*;[11] but compensation for indignity and for blemish[12] is in accordance with [the condition of life of] him that inflicts the indignity and her that suffers the indignity.

5. 'The law of him that *hath brought up an evil name* may sometimes bear leniently and sometimes stringently'—thus it is all one whether a man *hath brought up an evil name* against a woman from among the greatest of the priestly stock or against the least in Israel: he must pay a hundred *selas*.[13] Thus he that speaks with his mouth suffers more than he that commits an act. Thus also we find that the judgement was sealed against our fathers in the wilderness only by reason of their evil speaking, for it is written, *Yet have they tempted me these ten times, and have not hearkened to my voice*.[14]

4. 1. [When the priest shall value a man according to] his ability,[15] this shall be according to the ability of him that vows; [and when according to] the years of his age, this shall be according to the age of him [whose Valuation is] vowed; [and when according to] the Valuations [prescribed in the Law], this shall be according to him whose Valuation is vowed; and the Valuation [shall be paid at the rate prescribed] at the time of [the vow of] Valuation. '[When the priest shall value a man according to] his ability, this shall be according to the ability of him that vows'—thus if a poor man vowed the Valuation of a rich man, he need pay only the Valuation of a

---

[1] If it was a man between twenty and sixty years old.
[2] Which he had inherited.
[3] A place unidentified. Cf. Maksh. 3[4]. Other interpretations of this phrase are: a field 'in the surroundings of a town', or 'on the sands of the sea-shore'.
[4] The town built by Herod on the site of ancient Samaria.
[5] Lev. 27[16]. The *homer* is equal to the *kor* (App. II, D).
[6] Lev. 27[22].   [7] Both are valued at fifty shekels.   [8] Lev. 27[19]. See B.M. 4[8].
[9] The ox's owner.   [10] Ex. 21[32].   [11] Deut. 22[29].   [12] See Ket. 3[7].   [13] Deut. 22[19].
[14] Num. 14[22].   [15] Lev. 27[8].

poor man; but if a rich man vowed the Valuation of a poor man, he must pay the Valuation of a rich man.

2. But it is not so with offerings. If a man said, 'I take upon myself the offering of this leper', and the leper was poor,[1] he must bring the offering of a poor man; and if the leper was rich[2] he must bring the offering of a rich man. Rabbi says: I say that it is the same also with a vow of Valuation. Why should the poor man that vows the Valuation of a rich man pay only the Valuation of a poor man? Because the rich man had incurred no liability whatsoever. But if the rich man said, 'I vow my own Valuation', and the poor man heard and said, 'What this man has said, I take upon myself', then he must pay the Valuation of a rich man. If he was poor and then became rich, or rich and then became poor, he must nevertheless pay the Valuation of a rich man. R. Judah says: Even if he was poor and became rich and then again became poor he must pay the Valuation of a rich man.

3. But it is not so with offerings. Even if [when a man vowed] his father lay dying and left to him ten thousand, or if he had a ship on the sea and it brought to him ten thousand, the Temple has no claim at all on them.

4. '[And when according to] the years of his age, this shall be according to the age of him [whose Valuation is] vowed'—thus if a child vowed the Valuation of an old man, he pays the Valuation of an old man; and if an old man vowed the Valuation of a child, he pays the Valuation of a child. '[And when according to] the Valuations [prescribed in the Law], this shall be according to him whose Valuation is vowed'—thus if a man vowed the Valuation of a woman, he pays the Valuation of a woman, and if a woman vowed the Valuation of a man she pays the Valuation of a man. 'And the Valuation [shall be paid at a rate prescribed] at the time of [the vow of] Valuation'—thus if a man had vowed the Valuation of a child that was less than five years old and it then became more than five years old; or if of one that was less than twenty years old and he became more than twenty years old, he pays according to the time when he vowed the Valuation. Thirty days is accounted under this age; five years, or twenty years, is accounted under this age; for it is written, *And if it be from sixty years old and upward, if it be a male*;[3] thus we learn about the others from them that are sixty years old: as sixty years is accounted under this age, so, too, twenty years or five years must be accounted under this age. What! if [Scripture] has reckoned sixty years to be under this age, thereby acting the more stringently,[4] shall the fifth year or the twentieth year be reckoned under this age, thereby acting the more leniently?[5] But Scripture says, *Years*, in each case, to set forth the analogy: as the expression *years* used in *sixty years* means [that it is reckoned to him as if he was] under this age, so, too, the expression *years* used in *five years* and *twenty years* means [that it is reckoned to him as if he was] under this age, no matter whether it bears leniently or stringently. R. Eleazar says: [So is it even] until they are a month and a day more than the years prescribed.

5. 1. If a man said, 'I vow my weight', he must give his weight in silver if [he had said] 'in silver', or in gold if [he had said] 'in gold'. Once the mother of Yirmatia[6] said, 'I vow my daughter's weight', and she went up to

---

[1] Lev. 14²¹.   [2] Lev. 14¹⁰.   [3] Lev. 27⁷.
[4] Since under sixty the price is fifty shekels, and over sixty it is only fifteen.
[5] Since under twenty the price is only twenty shekels, and under five, five shekels.
[6] Cambridge text: 'Domitia.'

Jerusalem and weighed her and paid her weight in gold. [If a man said,] 'I vow my hand's weight', R. Judah says: He should fill a jar with water and put in his hand to the elbow; then he should weight out the flesh of an ass with its sinews and bones and put it in [the jar] until it is filled up again. R. Jose said: How is it possible to account one kind of flesh as like to another kind of flesh, and one kind of bones as like to another kind of bones!—but, rather, they estimate what the hand is likely to weigh.

2. [If he said,] 'I vow the worth of my hand', they estimate what his value is with a hand and what it is without a hand. Herein vows of worth bear more stringently than vows of Valuation; but vows of Valuation may bear more stringently than vows of worth; thus if a man said, 'I vow my Valuation', and he died, his heirs must pay it; but if [he said], 'I vow my worth', and he died, his heirs pay nothing, since the dead have no worth. [If a man said,] 'I vow the Valuation of my hand' or 'the Valuation of my foot', he has said nothing; but if [he said, 'I vow] the Valuation of my head' or 'the Valuation of my liver', he must pay the whole of his Valuation. This is the general rule: [If a man vows the Valuation of] aught whereon his life depends, he must pay the whole of his Valuation.

3. [If he said,] 'I vow the half of my Valuation', he need pay but the half of his Valuation; but if he said, 'I vow the Valuation of the half of me', he must pay the whole of his Valuation. This is the general rule: [If he vows the Valuation of] aught whereon his life depends, he must pay the whole of his Valuation.

4. If a man said, 'I vow the Valuation of such-a-one', and both he and he whose Valuation was vowed died, his heirs must pay it. And if [he said,] 'I vow the worth of such-a-one', and he that vowed died, his heirs must pay it; but if he died whose worth was vowed the heirs pay nothing, since the dead have no worth.

5. [If a man said,] 'Let this ox be a Whole-offering', or 'Let this house be an offering', and the ox died or the house fell down, he is not still bound to pay the like; [but if he had said,] 'I vow the worth of this ox as a Whole-offering', or 'the value of this house as an offering', and the ox died or the house fell down, he must pay the like.

6. Pledges must be taken from them that are bound by a vow of Valuation, but from them that are liable to Sin-offerings or Guilt-offerings pledges are not taken. A pledge must be taken from them that have bound themselves to bring Whole-offerings or Peace-offerings; although he cannot make atonement unless he acts of his own good will, since it is written, *At his good will*,[1] nevertheless they may compel him until he says, 'It is my will'. So, too, sayest thou, as touching women's bills of divorce:[2] they may compel him until he says, 'It is my will'.

6. 1. [The goods of] orphans that have been valued [by the court to meet the father's debt must be proclaimed for sale] during thirty days; and those of the Temple[3] during sixty days; and they must be proclaimed for sale in the morning and in the evening. If a man had dedicated his goods to the Temple and he was still liable for the payment of his wife's *Ketubah*,[4] R.

---

[1] Lev. 1³. R.V.: 'that he may be accepted'.
[2] When an illegal marriage must be set aside. A divorce is not valid except with the husband's consent.
[3] When a man would redeem a field (which he had bought and not inherited) which he had dedicated to the Temple.   [4] App. I. 16.

Eliezer says: When he divorces her he must vow to derive no further benefit from her.[1] R. Joshua says: He need not. Similarly[2] Rabban Simeon b. Gamaliel said: If a man was guarantor for a woman's *Ketubah* and her husband divorced her, the husband must vow to derive no further benefit from her, lest he make a conspiracy against the property of the guarantor and take back his wife again.

2. If a man dedicated his goods to the Temple while he was still liable for the payment of his [divorced] wife's *Ketubah* or indebted to a creditor, the wife cannot recover her *Ketubah* from what was dedicated nor the creditor his debt; but he that redeems them redeems them on the understanding that he must pay the wife her *Ketubah* or the creditor his debt. If he had dedicated goods worth ninety *minas*[3] and he owed a hundred *minas*, the creditor should lend him another *denar*,[4] and with this he may redeem the goods on the understanding that he must pay the wife her *Ketubah* or the creditor his debt.

3. Although they have said, 'Pledges must be taken from them that are bound by a vow of Valuation', they must leave him sustenance for thirty days and raiment for twelve months and bed and bedding and shoes and phylacteries[5]—for himself, but not for his wife or children. If he was a craftsman they must leave him two of every kind of the tools of his craft. If he was a carpenter they must leave him two axes and two saws. R. Eliezer says: If he was a husbandman they must leave him his yoke [of oxen], and if an ass-driver they must leave him his ass.

4. If he had many tools of one kind and few of another kind, they may not bid him sell of the many and buy some of the few, but they leave him two from every kind of which he has many and all that he has from them of which he has few. If a man dedicated all his property to the Temple, they take away[6] even his phylacteries.

5. It is all one whether a man dedicates his goods or vows his own Valuation: he[7] has no claim to his wife's raiment or his children's raiment, or to dyed clothes which he had dyed for their need, or to new sandals which he had bought for their need. Although it has been said, 'Slaves should be sold with their raiment to improve their value', since if raiment costing thirty *denars* was bought for a slave it improves him by a *mina's* worth[8] (so, too, if a cow is suffered to wait until market-day its value increases; so, too, if a pearl is brought to a great city its value increases), yet the Temple can claim the value of anything only in its own place and at that time.

7. 1. None may dedicate [the Field of his Possession][9] less than two years before the year of Jubilee or redeem it less than one year after the [beginning of the] year of Jubilee.[10] [In redeeming the field] they may not make reckoning of months to [the disadvantage of] the Temple,[11] but the Temple may make reckoning of months [to its own advantage].[12] If a man dedicated

---

[1] Lest his divorce was only a device to put a lien on certain property so that it could not be included in what was dedicated to the Temple.

[2] See B.B. 10[7].   [3] App. II, A.

[4] Since he had already dedicated all his property.   [5] See p. 104, n. 16.

[6] Rashi: 'put up to auction', so that he may redeem them.

[7] In paying his vow or redeeming what he has dedicated.

[8] But cf. B.M. 4[12] (end).   [9] Lev. 27[16ff].

[10] If he does, he must, when he redeems it, pay the full fifty shekels instead of, as in other years, a shekel and a *pondion* for each year before the year of Jubilee.

[11] e.g. two years and three months may not be reckoned as two years.

[12] e.g. one year and eleven months before the Jubilee cannot count as two full years to

his field at a time when the law of the year of Jubilee was binding,[1] he must pay[2] *the fifty shekels of silver* [for every part of a field that suffices for] *the sowing of a homer of barley*. If the field contained rifts ten handbreadths deep or rocks ten handbreadths high these are not included in the measure;[3] but if less than this they are included. If a man dedicated [his field] two years or three years before the year of Jubilee he must pay one *sela* and one *pondion*[4] for each year. If he said, 'I will pay for each year as it comes', they do not hearken to him, but he must pay for all the years together.

2. It is all one whether the owner or any other [redeems the field]. Wherein does the owner differ from any other? Only in that the owner must pay the [Added] Fifth[5] and any other does not pay the [Added] Fifth.

3. If a man dedicated a field and then redeemed it, it does not go out of his possession in the year of Jubilee. If his son redeemed it it reverts to his father in the year of Jubilee. If another, or a kinsman, redeemed it, and he[6] again redeemed it from his hand, it does not go out of his possession in the year of Jubilee. If one of the priests redeemed it,[7] and it was still in his possession [when the year of Jubilee began], he may not say, 'Since it goes out to the priests[8] in the year of Jubilee, and since it is now in my possession, therefore it belongs to me', but it goes out to all his brethren the priests.

4. If the year of Jubilee arrived and it was not yet redeemed, then the priests enter into possession of it and they pay its value.[9] So R. Judah. R. Simeon says: They enter into possession but they do not pay [its value]. R. Eleazar says: They neither enter into possession nor pay [its value], but it is called 'an abandoned field' until the second year of Jubilee; if the second year of Jubilee arrived and it was not redeemed, it is called 'a twice abandoned field' until the third year of Jubilee; the priests may never enter into possession until another has redeemed it.[10]

5. If a man bought a field from his father and his father died, and he afterward dedicated it, it is accounted a Field of his Possession.[11] If he dedicated it and afterward his father died, then it is accounted *a field which he hath bought*.[12] So R. Meir. R. Judah and R. Simeon say: [It is accounted] a Field of his Possession, for it is written, *And if a field which he hath bought which is not a field of his possession*—a field which was not such as might be a field of his possession; thus it excludes a field which is such as might be a field of his possession. *A field which he hath bought* does not go out to the priests in the year of Jubilee, for none can dedicate what he does not possess. Priests and levites may dedicate [their fields] at any time and redeem them at any time, whether before the Jubilee year or after it.

8. 1. If a man dedicated his field[13] at a time when the [law of the] year of

permit the field to be redeemed for two shekels and two *pondions*; the Temple can exact the full fifty shekels. See p. 549, n. 10.   [1] When all Israel lived in the Land of Israel.
   [2] At the beginning of the Jubilee cycle.   [3] Of a *homer's* sowing area.
   [4] A fraction more than one forty-ninth of the fifty shekels. The surplus is explained as surcharge (see Shek. 1[6]) to reimburse the Temple treasurer for any loss suffered by the Temple in changing the money.
   [5] Lev. 27[19]. This fifth is really a fourth; for if the estimation was twenty shekels he must pay twenty-five.
   [6] Who had dedicated it.   [7] From the Temple treasurer.
   [8] Lev. 27[21], 'holy to the Lord, the possession thereof shall be the priests'.
   [9] At the rate of fifty shekels for each *homer's* sowing space.
   [10] And at the next Jubilee it goes out of his possession and becomes the priests'.
   [11] Lev. 27[16].   [12] Lev. 27[22].   [13] His by inheritance.

Jubilee was no longer binding,[1] they say to him, 'Make thou first a begin-ning', for the owner pays the [Added] Fifth and none other pays the [Added] Fifth. Once a man dedicated his field because of its badness. They said to him, 'Make thou first a beginning', and he answered, 'I will take it for an *issar*'. R. Jose said: He said only 'for an egg' (for what is dedicated can be redeemed either by money or by money's worth). Whereupon they said to him, 'It is thine!' Thus he lost an *issar* and the field was still his.

2. If one man said, 'I bid ten *selas*', and another said 'twenty', and another 'thirty', and another 'forty', and another 'fifty', and then he that bid fifty recanted, they take pledges[2] from his property up to ten *selas*. If he that bid forty recanted, they take pledges from his property up to ten *selas*. If he that bid thirty recanted, they take pledges from his property up to ten *selas*. If he that bid twenty recanted, they take pledges from his property up to ten *selas*. If he that bid ten recanted, they sell the field for what it is worth, and exact the residue[3] from him that bid ten. If the owner bid twenty, and any other bid twenty, the owner's claim comes first, since he must add the Fifth.[4]

3. If [then] one said, 'I bid twenty-one', the owner must give twenty-six;[5] if [the other bid] twenty-two, the owner must give twenty-seven; if twenty-three, the owner must give twenty-eight; if twenty-four, the owner must give twenty-nine; if twenty-five, the owner must give thirty; since they do not add the Fifth to what the other bids more. If one man said, 'I bid twenty-six'[6] and the owner was willing to pay thirty-one and one denar,[7] the owner's claim comes first; but if not, they say to the other, 'It is thine'.

4. A man may devote[8] part of his flock or his herd or his Canaanitish bondmen and bondwomen, or the field of his possession; but if he devoted the whole of them they are not deemed [validly] devoted. So R. Eliezer. R. Eleazar b. Azariah said: If even to the Highest men may not devote all their property, how much the more then must men not squander their goods!

5. If a man devoted his son or his daughter, his Hebrew bondman or bondwoman, or the *field which he hath bought*, they are not deemed [validly] devoted, for a man may not devote what is not his.[9] Priests and levites cannot devote [their goods]. So R. Judah. R. Simeon says: Priests may not devote [their goods] since whatsoever is devoted falls to them; but levites may devote [their goods] since what is devoted does not fall to them. Rabbi says: The words of R. Judah are acceptable in cases of immovable property, for it is written, *For it is their perpetual possession*,[10] and the words of R. Simeon in cases of movable property, since what is devoted does not fall to them.

6. What is devoted [to the use] of the priests cannot be redeemed, but

---

[1] And the fixed valuation of fifty shekels for each *homer's* sowing space no longer applied, and a field must be redeemed at its market value.

[2] Since he has estimated the Temple's property at fifty, and by recanting and leaving it to him who bid forty he has involved the Temple in the loss of ten.

[3] The difference between ten and what was received from the next highest bidder.

[4] And pay twenty-five in all. See above, p. 550, n. 5.

[5] But this is not outbidding him who bid twenty-one, but a compulsory surcharge.

[6] Thereby outbidding the owner's original bid of twenty (plus the added fifth).

[7] The extra *denar* serves as an effective overbid.

[8] Lev. 27[28]. These, unlike what is dedicated, cannot be redeemed or sold again.

[9] He has the power to sell his daughter only when she is under age, and when she is of age she is free. A Hebrew slave is free after six years; a field that has been bought reverts to its original owner in the year of Jubilee.   [10] Lev. 25[34].

must be given to the priests. R. Judah b. Bathyra says: What is devoted without any condition falls to the Temple treasury, for it is written, *Every devoted thing is most holy to the Lord*.[1] But the Sages say: What is devoted without any condition falls to the priests, for it is written, *As a field devoted the possession thereof shall be the priest's*.[2] Then why is it written, *Every devoted thing is most holy unto the Lord*? [To show] that the prescription applies both to the Most Holy Things and to the Lesser Holy Things.

7. A man may devote what he had already set apart as animal-offerings whether they are Most Holy Things or Lesser Holy Things. If it was a vow[3] he must give [the priest] the value thereof. If it was a freewill-offering, he must give what it was worth to him; [thus if he had said,] 'Let this ox be a Whole-offering', they estimate what a man would pay for this ox in order to offer it as a Whole-offering for which he was not liable. A Firstling, whether unblemished or blemished, may be devoted. How is it redeemed? They that redeem it estimate what a man would pay for this Firstling in order to give it to the son of his daughter or to the son of his sister.[4] R. Ishmael says: One verse of Scripture says, [*All the firstling males*] *thou shalt sanctify*;[5] and another, [*The firstling among beasts*] *no man shall sanctify*.[6] It is not possible to say, Thou shalt sanctify, since it is written, *No man shall sanctify*; and it is not possible to say, Thou shalt not sanctify, since it is also written, *Thou shalt sanctify*. Say, rather, Thou mayest sanctify it as something whose estimated value falls to the Temple; but thou mayest not sanctify it as an offering that falls to the Altar.

9. 1. If a man sold his field[7] at a time when the law of the year of Jubilee was binding, he may not redeem it until after two years, for it is written, *According unto the number of years of the crops he shall sell unto thee*.[8] If there was a year of blight or mildew, or a Seventh Year, this is not included in the reckoning. If he only broke up the ground or left it fallow [for a year], that year is included in the reckoning. R. Eleazar says: If it was sold to him full of produce before the New Year, he will then enjoy three crops in two years.

2. If it was sold to the first for 100 *denars* and the first sold it to the second for 200 *denars*, he need take account only of the first buyer, for it is written, [*Let him . . . restore the overplus*] *unto the man unto whom he sold it*. If he sold it to the first for 200, and the first sold it to the second for 100, he need take account only of the last, for it is written, *Unto the man*; to the man that is in possession of it. A man may not sell a distant field in order to redeem one that is near by, or a poor field to redeem one that is good. He may not borrow money in order to redeem it, nor may he redeem it by halves. But with what has been dedicated all these things are permitted. Thus greater stringency applies to common property than to what has been dedicated.

3. If a man sold a house from among the houses in a walled city,[9] he may redeem it at once and at any time during twelve months. This is a kind of usury[10] which is yet not usury.[11] If he that sold it died, his son may redeem

---

[1] Lev. 27[28]. [2] Lev. 27[21].
[3] If he had vowed to offer a beast and had set it apart, he may still 'devote' it; he must then, besides offering it, give the priest its value.
[4] Who are priests and so have a right to Firstlings.
[5] Deut. 15[19]. [6] Lev. 27[26]. [7] His by inheritance.
[8] Lev. 25[15]. 'Years' cannot be less than two. [9] Lev. 25[29].
[10] The buyer having the use of the house in addition to having the purchase price returned.
[11] Since there was a valid purchase, and the seller was not certain to redeem it.

it; if he that bought it died it may be redeemed from his son. A man can only reckon the year from the time when he sold it,[1] for it is written, *Within the space of a full year*.[2] And in that it says a 'full' year, this is to include also an intercalary month.[3] Rabbi says: He is allowed a year and its intercalary [days].[4]

4. If the [last] day of the twelve months was come and it was not redeemed, it becomes his for ever, no matter whether he bought it or was given it was a gift, for it is written, *In perpetuity*.[5] Beforetime the buyer used to hide himself on the last day of the twelve months so that [the house] might be his for ever; but Hillel the Elder ordained that he [that sold it] could deposit his money in the [Temple] Chamber, and break down the door and enter, and that the other, when he would, might come and take his money.

5. Whatsoever is within the city wall is accounted *a dwelling house in a walled city*,[6] save only fields. R. Meir says: Even fields. If a house is built into the wall, R. Judah says: It is not accounted *a dwelling house in a walled city*. R. Simeon says: Its outer wall is deemed to be the city wall.

6. [A house within] a city whose house-roofs[7] form its city wall, or that was not encompassed by a wall in the days of Joshua the son of Nun, is not accounted *a dwelling house in a walled city*. [A house in any of these] is accounted *a dwelling house in a walled city*: [a city in which are not less than] three courtyards, having each two houses, which have been encompassed by a wall since the days of Joshua the son of Nun, such as the old castle of Sepphoris,[8] the fortress of Gush-Halab,[9] old Yodpat,[10] Gamala,[11] Gadwad,[12] Hadid,[13] Ono,[14] Jerusalem, and the like.

7. Houses in courtyards are given alike the rights of *a dwelling house in a walled city* and the rights that pertain to fields: they can be redeemed, and redeemed at once or redeemed any time during the twelve months—like dwelling houses [in a walled city]; and they go out [to their first owners] in the year of Jubilee, or [at an earlier time] by [payment of] a lessened price[15] —like fields. [The houses in any of] these are accounted but as houses in [open] courtyards: [a city in which are] two courtyards, having each two houses, even though they have been encompassed by a wall since the days of Joshua the son of Nun; they are accounted as but houses in [open] courtyards.

8. If an Israelite inherited [a house in a city of the levites] from his mother's father that was a levite, he cannot redeem it according to the order here prescribed.[16] So, too, if a levite inherited [a house in a city of Israelites] from his mother's father that was an Israelite, he cannot redeem it according to the order here prescribed, for it is written, *For the houses of the cities of the levites*;[17] [thus the order does not apply] unless he is a levite and in the

---

[1] To a first owner, and not from the time when it came into the possession of any later owner.   [2] Lev. 25[30].

[3] If Second Adar was intercalated he need not redeem it before thirteen months.

[4] The extra days by which the solar exceeds the lunar year.

[5] Lev. 25[30].   [6] Lev. 25[29].   [7] The Cambridge text reads: 'whose gardens'.

[8] In lower Galilee, ten miles west of mount Tabor.

[9] In upper Galilee. Cf. Gischala mentioned by Josephus (*Bell.*, II. xx. 6).

[10] In lower Galilee; the Yotapata of Josephus (*Vita*, 37).

[11] On the eastern shore of lake Galilee.

[12] Or Gadud. Variant: Gadur. Perhaps the same as Gadara, east of the Jordan.

[13] Cf. Ezra 2[33]; 1 Maccabees 12[38]; east of Lydda.

[14] Ezra 2[33]. The modern Kefr Auneh, three miles north of Lydda.

[15] A price determined by the years remaining in the Jubilee cycle. See above, 7[1]. Cf. Kidd. 1[2].   [16] Lev. 25[32].

[17] Lev. 25[33]. According to the Gemara 'the order' refers to the foregoing rules in the

cities of the levites. So Rabbi.[1] But the Sages say: It applies only to the cities of the levites. They may not turn a field into a city's outskirts[2] or a city's outskirts into a field, or a city's outskirts into a city, or a city into a city's outskirts. R. Eleazar said: It applies only to the cities of the levites; but in the cities of the Israelites they may turn a field into a city's outskirts, but not a city's outskirts into a field; a city's outskirts into a city, but not a city into a city's outskirts, that they destroy not the cities of Israel. The priests and the levites can sell [a house] at any time and redeem it at any time, for it is written, [*The houses of the cities of their possession*] *may the levites redeem at any time.*[3]

TEMURAH[4] ('THE SUBSTITUTED OFFERING')

1. 1. All, be they men or women, may substitute [another beast in the place of that which they first assigned for an offering]; howbeit none has the right to substitute [another beast], but if he has substituted it, it is substituted; and he incurs the Forty Stripes. Priests may substitute[5] [only] what belongs to themselves, and Israelites [only] what belongs to themselves. Priests may not substitute a Sin-offering or a Guilt-offering[6] or a Firstling.[7] R. Johanan b. Nuri said: Why may they not substitute a Firstling?[8] R. Akiba said to him: The Sin-offering and the Guilt-offering are a priest's due and the Firstling is a priest's due; and as they may not substitute a Sin-offering or a Guilt-offering, neither may they substitute a Firstling. R. Johanan b. Nuri answered: But why may not a priest substitute a Sin-offering or a Guilt-offering?—the priests have no claim to them while they are yet alive, and wouldest thou deduce aught therefrom touching the Firstling, to which they have a claim while it is yet alive? R. Akiba said to him: But is it not written, *Then both it and that for which it is changed shall be holy*?[9] Where does the holiness befall it?—in the owner's house; so, too, the Substitute becomes holy in the owner's house.[10]

2. They may[11] substitute oxen for small cattle, and small cattle for oxen, sheep for goats and goats for sheep, males for females and females for males, unblemished for blemished and blemished for unblemished, for it is written, *He shall not alter it nor change it, a good for a bad or a bad for a good.*[12] *A good for a bad* means [to bring a Substitute] for them that are blemished but that were consecrated before they suffered a blemish. They may substitute one beast in place of two, or two beasts in place of one; one

Mishnah, and the present passage should read: 'except according to the order here prescribed.' [1] Cambridge text reads: 'R. Meir'.

[2] Cf. M.Sh. 5[14]; Sot. 5[3]. A region extending a thousand cubits outside a town which was neither sown over nor built upon. [3] Lev. 25[32].

[4] Lev. 27[10] prescribes that a beast set apart and dedicated as an offering may *not* be replaced by another. If, however, another beast is brought in its stead the substitute is deemed a valid offering, yet the first beast still retains the sanctity which it acquired by its first dedication, and he who changes it for another has transgressed a negative command, and must suffer the Forty Stripes.

[5] The object (expressed or understood) of the verb 'substitute' is always the second, the beast that replaces, and not the first beast that is replaced.

[6] These belong to the priests only *after* they have been offered and their sacrificial portions burnt: as living beasts they do not belong to the priests.

[7] Given to him by an Israelite.

[8] Which is wholly the priest's. [9] Lev. 27[10].

[10] Therefore the priest may not offer what has not become holy in his own possession.

[11] Cambridge text reads: 'may not'. [12] Lev. 27[10].

in place of a hundred or a hundred in place of one.[1] R. Simeon says: They may only substitute a single beast in the place of another single beast, for it is written, *Then both it and that for which it is changed*; like as *it* means but one, so its Substitute must be but one.

3. They may not substitute members [of a beast] for unborn beasts, or unborn beasts for members [of a beast], or members and unborn beasts for whole beasts or whole beasts for them. R. Jose says: They may substitute members for whole beasts but not whole beasts for members. R. Jose said: Is it not so with animal-offerings that if a man says, 'Let the foot of this beast be a Whole-offering', the whole beast is a Whole-offering? So, too, if he says, 'Let the foot of this beast have the place of that beast', the whole beast shall be a Substitute in its stead.

4. What contains Heave-offering[2] renders [other produce] subject to the law of Heave-offering only if it is in the prescribed proportion. What is leavened [with Heave-offering][3] renders [other dough] leavened [as with Heave-offering] only if it is in the prescribed proportion. Drawn water renders the Immersion-pool invalid only if it is in the prescribed proportion.[4]

5. Sin-offering water can become [valid] Sin-offering water only by the putting in of the ashes [of the Red Heifer].[5] A Grave-area[6] cannot make [another field] into a Grave-area. Heave-offering is no Heave-offering if it is given from what has already given Heave-offering. A Substitute for a Substitute is no Substitute.[7] A Substitute for the young[8] [of an animal-offering] is no Substitute. R. Judah says: The Substitute for the young [of an animal-offering] is a [valid] Substitute. They said to him: Only a Substitute for what was itself dedicated[9] is valid; neither a Substitute for the young [of the beast] nor a Substitute for [another] Substitute is valid.

6. No Substitute is valid for Bird-offerings and Meal-offerings, for [the law of the Substitute] was written only of cattle. A Substitute brought by the congregation or by jointholders is not valid, for it is written, *He shall not*

---

[1] Lev. 27[10] 'beast for beast' is, literally, 'cattle for cattle'; the word 'cattle' (Heb. *behemah*) can be used either as a singular or as a collective noun.

[2] See Ter. 5[6]. If Heave-offering is mixed with common produce in the proportion of one in less than a hundred the mixture is forbidden to non-priests; if this mixture is mixed again with common produce the final mixture is forbidden only if the resultant proportion of original Heave-offering to common produce is still more than one in a hundred.

[3] If Heave-offering leaven fell into common dough and the dough was leavened by it, no matter what the proportion, the whole dough is forbidden to non-priests; if the resultant dough fell into other common dough the latter is forbidden only if, in what fell into it, there was enough of the original Heave-offering dough to leaven the latter dough.

[4] Unless the Immersion-pool (see tractate Mikwaoth) contains forty *seahs* of undrawn water it is invalid. If into less than forty *seahs* of undrawn water three *logs* of 'drawn' water (i.e. water that has remained standing in a vessel) fell or were poured, the Immersion-pool becomes invalid. The Gemara here explains the term 'prescribed proportion' differently: (*a*) if the pool held only twenty-one *seahs* of undrawn water it becomes permissible if nineteen *seahs* of other water were made to flow into it over the ground, but if the pool held less than twenty-one *seahs* the added water does not render it permissible; or (*b*) if into an Immersion-pool a total of three *logs* of drawn water fell in from three vessels or less, the pool becomes invalid; but if from more than three the pool remains valid.

[5] Cf. Par. 6[1ff]. It is deduced from Num. 19[17] that the living water was put into a vessel and the ashes put on the water, and not that the water was put into a vessel containing the ashes.   [6] See Ohol. 17[1, 2].

[7] i.e. though the sanctity of the original offering can pass also to what is substituted for it, the sanctity of the Substitute cannot pass to what is again substituted for the first Substitute so as to make the second Substitute a valid offering.

[8] Born after the dam was dedicated. It also is holy and must be offered, yet its sanctity cannot pass to what is substituted for it so as to make the Substitute a valid offering.

[9] Since it is written, 'It (i.e. only it) and that (i.e. only that) for which it is changed shall be holy'.

change it; only a single person may bring a Substitute, and a Substitute brought by the congregation or by jointholders is not valid. No Substitute may be brought for offerings[1] to the Temple treasury. R. Simeon said: Was not the Tithe [of Cattle] included [among the offerings for which a Substitute could be brought]?[2] Why was it mentioned in particular? To draw an analogy: as the Tithe [of Cattle] is the offering of the individual,[3] the offerings of the congregation are excluded; as the Tithe [of Cattle] is an offering that falls to the Altar, offerings to the Temple treasury are excluded.

2. 1. Some conditions apply to offerings of the individual and do not apply to the offerings of the congregation, and some conditions apply to offerings of the congregation and do not apply to the offerings of the individual. A Substitute may be brought for the offerings of the individual, but a Substitute may not be brought for the offerings of the congregation; for the offerings of the individual male or female beasts are brought, but for the offerings of the congregation only male beasts are brought; for the offerings of the individual he that offers them is answerable [and he must replace them if they are lost], and he is answerable for their drink-offerings,[4] but for the offerings of the congregation they are not answerable [and they need not be replaced if they are lost or delayed], and they are not answerable for their drink-offerings; but once the animal-offerings have been offered, they are answerable for their drink-offerings. Some conditions apply to offerings of the congregation and do not apply to the offerings of the individual. The offerings of the congregation override the Sabbath and [the laws of] uncleanness, but the offerings of the individual override neither the Sabbath nor [the laws] of uncleanness. R. Meir said: But are not the Baken Cakes[5] of the High Priest and the bullock offered on the Day of Atonement offerings of the individual?—yet they override the Sabbath and [the laws of] uncleanness? But [this is because] they must be offered at a fixed time.

2. The Sin-offerings of the individual whose owner has [otherwise] already made atonement[6] are left to die, but those of the congregation are not left to die. R. Judah says: They are left to die. R. Simeon said: Like as we find[7] in what concerns the young of a Sin-offering, the Substitute for a Sin-offering, and the Sin-offering whose owner has died, that the rule[8] applies only to the offerings of the individual and cannot apply to the offerings of the congregation,[9] so, too, in what concerns [the Sin-offering] whose owner has [otherwise] already made atonement, or [the Sin-offering] that has passed the age of a year, the rule applies to the offerings of the individual but not to the offerings of the congregation.

3. Greater stringency may apply to animal-offerings than to a Substitute, and greater stringency may apply to a Substitute than to animal-offerings; for a Substitute may be brought in the stead of animal-offerings but no Substitute may be brought in the stead of a Substitute; the congregation or

---

[1] Cf. Shek. 6[6]. Variant: Hallowed Things.   [2] See Lev. 27[33].
[3] It cannot be exacted from jointholders. Cf. Bekh. 9[3].
[4] The term includes also the prescribed Meal-offerings.
[5] Lev. 6[21]. Cf. Men. 4[5].
[6] i.e. the beast set aside as a Sin-offering was lost and only found after another had been offered in its stead.   [7] Cf. below, 4[1].
[8] That they shall be left to die.
[9] Since (*a*) the Sin-offerings of the congregation are male beasts, (*b*) these can be substitutes only for the offerings of individuals, and (*c*) the congregation cannot die.

jointholders may dedicate [a beast as an offering] but they cannot bring a Substitute; and they may dedicate the members of a beast or unborn young, but they cannot bring a Substitute [for them]. Greater stringency may apply to the Substitute: for the sanctity [that befalls the Substitute] can befall even a beast that has a lasting blemish and it cannot become unconsecrated, or be shorn or used for labour.[1] R. Jose b. R. Judah says: A beast becomes a [valid] Substitute alike whether he so dedicated it in error or wantonly, but a beast does not become a [valid] animal-offering alike whether he so dedicated it in error or wantonly.[2] R. Eleazar says: A beast that is cross-bred or *terefah* or born from the side [of the dam], or that is of doubtful or of double sex, cannot become holy[3] or render [its substitute] holy.[4]

3. 1. Of these animal-offerings what is born from them and what is substituted for them may be offered as the like kind of offering: the young and the Substitute of a Peace-offering, their young and their young's young until the end of the world—these may be offered as a Peace-offering, and they require the laying on of hands, drink-offerings, and waving; and the breast and the thigh [must be given to the priests]. R. Eliezer says: The young of a Peace-offering may not be offered as a Peace-offering.[5] But the Sages say: It may be so offered. R. Simeon said: They did not dispute whether the young's young of a Peace-offering or the young's young of a Substitute should be offered; but they disputed concerning the young itself—R. Eliezer said that it could not be offered, whereas the Sages said that it could be offered. R. Joshua and R. Papias testified[6] that the young of a Peace-offering could be offered as a Peace-offering. R. Papias said: I testify that we had a heifer that was offered as a Peace-offering; we consumed it at Passover and we consumed its young as a Peace-offering at the [next] Feast.

2. The young and the Substitute of a Thank-offering,[7] their young and their young's young until the end of the world—these [may be offered] as a Thank-offering, save only that they need no Bread-offering. The Substitute of a Whole-offering, the young of the Substitute, and its young's young until the end of the world—these [may be offered] as a Whole-offering, and they require flaying and cutting up, and they wholly fall to the Altar-fire.

3. If a man set apart a female beast as a Whole-offering and it bore a male, this must be left to pasture until it suffers a blemish, when it shall be sold and a Whole-offering brought with its price. R. Eleazar says: It can itself be brought as a Whole-offering. If a man set apart a female beast as a Guilt-offering,[8] it must be left to pasture until it suffers a blemish, when it may be sold and a Guilt-offering brought with its price; but if he had already brought his Guilt-offering, the price shall fall [to the Temple treasury] as a freewill-offering. R. Simeon says: It can be sold [forthwith] before it suffers a blemish. The Substitute of a Guilt-offering, the young

---

[1] 'Both it and that for which it is changed shall be holy.'

[2] e.g. if he designated one beast but had intended to designate another, it becomes a valid substitute, but not a valid offering. Here, too, greater stringency applies to a Substitute than to an animal-offering.

[3] Be brought as a Substitute.

[4] All these four kinds of beast can be holy if, e.g., the one became *terefah* after it was consecrated, or the other three were born of another beast that was already consecrated; but a Substitute for them is not valid.

[5] But must be left to die.   [6] Eduy. 7[6].

[7] Lev. 7[12f].   [8] For which only a male beast was valid.

of its Substitute, its young and its young's young until the end of the world, must be left to pasture until they suffer a blemish, when they shall be sold, and their price shall fall [to the Temple treasury] as a freewill-offering. R. Eliezer says: They must be left to die. But R. Eleazar says: Whole-offerings should be brought with their price. A Guilt-offering whose owner has died or [otherwise] already made atonement must be left to pasture until it suffers a blemish, when it shall be sold and its price shall fall [to the Temple treasury] as a freewill-offering. R. Eliezer says: It must be left to die. But R. Eleazar says: Whole-offerings should be brought with its price.

4. But is not [what falls to the Temple treasury as] a freewill-offering offered as a Whole-offering? How, then, do the words of R. Eleazar differ from those of the Sages? Only in that if it was an offering of obligation he must lay his hand upon it, and bring its drink-offerings, and he must bring the drink-offerings at his own charges; and if he is a priest he himself performs the offering and takes the hide; whereas if it was a freewill-offering he does not lay his hand upon it or bring its drink-offerings, and the drink-offerings are brought at the charges of the congregation, and even if he is a priest the offering is performed by the priests whose Course[1] it then is, who also takes the hide.

5. The Substitute for Firstlings or Tithe [of Cattle], their young and their young's young until the end of the world, can be offered as Firstlings or Tithe [of Cattle], and, if they are blemished, they may be consumed by their owners. Wherein do Firstlings and Tithe [of Cattle] differ from other animal-offerings? Other animal-offerings[2] can be sold and slaughtered in the market and weighed out by measure, save only Firstlings and Tithe [of Cattle]; and they may be redeemed and their Substitutes may be redeemed, save only Firstlings and Tithe [of Cattle]; and they may be brought to the Land [of Israel] from outside the Land, save only Firstlings and Tithe [of Cattle]. If these were brought [from thence] and they are without blemish, they may be offered; but if they are blemished they may be consumed, in that they are blemished, by their owners. R. Simeon said: Why [are not unblemished Firstlings and Tithe of Cattle brought from outside the Land]? Because Firstlings and Tithe [of Cattle] can be of avail[3] wheresoever they are; but other animal-offerings, even if a blemish arises in them, still continue in their sanctity.[4]

4. 1. The young of a Sin-offering, the Substitute for a Sin-offering, and the Sin-offering whose owner has died must be left to die.[5] If it passed the age of a year[6] or was lost and found blemished, and its owner had [otherwise] already made atonement, it must be left to die; a Substitute for it may not be brought, no use may be made of it, but the law of Sacrilege[7] does not apply to it. If the owner had not yet made atonement, it must be left to pasture until it suffers a blemish, when it shall be sold and another [Sin-offering] brought with its price; a Substitute for it may be brought, and the law of Sacrilege applies to it.

---

[1] Cf. p. 165, n. 12. [2] See Bekh. 5[1].
[3] Outside the Land they can be left to pasture until they incur a blemish, when they can be slaughtered and used for food.
[4] Even if they were blemished their money-value must be brought to the Land of Israel and another offering brought in their stead.
[5] Shut up and left without food. [6] And so became invalid as a Sin-offering.
[7] See p. 573, n. 2.

2. If a man set apart his Sin-offering and it was lost, and he offered another in its stead and the first was then found, it must be left to die. If a man set apart money for a Sin-offering, and the money was lost, and he offered another Sin-offering in its stead, and the money was then found, the money must be thrown into the Dead Sea.[1]

3. If a man set apart money for his Sin-offering and it was lost, and he set apart other money in its stead, and before he could buy a Sin-offering with this money the first money was found, he must bring a Sin-offering that was bought with both sums of money, and the residue shall fall [to the Temple treasury] as a freewill-offering. If a man set apart money for his Sin-offering and it was lost, and he set apart a Sin-offering in its stead, and before he could offer the Sin-offering the money was found, and the Sin-offering was blemished, it must be sold; and another Sin-offering must be brought from both this price and the first money, and the residue shall fall [to the Temple treasury] as a freewill-offering. If a man set apart a Sin-offering and it was lost, and he set apart money in its stead, and, before he could buy another Sin-offering with it, the first Sin-offering was found, and it was blemished, it must be sold, and another Sin-offering must be brought from both this price and the other money, and the residue shall fall [to the Temple treasury] as a freewill-offering. If a man set apart a Sin-offering and it was lost, and he set apart another Sin-offering in its stead, and, before he could offer it, the first was found, and both were blemished, both must be sold and another Sin-offering must be brought from the price of both, and the residue shall fall [to the Temple treasury] as a freewill-offering. If a man set apart a Sin-offering and it was lost, and he set apart another in its stead, and, before he could offer it, the first was found, and both were without blemish, one should be offered as a Sin-offering and the other left to die. So Rabbi. But the Sages say: No Sin-offering may be left to die save only that which is found after its owner had [otherwise] made atonement; and no money may be thrown into the Dead Sea unless it is found after its owner had already made atonement.

4. If a man set apart his Sin-offering and it was found to be blemished, he must sell it and bring another in its stead. R. Eleazar b. R. Simeon says: If the second was offered before the first was slaughtered, the first must be left to die, since its owner had already made stonement.

5. 1. How can the law of Firstlings be evaded?[2] If a beast that had not before borne young was pregnant, a man may say, 'What is within her, if a male, shall be a Whole-offering'; and if she bore a male it is brought as a Whole-offering. [Or he may say,] '. . . and if a female it shall be a Peace-offering', and if she bore a female it is brought as a Peace-offering. [Or he may say,] '. . . if a male it shall be a Whole-offering and if a female a Peace-offering', and if she bore a male and a female, the male is brought as a Whole-offering and the female as a Peace-offering.

2. If she bore two males, one should be brought as a Whole-offering and the other sold to any that were under obligation to bring a Whole-offering, and the price is free for common use. If she bore two females one should be brought as a Peace-offering and the other sold to any that were under obligation to bring a Peace-offering, and the price is free for common use.

---

[1] Lit. 'Sea of salt'. Cf. Naz. 4[4, 6]; A. Zar. 3[3, 9].   [2] Permissively.

If she bore offspring of double sex or of doubtful sex, Rabban Simeon b. Gamaliel says: No sanctity befalls them.

3. If a man said, 'The young of this [beast] shall be a Whole-offering and itself a Peace-offering', his words hold good.[1] If he said, 'This shall be a Peace-offering and her young a Whole-offering', it is accounted but the young of a Peace-offering.[2] So R. Meir. R. Jose said: If from the first his intention was such, his words hold good, since[3] it is not possible to assign them to two kinds of offering at the same time; but if after he said, 'This shall be a Peace-offering', he bethought himself and said, 'Its young shall be a Whole-offering', it is accounted but the young of a Peace-offering.

4. [If he said,] 'Let this beast be [both] a Substitute for a Whole-offering [and] a Substitute for a Peace-offering',[4] it is accounted but the Substitute for a Whole-offering.[5] So R. Meir. R. Jose said: If from the first his intention was such, his words hold good, since it is not possible to assign it to two kinds of offering at the same time; but if after he said, 'The Substitute for a Whole-offering', he bethought himself and said, 'The Substitute for a Peace-offering', it is accounted but the Substitute for a Whole-offering.

5. [If he said,] 'Let this be instead of this', [or] 'the Substitute for this', [or] 'in exchange for this', it is a valid Substitute. [If he said,] 'Let this become an unconsecrated beast by virtue of this', it is not a valid Substitute. If the consecrated beast was blemished it becomes an unconsecrated beast, but its full value must be made good.[6]

6. [If he said,] 'Let this be instead of a Sin-offering', or 'instead of a Whole-offering', he has said nothing; [but if] 'instead of this Sin-offering' or 'instead of this Whole-offering', or 'instead of the Sin-offering' or 'instead of the Whole-offering which I have in my house', and he had such, his words hold good. If he said of an unclean beast and of one that had a blemish, 'Let these be a Whole-offering', he has said nothing; [but if he said,] 'Let these be for a Whole-offering', they must be sold and a Whole-offering brought with their price.

6. 1. Beasts that may not be offered on the Altar render others forbidden [among which they are confused] no matter what their number; [namely][7] a beast that had committed or suffered an unnatural crime, or that had been set apart, or that had been worshipped, or that was *the hire* [*of a harlot*] *or the price* [*of a dog*], or that was cross-bred or that was *terefah*, or that was born from the side [of the mother-beast]. 'Set apart' means set apart for idolatry; the beast itself is forbidden, but what is upon it is allowed. 'Worshipped' means aught that has been worshipped [by the gentiles]. The beast itself and what is upon it are forbidden.[8] Both[9] alike are permitted for food.

2. What is accounted *the hire* [*of a harlot*]? If a man said to a harlot, 'Here is this lamb as thy hire', even though he gave her a hundred, they are all forbidden. So, too, if a man said to his fellow, 'Here is this lamb for

---

[1] Since the offspring's dedication preceded that of the dam.

[2] See above, 3[1]. Since it was unborn at the time of the dedication, the dam's dedication covered the offspring also.   [3] Variant: although.

[4] When he has a Whole-offering and a Peace-offering for which he wished to substitute a third beast.   [5] What he says first alone holds good.

[6] If it was replaced by a beast of less value the difference in value also falls to the Temple treasury.   [7] See Zeb. 8[1]; 9[3]; 14[2]; Par. 2[3].   [8] As offerings.

[9] What is 'set apart' and what is 'worshipped'.

thee so that thou suffer thy bondwoman to lodge with my bondman'. Rabbi[1] says: This is not accounted a hire. But the Sages say: It is accounted a hire.

3. What is accounted *the price of a dog*? If a man said, 'Take this lamb for this dog'; so, too, if two jointholders divided their goods, and one took ten [lambs] and the other took nine and one dog, those [lambs] that are set over against the dog are forbidden, but those that are together with the dog are permitted. The 'hire of a dog' and 'the price of a harlot' are permitted, for it is written, *Even both these*;[2] but not four.[3] Their young are permitted, for it is written, *these*; [themselves are forbidden,] but not their young.

4. If a man gave money to her, this is permitted; but if [he gave to her] wine, oil, meal, or aught the like of which can be offered on the Altar, these are forbidden. If he gave to her [beasts already set apart as] animal-offerings[4] these are permitted, but if Bird-offerings they are forbidden. It might have been inferred: if animal-offerings (which a blemish makes invalid) do not fall under the prohibition of *the hire of a harlot* and *the price of a dog*, how much more should Bird-offerings (which a blemish does not make invalid) not fall under the prohibition of *the hire of a harlot* and *the price of a dog*! But Scripture says: *For any vow*; to take into account even Bird-offerings.

5. Of all the beasts which may not be offered on the Altar, their young are permitted. R. Eliezer says: The young of a beast that is *terefah* may not be offered on the Altar. But the Sages say: It may be offered. R. Hanina b. Antigonus says: A valid beast that has drawn suck from another that is *terefah* is unfit to be offered on the Altar. All animal-offerings that have been rendered *terefah* may not be redeemed, since animal-offerings may not be redeemed in order to give them as food to the dogs.

7. 1. Some conditions apply to what is consecrated for the Altar and do not apply to what is consecrated for the Temple treasury, and some conditions apply to what is consecrated for the Temple treasury and do not apply to what is consecrated for the Altar. For what is consecrated for the Altar a Substitute may be brought and by reason of them punishment can be incurred through [transgression of the laws of] Refuse, Remnant, and uncleanness;[5] their young and their milk are forbidden after they have been redeemed, and if a man slaughtered them outside [the Temple Court] he is culpable; and they may not pay the [Temple] craftsmen their wages therewith. But it is not so with what is consecrated for the Temple treasury.[6]

2. Some conditions apply to what is consecrated for the Temple treasury and do not apply to what is consecrated for the Altar. Things consecrated without further assignment fall to the Temple treasury; all things may be consecrated to the Temple treasury; the law of Sacrilege[7] does not apply to what is produced from them,[8] and the priests have not the use of them.

3. It is all one whether they are consecrated for the Altar or for the

[1] Variant: R. Meir.   [2] Deut. 23[18].
[3] Namely the hire of a dog, and the hire of a harlot, and the price of a dog, and the price of a harlot.
[4] Only the like of Passover-offerings are here meant: if, e.g., as her hire he included her among those who should share in the eating of his Passover-lamb. 'For any vow' (Deut. 23[18]) is interpreted as covering only such beasts as are offered on the Altar.
[5] p. 471, nn. 9–11.   [6] Cf. Shek. 4[5].
[7] Lev. 5[15]; p. 573, n. 2.   [8] Such as milk, wool, or eggs.
3349

Temple treasury: none may make any change in their consecration;[1] one
may vow their estimated value[2] to the Temple, or devote them [to the
Temple]; and if they die they must be buried. R. Simeon says: If what is
consecrated for the Temple treasury dies, it may be redeemed.

4. These must be buried: miscarriages of animal-offerings must be
buried; if they cast an afterbirth it must be buried; the ox that is condemned to be stoned,[3] the heifer whose neck is to be broken,[4] [one of] the
Bird-offerings of the leper,[5] the hair of the Nazirite,[6] the Firstling of an
ass,[7] flesh seethed in milk,[8] and unconsecrated beasts slaughtered in
the Temple Court. R. Simeon says: Unconsecrated beasts slaughtered in the
Temple Court must be burnt; so, too, a wild animal that was slaughtered in
the Temple Court.

5. These must be burnt: whatsoever is leavened at Passover[9] must be
burnt; and unclean Heave-offering, *Orlah*-fruit,[10] and Diverse Kinds of the
Vineyard.[11] What it is the custom to burn must be burnt, and what it is the
custom to bury must be buried. Bread and Heave-offering oil may be used
for kindling.[12]

6. Animal-offerings that are slaughtered [with intent to perform an act]
outside its proper time or place must be burnt. A Suspensive Guilt-
offering[13] must be burnt.[14] R. Judah says: It must be buried. The Sin-
offering of a bird that was brought in a case of doubt[15] must be burnt. R.
Judah says: It should be cast into the [Temple-]gutter. What it is the
custom to burn should not be buried, and what it is the custom to bury
should not be burnt. R. Judah says: If a man was minded to apply to himself the greater stringency of burning what it is the custom to bury, he may
do so. They answered: He is not permitted to change the custom.

KERITHOTH[16] ('EXTIRPATION')

1. 1. For thirty-six transgressions is Extirpation prescribed in the Law: if
a man has connexion with his mother, his father's wife, his daughter-in-law;
or with a male or with a beast; if a woman has connexion with a beast; or if
a man has connexion with a woman and her daughter, with a married
woman, with his sister, his father's sister, his mother's sister, his wife's
sister, his brother's wife, or his father's brother's wife, or with a menstruous
woman;[17] if a man blasphemes,[18] commits idolatry,[19] offers of his seed to

---

[1] If dedicated to the Temple treasury they may not then be dedicated as an offering for
the Altar, and what is dedicated as a Whole-offering may not then be dedicated as a Sin-
offering.   [2] Cf. Arak. 8[7] (end).   [3] Ex. 21[28].
[4] Deut. 21[4].   [5] Lev. 14[6]. One of them is set free.
[6] If he has not completed his vow in cleanness. See Num. 6[9].
[7] Which is not redeemed with a lamb but has its neck broken. Ex. 34[20].
[8] See Hull. 8[1ff].   [9] But cf. Pes. 2[1].   [10] App. I. 32.   [11] Deut. 22[9].
[12] Cf. Ter. 11[10].   [13] Lev. 5[17f].   [14] Cf. Ker. 6[1].   [15] See Ker. 1[4].
[16] The tractate deals with those offences which are punishable by 'Extirpation', Heb.
kareth, pl. *kerithoth*, 'cutting off' (cf. the recurrent formula, 'that soul shall be cut off from
among his people'). This punishment is incurred in the cases cited in the first paragraph if
the transgression is committed deliberately ('with a high hand', Num. 15[31], and without
warning from witnesses; if witnesses warned the culprit yet he committed the transgression,
he is punishable in some cases by stoning, in others by burning, in others by strangling, and
in others by the Forty Stripes; cf. Makk. 3[15]). If the transgression is committed in error
the transgressor must bring a Sin-offering (Lev. 4[27ff].) if he comes to a knowledge of his
transgression; but if it is in doubt whether he has committed the transgression he must
bring a 'conditional' or 'suspensive' Guilt-offering (Lev. 5[17ff]).
[17] For these transgressions see Lev. 18[6ff] (cf. Lev. 18[29]).
[18] Num. 15[30]; cf. Sanh. 7[5].   [19] Cf. Sanh. 7[6].

Molech,[1] has a familiar spirit,[2] or profanes the Sabbath,[3] or eats what is consecrated while unclean[4] or enters the Temple while unclean,[5] or eats the fat,[6] or the blood,[7] or Remnant[8] or Refuse,[9] or slaughters[10] or offers up[11] [an offering] outside [the Temple Court]; or eats leavened bread during Passover,[12] or eats[13] or does any work[14] on the Day of Atonement, or compounds anointing oil[15] or compounds incense[16] [the like of what is compounded in the Temple], or anoints himself with the oil of unction;[17] or, from among positive commands,[18] [if he transgresses the laws of] the Passover[19] and circumcision.[20]

2. If in these things[21] he transgressed wantonly he is liable to Extirpation, and if in error to a Sin-offering; and if it was in doubt whether he had committed a transgression he is liable to a Suspensive Guilt-offering; howbeit, he that conveys uncleanness to the Temple or to its Hallowed Things is liable to a Rising and Falling [Sin-offering].[22] So R. Meir. And the Sages say: The blasphemer also,[23] for it is written, *Ye shall have one law for him that doeth aught unwittingly*;[24] thereby the blasphemer, who has done no deed, is excluded.

3. Some[25] women [after childbirth] bring an offering which is consumed [by the priests]; some bring one which is not consumed; and some bring no offering. These are they that bring an offering which is consumed: a woman that bears an abortion that is like to a beast or to a wild animal or to a bird (so R. Meir; but the Sages say: Only if it has somewhat of the human form), or an abortion like to a sandal, or an afterbirth or a fully-fashioned foetus, or young that needed to be cut up [during delivery].[26] So, too, if a bondwoman gives birth she brings an offering which is consumed.

4. These bring an offering which is not consumed:[27] a woman that bears something but it is not known what she bore; so, too, if of two women[28] the one bore what did not render her liable to an offering and the other what rendered her liable. R. Jose said: This applies only if they went the one to the east and the other to the west; but if they remained together they must [together] bring an offering which is consumed.

5. These are they that bring no offering: a woman that bears an abortion that is a foetus filled with water or filled with blood or variegated matter; or an abortion the like of fishes, locusts, insects, or creeping things; or that miscarries by the fortieth day or is delivered from the side.[29] R. Simeon declares her liable [to an offering] that is delivered from the side.

---

1 Lev. 20[5]; cf. San. 7[7]. · 2 Lev. 20[6]; cf. San. 7[7].
3 Ex. 31[14].   4 Lev. 22[3].   5 Lev. 15[31]; Num. 19[13, 20].   6 Lev. 7[25].
7 Lev. 7[26f].   8 Lev. 19[8].   9 Lev. 7[18].   10 Lev. 17[4].   11 Lev. 17[9].
12 Ex. 12[15].   13 Lev. 23[29].   14 Lev. 23[30].   15 Ex. 39[33].   16 Ex. 39[38].
17 Ex. 30[33, 38].
18 The foregoing all transgress negative commands, 'Thou shalt not . . .'
19 Num. 9[13].   20 Gen. 17[30].
21 Transgressions of the negative commands, i.e. sins of commission. No Sin-offering is required for sins of omission (cf. Shebu. 1[6]).
22 See p. 409, n. 4.
23 He is exempt from bringing a Sin-offering for unwitting transgression; and if he is exempt from a Sin-offering for a transgression that was known to him he is also exempt from a Suspensive Guilt-offering for a transgression unknown to him.
24 Num. 15[29], with emphasis on the 'doeth'. The quoted passage deals with those who must bring a Sin-offering (Num. 15[27]).
25 The following rules arise out of Lev. 12[6], the Sin-offering of a bird which, together with another bird as a Whole-offering, a woman must bring after childbirth at the end of her days of purifying.   26 Cf. Bekh. 8[1].
27 But burnt; cf. Tem. 7[6]. It is in doubt whether it can be deemed a birth.
28 Whose abortions were confused together.   29 See p. 479, n. 3.

6. If she miscarried in the night of the eighty-first day,[1] the School of Shammai declare her exempt from an offering,[2] but the School of Hillel declare her liable. The School of Hillel said to the School of Shammai: How does the night of[3] the eighty-first day differ from the eighty-first day? —if they are alike in what concerns uncleanness[4] are they not also alike in what concerns the offering? The School of Shammai answered: No! as thou arguest of her that miscarries on the eighty-first day (who was thus delivered at a time when it was fitting to bring an offering), wouldest thou likewise argue of her that miscarries on the night of the eighty-first day (who was thus delivered not at a time when it was fitting to bring an offering)? The School of Hillel answered: She that miscarries on an eighty-first day that falls on a Sabbath affords proof; for she was delivered not at a time when it was fitting to bring an offering, yet she is liable to bring an offering. The School of Shammai answered: No! as thou arguest of her that miscarries on an eighty-first day that falls on a Sabbath (when even if it is not fitting to bring the offering of the individual it is nevertheless fitting to bring the offering of the congregation) wouldest thou likewise argue of her that miscarries on the night of the eighty-first day (when it is not fitting to bring the offering either of the individual or of the congregation)? Her blood[-uncleanness] affords no proof, for if she miscarried before her days of uncleanness were fulfilled her blood is still unclean and she is not liable to bring an offering.

7. If a woman suffered five issues that were in doubt[5] or five miscarriages that were in doubt, she need bring but one offering, and she may then eat of the animal-offerings; and she is not bound to bring the other offerings. If she had suffered five miscarriages that were not in doubt[6] or five issues that were not in doubt, she need bring but one offering and she may then eat of the animal-offerings; and she is bound to bring the other offerings. Once in Jerusalem a pair of doves cost a golden *denar*.[7] Rabban Simeon b. Gamaliel said: By this Temple! I will not suffer the night to pass by before they cost but a [silver] *denar*. He went into the court and taught: If a woman suffered five miscarriages that were not in doubt or five issues that were not in doubt, she need bring but one offering, and she may then eat of the animal-offerings; and she is not bound to offer the other offerings.[8] And the same day the price of a pair of doves stood at a quarter-*denar* each.

2. 1. There are four whose atonement is yet incomplete,[9] and there are four which must bring an offering alike whether they transgressed wantonly or in error. These are they whose atonement is yet incomplete:[10] a man and a woman that have suffered a flux,[11] a woman after childbirth,[12] and a leper.[13] R. Eliezer b. Jacob says: A proselyte's atonement[14] is yet incomplete until

---

[1] i.e. the night following the eightieth day when (see Lev. 12[5]) after a previous birth of a female she ceases to 'continue in the blood of her purifying'.
[2] i.e. a second and separate offering for this birth.
[3] i.e. the night preceding. Cf. p. 136, n. 11.
[4] If she suffered a flow she would be unclean to her husband whether it was in the night or day of the eighty-first day.
[5] Whether they had befallen in the seven days of her menstrual separation or in the eleven days during which they must be reckoned fluxes (Lev. 15[26]).
[6] See above, 1[4]. [7] Twenty-five silver *denars*. [8] For the four other cases.
[9] Cf. Hag. 3[3]; Zeb. 2[1]; Meil. 2[1ff]; Kel. 1[5, 8].
[10] Who, though their period of uncleanness has expired, are still forbidden to eat of Hallowed Things or to enter the Temple until they bring the Sin-offering prescribed for them. [11] Lev. 15[2ff, 25ff]. [12] Lev. 12[2ff]. [13] Lev. 13[2ff].
[14] Who must be circumcised, undergo immersion, and bring an offering.

the blood [of his offering] has been tossed for him [against the base of the Altar]. And likewise a Nazirite[1] must abstain from wine, from cutting off his hair, and from contracting uncleanness [until he has brought his offerings].

2. These must bring an offering alike whether they transgressed wantonly or in error: he that has connexion with a bondwoman,[2] a Nazirite that has suffered uncleanness, he that utters a [false] oath of testimony,[3] and he that utters a [false] deposit-oath.[4]

3. There are five which need bring but one offering for many transgressions, and five which must bring a Rising and Falling Sin-offering.[5] These need bring but one offering for many transgressions: he that has connexion with a bondwoman many times, a Nazirite that suffers uncleanness many times, he that suspects his wife[6] of adultery with many men, and the leper who is marked by many [successive] leprosy-signs. If he brought his Bird-offerings[7] and was again marked by more leprosy-signs, they do not count to his credit unless he had brought his Sin-offering.[8] R. Judah says: Unless he had brought his Guilt-offering.[9]

4. If a woman had many miscarriages (if, namely, she bore a female within the eighty days[10] and bore yet another female within the [next] eighty days, or if she bore many at intervals) R. Judah says: She brings an offering for the first but not for the second; and for the third but not for the fourth. These five bring a Rising and Falling Sin-offering: [that are culpable] by reason of a [false] oath of testimony[11] or by reason of a rash oath,[12] or by reason of uncleanness that befalls the Temple or its Hallowed Things,[13] a woman after childbirth, and a leper. Wherein does [connexion with] a bondwoman differ from other forbidden connexions? They are unlike in both the punishment and the [prescribed] offering, in that for other forbidden connexions a Sin-offering is prescribed, but for connexion with a bondwoman a Guilt-offering;[14] for other forbidden connexions the man and the woman are alike liable to the Forty Stripes or to the offering [that is prescribed], but for connexion with a bondwoman the man is not like the woman liable to the Forty Stripes, and the woman is not like the man liable to the offering; in other forbidden connexions he that begins the act is as culpable as he that completes it, and he is liable for each connexion; and herein greater stringency applies in the case of a bondwoman in that he that transgresses wantonly or in error is alike liable [to a Guilt-offering].

5. What manner of bondwoman [is here spoken of in the Law]? She that is half bondwoman and half freedwoman, for it is written, *And she has not yet been altogether redeemed.*[15] So R. Akiba. R. Ishmael says: She that is wholly a bondwoman. R. Eleazar b. Azariah says: All other forbidden connexions are expressly set forth[16] and none is left save only connexion with her that is half bondwoman and half freedwoman.

6. In all forbidden connexions if the one was of full age and the other a minor, the minor is not culpable; if the one was awake and the other asleep the one that was asleep is not culpable; if the one acted in error and

---

[1] Num. 6[5, 6]. [2] Who is betrothed to another man. Lev. 19[20f].
[3] Lev. 5[1]. [4] Lev. 6[2]. [5] p. 409, n. 4. [6] Num. 5[14, 15].
[7] Lev. 14[4]. [8] Lev. 14[19]. [9] Lev. 14[12]. [10] See above, 1[6]. [11] Lev. 5[1].
[12] Lev. 5[4]. [13] See Shebu. 2[1].
[14] Some texts add: 'for other forbidden connexions (the offering of) a female beast is prescribed, but for connexion with a bondwoman a male beast'.
[15] Lev. 19[20]. [16] All were concerned with women wholly free.

the other wantonly the one that acted in error is liable to a Sin-offering and the one that acted wantonly is liable to punishment by Extirpation.

3. 1. If they said to a man, 'Thou hast eaten fat',[1] he must bring a Sin-offering.[2] If one witness said, 'He has eaten', and another said, 'He has not eaten', or if one woman said, 'He has eaten', and another woman said, 'He has not eaten', he must bring a Suspensive Guilt-offering.[3] If one witness said, 'He has eaten', and he said, 'I have not eaten', he is not culpable. If two said, 'He has eaten', but he said, 'I have not eaten', R. Meir declares him culpable. R. Meir said: If two witnesses suffice to bring upon him the graver penalty of death[4] should they not suffice to bring upon him the lighter penalty of an offering? They answered: But how if he would say, 'I acted wantonly'?[5]

2. If a man ate fat and again ate fat during one spell of forgetfulness,[6] he is liable only to one Sin-offering; but if he ate fat and blood and Remnant and Refuse during one spell of forgetfulness, he is liable on each count. Herein greater stringency applies to many kinds than to one kind; but greater stringency may apply to one kind than to many kinds; for if he ate a half-olive's bulk and then again ate a half-olive's bulk of the same kind, he is culpable; but had they been two kinds he would not have been culpable.

3. Within what time must he eat them? [The time that he would need] if he ate a like bulk of parched grains of corn. So R. Meir. But the Sages say: [He is not culpable] unless from beginning to end he ate them in the time that it takes to eat a half-loaf.[7] If a man ate unclean foods or drank unclean liquids, or if he drank a quarter-*log* of wine and entered the Temple, [the measure of time that renders him culpable is] if he stayed time enough to eat a half-loaf. R. Eleazar says: If he interrupted [the act of drinking] or put in any water at all, he is not culpable.

4. By but one act of eating a man may become liable to four Sin-offerings and one Guilt-offering; [namely,] if a man was unclean and he ate fat and it was Remnant from animal-offerings, and [he ate it] on the Day of Atonement. R. Meir says: If it was the Sabbath and he carried it forth in his mouth he is liable [to yet another Sin-offering]. But they said to him: This does not fall within the same class of transgression.[8]

5. By but one act of connexion a man may become liable to six Sin-offerings; [namely,] if he had connexion with his daughter[9] he may thereby become culpable by virtue of [the laws forbidding connexion with] his daughter, his sister, his brother's wife, his father's brother's wife, a married woman, and a menstruant. If[10] he had connexion with his daughter's daughter,[11] he may thereby become culpable by virtue of [the laws forbidding connexion with] his daughter's daughter, his daughter-in-law, his wife's sister, his brother's wife, his father's brother's wife, a married woman, and a

---

[1] Lev. 3[17]; 7[23].   [2] Lev. 4[28].   [3] See above, p. 562, n. 16 (end).
[4] In spite of what he may say contradicting their evidence.
[5] He would then be exempt from a Sin-offering and witnesses could not contradict him.
[6] Cf. Shab. 7[1].   [7] Cf. Erub. 8[2]; Neg. 13[9].   [8] Cf. Makk. 3[9f].
[9] Who was his sister through incestuous connexion with his mother, and married first to his brother and then to his uncle.
[10] Some texts omit this sentence.
[11] e.g. Jacob had connexion with his grand-daughter Rachel, who was the daughter of his daughter Dinah—Jacob being married to Leah the daughter of Laban, and Laban being married to Dinah the daughter of Jacob, by whom he begot Rachel; Rachel married Reuben son of Jacob; Reuben then died or divorced her, and Rachel married Jacob's brother Isaac; Isaac died or divorced her, and Rachel married Jacob's uncle.

menstruant. R. Jose says: If the grandfather[1] had committed transgression[2] and married her, he[3] may thereby become culpable by virtue of [the law of] the father's wife. So, too, if a man had connexion with his wife's daughter,[4] or his wife's daughter's daughter.[5]

6. If a man had connexion with his mother-in-law[6] he may thereby become culpable by virtue of [the laws forbidding connexion with] his mother-in-law, his daughter-in-law, his wife's sister, his brother's wife, his father's brother's wife, a married woman, and a menstruant. So, too, if a man had connexion with his mother-in-law's mother and his father-in-law's mother. R. Johanan b. Nuri says: If a man had connexion with his mother-in-law he may thereby become culpable by virtue of [the laws forbidding connexion with] his mother-in-law, his mother-in-law's mother, and his father-in-law's mother. They said to him: To all three applies a single prohibition.[7]

7. R. Akiba said: I asked Rabban Gamaliel and R. Joshua[8] in the market of Emmaus, where they went to buy a beast for the wedding-feast of the son of Rabban Gamaliel, [and I said,] If a man had connexion with his sister and his father's sister and his mother's sister during one spell of forgetfulness, what happens?—is he liable to one offering for them all or to one offering for each of them? They said to me, We have heard no tradition about this, but we have heard a tradition that if a man had connexion, during one spell of forgetfulness, with his five wives that were menstruants, he is liable for each one of them; and we consider that this applies still more so in the other case.

8. Moreover R. Akiba asked them, What happens if a member of a beast hangs loose?[9] They said to him, We have heard no tradition about this, but we have heard a tradition about a member of a man that hangs loose that it may be accounted clean; for thus used they to do in Jerusalem that were afflicted with boils: on the eve of Passover a man would go to the physician and he would cut [the boil] and leave but a hair's breadth;[10] he then stuck it on a thorn and drew himself [suddenly] away from it.[11] Thus the man was able to bring his Passover-offering and the physician was able to bring his Passover-offering. And we consider that this applies still more so in the other case.

9. Moreover R. Akiba asked them, If a man slaughtered five animal-offerings outside [the Temple Court] during one spell of forgetfulness, what happens?— is he liable to one offering for them all, or to one for each of them? They said to him, We have heard no tradition about this. R. Joshua said, I have heard a tradition about one who, during one spell of forgetfulness, ate of one animal-offering out of five dishes, that he was culpable on each count under the law of Sacrilege;[12] and I consider that this

---

[1] The father of Jacob.
[2] By marrying his son's daughter's daughter.   [3] Jacob.
[4] He can, in circumstances similar to the foregoing, become liable to six Sin-offerings.
[5] In circumstances similar to those in the other case he can become liable to seven Sin-offerings.
[6] e.g. if Leah had a daughter by incestuous connexion with her father, and he who marries Leah's daughter has connexion with Leah.
[7] All are included together in Lev. 18[17].   [8] Cf. Neg. 7[4].
[9] Does it convey uncleanness like a member from a living being? Cf. Hull. 9[7]; Ohol. 2[1].
[10] Since if it was completely severed it would be unclean and convey corpse-uncleanness both to patient and physician.
[11] So that when it was wholly severed he did not touch it.
[12] Lev. 5[15]; p. 573, n. 2.

is still more so in the other case. R. Simeon said: R. Akiba did not ask of such a case, but of one who ate Remnant[1] from five animal-offerings during one spell of forgetfulness. What happens?—is he liable to one Sin-offering for them all, or to one for each of them? They said to him, We have heard no tradition about this. R. Joshua said, I have heard a tradition about one who, during one spell of forgetfulness, ate of one animal-offering out of five dishes, that he was liable for each of them under the law of Sacrilege; and I consider that this applies still more so in the other case. R. Akiba said, If it is *Halakah* we must accept it, but if it is only an inference, there is a rebuttal. He said to him, Rebut it. He answered, As thou arguest of Sacrilege (whereby he that gives another to eat and he that eats, or he that gives it for another's use and he that uses it are alike culpable, even if what is needed to make up the forbidden quantity is consumed only after long time),[2] wouldest thou likewise argue of Remnant, to which none of these things apply?

10. R. Akiba said: I asked R. Eliezer, If a man did many acts of work of the like kind on many Sabbaths[3] during one spell of forgetfulness, what happens?—is he liable to one [Sin-offering] for all of them, or to one for each of them? He said to me, By an inference from the less to the greater he is liable to one for each; thus, If because of connexion with menstruants[4] (to which many classes [of work] and many ways of sinning do not apply) a man is still liable for every act, then because of [transgression of the laws of] the Sabbath (to which apply many classes [of work] and many ways of sinning) how much more must he be liable for every act? I said to him, No! as thou arguest of a menstruant (about whom is a twofold prohibition wherein a man is warned against the menstruant and the menstruant is warned against him)[5] wouldest thou argue likewise of the Sabbath (about which there is but the single prohibition)?[6] He said to me, The case of him that has connexion with [menstruants that are] minors affords proof, about whom there is but the single prohibition, yet a man becomes liable for every act. I said to him, No!—as thou arguest of one that has connexion with such as are minors (with whom though no prohibition now applies it will apply hereafter) wouldest thou likewise argue of the Sabbath, which he has now no right [to profane] nor may he have hereafter? He said to me, The case of him that has connexion with a beast affords proof. I said to him, What applies to [connexion with] a beast applies likewise to [the profaning of] the Sabbath.[7]

4. 1. If it was in doubt whether a man had eaten fat or had not eaten it, or, if he had eaten it, whether it contained the forbidden quantity[8] or not; or if forbidden fat and permitted fat[9] lay before him, and it is not known which of them he ate; or if his wife and his sister were with him in the house and he unwittingly had connexion with one of them and it is not known with which of them he unwittingly had connexion, or if he did an act of work on either a Sabbath or a weekday but it is not known on which he did the act, he must bring a Suspensive Guilt-offering.[10]

2. Like as a man is liable only to one Sin-offering if, during one spell of forgetfulness, he ate forbidden fat and again ate forbidden fat, so, too, when

---

[1] Lev. 7[15]; 19[6].   [2] Cf. Meil. 5[4, 5].   [3] Cf. Shab. 7[1].   [4] As in par. 7 above.
[5] Cf. Lev. 20[18].   [6] i.e. a prohibition directed against him alone.
[7] 'I doubt whether he is culpable for each act with the beast, just as I doubt whether he is culpable for each act of profaning the Sabbath.'
[8] An olive's bulk.   [9] Such as is covered by flesh.   [10] Lev. 5[17ff].

the transgression is not known of a certainty, he brings only one [Suspensive] Guilt-offering. If there was knowledge in the meantime, like as he must bring one Sin-offering for each act, so, too, [in like case] he must bring one Suspensive Guilt-offering for each act. Like as a man is liable on each count if he ate fat and blood and Remnant and Refuse during one spell of forgetfulness, so, too, [in like case] if the transgression was not known of a certainty, he must bring a Suspensive Guilt-offering for each act. If forbidden fat and Remnant lay before him and he ate one of them and it is not known which of them he ate; or if his wife was menstruous and his sister was in the house with him and he unwittingly had connexion with one of them and it is not known with which of them he unwittingly had connexion, or if he performed an act of work at sundown before the Sabbath or the Day of Atonement, and it is not known on which of the two days he did the act, R. Eliezer declares him liable to a Sin-offering, but R. Joshua declares him exempt. R. Jose said: They did not dispute about whether he that did an act of work at sundown was exempt; for I should assume that he did part of the work on the one day and part on the morrow. But about what did they dispute? About one that did work on the day itself and it is not known whether he did so on the Sabbath or whether he did so on the Day of Atonement (or about one that did work but it is not known what manner of work he did) whom R. Eliezer declares liable to a Sin-offering and R. Joshua declares exempt. R. Judah said: R. Joshua declared him exempt even from a Suspensive Guilt-offering.

3. R. Simeon of Shezur and R. Simeon say: They did not dispute about whether he was liable through a transgression falling within one class;[1] but about what did they dispute?—about a transgression falling within two classes,[2] for which R. Eliezer declares a man liable to a Sin-offering and R. Joshua declares him exempt. R. Judah said: Even if he intended to gather figs and he gathered grapes, or grapes and he gathered figs, black fruit and he gathered white, or white fruit and he gathered black, R. Eliezer declares him liable to a Sin-offering, but R. Joshua declares him exempt. R. Judah said: I marvel that R. Joshua declares him exempt in such case; if so why is it written, *Wherein he hath sinned*?[3] To exclude him that had occupied himself [otherwise and unintentionally committed transgression].

5. 1. [If a man consumed an olive's bulk of] blood[4] shed in the slaughtering[5] of cattle, wild animals, or birds, clean or unclean, or blood that had issued through stabbing or through tearing [the windpipe or gullet], or blood from the cutting of a vein by which the life-blood flowed away,[6] he thereby becomes liable;[7] but he does not become liable[8] because of blood from the spleen or from the heart or from the stones, or because of the blood of fishes or of locusts or blood that is squeezed forth.[9] But R. Judah declares a man liable in the case of blood that is squeezed forth.

2. R. Akiba declares a man liable to a Suspensive Guilt-offering for Sacrilege[10] that is in doubt; but the Sages declare him exempt. But R. Akiba agrees that a man need not make restitution for his Sacrilege until [his

---

[1] Doubt about alternatives which constituted a like transgression.
[2] e.g. whether he sowed or reaped, or whether he reaped wheat or barley.
[3] Lev. 4[23].   [4] Lev. 3[17]; 7[26]; 17[10, 14]; 19[26]; Deut. 12[16, 23]; 15[23].
[5] Killing in valid fashion.   [6] Killing in invalid fashion.
[7] To Extirpation.   [8] To Extirpation, but only to the Forty Stripes.
[9] Or that oozes.   [10] Lev. 5[15]; p. 573, n. 2.

offence] is known to him, when he must bring also an Unconditional Guilt-offering. R. Tarfon said: Why must he bring two Guilt-offerings?[1]—but, rather, he must make restitution for his Sacrilege and pay the [Added] Fifth,[2] and bring a Guilt-offering costing two *selas*,[3] and say, 'If of a truth I have committed Sacrilege, here is [restitution] for the Sacrilege and this is my Guilt-offering; but if it is in doubt let the money be a freewill-offering and the Guilt-offering a Suspensive Guilt-offering', since he must bring for what is unknown the same kind[4] of offering that he brings for what is known.

3. R. Akiba said to him: Thy words are acceptable if the Sacrilege is of small value; but if there befell at his hand Sacrilege wherein was doubt in value a hundred *minas*, is it not better for him to bring a Guilt-offering costing two *selas* rather than that he should make restitution for Sacrilege wherein was doubt in value a hundred *minas*? But R. Akiba agrees with R. Tarfon if the Sacrilege is of little value. If a woman, in a matter of doubt, brought a Sin-offering of a bird,[5] and before its head was wrung off it was known to her that it was a certain birth,[6] she may offer it as for a certain birth, since she brings for a certain birth the same kind of offering that she brings for an uncertain birth.

4. If there was a piece of unconsecrated flesh and a piece of consecrated flesh and a man ate one of them and it is not known which of them he ate, he is exempt. R. Akiba declares him liable to a Suspensive Guilt-offering. If he ate the second also, he must bring an Unconditional Guilt-offering;[7] if he ate the one and another came and ate the other, they must each bring a Suspensive Guilt-offering. So R. Akiba. R. Simeon says: They together bring one Guilt-offering. R. Jose says: Two cannot bring one Guilt-offering.[8]

5. If there was a piece of unconsecrated [and permitted] fat and a piece of [forbidden] fat and a man ate one of them and it is not known which of them he ate, he must bring a Suspensive Guilt-offering. If he ate the other also, he must bring a Sin-offering. If one person ate the one and another came and ate the other, each must bring a Suspensive Guilt-offering. So R. Akiba. R. Simeon says: They together bring one Sin-offering. R. Jose says: Two cannot bring one Sin-offering.

6. If there was a piece of [forbidden] fat and a piece of [permitted but] consecrated [fat], and a man ate one of them and it is not known which of them he ate, he must bring a Suspensive Guilt-offering. If he ate the second also, he must bring a Sin-offering and an Unconditional Guilt-offering. If one person ate the one and another came and ate the other, they must each bring a Suspensive Guilt-offering. R. Simeon says: They together bring one Sin-offering and one Guilt-offering. R. Jose says: Two cannot together bring one Sin-offering and one Guilt-offering.

7. If there was a piece of [forbidden] fat and a piece of consecrated fat and a man ate one of them and it is not known which of them he ate, he must bring a Sin-offering. R. Akiba says: He should bring a Suspensive Guilt-offering. If he ate the second also, he must bring two Sin-offerings and an

---

[1] A Suspensive Guilt-offering while he is in doubt; and an Unconditional Guilt-offering when he is certain.   [2] Lev. 5[16]. See B.M. 4[8].
[3] Lev. 5[15], 'by shekels'; therefore it must be at least two. On shekels and *selas* see p. 541, n. 5.
[4] A ram costing two *selas*.
[5] Lev. 12[6]. Cf. above, 1[4].   [6] Cf. above, 1[3].
[7] That prescribed in Lev. 5[15].   [8] But must each bring a Suspensive Guilt-offering.

Unconditional Guilt-offering. If he ate one of them and another came and ate the other, each must bring a Sin-offering. R. Akiba says: Each must bring a Suspensive Guilt-offering. R. Simeon says: Each must bring a Sin-offering and the two together one Guilt-offering. R. Jose says: Two cannot bring one Guilt-offering.

8. If there was a piece of fat and a piece of Remnant-fat,[1] and a man ate one of them and it is not known which of them he ate, he must bring a Sin-offering and a Suspensive Guilt-offering. If he ate the second also, he must bring three Sin-offerings. If one ate the one and another came and ate the other, each must bring a Sin-offering and a Suspensive Guilt-offering. R. Simeon says: Each must bring a Sin-offering, and the two together one Sin-offering. R. Jose says: No Sin-offering offered for a sin can be offered by two.

6. 1. If a man brought a Suspensive Guilt-offering, and it was then known to him that he had not sinned, if the beast was not yet slaughtered it may go forth and pasture among the flock. So R. Meir. But the Sages say: It must be left to pasture until it suffers a blemish, when it shall be sold and its price shall fall [to the Temple treasury] as a freewill-offering. R. Eliezer says: It should be offered, for if it was not offered for this sin it will have been offered for some other. But if it was known to him only after it was slaughtered, the blood must be poured away and the flesh taken to the place of burning. If the blood had already been tossed [against the Altar] the flesh may be eaten. R. Jose says: Even if the blood was yet only in the bason, it should be tossed and the flesh eaten.

2. But it is not so with an Unconditional Guilt-offering. If [it was known to him that he was not guilty] before the beast was slaughtered, it may go forth and pasture among the flock; if after it had been slaughtered, it must be buried; if after the blood was tossed, the flesh must be taken to the place of burning. But it is not so with the ox that is condemned to be stoned.[2] If [it was known that it was not guilty] before it was stoned it may go forth and pasture among the flock; if after it was stoned, its body may be used for [its owner's] profit. But it is not so with the heifer whose neck is to be broken.[3] If[4] [the slayer was found] before the heifer's neck was broken, it may go forth and pasture among the flock; but if after the heifer's neck was broken, it must be buried in the selfsame place; for in the beginning it was brought in a matter of doubt, it made atonement for what was in doubt, and so its purpose is fulfilled.

3. R. Eliezer says: A man may of his own free will offer a Suspensive Guilt-offering on any day and at any time he pleases, and this is called 'the Guilt-offering of the pious'. They told of Baba b. Buta that he offered of his own free will a Suspensive Guilt-offering every day save only the day after the Day of Atonement. He said, 'By this Temple! did they but suffer me I would bring one [even then], but they say to me, Wait until there befalls thee a matter of doubt'. But the Sages say: A man may bring a Suspensive Guilt-offering only for an act by which if he did it wantonly he is liable to Extirpation, and if in error to a Sin-offering.

4. They that are liable to Sin-offerings and to Unconditional Guilt-offerings, even if the Day of Atonement intervened, must bring them after

the Day of Atonement; but they that are liable to Suspensive Guilt-offer-ings are exempt.[1] If on the Day of Atonement there befell at a man's hand a transgression that is in doubt, even if it was at nightfall, he is exempt,[2] since any part of the day makes atonement.

5. If the Day of Atonement overtook a woman that was liable to a Sin-offering of a bird because of a matter of doubt, she must bring it after the Day of Atonement, since it is this offering that renders her fit to eat of the animal-offerings. If the Sin-offering of a bird was brought because of a matter of doubt and after it was killed it was known to her [that she need not offer it] it must be buried.

6. If a man set apart two *selas* for a Guilt-offering and bought two rams therewith for a Guilt-offering, and one of them was worth two *selas*, he may offer this alone; and the other must be left to pasture until it suffers a blemish, when it shall be sold and its price shall fall [to the Temple treasury] as a freewill-offering. If he had bought two rams therewith for common use, one worth two *selas* and the other ten *zuz*,[3] that worth two *selas* may be offered as a Guilt-offering and the other as restitution for his Sacrilege. But if [with the two *selas*] he had bought one ram for his Guilt-offering and one for common use, and the ram for the Guilt-offering was worth two *selas*, he may offer that as his Guilt-offering and the other as restitution for his Sacrilege, and bring with it another *sela* and the [Added] Fifth.

7. If a man set apart his Sin-offering and then died, his son after him may not offer it; nor may a man offer for one sin what was set apart because of another sin; he may not even offer it for the fat which he ate to-day as well as for the fat which he ate yesterday, for it is written, *His oblation for his sin*;[4] his offering must be only for that sin for which it was assigned.

8. [With money] dedicated to buy a lamb [as a Sin-offering] a man may buy a goat,[5] or a goat with what was dedicated to buy a lamb; or with what was dedicated to buy a goat or a lamb he may buy turtle-doves or young pigeons;[6] with what was dedicated to buy turtle-doves or young pigeons he may buy the Tenth of an Ephah.[7] Thus, if a man had set apart money for a lamb or a goat and he became poor, he may offer Bird-offerings; if he be-came still poorer he may offer the Tenth of an Ephah. If a man had set apart [money] for the Tenth of an Ephah and he then became rich he may offer Bird-offerings; and if he became still richer he may offer a lamb or a goat. If he had set apart a lamb or a goat and they suffered a blemish, he may if he is so minded offer Bird-offerings with their price. But if he had set apart Bird-offerings and they suffered a blemish he may not offer the Tenth of an Ephah with the price thereof, since Bird-offerings cannot be redeemed.

9. R. Simeon says: Everywhere Scripture speaks of sheep before goats. Is it because they are the choicer? But Scripture says, *And if*[8] *he bring a lamb as his oblation for a Sin-offering*;[9] to teach that both are equal. Every-where Scripture speaks of turtle-doves before young pigeons. Is it because they are the choicer? But Scripture says, *A young pigeon or a turtle dove for a Sin-offering*;[10] to teach that both are equal. Everywhere Scripture speaks of the father before the mother. Does the honour due to the father exceed

---

[1] Cf. Lev. 16[30].
[2] From a Suspensive Guilt-offering.
[3] Two *selas* and 2 half.
[4] Lev. 4[28]. [5] Both females. Cf. Lev. 5[6]. [6] Lev. 5[7]. [7] Lev. 5[11].
[8] Thus making the lamb only an alternative to the goat spoken of in the preceding verses.
[9] Lev. 4[32]. [10] Lev. 12[6].

the honour due to the mother? But Scripture says, *Ye shall fear every man his mother and his father*;[1] to teach that both are equal. But the Sages have said: Everywhere Scripture speaks of the father before the mother, because both a man and his mother are bound to honour the father. So, too, in the study of the Law, if the son gained much wisdom [the while he sat] before his teacher, his teacher comes ever before his father, since both he and his father are bound to honour the teacher.

MEILAH[2] ('SACRILEGE')

1. 1. If the Most Holy Things[3] were slaughtered on the south side[4] the law of Sacrilege still applies to them. If they were slaughtered on the south side and their blood received on the north or slaughtered on the north side and their blood received on the south, or if they were slaughtered during the day and their blood tossed[5] [against the Altar] by night, or slaughtered by night and the blood tossed by day, or if they were slaughtered [while an act was purposed] outside its proper time or outside its proper place, the law of Sacrilege still applies to them. R. Joshua laid down a general rule: The law of Sacrilege does not apply to whatsoever had at some time been permitted to the priests, and it applies to whatsoever had at no time been permitted to the priests. What is that which had at some time been permitted to the priests? That[6] which remained overnight or became unclean or was taken out [of the Temple Court]. What is that which had at no time been permitted to the priests? [Beasts] that were slaughtered [while an act was purposed] outside its proper time or outside its proper place, or whose blood was received or tossed by them that were unfit.[7]

2. If the flesh of the Most Holy Things was taken out [of the Temple Court] before the blood was tossed, R. Eliezer says: The law of Sacrilege applies to it, yet none thereby becomes culpable through [transgression of the laws of] Remnant, Refuse, or uncleanness.[8] R. Akiba says: The law of Sacrilege does not apply, but nevertheless men can thereby become culpable through [transgression of the laws of] Remnant, Refuse, or uncleanness. R. Akiba said: If a man set apart his Sin-offering and it was lost

---

[1] Lev. 19[3].

[2] Lit. 'trespass', or malappropriation of the property of the Temple. See Lev. 5[15f]. In applying this law the following general principles were adopted. If, in error, a *perutah's* worth or more of benefit was derived from Temple property (offerings, equipment, or money, whether in the Temple's possession or dedicated to the Temple) and it was such as to suffer corresponding deterioration by use, full restitution must be made for the benefit and the deterioration, together with the Added Fifth, and the prescribed Guilt-offering must be brought. If benefit was derived deliberately, full restitution must be made for the benefit and the deterioration, but neither the Added Fifth nor the Guilt-offering is exacted, but the offender, if he had been warned, incurs the Forty Stripes. The law of Sacrilege applies to what is to be burnt on the Altar from the moment it is dedicated until it has been finally consumed; it applies to what may be consumed by the priests (such as the residue of the Meal-offerings and the flesh of certain offerings) from the moment they are dedicated until the Handful has been burnt or the blood sprinkled on the Altar. It does not apply to the Lesser Holy Things, with the exception of their sacrificial portions between the moment of sprinkling the blood and burning the portions.

[3] Zeb.5[1-5]. Offerings (such as Whole-offerings, Sin-offerings, Guilt-offerings, and Peace-offerings of the congregation) which are consumed either on the Altar or by the priests within the Temple Court.   [4] Irregularly. See Zeb. 5[1].

[5] See p. 468, n. 15.

[6] Flesh of an offering whose blood had been sprinkled and whose flesh must be consumed by the priests during that day and the following night. If it is left longer it becomes 'Remnant' (Lev. 7[17]). In the three cases here specified the flesh was permissible for a time; but in the next three cases the flesh never was permissible since the offerings were never valid

[7] See Zeb. 2[1ff].   [8] See p. 471, nn. 9–11.

and he set apart another in its stead, and afterward the first was found and so they both remained [to be slaughtered], then like as the [tossing of the] blood [of the one beast] exempts its flesh [from the law of Sacrilege] so it exempts the flesh of the other beast; and if its blood exempts the flesh of the other beast from the law of Sacrilege how much more must it exempt its own flesh!

3. If the sacrificial portions of the Lesser Holy Things[1] were taken out before the tossing of the blood, R. Eliezer says: The law of Sacrilege does not apply to them, and none thereby becomes culpable through [transgression of the laws of] Remnant, Refuse, or uncleanness. R. Akiba says: The law of Sacrilege does apply, and men thereby become culpable through [transgression of the laws of] Remnant, Refuse, or uncleanness.[2]

4. The tossing of the blood of the Most Holy Things may have either a lenient or a stringent outcome, but with the Lesser Holy Things it has only a stringent outcome. Thus before the tossing of the blood of the Most Holy Things the law of Sacrilege applies both to the sacrificial portions and to the flesh; but after the tossing of the blood it applies to the sacrificial portions but not to the flesh; and because of either men may become culpable through [transgression of the laws of] Remnant, Refuse, or uncleanness. 'With the Lesser Holy Things it has only a stringent outcome'; thus before the tossing of the blood of the Lesser Holy Things the law of Sacrilege applies neither to the sacrificial portions nor to the flesh; but after the tossing of the blood it applies to the sacrificial portions but not to the flesh; and because of either men may become culpable through [transgression of the laws of] Remnant, Refuse, or uncleanness. Thus the tossing of the blood of the Most Holy Things may have either a lenient or a stringent outcome, but with the Lesser Holy Things it has only a stringent outcome.

2. 1. The law of Sacrilege applies to the Sin-offering of a bird so soon as it has been dedicated.[3] After its head has been wrung off it becomes susceptible so that it can be rendered invalid through [contact with] one that had immersed himself the selfsame day [because of uncleanness][4] or one whose atonement was yet incomplete,[5] or by remaining overnight. After its blood has been sprinkled men may thereby become culpable through [transgression of the laws of] Remnant, Refuse, or uncleanness, but the law of Sacrilege no longer applies to it.

2. The law of Sacrilege applies to the Whole-offering of a bird so soon as it has been dedicated. After its head has been wrung off it becomes susceptible so that it can be rendered invalid through [contact with] one that had immersed himself the selfsame day [because of uncleanness] or one whose atonement was yet incomplete, or by remaining overnight. After its blood has been squeezed out men may thereby become culpable through [transgression of the laws of] Remnant, Refuse, or uncleanness, and the law of Sacrilege applies to it until it is taken out to the place of ashes.[6]

3. The law of Sacrilege applies to the bullocks which are to be burnt and to the he-goats which are to be burnt,[7] so soon as they have been dedicated. After they have been slaughtered they become susceptible so that they can

---

[1] Zeb. 5[6-8]. Offerings whose flesh can be consumed by their owners anywhere in Jerusalem after the sprinkling of the blood. See also above, p. 573, n. 2 (end).
[2] Since the sprinkling of the blood is equally effective in rendering holy the sacrificial portions that are outside the Temple Court.   [3] Since it is one of the Most Holy Things.
[4] See p. 773, n. 6.   [5] See p. 564, n. 10.   [6] See p. 474, n. 2.
[7] p. 473, nn. 4–5. They are included among the Most Holy Things.

be rendered invalid through [contact with] one that had immersed himself the selfsame day [because of uncleanness] or one whose atonement was yet incomplete, or by remaining overnight. After their blood has been sprinkled men may thereby become culpable through [transgression of the laws of] Remnant, Refuse, or uncleanness, and the law of Sacrilege applies to them even in the place of ashes until the flesh is reduced to cinders.

4. The law of Sacrilege applies to the Whole-offering so soon as it has been dedicated. After it has been slaughtered it becomes susceptible so that it can be rendered invalid through [contact with] one that had immersed himself the selfsame way [because of uncleanness] or one whose atonement was yet incomplete, or by remaining overnight. After its blood has been tossed men may thereby become culpable through [transgression of the laws of] Remnant, Refuse, or uncleanness; the law of Sacrilege does not apply to its hide, but it applies to its flesh until the ashes are taken out to the place of ashes.

5. The law of Sacrilege applies to a Sin-offering, to a Guilt-offering, and to the Peace-offerings of the congregation so soon as they have been dedicated; after they have been slaughtered they become susceptible so that they can be rendered invalid through [contact with] one that had immersed himself the selfsame day [because of uncleanness] or one whose atonement was yet incomplete, or by remaining overnight. After their blood has been tossed men can thereby become culpable through [transgression of the laws of] Remnant, Refuse, or uncleanness; the law of Sacrilege does not apply to their flesh but it applies to their sacrificial portions until [their ashes are] taken out to the place of ashes.

6. The law of Sacrilege applies to the Two Loaves[1] so soon as they have been dedicated. After they have become crusted in the oven they become susceptible so that they can be rendered invalid through [contact with] one that had immersed himself the selfsame day [because of uncleanness] or one whose atonement was yet incomplete; and they may then slaughter the animal-offerings that pertain to them.[2] After the blood of the lambs has been tossed, men can by reason of the loaves become culpable through [transgression of the laws of] Remnant, Refuse, or uncleanness. But the law of Sacrilege does not apply to them.

7. The law of Sacrilege applies to the Shewbread[3] so soon as it has been dedicated. After it has become crusted in the oven it becomes susceptible so that it can be rendered invalid through [contact with] one that had immersed himself the selfsame day [because of uncleanness] or one whose atonement was yet incomplete; and it may then[4] be set in order on the table. After the dishes [of frankincense] have been brought, men can become culpable because of the Shewbread through [transgression of the laws of] Remnant, Refuse, or uncleanness; but the law of Sacrilege does not apply to it.[5]

8. The law of Sacrilege applies to the Meal-offerings so soon as they have been dedicated. After they have become holy in the vessel [of ministry] they become susceptible so that they can be rendered invalid through [contact with] one that had immersed himself the selfsame day [because of uncleanness] or one whose atonement was yet incomplete, or by remaining overnight. After the Handful has been offered, men may thereby become

---

[1] Lev. 23[17].   [2] Lev. 23[18].   [3] Lev. 24[5ff].
[4] 'After it has become crusted.'   [5] It can now be consumed by the priests.

culpable through [transgression of the laws of] Remnant, Refuse, or uncleanness, but the law of Sacrilege does not apply to their residue; but it applies to the Handful until it[1] is taken out to the place of ashes.

9. The law of Sacrilege applies to the Handful, the frankincense, the incense, the Meal-offering of the Priests, the Meal-offering of the anointed [High] Priest, and the Meal-offerings offered with drink-offerings,[2] so soon as they have been dedicated. After they have become holy in the vessel [of ministry] they become susceptible so that they can be rendered invalid through [contact with] one that had immersed himself the selfsame day [because of uncleanness] or one whose atonement was yet incomplete, or by remaining overnight; and men may thereby become culpable through [transgression of the laws of] Remnant or uncleanness, but the law of Refuse does not apply to them. This is the general rule: If any offering has that which renders it permissible[3] [for the Altar or for the use of the priests], none can thereby become culpable through [transgression of the laws of] Remnant, Refuse, and uncleanness, unless that which renders it permissible has been offered; whereas if any offering has not that which renders it permissible, men can thereby become culpable through [transgression of the laws of] Remnant and uncleanness so soon as it becomes holy in the vessel [of ministry], but the law of Refuse does not apply to it.

3. 1. The young of a Sin-offering,[4] the Substitute for a Sin-offering, and the Sin-offering whose owner has died must be left to die. If it passed the age of a year, or was lost and found blemished and its owner had already [otherwise] made atonement, it must be left to die; a Substitute for it may not be brought, no use may be made of it, but the law of Sacrilege does not apply to it. If the owner had not yet made atonement it must be left to pasture until it suffers a blemish when it shall be sold and another [Sin-offering] brought with its price; a Substitute for it may be brought and the law of Sacrilege applies to it.

2. If a man set apart money for his Nazirite-offerings[5] he may not make [other] use of it, yet the law of Sacrilege does not apply to it, since it may all be used to bring a Peace-offering. If he died and the money was not expressly assigned,[6] it falls [to the Temple treasury] as a freewill-offering; but if it was expressly assigned, the price of the Sin-offering is cast into the Dead Sea—no use may be made of it, but the law of Sacrilege does not apply to it; with the price of the Whole-offering a Whole-offering is brought, and the law of Sacrilege applies to it; with the price of the Peace-offering a Peace-offering is brought, and it is consumed the same day and it does not require the Bread-offering.[7]

---

[1] The ashes on the Altar.   [2] For the foregoing see Zeb. 4³.

[3] So that it is rendered 'acceptable' (Lev. 19⁷) and so can be offered on the Altar, or, in certain cases, be consumed by the Priests. See Zeb. 2³. With Sin-offerings, Guilt-offerings, and Peace-offerings the sprinkling of the blood renders their sacrificial portions permissible for the Altar and their flesh for the priests; likewise the sprinkling of the blood renders the flesh of the Whole-offerings of cattle or birds, the 'bullocks and he-goats that are to be burnt' permissible for the Altar; the Two Loaves are rendered permissble for the priests by the sprinkling of the blood of the lambs that pertain to them; and for all Meal-offerings (excepting those mentioned at the beginning of the verse, which are wholly burnt on the Altar) the taking and burning of the Handful renders the residue permissible for the priests.

[4] See Tem. 4¹.

[5] Num. 6¹⁴. He must, on the completion of his vow, bring a he-lamb as a Whole-offering, a ewe-lamb as a Sin-offering, and a ram as a Peace-offering. The law of Sacrilege only applies to the sacrificial portions of a Peace-offering (which is one of the Lesser Holy Things) and only after the blood has been sprinkled.

[6] Whether for Whole-offering, Sin-offering, or Peace-offering.   [7] See Num. 6¹⁹.

3. R. Ishmael[1] says: In what concerns the blood the law of Sacrilege bears leniently in the beginning and stringently in the end; in what concerns the drink-offerings it bears stringently in the beginning and leniently in the end. To the blood the law of Sacrilege does not apply in the beginning,[2] but after it has flowed away to the brook Kidron[3] the law of Sacrilege applies to it; to the drink-offerings the law of Sacrilege applies in the beginning, but after they have flowed down into the pits[4] the law of Sacrilege does not apply to them.

4. No use may be made of the ashes[5] from the inner Altar or [of the wicks that remained] from the Candlestick, but the law of Sacrilege does not apply to them. But if the ashes were dedicated in the beginning[6] the law of Sacrilege applies to them. No use may be made of turtle-doves that are not yet of prescribed age or of pigeons that are past the prescribed age,[7] but the law of Sacrilege does not apply to them. R. Simeon says: The law of Sacrilege applies to turtle-doves that are not yet of prescribed age; and no use may be made of young pigeons that are past the prescribed age, but the law of Sacrilege does not apply to them.

5. No use may be made of the milk of animal-offerings or of the eggs of the turtle-doves, but the law of Sacrilege does not apply to them. This applies only to what is consecrated for the Altar and not to what is consecrated for the Temple-treasury] but if a man had dedicated a hen [for the Temple treasury; the law of Sacrilege applies both to it and to its eggs; if an ass, the law of Sacrilege applies both to it and to its milk.

6. The law of Sacrilege applies to a thing whether it is fitting for the Altar but not for the Temple treasury, or fitting for the Temple treasury but not for the Altar, or to what is fitting neither for the Altar nor for the Temple treasury. Thus if a man dedicated a cistern full of water,[8] or a midden full of dung,[9] or a dovecot full of pigeons,[10] or a tree covered with fruit, or a field full of herbage, the law of Sacrilege applies both to the thing itself and to what is therein; but if he had dedicated a cistern and it was afterward filled with water, or a midden and it was afterward filled with dung, or a dovecot and it was afterward filled with pigeons, or a tree and it was afterward covered with fruit, or a field and herbage afterward grew up, the law of Sacrilege applies to the thing itself but not to what is therein. So R. Judah. But R. Simeon[11] says: If a man dedicated a tree or a field, the law of Sacrilege applies both to them and what grows from them, since their growth is from what belongs to the Temple. The young of the Tithe of Cattle may not draw suck from [beasts that have been made] Tithe [of Cattle];[12] but there are others that offer [their beasts] only on this condition.[13] The young[14] of animal-offerings may not draw suck from animal-offerings, but there are others that offer [their beasts] only on this condition.

---

[1] Variant: Simeon.   [2] Before it is sprinkled.
[3] See Yom. 5[6]; Midd. 3[2].   [4] Midd. 3[3]; cf. Sukk. 4[9].   [5] Of the incense.
[6] If, before the ashes were removed, some one had vowed to give the Temple their value.
[7] See p. 514, n. 4.
[8] Which cannot be used for the Altar but can be used or sold for the benefit of the Temple treasury.
[9] Which cannot be used for either Altar or treasury, but can be sold for their benefit.
[10] Which can be used for the Altar. The wood or stones of the dovecot can be used for Temple repairs.
[11] Some texts read 'Jose'.   [12] Cf. Bekh. 9[7].
[13] That if the Tithe of their cattle should be a female beast its milk should not be consecrated but permissible for its young.
[14] Born before the dam was dedicated.

Workmen[1] may not eat of dried figs which have been dedicated to the Temple; so, too, a cow[2] may not eat of vetches which have been dedicated.

7. If the roots of a tree in private ground spread into dedicated ground, or if the roots of a tree in dedicated ground spread into private ground, no use may be made of them, but the law of Sacrilege does not apply to them. If the source of a spring[3] was in a dedicated field no use may be made of it, but the law of Sacrilege does not apply to it. If it flowed outside the field use may be made of it. No use may be made of the water that is in the golden pitcher,[4] but the law of Sacrilege does not apply to it; but after it has been poured into the flagon[5] the law of Sacrilege applies to it. No use may be made of the willow-branches[6] [set beside the Altar], but the law of Sacrilege does not apply to them. R. Eliezer b. Zadok says: The old men used to take of them for their *Lulabs*.[7]

8. No use may be made of a nest on the top of a dedicated tree, but the law of Sacrilege does not apply to it; but one may flick off with a reed what is on the top of an *Asherah*.[8] If a man dedicated a wood the law of Sacrilege applies to the whole of it. If the [Temple] treasurers have bought the trees[9] the law of Sacrilege applies to the trees, but not to the chips or foliage.

4. 1. Hallowed Things that pertain to the Altar may be included together with one another to make up the quantity[10] forbidden by the law of Sacrilege, or to render a man liable through [transgression of the laws of] Remnant, Refuse, or uncleanness.[11] Hallowed Things that pertain to the Temple treasury may be included together with one another and Hallowed Things that pertain to the Altar may be included together with the Hallowed Things pertaining to the Temple treasury, to make up the quantity forbidden by the law of Sacrilege.

2. In a Whole-offering five things may be included together: the flesh, the fat, the fine flour, the wine, and the oil; and six in a Thank-offering: the flesh, the fat, the fine flour, the wine, the oil, and the bread. Heave-offering,[12] Heave-offering of Tithe,[13] Heave-offering of Tithe from *demai*-produce,[14] Dough-offering,[15] and First-fruits[16] may be included together to make up the quantity that renders them forbidden[17] and subject to the [law of the Added] Fifth.[18]

3. [To make up a prescribed forbidden quantity] the Refuse of any offerings may be included together; the Remnants of any offerings may be included together;[19] all kinds of carrion may be included together;[20] all creeping things[21] may be included together; the blood and the flesh of a creeping thing may be included together. R. Joshua laid down a general rule: All things that are alike in [the duration[22] of] their uncleanness and in

---

[1] Cf. B.M. 7[2].   [2] Deut. 25[4].

[3] Which had not been dedicated together with the field (Tif. Yis.).

[4] See Sukk. 4[10].   [5] Sukk. 4[9].   [6] See Sukk. 4[5].

[7] App. I. 20. They were saved the labour of going out to gather them at Motza, several miles away.   [8] App. I. 4.   [9] Cut down to be used for timber.

[10] One *perutah's* worth.

[11] If several portions of such offerings together make up an olive's bulk. Cf. Zeb. 3[4].

[12] Num. 18[8ff]. App. I. 48.   [13] Num. 18[25ff].

[14] See p. 20, n. 9.   [15] Num. 15[20]; p. 83, n. 1.

[16] Deut. 26[2ff].   [17] To non-priests.   [18] Lev. 22[14]. See B.M. 4[8].

[19] To make up an olive's bulk.   [20] Lev. 11[39]. An olive's bulk conveys uncleanness.

[21] Lev. 11[29f]. A lentil's bulk conveys uncleanness.

[22] e.g. uncleanness contracted from animal carcases lasts only until evening; that contracted from human corpses lasts seven days.

the quantity of them[1] [that is needful to convey uncleanness] may be included together; but if they are alike in [the duration of] their uncleanness but not in the quantity of them [that is needful to convey uncleanness], or if they are alike in the quantity of them [that is needful to convey uncleanness] but not in [the duration of] their uncleanness; or if they are alike neither in [the duration of] their uncleanness nor in the quantity of them [that is needful to convey uncleanness], they may not be included together.

4. Refuse and Remnant may not be included together since they are of two different classes.[2] A creeping thing and carrion (so, too, carrion and the flesh of a corpse) may not be included together to make up the quantity that is needful to convey uncleanness, even to convey the lesser degree[3] of uncleanness of the two. Food rendered unclean by a primary uncleanness[4] and other food rendered unclean by a derived uncleanness[5] can be included together and they convey the lesser degree of uncleanness of the two.

5. All foodstuffs[6] can be included together to make up the bulk of half a half-loaf that suffices to render the body unfit;[7] or to make up the food for two meals required for *Erub*;[8] or to make up the egg's bulk[9] that conveys food-uncleanness; or to make up the fig's bulk that it is forbidden to carry forth on the Sabbath[10] or to make up the date's bulk[11] that it is forbidden to eat on the Day of Atonement. All liquids can be included together to make up the quarter-*log* that suffices to render the body unfit, or to make up the mouthful that it is forbidden to drink on the Day of Atonement.

6. *Orlah*-fruit[12] and Diverse Kinds of the Vineyard[13] can be included together.[14] R. Simeon says: They cannot be included together. Cloth[15] and sacking, sacking and leather, leather and matting, can be included together,[16] the one with the other. R. Simeon says:[17] Because they are such that contract uncleanness by being sat upon.

5. 1. If a man enjoyed a *perutah's* worth of use of what pertains to the Temple, even though he did not lessen its value, he is guilty of Sacrilege. So R. Akiba. But the Sages say: Whatsoever deteriorates by use, the law of Sacrilege applies to it only if it has suffered deterioration; and whatsoever

1 e.g. a lentil's bulk of human corpse and an olive's bulk of animal carcase are the minimum quantities which convey uncleanness.
2 Separately forbidden, the one in Lev. 7[18] as an 'abomination', and the other in Ex. 29[34] 'because it is holy'.
3 The 'evening-uncleanness' conveyed by an olive's bulk of carrion.
4 Lit. 'father of uncleanness'; see p. 424, n. 8. Such food counts as suffering 'first-grade uncleanness', i.e. uncleanness suffered at a single remove from a 'father of uncleanness'.
5 Lit. 'offspring of uncleanness'. It counts as suffering 'first-grade uncleanness', and what it renders unclean counts as suffering 'second-grade uncleanness'. The two unclean foods can combine to make up the egg's bulk that suffices to convey food-uncleanness. But combined they count as suffering 'second-grade uncleanness' only, and what they touch suffers only 'third-grade uncleanness'. 6 Mikw. 10[7].
7 Not 'unclean' but 'unfitted' (if he is a priest) to eat of Heave-offering. The half of a half-loaf (cf. Toh. 1[3]) is variously explained as either two, or one and a half, eggs' bulk. Cf. Erub. 8[2]. 8 App. I. 8. See Erub. 8[1f].
9 Food can convey uncleanness only if it is at least an egg's bulk in quantity.
10 See Shab. 7[4]. 11 Yom. 8[2]. 12 App. I. 32.
13 See p. 28, n. 1.
14 So that if a man ate an olive's bulk of the two combined he incurs the Forty Stripes.
15 The following rule is explained in Kel. 27[2, 3].
16 So that they shall be considered large enough to be susceptible to *midras*-uncleanness (see App. I. 26).
17 Wishing to show that there is no analogy between the combining of *Orlah*-fruit with Diverse Kinds of the Vineyard, and the combining of these other materials, since the ruling concerning the combination of the latter deals only with their susceptibility to *midras*-uncleanness.

does not deteriorate by use, the law of Sacrilege applies to it so soon as use is made of it. Thus, if [a woman] wore a chain around her neck or a ring on her hand or drank from a golden cup,[1] she is guilty of Sacrilege so soon as she has made use of them; but if any one wore a shirt, or clothed himself with a cloak, or used an axe to split wood, he is not guilty of Sacrilege unless it suffers deterioration. If a man plucked wool from a Sin-offering while it was yet alive, he is guilty of Sacrilege only if it suffered deterioration; but if after it was dead, he is guilty of Sacrilege so soon as he has made use of it.

2. If he enjoyed half a *perutah's* worth of use and lessened its value by half a *perutah*, or if he enjoyed a *perutah's* worth of use from one thing and lessened by a *perutah* the value of something else, he is not thereby guilty of Sacrilege; but only after he has enjoyed a *perutah's* worth of use and lessened by a *perutah* the value of the selfsame thing.

3. Sacrilege cannot twice be committed with [the same] Hallowed Things, save only with cattle and the vessels of ministry. Thus, if one man rode on a beast and another came and rode on it, and yet another came and rode on it; or if one drank from the golden cup, then another came and drank, and yet another came and drank; or if one plucked wool from a Sin-offering, and then another came and plucked and then yet another came and plucked, all are guilty of Sacrilege. Rabbi says: Sacrilege can be committed repeatedly with aught that is not subject to redemption.

4. If a man took away a stone or a beam from what belongs to the Temple he is not guilty of Sacrilege; but if he gave it to his fellow he himself is guilty of Sacrilege but his fellow is not guilty. If he built it into his house he is not guilty of Sacrilege unless he dwells under it [and enjoys the use of it] to the value of one *perutah*. If he took away a *perutah* belonging to the Temple, he is not guilty of Sacrilege; but if he gave it to his fellow he himself is guilty of Sacrilege but his fellow is not guilty. If he gave it to a bath-keeper even though he did not bathe he is guilty of Sacrilege, since the other [as it were] says to him, 'The bath is open: go and bathe'.

5. What he has eaten and what his fellow has eaten, what he has used and what his fellow has used, what he has eaten and what his fellow has used, what he has used and what his fellow has eaten, these can be included together[2] even though long time intervened.

6. 1. If an agent performed his appointed errand [and thereby committed an act of Sacrilege] it is the householder that is guilty; but if he had not performed his appointed errand, it is the agent that is guilty of the Sacrilege.[3] Thus if he said to him, 'Give the guests flesh', and he gave them liver,[4] or '[Give them] liver', and he gave them flesh, it is the agent that is guilty of Sacrilege. If he said to him, 'Give each one piece',[5] but he said [to them], 'Take ye each two pieces', and they each took three, they are all guilty of Sacrilege. If he said to him, 'Bring [such a thing] to me from the wall-niche', or 'from the chest', and he brought aught to him,[6] even though the householder said, 'I had meant only from thence' and he

---

[1] All three things belonging to the Temple.
[2] To make up the forbidden *perutah's* worth.
[3] Thus the rule prevailing with non-sacred property, that none may plead agency in excuse for transgression, does not apply to what is consecrated. See B.K. 8[7] (end).
[4] Both of which belonged to the Temple.
[5] From a dish the whole contents of which belonged to the Temple.
[6] Thereby committing an act of Sacrilege.

brought it to him from elsewhere, the householder is guilty of Sacrilege. But if he said, 'Bring me [such a thing] from the wall-niche', and he brought to him aught from the chest, or 'from the chest', and he brought to him aught from the wall-niche, it is the agent that is guilty of Sacrilege.

2. If he sent as his agent[1] a deaf-mute, an imbecile, or a minor, and they performed their appointed errand, it is the householder that is guilty of Sacrilege. If they did not perform their appointed errand it is the shop-keeper that is guilty of Sacrilege. If he sent by one of sound senses and he[2] bethought himself before he reached the shopkeeper, it is the shopkeeper that is guilty of Sacrilege when he delivers [his wares].[3] What should [the householder] do? He should take a *perutah* or any article and say, 'The *perutah* which belongs to the Temple, wheresoever the *perutah* may be, let it be redeemed with this', for what belongs to the Temple can be re-deemed either by money or by money's worth.[4]

3. If he gave him a *perutah*[5] and said to him, 'Bring me lamps[6] for half of it and wicks for the other half', and he went and brought him lamps with the whole of it, or wicks with the whole of it; or if he said to him, 'Bring me lamps for the whole of it' or 'wicks for the whole of it', and he went and brought him lamps with the half of it and wicks with the other half, neither of them[7] is guilty of Sacrilege. But if he said to him, 'Bring me with half of it lamps from such a place, and with the other half wicks from such a place', and he went and brought him lamps from where he should have brought wicks and wicks from where he should have brought lamps, it is the agent that is guilty of Sacrilege.[8]

4. If he gave him two *perutahs*[5] and said, 'Bring me a citron', and he went and brought him a citron for the one *perutah* and a pomegranate for the other, they are both guilty of Sacrilege. R. Judah says: The householder is not guilty of Sacrilege, since he could say, 'I wished for a large citron and thou hast brought me one that is small and bad'. If he gave him a golden *denar*[9] and said to him, 'Bring me a shirt', and he went and brought him a shirt for three *selas*[10] and a cloak for three *selas*, they are both guilty of Sacrilege. R. Judah says: The householder is not guilty of Sacrilege, for he could say, 'I wished for a big shirt and thou hast brought me one that is small and bad'.

5. If a man deposited money[11] with a money-changer and it was tied up, he may not make use of it; therefore if he paid it out he is guilty of Sacri-lege; but if it was loose, he may make use of it; therefore if he paid it out he is not guilty of Sacrilege. If he deposited it with a householder, in neither case should he make use of it; therefore if he paid it out he is guilty of Sacrilege. The shopkeeper counts as a householder. So R. Meir. R. Judah says: As a money-changer.[12]

---

[1] To buy food with money belonging to the Temple.   [2] The householder.
[3] Thereby acquiring the Temple's money. The law of Sacrilege does not now apply to the householder who, by remembering that the money is the Temple's, ceases to be a trans-gressor by error; and only he who acts in error can take advantage of the law of Sacrilege and atone for his offence.   [4] Cf. Arak. 8[1].
[5] Which belonged to the Temple.
[6] They were a species of small, roofed-in saucer, made of baked clay, with an aperture at the top to pour in oil and a spout or nozzle at the side which carried the wick.
[7] Some texts read 'both of them'. According to the ordinary reading the householder is guiltless since his errand was not fulfilled, and the agent is guiltless since he only half ful-filled (i.e. to only half a *perutah*'s worth) his appointed errand.
[8] He has not fulfilled his errand at all.   [9] Twenty-five silver *denars*
[10] Twelve *denars*.   [11] Belonging to the Temple.   [12] Cf. B.M. 3[11].

6. If a *perutah* that belonged to the Temple fell into a bag of other money; or if a man said, 'One *perutah* in this bag belongs to the Temple', so soon as he pays out the first *perutah* he has committed Sacrilege. So R. Akiba. But the Sages say: Only after he has paid out all that is in the bag. R. Akiba agrees that if a man said, 'One *perutah* from this bag shall belong to the Temple', he may go on paying out of the bag [and not be guilty of Sacrilege] until he pays out all that is in the bag.

TAMID[1] ('THE DAILY WHOLE-OFFERING')

1. 1. The priests kept watch at three places in the Temple: at the Chamber of Abtinas,[2] at the Chamber of the Flame,[3] and at the Chamber of the Hearth.[4] The Chamber of Abtinas and the Chamber of the Flame were on the upper story[5] and there the young men [from among the priests] kept watch. The Chamber of the Hearth was vaulted; it was a large chamber and around it ran a raised stone pavement; and there the eldest of the father's house[6] used to sleep with the keys of the Temple Court in their hand. The young priests had each his mattress on the ground. They did not sleep in the sacred garments but stripped them off, folded them up and put them under their heads and dressed themselves in their own clothes. If one[7] of them suffered a pollution he would go out and go along the passage that leads below the Temple building,[8] where lamps were burning here and there, until he reached the Chamber of Immersion. There was a fire there and a privy, and this was its seemly use: if he found it locked he knew that some one was there; if open he knew that no one was there. He went down and immersed himself,[9] came up and dried himself, and warmed himself before the fire. He returned and lay down beside his brethren the priests until the gates were opened, when he went out and left the Temple.[10]

2. He that was minded to clean the Altar of ashes rose up early and immersed himself before the officer[11] came. At what time did he come? Not always at the same time. Sometimes he came at cockcrow and sometimes a little sooner or later. The officer came and knocked [on the door] where they were, and they opened to him. He said, 'Let him that has immersed himself come and cast lots'. And they cast lots and the lot fell upon whom it fell.

3. He took the key and opened the wicket and entered the Temple Court by the Chamber of the Hearth.[12] The priests entered after him carrying two lighted torches and they separated into two parties, the one going along the colonnade eastwards and the other going along the colonnade westwards. As they went they kept diligent watch until they came to the place where the Baken Cakes[13] were made.[14] When both were come thither they called [one to the other], 'Is all well?' 'All is well!' There they left them that made the Baken Cakes to make the Baken Cakes.

---

1 Lit. 'continual', i.e. the continual or Daily Whole-offering, brought every day throughout the year, morning and evening (Ex. 29[38-42]; Num. 28[1-8]).
2 See Shek. 5[1]; Yom. 1[5]; 3[11]; Midd. 1[1]. It was in the upper story, on the south side of the 'Court of the Priests'.   3 See Midd. 1[5].   4 Midd. 1[6].
5 It was built above the colonnade which surrounded the inner court of the Temple.
6 See p. 165, n. 11.   7 Midd. 1[9].
8 The *Birah*. See p. 140, n. 3.   9 Cf. Mikw. 8[4].
10 He could not be accounted clean and fit to minister in the Temple or eat of Hallowed Things (cf. Ber. 1[1]) until sunset. See p. 77[3], n. 6.
11 Who 'was over the lots'. Cf. Shek. 5[1] (Mattithiah b. Samuel); Yom. 3[1].
12 i.e. north of the space that lay between the Porch and the Altar.
13 See Men. 4[5]; Lev. 6[21].   14 The south-east corner of the Temple Court.

4. He whose lot it was to clear the Altar of ashes went to clear the Altar of ashes, while they said to him, 'Take heed that thou touch not the vessel[1] before thou hast sanctified thy hands and feet in the laver;[2] and lo, the firepan lies in the corner between the Ramp and the Altar, on the western side of the Ramp'.[3] None went in[4] with him and he carried no lamp, but he walked in the light of the Altar fire. They neither saw him nor heard the sound of him until they heard the noise of the wooden device which Ben Katin[5] had made for the laver; and then they said, 'The time is come!' He sanctified his hands and feet at the laver, took the silver firepan and went up to the top of the Altar and cleared away the cinders to this side and to that, and scooped up the innermost burnt [cinders] and came down again. When he reached the pavement he turned his face to the north and went some ten cubits to the east of the Ramp. He heaped the cinders together on the pavement three handbreadths away from the Ramp at the place where they throw the crops of the birds[6] and the ashes from the inner Altar and the Candlestick.

2. 1. When his brethren saw that he was come down they came running and hastened and sanctified their hands and their feet at the laver, and they took the shovels and the rakes and mounted to the top of the Altar. Any members [of the animal-offerings] and fat pieces that had not been consumed since the evening they raked to the sides of the Altar, and if the sides could not contain them they put them in order on the Circuit[7] by the Ramp.

2. They began to heap up the ashes above the ash-pile, and the ash-pile was in the middle of the Altar; sometimes there were about three hundred *kors*[8] [of ashes] upon it; and at the Feasts[9] the priests did not clear away the ashes since they were an adornment to the Altar: [when the ashes remained] it was never through negligence of the priest to clear away the ashes.

3. They began to bring up faggots to set in order the Altar fire. Were all kinds of wood valid for use in the Altar fire? Yea, all kinds of wood were valid for use in the Altar fire save only olive-wood and the wood of the vine; but their custom was to use only boughs of the fig-tree or the walnut-tree or of oleaster-wood.

4. He[10] set in order the greater of the Altar fires to the east side; and its fore side[11] was to the east, and the inner ends of the faggots touched the ash-pile, and there was a space between the faggots through which they set fire to the kindling-wood.

5. They chose from thence fine pieces of fig-tree wood wherewith to set in order the second fire appointed for the incense, over against the south-western corner, but distant four cubits to the north of this corner; [on weekdays they took wood sufficient to give] about five *seahs* of cinders, and on the Sabbath sufficient to give about eight *seahs* of cinders, for there they used to put the two dishes of frankincense that pertained to the Shew-bread.[12] Then they put back on the fire the members [of the animal-offerings] and the fat pieces that had not been consumed since the evening.

They kindled the two fires and came down and betook themselves to the Chamber of Hewn Stone.[1]

3. 1. The officer said to them, 'Come and cast lots',[2] [to decide] which of them should slaughter, which should sprinkle the blood, which should clear the inner Altar[3] of ashes, which should trim the Candlestick, and which should take up the Ramp the members [of the Daily Whole-offering, namely] the head and the [right] hind-leg, and the two fore-legs, the rump and the [left] hind-leg, the breast and the neck, and the two flanks, the inwards, and the fine flour, the Baken Cakes and the wine. They cast lots, and the lot fell upon whom it fell.

2. The officer said to them, 'Go and see if the time is come for slaughtering'. If it was come, he that perceived it says, 'It is daylight'. Mattithiah b. Samuel[4] used to say: [He that perceived it says,] 'The whole east is alight'. 'As far as Hebron?' and he answered, 'Yea!'

3. He said to them, 'Go and bring a lamb from the Chamber of Lambs'.[5] Now the Chamber of Lambs was in the north-western corner. Four chambers were there:[6] one was the Chamber of Lambs, one the Chamber of Seals,[7] one the Chamber of the Hearth, and one the chamber wherein they made the Shewbread.

4. They went into the Chamber of Utensils[8] and brought forth ninety-three vessels of silver and vessels of gold; and they gave [the lamb that was to be] the Daily Whole-offering to drink from a cup of gold. Although it had been inspected in the evening of the day before, they inspect it again by the light of torches.

5. He to whom it fell to slaughter the Daily Whole-offering dragged it along to the shambles,[9] and they to whom it fell to carry the members followed after. The shambles lay north of the Altar and there stood there eight short pillars; upon these were four-sided blocks of cedar-wood into which were fixed iron hooks,[10] three rows to each, whereon they used to hang [the slaughtered beasts]. They used to flay them on marble tables[11] between the pillars.

6. They to whom it fell to clear the inner Altar of ashes and to trim the Candlestick had already gone, bearing four utensils in their hands: an ash-bin, an oil-jar, and two keys. The ash-bin was like a large golden three-*kab* measure and it held two and a half *kabs*; and the oil-jar was like a large golden flagon; and as for the two keys, one was thrust into the lock as far as the armpit, and the other opened [the door] forthwith.

7. He reached the northern wicket.[12] The great gate[13] had two wickets, one to the north and another to the south. By that to the south none ever entered, whereof it is expressly said by Ezekiel, *And the Lord said unto me, This gate shall be shut, it shall not be opened, neither shall any man enter in by it, for the Lord, the God of Israel, hath entered in by it; therefore it shall be shut.*[14] He took the key and opened the wicket. He entered into a cell, and from the cell into the Sanctuary, until he reached the great gate.[15] When he reached the great gate he drew back the bolt and the locks and

---

[1] Sanh. 11[2]; Midd. 5[4].   [2] Cf. Yom. 2[1ff].   [3] Cf. Yom. 5[5].
[4] See above, p. 582, n. 11.   [5] Cf. Arak. 2[5].   [6] See Midd. 1[6].   [7] See Shek. 5[3f].
[8] See Shek. 5[6].   [9] Midd. 3[5].   [10] Cf. Pes. 5[9].   [11] Cf. Shek. 6[4].
[12] A small door to the right of the main door leading from the Porch into the Sanctuary.
[13] Midd. 4[2].   [14] Ezek. 44[2].   [15] From the inside.

opened it. He that slaughtered never slaughtered until he heard the noise of the opening of the great gate.

8. From Jericho they could hear the noise of the opening of the great gate; from Jericho they could hear the sound of the 'Shovel';[1] from Jericho they could hear the noise of the wooden device which Ben Katin made for the laver;[2] from Jericho they could hear the voice of Gabini the herald;[3] from Jericho they could hear the sound of the flute; from Jericho they could hear the noise of the cymbal;[4] from Jericho they could hear the sound of the singing; from Jericho they could hear the sound of the *Shofar*; and some say, even the voice of the High Priest when he pronounced the Name on the Day of Atonement;[5] from Jericho they could smell the smell at the compounding of the incense. R. Eleazar b. Diglai said: My father's house kept goats in the mountain of Machwar,[6] and they used to sneeze from the smell of the compounding of the incense.

9. He to whom it fell to clean the inner Altar of ashes went in and took the ash-bin, set it down before him, scooped up the ashes with both hands and put them into it; what was left at the last he swept into it; there he left it and came away. He to whom it fell to trim the Candlestick went in, and if he found the two easternmost lamps[7] burning he trimmed the rest, but left them burning as they were. If he found that they had gone out, he trimmed them and kindled them from those that were still alight, and then trimmed the rest. There was a stone before the Candlestick in which were three steps; on this the priest stood to trim the lamps. He left the oil-jar on the second step and came away.

4. 1. The lamb was not [wholly] bound up but [only] tied, and they to whom it fell to take the members [of the lamb] laid hold on it. And thus was it tied up—with its head to the south and its face to the west. He that slaughtered it stood to the east with his face to the west. [The Daily Whole-offering] of the morning was slaughtered at the north-western corner at the second ring;[8] that of the afternoon was slaughtered at the north-eastern corner at the second ring. He whose lot it was to slaughter slaughtered it; and he whose lot it was to receive [the blood][9] received the blood and came to the north-eastern corner [of the Altar] and sprinkled it to the east and to the north; then he came to the south-western corner and sprinkled it to the east and to the south.[10] The residue of the blood he poured out at the base [of the Altar] on the south side.

2. He [that slaughtered it] did not break its hind-leg but pierced the knee-joint and so hung it up; he flayed it downwards as far as the breast; when he reached the breast he cut off the head and gave it to him whose lot it was to take it. He cut off the shanks and gave them to him whose lot it was to take them. He stripped off all the hide, slit the heart and let out its blood. He cut off the fore-legs and gave them to him whose lot it was to take them. He came up to the right hind-leg, cut it off, and gave it with the two stones

---

[1] Heb. *Magrefah*. Cf. below, 5[6]. It is explained as being an instrument having ten pipes, ten holes in each pipe, and made in the shape of a shovel. It is not identified with the shovel mentioned below, 5[6].

[2] See above, 1[4]. It was a device for lowering the water into a well below. See p. 165, n. 15.   [3] Shek. 5[1].   [4] Arak. 2[5].

[5] Cf. p. 165, n. 8; Sot. 7[6].   [6] East of the Dead Sea.

[7] The 'candlestick' was a large seven-armed candelabrum, carrying a lamp (cf. p. 581, n. 6) on each arm. The lamps were in line, running east and west (cf. Men. 11[6]).

[8] See Midd. 3[5]; Sukk. 5[8].   [9] Cf. Pes. 5[5].   [10] Zeb 5[4·].

to him to whose lot they fell. He slit [the carcase] so that all the inward parts lay open before him. He removed the fat and put it above where the head was cut off. He removed the inward parts and gave them to him whose lot it was to swill them. The stomach was swilled as many times as it needed in the swilling chamber, and the inwards were rinsed at least three times on the marble tables between the pillars.[1]

3. He took the knife and cut asunder the lungs from the liver, and the lobe of the liver from the liver itself, but he did not remove it. He cut open the breast and gave it to him to whose lot it fell. He came up to the right flank and cut downwards as far as the backbone; he did not touch the backbone itself until he came to the two small ribs; he then cut off the flank and gave it to him to whose lot it fell, with the liver attached thereto. He came to the neck and left with it two ribs on either side; he cut it off and gave it to him to whose lot it fell, with the windpipe, heart, and lungs attached thereto. He came to the left flank and he left with it two thin ribs above and two below; and in like manner he left them on the other flank; thus with both flanks he left two each above, and two each below. Then he cut it off and gave it to him to whose lot it fell, with the backbone and spleen attached thereto. This was the larger portion; but they used to call the right flank the larger, since the liver was attached thereto. He came to the rump and cut it off and gave it to him to whose lot it fell, with the fat tail, the lobe of the liver, and the two kidneys attached thereto. He took the left hind-leg and gave it to him to whose lot it fell. So they all stood in line with the members [of the lamb] in their hands: the first bore the head and a hind-leg, the head in his right hand, its muzzle along his arm, and its horns in his fingers, and the place where it was slaughtered upwards, with the fat thereon, and the right hind-leg in his left hand with the flayed end outermost; the second bore the two fore-legs, the right leg in his right hand, the left leg in his left hand, with the flayed end outermost; the third bore the rump and the [other] hind-leg, the rump in his right hand and the fat tail hanging down between his fingers, and the lobe of the liver together with the two kidneys, while the left hind-leg was in his left hand, with its flayed end outermost; the fourth bore the breast and the neck, the breast in the right hand, and the neck in the left, and the ribs thereof between his fingers; the fifth bore the two flanks, the right flank in his right hand and the left in his left, with their flayed end outermost; the sixth bore the inwards in a dish with the shanks set on top; the seventh bore the fine flour; the eighth bore the Baken Cakes; and the ninth bore the wine. They went along and put them on the lower half of the Ramp and on the west side of it, and salted them; then they came down and betook themselves to the Chamber of Hewn Stone to recite the *Shemaʿ*.[2]

5. 1. The officer said to them, 'Recite ye a Benediction!' They recited a Benediction, and recited the Ten Commandments, the *Shemaʿ*,[3] and the *And it shall come to pass if ye shall hearken*,[4] and the *And the Lord spake unto Moses*.[5] They pronounced three Benedictions with the people: 'True and sure',[6] and 'Abodah',[7] and the Priestly Blessing;[8] and on the

---

[1] Cf. Shek. 6[4].   [2] App. I. 38.   [3] Deut. 6[4–9].   [4] Deut. 11[13–21].   [5] Num. 15[37–41].
[6] See Ber. 1[4]; 2[2] (Singer, p. 42, 'True and firm').
[7] The (Temple-)service. One of the 'Eighteen Benedictions'. See Singer, p. 50 ('May the service of thy people Israel be ever acceptable unto thee!')
[8] Num. 6[24–6].

Sabbath they pronounced a further Benediction for the outgoing Course of priests.[1]

2. He said to them, 'Ye that are new[2] to the incense preparation, come and cast lots', and they cast lots, and the lot fell upon whom it fell. 'Both ye that are new to it and ye that are not, come and cast lots, which of you shall take up the members from the Ramp to the Altar'. R. Eliezer b. Jacob says: He that takes up the members to the Ramp takes them up also upon the Altar.

3. The other priests[3] they delivered to the ministers of the Temple.[4] These stripped them of their raiment and left them with their drawers only. There were wall-niches[5] there whereon was written [the names of] the several articles of raiment.

4. He to whom fell the lot of [offering] the incense took the ladle. The ladle was like a large golden three-*kab* measure, holding three *kabs*; within it was a dish, heaped up full of incense. It had a lid and over this a kind of covering.[6]

5. He whose lot it was to bear the firepan took the silver firepan and went to the top of the Altar and cleared away the cinders on this side and on that, scooped up fire with the firepan, came down and emptied it out into the golden [firepan]; there were spilled from it about a *kab* of cinders which he swept away into the water-channel.[7] On the Sabbath he put an upturned psykter[8] over them. The psykter was a large vessel holding a *lethek*,[9] and on it were two chains; with one of them they pulled to lower it, and with the other it was held firm from above so that it should not roll. It was used for three things: it was put upside down over the cinders or over a creeping thing on the Sabbath, and with it they lowered the ashes from upon the Altar.

6. When they reached the space between the Porch and the Altar, one of them took the 'Shovel'[10] and cast it between the Porch and the Altar, and in Jerusalem none could hear his fellow's voice by reason of the noise of the 'Shovel'. It was used for three things: when a priest heard the noise of it he knew that his brethren the priests had entered in to prostrate themselves, and he ran and came also; and when a levite heard the noise of it he knew that his brethren the levites were gone in to sing, and he ran and came also; and [when he heard the noise of it] the chief of the *Maamad*[11] made the unclean[12] to stand at the Eastern Gate.

6. 1. Then they[13] began to go up the steps of the Porch.[14] They went first whose lot it was to clear the ashes from the inner Altar and the Candlestick.[15]

---

[1] Cf. Sukk. 5[8].   [2] i.e. 'Ye to whose lot it has never yet fallen to offer the incense'.
[3] Who were allotted no part in the service for the day.
[4] Namely to the servants of Phineas, the officer in the Temple (Shek. 5[1]) who 'was over the vestments'. Cf. Midd. 1[4].   [5] Cf. Sukk. 5[8].
[6] Or 'hanger'. Heb. *m'toteleth*. Cf. p. 104, n. 3.
[7] Midd. 3[2].   [8] See Erub. 10[15].   [9] App. II, D.
[10] Most commentators hold that this was not the 'shovel' of 3[8], but was a utensil shaped like a shovel and serving the purpose of a signal-gong. On the other hand the verb rendered 'throw' may here have the sense of 'making a noise on' the organ-like instrument called the *Magrefah* or 'Shovel'.   [11] See Taan. 4[1]. App. I. 21.
[12] According to Maimonides these were the lepers who had been pronounced clean, and who were set in readiness at the Eastern or Nicanor Gate to bring their offerings and to be sprinkled. See Neg. 14[8f]. Others suppose them to be priests who were stationed there to shame them for their remissness in contracting uncleanness; or priests who were made to stand there to show that it was not from idleness that they were not serving in the Temple.
[13] See above, 5[4f].   [14] See Midd. 3[6].   [15] See above, 3[9].

He whose lot it was to clear the ashes from the inner Altar went in and took the ash-bin, prostrated himself, and came out. He whose lot it was to trim the Candlestick entered in, and if he found the two easternmost lamps burning, he trimmed the easternmost one and left burning that to the west, since with that he lighted the Candlestick in the afternoon. If he found it extinguished he trimmed it and then lighted it from the Altar of the Whole-offering. He then took the oil-jar from the second step, prostrated himself, and came out.

2. He whose lot it was to bear the firepan piled up the cinders on the [inner] Altar, smoothed them with the back of the firepan, prostrated himself, and came out.

3. He whose lot it was to bring the incense took the dish from the midst of the ladle[1] and gave it to his friend or kinsman. If aught was spilled from the firepan into the ladle he gave it to him into his two hands. They used to teach him,[2] 'Take heed that thou begin not in front of thee lest thou be burnt'.[3] He began to smooth it down and came out. He that offered the incense did not offer it until the officer said to him, 'Offer the incense!' If it was the High Priest he used to say, 'My lord High Priest, offer the incense!' When all were gone away he offered the incense and prostrated himself and came away.

7. 1. When the High Priest came in [to the Sanctuary] to prostrate himself, three [priests] held him, one by his right hand and one by his left hand, and one by the precious stones;[4] and when the officer heard the sound of the High Priest's feet as he came out,[5] he raised the curtain for him, and he went in and prostrated himself and came out. Then his brethren the priests went in and prostrated themselves and came out.

2. They came[6] and stood on the steps of the Porch. They that came first stood to the south of their brethren the priests; and they bore five utensils in their hands, one having the ash-bin, another the oil-jug, another the firepan, another the [incense] dish, another the ladle and its cover. They then pronounced the Blessing [of the Priests] over the people as a single Blessing;[7] in the provinces it was pronounced as three Blessings, but in the Temple as a single Blessing. In the Temple they pronounced the Name as it was written, but in the provinces by a substituted word. In the provinces the Priests raised their hands as high as their shoulders, but in the Temple above their heads, excepting the High Priest, who raised his hands only as high as the frontlet. R. Judah says: The High Priest also raised his hand above the frontlet, for it is written, *And Aaron lifted up his hands towards the people and blessed them.*[8]

3. When the High Priest was minded[9] to burn the offering, he used to ascend the Ramp having the Prefect[10] at his right hand. When he had reached half way, the Prefect took him by the right hand and led him up. The first priest stretched out to him the head and the hind-leg, and he laid his hands on them and threw them [into the Altar fire]. The second priest

---

[1] See above, 5[4].   [2] Since he had never offered the incense before (cf. above, 5[2]).
[3] The incense must be burnt over the whole Altar; therefore to prevent himself from being burnt by the burning incense he is advised to begin with the farthermost portion of the Altar's surface.
[4] See Ex. 28[9ff]. Cf. p. 305, n. 10.   [5] Of his own chamber. See Midd. 5[4].
[6] The priests who had completed their allotted tasks.
[7] See Sot. 7[6].   [8] Lev. 9[22].   [9] Cf. Yom. 1[2].
[10] Cf. Yom. 3[9]; 4[1]; 7[1]; Sot. 7[7, 8]. The chief of the priests.

then gave the first one the two fore-legs and he gave them to the High Priest who laid his hands upon them and threw them. The second priest then slipped away and departed. In like manner[1] they held out to him the rest of the members [of the offering] and he laid his hands on them and threw them. When he was so minded he only laid his hands on them while others threw them. Then he walked around the Altar. Where did he begin? From the corner at the south-east, and so to the north-east and to the north-west and to the south-west. They gave him the wine for the drink-offering, and the Prefect stood by each horn of the Altar with a towel in his hand, and two priests stood at the table of the fat pieces with two silver trumpets in their hands. They blew a prolonged, a quavering, and a prolonged blast.[2] Then they came and stood by Ben Arza,[3] the one on his right and the other on his left. When he stooped to pour out the drink-offering the Prefect waved the towel and Ben Arza clashed the cymbal and the levites broke forth into singing. When they reached a break in the singing they blew upon the trumpets and the people prostrated themselves; at every break there was a blowing of the trumpet and at every blowing of the trumpet a prostration. This was the rite of the Daily Whole-offering in the service of the House of our God. May it be his will that it shall be built up again, speedily, in our days. Amen.

4. This was the singing which the levites used to sing in the Temple. On the first day they sang *The earth is the Lord's and all that therein is, the round world and they that dwell therein*;[4] on the second day they sang *Great is the Lord and highly to be praised in the city of our God, even upon his holy hill*;[5] on the third day they sang *God standeth in the congregation of God, he is a judge among the gods*;[6] on the fourth day they sang *O Lord God to whom vengeance belongeth, thou God to whom vengeance belongeth show thyself*;[7] on the fifth day they sang *Sing we merrily unto God our strength, make a cheerful noise unto the God of Jacob*;[8] on the sixth day they sang *The Lord is king, and hath put on glorious apparel*.[9] On the Sabbath they sang *A Psalm: a Song for the Sabbath Day*;[10] a Psalm, a song for the time that is to come, for the day that shall be all Sabbath and rest in the life everlasting.

MIDDOTH[11] ('MEASUREMENTS')

1. 1. The priests kept watch[12] at three places in the Temple: at the Chamber of Abtinas, at the Chamber of the Flame, and at the Chamber of

---

[1] Each priest in turn gave to the first priest the parts of the offering which he was carrying, the first priest gave them to the High Priest while each priest, except the first, went away.   [2] Cf. Sukk. 5⁵.   [3] Shek. 5¹.   [4] Ps. 24.   [5] Ps. 48.
[6] Ps. 82.   [7] Ps. 94.   [8] Ps. 81.   [9] Ps. 93.   [10] Ps. 92.
[11] Lit. 'measurements', of the Temple, as it was before its destruction in 70 A.D. The whole was contained in an area (the 'Temple Mount') 500 cubits square. Within the northern half of this square (and bearing to the west) was a rectangle having its west and east sides 135 cubits, and its north and south sides 322 cubits long. The space in the main square not covered by this rectangle was the 'Court of the Gentiles'. The eastern portion of the rectangle was the 'Court of the Women', 135 cubits square. The rest of the rectangle (187 cubits east to west by 135 cubits north to south) was the 'Temple Court' (*Azarah*) within which alone the Most Holy Things could be consumed. Of the 'Temple Court' the easternmost strip (measuring 11 cubits east to west) was called the 'Court of the Israelites' (i.e. males who were not priests could enter there); west of this was a strip of equal breadth, called the 'Court of the Priests'. Standing between these two strips was the levites' 'platform'. West of this was the great outer Altar, with the Ramp to the south of it and the shambles to the north. West of the outer Altar was the actual Temple structure, consisting of (east to west) the Porch, the Sanctuary, and the Holy of Holies. For the ascending degrees of sanctity attaching to the several parts of the Temple, see Kel. 1⁸ᶠ. *J. E.* xii, 94–5 gives plans of the Temple based on this tractate.   [12] Tam. 1¹.

the Hearth; and the levites at twenty-one places: five at the five gates of the Temple Mount, four at its four corners inside, five at five of the gates of the Temple Court, four at its four corners outside, and one at the Chamber of Offerings,[1] and one at the Chamber of the Curtain,[2] and one behind the place of the Mercy Seat.[3]

2. The officer of the Temple Mount used to go round to every watch with lighted torches before him, and if any watch did not stand up and say to him, 'O officer of the Temple Mount, peace be to thee!'[4] and it was manifest that he was asleep, he would beat him with his staff, and he had the right to burn his raiment. And they would say, 'What is the noise in the Temple Court?' 'The noise of some levite that is being beaten and having his raiment burnt because he went to sleep during his watch.' R. Eliezer b. Jacob said: They once found my mother's brother asleep and burnt his raiment.

3. There were five gates to the Temple Mount:[5] the two Huldah Gates on the south, that served for coming in and for going out; the Kiponus Gate on the west, that served[6] for coming in and for going out; the Tadi Gate[7] on the north which was not used at all; the Eastern Gate on which was portrayed the Palace of Shushan.[8] Through this the High Priest that burned the [Red] Heifer,[9] and the heifer, and all that aided him went forth to the Mount of Olives.

4. There were seven gates to the Temple Court, three to the north and three to the south and one to the east. Those to the south were[10] the Kindling Gate,[11] next to it the Gate of the Firstlings, and the third was the Water Gate.[12] That to the east was the Nicanor Gate[13] beside which were two Chambers, one to the right[14] and one to the left; the one was the Chamber of Phineas,[15] the keeper of the vestments, and the other the chamber of them that made the Baken Cakes.[16]

5. And those to the north were the Gate of the Flame,[17] which was a kind of portico over which an upper chamber was built, so that the priests might keep watch above and the levites below, and it had a door[18] towards the Rampart; next to it was the Gate of the Offering;[19] and the third was the [Gate of the] Chamber of the Hearth.

6. There were four rooms in the Chamber of the Hearth, like cells

---

[1] The Chamber of Lambs, north of the Porch and south-west of the Chamber of the Hearth.

[2] Supposed to be the place where they wove the veil which separated the Holy of Holies from the Sanctuary (cf. Shek. 8[5]). The position is unknown.

[3] i.e. outside the western wall of the Holy of Holies. See below, 5[1].

[4] Variant: The officer of the Temple Mount would say to him, 'Peace be to thee'.

[5] i.e. in the wall surrounding the entire square of the Temple Area.

[6] Some texts omit this clause.   [7] Variant: Tari.

[8] Cf. Kel. 17[9].   [9] Num. 19[2ff]. Cf. below, 2[4], and Par. 3[6].

[10] Counting from the west.

[11] Through which the wood was brought for the Temple fires.

[12] See below, 2[6].   [13] See Yom. 3[10].

[14] i.e. the north; cf. p. 181, n. 10.

[15] Shek. 5[1]; Tam. 5[3].   [16] Cf. Tam. 1[3]; see Men. 4[5].

[17] So called, according to the commentators, because in the chamber above it a flame was continually kept burning whereby to rekindle the fire in the Chamber of the Hearth where it was the custom of the priests to resort to restore their warmth after a spell of service bare-footed.

[18] The upper Chamber of the Hearth could be entered both from the Temple Court and from the Rampart, the high causeway that surrounded the rectangle containing the Temple Court and the Court of the Women.

[19] Beasts, especially the Most Holy Things, were brought in from that side since (Zeb. 5[1]) they must be slaughtered on the north side of the Altar.

opening into a hall, two within holy ground and two outside holy ground,[1] and the ends of flagstones divided the holy from what was not holy. And what was their use? That to the south-west was the Chamber of the Lamb-offerings;[2] that to the south-east was the Chamber of them that made the Shewbread;[3] in that to the north-east the sons of the Hasmoneans had hidden away the stones of the Altar which the Grecian[4] kings had defiled;[5] and by that to the north-west they went down to the Chamber of Immersion.[6]

7. There were two gates to the Chamber of the Hearth: one opened towards the Rampart and one opened towards the Temple Court. R. Judah said: In that which opened towards the Temple Court was a small wicket by which they went in to inspect the Temple Court.

8. The Chamber of the Hearth[7] was vaulted; it was a large chamber and around it ran a raised stone pavement; and there the eldest of the father's house used to sleep with the keys of the Temple Court in their hand. The young priests had each his mattress on the ground.

9. And there was a place there, one cubit square, whereon lay a slab of marble in which was fixed a ring and a chain on which hung the keys. When the time was come to lock up [the Temple Court] he lifted up the slab by the ring and took the keys from the chain. And the priest locked [the gates] from inside while a levite slept outside. When he had finished locking [the gates] he put back the keys on the chain and the slab in its place, put his mattress over it, and went to sleep. If one of them suffered a pollution he would go out and go along the passage that leads below the Temple building, where lamps were burning here and there, until he reached the Chamber of Immersion. R. Eliezer b. Jacob said: He used to go out by the passage that leads below the Rampart and so he came to the Tadi Gate.[8]

2. 1. The Temple Mount measured five hundred cubits by five hundred cubits. Its largest [open] space was to the south, the next largest to the east, the third largest to the north, and its smallest [open space] was to the west;[9] the place where its measure was greatest was where its use was greatest.[10]

2. Whosoever it was that entered the Temple Mount came in on the right and went round and came out on the left, save any whom aught befell, for he went round to the left. 'What aileth thee that thou goest to the left?' 'Because I am a mourner'.[11] 'May he that dwelleth in this House give thee comfort!' 'Because I am under a ban.' 'May he that dwelleth in this House put it into their hearts to bring thee near again!' So R. Meir. R. Jose said to him: Thou wouldest make it as though they[12] had transgressed

---

1 i.e. the Chamber of the Hearth extended north and south. The two cells to the south stood over the area of the Temple Court and so counted as in holy ground; and the two to the north stood over the area that pertained to the non-holy ground of the Court of the Gentiles. Cf. M. Sh. 3[8].   2 Cf. Arak. 2[5].

3 Cf. Tam. 3[3].   4 i.e. Syrian.   5 Cf. 1 Maccabees 4[44-6].

6 Cf. Tam. 1[1]. See below, 1[9].   7 Tam. 1[1].

8 In opposition to Tam 1[1], according to which he returned to his fellow-priests in the Chamber of the Hearth.

9 Cf. above, p. 589, n. 11. The free space to the south was 265 by 500 cubits; to the east of the inner rectangle was a space of 115 cubits; to the north was a space of 100 cubits; while west of the Temple structure there was only 63 cubits.

10 Public access and egress was by the two Huldah Gates, south of the Temple Area.

11 And, as such, forbidden to bring any offering (cf. Deut. 26[14]).

12 Who had pronounced a ban against him.

against him in judgement!—but, rather, [they say], 'May he that dwelleth in this House put it into thy heart to listen to the words of thy fellows that they may bring thee near again.'

3. Inside the Temple Mount[1] was a latticed railing (the *Soreg*), ten hand-breadths high. It had thirteen breaches which the Grecian kings had made; these were fenced up again, and over against them thirteen prostrations were decreed.[2] Inside this was the Rampart (the *Hel*),[3] ten cubits broad. And there were twelve steps there;[4] the height of each step was half a cubit and the tread thereof was half a cubit. All the steps that were there [within the Temple Mount], the height thereof was half a cubit and the tread thereof was half a cubit, save only those of the Porch.[5] All the entrances and gates that were there were twenty cubits high and ten cubits wide, save only those of the Porch. All the entrances that were there had doors save only those of the Porch. All the gates that were there had lintels, save only the Tadi Gate over which two stones leaned the one against the other.[6] All the gates that were there had been changed [and overlaid] with gold, save only the doors of the Nicanor Gate, for with them a miracle had happened;[7] and some say, because their bronze shone like gold.

4. All the walls there were high, save only the eastern wall, because the [High] Priest that burns the [Red] Heifer and stands on the top of the Mount of Olives should be able to look directly into the entrance of the Sanctuary when the blood is sprinkled.[8]

5. The Court of the Women was one hundred and thirty-five cubits long and one hundred and thirty-five cubits wide. At its four corners were four chambers each of forty cubits; and they had no roofs. And so shall they be hereafter, for it is written, *Then he brought me forth into the outer court and caused me to pass by the four corners of the court; and behold, in every corner of the court there was a court. In the four corners of the court there were courts inclosed*;[9] and *inclosed* means only that they were not roofed. And what was their use? That to the south-east was the Chamber of the Nazirites, for there the Nazirites cooked their Peace-offerings and cut off their hair and threw it under the pot.[10] That to the north-east was the Chamber of the Wood-shed,[11] for there the priests that were blemished[12] examined the wood for worms, since any wood wherein was found a worm was invalid [and could not be burnt] upon the Altar. That to the north-west was the Chamber of the Lepers.[13] That to the south-west—R. Eliezer b. Jacob said: I forget for what it was used. Abba Saul [b. Batnith] said: There they put the wine and the oil, and it was called the Chamber of the House of Oil. Beforetime [the Court of the Women] was free of buildings, and [afterward] they surrounded it with a gallery,[14] so that the women should behold from above and the men from below and that they should not mingle together. Fifteen steps led up from within it to the Court of the Israelites,[15]

---

[1] Surrounding the inner precincts which contained the Court of the Women and the Temple Court.

[2] In thanksgiving for the deliverance of the Temple from the hands of gentiles.

[3] A raised causeway going around the inner precincts.

[4] Leading up from the Court of the Gentiles (or from the level of the top of the Rampart) to the entrance of the Court of the Women, on the eastern side, through the 'Lower Gate'.   [5] See below, 3[6].   [6] In the fashion of a pointed arch.

[7] See p. 166, n. 3.   [8] See Par. 4[2].   [9] Ezek. 46[22].

[10] See Num. 6[17, 18].   [11] Cf. Ned. 1[3].

[12] See Lev. 21[17]; Bekh. 7[1ff]. They could take no part in the sacrificial service of the Temple.   [13] See Neg. 14[8].   [14] Cf. Sukk. 5[2].

[15] i.e. male Israelites who were not priests.

corresponding to the fifteen Songs of Ascents in the Psalms,[1] and upon them the levites used to sing. They were not four-square,[2] but rounded like the half of a round threshing-floor.

6. And there were chambers beneath the Court of the Israelites which opened into the Court of the Women, and there the levites played upon harps and lyres and the cymbals and all instruments of music.[3] The Court of the Israelites was one hundred and thirty-five cubits long and eleven wide; so, too, the Court of the Priests was one hundred and thirty-five cubits long and eleven wide, and the ends of flagstones separated the Court of the Israelites from the Court of the Priests. R. Eliezer b. Jacob said: There was a step one cubit high, and the Platform[4] was set thereon, and on it were three [other] steps each half a cubit high; thus the Court of the Priests was two cubits and a half higher than the Court of the Israelites. The whole of the Temple Court was a hundred and eighty-seven cubits long and a hundred and thirty-five cubits wide. And thirteen prostrations[5] were made there.[6] Abba Jose b. Hanin said: Opposite the thirteen gates.[7] The southern [gates] were [thus] reckoned counting from the west: the Upper Gate, the Kindling Gate, the Gate of the Firstlings, and the Water Gate. And why was it called the Water Gate? Because through it they brought in the flagon of water for the libation at the Feast [of Tabernacles].[8] R. Eliezer b. Jacob said: Through it *the waters trickle forth*,[9] and hereafter they will *issue out from under the threshold of the House*.[10] And opposite them on the north, counting from the west: the Gate of Jeconiah, the Gate of the Offering, the Gate of the Women, and the Gate of Singing. And why was it called the Gate of Jeconiah? Because through it Jeconiah went forth when he went into exile.[11] To the east was the Nicanor Gate, and it had two wickets, one to the right and one to the left. And there were two [gates] to the west which had no name.[12]

3. 1. The Altar was[13] thirty-two cubits long and thirty-two cubits wide. It rose up one cubit and drew in one cubit:[14] this formed the Base;[15] thus there was left thirty cubits by thirty. It rose up five cubits and drew in one cubit: this formed the Circuit;[16] thus there was left twenty-eight cubits by twenty-eight. The place of the horns was one cubit on every side; thus there was left twenty-six cubits by twenty-six. The place on which the feet of the priests trod was one cubit on every side; thus there was left twenty-four cubits by twenty-four, the place for the [Altar] fire. R. Jose said: At first[17] it was only twenty-eight[18] cubits by twenty-eight; it rose up and drew in in the selfsame measure, until the place for the [Altar] fire was twenty cubits by twenty; but when the children of the Exile came up they added to it four more cubits to the south and four more cubits to the west, in the form of [the Greek letter] *Gamma*; for it is written, *And the*

---

[1] Pss. 120–34.   [2] In plan.   [3] Cf. Arak. 2[3ff].
[4] Kidd. 4[5]; Arak. 2[6]. Here the levites stood to sing the daily psalm. It was also probably used by the priests when (Tam. 7[2]) they blessed the congregation.
[5] Cf. above, 2[3]; Shek. 6[3].
[6] By all who came in and went round the Temple Area.
[7] Above, 1[4], only seven gates are assigned to the Temple Court.
[8] Sukk. 4[9].   [9] Ezek. 47[2].   [10] Ezek. 47[1].   [11] 2 Kings 24[12].
[12] Cambridge text omits 'which had no name'.
[13] At its base.   [14] On every side.
[15] It was not, however (see end of paragraph), a regular plinth.
[16] This formed a ledge all round the Altar.
[17] In Solomon's Temple.   [18] At its base.

altar hearth shall be twelve cubits long by twelve broad, square;[1] and can it be that it was only twelve cubits by twelve?—but when it [also] says, *in the four quarters thereof*, it teaches that one must measure from the middle twelve cubits in every direction.[2] And a red line[3] went around it in the middle to separate between blood that must be sprinkled above and blood that must be sprinkled below. And the Base [of the Altar] extended all the length of the north side and all the length of the west side, and projected[4] one more cubit to the south and one more cubit to the east.

2. And at the south-western corner there were two holes like two narrow nostrils by which the blood that was poured over the western base and the southern base used to run down and mingle in the water-channel and flow out into the brook Kidron.[5]

3. At the same corner in the pavement below was a place one cubit square where was a slab of marble on which a ring was fixed; by it they used to go down to the pit[6] and clean it. To the south of the Altar was an incline, [the Ramp,] thirty-two cubits long and sixteen wide, and on its western side was a hollow into which they cast the Sin-offerings of birds that became invalid.

4. The stones of the Ramp and the stones of the Altar were alike taken from the valley of Beth Kerem,[7] where they were quarried from below virgin soil and brought from thence as whole stones upon which no [tool of] iron had been lifted up.[8] For iron renders [the stones] invalid [for the Altar] even by a touch, and by a blemish[9] [it renders them invalid] in every respect.[10] If one of the stones was blemished it becomes invalid, but the rest remain valid. They used to whiten them twice in the year, once at Passover and once at the Feast [of Tabernacles], and the Sanctuary once [in the year] at Passover. Rabbi said: They whitened them with a cloth on the eve of every Sabbath because of the blood. They did not plaster them with an iron trowel lest it should touch [the stones] and render them invalid; for iron was created to shorten man's days, while the Altar was created to lengthen man's days: what shortens may not rightly be lifted up against what lengthens.

5. To the north of the Altar were rings, six rows of four each[11] (and some say four rows of six each) at which they slaughtered the animal-offerings. The shambles[12] lay north of the Altar, and there stood there eight short pillars; upon these were four-sided blocks of cedar-wood into which were fixed iron hooks, three rows to each, whereon they used to hang [the slaughtered beasts]. They used to flay them on marble tables between the pillars.

6. The laver[13] stood between the Porch and the Altar, towards the south. Between the Porch and the Altar was twenty-two cubits, and there were twelve steps there, the height of every step was half a cubit and the tread

[1] Ezek. 43[16].
[2] i.e. the four quarters of its top surface must each measure twelve cubits by twelve; therefore the whole top surface (i.e. that available for the Altar fire) must be twenty-four cubits by twenty-four.
[3] Cf. p. 469, n. 8; Zeb. 7[1]; Kinn. 1[1].   [4] i.e. it jutted out an extra cubit.
[5] Cf. Yom. 5[6]. Meil. 3[3].   [6] Cf. Meil. 3[3].
[7] Jer. 6[1]. See Neub., p. 131.   [8] Ex. 20[25]; Deut. 27[5].
[9] Some texts read 'a blemish (renders them invalid) in every respect'.
[10] Not only unfit for the Altar or the Ramp but even for any building within the Temple Court (Tif. Yis.).
[11] Twenty-four according to the number of the Courses of the priests.
[12] Tam. 3[5].   [13] Ex. 39[18].

thereof was [first] one cubit, [then another of] one cubit, [and another of] one cubit, [then] a terrace[1] of three cubits, then two steps each of one cubit's tread, then a terrace of three cubits, and at the top were two steps each of one cubit's tread and a terrace of four cubits. R. Judah says: At the top were two steps each of one cubit's tread and a terrace of five cubits.

7. The entrance to the Porch was forty cubits high and twenty cubits wide, and above it were five carved oak beams; the lowest one projected beyond the entrance one cubit to either side, the one above it projected beyond it one cubit to either side, [and so on]; thus the uppermost was thirty cubits long. Between every two beams was a course of stones.

8. And cedar posts were fixed between the wall of the Sanctuary and the wall of the porch that it might not bulge. And golden chains were fixed to the roof-beam of the Porch by which the young priests could climb up and see the crowns,[2] as it is written, *And the crowns shall be to*[3] *Helem, and to Tobijah, and to Jedaiah, and to Hen the son of Zephaniah for a memorial in the temple of the Lord.*[4] A golden vine stood over the entrance to the Sanctuary, trained over posts; and whosoever gave a leaf, or a berry, or a cluster[5] as a freewill-offering, he brought it and [the priests] hung it thereon.[6] R. Eliezer b. R. Zadok said: It once happened that three hundred priests were appointed thereto.[7]

4. 1. The entrance to the Sanctuary was twenty cubits high and ten cubits wide. It had four doors, two within and two without,[8] as it is written, *The temple and the sanctuary had two doors.*[9] The outer doors opened into the inside of the entry[10] and covered[11] the thickness of the wall, and the inner doors opened into the inside of the House and covered the space behind the doors,[12] for all the House was overlaid with gold, save only behind the doors. R. Judah says: They[13] stood inside the entry and were in the form of folding doors which doubled back upon themselves; these [covered] two cubits and a half and those two cubits and a half; and the door-post was half a cubit thick on the one side and the door-post was half a cubit thick on the other side,[14] as it is written, *And the doors had two leaves apiece, two turning leaves, two leaves for the one door and two leaves for the other.*[15]

2. The great gate had two wickets,[16] one to the north and another to the south. By that to the south none ever entered, whereof it is expressly said by Ezekiel, *And the Lord said unto me, This gate shall be shut, it shall not be opened, neither shall any man enter in by it, for the Lord, the God of Israel,*

---

[1] Cf. Yom. 4³.
[2] The Cambridge text and some printed editions add: 'in the windows'. They were crown-shaped ornaments set over the Sanctuary (or Porch) windows.
[3] Their donors.   [4] Zech. 6¹⁴.   [5] Of gold, so shaped.
[6] And when the Temple treasury was in need the treasurer took from the vine as much as was required.
[7] Some texts add: 'to clear it (of its golden leaves, berries, and clusters)'.
[8] The wall was six cubits thick and two sets of double doors enclosed the space corresponding to the wall's thickness.   [9] Ezek. 41²³.
[10] The cell, six cubits by ten, enclosed within the two sets of doors.
[11] Each wing of the door, folded back, sufficed to cover up five of the six cubits of the wall-thickness.
[12] The inner set of double doors were swung inwards 180 degrees, and so covered the adjacent walls to either side.
[13] Both the inner and outer sets of doors.
[14] Therefore within the door-cell there was only five cubits of wall surface, and when the folding wings of both sets of doors were folded back (each then measuring two and a half cubits) and turned all of them inwards in the direction of the door-cell, they exactly covered the wall-space of the cell.   [15] Ezek. 41²⁴.   [16] Tam. 3⁷.

hath entered in by it, therefore it shall be shut.[1] He[2] took the key and opened the wicket. He entered into a cell, and from the cell into the Sanctuary. R. Judah says: He went along the thickness of the wall[3] until he found himself standing between both gates; then he opened the outer doors from within and the inner doors from without.

3. And there were thirty-eight cells there, fifteen to the north, fifteen to the south, and eight to the west. Those to the north and those to the south were [built] five over five, and five over them;[4] and those to the west, three over three and two over them.[5] And to every one were three entrances, one into the cell on the right, and one into the cell on the left, and one into the cell above it. And in the one at the north-eastern corner[6] were five entrances: one into the cell on the right,[7] and one into the cell above it, and one into the passage-way, and one into the wicket, and one into the Sanctuary.

4. The lower [story of cells] was five cubits wide and the floor above it six; the middle one was six cubits and the floor above it seven; and the upper one was seven,[8] as it is written, *The nethermost story was five cubits broad and the middle was six cubits broad and the third was seven cubits broad.*[9]

5. And a passage-way went up from the north-eastern corner to the north-western corner, whereby they could go up to the roofs of the cells. [The priest] went up by the passage-way facing westward, and went the whole length of the northern side until he reached the west; after he had reached the west he turned his face to the south, and went the whole length of the western side until he reached the south; after he had reached the south he turned his face to the east and went along the southern side until he reached the entrance to the upper chamber,[10] for the entrance to the upper chamber opened towards the south. And at the entrance to the upper chamber were two cedar posts by which they could mount to the roof of the upper chamber. And in the upper chamber the ends of flagstones marked where was the division between the Sanctuary and the Holy of Holies. And in the upper story were openings into the Holy of Holies by which they used to let down the workmen in boxes, so that they should not feast their eyes on the Holy of Holies.

6. The Sanctuary[11] was a hundred cubits square and a hundred cubits in height. The solid basement[12] was six cubits, and the height [of wall built thereon] forty cubits, the wall-frieze[13] one cubit, the place of drippings[14]

[1] Ezek. 44[2].   [2] The priest charged with opening the doors.
[3] i.e. the wicket to the right did not lead into the Sanctuary but only to a corridor which, by turning to the left, led to the door-cell between the two sets of Sanctuary doors.
[4] There were three stories of five each.
[5] The two lower stories had three cells each and the highest story two.
[6] i.e. the cell into which the priest had entered from the northern wicket (on the right of the Sanctuary entrance) on his way in to open the Sanctuary doors.
[7] The priest is supposed to be facing south.
[8] i.e. the outer wall of the higher stories was thinner than that of the lower stories.
[9] 1 Kings 6[6].   [10] Over the Sanctuary and Holy of Holies.
[11] Here meaning the entire block of buildings, including the Porch, side-cells, and passage-way.
[12] Of the walls; the lowest section of the wall above ground before its thickness was reduced to lighten the upper works and to leave room for the larger cells of the upper stories. According to Maimonides this basement was the underground foundation.
[13] Some kind of ornamental plasterwork surmounting the actual wall (Tif. Yis.); or the lowest set of roof-beams, which were carved and gilded (Bert.).
[14] The sense is obscure. According to Maimonides it was an upper portion of the wall so constructed as to carry off water and prevent its leaking inside the Sanctuary. According to Bert. and Tif. Yis. it was a second set of rafters with broad sides, placed perpendicularly, and sustaining the uppermost rafters, which held the plasterwork of the ceiling.

two cubits, the roof-beams one cubit, and the plasterwork one cubit; and the height of the upper chamber was forty cubits, the wall-frieze one cubit, the place of drippings two cubits, the roof-beams one cubit, and the plasterwork one cubit; and the parapet three cubits and the scarecrow[1] one cubit. R. Judah says: The scarecrow was not taken into account; but the parapet was four cubits.

7. From east to west was one hundred cubits. The [thickness of the] wall of the Porch was five and the Porch eleven; the wall of the Sanctuary six and its interior forty cubits; the dividing space[2] was one cubit and the Holy of Holies twenty cubits; the wall of the Sanctuary six, the cell six, and the wall of the cell five. From north to south was seventy cubits. The wall of the passage-way was five and the passage-way three; the wall of the cell five and the cell six; the wall of the Sanctuary six and its interior twenty cubits; the wall of the Sanctuary six and the cell six; the wall of the cell six, the space for draining away the water was three cubits, and the wall five cubits. The Porch projected fifteen cubits to the north, and fifteen cubits to the south, and this was called the Chamber of the Slaughter-knives, for there they used to keep the knives. The Sanctuary was narrow behind and wide in front, and it was like to a lion, as it is written, *Ho, Ariel, Ariel, the city where David encamped*;[3] as a lion is narrow behind and wide in front so the Sanctuary was narrow behind and wide in front.

5. 1. The Temple Court was in all a hundred and eighty-seven cubits long and a hundred and thirty-five cubits wide. From east to west it was a hundred and eighty-seven cubits: the place which the Israelites trod[4] was eleven cubits; the place which the priests trod[5] was eleven cubits; the Altar thirty-two; between the Porch and the Altar was twenty-two cubits; the Sanctuary a hundred cubits, and eleven cubits behind the place of the Mercy Seat.

2. From north to south was a hundred and thirty-five cubits: the Ramp and the Altar measured sixty-two; from the Altar to the rings was eight cubits; the place of the rings was twenty-four; from the rings to the tables was four cubits; from the tables to the pillars four; from the pillars to the wall of the Temple Court was eight cubits; and the remainder[6] lay between the Ramp and the wall and in the place of the pillars.

3. There were six chambers in the Temple Court, three to the north and three to the south. Those to the north were the Salt Chamber, the Parwah Chamber,[7] and the Rinsing Chamber. In the Salt Chamber they put the salt for the offerings; in the Parwah Chamber they salted the hides of the animal-offerings, and on its roof was the place of immersion for the High Priest on the Day of Atonement. The Rinsing Chamber [was so named] because there they rinsed the inwards of the animal-offerings; and a passage-way led from it to the roof of the Parwah Chamber.

4. Those to the south were the Wood Chamber, the Golah Chamber, and the Chamber of Hewn Stone. 'The Wood Chamber'—R. Eliezer b. Jacob said: I forget what was its use. Abba Saul [b. Batnith] said: It was the chamber of the High Priest and it lay behind the other two; and the roof of the

---

[1] Sharp-edged rims set round the parapet which served to prevent birds perching there and bringing uncleanness.
[2] Between the two curtains. See Yom. 5[1].   [3] Is. 29[1]. 'Ariel' means 'lion of God'.
[4] The Court of the Israelites.   [5] The Court of the Priests.
[6] Twenty-five cubits.   [7] Yom. 3[3, 6].

three of them was on the same level. 'The Golah Chamber'—the Golah cistern[1] was there, and a wheel was set over it, and from thence they drew water enough for the whole Temple Court. 'The Chamber of Hewn Stone'—there used the Great Sanhedrin[2] of Israel to sit and judge the priesthood; and if in any priest a blemish was found he clothed himself in black and veiled himself in black and departed and went his way; and he in whom no blemish was found clothed himself in white and veiled himself in white, and went in and ministered with his brethren the priests. And they kept it as a festival-day for that no blemish was found in the seed of Aaron the priest. And thus used they to say: 'Blessed be God, blessed be he! for that no blemish has been found in the seed of Aaron. And blessed be he that chose Aaron and his sons to stand and serve before the Lord in the House of the Holy of Holies!'

KINNIM[3] ('THE BIRD-OFFERINGS')

1. 1. [The blood of] a bird that is a Sin-offering is sprinkled below [the red line][4] and [the blood of] a beast that is a Sin-offering is sprinkled above. [The blood of] a bird that is a Whole-offering[5] is sprinkled above [the red line], and [the blood of] a beast that is a Whole-offering is sprinkled below. If [the blood of] either of them was sprinkled otherwise the offering is invalid. This is the rite prescribed in the offering of a pair of birds: if they were an offering of obligation the one must be offered in the manner prescribed for a Sin-offering and the other in the manner prescribed for a Whole-offering; but if they were Vow-offerings or freewill-offerings both must be offered in the manner prescribed for Whole-offerings. When are they accounted Vow-offerings? When he says, 'I pledge myself to a Whole-offering'. And when are they accounted freewill-offerings? When he says, 'This shall be a Whole-offering'. Wherein do Vow-offerings differ from freewill-offerings? [In nothing] save that with Vow-offerings he is answerable for them [and must replace them] if they die or are stolen, but with freewill-offerings he is not answerable for them if they die or are stolen.[6]

---

[1] See p. 136, n. 5.   [2] Cf. Sanh. 11[2].

[3] Lit. 'nests'. It is used of the pairs of birds, 'two turtle doves or two young pigeons', prescribed as obligatory offerings in expiation of certain offences and of certain conditions of uncleanness: Lev. 5[1-10] (transgression arising out of the 'oath of testimony', or contact with carrion or dead creeping things, or with uncleanness issuing from humankind, or rash vows); Lev. 12[8] (a woman after childbirth); Lev. 14[22], [30f] (the Bird-offerings of the leper); Lev. 15[14f], [29f] (a man and a woman who have suffered a flux); and Num. 6[9ff] (a Nazirite who has failed to fulfil his vow in cleanness). One bird of each pair must be specially assigned and offered as a Whole-offering (see Zeb. 6[5]; 7[2]; 7[4]) and the other must be specially assigned and offered as a Sin-offering (see Zeb. 6[2, 4, 7]; 7[1]), and they must each be killed, and the blood sprinkled and the bodies disposed of in the manner specially prescribed for each of these two categories of offering; otherwise the offering is invalid. Birds singly or in one or more pairs could also be brought as a freewill-offering or in fulfilment of vows, when they must be dealt with in the manner prescribed for Whole-offerings (Lev. 1[14]). Confusion was easily possible between the birds assigned to the three categories of (a) Whole-offering (voluntary), (b) Whole-offering (obligatory), and (c) Sin-offering (obligatory). Cases of such confusion present complicated problems (cf. p. 157, n. 7, on Petahiah who 'was over the Bird-offerings'; see also Ab. 3[19]). The tractate Kinnim gives only the bare answers to some of these problems and does not provide the arguments leading to their solution. The attempts of the commentators to expound the text of the Mishnah (particularly ch. 3) are lengthy, laborious, and sometimes tentative and uncertain; and since they are incapable of being summarized lucidly they are here omitted in the annotations.

[4] See Midd. 3[1]; cf. Zeb. 7[1].   [5] See Zeb. 7[2].   [6] Meg. 1[6].

2. If a Sin-offering was confused with a Whole-offering or a Whole-offering with a Sin-offering, even if it was but one [of the one kind] among ten thousand [of the other kind], they must all be left to die. If [a bird that was assigned as] a Sin-offering was confused with [unassigned birds that were] offerings of obligation, there remain valid only as many as the number of Sin-offerings among the offerings of obligation; so, too, if [a bird that was] a Whole-offering was confused with [unassigned birds that were] offerings of obligation, there remain valid only as many as the number of Whole-offerings among the offerings of obligation, no matter whether the offerings of obligation were the more and the freewill-offerings the fewer, or the freewill-offerings the more and the offerings of obligation the fewer, or whether they were equal.

3. This applies only when offerings of obligation and freewill-offerings are confused one with the other; but if offerings of obligation only are confused one with another, the one [pair] belonging to one [woman] and the other to another, or two [pairs] to one [woman] and two to another, or three [pairs] to one [woman] and three to another, then half of them remain valid and half become invalid. If one [pair] belonged to one [woman] and two to another, or even three to another or ten to another or a hundred to another, only the lesser number [among the two groups that are confused] remain valid, no matter whether they are of a single class or of two classes, or whether they belonged to one woman or to two women.

4. What is meant by 'a single class'? [If one pair of birds was brought by a woman because of] a birth,[1] and [the other pair by the same woman because of] another birth; or [if one pair was brought because of] an issue,[2] and [the other pair by the same woman because of] another issue, they count as 'a single class'. What is meant by 'of two classes'? [If two pairs were brought by the same woman because of] a birth and an issue. What is meant by 'two women'? [If the several pairs were brought] by the one woman because of a birth and by the other woman because of a birth, or by the one woman because of an issue and by the other woman because of an issue, they count as 'a single class'. 'Of two classes'? [If the several pairs were brought] by the one woman because of a birth and by the other woman because of an issue. R. Jose says: If two women bought their pairs of birds jointly or gave the price of the pairs of birds to the priest, he may offer which he will as a Sin-offering and which he will as a Whole-offering, no matter whether [the pairs of birds were brought because of occasions that fall] within one class or two classes.

2. 1. If a single bird from a pair that were yet unassigned flew away, or if it flew among other birds that had been left to die,[3] or if one of the pair died, another may be taken to complete the pair. If it flew among another pair [yet unassigned] that were set aside as offerings, it becomes itself invalid and renders invalid also its fellow in the pair; for the pigeon that flies away becomes itself invalid and renders invalid also its fellow in the pair.

. 2. Thus if two women had each two pairs and the one that belonged to the first woman flew among them that belonged to the second, by its flying away it renders invalid one [of the birds from which it flew]; if it flew back, by its flying back it renders invalid yet another. If it again flew away and then flew back, and yet again flew away and then flew back, it can effect no further loss, since even if they were all confused together, there are never less than two pairs [which may validly be offered].

3. If one woman had one pair, another two, another three, another four, another five, another six, and another seven, and one [bird] flew from the first to the second, then one from thence to the third, then one from thence to the fourth, then one from thence to the fifth, then one from thence to the sixth, then one from thence to the seventh, and then [one from each] flew back [in like order], each renders one other invalid by flying away and one by flying back; thus the first [woman] and the second will have none left [that can validly be offered]; the third will have one pair, the fourth will have two, the fifth will have three, the sixth will have four, while the seventh will have six. If again one [from each] flew away, and one flew back [in like order], each renders one other invalid by flying away, and one by flying back; thus the third [woman] and the fourth will have none left [that can validly be offered], the fifth will have one pair, the sixth will have two, and the seventh will have five. If again one [from each] flew away and one flew back [in like order], each renders one other invalid by flying away and one by flying back; thus the fifth [woman] and the sixth will have none left [that can validly be offered], and the seventh will have four pairs. But some say that the seventh woman [this third time] has suffered no further loss. But if one from among birds that had been left to die flew among any of these, all must be left to die.

4. If one bird from a pair that were yet unassigned flew among a pair that were assigned, another may be taken to complete the pair. If one [from the pair that were assigned] flew back, or if, at the first, one from the pair that were assigned flew [among the other pair], all must be left to die.

5. If at the one side were Sin-offerings and at the other Whole-offerings, and in the middle [birds] yet unassigned, and from the middle one flew to the one side and one to the other, no loss ensues, since it can be said that the bird [from the middle] that flew to the Sin-offerings was to be a Sin-offering, and that [which flew from the middle] to the Whole-offerings was to be a Whole-offering. If [one from the side] flew back to the middle, those that are in the middle must be left to die, but those on the one side can still be offered as Sin-offerings and those on the other as Whole-offerings. If it returned, or if another bird flew from the middle to the sides, then all must be left to die. They may not use turtle-doves to make up pairs with young pigeons, or young pigeons to make up pairs with turtle-doves. Thus if a woman offered a turtle-dove as her Sin-offering and a young pigeon as her Whole-offering, she must bring another turtle-dove as her Whole-offering; if she had offered a turtle-dove as her Whole-offering and a young pigeon as her Sin-offering, she must bring another young pigeon as her Whole-offering. Ben Azzai says: They should decide by what is first offered. If a woman had offered her Sin-offering and then died, her heirs must bring her Whole-offering; but if she had [first] offered her Whole-offering and then died, her heirs need not bring her Sin-offering.

3. 1. This[1] applies only if the priest had inquired;[2] but if the priest had not inquired and one pair belonged to one woman and one to another, or two to one woman and two to another, or three to one and three to another,

---

[1] Namely the substance of paragraphs 2 and 3 of ch. 1.
[2] Lit. 'If he had bethought himself', namely, to ask the women which pair belonged to which, and which of the pair was assigned as the Sin-offering and which the Whole-offering.

if he sprinkled the blood of them all above [the red line], half are valid and half invalid; if below [the red line], half are valid and half invalid; if [he sprinkled the blood of] half of them above and the other half below, half of them [whose blood was sprinkled] above are invalid and half are valid, and half of them [whose blood was sprinkled] below are valid and half are invalid.

2. If one pair belonged to one and two to another, or even three to another or ten to another or a hundred to another, and he sprinkled the blood of them all above [the red line], half are valid and half invalid; if below, half are valid and half invalid; but if [he sprinkled the blood of] half of them above and of half of them below, the greater part are valid. This is the general rule: If the pairs of birds can be divided into two equal parts so that some of those belonging to one woman do not perforce have their blood sprinkled above and some of them below, half are valid and half invalid; but if the pairs of birds can only be divided into two equal parts in such a way that some of those belonging to one woman must perforce have their blood sprinkled above and some [perforce] below, the greater part are valid.

3. If the Sin-offerings belonged to one woman and the Whole-offerings belonged to the other, and he sprinkled the blood of them all above [the red line], half are valid and half invalid; if he sprinkled the blood of them all below, half are valid and half invalid; if the blood of half of them was sprinkled above and the blood of half of them below, both are invalid, for I can suppose that the Sin-offering had been offered above and the Whole-offering below.

4. If there was a Sin-offering and a Whole-offering and one pair of birds unassigned and one assigned, and he sprinkled the blood of them all above [the red line], half are valid and half invalid; if below the line, half are valid and half invalid; if [he sprinkled the blood of] half of them above and the blood of half of them below, none is valid excepting what was un-assigned; and this pair must be shared between them.

5. If [birds assigned as] Sin-offerings were confused with [unassigned birds that were] offerings of obligation, there remain valid only as many as the number of the Sin-offerings among the offerings of obligation. If the [unassigned] offerings of obligation were twice the number of the Sin-offerings, half are valid and half invalid; if the Sin-offerings were twice the number of the [unassigned] offerings of obligation, there remain valid as many as the number of the [unassigned] offerings of obligation. So, too, if [birds assigned as] Whole-offerings were confused with [unassigned birds that were] offerings of obligation, there remain valid only as many as the number of Whole-offerings among the offerings of obligation. If the [unassigned] offerings of obligation were twice the number of the Whole-offerings, half are valid and half invalid; if the Whole-offerings were twice the number of the [unassigned] offerings of obligation, there remain valid as many as the number of the [unassigned] offerings of obligation.

6. If a woman said, 'I pledge myself to a pair of birds if I bear a son', and she bore a son, she must bring two pairs, one for her vow and one[1] as her offering of obligation. If [before she had assigned them][2] she gave

---

[1] In fulfilment of Lev. 12[6].
[2] Which two out of the four birds were to be Whole-offerings in fulfilment of her vow, and which of the remaining two was to be the Sin-offering and which the Whole-offering.

them to the priest, who should sprinkle the blood of three of the birds above the line and one below, and he did not do so but sprinkled the blood of two of them above and the blood of two of them below, and he had not [first] inquired, she must bring another bird of like kind[1] which he must offer above. If she brought one of a different kind she must then bring a second of that kind. If she had said expressly which kind she would offer for her vow, she must bring three more of like kind. If she brought them of a different kind she must bring still four more. If she had determined in her vow [to bring her offering of obligation and her Vow-offering at the same time and of the same kind] she must bring five more of like kind. If she brought them of a different kind she must bring six more. If she gave them to the priest and it was not known what she gave and the priest went and sprinkled their blood and he did not know in what manner he had sprinkled it, she must bring four more birds for the Vow-offering and two more for her offering of obligation, and one more as the Sin-offering. Ben Azzai says: Two more as Sin-offerings. R. Joshua says: This it is of which they have said, 'While [a beast] lives it has but one voice; after it is dead its voice is multiplied sevenfold'. How is its voice multiplied sevenfold? Its two horns become two trumpets, its two leg-bones become two flutes, its hide becomes a drum, its entrails are used for lyres, and its chitterlings for harps. Moreover some say: Also its wool is used for the [High Priest's] blue pomegranates.[2] R. Simeon b. Akashya says: The older the elders of the ignorant grow, the more they lose their understanding; as it is written, *He removeth the speech of the trusty and taketh away the understanding of the elders.*[3] But it is not so with the elders that are learned in the Law, for the older they grow the more stable grows their understanding, as it is written, *With aged men is wisdom and in length of days understanding.*[4]

---

[1] A turtle-dove if the others had been turtle-doves, or a pigeon if the others had been pigeons.
[2] Ex. 28[33].   [3] Job 12[20].   [4] Job 12[12].

SIXTH DIVISION

TOHOROTH

('CLEANNESSES')

KELIM

OHOLOTH

NEGAIM

PARAH

TOHOROTH

MIKWAOTH

NIDDAH

MAKSHIRIN

ZABIM

TEBUL YOM

YADAIM

UKTZIN

KELIM[1] ('VESSELS')

1. 1. These Fathers[2] of Uncleanness, [namely] a [dead] creeping thing, male semen, he that has contracted uncleanness from a corpse, a leper in his days of reckoning,[3] and Sin-offering water too little in quantity to be sprinkled,[4] convey uncleanness to men and vessels by contact and to earthenware vessels by [presence within their] air-space;[5] but they do not convey uncleanness by carrying.[6]

2. They are exceeded by carrion and by Sin-offering water sufficient in quantity to be sprinkled, for these convey uncleanness to him that carries them, so that he, too, conveys uncleanness to garments by contact,[7] but the garments do not become unclean by contact [alone].[8]

3. They are exceeded by him that has connexion with a menstruant, for he conveys uncleanness to what lies beneath him in like degree as [he that has a flux conveys uncleanness] to what lies above him.[9] They are exceeded by the issue of him that has a flux, by his spittle, his semen, and his urine, and by the blood of a menstruant, for they convey uncleanness both by contact and by carrying. They are exceeded by [the uncleanness of] what is ridden upon [by him that has a flux], for it conveys uncleanness even to what lies beneath a heavy stone. [The uncleanness of] what is ridden upon [by him that has a flux] is exceeded by what he lies upon,[10] since [the uncleanness caused by] contact with it is equal to [the uncleanness caused by] carrying it. [The uncleanness of] what he lies upon is exceeded by [the uncleanness of] him that has a flux; for it is he that conveys uncleanness to what he lies upon, while what he lies upon does not convey the like uncleanness to that upon which it lies.

4. [The uncleanness of] the man that has a flux is exceeded by the uncleanness of the woman that has a flux, for she conveys uncleanness to him that has connexion with her. [The uncleanness of] the woman that has a flux is exceeded by [the uncleanness of] the leper, for he renders [a house] unclean by entering into it.[11] [The uncleanness of] the leper is exceeded by [the uncleanness of] a barleycorn's bulk of bone [from a corpse], for it conveys seven-day uncleanness.[12] These are all exceeded by [the unclean-

[1] Usually rendered 'vessels'. The word has, however, the wider sense of 'articles of utility', including clothing, implements, and utensils of all kinds. The tractate deals with every kind of vessel's susceptibility to uncleanness, at what stage in their manufacture they become susceptible, and how damaged they must be to be regarded as insusceptible to uncleanness.

[2] i.e. such that cause uncleanness in other things which thereby become 'offspring of uncleanness'. 'Fathers of uncleanness' can convey uncleanness to men and vessels; whereas 'offspring of uncleanness' can convey uncleanness only to foodstuffs and liquids. For the general principles underlying paragraphs 1 to 4, and for a summary classification of all the uncleannesses dealt with throughout this Sixth Division of the Mishnah, see Appendix IV.

[3] Lev. 14[8].   [4] Par. 12[5].

[5] i.e. the contained hollow within a jar or other earthenware utensil; whereas what touches the outside of an earthenware jar does not render the inside unclean.

[6] Even without contact. Moving and not merely supporting the burden is meant by the term 'carrying'. The uncleanness is conveyed even if the object is only moved by a stick.

[7] Some texts omit 'by contact'.

[8] i.e. they do not become unclean except at the time when he is actually carrying the uncleanness.

[9] i.e. what lies beneath him suffers the lesser degree of uncleanness (derived uncleanness of first grade) suffered by what lies above (without touching) him who has a flux, whereas what the latter lies on becomes itself a primary uncleanness or 'father of uncleanness' (App. IV. 3a).   [10] Cf. below, 23[3].

[11] App. IV. 12c. This applies to a leper certified unclean or not yet pronounced clean, and not (as in par. 1) to the leper who counts the seven days before bringing his offerings (Lev. 14[8]).   [12] App. IV. 2.

ness of] a corpse, for it conveys uncleanness by overshadowing,[1] which uncleanness is conveyed by naught else.

5. There are ten several degrees of uncleanness in men. He whose
atonement is yet incomplete[2] is forbidden [to eat of] Hallowed Things
but permitted Heave-offering and [Second] Tithe; he that had immersed
himself the selfsame day [because of uncleanness][3] is forbidden Hallowed
Things and Heave-offering, but permitted [Second] Tithe; he that has
suffered a pollution[4] is forbidden all three; he that has connexion with a
menstruant conveys uncleanness to what lies beneath him in like degree as
[he that has a flux conveys uncleanness] to what lies above him; he that
has a flux and has suffered two issues conveys uncleanness to what he lies
upon and to what he sits upon, and he must bathe in running water[5] but
he is exempt from the offering; if he suffered three issues he must bring
the offering; he that is a leper but only shut up[6] renders [a house] unclean
by entering into it, but he is exempt from the obligations of loosening his
hair, rending his clothes[7] and cutting off his hair and from the Bird-
offerings,[8] but after he is pronounced free of leprosy he is liable to them all;
if a member is severed [from a man] and it does not bear its proper flesh,[9]
it conveys uncleanness by contact and carrying but it does not convey
uncleanness by overshadowing; if it bears its proper flesh it conveys uncleanness by contact and carrying and it also conveys uncleanness by overshadowing. The measure of 'its proper flesh' is such that is capable of
healing. R. Judah says: If in one place there is [flesh] sufficient to surround
the member with [the thickness of] the thread of the woof, there is there
such that is capable of healing.

6. There are ten degrees of holiness. The Land of Israel is holier than
any other land. Wherein lies its holiness? In that from it they may bring
the *Omer*,[10] the Firstfruits,[11] and the Two Loaves,[12] which they may not
bring from any other land.

7. The walled cities[13] [of the Land of Israel] are still more holy, in that
they must send forth the lepers from their midst; moreover they may carry
around a corpse therein wheresoever they will, but once it is gone forth
[from the city] they may not bring it back.

8. Within the wall [of Jerusalem] is still more holy, for there [only] they
may eat the Lesser Holy Things[14] and the Second Tithe. The Temple
Mount[15] is still more holy, for no man or woman that has a flux, no menstruant, and no woman after childbirth may enter therein. The Rampart[16]
is still more holy, for no gentiles and none that have contracted uncleanness
from a corpse may enter therein. The Court of the Women is still more
holy, for none that had immersed himself the selfsame day [because of
uncleanness] may enter therein, yet none would thereby become liable to

---

[1] App. IV. 6. See p. 649, n. 3.
[2] See Ker. 2[1]. He counts as still suffering 'third-grade' derived uncleanness, and so
renders Hallowed Things invalid by causing them to suffer 'fourth-grade uncleanness'.
Cf. App. IV. 17.
[3] See p. 773, n. 6. He is still suffering the equivalent of 'second-grade uncleanliness' and
can convey 'third-grade uncleanness' to Heave-offering, so rendering it invalid.
[4] And has not yet undergone immersion. Lev. 15[16ff].
[5] See Zab. 1[1]; Lev. 15[13].   [6] Cf. Lev. 13[4].   [7] Lev. 13[45].   [8] Cf. Lev. 14[4, 8].
[9] App. IV. 5a.   [10] Lev. 23[10f]; App. I. 31.   [11] Deut. 26[2ff].
[12] Of Pentecost. Lev. 23[17].   [13] See Arak. 9[6].   [14] See Zeb. 5[6ff]; 14[8].
[15] The whole square (see p. 589, n. 11) of the Temple Area.
[16] Surrounding the rectangular group of inner courts, containing the Temple structure
to the west and the Court of the Women to the east (see Midd. 2[3]).

a Sin-offering. The Court of the Israelites[1] is still more holy, for none whose atonement is yet incomplete may enter therein, and they would thereby become liable to a Sin-offering.[2] The Court of the Priests is still more holy, for Israelites may not enter therein save only when they must perform the laying on of hands,[3] slaughtering, and waving.[4]

9. Between the Porch and the Altar is still more holy, for none that has a blemish or whose hair is unloosed may enter there. The Sanctuary is still more holy, for none may enter therein with hands and feet unwashed. The Holy of Holies is still more holy, for none may enter therein save only the High Priest on the Day of Atonement at the time of the [Temple-] service. R. Jose said: In five things is the space between the Porch and the Altar equal to the Sanctuary: for they may not enter there that have a blemish, or that have drunk wine, or that have hands and feet unwashed, and men must keep far from between the Porch and the Altar at the time of burning the incense.[5]

2. 1. Utensils[6] of wood, leather, bone, or glass that are flat are not susceptible to uncleanness. If they form a receptacle they are susceptible. After they are broken they become clean, but if again utensils are made of them they once more become susceptible. Earthenware vessels and vessels of alum-crystal are alike in what concerns uncleanness: they contract uncleanness and convey uncleanness through their air-space, and they contract uncleanness [when upturned] from what touches their [concave] bottoms but not from what touches their outer sides; and when they are broken they become insusceptible to uncleanness.

2. The smallest remnants of earthenware vessels and the bottoms and sides [of broken vessels] that can stand without support [remain susceptible to uncleanness] if, [having when unbroken held] as much as a *log*,[7] they can still hold enough [oil] to anoint the little finger [of a child]; or if, [having when unbroken held] from one *log* to one *seah*,[7] they can still hold a quarter-*log*; or if, [having when unbroken held] from one to two *seahs*, they can still hold a half-*log*; or if, [having when unbroken held] from two to three or up to five *seahs*, they can still hold one *log*. So R. Ishmael. But R. Akiba says: I would not prescribe any measure for [the unbroken] vessels; [but, rather, the rule should be]: The smallest remnants of earthenware vessels and the bottoms and sides [of broken vessels] that can stand without support [are still susceptible to uncleanness] if after having been as large as small cooking-pots, they can still hold [oil] enough to anoint the little finger [of a child]; or if after having been as large as Lydda jars, they can still hold a quarter-*log*; or if after having been of a size between Lydda jars and Bethlehem jars, they can still hold a half-*log*; or if after having been of a size between Bethlehem jars and large store-jars, they can still hold one *log*. R. Johanan b. Zakkai says: The capacity of the fragments from large store-jars is two *logs*; the capacity of the bottoms of [broken] Galilean cruses and of little jars may be aught soever; but their [broken] sides are not susceptible to uncleanness.

3. Among earthenware utensils these are not susceptible to uncleanness: a tray without a rim, a breached fire-pan, a tube for parched corn,[8] gutter

---

[1] Midd. 2[5].　　　　[2] See Shebu. 2[1].　　　　[3] Lev. 3[2].　　　　[4] Lev. 7[30].
[5] See Tam. 6[3] (end).　　　　　　　　[6] See App. IV. 16. Cf. below, 11[1]; 15[1].
[7] See App. II, D.　　　　　　　　　　[8] Cf. Men. 10[4].

spouts, even if they are bent or even if they are hollowed out,[1] a basket-top
that is used as a bread-basket, a ewer that has been fashioned so as to cover
up grapes, a [stopped-up] jar for swimmers, a [small] jar let into the sides
of a ladling-jar,[2] a bed, a stool, a bench, a table, a ship,[3] an earthenware
lamp-stand; these[4] are not susceptible to uncleanness. This is the general
rule:[5] Among all earthenware utensils that have no inner part no regard is
paid to their outer part.

4. If a lantern has a container for oil it is susceptible to uncleanness; if
it has not, it is not susceptible. A potter's mould with which he begins
to shape the clay is not susceptible to uncleanness; but that with which he
finishes it is susceptible. A funnel belonging to householders is not
susceptible to uncleanness, but one that belongs to pedlars is susceptible,
since it serves also as a measure. So R. Judah b. Bathyra. But R. Akiba
says: Because he lays it on its side to let the buyer smell it.

5. The cover of wine-jars and oil-jars and the cover of papyrus jars[6] are
not susceptible to uncleanness, but if they were adapted for other use they
are susceptible. If the cover of a stewpan has a hole in it or if it has a
pointed top, it is not susceptible to uncleanness; if there is no hole in it or
if it has not a pointed top, it is susceptible, because the housewife drains
the vegetables into it. R. Eliezer b. Zadok says: Because she turns out the
[stewpan's] contents on to it.

6. If a spoilt jar was found in the [potter's] furnace before its manufacture was complete it is not susceptible to uncleanness; but if after its
manufacture was complete, it is susceptible. A sprinkler[7] R. Eliezer b.
Zadok declares insusceptible to uncleanness, but R. Jose declares it susceptible because it only lets the liquid out in drops.

7. Among earthenware vessels these are susceptible to uncleanness: a
tray with a rim, an unbroken firepan, and a tray that is made up of several
dishes. If one of them was rendered unclean by a [dead] creeping thing,
they are not all rendered unclean; but if the tray had a rim that exceeded
[the height of the rims of the contained dishes], and one dish was rendered
unclean, all become unclean. So, too, with an earthenware spice-pot, or
a double inkstand. But if one part in a wooden spice-pot is rendered unclean by a liquid,[8] the other is not rendered unclean. R. Johanan b. Nuri
says: They divide the thickness of the partition and the half that serves
the unclean part is accounted unclean, and the half that serves the clean
part is accounted clean. But if its rim exceeded [the height of the rims of
the contained parts], and one part was rendered unclean, the other parts
become unclean also.

8. A torch is susceptible to uncleanness, and the reservoir of a lamp is
susceptible to uncleanness from [an uncleanness within] its air-space.[9]
The comb-shaped filter of a water-cooler R. Eliezer declares insusceptible
to uncleanness; but the Sages declare it susceptible.

---

[1] By the dripping of water, so that a cavity is formed.

[2] Cf. Par. 5[5]; Toh. 10[7]; Yad. 1[2]. The large earthenware bucket used to draw up water
out of a well. This 'small jar let into the sides' is in Par. 5[3] and Yad. 1[2] referred to as 'the
flanks'; it was some appendage to facilitate the handling of the large jar.

[3] Cf. Shab. 9[2].   [4] Even if they have a cavity.   [5] Cf. below, 25[1]; 27[1].

[6] Or 'papyrus jar-covers'. Some explain the adjective, *nayyaroth*, as a place-name.

[7] So devised that water in a sieve-like receptacle could be retained or released by
closing or opening a hole above by means of the finger.

[8] Which, of itself, cannot render anything else unclean (see App. IV. 18b), though
(cf. Maksh. 6[4]) it renders foodstuffs susceptible to uncleanness.   [9] See p. 604, n. 5.

3. 1. What is the measure of the breach that suffices in an earthenware vessel to render it insusceptible to uncleanness?[1] If it was used for food-stuffs the breach must be large enough for an olive to fall through; if for liquids, large enough for liquids to run through; and if for either, the more stringent condition applies: a hole large enough for an olive to fall through.

2. In a jar the measure of the breach is such that a dried fig [will fall through]. So R. Simeon. But R. Judah says: A walnut.[2] R. Meir says: An olive. In a stewpan or cooking-pot the measure is an olive; in a cruse or ewer the measure is such that oil will drip through; in a water-cooler the measure is such that water will drain through. R. Simeon says: For all three of them the measure is such that seeds will fall through. In a lamp[3] the measure is such that oil will drip through. R. Eliezer says: A small coin. If a lamp has lost its nozzle it is not susceptible to uncleanness. A lamp of unbaked clay that has its nozzle burnt by the wick is not susceptible to uncleanness.

3. If a hole was made in a jar and it was mended with pitch and it was broken again but the part mended with pitch can still hold a quarter-*log*, it remains susceptible to uncleanness since it has never ceased to belong to the category of 'vessel'. If a hole was made in a potsherd and it was mended with pitch, even if it will hold a quarter-*log* it is not susceptible to uncleanness since it had ceased to belong to the category of 'vessel'.

4. If a jar was cracked and it was plastered over with cattle-dung, even though the potsherds would fall apart if the cattle-dung was taken away, it is still susceptible to uncleanness since it has never ceased to belong to the category of 'vessel'. If it was broken in pieces and its sherds were stuck together again or if potter's clay was brought from elsewhere [to stick them together], and it was plastered over with cattle-dung, even though the sherds held together when the cattle-dung was taken away, it is no longer susceptible to uncleanness since it had ceased to belong to the category of 'vessel'; yet if there was in it one sherd that could hold a quarter-*log* every part is susceptible to uncleanness by contact, but only the part adjacent can suffer uncleanness from [uncleanness within] the air-space.

5. If a man plastered [a layer of cattle-dung] over a sound vessel [and the vessel became unclean], R. Meir and R. Simeon declare the plastering unclean. But the Sages say: If a man plastered over what was sound, the plastering is not susceptible to uncleanness; but if over what was cracked, the plastering is susceptible. And the same applies also to the hoop bound round a gourd-shell.

6. If a man touched the scutchgrass that was smeared over a pithos[4] [and the pithos was unclean], he becomes unclean. The clay plug of a jar does not serve as a connective.[5] If a man touched the plastering of a baking-oven [that was unclean] he becomes unclean.

7. If a kettle was plastered over with both mortar and potter's clay and a man touched the mortar, he becomes unclean, but if the potter's clay, he remains clean.[6] If a cauldron had a hole in it and it was mended with pitch, R. Jose declares it insusceptible to uncleanness, since it cannot hold

---

[1] Which it becomes so soon as it cannot fulfil its proper purpose.
[2] Which is larger.   [3] See p. 581, n. 6.
[4] The largest type of store-jar. Cf. R.Sh. 3[7].
[5] So that if either the plug or the jar became unclean the other becomes unclean also.
[6] If the kettle was unclean. The potter's clay does not adhere thoroughly and so does not count as a connective.

hot water as well as cold. And he used to say the same of a vessel made of pitch. If copper vessels[1] were mended with pitch they become insusceptible to uncleanness; but if they were used for wine they are still susceptible.

8. If a hole was made in a jar and it was mended with more pitch than was needful, what touches the pitch that was needful becomes unclean, but what touches the pitch that was not needful remains clean. If pitch dripped on to a jar, what touches the pitch remains clean. If a wooden or earthenware funnel was stopped up with pitch, R. Eleazar b. Azariah declares it susceptible[2] to uncleanness. R. Akiba declares it susceptible if it was of wood[3] but insusceptible if it was of earthenware. R. Jose declares both susceptible.[4]

4. 1. If a potsherd cannot stand of itself because of a handle-piece on it, or because its bottom is pointed and the point overbalances it, it is not susceptible to uncleanness. If the handle was taken away or the point broken off it is still insusceptible. R. Judah declares it susceptible. If a jar was broken but could still hold something in its sides, or if it was split as it were into two troughs, R. Judah declares it insusceptible to uncleanness, but the Sages declare it susceptible.

2. If a jar was so cracked that it could not be moved about with even half a *kab* of dried figs in it, it is not susceptible to uncleanness. If a flawed earthenware vessel became so cracked that it could not hold any liquid, even if it could hold foodstuffs, it is not susceptible to uncleanness, since there can be no remnants of remnants.

3. What counts as a flawed earthenware vessel? Any that has lost even its handle only. If the sharp broken ends stuck out [at the top of a broken vessel], all those that [stand close enough together to] contain olives are susceptible to uncleanness by contact, and what lies over against them is susceptible to uncleanness from [uncleanness within] the contained air-space; but those that do not [stand close enough together to] contain olives are susceptible to uncleanness only by contact, and what lies over against them is not susceptible to uncleanness from [uncleanness within] the contained air-space. If it leans on its side like a kind of throne, any part that can contain olives is susceptible to uncleanness by contact, and what lies over against it is susceptible to uncleanness from [uncleanness within] the contained air-space; but any part that cannot contain olives is susceptible to uncleanness only by contact, and what lies over against it is not susceptible to uncleanness from [uncleanness within] the contained air-space. The bottoms of pointed-bottomed jugs[5] and the bottoms of Sidonian bowls, although they cannot stand unsupported, are susceptible to uncleanness, because they were made after this fashion from the first.

4. If an earthenware vessel has three rims and the innermost exceeds the others in height, all [outside it] remain clean;[6] if the outermost rim exceeds the others in height the whole becomes unclean; if the middle one exceeds the others in height, what is within it is unclean, and what is outside it remains clean. If all three are equal, R. Judah says: They divide [the thickness of] the middle rim. But the Sages say: [If what is within one rim

---

[1] Used for heating liquids.   [2] It will contain liquids.
[3] To which the pitch will adhere tightly, whereas it will easily fall away from earthenware.
[4] The pitch will hold tight to the broken edges if not to a smooth earthenware surface.
[5] Some explain the word *korfiyoth* as the adjectival form of a place-name, 'Korfian'.
[6] They count only as part of the outside of the vessel, which does not become unclean if the inside becomes unclean.

becomes unclean] all [the rest] remain clean. After what time does an earthenware vessel become susceptible to uncleanness? From the time that it is fired in the furnace, for that is the completion of its manufacture.

5. 1. [To be susceptible to uncleanness] a baking-oven[1] must, in its first state, be [at least] four [handbreadths high] and [it is still susceptible if] what is left[2] of it is four [handbreadths high]. So R. Meir. But the Sages say: This applies only to a large oven, but if it is a small one [it is susceptible] in its first state no matter what its height, and [it is still susceptible] if what is left of it is the greater part of it. [It becomes susceptible] after its manufacture is complete. What counts as the completion of its manufacture? When it has been heated to a degree sufficient to bake spongy cakes. R. Judah says: When a new oven has been heated to a degree sufficient to bake spongy cakes in an old oven.[3]

2. [To be susceptible to uncleanness] a double stove[4] must, in its first state, be [at least] three [handbreadths high], and [it is still susceptible if] what is left of it is three [handbreadths high]. [It becomes susceptible] after its manufacture is complete. What counts as the completion of its manufacture? When it has been heated to a degree sufficient to cook thereon the lightest of eggs when broken and put in a saucepan. If a single stove[5] was made for baking, its prescribed measure[6] is like that for an oven; if it was made for cooking, its prescribed measure is like that for a double stove. A stone that projects[7] one handbreadth from an oven or three fingerbreadths from a double stove serves as a connective.[8] If it projects from a single stove that was made for baking, the prescribed measure is like that for an oven; if it was made for cooking, the prescribed measure is like that for a double stove. (R. Judah said: They have spoken of the measure of a handbreadth only [in what concerns a stone] between the oven and the wall[9] of the house]). If there were two ovens side by side [and joined together by a stone], one handbreadth is allotted to each, and the residue between is not susceptible to uncleanness.

3. The crown[10] of a stove is not susceptible to uncleanness. If the fender around an oven is four handbreadths high it is susceptible to uncleanness by contact and from [uncleanness within] its contained air-space; but if it is less than this it is not susceptible. If it was joined to the oven, if only by three stones,[11] it is susceptible to uncleanness. The places on a stove[12] for the oil-cruse, spice-pot, and lamp are susceptible to uncleanness by contact but not from their air-space. So R. Meir. But R. Ishmael[13] declares them insusceptible.

---

[1] Made of clay, pot-shaped, narrow above and wide below, like a truncated cone. It has no bottom but is fixed to the ground with fresh clay. Cf. below, 5⁷.

[2] After it had been broken because it had contracted uncleanness.

[3] Which needs less heat than the new oven.

[4] Shab. 3¹. A utensil for containing fire. It has two holes above, over which the cooking-pots are set.

[5] Shab. 3². Similar to the ordinary stove except that it has but one hole above.

[6] When its height is enough for it to be susceptible to uncleanness; and also the prescribed degree of heating which marks the end of its manufacture.   [7] To serve as a handle.

[8] If the oven or stove is unclean, what touches the stone becomes unclean; and if anything unclean touches the stone, the oven or stove becomes unclean.

[9] Where one handbreadth suffices to isolate the wall from the oven. But if the stone projects in the other direction it counts as a handle, and therefore a connective, even if it is longer than one handbreadth.

[10] A high, and apparently detachable, rim around the stove's open top; it does not contract uncleanness from uncleanness in the stove.

[11] The meaning is obscure. Some temporary or insecure connexion is implied.

[12] A kind of 'hob' is intended.   [13] Some texts read 'Simeon'.

4. If an oven was heated from without or unwittingly or while yet in the craftsman's house, it becomes susceptible to uncleanness. Fire once broke out among the ovens at Kefar Signah,[1] and when the case was brought [for decision] to Jabneh, Rabban Gamaliel declared them susceptible to uncleanness.[2]

5. The chimney-piece on a householder's oven is not susceptible to uncleanness, but that of bakers is susceptible because the baker rests the roasting-spit[3] on it. R. Johanan the Sandal-maker says: Because he bakes thereon[4] in time of need. So, too,[5] the rim around the boiler belonging to olive-seethers is susceptible to uncleanness, but that belonging to dyers is not susceptible.

6. If an oven was half filled up with earth, that part from the earth downwards can contract uncleanness only by contact,[6] but the part from the earth upwards also from [uncleanness within] its contained air-space. If an oven was put over the mouth of a cistern or cellar, and a stone was laid there,[7] R. Judah says: If by being heated below it was also heated above, it is susceptible to uncleanness. But the Sages say: Since it has been heated it is susceptible, no matter whence [it was heated].[8]

7. If an oven had become unclean how is it made clean again? It is divided[9] into three parts and the plastering scraped off down to the earth bottom. R. Meir says: The plastering need not be scraped off, still less to the earth bottom; but it need only be cut down so that on the inner side[10] it is less than four handbreadths high. R. Simeon says: And it must be removed from its place. If it was divided into two parts, one large and the other small, the larger remains unclean and the smaller becomes clean. If it was divided into three parts one as big as the other two together, the big part remains unclean and the two small parts become clean.

8. If it was cut up breadthwise into rings, so that each is less than four handbreadths high, it becomes clean. If it was again [set up and] plastered over with clay it becomes susceptible to uncleanness after it has been heated to a degree sufficient to bake spongy cakes. If the plastering was built [around the oven] at a distance, and sand or gravel put between, of such they have said, 'Be it a menstruant or she that is clean that bakes therein, it continues clean'.[11]

9. If an oven was brought in pieces from the craftsman's house and hoops were made for it and fastened around it while it was yet clean, and it then became unclean, it again becomes clean if the hoops are taken off; if they are fastened on again it continues clean. If it was now plastered with clay it [forthwith] becomes susceptible to uncleanness; for it needs not to be fired since it has been fired already.

10. If it was cut up[12] into rings and sand put between each ring, R. Eliezer declares it insusceptible to uncleanness, but the Sages declare it susceptible. Such was the [kind of] oven made by Achinai. As for the

cauldrons of the Arabs,[1] which are hollows dug in the ground and plastered with clay, if the plastering can stand of itself it is susceptible to uncleanness; otherwise it is not susceptible. Such was the [kind of] oven made by Ben Dinai.[2]

11. An oven of stone or of metal is not susceptible to uncleanness; yet this last[3] is susceptible by virtue of being a vessel of metal.[4] If a hole was made in it, or if it was damaged or split, and it was mended by plastering or patched with clay, it becomes susceptible to uncleanness.[5] How big must the hole be? So big that the flame comes through. So, too, with a stove. A stove of stone or of metal is not susceptible to uncleanness; yet this last[3] is susceptible by virtue of being a vessel of metal. If a hole was made in it or if it was damaged or split and[6] it was mended by plastering, or if clay props were made on it,[7] it becomes susceptible to uncleanness. If it was smeared over with clay, whether inside or outside, it remains insusceptible to uncleanness. R. Judah says: If inside, it becomes susceptible, but if outside, it remains insusceptible.[8]

6. 1. If a man made three clay props on the ground and joined them together with clay so that he could set the cooking-pot thereon, it[9] is susceptible to uncleanness. If he fixed three nails in the ground so that he could set the cooking-pot thereon, even if he so fashioned them to make a place for the cooking-pot to rest upon, it remains insusceptible to uncleanness. If he used two stones as a stove and joined them together with clay, it is susceptible to uncleanness. R. Judah declares it insusceptible unless a third stone is used, or unless it is made to lean against a wall. If one stone was joined [to the other] with clay, and the [third] one not joined with clay, it remains insusceptible to uncleanness.

2. A stone on which a cooking-pot is so set that it rests both on the stone and on an oven or a double stove or a single stove, is susceptible to uncleanness. If the cooking-pot rested on this stone and also on another stone or on a rock or on a wall, such is not susceptible to uncleanness. This was the [kind of] stove put against a rock used by the Nazirites[10] in Jerusalem. If stones were set side by side for a butcher's stove, and one of them became unclean, all of them do not become unclean.

3. If three stones were used to make two stoves, and one of the outer stones became unclean, the [half of the] middle stone that serves the unclean stone becomes unclean, but [the half] that serves the clean stone remains clean. If the clean stone was taken away, the middle stone pertains wholly to the unclean stone. If the unclean stone was taken away, the middle stone pertains wholly to the clean stone. If both outer stones became unclean and the middle stone was a large one, as much of it as is required to support the cooking-pot is reckoned to one [of the outer stones], and as much of it as is required to support the cooking-pot is reckoned to the other, and the residue between is deemed clean. But if it was a small stone,

---

[1] Men. 5[9].   [2] Sot. 9[9]. Cf. Josephus, *Ant.* xx. vi. 1; viii. 5; *Bell.* II. xii. 4.
[3] It is not susceptible through its air-space like an earthenware vessel; and it can be made clean by immersion.
[4] See App. IV. 16. Also, as distinct from an earthenware vessel, it can contract uncleanness from its outer side.
[5] It then takes on the qualities of an earthenware oven.
[6] Some texts omit this clause.
[7] On top of it, on which to set the cooking-vessels.
[8] On the ground that it derives no effective benefit.
[9] Such an earthenware tripod counts as an earthenware stove.   [10] Cf. Midd. 2[5].

all of it becomes unclean. If the middle stone was taken away and the other stones were near enough to support a large cauldron, they are susceptible to uncleanness. If the stone was put back again the whole becomes again clean. If it was plastered with clay it becomes susceptible to uncleanness after it has been heated to a degree sufficient to cook an egg thereon.

4. If two stones were used to make a stove and they became unclean and another stone was set up on the one side and another stone set up on the other side, a half of each [inner] stone remains unclean, and a half clean. If the clean [outer] stones were taken away, the others again become [wholly] unclean.

7. 1. If the bottom of the fire-basket[1] of householders was hollowed out to a depth of less than three handbreadths[2] it is still susceptible to uncleanness, since when it is heated from below the cooking-pot above will still boil; but if [it is hollowed out] more deeply it is not susceptible[3] to uncleanness. If [then] stone[4] or gravel was put in [to fill up the hole] it still remains insusceptible.[5] If [the stone] was plastered over with clay, it is thereafter susceptible to uncleanness. This was the answer of R. Judah[6] about the oven that was set over the mouth of a cistern or cellar.

2. If the hob[7] [of a stove] has a cavity in which to hold cooking-pots, it is not susceptible to uncleanness by virtue of conditions applying to a stone,[8] but it is susceptible by virtue of being a vessel having a cavity. What touches the [outer] sides [of it] does not become unclean by virtue of conditions applying to a stove. Its flat expanse R. Meir declares insusceptible to uncleanness, but R. Judah declares it susceptible. So, too, if a [wooden] basket was turned upside down and a stove made above it.[9]

3. If a stove is divided into two lengthwise it becomes clean; if breadthwise it remains unclean. If a single stove is divided into two lengthwise or breadthwise it becomes unclean. If a fender around a stove is three finger-breadths high it is susceptible to uncleanness both by contact and from [uncleanness within] its contained air-space; but if it is less than this it is only susceptible to uncleanness by contact and not from [uncleanness within] its contained air-space. How is the measure of the contained air-space determined? R. Ishmael says: They stretch the spit from above [the brim of the stove] downwards [to the brim of the fender], and whatsoever is thereby enclosed can convey uncleanness through the contained air-space. R. Eliezer b. Jacob says: If the stove becomes unclean the fender becomes unclean; but if the fender becomes unclean the stove does not become unclean.[10]

4. If the fender was detached from the stove and was three finger-breadths high, it is susceptible to uncleanness both by contact and from [uncleanness within] its contained air-space; if it was lower than this, or had

---

[1] A movable earthenware stove with very thick bottom, open at the top, where a pot could be set. According to Maim. it is the masonry under a stationary stove.

[2] Lowering by so much the level of the fire.

[3] The fire would be too low down and the heat would be dissipated.

[4] Variant: lead.

[5] Since the filling substance does not count as part of the vessel.

[6] See above, 5[6].

[7] But according to Maim. it is a chest filled with hot ashes; on the top of the chest are holes to take pots in which food can be kept warm.

[8] Cf. above, 5[2]. When attached to the ground it is insusceptible, and if it becomes unclean it can be made clean in the conditions prescribed above, 3[1f].

[9] The conditions applying to the stove do not apply to it.

[10] The fender is but an adjunct.

no rim at all, it is not susceptible to uncleanness. If the three clay props [that bear the cooking-pot] were three fingerbreadths long, they are susceptible to uncleanness both by contact and from [uncleanness within] their contained air-space; if they were shorter they are the more susceptible,[1] even if they were four[2] in number.

5. If one [of the three] was taken away they are still susceptible to uncleanness by contact[3] but not from [uncleanness within] their contained air-space. So R. Meir. But R. Simeon declares them insusceptible. If it was made with only two props, one opposite the other,[4] they are susceptible to uncleanness both by contact and from [uncleanness within] their contained air-space. So R. Meir. But R. Simeon declares them insusceptible. If they were more than three fingerbreadths high, the part [of the props] three fingerbreadths high and downwards is susceptible to uncleanness both by contact and from [uncleanness within] their contained air-space; and the part higher than three fingerbreadths is susceptible to uncleanness by contact but not from [uncleanness within] their contained air-space. So R. Meir. But R. Simeon declares them insusceptible. If the props were removed less than three fingerbreadths from the rim of the [mouth of the] stove, they are still susceptible to uncleanness by contact and from [uncleanness within] their contained air-space; but if more[5] than three fingerbreadths they are susceptible by contact and not from [uncleanness within] their contained air-space. So R. Meir. But R. Simeon declares them insusceptible.

6. How is the measure of the contained air-space determined?[6] Rabban Simeon b. Gamaliel says: A measuring-rod is stretched from one to the other;[7] what is outside the measuring-rod is clean and what is inside the measuring-rod, and the place occupied by the measuring-rod itself, is unclean.

8. 1. If an oven was divided [into two parts] by boards or hangings and a creeping thing was found in one part, the whole becomes unclean. If a broken-down hive that was patched with straw[8] hung down within the air-space of the oven, and had within it a creeping thing, the oven becomes unclean. If the creeping thing was found in the oven, food in the hive becomes unclean. R. Eliezer declares it clean. R. Eliezer said, If the hive affords protection in the graver matter of corpse[-uncleanness],[9] should it not also afford protection in the lighter matter of [uncleanness contracted from] an earthenware vessel? They answered, If it affords protection in the graver matter of corpse[-uncleanness] (respecting which partitions afford protection in a 'Tent'),[10] does it therefore follow that it will also afford protection in the lighter matter of [uncleanness contracted from] an earthenware vessel (respecting which partitions afford no protection)?

2. If the hive was undamaged (and the same applies to a hamper or a

---

[1] They are more nearly portions of the stove itself.
[2] And one was superfluous for bearing the pot.
[3] As being usable as handles.   [4] But broad enough to bear the pot.
[5] The surplus ceases to count as part of the stove and to suffer the conditions peculiar to a stove.
[6] What space counts as contained within the three props?
[7] So describing a triangle (Bert., Tif. Yis.).
[8] It does not count as a vessel at all and so does not afford the protection which is afforded to its contents by a sound vessel (see below, 8³).   [9] See Ohol. 9³, ⁷.
[10] Referring to corpse-uncleanness conveyed by 'overshadowing' (see App. IV. 6) based on Num. 19¹⁴. See Ohol. 15⁴.

goatskin) and the creeping thing was found in it, the oven remains clean. If the creeping thing was found in the oven, food in the hive remains clean. If there was a hole in them[1] [what they contain becomes unclean] when, if the vessel was used for foodstuffs, the breach was large enough for olives to fall through, and if for liquids, large enough for liquids to drain through; and if for either, the more stringent condition applies—a breach large enough for a liquid to filter in.

3. If a colander[2] was put over the mouth of the oven and it sank therein[3] and it had no rims, and the creeping thing was found in it, the oven becomes unclean; if the creeping thing was in the oven, food in the colander becomes unclean, since only vessels[4] afford protection against [uncleanness within] earthenware vessels.[5] If a jar was full of clean liquid and it was put beneath the bottom of the oven, and the creeping thing was in the oven, the jar and the liquid remain clean. If a jar was held upside down with its mouth within the air-space of the oven, and the creeping thing was in the oven, the dripping liquid [still] at the bottom of the jar remains clean.

4. If a cooking-pot was put in the oven and the creeping thing was in the oven, the cooking-pot remains clean, since an earthenware vessel cannot convey uncleanness to other vessels.[6] If it contained dripping liquid this becomes unclean and renders the pot unclean. Thus the pot may say,[7] 'What renders thee[8] unclean does not render me unclean, but thou hast rendered me unclean'.

5. If a cock swallowed a creeping thing and fell within the air-space of an oven, the oven remains clean; but if the cock died there the oven becomes unclean.[9] If a creeping thing was found in an oven, the bread in it suffers second-grade uncleanness because of the oven's first-grade uncleanness.[10]

6. If a leaven-pot [of earthenware] having a tightly stopped-up cover[11] was put inside an oven, and in the pot was leaven and a creeping thing separated by a partition [within the pot], the oven becomes unclean but the leaven remains clean.[12] But if it was an olive's bulk of corpse both the oven and the house become unclean but the leaven remains clean.[13] But if there was an opening [in the partition] one handbreadth square,[14] all becomes unclean.

7. If a creeping thing was found in the outlet[15] of an oven or of a double stove or of a single stove, and it was outside the inner edge, the oven remains clean. If it[16] was in the open air, even if an olive's bulk of corpse [was in its outlet], it remains clean; but if there was [in the outlet] an opening one handbreadth square,[17] all becomes unclean.

---

[1] A hive, hamper, or goatskin suspended in the air-space of an oven in which was a dead creeping thing.

[2] A tablet with perforations and made of earthenware (so Maim.). Bert. and Tif. Yis: a small earthenware slab having no cavity, used by bakers to knead on.

[3] It was in part lower than the level of the oven's opening.

[4] And a flat, rimless sieve is not accounted a vessel.   [5] Cf. Par. 5[5]; Yad. 1[2].

[6] i.e. it can never become a 'father of uncleanness' (App. IV. 16 b).

[7] To the liquid.   [8] The uncleanness of the earthenware vessel. Cf. Par. 8[2ff]; Toh. 8[7].

[9] From the creeping thing. On the carrion of 'clean birds' see App. IV. 14 c.

[10] The creeping thing is a 'father of uncleanness' and conveys 'derived uncleanness' of 'first grade' to the vessel; and the food thereby suffers 'second-grade' uncleanness from the oven. See App. IV. 8 b, 17 d.   [11] See below, 10[2].

[12] Because in an earthenware vessel the effect of a 'tightly stopped-up cover' is to prevent the entrance of uncleanness; it does not prevent its egress.   [13] Cf. Num. 19[15].

[14] The minimum opening which suffices to afford passage to corpse-uncleanness. See Ohol. 3[6].

[15] A hole low down in the stove- or oven-side, to let out smoke or let in air.

[16] The oven or stove.   [17] And one handbreadth deep. See Ohol. 3[7].

8. If the creeping thing was found in the opening at which the wood was put in, R. Judah says: If it was within the outer edge the stove becomes unclean. But the Sages say: If it was outside the inner edge it remains clean. R. Jose says: [If the creeping thing was found] directly beneath where the cooking-pot is set and inwards, the oven becomes unclean; but if directly beneath where the cooking-pot is set and outwards it remains clean. If it was found [on that part of the stove] where the bath-keeper sits, or where the dyer sits, or where the olive-seethers sit, the stove remains clean; it becomes unclean only [if the creeping thing is found] inside that part of the stove which is blocked up [by the cooking-pot].

9. If an earth-oven[1] has some place whereon to set a pot, it is susceptible to uncleanness; also that of glass-blowers, if it has some place whereon to set a pot, is susceptible to uncleanness. The furnace of lime-burners or of potters is not susceptible. A big baking-oven, if it has a rim, is susceptible to uncleanness. R. Judah says: If it is roofed. Rabban Gamaliel says: If it has a border.

10. If a man touched one that had contracted uncleanness from a corpse, and he had foodstuffs or liquids in his mouth, and he put his head into the air-space of an oven that was clean, they render the oven unclean.[2] If a man was clean and had foodstuffs or liquids in his mouth, and he put his head into the air-space of an oven that was unclean, they become unclean.[3] If a man ate fig-cakes[4] with unwashed hands[5] and put his hand into his mouth to take out the small stones, R. Meir declares [the fig-cake] unclean, and R. Judah declares it clean. R. Jose says: If he turned it over in his mouth it becomes unclean; otherwise it remains clean. If he had a *pondion*[6] in his mouth, R. Jose says: If it was to relieve his thirst, it becomes unclean.

11. If milk from the breasts of a woman [who was unclean] dropped into the air-space of an oven, the oven becomes unclean, since a liquid [that is unclean] conveys uncleanness whether [its presence is] acceptable or not acceptable.[7] If she was cleaning out the oven and a thorn pricked her so that she bled, or if she burnt herself and put her finger into her mouth, the oven is rendered unclean.

9. 1. If a needle or a ring[8] were found embedded in the bottom[9] of an oven and they were visible but did not project, and if, in baking, the dough would touch them, the oven is unclean. This applies to dough that is neither too soft nor too hard. If they were found in the [outer] plastering of an oven[10] with a tightly stopped-up cover, and the oven was unclean, they also are unclean; if it was clean, they also are clean.[11] If they were found at the sides of the [clay] plug of a jar,[12] they are unclean; but if opposite the mouth

---

[1] Such as that of Ben Dinai, 5[10].
[2] Although they suffer only 'derived uncleanness'; see App. IV. 18 b. Par. 8[5].
[3] His mouth does not count as 'a vessel having a tightly stopped-up cover' (see 10[1f]).
[4] That were Heave-offering. See p. 714, n. 3.
[5] These count as suffering 'second-grade uncleanness'; therefore they render Heave-offering (see App. IV. 17) unclean and invalid with 'third-grade uncleanness'. But dry food is only susceptible to uncleanness when moistened by a liquid (p. 758, n. 1.)
[6] App. II, A.   [7] Cf. Maksh. 1[1]; 4[8]; Teb. Y. 2[1].
[8] Metal objects found by chance are in any case deemed to be suffering corpse-uncleanness.
[9] The ground on which the oven was fixed. If the objects were in the ground before the oven was put there they cannot count as part of the oven.
[10] In a 'tent' wherein was a corpse.
[11] They count as part of the plastering which is a part of the oven.
[12] The plug was cone-shaped and thrust, narrow end down, into the jar's mouth; therefore part of the sides of the plug was within the jar's air-space, part 'opposite' the mouth of

of the jar, they are clean. If they were visible from within but do not project into the air-space of the jar, they are clean. If they sank into [the air-space of the jar] but beneath them was still [clay] thin as garlic-peel [between them and the air-space], they are clean.

2. If there was a jar[1] full of clean liquids with a siphon inside it and the jar had a tightly stopped-up cover, and it was put in a 'Tent' wherein was a corpse, the School of Shammai say: The jar and the liquids remain clean but the siphon is unclean. The School of Hillel say: The siphon also is clean. But the School of Hillel changed their opinion and taught according to the opinion of the School of Shammai.

3. If a creeping thing was found beneath the bottom of an oven, the oven remains clean, since I may suppose that it was still alive when it fell,[2] and is only now dead. If a needle or a ring were found beneath the bottom of an oven, it remains clean, since I may suppose that they were there before the oven was brought there. If they were found in the wood ashes, the oven is unclean, since there is naught whereon to rely [in deeming it clean].

4. If a sponge had soaked up unclean liquids and its surface became dry, and it fell into the air-space of an oven, the oven becomes unclean, since the [absorbed] liquid will in the end emerge. So, too, if a piece of turnip or reed-grass [had absorbed unclean liquids]; but in these two cases R. Simeon declares [the oven] clean.

5. If potsherds that had been used for unclean liquids fell into the air-space of an oven, and the oven was heated, it becomes unclean, since the [absorbed] liquid will in the end emerge. So, too, with fresh olive-peat; but if the peat was old the oven remains clean. But if it was known that liquid emerged, even if the peat was three years old, the oven becomes unclean.

6. If olive-peat or grape-skins had been pressed out in conditions of cleanness[3] and unclean persons trod upon them and liquid emerged therefrom, they remain clean since they had at first been prepared in conditions of cleanness.[4] If while they were yet clean the spindle-hook was wholly sunk into the spindle, or the iron point into the ox-goad, or a ring into a clay brick, and they were then brought into a 'Tent' wherein was a corpse,[5] they become unclean.[6] If one that had a flux[7] shifted them they become unclean. If they then fell into the air-space of an oven that was clean they render it unclean; but if a loaf of Heave-offering touched them it remains clean.

7. If a colander[8] was put over the mouth of an oven, forming a tightly stopped-up cover,[9] and there was [in the plastering] a split between the oven and the colander, [it no longer serves as a tightly stopped-up cover] even if the split is so small in size that the tip of an ox-goad cannot enter.

the jar, and the thickest part was outside. If the ring or needle were in the first two parts they have the benefit of the protection of the 'tightly stopped-up cover'.

[1] Belonging to an *Am-haaretz* (App. I. 3). The present case is supposed to be the same as that dealt with in Eduy. i[14].

[2] And so did not render the oven unclean through the contained air-space.

[3] By clean persons and in clean vessels.

[4] The liquid was not intentionally trodden out and so could not render the solid olive- and grape-skins susceptible to uncleanness. See p. 758, n. 1.

[5] See p. 614, n. 10.

[6] Only objects 'swallowed' by living creatures are protected against corpse-uncleanness. Cf. above, 8[5].   [7] See App. IV. 1, 12 a. Cf. above, p. 604, n. 6.

[8] See above, 8[3].   [9] See below, 10[2].

R. Judah says: [It is valid unless it is such that] it can enter. If there was a
split in the colander itself [it no longer serves as a tightly stopped-up cover]
if the size [of the split] is such that the tip of an ox-goad can enter. R.
Judah says: [Even if it is such that] it cannot enter. If the split was curved
it is not measured lengthwise; but [they take account only of] whether its
size is such that the tip of an ox-goad can enter.

8. If a hole was made in the [stopped-up] outlet of an oven [it no longer
acts as a tightly stopped-up cover] if its size is such that a spindle-staff
can enter in and come out burning. R. Judah says: [Even if it comes out]
not burning. If a hole is made in [the plastering] at the side of it [it no
longer acts as a tightly stopped-up cover] if its size is such that a spindle-
staff can enter in and come out, but not burning. R. Judah says: [It must
be such that it will come out] burning. R. Simeon says: If [the hole was]
in the middle, [the prescribed size is such that a spindle-staff] can enter;
but if at the side, such even that it cannot enter. So, too, he used to say of
a jar's plug in which was a hole, of which the prescribed size is the thickness of the second knot in an oat-stalk, that if [the hole was] in the middle,
the stalk should be able to enter; if at the side it need not be able to enter.
So, too, he used to say of large store-jars in which was a hole, of which
the prescribed size is the thickness of the second knot in a reed, that if
[the hole was] in the middle [of the plug] the reed should be able to enter;
if at the side, it need not be able to enter. This applies only if they were
made to store wine; but if they were made for other liquids, however small
the hole, [the contents] are subject to uncleanness.[1] This applies only if
[the holes] were not made at man's hand; if they were made at man's hand,
however little the hole, [the contents] are subject to uncleanness. If a hole
appeared [not caused by man's hand], and the vessel was used for foodstuffs, the prescribed size of the hole[2] is such that olives will fall through;
if for liquids, such that liquids will drip through; if for either, the more
stringent condition applies—that of the tightly stopped-up cover—such
that liquids can filter into it.

10. 1. These vessels afford protection [in the 'Tent' wherein is a corpse]
when they have a tightly stopped-up cover:[3] vessels made from cattle-
dung, stone, [unburnt] clay, earthenware, or alum-crystal; also[4] from fish-
bones or fish-skin, the bones and skin of animals that live in the sea, and
wooden vessels that are not susceptible to uncleanness.[5] They afford
protection whether [the tightly stopped-up cover] is above or at the side,
whether they stand on their bottom or lean on their sides. If they are
turned upside down they afford protection to all that is beneath them to the
nethermost deep. R. Eliezer declares unclean [what is beneath them].
They[6] afford protection to everything save that an earthenware vessel can
afford protection only to foodstuffs, liquids, and [other] earthenware
vessels.[7]

2. With what may they stop them up? With lime or gypsum, pitch
or wax, mud or excrement, crude clay or potter's clay, or aught used for

---

[1] In the 'tent' wherein is a corpse.
[2] When the contents are no longer preserved from corpse-uncleanness, even if the vessel
has a tightly stopped-up cover.
[3] See Num. 19[15].   [4] See below, 17[13].
[5] Those big enough to hold forty *seahs*. See below, 15[1]
[6] Such vessels having tightly stopped-up covers.   [7] Cf. Eduy. 1[14].

plastering. They may not stop them up with tin or lead, for though they serve as a covering they cannot serve as a cover that is tightly stopped up. They may not stop them up with swollen fig-cakes or dough kneaded with fruit-juice, lest they make unfit[1] what is in the vessel. But if a vessel was so stopped up it affords protection.

3. If the plug of a jar became loose but did not fall out, R. Judah says: It affords protection. But the Sages say: It does not afford protection. If its finger-hold[2] was sunk below [the level of the top of] the jar and had a creeping thing therein, the jar becomes unclean. If the creeping thing was in the jar food within the finger-hold becomes unclean.

4. If a ball or coil of reed-grass was put over the mouth of the jar and only the sides of it were plastered down, it does not afford protection—but it must be plastered above and below. So, too, with a patch of woven stuff. If [the covering was] of paper or leather, and it was bound round with a cord, it affords protection only if it is plastered at the sides.

5. If the earthenware of a jar had scaled off but the pitch [lining] remained (so, too, pots of fish-brine which are lined with gypsum up to the brim) R. Judah says: Such do not afford protection. But the Sages say: They do afford protection.

6. If a jar had a hole in it, but the wine-lees blocked it up, they afford protection. If it was corked up with a vine-shoot [it affords protection] only if it was plastered at the sides. If it was corked up with two vine-shoots [they afford protection] only if it was plastered at the sides and between the one vine-shoot and the other. If a board was put over the mouth of an oven, and it was plastered at the sides, it affords protection; if two boards, [they afford protection] if they were plastered at the sides and between the one board and the other. If they were fastened together with pegs or joints they need not be plastered in the middle.

7. If[3] an old oven[4] was within a new oven,[5] and a colander lay over the mouth of the old oven and was such that if the old one was removed the colander would fall, the whole becomes unclean; if it would not fall the whole remains clean.[6] If a new oven was within an old oven, and a colander lay over the mouth of the old oven, and the space between the new oven and the colander was less than one handbreadth, whatsoever is in the new oven remains clean.[7]

8. If many saucepans stood one within the other, yet their rims were at the like level, and there was a creeping thing in the uppermost one or in the lowest one, that one alone becomes unclean and the others remain clean. If they were so [damaged] that liquids could penetrate into them, and the creeping thing was in the uppermost saucepan, all become unclean; if it was in the lowest, that one is unclean but the rest remain clean. If the creeping thing was in the uppermost saucepan and the lowest was highest [in the brim], these both become unclean. If it was in the upper-

---

[1] By means of their liquid matter (cf. Maksh. 6[4]) they may render the food within susceptible to uncleanness (Lev. 11[34]).

[2] A cavity in the plug to help the fingers to draw out the plug.

[3] In the 'tent' wherein is a corpse.

[4] Properly fired, thereby counting as a 'vessel' and requiring a tightly stopped-up cover to protect it.

[5] Not yet properly fired; it is therefore not a finished 'vessel', is insusceptible to uncleanness, and can serve as a 'screen' against corpse-uncleanness.

[6] The colander serves as a valid screen. Cf. Ohol. 12[1].

[7] It can be regarded as though the colander lay over the top of the new oven, so affording t protection.

most saucepan, and the lowest was highest [in the brim], all of them in the middle that drip with liquid become unclean.

11. 1. Utensils[1] of metal are susceptible to uncleanness whether they are flat or whether they form a receptacle; after they are broken they become insusceptible; but if again utensils are made of them they once more become susceptible. Rabban Simeon b. Gamaliel says: This does not apply to every uncleanness but only to uncleanness from a corpse.

2. Any article of metal that has a name of its own[2] is susceptible to uncleanness, excepting a door, bolt, lock, hinge-socket, hinge, clapper, or [threshold] groove, since these are made to be joined to the ground.[3]

3. Articles made from iron ore, or a piece of [unshaped] smelted iron, or the iron hoop of a wheel, or of sheet-metal, or metal plating, or the bases or rims or handles of other vessels, or metal chippings or filings, are not susceptible to uncleanness. R. Johanan b. Nuri says: Also [such as are made] from broken up [metal] articles. If they were made from the fragments of [other] articles or from the refuse, or from nails known to have been made from other articles, they are unclean. If [they were made] from common nails the School of Shammai declare them unclean, but the School of Hillel declare them clean.

4. If iron from an unclean article was smelted together[4] with clean iron and the greater part was from the unclean iron, the whole is unclean; if the greater part was from the clean iron, the whole is clean; if the two were equal the whole is unclean. So, too, if an article was made of both cement and cattle-dung.[5] A door-bolt[6] is susceptible to uncleanness, but if it was only [wood] plated [with metal], it is not susceptible. The clutch and the cross-piece of a lock are susceptible to uncleanness. R. Joshua says: A door-bolt may be drawn off one door and hung on another on the Sabbath. R. Tarfon says: It can be dealt with like all other articles and moved about within the courtyard.

5. The scorpion-bit of a bridle is susceptible to uncleanness, but the cheek-pieces are not susceptible. R. Eliezer declares the cheek-pieces also susceptible, but the Sages say: The scorpion-bit alone is susceptible to uncleanness, but while they are joined together the whole is susceptible.

6. A metal spindle-knob R. Akiba declares susceptible to uncleanness, but the Sages declare it insusceptible. If it is only plated it is insusceptible. If a spindle, distaff, rod, double flute, or pipe are made of metal they are susceptible to uncleanness; but if they are only plated they are not susceptible; but in either case if the double flute has a groove for the 'wing'[7] it is susceptible.

7. A curved horn is susceptible to uncleanness and a straight one is insusceptible, but if its mouthpiece is of metal it is susceptible. Its wide [metal] end R. Tarfon declares susceptible, but the Sages declare it insusceptible. When they are joined together the whole is susceptible. So, too, [they have taught that] the branches of a candlestick are not susceptible to uncleanness, but the cups and the base are susceptible; and when they are joined together the whole is susceptible.

---

[1] Cf. 2[1]; 15[1].   [2] i.e. it is not merely part of another utensil.
[3] And remain insusceptible even if they are not yet attached to the ground.
[4] Maksh. 2[3].
[5] If this is the greater part the whole is insusceptible. See App. IV. 16 c.
[6] Often used as a pestle.
[7] Perhaps a cavity containing a vibrating tongue of reed is intended.

8. A helmet is susceptible to uncleanness but the cheek-pieces are not susceptible; but if they have a cavity that will hold water they are susceptible. All weapons of war are susceptible: the javelin, spear-head, greaves, and breastplate are susceptible to uncleanness. All women's adornments are susceptible to uncleanness: the 'golden city',[1] necklace, ear-rings, finger-rings, rings with a seal or without a seal, and nose-rings. If a necklace has metal beads on a thread of flax or wool and the thread breaks, the beads are still susceptible to uncleanness, since each one is an article in itself. If the necklace has a thread of metal, with beads of precious stones and pearls or glass, and the beads are broken and the thread alone remains, it is still susceptible to uncleanness. The remnants of a necklace [are still susceptible] if enough to encompass the neck of a little girl. R. Eliezer says: Even if only a single link remains it is susceptible to uncleanness since the like of it is hung around the neck.

9. If an ear-ring is made with a pot-shaped bottom and a lentil-shaped top and the pieces fall apart, the pot-shaped piece is susceptible to uncleanness by virtue of being an article forming a receptacle, and the lentil-shaped piece is susceptible to uncleanness in itself. The hooklet [of the ear-ring] is not susceptible. If the pieces [of a pendant] made in the shape of a grape-cluster fall apart, it is not susceptible to uncleanness.

12. 1. A ring[2] worn by men is susceptible to uncleanness, but a ring for cattle or for utensils and all other rings are not susceptible. The [iron-shod] beam [used as a target] for arrows is susceptible to uncleanness, but that [used as a foot-stock] for prisoners is not susceptible. A neck-iron is susceptible. A chain that has a lock-piece is susceptible, but if it is used [only] to tie up [a beast] it is not susceptible. The chain belonging to corn-merchants is susceptible, but that belonging to householders is not susceptible. R. Jose said: This applies only if it has but one link; if it has two, or if it has a slug-piece on the end, it is susceptible.

2. The [wooden] beam of the wool-comber's balance is susceptible to uncleanness by reason of the hooks; that of householders, if it has hooks, is also susceptible. The lading-hooks of porters are not susceptible, but those of pedlars are susceptible. R. Judah says: Only the hook that is carried in front of pedlars is susceptible; that behind is not susceptible. The hooks of a bed-frame are susceptible, but those on the bed-poles[3] are not susceptible. [The hook] of a box is susceptible to uncleanness but that of a fish-trap is not susceptible. That of a table is susceptible, but that of a wooden candlestick is not susceptible. This is the general rule: Any hook that is joined to what is susceptible is itself susceptible, and what is joined to what is not susceptible is itself not susceptible; but by themselves they are all insusceptible.

3. The metal covering of a basket belonging to householders Rabban Gamaliel declares susceptible to uncleanness, and the Sages declare it not susceptible; but that of physicians is susceptible. The [metal] door to the cupboard belonging to householders is not susceptible, but that of physicians is susceptible. Smelters' tongs are susceptible, but fire-bars are

---

[1] Cf. Shab. 6[1]; Eduy. 2[7].

[2] The objects specified in the following paragraphs are susceptible or insusceptible to uncleanness according to whether they can be accounted 'utensils in their own right' and not merely subsidiary parts.

[3] One at the head and one at the foot of the bed. Cf. Sukk. 1[3].

not susceptible. The scorpion-shaped hook in the olive-press is susceptible, but hooks in walls are not susceptible.

4. The blood-letter's lancet is susceptible to uncleanness, but the point of a sundial is not susceptible. R. Zadok declares it susceptible. A weaver's pin is susceptible; the grist-dealer's chest R. Zadok declares susceptible, but the Sages declare it insusceptible, though if its wagon was made of metal it is susceptible.

5. If a nail is fashioned so that it will open or shut a lock it is susceptible to uncleanness; but if it was only used as a safeguard[1] it is not susceptible. If it is fashioned so that it will open a jar R. Akiba declares it susceptible, but the Sages declare it not susceptible unless it was forged [anew]. The nail of a money-changer is not susceptible, but R. Zadok declares it susceptible. Three things[2] did R. Zadok declare susceptible to uncleanness and the Sages declared them not susceptible: the nail of a money-changer, a grist-dealer's chest, and the point of a sundial. R. Zadok declared them susceptible and the Sages declared them not susceptible.

6. Four things[3] did Rabban Gamaliel declare susceptible to uncleanness and the Sages declared them not susceptible: the metal basket-cover belonging to householders, the hanger of a strigil, unfinished metal vessels, and a plate broken into two [equal] pieces. But the Sages agree with Rabban Gamaliel that if the plate was broken into two pieces, the one large and the other small, the large is susceptible to uncleanness and the smaller becomes insusceptible.

7. If a *denar*[4] had become defective and was fashioned for hanging around a young girl's neck, it is susceptible to uncleanness. So, too, if a *sela*[4] had become defective and was fashioned for use as a weight, it is susceptible to uncleanness. How defective[5] may it become and yet be fit for use [as a coin]? So long as it is still worth two *denars*; if it is worth less than this it should be cut up.

8. The penknife, pen, plummet, weights, pressing-plates, measuring-rod, and measuring-tables are susceptible to uncleanness. And all unfinished utensils of wood are susceptible excepting those of box-wood. R. Judah says: What is made from olive-tree branches is also not susceptible unless [the wood] has been heated [to drive out moisture].

13. 1. The sword, knife, dagger, spear, hand-sickle, harvest-sickle, razor, and barbers' scissors (even if the two parts are sundered) are susceptible to uncleanness. R. Jose says: The part near the hand is susceptible, but that nearer the point is not susceptible. Shears whose two parts are sundered R. Judah declares still susceptible to uncleanness, but the Sages declare them insusceptible.

2. If a shovel-fork has lost its shovel-end, it is still susceptible to uncleanness because of its pointed end; if it has lost its pointed end it is still susceptible because of its shovel-end. If a kohl-stick[6] has lost its ear-spoon it is still susceptible because of its point; if it has lost its point it is still susceptible because of its ear-spoon. If a stylus has lost its writing point it is still susceptible because of its eraser;[7] if it has lost its eraser it is still

---

[1] To serve as an indication whether any one has entered the house.   [2] Eduy. 3[8].
[3] Eduy. 3[9].   [4] App. II, A.   [5] Cf. B.M. 4[5].
[6] Used in applying stibium to blacken the eyelids; it has one end shaped for cleaning out the ears.
[7] For smoothing over the wax that has been written on.

susceptible because of its writing point. If a soup-ladle has lost its spoon it is still susceptible because of its forked end; if it has lost its forked end it is still susceptible because of its spoon. So, too, with the prongs of the mattock. [To be still susceptible to uncleanness], the size of [what remains] of them must in every case be such that they can do their wonted work.

3. If a coulter is damaged it still remains susceptible to uncleanness until it has lost its greater part; but if its shaft-socket is broken it becomes insusceptible. If a hatchet-head has lost its cutting edge it still remains susceptible because of its splitting edge; if it has lost its splitting edge it still remains susceptible because of its cutting edge; but if its shaft-socket is broken it becomes insusceptible to uncleanness.

4. If a shovel has lost its blade it still remains susceptible to uncleanness because it is become the like of a hammer. So R. Meir. But the Sages declare it insusceptible. If a saw has lost one tooth in every two it becomes insusceptible; but if there is left a length of one *sit*[1] of teeth at any one place it remains susceptible. If an adze, scalpel, plane, or drill is damaged it remains susceptible to uncleanness, but if it lost its sharp edge it becomes insusceptible. If any of them was split into two they remain susceptible, excepting the drill. The block of a plane is not susceptible by itself.

5. If a needle has lost its eye or its point it becomes insusceptible to uncleanness; but if it was then fashioned to be a stretching-pin it remains susceptible. If a pack-needle has lost its eye it still remains susceptible since one may write with it; but if it has lost its point it becomes insusceptible. If a stretching-pin lost either, it remains susceptible to uncleanness. If a needle has become rusty and this hinders it from sewing, it is not susceptible; otherwise it remains susceptible. If a hook is straightened out it is insusceptible to uncleanness; if it is bent back it again becomes susceptible.

6. Wood that serves as a part of a metal utensil is susceptible to uncleanness, but metal that serves as a part of a wooden utensil is not susceptible. Thus if a lock is of wood and its clutches of metal, or even one only of them, it is susceptible to uncleanness; but if the lock is of metal and its clutches of wood, it is not susceptible. If a ring is of metal and its seal of coral, it is susceptible to uncleanness, but if the ring is of coral and its seal of metal it is not susceptible. The teeth of the plate in a lock or in a key are susceptible in themselves.

7. If Ashkelon grappling-irons were broken yet their hooks remained, they are still susceptible to uncleanness. If a [wooden] pitch-fork, winnowing-fan, or rake (so, too, a hair-comb) lost one of its teeth and another of metal was made for it, they become susceptible to uncleanness. Concerning all these, R. Joshua said: The Scribes have invented a new thing, and I cannot make answer [to them that would gainsay them].[2]

8. If a flax-comb has lost its teeth and but two are left, it is still susceptible to uncleanness; if one only, it is not susceptible. Each tooth in itself is susceptible. If a wool-comb has lost one tooth in every two, it becomes insusceptible, but if three are left together in any one place it remains susceptible. But if one of them was the outermost[3] [of the comb] it is not

---

[1] The distance between the tips of the outstretched thumb and forefinger. According to Maim. it is the distance between the outstretched fore- and middle fingers, or four thumbs' breadth.
[2] Since such wooden vessels are flat and therefore by rule insusceptible to uncleanness. See below, 15[1].   [3] Which was made broad in shape and was unsuited for combing.

susceptible. If two teeth were taken from the comb and made into a pair of forceps they are susceptible to uncleanness; if one [only was taken] and fashioned to be used for a lamp or as a stretching-pin, it is susceptible to uncleanness.

14. 1. [If] metal vessels [have been broken because of their uncleanness] how large must they be [so that they still remain susceptible to uncleanness or retain their old uncleanness]? A bucket must still be of a size such that it can draw water; a boiler, such that water can still be heated in it; a kettle, such that it can hold *selas*;[1] a cauldron, such that it can hold jugs; jugs, such that they can hold *perutahs*;[1] wine-measures and oil-measures, such that they can still measure wine and oil. R. Eliezer says: With all of them the size must be such that they can hold *perutahs*. But R. Akiba says: Any vessel that lacks but trimming [to make it of use] is susceptible to uncleanness, but what needs polishing is not susceptible.[2]

2. A staff that has a club-headed nail fashioned on its end is susceptible to uncleanness. One that is studded with nails is susceptible. R. Simeon says: Only if three rows [of nails] are put in it. But whensoever they are put in only for adornment [the staff] remains insusceptible. If a tube was put on the end (so, too, in the case of a door) it remains insusceptible. But if [the tube] had already served as some utensil and was fastened to it, it remains susceptible. When does it become insusceptible? The School of Shammai say: So soon as it has suffered damage. And the School of Hillel say: So soon as it is fastened on.

3. A builder's crowbar and a carpenter's pick are susceptible to uncleanness. Tent-pegs and surveyors' pegs are susceptible. A surveyor's chain is susceptible; but a chain used for [binding up] faggots is not susceptible. The chain of a big bucket [is susceptible to uncleanness to a length of] four handbreadths [from the bucket], and that of a little bucket [to a length of] ten handbreadths.[3] A blacksmith's jack is susceptible. A saw in which the teeth are set in sockets is susceptible, but if they were put in upside down it is not susceptible.[4] All covers are insusceptible to uncleanness excepting that of a kettle.[5]

4. These parts in a wagon are susceptible to uncleanness: the metal [cattle-]yoke, the cross-bar, the side-pieces which hold the straps, the iron piece that comes under the neck of the cattle, the pole-pin, the metal girth, the trays, the clapper, the hook, and any nail that holds the parts together.

5. These parts in a wagon are not susceptible to uncleanness: the [cattle-]yoke that is [only] plated with metal, side-pieces made for adornment, tubes that give out a noise, the lead by the side of the necks of the cattle, the rim of the wheel, the metal plates and mountings, and any other nails—these are not susceptible to uncleanness. The metal shoes of the cattle are susceptible to uncleanness but those made of cork are not susceptible. When is a sword susceptible to uncleanness? So soon as it is polished. And a knife? So soon as it is whetted.

---

1 App. II, A.
2 The first can be done by the householder, while the second requires a skilled craftsman.
3 As much as is used in the handling of it.
4 So Maim. Bert. and Tif. Yis. would render: 'If a saw (had become unclean and) its teeth were put in a hole (of a door, with the teeth outermost, to serve as a door-jamb), it remains susceptible; but if the teeth were put in the reverse way, &c.'
5 Since this alone is used as a utensil in itself.

6. If a mirror is made from a metal basket-cover, R. Judah declares it insusceptible to uncleanness, but the Sages declare it susceptible.[1] If a mirror is broken and does not reflect the greater part of the face, it is not susceptible to uncleanness.

7. Vessels of metal[2] can be rendered unclean and be again made clean even when they are broken. So R. Eliezer. But R. Joshua says: They can only be made clean while they are whole. Thus[3] if they were sprinkled[4] and broken on the same day and recast and sprinkled a second time the same day, then they are clean. So R. Eliezer. But R. Joshua says: They may not be sprinkled earlier than the third day [for the first sprinkling] and the seventh day [for the second sprinkling].

8. If a knee-shaped key is broken at its joint it becomes insusceptible to uncleanness. R. Judah declares it susceptible since one may still open [the door] with the inner portion. If a *gamma*-shaped[5] key was broken off at its bend it becomes insusceptible.[6] If [what remained] still retained the teeth and gaps it remains susceptible. If a key has lost its teeth it is still susceptible because of the gaps; if the gaps were blocked up it is still susceptible because of the teeth. If the teeth were lost and the gaps blocked up or merged into one another, the key becomes insusceptible. If three holes in the bottom of a mustard-strainer merged into one another, it becomes insusceptible to uncleanness, but a metal mill-funnel [in like condition] remains susceptible.

15. 1. Utensils of wood, leather, bone, or glass that are flat are not susceptible to uncleanness. If they form a receptacle they are susceptible. After they are broken they become clean, but if again utensils are made of them they once more become susceptible to uncleanness.[7] A chest, a box, a cupboard, a straw basket,[8] a reed basket, or the tank of an Alexandrian ship that have [flat] bottoms and that hold [not less than] forty *seahs*[9] of liquid, or two *kors*[9] of dry wares, are not susceptible to uncleanness. All other vessels, whether they can hold [such measure] or not, are susceptible to uncleanness. So R. Meir. But R. Judah says: The tub of a [water-] wagon, the food-chests of kings, a tanner's trough or the tank of a small ship, or an ark, even if they hold [forty *seahs*] are susceptible to uncleanness since they have no other use than to go about carrying what is in them. All other vessels that can hold [the like measure] are not susceptible to uncleanness, while those that cannot hold [the like measure] are susceptible. The words of R. Meir differ from the words of R. Judah only in what concerns the baking-trough that belongs to a householder.

2. The baking-boards of bakers are susceptible to uncleanness, but those of householders are not susceptible.[10] If they have been coloured red or saffron they are susceptible. The baker's shelf that is fixed to the wall R. Eliezer declares insusceptible to uncleanness, but the Sages declare it susceptible. The baker's frame is susceptible to uncleanness, but that

---

[1] Since it is always available for its former purpose.
[2] See above, 11[1].
[3] Many texts omit 'thus'; the following sentence is not part of the preceding rule.
[4] See Num. 19[18].
[5] Like a right-angle with one arm shorter than the other.
[6] Apparently the latter type of key needed to be thrust in deeper than the former.
[7] Cf. above, 11[1].
[8] A large round basket; the same word is used for a hive (Shebi. 10[7]; B.B. 5[3]; Kel. 8[1]; 22[10]; Ohol. 5[6]; 9[1]).   [9] App. II, D.
[10] They are not fashioned as special utensils. See Eduy. 7[7].

which belongs to householders is not susceptible. If it is shut in on all four sides it is susceptible to uncleanness, but if one side is open it is not susceptible. R. Simeon says: If he had arranged it so that he could cut [the dough] thereon it is susceptible to uncleanness. So, too, the rolling-pin is susceptible.

3. The container of the flour-dealer's sifter is susceptible to uncleanness, but that which belongs to householders is not susceptible. R. Judah says: Also that which belongs to hairdressers is susceptible to uncleanness as being something that is sat upon,[1] since girls sit in it to have their hair dressed.

4. All hangers are susceptible to uncleanness excepting that of a house-holder's sifter or riddle. So R. Meir. But the Sages say: They are none of them susceptible excepting the hanger of the sifter belonging to flour-dealers, and the riddle that belongs to threshing-floors, and the hanger of a hand-sickle and the hanger of the exciseman's staff, since they aid the implement at its time of use. This is the general rule: Any hanger made to aid the implement at its time of use is susceptible to uncleanness, but if it was made as a hanger alone, it is not susceptible.

5. The grist-dealer's shovel is susceptible to uncleanness, but that of store-rooms [for grain] is not susceptible; that of winepresses is susceptible, but that of threshing-floors is not susceptible. This is the general rule: Any shovel made to hold anything is susceptible to uncleanness, but if it was made only to heap stuff together it is not susceptible.

6. The harps whereto they sing are susceptible to uncleanness; but the harps of the sons of Levi are not susceptible.[2] All liquids[3] are susceptible to uncleanness, but the liquid in the shambles [of the Temple] is not susceptible. All scrolls [of Scripture] render the hands unclean[4] excepting the scroll used in the Temple Court.[5] The *markof*[6] is not susceptible to uncleanness. The lute, the *niktimon*,[7] and the drum are susceptible to uncleanness. R. Judah says: The drum is susceptible to uncleanness as being something that is sat upon,[8] since the wailing woman sits thereon. A weasel-trap is susceptible, but a mouse-trap is not susceptible.[9]

16. 1. Any utensil of wood [that had become unclean] becomes clean after it is broken into two pieces, excepting a folding table, a dish made with several partitions for food, and the footstool belonging to house-holders.[10] R. Judah says: The same also applies to a [double] dish and a Babylonian tray. When do utensils of wood become susceptible to un-

---

[1] i.e. it is susceptible to *midras*-uncleanness. See App. I. 26, App. IV. 17 b.
[2] They were only used in the Temple and had no metal pieces.
[3] Those enumerated in Maksh. 6[4].
[4] See Zab. 5[12]; Yad. 3[2]; 4[5]. The reason given for this rabbinical rule is that it used to be the custom to store the Heave-offering with the scrolls, and the mice among the Heave-offering produce destroyed the scrolls; therefore it was ruled that the scrolls rendered the Heave-offering invalid by contact; in other words (see App. IV. 17; cf. p. 714, n. 3) the scrolls suffered 'second-degree uncleanness'; similarly the hands which touched the scrolls were deemed to suffer the same 'second-grade uncleanness'.
[5] Yom. 7[1]; Sot. 7[8]. Instead of 'Temple Court' (*Azarah*), the Tosefta here reads 'The Book of Ezra'. Cf. p. 210, n. 15.
[6] Explained as a wooden horse; also as the wooden arm of a harp around which the strings were bound. Cf. 16[7].
[7] See Shab. 6[8] ('clogs'); Sot. 9[14] ('drum').   [8] See above, n. 1.
[9] Since the weasel is caught for its skin and the trap is hollowed out to preserve it; but a mouse-trap aims only at crushing the mouse, and has only flat boards.
[10] Made to take to pieces.

cleanness?[1] Beds and cots [become susceptible] after they are rubbed over with fish-skin.[2] If it was determined not to rub them over, they are [forthwith] susceptible. R. Meir says: A bed [becomes susceptible] after three rows of meshes[3] have been knit together.

2. Wooden baskets [become susceptible to uncleanness] after their rims are bound round and the rough ends smoothed off; but baskets of palm-branches, even if the ends are not smoothed off inside, become susceptible, for thus they are suffered to remain. A big basket [becomes susceptible] after its rim is bound round and the rough ends smoothed off and its hanger finished. A wicker case for flagons or for cups, even if the rough ends are not smoothed off inside, becomes susceptible to uncleanness, for thus they are suffered to remain.

3. Small food-baskets and hand baskets [become susceptible to uncleanness] after their rims are bound round and the rough ends smoothed off; large food-baskets and large hampers, after two circling bands have been made around their sides; the container of a sifter or sieve and the cup for balances, after one circling band has been made around their sides; a willow basket, after two twists have been made around its sides; a rush basket, after one twist has been made around its sides.

4. When do leathern articles become susceptible to uncleanness? A shepherd's bag [becomes susceptible] after its hem has been stitched and its rough ends trimmed and its thongs sewn on. R. Judah says: After its ears[4] have been been sewn on. A leathern apron [becomes susceptible] after its hem has been stitched and the rough ends trimmed and its strings sewn on. R. Judah says: After its loops have been sewn on. A leathern bed-cover [is susceptible] after its hem has been stitched and its rough ends trimmed. R. Judah says: After its thongs have been sewn on. Leathern cushions or mattresses [become susceptible] after their hems have been stitched and their rough ends trimmed. R. Judah says: After they have been sewn up and less than five handbreadths is left open.

5. A fig-basket is susceptible to uncleanness, but a rubbish-basket is not susceptible. Little fruit-baskets made of leaves are not susceptible, but those made of twigs are susceptible. The wicker wrapping [in which the dates are left to ripen and] whose contents can be put in or taken out [without tearing it] is susceptible to uncleanness; but if they cannot be put in or taken out without tearing it or unbinding it, it is not susceptible.

6. The leathern glove[5] of winnowers, travellers, or flax-workers is susceptible to uncleanness; but that of dyers or blacksmiths is not susceptible. R. Jose says: The same also applies to the glove of grist-dealers. This is the general rule: What is used to seize hold with is susceptible to uncleanness; but what is worn because of sweat is not susceptible to uncleanness.

7. A bag [to hold the dung] of a bullock, its muzzle, a bee-smoker, and a fan are not susceptible to uncleanness. The cover of a casket is susceptible; the cover of a clothes-chest is not susceptible. The cover of an ark, the cover of a basket, a carpenter's vice, the cushion under an ark and its arched cover, the reading-desk for a book, the bolt-socket, the lock-socket, the

---

[1] At what stage in their manufacture do they become fit for use and so become exposed to uncleanness?   [2] To rid the surface of splinters.
[3] Of the under-webbing.   [4] Flaps to facilitate handling.
[5] Also explained as a protective apron or head-gear.

Mezuzah-case,[1] the viol-case and lyre-case, the turban-maker's block, the singer's *markof*,[2] the clappers of the wailing women, the poor man's parasol, the bed-struts, the phylactery-mould,[3] and the cloak-maker's block—these are not susceptible to uncleanness. This, said R. Jose, is the general rule: Such as are accessory to what a man uses both during his work and not during his work are susceptible to uncleanness; but if only during his work they are not susceptible.

8. The sheath of a sword or knife or dagger, the case for scissors or shears or razors, the case for kohl-[4]sticks, the kohl-box, the stylus-box, the box with many partitions, the tablet-case, the leathern apron, the quiver, and the javelin-case—these are susceptible to uncleanness. The case for the double flute, if this is put in from above, is susceptible to uncleanness; if from the side it is not susceptible. The case for pipes R. Judah declares not susceptible, since they are put in from the side. The covering for a club, bow, or spear is not susceptible to uncleanness. This is the general rule: What is made as a case is susceptible to uncleanness; what is made only as a covering is not susceptible.

17. 1. [Wooden] vessels that belong to householders [and that are broken because of their uncleanness become clean if the breaches therein are] such a size that pomegranates will drop through them; but R. Eliezer says: If aught soever will drop through. Gardeners' baskets [become clean] if [the rents are such] that bundles of vegetables will drop through; and the baskets of householders, if bundles of straw will drop through; and the baskets of bath-keepers, if bundles of shavings will drop through. R. Joshua says: In every case [they become clean if the breaches therein are] such that pomegranates will drop through.

2. A goatskin [becomes clean if it has holes] such that anything the size of warp-clews will pass through; if it will not hold [aught small as] warp-clews but will at least hold [what is the size of] woof-clews, it is still susceptible to uncleanness. A dish-holder that will not hold dishes but will at least hold trays is susceptible to uncleanness. A chamber-pot that will not hold liquids but will at least hold excrement is susceptible to uncleanness. Rabban Gamaliel declares it not susceptible, since men do not suffer it to remain so.

3. Bread-baskets [become clean if they have breaches] such that loaves will fall through. A [wide-meshed] basket made of papyrus, although reeds have been tied below it and above it to strengthen it, remains insusceptible to uncleanness; but if any manner of handles were made for it it becomes susceptible. R. Simeon says: If it cannot be taken away by the handles it remains insusceptible.

4. The pomegranates of which they have spoken are three fastened together. Rabban Simeon b. Gamaliel says: In a sifter or sieve [the hole must be] such that they will fall through when it is taken and shaken; and in a hamper, such [that they will fall through] when a man hangs it behind him. All other vessels which cannot hold pomegranates, such as the quarter-*kab*[5] [measure] and the half quarter-*kab*, and small baskets, [become clean] when the greater part of them [is defective]. So R. Meir. R. Simeon says: [If] olives [will fall through]. If [their sides] are broken through [they

---

become clean] if olives will fall through. If they are worn away [so that little remains of the sides], [they are still susceptible to uncleanness] if they can hold aught soever.

5. The [measure of the] pomegranate of which they have spoken applies to one that is neither big nor little, but of middle size. And why were the pomegranates of Baddan spoken of?[1] Because [when they are *Orlah*-fruit[2] or are otherwise forbidden] in any quantity soever they render forbidden [other pomegranates with which they are confused]. So R. Meir. R. Johanan b. Nuri says: To measure therewith [the breaches in] vessels. R. Akiba says: They are spoken of for both reasons—to measure therewith [the breaches in] vessels and because in any quantity soever they render other fruit forbidden. R. Jose[3] said: Pomegranates of Baddan and leeks of Geba[4] were spoken of only because Tithes must everywhere be given from them as being certainly untithed.[5]

6. The [measure of the] egg of which they have spoken[6] applies to one that is neither big nor little, but of middle size. R. Judah says: They should bring the largest and the smallest and put them in water and divide the [volume of] water [that is displaced]. R. Jose said: But who can tell me which is the largest and which the smallest?—but, rather, it is all in accordance with the impression of the eye.

7. The [measure of the] dried fig of which they have spoken[7] applies to one that is neither big nor little, but of middle size. R. Judah says: What is big in the Land of Israel is but of middle size in other lands.

8. The [measure of the] olive of which they have spoken[8] applies to one that is neither big not little, but of middle size, such as an olive fit for storing. The [measure of the] barleycorn of which they have spoken[9] applies to one that is neither big nor little, but of middle size, such as barley that grows in the wilderness. The [measure of the] lentil of which they have spoken[10] applies to one that is neither big nor little, but of middle size, such as an Egyptian lentil. Any[11] movable object conveys the uncleanness[12] if it is as thick as an ox-goad—this applies to one that is neither big nor little, but of middle size. Which is accounted of middle size? One that is a handbreadth round.

9. The [measure of the] cubit of which they have spoken[13] applies to the cubit of middle size.[14] There were two cubits[15] by the Palace of Shushan [Gate],[16] one at the north-eastern corner and another at the south-eastern corner. That at the north-east was longer than the cubit of Moses[17] by half a fingerbreadth; that at the south-east was longer than the other by half a fingerbreadth; thus it was one fingerbreadth longer than the cubit of Moses. And why was there ordained a larger cubit and a smaller cubit? So that the craftsmen might undertake their tasks according to the measure of the

---

[1] Orl. 3[7].　　　　[2] App. I. 32.　　　　[3] Variant: Judah.　　　　[4] In Samaria.
[5] And if offered for sale by an *Am-haaretz* must, by an 'Associate', be deemed not merely *demai*-produce (see p. 20, n. 9) from which First Tithe and Poorman's Tithe need not be set apart, but as produce from which these two Tithes also must be set apart.
[6] Cf. Ber. 7[2]; Ter. 5[1]; Orl. 2[4]; Pes. 3[8]; Sukk. 3[7]; Meil. 4[5]; Ohol. 13[5]; Toh. 1[5].
[7] Cf. Shab. 7[4]; 9[7]; Erub. 7[8]; Meil. 4[5].
[8] Cf. Ber. 7[1]; Kil. 8[5]; Hall. 1[2]; Pes. 3[2], and frequently.
[9] Cf. Naz. 7[2]; Eduy. 6[3]; Kel. 1[4]; Ohol. 2[3].
[10] Cf. Kil. 8[5]; Ohol. 1[7]; 13[5]; Neg. 4[6]; Mikw. 6[7].　　　[11] Quoting from Ohol. 16[1].
[12] By overshadowing both a man and something that conveys corpse-uncleanness.
[13] Cf. Kil. 3[6]; Erub. 1[1]; Shek. 8[5]; Yom. 5[1]; Sukk. 1[1]; R.Sh. 2[5]; Ohol. 16[3].
[14] Six handbreadths.　　　　[15] As deposited standards.　　　　[16] Midd. 1[3].
[17] Used in building the Tabernacle. This, according to Maim., was six handbreadths.

smaller cubit and fulfil them according to the measure of the larger cubit, and thereby escape the guilt of Sacrilege.[1]

10. R. Meir says: All [the measurements in the Temple] were according to the cubit of middle size excepting those of the Golden Altar[2] and the horns and the Circuit and the Base [of the Altar].[3] R. Judah says: The [standard of the] cubit used for the [Temple] building was six handbreadths and that for the utensils five handbreadths.

11. Sometimes they have prescribed a smaller measure: [thus] for liquids and dry wares [they sometimes prescribed] Italian measure;[4] such is the measure of [the time of] the wilderness. Sometimes they have prescribed a measure that is in accordance with the measure of the man himself, like as when he is bidden to take a 'handful' of the Meal-offering,[5] or 'both hands full' of the incense,[6] or [forbidden] to drink a 'mouthful'[7] on the Day of Atonement, or [like as when it is enjoined to prepare] 'food enough for two meals'[8] for the *Erub*,[9] fare such as he would eat on weekdays and not on the Sabbath. So R. Meir. But R. Judah says: Such as he would eat on the Sabbath and not on weekdays. And they were each minded to give the more lenient ruling. R. Simeon says: [It should consist] of two-thirds of a loaf of [a size] three to the *kab*.[10] R. Johanan b. Baroka says: [Not less than] one loaf worth a *pondion*[11] [from wheat costing] one *sela* for four *seahs*.

12. Sometimes they have prescribed a large measure: [thus] 'a ladleful of corpse-mould'[12] is according to the big ladle of physicians; the 'split bean' spoken of in leprosy-signs[13] is the Cilician bean; [and it is enjoined that he is culpable] who eats on the Day of Atonement a large date's bulk[14] the like of it together with its stone; in skins of wine and oil, the measure [of the rent by which they are rendered clean] is according to their large stopper; the prescribed measure of the light-hole[15] not made by man's hands is that of a large fist, a fist like that of Ben Batiach[16] (R. Jose said: That is the size of a large head of a man), [and that of the light-hole] made by man's hands is that of a hole made by the large drill that lay in a chamber of the Temple,[17] which is the size of an Italian *pondion* or a Neronian *sela*, or like the hole in a yoke.

13. All [utensils made of the skin of creatures that live] in the sea are insusceptible to uncleanness excepting [what is made from] the sea-dog, since this seeks refuge on dry land. So R. Akiba. If a man made utensils from what grows in the sea and joined to them[18] aught that grows on land, even if it is but a thread or a cord, yet something that is susceptible to uncleanness, it, too, becomes susceptible.

14. Uncleanness can arise in what was created on the First Day;[19] no uncleanness can arise in what was created on the Second Day;[20] uncleanness can arise in what was created on the Third day;[21] no uncleanness can arise in what was created on the Fourth Day[22] and on the Fifth day,[23] excepting [what is made from] the wing of the vulture and the plated egg of an

---

[1] Profiting from labour or material that belongs to the Temple; cf. Lev. 5[15]; p. 573, n. 2.
[2] Within the Sanctuary. [3] See Midd. 3[1].
[4] Shebi. 1[2, 3]. Kidd. 1[1] (Eduy. 4[7]); Hull. 3[2]. [5] Lev. 2[2]. [6] Lev. 16[12].
[7] Yom. 8[2]. [8] Erub. 8[2]. [9] App. I. 8. [10] App. II, D.
[11] App. II, A. Cf. Peah 8[7]. [12] Ohol. 2[1]. [13] Neg. 1[5]; 6[1]. [14] Yom. 8[2].
[15] Ohol. 13[1].
[16] A giant who lived at the time of the destruction of the Temple; said to have been the nephew of R. Johanan b. Zakkai. [17] Ohol. 2[3]. [18] Cf. Neg. 11[1].
[19] What is made from the sea (Maim.) or (Bert.) from the products of the earth.
[20] Anything in heaven. [21] The ground and plants.
[22] The sun, moon, and stars. [23] Birds and beasts of the sea.

ostrich (R. Johanan b. Nuri said: How does the wing of the vulture differ
from other wings?); and everything that was created on the Sixth Day[1] is
susceptible to uncleanness.

15. If a man made an article that could in any wise be a receptacle it is
susceptible to uncleanness. If he made an article that could in any wise be
lain upon or sat upon it is susceptible to uncleanness.[2] If he made a purse
of untanned hide or paper it is susceptible to uncleanness. If children
hollowed out a pomegranate, acorn, or nut wherewith to measure dust, or
fashioned them into a pair of scales, they are susceptible to uncleanness,
because with children only the act is of consequence while the intention is
of no consequence.[3]

16. A beam of a balance or a levelling-rod that contains a [secret]
receptacle in which to load it with metal, or a carrying-yoke wherein is a
[secret] receptacle for [stolen] money, or a beggar's cane that has a receptacle
for water,[4] or a stick that has a receptacle for a *Mezuzah* and for pearls[5]—
these are susceptible to uncleanness. And of all these Rabban Johanan b.
Zakkai said: Woe is me if I speak of them and woe is me if I speak not
of them.[6]

17. The base of a goldsmith's anvil is susceptible to uncleanness, but
that of a blacksmith is not susceptible.[7] If a whetstone has a receptacle for
oil it is susceptible; otherwise it is not susceptible. If a writing-tablet has
a receptacle for wax it is susceptible; otherwise it is not susceptible. Matting of straw or a tube of straw R. Akiba declares susceptible to uncleanness, but R. Johanan b. Nuri declares them not susceptible. R. Simeon
says: The same also applies to the hollow stalk of colocynth. Matting of
reed or of rushes is not susceptible to uncleanness. A reed-tube which was
cut in order to hold anything remains insusceptible to uncleanness until
all the pith has been taken away.

18. 1. The School of Shammai say: A chest[8] should be measured on the
inside [to determine its capacity].[9] And the School of Hillel say: On the
outside. But they agree that the thickness of the legs and the thickness of
the rim should not be included in the measurement. R. Jose says: They
agree that the thickness of the legs and of the rim should be included, but
that the space between them should not be included. R. Simeon of Shezur
says: If the legs were a handbreadth high the space between them should not
be included in the measurement; but if less than this, the space between
them should be included.

2. If the device[10] thereof can be slipped off it does not count as a connective[11] nor is it included in its measurement nor does it afford protection
together with it[12] in the 'Tent' wherein lies a corpse; and it may not be

---

1 Animals living on dry land, and human kind.
2 By *midras*-uncleanness. App. I. 26.   3 Cf. Toh. 8[6]; Maksh. 3[8]. See below, 25[9].
4 Cf. p. 115, n. 8.   5 App. I. 25. The *Mezuzah* is used as a device for smuggling pearls.
6 'Since if I speak of them I teach men how to deceive, and if I do not speak of them they
will offend against the laws of uncleanness.'
7 The former is made to catch scraps of metal, but not the latter.   8 Cf. above, 15[1].
9 Whether it can contain forty *seahs* (or three cubic cubits) or more; and so be accounted
insusceptible to uncleanness.
10 Cf. Ohol. 4[3]. The Hebrew (also in Yom. 3[10]; Tam. 1[4]; 3[8]) is a transliteration of
μηχανή, and probably denotes here a low carriage on rollers.
11 So that it shares uncleanness with the chest.
12 If it partly blocked up a hole (one handbreadth square) in the chest (which was otherwise tightly sealed up) it does not serve to protect it against the ingress of corpse-uncleanness.

drawn along on the Sabbath if there is money therein.[1] But if it cannot be slipped off it counts as a connective and it is included in its measurement and it affords protection together with it in the 'Tent' wherein lies a corpse; and it may be drawn along on the Sabbath even if there is money therein. If the arched top of the chest is fixed, it counts as a connective and it is included in its measurement; but if it is not fixed it does not count as a connective nor is it included in its measurement. How is it measured? Ox-head fashion.[2] R. Judah says: If the chest cannot stand of itself it is not susceptible to uncleanness.

3. A chest, a box, or a cupboard that has lost one of its legs, even if it can still contain aught, is not susceptible to uncleanness, since[3] it cannot contain it after its usual fashion; but R. Jose declares it susceptible. The bed-poles, the bed-base, and the wrapper are not susceptible to uncleanness. Only the bed itself and the bed-frame are susceptible; but the bed-frames of the sons of Levi are not susceptible.[4]

4. If a bed-frame is set up on [movable] props R. Meir and R. Judah declare it susceptible to uncleanness, but R. Jose and R. Simeon declare it insusceptible. R. Jose said: Wherein does this differ from the bed-frames of the sons of Levi?—for the bed-frames of the sons of Levi are not susceptible.

5. If a bed had contracted *midras*-uncleanness[5] and one of the short sides and two bed-legs were taken off, it remains unclean;[6] but if one of the long sides and two bed-legs were taken off it becomes clean. R. Nehemiah declares it still unclean. If the two stays at opposite corners were cut off, or if a handbreadth was cut off from the two legs at opposite corners, or if [the whole bed] was reduced to [a level of] less than one handbreadth, it becomes clean.

6. If a bed had contracted *midras*-uncleanness and one of the long sides was broken and then mended, it retains its *midras*-uncleanness; but if the second side also was broken and then mended it becomes free of *midras*-uncleanness, but it remains unclean from contact with[7] *midras*-uncleanness. But if the second was broken before the first could be mended the bed becomes clean.

7. If a bed-leg had contracted *midras*-uncleanness and was then joined to a bed [that was clean], the whole bed contracts *midras*-uncleanness; if it was taken off again the bed-leg retains its *midras*-uncleanness, but the bed is unclean from contact with *midras*-uncleanness. If the bed-leg had contracted seven-day uncleanness[8] and was then joined to a bed [that was clean], the whole bed contracts seven-day uncleanness; if it was taken off again the bed-leg still suffers seven-day uncleanness and the bed suffers only evening-uncleanness. If the bed-leg had contracted evening-uncleanness[9] and it was then joined to a bed [that was clean], the whole bed contracts evening-uncleanness. If it was taken off again the bed-leg still

---

[1] Cf. Shab. 21[2].
[2] An isosceles triangle is described, the apex being the highest point in the arch; the volume contained within the triangle is added to the bulk of the chest.
[3] Variant: And if it cannot hold (the forty *seahs*) in its usual fashion (but needs to be propped up), R. Jose declares it susceptible.
[4] They were easily detachable and not accounted part of the bed.
[5] See App. I. 26; App. IV. 3.
[6] It is not deemed properly broken since it is still usable to lie upon; therefore it is still deemed to be suffering *midras*-uncleanness.
[7] It is not a 'father of uncleanness' but only a 'derived uncleanness' of first grade.
[8] See Num. 19[11]; App. IV. 2.   [9] Num. 19[22].

suffers evening-uncleanness and the bed becomes clean.[1] So, too, with the prong of a mattock.[2]

8. A phylactery[3] counts as four separate objects. If [it had contracted corpse-uncleanness and] the first section was unloosed and then mended,[4] the phylactery still retains its corpse-uncleanness; so, too, if the second and the third [sections were then unloosed and then mended]. If the fourth also was unloosed, the phylactery becomes free of corpse-uncleanness but it remains unclean from contact with corpse-uncleanness. If, now, the first section was again unloosed and then mended, it continues unclean from contact; so, too, if the second [was again unloosed and then mended]. If, then, the third was unloosed, the whole becomes clean, since the fourth was only unclean from contact; and what is unclean from contact cannot convey uncleanness by contact.

9. If the half of a bed [that was unclean] was stolen or if the half was lost, or if brothers or jointholders had divided it between them, it becomes clean. If it was brought back again it thereafter becomes susceptible to uncleanness. A bed can contract uncleanness [only] when [all its parts are] bound together and be rendered clean[5] again [only] when [all its parts are] bound together. So R. Eliezer. But the Sages say: It can contract uncleanness in single parts and be rendered clean again in single parts.

19. 1. If a man took a bed[6] to pieces to immerse it, he that touches the ropes [of the webbing] remains clean.[7] When[8] does the rope count as a connective with the bed? After three [rows of] meshes of it have been knotted; then he that touches the rope from the knot inwards[9] becomes unclean; but if from the knot outwards, he remains clean. If he touched the loose ends of a knot that are needed for the knot he becomes unclean. How much [loose end] is needed for the knot? R. Judah says: Three fingerbreadths.

2. If the rope that hangs over from the [webbing of the] bed[10] is shorter than five handbreadths it is not susceptible to uncleanness; if it is from five to ten handbreadths long it is susceptible, and what is over the ten handbreadths is not susceptible to uncleanness. With this[11] they tie up the Passover-lambs and hang up the beds.

3. Aught soever of the bed-girth[12] that hangs over [is susceptible to uncleanness]. So R. Meir. But R. Jose says: Only such as is shorter than ten handbreadths. The remnants of a bed-girth [are susceptible] if they are seven handbreadths long, enough to use as an ass's girth.

4. If a man with flux was borne on a bed and [he lay] on the bed-girth, this can convey uncleanness at two removes and can render [Heave-offering] invalid at the third remove.[13] So R. Meir. But R. Jose says: If

---

1 Since the leg, being only a 'derived uncleanness', cannot (after being severed) transmit uncleanness to another utensil (cf. p. 604, n. 2).

2 If one prong suffering evening-uncleanness was secured to a mattock that was clean, the mattock suffers evening-uncleanness; if the prong was removed the prong still suffers evening-uncleanness but the mattock becomes clean again.

3 See p. 104, n. 16. Cf. Men. 4[1].   4 Replaced by a new one.

5 By immersion or, in case of corpse-uncleanness, by sprinkling with Sin-offering water (Num. 19[19]).   6 Suffering *midras-* or corpse-uncleanness.

7 After the bed is dismantled the ropes are not in themselves susceptible to uncleanness.

8 When a man makes a new bed.   9 Towards the already knotted webbing.

10 Rope ends left over after finishing the necessary webbing, but not yet cut off.

11 The length under ten handbreadths.   12 Too short to bind round a bed.

13 The bed and the girth are (App. IV. 3) 'fathers of uncleanness'. What touches the girth thereby becomes a 'derived uncleanness', and such can render common food invalid by touching it (giving it 'second-grade uncleanness'), and this again can render Heave-offering invalid (with 'third-grade uncleanness'). See App. IV. 17 b.

a man with flux was borne on a bed and [he lay] on the bed-girth, less than ten handbreadths [of the bed-girth] can convey uncleanness at two removes and can render [Heave-offering] invalid at the third remove; but what is over the ten handbreadths[1] can convey uncleanness only at one remove and render [Heave-offering] invalid only at the second remove. If he was borne on the bed-girth [on the overhanging part] within the ten hand-breadths, the bed becomes unclean; but if [on the overhanging part] out-side the ten handbreadths, the bed remains clean.

5. If a bed-girth was wrapped around a bed that had contracted *midras*-uncleanness, the whole contracts *midras*-uncleanness;[2] if it was removed, the bed retains its *midras*-uncleanness and the bed-girth is unclean from contact with *midras*-uncleanness. If a bed-girth was wrapped around a bed that had contracted seven-day uncleanness, the whole contracts seven-day uncleanness; if it was removed, the bed retains its seven-day uncleanness, and the bed-girth suffers evening-uncleanness. If a bed-girth was wrapped around a bed that had contracted evening-uncleanness, the whole contracts evening-uncleanness; if it was removed, the bed retains its evening-uncleanness, but the bed-girth becomes clean.

6. If a bed-girth was wrapped around a bed and a corpse touched them, they contract seven-day uncleanness; when they are taken apart they retain seven-day uncleanness. If it was a [dead] creeping thing that touched them, they contract evening-uncleanness; when they are taken apart they retain evening-uncleanness. If from a bed [that was unclean] two longer sides were taken away and two new ones were made for it, yet the sockets re-mained unchanged, if the new sides are broken the bed still remains un-clean; but if the old sides are broken, the bed becomes clean, since all is determined by the old sides.

7. A box whose opening is at the top is susceptible to corpse-uncleanness. If [after contracting corpse-uncleanness] it was damaged above, it still retains its corpse-uncleanness. If it was damaged below it becomes clean, but the partitions within it [if they were not broken] remain unclean, and they do not count as a connective with it.

8. If a shepherd's bag was damaged [after contracting uncleanness] its inner pocket remains unclean and it does not count as a connective with it. If the testicle-bags of a goatskin also hold water, and they were damaged, they become clean, since they will no longer hold water after their usual fashion.

9. A box whose opening is at the side is susceptible both to *midras*-uncleanness[3] and to corpse-uncleanness. R. Jose said: This applies only if it is less than ten handbreadths high or has not a rim one handbreadth deep. If it was damaged above it is still susceptible to corpse-uncleanness; if it was damaged below,[4] R. Meir declares it [still] susceptible [to *midras*-uncleanness], but the Sages declare it insusceptible, since if the primary purpose[5] is annulled the secondary purpose[6] is annulled also.

10. If a dung-basket was so damaged that it will not hold pomegranates, R. Meir declares it [still] susceptible [to *midras*-uncleanness], but the Sages declare it insusceptible, since if the primary purpose is annulled the secondary purpose[6] is annulled also.

---

[1] Such counts only as suffering from contact with *midras*-uncleanness, and itself only suffers 'first-grade uncleanness'. [2] As in the examples given above, 18[7].
[3] It can be sat upon and still do its normal work. [4] Yet its top could still be sat upon.
[5] As a receptacle. [6] As something that can be sat upon.

20. 1. Mattresses, pillows, sacks, and packing-bags, although they have been damaged,[1] are still susceptible to *midras*-uncleanness.[2] A fodder-bag holding four *kabs*,[3] a shepherd's wallet holding five *kabs*, a travelling-bag holding a *seah*,[3] a goatskin holding seven *kabs* (R. Judah says: Also a spice-bag and a food-wallet, however little they hold) are susceptible to *midras*-uncleanness;[4] but if any of them are damaged, they are insusceptible to uncleanness, since if the primary purpose is annulled the secondary purpose is annulled also.

2. Bagpipes are not susceptible to *midras*-uncleanness; a trough for mixing mortar the School of Shammai declare susceptible to *midras*-uncleanness, and the School of Hillel declare it susceptible to corpse-uncleanness alone. If a trough that holds from two *logs* to nine *kabs* is split, it becomes susceptible to *midras*-uncleanness; if it was left in the rain so that it swelled, it becomes susceptible to corpse-uncleanness only;[5] if it was left out during the east wind so that it split again, it becomes susceptible to *midras*-uncleanness. Herein greater stringency applies to the remnants of wooden vessels than applies to them in the beginning; also greater stringency applies to the remnants of wicker vessels than applies to them in the beginning, for they are not susceptible to uncleanness in the beginning until their rim is finished; but once their rim has been finished, even if their edges fall away leaving aught soever, they remain susceptible to uncleanness.

3. If a staff was used as a haft for a hatchet, it counts as a connective for uncleanness at the time of use.[6] A yarn-winder counts as a connective[7] for uncleanness at the time of use. If it was fixed to a post it is susceptible[8] to uncleanness, but the post does not count as a connective. If the post itself was used[9] to make a yarn-winder, only so much of the post is susceptible to uncleanness as is needful for use. If a seat was fixed to the post the seat is susceptible to uncleanness but the post does not count as a connective with it; if the post was used as a seat, only that part that is sat upon is susceptible to uncleanness. If a seat was fixed to the beam in an olive-press, the seat is susceptible to uncleanness, but the beam does not count as a connective with it; if the end of the beam was used as a seat, it is not susceptible to uncleanness, because they say to him [that sits upon it], 'Get up and let us do our work!'

4. If a large trough was so damaged that it could not contain pomegranates and was made into a seat, R. Akiba declares it susceptible to uncleanness, but the Sages declare it insusceptible unless its rough parts have been smoothed. If it was used as a feeding-trough for cattle, even if it was fastened to the wall, it is susceptible to uncleanness.

5. If a wooden block was fixed to a course of a wall, whether it was fixed in but not built upon, or built upon but not fixed in, it is susceptible to uncleanness. If it was both fixed in and built upon, it is not susceptible.[10] If

---

1 So that they can no longer serve as receptacles.
2 So long as they can serve as seats for one that has a flux or a menstruant or a woman after childbirth.   3 App. II, D.
4 If they hold that minimum quantity they are large enough to sit upon.
5 It becomes fit for its proper work; it is not susceptible to *midras*-uncleanness since it only counts as a seat if it is unfitted for its proper work (see par. 3, end).
6 Even though, as a flat wooden utensil, it is not susceptible to uncleanness.
7 With the metal end cross-pieces, temporarily attached.
8 Since the metal ends are then left on it permanently.
9 The metal pieces were put directly on to the post.
10 It then counts as part of the wall and as fixed to the ground.

matting was spread over the roof-beams, whether it was fixed on but no plasterwork laid over it, or whether plasterwork was laid over it but it was not fixed on, it is susceptible to uncleanness.[1] But if it was both fixed on and plasterwork laid over it, it is not susceptible. If a dish was fixed to a chest, a box, or a cupboard so that it can contain aught after its usual fashion, it is still susceptible to uncleanness; but if so that it cannot contain aught after its usual fashion, it is not susceptible.

6. If a sheet that was susceptible to *midras*-uncleanness was used as a curtain it becomes insusceptible to *midras*-uncleanness, but it is still susceptible to corpse-uncleanness. When does it cease to be susceptible to *midras*-uncleanness? The School of Shammai say: After it has been sewn up. And the School of Hillel say: After it has been tied up. R. Akiba says: After it has been fixed up [in its new place].

7. A piece of matting whereon reeds[2] are laid lengthwise is not susceptible to uncleanness; but the Sages say: Only if they are laid crosswise.[3] If they were laid along the breadth of the matting and there was less than four handbreadths between each, it is not susceptible to uncleanness. If a piece of matting is divided along its breadth, R. Judah declares it insusceptible. So, too, if the end-knots of a reed mat are untied, it becomes insusceptible. If it was divided along its length, but there were still left three end-knots, six handbreadths in all, it remains susceptible to uncleanness. When does a mat become susceptible to uncleanness? After its rough ends have been trimmed; and that is the completion of its manufacture.

21. 1. If[4] a man touched the upper beam[5] [of a loom] or the lower beam, or the heddles[6] or the sley or the thread that is drawn over fine purple, or a spool which is not to be shot back again [into the web], he remains clean; [but if he touched] the shedded weft or the standing warp or the double thread that is drawn over fine purple, or a spool which is to be shot back again, he becomes unclean. If a man touched the wool that is on the distaff or spool, he remains clean; but if he touched the spinner before it is laid bare, he becomes unclean; but if after it is laid bare he remains clean.[7]

2. If[8] a man touched the yoke [of the wagon], the cross-bar, the collar-piece, or the thick ropes [of the plough], even at the time of use, he remains clean; [but if he touched] the tail-piece, knee, or handle of the plough, he becomes unclean. If he touched the metal rings or the plough-guides or the plough-flanks, he becomes unclean; but R. Judah declares him clean if he touched the plough-guides, since these are used only to increase the soil.[9]

3. If[10] a man touched either end of a saw handle, he becomes unclean; but if he touched the string, cord, cross-piece, or side-pieces, or a carpenter's press, or the bow-handle of a drill, he remains clean. R. Judah says: Also, if he touched the frame of a large saw he remains clean. If he touched the bow-strings or the bow, even when it was stretched, he remains clean. The

---

1 It is still possible to take it and use it to lie on.
2 Too hard for a man to lie on comfortably.
3 Lit. 'in the form of (the Greek letter) *chi*'. Cf. Men. 6³.
4 The case is concerned with a piece of stuff partially woven on a loom. The woven portion had contracted corpse-uncleanness. Whatever is in contact with this woven portion becomes unclean.   5 Neg. 11⁹.   6 Cf. Shab. 13².
7 It then no longer counts as a part of the spindle.
8 If the ploughshare was unclean.
9 Variant: to break up the soil. The meaning intended in either case is that it is not concerned in the actual process of ploughing.
10 If the saw-blade was unclean, or the metal parts of the other implements.

mole-trap is not susceptible to uncleanness. R. Judah says: So long as it is set [the iron spring] serves as a connective.

22. 1. If a table or a side-table[1] [that had contracted uncleanness] was damaged or was overlaid with marble[2] yet room enough was left to set cups thereon, it still remains susceptible to uncleanness. R. Judah says: Even if there is only room to set pieces [of food] thereon.

2. If a [three-legged] table lost one of its legs it becomes insusceptible to uncleanness;[3] if it lost a second leg it is still insusceptible; but if it lost the third it again becomes susceptible to uncleanness if a man has the intention[4] to use it [in such condition]. R. Jose says: Not even intention is necessary. So, too, in the case of a side-table.

3. If a bench lost one of its [two upright] ends it becomes susceptible to uncleanness;[5] if it lost the second it is still insusceptible; but if it was still one handbreadth high it is susceptible. If a footstool lost one of its [two] feet it is still susceptible to uncleanness; so, too, the stool in front of a throne.

4. If[6] a bride's stool lost its seat-boards, the School of Shammai declare it still susceptible to uncleanness, and the School of Hillel declare it not susceptible. Shammai says: Even the frame of the stool remains susceptible to uncleanness. If a stool is fixed to a baking-trough, the School of Shammai declare it susceptible to uncleanness, and the School of Hillel declare it not susceptible.[7] Shammai says: Even one that was made [to be used] inside it [is susceptible].

5. If the seat-boards of a stool do not extend beyond the sides, and they are removed, it is still susceptible to uncleanness since it is usual to turn it on its side and sit on it.

6. If a stool lost its middle seat-board but the outer ones remain, it is still susceptible to uncleanness; if the outer ones were lost but the centre one remains, it is still susceptible to uncleanness. R. Simeon says: Only if it is a handbreadth wide.

7. If[8] a stool lost two adjacent seat-boards, R. Akiba declares it still susceptible, but the Sages declare it insusceptible. R. Judah said: Even if a bride's stool lost its seat-boards though there still remained the under-receptacle, it becomes insusceptible, since once the primary purpose is annulled the secondary purpose is annulled also.[9]

8. If a chest[10] lost its top part it remains susceptible to uncleanness because of its bottom part; and if it lost its bottom part it remains susceptible because of its top part. If it lost both the top and the bottom part, R. Judah declares it susceptible to uncleanness because of its sides; but the Sages declare it insusceptible. What a stone-cutter sits upon[11] is susceptible to *midras*-uncleanness.

9. If a wooden block was stained red or saffron, or was polished, R. Akiba declares it susceptible to [*midras*-]uncleanness, but the Sages declare

---

[1] *Delphica.* See A. Zar. 5[5]. Although the table is a flat wooden utensil (15[1]) not susceptible to uncleanness by virtue of containing a receptacle, it is susceptible as being an object leaned against (and so susceptible to *midras*-uncleanness), and as an object which serves objects which serve a man. [2] Which is not susceptible to uncleanness.
[3] It can no longer serve its purpose. [4] Cf. below, 25[9].
[5] It is impossible to sit on it. [6] Eduy 1[11].
[7] It is reckoned only as an adjunct to the trough which is not susceptible to *midras*-uncleanness. [8] Eduy. 2[8]. [9] Cf. 19[9].
[10] Holding less than forty *seahs*; cf. 15[1]. The present chest has an upper and a lower container.
[11] Small block of wood.

it insusceptible unless it was hollowed out. If a small or big basket was filled with straw or flocking and fashioned as a seat, it remains insusceptible to uncleanness; but if it was plaited over with reed-grass or cords it becomes susceptible.

10. A night-stool is susceptible both to *midras*-uncleanness and to corpse-uncleanness. If it is taken apart the leather [seat] is susceptible to *midras*-uncleanness, and the iron base to corpse-uncleanness. A tripod stool that is covered with leather is susceptible both to *midras*-uncleanness and to corpse-uncleanness; if it is taken apart the leather is susceptible to *midras*-uncleanness but the tripod itself is not susceptible to any uncleanness. A bath-house bench[1] that has two wooden legs is susceptible to uncleanness; if one leg is of wood and the other of stone, the bench is not susceptible. If the boards in a bath-house were joined together, R. Akiba declares them susceptible to uncleanness, and the Sages declare them insusceptible,[2] since they are used only for the water to flow away beneath them. A fumigation-cage wherein is a receptacle for garments is susceptible to uncleanness, but if it is made like a bee-hive[3] it is not susceptible.

23. 1. If a ball, a shoe-last, an amulet, or a phylactery[4] [contracted corpse-uncleanness and] were torn, he that touches them becomes unclean;[5] but if he touched what was within them he remains clean.[6] If a saddle was torn open, he that touches what is within it becomes unclean, since the stitching joins together [the cover and the stuffing].

2. These are susceptible to [*midras*-]uncleanness as things used for riding upon: an Ashkelon girth, a Median 'mortar',[7] a camel's pack-saddle, and a horse-cloth. R. Jose says: A horse-cloth is also susceptible to [*midras*-] uncleanness as a thing used for sitting upon, since they rest thereon in the arena; but the saddle of a female camel is susceptible to uncleanness [only as a thing used for riding upon].

3. Wherein does [the uncleanness of] what is ridden upon differ from [the uncleanness of] what is sat upon? The effect of contact with [the uncleanness of] what is ridden upon is different from the effect of carrying [such uncleanness];[8] but there is no difference between the effect of contact with [the uncleanness of] what is sat upon and that of carrying [such uncleanness]. An ass's pack-frame, whereon [in time of need] a man may sit, is not susceptible to uncleanness; but if he changed the width between its spaces or broke them one into another,[9] it becomes susceptible to uncleanness.

4. The bier, mattress, and pillow of a corpse are susceptible to *midras*-uncleanness. A bride's stool, a midwife's travailing-stool, and a washerman's stool on which he piles the clothes—R. Jose said: They do not come within the class of what is sat upon.[10]

---

1 Which usually has a marble seat.
2 Too dirty to sit on.
3 Without a bottom or a receptacle and open at both ends.
4 Cf. above, 18⁸.   5 They are still serviceable as receptacles.
6 The contents do not count as connectives.
7 A wooden saddle hollowed out like a mortar.
8 See App. IV. 3 a (iii); cf. Kel. 1³. He who carries what has been ridden upon by one who has a flux becomes a 'father of uncleanness', and, while still carrying it, can convey uncleanness to garments and vessels; but he who touches it suffers only 'first-grade uncleanness', and does not convey the uncleanness to anything except foodstuffs. Both he who touches and he who carries what has been sat upon by one who has a flux becomes a 'father of uncleanness'.   9 Making it more suitable for riding upon.
10 But are set apart for their own specialized use.

5. A fishing-net is susceptible to uncleanness because of its net-work bag.[1] Nets, snares, bird-traps, slings, and fishermen's snares are susceptible to uncleanness.[2] A fish-trap, a bird-basket, and a bird-cage are not susceptible.[3]

24. 1. There are three kinds of shield: the bent shield which is susceptible to *midras*-uncleanness; the shield with which they play in the arena, which is susceptible to corpse-uncleanness; and the toy shield of the Arabs, which is not susceptible to any uncleanness.

2. There are three kinds of wagon: that made like a throne, which is susceptible to *midras*-uncleanness; that made like a bed, which is susceptible to corpse-uncleanness; and that made for carrying stones, which is not susceptible to any uncleanness.

3. There are three kinds of baking-trough: that holding from two *logs*[4] to *nine* kabs,[4] which, when split, is susceptible to *midras*-uncleanness; and the same, when whole, which is susceptible [only] to corpse-uncleanness; and that holding the prescribed measure,[5] which is not susceptible to any uncleanness.

4. There are three kinds of box: that with its opening at the side, which is susceptible to *midras*-uncleanness; that with its opening on top, which is susceptible to corpse-uncleanness; and that holding the prescribed measure, which is not susceptible to any uncleanness.

5. There are three kinds of leathern cover: that of barbers, which is susceptible to *midras*-uncleanness; that off which men eat, which is susceptible to corpse-uncleanness; and that for spreading out olives, which is not susceptible to any uncleanness.

6. There are three kinds of dais:[6] that which lies before a bed or before scriveners, which is susceptible to *midras*-uncleanness; that of a side-table,[7] which is susceptible to corpse-uncleanness; and that of a cupboard, which is not susceptible to any uncleanness.

7. There are three kinds of writing-tablet: that of papyrus, which is susceptible to *midras*-uncleanness; that which has a receptacle for wax, which is susceptible to corpse-uncleanness; and that which is polished, which is not susceptible to any uncleanness.

8. There are three kinds of bed: that used for lying upon, which is susceptible to *midras*-uncleanness; that of the glass-makers, which is susceptible to corpse-uncleanness; and that of harness-makers, which is not susceptable to any uncleanness.

9. There are three kinds of refuse-basket: that for dung,[8] which is susceptible to *midras*-uncleanness; that for straw, which is susceptible to corpse-uncleanness; and a camel's rope-bag, which is not susceptible to any uncleanness.

10. There are three kinds of mat: that used for lying upon, which is susceptible to *midras*-uncleanness; that of dyers, which is susceptible to corpse-uncleanness; and that used in winepresses, which is not susceptible to any uncleanness.

11. There are three kinds of water-skin[9] and three kinds of shepherd's wallet: those holding the prescribed quantity, which are susceptible to

---

1 As woven work. See 27[1]. Cf. 28[9].   2 As having containers.
3 They do not count as vessels with receptacles.
4 App. II, D.   5 See 15[1].   6 Heb. *basisiyah*.
7 22[1]. Its dais is also used for setting out vessels of food.   8 Shebi. 3[2].   9 Cf. 20[1].

midras-uncleanness; those that do not hold the prescribed quantity, which are susceptible to corpse-uncleanness; and those made of fish-skin, which are not susceptible to any uncleanness.

12. There are three kinds of hide:[1] that used as a rug, which is susceptible to *midras*-uncleanness; that used as a wrapper for utensils, which is susceptible to corpse-uncleanness; and that used for straps and sandals, which is not susceptible to any uncleanness.

13. There are three kinds of sheet: that used for lying upon, which is susceptible to *midras*-uncleanness; that used as a curtain, which is susceptible to corpse-uncleanness; and that whereon images are portrayed, which is not susceptible to any uncleanness.

14. There are three kinds of napkin: that for the hands, which is susceptible to *midras*-uncleanness; that for covering books, which is susceptible to corpse-uncleanness; and that used as a wrapper and that used for the harps of the sons of Levi,[2] which are not susceptible to any uncleanness.

15. There are three kinds of leathern glove:[3] that of them that hunt wild animals and birds, which is susceptible to *midras*-uncleanness; that of the locust-catcher, which is susceptible to corpse-uncleanness; and that of fruit-pickers, which is not susceptible to any uncleanness.

16. There are three kinds of head-net: that of a girl, which is susceptible to *midras*-uncleanness; that of an old woman, which is susceptible to corpse-uncleanness; and that of a harlot, which is not susceptible to any uncleanness.

17. There are three kinds of store-basket: if a worn-out basket is patched on to one that is sound, all is decided [in what concerns cleanness and uncleanness] by the sound one; if a small one is patched on to a large one, all is decided by the large one; if they are equal, all is decided by the inner one. R. Simeon says: If the cup of a balance [that was unclean] is patched on to the bottom of a cauldron on the inside, the cauldron becomes unclean; but if on the outside it remains clean. But if it is patched on to the side, whether inside or outside, it remains clean.

25. 1. In all utensils an outer and an inner part are distinguished,[4] as in mattresses, pillows, sacks, and packing-bags. So R. Judah. R. Meir says: In such as have hangers an outer and an inner part are distinguished, but in such as have not hangers an outer and an inner part are not distinguished. In a table or side-table an outer and an inner part are distinguished. So R. Judah. R. Meir says: An outer and an inner part are not distinguished. So, too, in a rimless tray.

2. In an ox-goad an outer and an inner part are distinguished; [to the outer part belongs that part of the shaft that lies between] seven handbreadths from the broad blade and four handbreadths from the point. So R. Judah. R. Meir says: [An outer and an inner part] are not distinguished: they have spoken of four and seven handbreadths only in what concerns the remnants [of an ox-goad].[5]

---

[1] Cf. 26[5].   [2] Cf. 15[6].   [3] Cf. 26[3].

[4] If the inner part is rendered unclean by an unclean liquid the outside becomes unclean also; but if the outer part is rendered unclean by an unclean liquid the inner part remains clean.

[5] That if an ox-goad was broken and four handbreadths of shaft were still joined to the pointed end, or seven to the broad blade, such is still susceptible to uncleanness as a usable implement. Cf. below, 29[7, 8].

3. In a wine-measure, an oil-measure, a soup-ladle, a mustard-strainer, and a wine-filter an outer and an inner part are distinguished. So R. Meir. R. Judah says: They are not distinguished. R. Simeon says: They are distinguished, because if the outer part contracts uncleanness the inner part remains clean; howbeit the whole vessel must be immersed.

4. If in the Quarter and Half-quarter measure[1] the Quarter contracted uncleanness, the Half-quarter does not also become unclean; if the Half-quarter contracted uncleanness the Quarter does not also become unclean. They said before R. Akiba, Since the Half-quarter counts as the outer part of the Quarter, then if the inner part of the vessel contracts uncleanness does not the outer part become unclean too? He said to them, Is this among the class of them that have precedence? Or perchance [may we not likewise say], the Quarter counts as the outer part of the Half-quarter, and if the outer part of the vessel contracts uncleanness its inner part does not also become unclean!

5. If the Quarter contracted uncleanness, the Quarter and its outer part are unclean; but the Half-quarter and its outer part remain clean. If the Half-quarter contracted uncleanness, the Half-quarter and its outer part are unclean, but the Quarter and its outer part remain clean. If the outer part of the Quarter contracted uncleanness, the outer part of the Half-quarter remains clean. So R. Meir. But the Sages say: The hinder part [of a vessel] is not divisible; and he that immerses it must immerse the whole of it.

6. If [unclean] liquid fell on to the bases, rims, hangers, or handles of vessels that have a receptacle, they need but to be dried and they are clean. But if [unclean] liquid fell on part of any other vessel (which cannot contain pomegranates)[2] in which an outer part and an inner part are not distinguished, the whole becomes unclean. If a vessel's outer part was rendered unclean by [unclean] liquid, its inner part, rims, hangers and handles remain clean. But if its inner part becomes unclean the whole is unclean.

7. In all utensils an outer part and an inner part are distinguished, and also a part by which they are held.[3] R. Tarfon says: [This applies only] to a large wooden baking-trough. R. Akiba says: To cups. R. Meir says: To unclean and clean hands.[4] R. Jose said: What they have said applies only to clean hands.

8. Thus if a man's hands were clean and the outer part of the cup was unclean, and he held it by its holding-place, he need not scruple lest his hands be made unclean by the outer part of the cup. If a man was drinking from a cup whose outer part was unclean, he need not scruple lest the liquid in his mouth be made unclean by the outer part of the cup and that so he will render the cup unclean [within]. If a kettle[5] boils none need scruple lest liquid should come out and touch the outer part and return again within.

9. In the holy vessels an outer part and an inner part are not dis-

---

[1] A single utensil, the concave bottom measuring a half quarter-*log* of liquid, and the main receptacle a quarter-*log*. The double measure is also explained as having the two receptacles side by side, like a double ink-pot. [2] Cf. 17[1].

[3] And this part does not become unclean if the outer part becomes unclean.

[4] If a man touched the outer part with unclean hands he does not render the 'holding part' unclean, and *vice versa*; or if clean hands touched one of the parts, and the other part was unclean, the hands do not become unclean. According to R. Jose it is only for this latter case that provision is made in distinguishing an outer part and a holding part.

[5] Whose outer part is unclean.

3349

tinguished,[1] nor a part by which they are held. Vessels that are used for the Hallowed Things may not be immersed while the one is within the other.[2] All articles can be rendered susceptible to uncleanness through intention;[3] and they cannot be rendered insusceptible except by an act[4] which changes their use. For an act of use can disannul both an [earlier] act of use and also an [earlier] intention; but an intention cannot disannul either a [present] act of use or a [former] intention.

26. 1. An Amki[5] sandal or a laced-up bag (R. Judah says: Also an Egyptian basket; and R. Simeon b. Gamaliel says: The same applies also to a Laodicean sandal) can be made susceptible to uncleanness and again be made insusceptible without the aid of the craftsman.[6] R. Jose said: But cannot all articles be made susceptible to uncleanness and again be made insusceptible without the aid of the craftsman?—but these, even when they are unlaced, are susceptible to uncleanness since a common person can restore them to what they were. What they have said applies only to an Egyptian basket[7] which even the craftsman cannot restore to what it was.[8]

2. If a laced-up bag has lost its laces it is still susceptible to uncleanness; but if it is made flat, it becomes insusceptible. If it had been patched below it remains susceptible. If a bag is contained within another bag and one is made unclean by an [unclean] liquid, the other does not become unclean. A pearl-pouch is susceptible to uncleanness. A money-pouch R. Eliezer declares susceptible, but the Sages declare it insusceptible.

3. The glove of a thorn-picker is not susceptible to uncleanness. The leathern girdle and leg-guards are susceptible. Leathern sleeves are susceptible, but leathern gloves are not susceptible. All finger-stalls are insusceptible excepting those of fruit-pickers, since such are used to hold sumach-berries; but if they are torn and cannot hold the greater part of a sumach-berry they become insusceptible to uncleanness.

4. If one of the straps of a sandal [that had contracted *midras*-uncleanness] was torn off and mended again, it retains its *midras*-uncleanness. If the second strap was torn off and mended again it becomes free from *midras*-uncleanness, but it remains unclean from contact with *midras*-uncleanness. If the second was torn off before the first strap could be mended, it becomes clean. If the heel was torn off or if the toe-piece was taken away, or if it was torn in two, the sandal becomes clean. Heelless slippers that are torn anywhere become clean. If a shoe was so damaged that it could not contain the greater part of the foot, it becomes clean. A shoe that is still on the last R. Eliezer declares insusceptible to uncleanness, but the Sages declare it susceptible. Water-skins [that have been pierced because of their uncleanness and] that have been tied up again with a knot, are not susceptible to uncleanness, excepting those tied up with an Arab knot. R. Meir says: If [they are tied up] with a knot that will not endure, they are insusceptible to

---

1 i.e. if the outer part is unclean the inner side becomes unclean also. Cf. Par. 12[8].
2 See Hag. 3[1]. One of the vessels may thus hinder access of water to part of the other vessel.
3 Cf. Kel. 17[15]; 26[7, 8]. If, e.g., a man took the ring round the neck of a beast (cf. 12[1]) intending to use it for a man.
4 The intention is not enough.   5 North-east of Acre. Cf. Josh. 19[27].
6 They are in themselves flat objects, and so insusceptible; but they can be laced or sewn up to form a receptacle, so becoming susceptible, and again unlaced or unsewn, becoming again insusceptible.
7 Or, 'basket of palm-twigs' or rushes. Cf. Shab. 20[2]; Sot. 2[1]; 3[1].
8 Once the binding strips have been unloosed.

uncleanness; but if with a knot that will endure they remain susceptible.[1] R. Jose says: All water-skins that have been tied up with a knot are insusceptible to uncleanness.

5. These hides[2] are susceptible to *midras*-uncleanness: a hide that it is intended to use as a rug, a tanner's apron, the hide used as the lower covering of a bed,[3] a hide used by an ass-driver or flax-worker or porter or physician,[4] a hide used for a cot, or a hide put over a child's heart,[5] and the hide of a mattress or cushion; [all these are susceptible to] *midras*-uncleanness. A hide used to wrap up combed wool and a hide worn by the wool-comber R. Eliezer declares susceptible to *midras*-uncleanness, but the Sages declare them susceptible [only] to corpse-uncleanness.

6. A leathern bag or wrapper for garments is susceptible to *midras*-uncleanness. A leathern bag or wrapper for purple wool the School of Shammai declare susceptible to *midras*-uncleanness, and the School of Hillel declare it susceptible [only] to corpse-uncleanness. A hide used as a covering for utensils is not susceptible to uncleanness; but if it is used for weights[6] it is susceptible; but R. Jose, in the name of his father, declares it insusceptible.

7. What suffers no lack in its readiness for use, intention to use it makes it susceptible to uncleanness; but what suffers any lack in its readiness for use, intention to use it does not make it susceptible to uncleanness, excepting only fur skins.[7]

8. Intention to use them makes hides belonging to a householder susceptible to uncleanness, but intention does not make hides belonging to a tanner susceptible; intention makes those taken by a thief susceptible, but intention does not make those taken by a robber susceptible.[8] R. Simeon says: The rule is to the contrary:[9] intention makes those taken by a robber susceptible, but intention does not make those taken by a thief susceptible, since the owner still cherishes hope of regaining them.

9. If a hide had contracted *midras*-uncleanness, and a man had the intention to use it for straps and sandals, so soon as he puts the knife into it it becomes clean. So R. Judah. But the Sages say: Not until he has reduced its size to less than five handbreadths. R. Eliezer b. R. Zadok says: Even if a man made a napkin from [such] a hide, it remains unclean;[10] but if from a pillow, it becomes clean.

27. 1. Cloth is susceptible to uncleanness by virtue of five things,[11] sacking by virtue of four, leather by virtue of three, wood by virtue of two, and an earthenware vessel by virtue of one. An earthenware vessel is susceptible to uncleanness in that it is a vessel having a receptacle. In all earthenware vessels that have no inner part, no regard is paid to their outer part.[12] [What is made from] wood is, moreover, susceptible to uncleanness in that it may be sat upon; thus a plate that has no rim is susceptible to uncleanness if it is of wood but insusceptible if it is of earthenware. [What is made

1 Cf. Eduy. 5[1].   2 Cf. above, 24[12].   3 Cf. above, 16[4].
4 A protection against blood.   5 A protection against cats.
6 To prevent them rubbing. Such a hide forms cavities by use.
7 It can be used without any trimming or treatment.
8 The difference is that the thief steals secretly and the robber openly; recovery from the former is impossible since he is not known.
9 There is less hope of recovery from the robber since he is the stronger of the two.
10 Since the change in use is but slight.
11 Lit. 'names' or categories.
12 Cf. above, 2[3]; 25[1].

from] leather is, moreover, susceptible to uncleanness by overshadowing.[1] [What is made from] sacking[2] is, moreover, susceptible to uncleanness in that it is woven work. [What is made from] cloth is, moreover, susceptible to uncleanness when it is but three fingerbreadths square.

2. Cloth that is three handbreadths square is susceptible to *midras*-uncleanness, and to corpse-uncleanness when it is three fingerbreadths square. Sacking four handbreadths square, leather five handbreadths square, and matting six handbreadths square are susceptible both to *midras*-uncleanness and to corpse-uncleanness alike. R. Meir says: Sacking [is susceptible to uncleanness] when there still remains of it four handbreadths, and in its first condition [it becomes susceptible] so soon as its manufacture is complete.

3. If a man used together two handbreadths of cloth and one of sacking; or three handbreadths of sacking and one of leather; or four handbreadths of leather and one of matting, it is not susceptible to uncleanness. But if he used five handbreadths of matting and one of leather; or four handbreadths of leather and one of sacking; or three handbreadths of sacking and one of cloth, it is susceptible to uncleanness. This is the general rule: If to one stuff another stuff is joined to which greater stringency applies, it[3] becomes susceptible to uncleanness; but if to one stuff another stuff is joined to which lesser stringency applies, it does not become susceptible.

4. If from any of these [four stuffs] a piece one square handbreadth was cut, it is susceptible[4] to uncleanness. If from the bottom of a basket a piece one square handbreadth was cut, it is susceptible to uncleanness; but if [it was cut off] from the sides of a basket, R. Simeon declares it not susceptible, but the Sages say: No matter where the square handbreadth is cut off it is susceptible to uncleanness.

5. If worn-out pieces of a sifter or sieve were fashioned for use as a seat, R. Akiba declares them susceptible to uncleanness, but the Sages declare them insusceptible unless their rough ends are cut off. A child's stool that has legs, even if it is less than a handbreadth high, is susceptible to uncleanness. A child's shirt, however small, R. Eliezer declares susceptible; but the Sages say: Only if it is of the prescribed size; and it should be measured double.

6. These are measured double: socks, long stockings, drawers, caps, and money-belts. If a patch is sewn on the hem,[5] if it is undoubled it is measured undoubled; if it is doubled it is measured double.

7. If a man wove cloth three handbreadths square and it contracted *midras*-uncleanness, and he finished the piece of cloth,[6] if he then took away one thread from the first part it becomes free[7] of *midras*-uncleanness but unclean from contact with *midras*-uncleanness. If he [first] took away one thread from the first part and afterward finished the whole piece of cloth, it is [still] unclean from contact with *midras*-uncleanness.

8. So, too, if a man wove cloth three fingerbreadths square and it con-

---

[1] Or being itself overshadowed. App. IV. 6; p. 649, n. 3; Lev. 11³²; Num. 19¹⁴.

[2] Made of goat-hair or hair of other animals.

[3] The total area, when it equals that prescribed as susceptible in the case of the stuff to which the lesser stringency applies. Cf. Meil. 4⁶.

[4] As something to be sat on. If it was cut off to be lain on it is not susceptible unless it is the size prescribed in par. 2 for the several stuffs.   [5] The neck-band.

[6] Some texts add: 'the whole piece of cloth contracts *midras*-uncleanness'.

[7] Since the first portion is now less than the measure prescribed as susceptible to *midras*-uncleanness.

tracted corpse-uncleanness, and he finished the whole piece of cloth,[1] if he then took away one thread from the first part, it becomes free[2] from corpse-uncleanness, but unclean from contact with corpse-uncleanness. If he [first] took away one thread from the first part and afterward finished the whole piece of cloth, it becomes clean, for they have said, 'If a piece three fingerbreadths square is lessened, it becomes clean'. But if a piece three handbreadths square is lessened, though it is not susceptible to *midras*-uncleanness it is susceptible to any other uncleanness.

9. If a sheet that had contracted *midras*-uncleanness was used as a curtain,[3] it becomes free of *midras*-uncleanness but remains unclean from contact with *midras*-uncleanness. R. Jose said: What *midras*-uncleanness has it touched![4] but if so be that one with a flux had touched it,[5] then it will be unclean from contact with one with a flux.

10. If a piece of cloth three handbreadths square [that had contracted *midras*-uncleanness] was divided, it is free of *midras*-uncleanness, but unclean from contact with *midras*-uncleanness. R. Jose said: What *midras*-uncleanness has it touched!—but if so be that one with a flux had touched it, then it will be unclean from contact with one with a flux.

11. If a piece of cloth three handbreadths square was found on a dungheap [it is susceptible to *midras*-uncleanness] if it was both sound and able to wrap up salt; but if it was found in the house [it is susceptible to *midras*-uncleanness] if it is either sound or able to wrap up salt. How much salt should it be able to wrap up? A quarter-*kab*.[6] R. Judah says: Fine salt.[7] But the Sages say: Coarse salt. Both were minded to give the more lenient ruling.[8] R. Simeon says: A piece three handbreadths square found on a dungheap is [in effect] equal to a piece three fingerbreadths square found in the house.[9]

12. If a piece of cloth three handbreadths square was torn[10] and put on a stool, and the flesh [of him that sits on it] touches the stool, it is not susceptible to uncleanness; but if it does not touch the stool it is susceptible. If from a piece of cloth three fingerbreadths square one thread was worn away, or if a knot was found in it, or if two threads ran alongside each other, it is not susceptible to uncleanness. If a piece of stuff three fingerbreadths square was thrown on the dungheap, it is not susceptible to uncleanness. If it was brought back again it becomes susceptible. Throwing it away always renders it insusceptible to uncleanness, and bringing it back renders it again susceptible, save only purple or fine crimson stuff.[11] R. Eliezer says: The same applies also to a patch of new cloth. R. Simeon says: They all[12] become insusceptible: these were spoken of only concerning the obligation to return lost property.[13]

---

[1] Some texts add: 'the whole piece of cloth contracts corpse-uncleanness'.
[2] Since it is less than the measure prescribed as susceptible.
[3] See above, 20[6].
[4] He holds that in its present form, in which it is not susceptible to *midras*-uncleanness, it is in no way unclean from *midras*-uncleanness.
[5] With his naked flesh, and had not merely exerted pressure (*midras*) on it.
[6] App. II, D.
[7] It is the heavier, but coarse salt is more likely to tear the stuff.
[8] That only the stronger material was susceptible.
[9] And is only susceptible to corpse-uncleanness.
[10] Less than half way across. See 28[8].
[11] Which, even thrown away on the dungheap, remain susceptible.
[12] Even purple and fine crimson.
[13] See B.M. 2[1]. If any one finds them he may not keep them until he has discovered whether they have any claimant.

28. 1. If a piece of cloth three fingerbreadths square[1] was used to stuff a ball or was itself made into a ball, it becomes clean; but if a piece three handbreadths square[2] was used to stuff a ball it remains unclean;[3] if it was itself made into a ball it becomes clean, since the sewing diminishes it.

2. If a piece of cloth less than three handbreadths square was used to block up [a hole in] the bath-house or [to hold and] empty out a cooking-pot, or to wipe the mill-stones, whether it was kept in readiness [for such use] or whether it was not kept in readiness, it is susceptible to uncleanness.[4] So R. Eliezer. R. Joshua says: Whether it was kept in readiness or whether it was not kept in readiness, it is not susceptible. R. Akiba says: If it was kept in readiness it is susceptible to uncleanness; if it was not kept in readiness it is not susceptible.

3. If a man made a plaster of cloth or leather, it is not susceptible to uncleanness.[5] If he made a poultice of cloth it is not susceptible to uncleanness; but if of leather it is susceptible. Rabban Simeon b. Gamaliel says: Even if of cloth it is susceptible, since [the contents, when they are dried] can be shaken off [and it can be used again].

4. Scroll-wrappers, whether figures are portrayed on them or not, are susceptible to uncleanness. So the School of Shammai. And the School of Hillel say: If figures are portrayed on them they are not susceptible to uncleanness;[6] if figures are not portrayed on them they are susceptible. Rabban Gamaliel says: In either case they are not susceptible to uncleanness.

5. If a head-wrap that had contracted *midras*-uncleanness was used to wrap around a scroll it becomes free of *midras*-uncleanness but it remains susceptible to corpse-uncleanness. If a water-skin was used as a rug, or if a leathern rug was used as a water-skin, it becomes clean. If a water-skin was used as a shepherd's wallet or a shepherd's wallet as a water-skin; or if a mattress was used as a sheet, or a sheet as a mattress; or if a cushion [-cover] was used as a napkin or a napkin as a cushion[-cover], they remain unclean. This is the general rule: If an article's use is changed into a use of like category, it remains unclean; but if into a use of different category, it becomes clean.

6. If a patch [three handbreadths square that had contracted *midras*-uncleanness] was sewn on to a basket, the basket can convey uncleanness at a first remove and render [Heave-offering] invalid at a second remove.[7] If the patch was then severed from the basket,[8] the basket can convey uncleanness at one remove and render [Heave-offering] invalid at a second remove; but the patch is clean.[9] If it is sewn on to cloth,[10] the cloth can

---

[1] That had contracted corpse-uncleanness.
[2] That had contracted *midras*-uncleanness.
[3] It may still be used for its former purpose.   [4] Other than *midras*-uncleanness.
[5] Its condition is too filthy for further use. Some texts here add: 'R. Jose says: If on leather it is not susceptible', apparently copied from par. 6 below.
[6] Since the embroidery proves that the wrappers were for ornament only and not for use.
[7] See App. IV. 17 b. The basket suffers 'first-grade uncleanness' and can make food unclean by 'second-grade uncleanness', and affect Heave-offering at one further remove, thereby rendering it invalid.
[8] It is as though any other part of the basket was severed. So that the basket's degree of uncleanness remains unchanged.
[9] Since a piece from the side of a basket is not susceptible, unless it was intended to sit on it; cf. above, p. 644, n. 4.
[10] Which is itself susceptible to *midras*-uncleanness. This cloth itself becomes a 'father of uncleanness'. After the patch is removed it remains unclean from contact with *midras*-uncleanness.

convey uncleanness at two removes and render [Heave-offering] invalid at a third remove. If the patch was then severed from the cloth, the cloth can convey uncleanness at one remove and render [Heave-offering] invalid at a second remove; and the patch can convey uncleanness at two removes and render [Heave-offering] invalid at a third remove. So, too, if the patch was sewn on to sacking or leather. So R. Meir. R. Simeon declares them clean.[1] R. Jose says: If [the patch was sewn] on leather, it is clean, but if on sacking it is unclean, since this is woven stuff.

7. The measurement three fingerbreadths square of which they have spoken does not include a hem. So R. Simeon. But the Sages say: It means three fingerbreadths square exactly. If a patch [three handbreadths square that had contracted *midras*-uncleanness] was sewn on to [other] cloth by [but] one of its [four] sides, this does not serve as a connective;[2] if it was sewn on by its two opposite sides, it serves as a connective. If it was sewn *gamma*-wise,[3] R. Akiba declares [the cloth] unclean, but the Sages declare it clean. R. Judah said: This[4] applies only in the case of a cloak;[5] but in the case of a shirt[6] if the patch was so sewn on above it serves as a connective, but if underneath it does not serve as a connective.[7]

8. The pieces of cloth [in the garments] of poor folk, even if none measures three fingerbreadths square, are susceptible to *midras*-uncleanness. If a man had begun to tear a cloak [that had contracted uncleanness], so soon as the greater part is torn the halves are not deemed to be bound together.[8] The rules touching cloth that measures three fingerbreadths square do not apply to cloth that is very thick or very thin.[9]

9. A porter's pad[10] is susceptible to *midras*-uncleanness. A wine-filter[11] is not susceptible to uncleanness as a thing that is sat upon. An old woman's head-net[12] is susceptible to uncleanness in that it can be sat upon. A harlot's shift that is made like network is not susceptible to uncleanness. If a garment is made out of a fishing-net it is not susceptible to uncleanness; if out of its network bag, it is susceptible. R. Eliezer b. Jacob says: Also if a garment is made of a fishing-net and made double, it is susceptible to uncleanness.

10. If a man made a head-net beginning with the hem,[13] it remains insusceptible to uncleanness until he finishes the bottom part; if he began with the bottom part it remains insusceptible until he finishes the hem. Its head-band is susceptible to uncleanness in itself. Its strings are susceptible in that they are connectives. If a head-net is torn and cannot contain the greater part of the hair it is not susceptible to uncleanness.

29. 1. The fringes[14] of a sheet, neckcloth, head-wrap, or cap [serve as

---

[1] It is a different species of stuff, therefore the same conditions apply as when it was sewn on to a basket.   [2] Therefore the other cloth remains clean.

[3] By two of its adjacent sides, forming a *gamma*, or a right angle.

[4] That, being sewn by but one side, it forms no connective.

[5] With which a man may wrap himself round while it is upside-down.

[6] Always worn with the same side uppermost.

[7] In the former case it hangs down and covers the rent, but not in the latter case.

[8] The garment is deemed completely torn and unfit for its purpose, and therefore clean. Bert. and Tif. Yis. understand the passage to mean that if one fragment becomes unclean the other remains clean.

[9] e.g. felt or fine linen.   [10] That protects his head or shoulders.

[11] A piece of felt.

[12] But cf. above, 24[16]. Here it is explained as a net that is intended for sitting on.

[13] That part that goes round the forehead.

[14] The warp threads left hanging at opposite ends after a length of stuff is woven.

connectives] [up to a length of] six fingerbreadths;[1] those of an under-garment [to a length of] ten fingerbreadths; the fringes of a thick cloak, a veil, a shirt, or mantle [to the length of] three fingerbreadths; the fringes of an old woman's head-cloth, an Arab's mouth-wrap, a Cilician goat-hair cloth, a money-belt, turban, or curtain [serve as connectives] whatsoever their length.

2. Three woollen cushions, or six linen cushions, or three sheets, or twelve napkins, or two arm-cloths, or one shirt, or one cloak, or one winter cloak serve as connectives both when they contract uncleanness and when they are sprinkled;[2] if they are more in number than this, they serve as connectives when they contract uncleanness, but not when they are sprinkled. R. Jose says: Nor even when they contract uncleanness.

3. The cord[3] of a plummet [serves as a connective up to a length of] twelve handbreadths; that of a carpenter's plummet, up to eighteen; that of a builder's plummet, up to fifty cubits. What is more than this, even if a man is minded to leave it so,[4] is not susceptible to uncleanness. The cord of the plummet of plasterers or moulders [is susceptible to uncleanness] whatsoever its length.

4. The cord that holds the balances of goldsmiths or dealers in fine purple [serves as a connective up to a length of] three fingerbreadths. [The length] behind [the grip in] the haft of an axe [that serves as a connective] is three fingerbreadths; but R. Jose says: If there is as much as one hand-breadth [behind the grip] it is not susceptible to uncleanness.

5. The cord that holds the balances of shopkeepers or householders [serves as a connective up to a length of] one handbreadth. [The length] in front of [the grip in] the haft of an axe [that serves as a connective] is one handbreadth; of the shaft of a pair of compasses, one handbreadth; of the shaft of a stonemason's chisel, one handbreadth.

6. The cord that holds the balances of wool-dealers and glass-weighers [serves as a connective up to a length of] two handbreadths; [the length of] the shaft of a millstone chisel [that serves as a connective] is two handbreadths; of the battle-axe of the legions, two handbreadths; of a goldsmith's hammer, two handbreadths; of a blacksmith's hammer, two handbreadths.

7. The length of the remnants [of the shaft] above the point of an ox-goad [that serves as a connective] is four handbreadths;[5] of the shaft of a spade, four handbreadths; of the shaft of a weeding-spade, five handbreadths; of the shaft of a small hammer, five handbreadths; of a common hammer, six handbreadths; of the shaft of an axe used to split wood or to dig, six hand-breadths; and of the shaft of a stone-trimmer's axe, six handbreadths.

8. The length of the remnants [of the shaft] below the broad blade of the ox-goad [that serves as a connective] is seven handbreadths;[5] of the shaft of a householder's trowel—the School of Shammai say seven, and the School of Hillel say eight handbreadths; of the shaft of a plasterer's trowel

---

[1] If uncleanness touched any portion beyond this length the uncleanness is not conveyed to the main portion of the article.

[2] If such were stitched together by the washerman, or kept combined in the weaving, and one suffered uncleanness, the others suffer uncleanness also; and if they were sprinkled with the Sin-offering water (Num. 19[18]) to free them from corpse-uncleanness, if one was made clean the others are made clean also.

[3] In the following cases that length of cord (or of handle-shaft) which is essential in use serves as a connective and is susceptible to uncleanness.

[4] i.e. in his opinion such greater length was necessary in practice.   [5] Cf. above, 25[2].

—the School of Shammai say nine, and the School of Hillel say ten hand-breadths. If there is left more than this and a man is minded to leave it so, it is still susceptible to uncleanness. The shafts of fire implements, what-soever their length, [are susceptible to uncleanness].

30. 1. Utensils[1] of glass that are flat are not susceptible to uncleanness. If they form a receptacle they are susceptible. After they are broken they become clean, but if again utensils are made of them they once more become susceptible to uncleanness. A glass plate or a flat dish are not susceptible to uncleanness; if they have a rim they are susceptible. If the [broken] bottoms of a glass bowl or plate were fashioned to some use, they remain insusceptible to uncleanness. If they were scraped or filed they become susceptible.

2. A mirror is not susceptible to uncleanness; a tray that has been turned into a mirror is still susceptible, but if it was made for a mirror in the beginning it is not susceptible. If a [glass] spoon when laid on the table can hold aught soever it is susceptible to uncleanness; if it can hold nothing, R. Akiba declares it susceptible, but R. Johanan b. Nuri declares it not susceptible.

3. If the greater part of a [glass] cup is broken off it is not susceptible to uncleanness; if it was broken in three [places, extending] over the greater part of it, it is not susceptible to uncleanness. R. Simeon says: If it lets the greater part of the water leak out, it is not susceptible to uncleanness. If there was a hole in it, and it was mended with tin or pitch, it is still insusceptible. R. Jose says: If with tin it is susceptible; if with pitch it is not susceptible.

4. If a small flask has lost its neck it is still susceptible to uncleanness;[2] but if a large one has lost its neck it is not susceptible. If a flask of spike-nard oil has lost its neck, it is not susceptible to uncleanness, since it scratches the hand. If large [glass] flagons have lost their necks, they are still susceptible to uncleanness since they can be made to hold pickled produce. A glass mill-funnel always continues 'clean'.

R. Jose said: Blessed art thou, O Kelim, for thou didst enter in in un-cleanness, but art gone forth in cleanness!

OHOLOTH[3] ('TENTS')

1. 1. [Sometimes] two things contract uncleanness from a corpse, one of them seven-day uncleanness and the other evening-uncleanness; [some-times] three things contract uncleanness from a corpse, two of them seven-day uncleanness and the third evening-uncleanness; [sometimes] four

---

[1] Cf. 2¹; 15¹.   [2] It is still usable since liquids can be carried in it, although it is not used as a drinking-utensil.

[3] Lit. 'tents' or 'overshadowings'. The tractate assumes the following principles: (a) From Num. 19¹⁴ it is inferred that all (men and utensils) who are under the same 'tent' or roof as a corpse (i.e. a dead human body or a part of it), or who are overshadowed by something which also overshadows a corpse (and the same also applies to a person or utensil which overshadows or is overshadowed by a corpse) suffer corpse-uncleanness and remain unclean for seven days. (b) Num. 19²² enjoins that whatever touches that which suffers corpse-uncleanness is unclean until evening. (c) From the, apparently superfluous, use of 'sword' in Num. 19¹⁶ it is inferred that the sword suffers the same degree of uncleanness as the dead body which it has touched; therefore as a corpse can convey seven-day uncleanness, so the sword (and by inference any other utensil—except an earthenware vessel—which has touched the corpse) can convey seven-day uncleanness. (d) Like as the utensil which touches the corpse suffers the same degree of uncleanness, so the utensil which touches him who has

things contract uncleanness from a corpse, three of them seven-day uncleanness and the fourth evening-uncleanness. How [does this befall] the two things? If a man touches a corpse[1] he contracts seven-day uncleanness, and if a man touches him[2] he contracts evening-uncleanness.[3]

2. How [does this befall] the three things? If vessels touch a corpse, and vessels touch these vessels,[4] they all contract seven-day uncleanness; the third, be it man or vessel, [that touches these] contracts evening-uncleanness.[5]

3. How [does this befall] the four things? If vessels touch a corpse and a man touches the vessels, and then vessels touch this man, they all contract seven-day uncleanness;[6] the fourth, be it man or vessel, [that touches these] contracts evening-uncleanness. R. Akiba said: I can cite a case where a fifth [can contract uncleanness]: if a [metal] tent-peg was stuck into the tent,[7] the tent, the peg, the man that touches the peg, and the vessels that touch the man contract seven-day uncleanness; and the fifth, be it man or vessel, [that touches these] contracts evening-uncleanness. They said to him: The tent cannot be included in the reckoning.

4. Both men and vessels can contract uncleanness from a corpse. This may bear with greater stringency on men than on vessels, and it may also bear with greater stringency on vessels than on men. [Thus] if vessels [first touched the corpse] three things[8] [in all can contract uncleanness], but if a man [first touched the corpse] only two[9] [in all can contract uncleanness]. It may bear with greater stringency on men in that when a man intervenes, four things[10] [in all] can contract uncleanness, but when he does not intervene only three things [in all can contract uncleanness].

5. Men and garments can contract uncleanness from a man that has a flux.[11] This may bear with greater stringency on men than on garments, and it may also bear with greater stringency on garments than on men. [Thus] if a man touched him that has a flux he renders garments unclean,[12] but the garments which touch him that has a flux do not render other garments unclean.[13] And it may bear with greater stringency on garments, in that the garments that carry him[14] that has a flux can render a man un-

---

touched a corpse suffers his degree of uncleanness. This is an exception to the rule that uncleanness, when it is transferred, becomes uncleanness of a lower grade. (e) In 'the tent wherein lies a corpse', passage for the uncleanness is afforded by any aperture every dimension of which is not less than one handbreadth. (f) If the uncleanness has no such egress, but is in a confined space of less than one cubic handbreadth's capacity, it will cleave through solid matter, but only perpendicularly upwards and downwards. (g) If the confined space is of one cubic handbreadth's capacity the uncleanness is regarded as being within a closed-up grave, with the result that its uncleanness spreads to everything in every direction until it comes to a space of more than one cubic handbreadth's capacity. (h) If the uncleanness is in the open air it 'cleaves perpendicularly upwards', and downwards only to ground level (or until it is stopped by a valid screen—cf. 8[1]). (i) In a 'tent' the uncleanness is not confined to the contained space, but it penetrates to everything underground below the space of the tent. [1] Num. 19[16]. [2] Num. 19[22].

[3] The corpse itself is a 'father of fathers of uncleanness'; what it touches becomes itself a 'father of uncleanness', and what touches this suffers 'derived uncleanness' ('first-grade uncleanness' or 'uncleanness at a first remove'). But if the third party touched the second while the second was still in contact with the corpse, the third party also counts as a 'father of uncleanness'. [4] See p. 649, n. 3 (c).

[5] In virtue of Num. 19[22]. [6] See p. 649, n. 3 (d).

[7] Which, like the corpse, is a 'father of fathers of uncleanness'; and the peg counts as part of the tent. [8] See par. 2.

[9] See par. 1 (end). [10] See par. 3. [11] See App. IV. 1 a, 3 a.

[12] Such time as he is in contact with him that has a flux.

[13] They suffer only 'derived uncleanness', and only 'fathers of uncleanness' can convey uncleanness to men and garments (or utensils).

[14] i.e. what he sits on. They are (App. IV. 3) 'fathers of uncleanness'.

clean, but a man that carries him that has a flux cannot render other men unclean.

6. A man conveys uncleanness [as a corpse] only after his soul is gone forth; even when he is mortally wounded[1] or in the last death-agony [he is still deemed to be living and] he can bind [his childless brother's widow] to the obligation of levirate narriage,[2] and he can free her[3] from the obligation; he can qualify[4] [a woman] to eat of Heave-offering and he can disqualify[5] [a woman] from eating of Heave-offering. So, too, cattle and wild animals convey uncleanness only after their soul is gone forth. If their heads have been cut off, even if their limbs still jerk, they become unclean —like the lizard whose tail still jerks [after it is cut off].

7. The members[6] [of the body] have no prescribed bulk: even less than an olive's bulk of a corpse, and less than an olive's bulk of carrion, or less than a lentil's bulk of a creeping thing, suffice to convey their several uncleannesses.[7]

8. There are 248 members in a man: thirty in the foot, six to every toe, ten in the ankle, two in the lower leg, five in the knee, one in the thigh, three in the hip, eleven ribs, thirty members in the hand, six to every finger, two in the fore-arm, two in the elbow, one in the upper arm, and four in the shoulder, [thus there are] 101 on the one side [of the body] and 101 on the other; also there are eighteen links in the spine, nine members in the neck, eight in the neck, six in the breast,[8] and five in the holes. Each single member can convey uncleanness by contact, by carrying, and by overshadowing. Howbeit this applies only when they bear their proper flesh; if they do not bear their proper flesh they convey uncleanness by contact and by carrying but they do not convey uncleanness by overshadowing.

2. 1. These[9] convey uncleanness by overshadowing: a corpse, or an olive's bulk [of the flesh] of a corpse, or an olive's bulk of corpse-dregs,[10] or a ladleful[11] of corpse-mould, or the backbone, or the skull, or any [severed] member of a corpse or any [severed] member from a living man that still bears its proper flesh, or a quarter-kab[12] from the larger bones or the greater number of the bones; and the greater part of a corpse, or the greater number of its members, even if they are less than a quarter-kab, are unclean. How many is 'the greater number'? A hundred and twenty-five.

2. A quarter-log[13] of blood,[14] a quarter-log of mingled blood[15] from the one corpse (R. Akiba says: Even from two corpses), the blood of a new-born child all of which has flowed out (R. Akiba says: Any quantity soever. But the Sages say: A quarter-kab). An olive's bulk of a living or a dead

---

[1] Lit. 'has his tendons cut'. Cf. Yeb. 16[3].   [2] See p. 218, n. 1.
[3] If he was the sole son he still has power to save his widowed mother from the obligation of marrying her dead father's brother.
[4] If his mother (the daughter of a non-priest) was married to a priest who died, if she had a son by him she has the right to eat of Heave-offering (cf. Yeb. 7[1ff]).
[5] If his mother (the daughter of a priest) was married to a non-priest who died, if she had a son by him she may not return to her father's house, there to eat of Heave-offering.
[6] A portion of a body that still retains its proper flesh, bones, and sinews.
[7] In the manner peculiar to them—the member of a corpse by contact, carrying, and overshadowing; a member from carrion by contact and carrying; and a member of a creeping thing by contact.
[8] Lit. 'key of the heart'.
[9] Cf. Naz. 7[2].   [10] Flesh that has rotted and liquefied and then congealed.
[11] See Kel. 17[12].   [12] App. II, D.   [13] App. II, D.
[14] That has issued after death.   [15] See below, 3[5].

worm [from a corpse] R. Eliezer declares unclean like the flesh of the corpse, but the Sages declare it clean. The ash of burnt corpses R. Eliezer declares unclean if it is a quarter-*kab* in quantity, but the Sages declare it clean. A ladleful and more of grave-dust[1] is unclean; but R. Simeon declares it clean. If a ladleful of corpse-mould is kneaded with water it does not serve as a connective for uncleanness.[2]

3. These convey uncleanness by contact and carrying, but not by over-shadowing: a barleycorn's bulk of bone, earth from a foreign country, [earth from] a grave-area,[3] a member from a corpse or a member from a living man that no longer bears its proper flesh, a backbone or a skull in which aught is lacking. How much must be lacking in the backbone?[4] The School of Shammai say: Two links. And the School of Hillel say: Even one link. And in the skull? The School of Shammai say: As much as [a hole made by] a drill. And the School of Hillel say: So much that, if it was taken from a living man, he would die.[5] Of what kind of drill did they speak? A physician's small drill. So R. Meir. But the Sages say: The large drill that lay in a chamber in the Temple.[6]

4. The stone that seals a grave[7] and its buttressing stone convey un-cleanness by contact and by overshadowing but not by carrying. R. Eliezer says: They convey uncleanness by carrying. R. Joshua says: If there is grave-dust beneath them they convey uncleanness by carrying, otherwise they do not convey uncleanness by carrying. What is the buttressing stone? That against which the stone leans that seals the grave. But a stone that serves as a buttress to the buttressing stone is clean.

5. If these lack aught of the prescribed measure they are clean: an olive's bulk [of the flesh] of a corpse, an olive's bulk of corpse-dregs, a ladleful of corpse-mould, a quarter-*log* of blood, a barleycorn's bulk of bone, and a member from a living man of which aught of the bone is lacking.

6. A backbone or a skull [made up from the bones] of two corpses, a quarter-*log* of blood from two corpses, a quarter-*kab* of bones from two corpses, a member from a corpse or from a living man [that is made up] from two corpses or from two [living] men, these R. Akiba declares unclean, but the Sages declare them clean.

7. If a barleycorn's bulk of bone is divided into two, R. Akiba declares it unclean, but R. Johanan b. Nuri declares it clean. R. Johanan b. Nuri said: They did not say 'bones' of a barleycorn's bulk, but 'a bone'[8] of a barleycorn's bulk. If a quarter-*kab* of bones has been crushed so fine that there is no piece left of a barleycorn's bulk, R. Simeon declares it clean, but the Sages declare it unclean. If a member from a living man is divided into two, it is clean. R. Jose declares it unclean; but he agrees that if it is taken away by halves it is clean.

3. 1. If[9] aught that conveys uncleanness by overshadowing was divided and brought into a house, R. Dosa b. Harkinas declares clean [whatsoever

---

[1] Some texts read: 'a ladleful of corpse-mould and some grave-dust'.
[2] So that if part of it was overshadowed it is not as though the whole were overshadowed, since (see below, 3⁴) 'connexion effected by the hands of men does not count as a connexion'.
[3] See below, 17¹ff; App. IV. 19 c.
[4] So that it shall not convey uncleanness by overshadowing.
[5] Defined as a portion equal to the size of a *sela*, or the third of a handbreadth.
[6] See Kel. 17¹².   [7] Erub. 1⁷; Naz. 7³; Ohol. 15⁹. Lit. 'such that can be rolled'.
[8] Cf. Shab. 9²; Sanh. 4⁵.   [9] Eduy. 3¹.

is found in the house], but the Sages declare it unclean. Thus if a man touched or carried two pieces of carrion, each a half-olive's bulk; or if he touched one half-olive's bulk of a corpse and overshadowed another half-olive's bulk; or if he touched one half-olive's bulk and another half-olive's bulk overshadowed him; or if he overshadowed two [pieces each of a] half-olive's bulk; or if he overshadowed one half-olive's bulk and another half-olive's bulk overshadowed him—R. Dosa b. Harkinas declares him clean, but the Sages declare him unclean. But if he touched one half-olive's bulk and some other thing overshadowed both him and another half-olive's bulk; or if he overshadowed a half-olive's bulk and some other thing overshadowed both him and another half-olive's bulk, he remains clean. R. Meir said: Here, too, R. Dosa b. Harkinas declared him clean and the Sages declared him unclean. All such conditions render a man unclean save where there is both contact and carrying, or both carrying and overshadowing. This is the general rule: If the means of conveying the uncleanness fall within a single category[1] they convey uncleanness; but if within two categories they do not convey uncleanness.

2. If a ladleful of corpse-mould was strewed about in a house, the house is unclean; but R. Simeon declares it clean. If a quarter-*log* of blood was soaked up in a house the house is clean. If it was soaked up in a garment and, when this was washed, a quarter-*log* of blood came from it, it is unclean;[2] otherwise it is clean, since aught that is soaked up and cannot come forth is clean.

3. If it[3] was poured out in an open place and on an incline, and a man overshadowed part of it, he remains clean; but if it was in a hollow, or if the blood congealed, he becomes unclean. If the blood was poured out over the threshold and this inclined inwards or outwards, and the house overshadowed [part of] it, aught found in the house remains clean; but if [the threshold was] in a hollow place or if the blood congealed, it becomes unclean. Whatsoever pertains to a corpse is unclean excepting the teeth, the hair, and the nails; but so long as they are joined to the corpse they are all unclean.

4. Thus if the corpse lay outside and its hair [stretched] inside, the house is unclean. If of a bone that bore an olive's bulk of flesh a part was brought within and the house overshadowed it, the house becomes unclean; if of two bones that bore each a half-olive's bulk of flesh a part was brought within and the house overshadowed them, the house becomes unclean;[4] but if [the pieces of flesh] were stuck on by the hands of men, it remains clean, since a connexion effected by the hands of men does not count as a connexion.

5. What counts as 'mingled blood?'[5] [Blood from] a corpse from which an eighth part of a *log* issued while he was yet alive and an eighth part after his death. So R. Akiba. But R. Ishmael says: [Blood of which] a quarter-*log* [issued] while he was yet alive and a quarter after his death, and a quarter-*log* was taken from the two together. R. Eleazar b. R. Judah says: These both alike are but as water. What counts as 'mingled blood?' If beneath a man that was crucified, whose blood gushes out, there was found

---

[1] Overshadowing only, or contact only, or carrying only.
[2] And renders the house unclean by overshadowing. Texts vary in making 'it' the blood or the garment. [3] A quarter-*log* of blood from a corpse.
[4] The bone or bones serve as connectives to the olive's bulk of flesh.
[5] Of which a quarter-*log* conveys uncleanness by overshadowing (2²).

a quarter-*log* of blood, it is unclean; but if beneath a corpse, whose blood drips out, there was found a quarter-*log* of blood, this is clean. R. Judah says: It is not so, but the blood that gushes out is clean and that which drips out is unclean.[1]

6. For an olive's bulk from a corpse an opening [in a room] of one handbreadth [square], and for a corpse an opening of four handbreadths [square, suffices] to protect other openings from the uncleanness;[2] howbeit to give passage[3] to the uncleanness, an opening of one handbreadth [square suffices[4]]. More than an olive's bulk counts as a [whole] corpse. R. Jose says: The backbone and the skull count as a [whole] corpse.

7. [A space[5]] one handbreadth square and one handbreadth high,[6] in the form of a cube,[7] serves both to give passage[8] to the uncleanness and to afford a screen[9] against the uncleanness. How [does it afford a screen]? If beneath the house there was an arched-in drain one handbreadth wide with an outlet one handbreadth wide, and there was uncleanness[10] within it, the house remains clean;[11] if there was uncleanness in the house, what is in the drain remains clean, since it is the way of uncleanness to issue forth and not to enter in.[12] If the drain was one handbreadth wide and had not an outlet one handbreadth wide, and there was uncleanness in the drain, the house also becomes unclean; but if there was uncleanness in the house, what is in the drain remains clean, since it is the way of uncleanness to issue forth and not to enter in. If the drain was not one handbreadth wide and had not an outlet one handbreadth wide, and there was uncleanness in it, the house becomes unclean; if there was uncleanness in the house, what is in the drain also becomes unclean.[13] It is all one whether such space is a hole bored by water or by creeping things or eaten through by saltpetre; so, too, with a row of stones, or a pile of beams.[14] R. Judah says: Any 'Tent'

---

1 According to one view, in the intermittent dripping of the blood the uncleanness of each drop in turn is nullified by its smallness in quantity; therefore the whole quarter-*log* is clean. According to the other view the slowness of its dripping is proof that it issued after death, and it is therefore unclean.

2 The principle implied is stated more fully in 7³. Not only what is within the room suffers corpse-uncleanness but even what is outside a shut door becomes unclean if it is beneath the lintel of the entrance, since uncleanness is ascribed to that doorway through which the corpse will be brought out. If there are more entrances to the room, the same applies to them also, unless it has been specifically determined through which of the entrances the uncleanness shall be taken out. This 'protects' the other openings. But such a specified opening must be not less than one square handbreadth for an olive's bulk of corpse, and not less than four cubits square for a whole corpse.

3 Cf. p. 121, n. 10. So that what is in an adjoining room also becomes unclean.

4 Whether it is a whole corpse or but an olive's bulk.

5 Between the uncleanness and what lies horizontally above it.

6 Above the uncleanness.

7 No dimension may be less than one handbreadth.

8 So that it can pass under the whole of that roof and convey uncleanness to what that same roof overshadows.

9 If that roof is the prescribed handbreadth above the uncleanness, what lies above the roof is protected from what is beneath the roof. But if the uncleanness is in a space more confined than the prescribed cubic handbreadth it will cleave through solid matter upwards and downwards (see below, 6⁶; 7¹, ²; 9¹³, ¹⁴, ¹⁶; 10⁶, ⁷; 12⁶, ⁷; 15¹, ³, ⁷).

10 An olive's bulk of a corpse. Cf. below, 18⁷, ⁸.

11 Everything in the house is protected since the uncleanness has the necessary space for passage out of the drain and the outlet. It is assumed that the other end of the drain leading into the house is less than one handbreadth square.

12 The uncleanness would spread not into the drain, but outside the house through the door.

13 In such cases the drain counts as part of the ground of the house into which the restricted uncleanness penetrates.

14 Which form a 'tent' or roof over uncleanness. If the space is restricted to less than the cubic handbreadth the uncleanness will cleave upwards and downwards.

that is not made by the hands of man does not count as a 'Tent'. But he agrees that the rules apply to clefts and overhanging rocks.[1]

4. 1. If a cupboard stood in an open place and there was some uncleanness within it, any articles contained within the thickness of its sides[2] remain clean. If there was some uncleanness in the thickness of its sides, the articles inside the cupboard remain clean. R. Jose says: [The thickness of the sides should be divided], a half [pertaining to the inside] and a half [pertaining to the outside]. If the cupboard stood inside the house, and there was some uncleanness within it, the house is unclean; if there was some uncleanness in the house, what is in the cupboard remains clean, since it is the way of uncleanness to issue forth and not to enter in. If there were articles between the cupboard and the ground, or between it and the wall, or between it and the roof-beams, and there was a space there of one cubic handbreadth,[3] they become unclean; if there was less space[4] they remain clean. If there was some uncleanness there,[5] the house becomes unclean.[6]

2. If a box[7] in the cupboard measured one cubic handbreadth within, and its outlet was less than one handbreadth [square], and there was some uncleanness within it, the house becomes unclean; if there was some uncleanness in the house, what is within the box remains clean, since it is the way of uncleanness to issue forth and not to enter in. R. Jose declares the house clean, since a man could remove the uncleanness by halves, or burn it where it lies.

3. If the cupboard stood in the doorway of a house and opened outwards, and there was some uncleanness within it, the house remains clean; if there was some uncleanness within the house, what is in the cupboard becomes unclean,[8] since it is the way of uncleanness to issue forth and not to enter in. If the device[9] beneath the cupboard extended backwards [into the house] by three fingerbreadths and it contained some uncleanness directly under the roof-beams, the house remains clean. Howbeit this applies only when [in the device] there is a space of one cubic handbreadth, and when it is not separable [from the cupboard], and when the cupboard is of the prescribed measure.[10]

5. 1. If a baking-oven stood within the house[11] and it had an arched outlet that projected outside [the house], and corpse-bearers overshadowed it [with the corpse], the School of Shammai say: All becomes unclean. The School of Hillel say: The oven becomes unclean but the house remains clean. R. Akiba says: Even the oven remains clean.

2. If over a hatchway between a house[11] and the upper room there was set a cooking-pot which had a hole such that liquid could filter into it, the

---

1 Cf. below, 8[2].
2 These cupboards are described as having niches in the thickness of their walls, opening both inwards and outwards. They measured less than a cubic handbreadth (but according to Maim. and Tif. Yis. they contained such a measure).
3 And there was a corpse in the room.   4 The uncleanness cannot enter there.
5 Between the cupboard and the floor, wall, or roof.
6 The rule of cleaving upwards and downwards does not here apply, since a 'tent' within a 'tent' cannot protect the rest of the 'tent'. Cf. Kel. 8[6].
7 Or drawer; within the cupboards according to some commentators; underneath according to others.   8 Some texts read 'clean'.
9 Cf. p. 631, n. 10. The base here spoken of has a container.
10 A wooden article, holding forty *seahs*, is not susceptible to uncleanness. See Kel. 15[1].
11 In which was a corpse.

School of Shammai say: All becomes unclean. The School of Hillel say: The cooking-pot becomes unclean but the upper room remains clean. R. Akiba says: Even the cooking-pot remains clean.

3. If the cooking-pot was sound, the School of Hillel say: It protects all [from uncleanness]. The School of Shammai say: It protects only food, liquids, and [other] earthenware vessels.[1] The School of Hillel changed their opinion and taught according to the opinion of the School of Shammai.

4. If there was a flagon[2] full of clean liquid [in the upper room],[3] the flagon contracts seven-day uncleanness,[4] and the liquid remains clean; but if the liquid was emptied out into another vessel[5] it becomes unclean. If a woman [in the upper room] was kneading in a trough, the woman and the trough contract seven-day uncleanness, and the dough remains clean; but if she emptied it into another vessel it becomes unclean. The School of Hillel changed their opinion and taught according to the opinion of the School of Shammai.

5. If [blocking up the hatchway] there were vessels of cattle-dung, stone or [unburnt] clay,[6] all remains clean; if it was a clean vessel[7] to be used for Hallowed Things[8] or for Sin-offering [water],[9] all remains clean (for all are accounted trustworthy[10] in what concerns the Sin-offering), since vessels that are not susceptible to uncleanness and clean earthenware vessels, together with the walls of the 'Tent', protect[11] [against corpse-uncleanness].

6. Thus if there was a cistern or cellar[12] in the house,[13] and an olive-basket[14] was put over it, [whatsoever is beneath] remains clean. If the olive-basket was laid over a well whose banks were levelled to the ground, or over a broken-down[15] hive, [whatsoever is therein] becomes unclean.[16] If a smooth board or a colander without rims was put over them, [whatsoever is therein] remains clean.[17] For vessels can only protect [against uncleanness] together with the walls of the 'Tent' if they themselves have walls. How high should the wall be? One handbreadth. If it is a half-handbreadth high here, and a half-handbreadth high there,[18] it does not count as a wall; but only if there is a whole handbreadth to one or the other of them.

7. Like as they[19] protect [against uncleanness] within [the 'Tent'] so do they protect [from uncleanness] outside. Thus if an olive-basket[20] was laid on the tent-pegs[21] outside, and there was uncleanness beneath it, the vessels in the olive-basket remain clean; [but if it was laid on] the wall of a court-

---

[1] Cf. Eduy. 1[14].   [2] Of wood or metal.   [3] With the pot set over the hatchway.
[4] The pot affords no protection to vessels not of earthenware, but only to foods and liquids.
[5] Of wood or metal, which had already contracted corpse-uncleanness.
[6] App. IV. 16 c.   [7] Of earthenware.
[8] Foodstuffs, oil, or wine dedicated to the Temple.
[9] Num. 19[17]. Cf. Par. 5[1].   [10] Cf. Par. 5[1].
[11] Making together a single roof to afford protection to what is above.
[12] Each surmounted by a coping at least one handbreadth high.
[13] And a corpse lay in the house and vessels in the cistern or cellar.
[14] A flat-shaped, round wooden receptacle in which olives are left to soften, and which holds more than forty *seahs* and so (Kel. 15[1]) is insusceptible to uncleanness.
[15] Variant: 'open', not blocked up.
[16] Since they neither of them have 'walls of the tent' to serve, with the olive-basket, as a screen against the uncleanness.
[17] The rule does not now apply to these, since they do not count as vessels.
[18] i.e. if the well-wall is half, and the covering vessel half a handbreadth high.
[19] These vessels in conjunction with the walls of the 'tent'.
[20] With 'walls' one handbreadth high.
[21] Which must be at least one handbreadth high; otherwise the uncleanness will cleave upwards and downwards.

yard or the wall of a garden,[1] it does not afford protection. If a beam[2] stretched from one wall to another,[3] and a cooking-pot was hung from it[4] and uncleanness lay under it,[5] the vessels in the cooking-pot R. Akiba declares clean, but the Sages declare them unclean.[6]

6. 1. Men and vessels can serve as 'tents'[7] in such wise as to give passage to uncleanness, but not in such wise as to protect[8] from uncleanness. Thus if four men carried a large stone[9] and there was some uncleanness beneath it, the vessels on the stone become unclean. If there was uncleanness upon it, vessels beneath it become unclean. R. Eliezer declares them clean.[10] If it was set down on four vessels, even on vessels made of cattle-dung, stone, or [unburnt] clay, and there was some uncleanness beneath it, vessels upon it become unclean; and if there was some uncleanness upon it, vessels beneath it become unclean. If it was set down on four stones, or on some living creature, and there was some uncleanness beneath it, vessels that are upon it remain clean; and if there was some uncleanness upon it, vessels beneath it remain clean.

2. If corpse-bearers passed through the portico [before a house] and some one shut the door and fastened it with the key, if the door was able to stand of itself [whatsoever is within the house] remains clean; but if it could not stand of itself [whatsoever is in the house] becomes unclean. So, too, if a jar of dried figs or a basket of straw was set in a window,[11] and the figs or straw could stand of themselves, [what is in the room behind] remains clean; but if not, [what is in the room behind] becomes unclean. If a man separated part of a house with a partition of jars and plastered them with clay, and the plastering was able to stand of itself, [the space behind them] remains clean; if not, it becomes unclean.

3. A wall that belongs to a house is deemed to be divided into halves. Thus if a wall looked towards an open space and there was some uncleanness within the wall in its inner half, the house is unclean, whereas what is above [the uncleanness] is clean; but if the uncleanness was within the wall in its outer half, the house is clean, and what is above [the uncleanness] is unclean. If the uncleanness was in the middle, the house becomes unclean; and what is above [the uncleanness] R. Meir declares unclean, but the Sages declare it clean. R. Judah says: The entire wall is deemed to belong to the house.

4. If the uncleanness was in a wall that is between two houses, the house nearer to the uncleanness is unclean, and the house nearer to the clean part is clean. If it was in the middle, both houses are unclean. If the uncleanness

---

[1] Where it is not conjoined to what forms the wall of a house or 'tent'.
[2] At least one handbreadth wide and one handbreadth from the ground.
[3] From one house to another.   [4] With less than one handbreadth between the pot and the beam.   [5] The beam; not the pot.
[6] The uncleanness and the vessels in the pot are jointly overshadowed by the beam; but according to R. Akiba the conditions apply as in a room, when the uncleanness could not pass through any space less than a handbreadth; whereas according to the Sages the pot is not regarded as conjoined with 'tent-walls' or a roof, therefore the conditions protecting the contents of the pot cannot apply.
[7] As when some manner of 'tent' is supported by men.
[8] i.e. to isolate what is above them from uncleanness that is below them, as can 'clean vessels together with the walls of the tent'.
[9] Variant: 'bier' (but not with a corpse on it).
[10] In both cases, provided that the men are clean. This will be so (cf. 16[1]) if the bearing-rods are less than the third of a handbreadth thick.
[11] Not less than one handbreadth square that communicates between two rooms in one of which lies a corpse.

was in one of the houses, and there were vessels within the thickness of the wall, the vessels that are in the half of the wall nearer the uncleanness are unclean, and they that are in the half nearer the clean house are clean; and they that are in the middle are unclean. If there was uncleanness in the plasterwork between the house and the upper room, and it was within the lower half, the house below is unclean and the upper room is clean; if it was within the upper half, the upper room is unclean and the house below is clean; but if it was in the middle, both are unclean. If there was uncleanness either in the house below or in the upper room and there were vessels within the plasterwork, they that are in the half nearer the uncleanness are unclean and they that are in the half nearer the clean room are clean; and they that are in the middle are unclean. R. Judah says: The whole plasterwork is deemed to belong to the upper room.

5. If there was uncleanness between the roof-beams, with plaster beneath it thin as garlic-peel,[1] and there was an open space there[2] measuring one cubic handbreadth, all becomes unclean.[3] If there was not an open space there measuring one cubic handbreadth, the uncleanness is deemed to be in a closed-up place.[4] In either case if it is visible from within the house the house becomes unclean.[5]

6. If a house forms part of a wall the principle of the garlic-peel applies. Thus if there was a [rock-]wall between two tomb-niches or two caverns, and uncleanness was found within the niches or caverns, and there were vessels in the wall with aught covering them thin as garlic-peel, the articles remain clean. If uncleanness was found in the wall, and there were vessels in the niches or caverns, and over the uncleanness was a covering thin as garlic-peel, the vessels remain clean. If uncleanness was under a pillar, the uncleanness cleaves [through the solid matter] upwards and downwards.[6]

7. If there were vessels under the capital of the pillar they remain clean. R. Johanan b. Nuri declares them unclean. If the uncleanness and the vessels were both found beneath the capital and there was a space one cubic handbreadth [over which the capital projected], the vessels become unclean; if [there was] not [a space of one cubic handbreadth] they remain clean. If there were two wall-cupboards one beside the other, or one above the other, and one of them was opened, both it and the house are unclean; but [what is in] the other remains clean. A wall-cupboard is deemed a closed-up space, and in what concerns conveying uncleanness to the house the principle of [dividing the wall into] halves applies to it.[7]

7. 1. If there was uncleanness within the wall, in a space measuring one cubic handbreadth, all upper rooms above it, even if they are ten in number, become unclean. If a single upper room was built over two houses, it becomes unclean, but all the upper rooms above it remain clean. In a rock-wall the uncleanness cleaves [through the solid matter] upwards and downwards. If a man touches the sides of a solid tomb-monument,[8] he remains clean, since the uncleanness cleaves [through the solid matter] upwards and downwards; but if where the uncleanness lay there was a space measuring

---

[1] Cf. Kel. 9[1].   [2] Where the uncleanness lay.
[3] It counts as a closed-up grave which spreads its uncleanness all around in every direction.   [4] And cleaves upwards and downwards.
[5] As though it lay in the house.   [6] See above, p. 654, n. 9.
[7] As described above, par. 3.
[8] Cf. Erub. 5[1]; Shek. 2[5].

one cubic handbreadth, no matter where he touches it he becomes unclean, since it is deemed a closed-up grave. If booths were built up against it they become unclean; but R. Judah declares them clean.

2. All sloping parts of tents count as the tents themselves. If the [wall of the] 'Tent' sloped down and was but one fingerbreadth at the bottom, and there was some uncleanness in the tent, vessels beneath the slope become unclean. If there was uncleanness under the slope, vessels which are in the tent become unclean. If there was some uncleanness within and a man touched the tent from the inner side,[1] he contracts seven-day uncleanness; but if from the outer side,[2] he contracts evening-uncleanness only. If the uncleanness was on the outer side and a man touched the tent from the outer side, he contracts seven-day uncleanness; but if from the inner side, he contracts evening-uncleanness only. If there was a half-olive's bulk on the inner side and a half on the outer side, and he touched the tent either from the inner side or the outer side, he contracts evening-uncleanness. If part of the tent-cover lay flat on the ground and there was some uncleanness beneath it or above it, the uncleanness cleaves through [the solid matter] upwards and downwards. If a tent was stretched in an upper room and a part of the tent-cover lay flat over the hatchway that was between the upper room and the house [in which lay the uncleanness], R. Jose says: It protects [the upper room against the uncleanness]. R. Simeon says: It protects [against the uncleanness] only when it is stretched out in the manner of a tent.

3. If a corpse lay in a room to which were many entrances,[3] they are all[4] unclean; if one entrance was opened it alone is unclean and the rest are clean. If there was intention to take out the corpse through one of them, or through a window which measures four handbreadths square, this affords protection to all other entrances. The School of Shammai say: The intention must have been formed before the corpse was dead. The School of Hillel say: [It suffices] even after it was dead. If an entrance had been blocked up and it was determined to open it, the School of Shammai say: [It affords protection to all other entrances only] after it has been opened as much as four handbreadths square. The School of Hillel say: So soon as they begin to open it. But they agree that if an opening was here made for a first time the opening must be as much as four handbreadths [before it can afford protection].

4. If a woman was in hard travail and was taken out from one house into another [and there bore a child that was dead], the first house is unclean because of doubt,[5] and the second is unclean of a certainty. R. Judah said: This applies only if she needed to be supported by the arms; but if she was able to walk [without help] the first house is clean, since after the opening of the 'tomb' it is not possible that she can walk. When a woman miscarries it is not deemed an opening of the 'tomb' unless the head is already rounded like a spindle-knob.

5. If [at the birth of twins] the first was born dead and the second alive,

---

[1] After the corpse is removed the 'tent' still suffers seven-day uncleanness.

[2] The outer side is deemed distinct from the inside; it is only 'a father' and not 'a father of fathers' of uncleanness; therefore he that touches it suffers only a 'derived' uncleanness.

[3] See above, 3[6]. All the entrances are closed.

[4] Everything, the door itself, and even what is outside it under the same lintel.

[5] Whether or not the head of the child had protruded before she left that house. An unborn dead child cannot convey uncleanness; but if its head had emerged it is deemed fully born.

this one is clean.[1] If the first was born alive and the second dead, the first is unclean.[2] R. Meir says: If both lay within the one membrane the [living] child is unclean; but if in separate membranes it is clean.

6. If a woman was in hard travail, the child must be cut up while it is in the womb and brought out member by member, since the life of the mother has priority over the life of the child; but if the greater part of it was already born, it may not be touched, since the claim of one life cannot override the claim of another life.

8. 1. Some things give passage to uncleanness and serve for a screen against it; some give passage to uncleanness and do not serve for a screen against it; some serve for a screen and do not give passage to uncleanness; and some neither give passage to uncleanness nor serve for a screen against it. These[3] give passage to the uncleanness and serve for a screen against it: a chest, a box, a cupboard, a straw basket, a reed basket, or the tank of an Alexandrian ship that have [flat] bottoms and that hold [not less than] forty *seahs* of liquid or two *kors* of dry wares; a curtain, a leathern apron, a bed-undercover, a sheet, matting or a mat that are spread out tentwise; a herd of cattle, clean or unclean, a pack[4] of wild animals or birds, a sitting bird, or the shelter that a woman makes for her child among the ears of corn; the iris, ivy, squirting-cucumber, Greek gourds, and foodstuffs that are not susceptible to uncleanness (R. Johanan b. Nuri did not agree to foodstuffs that are not susceptible to uncleanness, save cakes of dried figs alone);

2. also wall-projections, balconies, dovecotes, overhanging crags and rocks, grottoes and cliffs, interlaced foliage and protruding stones that can hold a thin layer of plaster. So R. Meir. But the Sages say: A layer of plaster of moderate thickness. 'Interlaced foliage' means the foliage of a tree that affords a covering over the ground; and 'protruding stones' means [small] stones [or thorns] that project from a wall.

3. These[5] give passage to uncleanness and do not serve for a screen against it: a chest, a box, a cupboard, a straw basket, a reed basket, or the tank of an Alexandrian ship that have not [flat] bottoms or that do not hold forty *seahs* of liquid or two *kors* of dry wares; a curtain, a leathern apron, a bed-undercover, a sheet, matting or a mat that are not spread out tentwise; cattle or wild animals that have died, and foodstuffs that are susceptible to uncleanness. Added to these are mill-stones worked by hand.

4. These[6] serve for a screen and do not give passage to uncleanness: stretched-out warp-threads, bed-ropes, refuse baskets, and lattice-work of windows.

5. These neither give passage to uncleanness nor serve for a screen against it: seeds, vegetables, what still grows in the ground (excepting the vegetables that they have recounted),[7] hail-stones, snow, frost, ice and salt, and what hops from place to place, or what leaps from place to place, a flying bird, a flapping cloak, or a ship moving on the water; but if the ship was tied to aught that holds it still, or if the cloak was held down with

---

[1] It could not contract uncleanness in the womb, and before it was born the other birth had been removed from the house.

[2] By the application of the rule of par. 3: the living child passed through the opening by which the dead child must pass.

[3] Which (Kel. 15[1]) are not susceptible to uncleanness.

[4] So Maim. Others explain as 'lair' or 'nest'.   [5] Which are susceptible to uncleanness.

[6] Which offer a surface in which are holes, but none of them one handbreadth square. See introductory note (*e*).   [7] Above, par. 1 (end).

a stone, it can convey uncleanness. R. Jose says: A house on a ship does not convey uncleanness.

6. If two jars, each containing a half-olive's bulk [of a corpse] and having a tightly stopped-up cover, were put in a house, they are clean but the house is unclean; if one of them was opened, it and the house are unclean, but the other remains clean; and the like applies to two chambers that open into a house.[1]

9. 1. If a hive[2] lay within the entrance of a house with its open end outside, and an olive's bulk of corpse lay below it or above it outside, whatsoever is above or below the olive's bulk is unclean;[3] and whatsoever is not immediately above or below the olive's bulk and what is within the hive[4] and within the house is clean. If the uncleanness lay in the house, the house alone is unclean; but if it lay within the hive all is unclean.

2. If the hive was raised one handbreadth above the ground and the uncleanness lay below it or within the house or above it, all is unclean save what is within the hive; but if it lay within the hive all is unclean.

3. When does this apply? When the hive is still a usable vessel and lies loosely[5] [in the entrance]. If it was wholly broken and stopped up with straw or if it was fixed tightly (what means 'tightly'?—that there is nowhere a gap one handbreadth square) and an olive's bulk of corpse lay below it, what is directly below it down to the nethermost deep is unclean. If it lay above it, what is directly above it up to the sky is unclean. If it lay in the house, the house alone is unclean; but if it lay within the hive, what is within the hive alone is unclean.

4. If the hive was raised one handbreadth above the ground, and the uncleanness lay below it or within the house, what is below it and what is within the house is unclean; but what is within it and what is above it is clean; if the uncleanness was within it, what is within it alone is unclean; if the uncleanness was above it, what lies directly above it, up to the sky, is unclean.

5. When does this apply? When the hive's open end is turned outwards. If it is turned inwards and an olive's bulk of corpse lay below it or above it outside, whatsoever is directly above or below the olive's bulk[6] is unclean; but what is not directly above or below the olive's bulk, and what is within the hive and the house itself, remains clean. But if it lay within the hive or within the house, all is unclean.

6. If the hive was raised one handbreadth above the ground, and there was uncleanness below it or within the house, or within the hive or above it, all is unclean.

7. When does this apply? When the hive is a usable vessel and lies loosely [in the entrance]. If it was wholly broken and stopped up with

---

[1] If a half-olive's bulk was in each, and they were shut up, the house (i.e. the room into which the two cells opened) is unclean, since the uncleanness must in the end go out through it.

[2] A wooden cylindrical vessel, open at the bottom so that honey can be scraped out, and pierced with small holes to give passage to the bees. It is not susceptible to uncleanness but it is not such that can serve as a screen. It is here thought of as lying on its side, with its open end outwards, and partly inside and partly outside the house.

[3] See introductory note, p. 650, n. 3 (f) and (h).

[4] As a vessel insusceptible to uncleanness it protects what is within it.

[5] Not so tightly that it can protect against uncleanness together with the walls of the 'tent' (as taught above, 5[5f]). So the more recent commentators. The same term is used (Kel. 10[3]) of a loose jar plug. Earlier commentators render the text 'pierced with holes', for the bees.

[6] Some texts here add 'or within the hive'.

straw, or if it was fixed tightly (what means 'tightly'?—that there is nowhere a gap one handbreadth square) and an olive's bulk of corpse lay below it, what is directly below it down to the nethermost deep is unclean. If it lay above it, what is directly above it up to the sky is unclean. If it lay within it or within the house, what is within it and within the house is unclean.

8. If it was raised one handbreadth above the ground and the uncleanness lay below it or within the house or within the hive, all is unclean save what is above the hive. If it lay above the hive, all that is directly above it up to the sky is unclean.

9. If the hive filled the whole house and there was not the space of a handbreadth between it and the roof-beams, and the uncleanness lay within the hive, the house is unclean; if the uncleanness lay in the house what is within the hive is clean, since it is the way of uncleanness to issue forth and not to enter in. It is all one whether the hive was upright or turned on its side, or whether there was one hive or two [one above the other].

10. If it was upright within the entrance and between it and the lintel there was not the space of a handbreadth, and the uncleanness lay in the house, what is in the hive is unclean, since it is the way of uncleanness to issue forth and not to enter in.

11. If it was turned on its side in the open air and an olive's bulk of corpse lay below it or above it, all that is directly above or below the olive's bulk is unclean; and all that is not directly above or below the olive's bulk and what is within the hive remains clean. If the uncleanness lay within the hive all is unclean.

12. If the hive was raised one handbreadth above the ground and the uncleanness lay below it or above it, all is unclean save what is within it. If uncleanness lay within it, all is unclean. When does this apply? When the hive is a usable vessel. If it was wholly broken and stopped up with straw, or (according to the Sages) if it held forty *seahs*,[1] and an olive's bulk of corpse lay below it, what is directly below it down to the nethermost deep is unclean. If it lay above it, what is directly above it up to the sky is unclean. If it lay within it, what is within it alone is unclean. If it was raised one handbreadth above the ground, and the uncleanness lay below it, what is below it is unclean; if it lay within it, what is within it is unclean; if it lay above it, what is directly above it up to the sky is unclean.

13. If it was standing on its bottom[2] and it was a usable vessel, and the uncleanness lay below it or within it or above it, the uncleanness cleaves through [the solid matter] upwards and downwards. If it was raised one handbreadth above the ground or if it was closed up, or turned with its opening to the ground, and the uncleanness lay below it or within it or above it, all is unclean.

14. When does this apply? When it is a usable vessel. If it was wholly broken and stopped up with straw or (according to the Sages) if it held forty *seahs*, and the uncleanness lay below it or within it or above it, the uncleanness cleaves upwards and downwards. R. Eliezer and R. Simeon say: The uncleanness penetrates neither above it nor below it. If the hive

---

[1] See Kel. 15[1]. 'According to the Sages' refers to a ruling (t. Kel. B.M. 5[1]) in which the Sages decided, as against R. Meir, that such a vessel could be treated according to the conditions applying to a 'tent'. [2] Mouth upwards.

was raised one handbreadth above the ground and the uncleanness lay below it, what is below it is unclean. If it lay within it or above it, what is directly above it up to the sky is unclean.

15. If a tomb[1] was broad below and narrow above[2] and a corpse lay within it, he that touches [the rock] below[3] remains clean and he that touches it above becomes unclean. If it was wide above and narrow below, he that touches it anywhere becomes unclean. If it was equally wide above and below, he that touches it anywhere becomes unclean. So R. Eliezer. R. Joshua says: [He that touches the rock] more than a handbreadth below remains clean; but he that touches it less than a handbreadth below becomes unclean.[4] If it was made in the form of a clothes-chest,[5] what touches it anywhere becomes unclean; if it was made in the form of a case,[6] he that touches it anywhere, excepting at the place where it opens, remains clean.

16. If a jar[7] rested on its bottom in the open air, and an olive's bulk of corpse lay below it or within it directly opposite its bottom, the uncleanness cleaves through [the solid matter] upwards and downwards, and the jar[8] is unclean. [If it lay] outside it below its [convex] side, the uncleanness cleaves through [the solid matter] upwards and downwards, but the jar remains clean.[9] [If it lay] within it, below the [concave] sides of the jar, and within the [concavity of the] sides of the jar was a space of one cubic handbreadth, all becomes unclean; but what lies directly opposite the mouth of the jar remains clean.[10] But if there was not [a space of one cubic handbreadth] the uncleanness cleaves through [the solid matter] upwards and downwards. When does this apply? When the jar is clean. If it was unclean, or if it was raised one handbreadth above the ground, or if its mouth was closed, or if it was turned upside down on its mouth, and uncleanness was found below it or within it or above it, all is unclean.

10. 1. If there was a hatchway one handbreadth square in [the roof of] a house[11] and uncleanness lay in the house, what is directly below the hatchway is clean.[12] If the uncleanness lay directly below the hatchway, the house is clean. If the uncleanness lay [elsewhere] in the house or directly below the hatchway and any one set his foot above the hatchway, he has combined[13] [with the roof to spread] the uncleanness. If part of the

---

[1] Carved out of an outcrop of rock. The rock was cut away, leaving the structure above ground.
[2] The movable lid over the cavity containing the corpse was narrower than the rock mass below it.
[3] The portions of the tomb which lie outside the area of rock over which the lid was superimposed. Only that portion of the rock directly below the covering stone is deemed unclean as being the portion acting the part of 'buttressing-stone'; cf. above, 2[4]. The rest of the rock is deemed to be part of the actual earth and insusceptible to uncleanness; whereas the uncleanness of the lid strikes perpendicularly upwards and downwards.
[4] Only the one handbreadth of rock immediately below the lid is reckoned as belonging to the tomb.
[5] Cf. Kel. 16[7]. The lid is superimposed over the whole area covered by the thickness of the tomb's sides.
[6] Heb. glosokos (or glosokom); perhaps γλωσσόκομον. It is explained as a box into which the lid sinks without touching the tops of the sides.
[7] It is presupposed to be of unburnt clay, stone, or cattle-dung, and insusceptible to uncleanness, narrow at the bottom and top, with its middle bulging out less than one handbreadth beyond its base (otherwise it would serve as a 'tent' to give passage to the uncleanness).   [8] i.e. vessels within the jar directly opposite the olive's bulk of uncleanness.
[9] Since it cannot contract uncleanness from its outer side.   [10] Cf. below, 10[1].
[11] As generally in the Mishnah, 'house' is used in the sense of a single room on the ground floor.   [12] It is not 'overshadowed'.
[13] See 6[1], above. The uncleanness has no longer free egress through a hole one handbreadth square. The man serves with the roof to make a 'tent', causing the uncleanness to disseminate throughout the room.

uncleanness lay in the house and part directly below the hatchway, the house becomes unclean and what is directly above the uncleanness [and opposite the hatchway] is unclean.[1]

2. If the hatchway was less than one handbreadth square and uncleanness lay in the house, what is directly below the hatchway is clean. If the uncleanness lay directly below the hatchway, the house is unclean. If the uncleanness lay in the house and any one set his foot above the hatchway, he remains clean. If the uncleanness lay directly below the hatchway and any one set his foot above the hatchway, R. Meir declares him unclean, but the Sages say: If the uncleanness was there before his foot, he becomes unclean; but if his foot was there before the uncleanness, he remains clean. R. Simeon says: If two [men's] feet, one on top of the other, were there before the uncleanness, and the first withdrew his foot so that the foot of the other person was found there, the second person remains clean, since the foot of the first person was there before the uncleanness.

3. If part of the uncleanness lay in the house and part directly below the hatchway, the house is unclean and what is directly above the uncleanness [and directly below the hatchway] is unclean. So R. Meir. R. Judah says: The house is unclean, but what is directly above the uncleanness [and directly below the hatchway] is clean. R. Jose says: If there was enough of the uncleanness to be divided and [still] to convey uncleanness to the house and [to what is directly below the hatchway and] directly above the uncleanness, [then all] is unclean; if not, the house is unclean and what is [directly below the hatchway and] directly above the uncleanness is clean.

4. If there were many hatchways, one above the other, each one handbreadth square, and uncleanness lay in the house,[2] what lies directly below the hatchways remains clean. If the uncleanness lay directly below the hatchways the house remains clean. If the uncleanness lay either in the house or directly below the hatchways, and any one set aught that is susceptible to uncleanness over an upper or a lower hatchway, all is unclean; if it was aught that was not susceptible to uncleanness, what is below it is unclean, but what is above remains clean.

5. If the hatchways were less than one handbreadth square, and uncleanness lay in the house, what is directly below the hatchways remains clean. If the uncleanness lay directly below the hatchways, the house remains clean. If the uncleanness lay in the house and any one set aught that was susceptible or that was not susceptible to uncleanness over either an upper or a lower hatchway, only the lower house is unclean. If, when the uncleanness lay directly below the hatchways, any one set aught that was susceptible to uncleanness over either an upper or a lower hatchway, all is unclean; if he set aught that is not susceptible to uncleanness either over an upper or a lower hatchway, the lower house alone is unclean.

6. If there was a hatchway in the house and a cooking-pot beneath it so set that if it rose [straight up] its rims would not touch the [edges of the] hatchway, and uncleanness lay below it or within it or above it, the uncleanness cleaves upwards and downwards. If the cooking-pot was raised one handbreadth above the floor and uncleanness lay below it or [elsewhere] in the house, what is below it and what is in the house is unclean, and what

---

[1] According to the principle laid down above, 3[4].
[2] In the bottom room and not perpendicularly below the hatchways opening into the various stories above.

is within it and above it remains clean. [If the uncleanness lay] within it or above it, all is unclean.

7. If the cooking-pot was set at the side of the threshold so that if it rose up it would touch a handbreadth of the lintel, and uncleanness lay below it or within it or above it, the uncleanness cleaves upwards and downwards. If the cooking-pot was raised one handbreadth above the ground and the uncleanness lay below it or [elsewhere] in the house, what is below it and the house are unclean, and what is within it and what is above it are clean. If the uncleanness lay within it or above it, all is unclean. [But if the cooking-pot was so set that] if it rose up it would not touch a handbreadth of the lintel, or if it was fastened to the lintel, and uncleanness lay beneath it, naught is unclean save the space beneath it.

11. 1. If [the whole roof of] a house was split and uncleanness lay [in the house] in the outer side,[1] the vessels [in the house] on the inner side remain clean.[2] If the uncleanness was within, the vessels outside remain clean if, according to the School of Shammai, the split is four handbreadths wide; but the School of Hillel say: [They remain clean] however wide it is. R. Jose says in the name of the School of Hillel: If it is one handbreadth wide.

2. If [the whole roof of] a portico[3] was split and uncleanness lay in it to the one side, the vessels on the other side remain clean. If any one set his foot or a reed above the split he has combined[4] the uncleanness. If he set the reed on the ground [directly below the split],[5] it does not give passage to the uncleanness unless it is raised one handbreadth above the ground.[6]

3. [If he set there] a thick cloak[7] or a thick wooden block, they do not give passage to the uncleanness unless they are raised one handbreadth above the ground. If garments lay folded one above the other, they give passage to the uncleanness so soon as the upper one is raised one handbreadth above the ground. If[8] a man was put there [below the split], the School of Shammai say: He does not give passage[9] to the uncleanness. And the School of Hillel say: A man is hollow, and his upper side gives passage to the uncleanness.

4. If a man looked out of the window and overshadowed the corpse-bearers, the School of Shammai say: He does not give passage to the uncleanness.[10] And the School of Hillel say: He gives passage to the uncleanness. But they agree that if he was wearing his clothes, or if there were two men one above the other, these give passage to the uncleanness.

5. If a man lay over the threshold and the corpse-bearers overshadowed

---

[1] The side of the room nearer the entrance, the split being parallel to the entrance.

[2] The two sections of the house count as two separate 'tents'; furthermore 'it is the way of uncleanness to issue forth and not to enter in'.

[3] A vestibule open on one of its four sides. The roof was split across at right angles to the open side, the split stretching to the inner wall.

[4] He has made what were two 'tents' into one, and the uncleanness is given passage from the one to the other. See above, 10[1]; cf. 6[1].

[5] Coinciding with the non-overshadowed part of the pavement.

[6] So that the uncleanness can pass underneath it from one 'tent' to the other.

[7] The passage is repeated below, 15[1].   [8] Eduy. 4[12].

[9] Since between him and the ground there is not the necessary space of one handbreadth, the uncleanness cannot pass beneath him from the one side of the portico to the other.

[10] So that the uncleanness enters the house. According to the School of Shammai there is not room for the uncleanness to pass *under* the man into the room behind, whereas the School of Hillel argue that it can pass through him since he is hollow. The same principles apply in the three following paragraphs.

him, the School of Shammai say: He does not give passage to the uncleanness. And the School of Hillel say: He gives passage to the uncleanness.

6. If there was uncleanness within the house and they that overshadowed him were clean, the School of Shammai declare them clean, and the School of Hillel declare them unclean.

7. If a dog ate the flesh of a corpse and it died and lay over the threshold,[1] R. Meir says: If its neck was one handbreadth wide, it conveys the uncleanness; but if not, it does not convey the uncleanness. R. Jose says: They see where is the uncleanness: if it lies opposite the lintel inwards, the house is unclean; but if opposite the lintel outwards the house remains clean. R. Eliezer says: If its mouth was towards the inside the house remains clean; if towards the outside, the house becomes unclean, since the uncleanness issues forth by way of its hinder parts. R. Judah b. Bathyra says: Whichever way it may be, the house becomes unclean. How long[2] should it have remained in its entrails [so that it no more conveys uncleanness]? Three times twenty-four hours; and if [it was in the entrails of] birds or fishes,[3] time enough for it to be burnt if it had fallen into a fire. So R. Simeon. R. Judah b. Bathyra says: If it was [in the entrails of] birds or fishes, it should have remained twenty-four hours.

8. If a candlestick stood in the cistern of a house,[4] and its cup projected,[5] and over it was an olive-basket so placed[6] that if the candlestick was taken away the olive-basket would still stay over the mouth of the cistern, the School of Shammai say: The cistern remains clean but the candlestick is unclean.[7] The School of Hillel say: The candlestick also remains clean. But they agree that if the olive-basket would fall in if the candlestick was taken away, all is unclean.

9. Vessels lying between the rims of the olive-basket[8] and the rims of the cistern,[9] down to the nethermost deep, remain clean. If there was uncleanness [in the cistern] the house is unclean. If there was uncleanness in the house, vessels that are in the walls of the cistern remain clean if they have a space measuring one cubic handbreadth; otherwise they are unclean. But if the walls of the cistern were wider than those of the house, in either case the vessels remain clean.

12. 1. If a board lay over the mouth of a new oven[10] and projected one handbreadth on every side, and there was uncleanness below [the projecting sides of the board], vessels that are above it remain clean; if there was uncleanness above it, vessels that are beneath it remain clean. If it was an old oven, all become unclean; but R. Johanan b. Nuri declares them clean. If the board was put over the mouth of two ovens,[11] and there was

---

[1] With its head pointing towards the house.
[2] Before the dog died, so that it would have time to be digested.
[3] That ate the flesh of the corpse.   [4] Where lay a corpse.
[5] As high as the cistern's lower rim.
[6] The candlestick-top was visible between the rim of the cistern and the rim of the basket.
[7] Since it projected outside.   [8] That was not supported by the candlestick.
[9] The olive-basket being round and the cistern mouth square, the corners of the cistern mouth remain uncovered; yet if none of them measures a square handbreadth, the olive-basket suffices to protect whatsoever is below.
[10] Not yet heated (cf. Kel. 5[1ff]) and therefore not deemed a 'vessel'; hence it may form the 'wall of a tent' and protect against uncleanness. If it was an old (burnt) oven it counts as a 'vessel' and the rule applies (see above, 6[1]) by which it can act as a 'tent' only in respect of giving passage to uncleanness, but not in protecting against it.
[11] Old ovens.

uncleanness between them, they become unclean; but R. Johanan b. Nuri declares them clean.

2. If a colander[1] lay over the mouth of an oven [and projected one hand-breadth on every side], closing it with a tightly stopped-up cover,[2] and there was uncleanness below [the projecting sides of the board] or above it, all[3] becomes unclean; but what is directly above the air-space of the oven remains clean. If the uncleanness lay directly above the air-space of the oven, all that is directly above it even to the sky is unclean.

3. If a board lay over the opening of an old oven and projected one handbreadth at the two ends, but not at the sides, and there was unclean-ness [under the projecting part] at the one end, the vessels [under the projecting part] at the other end remain clean; but R. Jose declares them unclean. A projecting window-sill[4] does not give passage to uncleanness [that lies beneath it outside, so that it enters the house]. If there was a projection [above the window], R. Eliezer says: It does not give passage to the uncleanness. But R. Joshua says: The window-sill is regarded as though it was not, and the upper projection gives passage to the uncleanness [into the house].

4. If a hole was made for the sandal[5] of a cradle [in the plasterwork in the floor of an upper room], such that it penetrated into the house below,[6] and the hole was one handbreadth square, all is unclean;[7] but if [the hole was] not [one handbreadth square], they reckon [the degree of uncleanness] after the manner prescribed for corpse-uncleanness.[8]

5. If on the roof-beams of a house and of its upper room there is no plasterwork, and they lie exactly one above the other, and uncleanness lay below one [of the lower beams], only the space below this is unclean; if it lay between a lower and an upper beam, only the space between them is unclean; if it lay above an upper beam, what is directly above it up to the sky is unclean. But if the upper beams lay opposite the gaps between the lower beams, and uncleanness lay below one of the beams, the space below them all is unclean; and if it lay above one of the beams, what is directly above it up to the sky is unclean.

6. If a beam stretched from one wall to the other and uncleanness lay below it, and the beam was one handbreadth wide, it gives passage to the uncleanness below the whole of it; but if [it was] not [one handbreadth wide], the uncleanness cleaves upwards and downwards. How much must be its circumference so that it measures one handbreadth wide? If it was round, its circumference must be three handbreadths; if square, four hand-breadths, since if it is square, its circumference is one quarter greater than it is when it is round.[9]

7. If a column lay in the open air, and its circumference was twenty-four handbreadths, it gives passage to uncleanness under its entire side;[10] but if it was not, the uncleanness cleaves upwards and downwards.

---

[1] See Kel. 8³.   [2] In the manner prescribed in Kel. 9⁷.
[3] Above or below the projecting sides.
[4] So Maim. It is also explained as a bath-tub fixed to the ground, over which a board is laid in the same way as over the oven.
[5] A metal ornament or protection for the cradle-legs.   [6] Where lay a corpse.
[7] Variant: it gives passage to the uncleanness.
[8] i.e. 'sandal' and cradle will suffer seven-day uncleanness, and the child in the cradle evening-uncleanness (see p. 650, n. 3 (a) and (b)).
[9] Cf. Erub. 1⁵ for the same simplified calculation.
[10] Its diameter would be reckoned as eight handbreadths. If, then, C is the point where the circle of the pillar touches the ground, and a perpendicular line, AB, is dropped from

8. If an olive's bulk of corpse cleaved to the threshold,[1] R. Eliezer declares the house unclean. R. Joshua declares it clean. If it lay below the threshold, [the thickness of threshold] is deemed to be divided into halves.[2] If it cleaved to the lintel, the house is unclean. R. Jose declares it clean. If it lay within the house and any one touched the lintel[3] he becomes unclean.[4] If he touched the threshold, R. Eliezer declares him unclean; but R. Joshua says: If he touched a part [of the outer side of the threshold] less than one handbreadth from the ground, he remains clean; if higher than one handbreadth he becomes unclean.[5]

13. 1. If a light-hole is newly made, its measure [that suffices to give passage to uncleanness] is that of a hole made by the drill that lay in the chamber [in the Temple].[6] The measure of the residue[7] of a light-hole is two fingerbreadths high and one thumb-breadth wide. By 'the residue of a light-hole' is meant [also] any window which a man blocked up but was not able to finish. If water had bored the hole, or creeping things, or if it had been eaten through by saltpetre, its measure must be the size of a fist;[8] if a man had intended to make use of it, its measure must be one handbreadth square; and if to make use of it as a light-hole, its measure must be that of a hole made by the drill. If it is a light-hole covered with grating or lattice-work, the several holes are included together to make up the measure of the hole made by the drill. So the School of Shammai. And the School of Hillel say: There must be one hole having the measure of a hole made by the drill. [A light-hole that is of such a measure suffices] both to let in uncleanness and to let out uncleanness. R. Simeon says: [This suffices] to let in uncleanness; but to let out uncleanness it must measure one handbreadth square.[9]

2. If a window was made to let in air, its measure [that suffices to give passage to uncleanness] must be that of a hole made by the drill; if a house was built outside it, the measure of the hole must be one handbreadth square; if the roof-beam [of a house built outside it] was set against the middle of the window,[10] the part below [the beam] must be one handbreadth square, and the part above, the measure of a hole made by the drill.

3. A hole in the door must be the size of a fist. So R. Akiba. R. Tarfon says: One handbreadth square. If the carpenter had left a hole at the top or at the bottom of the door, or if one shut the door and did not close it tightly, or if the wind blew it open, the measure of the opening [that suffices to give passage to uncleanness] must be the size of a fist.[11]

4. If a man made a place[12] for a rod or a [weaver's] stave[13] or for a lamp, its measure may be whatsoever is needful. So the School of Shammai. And the School of Hillel say: One handbreadth square. If a man made a hole through which to look out or to speak to his fellow, or for other use, its measure must be one handbreadth square.

A, the outermost point of the pillar's circle, a complete square with an area of approximately one square handbreadth may be described within the section *ABC*.

[1] To the outer side of the door-jamb.
[2] And only if the uncleanness lay below the inner half is the house unclean.
[3] Under the outer half.   [4] Cf. above, 3[6]; 7[3].
[5] The same conditions apply as in 9[15].
[6] Kel. 17[12].   [7] Still unblocked.   [8] See Kel. 17[12].   [9] Cf. 3[6]; 7[3].
[10] Blocking it up, but still leaving a hollow space corresponding to the thickness of the wall.   [11] They count as holes not made at the hands of man.
[12] By piercing through the wall.
[13] The σπάθη with which the weaver at an upright loom beats together the newly woven woof-threads.

5. These serve to lessen the size of what is one handbreadth square: less than an olive's bulk of flesh lessens the space so that uncleanness arising from a quarter-*kab* of bones cannot pass through; and less than a barley-corn's bulk of bone [from a corpse] lessens the space so that uncleanness arising from an olive's bulk of flesh from a corpse cannot pass through; less than an olive's bulk of flesh from a corpse, less than an olive's bulk of carrion, less than a lentil's bulk of a [dead] creeping thing, less than an egg's bulk of food, grain growing against the window, reed-pith with any substance in it, the carcase of a clean bird which is not intended to be eaten, or the carcase of an unclean bird which is intended to be eaten but which has not been rendered susceptible to uncleanness,[1] or which has been rendered susceptible to uncleanness but which is not intended to be eaten.

6. These do not lessen [the measure of one handbreadth square]: bone from a corpse does not lessen [the space so that it protects] against [unclean-ness arising from other] bones from a corpse; nor corpse-flesh against other corpse-flesh; nor does a whole olive's bulk of a corpse, nor an olive's bulk of carrion, nor a lentil's bulk of a [dead] creeping thing, nor an egg's bulk of food, nor grain growing against the windows,[2] nor reed-pith that lacks substance, nor the carcase of a clean bird which is intended to be eaten, nor the carcase of an unclean bird which is intended to be eaten and which has been rendered susceptible to uncleanness; nor warp and woof threads that have contracted leprosy,[3] nor a brick from a grave-area.[4] So R. Meir. But the Sages say: The brick lessens [the space] since its dust is clean. This is the general rule: What is clean lessens the space, and what is unclean does not lessen it.

14. 1. A wall-projection, whatsoever its depth, gives passage [into the house] to uncleanness [that it overshadows]; but a pointed moulding or a rounded moulding [only] if they are a handbreadth in depth. By a wall-projection is meant a projection whose lower face is inclined downwards; and by a pointed moulding, a projection whose lower face is inclined upwards. And of what manner of projection did they speak [saying], 'Whatsoever its depth it gives passage to uncleanness'? A wall-projection that is three courses, or twelve handbreadths, higher than the doorway. If it is higher than this, it gives passage to the uncleanness only if it is a hand-breadth in depth. Cornices and carvings give passage to the uncleanness only if they are a handbreadth in depth.

2. A wall-projection above a doorway gives passage to the uncleanness if it is a handbreadth in depth;[5] if it is above a window two fingerbreadths high or above a window the size of a hole made by the drill, [it gives passage to the uncleanness] whatsoever its depth. R. Jose says: Only if it is of equal measure [to the window].[6]

3. A rod above a doorway[7] gives passage to the uncleanness even if it is higher by one hundred cubits, whatsoever its depth. So R. Joshua. R. Johanan b. Nuri says: Let not greater stringency apply to this than to the wall-projection.

---

[1] See Toh. 1[1].
[2] But which it is not intended (contrary to the case in the preceding paragraph) to suffer to grow.   [3] See Neg. 11[8].   [4] See below, 17[1ff].
[5] This contradicts the previous paragraph. According to Bert. the Mishnah speaks here in particular of a door that is closed.   [6] Two fingerbreadths.
[7] Fixed parallel to the top of the entrance.

4. If a wall-projection[1] surrounds the whole house, and extends but three fingerbreadths over the doorway, and there was uncleanness in the house, vessels under the wall-projection are unclean. If there was uncleanness under the wall-projection, R. Eliezer declares the house unclean, but R. Joshua declares it clean. So, too, if a courtyard was surrounded by a colonnade.[2]

5. If there were two wall-projections, one above the other, each a handbreadth deep, with a space between them a handbreadth wide, and there was uncleanness below them, what is below them is unclean; if it lay between them, what is between them is unclean; if above them, what is directly above it up to the sky is unclean. If the upper one projected beyond the lower one by a handbreadth, and there was uncleanness below the lower one, or between them, the space below them and between them is unclean. If the upper one projected beyond the lower one by less than a handbreadth and there was uncleanness below the lower one, the space below them and between them is unclean. If it was between them or below that part [of the upper one] that projected, R. Eliezer says: Both what is below them and what is between them is unclean. But R. Joshua says: What is between them and below the part that projected is unclean, but what is below the lower one remains clean.

6. If the two wall-projections were a handbreadth deep, but the space between them was less than a handbreadth, and there was uncleanness below the lower one, what is below is unclean. If there was uncleanness between them[3] or above the higher one, what lies directly above up to the sky is unclean.[4]

7. If they were not a handbreadth deep, whether the space between them was a handbreadth or whether it was not a handbreadth, and there was uncleanness below them, between them, or above them, the uncleanness penetrates upwards and downwards. So, too, if there were two outspread curtains raised a handbreadth above the ground.[5]

15. 1. A thick cloak[6] or a thick wooden block do not give passage to the uncleanness unless they are raised one handbreadth above the ground. If garments lay folded one above the other, they give passage to the uncleanness so soon as the upper one is raised one handbreadth above the ground. Tablets of wood, one above the other, do not give passage to the uncleanness unless the upper one is raised a handbreadth above the ground.[7] If they were of marble,[8] the uncleanness cleaves upwards and downwards.

2. If wooden tablets touched each other at their corners, and were raised

---

[1] One handbreadth deep.

[2] And the roofed portion of the colonnade extended only three fingerbreadths over the doorway of a house in the courtyard.

[3] Not having its minimum space of a cubic handbreadth it cleaves upwards and downwards (see p. 650, n. 3 (f)).

[4] Variant: 'If the wall-projections were one handbreadth deep but the spaces between them (i.e. the space between the ground and the lower projection, and the space between the two projections themselves) were less than one handbreadth, and there was uncleanness below them or between them, both what is below them and what is between them is unclean (i.e. the two spaces in either case combine to form but a single "tent", the lower projection counting as non-existent); if the uncleanness was above them what is directly above up to the sky is unclean.'

[5] In similar conditions the same rules apply as in the three preceding paragraphs.

[6] The first part of this paragraph is repeated from 11³.

[7] Then, although there is less than a free space of a cubic handbreadth, the lower tablets count as non-existent. Cf. above, 14⁶ (variant).   [8] And uncleanness lay beneath them

a handbreadth above the ground, and there was uncleanness beneath one of them, if any one touched the second tablet he contracts seven-day uncleanness; vessels that are below the one table become unclean, but those that are below the other remain clean.[1] A table does not give passage to the uncleanness unless a square of one handbreadth's extent is contained therein.[2]

3. If jars standing on their bottoms or lying on their sides in the open air touched one another to the extent of a handbreadth, and there was uncleanness below one of them, the uncleanness cleaves upwards and downwards. This applies only to clean jars. If they were unclean or raised a handbreadth above the ground and there was uncleanness below one of them, all that is below them both is unclean.

4. If part of a house[3] was separated off by boards or curtains, from the sides[4] or from the roof-beams,[5] and there was uncleanness in the house, vessels that are in the part that was separated off remain clean. If there was uncleanness in the part that was separated off, vessels that are in the [rest of] the house are unclean.[6] Vessels that are in the part that was separated off[7] are unclean if there was a space there of one cubic handbreadth; otherwise they remain clean.[8]

5. If a [horizontal] partition was made over the floor, and there was some uncleanness beneath the partition, vessels in the house become unclean;[9] if the uncleanness was in the house, vessels under the partition remain clean if there was a space there of one cubic handbreadth; otherwise they became unclean, since the floor of the house down to the nethermost deep is reckoned like to the room itself.[10]

6. If a house was filled with chopped straw so that there was a space of less than a handbreadth between the straw and the roof-beams, and there was some uncleanness inside the straw, vessels over against the entrance[11] become unclean; if the uncleanness was outside [the straw][12] and the vessels inside it, they remain clean if there was around them one cubic handbreadth of space; otherwise they become unclean. In either case, if between the straw and the roof-beams there was a space of a handbreadth, the vessels become unclean.

7. If a house was filled with earth[13] or with gravel and it was purposed to abandon it (so, too, if it was a heap of grain or a heap of gravel, even like the stone-heap of Achan)[14] even if the uncleanness lay by the side of vessels, it cleaves only upwards and downwards.

8. If a man stood in the middle of the forecourt of a tomb-vault, he remains clean if the space was not less than four cubits square. So the School of Shammai. And the School of Hillel say: [He remains clean if it measures only] four handbreadths [square]. If a beam was used instead

---

[1] The connexion between the tablets suffices to convey uncleanness by contact but not by overshadowing.
[2] This is explained as meaning that a *round* table is deemed to have the area necessary for giving passage to uncleanness only if, within its circle, a square can be described with sides of one handbreadth.   [3] Having a single room.
[4] By a perpendicular screen parallel to the wall.
[5] By a horizontal screen parallel to the floor.
[6] Since the way of uncleanness is not to enter in but to issue forth.
[7] If the uncleanness was on their side of the partition.
[8] The uncleanness cleaves upwards and downwards without affecting what is by its side.
[9] The uncleanness has no other way out.   [10] See introd. note (j).
[11] Space within the doorway of the house that is clear of straw.
[12] In the empty space within the doorway.   [13] Variant: chopped straw.
[14] Josh. 7[26].

of a stone to seal the tomb, either upright or on its side, only that part is unclean that lies opposite the opening. If its end was used to seal the tomb, only four handbreadths [near the opening] are unclean. But if [the rest of it] was about to be cut off, R. Judah says: The whole of it counts as a connective [with the uncleanness in the tomb].

9. If a jar was filled with clean liquid and fastened with a tightly stopped-up cover,[1] and this was used instead of a stone to seal the tomb, and a man touched it, he contracts seven-day uncleanness, while the jar and the liquid within it remain clean. If a [living] beast[2] was used instead of a stone to seal a tomb, he that touched it contracts seven-day uncleanness. R. Meir says: Whatsoever has in it the spirit of life cannot convey uncleanness by being used as the stone that seals the tomb.[3]

10. If a man touched a corpse and then touched any vessels, or if he overshadowed a corpse and then touched any vessels, these become unclean. If he overshadowed a corpse and then overshadowed any vessels, or if he touched a corpse and then overshadowed any vessels, these remain clean. If his hand was a handbreadth square, the vessels become unclean. If there were two pieces of corpse, each a half-olive's bulk, in two houses, and a man stretched his two hands into each of them, and his hands were one handbreadth wide, he conveys the uncleanness; otherwise he does not convey the uncleanness.

16. 1. Any movable object conveys the uncleanness[4] if it is as thick as an ox-goad. R. Tarfon said: May I bury my children if this is not a perverted *Halakah* which the hearer heard wrongly: when a husbandman passed by [a tomb] with the ox-goad over his shoulder and one end of it overshadowed the tomb, they declare him unclean[5] by virtue of the law of vessels which overshadow a corpse. R. Akiba said: I will amend [this *Halakah*] so that the words of the Sages shall remain valid: Any movable object conveys uncleanness to him that carries the object if it is as thick as an ox-goad; and the object conveys the uncleanness to itself whatsoever its thickness, but to other men and vessels only if it is one handbreadth wide.

2. Thus if a spindle was thrust into the wall, and there was a half-olive's bulk [of uncleanness] beneath it, and a half-olive's bulk above it, even if they were not directly opposite each other, the spindle becomes unclean. Thus the spindle conveys the uncleanness to itself, no matter what its size. If a pot-seller passed [a tomb] with his carrying-yoke on his shoulder, and one end of it overshadowed a tomb, the vessels on the other side remain clean. But if the yoke was one handbreadth wide, all are unclean. Mounds which are near to a town or to a road, whether they are new or old, are unclean.[6] Mounds far off that are new are clean; if they are old they are unclean. 'Near' means within fifty cubits; and 'old' means sixty years old [or more]. So R. Meir. R. Judah says: 'Near' means that there is none nearer; and 'old' means that none remembers [when it was made there].

3. If[7] for a first time[8] a man found a corpse lying in usual fashion, he

---

1 Kel. 10².   2 Erub. 1⁷.   3 Ohol. 2⁴.

4 Serves as a temporary 'tent' or roofing, transferring uncleanness from an uncleanness which it overshadows, to a man or vessel which it simultaneously overshadows.

5 Not because he was overshadowed by, but because he was in contact with, an object that suffered corpse-uncleanness by overshadowing.

6 Because of the possibility that human abortions have been buried there.

7 In ploughing his field. Naz. 9³.

8 It was not before known that there was a grave there.

may remove it and the soil about it[1] [for burial elsewhere]; if he found two, he may remove them and the soil about them. If he found three and a space of four to eight cubits between them (space enough for the bier and its bearers),[2] this must be accounted a graveyard, and he must examine the ground over a further twenty cubits. If he found another corpse twenty cubits away, he must examine yet another twenty cubits from that point, since there is proof whereon to rely [that this is indeed a graveyard]; although if for a first time a man found a corpse, he may remove it and the soil about it.

4. He that examines should examine one square cubit and then leave a cubit, until he reaches solid rock or virgin soil. He that takes away earth from a place of uncleanness[3] may still eat of his Heave-offering,[4] but he that clears away a ruin[5] may not eat of his Heave-offering.

5. If when he was examining he reached a brook or pool of water or a public road, he may make an end [of examining]. In a field where men have been slain, the bones may be gathered together one by one, and all may be accounted clean. If a man would remove from his field a tomb that belongs to him, he may collect together the bones one by one, and all may be accounted clean. If abortions, or men that had been slain, were thrown into a cistern, the bones may be collected one by one, and all may be accounted clean. R. Simeon says: If from the first it was prepared to be a burying-place, its soil must be deemed soil wherein a corpse has lain.

17. 1. If a man ploughed up a grave, the field is accounted a Grave-area.[6] How great is the space [so accounted]? A furrow's length, one hundred [square] cubits, a space of four *seahs*.[7] R. Jose says: A space of five *seahs* if the land slopes downwards;[8] but if it slopes upwards, a quarter-*kab*[9] of vetch-seed should be put on the knee of the plough,[10] and as far as where three vetches spring up together, thus far is the field accounted a Grave-area. R. Jose says: [The rule of the Grave-area applies only] where the ground slopes downwards, and not where it slopes upwards.

2. If a man was ploughing and he struck against a rock or a wall, or if he shook off the soil from the plough, thus far only is the field accounted a Grave-area. R. Eliezer says: One Grave-area may make another Grave-area.[11] R. Joshua says: Sometimes it may, but other times it may not. Thus if a man ploughed a half-furrow and then returned and ploughed a half-furrow, and then ploughed to the side, this is accounted a Grave-area. But if he ploughed a whole furrow, and then ploughed from that point onwards, beyond this [first furrow] is not accounted a Grave-area.

3. If a man ploughed from a pit filled with bones, or from a heap of bones, or from a field in which was a lost grave or in which a grave was afterward found, or if he ploughed in a field which did not belong to him,

---

[1] i.e. the clotted earth beneath the corpse with which matter that had issued from the corpse was mingled.

[2] The bracketed words are lacking in some texts. They are taken from B.B. 6[8], where the size of the forecourt to a rock sepulchre is prescribed.

[3] This field in which corpses have been found.   [4] If he is a priest.

[5] A house that has fallen upon a man and it is in doubt whether he is alive or dead.

[6] See App. IV. 19 c.   [7] App. II, E.

[8] When there is a likelihood of the plough carrying portions of the corpse a longer distance.

[9] App. II, D.

[10] Kel. 21[2]. Some part of the plough forming a shallow cavity where seed could be placed. The seed was automatically and gradually thrown out by the shaking of the plough.

[11] Cf. Tem. 1[5]. If a new furrow is begun anywhere within the hundred cubits of the Grave-area, the whole of the hundred cubits from that beginning is accounted a Grave-area.

or if a gentile ploughed, the field cannot be accounted a Grave-area; for the rule of the Grave-area does not apply even to Samaritans.

4. If there was a Grave-area on higher ground adjoining a clean field, and the rain washed down soil from the Grave-area into the clean field, even if this was of reddish soil and the other turned it white, or if this was white and the other turned it red, it is not accounted a Grave-area.

5. If there was a field in which was a lost grave and a house was built thereon and an upper room above it, if the door of the upper room was directly above the door of the house, the upper room remains clean;[1] otherwise the upper room is deemed unclean.[2] If soil from a Grave-area or soil from a foreign country[3] was brought in with vegetables, the [several pieces of] soil are included together to make up the bulk equal to the seal of packing-bags [that suffices to convey uncleanness]. So R. Eliezer. But the Sages say: [It conveys uncleanness] only if in one place there was a bulk equal to the seal of packing-bags. R. Judah said: Letters once came from beyond the sea to the Sons of the High Priests,[4] and there was on them about a *seah*[5] or two *seahs* of seals, yet the Sages were not scrupulous about them[6] on account of uncleanness.

18. 1. How can they gather the grapes in a Grave-area?[7] Men and vessels must be sprinkled[8] the first and the second time; then they gather the grapes and take them out of the Grave-area; others[9] receive the grapes from them and take them to the winepress. If these others touched the grape-gatherers they become unclean. So the School of Hillel. The School of Shammai say: They should hold the sickle with a wrapping of bast, or cut the grapes with a sharp flint, and let them fall into a large olive-basket and bring them to the winepress. R. Jose said: This applies only to a vineyard that later became a Grave-area; but if a man planted vines in a Grave-area, the grapes should be sold in the market [and not made into wine].

2. There are three kinds of Grave-area. If a man ploughed over a grave, the field may be planted with any kind of tree; but it may not be sown with any kind of seed excepting that of plants which are cut [and not plucked]. If a man plucked such plants, he must heap up the threshing-floor within the field itself and sift the grain through two sieves. So R. Meir. But the Sages say: Grain should be sifted through two sieves, but pulse through three sieves. The stubble and stalks must be burnt. These convey uncleanness by contact and carrying but not by overshadowing.

3. A field in which is a lost grave may be sown with any kind of seed, but it may not be planted with any kind of plants, nor may trees be suffered to grow there save only such that bear no fruit.[10] It[11] conveys uncleanness by contact and carrying and by overshadowing.

4. A field of mourners[12] may neither be planted nor sown; but its soil

---

[1] If the uncleanness is within the area covered by the inner space of the house the upper story is protected by its floor; if it is under the doorway it enters under the lintel of the lower doorway which saves the upper doorway, and if it was under the walls it cleaves upwards perpendicularly, leaving both house and upper story clean.

[2] On the assumption that the uncleanness is directly under the lintel of the upper story's doorway.   [3] See above, 2³.   [4] See Ket. 13¹; cf. p. 245, n. 14.   [5] App. II, D.

[6] Since none was alone as large as a packing-bag seal.

[7] So that the wine may be accounted clean.   [8] Num. 19¹⁸ᶠ.

[9] Who have not been rendered unclean by the Grave-area.   [10] *Serak* trees. Cf. Kil. 6⁵.

[11] Such a field and soil from it.

[12] A field where they bewail the dead (cf. Meg. 4³; Ket. 2¹⁰; B.B. 6⁷), near to the tombs themselves. For 'mourners' (*bokim*) the Tosefta has 'tomb-niches' (*kokim*). Cf. App. IV. 19 c.

is clean and may be used for making ovens meet for the Hallowed Things.[1] The School of Shammai and the School of Hillel agree that a Grave-area needs to be examined[2] on behalf of him that would bring his Passover-offering,[3] but not on behalf of him that would eat Heave-offering. For a Nazirite,[4] the School of Shammai say: It must be examined. And the School of Hillel say: It need not be examined. How is the field examined? Earth that is easily shifted is taken and put in a sieve that has narrow meshes, and rubbed. If a barleycorn's bulk of bone is found there [he that has been there] is accounted unclean.

5. How is a Grave-area rendered clean? The soil is taken away to a depth of three handbreadths;[5] or[6] soil is added thereon to a height of three handbreadths. If from half of the field soil was taken away to a depth of three handbreadths, and to the other half soil was added to a height of three handbreadths, it becomes clean. R. Simeon says: Even if a handbreadth and a half was taken away and soil from elsewhere was added to a height of a handbreadth and a half, it becomes clean. If a Grave-area was paved with stones that cannot easily be shifted, it becomes clean. R. Simeon says: Even if a Grave-area was cleared of stones, it becomes clean.

6. If a man walked through a Grave-area over stones that cannot easily be shifted or rode upon a man or beast whose strength was great, he remains clean; but if [he walked] over stones that can easily be shifted, or [rode] upon a man or beast whose strength was small, he becomes unclean.[7] If a man went through the country of the gentiles[8] in hilly or rocky country, he becomes unclean; but if by the sea or along the strand, he remains clean. What is 'the strand'? Any place over which the sea rolls during a storm.

7. If a man bought a field in Syria that lies close to the Land of Israel and he can enter it in cleanness,[9] it is clean, and it is subject to the laws of Tithes and Seventh Year produce; but if he cannot enter it in cleanness it is deemed unclean, yet it is still subject to the laws of Tithes and Seventh Year produce. The dwelling-places of gentiles are unclean.[10] How long must a gentile have lived in them so that examination becomes needful? Forty days,[11] even though he had no woman with him; but if a slave or [an Israelitish] woman watched over the dwelling, no examination is needful.

8. What do they examine? The deep drains and the foul water. The School of Shammai say: Also the dunghill and loose earth. The School of Hillel say: Wheresoever a pig or weasel can penetrate no examination is needful.

9. The rules about the dwelling-places of gentiles do not apply to colonnades. R. Simeon b. Gamaliel says: The rules about the dwelling-places of gentiles do not apply to a city of the gentiles that is in ruins. The east side of Kesrin[12] and the west side of Kesrin[13] are graveyards. The east side of Acre was in doubt, but the Sages have declared it clean. Rabbi and his court voted on Keni[14] and declared it clean.

[1] Baking the bread used for the various Meal-offerings in the Temple.
[2] When one who may not become unclean has been there, and it is in doubt whether it may not be a Grave-area.   [3] See Num. 9[6].   [4] Num. 6[6].
[5] The maximum depth penetrated by the plough.
[6] Some texts prefix 'Rabbi (Judah the Patriarch) says'.
[7] He can be assumed to have shared in moving the uncleanness on the ground.
[8] Cf. above, 2[3]; 17[5].   [9] i.e. no gentile land intervened.
[10] Because they throw abortions down their drains.   [11] Cf. Nidd. 3[7].
[12] Caesarea maritima.   [13] Variant: *Kesarion*, Caesarea Philippi.
[14] Identifications have been suggested with Wady Kanah (in Samaria), or Ain Keni (near Lydda).

10. To ten places the rules about the dwelling-places of gentiles do not apply: the tents of the Arabs, field-huts, simple tents, fruit-shelters, summer houses, a gate-house, the open space in a courtyard, a bath-house, an armoury, and the camping-grounds of the legions.

NEGAIM[1] ('LEPROSY-SIGNS')

1. 1. The colours of leprosy-signs[2] are two,[3] which are, indeed, four[4]: the Bright Spot, which is bright white like snow—and the second shade of it is [as white] as the lime used in the Sanctuary;[5] and the Rising, which is [as white] as the skin in an egg—and the second shade of it is [as white] as white wool. So R. Meir. But the Sages say: The Rising is [as white] as white wool and the second shade of it is [as white] as the skin in an egg.[6]

2. Where there is a [reddish] mixture[7] in the snow-like whiteness, [the colour] is like wine mingled with snow; in the lime-like whiteness [the colour] is like blood mingled with milk. So R. Ishmael. R. Akiba says: In either of them the reddishness is like wine mingled with water, save only that in the snow-like whiteness [the colour] is bright, and in the lime-like whiteness [the colour] is duller.

3. [Any among] these four colours may be included together to make up [the prescribed measure][8] whether to pronounce [a leprosy-sign] clean,[9] or to certify it unclean,[10] or to cause it to be shut up.[11] 'To cause it to be shut up'—namely, such that continues unchanged by the end of the first week; 'to pronounce it clean'—namely, such that continues unchanged by the end of the second week; 'to certify it unclean'—namely, that wherein has arisen quick flesh or white hair, whether in the beginning, or by the end of the first week, or by the end of the second week, or even after it had been pronounced clean; or [again] 'to certify it unclean'—namely, that wherein has arisen a spreading by the end of the first week, or by the end of the second week, or even after it had been pronounced clean; 'to certify it unclean'—if the whole [skin of his flesh] turned white after the leprosy-sign had been pronounced clean; or 'to pronounce it clean'—if the whole [skin of his flesh] turned white after the leprosy-sign had been certified unclean, or after it had been kept shut up. These are the colours of leprosy-signs whereon depend all [the prescriptions concerning] leprosy-signs.

4. R. Hanina[12] the Prefect of the Priests says: The colours of leprosy-signs are sixteen. R. Dosa b. Harkinas says: The colours of leprosy-signs are thirty-six. Akabya b. Mahalaleel says: Seventy-two.[13] R. Hanina the Prefect of the Priests says: They may not inspect leprosy-signs for the first time the day after the Sabbath since the end of that week[14] will fall on the

[1] Lit. 'plagues'. The tractate is based on Lev. 13-14. It elaborates the details there given concerning the various symptoms of the so-called leprosy as they appear in men, garments, and houses.
[2] Such as appear 'in the skin of the flesh' (Lev. 13²), i.e. the bare flesh as distinct from parts covered by hair.   [3] The Bright Spot and the Rising (Lev. 13²).
[4] The word *sappahath* (Lev. 13²; R.V. 'scab') is interpreted as meaning something 'joined' or 'attached to'; hence a secondary shade of colour of the main symptoms. Cf. below, 7².   [5] Cf. Midd. 3⁴.
[6] Of these four shades the whitest is snow, the next lime, the next white wool, and the dullest white is that of the skin in an egg.   [7] See Lev. 13¹⁹.
[8] To make up the size of a split bean (see below, 4⁵; 6¹).   [9] Lit. 'acquit'.
[10] Lit. 'determine.'   [11] See Lev. 13⁴.   [12] Some texts omit this sentence.
[13] These totals are reached by various possible combinations of some or all of the simple colours, mixed colours, the boil and the burn, the scalp and forehead baldness, the scall, and also the reddishness and greenishness in garments and houses.
[14] Following the seven days during which the symptom is 'shut up'.

Sabbath; nor yet on the second day of the week since the end of the Second week will fall on the Sabbath; nor [do they inspect leprosy-signs] in houses on the third day of the week since the end of the third week will fall on the Sabbath. R. Akiba says: They may inspect them at any time; and if [the time for inspection at the end of the seven days] falls on a Sabbath they leave it until after the Sabbath. This may bear either with leniency or with stringency.[1]

5. How can it bear with leniency? If [on the Sabbath] there was white hair[2] in the leprosy-sign but [the next day] the white hair was gone; or if the hairs were white but [the next day] they turned black, whether one was white and the other black, or both black; or if [on the Sabbath] they were long but [the next day] they became short,[3] whether one was short and the other long, or both short; or if [after the Sabbath] a boil[4] adjoined both hairs or one of them; or if the boil encompassed both hairs or one of them; or if they were sundered by a boil or the quick flesh[5] of a boil, or by a burning or the quick flesh of a burning, or by a tetter;[6] or if [on the Sabbath] there was quick flesh but [the next day] the quick flesh was gone; or if it was four-sided but [the next day] it became round or long; or if it was encompassed but [the next day] it appeared only to the side; or if it was united but [the next day] it was dispersed; or if [the next day] a boil came and entered therein; or if [the next day] it was encompassed or sundered or lessened by a boil or the quick flesh of a boil, or by a burning or the quick flesh of a burning, or by a tetter; or if [on the Sabbath] there was a spreading but [the next day] the spreading was gone; or if the first sign itself was gone or so lessened that both it and the spreading were less than a split bean;[7] or if the first sign and the spreading were sundered by a boil or the quick flesh of a boil, or by a burning or the quick flesh of a burning, or by a tetter;—then the rule bears with leniency.

6. How can it bear with stringency? If [on the Sabbath] there was no white hair therein but [the next day] white hair appeared; or if they were black but [the next day] they turned white, or if one was white and the other black but [the next day] they were both white; or if they were short but became long, or if one was short and the other long, but [the next day] they were both long; or if a boil adjoined them both or one of them; or if the boil encompassed them both or one of them; or if [on the Sabbath] it was sundered by a boil or the quick flesh of a boil, or by a burning or the quick flesh of a burning, or by a tetter, but [the next day] they were gone; or if there was no quick flesh therein [on the Sabbath] but [the next day] quick flesh arose; or if it was round or long but became four-sided; or if [on the Sabbath] it was at the side but [the next day] it was encompassed; or if it was dispersed but became united; or if a boil came and entered therein; or if a boil or the quick flesh of a boil, a burning or the quick flesh of a burning, or a tetter encompassed, sundered, or lessened it, but [the next day] they were gone; or if [on the Sabbath] there was no spreading therein but [the next day] a spreading arose; or if [on the Sabbath] a boil or the quick flesh of a boil, a burning or the quick flesh of a burning, or a tetter sundered the first sign and the spreading, but [the next day] they were gone;—then the rule bears with stringency.

---

[1] Cf. M. Kat. 1⁵.   [2] Which would certify the leprosy-sign to be unclean. Lev. 13³.
[3] They became too short to be taken account of. See Nidd. 6¹².
[4] Lev. 13¹⁸. See below, 8⁷.   [5] Cf. Lev. 13¹⁰, ¹⁴, ²⁴.   [6] Lev. 13³⁹.   [7] See Kel. 17¹².

2. 1. In a German the Bright Spot appears as dull white, and in an Ethiopian[1] what is dull white appears as bright white. R. Ishmael says: The Children of Israel (may I make atonement for them!) are like boxwood, neither black nor white, but of the intermediate shade. R. Akiba says: Painters have colours wherewith they depict figures in black and white and in the intermediate shade. A man should bring paint of an intermediate shade and encompass the leprosy-sign therewith, and it will then appear as on one [whose skin is] of the intermediate shade. R. Judah says: The [rules concerning] the colours of leprosy-signs should be applied leniently and not stringently: let a German be judged leniently by [the standard of the colour of] his own skin, and let an Ethiopian be judged leniently by [the standard of colour of] the intermediate shade. But the Sages say: Let both be judged by [the standard of colour of] the intermediate shade.

2. They may not inspect leprosy-signs in the early morning or in the evening or within the house or on a cloudy day, for then the dull white would appear bright white; or at mid-day, for then the bright white would appear dull white. When should they inspect them? At the third, fourth, fifth, seventh,[2] eighth, or ninth hour. So R. Meir. R. Judah says: At the fourth, fifth, eighth, or ninth hour.

3. A priest that is blind in one eye or the light of whose eyes is dim may not inspect leprosy-signs, for it is written, *As far as appeareth in the eyes of the priest.*[3] They may not open up windows in a dark house to inspect the leprosy-signs thereof.

4. After what fashion is the inspection of leprosy-signs? The man is inspected [while he stands] like one that hoes, and like one that gathers olives, and the woman [while she stands] like one that rolls out bread, and like one that gives suck to her child, and like one that weaves at an upright loom if the sign is within the right armpit. R. Judah says: Also like one that spins flax if the sign is within the left [armpit]. As the inspection of leprosy-signs in a man applies only to what is visible, so the cutting off of his hair[4] applies only to what is visible.

5. A man may examine any leprosy-signs[5] excepting his own leprosy-signs. R. Meir says: Excepting also those in his near of kin. A man[6] may annul all vows excepting his own. R. Judah says: But not his wife's vows that rest between herself and others. A man may inspect any Firstlings[7] excepting his own Firstlings.

3. 1. All can contract uncleanness from leprosy-signs excepting gentiles and resident aliens.[8] All are qualified to inspect leprosy-signs, but only a priest may pronounce them unclean or clean. They [that are skilled] say to a priest, 'Say, Unclean!' and he shall say 'Unclean!' or [they say to him], 'Say, Clean!' and he shall say 'Clean!' They may not inspect two leprosy-signs at the same time whether in the one man or in two men; but they must inspect the one, and shut him up or certify him unclean or pronounce him clean, and then turn to the second. [Because of a second leprosy-sign] they cannot shut up him that is already shut up or certify him unclean that is already certified unclean, or shut up him that is already certified unclean,

---

[1] Lit. 'Kushite.' Cf. Sukk. 3[6]; Bekh. 7[6].   [2] Some texts omit 'seventh'.
[3] Lev. 13[12].   [4] Lev. 14[9].   [5] Even those of his near of kin.
[6] A sage, who had authority to release a man from his vow. Cf. Ned. 9[1ff].
[7] To find whether they have a blemish. See Bekh. 6[1ff].
[8] See p. 356, n. 9.

or certify unclean him that is already shut up; but in the beginning, or by the end of the week the priest may shut him up [because of the one sign] and shut him up [because of the other also], or certify the one unclean and certify the other unclean also, or shut him up [because of the one] and pronounce the other clean, or certify the one unclean and pronounce the other clean.

2. If a leprosy-sign appeared in a bridegroom they must suffer him to remain free [before inspection] during the seven days of the marriage feast, whether it appeared in his person, in his house, or in his garment; so, too, [if it appeared in any man] during a Feast, they must suffer him to remain free all the days of the Feast.[1]

3. The skin of the flesh[2] may be certified unclean within two weeks and by three tokens: by white hair[3] or by quick flesh[4] or by a spreading.[5] 'By white hair or by quick flesh'—in the beginning, or by the end of the first week, or by the end of the second week, or even after it had been pronounced clean. 'Or by a spreading'—by the end of the first week or by the end of the second week, or even after it had been pronounced clean. It may be certified unclean within two weeks, that are but thirteen days.

4. A boil[6] or a burning[7] may be certified unclean within one week and by two tokens: by white hair[8] or by a spreading.[9] 'By white hair'—in the beginning, or by the end of the week, or even after it had been pronounced clean. 'Or by a spreading'—by the end of the week, or even after it had been pronounced clean. They may be certified unclean within one week, that is of seven days.

5. Scalls[10] may be certified unclean within two weeks and by two tokens: by yellow thin hair[11] or by a spreading.[12] 'By yellow thin hair'—in the beginning, or by the end of the first week, or by the end of the second week, or even after they had been pronounced clean. 'By a spreading'—by the end of the first week, or by the end of the second week, or even after they had been pronounced clean. They may be certified unclean within two weeks, that are but thirteen days.

6. Scalp-baldness or forehead-baldness[13] may be certified unclean within two weeks and by two tokens: by quick flesh or by a spreading. 'By quick flesh'—in the beginning, or by the end of the first week, or by the end of the second week, or even after they had been pronounced clean. 'Or by a spreading'—by the end of the first week, or by the end of the second week, or even after they had been pronounced clean. They may be certified unclean within two weeks, that are but thirteen days.

7. Garments[14] may be certified unclean within two weeks, and by three tokens: by a greenish colour or by a reddish colour or by a spreading. 'By a greenish colour or by a reddish colour'—in the beginning, or by the end of the first week, or by the end of the second week, or even after they had been pronounced clean. 'Or by a spreading'—by the end of the first week or by the end of the second week, or even after they had been pronounced clean. They may be certified unclean within two weeks, that are but thirteen days.

8. Houses may be certified unclean within three weeks, and by three

---

[1] Cf. M. Kat. 1[5].   [2] In which any of the four shades of white had appeared.
[3] Lev. 13[3].   [4] Lev. 13[10, 14, 24].   [5] Cf. Lev. 13[8, 22].   [6] Lev. 13[18].
[7] Lev. 13[24].   [8] Lev. 13[20, 25].   [9] Lev. 13[22, 27].   [10] Lev. 13[30].   [11] Lev. 13[30].
[12] Lev. 13[35].   [13] Lev. 13[40f].   [14] Lev. 13[47ff].

tokens: by a greenish colour or by a reddish colour or by a spreading. 'By a greenish colour or by a reddish colour'—in the beginning, or by the end of the first week, or by the end of the second week, or by the end of the third week, or even after they had been pronounced clean. 'Or by a spreading'—by the end of the first week, or by the end of the second week, or by the end of the third week, or even after they had been pronounced clean. They can be certified unclean within three weeks, that are but nineteen days. No leprosy-signs are shut up less than one week and none more than three weeks.[1]

4. 1. Conditions pertain to the white hair which do not pertain to the spreading, and conditions pertain to the spreading which do not pertain to the white hair. Thus white hair certifies uncleanness in the beginning, it certifies uncleanness no matter what its degree of whiteness, and it can never be a token of cleanness. But it pertains to the spreading that the spreading certifies uncleanness no matter what its extent, and it certifies uncleanness in all other leprosy-signs though it is outside the sign itself; whereas not so is it with the white hair.

2. Conditions pertain to the quick flesh which do not pertain to the spreading, and conditions pertain to the spreading which do not pertain to the quick flesh. Thus quick flesh certifies uncleanness in the beginning, it certifies uncleanness no matter what its colour, and it can never be a token of cleanness. But it pertains to the spreading that the spreading certifies uncleanness no matter what its extent, and it certifies uncleanness in all other leprosy-signs though it is outside the sign itself; whereas not so is it with the quick flesh.

3. Conditions pertain to the white hair which do not pertain to the quick flesh and conditions pertain to the quick flesh which do not pertain to the white hair. Thus white hair certifies uncleanness in a boil or a burning or any leprosy-sign that is united or dispersed, encompassed or unencompassed; but it pertains to quick flesh that quick flesh certifies uncleanness in scalp-baldness or forehead-baldness, whether the quick flesh came after or whether the quick flesh came before; and it hinders [the cleanness] in him who is all turned white,[2] and it certifies uncleanness no matter what its colour; whereas not so is it with the white hair.

4. If two hairs [in the leprosy-sign] were black at the root and white at the tip, he is clean; if they were white at the root and black at the tip, he is unclean. How much thereof must be coloured white? R. Meir says: Aught soever. R. Simeon says: Enough to be cut with a pair of scissors.[3] If it was single at the root but split at the tip and like two hairs in appearance, he is clean. If there was a Bright Spot wherein was a white hair or a black hair, he is unclean. They need not scruple lest the place of the black hair lessens the space of the Bright Spot since it scarce counts.

5. If from a Bright Spot the size of a split bean there extended a streak that was two hairs in breadth, it serves to link the Bright Spot with white hair or a spreading, but not with quick flesh. If there were two Bright Spots and a streak extended from one to the other, it makes them to be included together if it is two hairs in breadth; but if it is not, it does not make them to be included together.

6. If a Bright Spot the size of a split bean had within it quick flesh the

[1] Arak. 2[1].   [2] Lev. 13[13f].   [3] Cf. Nidd. 6[12].

size of a lentil and there was white hair within the quick flesh, if the quick flesh disappeared it is unclean by reason of the white hair; if the white hair disappeared it is unclean by reason of the quick flesh. R. Simeon declares it clean, since it did not turn white while in the Bright Spot. If the Bright Spot and the quick flesh together were the size of a split bean and there was white hair within the Bright Spot, if the quick flesh disappeared it is unclean by reason of the white hair; if the white hair disappeared it is unclean by reason of the quick flesh. R. Simeon declares it clean since it did not turn white while in a Bright Spot the size of a split bean. But he agrees that it is unclean if the place of the white hair was the size of a split bean.

7. If within the Bright Spot was quick flesh and a spreading, and the quick flesh disappeared, it is unclean by reason of the spreading; if the spreading disappeared it is unclean by reason of the quick flesh; so, too, if there was white hair and a spreading. If the Bright Spot disappeared and appeared again by the end of the week, it is regarded as though it had remained as it was; [but if it appeared] after it had already been pronounced clean, it must be inspected anew. If it had been bright white but was now dull white, or dull white but was now bright white, it is regarded as though it had remained as it was; provided that it does not become less white than the four colours.[1] If it contracted and then spread or if it spread and then contracted, R. Akiba declares it unclean but the Sages declare it clean.

8. If a Bright Spot the size of a split bean spread as much as another half a split bean, and from the first spot there disappeared as much as half a split bean, R. Akiba says: It must be inspected anew. But the Sages declare it clean.

9. If a Bright Spot the size of a split bean spread as much as another half a split bean and more, and from the first spot there disappeared as much as half a split bean, R. Akiba declares it unclean but the Sages declare it clean. If a Bright Spot the size of a split bean spread as much as another split bean and more and the first spot disappeared, R. Akiba declares it unclean, but the Sages say: It must be inspected anew.

10. If a Bright Spot the size of a split bean spread as much as another split bean, and there appeared in the spreading quick flesh or white hair and the first spot disappeared, R. Akiba declares it unclean, but the Sages say: It must be inspected anew. If in a Bright Spot the size of half a split bean naught else appeared, but [beside it] there arose a Bright Spot the size of half a split bean and in it a single hair, it must be shut up. If in a Bright Spot the size of half a split bean there was a single hair, and another Bright Spot the size of half a split bean appeared, in which was a single hair, it must be shut up. If in a Bright Spot the size of half a split bean there were two hairs, and another Bright Spot the size of half a split bean appeared in which was a single hair, it must be shut up.

11. If in a Bright Spot the size of half a split bean naught else appeared but [beside it] arose a Bright Spot the size of half a split bean in which were two hairs, it must be certified unclean, since they have said: If the Bright Spot came before the white hair, he is unclean; but if the white hair came before the Bright Spot he is clean; and if it is in doubt, he is unclean. But [to this] R. Joshua demurred.

5. 1. Any condition of doubt in what concerns leprosy-signs is deemed clean, save only in this case[2] and one other. Which is that? If a man had

---

[1] See above, 1[1].   [2] That recorded above, 4[11].

a Bright Spot the size of a split bean and it was shut up, and by the end of the week it was as large as a *sela*,[1] and it is in doubt whether it is the same or whether another has arisen in its place, he is nevertheless unclean.

2. If he had been certified unclean because of white hair, and the white hair disappeared and other white hair appeared (so, too, with quick flesh or a spreading, in the beginning, or by the end of the first week, or by the end of the second week, or after he had been pronounced clean) it remains as it was before. If he had been certified unclean because of quick flesh, and the quick flesh disappeared and other quick flesh appeared (so, too, with white hair or a spreading, in the beginning, or by the end of the first week, or by the end of the second week, or after he had been pronounced clean), it remains as it was before. If he had been certified unclean because of a spreading, and the spreading disappeared and another appeared (so, too, with white hair by the end of the first week, or by the end of the second week, or after he had been pronounced clean), it remains as it was before.

3. Residuary hair[2] Akabya b. Mahalaleel declares unclean, but the Sages declare it clean. What is residuary hair? If a man had a Bright Spot in which was white hair, and the Bright Spot disappeared and left the hair where it was, and it afterward returned, Akabya b. Mahalaleel declares him unclean, but the Sages declare him clean. R. Akiba said: I agree that such a one is clean. But what is residuary hair?[3] If a man had a Bright Spot the size of a split bean in which were two hairs, and as much as half a split bean disappeared but left the white hair in the place of the Bright Spot, and it afterward appeared again [such is deemed unclean]. They said to him: Like as they made void[4] the words of Akabya, so are thy words not to be accepted as valid.

4. Any condition of doubt[5] in the beginning in what concerns leprosy-signs is deemed clean if it had not already come within the bonds of uncleanness; if it had come within the bonds of uncleanness its condition of doubt is deemed unclean. Thus if two men came to the priest, one with a Bright Spot the size of a split bean and the other with one the size of a *sela*, and at the end of the week that of each was the size of a *sela*, and it is not known in which of them was the spreading ([and it is all one] whether this befell one man or two men), he is clean. R. Akiba says: If there was but one man he is unclean; but if there were two he is accounted clean.

5. 'If it had come within the bonds of uncleanness its condition of doubt is deemed unclean'—thus if two men came to the priest, one with a Bright Spot the size of a split bean and the other with one the size of a *sela*, and at the end of the week that of each was the size of a *sela* and more, both are unclean; and even if both return to the size of a *sela* they both are unclean; [both are unclean] unless they [both] return to the size of a split bean. This it is whereof they have said, 'If it had come within the bonds of uncleanness its condition of doubt is deemed unclean'.

6. 1. The space of a Bright Spot must be [not less than] a square with sides the length of a Cilician split bean.[6] A space the size of a split bean equals that of nine lentils, and a space the size of a lentil equals that of four hairs;[7] thus [the space of the Bright Spot] equals thirty-six hairs.

---

[1] App. II, A.   [2] Eduy. 5⁶.   [3] That must be deemed unclean.
[4] Variant: Like as thou hast made void.
[5] Naz. 9⁴.   [6] Kel. 17¹². If it is smaller it is deemed clean.
[7] i.e. the space they occupy when growing elsewhere than on the head or beard.

2. If in a Bright Spot the size of a split bean was quick flesh the size of a lentil, and the Bright Spot grew larger, it is unclean; if it grew smaller it is clean; if the quick flesh grew larger it is unclean; if it grew smaller it is clean.

3. If in a Bright Spot the size of a split bean there was quick flesh less in size than a lentil, and the Bright Spot grew larger, it is unclean; if it grew smaller it is clean; if the quick flesh grew larger it is unclean; if it grew smaller, R. Meir declares it unclean, but the Sages declare it clean, since the leprosy-sign cannot spread within itself.

4. If in a Bright Spot larger in size than a split bean there was quick flesh larger than a lentil and they increased or decreased, they are unclean provided that they do not grow smaller than the prescribed measure.

5. If a Bright Spot the size of a split bean was encompassed by quick flesh the size of a lentil, and outside the quick flesh was [another] Bright Spot, the inner Bright Spot must be shut up and the outer one must be certified unclean. R. Jose says: Quick flesh is not a token of uncleanness for the outer one, since the [inner] Bright Spot is encompassed by it. If the quick flesh decreased or disappeared, Rabban Gamaliel says: If it fell away from the inner side it is a token of a spreading in the inner Bright Spot, and the outer one becomes clean; but if it fell away from the outer side, the outer Bright Spot is clean and the inner one must be shut up. R. Akiba says: In either case it is clean.

6. R. Simeon said: This applies only if the quick flesh was the very size of the lentil applied thereto; if it exceeded the size of a lentil the excess betokens a spreading of the inner Bright Spot, and the outer one is unclean. If a tetter was there[1] less in size than a lentil, it betokens a spreading of the inner Bright Spot and not a spreading of the outer one.

7. In a man's body are twenty-four tips of members that may not be deemed unclean[2] by reason of quick flesh: the tips of the fingers and the toes, the tips of the ears and the tip of the nose, and the tip of the male organ; and the nipples in a woman. R. Judah says: The nipples in men also. R. Eliezer says: Nor may warts or wens be deemed unclean by reason of quick flesh.

8. These places[3] in men may not be deemed unclean by reason of a Bright Spot: inside the eye, inside the ear, inside the nose, inside the mouth, wrinkles, wrinkles in the neck, under the breast, and the armpit, the sole of the foot, the nails, the head and the beard, or a festering boil, burning, or blister; these cannot be deemed unclean by reason of leprosy-signs, nor can they be included together with other leprosy-signs, nor can a leprosy-sign spread into them, nor do they render other signs unclean by reason of being quick flesh, nor do they hinder [cleanness] in him who is all turned white.[4] If a bald spot arose in the head or beard, or if the boil, burning, or blister formed a scar,[5] they may be deemed unclean by reason of leprosy-signs, but they cannot be included together with other leprosy-signs, nor can other leprosy-signs spread into them, nor do they become unclean by reason of being quick flesh, but they hinder [cleanness] in him who is all turned white. The head and the beard before they have grown hair, and wens on the head or the beard, are deemed like to *the skin of the flesh*.[6]

---

1 Between the inner and outer spots.
2 i.e. if the raw flesh (Lev. 13[14]) appears on any of these alone, the terms of Lev. 13[15] do not apply, since the sign, appearing on a convex area, is not all visible at once.
3 They are excluded as not falling within the definition 'the skin of his flesh' (Lev. 13[2]).
4 Except for any of these places. Lev. 13[13ff].   5 Lev. 13[23].   6 Lev. 13[3].

7. 1. These Bright Spots are clean: any that were on a man before the Law was given,[1] or that were on a gentile when he became a proselyte, or that were on a child when it was born, or that were in a crease and were later laid bare. If they were on the head or the beard, on a festering boil, burning, or blister, and the head or the beard then became bald, and the boil, burning, or blister formed a scar, they are clean. If they were on the head or the beard before these grew hair, and they then grew hair and again became bald, or if the boil, burning, or blister had not formed a scar and afterward formed a scar, and again became quick flesh, R. Eliezer b. Jacob declares them unclean, since both in the beginning and at the end they were unclean; but the Sages declare them clean.

2. If their colour changed, whether after a fashion that effects leniency or after a fashion that effects stringency—(How could it effect leniency? If, namely, the colour of the leprosy-sign had been white as snow and it became white as the lime used in the Sanctuary or as white wool or as the skin in an egg, or if its colour turned to the second shade of the Rising or to the second shade of bright white.[2] How could it effect stringency? If, namely, its colour had been white as the skin in an egg and it became white as white wool or as the lime used in the Sanctuary or as snow)— R. Eleazar b. Azariah declares them clean. R. Eleazar Hisma says: If the leprosy-sign changed after a fashion that effects leniency it is clean, but if after a fashion that effects stringency it must be inspected anew. R. Akiba says: Whether it changed after a fashion that effects leniency or after a fashion that effects stringency it must be inspected anew.

3. If in a Bright Spot naught else appears, whether in the beginning, or by the end of the first week, it must be shut up; if [naught else appears] by the end of the second week, or after it had been pronounced clean, it may be pronounced clean. If the priest had not yet shut it up or pronounced it clean, and tokens of uncleanness[3] arose, he must certify it to be unclean. If in a Bright Spot appeared tokens of uncleanness, he must certify it to be unclean; if he had not yet certified it to be unclean and the tokens of uncleanness disappeared, whether in the beginning, or by the end of the first week, he must shut it up; if [they disappeared] by the end of the second week or after it had been pronounced clean,[4] he must pronounce it clean.

4. If a man plucked out the tokens of uncleanness or cauterized quick flesh, he transgresses a negative command.[5] In what concerns his cleanness, [if he removed the tokens] before he came to the priest, he is clean; but if after he had been certified unclean, he is still unclean. R. Akiba said: I asked Rabban Gamaliel and R. Joshua[6] when they were on the way to Narwad,[7] 'What would befall [if he removed the tokens of uncleanness] while he was shut up?' They said to me, 'We have heard no tradition about this, but we have heard that if he did so before he came to the priest, he is clean; but if after he had been certified unclean, he is still unclean'. I began to bring them proofs: It is all one whether he stand before the priest or whether he is shut up: he is clean, unless the priest has certified him to be unclean. From what time does he [again] become clean? R. Eliezer

---

[1] Although they continued after the Law was given.   [2] See above 1[1].
[3] White hair and 'plague . . . deeper than the skin of his flesh'.
[4] e.g. if after being pronounced clean, tokens of uncleanness appeared but, before they were certified unclean, they disappeared, the priest must pronounce the Bright Spot clean.
[5] Cf. Deut. 24[8].   [6] Cf. Ker. 3[7].
[7] Variants: Nadwad, Nadabah, Gadwad. Cf. Arak. 9[6].

says: After another leprosy-sign has arisen in him and he has become clean again after it. But the Sages say: Only after it has spread over his whole body or until the Bright Spot grows smaller than a split bean.

5. If a man had a Bright Spot and it was cut off, he becomes clean; but if he cut it off intentionally, R. Eliezer says: [He does not become clean] until after another leprosy-sign has arisen in him and he has become clean again after it. But the Sages say: Only after it has spread over his whole body. If it is upon the tip of the foreskin, he may nevertheless be circumcised.[1]

8. 1. If it broke out abroad[2] [and covered all his skin, beginning] from a leprosy-sign that was certified unclean,[3] he becomes clean; but if it receded from but the ends of his members[4] he becomes unclean until the Bright Spot is become less than the size of a split bean. [If it broke out abroad, beginning] from a leprosy-sign that was pronounced clean, he becomes unclean; and if it receded from the ends of his members he remains unclean until his Bright Spot becomes again what it was before.

2. If a Bright Spot the size of a split bean, wherein was quick flesh the size of a lentil, broke out abroad and covered all his skin, and the quick flesh afterward disappeared; or if the quick flesh disappeared and the Bright Spot afterward broke out abroad and covered all his skin, he is clean. If quick flesh then arose he is unclean. If white hair arose, R. Joshua declares him unclean but the Sages declare him clean.

3. If a Bright Spot wherein was white hair broke out abroad and covered all his skin, although the white hair continued in its place, he is clean. If a Bright Spot wherein was a spreading broke out abroad and covered all his skin, he is clean. But with them all, if it receded from but the ends of the members, they[5] are unclean. If it broke out abroad and covered but part of his skin, he is unclean; if it broke out abroad and covered all his skin, he is clean.

4. Whenever, by reason of the spreading [of the Bright Spot] to the ends of the members, they have pronounced clean him that was unclean, if the spreading recedes they become again unclean. Whenever, by reason of the receding [of the leprosy] from the ends of the members, they have pronounced unclean him that was clean, if they again become covered he becomes clean, and if they again become uncovered he becomes unclean, even a hundred times.

5. Any part of the skin that can suffer uncleanness[6] by reason of the leprosy-sign of a Bright Spot, can impair the breaking out abroad [of the leprosy over all his skin];[7] but any part that cannot suffer uncleanness by reason of the leprosy-sign of a Bright Spot cannot impair the breaking out abroad [of the leprosy over all his skin]. Thus, if it broke out abroad and covered all his skin, but it did not cover the head or the beard, or a festering boil, burning, or blister, and the head or the beard then became bald, or the boil, burning, or blister formed a scar, he is nevertheless clean. But if it broke out abroad and covered all his skin excepting half a lentil's space [where was quick flesh] near the head or the beard, near a boil, burning,

---

[1] The law of circumcision overrides the prohibition (cf. above, 7[4]) against removing the tokens of uncleanness. Cf. Ned. 3[11] (R. Nehemiah).
[2] Lev. 13[12f].   [3] Or that was shut up.
[4] i.e. if raw flesh appeared (Lev. 13[14]).   [5] The cases cited in paragraphs 2 and 3.
[6] Thereby excluding the parts specified above, 6[8].   [7] Whereby he becomes clean.

or blister, and the head or the beard became bald, or the boil, burning, or blister formed a scar, even if the place of the quick flesh became a Bright Spot, he is unclean; [he does not become clean] until it breaks out abroad and covers all his skin.

6. If there were two Bright Spots, the one unclean and the other clean, and [the leprosy] broke out from the one to the other, and then broke out abroad and covered all his skin, he becomes clean. [If there were two Bright Spots, each the size of half a split bean], the one on the upper lip and the other on the lower lip, or on two fingers or on the two eyelids, although when they cleave together they appear as one, he is nevertheless clean. If it broke out abroad and covered all his skin, save only a tetter, he is unclean. If[1] it receded from the ends of the members leaving a kind of a tetter, he still remains clean. If it receded from the ends of the members less than the space of a lentil, R. Meir declares him unclean; but the Sages say: A tetter less than the space of a lentil is a token of uncleanness in the beginning, but it is not a token of uncleanness at the end.

7. If a man came [before the priest in the beginning] with his whole body white, he must be shut up; if, then, white hair arose he must be certified unclean; if [afterward] both hairs or one of them turned black, if both of them or one of them became short,[2] if a boil adjoined both hairs or one of them, if the boil encompassed both hairs or one of them, or if they were sundered by a boil or the quick flesh of a boil, or a burning or the quick flesh of a burning, or by a tetter, and then there arose quick flesh or white hair, he is unclean; but if no quick flesh or white hair arose he is clean. But with them all if it receded from but the ends of the members, he remains as he was before. If it broke out abroad and covered but part of his skin, he is unclean; if it broke out abroad and covered all his skin, he is clean.

8. If it broke out abroad and covered all his skin at once, after that he was become clean, he is unclean; but if after he had been certified unclean, he is clean. He that is pronounced clean after that he was shut up, is exempt from the law of loosening the hair and rending the clothes,[3] and also from cutting off the hair[4] and from bringing the pair of birds;[5] but he that is pronounced clean after that he had been certified unclean is liable to all these; and both alike convey uncleanness by entering in.[6]

9. If a man came [before the priest] with his whole body white, and there was upon him quick flesh of the space of a lentil, and the leprosy broke out and covered all his skin, and it afterward receded from the ends of the members, R. Ishmael says: It is as though it had receded from the ends of the members as when there had been a great Bright Spot.[7] But R. Eleazar b. Azariah says: It is as though it had receded from the ends of the members as when there had been a little Bright Spot.[8]

10. Sometimes a man may show his leprosy-sign to the priest to his gain and sometimes he may show it to his loss. Thus if he had been certified unclean and the tokens of his uncleanness disappeared, and before he could show himself to the priest the leprosy broke out abroad and covered all his skin, he is clean; whereas if he had already shown it to the priest he would have become unclean.[9] If he had a Bright Spot wherein naught else arose,

---

[1] After being declared clean because the leprosy wholly covered him.
[2] See p. 677, n. 3.   [3] Lev. 13[45].   [4] Lev. 14[8].   [5] Lev. 14[4].   [6] See below, 13[11].
[7] Such that covered the whole body.   [8] Confined to a part of the skin.
[9] See above, 8[1].

and before he could show himself to the priest[1] the leprosy broke out abroad and covered all his skin, he is unclean; whereas if he had already shown it to the priest he would have become clean.

9. 1. A boil or a burning can be certified unclean within one week and by two tokens: by white hair or by a spreading. What is a boil? If a man suffered hurt from wood or stone or olive-peat or Tiberias water; any hurt that is not caused by fire is a boil. What is a burning? If a man was burnt by burning coal or by embers; any hurt that is caused by fire is a burning.

2. A boil and a burning cannot be included together;[2] a spreading from one to the other, or from them to the skin of the flesh, or from the skin of the flesh to them, does not count as a spreading. If they fester they are clean; if they form a scale as thick as garlic peel, such is the *scar of the boil* spoken of in the Law[3]. If again they become quick flesh, although there is a cicatrix in the place thereof, they count as *the skin of the flesh*.[4]

3. They asked R. Eliezer, [What befalls] if there arose on the inside of a man's hand a Bright Spot the size of a *sela*, and the place thereof becomes the *scar of the boil*?[5] He said to them, It must be shut up. They said to him, Why?[6] The place is not such that white hair can arise there; there can be no spreading there; and quick flesh[7] does not render it unclean. He said to them, Perchance it will contract and spread again. They said to him, But does not the question[8] still stand even if [the scar contracts and] its place is but the space of a split bean? He said to them, I have heard no tradition about this. R. Judah b. Bathyra said to him, I will expound it. He said to him, If it be to confirm the words of the Sages, be it so. He said to him, Perchance another boil may arise outside it, and spread into it. He said to him, Thou art a great Sage in that thou hast confirmed the words of the Sages.

10. 1. Scalls[9] can be certified unclean within two weeks and by two tokens: by yellow thin hair or by a spreading. 'By yellow thin hair'—if it is so diseased that it is short. So R. Akiba. R. Johanan b. Nuri says: Even though it is long. R. Johanan b. Nuri said: What does the expression mean when they say, 'This stick is thin', or 'This reed is thin'?—does it mean that it is unusually thin and short, or[10] unusually thin and long? R. Akiba said to him, Before we learn from the reed let us learn from the hair!—[for if we say,] 'The hair of such-a-one is thin', 'thin' means that it is unusually thin and short, not that it is unusually thin and long.

2. Yellow thin hair betokens uncleanness whether it is clustered together or dispersed, whether it is encompassed or unencompassed, whether it came after[11] or before. So R. Judah. R. Simeon says: It betokens uncleanness only if it came after. R. Simeon said: It is a logical inference: if white hair (against whose effect other hair cannot afford protection)[12] betokens uncleanness only if it comes after, must we not infer that yellow thin hair (against whose effect other hair can afford protection) betokens uncleanness

---

1 Who would have shut him up.
2 To make up the space of a split bean.   3 Lev. 13[23].
4 Lev. 13[3].   5 The scar covers the entire Bright Spot.
6 The tokens of uncleanness cannot arise there.
7 This is not prescribed (Lev. 13[18ff, 24ff]) as a token of uncleanness in a boil or burning.
8 Why should it be shut up?
9 See above, 3[5].   10 Variant: and not, rather, . . .
11 The scall.   12 In the case of leprosy symptoms in 'the skin of the flesh'; whereas in a scall in the head or beard two black hairs nullify the yellow hairs (Lev. 13[31, 37]).

only if it comes after? R. Judah says: If ever it was needful to say 'If it comes after' [Scripture] has said 'If it comes after'; but the scall, whereof it is said, *And there be in it no yellow hair*,[1] betokens uncleanness whether it came before or after.

3. Any [black hair][2] that grows up affords protection against the yellow hair and against the spreading, whether it is clustered together or dispersed, whether it is encompassed or unencompassed. Any [black hair][2] that is left affords protection against the yellow hair and against the spreading, whether it is clustered together or dispersed, or whether it is encompassed; but it does not afford protection if it is at the side [of the scall] unless it is distant by two hairs from the surrounding growth of hair. If one of the hairs was yellow and the other black, or if one was yellow and the other white, they do not afford protection.

4. If a yellow hair was there before the scall it is clean. R. Judah declares it unclean. R. Eliezer b. Jacob says: It neither betokens uncleanness nor affords protection. R. Simeon says: Aught in the scall that is not a token of uncleanness is a token of cleanness in the scall.

5. How is he shaven[3] that has a scall? They shave the space outside it but leave [a circle] two hairs [deep] next to it so that it shall be manifest if it spreads. If he was certified unclean because of yellow hair and the yellow hair disappeared and other yellow hair appeared (so, too, if there was a spreading, whether in the beginning, or by the end of the first week, or by the end of the second week, or even after he had been pronounced clean), he remains as he was before. If he was certified unclean because of a spreading, and the spreading disappeared and appeared again (so, too, if there was yellow hair, whether by the end of the first week, or by the end of the second week, or even after he had been pronounced clean), he remains as he was before.

6. If there were two scalls side by side and a line of hair separated them, if a gap appeared in one place the scall is unclean; but if in two places, it is clean.[4] How great should be the gap? The space of two hairs. If there was a gap in one place the size of a split bean, it is unclean.

7. If there were two scalls one within the other, and a line of hair separated them, and there was a gap in one place, the [inner] scall is unclean; if in two places, it is clean. How great should be the gap? The space of two hairs. If there was a gap in one place the size of a split bean, it is clean.

8. If a man had a scall wherein was yellow hair, it is unclean; if black hair grew therein, it is clean; even if the black hair disappeared again it remains clean. R. Simeon b. Judah in the name of R. Simeon says: Any scall that has once been pronounced clean can never again become unclean. R. Simeon says: Any yellow hair that has once been pronounced clean can never again become unclean.

9. If a man had a scall the size of a split bean and it spread over his whole head, he is clean.[5] The head and the beard cannot hinder one another [from being pronounced clean].[6] So R. Judah. But R. Simeon says: They

---

[1] Lev. 13[32].   [2] If there are not less than two hairs.   [3] See Lev. 13[33].
[4] The two scalls are then deemed a single scall, and the residue of the dividing hair is a token of cleanness in the scall (Lev. 13[31]).
[5] Or over his whole beard; on the analogy of the Bright Spot that breaks out abroad and covers the whole of his skin, whereby he becomes clean.
[6] The scall is to be accounted clean if it spreads only over the whole head, or only over the whole beard.

can hinder one another. R. Simeon said: It is a logical inference: if the skin of the face and the skin of the body (which have that which keeps them asunder)[1] hinder one another, must we not infer that the head and the beard (which have naught that keeps them asunder) hinder one another? [A scall in] the head and [a scall in] the beard cannot be included together, nor can a scall spread from the one to the other. What counts as the beard? From the bend of the jaw to the knob of the windpipe.[2]

10. Scalp-baldness or forehead-baldness[3] may be certified unclean within two weeks and by two tokens: by quick flesh or by a spreading. What counts as baldness? If a man had eaten *neshem*[4] or smeared himself with *neshem*, or suffered a wound from which hair can no more grow. What counts as scalp-baldness? [Lack of hair] from the crown sloping backwards to the protruding bone of the neck. What counts as forehead-baldness? [Lack of hair] from the crown sloping forwards over against the hair above [the face]. Scalp-baldness and forehead-baldness cannot be included together, nor can they spread from one into the other. R. Judah says: If there is hair between them they cannot be included together, but if there is none they can be included together.

11. 1. All garments[5] may contract uncleanness from leprosy-signs, excepting those of gentiles.[6] If a man bought garments from gentiles [the leprosy-signs in them] must be inspected [as if they had arisen] anew. The hides of [creatures that live in] the sea cannot contract uncleanness from leprosy-signs, but if a man joined[7] to them aught that grows on land, even if it is but a thread or a cord, yet something that is susceptible to uncleanness, they, too, become susceptible.

2. If camel's hair and sheep's wool have been hackled together[8] and the greater part is camel's hair, they cannot contract uncleanness from leprosy-signs; but if the greater part is sheep's wool, they can contract uncleanness from leprosy-signs; if they are in equal parts, they can contract uncleanness from leprosy-signs. So, too, if flax and hemp have been hackled together.[9]

3. Coloured hides and garments cannot contract uncleanness from leprosy-signs; houses,[10] whether they are coloured or not coloured, can contract uncleanness from leprosy-signs. So R. Meir. R. Judah says: [In this] hides are like to houses. R. Simeon says: Such as are coloured by heaven can contract uncleanness but such as are coloured by man cannot contract uncleanness.

4. If in a garment the warp was coloured but the woof was white, or if the woof was coloured but the warp was white, all is according to what is the more apparent. Garments contract uncleanness by an intense green or an intense red colour. If [the leprosy-sign] was green and it spread out red, or if it was red and it spread out green, it is unclean. If its colour changed and [afterward] spread, or changed but did not spread, it is accounted as if it had not changed. R. Judah says: It must be inspected anew.

5. If [the leprosy-sign] continued unchanged throughout the first [week] it must be washed and kept shut up; if it continued unchanged throughout the second week it must be burned; if it spread, whether in the first week

---

[1] The growth of hair on the chin and head.   [2] Cf. Hull. 10⁴.   [3] Lev. 13⁴⁰ᶠ.
[4] Or *nesem*. A drug used, internally or externally, to hinder the growth of hair.
[5] Lev. 13⁴⁷.   [6] Cf. above, 3¹.   [7] Kel. 17¹³.
[8] And a garment woven from them.   [9] Cf. Kil. 9¹.   [10] Lev. 14³⁴.

or in the second, it must be burnt. If it was faint in the beginning, R. Ishmael says: It must be washed and kept shut up. But the Sages say: It does not require this.[1] If it grew fainter after the first week it must be washed and kept shut up; if it grew fainter after the second week it may be torn out and what is torn out [alone] need be burnt, and a patch must be put thereon. R. Nehemiah says: A patch need not be put thereon.

6. If the leprosy-sign came again [elsewhere] in the garment, the patch is free;[2] if it came again in the patch, the [whole] garment must be burnt. If a man used [part of] what had been shut up to patch a garment that was clean, and the leprosy-sign came again in the first garment, he must burn the patch. If the leprosy-sign came again in the patch, the first garment must be burnt, and the patch serves the second garment [only] while the tokens are under inspection[3] [and then it must be burnt].[4]

7. In a summer garment[5] that has coloured and white checks [the leprosy-sign] may spread from one [white check] to another.[6] They asked R. Eliezer, What if [the white colour] is on one check only? He replied, I have heard no tradition about this. R. Judah b. Bathyra said to him, I will expound it. He said to him, If it be to confirm the words of the Sages, be it so. He said to him, Perchance it will remain unchanged therein for two weeks, and what remains unchanged in garments throughout two weeks is unclean.[7] He said to him, Thou art a great Sage in that thou hast confirmed the words of the Sages. A spreading that adjoins [the first leprosy-sign counts as a spreading] however small it is; if it is distant, it must be the size of a split bean; and if it returns it must be the size of a split bean.

8. The warp and woof as soon as they are woven may contract uncleanness from leprosy-signs. R. Judah says: The warp, after it has been boiled; the woof, forthwith; and bundles of flax, after they have been bleached. How much must there be in a coil [of thread] for it to be able to contract uncleanness from leprosy-signs? Enough wherewith to weave a piece three fingerbreadths square, either warp or woof, even if it is all warp or all woof. If they were broken threads it cannot contract uncleanness from leprosy-signs. R. Judah says: Even if the thread was broken only in one place and it was knotted together it cannot contract uncleanness.

9. If the thread was wound from one coil to another, or from one spool to another or from the upper beam to the lower (so, too, with the two wings of a shirt) if a leprosy-sign appeared on the one, the other remains clean. If it was in the shedded weft[8] or in the standing warp, these can forthwith contract uncleanness from leprosy-signs. R. Simeon says: Only if the warp is closely ordered can it contract uncleanness.

10. If [the leprosy-sign appeared] in the standing warp the web is clean. If it appeared in the web the standing warp is clean. If it appeared in a sheet the fringes must be burnt [also], but if it appeared in the fringes the sheet remains clean. If the leprosy-sign appeared in a shirt, the hems thereof can be set free even if they are of purple wool.

11. Whatsoever is susceptible to corpse-uncleanness though not sus-

---

[1] But it is accounted clean.   [2] If the rest of the garment needs to be burnt.
[3] It, together with the second garment, is shut up, to see whether the leprosy sign spreads in the second garment.   [4] Cf. below, 13[5].
[5] Also explained as a patchwork curtain.
[6] Though coloured checks intervened and the combined space of the affected white checks can be included together to determine whether the colour has spread or grown fainter.   [7] Lev. 13[55].   [8] Cf. Kel. 21[1].

ceptible to *midras*-uncleanness,[1] can contract uncleanness from leprosy-signs—like the sail of a ship, a curtain, the forehead-band of a hair-net, the wrappings of scrolls, a girdle, the straps of a shoe or sandal; if they are as wide as a split bean, they can contract uncleanness from leprosy-signs. If the leprosy-sign appeared in a thick cloak, R. Eliezer b. Jacob says: It remains clean unless it appears in the texture and the soft [surface] wool. A water-skin or shepherd's leather wallet are examined in the manner in which they are carried,[2] and a spreading is so accounted whether it be from its inner to its outer side, or from its outer to its inner side.

12. If a garment that had been shut up was confused with others, all are accounted clean. If it was cut up and made into woollen shreds it becomes clean and use may be made of it. But if a garment that had been certified unclean was confused with others all are accounted unclean. If it was cut up and made into woollen shreds, it is [still] unclean and no use may be made of it.

12. 1. All houses can contract uncleanness from leprosy-signs excepting those of gentiles. If a man bought houses from gentiles [the leprosy-signs in them] must be inspected [as if they had arisen] anew. A round house or a three-cornered house or a house built on a ship or on a raft or on four beams, cannot contract uncleanness from leprosy signs. But if it was four-sided, even if it was built on four pillars, it can contract uncleanness.

2. If a house has one of its sides overlaid with marble, or one with rock, or one with bricks, or one with earth, it is not susceptible to uncleanness [from leprosy-signs]. If a house had not in it stones and wood and earth,[3] and a leprosy-sign appeared in it, and they afterward brought into it stones and wood and earth, it remains clean. So, too, if a garment had not in it woven work three fingerbreadths square, and a leprosy-sign appeared in it, and there was afterward woven into it a piece three fingerbreadths square, it remains clean. A house cannot contract uncleanness from leprosy-signs unless there is in it stones and wood and earth.

3. How many stones must there be in it? R. Ishmael says: Four. R. Akiba says: Eight. For R. Ishmael used to say: [The leprosy-sign] must appear two split beans in size on two stones or on one stone.[4] R. Akiba says: It must appear two split beans in size on two stones,[4] and not on one stone. R. Eleazar b. Simeon says: It must appear two split beans in size on two stones on two walls at a corner, and it must be two split beans in length and one in breadth.

4. Of wood[4] there must be as much as suffices to set under the lintel. R. Judah says: Enough to make the support[5] at the back of the lintel. Of earth there must be enough to fill up the space between one row of stones[6] and another. The walls of a cattle-stall or partition-walls cannot contract uncleanness from leprosy-signs. [Houses in] Jerusalem and [in places] outside the Land [of Israel] cannot contract uncleanness from leprosy-signs.[7]

---

[1] See Kel. 27[2].

[2] Those parts are deemed joined together (so that leprosy-signs on various parts can be included together to make up the prescribed bulk that betokens uncleanness) which are in contact when the bag is carried, even though they lie apart when it is not carried.

[3] Lev. 14[45].   [4] In each wall.

[5] Lit. 'sandal'. A block of wood placed to protect the lintel against the knocking of the door.   [6] So Tif. Yis. Others 'boards'; and so Tif. Yis. in Shab. 8[7].

[7] Since it is written, 'Which I give to you for a possession' (Lev. 14[34]), which excludes

5. How do they fulfil the inspection of a house? *Then he that owneth the house shall come and tell the priest, saying, There seemeth to me to be as it were a plague in the house.*[1] Even if he was a learned Sage and knew of a truth that it was a leprosy-sign, he may not decide and say, 'A leprosy-sign has been seen of me in my house', but [only], *There seemeth to me to be as it were a plague in the house. And the priest shall command that they empty the house before the priest go in to see the plague, that all that is in the house be not made unclean; and afterward the priest shall go in to see the house*; even bundles of wood and even bundles of reeds[2] [must be taken out]. So R. Judah. R. Simeon says: That is [only] a business for such as have no occupation. R. Meir said: And which of his goods would it render unclean? If thou wouldest say, 'His articles of wood or of cloth or of metal', these he may immerse and they become clean. For what has the Law taken thought? For his earthenware vessels,[3] even his cruse and his ewer.[4] If the Law thus takes thought for that property of a man that is of least worth, how much more for property that he prizes most! And if for his property how much more for the life of his sons and daughters! And if for what belongs to the wicked how much more for what belongs to the righteous!

6. He does not go[5] within his own house to shut up [the other house], or inside the house wherein is the leprosy-sign to shut it up; but he stands at the door of the house wherein is the leprosy-sign, and [there] shuts it up, for it is written, *Then the priest shall go out of the house to the door of the house and shut up the house seven days.*[6] And he shall come at the end of the week and inspect it, and if it has spread, *then the priest shall command that they take out the stones in which the plague is and cast them into an unclean place without the city . . . and they shall take other stones and put them in the place of those stones, and he shall take other mortar and shall plaister the house.* He may not take stones from the one side and bring them to the other; or earth from one side and bring it to the other, or lime from anywhere. He may not bring one stone in place of two, or two in place of one, but he must bring two in the place of two, or in the place of three or in the place of four. From this verse[7] they have said: Woe to the wicked, woe to his neighbour!—they both must take out the stones, they both scrape the walls, and they both must bring the [new] stones;[8] but he alone brings the earth, for it is written, *And he shall take other mortar and plaister the house*; his fellow does not join with him in the plastering.

7. He shall come at the end of [another] week and inspect it, and if it has returned, *he shall break down the house, the stones of it, and the timber thereof, and all the mortar of the house, and he shall carry them forth out of the house into an unclean place.*[9] A spreading that adjoins [the first leprosy-sign counts as a spreading] however small it is; if it is distant, it must be the size of a split bean. And, in houses, [the leprosy-sign] when it returns, must be the size of two split beans.

foreign lands, and also Jerusalem, since this was not divided for a possession among the tribes.
  [1] Lev. 14[35]. This and the following verses from Leviticus are treated *Midrash*-fashion (App. I. 27). Cf. Sot. 8[1]; Sanh. 2[4]; 10[4ff].
  [2] Although these are not susceptible to uncleanness.
  [3] Which cannot be made clean again by immersion, but must be broken.
  [4] Cf. Kel. 3[2]   [5] Variant: stand.   [6] Lev. 14[38].
  [7] Where certain acts are ordained with the subject in the plural, implying that both the occupant of the leprous house and his neighbour share in pulling down and rebuilding; whereas the plastering is enjoined in the singular.
  [8] To rebuild their common wall.   [9] Lev. 14[45].

13. 1. Ten cases arise in houses [wherein a leprosy-sign appears]. If during the first week it became faint, or if it disappeared, it needs but to be scraped and is then clean. If during the second week it became faint or if it disappeared, it needs but to be scraped, and the [pair of] birds[1] must be brought. If it spread during the first week, the stone must be taken out and the wall scraped and [another stone put in its stead and] plastered, and it must be left during another week; if then it returned the house must be pulled down; if it did not return, the [pair of] birds must be brought. If it remained unchanged during the first week and spread during the second week the stone must be taken out and the wall scraped and [another stone put in its stead and] plastered, and it must be left during another week; if then it returned the house must be pulled down; if it did not return, the [pair of] birds must be brought. If it remained unchanged during both the weeks, the stone must be taken out and the wall scraped and [another stone put in its stead and] plastered, and it must be left during another week; if then it returned the house must be pulled down; if it did not return the [pair of] birds must be brought. If the leprosy-sign appeared therein before it was made clean through the [pair of] birds, the house must be pulled down, and if it appeared after it was made clean through the [pair of] birds, it must be inspected anew as at the beginning.

2. When a stone that is in a corner is taken out it must be taken out wholly;[2] but when a house must be pulled down a man need pull down only what belongs to him and may leave what belongs to his fellow. Thus greater stringency applies to taking out than to pulling down. R. Eliezer says: If the house was built with [walls having alternate courses of] great stones and small stones,[3] and the leprosy-sign appeared on a great stone, he must take it out wholly; but if on the small stones he need take out only what belongs to him and may leave what belongs to his fellow.

3. If the leprosy-sign appeared in a house that had an upper room above it, the roof beams must be left for the upper room; if it appeared in the upper room the beams must be left for the lower house. If it had no upper room, its stones and wood and earth must all be pulled down with it; but a man may save the frames and the window lattices. R. Judah says: The frame [for the beams] built over it must be pulled down with it. Its stones and wood and earth convey uncleanness if they are of an olive's bulk. R. Eleazar Hisma says: Whatsoever their bulk.

4. A house that is shut up conveys uncleanness from its inner side, and one that has been certified unclean both from its inner side and from its outer side. Both alike convey uncleanness by entering in.[4]

5. If a man used stones from a house that was shut up[5] to build into a house that was clean, and the leprosy-sign came back to the [first] house, he must pull out the stones. If it came again upon the stones, the first house must be pulled down, and the stones serve the second house [only] while the tokens are under inspection.[6]

6. If a house overshadowed another house that was afflicted with leprosy (so, too, if a tree overshadowed a house that was afflicted with leprosy),

---

[1] Lev. 14[49].   [2] Although it forms part of his neighbour's house.
[3] The great stones can be seen on either side of the common wall, whereas the small stones face only to the one side.   [4] Lev. 14[46]. See below, par. 9.
[5] The case is analogous with that cited above, 11[6].
[6] The second house is shut up to see whether the leprosy sign spreads in the second house, and then the stones from the first house must be taken out.

and a man entered within the outermost of the two, he remains clean. So R. Eleazar b. Azariah. R. Eliezer said: If one stone of the house can convey uncleanness by entering in, shall not the house itself convey uncleanness by entering in?

7. If a man unclean [from leprosy] stood beneath a tree and one that was clean passed by, he becomes unclean; if he that was clean stood beneath the tree and he that was unclean passed by, he remains clean; but if [he that was unclean] stood still the other becomes unclean. So, too, if a man carried [beneath a tree] a stone afflicted with leprosy, he [that was standing beneath the tree] remains clean; but if he set it down the other becomes unclean.

8. If a man that was clean put his head and the greater part of his body inside a house that was unclean, he becomes unclean; and if a man that was unclean put his head and the greater part of his body inside a house that was clean he renders it unclean. If a piece, three fingerbreadths square, of a cloak that was clean was put inside a house that was unclean, it becomes unclean; and if an unclean cloak, even an olive's bulk of it, was put inside a clean house, it renders it unclean.

9. If a man entered a house afflicted with leprosy, bearing his garments on his shoulder and his sandals and rings in his hands, he and they forthwith become unclean; but if he was clothed with his garments and had his sandals on his feet and his rings on his hand, he forthwith becomes unclean but they remain clean, unless he stayed there time enough to eat a half-loaf[1] of bread—wheaten bread and not barley bread, and while in a reclining position and eating the bread with condiment.

10. If he was standing inside with his hand stretched outside and with his rings on his hands, and he stayed time enough to eat a half-loaf, they become unclean. If he was standing outside with his hand stretched inside and with his rings on his hands, R. Judah declares him forthwith unclean. But the Sages say: [Only] after he shall have stayed time enough to eat a half-loaf. They said to R. Judah: If, when his whole body is unclean, he does not render what is upon him unclean until he has stayed long enough to eat a half-loaf, is not the inference that, when only part of his body is unclean, he does not render what is upon him unclean until he shall have stayed long enough to eat a half-loaf?

11. If a leper enters a house every vessel therein becomes unclean, even to the height of the roof beams. R. Simeon says: Only to a height of four cubits. The vessels become unclean forthwith. R. Judah says: Only if he stayed time enough for to light a lamp.

12. When he enters a synagogue they must make for him a partition ten handbreadths high and four cubits wide. He must enter in first and come forth last. Whatsoever by having a tightly stopped-up cover affords protection [from uncleanness] in the 'Tent' wherein lies a corpse,[2] likewise affords protection by having a tightly stopped-up cover in a house that is afflicted with leprosy. And whatsoever, when covered, affords protection from uncleanness in the 'Tent' wherein lies a corpse,[3] also, when covered, affords protection in a house afflicted with leprosy. So R. Meir. R. Jose says: Whatsoever by having a tightly stopped-up cover affords protection in the 'Tent' wherein lies a corpse, will, even if only covered, afford protection in a house afflicted with leprosy; and whatsoever, when covered,

---

[1] Cf. Erub. 8[2]; Ker. 3[3].   [2] See Kel. 10[1].   [3] See Ohol. 5[6].

affords protection in the 'Tent' wherein lies a corpse, remains clean even when uncovered in a house afflicted with leprosy.

14. 1. How did they cleanse the leper?[1] He brought a new earthenware flask and put therein a quarter-*log*[2] of living water; and he brought two birds that had lived in freedom. The priest slaughtered one of them over the earthenware vessel and over the living water, and dug a hole and buried it in his presence. He took cedarwood and hyssop and scarlet wool and bound them together with the ends of the strip [of wool]; and brought near to them the tips of the wings and the tip of the tail of the second bird; and dipped them [in the blood of the slaughtered bird] and sprinkled [the blood] seven times on the back of the leper's hand; and some say, also on his forehead. So likewise used they to sprinkle the lintel of the house from outside.

2. He then came to set free the living bird. He used not to turn his face toward the sea or toward the city or toward the wilderness, for it is written, *But he shall let go the living bird out of the city into the open field.*[3] He then came to cut off the hair of the leper. He passed the razor over the whole of his skin[4] and washed his garments and immersed himself; and thus he became so clean that he no more conveyed uncleanness by entering in, yet he [still] conveyed uncleanness like a creeping thing:[5] he could enter within the city wall but he was forbidden to enter into his house for seven days,[6] and he was not allowed marital connexion.

3. On the seventh day he cut off his hair a second time after the manner of the first cutting. He washed his garments and immersed himself; and thus he became clean so that he no more conveyed uncleanness like a creeping thing but was become like one that had immersed himself the selfsame day [because of uncleanness],[7] and so could eat of [Second] Tithe. After he had awaited sunset he could eat of Heave-offering; and after he had brought his offering of atonement he could eat of the Hallowed Things. Thus there are three stages in the purification of the leper; so, too, there are three stages in the purification of a woman after childbirth.[8]

4. There are three that must cut off the hair, and their cutting it off is a religious duty: the Nazirite,[9] the leper,[10] and the levites;[11] and if any of these cut it off but not with a razor, or left two hairs remaining, they have done nothing.

5. The two birds should be alike in appearance, in size and in value and have been bought at the same time;[12] yet even if they are not alike they are valid and if one was bought one day and the other on the morrow they are valid. If one was slaughtered and it was found that it had not lived in freedom, a fellow may be bought for the second, and the first is permitted to be eaten. If one was slaughtered and it was found to be *terefah*,[13] a fellow may be bought for the second and the first is permitted for use. If the blood

---

[1] See Lev. 14[2ff].   [2] App. II, D.   [3] Lev. 14[53].

[4] But cf. above, 2[4] (end).   [5] Lev. 11[29-31]. See App. IV. 8b, 12a, 17d.

[6] Lev. 14[8]. See Kel. 1[1], 'a leper in his days of reckoning'.

[7] He does not render ordinary food unclean, but only Heave-offering and Hallowed Things. Cf. p. 773, n. 6.

[8] Lev. 12[1ff]. After seven days (from the birth of a male, or fourteen from the birth of a female) she is clean for her husband; after immersion after forty days (from the birth of a male, or eighty from the birth of a female), and awaiting sunset, she is of such a degree of cleanness that she may eat of Heave-offering; and after she has brought the prescribed offerings she may eat of Hallowed Things.   [9] Num. 6[18].

[10] Lev. 14[8]   [11] Num. 8[7].   [12] Cf. Yom. 6[1].   [13] App. I. 47.

had been poured away [before the sprinkling] the one that was to be let loose must be left to die. If the one that was to be let loose died, the blood [of the other] must be poured away.

6. The cedar wood should be one cubit in length, and its thickness the quarter of the thickness of the leg of a bed—one [leg] divided into two, and these two into four. The hyssop should not be Greek hyssop or stibium-hyssop or Roman hyssop or wild hyssop or any kind of hyssop to which a special name is given.[1]

7. On the eighth day[2] he brought three beasts: a Sin-offering, a Guilt-offering and a Whole-offering. If he was poor,[3] he brought a Sin-offering of a bird and a Whole-offering of a bird.

8. He came to the Guilt-offering, put his two hands thereon; and it was slaughtered. Two priests received its blood, the one in a vessel and the other in his hand. He that received it in a vessel went and tossed it against the front of the Altar. And he that received it in his hand came to the leper. And the leper had immersed himself in the Chamber of the Lepers,[4] and he came and stood at the Nicanor Gate.[5] R. Judah says: He did not need to immerse himself.

9. He put his head inside [the Temple Court] and [the priest] put [the blood] on the tip of his ear; then [he put in] his hand, and the priest put the blood on the thumb of his hand; then [he put in] his foot—and he put the blood on the great toe of his foot. R. Judah says: He put them in all three together. If he had not a thumb on his hand or a great toe on his foot, or a right ear, he could never have purification. R. Eliezer says: The blood may be put in the place where they were. R. Simeon says: If it was put on the left side, he has fulfilled his obligation.

10. The priest took of the *log* of oil[6] and poured it into his fellow's hand; but if he poured it into his own hand that suffices. He dipped [his finger in the oil] and sprinkled it seven times toward the Holy of Holies, dipping anew for every sprinkling. He came to the leper; in the places where he put the blood there also he put the oil, for it is written, *Upon the place of the blood of the Guilt-offering; and the rest of the oil that is in the priest's hand he shall put upon the head of him that is to be cleansed to make atonement.*[7] If he put it thereon it made atonement; if he did not put it thereon it did not make atonement. So R. Akiba. R. Johanan b. Nuri says: These are but the residue[8] of the ordinance: whether he put it thereon or did not put it thereon, it has made atonement, yet to him it is reckoned as though he had not made atonement.[9] If the *log* was found to lack aught before it was poured out, its measure may be filled up; but if after it was poured out, other oil must be brought anew. So R. Akiba. R. Simeon says: If the *log* was found to lack aught before it was put [on the members of the leper] its measure may be filled up; but if after it was put thereon, other oil must be brought anew.

11. If a leper brought his offering as a poor man[10] and he became rich, or as a rich man and he became poor, all must follow according to what the Sin-offering was.[11] So R. Simeon. But R. Judah says: According to what the Guilt-offering was.

---

[1] Cf. Ned. 6[9]; Par. 11[7].   [2] Lev. 14[10].   [3] Lev. 14[21].   [4] Midd. 2[5].
[5] p. 166, n. 3; Midd. 2[3].   [6] Lev. 14[21].   [7] Lev. 14[28f].
[8] Cf. p. 505, n. 7.   [9] In the rightful and prescribed fashion.
[10] Lev. 14[21].
[11] The order of the offerings was (Lev. 14[19, 21]) Guilt-offering, Sin-offering, and

12. If a poor leper brought the offering of a rich leper he has fulfilled his obligation; if a rich leper brought the offering of a poor leper he has not fulfilled his obligation. A man may bring a poor man's offering on behalf of his son or daughter or his bondman or bondwoman, and so enable them to eat of the animal-offerings.[1] R. Judah says: But he must bring a rich man's offering on behalf of his wife; and the same applies to whatsoever other offering she may be liable.[2]

13. If the offerings of two lepers were confused, and the offering of one of them was offered, and then one of them died—this is what the men of Alexandria asked of R. Joshua. He said to them: Let him assign his property to another, and bring a poor man's offering.

PARAH[3] ('THE RED HEIFER')

1. 1. R. Eliezer says: The heifer [whose neck is to be broken][4] must be [not more than] one year old; and the [Red] Heifer [not more than] two years old. But the Sages say: The heifer may be two years old and the Red Heifer three years old or four. R. Meir says: Even five years old. An older heifer is valid, but they may not suffer it to wait so long lest any hair in it turns black, and that it may not [otherwise][5] become invalid. R. Joshua said: I have never heard that any [was valid] save a 'three-year-old' (*sheloshith*). They said to him, Why dost thou use the term *sheloshith*? He said to them, Thus have I heard it[6] but without explanation. Ben Azzai said, I will explain it: When thou sayest *shelishith* it means 'the third' in number in relation to others; but when thou sayest *sheloshith* it means something that is three years old. In like manner have they spoken of a 'four-year-old' (*reba'i*) vineyard. They said to him, Why dost thou use the term *reba'i*? He said to them, Thus have I heard it without explanation. Ben Azzai said, I will explain it: When thou sayest *rebi'i* it means 'the fourth' in number in relation to others; but when thou sayest *reba'i* it means something that is four years old. In like manner they have said: If a man ate in a house afflicted with leprosy [he becomes unclean if he stayed time enough to eat] a half-loaf,[7] [the size] of which is three to the *kab*.[8] They said to him, 'Say, rather, eighteen to the *seah*'.[8] He said to them, Thus have I heard it but without explanation. Ben Azzai said, I will explain it: When thou sayest 'three to the *kab*' it means that it had not been liable to

---

Whole-offering; if his condition changed after he had brought a bird as a Sin-offering, his Whole-offering must be a bird; if, as a rich man, his Sin-offering had been a ewe-lamb, his Whole-offering, even if he becomes poor, must be a he-lamb.

1 i.e. complete the third stage in their purification; cf. above, 14[3].
2 Her offering must be according to her husband's condition in life.
3 Lit. 'heifer', namely the Red Heifer which, in accordance with the prescriptions of Num. 19[1-22], is to be burnt, its ashes collected together and laid up 'without the camp in a clean place'. These ashes were to be mixed with water 'for a water of separation: it is a sin offering' (19[9]). This water is called throughout the Mishnah 'the water of the Sin-offering' (cf. Num. 8[7]; R.V. 'water of expiation'). If men or utensils contracted 'corpse-uncleanness' (thereby becoming unclean for seven days) this 'Sin-offering water' must be sprinkled on them on the third and seventh days; they must afterwards be immersed and at sunset they become clean (Num. 19[19]). See App. IV. 1 c (i), 9, 12 a, 15. From Num. 19[9] it is inferred that the Sin-offering water requires conditions of cleanness a grade higher even than is required for Hallowed Things; thus what is accounted clean so far as Heave-offering and Hallowed Things are concerned, is uncleanness in what concerns Sin-offering water and those who are engaged with it.   4 See Deut. 21[1ff].
5 By bearing the yoke or suffering a blemish (Num. 19[2]).
6 Cf. p. 422, n. 7.   7 See Neg. 13[9].
8 See App. II, D. There are six *kabs* to the *seah*.

Dough-offering;[1] but when thou sayest 'eighteen to the *seah*' it means that the Dough-offering that was taken from it has lessened the loaf [somewhat].

2. R. Jose the Galilean says: Bullocks must be [not more than] two years old, for it is written, *And 'a second [year]' bullock of the herd shalt thou take for a Sin-offering.*[2] But the Sages say: They may even be three years old. R. Meir says: Even if they are four years old or five they are valid; but they do not offer them that are old out of reverence [towards the Altar].

3. Lambs must be [not more than] one year old, and rams [not more than] two years old; and always the year is reckoned from day to day.[3] What is thirteen months old is not valid whether as a ram or as a lamb. R. Tarfon calls such a one a *pallax*;[4] Ben Azzai calls it a *noked*;[5] R. Ishmael calls it a *parakhadeigma*.[6] If a man offered it he must bring for it the Drink-offerings of a ram, but it is not accounted to his credit as his prescribed animal-offering.[7] If it was thirteen months old and a day it counts as a ram.

4. The Sin-offerings of the congregation[8] and their Whole-offerings,[9] the Sin-offerings of an individual, the Guilt-offering of a Nazirite[10] and the Guilt-offering of a leper[11] are valid from the time that they are thirty days old and upwards, and even on the thirtieth day. And if they were offered on the eighth day they are valid. Vow-offerings and freewill-offerings, Firstlings[12] and Tithe [of Cattle][13] and the Passover-offering are valid from the eighth day onwards, and even on the eighth day.

2. 1. R. Eliezer says: If the [Red] Heifer for the Sin-offering was with young it is valid. But the Sages declare it invalid. R. Eliezer says: It may not be bought from gentiles. But the Sages declare such a one valid; and not only this, but any of the offerings of the congregation and of the individual may be brought from within the Land [of Israel] or from outside of it, from new produce or from old, save only the *Omer*[14] and the Two Loaves,[15] which may be brought only from new produce and from within the Land [of Israel].

2. If the horns and hoofs of the Heifer were black they may be chopped off. [If there was a blemish] in the eye-socket or the teeth or the tongue they do not render the heifer invalid. If it was dwarflike it is still valid. If there was a wen on it and this was cut off, R. Judah declares it invalid. R. Simeon says: If it grew no red hair at the place whence it was removed it is invalid.

3. If it was born from the side or was *the hire [of a harlot] or the price [of a dog]* it is invalid. R. Eliezer declares it valid, for it is written, *Thou shalt not bring the hire of a harlot or the price of a dog into the house of the Lord thy God;*[16] whereas the Heifer was not brought into the Temple.

---

[1] Num. 15[18ff]. Dough is liable to Dough-offering if it is made from more than five quarter-*kabs* of flour (Hall. 1[4]).

[2] Num. 8[8]. R.V. 'another young bullock'. But if the word means only 'another' it is superfluous.

[3] i.e. a full calendar year: from the day in the one year to the corresponding day of the next year.　　　　[4] πάλλαξ, a youth, or maiden.

[5] In Amos 1[1]; 2 Kings 3[4], the word is used in the sense of herdsman.

[6] Variant: *parakharigma.* Cf. παραχάραγμα, a counterfeit coin. All three terms, although their precise application in the circumstances is uncertain, are intended to illustrate the fact that at the age of thirteen months they are useless.

[7] Whether his offering should have been a 'he-lamb' or a 'ram'.

[8] Lev. 4[14].　　　　　　　　　　　　　[9] Whether lambs or he-goats.

[10] Num. 6[14].　　　　[11] Lev. 14[12].　　　[12] Ex. 22[30].　　　[13] Lev. 17[32].

[14] App. I. 31.　　　[15] Of Pentecost. Lev. 23[17].　　　[16] Deut. 23[18]. Cf. Tem. 6[1ff].

Any blemish that renders animal-offerings invalid renders the Heifer invalid.[1] If a man had ridden thereon or leaned thereon or if aught had been hung on its tail or if any had crossed a river by its help or doubled its leading-rope on its back or set his cloak on it, it is invalid.[2] But if he had fastened it by its leading-rope or made sandals for it lest it slip or spread his cloak over it because of flies, it remains valid. This is the general rule: if aught was done for the sake of the Heifer it remains valid; but if for the sake of any other, the Heifer becomes invalid.

4. If a bird alighted on it it remains valid. If a male beast mounted it it becomes invalid. R. Judah says: If it was made to mount it becomes invalid; but if it acted of itself it remains valid.

5. If it had two black or white hairs [growing] from within a single hole it is invalid. R. Judah says: Or even from within a single hollow. If they grew from within two hollows that were adjacent, it is invalid. R. Akiba says: Even though there were four or even five but they were dispersed, they may be plucked out. R. Eliezer says: Or even fifty. R. Joshua b. Bathyra says: Even though it has but one on its head and one on its tail, it is invalid. If there were two hairs with their roots black but their tips red, or their roots red but their tips black, all is according to what is the more manifest. So R. Meir. But the Sages say: According to the root.

3. 1. Seven days before the burning of the Heifer the priest that was to burn the Heifer was taken apart from his house[3] to a chamber that was opposite the north-eastern corner of the Temple-building; and it was called the House of Stone. And throughout the seven days they sprinkled him [with water] from [the ashes of] all the Sin-offerings that were there.[4] R. Jose says: They sprinkled him only on the third and seventh days. R. Hanina the Prefect of the Priests says: They sprinkled the priest that was to burn the Heifer on each of the seven days, but the priest that was set apart for the Day of Atonement they sprinkled only on the third and seventh days.

2. There were courtyards in Jerusalem built over the rock,[5] and beneath them the rock was hollowed for fear of any grave down in the depths;[6] and they used to bring women while they were pregnant and there they bore their children and reared them. And they brought oxen with doors laid upon their backs, and on these the children sat[7] bearing in their hands cups of stone.[8] When they reached Siloam they alighted and filled the cups with water and got up again and sat upon the boards. R. Jose says: The child used to let down his cup and fill it without alighting.

3. When they came to the Temple Mount they alighted. Beneath both the Temple Mount and the courts of the Temple[9] was a hollowed space for fear of any grave down in the depths. At the entrance[10] of the Temple Court was set ready a jar of the [ashes of the] Sin-offering.[11] They brought a male from among the sheep, tied a rope between its horns, and tied a stick and

---

[1] Num. 19[2], 'wherein is no blemish'.   [2] Num. 19[2], 'and upon which never came yoke'.   [3] Cf. Yom. 1[1].   [4] See below, 3[5,11].
[5] For fear of danger of uncleanness from unknown graves below.
[6] As a further precaution, since if by chance there was corpse-uncleanness below, and it had not sufficient space (see p. 649, n. 3) it would cleave upwards through the solid rock.
[7] Therefore if they passed over any corpse-uncleanness on the way, the children themselves would not overshadow it, but would be protected by the doors over which they sat.
[8] Which are not susceptible to uncleanness.
[9] See p. 589, n. 11.   [10] Between the Rampart and the Court of the Women (Midd. 2[3]).   [11] Reserved from the ashes of previously burnt Red Heifers.

wound it about[1] with the [other] end of the rope, and threw it into the jar.
The sheep was smitten so that it started backward [and spilled the ashes],[2]
and the child took of the ashes and mixed[3] enough to be visible on the
water. R. Jose says: Give not the Sadducees occasion to cavil![4] but, rather,
one [of the children] took [the ashes directly] from the jar and mixed
them.

4. They might not bring another [heifer for a] Sin-offering by virtue of
[the purifications made for] the [first] Sin-offering, or another child by
virtue of [the purifications made for] his fellow.[5] Even the children needed
to be sprinkled. So R. Jose the Galilean. R. Akiba says: They needed not
to be sprinkled.

5. If they did not find the ashes from the seven [earlier] Sin-offerings,
they could use them from six, or from five, or from four, or from three, or
from two, or from one. Who had prepared them? Moses prepared the first,
Ezra prepared the second, and five were prepared after Ezra. So R. Meir.
But the Sages say: Seven since Ezra. And who prepared them? Simeon
the Just and Johanan the High Priest prepared two each, and Eliehoenai[6]
the son of Hakkof[7] and Hanamel the Egyptian and Ishmael the son of Piabi[8]
prepared one each.

6. They made a causeway[9] from the Temple Mount to the Mount of
Olives, an arched way built over an arched way, with an arch directly above
each pier [of the arch below], for fear of any grave in the depths below.[10]
By it the priest that was to burn the Heifer, and the Heifer, and all that
aided him went forth to the Mount of Olives.

7. If the Heifer refused to go forth they may not send out with her a
black heifer lest any say, 'They slaughtered a black heifer'; nor another
red heifer, lest any say, 'They slaughtered two'. R. Jose says: It was not
for this reason, but because it is written, *And he shall bring her forth*;[11] by
herself. And the elders of Israel used to go forth before them on foot to
the Mount of Olives. There was a place of immersion there; and they had
[first] rendered unclean the priest that should burn the Heifer, because of
the Sadducees: that they should not be able to say,[12] 'It must be performed
only by them on whom the sun has set'.[13]

8. They laid their hands upon him and said, 'My lord the High Priest,
immerse thyself this once'. He went down and immersed himself and came
up and dried himself. Wood was set in order there: cedarwood and pine
and spruce and pieces of smooth fig-tree wood; and they built up [the pile]

---

[1] The text is doubtful. There is a variant: 'and tied a stick and (or) a bushy twig (?pine-cone)'.
[2] So avoiding the risk of rendering them unclean by taking them out by hand.
[3] Lit. 'sanctified'; this verb is consistently used where the reference is to mixing the ashes of the Red Heifer with water.
[4] At such excessive scruples. According to some commentators this complicated proce-dure was essential when the exiles returned from Babylon (where they had had no means of freeing themselves from corpse-uncleanness) and wished to make use of the ashes of the Red Heifer that had been left in the Temple, safely hidden, when the nation went into exile.
[5] But if the Red Heifer died or became invalid, or if the child became unclean, all the preparations must be carried out afresh for another Red Heifer, or for another child.
[6] Cf. Ezra 8[4].   [7] Variant: *ha-Kayyaf* (cf. the name 'Caiaphas').
[8] Sot. 9[15]. Variant: Fabi.   [9] Cf. Shek. 4[2]; Yom. 6[4].
[10] If there was only solid structure between those who crossed the causeway and any corpse-uncleanness below, the uncleanness, if confined in less than a cubic handbreadth's space, would cleave perpendicularly upwards; but if a hollow space intervened, measuring a cubic handbreadth or more, the uncleanness penetrates no farther (p. 649, n. 3 f.).
[11] Num. 19[3].   [12] Variant: For they used to say....
[13] i.e. he must be wholly clean. See p. 773, n. 6.

in the fashion of a tower and opened [as it were] windows in it; and its fore side was to the west.[1]

9. They bound the Heifer with a rope of bast[2] and set it on the pile [lying] with its head to the south and its face to the west. The priest stood to the east with his face to the west. He slaughtered with his right hand and received the blood with his left. R. Judah says: He used to receive the blood on his right hand, put it on his left hand and sprinkle with his right. He dipped his hand and sprinkled the blood seven times towards the Holy of Holies,[3] dipping anew for each sprinkling. When he made an end of sprinkling he wiped his hand on the Heifer's body. He came down and kindled the fire with small chips of wood. R. Akiba says: With branches of date palm.

10. When the Heifer burst he stood outside the pit. He took cedarwood, hyssop and scarlet wool and said to them, 'Is this cedarwood?' 'Is this cedarwood?' 'Is this hyssop?' 'Is this hyssop?' 'Is this scarlet wool?' 'Is this scarlet wool?'—asking three times for each; and they answered, 'Yea! Yea!'—three times for each.

11. He wrapped them together with the ends of the strip of wool and cast them inside the burning [Heifer]. When it was burnt up they beat the cinders with rods and sifted the ashes with sieves. R. Ishmael says: They used stone hammers and stoneware sieves. If a black cinder had ashes thereon it was beaten up small; otherwise it was suffered to remain; in either case if it was a bone it was beaten up small. The ashes were divided into three: one part was kept on the Rampart, one on the Mount of Olives, and one was divided among the Courses of the priests.[4]

4. 1. If the Heifer for the Sin-offering was slaughtered under some other name,[5] or if its blood was received or sprinkled under some other name, or under its own name and then under another name, or under another name and then under its own name, it is invalid; but R. Eliezer declares it valid. If it was slaughtered by one with hands and feet unwashed it is invalid; but R. Eliezer declares it valid. If it was slaughtered not by the High Priest it is invalid; but R. Judah declares it valid. If [it was slaughtered] by one that had not on the proper garments, it is invalid; for the rite was performed in a white garment.

2. If it was burnt outside its [appointed] pit, or in two pits, or if two beasts were burnt in the same pit, it is invalid. If the blood was sprinkled not in the direction of the entrance [of the Holy of Holies] it is invalid. If he sprinkled as if for a seventh time instead of a sixth time, and then sprinkled again a seventh sprinkling, it is invalid; but if he sprinkled as if for an eighth time instead of the seventh time, and then sprinkled again an eighth sprinkling, it remains valid.

3. If it was burnt but not with wood, or with any [other than the prescribed] wood, or with straw or stubble, it remains valid. If it was flayed and cut up it remains valid. If it was slaughtered with an intention of eating its flesh or drinking its blood, it is valid. R. Eliezer says: No [wrong] intention can render invalid aught that concerns the [Red] Heifer.

4. All that engage in the rite of the [Red] Heifer, from the beginning until the end, render garments unclean;[6] and they render it invalid if they

[1] Cf. Tam. 2[4].   [2] A material not susceptible to uncleanness.   [3] See Midd. 2[4].
[4] See p. 165, n. 12.   [5] Cf. Zeb. 1[ff].   [6] See Num. 19[7, 8, 10, 21].

do then any [other] act of work. If aught befell that rendered it invalid when it was slaughtered it does not render garments unclean. If aught rendered it invalid while the blood was being sprinkled, for all them that engaged in the rite before the Sin-offering became invalid, it renders the garments unclean; but for them that engaged in the rite after it was rendered invalid it does not render the garments unclean. Thus wherein stringency applies[1] leniency applies[2] also. The law of Sacrilege[3] applies throughout. They may continue to add wood [to the fire]. Its every act must be carried out by day and by a priest. Any act of work renders it invalid until it becomes ashes; and any act of work[4] renders the water invalid until the ashes are put into it.

5. 1. He that brings the earthenware vessel for [the water or the ashes of] the Sin-offering must immerse himself, and spend the night by the furnace.[5] R. Judah says: He may bring it from the house [of the potter] and it will still be valid, for all are accounted trustworthy[6] in what concerns the Sin-offering. For a jar that is to contain Heave-offering, the potter may open the furnace and [forthwith] take out [any jar]. R. Simeon says: Only from the second row. R. Jose says: Only from the third row.

2. If the vessel for the Sin-offering water was immersed in water that was not fit[7] for mixing [the ashes],[8] it must be dried; but if in water that was fit for mixing the ashes it need not be dried; but if [it was immersed] to collect therein water that was already mixed with the ashes, it must be dried in either case.[9]

3. If a gourd-shell was immersed in water that was not fit for mixing the ashes, they may mix[10] the ashes therein if it had never before contracted uncleanness; if it had before contracted uncleanness, the ashes may not be mixed therein. R. Joshua says: If the ashes may be mixed therein in the beginning they may also be mixed therein at the end; but if they cannot be mixed therein at the end neither can they be mixed therein in the beginning. But whether it had before contracted uncleanness or not, water may not be collected therein that was already mixed with the ashes.

4. If a [reed] pipe[11] was cut[12] for the sake of [containing the water or the ashes of] the Sin-offering, R. Eliezer says: It should be immersed forthwith. R. Joshua says: Let it be rendered unclean and then let it be immersed.[13] All are qualified to mix the ashes excepting a deaf-mute, an imbecile or a minor. R. Judah declares a minor qualified but not a woman or one that is of double sex.

5. They may[14] mix the ashes in any vessel, even in vessels made from cattle-dung or vessels of stone or vessels of unbaked clay;[15] and they may

---

[1] In that engagement with other work renders the Heifer invalid.

[2] In that after it becomes invalid it does not render garments unclean.

[3] Lev. 5[15f]; p. 573, n. 2.

[4] Engagement with other work, while drawing, carrying or pouring out the water intended for mixing with the ashes of the Red Heifer.

[5] Where new earthenware vessels are being burnt, so that no other, who may be unclean, shall have touched the vessel intended for the Sin-offering water.

[6] Cf. Ohol. 5[5].

[7] It must be 'running water' (Num. 19[17]). See below, 8[8–11].

[8] Lit. 'sanctifying'. See above, p. 700, n. 3.

[9] Whether the water of immersion was or was not fit for mixing the ashes; for even water fit for mixing renders invalid water that is already mixed (cf. below, 6[2]).

[10] After it has been dried, even though the unfit water may have soaked into the surface of the gourd.   [11] Cf. Kel. 17[17].

[12] Freshly from the ground.   [13] On the grounds states in 3[7].

[14] Cf. the parallel paragraph, Yad. 1[2].   [15] Lit. 'earth'. Cf. App. IV. 16 c.

mix the ashes in a ship.[1] But they may not mix the ashes in the sides of [broken] vessels,[2] or in the flanks of a ladling-jar,[3] or in the plug of a jar, or in the cupped hands, since they may not draw the water or mix the ashes or sprinkle the Sin-offering water save only in a vessel. Only vessels that have a tightly stopped-up cover[4] afford protection [against uncleanness in the 'Tent' wherein lies a corpse]; and only vessels afford protection against [uncleanness present in] earthenware vessels.[5]

6. A potter's 'egg'[6] is valid; but R. Jose declares it invalid. A hen's egg R. Meir and R. Judah declare valid, but the Sages declare it invalid.

7. A trough[7] hewn in the rock—they may not gather the water into it or mix the ashes therein or sprinkle from it; it does not need a tightly stopped-up cover,[8] nor does it render an Immersion-pool invalid.[9] If it was a movable vessel, although it had been joined [to the ground] with lime, they may gather water into it or mix the ashes therein or sprinkle from it; and it needs a tightly stopped-up cover, and it renders an Immersion-pool invalid. If there was a hole in it below and this was stopped up with rags, the water therein is invalid [for mixing the ashes] since it is not wholly enclosed by the vessel; but if the hole was in the side and it was stopped up with rags, the water therein is valid since it is wholly enclosed by the vessel. If the vessel was crowned with a brim of clay and the water reached it, it[10] is invalid; but if the brim was firm enough for the vessel to be moved therewith, the water remains valid.

8. If there were two troughs hewn out in the same stone[11] and the ashes were mixed in one, the water in the other is not thereby sanctified.[12] If there was a hole passing from one to the other, as large as the spout of a water-skin,[13] or if the water washed over [from one to the other] if only to a depth the thickness of garlic peel, and the ashes were mixed in one of them, the water also in the other is thereby sanctified.

9. If two stones were set closely together and made into a rock-trough (so, too, if there were two kneading-troughs;[14] so, too, if a rock-trough was split [and ashes were mixed in the water therein]), water that lies between them is not thereby sanctified, but if they were joined together with lime or gypsum and they could be moved together, water that lies between them is thereby sanctified.

6. 1. If a man was mixing the ashes [with the water in the stone trough] and the ashes[15] fell on his hand or on the side [of the trough] and then fell into the [water of the] trough, [the water] is not valid.[16] If the ashes fell [of themselves] into the trough from the pipe,[17] the water is not valid. If he

---

[1] Cf. Shab. 9[2]; Kel. 2[3]. See below, 9[6].   [2] Cf. Kel. 4[1].
[3] See p. 607, n. 2; Toh. 10[7]; Yad. 1[2].   [4] See Kel. 10[1].   [5] Kel. 8[3]; Yad. 1[2].
[6] The hollowed-out lump of clay out of which the pot is shaped.
[7] Mikw. 4[5]. It does not constitute a 'vessel'.
[8] But it affords protection from corpse-uncleanness if it has a simple cover; see Ohol. 5[6].
[9] If water from it flowed into an Immersion-pool (see p. 732, n. 5) which did not yet contain the prescribed forty *seahs*, such water is not deemed 'drawn water' which would render the pool invalid for immersion.
[10] i.e. such of the water as reaches the clay brim.
[11] Which was not fixed to the ground.
[12] Mixed with the ashes in such fashion that the water can be used efficaciously for sprinkling.   [13] Wide enough for two fingers to pass into it.
[14] Set side by side, forming one large receptacle, but with an accidental gap between.
[15] Lit. 'the sanctification'.
[16] From Num. 19[17] it is inferred that the ashes must 'be put thereto in a vessel', and not fall in of themselves.   [17] In which the ashes were kept.

took [the ashes] from the pipe and then covered up [the pipe], or if he shut the door,[1] the ashes remain valid but the water becomes invalid.[2] If he set it[3] upright on the ground, the water becomes invalid; if he set it upright in his hand it remains valid because it is possible so to do.[4]

2. If the ashes floated on the water, R. Meir and R. Simeon say: He may take [some of] them off and mix them with other water. But the Sages say: What has once touched water they may not mix with other water. If the water was emptied out and ashes were found at the bottom, R. Meir and R. Simeon say: They may be dried and used to mix with other water. But the Sages say: What has once touched water they may not mix with other water.

3. If a man was mixing the ashes in [the water of] a stone trough and a ewer was therein, however narrow its neck, water therein is thereby sanctified. If there was a sponge [in the trough] water that is in the sponge is not valid.[5] What should be done? The water [in the trough] may be emptied out[6] until the sponge is reached; when once the sponge is reached, however much water still washes over it, the water is not valid.

4. If a man so placed his hand or his foot or leaves of vegetables as to direct water[7] into the jar, the water is not valid; but if he used leaves of reeds or nuts in like fashion,[8] it remains valid. This is the general rule: [If he used] aught that is susceptible to uncleanness, the water is invalid; but if aught that is not susceptible to uncleanness it remains valid.

5. If water from a well was made to flow into a wine vat or into rain-cisterns, the water is not valid[9] for such as have a flux or for lepers or for mixing the ashes of the Sin-offering,[10] since the water was not drawn into a vessel.

7. 1. If[11] five men had drawn water into five jars purposing to mix the ashes therein by five several acts of mixing, [each for himself,] but they bethought themselves and mixed therein by one single act of mixing [in a single vessel]; or if they purposed to mix the ashes therein by one single act of mixing [in a single vessel], but they bethought themselves and mixed therein by five several acts of mixing, [each for himself], the whole water remains valid. But if one man drew water into five jars purposing to mix the ashes therein by five several acts of mixing, but he bethought himself and mixed therein by one single act of mixing, the water in the last jar alone is valid; or if he purposed to mix the ashes by one single act of mixing, but he bethought himself and mixed therein by five several acts of mixing, the water in the first jar alone is valid; if he said to another,[12] 'Do thou mix these for thyself', the water in the first jar alone is valid; [and if he said,] 'Do thou mix these for me', the water in them all is valid.

---

[1] After taking the ashes from the pipe and before mixing them.
[2] See above, 4[4] (end).   [3] The pipe containing the rest of the ashes.
[4] The act of holding it safely is so simple as not to count as a distraction or an act of work. A variant reads: 'Because it is impossible (to do otherwise)'.
[5] Since a sponge does not count as a vessel.
[6] Into another vessel; and this water is valid for sprinkling.
[7] 'Living water' intended for mixing with the ashes. The vessel must be filled directly from the water source.
[8] Cf. Eduy. 7[4]. They are not edible and so cannot contract food-uncleanness.
[9] It ceases to count as 'living water'.
[10] For all three 'living water' (Lev. 15[13]; 14[5]; Num. 19[17]) is prescribed.
[11] The cases cited in this chapter deal with the application of the rule against doing other work while engaged in the act of mixing the ashes or drawing the water.
[12] When he drew the water into five vessels purposing to mix the ashes by one single act of mixing.

2. If he drew the water with one hand and did other work with the other hand; or if he drew water both for himself and for another; or if he drew water into two [jars] at the same time, the water of both is invalid, since an act of work renders the water invalid whether he drew it for himself or for another.

3. If he mixed the ashes with one hand and did other work with the other hand and he mixed them for himself, it is invalid; but if for another it is valid. If he mixed the ashes both for himself and for another, his own is invalid but that of the other is valid. If he mixed the ashes for two [others] at the same time both are valid.

4. [If a man said,] 'Mix the ashes for me and I will mix the ashes for thee', the first [alone] is valid. [If he said,] 'Draw water for me and I will draw water for thee', the last is valid. [If he said,] 'Mix the ashes for me and I will draw the water for thee', both are valid. [If he said,] 'Draw the water for me and I will mix the ashes for thee', both are invalid.

5. If a man drew water both for his own [common] needs and for the [ashes of the] Sin-offering, he must draw for himself first and fasten [the bucket to] the carrying-yoke and then draw the water for the Sin-offering. If he drew first the water for the Sin-offering and afterward drew the water for himself, it is invalid. He must bear his own behind him and that for the Sin-offering before him, and if he bore that for the Sin-offering behind him it is invalid. If both were for the Sin-offering, he may bear one before him and one behind him; because it is possible [so to do].[1]

6. If a man could carry back in his hand a [borrowed] rope [to its owner] without turning off his path, the water remains valid; but if not without turning off his path it becomes invalid. Three times was this matter brought [for decision] to Jabneh and the third time they declared it valid but as a special dispensation.[2]

7. If he coiled the rope little by little [while he drew up the water] the water remains valid; but if he coiled it afterward it is invalid. R. Jose said: This too they declared valid but as a special dispensation.

8. If he [afterward] hid away the jar lest it be broken, or turned it upside down to dry it that he might draw [other] water therein, [the water that he had already drawn] remains valid; but if to carry the sanctified water therein, it becomes invalid. If he cleared out potsherds from the trough [before he mixed the ashes] that it might hold the more water, the water remains valid; but if that it might not hinder him when he empties out the water [for sprinkling], it becomes invalid.

9. If a man was carrying his water on his shoulder and he [stopped and] decided a matter of the Law or showed others the way or killed a serpent or a scorpion or removed food to a place of safety, the water becomes invalid; but if he took the food to eat it, the water remains valid; or [if he killed] the serpent or the scorpion because they hindered him, it remains valid. R. Judah said: This is the general rule: If his act was of the nature of work, whether he stayed to do it or not, the water becomes invalid; if it was not of the nature of work, yet he stayed to do it, the water becomes invalid; if he did not stay, it remains valid.

10. If a man gave the water into the keeping of one that was unclean, it becomes invalid; if of one that was clean it remains valid. R. Eliezer says:

---

[1] Variant: 'Because it is impossible (to do otherwise)'. The grounds are the same as above, 6[1].   [2] Lit. 'instruction of the hour'.

It remains valid even if he gave it into the keeping of one that was unclean, provided that [meanwhile] the owner did no act of work.

11. If two were drawing the water for the Sin-offering and they helped each other to raise it, or one pulled out a thorn for the other, and the water was intended for one single act of mixing the ashes, it remains valid; but if it was for two several acts, it becomes invalid. R. Jose says: Even if it was for two several acts, it remains valid if they had made terms between them.[1]

12. If [while he bore the water] he broke down a wall with the intention of building it up again, the water remains valid; but if he did build it up it becomes invalid. If [after he had drawn the water] he ate [of figs] and had the intention of storing them, it remains valid; but if he did store them, it becomes invalid. If he ate some and left some over and cast what was in his hand under the fig-tree or into the storing-place lest it be wasted, the water becomes invalid.

8. 1. If two kept watch over the stone trough[2] and one of them became unclean, the water remains valid, since it is yet in the keeping of the other; if the first became clean again and the other became unclean it still remains valid since it is in the keeping of the first; but if they both at one time became unclean it becomes invalid. If one of them did an act of work, it remains valid since it is yet in the keeping of the other; if the first ceased from the work and the other did an act of work it still remains valid since it is in the keeping of the first; but if they both at one time did an act of work it becomes invalid.

2. He that mixes[3] the Sin-offering water may not wear his sandals, for if the liquid fell on his sandal, his sandal becomes unclean and renders him unclean. Thus he may say, 'What renders thee unclean does not render me unclean, but thou hast rendered me unclean'.[4] If the liquid fell on his flesh he remains clean; but if it fell on his garment it becomes unclean and renders him unclean. Thus he may say, 'What renders thee unclean does not render me unclean, but thou hast rendered me unclean'.

3. He that burns the [Red] Heifer or the bullocks,[5] and he that takes away the Scape-goat,[6] render garments unclean; but the [Red] Heifer and the bullocks and the Scape-goat cannot themselves render garments unclean. Thus they may say,[7] 'What renders thee unclean does not render me unclean, but thou hast rendered me unclean'.

4. If a man ate of the carrion of a clean bird and it is yet in his gullet,[8] he renders garments unclean; but the carrion itself does not render garments unclean. Thus they may say, 'What renders thee unclean does not render me unclean, but thou hast rendered me unclean'.

5. A derived uncleanness cannot convey uncleanness to a vessel but only to a liquid; howbeit if a liquid becomes unclean it can render vessels unclean. Thus they may say,[9] 'What renders thee unclean does not render me unclean, but thou hast rendered me unclean'.

6. An earthenware vessel cannot convey uncleanness to another vessel,

---

1 If, e.g., one said to the other, Only if thou helpest me to raise my water will I help thee to raise thine.
2 In which was water in readiness for mixing with the ashes.
3 So, too, he that sprinkles it.　　　　4 Cf. Kel. 8⁴; Toh. 8⁷.
5 Whose flesh is not burnt on the Altar. Cf. App. IV. 1 c.　　　6 Lev. 16²⁶.
7 The garments to the man.　　　8 See Zeb. 7³, ⁵, ⁶; Toh. 1¹, ³; Zab. 5⁹. See App. IV.
14 c.　　　　　　　　　　　　9 The vessels to the liquid.

but only to a liquid; howbeit if the liquid becomes unclean it can render the other vessel unclean. Thus it may say,[1] 'What renders thee unclean does not render me unclean, but thou hast rendered me unclean'.

7. Whatsoever renders Heave-offering invalid[2] conveys uncleanness to liquids[3] so that they suffer first grade uncleanness, whereby they can convey uncleanness[4] at one remove and render [Heave-offering] invalid at a second remove (excepting only him that had immersed himself the selfsame day [because of uncleanness]).[5] Thus they may say,[6] 'What renders thee unclean does not render me unclean,[7] but thou hast rendered me unclean'.

8. All seas[8] are valid as an Immersion-pool (*Mikweh*),[9] for it is written, *And the* Mikweh[10] *of the waters called he Seas*.[11] So R. Meir. R. Judah says: The Great Sea[12] is valid as an Immersion-pool, and it is written, *Seas*, only because there are in it many kinds of seas. R. Jose says: All seas render clean by virtue of being flowing waters; but they are not valid for them that have a flux or for lepers or for mixing therein the ashes of the Sin-offering.

9. Smitten waters[13] are not valid.[14] They are deemed smitten waters that are salty or warm. Intermittent waters[15] are not valid. They are deemed intermittent waters that fail [even] once in a week of years; but they that have failed only in times of war or in years of drought are valid. R. Judah declares them invalid.

10. The waters of the Keramiyon[16] and the Puga[17] are invalid because they are miry waters. The waters of the Jordan and the Yarmuk are invalid because they are mixed waters.[18] They are deemed mixed waters whereof the one is valid and the other invalid and they mingle together; if they both are valid and they mingle together they remain valid. R. Judah declares them invalid.

11. The Well of Ahab and [the pool in] the Cave of Pamias[19] are valid. If the colour of the water changed but the change arose from itself, it remains valid. A water-channel[20] that comes from far is valid, if only they take heed that none interrupts its flow. R. Judah says: Even so the presumption is that its water is permitted. If clay or earth fell into a well a man must wait until it becomes clear. So R. Ishmael. R. Akiba says: There is no need to wait.

9. 1. If there fell into a flask[21] any water soever, R. Eliezer says: Let it be

---

[1] The other vessel to the liquid.
[2] Namely whatever suffers second-grade uncleanness, and the hands, and those enumerated in Zab. 5[12].   [3] See Toh. 2[6].   [4] To foodstuffs.
[5] Who does not render common foodstuffs and liquids unclean. See p. 773, n. 6.
[6] The common foodstuffs that have been rendered unclean, to the liquids.
[7] Since common foodstuffs cannot suffer third-grade uncleanness.   [8] Mikw. 5[4].
[9] i.e. they are valid for immersion in cases of uncleanness; but they do not count as 'living water' prescribed (see above, 6[5]) for them that have a flux, for the leper, and for mixing the Sin-offering ashes.   [10] R.V. 'the gathering together'.   [11] Gen. 1[10].
[12] The Mediterranean Sea, and not small inland seas.   [13] Cf. Ex. 7[17].
[14] For use in the cases where 'living water' is prescribed.
[15] Lit. 'disappointing waters' whose flow is not to be relied upon. The term is derived from Is. 58[11].
[16] Identifications with the rivers Kishon or Amana have been suggested.
[17] Or Piga. The Belus (a few miles north of the Kishon) has been suggested; also the Biblical Pharpar.
[18] Fed by tributary streams of which some are 'smitten' or 'disappointing'.
[19] Banias, at the source of the Jordan.
[20] By which spring-water is conducted from a distance. Cf. above, 6[5].
[21] Meaning, as often in this and the succeeding chapters, a flask containing the ashes of the Red Heifer mixed with water and ready for sprinkling.

sprinkled twice over. But the Sages declare it[1] invalid. If dew dropped into it, R. Eliezer says: Let it be left out in the sun and the dew will go up from it. But the Sages declare it invalid. If liquid or fruit juice fell into it, all must be poured away and the vessel must be dried;[2] but if it was ink or gum or copperas[3] or aught that leaves a trace, all must be poured away, but the vessel need not be dried.

2. If insects or creeping things fell therein, and they broke asunder or the colour of the water changed, it becomes invalid. If it was a beetle [that fell therein] it in any wise renders the water invalid since it is as it were a tube. R. Simeon and R. Eliezer b. Jacob say: If a maggot or a weevil from out of the corn [fell therein], they are valid[4] since they contain no moisture.

3. If cattle or wild animals drank thereof it becomes invalid. All birds render it invalid excepting the dove, since it sucks up the water. No creeping things render it invalid excepting the weasel, since it laps up the water. Rabban Gamaliel says: The serpent also, since it vomits. R. Eliezer says: The mouse also.

4. If a man had the intention[5] to drink the Sin-offering water, R. Eliezer says: It becomes invalid. But R. Joshua says: Only after he turns up [the flask to drink out of it]. R. Jose said: This only applies to the water before the ashes are mixed in it; but if the ashes have been mixed with the water, R. Eliezer says, [It becomes invalid] after he turns up [the flask to drink out of it]; and R. Joshua says, [It first becomes invalid] only when he drinks. But if he poured it into his throat[6] it remains valid.

5. If the Sin-offering water becomes invalid it may not be trampled into the mud lest it become a snare for others;[7] but R. Judah says: It becomes harmless. If a heifer drank of the Sin-offering water, its flesh becomes unclean for a space of twenty-four hours. R. Judah says: It becomes harmless in its bowels.

6. Sin-offering water or the ashes of the Sin-offering may not be taken over a river in a ship, nor may they be floated over the water, nor may a man stand on one side and throw them to the other side; but he may cross over [on his feet] with water up to the neck. Yet he that is clean for the Sin-offering water may cross over bearing in his hands an empty vessel that is clean for the Sin-offering water or with water that has not yet been mixed with the ashes.

7. If ashes that were valid were confused with ashes from a stove, whether they convey uncleanness is determined by which of them is greater in quantity; but they may not sanctify water therewith.[8] R. Eliezer says: They may use them all together[9] to sanctify water therewith.

8. Sin-offering water even when it is invalid still conveys uncleanness to him that is clean for Heave-offering[10] whether it touched his hands or his body, but it conveys no uncleanness to him that is clean for the Sin-offering whether it touched his hands or his body. [Sin-offering water] that is become unclean conveys uncleanness to him that is clean for Heave-offering

---

[1] The contents of the flask.   [2] Before other Sin-offering water can be put in.
[3] See p. 203, n. 15. Cf. Sot. 2[4].
[4] i.e. they do not render the Sin-offering water invalid.   [5] And said so.
[6] So that his mouth did not touch the flask.
[7] Who unsuspectingly touched it while it was yet moist, since it still conveys uncleanness; cf. below, par. 8.
[8] Even if the greater part is valid ashes.
[9] Ensuring the presence of valid ashes.
[10] But he that is clean only for common food is not affected.

whether it touched his hands or his body, and also to him that is clean for the Sin-offering if it touched his hands, but not if it touched his body.

9. If ashes that were valid were put on water that was not fit for mixing the ashes therewith, the water conveys uncleanness to him that is clean for Heave-offering whether it touched his hands or his body; but it conveys no uncleanness to him that is clean for the Sin-offering, whether it touched his hands or his body.

10. 1. Whatsoever is susceptible to *midras*-uncleanness,[1] whether it is unclean or clean, is deemed to be unclean with *maddaf*-uncleanness[2] for them that occupy themselves with the Sin-offering water.[3] And the like applies also to men.[4] Whatsoever is susceptible [only] to corpse uncleanness, whether it is unclean or clean, R. Eliezer says: It is not deemed to be unclean with *maddaf*-uncleanness. And R. Joshua says: It is deemed to be unclean with *maddaf*-uncleanness. But the Sages say: It can convey *maddaf*-uncleanness if it is unclean, but not if it is clean.

2. If he that was clean for the Sin-offering water touched him that suffered *maddaf*-uncleanness, he becomes unclean; if a flagon appointed for Sin-offering water touched aught that suffered *maddaf*-uncleanness, it becomes unclean. If he that was clean for the Sin-offering water touched foodstuffs or liquid with his hand, he becomes unclean; if [he touched them] with his foot he remains clean. If he shifted them with his hand R. Joshua declares him unclean, but the Sages declare him clean.

3. If the jar containing the [ashes of the] Sin-offering, touched a [dead] creeping thing, the jar remains clean;[5] if the jar was set above it, R. Eliezer declares it clean, but the Sages declare it unclean.[6] If the jar touched [unclean] foodstuffs or liquids or the Holy Scriptures,[7] it remains clean; if it was put above them, R. Jose declares it clean, but the Sages declare it unclean.

4. If he that was clean for the Sin-offering water touched an oven with his hand he becomes unclean; but if with his foot he remains clean. If he stood over the oven and stretched his hand beyond the oven with the flagon[8] in his hand (so, too, if a carrying-yoke was set over the oven with two jars hanging from either end), R. Akiba declares them clean, but the Sages declare them unclean.

5. If he stood away from the oven and stretched out his hand to the window and took the flagon [therefrom] and passed it over the oven, R. Akiba declares it unclean, but the Sages declare it clean. Yet he that is clean for the Sin-offering water may stand over the oven bearing in his hands an empty vessel that is clean for the Sin-offering water or with water that has not yet been mixed with the ashes.

6. If the flagon containing the Sin-offering water touched another

---

[1] See App. I. 26.   [2] App. I. 22.

[3] Cf. Hag. 2⁷. If he that is 'clean for Sin-offering water' touched, carried or shifted any object liable to contract *midras*-uncleanness, whether or not it was unclean, he is deemed to suffer uncleanness from it to the same degree that one who was 'clean for Heave-offering' would suffer uncleanness from an object that, in fact, suffered *midras*-uncleanness.

[4] If he that was 'clean for Sin-offering water' touched, carried or shifted a man who was 'clean for Heave-offering', the latter is deemed as unclean as if he had a flux and renders the former unclean in what concerns the Sin-offering water.

[5] Since the inner part of an earthenware jar cannot contract uncleanness from its outer part.   [6] Num. 19⁹ ordains that the ashes must be set 'in a clean place'.

[7] p. 626, n. 4; Zab. 5¹²; Yad. 4⁵.

[8] Containing the water intended for mixing with the ashes.

containing Hallowed Things or Heave-offering, that containing Sin-offering water becomes unclean, and that containing Hallowed Things or Heave-offering remains clean. If he held them one in each of his two hands, they both become unclean; if they were each wrapped in paper they both remain clean; if the one containing the Sin-offering water was wrapped in paper and that containing Heave-offering was in his [bare] hand, they both become unclean; if that containing Heave-offering was wrapped in paper and that containing the Sin-offering water was in his [bare] hand, they both remain clean. R. Joshua says: That containing the Sin-offering water becomes unclean. If they were set on the ground and he touched them, that containing the Sin-offering water becomes unclean and that containing Hallowed Things or Heave-offering remains clean. If he shifted them, R. Joshua declares them unclean, but the Sages declare them clean.

11. 1. If a man left uncovered a flask [containing the Sin-offering water] and came and found it covered, it is invalid.[1] If he left it covered and came and found it uncovered and a weasel could have drunk from it or, according to Rabban Gamaliel,[2] a serpent, or if dew fell into it in the night, the water is invalid. Sin-offering water is not protected [from uncleanness in the 'Tent' wherein lies a corpse] by a tightly stopped-up cover;[3] but water that has not yet been mixed with the ashes is protected by a tightly stopped-up cover.

2. Any condition of doubt that is deemed clean when it concerns Heave-offering is also deemed clean when it concerns the Sin-offering water. Any condition in which the decision is left in suspense when it concerns Heave-offering,[4] in like condition the Sin-offering water must be poured away. If acts that must be done in cleanness were done after sprinkling by such Sin-offering water, their validity must be left in suspense. Wooden lattice work is clean[5] in what concerns Hallowed Things or Heave-offering or the Sin-offering water. R. Eliezer says: Loosely fastened boards are unclean in what concerns the Sin-offering water.[6]

3. If pressed figs that were Heave-offering fell into Sin-offering water, and were taken out and eaten, and there was an egg's bulk[7] of them, whether they were unclean or clean the water becomes unclean[8] and he that ate of them is guilty of death.[9] If[10] there was not an egg's bulk of them the water remains clean, yet he that ate of them is guilty of death. R. Jose says: If the pressed figs were clean the water remains clean.[11] If he that was clean for the Sin-offering water put in his head and the greater part of his body into the Sin-offering water, he becomes unclean.

---

[1] It must have been touched by a man; and he may be assumed not to have been 'clean for Sin-offering water'.   [2] See above, 9[3].

[3] Since such a place does not conform to the rule of Num. 19[9]; cf. above, 10[3].

[4] Cf. Ter. 8[8]; Toh. 4[5].

[5] Since such cannot count as vessels, and they cannot contract *midras*-uncleanness or corpse-uncleanness.

[6] They may be used to sit or lie upon; therefore they are susceptible to *midras*-uncleanness, and even when clean (cf. 10[1]) count as suffering '*maddaf*-uncleanness' so far as concerns the cleanness required for the Sin-offering water.

[7] The minimum quantity in foodstuffs that conveys uncleanness.

[8] Since the degree of cleanness required in Heave-offering is uncleanness in what concerns Sin-offering water.

[9] Because of eating Heave-offering while his person is unclean from the Sin-offering water.   [10] Some texts omit this sentence.

[11] He is not of the opinion that the condition of cleanness required in Heave-offering is uncleanness in what concerns the Sin-offering water.

4. Whosoever according to what is prescribed in the Law requires immersion,[1] conveys uncleanness to Hallowed Things, to Heave-offering, to common food, and to [Second] Tithe, and he is forbidden to enter into the Temple. After he has immersed himself he still conveys uncleanness to Hallowed Things and renders Heave-offering invalid. So R. Meir. But the Sages say: He renders Hallowed Things and Heave-offering invalid; but common food and [Second] Tithe are permitted to him. But if he entered the Temple, whether before or after he had immersed himself, he is culpable.

5. Whosoever according to the words of the Scribes requires immersion,[2] conveys uncleanness to Hallowed Things and renders Heave-offering invalid; but common food and [Second] Tithe are permitted to him. So R. Meir. But the Sages say: He is forbidden [Second] Tithe. But after he has immersed himself they are all permitted to him; and if he entered the Temple, whether before or after he had immersed himself, he is not culpable.

6. Whosoever, whether according to what is prescribed in the Law or according to the words of the Scribes, requires immersion, conveys uncleanness, whether by contact or by carrying, to the Sin-offering water and to the ashes of the Sin-offering, and to him that sprinkles the water of the Sin-offering. Moreover [he conveys uncleanness], whether by contact or by carrying, to the hyssop[3] that has been rendered susceptible to uncleanness,[4] and to the water that has not yet been mixed with the ashes, and to an empty vessel that is clean for the Sin-offering water. So R. Meir. But the Sages say: [He conveys uncleanness] by contact but not by carrying.

7. Any kind of hyssop that is given a special name[5] is invalid, but hyssop, simply so called, is valid; Greek hyssop, stibium hyssop, Roman hyssop or wild hyssop are invalid; if it is unclean Heave-offering it is invalid, and even if it is clean Heave-offering it should not be used for sprinkling, but if they sprinkled with it it is valid. They may not sprinkle with the young shoots or with the berries [of the hyssop]. But if a man was sprinkled with the young shoots he is not culpable if he enters the Temple. R. Eliezer says: Nor if he was sprinkled with the berries. By young shoots is meant [the hyssop] before the buds have ripened.

8. Hyssop that was used for sprinkling the Sin-offering water is valid for the cleansing of the leper.[6] If it was gathered for firewood and liquid fell thereon it must be dried and it is then valid. If it was gathered for food and liquid fell thereon, even though it is dried, it is invalid. If it was gathered for the Sin-offering water, it is regarded as if it had been gathered for food. So R. Meir. R. Judah, R. Jose, and R. Simeon say: As if it had been gathered for firewood.

9. The [bunch of] hyssop should be made up from three stalks having [in all] three buds. R. Judah says: Three to each. If the hyssop had three stalks [from the one root] these are severed and then bound up; yet if they were severed and not bound up or bound up and not severed, or neither

---

[1] i.e. men and vessels that have been rendered unclean by a 'father of uncleanness'. They therefore suffer first-grade uncleanness, which suffices to render common food and Second Tithe unclean at one remove, and Heave-offering invalid at the second remove, and Hallowed Things unclean even at the third remove.
[2] They who eat or drink what is unclean, vessels that have touched unclean liquids, and the hands. These suffer 'second-grade uncleanness'. See Zab. 5[12].
[3] Num. 19[18].   [4] Lev. 11[34, 38]. See p. 758, n. 1.
[5] Cf. Ned. 6[9]; Neg. 14[6].   [6] Lev. 14[4].

severed nor bound up, the hyssop is still valid. R. Jose says: The [bunch of] hyssop should be made up from three stalks having [in all] three buds; and its remnants[1] [continue valid] if there are [at least] two stalks and if there is aught soever of the stumps thereof.

12. 1. If the hyssop was too short[2] it may be made to suffice with thread and a spindle-reed, and thus it may be dipped in and brought up again; yet a man must hold it by the hyssop [itself] when he sprinkles. R. Judah and R. Simeon say: As the sprinkling must be with the hyssop alone, so must the dipping be with the hyssop alone.

2. If he sprinkled and it is in doubt whether it was from the thread or the spindle-reed or the buds, his sprinkling is invalid. If he sprinkled two vessels and it is in doubt whether he sprinkled them both or whether water from the one dripped on to the other, his sprinkling is invalid. If there was a needle fixed in the earthenware and he sprinkled thereon and it is in doubt whether he sprinkled the needle or whether water from the earthenware dripped thereon, his sprinkling is invalid. If the mouth of the flask[3] was narrow, he may dip in the hyssop and draw it out in usual fashion.[4] R. Judah says: [Only] at the first sprinkling. If there was but little remaining of the Sin-offering water it suffices to dip only the tips of the buds and then to sprinkle, provided that [the hyssop] is not dried [by the inner sides of the neck]. If a man intended to sprinkle in front of him and he sprinkled behind him, or behind him and he sprinkled in front of him, his sprinkling is invalid; but if [he intended to sprinkle] in front of him and he sprinkled to the sides, his sprinkling that is in front of him is still valid. They may sprinkle a man with his knowledge or without his knowledge; they may sprinkle a man and vessels together even though there be a hundred of them.

3. If he intended to sprinkle what was susceptible to uncleanness and he sprinkled what was not susceptible to uncleanness, and there was still water enough on the hyssop he need not dip again. But if [he intended to sprinkle] what was not susceptible to uncleanness and he sprinkled what was susceptible to uncleanness, even if there was still water enough on the hyssop he must dip again. If [he intended to sprinkle] a man and he sprinkled a beast, and there was still water enough on the hyssop he need not dip again; but if [he intended to sprinkle] a beast and he sprinkled a man, even if there was still water enough on the hyssop he must dip again. Water that drips [off the hyssop] is valid; therefore it still conveys uncleanness as Sin-offering water.

4. If a man sprinkled from [Sin-offering water standing in] a wall-niche in a public place and [an unclean person so sprinkled] entered the Temple, and the water was found to be invalid, he is not culpable; but if it was from a wall-niche belonging to a private person and he entered the Temple, and the water was found to be invalid, he is culpable. But if it was the High Priest, whether it was from a wall-niche belonging to a private person or from a wall-niche in a public place, he is not culpable, since the High Priest is never subject to penalty for entering the Temple. They used to slip before such a wall-niche in a public place [because of the much water

---

[1] After it has become broken up by use.
[2] To be dipped into the flask containing the Sin-offering water.
[3] Containing the Sin-offering water.
[4] Not scrupling lest the bunch be squeezed dry in drawing it out of the narrow neck.

that was sprinkled there,] but they could still go their way [into the Temple] and not refrain, for they have said, 'The water of the Sin-offering that has fulfilled its purpose does not convey uncleanness'.[1]

5. He that is clean may hold in his skirt an unclean axe and sprinkle it; and although there is thereon sufficient for a sprinkling, he remains clean. How much water should there be to be sufficient for a sprinkling? Sufficient for the buds to be dipped therein and [water sufficient] to be sprinkled. R. Judah says: The buds are regarded as though they were on brazen hyssop.[2]

6. If a man sprinkled with unclean hyssop and there was an egg's bulk [of the hyssop] the water is invalid and his sprinkling is invalid; if there was less than an egg's bulk the water remains valid but his sprinkling is invalid. Such [hyssop] renders other hyssop unclean, and this other [hyssop] renders other [hyssop] unclean, even though they be a hundred.

7. If the hands of one that was clean for the Sin-offering water became unclean, his body becomes unclean, and he conveys uncleanness to his fellow, and he to his fellow, even though they be a hundred.

8. If the outer part of the flagon[3] containing the Sin-offering water became unclean, its inner part becomes unclean also,[4] and it conveys uncleanness to another flagon, and this to another, even though they be a hundred. A bell and clapper count as connectives[5] with each other. In sprinkling a spindle used for spinning coarse stuff, they should not sprinkle the spindle-rod or the spindle ring [since they do not count as connectives with the spindle-hook], but if it was so sprinkled it is valid; but in a spindle used for spinning flax they count as connectives. If the leathern cover of a cot was fastened on to the knobs [of the cot], it counts as a connective. The base [on which a bed stands] does not count as a connective whether in contracting uncleanness or in being rendered clean. Handles of utensils in which is drilled a hole [to fasten them to the utensils] count as connectives. R. Johanan b. Nuri says: Also when [the handles] are wedged [into the utensils].

9. The several baskets of a pack-saddle, the bed of a harrow,[6] the [iron] corner[7] of a bier, the [drinking] horns[8] of wayfarers, a key-chain,[9] the loose stitches of the washermen, or a garment stitched together with threads of mixed stuff—these count as connectives in contracting uncleanness, but not in being rendered clean.

10. If the lid is joined to the kettle by a chain, the School of Shammai say: It counts as a connective in contracting uncleanness but not when it is sprinkled. The School of Hillel say: If a man sprinkled the kettle he has sprinkled the lid also; but if he sprinkled the lid he has not sprinkled the kettle. All are qualified to sprinkle excepting one that is of doubtful sex or of double sex, a woman or a child that is without understanding. A woman may aid a man when he sprinkles and hold the water for him while he dips

---

[1] Cf. Eduy. 5[3].

[2] i.e. no account is taken of the water they soak up in measuring whether there remains in the flask sufficient for a sprinkling. [3] It was of wood or metal.

[4] Cf. Kel. 25[9].

[5] So that if but the one was sprinkled the other also is rendered clean, and if the one contracted uncleanness the other also becomes unclean.

[6] Made up of detachable links.

[7] Some detachable device for holding the corpse in position.

[8] Made out of a series of links which are extended telescope-wise when in use; and which can be made to collapse one within the other when not required for use.

[9] Holding many separable keys.

and sprinkles; but if she held his hand, even at the moment of sprinkling, it is invalid.[1]

11. If a man dipped the hyssop during the day and sprinkled the same day it is valid. But if he dipped during the day and sprinkled at night, or dipped at night and sprinkled during the [next] day,[2] it is invalid. But a man may immerse himself by night and be sprinkled during the [next] day, for they may not sprinkle until the sun is risen; yet if any have done so at the rise of dawn [only] it is valid.

TOHOROTH[3] ('CLEANNESSES')

1. 1. Thirteen things apply to carrion of a clean bird.[4] [Before it can contract or convey uncleanness] there must be intention [to use it for food], but it does not need[5] to be rendered susceptible [to uncleanness by contact with a liquid]; an egg's bulk of it conveys food uncleanness;[6] and an olive's bulk when in the [eater's] gullet;[7] he that eats it remains unclean until sunset;[8] because of it they are culpable that enter the Temple; because of it[9] Heave-offering[10] must be burnt; he that eats a member from the living bird incurs the Forty Stripes; slaughtering it or wringing its neck makes it to be no longer *terefah*[11] (so R. Meir; R. Judah says: This does not render it clean; R. Jose says: Slaughtering it renders it clean but not wringing its neck);

2. the small feathers and down[12] contract uncleanness and convey uncleanness but they are not included together [with the flesh to make up the prescribed bulk[13] that suffices to convey uncleanness] (R. Ishmael says: The down is also[14] included together [with the flesh]); the beak and claws contract uncleanness and convey uncleanness, and they are included together [with the flesh] (R. Jose says: Also the ends of the wings and the end of the tail[15] are included together [with the flesh], since they are suffered to remain on fattened birds).

---

[1] Num. 19[18] ordains explicitly that a 'clean man' shall take the hyssop and dip and sprinkle.   [2] Some texts add: 'or dipped one day and sprinkled the next day'.
[3] 'Cleannesses', euphemistic for 'uncleannesses'. The tractate deals with the suscepti-bility to uncleanness of foodstuffs and liquids used for food, and the conditions in which they are rendered unclean from contact with human beings, with utensils, and with other food-stuffs, and the degree of uncleanness to which they are liable. Common food can suffer uncleanness from 'a father of uncleanness' (see Kel. 1[1ff.]) at one remove ('first-grade un-cleanness') and at a second remove ('second-grade uncleanness'); Heave-offering, with its special sanctity, is one degree more highly susceptible, and can suffer uncleanness at one farther remove ('third-grade uncleanness', whereby it becomes *pasul*, unfit or invalid, and must be burnt); 'Hallowed Things' (i.e. flesh, meal-offerings and drink-offerings, which have been brought as offerings in the Temple) are susceptible to a still higher degree, and can be rendered unclean even at a fourth remove ('fourth-grade uncleanness'). See App. IV.
[4] See App. IV. 14 c.
[5] Like other dry foodstuffs, which only contract and convey uncleanness when purposely made wet (see p. 758, n. 1; Maksh. 6[4]).
[6] i.e. if it is an egg's bulk in quantity it is like other unclean foodstuffs and conveys uncleanness to clean foodstuffs, making them suffer 'second-grade uncleanness'.
[7] At the moment when an olive's bulk is in contact with his gullet he becomes a 'father of uncleanness' so that he (at that moment) conveys first-grade uncleanness to garments or vessels which he touches or carries. After the olive's bulk is swallowed he suffers only first-grade uncleanness.   [8] See Lev. 17[15].
[9] After having eaten of it.
[10] If the carrion, or a man who ate the carrion, touched it.   [11] See Zeb. 7[6].
[12] So Maim. Others: 'the large feathers and the small feathers'.
[13] The egg's bulk, or the olive's bulk in the gullet.
[14] Cf. Uktz. 1[1], where the principle is stated that what 'serves as a protection' is included with the rest to make up the prescribed bulk that is susceptible to uncleanness.
[15] The (sometimes) edible portions nearest the body.

3. As for the carrion of an unclean bird, [before it can contract or convey uncleanness] there must be intention [to use it as food] and it needs to be rendered susceptible [to uncleanness by contact with a liquid]; an egg's bulk of it conveys food uncleanness;[1] he that eats half a half-loaf's bulk of it becomes unfit[2] [to eat of Heave-offering]; an olive's bulk in the gullet does not convey uncleanness; he that eats of it does not remain unclean until sunset; because of it they are not culpable that enter the Temple; but because of it Heave-offering must be burnt; he that eats a member from the living bird does not incur the Forty Stripes; slaughtering it does not render it clean; the small feathers and down contract uncleanness and convey uncleanness, and they are included together [with the flesh]; the beak and claws contract uncleanness and convey uncleanness, and they are included together [with the flesh].

4. In cattle,[3] the hide, grease, sediment, flayed-off flesh, bones, sinews, horns and hoofs are included together [to make up the egg's bulk that suffices] to convey food uncleanness, but not [to make up the olive's bulk that suffices to convey] carrion uncleanness. In like manner if a man slaughtered an unclean beast for a gentile and it still jerks [its limbs] it can convey food uncleanness but it only conveys carrion uncleanness after it is dead or has its head chopped off. [Scripture] has prescribed more conditions that convey food uncleanness than that convey carrion uncleanness.[4]

5. Food rendered unclean by a Father of Uncleanness[5] and food rendered unclean by an Offspring of Uncleanness[6] may be included together so as to convey uncleanness according to the lighter degree of uncleanness of the two. Thus if a half-egg's bulk of food suffering first-grade uncleanness and a half-egg's bulk of food suffering second-grade uncleanness were mixed together, they together count as suffering only second-grade uncleanness; if a half-egg's bulk of food suffering second-grade uncleanness and a half-egg's bulk of food suffering third-grade uncleanness were mixed together, they together count as suffering only third-grade uncleanness. If an egg's bulk of food suffering first-grade uncleanness and an egg's bulk of food suffering second-grade uncleanness were mixed together, they together count as suffering first-grade uncleanness;[7] if they were then divided, each part counts as suffering only second-grade uncleanness.[8] If each by itself fell on a loaf of Heave-offering, they only render it invalid; but if they fell both together, they convey to it second-grade uncleanness.

6. If an egg's bulk of food suffering second-grade uncleanness and an egg's bulk of food suffering third-grade uncleanness were mixed together, they together count as suffering second-grade uncleanness; if they were then divided, each part counts as suffering only third-grade uncleanness. If each by itself fell on a loaf of Heave-offering, they do not render it invalid;[9] but if they fell both together they convey to it third-grade uncleanness.[10] If an egg's bulk of food suffering first-grade uncleanness and an egg's bulk of

---

[1] If there is already 'intention' and it has been rendered susceptible (cf. Uktz. 3[1ff.]).
[2] Cf. Meil. 4[5]. He suffers second-grade uncleanness, and so would render Heave-offering *pasul*, unfit or invalid.   [3] See Hull. 9[1]. Cf. Zeb. 3[4].
[4] In the cases cited in the preceding rules.   [5] And so suffering first-grade uncleanness.
[6] By first grade uncleanness, and so suffering second-grade uncleanness.
[7] Since there is now in the mixture a complete egg's bulk suffering first-grade uncleanness.
[8] Since in neither of the halves would there be a complete egg's bulk suffering first-grade uncleanness.
[9] Since they convey fourth-grade uncleanness to which Hallowed Things alone are susceptible.   [10] Which renders Heave-offering invalid so that it must be burnt.

food suffering third-grade uncleanness were mixed together, they together count as suffering first-grade uncleanness; if they were then divided each part counts as suffering second-grade uncleanness; for third-grade uncleanness, if it has touched first-grade uncleanness, counts as suffering second-grade uncleanness. If two eggs' bulk of food suffering first-grade uncleanness and two eggs' bulk of food suffering second-grade uncleanness were mixed together, they together count as suffering first-grade uncleanness; if they were then divided each counts as suffering first-grade uncleanness; but if [they were divided] into three parts or four, they each count as suffering second-grade uncleanness only. If two eggs' bulk of food suffering second-grade uncleanness and two eggs' bulk of food suffering third-grade uncleanness were mixed together, they together count as suffering second-grade uncleanness; if they were then divided, each part counts as suffering second-grade uncleanness; but if [they were divided] into three parts or four, they each count as suffering only third-grade uncleanness.

7. If pieces of dough [that were Heave-offering] were stuck together or if loaves were stuck together, and one of them was rendered unclean by a [dead] creeping thing,[1] they all count as suffering first-grade uncleanness; if they were separated each counts as suffering first-grade uncleanness. If one of them was rendered unclean by a liquid[2] they all count as suffering second-grade uncleanness; if they were separated each counts as suffering second-grade uncleanness. If [one of them was rendered unclean] by hands,[3] all count as suffering third-grade uncleanness; if they were separated, each counts as suffering third-grade uncleanness.

8. If to a piece of dough already suffering first-grade uncleanness others were made to stick, all count as suffering first-grade uncleanness; if they were separated, the first still suffers first-grade uncleanness but the others only second-grade uncleanness. If to a piece suffering second-grade uncleanness others were made to stick, all count as suffering second-grade uncleanness; if they were separated, the first still suffers second-grade uncleanness, but the others only third-grade uncleanness. If to a piece suffering third-grade uncleanness others were made to stick, it suffers third-grade uncleanness, but the others remain clean,[4] whether they were separated or whether they were not separated.

9. If in the hollows of loaves that were Hallowed Things[5] was water that was holy, and one of them was rendered unclean by a creeping thing, they all become unclean.[6] If the loaves were Heave-offering, [the creeping thing] renders the first and the second unclean and the third invalid.[7] But

---

[1] App. IV. 8 b.   [2] Unclean liquids themselves suffer only first-grade uncleanness; they are not fathers of uncleanness (cf. App. IV. 8 b).

[3] Which, unless intentionally cleaned for the purpose of touching food, always count as suffering second-grade uncleanness.

[4] Since third-grade conveys fourth-grade uncleanness, to which not even Heave-offering is susceptible.   [5] And that touched each other.

[6] The first loaf suffers first-grade uncleanness, the one that touches this suffers second-grade, and so up to the fourth. But (see below, 2[b]; cf. Par. IV. 8[7]) the liquid on being rendered unclean by third-grade uncleanness suffers first-grade uncleanness, thereby having the power to convey second-grade uncleanness to that loaf; and so the process can continue without end.   [7] i.e. the first suffers first-grade uncleanness, the one that touches this suffers second-grade, and the next third grade; but Heave-offering is not susceptible to lighter grades of uncleanness. But if liquid was present this contracts first-grade uncleanness even from the loaves suffering the lighter grade of uncleanness, so conveying the uncleanness indefinitely.

if there was dripping liquid between them, even among Heave-offering all become unclean.

2. 1. If a woman was preparing preserved vegetables [of Heave-offering] in a pot, and she touched a leaf [that projected] outside the pot at a place that was dry, although there was an egg's bulk[1] [in the leaf] the leaf alone becomes unclean but the rest [that is in the pot] remains clean;[2] but if she touched it at a wet spot[3] and there was an egg's bulk [in the whole leaf] all [that is in the pot] becomes unclean; if there was not an egg's bulk it becomes unclean but the rest remains clean. If [the part of the leaf that was wet] returned into the pot the whole is unclean. If she had had contact with one that suffered corpse uncleanness,[4] and she touched the leaf either at a dry spot or a wet spot, and there was an egg's bulk [in the leaf,] all [in the pot] becomes unclean; but if there was not an egg's bulk, the leaf itself becomes unclean but the rest remains clean. If a woman that had immersed herself the selfsame day[5] [because of uncleanness] emptied out the pot while her hands were unwashed, and she saw liquid on her hands, and it is in doubt whether it was splashed from the pot or whether a stalk of the vegetables had touched her hands, the vegetables become invalid, but the pot remains clean.

2. R. Eliezer says: He that eats food of first-grade uncleanness suffers first-grade uncleanness; if it was food of second-grade uncleanness, he suffers second-grade uncleanness; if it was food of third-grade uncleanness, he suffers third-grade uncleanness. R. Joshua says: He that eats food of first-grade uncleanness or food of second-grade uncleanness suffers second-grade uncleanness; if [it was food of] third-grade uncleanness he suffers second-grade uncleanness in what concerns Hallowed Things,[6] but not second-grade uncleanness in what concerns Heave-offering. [This applies only] to common food that is kept in the cleanness proper to Heave-offering.[7]

3. First-grade uncleanness in common food is unclean and renders [Heave-offering] unclean; second-grade uncleanness renders [Heave-offering] invalid, but not unclean; while [common food suffering] third-grade uncleanness may be consumed in pottage containing Heave-offering.

4. First-grade uncleanness and second-grade uncleanness in Heave-offering are unclean and render [Hallowed Things] unclean; third-grade uncleanness renders [Hallowed Things] invalid but not unclean; while [Heave-offering suffering] fourth-grade uncleanness may be consumed in pottage containing Hallowed Things.

5. The first, second and third grades of uncleanness in Hallowed Things are unclean and render [Hallowed Things] unclean; the fourth grade of uncleanness is invalid and does not render [Hallowed Things] unclean; while [Hallowed Things suffering] fifth-grade uncleanness may be consumed in pottage containing Hallowed Things.

---

[1] Which suffices to convey uncleanness.

[2] Her hands are deemed to suffer second grade, and what she touches contracts only third-grade uncleanness which (in Heave-offering) cannot convey further uncleanness.

[3] The liquid (see below, 2[6]) contracts first-grade uncleanness, sufficing to give the leaf second-grade uncleanness, which conveys to the rest of the contents third-grade uncleanness.

[4] And she was therefore suffering first-grade uncleanness.

[5] Such a one is deemed to suffer second-grade uncleanness until sunset.

[6] And so capable of rendering them unclean at a first and also at a second remove.

[7] Since common food can contract uncleanness only from what suffers first-grade uncleanness.

6. Second-grade uncleanness in common food renders unclean liquid[1] that is common food, and renders invalid foods that are Heave-offering. Third-grade uncleanness in Heave-offering renders unclean liquid pertaining to Hallowed Things, and renders invalid food pertaining to Hallowed Things if it was kept in the cleanness proper to Hallowed Things; but if it was esteemed according to the clean conditions proper to Heave-offering, it conveys uncleanness at the first and second removes, and renders Hallowed Things invalid at the third remove.

7. R. Eliezer says: The three of them are equal:[2] Hallowed Things, Heave-offering and common food that suffer first-grade uncleanness convey uncleanness to Hallowed Things at a first and a second remove, and render them invalid at a third remove; and they convey uncleanness at a first remove to Heave-offering and render it invalid at a second remove; while they do but render common food invalid. The three of them, when they suffer second-grade uncleanness, convey uncleanness at a first remove to Hallowed Things and render them invalid at a second remove; they convey uncleanness to liquid that is common food and render invalid food that is Heave-offering. The three of them, when they suffer third-grade uncleanness, convey uncleanness to a liquid pertaining to Hallowed Things, and render invalid food pertaining to Hallowed Things.

8. He that eats food suffering second-grade uncleanness may not labour in an olive press.[3] Common food kept in the cleanness proper to Hallowed Things counts still as common food. R. Eliezer b. Zadok says: It counts as Heave-offering, in that it conveys uncleanness at a first and a second remove and renders [Hallowed Things] invalid at the third remove.

3. 1. If grease, bean-mash or milk are in the form of running liquid, they suffer[4] first-grade uncleanness;[5] if then they turn solid they suffer second-grade uncleanness.[6] If they again become liquid and are [no more than] an egg's bulk exactly, they are clean;[7] but if they are more than an egg's bulk they remain unclean, for then so soon as the first drop has come forth they are unclean if they are as much as an egg's bulk.

2. R. Meir says: [Unclean] oil always suffers first-grade [uncleanness]. The Sages say: Honey also. R. Simeon of Shezur says: Wine also. If a mass of [unclean] olives fell into an oven and were burnt,[8] and they were [no more than] an egg's bulk exactly, they are clean; but if they were more than an egg's bulk they remain unclean, for then so soon as the first drop has come forth they are unclean if they are as much as an egg's bulk. But if they were separate olives they are clean, even though there was a *seah* of them.

3. If one that suffered corpse uncleanness pressed out the juice of olives or grapes that were [no more than] an egg's bulk exactly, they remain clean, provided that he does not touch the place where is the liquid; if they were more than an egg's bulk they become unclean, for then so soon as the first

---

[1] With first grade uncleanness. See Par. 8[7]. Cf. above, 1[9].
[2] i.e. they can be compared after the manner that follows.
[3] In pressing out the oil. He would convey third-grade uncleanness and so render invalid the portion destined to be Heave-offering.
[4] If they touch what is unclean.   [5] As is the rule with liquids.
[6] As having touched first-grade uncleanness.
[7] Since at the moment the first drop of liquid is fashioned, there is not left an egg's bulk still solid, which alone suffices to convey the uncleanness to the drop of liquid.
[8] So that some liquid flowed out.

drop has come forth they become unclean, if they are as much as an egg's bulk. If it was a man or woman that had a flux, and but a single berry [was squeezed out], it becomes unclean, for then so soon as the first drop has come forth it becomes unclean by carrying.[1] If one that had a flux milked a goat, the milk becomes unclean, for then so soon as the first drop has come forth, it becomes unclean by carrying.

4. If an egg's bulk of food was left in the sun and shrank (so, too, if it was[2] an olive's bulk of corpse or an olive's bulk of carrion, or a lentil's bulk of a creeping thing, an olive's bulk of Refuse,[3] an olive's bulk of Remnant,[4] or an olive's bulk of fat), they become clean, and none thereby becomes liable through [transgression of the laws of] Refuse, Remnant and uncleanness.[5] If they were left in the rain and swelled, they become unclean, and one may become liable thereby through [transgression of the laws of] Refuse, Remnant, and uncleanness.

5. Conditions of uncleanness are so accounted of as they appear at the time when they are found:[6] if they were [found] unclean they are [assumed to have been already] unclean [if one had touched them before]; if they were [found] clean they are [assumed to have been] clean [before]; if they were [found] covered they are [assumed to have been] covered [before]; if they were [found] uncovered they are [assumed to have been] uncovered [before]; if a needle was found full of rust or broken,[7] it is [assumed to have been] clean [if one had touched it before], since conditions of uncleanness are so accounted of as they appear at the time when they are found.

6. If a deaf-mute, an imbecile or a minor was found in an alley-way[8] wherein was uncleanness, he can be assumed to be clean, but one of sound senses must be assumed to be unclean.[9] If any one lacks understanding to be inquired of, a condition of doubt affecting him must be deemed clean.

7. If a child was found beside a cemetery with lilies in his hand, and the lilies grew only in a place of uncleanness, he is deemed to be clean, since I might suppose that another gathered them and gave them to him. So, too, if an ass was found among the tombs, its harness is deemed to be clean.[10]

8. If a child [that was unclean] was found beside unbaked bread with a piece of dough in his hand, R. Meir declares the unbaked bread clean, but the Sages declare it unclean, since it is the way of a child to slap [dough]. If dough had on it the marks of a hen's beak, and there was unclean liquid in the house, and the distance between the liquid and the loaves was enough for the hens to dry their mouths on the ground, the loaves are deemed to be clean; or, in the case of a cow or a dog, if the distance was enough for it to lick its tongue; or, in the case of other beasts, if the distance was enough for their tongue to dry. R. Eliezer b. Jacob declares the dough

---

[1] See App. IV. 1a, 12.

[2] The quantities here cited are the minimum in each case that conveys uncleanness.

[3] See p. 470, n. 1.   [4] See p. 471, n. 10.   [5] Lev. 7[20].   [6] Cf. 4[12]; 5[7]; 9[9].

[7] In which condition, as the useless remains of a utensil, it can no longer contract or convey uncleanness.

[8] The side street, leading from the public street to a series of courtyards and houses. It counts as the private domain of the neighbouring occupants, who include it in their *shittuf* (see App. I. 39).

[9] The principle here introduced is that where a condition of doubt arises in a question of uncleanness in a private domain it must be deemed unclean; and if in the public domain, it may be deemed clean.

[10] If its trappings were not found at the time overshadowing a grave (App. IV. 4, 6) it need not be assumed that they had earlier overshadowed a grave.

clean in the case of a dog, since it is cunning and will not leave food and go after water.

4. 1. If a man threw aught unclean from one place to another,[1] or [if he threw] a [clean] loaf between [unclean] keys, or an [unclean] key between [clean] loaves, [what was clean] is still accounted clean. R. Judah says: [If he threw] a [clean] loaf between [unclean] keys it becomes unclean; and if an [unclean] key between [clean] loaves, they are still accounted clean.

2. If a weasel[2] had a [dead] creeping thing in its mouth and passed over loaves of Heave-offering, and it is in doubt whether [the creeping thing] touched them or whether it did not touch them, their condition of doubt is deemed clean.

3. If a weasel had a creeping thing in its mouth, or if a dog had carrion in its mouth, and they passed between things that were clean, or if they that were clean passed between them, their condition of doubt is deemed clean, since the uncleanness had no abiding place. If they[3] picked at them [while these lay] on the ground, and a man said, 'I went to that place but I do not know whether I touched it or whether I did not touch it', his condition of doubt is deemed unclean, since the uncleanness had an abiding place.

4. If a raven had an olive's bulk of corpse in its beak, and it is in doubt whether it overshadowed a man or vessels, and it was in a private domain, the man's condition of doubt is deemed unclean, but the vessels' condition of doubt is deemed clean.[4] If a man drew water into ten buckets and a creeping thing was found in one of them, this is deemed unclean but the rest clean. If a man poured out from one vessel into another and a creeping thing was found in the lower vessel, the upper one is deemed clean.

5. Because of six uncleannesses whereof there is doubt, Heave-offering must be burnt: because of what was perhaps a Grave-area, or because of what was perhaps earth from the land of gentiles, or because of the garments of an *Am-haaretz* that were perhaps unclean, or because of vessels found by chance that were perhaps unclean, or because of spittle encountered by chance that was perhaps unclean, or because of urine of a man that was near by the urine of a beast; if these have of a certainty touched [the Heave-offering] and so conveyed an uncleanness which is in doubt, the Heave-offering must be burnt. R. Jose says: [The same applies] in a private domain even when the contact itself was in doubt. But the Sages say: In a private domain it[5] is left in suspense; and in the public domain the condition of doubt is deemed clean.

6. If there were two drops of spittle, the one unclean and the other clean, [and a man touched one of them and it is not known which,] the matter is left in suspense if, being in a private domain, he touched, carried or shifted [one of them], or, being in the public domain, he touched one of them that was moist, or carried one of them, whether it was wet or dry. If there was but one drop of spittle and he touched, carried or shifted it in the public domain, Heave-offering must be burnt by reason of it; still more so if it was in a private domain.

7. These conditions of doubt[6] the Sages have declared clean: if there is

---

[1] And it is in doubt whether it touched anything clean on its way.
[2] Eduy. 2[7].
[3] The weasel or dog; it is assumed that it was in a private domain. Cf. above, p. 719, n. 9.
[4] Applying the principle of 3[6]; the man has 'understanding to be inquired of', the vessels have not.   [5] A case where there is the double doubt.
[6] Whether they befell in the public or a private domain.

doubt about drawn water that falls into an Immersion-pool,[1] or doubt about aught unclean that floats on the water;[2] if it is in doubt whether a liquid has contracted uncleanness, it is deemed unclean, but if whether it has conveyed uncleanness, it is deemed clean;[3] if there is doubt about the hands, whether they have contracted uncleanness or have conveyed uncleanness or have become clean, they are deemed clean.[4] [Moreover they have declared clean] a condition of doubt that arises in the public domain,[5] or about what is enjoined by the Scribes,[6] or about common food,[7] or about creeping things,[8] or about leprosy-signs,[9] or about the Nazirite-vow,[10] or about Firstlings[11] or about offerings.[12]

8. 'If there is doubt . . . about aught unclean that floats on the water'—[it is deemed clean] whether [the water was] in vessels or upon the ground. R. Simeon says: If in vessels [and it is in doubt whether a man touched it or not] he is deemed unclean; but if upon the ground, he is deemed clean. R. Judah says: If it is in doubt [whether he touched it] when he went down into the water, he is deemed unclean; but if when he came up, he is deemed clean.[13] R. Jose says: Even if there was there [in the water] only space enough for the man and the uncleanness, he is still deemed clean.

9. 'If it is in doubt whether a liquid has contracted uncleanness, it is deemed unclean'—thus if one that was unclean stretched his foot between clean liquids and it is in doubt whether he touched them or not, the condition of doubt is deemed unclean. If he had an unclean loaf in his hand and he threw it[14] between clean liquids, and it is in doubt whether he touched them or not, the condition of doubt is deemed unclean. ['If it is in doubt] whether it conveyed uncleanness it is deemed clean'—thus if a man had a stick in his hand and there was unclean liquid on the end of it and he threw it between clean loaves and it is in doubt whether it touched them or not, the condition of doubt is deemed clean.

10. R. Jose says: Where a condition of doubt arises about the cleanness of liquids, it is deemed unclean in what concerns foodstuffs and clean in what concerns vessels. Thus if there were two jars [of water], the one unclean and the other clean, and a man kneaded dough [with water] from one of them, but it is in doubt whether he kneaded it [with water] from the unclean jar or from the clean jar, such is a case where a condition of doubt about liquids is deemed unclean in what concerns foodstuffs and clean in what concerns vessels.[15]

11. 'If there is doubt about the hands, whether they have contracted uncleanness or have conveyed uncleanness or have become clean', the condition of doubt is deemed clean. A condition of doubt that arises in the public domain is deemed clean. A condition of doubt that arises about aught enjoined by the Scribes—[namely, if it is in doubt] whether a man ate unclean food or drank unclean liquid, or whether he immersed his head and the greater part of his body in drawn water,[16] or whether there fell on

---

[1] See Mikw. 2³.   [2] See the following paragraph.   [3] See below, 4⁹ᶠ.
[4] Yad. 2⁴.   [5] Even if it was an uncleanness explicitly declared unclean in the Law.   [6] See App. IV. 13, 19, 20, 22.   [7] See below, 4¹².
[8] See below, 4¹².   [9] See below, 4¹².   [10] Cf. Naz. 3⁷.
[11] See below, 4¹².   [12] See below, 4¹³.
[13] Since it is the nature of floating matter to be drawn to him when he goes into the water and to be propelled away from him when he rises out of the water.
[14] There is a variant: 'stretched it out', the preferable reading. Cf. above, 4¹
[15] The dough is deemed unclean whereas the vessels containing it are deemed clean.
[16] Cf. Zab. 5¹².

his head and the greater part of his body three *logs* of drawn water, such a
condition of doubt is deemed clean; but if it was a doubt about 'a father of
uncleanness', even one that is enjoined by the Scribes,[1] such a condition of
doubt is deemed unclean.

12. 'A condition of doubt about common food'—this concerns the
cleanness practised by the Pharisees.[2] 'A condition of doubt about creeping
things'—this is determined according to their condition at the time when
they are found.[3] 'A condition of doubt about leprosy-signs'—in the beginning it is deemed clean if it had not yet come within the bonds of uncleanness, but after it has come within the bonds of uncleanness the
condition of doubt is deemed unclean.[4] If there is a doubt about the
Nazirite-vow[5] the vow is not binding. If there is doubt about a Firstling—
it is all one whether it is the firstborn of man or beast, or whether it is a
thing unclean or clean: [the priest can claim nothing], for on him that would
exact aught from his fellow lies the burden of proof.[6]

13. 'A condition of doubt about offerings'; thus,[7] if a woman suffered
five miscarriages that were in doubt or five issues that were in doubt, she
need bring but one offering, and she may then eat of the animal-offerings;
and she is not bound to bring the other offerings.

5. 1. If there was a creeping thing[8] and a frog[9] in the public domain (so,
too, if there was an olive's bulk of corpse[10] and an olive's bulk of carrion,[11]
or a bone of a corpse[12] and a bone of carrion,[13] or a clod of clean earth
and a clod from a Grave-area,[14] or a clod of clean earth and a clod
from the land of gentiles,[14] or if there were two paths, the one unclean[15] and
the other clean), and a man walked by one of them but it is not known
which, or overshadowed one of them[16] and it is not known which, or shifted
one of them and it is not known which, R. Akiba declares him unclean,
but the Sages declare him clean.

2. If a man said, 'I touched this[17] and I know not whether it is unclean
or clean', or 'I touched one but I know not which of the two I touched',
R. Akiba declares him unclean, but the Sages declare him clean. R. Jose
declares him unclean in every case[18] excepting the case of the path, since
men usually go their way and do not usually touch.

3. If there were two paths, the one unclean and the other clean,[19] and
a man walked by one of them and afterward prepared foodstuffs in conditions of cleanness and they were consumed, and he then sprinkled himself
a first and a second time and immersed himself and became clean;[20] if he

---

1 See above, 4[7].
2 For whom the clothes of an *Am-haaretz* were deemed to suffer *midras*-uncleanness (cf.
Hag. 2[7]); and if it is in doubt whether the Pharisee touched the clothes of an *Am-haaretz*,
the condition of doubt is deemed clean and the Pharisee may eat of common food.
3 Cf. above, 3[5]. If such was thrown among clean foodstuffs but was not found touching
them, it need not be assumed that it had touched them and that they are unclean.
4 See Neg. 5[4f].   5 Whether a man did or did not vow to become a Nazirite.
6 Cf. Bekh. 3[6ff].   7 Ker. 1[7].
8 Any one of the eight specified in Lev. 11[29]. It is a father of uncleanness and conveys
uncleanness by contact.   9 Which does not convey uncleanness at all.
10 Which conveys uncleanness by contact, carrying, and overshadowing.
11 Conveys uncleanness by contact and carrying.
12 Conveys uncleanness by contact and carrying.
13 Which does not convey uncleanness at all.   14 Conveys uncleanness by contact and
carrying.   15 Passing over a grave.
16 The olive's bulk of corpse or of carrion.   17 The creeping thing or the frog.
18 Of those cited in these two paragraphs.   19 But it was unknown which was which.
20 Fulfilling the injunctions of Num. 19[19], for becoming clean from corpse-uncleanness.

then walked by the other path and prepared foodstuffs in conditions of cleanness, these are clean; but if the first foodstuffs still remained, both alike are left in suspense. If he had not become clean in the meantime, the first foodstuffs are left in suspense, but the second must be burnt.

4. If there was a creeping thing and a frog in the public domain,[1] and a man touched one of them and then prepared foodstuffs in conditions of cleanness and they were consumed; and he immersed himself and then touched the other and afterward prepared foodstuffs in conditions of cleanness, these are clean. If the first still remained, both alike are left in suspense; if he did not immerse himself in the meantime, the first are left in suspense, but the second must be burnt.

5. If there were two paths, the one unclean and the other clean, and a man walked by one of them and afterward prepared foodstuffs in conditions of cleanness, and his fellow came and walked by the second path, and prepared foodstuffs in conditions of cleanness, R. Judah says: If each inquired[2] by himself, each is declared clean; but if they inquired together, they are both declared unclean. R. Jose says: In either case they are both declared unclean.

6. If there were two loaves, the one unclean and the other clean, and a man ate one of them and afterward prepared foodstuffs in conditions of cleanness, and his fellow came and ate the other loaf and afterward prepared foodstuffs in conditions of cleanness, R. Judah says: If each inquired by himself, each is declared clean; but if they inquired together, both are declared unclean. R. Jose says: In either case both are declared unclean.

7. If one man sat in the public domain and another came and pressed against his clothes, or if he spat and the other touched his spittle, because of the spittle the Heave-offering[3] must be burnt, and as for his garments, they decide[4] according to [whether] the greater number [of the people of the place suffered from flux].[5] If a man slept in the public domain, when he is risen his garments are deemed unclean from *midras*-uncleanness. So R. Meir. But the Sages declare them clean. If he touched some one in the night and it is not known whether it was one that was alive or dead, and in the morning he arose and found him dead, R. Meir declares him clean, but the Sages declare him unclean, for conditions of uncleanness are so accounted of as they appear at the time when they are found.[6]

8. If there was in the town a woman that was an imbecile[7] or a woman that was a gentile or a Samaritan,[8] all spittle found in the town is unclean. If a woman pressed against a man's garments or sat with him in a boat,[9] if she perceived that he was one that ate Heave-offering[10] his garments remain clean; if not, he must inquire of her.

9. If a witness said, 'Thou hast become unclean', but he said, 'I have not become unclean', he is accounted clean. If two said, 'Thou hast become unclean', but he said, 'I have not become unclean', R. Meir declares him unclean, but the Sages say: He may be believed concerning himself. If one witness said, 'He has become unclean', but two witnesses said, 'He has

---

[1] And they cannot be distinguished one from the other.
[2] Asked the Sages for a ruling about their cleanness.
[3] Which the first man touches. See above, 4[5].
[4] As to whether the first man is to be accounted unclean from *midras*-uncleanness.
[5] See App. IV. 10.   [6] See above, 3[5].
[7] And careless of her conduct and of the onset of her periods.
[8] See App. IV. 10, 20.   [9] See Zab. 3[1].
[10] A priest; she would therefore not press against his garments or sit with him in a boat.

not become unclean', whether it was in the public domain or in a private domain, he is accounted clean. If two witnesses said, 'He has become unclean', but one said, 'He has not become unclean', whether it was in the public domain or in a private domain he is accounted unclean. If one witness said, 'He has become unclean', and another witness said, 'He has not become unclean', or if one woman said, 'He has become unclean', and another woman said, 'He has not become unclean', and it was in a private domain, he is accounted unclean; but if it was in the public domain he is accounted clean.

6. 1. If a place was a private domain and was made a public domain and then became again a private domain,[1] such time as it was a private domain any condition of doubt concerning it is deemed unclean, but such time as it was a public domain any condition of doubt concerning it is deemed clean. If a man at the point of death was in a private domain, and they took him out into the public domain and then brought him again into a private domain [and he was found to be dead], such time as he was in a private domain his condition of doubt[2] is deemed unclean, but such time as he was in the public domain his condition of doubt is deemed clean. R. Simeon says: The public domain intervenes.[3]

2. In four conditions of doubt R. Joshua declares a man unclean, but the Sages declare him clean. Thus if one that is unclean[4] stands still[5] and one that is clean passes by,[6] or if one that is clean stands still and one that is unclean passes by; or if what is unclean is in a private domain and what is clean is in the public domain, or if what is clean is in a private domain and what is unclean is in the public domain, and it is in doubt whether one touched the other or not, or whether one overshadowed the other or not, or whether one shifted [what was unclean] or not, R. Joshua declares a man unclean, but the Sages declare him clean.

3. If a tree stood in the public domain and there was aught unclean within it, and a man climbed to the top of it and it is in doubt whether he touched [the uncleanness] or not, his condition of doubt is deemed unclean; if he put his hand into a hole wherein was aught unclean and it is in doubt whether he touched it or not, his condition of doubt is deemed unclean.[7] If a shop that was unclean was open toward the public domain, and it is in doubt whether a man entered it or not, his condition of doubt is deemed clean. If it is in doubt whether he touched aught or not, his condition of doubt is deemed clean.[8] If there were two shops, the one unclean and the other clean, and it is in doubt whether he entered the unclean or the clean, his condition of doubt is deemed unclean.[9]

4. Where thou canst multiply doubts and doubts about doubts, if it concerns a private domain the condition is deemed unclean; if it concerns

---

[1] e.g. a valley which in the rainy season is watched over only by the owner, but at harvest time is frequented by many labourers. Cf. below, 6⁶.

[2] i.e. those who touched him while he was in the private domain, before and after his passing through the public domain, are deemed unclean.

[3] i.e. if they are deemed clean who touched him in the public domain, they who touched him before he was brought out into the public domain must also be deemed clean.

[4] With leprosy. See Neg. 13⁷.   [5] Under a roof or tree.

[6] And it is in doubt whether the unclean touched him or whether he at all remained stationary and the clean person thereby became unclean.

[7] In both cases it is deemed to be private domain.

[8] The case is parallel to that of the creeping thing and the frog, 5¹ᶠ.

[9] Since he certainly entered a private domain.

the public domain it is deemed clean. Thus if a man entered an alley-entry[1] and there was aught unclean in the courtyard, and it is in doubt whether he entered or not; or if there was aught unclean in a house and it is in doubt whether he entered or not; or if, though he entered, it is in doubt whether the uncleanness was there or not; or if, though it was there, it is in doubt whether the uncleanness was of the prescribed bulk or not; or if, though it was of the prescribed bulk, it is in doubt whether it was unclean or clean; or if, though it was unclean, it is in doubt whether he touched it or not, such a condition of doubt is deemed unclean. R. Eleazar says: If it is in doubt whether he entered in, he is deemed clean; if it is in doubt whether he touched what was unclean, he is deemed unclean.

5. If in the rainy season[2] a man entered [the fields in] a valley, and there was an uncleanness in a certain field, and he said, 'I went into that place but I do not know whether I entered that field or not', R. Eleazar declares him clean, but the Sages declare him unclean.

6. A condition of doubt concerning a private domain is accounted unclean unless a man can say, 'I did not touch'. A condition of doubt concerning the public domain is accounted clean unless a man can say, 'I did not touch'. What is accounted public domain? The paths of Beth Gilgul, and the like of them, are accounted private domain[3] in what concerns the [laws of the] Sabbath, and public domain in what concerns [the laws of] uncleanness. R. Eleazar said: The paths of Beth Gilgul were spoken of only in that they are accounted private domain in what concerns both the [laws of the] Sabbath and [the laws of] uncleanness. Paths that lead [only] towards cisterns, pits, caverns, and winepresses are accounted private domain in what concerns the [laws of the] Sabbath and public domain in what concerns [the laws of] uncleanness.

7. In the summer time[4] a [field in a] valley is accounted private domain in what concerns the [laws of the] Sabbath and public domain in what concerns [the laws of] uncleanness; and in the rainy season private domain in what concerns both.

8. A basilica[5] is accounted private domain in what concerns [the laws of] the Sabbath and public domain in what concerns [the laws of] uncleanness. R. Judah says: If a man stands at the one entrance and can see[6] persons entering and leaving at the other entrance, it is accounted private domain in what concerns both the [laws of the] Sabbath and [the laws of] uncleanness; otherwise, it is accounted private domain in what concerns the [laws of the] Sabbath and public domain in what concerns [the laws of] uncleanness.

9. A forum[7] is accounted private domain in what concerns the [laws of the] Sabbath and public domain in what concerns [the laws of] uncleanness; so, too, the sides[8] thereof. R. Meir says: The sides are accounted private domain in what concerns both.

10. Colonnades[9] are accounted private domain in what concerns the

---

[1] Which counts as private domain.   [2] When the field is accounted private domain.
[3] Here used in the sense of *karmelith*, neither public nor private. Cf. p. 133, n. 1; Erub. 9[2].
[4] When it is frequented by the harvesters.
[5] A building frequented for public functions but not a thoroughfare (t. Toh. 7[12] reads 'which they open by day and close by night').
[6] *Eliyahu Rabba* prefers the reading 'cannot see'.
[7] Heb. *faron*. It is explained as like the basilica except that it has doors at either side directly opposite one another.   [8] The parts of the enclosure not opposite the doors.
[9] The covered thoroughfares in front of shops.

[laws of the] Sabbath and public domain in what concerns [the laws of] uncleanness. A courtyard which the many enter by one entrance and leave by another, is accounted private domain in what concerns the [laws of the] Sabbath and public domain in what concerns [the laws of] uncleanness.

7. 1. If a seller of pots set down his pots [in the public domain] and went down to drink, the innermost pots remain clean but the outer ones become unclean. R. Jose said: This applies only if they were not tied together; but if they were tied together, all remain clean.[1] If a man gave his key into the keeping of an *Am-haaretz*,[2] his house still remains clean, since he only gave him the charge of guarding the key.[3]

2. If a man left an *Am-haaretz* within his house awake and found him awake, or asleep and found him asleep, or awake and found him asleep, the house remains clean; but if he left him asleep and found him awake, the house is unclean. So R. Meir. But the Sages say: Only that part is unclean which he could touch by stretching out his hand.

3. If a man left craftsmen within his house, the house becomes unclean. So R. Meir. But the Sages say: Only that part becomes unclean which they could touch by stretching out their hands.

4. If the wife of an Associate[4] left the wife of an *Am-haaretz* grinding flour within her house and she ceased from the grinding, the house becomes unclean; if she did not cease from the grinding, only that part of the house is unclean which she could touch by stretching out her hand. If there were two of them the house becomes unclean in either case, since the one can go about and touch while the other grinds. So R. Meir. But the Sages say: Only that part of the house becomes unclean which they could touch by stretching out their hands.

5. If a man left an *Am-haaretz* within his house to guard it, such time as he[5] can see them that go in and out, [only] foodstuffs and liquids and open earthenware vessels become unclean, but couches and seats and earthenware vessels having a tightly stopped up cover remain clean; if he could not see them that go in and out,[6] even though the *Am-haaretz* could not move himself or was tied up, all becomes unclean.

6. If[7] taxgatherers entered a house [all that is within it] becomes unclean; even if a gentile was with them they may be believed if they say ('We did not enter'; but they may not be believed if they say)[8] 'We entered but we touched naught'. If thieves entered a house, only that part is unclean that was trodden by the feet of the thieves. What do they render unclean? Foodstuffs and liquids and open earthenware vessels; but couches and seats and earthenware vessels having a tightly stopped-up cover remain clean. If a gentile or a woman was with them all becomes unclean.[9]

7. If a man left his vessels in a wall-niche of a bath-house,[10] R. Eleazar b. Azariah declares them clean. But the Sages say: Only if he[11] gave him the key, or the seal, or if he left some sign thereon. If a man[12] left his vessels

---

[1] They would not then be handled by any *Am-haaretz* or unclean person passing by. Maim., however, reads 'all become unclean'.   [2] App. I. 3.
[3] He would not enter the house from fear of being thought a thief.
[4] See Dem. 2³; App. I. 6.   [5] The householder.
[6] Bert. reads 'that go in and that sit down'.   [7] Hag. 3⁶.
[8] Some texts omit the bracketed passage.   [9] See App. IV. 10.
[10] Or: bath-attendant. Heb. *odiarin*; variant, *oriarin*. It may represent the *olearius*, the attendant whose function it was to rub the bodies of the bathers with oil.
[11] The bath-keeper or the bath-attendant.
[12] An Israelite who gathered grapes in the vineyard of a gentile.

from one vintage until the next,[1] his vessels remain clean; but if with an Israelite[2] [they remain clean] only if he says, 'I was at pains to guard them'.

8. If [a priest] that was clean had given up the thought of eating [his Heave-offering], R. Judah declares [the Heave-offering still] clean, since it is the way of the unclean to keep themselves apart from him. But the Sages declare it unclean. If his hands were clean and he had given up the thought of eating [his Heave-offering], even though he says, 'I know that my hands have not become unclean', his hands are nevertheless deemed unclean, for the hands are ever busy.

9. If a woman went in to bring out bread to a poor man and she came out and found him standing beside loaves of Heave-offering (so, too, if a woman went out and found her neighbour raking out coals under a cooking-pot in which was Heave-offering), R. Akiba declares it unclean, but the Sages declare it clean. R. Eleazar b. Pila[3] said: But why did R. Akiba declare it unclean and the Sages clean?—because women are gluttonous; for a woman is suspected of uncovering her neighbour's cooking-pot to know what she is cooking.

8. 1. If a man dwelt in the same courtyard with an *Am-haaretz*, and he forgot vessels and left them in the courtyard, even if they were jars having a tightly stopped-up cover, or an oven having a tightly stopped-up cover, they become unclean.[4] R. Judah declares clean an oven[5] having a tightly stopped-up cover. R. Jose says: The oven also becomes unclean unless a screen ten handbreadths high was made for it.

2. If a man deposited vessels with an *Am-haaretz*, they become unclean with corpse-uncleanness and *midras*-uncleanness. If the *Am-haaretz* knew him to be one that ate of Heave-offering,[6] they do not become unclean with corpse-uncleanness, but they still become unclean with *midras*-uncleanness.[7] R. Jose says: If he gave into his keeping a chest full of clothes tightly packed,[8] they become unclean with *midras*-uncleanness; if it was not tightly packed they still become unclean with *maddaf*-uncleanness,[9] even though the key was in the hand of the owner.

3. If a man lost aught and found it the same day, it remains clean. If he lost it during the day and found it during the night, or lost it during the night and found it the next day, or lost it on one day and found it on the next, it becomes unclean. This is the general rule: If a night or part of a night has passed over it, it becomes unclean. If a man spread out garments to dry in the public domain, they remain clean; but if in a private domain they become unclean; though if he guarded them they remain clean. If they fell down and he went to fetch them in, they become unclean. If his bucket fell into the cistern of an *Am-haaretz*, and he went to fetch something to draw it up, it becomes unclean, since it was left for a time in the domain of an *Am-haaretz*.

---

[1] Bert. gives the added clause: 'in the vineyard of a gentile'.
[2] Who is an *Am-haaretz* and more prying (Bert.).   [3] i.e. Philo. Variant: Piabi.
[4] A menstruant may have moved them or sat on them (App. IV. 3 b).
[5] Since it is fixed to the ground and could not be moved.   [6] A priest.
[7] He himself would be mindful of them but his wife might still sit on them.
[8] So that they are pressed by any one who sits on the lid.
[9] Uncleanness sustained by objects lifted by one with a flux though he has not touched them; they suffer only 'derived uncleanness'; i.e. they do not become 'fathers of uncleanness' (cf. App. IV. 3 a), and so can convey uncleanness only to foodstuffs and liquids, i.e. to what is susceptible to 'second-grade uncleanness'.

4. If a man left his house open and found it open, or shut and found it shut, or open and found it shut, it is clean; but if he left it shut and found it open, R. Meir declares it unclean, but the Sages declare it clean, since it may have been that thieves had gone there but had bethought themselves and gone away.[1]

5. If the wife of an *Am-haaretz* entered the house of an Associate[2] to fetch out his son or his daughter or his cattle, the house remains clean, since she had entered without permission.[3]

6. They laid down a general rule about clean food: Whatsoever is food for man in particular is susceptible to uncleanness unless it is rendered unfit to be food for dogs; and whatsoever is not food for man in particular is not susceptible to uncleanness unless it is made food for man[4] in particular. Thus[5] if a young pigeon fell into the winepress[6] and one formed the intention to pick it out to give to a gentile to eat, it becomes susceptible to uncleanness; but if to give it to a dog, it is insusceptible (R. Johanan b. Nuri declares it susceptible); if he was a deaf-mute, an imbecile or a minor [that formed the intention] it is insusceptible; yet if they picked it out to give it to a gentile to eat, it becomes susceptible; for with them only the act is of consequence while the intention is of no consequence.[7]

7. If the outer parts[8] of vessels were rendered unclean by a liquid, R. Eliezer says: They render liquids unclean, but they do not render foodstuffs invalid. R. Joshua says: They render liquids unclean and foodstuffs invalid. Simeon the brother of Azariah says: They do neither the one nor the other: but liquids that are rendered unclean by the outer parts of vessels convey uncleanness at one remove[9] and render [Heave-offering] invalid at a second remove. Thus these may say,[10] 'What renders thee unclean[11] does not render me unclean, but thou hast rendered me unclean'.

8. If a kneading-trough lay on an incline, and there was [unclean] dough in the higher part and dripping moisture in the lower part, if there were three pieces of dough[12] making up an egg's bulk, they cannot [all three][13] be included together [so that they render the liquid unclean];[14] but [if they were but] two pieces they can be included together. R. Jose says: Neither can two be included together unless they confine the liquid closely.[15] But if it was standing liquid,[16] even if [the pieces of dough that made up the egg's bulk were] small [and numerous] as mustard seed, they are included together. R. Dosa says: Food broken into crumbs may not be included together [to make up the egg's bulk].

9. If a stick was wholly covered with unclean liquid,[17] so soon as it has touched the Immersion-pool it becomes clean.[18] So R. Joshua. But the Sages say: Not until the whole of it is immersed. A jet of liquid,[19] [water

---

[1] Touching nothing.   [2] See Dem. 2³; App. I. 6.   [3] And would be unlikely to linger there.
[4] By a man's deliberate proposal to eat it (see Uktz. 3¹ᶠᶠ.).   [5] Referring to the last clause.
[6] And died, and so was not deemed fit for human food.   [7] Cf. Kel. 17¹⁵; Maksh. 3⁸.
[8] Kel. 25¹   [9] To Heave-offering, and they can render other Heave-offering invalid.
[10] Heave-offering foodstuffs to the liquids that have rendered them unclean.
[11] Outer parts of vessels. Cf. Kel. 8⁴; Par. 8²ᶠᶠ.
[12] Which were unclean and which touched each other, two being on the dry part of the trough and, touching one of them, a third in contact with the liquid.
[13] But only the lower piece, and the piece in contact with it.
[14] Which in turn renders the trough unclean.   [15] Surround it and, as it were, press upon it.   [16] If the trough lay level.
[17] The rule applies to water only.
[18] The water on an inclined plane serves as a connective.
[19] The unbroken column of water formed by pouring liquid from a clean to an unclean vessel does not communicate the uncleanness of the lower vessel to the other.

on] an incline, and dripping moisture, do not serve as a connective for uncleanness or for cleanness;[1] but a pool of water serves as a connective for uncleanness and for cleanness.

9. 1. From what time do olives become susceptible[2] to uncleanness? After they exude the moisture that comes out of them when they are in the vat, but not the moisture that comes out of them when they are yet in the store-basket.[3] So the School of Shammai. R. Simeon says: The prescribed time for the moisture [before it renders the olives susceptible to uncleanness] is three days. The School of Hillel say: After there is moisture enough for three olives to stick together. Rabban Gamaliel says: After the preparation is finished.[4] And the Sages agree with his words.

2. If a man had finished gathering them, but intended to buy still more, if he had finished buying but intended to borrow[5] still more, if there befell him a time of mourning or a wedding feast, or unavoidable hindrance,[6] then even if men or women that had a flux walked over them, the olives remain clean. If unclean liquid fell upon them only the place where it touches them becomes unclean, and any sap that comes forth from them does not render them susceptible to uncleanness.

3. But after their preparation is finished, they become susceptible to uncleanness. If unclean liquids fell upon them [they become unclean]. If sap came forth from them, R. Eliezer declares it clean,[7] but the Sages declare it unclean. R. Simeon said: They did not dispute about the sap that came forth from the olives, whether it was clean; but about what did they dispute?—about what comes forth from the [oil] vat,[8] which R. Eliezer declares clean and the Sages declare unclean.

4. If a man had finished [gathering together] his olives but had one basketful set aside,[9] let him give it to a priest that is poor.[10] So R. Meir. R. Judah says: He should give him the key at once.[11] R. Simeon says: Within twenty-four hours.

5. If a man left his olives in the basket[12] to grow soft so that they may be easy to press, they then become susceptible to uncleanness; but if to grow soft so that they may be salted, the School of Shammai say: They become susceptible. And the School of Hillel say: They do not become susceptible. If a man crushed olives[13] with unclean hands he renders them unclean.

---

1 So that if one thing, or part of a thing, with which they are joined becomes unclean (or is made clean), then the other thing or part of a thing with which they are joined becomes unclean (or is made clean).   2 See p. 758, n. 1; Maksh. 6[4]; Lev. 11[34, 38].
3 The rule (see Maksh. 1[1]) is that only that liquid renders foodstuffs susceptible that is put on deliberately or whose presence is in any way desirable.
4 i.e. so soon as a batch of olives is finally harvested and deemed ready to have the oil extracted.   5 Variant: 'gather'.
6 When it was in his mind still to increase his batch of olives.
7 Since, according to him, the moisture is not deemed 'oil', and so is not one of the 'seven liquids' (Maksh. 6[4]).   8 After all the oil has been removed.
9 After the season of olive-gathering was over, after which (Hag. 3[4]) an Am-haaretz was not to be trusted to prepare his olives in cleanness, so that Heave-offering could without scruple be accepted by a priest. Variant: 'Let him leave . . . and let him give'.
10 Variant: 'in the presence of the priest'. The priest should himself press out the oil in the necessary conditions of cleanness and take his Heave-offering.
11 So that the priest can be assured that the oil shall not be rendered unclean.
12 Variant: 'press'.
13 That were Heave-offering. His hands suffer second-grade uncleanness; the olives thereby become invalid (with third grade uncleanness); they convey first-grade uncleanness (see above, p. 718, n. 1) to the exuding moisture (which had rendered them, in the first place, susceptible to uncleanness—Lev. 11[34, 38]), and this moisture conveys second-grade uncleanness to the olives.

6. If a man left his olives on the roof to dry them, even though they are a cubit high,[1] they do not become susceptible.[2] If he put them in the house so that they might putrify and intended afterward to take them up on the roof; or if he put them on the roof so that they might be bruised or made to open,[3] they become susceptible. If he put them in the house until he could keep watch over his roof, or until he could take them elsewhere, they do not become susceptible.

7. If he was minded to take from them[4] [only] enough for one pressing or for two, the School of Shammai say: He may set apart [what he needs] in a condition of uncleanness,[5] but he must cover up [what he takes] in a condition of cleanness. The School of Hillel say: He may also cover it up in a condition of uncleanness. R. Jose says: He may [even] dig out [what he needs] with a metal axe and take the olives to the press in a condition of uncleanness.

8. If a creeping thing was found in the milling stones only the part that it has touched becomes unclean. If there was dripping moisture there, all becomes unclean. If it was found on the leaves,[6] they inquire of the olive-press workers whether they can say, 'We did not touch'; but if it touched the mass [of olives], if it be but a barleycorn's bulk, the mass becomes unclean.

9. If it was found on broken-off blocks [of olives][7] and it had touched so much as an egg's bulk, the mass becomes unclean; but if [it had touched] broken-off blocks that lay upon other broken blocks,[8] only the part it touches becomes unclean. If it was found between the wall and the olives, the olives are deemed clean. If it was found on [olives taken from the vat to] the roof, the others still in the vat are deemed clean. If it was found in the vat, the olives on the roof [also] are deemed unclean. If it was found burnt[9] upon the olives (so, too, if a scorched rag was found there) they remain clean, since conditions of uncleanness are so accounted of as they appear at the time when they are found.[10]

10. 1. If a man locked in the workers in the olive-press[11] and there were articles there that were unclean with *midras*-uncleanness, R. Meir says: The olive-press becomes unclean. R. Judah says: The olive-press remains clean.[12] R. Simeon says: If to their mind the articles were clean, the olive-press becomes unclean; but if to their mind they were unclean, the olive-press remains clean. R. Jose said: But why are they accounted unclean?— only because the *Amme-haaretz* are not versed in the rules concerning the shifting of what is unclean.[13]

2. If the workers in the olive-press went in and out, and there was unclean liquid in the olive-press, and there was space enough between the liquid and the olives for their feet to get dry on the ground, they remain

---

[1] So that moisture is surely pressed out from the lower layers because of the weight of those above.   [2] Variant: 'they are susceptible'.
[3] Variant: 'so that they might be made to open, or so that he could salt them'.
[4] A batch of olives not yet ready in their entirety.
[5] Since the batch is not susceptible.   [6] With which the mass of olives was covered.
[7] Each less than an egg's bulk. And they lie on the main mass.
[8] And not on the main mass.   [9] When it does not convey uncleanness.   [10] See 3[5].
[11] They were *Amme-haaretz*, and after making them clean he shut them in so that they should not come out and contract uncleanness, and that others who were unclean should not come in.   [12] The workers, after being made clean, could be trusted to be scrupulous and to refrain from contracting uncleanness from them.
[13] i.e. ignorant of the fact that they would contract *midras*-uncleanness by moving the uncleanness even though they did not touch it.

clean. If uncleanness was found in the front of workers in the olive-press
and grape-gatherers, they are to be believed if they say, 'We touched it
not'. So, too, the children among them may go outside the door of the
olive-press and relieve themselves behind the wall and still be deemed
clean. How far off may they go and still be deemed clean? Only so far
that they can still be seen.

3. If workers in the olive-press and grape-gatherers are brought to the
cavern,[1] that suffices. So R. Meir. R. Jose says: One must needs stand
over them until they immerse [themselves, or the vessels]. R. Simeon says:
If to their mind the vessels were clean one must needs stand over them
until they immerse them; but if to their mind they were unclean, one needs
not to stand over them until they immerse them.

4. If a man put [grapes into the wine-press] from what was [stored] in
baskets or from what was spread out on the ground, the School of Shammai say: He must put them in with clean hands; if he put them in with unclean hands he renders them unclean. And the School of Hillel say: [He may
put them in] with unclean hands; yet he must set apart the Heave-offering
in cleanness. It is all one [whether he takes them] from the grape-basket
or from what are spread out on leaves: he must put them into the winepress with clean hands. If he put them in with unclean hands, he renders
them unclean.

5. If a man ate of the grapes out of the baskets or from those spread out
on the ground, although their skins were burst open or although they were
dripping into the wine-press, the wine-press remains clean.[2] If he took
grapes that were in the grape-baskets or spread out on leaves, and a single
berry fell back,[3] if it was still sealed up [by the stalk] what is in the basket
remains clean. If it was not still sealed up, what is in the basket becomes
unclean. If he dropped some of the grapes and trampled them in an empty
part [of the winepress] and there was no more than an egg's bulk exactly, it
remains clean; if there was more, it becomes unclean, for then, so soon as
the first drop has come forth it becomes unclean, in that the rest is as much
as an egg's bulk.[4]

6. If a man stood and spoke by the edge of the cistern and spittle spirted
from his mouth, and it is in doubt whether it reached the cistern or not,
the condition of doubt is deemed clean.

7. If a man emptied out the cistern and in the first jarful was found a
creeping thing, all that is in the cistern is accounted unclean; if it was
found in the last, that is unclean but the other are accounted clean. This
applies only when he drew out the wine into each single jar; but if he
emptied it out with a ladling-jar,[5] and the creeping thing was found in one
of the jars, it alone is accounted unclean. This applies only if he examined
[the vessels] but did not cover up [the jars and the cistern], or if he covered
them up but did not examine them. If he both examined them and covered
them up, and the creeping thing was found in one jar, all is accounted
unclean; all that is in the cistern is unclean, and all that is in the ladling-
jar is unclean.

---

[1] Where is the water in which they must immerse themselves or the vessels to become
clean before they touch the fruit.
[2] Since such liquid was not intended or desired (Maksh. 1[1]), and so does not render the
grapes susceptible to uncleanness.
[3] After its gathering had been completed and it was therefore susceptible to uncleanness
(if made wet) from contact with hands.   [4] Cf. above, 3[1ff].
[5] p. 607, n. 2. Par. 5[5]; Yad. 1[2].

8. The space between the rollers[1] and the grape skins counts as public domain,[2] the part of the vineyard in front of the grape-gatherers[3] counts as private domain, and that behind them public domain. This applies only when the many enter in at the one end and go out at the other. The vessels of the olive-press and the wine-press and the olive-truss,[4] if they are of wood, need but to be dried and they are clean; if they are of reed-grass, they must be left unused for the twelve months, or scalded in hot water. R. Jose says: It suffices if they are dipped in the stream of a river.

MIKWAOTH[5] ('IMMERSION-POOLS')

1. 1. There are six grades among pools of water, one more excellent than another.[6] The water in ponds[7]—if a man that was unclean drank from it and afterward a man that was clean drank from it, he becomes unclean; if a man that was unclean drank from it and afterward drew water into a clean vessel, it becomes unclean;[8] if a man that was unclean drank from it and afterward a loaf of Heave-offering fell therein and he rinsed it,[9] it becomes unclean; if he did not rinse it, it remains clean.[10]

2. If a man drew water from it into an unclean vessel and afterward a man that was clean drank [from the pond] he becomes unclean; if a man drew water from it into an unclean vessel and afterward drew water from it into a clean vessel it becomes unclean; if he drew water into an unclean vessel and a loaf of Heave-offering fell [in the pond], and he rinsed it, it becomes unclean; if he did not rinse it, it remains clean.

3. If unclean water fell into it, and a man that was clean drank from it he becomes unclean; if unclean water fell into it and a man drew water from it into a clean vessel, it becomes unclean; if unclean water fell into it and a loaf of Heave-offering fell in and he rinsed it, it becomes unclean; if he did not rinse it, it remains clean. R. Simeon says: Whether he rinsed it or not it becomes unclean.[11]

4. If a corpse fell therein or a man that was unclean walked into it, and a clean person drank from it, he still remains clean.[12] The water in ponds, the water in cisterns, the water in ditches, the water in caverns, rain-ponds after the rain-stream has stopped, and pools holding less than forty

---

[1] The beams for squeezing the grapes.
[2] For purposes of applying the rule that in the public domain a doubtful condition of uncleanness is deemed clean, and in a private domain unclean.
[3] Where the grapes are still ungathered.   [4] See p. 68, n. 1.
[5] Lit. 'pools of water'; generally used in the Mishnah in the technical sense of pools in which men and vessels suffering certain kinds of uncleanness must be totally immersed. To be sufficient for total immersion and free from contracting any uncleanness, the pool must contain forty *seahs* (approximately 60 gallons or 270 litres) of water, and at the same time be of such depth that the whole body can be covered. Forty *seahs* is, traditionally, three cubic cubits. Such water may not be 'drawn' (i.e. it may not be taken from water that has been standing in a vessel or any kind of receptacle) but must be taken directly from a river or a spring, of from rain-water that is led directly into the Immersion-pool.
[6] i.e. they are here given in ascending order of efficacy.
[7] Containing less than the 40 *seahs* of undrawn water.
[8] Although the pool itself, as being joined directly to the ground, is not susceptible to uncleanness, the clean person or vessel may have touched an unclean drop that had fallen from the mouth of the unclean drinker (App. IV. 3 a ii).
[9] He may make use of the unclean drop.
[10] There being no intention to use part of the water separated from the pool (as in the previous cases) the unclean drop is deemed to be neutralized and ineffective.
[11] It cannot be assumed that the unclean drop was rendered ineffective.
[12] There is here no case of swallowing or intentionally using water that may contain the unclean drop.

seahs are alike in this, that while the rain continues all are deemed clean;[1] but after the rain has stopped they that lie near to a city or pathway are deemed unclean, and they that lie far off are deemed clean unless a multitude of men have passed by.

5. When are they again deemed clean? The School of Shammai say: After they have been increased [by more than the like quantity of rain] and overflowed. The School of Hillel say: After they have been increased [by more than the like quantity of rain] even though they have not overflowed. R. Simeon says: Even though they have not been so increased they are valid for preparing Dough-offering,[2] and for the washing of hands.[3]

6. More excellent is the water of a rain-pond before the rain-stream has stopped.[4] If a man that was unclean drank from it and afterward a man that was clean drank from it, he remains clean; if a man that was unclean drank from it and afterward drew water into a clean vessel, it remains clean; if a man that was unclean drank from it and a loaf of Heave-offering fell therein, although he rinsed it it remains clean; if a man drew water from it into an unclean vessel and afterward a clean person drank [from the pond], he remains clean; if a man drew water from it into an unclean vessel and afterward drew water from it into a clean vessel, it remains clean; if he drew water into an unclean vessel and a loaf of Heave-offering fell [into the pond], although he rinsed it, it remains clean; if unclean water fell into it and a man that was clean drank from it, he remains clean; if unclean water fell into it and a man drew water into a clean vessel, it remains clean; if unclean water fell into it and a loaf of Heave-offering fell in, although he rinsed it, it remains clean. Such water is valid for [cooking] Heave-offering and for the washing of hands.[5]

7. More excellent is a pool of water containing forty *seahs*; for in them men[6] may immerse themselves and immerse other things.[7] More excellent is a well whose own water is little in quantity and which is increased by a greater part of drawn water: it is the equal of the pool as standing water in that it can render clean [what is immersed therein], and of the well in that vessels[8] may be immersed therein however little its quantity.

8. More excellent are smitten waters[9] which render clean such time as they are flowing water. More excellent than they are living waters, for they serve for the immersion of them that have a flux[10] and for the sprinkling of lepers,[11] and are valid for mixing with the ashes of the Sin-offering.[12]

2. 1. If an unclean person went down to immerse himself and it is in doubt whether he immersed himself or not; or if, even though he immersed himself, it is in doubt whether there was forty *seahs* [of water] or not; or if there were two pools, the one holding forty *seahs* but not the other; and he immersed himself in one of them but he does not know in which of them he immersed himself, his condition of doubt is deemed unclean.

[1] None need fear to use them because of an unneutralized unclean drop.
[2] Num. 15[18ff]. Cf. p. 83, n. 1.   [3] Cf. Yad. 1[3].
[4] Such can never be deemed unclean.
[5] For the water to be poured over the hands out of a vessel; but not for making men, vessels, or hands clean by immersion.
[6] That are unclean, excepting the man with flux, who requires 'living water' (Lev. 15[13]).
[7] Vessels and the hands.
[8] According to some commentators men also, provided that the water is deep enough for total immersion.   [9] Water that is salty or from a hot spring. Cf. Par. 8[9].
[10] Lev. 15[13].   [11] Lev. 14[5]; Neg. 14[1].
[12] Num. 19[17]; Par. 3[2].

2. If an Immersion-pool was measured and found lacking,[1] any acts requiring cleanness that had theretofore been done following immersion therein, are deemed to have been done in uncleanness, whether [the condition of doubt arising thereby concerned] a private domain or the public domain. This applies only to graver uncleanness;[2] but if it was a lighter uncleanness, to wit, if a man ate unclean foods or drank unclean liquids, or if his head and the greater part of him entered drawn water, or if three *logs* of drawn water fell on his head and the greater part of him—if then he went down to immerse himself, and it is in doubt whether he immersed himself or not; or if, even though he immersed himself, it is in doubt whether there was forty *seahs* [of water] or not; or if there were two pools, the one holding forty *seahs* but not the other, and he immersed himself in one of them but he does not know in which of them he immersed himself, his condition of doubt is deemed clean. R. Jose declares him unclean; for R. Jose used to say: [If he was rendered unclean by] aught that must be assumed to be unclean, his unfitness continues until he knows that he is become clean; but if it is in doubt whether he became unclean or whether he [afterward] conveyed uncleanness, he is deemed clean.[3]

3. In a case of doubt concerning drawn water, such as the Sages have declared clean,[4] if it is in doubt whether [three *logs* of drawn water] fell [into the Immersion pool] or not; or if, even though it fell therein, it is in doubt whether the pool held forty *seahs* or not, or, if there were two pools, the one holding forty *seahs* but not the other, and it fell into one of them but it is not known into which of them it fell, then its condition of doubt is deemed clean, since there is that whereon to rely [in deeming it clean]. But if they each held less than forty *seahs*, and [the drawn water] fell into one of them and it is not known into which, its condition of doubt is deemed unclean, since there is naught whereon to rely [in deeming it clean].[5]

4. R. Eliezer says: A quarter-*log* of drawn water in the beginning[6] renders the Immersion-pool invalid, or three *logs* on the surface.[7] But the Sages say: Whether in the beginning or at the end, the prescribed quantity [that renders it invalid] is three *logs*.

5. If in [the bottom of] a pool were three hollows, each containing one *log* of drawn water, and it is known that forty *seahs* of valid water fell into the pool before the water spread to the third hollow, it is valid; but if this is not known, it is invalid. But R. Simeon declares it valid, since it may be likened to one [valid] Immersion-pool adjoining another [invalid] Immersion-pool.

6. If the mud was scraped up [from the pool and heaped] by the sides, and three *logs* of water drained down therefrom, it remains valid; but if the mud was removed away [from the pool] and three *logs* drained down therefrom [into the pool] it becomes invalid. But R. Simeon declares it valid, since it was not drawn of set purpose.

7. If [empty] wine-jars were left on the roof to dry and [because of the rain] they became filled with water, R. Eliezer says: If it was the rainy season and[8] there was in them as little water as was in the cistern, they may

---

[1] Not fully forty *seahs*.
[2] i.e. from 'a father of uncleanness', whether this be one that is specified in the Law (App. IV. 1) or in the words of the Scribes (App. IV. 13, 22).   [3] Cf. Yad. 2[4].
[4] See Toh. 4[7].   [5] Cf. Kel. 9[3].
[6] The rest of the forty *seahs* being made up afterwards of valid rain water.
[7] Of a pool of valid rain water that lacks aught of the forty *seahs*.   [8] Variant: 'or if'.

be broken [that the water may flow into the cistern];[1] but if there was not, they may not be broken. R. Joshua says: In either case they may be broken or turned upside down; but they may not be taken and emptied [into the cistern].

8. If the plasterer forgot his lime-pot and left it behind in the cistern and it became filled with water, if the water at all floated over it it may be broken; but if not, it may not be broken. So R. Eliezer. But R. Joshua says: In either case it may be broken.

9. If [empty] wine-jars were set in the cistern [for their sides to become saturated][2] and they became filled with water, although the water of the cistern was all soaked up, they may be broken.[3]

10. If an Immersion-pool held forty *seahs* of water and mud together, R. Meir says: Vessels may be immersed in the water but not in the mud. R. Joshua says: Either in the water or in the mud. In what mud may they be immersed? In mud over which water floats. But if the water was at the one side only, R. Joshua agrees that vessels must be immersed in the water and may not be immersed in the mud. Of what kind of mud did they speak? Such that a reed will sink into it of itself. So R. Meir. R. Judah says: Such that the measuring rod will not stand there of itself. Abba Eleazar b. Dula'i says: Such that a plummet will sink there. R. Eliezer says: Such that will go down through the [narrow] neck of a jar. Rabbi[4] says: Such that will go into the spout of a water-skin. R. Eliezer b. Zadok says: Such as can be measured in a *log*-[measure].

3. 1. R. Jose says: If into each of two pools, neither containing forty *seahs*, there fell a *log* and a half [of drawn water], and [the two pools] were mingled together, they are valid, since they never came within the category of what was invalid. But if three *logs* fell into one pool that did not contain forty *seahs*, and it was then divided into two, it is invalid, since it had already come within the category of what was invalid. R. Joshua declares it valid; for R. Joshua used to say: If into any pool containing less than forty *seahs* there fell three *logs* less but a *kortab*,[5] it remains valid, since it lacks the full three *logs*. But the Sages say: It continues invalid until all that was before in it is taken from it and somewhat more.[6]

2. Thus if into a cistern that was in a courtyard there fell three *logs*, it continues invalid until all that was before in it is taken from it and somewhat more, or until [another pool holding] forty *seahs* is made in the courtyard [below the first and connected with it], so that the upper [water] shall be made clean by the lower. R. Eleazar b. Azariah declares it invalid until all its water comes to an end.[7]

3. If a cistern was full of drawn water and a channel [of rain water] led into it and [a channel] led out of it, it continues invalid until it is estimated that there does not remain three *logs* from the first water. If two persons each poured into a pool a *log* and a half of water; or if one squeezed out his

[1] And the water will be accounted valid and not 'drawn water'.
[2] So that their porous sides will not afterwards soak up the wine.
[3] And the water will still be accounted valid for the Immersion-pool, since there was no intention to collect it into the jars.   [4] Variant: 'R. Simeon'.
[5] One sixty-fourth of a *log*.
[6] i.e. all the original water that was invalid and the 'somewhat more' to reduce the full measure of the invalidating three *logs*.
[7] Variant: 'unless it (the new pool) is stopped up', so that the water of the first cannot enter into it.

raiment pouring in water from many places, or emptied out a water-cooler[1] pouring in water from many places,[2] R. Akiba declares the pool valid, but the Sages declare it invalid. R. Akiba said: They said not, 'If many pour', but 'If one pours'.[3] They replied: They have said neither the one thing nor the other, but 'If there fell therein three *logs* [of drawn water].'

4. [If three *logs* fell therein] from one vessel or from two or from three, they can be included together; if from four, they cannot be included together. If one that suffered a pollution lay sick[4] and there fell on him nine *kabs* of water;[5] or if on one that was clean there fell on his head and the greater part of him three *logs* of drawn water, from one vessel or from two or from three, they can be included together; but if from four they cannot be included together. This applies only if the second began before the first ceased; and it applies only when there was no intention to add more; but if there was intention to add more, even but one *kortab* in a whole year, it can be included together to make up the three *logs*.

4. 1. If a man put vessels under the water-spout[6] [that feeds the Immersion-pool] (it is all one whether they are large vessels or small vessels or even vessels of cattle-dung, vessels of stone or vessels of [unburnt] clay), they render the Immersion-pool invalid. It is all one whether they were set there or left in forgetfulness. So the School of Shammai. But the School of Hillel declare it clean[7] if they were left in forgetfulness. R. Meir said: They voted and the School of Shammai outnumbered the School of Hillel; but they agree that if they were left in forgetfulness in the courtyard [and not under the water-spout], it remains clean. R. Jose said: The dispute still stands where it was.

2. If a man left a tray beneath the water-pipe, and it had a rim, it renders the Immersion-pool invalid, but if it had not, it does not render it invalid. If it was set upright to be rinsed, in neither case does it render the Immersion-pool invalid.

3. If a cavity was made in a water-pipe to catch the gravel, it renders the Immersion-pool invalid if, being of wood, it holds aught soever, or, being of earthenware, it holds a quarter-*log*. R. Jose says: [Also] if, being of earthenware, it holds aught soever: they have spoken of 'a quarter-*log*'[8] only in what concerns the broken sherds of an earthenware vessel. If the gravel [even after it had filled up the cavity] rolled about within it, it renders the Immersion-pool invalid.[9] If earth fell therein and it was pressed tight, the Immersion-pool remains valid. If the water-pipe was narrow at either end and wide in the middle, it does not render the Immersion-pool invalid, since it was not fashioned as a receptacle.

4. If drawn water and rain water were mingled together in a courtyard or in a hollow or on the steps of a cavern, and the greater part was water that was valid, the whole is valid; if the greater part of it was water that was invalid, the whole is invalid; if they were in equal parts the whole is invalid. This applies only if they were mingled together before they reached

---

[1] Kel. 2[8]; 3[2]. This vessel had a comb-like cover.   [2] And three *logs* altogether.
[3] In this form of words R. Akiba had received the tradition. Cf. Eduy. 1[3].
[4] And so was not able to immerse himself.   [5] Ber. 22 a.
[6] The water is thereby made to remain in a receptacle; such water if used in an Immersion-pool counts as 'drawn water'.
[7] i.e. valid, so that it can render clean what is immersed therein.   [8] See Kel. 2[2].
[9] Since this means that water is still contained in it, so coming within the category of 'drawn water'.

the Immersion-pool. If they flowed in an unbroken stream into the water [of the pool], and it was known that there fell therein forty *seahs* of water that was valid before there came down into it three *logs* of drawn water, it is valid, otherwise it is invalid.

5. A trough[1] hewn in the rock—they may not gather the water into it, or mix [the ashes] therein, or sprinkle from it; it does not need a tightly stopped-up cover, nor does it render an Immersion-pool invalid. If it was a movable vessel, although it had been joined [to the ground] with lime, they may gather water into it or mix the ashes therein or sprinkle from it; and it needs a tightly stopped-up cover, and it renders an Immersion-pool invalid. If there was a hole in it below or at the side such that it can hold no water at all, the water is valid.[2] How large need the hole be? As large as the spout of a water-skin. R. Judah b. Bathyra said: It once happened that the Trough of Jehu in Jerusalem had in it a hole as big as the spout of a water-skin, and all the acts in Jerusalem requiring cleanness were done after immersing [the vessels] therein. But the School of Shammai sent and broke it down, for the School of Shammai say: [It is still to be accounted a vessel] until the greater part of it is broken down.

5. 1. If [the water of] a well was made to flow through a stone trough[3] the water becomes invalid. If it was made to flow over[4] its rim at all, what flows out [of the trough] is valid,[5] for [the water of] a well renders clean whatsoever its quantity. If it was made to flow over a pond and then its flow was stopped, the pond counts [only] as a pool [of standing water]; if it was made to flow once more, it is still invalid for them that have a flux and for lepers, and for mixing therein the ashes of the Sin-offering,[6] until it is known that the first water has flowed away.[7]

2. If the water was made to flow over [the outsides of] vessels or over a bench, R. Judah says: It still remains as it was before.[8] R. Jose says: It counts then [only] as [the water of] a pool[9] [of standing water], save that naught may be immersed above the bench.

3. If the water of a well was diverted into many different channels[10] and [drawn] water was added and it was made to flow farther, it remains [as valid] as it was before; if it stood still and [drawn] water was added and it was made to flow farther, it is the equal of the pool as standing water, in that it can render clean [what is immersed therein], and of the well in that vessels may be immersed therein however little its quantity.[11]

4. All seas[12] are valid as an Immersion-pool (*Mikweh*), for it is written, *And the Mikweh of the waters called he Seas*.[13] So R. Meir. R. Judah says: The Great Sea is valid as an Immersion-pool, and it is written, *Seas*, only because there are in it many kinds of seas. R. Jose says: All seas render

1 Repeated in Par. 5[7]. If it was hewn out of the rock, water collected in it does not count as 'drawn water', since the trough counts not as a 'vessel' but part of the earth itself. But if it was only made fast to the rock it counts as a vessel and a receptacle, and water used from it is 'drawn' and invalid for an Immersion-pool.

2 Since it is only an avenue for the water and not a container.

3 A separate receptacle not hewn in the rock.

4 The level of the stream of water was higher than the rim of the trough.

5 But what is inside is valid only if there is a hole, the size of a water-skin spout, in its bottom or side.   6 See above, 1[8].

7 It can be accounted 'running' or 'living water' only after there is nothing left of that water which, for a time, had been standing water.

8 It still had the efficacy of 'living water' and could render clean whatever its quantity.

9 And must be forty *seahs* in quantity.   10 Lit. 'centipede-wise'.

11 Cf. 1[7].   12 See Par. 8[8].   13 Gen. 1[10].

clean by virtue of being flowing waters, but they are not valid for them that have a flux[3] or for lepers or for mixing therein the ashes of the Sin-offering.

5. Flowing water counts as [the water of] a well;[1] dripping water counts as [the water of] an Immersion-pool.[2] R. Zadok[3] testified that if flowing water was more than the dripping water [with which it was mingled] it was still valid [as flowing water]; and that if dripping water was made into flowing water,[4] even if its flow was stayed by a rod or reed, or by a man or a woman that had a flux,[5] [it was still valid as an Immersion-pool and] men might go down and immerse themselves therein. So R. Judah. R. Jose says: They may not stay flowing water with aught susceptible to uncleanness.

6. If a wave was sundered [from the face of the sea] and contained forty *seahs* and it fell upon a man or upon vessels [that were unclean], they become clean. Any pool wherein is forty *seahs* is valid for the immersion of men or vessels. They may immerse vessels in trenches or ditches or even in donkey-tracks in the valley that are mingled[6] [with water from a valid Immersion-pool]. The School of Shammai say: They may immerse vessels in a rain-stream.[7] The School of Hillel say: They may not do so. But they agree that a man may dam it with vessels and immerse himself therein, but the vessels by which he dammed it are not thereby immersed.

6. 1. Any [pool of water] that is mingled with [water from] an Immersion-pool is deemed like to the Immersion-pool itself. Vessels may be immersed in [water in] holes and clefts [that mingles with the water of an Immersion-pool] in a cavern, however small[8] [the stream by which they mingle]; but they may not be immersed in a pit beside the cavern,[9] unless the hole between them is as large as the spout of a water-skin. R. Judah said: This applies only when it is self-contained;[10] but if it is not self-contained they may be immersed therein however small [the connecting stream].

2. If a bucket[11] filled with vessels was immersed, they also become clean;[12] but if the bucket[13] itself was not [wholly] immersed, the water [within it] does not count as mingled [with the water of the Immersion-pool] unless [the water within the bucket] mingled [with the water of the pool] by a stream the size of the spout of a water-skin.

3. If there were three pools, two containing each twenty *seahs* [of undrawn water] and the third twenty *seahs* of drawn water, and that which held drawn water was at the side, if three went down and immersed themselves therein and the water [of the three pools overflowed and] mingled together, the pools are accounted clean, and they that immersed themselves become clean. If that which held drawn water was in the middle, and three went down and immersed themselves therein and the water [of the three pools overflowed and] mingled together, the pools remain as they were before, and they that immersed themselves remain as they were before.

4. If a sponge or a bucket which held three *logs* of [drawn] water fell

---

1 And renders clean whatever its quantity.   2 And must be forty *seahs* in quantity.
3 Eduy. 7³.   4 Turned into a water-channel.
5 If they stopped the flow, turning it into standing water.
6 Joined, by means of 'a hole the size of a water-skin spout' to a valid Immersion-pool.
7 Which is not 'standing water'.
8 Even if it is less than a hole the size of a water-skin spout.
9 A rock-wall standing between them.
10 Wholly distinct from the Immersion-pool in the cavern.
11 Unclean.   12 Even if its neck is narrower than a water-skin spout.
13 This time a clean vessel, used to immerse within it smaller vessels at one and the same time.

into an Immersion-pool[1] they do not render it invalid, since they have said, 'If there fell therein three *logs* [of drawn water]'.[2]

5. Vessels may not be immersed in a box or a chest that is in the sea unless there was in them a hole the size of the spout of a water-skin. R. Judah says: If it was a large vessel [the hole must be] four handbreadths; and if a small vessel [the hole should be equal] to the greater part of it. If a sack or a basket [was in the sea] vessels may be immersed in them like as they are already, since the water [in them and in the sea] is mingled together. If such as these were put under a water-spout[3] they do not render the Immersion-pool invalid; and they may be immersed and brought up [while they are held] in their usual fashion.[4]

6. If there was a defective earthenware vessel[5] in the Immersion pool and other vessels were immersed therein, they are rendered clean from their [former] uncleanness, but they become unclean [again] by reason of the [unclean] earthenware vessel; if any water soever floated over the top of it, they become clean. If [the water of] a well came up out of an oven[6] and a man went down and immersed himself therein, he becomes clean, but his hands become unclean [again];[7] but if the water was higher than the level of the oven by the height of his hands, his hands also continue clean.

7. Two pools may be combined together [to make up the prescribed forty *seahs*] if the stream that joins them together has the thickness and the space of the spout of a water-skin, [namely, if it is big enough to contain] two fingers doubled up. If it is in doubt whether it is as big as the spout of a water-skin or not, it is invalid, since [the immersion of what is unclean] is a thing enjoined in the Law;[8] so, too, in what concerns the olive's bulk of a corpse, and the olive's bulk of carrion, and the lentil's bulk of a [dead] creeping thing.[9] If aught lies in the [space the size of the] spout of the water-skin, it makes it less than the prescribed measure.[10] Rabban Simeon b. Gamaliel says: If it is a creature that lives in the water [that lies in the spout] whatsoever its size, the pool is accounted clean.[11]

8. They may render Immersion-pools clean [by mingling the drawn water in] a higher pool [with undrawn water] from a lower pool, or [the drawn water in] a distant pool [with undrawn water] from a pool that is near by. Thus a man may bring a pipe of earthenware or lead, and keep his hand beneath it until it is filled with water, and draw it along until the

---

[1] Containing less than forty *seahs*.   [2] Cf. 3³.   [3] See above, 4¹.

[4] See 7⁶, where it is taught that vessels having receptacles must be lifted out upside down lest they retain some of the water, thereby rendering it 'drawn water'; in the present case, however, the vessels are not in a condition to contain any water. Cf. 10¹.

[5] It was unclean and its rim was broken, and though water entered the breach, part of its broken rim protruded out of the pool, and it therefore remains unclean, and it can convey uncleanness through its contained airspace (p. 604, n. 5).

[6] A cylindrical, bottomless vessel, made of clay, hardened by the fire kindled inside it; it was fixed to the ground with clay. It was open at the top and was narrower at the top than at the bottom. The oven is here thought of as big enough to contain a man's body. It is assumed to be unclean.

[7] They contract uncleanness from the oven's contained airspace. Even the water within the contained space does not nullify the uncleanness of the contained space; therefore the hands become clean only if they pass through water that is not contained within the oven.

[8] And a condition of doubt about uncleanness in a matter enjoined in the Law must be deemed unclean.

[9] If it is in doubt whether they are of the prescribed bulk which is the minimum quantity to convey their particular uncleanness, they must be deemed unclean.

[10] So that the adjoining pools are not a valid ('clean') Immersion-pool.

[11] It is deemed to be like the water itself and does not lessen the space of the opening.

surface of this water is made to touch the surface of the other water; if it touches by a hair's breadth it suffices. If there were forty *seahs* [of undrawn water] in the upper pool and nothing at all in the lower, water may be drawn [into vessels and carried] on the shoulder and put into the upper pool until forty *seahs* flows down into the lower pool.[1]

9. If between two Immersion-pools [of which one lacked aught of the forty *seahs*] there was a wall in which was a perpendicular crack, they may be included together; but if it was a horizontal crack they may not be included together unless in one place there was a hole the size of the spout of a water-skin. R. Judah says: The rule is to the contrary. If they flow together through a breach [in the top of the dividing wall, they can be included together] if the height [of the connecting stream] is but the thickness of garlic peel and its width that of the spout of a water-skin.

10. If the outlet of a bath is in the middle, it renders the bath invalid [as an Immersion-pool]; if it is at the side it does not render it invalid, since it is then like to one Immersion-pool that adjoins another. So R. Meir. But the Sages say: If the bath holds a quarter-*log* before the water reaches the outlet, it is valid; otherwise it is invalid. R. Eliezer b. R. Zadok says: If the outlet holds any water at all it is invalid.

11. If the lower pipe of a bath's filter[2] was full of drawn water and the upper one was full of undrawn water,[3] and there were three *logs*[4] [of drawn water] opposite the hole, the bath is invalid [as an Immersion-pool]. How large must the hole be so that it shall contain three *logs*? A three-hundred-and-twentieth part of the pool.[5] So R. Jose. R. Eliezer says: Even if the lower pipe was full of undrawn water and the upper full of drawn water and there were three *logs* by the side of the hole, the bath is valid, for they have said, 'If there fell therein three *logs* [of drawn water]'.

7. 1. Some things there are that serve to fill up the Immersion-pool [to its prescribed measure of forty *seahs*] and do not render it invalid; some that render it invalid and do not serve to fill up its measure; and some that neither fill up its measure nor render it invalid. These serve to fill up its measure and do not render it invalid: snow, hail, hoar-frost, ice, salt, and thin mud. R. Akiba said: R. Ishmael was arguing before me, saying, 'Snow does not serve to fill up the measure of an Immersion-pool', and the men of Madeba testified in his name that he had said to them, 'Go and bring snow, and make of it the beginning of an Immersion-pool'. R. Johanan b. Nuri says: Hailstones are like to [drawn] water. How do they serve to fill up the measure and not render it invalid? If an Immersion-pool held forty *seahs* less one and a *seah* of hailstones fell therein and filled it up, they thus serve to fill up its measure and do not render it invalid.

2. These render the Immersion-pool invalid and do not serve to fill up its measure: [drawn] water, whether clean or unclean, water in which food has been pressed or seethed; unfermented grape-skin wine.[6] How do they

---

[1] Since if an Immersion-pool contains forty *seahs* no quantity whatsoever of drawn water can ever render it invalid.

[2] Lit. 'purifier'. This consisted of two pipes one above the other, the bottom of the one forming the top of the other; the top one led in fresh water and the bottom one let out the used water. The top pipe contained a hole on its bottom surface so that foreign matter fell into the lower pipe.   [3] But less than forty *seahs*.

[4] Collected in the lower pipe, while forty *seahs* was poured in from the upper pipe.

[5] Which is the proportion of three *logs* to forty *seahs*.

[6] Cf. Maas. 5[6].

render the pool invalid and do not serve to fill up its measure? If an Immersion-pool held forty *seahs* less a *kortab* and a *kortab* from any of these fell therein, it does not serve to fill up its measure, and if it was three *logs* in quantity it renders it invalid; but other liquids, fruit-juice, brine and fish-brine and fermented grape-skin wine sometimes serve to fill up the measure and sometimes they do not; thus, if an Immersion-pool held forty *seahs* less one, and a *seah* from any of these fell therein, it does not serve to fill up its measure; but if it held already forty *seahs*, and a *seah* from any of these was put in and then one *seah* was taken away, it would remain valid.

3. If baskets of olives or baskets of grapes were rinsed therein and they changed the colour of the water, it remains valid. R. Jose says: Dye-water, if it is three *logs* in quantity, renders it invalid, but it does not render it invalid by changing the colour. If wine fell therein or olive sap and changed its colour, it becomes invalid. What should be done [to make it clean]? It should be left until the rains fall and its colour returns to the colour of water. If there was in it already forty *seahs*, water may be drawn [and borne] on the shoulder and poured therein until its colour returns to the colour of water.[1]

4. If wine or olive sap fell therein and changed its colour at one place and there nowhere remained forty *seahs* having the colour of water, none may immerse therein.

5. If into three *logs* of water there fell a *kortab* of wine, and their colour became like the colour of wine, and they fell into an Immersion-pool, they do not render it invalid. If into three *logs* of water all but one *kortab*, there fell a *kortab* of milk, and their colour remained the colour of water, and they fell into an Immersion-pool, they do not render it invalid. R. Johanan b. Nuri says: All is determined in accordance with the colour.

6. If an Immersion-pool held forty *seahs* exactly and two went down and immersed themselves, the one after the other, the first becomes clean, but the second remains unclean.[2] R. Judah says: If the feet of the first were still touching the water, the second, too, becomes clean. If a man immersed his thick mantle therein and brought it up but part still touched the water, [and another immersed himself therein] he becomes clean. If a leathern cushion or mattress was lifted out of the water by its upper edges, the water contained therein is drawn water. What should be done? They should be immersed and lifted out by their bottoms.[3]

7. If a bed was immersed therein even if its legs sank into the thick mud, it becomes clean, since the water first touched them. If the water of an Immersion-pool was too shallow it may be dammed [to one side] even with bundles of sticks or reeds, that the level of the water may be raised and so he may go down and immerse himself. If a needle was put on the ledge of [an Immersion-pool in] a cavern and [its owner] stirred the water to and fro, after a wave has passed over it, it becomes clean.

8. 1. The Land of Israel is clean and the Immersion-pools thereof are clean. The pools of the gentiles outside the Land [of Israel] are valid for such as have suffered a pollution, even though they are filled with water

---

[1] Cf. above, 6[8].
[2] The water taken away on the body of the first would cause the pool to lack part of the forty *seahs*.   [3] And so no water can be contained in their cavities. Cf. above, p. 739, n. 4.

from a swape-well,[1] while those within the Land [of Israel] when they are outside the town-gate are valid also for menstruants, and when they are inside the town-gate they are valid for such as have suffered a pollution; but they are invalid for all [others] that are unclean. R. Eliezer says: Those near to the city or to a pathway are unclean because of the washing [of clothes], but those far off are clean.

2. These that have suffered a pollution need immersion: if in the beginning his urine issued in drips or was turbid, he is clean; if it did so in the middle and at the end he is unclean; if from the beginning to the end, he is clean. If it was white and continuous he is unclean. R. Jose says: The white is accounted like to what is turbid.

3. If he discharged thick drops from the member, he is unclean. So R. Eleazar Hisma. If he suffered impure thoughts in the night and rose up and found his flesh heated, he is unclean. If a woman discharged semen on the third day she is clean.[2] So R. Eleazar b. Azariah. R. Ishmael says: Sometimes there are four seasons[3] and sometimes five and sometimes six. R. Akiba says: They are always five.

4. If a gentile woman discharged seed from an Israelite it is unclean; if the daughter of an Israelite discharged seed from a gentile it is clean. If a woman had connexion and then went down and immersed herself but had not cleansed 'the house', it is as though she had not immersed herself. If he that suffered a pollution immersed himself but had not first made water,[4] when he makes water he [again] becomes unclean. R. Jose says: If he was sickly or aged he is unclean, but if youthful or healthy he is clean.

5. If a menstruant put coins in her mouth and went down and immersed herself she is clean of her uncleanness but unclean from her saliva. If she put her hair in her mouth or closed her hand or pressed her lips together, it is as though she had not immersed herself at all. If one kept hold on a man or on vessels and immersed them they remain unclean, but if one had before rinsed his hand in the water they become clean. R. Simeon says: He should loose his hold on them so that the water can come into them. It is not needful that the water should enter into every orifice and wrinkle [in the body].

9. 1. These interpose[5] in the case of a human creature: strips of wool or strips of flax; and the ribbons on the heads of girls (R. Judah says: Strips of wool or of hair do not interpose, since the water can penetrate them);

2. the matted hair over the heart and the hair of the beard and of the secret parts of a woman; the rheum outside the eye, the dried pus outside a wound and the plaster thereon, dried juice, clots of excrement on the skin, dough under the fingernail, dirt from sweatings, miry clay, potter's clay and road-clay. What is miry clay? Such is the clay in pits, as it is written, *He brought me up also out of an horrible pit, out of the miry clay*.[6] And potter's clay? It is according to its common meaning. R. Jose declares potter's clay insusceptible to uncleanness, but the clay used for putty he declares susceptible. And road-clay? [This it is from which they make] the pegs by the road-sides; in such mud none may immerse himself,

---

[1] M.Kat. 1[1]; Maksh. 4[9].   [2] See Shab. 9[3].
[3] Occasions of intercourse within the three days.   [4] Tam. 1[1].
[5] Between the body and the water. For immersion to be valid, no part of the body's surface may be untouched by the water.   [6] Ps. 40[2].

nor may he immerse himself while it is on his skin. But vessels may be immersed in any other kind of mud when it is wet. None may immerse himself with the dust on his feet. A kettle may not be immersed with the soot that is thereon unless it has been scraped.

3. These do not interpose [between the water and the body]: the matted hair of the head and armpits and of the secret parts of a man. R. Eliezer says: It is all one whether it be a man or a woman: aught concerning which a person is fastidious, this interposes; but aught concerning which a person is not fastidious, this does not interpose.

4. Dried rheum within the eye, the dried pus over a wound, juice that is moist, undried excrement on the skin, excrement that is under the finger-nail, a loosened fingernail and the downy hair of a child—these are not susceptible to uncleanness and do not convey uncleanness. The skin that grows over a wound is susceptible to uncleanness and conveys uncleanness.

5. These interpose in vessels:[1] in vessels of glass, pitch, and the gum of myrrh,[2] whether inside or outside; [if they are found] on a table or on a tablet or on a couch that are kept unsoiled, they interpose; but if these are [usually] suffered to remain dirty, they do not interpose. [If they are found] on beds belonging to a householder they interpose; but if on a bed belonging to a poor man they do not interpose. [If they are found] on a saddle belonging to a householder they interpose; but if on that of water-skin carriers, they do not interpose. [If they are found] on a packsaddle they interpose.[3] Rabban Simeon b. Gamaliel says: [They interpose only] if the spots are as big as an Italian *issar*.[4]

6. [If they are found] on clothes, on one side only, they do not interpose; but if on both sides, they interpose. R. Judah in the name of R. Ishmael says: Even on one side only. R. Jose says: [They interpose in] the clothes of the edifiers[5] if on one side only; but in [the clothes of] the boorish, only if on both sides.

7. [If the pitch or gum is found on] the aprons of pitch-workers or potters or tree-trimmers, they do not interpose. R. Judah says: Nor on those of fruit-driers. This is the general rule: Aught concerning which a person is fastidious, this interposes; but aught concerning which a person is not fastidious, this does not interpose.

10. 1. Any handles of utensils that are not fixed in in their usual fashion, or, if they are fixed in in their usual fashion, that have not been properly finished, or, if they have been properly finished, that have been broken—these interpose [between the water and the utensil]. If a vessel was immersed mouth downwards[6] it is as though it had not been immersed at all. If it was immersed [and held] in its usual way without [immersing] the handle,[7] [it does not become clean] unless it is turned on its side. If a vessel is narrow at either end and wide in the middle, it does not become clean unless it is turned on its side. A bottle whose mouth is turned downwards[8] does not become clean unless a hole is made at the side. The ink-

---

[1] Including utensils and garments.
[2] Variant: 'Bitumen'.
[3] Some texts omit this sentence.
[4] See App. II, A.
[5] Lit. 'builders'. 'Disciples of the Sages who are engaged all their days in the building up of the world' and who are scrupulous about spots of filth on their clothes (Shab. 114 a).
[6] The air could not escape and the water could not touch the inner surfaces. Cf. above, 6[5]; 7[6].
[7] The word is uncertain. Some commentators explain it as the long neck of a vessel.
[8] And inwards to prevent the escape of liquid if it is overturned.

pot of ordinary folk does not become clean unless a hole is made at the side; and the inkpot of Joseph the priest[1] had a hole at the side.

2. A cushion or mattress of leather requires that the water shall enter inside it; but a round cushion, a ball, a block, an amulet or a phylactery[2] does not require that the water shall enter inside it. This is the general rule: Aught whose contents it is not usual to put in and take out, may be immersed sealed up.

3. These do not require that the water shall enter inside them: the knot [in the rags] of a poor man, or in fringes, the knotted thong of a sandal, or that of a head-phylactery if it is tight, or that of the arm-phylactery if it will not move up and down, or the handgrip of a water-skin or of a shepherd's wallet.

4. These require that the water shall enter inside them: the shoulder-knot of undergarments (the hem, also, of a sheet must be opened out) and [the knot of] a head-phylactery if it is not tight, and that of the arm-phylactery if it will move up and down, and the straps of a sandal. If garments are immersed when they are already wet from being washed [they need remain in the water only] until they bulge; but if they are dry [they must remain] until they bulge and until they cease from bulging.

5. Handles of utensils which are [too] long[3] and which it is intended to cut down, need to be immersed [only] as far as the [appointed] length. R. Judah says: [They do not become clean] unless the whole is immersed. The chain of a big bucket[4] [is susceptible to uncleanness to a length of] four handbreadths [from the bucket], and that of a little bucket [to a length of] ten handbreadths; they need to be immersed [only] as far as the [appointed] length. R. Tarfon says: The whole of a ring [in the chain, if but part of it comes within the appointed length], needs to be immersed. A rope that is fastened to a basket does not count as a connective unless it is sewn on.

6. The School of Shammai say: They may not immerse hot water in cold, or cold water in hot, or fresh water in foul, or foul water in fresh. And the School of Hillel say: They may do so. If a vessel full of liquid was immersed, it is as though it was not immersed at all. If it was full of urine, it is looked upon as though it was water. If it was full of Sin-offering water[5] [it is unclean] unless the water [from the Immersion-pool that flows into the vessel] is more than the Sin-offering water. R. Jose says: Even if the vessel could hold a *kor*[6] and there was in it but a quarter-*log*, it is as though it was not immersed at all.

7. All[7] foodstuffs can be included together to make up the bulk of half a half-loaf[8] that suffices to render the body unfit [to eat of Heave-offering]. All liquids can be included together to make up the quarter-*log* that renders the body unfit. Herein greater stringency applies to him that drinks unclean liquids than to the Immersion-pool, since for him they have made all other liquids to be like to water.

8. If a man ate unclean food or drank unclean liquid and immersed himself and vomited them forth, they remain unclean since they have not become clean with the body; but if he drank unclean water and immersed himself and vomited it forth, it is clean, since it became clean with the

[1] Hall. 4[11].   [2] See p. 104, n. 16.   [3] Cf. Kel. 29[3ff].
[4] See Kel. 14[3].   [5] Num. 19[9]; p. 697, n. 3.   [6] App. II, D.
[7] See Meil. 4[5].   [8] Ker. 3[3]; Meil. 4[5]; Neg. 13[9, 10]; Toh. 1[3].

body. If a man swallowed a clean ring and entered a 'Tent' wherein lies a corpse,[1] and he sprinkled himself a first and a second time,[2] and then immersed himself and vomited forth the ring, it remains as it was before. If he swallowed an unclean ring and immersed himself, he may eat of Heave-offering [at sunset]; if he vomited forth the ring, it is [still] unclean and it renders him unclean. If an arrow was thrust into a man and it is still visible, it interposes [between the water and his flesh]; but if it is not visible, he may immerse himself and eat of Heave-offering.

NIDDAH[3] ('THE MENSTRUANT')

1. 1. Shammai says:[4] For all women it is enough for them [that they be deemed unclean only from] their time [of suffering a flow]. Hillel says: [A woman is deemed to have been unclean] from [the previous] examination to [the present] examination, even if [the interval is of] many days. But the Sages say: It is not according to the opinion of either; but [she is deemed to have been unclean] during the preceding twenty-four hours if this is less than [the time] from [the previous] examination to [the present] examination, or else from [the previous] examination to [the present] examination if this is less than twenty-four hours. If a woman has fixed periods it is enough for her [that she be deemed unclean only from] her time [of suffering a flow]. If she had connexion and used the test-rags, this counts as an examination, and may lessen either the interval of twenty-four hours, or the interval from [the previous] examination to [the present] examination.

2. '[If a woman has fixed periods] it is enough for her [that she be deemed unclean only from] her time [of suffering a flow]'—thus if she was sitting on a bed and was occupied in matters requiring conditions of cleanness and she went apart and suffered a flow, she is unclean but the other things remain clean. Although they have said that she conveys uncleanness 'during the preceding twenty-four hours', she may take count [of the seven days prescribed in the Law][5] only from the time that she suffered a flow.

3. R. Eliezer says: For four kinds of women it is enough for them [that they be deemed unclean only from] their time [of suffering a flow]: a virgin (*bethulah*), a woman that is pregnant, one that gives suck, and an old woman. R. Joshua said: I have only heard [that such a rule applies to] a virgin. But the *halakah*[6] is according to R. Eliezer.

4. Who is accounted a *bethulah*? She that has never yet suffered a flow, even though she was married. And [who is accounted] pregnant? She in whom the young is manifest. And [who is accounted] one that gives suck? She that has not yet weaned her child. If she gave her child to another that should suckle it, or if she had weaned it,[7] or if it died, R. Meir says: She conveys uncleanness during the preceding twenty-four hours. But the Sages say: It is enough for her [that she be deemed unclean only from] her time [of suffering a flow].

5. Who is accounted an old woman? She over whom three periods have

---

[1] Num. 19[14f].   [2] Num. 19[19].
[3] The main subject of the tractate is that of Lev. 15[19-24]. *Niddah* is, literally, 'impurity' or 'separation'. The word has acquired the more specialized senses of (*a*) a menstruous woman, (*b*) menstrual impurity.   [4] Eduy. 1[1].
[5] Lev. 15[19].   [6] App. I. 11.   [7] Prematurely.

passed [without her suffering a flow] about the time of her old age. R. Eliezer says: She over whom three periods have passed, it is enough for her [that she be deemed unclean only from] her time [of suffering a flow]. R. Jose says: If over her that is pregnant or that gives suck, three periods have passed, it is enough for her [that she be deemed unclean only from] her time [of suffering a flow].

6. And of what did they speak[1] when they said, 'It is enough for her [that she be deemed unclean only from] her time [of suffering a flow]'? Of a first flow; but if it was a second flow, she conveys uncleanness during the twenty-four hours that have gone before. Yet if she suffered the first flow by reason of constraint,[2] then, even for the second flow, it is enough for her [that she be deemed unclean only from] her time [of suffering a flow].

7. Although they have said,[3] 'It is enough for her [that she be deemed unclean] only from her time [of suffering a flow]', she must needs make examination, unless she is a menstruant [and making count of her prescribed seven days of uncleanness], or is abiding *in the blood of her purifying*[4] [after giving birth], or has connexion and uses the test-rags (unless she is abiding *in the blood of her purifying*), or is a virgin (*bethulah*) whose blood is clean. Twice must she make examination: in the morning and in the evening, and again at the time that she prepares for connexion; moreover women of the priestly stock [must make examination] when they eat of Heave-offering. R. Judah says: Also when they have ceased to eat of Heave-offering.

2. 1. The hand that oftentimes makes examination is, among women, praiseworthy; but among men—let it be cut off! If a woman was a deaf-mute or an imbecile or blind or not conscious, and there were at hand women of sound senses, these may do for her what is needful, and then she may eat of Heave-offering. It is the way of the daughters of Israel when they have connexion to use two test-rags, one for him and one for her; the more pious make ready a third wherewith they set in order 'the house'.

2. If the blood was found with him, both are unclean and liable to an offering.[5] If it was found with her at the time itself, both are unclean and liable to an offering; but if it was found with her after a time, their uncleanness remains in doubt and they are exempt from the offering.

3. How long is meant by 'after a time'? Time enough for her to get down from the bed and rinse her face;[6] if after this [she suffered a flow] she is deemed to have conveyed uncleanness during the preceding twenty-four hours; but she has not rendered unclean him that has connexion with her. But the Sages agree with R. Akiba that if she observes a blood-stain she renders unclean him that has connexion with her.[7]

4. Women may always be assumed clean in readiness for their husbands. When men have come from a journey their wives may be assumed clean in readiness for them. The School of Shammai say: She needs two test-rags for every act; or else [on every occasion] she should examine it by the light of a lamp. And the School of Hillel say: Two test-rags suffice her throughout the night.

---

[1] In the case of the four cited above, par. 3.
[2] Through abnormal or unnatural causes.
[3] Of her that has fixed periods.   [4] Lev. 12^4.
[5] A Sin-offering (Lev. 4^{27}) in expiation of a transgression against Lev. 18^{19}; 20^{18}.
[6] Euphemism.   [7] With seven-day uncleanness (Lev. 15^{24}).

5. The Sages spoke in a parable about woman: [There is in her] a chamber, an ante-chamber, and an upper-room: blood in the chamber is unclean; if it is found in the ante-chamber, its condition of doubt is deemed unclean, since it is presumed to be from the fountain.

6. Five kinds of blood in a woman are unclean: red and black and bright crocus colour and a colour like earthy water and like mixed [water and wine]. The School of Shammai say: Also a colour like water in which fenugreek had been soaked and a colour like the juice that comes out of roast flesh. But the School of Hillel declare these clean. If it is yellow, Akabya b. Mahalaleel[1] declares it unclean, but the Sages declare it clean. R. Meir said: Even if it does not convey uncleanness by virtue of being a blood-stain, it conveys uncleanness by virtue of being a liquid.[2] R. Jose says: In neither case does it convey uncleanness.

7. What colour is meant by 'red'? Like the blood of a wound. 'Black' means like ink sediment; if it is darker than this it is unclean, but if lighter it is clean. 'Bright crocus colour' means like the brightest shade in it. 'Like earthy water' means [a colour like that] when water is made to float over earth from the valley of Beth Kerem.[3] And 'like mixed [water and wine]' [means a colour like as] when two parts of water [are mixed] with one part of wine, or the wine of Sharon.

3. 1. If a woman suffered a miscarriage and there was blood with it, she becomes unclean; but if there was not, she remains clean. R. Judah says: In either case she is unclean.[4]

2. If the abortion was the like of rind, or hair, or dust, or red flies, let her cast them into water: if they dissolve she is unclean, but if they do not, she is clean. If the abortion was the like of fishes, locusts, insects, or creeping things,[5] and there was blood with them she is unclean; but if there was not, she is clean. If the abortion was like to a beast, a wild animal or a bird, be they clean or unclean, and it was a male, she must continue [unclean[6] the number of days prescribed] for a male; and if it was a female she must continue [unclean the number of days prescribed] for a female; if the sex is not known she must continue [unclean the number of days prescribed] both for a male and for a female. So R. Meir. But the Sages say: What is not of the form of man is not accounted [human] young.

3. If the abortion was a foetus filled with water or filled with blood or filled with variegated matter,[7] she need not take thought for it as for [human] young; but if its [human] parts were fashioned, she must continue [unclean the number of days prescribed] both for a male and for a female.

4. If the abortion was like to a sandal or an afterbirth, she must continue [unclean the number of days prescribed] both for a male and for a female. If there was an afterbirth in a house, the house becomes unclean; it is not because the afterbirth counts as [human] young, but because there can be no afterbirth without young.[8] R. Simeon says: The young may have melted away before it came forth.

5. If the abortion was of doubtful sex or of double sex she must continue [unclean the days prescribed] both for a male and for a female. [If she bore] a thing of doubtful sex and a male, or a thing of double sex

[1] See Eduy. 5[6].   [2] Maksh. 6[4].   [3] See Midd. 3[4].
[4] Since it was impossible that blood should not have issued even if it was not seen.
[5] Cf. Ker. 1[5].   [6] Lev. 12[4f].   [7] Cf. Ker. 1[5].
[8] Cf. Bekh. 3[1]; 8[1]; Ker. 1[3].

and a male, she must continue [unclean the days prescribed] both for a male
and for a female; but if it was a thing of doubtful sex and a female, or a
thing of double sex and a female, she need continue [unclean the days
prescribed] for a female only. If it came forth in pieces or with feet foremost, it is deemed born after the greater part is come forth. If it came
forth in its ordinary way [it is not deemed born] until the greater part of
its head has come forth. And what is deemed the greater part of its head?
When its forehead has come forth.

6. If she suffered a miscarriage and it is not known what it was, [whether
male or female], she must continue [unclean the days prescribed] both for a
male and for a female. If it is not known whether it was [human] young
or not, she must continue [unclean the days prescribed] both for a male and
for a female, and also for a menstruant.

7. If she suffered a miscarriage on the fortieth day, she need not take
thought for it as for [human] young; if on the forty-first day, she must
continue [unclean the days prescribed] both for a male and for a female,
and also for a menstruant. R. Ishmael says: If [she suffered a miscarriage]
on the forty-first day, she must continue [unclean the days prescribed]
for a male and for a menstruant; but if on the eighty-first day, she must
continue [unclean the days prescribed] both for a male and for a female,
and for a menstruant, since a male is fully fashioned after forty-one days,
but a female only after eighty-one days. But the Sages say: The creation
of a male and the creation of a female are alike: each [is fully fashioned]
after forty-one days.

4. 1. The daughters of the Samaritans are [deemed unclean as] menstruants from their cradle; and the Samaritans convey uncleanness to
what lies beneath them in like degree as [he that has a flux conveys un-
cleanness] to what lies above him,[1] since they have connexion with menstruants. Moreover the daughters of the Samaritans continue [unclean
for seven days] by reason of any kind of blood.[2] Because of [uncleanness
incurred from] them, none becomes culpable by entrance into the Temple,
and Heave-offering need not be burnt, since their uncleanness remains
in doubt.

2. The daughters of the Sadducees, if they follow after the ways of their
fathers, are deemed like to the women of the Samaritans; but if they have
separated themselves and follow after the ways of the Israelites, they are
deemed like to the women of the Israelites. R. Jose says: They may ever
be deemed like to the women of the Israelites unless they separate themselves and follow after the ways of their fathers.

3. The blood[3] of a gentile woman and the blood of the purifying[4] of a
woman that is a leper, the School of Shammai declare clean, but the School
of Hillel say: It is like to her spittle or her urine.[5] The blood of a woman
that has not yet immersed herself after childbirth,[6] the School of Shammai
say: It is like to her spittle or her urine. But the School of Hillel say: It
conveys uncleanness whether it is wet or dried up. But they agree that if
a woman gave birth while she had a flux, it conveys uncleanness whether
it is wet or dried up.

[1] See p. 604, n. 9.   [2] i.e. their custom is to deem unclean such blood as the
Sages have taught to be clean; cf. above, 2⁶. See also 7³.
[3] Lev. 15¹⁹, or 15²⁵.   [4] Lev. 12⁴.   [5] Eduy. 5¹.
[6] Lev. 12²ᶠᶠ. Cf. Eduy. 5⁴.

4. If a woman was in hard travail during [her seven days of] menstruation, [blood that flows is deemed unclean as menstrual blood]. If she was in hard travail three days of the eleven days,[1] and she had relief [from her pains] for twenty-four hours and then gave birth, such is one that has given birth while she had a flux. So R. Eliezer. R. Joshua says: [She must have had relief for] a [whole] night and a [whole] day, like the night of the Sabbath and the day thereof; for she may have had relief from the pain but not from the blood.

5. How long may her hard travail endure?[2] R. Meir says: Even forty days or fifty days. R. Judah says: It is enough for her [that the blood be deemed clean that issues during] her [ninth] month. R. Jose and R. Simeon say: The time of hard travail [when the blood may be deemed clean] may not exceed two weeks.

6. If a woman was in hard travail during the eighty days [that she continues unclean after the birth] of a daughter,[3] any issue of blood that she suffers is clean until the young comes forth. But R. Eliezer declares her unclean.[4] They said to R. Eliezer, If, where stringency applies to blood discharged without travail, leniency applies to blood discharged during travail, must we not, then, infer that, where leniency applies to blood discharged without travail, leniency applies still more to blood discharged during travail? He answered, It is enough if the inferred law is as strict as that from which it is inferred.[5] Touching what does leniency apply to her? Touching the uncleanness from flux. But she is still unclean because of the uncleanness of the menstruant.

7. Throughout the eleven days [that follow the seven days of her uncleanness as a menstruant] she can be presumed clean; and if she sat herself down and had not examined herself, or did aught in error, or through constraint, or wantonly, and had not examined herself, she may be deemed clean. But if the time of her fixed period was come and she had not examined herself, she is deemed unclean. R. Meir says: If she was in hiding and the time of her fixed period was come and she had not examined herself she may be deemed clean, since fearfulness suspends the blood-flow. But during the [seven clean] days [that must be taken count of] by the man or the woman that has a flux, or [the one day of cleanness to be taken count of] by her that awaits day against day,[6] [during such time] they must be presumed to be unclean.

5. 1. By reason of what was born from the side[7] they need not continue [apart] during the [prescribed] days of uncleanness[8] and the days of purifying,[9] nor are they liable to an offering[10] because of it. R. Simeon says: Such is reckoned a valid birth. All women convey uncleanness [by reason of blood] in the antechamber,[11] for it is written, *And her issue in her flesh be blood.*[12] But he that has a flux and he that suffers a pollution do not convey uncleanness unless their uncleanness is come forth.

1 The period of time between the periods. A flow during these intervening eleven days is deemed a flux (Lev. 15²⁵ᶠᶠ.).
2 Without her being deemed unclean from a flow of blood, i.e. the blood not coming within either of the categories of Lev. 15¹⁹ or 15²⁵.   3 Lev. 12⁵.
4 If she was in hard travail during the seven days of menstruation.
5 See p. 333, n. 3.   6 Pes. 8⁵; Meg. 2⁴; Hor. 1³; Zab. 1¹.
7 Young cut out of the parent's side. See p. 479, n. 3.
8 Seven days for a male and fourteen for a female. See Lev. 12²ᶠᶠ.
9 Thirty-three for a male and sixty-six for a female.   10 See Lev. 12⁶.
11 See above, 2⁵.   12 Lev. 15¹⁹.

2. If a man was eating Heave-offering and he felt his limbs tremble, he must lay hold on the member and swallow the Heave-offering. And [the discharge] renders him unclean whatsoever its bulk, even though it be like to a grain of mustard, or less than this.

3. A girl one day old[1] can become unclean by virtue of being a menstruant. A girl ten days old[2] can become unclean by reason of a flux. A boy one day old can become unclean by reason of a flux, and he can become unclean from leprosy-signs, and he can become unclean from corpse-uncleanness; he suffices to hold [his childless brother's widow] in the bonds of levirate marriage,[3] and to exempt [his mother] from levirate marriage;[4] he suffices to render [his mother] qualified to eat Heave-offering, or to render her unqualified to eat Heave-offering;[5] and he can inherit property and bequeath it;[6] he that kills him is culpable; and he counts as a full relative[7] to his father and his mother and to all his kinsfolk.

4. A girl three years old and one day may be betrothed by intercourse;[8] her deceased childless husband's brother can acquire her[9] by intercourse; and by connexion with her a man can be culpable by virtue of the law of a married woman;[10] and him that has connexion with her [while she is a menstruant] she renders unclean so that he conveys uncleanness to what is beneath him in like degree as [he that has a flux conveys uncleanness] to what lies above him;[11] if she is married to a priest she may eat of Heave-offering;[12] if one that is ineligible[13] has connexion with her he renders her ineligible for marriage with a priest; if any of the forbidden degrees[14] prescribed in the Law had connexion with her they are put to death on her account, but she is not culpable. If she is younger than this, it is as one that puts a finger in the eye.

5. If a boy nine years old and one day had connexion with his childless brother's widow, he has acquired her to wife, and he cannot give her a bill of divorce until he comes of age; he can contract uncleanness by [connexion with] a menstruant so that he conveys uncleanness to what is beneath him in like degree as [he that has a flux conveys uncleanness] to what lies above him; he can render [a woman] unqualified[15] but cannot render [a woman] qualified[16] to eat of Heave-offering; he can render cattle invalid for the Altar;[17] and a beast can be stoned[18] because of him; and if he has connexion with any of the forbidden degrees prescribed in the Law they are put to death on his account, but he is not culpable.

6. A girl eleven years old and one day—her vows must be examined;[19] if she is twelve years old and one day her vows are valid, but they must be

---

[1] If she suffers a flow.

[2] If she had passed her first seven days in the uncleanness of a menstruant, and then suffered flows on the next three consecutive days.

[3] If he lived within the lifetime of his childless brother (cf. Yeb. 2[1]).

[4] If he was born after the death of the father, and then died, the mother is exempt from levirate marriage with her brother-in-law.

[5] See p. 651, n. 5.   [6] e.g. if his mother died he can inherit her goods, and if then he died his brothers by the same father (and another mother) inherit from him.

[7] Lit. 'bridegroom' or 'son-in-law'. Cf. Ex. 4[25].

[8] See Kidd. 1[1].   [9] Consummate levirate marriage.

[10] Lev. 18[20].   [11] See above, 4[1]. Cf. p. 604, n. 9.

[12] See Lev. 22[10ff].   [13] See Kidd. 4[1].   [14] Lev. 18[6ff].

[15] If, not being eligible for marriage with priestly stock, he had connexion with a woman of priestly stock.

[16] If he was of priestly stock and consummated levirate marriage with one who was not. He cannot validly marry.   [17] By unnatural crime. See Zeb. 8[1].   [18] Lev. 20[15].

[19] Whether she knew the nature of her vow.

examined throughout the twelfth year. A boy twelve years old and one day
—his vows must be examined; if he is thirteen years old and one day, his
vows are valid, but they must be examined throughout the thirteenth year.
When they are younger than this, even though they say, 'We know in
whose name we have vowed it' or 'in whose name we have dedicated it',
their vow is no vow and what they dedicate is not dedicated. But when they
are older than this, even though they say, 'We know not in whose name
we vowed it', or 'in whose name we dedicated it', their vow is a valid one,
and what they dedicate is validly dedicated.

7. The Sages spoke in a parable about woman: [She is like] an unripe
fig,[1] or a ripening fig,[2] or a fully ripe fig:[3] 'an unripe fig'—while she is yet
a child; and 'a ripening fig'—these are the days of her girlhood[4] (and during
both times her father is entitled to aught that she finds and to the work
of her hands,[5] and he can annul her vows);[6] and 'a fully ripe fig'—after she
is past her girlhood, when her father no more has any rights over her.

8. What are the tokens in her [that she is past her girlhood]? R. Jose the
Galilean says: When the wrinkle appears beneath the breast. R. Akiba says:
When the breasts hang down. Ben Azzai says: When the ring around the
nipple turns dark. R. Jose says: [When the breast is so grown] that if the
hand is put on the ring around the nipple it sinks and slowly returns.

9. If a woman twenty years old has not grown two hairs she must bring
proof that she is twenty years old; she is reckoned sterile, and she may not
perform *halitzah* nor may she contract levirate marriage.[7] If a man twenty
years old has not grown two hairs he must bring proof that he is twenty
years old; he is reckoned a eunuch, and he may neither submit to *halitzah*
nor may he contract levirate marriage. So the School of Hillel. The School
of Shammai say: In either case [this applies] when they are eighteen years
old. R. Eliezer says: For a male the rule is according to the School of
Hillel, and for a female it is according to the School of Shammai, since the
growth of a woman is more speedy than that of a man.

6. 1. If the lower token was come but the upper token was not yet come
she may perform *halitzah* or contract levirate marriage; if the upper token
was come but the lower token was not yet come (though this is not possible),
R. Meir says: She may neither perform *halitzah* nor may she contract
levirate marriage. But the Sages say: She may either perform *halitzah* or
contract levirate marriage. Since[8] they have said: The lower [token] may
come before the upper [token] is come, but it is not possible for the upper
[token] to come before the lower [token] is come.

2. In like manner: any earthenware vessel that will let in [a liquid] will
also let it out; but there are some that will let out a liquid and will not let
it in. Any member [of the body] that grows a claw must have a bone in it;
but some members have a bone in them and do not grow a claw.

3. Whatsoever is susceptible to *midras*-uncleanness is susceptible to
corpse-uncleanness, but some things are susceptible to *corpse*-uncleanness
and are not susceptible to *midras*-uncleanness.[9]

4. Whosoever is fit to judge capital cases is fit to judge non-capital

---

1 *Paggah.*   2 *Bohel.*
3 *Tzemel.*   4 Between twelve years and twelve years and a half.
5 Ket. 4[1].   6 Num. 30[3ff].   7 See p. 218, n. 1.
8 This is in continuation of the previous interpolation 'though this is not possible'.
9 Namely things which are not such that can be sat upon. See Kel. 24[1ff]. App. I. 26.

cases; but some are fit to judge non-capital cases and are not fit to judge capital cases.[1] Whosoever is eligible to judge is eligible to bear witness; but some are eligible to bear witness and are not eligible to judge.[2]

5. Whatsoever is subject to Tithes can contract food-uncleanness; but there is produce that can contract food uncleanness and is not subject to Tithes.[3]

6. Whatsoever is subject to the laws of Gleaning (*Peah*) is subject to Tithes; but some things are subject to Tithes and are not subject to the laws of Gleaning.[4]

7. Whatsoever beasts are subject to the law of *the first of the fleece*[5] are subject to the law of the [Priests'] Dues;[6] but some beasts are subject to the law of the [Priests'] Dues and are not subject to the law of *the first of the fleece*.[7]

8. Whatsoever crop is subject to the law of Removal[8] is subject to the law of Seventh Year produce; but there are crops that are subject to the law of Seventh Year produce and are not subject to the law of Removal.[9]

9. All fishes that have scales have fins; but not all fishes that have fins have scales. All animals that have horns have hoofs; but not all animals that have hoofs have horns.

10. Whatsoever requires a Benediction after it requires a Benediction before it; but there are things that require a Benediction before them and do not require a Benediction after them.[10]

11. If a girl has grown two hairs she is subject to all the commands prescribed in the Law, and she may perform *halitzah* or contract levirate marriage. So, too, if a boy has grown two hairs he is subject to all the commands prescribed in the Law; and he is fitted to become a stubborn and rebellious son[11] from the time that he has grown two hairs until he has grown an encircling beard (the lower and not the upper one [is meant], for the Sages spoke in modest language). If a girl has grown two hairs she cannot exercise the right of Refusal.[12] R. Judah says: [She may do so] until the dark [hair] is become widespread.

12. The two hairs spoken of in Parah and Negaim[13] and that are spoken of in any [other] place, must be long enough for their tip to be bent to their root. So R. Ishmael. R. Eliezer says: To be grasped by the finger-nails. R. Akiba says: To be taken off with scissors.

13. If a woman observed a blood-stain [in her shift] she is in ill plight, and she must fear lest she has suffered a flux. So R. Meir. But the Sages say: Blood-stains are not accounted of as being of the nature of flux.

14. If a woman suffered an issue on the eleventh day[14] at twilight, or at the beginning of [the period of] menstruation, or at the end of [the period] of menstruation, or at the beginning of [the period of] a flux, or at the end of [the period of] a flux,[15] or on the fortieth day [of the days of purifying prescribed after the birth] of a male, or on the eightieth day [after the days of purifying prescribed after the birth] of a female, in every case at twilight—

---

[1] e.g. a bastard.   [2] e.g. such as are blind in one eye.
[3] Foodstuffs which do not grow from the soil.
[4] Certain crops, e.g. figs, which are not all gathered at the same time.
[5] See Hull. 11[1ff].   [6] See Hull. 10[1ff].   [7] e.g. oxen and goats.
[8] See p. 49, n. 4.
[9] Certain plants whose growth continues summer and winter, and whose roots are not perishable.   [10] Putting on the phylacteries or taking the *Lulab*.
[11] See Sanh. 8[1].   [12] See Yeb. 13[1ff].   [13] See Par. 2[5]; Neg. 1[5].
[14] The end of the period when a flow may be a case of flux (Lev. 15[25ff].) and the beginning of the seven days when it may be a menstrual flow (Lev. 15[19ff].).
[15] i.e. the time when a flow can be regarded as a flux.

such will be at fault in their reckoning.[1] R. Joshua said: Before ye order the affairs of women that are foolish, come and order the affairs of women that are wise![2]

7. 1. The blood of a menstruant and the flesh of a corpse convey uncleanness when wet and they convey uncleanness when dry. But flux, phlegm, spittle, a [dead] creeping thing, carrion and semen convey uncleanness when wet but they do not convey uncleanness when dry; but if, when they are soaked, they return to their former bulk they convey uncleanness when wet and they convey uncleanness when dry. How long must they be soaked? For twenty-four hours in lukewarm water. R. Jose says: If the flesh of a corpse is dry, and cannot, when it is soaked, return to its former bulk, it is clean.[3]

2. If a creeping thing is found in an alley-way, it is assumed to have conveyed uncleanness in the past to such time as it can be said, 'I examined this alley-way and there was no creeping thing in it', or to such time as it was last swept. So, too, if a blood-stain was found on a shift, it is assumed to have conveyed uncleanness in the past to such time as it can be said, 'I examined this shift and there was no stain on it', or to such time as it was last washed; and it conveys uncleanness both when wet and when dry. R. Simeon says: What is dry conveys uncleanness in time that is past, but what is wet only to a time when it could have been wet.

3. All blood-stains that come from Rekem[4] are clean. R. Judah declares them unclean since they are proselytes there and liable to err. Those that come from the gentiles are clean. If they come from among Israelites or Samaritans, R. Meir declares them unclean, but the Sages declare them clean, since they are not under suspicion concerning their stains.

4. All blood-stains wheresoever they are found are deemed clean excepting those found in rooms or round about places of uncleanness. Places of uncleanness that belong to Samaritans convey uncleanness by overshadowing, since they bury abortions there.[5] R. Judah says: They did not bury them but only threw them away, and the wild animals dragged them off.

5. They[6] may be believed when they say, 'We buried abortions there', or 'We did not bury them'. They may be believed when they tell of a beast whether it had borne a firstling or had not borne a firstling. They may be believed in the pointing out of graves. But they may not be believed in what concerns interlaced foliage or protruding stones,[7] or Grave-areas.[8] This is the general rule: In any matter concerning which they are under suspicion they may not be believed.

8. 1. If a woman saw a blood-stain on her flesh and it was near her secret parts, she is unclean; but if it was not, she remains clean. If it was on her heel or on the end of her great toe, she is unclean. If it was on the inner side of the thigh or of the feet, she is unclean; but if on the outer side, she remains clean. If it was on the flanks at either side, she remains clean. If she saw it on her shift below the girdle, she is unclean; but if above the

---

[1] Cf. Arak. 2[1].

[2] i.e. there are problems of far greater complexity arising out of the calculations concerning a woman's periods. Cf. Ab. 3[19].

[3] i.e. an olive's bulk of it as flesh no longer conveys corpse-uncleanness; but a ladleful of it as corpse dust still conveys corpse-uncleanness. Cf. Ohol. 2[1].   [4] Gitt. 1[1,2].

[5] Cf. Ohol. 18[7] (of places belonging to gentiles).   [6] The Samaritans.

[7] Cf. Naz. 7[3]; Ohol. 8[2].   [8] See Ohol. 17[1ff].

girdle, she remains clean. If she saw it on the sleeve of the shift and [the place where it was found] could reach as far as the secret parts, she is unclean; but if it could not, she remains clean. If she had stripped it off or put it on in the night, wheresoever the stain may be found, she is unclean, since it can have been turned about. So, too, in the case of a pallium.[1]

2. She may set it down to any cause to which she is able to set it down. If she had slaughtered a beast, a wild animal or a bird, or if she had engaged in [aught that occasions] blood-stains, or sat beside them that had so engaged, or if she had killed a louse, she may set down [the blood-stain] to them. How large a stain may she set down to the louse? R. Hanina b. Antigonus says: [A stain] the size of a split bean. And [she may set it down to it] even though she did not kill it. She may set it down to her son or her husband. If she had a wound in her that could open again and bleed, she may set it down to that.

3. A woman once came to R. Akiba and said to him, ' I have found a stain'. He said to her, 'Perhaps thou hast a wound in thee?' She said to him, 'Yea, but it has healed'. He said to her, 'Perhaps it may have opened again and bled?' She said to him, 'Yea'. And R. Akiba declared her clean. He saw his disciples gazing at one another [in wonder]. He said, 'Why is the matter difficult in your eyes?—for the Sages have not enjoined this rule for the sake of stringency, but for the sake of leniency, for it is written, *And if a woman have an issue and her issue in her flesh be blood*[2]—not a stain, but blood.

4. If blood was found in the test-rag[3] that was put under the pillow, and it was a round [stain], this is clean; but if it was long, it is unclean. So R. Eliezer b. R. Zadok.

9. 1. If a woman suffered a flow of blood when she made water, R. Meir says: If she was standing she is unclean, but if sitting she remains clean. R. Jose says: In either case she remains clean.

2. If a man and a woman had made water in the pot and blood was found on the water, R. Jose declares it clean, but R. Simeon declares it unclean, for it is not the way of the man to discharge blood; but the presumption is that the blood is from the woman.

3. If she lent her shift to a gentile woman or to a menstruant, she may set down [the stain] to them. If three women had worn the same shift or had sat on the same bench, and blood was found thereon, all are accounted unclean. If they had sat on a stone bench or on the bench in a bath-house, R. Nehemiah declares them clean; for R. Nehemiah used to say: Aught that is not susceptible to uncleanness is not susceptible [to uncleanness] from stains.

4. If three women were sleeping in one bed, and blood was found under one of them, all are deemed unclean. If one of them examined herself and she was found unclean, she alone is unclean and the two [others] remain clean. Or they may set it down the one to the other. If none was like to suffer a flow, they must be looked upon as though they were like to suffer it.

5. If three women were sleeping in one bed, and blood was found under her that was in the middle, they are all deemed unclean; if under her that was on the inner side, the two to the inner side are deemed unclean, and

---

[1] A large, square mantle. Any part of it in turn could be worn in such a way as to reach the lower parts of the body.　　　[2] Lev. 15[19].　　　[3] Cf. above, 1[7].

she on the outer side remains clean; if under her that was on the outer side, the two to the outer side are deemed unclean, and she on the inner side remains clean. R. Judah said: This applies only if they passed [into the bed] by way of the foot of the bed; but if the three had all passed over the upper part, all are deemed unclean. If one of them examined herself and she was found clean, she is clean and the other two unclean. If two of them examined themselves and they were found clean, they are clean and the third unclean; if all three [examined themselves] and they were found clean, then all are unclean. To what is it like? It is like an unclean heap that was confused among two clean heaps. If they examined one of them and found it clean, then it is clean and the other two unclean; if they examined two and they were found clean, they are clean and the third unclean; if they examined all three and they were found clean, then all are unclean. So R. Meir; for R. Meir used to say: If aught is in a condition of presumed uncleanness, it continues in its condition of uncleanness until it is known to thee where is the uncleanness. But the Sages say: Examination must be made until bedrock or virgin soil is reached.

6. Seven substances must be rubbed over a [blood-]stain: tasteless spittle, water from boiled grits, urine, nitre, soap, Cimolian earth, and lion's leaf. If after it was immersed and washed and rubbed with these seven substances it is not rubbed off, then it is but some dye: aught requiring conditions of cleanness [that has touched it] remains clean, and it needs not to be immersed. If it disappeared or grew fainter, then it is a [blood-]stain: aught requiring conditions of cleanness [that has touched it] becomes unclean and it needs to be immersed.

7. What manner of tasteless spittle is meant? [That of a man] who has tasted nothing. 'Water from boiled grits'?—paste made from grits of peeled beans. 'Urine'?—such that has fermented. [The stain] must be scoured with each of them three times. If they were rubbed over it in different order, or if the seven were rubbed over it together, [it is as if] one has done nothing at all.

8. If a woman has fixed periods, it is enough for her [that she be deemed unclean only from] her time [of suffering a flow].[1] And these are [the tokens of] fixed periods: if she yawned or sneezed or felt pain in the top of her stomach or the bottom of her bowels, or if she discharges, or if a kind of shuddering took hold on her, or other tokens the like of these. If ever the like of these have befallen her regularly three times, they are deemed [the tokens of] a fixed period.

9. If her use was to suffer the flow at the onset of these tokens, any foods requiring conditions of cleanness that she prepared while the tokens were upon her are deemed unclean; but if only at the end of these tokens, any foods requiring conditions of cleanness that she prepared while the tokens were upon her remain clean. R. Jose says: The fixed periods may also be according to certain days or hours: [thus] if her use was to suffer the flow after sunrise, she becomes forbidden only after sunrise. R. Judah says: [She is permitted] the whole of that day [should no token befall her].

10. If her use was to suffer the flow on the fifteenth day and the habit changed and she suffered it on the twentieth day, both are forbidden times. If the habit changed and she twice suffered the flow on the twentieth day, both are still forbidden times to her. If the habit changed and she three

---

[1] Quoting from 1[1], above.

times suffered the flow on the twentieth, then the fifteenth becomes a permitted time, and she has made the twentieth day her fixed period; for no woman may deem her period fixed unless it has befallen her regularly three times, nor may she account herself clean at [what had been] a fixed period until it has three times ceased to befall her.

11. Women, as touching [the blood of] virginity[1] are like vines: one vine has red wine, another black; one vine gives much wine, another little. R. Judah says: Every vine has its wine; and that which has no wine is called a *dorketi* vine.[2]

10. 1. If a girl was married that had not yet suffered a flow, the School of Shammai say: They allow her four nights. And the School of Hillel say: Until the wound heals.[3] If her time was come to suffer a flow, and she was married, the School of Shammai allow to her the first night; and the School of Hillel say: Until the outgoing of the Sabbath: four nights.[4] If she suffered a flow while yet in her father's house, the School of Shammai says: She is allowed but the coition of obligation. And the School of Hillel say: The whole night.

2. If a menstruant examined herself on the morning of the seventh day and found herself clean, but at twilight did not mark her separation[5] [from uncleanness], and after certain days she examined herself and found herself unclean, then [in the days between] she was in a condition of presumed cleanness. If she examined herself and found herself unclean in the morning of the seventh day, but at twilight did not mark her separation [from uncleanness], and after some time she examined herself and found herself clean, then [in the days between] she was in a condition of presumed uncleanness, and she conveys uncleanness both during the twenty-four hours that have gone before, and the time between [the present] examination and [the previous] examination. But if she has a fixed period it is enough for her [that she be deemed unclean only from] her time [of suffering a flow]. R. Judah says: She that has not marked her separation [from uncleanness] after the afternoon is in a condition of presumed uncleanness. But the Sages say: Even if she examined herself on the second day of her menstruation and found herself clean, and at twilight did not mark her separation [from uncleanness], and afterward found herself unclean, then [in the days between] she was in a condition of presumed cleanness.

3. If a man or a woman that had a flux examined themselves on the first day and found themselves clean, and again on the seventh day and found themselves clean, yet did not examine themselves in the days between, R. Eliezer says: They were in a condition of presumed cleanness. R. Joshua says: They can reckon [as days of uncleanness] the first and the seventh days only. R. Akiba says: The seventh day only.

4. If a man or a woman that had a flux, or a menstruant, or a woman after childbirth, or a leper have died, they convey uncleanness by carrying, until the flesh has decayed. A gentile that has died does not convey uncleanness by carrying. The School of Shammai say: All women that die

---

[1] See Deut. 22[14].
[2] Apparently a corrupted form of τρωκτή, an adjective applied to grapes used for eating only and not for making wine.
[3] Until then any blood is not deemed unclean menstrual blood.
[4] The marriage of a virgin must be performed on a Wednesday. See Ket. 1[1].
[5] Examine herself finally to mark the close of her seven prescribed days of uncleanness.

are deemed [to have died while they were] menstruants. And the School of Hillel say: Only she that dies while she was a menstruant is deemed a menstruant.

5. If a woman died and a quarter-*log* of blood issued from her, she conveys uncleanness by virtue of the blood-stain, and also by overshadowing.[1] R. Judah says: She does not convey uncleanness by virtue of the blood-stain, since [her period] ceased to befall her after she died. But R. Judah agrees that if a woman was sitting on the travailing stool and died, and a quarter-*log* of blood issued from her, she conveys uncleanness by virtue of the blood-stain. R. Jose said: Therefore she does not convey uncleanness by overshadowing.

6. Beforetime they used to say: She that continues in *the blood of her purifying*[2] was permitted to pour out water for [washing] the Passover-offering.[3] But they changed their opinion and said: For the Hallowed Things she is as one that has had contact with one that suffered corpse-uncleanness.[4] So the School of Hillel. The School of Shammai say: Even as one that suffered uncleanness from a corpse.[5]

7. But they agree that she may eat of [Second] Tithe[6] and set apart Dough-offering[7] and bring near [to the other dough the vessel wherein she has put the portion set apart as Dough-offering] to designate it as Dough-offering, and that if any of her spittle or of *the blood of her purifying* fell on a loaf of Heave-offering, it remains clean. The School of Shammai say: She needs immersion at the end [of the days of her purifying]. But the School of Hillel say: She does not need immersion at the end.

8. If she suffered a flux on the eleventh day[8] and immersed herself at nightfall and then had connexion, the School of Shammai say: [Both] convey uncleanness to what they lie upon or sit upon, and they are liable to an offering. And the School of Hillel say: They are not liable to an offering. If she immersed herself the next day, and she had connexion and afterward suffered a flux, the School of Shammai say: They convey uncleanness to what they lie upon or sit upon, but they are not liable to an offering. And the School of Hillel say: Such a one is gluttonous [yet is he not culpable]. But they agree that if she suffered a flux during the eleventh day and immersed herself at evening and then had connexion, they convey uncleanness to what they lie upon or sit upon, and they are liable to an offering. If she immersed herself the next day and then had connexion, such is evil behaviour, and [whether] their contact [conveys uncleanness] or their connexion [is culpable] is left in suspense.

---

[1] See Ohol. 2¹.   [2] Lev. 12⁴ᶠᶠ. She had immersed herself after the prescribed seven (or fourteen) days of uncleanness. She was deemed to be suffering second-grade uncleanness only (see p. 714, n. 3; p. 773, n. 6.)
[3] But not to touch it.   [4] i.e. she is deemed to suffer first-grade uncleanness.
[5] She is deemed a 'father of uncleanness'; she renders even vessels unclean.
[6] See p. 73, n. 6.   [7] See p. 83, n. 1.
[8] See above, p. 752, n. 14.

MAKSHIRIN[1] ('PREDISPOSERS')

1. 1. If any liquid was acceptable in the beginning even though it was not acceptable in the end, or if it was acceptable in the end even though it was not acceptable in the beginning, the law *If water be put on* applies.[2] Liquids that are unclean [forthwith] convey uncleanness whether [their presence is] acceptable or not acceptable.

2. If a man shook a tree to bring down fruit or some uncleanness [and he brought down also drops of rain and these fell upon the fruit], the law *If water be put on* does not apply; but if [he shook it] to bring down the drops of rain, the School of Shammai say: The law *If water be put on* applies to the drops that fell and to them that remained [and that fell later]. And the School of Hillel say: The law *If water be put on* applies to the drops that fell but not to them that remained, since his purpose was that all should fall off together.

3. If he shook a tree and the drops of rain fell on another tree; or a bush, and the drops of rain fell on another bush,[3] and beneath them were seeds or unplucked vegetables, the School of Shammai say: The law *If water be put on* applies. And the School of Hillel say: It does not apply. R. Joshua said in the name of Abba Jose Holi Kufri of Tibeon: Marvel at thyself if anywhere the Law prescribes that a liquid can render aught susceptible to uncleanness unless it was applied of set purpose, for it is written, *But if water be put upon the seed.*[4]

4. If a man shook a bunch of herbs and [the drops of rain thereon] fell from the top side to the bottom, the School of Hillel say: The law *If water be put on* applies. And the School of Hillel say: It does not apply. The School of Hillel said to the School of Shammai: If a man shakes the stalk [of a plant] do we take thought lest the drops fall from one leaf to another? The School of Shammai said to them: A stalk is but a single thing, but a bunch of stalks is many things. The School of Hillel said to them: If a man pulled out a sack full of fruit [that had fallen into the river] and put it on the river bank, do we take thought lest water falls from the top to the bottom?—yet if he had pulled out two sacks and put them one above the other, the law *If water be put on* applies to the lower sack. R. Jose says: Here also the lower one is not rendered susceptible.

5. If a man rubbed [the wetness] from off a leek or squeezed [the wetness] out of his hair with his garment, R. Jose says: The law *If water be put on* applies to the drops that fall but not to them that remain, since his purpose was that all should fall off together.

6. If a man blew on lentils to test whether they were good [and his spittle fell thereon], R. Simeon says: The law *If water be put on* does not apply. But[5] the Sages say: It does apply. If a man ate sesame with his [wet] finger,

---

[1] Lit. 'predisposers', or 'means which render (foodstuffs) susceptible (to uncleanness)'. From Lev. 11[38] ('But if water be put upon the seed and aught of their carcase fall thereon, it is unclean unto you') is deduced the rule that foodstuffs become susceptible to uncleanness after they are made wet by water or the like of water (see 6[4]), provided that such liquid was applied purposely, or, if, when not applied purposely, such liquid's presence was acceptable.

[2] This formula is used throughout the tractate with the meaning 'it is made susceptible to uncleanness' by virtue of the law of Lev. 11[38].

[3] And so fell indirectly upon foodstuffs lying below.   [4] Lev. 11[38].

[5] Some texts omit this sentence.

R. Simeon says: The law *If water be put on* does not apply to the liquid that is on his hand. But the Sages say: It does apply. If a man hid away his fruit in the water because of thieves, the law *If water be put on* does not apply. It once happened that the men of Jerusalem hid their fig-cakes in the water because of usurping owners;[1] and the Sages declared them not susceptible.[2] If a man floated his fruit on the stream of the river to bear it along with him, the law *If water be put on* does not apply.

2. 1. The drippings [of damp walls] in houses, cisterns, trenches, or caverns do not render food susceptible to uncleanness. A man's sweat does not render food susceptible to uncleanness. If he drank unclean water and sweated, his sweat is clean; but if he had been into drawn[3] water and sweated, his sweat is unclean; if he dried himself and afterwards sweated, his sweat is clean [and does not render food susceptible to uncleanness].[4]

2. If [the water of] a bath-house was unclean[5] the drippings [of the walls] are unclean; and if it was clean, the law *If water be put on* applies to the drippings thereof. If there was a pool within the house and the [walls of the house] dripped moisture by reason of it, and the pool was unclean,[6] the drippings of the whole house that are caused by the pool are unclean.

3. If there were two pools, the one clean and the other unclean, the drippings of the walls near to the unclean pool are unclean, and those near to the clean pool are clean; and those that are midway are unclean. If unclean iron[7] was smelted with clean iron, and the greater part was unclean iron, the whole is unclean; if the greater part was clean iron, the whole is clean; if they were equal, the whole is unclean. If in pots[8] wherein Israelites and gentiles have made water the greater part was from the clean persons, the whole is clean; if the greater part was from the unclean persons,[9] the whole is unclean; if they were equal, the whole is unclean. If rain had fallen into dirty water and the greater part was from the clean [water], the whole is clean; if the greater part was from the unclean [water] the whole is unclean; if they were equal, the whole is unclean. This applies only if the dirty water came first; but if the rain water, however great in quantity, came before the dirty water, it becomes unclean.

4. If a man was plastering his roof [with dirty water and clay] or washing his raiment, and rain came down [on the dirty water], if the greater part was from the unclean [water], the whole is unclean; if the greater part was from the clean, the whole is clean; if they were equal the whole is unclean. R. Judah says: If the rain continued falling [the whole is clean].

5. If both Israelites and gentiles dwelt in a city and in it was a bath-house which was open and heated for bathing on the Sabbath, if most [of the people in the city] were gentiles [an Israelite] may bathe there at once [after the close of the Sabbath]; but if most of them were Israelites, he must wait time enough for the water to be heated; if they were equal, he must wait time enough for the water to be heated. R. Judah says: If it was a small bath

---

[1] See Gitt. 5[6].
[2] Though the water was applied purposely it was 'not acceptable' for its own sake.
[3] p. 732, n. 5.
[4] Throughout the tractate the terms 'unclean' and 'clean' frequently convey the supplementary sense of 'render susceptible to uncleanness' and 'not render susceptible' respectively.   [5] i.e. whose water is 'drawn' (p. 732, n. 5).
[6] Full of drawn water.   [7] Cf. Kel. 11[4].
[8] The word is that rendered 'flawed earthenware vessel' in Kel. 4[3].
[9] See App. IV. 10 (cf. 3*a* ii).

and there was there some [gentile] of high estate, an Israelite may wash therein at once.[1]

6. If vegetables [gathered on the Sabbath] were sold in the city [at the close of the Sabbath] and most of the people were gentiles, an Israelite may buy them at once; if most of them were Israelites he must wait time enough for others to come [with vegetables gathered after the Sabbath] from a place near by; if they were equal he must wait time enough for others to come from a place near by. But if there was there some [gentile] of high estate, an Israelite may buy them at once.

7. If he found an abandoned child in the city and most of the people were gentiles, it may be deemed a gentile child; if most of them were Israelites, it may be deemed an Israelitish child; if they were equal, it may be deemed an Israelitish child. R. Judah says: It should be determined by which are more wont to abandon children.

8. If he found lost property in the city and most of the people were gentiles, he need not proclaim it; if most of them were Israelites he must proclaim it; if they were equal he must proclaim it. If he found any bread in the city, they determine [whether it is the bread of Israelites or gentiles] by which of them have the greater number of bakers; if the bread was made of pure flour, it is determined by which [of the two] are more wont to eat bread of pure flour. R. Judah says: [Only] if it was bread of coarse meal should it be determined by which [of the two] are more wont to eat bread of coarse meal.

9. If he found any flesh in the city, they determine [whether it is flesh belonging to Israelites or gentiles] by which of them have the greater number of butchers; if it was boiled flesh it is determined by which [of the two] are more wont to eat boiled flesh.

10. If he found produce by the wayside[2] and the greater number of the people were wont to store up their fruit in their houses,[3] he is not liable [to give Tithes from it]; but if [the greater number were wont to take it] to sell it in the market, he is liable [to give Tithes from it]; if they were equal, it must be accounted *demai*-produce.[4] If there was a store-house into which both Israelites and gentiles cast their produce, and most of them were gentiles, it must be deemed produce certainly untithed; if most of them were Israelites it must be deemed *demai*-produce; if they were equal it must be deemed produce certainly untithed. So R. Meir. But the Sages say: Even though all were gentiles and but one Israelite cast his produce therein the whole may be deemed *demai*-produce.

11. If fruit of the second year exceeded in quantity the fruit of the third year, or fruit of the third year the fruit of the fourth, or fruit of the fourth year the fruit of the fifth, or fruit of the fifth year the fruit of the sixth, or fruit of the sixth year the fruit of the seventh year, or fruit of the seventh year the fruit of the year after the seventh year, they determine [under what obligations[5] the fruit lies] by which [of the two] is the greater in

---

[1] The principle implied is that the Israelite may not bathe in water specially heated on the Sabbath for the benefit of Israelites.

[2] Between the field where it was harvested and the town to which it was being taken to be stored up.

[3] So that the produce was not fully harvested, and therefore not liable to tithes (see Maas. 1[5], end).

[4] p. 20, n. 9; App. I. 6.

[5] In the first, second, fourth, and fifth years the produce is subject to First Tithe and Second Tithe; in the third and sixth years it is subject to First Tithe and Poorman's Tithe.

quantity; if they were equal they must apply the more stringent of the rules [governing the two years].[1]

3. 1. If a sack that was full of produce was put on a river-bank or over the mouth of a cistern or on the ledge of a [pool in a] cavern, and it absorbed [any water], the law *If water be put on* applies to [any of the produce] that absorbed the water. R. Judah says: It applies to what is over against the water but not to what is not over against the water.[2]

2. If a jar[3] that was full of produce was put into liquid, or if a jar that was full of liquid was put into produce, and the produce absorbed [any of the liquid], the law *If water be put on* applies to any produce that has absorbed [the liquid]. These are the liquids of which they have spoken: water, wine, or vinegar; but with other of the liquids[4] that can render [dry foodstuffs] susceptible, the produce would remain insusceptible to uncleanness. R. Nehemiah declares pulse insusceptible, since pulse does not absorb moisture.

3. If a man took off hot bread[5] [from the oven's side] and put it over the mouth of a jar of wine, R. Meir declares it thereby susceptible to uncleanness, but R. Judah declares it insusceptible. R. Jose declares it insusceptible if it was wheaten bread but susceptible if it was barley bread, since barley absorbs moisture.

4. If a man besprinkled his house with water and put wheat therein, and the wheat grew damp, if it was by reason of the water, the law *If water be put on* applies to it; but if by reason of the rock-floor, it does not apply. If a man washed his clothes in a trough and afterward put wheat therein, and it became damp, if it was by reason of the water, the law *If water be put on* applies to it, but if it grew damp of itself, it does not apply. If wheat was made damp with sand, the law *If water be put on* applies. It once happened to the men of Machuz[6] who used to damp their grain with sand that the Sages said to them: If thus ye have been wont to do, never in your lives have ye prepared food in conditions of cleanness.

5. If grain was damped with dried clay, R. Simeon says: If there was still dripping moisture in it, the law *If water be put on* applies to it; but if there was not, it does not apply. If a man besprinkled his threshing-floor, he need not scruple lest wheat be put therein and it be made damp. If a man gathered grass to moisten wheat, and the dew was still on it, the law *If water be put on* does not apply; but if it was his purpose that the dew should moisten it, the law *If water be put on* does apply. If a man took his wheat to the miller and rain fell on it and he rejoiced thereat, the law *If water be put on* applies to it. R. Judah says: It is impossible that he should not rejoice; but, rather, the law applies only if he stood still.

6. If his olives were put out on the roof and rain fell on them and he rejoiced thereat, the law *If water be put on* applies. R. Judah says: It is

---

[1] e.g. if it is in doubt whether it should come under the Seventh-Year produce restrictions, it is liable to 'removal' (i.e. it must be forthwith consumed or destroyed if that same produce is no longer growing in the fields; Shebi. 9[2]), and also to tithes (from which Seventh Year produce is exempt); and in the years when it is in doubt whether the produce is liable to Second Tithe or Poorman's Tithe, the tithe must be given to the poor, and the value of it must also be consumed by the owner in Jerusalem in the conditions required for Second Tithe (see p. 73, n. 6).

[2] The water is 'acceptable' as a means of freshening the produce.

[3] Of earthenware, which absorbs moisture through its sides, and from which the liquid slowly percolates.   [4] See below, 6[4]. These others are less easily absorbed.

[5] Cf. Ter. 10[3].   [6] See Arak. 3[2].

impossible that he should not rejoice; but, rather, the law applies only if he stopped up the water-spout or soaked the olives in the rain.

7. If ass-drivers were crossing a river and their sacks fell into the water and they rejoiced thereat, the law *If water be put on* applies. R. Judah says: It is impossible that they should not rejoice; but, rather, it applies only if the sacks were turned over. If a man's feet were covered with mud (so, too, the feet of his beast) and he crossed through a river, and rejoiced thereat, the law *If water be put on* applies. R. Judah says: It is impossible that he should not rejoice; but, rather, it applies only if he stood still and rinsed them. But in the case of the man or an unclean beast, the water always makes them susceptible to uncleanness.

8. If a man took wagon-wheels and cattle-yokes down to the water at the time of the east wind[1] for the cracks to swell out, the law *If water be put on* applies. If he took down his beast to drink, the law *If water be put on* applies to the water that comes up on its mouth, but not to the water on its legs; yet if his purpose was that its legs should be rinsed, the law *If water be put on* applies also to the water on its legs; and in times of footsoreness or threshing, [the water on its legs] always renders them susceptible to uncleanness. If a deaf-mute, an imbecile, or a minor led down the beast, even if its owner's purpose was that its feet should be rinsed, the law *If water be put on* does not apply, because with them only the act is of consequence, while the intention is of no consequence.[2]

4. 1. If a man stooped down to drink [from a river] the law *If water be put on* applies to the water that comes up to his mouth or on his moustache, but not to what comes up in his nose or on his head or his beard. If a man drew water [from a well] in a jar, the law *If water be put on* applies to the water that is brought up on its outside and on the rope wound round its neck and on the [part of the] rope needful in handling it. How much is needful in handling it?[3] R. Simeon b. Eleazar says: One handbreadth. If it was put beneath a water-spout, the law *If water be put on* does not apply [to the water on its outside and on the rope].

2. If rain fell on a man, even though he was a Father of Uncleanness,[4] the law *If water be put on* does not apply.[5] But if he shook off [the rain] the law *If water be put on* applies. If he stood beneath a water-spout to cool himself or to rinse himself and he was unclean, the water becomes unclean;[6] even if he was clean, the law *If water be put on* applies.

3. If a man put a dish on end against a wall that it might be rinsed, the law *If water be put on* applies; but if that the wall might not suffer hurt, it does not apply.

4. If water leaking from the roof dripped into a jar,[7] the School of Shammai say: It must be broken.[8] And the School of Hillel say: It may be emptied out. But they agree that a man may put forth his hand inside and take out produce, and that this is not susceptible to uncleanness.

---

[1] The very hot, dry wind common in Palestine in May and October.
[2] Cf. Kel. 17[15]; Toh. 8[6]; Maksh. 6[1].
[3] Cf. Kel. 14[3].   [4] See p. 604, n. 2.   According to the rule in 1[1], unclean liquids render susceptible whether their presence is acceptable or not.
[5] To foodstuffs on which the drops fell, since the rain, in the first place, was not acceptable to him.   [6] Besides rendering susceptible foodstuffs on which it falls.
[7] Filled with produce, and the lesser part of the produce was made wet.
[8] And not emptied out in the ordinary way; since if the produce was emptied out all the produce would be rendered susceptible by contact with the water.

5. If water leaking from the roof dripped into a trough, the law *If water be put on* does not apply to the water that splashed out or overflowed.[1] If the trough was taken away to pour out [the water elsewhere], the School of Shammai say: The law *If water be put on* applies to it.[2] And the School of Hillel say: It does not apply. If it had been so set that the water leaking from the roof should fall into it, the School of Shammai say: The law *If water be put on* applies to what splashes out or overflows. And the School of Hillel say: It does not apply. But they agree that if it was taken away to pour out [the water elsewhere], the law *If water be put on* applies to it.[3] If a man immersed vessels or washed his raiment in a [pool in a] cavern, the law *If water be put on* applies to the water that comes up on his hands, but not to what comes up on his legs. R. Eliezer says: If it was impossible for him to go down without his feet becoming muddy, the law *If water be put on* applies also to the water that comes up on his feet.

6. If a basket full of lupines was put in an Immersion-pool, a man [that is unclean] may put out his hand and take lupines therefrom and they will remain clean;[4] but if he raised them[5] out of the water, those that touch the basket are unclean, but all the other lupines remain clean.[6] A menstruant may rinse a radish in [a pool in] a cavern and it remains clean, but if she lifted it at all out of the water it becomes unclean.

7. If produce had fallen into a channel of water, and one whose hands were unclean put out [his hands] and took it, his hands become clean and the produce remains clean; if his purpose was that his hands should be rinsed, his hands become clean, but the law *If water be put on* applies to the produce.

8. If a pot full of water was put in an Immersion-pool and a Father of Uncleanness thrust his hand into the jar, it becomes unclean; but if he was unclean only from contact with uncleanness,[7] it remains clean,[8] but any other liquids [than water] become unclean, since water cannot render other liquids clean.

9. If a man had drawn water from a swape-well [and produce fell into the water in the bucket] it is susceptible to uncleanness during three days. R. Akiba says: If [the bucket] had been dried, the produce is forthwith deemed insusceptible to uncleanness, but if it was not dried, it remains susceptible even for thirty days.

10. If [unclean] liquid fell on pieces of wood, and rain fell on them, and the rain was more [than the unclean liquid], they become clean; but if they had been taken outside so that rain should fall on them, even if the rain was more [than the unclean liquid] they remain unclean;[9] if they had absorbed the unclean liquid, even if they were taken out so that rain should fall on them, they become clean;[10] but they may not be set alight

---

1 Nor to what is in the trough, since the trough was not put there to catch the water.
2 Until it is brought to the place where it is to be poured out; the presumption is that until it is poured away its presence is acceptable.
3 Since the water's presence in the trough was from the first acceptable.
4 Since water in a pool (i.e. water still connected with the ground) does not render susceptible.   5 In their basket.
6 The basket suffers first-grade uncleanness, the lupines that touch it suffer second-grade uncleanness; and the uncleanness cannot be further transferred in the case of common food (p. 714, n. 3).
7 i.e. he suffered first grade uncleanness.
8 Since a vessel can contract uncleanness only from a Father of Uncleanness.
9 The raindrops themselves become unclean since it was intended that they should fall on the uncleanness.   10 Since the two liquids did not come into contact.

[to heat the oven] save only with clean hands.[1] R. Simeon says: If they were still wet and were set alight, and more liquid came out of them than the [unclean] liquid which they had absorbed, then they are clean.

5. 1. If a man immersed himself in a river[2] and before him was another river and he passed through it, the second water[3] makes the first water clean. If by reason of his drunkenness another had pushed him in [a second time][4] (so, too, if he had pushed in his beast), the second water makes the first water clean; but if he had done so in play, the law *If water be put on* applies.

2. If a man was swimming in the water, the law *If water be put on* does not apply to water that is splashed;[5] but if it was his purpose to splash his fellow, the law *If water be put on* applies. If he made 'a bird'[6] in the water, the law *If water be put on* does not apply to what is splashed[7] and what is left therein.

3. If water leaking from a roof fell among fruits, and they were mixed up together to dry them, R. Simeon says: The law *If water be put on* applies. But the Sages say: It does not apply.

4. If a man measured a cistern, the law *If water be put on* applies [to the water that comes up on the measuring rod] whether he measured the depth thereof or the breadth thereof. So R. Tarfon. R. Akiba says: It applies to [the water that comes up when he measures] the depth thereof, but not [when he measures] the breadth thereof.

5. If he thrust his hand or his foot or a reed into a cistern to find out whether there was water in it, the law *If water be put on* does not apply to the water [that comes up]; but if it was to find out how much water there was in it, the law *If water be put on* applies. If he threw a stone into the cistern to find out whether there was water in it, the law *If water be put on* does not apply to the water that is splashed; and the water that is on the stone is clean.[8]

6. If a man beat upon a [wetted] pelt beyond the wetness,[9] the law *If water be put on* applies; but if amid the wetness it does not apply. R. Jose says: Even if he beat it amid the wetness the law *If water be put on* applies, since his purpose was that it should flow off together with the offscourings.

7. To water that comes up on a ship's hull or in its bilge or on its oars, the law *If water be put on* does not apply. The law *If water be put on* does not apply to water in snares, gins, or nets; but it applies [to water that comes out of them] if they are shaken. If a man took out a ship into the Great Sea to tighten [the seams], or took out a nail into the rain to temper it, or left a burning brand out in the rain to quench it, the law *If water be put on* applies.

8. To [any water that falls on] the covering that is stretched over tables [whereon food is laid], or on the matting that is stretched over bricks, the law *If water be put on* does not apply; but if they were shaken it does apply.

9. Any unbroken stream of liquid [that is poured from a clean to an

---

[1] Unclean hands would render the clean liquid unclean (with first-grade uncleanness) and so render his food in the oven unclean.

[2] The water on him (cf. above, 4²) renders susceptible what it falls upon, since its presence was acceptable.   [3] Which was not acceptable.

[4] Into a pool in which he had intentionally immersed himself.   [5] Accidentally.

[6] Explained as a device for making bubbles. Variant: 'squirt', 'water-spout'.

[7] Accidentally.   [8] i.e. is not such as to be susceptible to uncleanness.

[9] As a means of drying it.

unclean vessel] remains clean, save only a stream of thick honey or batter.[1] The School of Shammai say: Also one of porridge made from grits or beans, since [at the end of its flow] it shrinks backwards.[2]

10. If hot water was emptied out into hot water [from a clean into an unclean vessel], or cold into cold, or hot into cold, [the liquid stream] remains clean; but if cold [water was emptied out] into hot, the stream becomes unclean.[3] R. Simeon says: Moreover if hot water was emptied out into hot, and the heat of the lower water was more than the heat of the upper, the stream becomes unclean.

11. If a woman whose hands were clean stirred up a cooking-pot that was unclean, and her hands sweated [by reason of the steam], they become unclean. If her hands were unclean and she stirred up a cooking-pot[4] and her hands sweated, the pot becomes unclean. R. Jose says: [Only] if they dripped [does the pot become unclean]. If grapes were weighed in the cup of a balance, the wine [that remains] in the cup does not make anything susceptible unless it is emptied out into a vessel.[5] In this it is like to a basket of olives or grapes when moisture drips from them.

6. 1. If a man took his produce up to the roof to keep it free from maggots and dew fell upon it, the law *If water be put on* does not apply; but if such had been his purpose, the law *If water be put on* does apply. If a deaf-mute, an imbecile, or a minor took it up, even if his purpose was that the dew should fall upon it, the law *If water be put on* does not apply, because with them only the act is of consequence, while the intention is of no consequence.[6]

2. If a man took up to the roof bundles of vegetables or blocks of figs or garlic to keep them fresh, the law *If water be put on* does not apply [if dew fell upon them]. All bundles of vegetables in the market places are unclean.[7] R. Judah declares them clean if they were fresh. R. Meir said: Then why have they declared them unclean?—only because of liquid from the mouth.[8] All kinds of meal and flour in the market places are unclean. Pounded wheat, groats, and grits are everywhere unclean.[9]

3. All eggs can be presumed clean excepting those that belong to sellers of liquids; but if they sold dry produce also they are clean. All fish can be presumed unclean. R. Judah says: Pieces of Iltith fish, Egyptian fish that is brought packed in baskets, and Spanish tunny fish, can be presumed clean. All manner of brine can be presumed to be unclean. And concerning any of them an *Am-haaretz*[10] may be believed if he says that they are clean,[11] excepting the brine of fish, since such is left in the care of any *Am-haaretz*. R. Eliezer b. Jacob says: If any water at all fell into brine that had been made clean, it becomes susceptible to uncleanness.

4. There are seven liquids [to which applies the law *If water be put on*]:

---

[1] Maim. renders 'honey from Zifin or Tsappahath'. Cf. Sot. 9[12].
[2] A thick, glutinous tongue of it has such elasticity that after touching the lower vessel it can spring back to the upper vessel.
[3] Since the cold water causes steam to rise from the lower, unclean, hot liquid, and this steam mixes with the unbroken liquid stream, so communicating the uncleanness to the upper vessel. [4] Some texts add: 'that was clean'.
[5] Only then is it regarded as a liquid in its own right.
[6] See above, 3[8]. [7] They have been purposely wetted to keep them fresh, and have contracted uncleanness by handling. [8] The bundles were untied with the teeth.
[9] Because they have been moistened in their preparation. These three varieties are explained as grain split into two, three, and four parts, respectively. [10] App. I. 3.
[11] i.e. have not been rendered susceptible.

dew, water, wine, oil, blood, milk, and bees' honey. Hornets' honey does not render anything susceptible, and it is permitted to be eaten.

5. Under water is included any liquid that comes forth from the eye, ear, nose, or mouth; liquid excrement and urine,[1] whether it issues intentionally or unintentionally. Under blood is included blood that flows in the slaughtering of clean beasts, wild animals, or birds, blood let out from the veins to be given as a drink. Water that comes from milk counts as milk, and the sap of olives counts as oil, since it has never departed out of the category of oil. So R. Simeon. R. Meir says: Even if there is no oil in it. The blood of a creeping thing is like to its flesh: it conveys uncleanness but, [as a liquid], it does not render anything susceptible to uncleanness; and there is naught that is like to it.[2]

6. These alike convey uncleanness and render susceptible to uncleanness: the issue of one that has a flux and his spittle, semen and urine; a quarter-*log* [of blood] from a corpse, and the blood of a menstruant. R. Eliezer says: Semen does not render anything susceptible. R. Eleazar b. Azariah says: Nor the blood of a menstruant. R. Simeon says: The blood of a corpse does not render anything susceptible; and if it fell on a gourd, this may be scraped and is forthwith clean.

7. These neither convey uncleanness nor render anything susceptible to uncleanness: sweat, foul secretion, excrement, the blood that comes forth with them, any liquid pertaining to an eight months' abortion (R. Jose says: Excepting its blood); [the excrement of him] that drinks the water of Tiberias though it comes forth clean, the blood of unclean beasts, wild animals, and birds, and the blood that is let for healing. R. Eliezer declares these unclean. R. Simeon b. Eleazar says: The milk of a male is clean.

8. A woman's milk[3] renders anything susceptible to uncleanness whether it is drawn purposely or not purposely. The milk of cattle renders anything susceptible to uncleanness only if it is drawn purposely. R. Akiba said: It is an argument from the less to the greater: If a woman's milk (which is intended for children alone) renders anything susceptible to uncleanness whether it is drawn purposely or not purposely, how much more must the milk of cattle (which is intended both for children and for them that are fully grown) render anything susceptible to uncleanness whether it is drawn purposely or not purposely! [The Sages] said to him, No!—if the milk that is not drawn purposely is unclean in the case of a woman (of whom the blood from a wound is unclean), [wouldest thou argue that] the milk that is not drawn purposely is unclean in the case of cattle (of which the blood from a wound is clean)! He said to them, I would apply to milk a more stringent ruling than to blood; for if milk is drawn for healing it is unclean; but blood that is let for healing is clean. They answered, Let baskets of olives or grapes afford proof: for the liquid that is drawn from them purposely is susceptible to uncleanness, but what is not drawn purposely is not susceptible to uncleanness. He said to them, No!—as ye argue of baskets of olives or grapes (whose first state is [solid] food and their last state a liquid), would ye likewise argue of milk (whose first state and last state are both a liquid)? Thus far is the answer. R. Simeon said: From this

---

1 So Bert. Others render more literally: Urine, whether of grown men or children.
2 Where blood and flesh alike render unclean and in like bulk. Cf. Meil. 4³.
3 Cf. Kel. 8¹¹.

point we used to make answer before him, Let rain afford the proof: both in its first state and in its last state it is a liquid, but it only renders anything susceptible to uncleanness if it is used purposely. He said to us, No!—as ye argue of rain, of which the greater part is intended not for man but for the ground and the trees, [would ye likewise argue of milk] when the greater part of milk is intended for man!

ZABIM[1] ('THEY THAT SUFFER A FLUX')

1. 1. If a man has suffered one issue of flux the School of Shammai say: He is like to the woman that awaits day against day.[2] And the School of Hillel say: Like to one that has suffered a pollution.[3] If he suffered one issue and on the second day it ceased, and on the third day he suffered two issues, or one as profuse as if it were two, the School of Shammai say: He is wholly a Zab. And the School of Hillel say: He conveys uncleanness to what he lies upon or sits upon, and he must bathe in running water,[4] but he is exempt from the offering.[5] R. Eleazar b. Judah said: The School of Shammai agreed that such a one was not wholly a Zab; and about what did they dispute?—about him that suffered two issues, or one as profuse as two, but suffered none on the second day, and on the third day again suffered an issue; [of such a one] the School of Shammai say: He is wholly a Zab. And the School of Hillel say: He conveys uncleanness to what he lies upon or sits upon, and he must bathe in running water, but he is exempt from the offering.

2. If he suffered an issue of semen on his third day of reckoning after his flux, the School of Shammai say: It makes void[6] the two clean days that went before. And the School of Hillel say: It makes void that day only.[7] R. Ishmael says: If he suffered it on the second day it makes void the [clean] day that went before. R. Akiba says: It is all one whether he suffered it on the second or on the third day. For the School of Shammai used to say: It has made void the two days that went before. And the School of Hillel used to say: It has made void that day only. But they agree that if he suffered it on the fourth day it makes void that day only if it was an issue of semen; but if he suffered a flux, even on the seventh day, it makes void [all] the days that went before.

3. If he suffered one [issue of flux] on one day and two on the morrow, or two on the one day and one on the morrow, or three in three days or in three nights, he is wholly a Zab.

4. If he suffered one issue and it then ceased time enough for him to immerse himself and dry himself, and he then suffered two issues, or one as profuse as two; or if he suffered two issues or one as profuse as two, and it then ceased time enough for him to immerse himself and dry himself, and he again suffered an issue, he is wholly a Zab.

[1] The subject is that of Lev. 15[1-15] ('when any man hath an issue out of his flesh') and 15[25-30] ('if a woman have an issue of her blood any days not in the time of her impurity'). Such a man is called a Zab, and the woman a Zabah. For the nature and intensity of their uncleanness, and the means by which it can be conveyed to others, see App. I. 26, and App. IV. 1 a i, ii; 2 i, ii; 3 a, b; 17 b; 18 b; 20; 21. To be subject to the laws affecting the Zab there must have been three issues on one day or on consecutive days. After the issues have ceased he must wait until seven 'clean days' have passed, when he must wash his clothes and immerse himself in 'living' (running) water. On the eighth day he must bring two turtle doves or two young pigeons, which the priest shall offer, the one for a Sin-offering and the other for a Whole-offering.   [2] See Pes. 8[5]; Meg. 2[4]; Hor. 1[3]; Nidd. 4[7].
[3] Lev. 15[16ff].   [4] Lev. 15[13].   [5] Lev. 15[14f].
[6] He must wait still another seven days.   [7] He need wait but five days more.

5. If he suffered an issue as profuse as three, continuing time enough [for a man to go] from Gad-Yavan[1] to Siloam[2] (which is time enough for two immersions and two dryings), he is wholly a Zab. If he suffered an issue as profuse as two, he conveys uncleanness to what he lies upon or sits upon, and he must bathe in running water, but he is exempt from the offering. R. Jose said: They have not spoken of one issue that was profuse unless it was enough to make up three.

6. If he suffered an issue on the one day and one at twilight, or one at twilight and one on the morrow, and it was known that part of the issue [at twilight] was on the one day and part on the morrow, his condition is certain as touching uncleanness and he is liable to the offering; but if it is in doubt whether part of the issue was on the one day and part on the morrow, then his condition is certain as touching uncleanness, but in doubt as touching the offering. If he suffered issues on two days at twilight, his condition is in doubt as touching uncleanness and the offering; if one at twilight, his condition is in doubt as touching uncleanness.

2. 1. All are susceptible to uncleanness by reason of a flux, even proselytes, even slaves, whether freedmen or not, a deaf-mute, an imbecile or a minor, a eunuch of man's making or a eunuch by nature.[3] To one that is of doubtful sex or of double sex the stringencies that bear in the case of a man and the stringencies that bear in the case of a woman both apply: they convey uncleanness through blood like a woman, and through semen like a man; but their uncleanness remains in doubt.

2. Along seven lines[4] do they examine a Zab if he has not already come within the bonds of uncleanness[5] as a Zab: concerning what he had eaten, what he had drunk, what he had carried, whether he had jumped, whether he had been sick, what he had seen, or whether he had had impure thoughts: whether he had had impure thoughts before he saw [a woman] or saw [the woman] before he had had impure thoughts. R. Judah says: Even whether he had seen beasts, wild animals, or birds engaged with each other, even whether he had seen a woman's coloured garments. R. Akiba says: Even whether he had eaten any food, good or bad, or had drunk any liquid. They said to him, If so there would henceforward be no Zabs. He said to them, Ye are not answerable for them that must be deemed Zabs. After he has already come within the bonds of uncleanness as a Zab they do not examine him; for any flux that he suffers from inadvertence, or a flux that is in doubt, or a discharge of semen, these are accounted unclean, since there is whereon to rely. If he suffered a first issue, they must examine him; if he suffered a second, they must examine him; but if he suffered a third issue they need not examine him. R. Eliezer says: Even if he suffered a third issue they must examine him to determine whether he is liable to the offering.

3. If he suffered an issue of semen[6] he does not convey uncleanness as if it was a flux, nor for twenty-four hours. R. Jose says: For that day alone. If a gentile suffered an issue of semen and became a proselyte, he forthwith conveys uncleanness as if it was a flux. If a woman suffered a flow of blood,[7]

---

[1] Lit. 'Gad (the god of fortune; cf. Is. 65[11]) of the Greeks'.　　[2] Sukk. 4[9, 10]; Par. 3[2].
[3] See Yeb. 8[4].　　　　　　　[4] Naz. 9[4].
[5] i.e. if he had not yet suffered the three issues which render him 'wholly a Zab'.
[6] See Lev. 15[16].　　　　　　　[7] Nidd. 1[1].

or was in hard travail,[1] [the time prescribed[2] is] twenty-four hours. If a man strikes his servant, the *day or two*[3] is twenty-four hours. If a dog ate the flesh of a corpse, it continues in its natural state during three days, each of twenty-four hours.[4]

4. By five means the Zab conveys uncleanness to what he lies upon, so that it conveys uncleanness to men and to garments: by standing, sitting, lying, hanging, or leaning. By seven means what he lies upon conveys uncleanness to a man so that he conveys uncleanness to garments: if he stands, sits, lies, hangs, or leans upon it, or touches or carries it.

3. 1. If a Zab and one that was clean sat together in a boat or on a raft or rode on a beast, even if their garments do not touch, [he that was clean and his garments] suffer *midras*-uncleanness.[5] If they sat on a plank, or bench, or bed-frame, or beam, when these were not secured tightly, or if they mounted a tree that was infirm, or an infirm branch in a firm tree, or an Egyptian ladder[6] when it was not secured with a nail, or a bridge, rafter, or door, when they were not held firm with clay, [he that was clean and his garments] become unclean. R. Judah declares them clean.

2. If they were both closing or opening a door, the Sages say: [The uncleanness is not conveyed] unless the one was shutting and the other opening it.[7] If the one lifted the other out of the cistern, R. Judah says: [The uncleanness is not conveyed] unless he that is clean lifted out him that was unclean. If they were twisting ropes together, the Sages say: [The uncleanness is not conveyed] unless the one pulled one way and the other pulled the other. If they were weaving together, whether standing or sitting, or grinding wheat together, in every case R. Simeon declares clean [him that was before clean], save only when they were grinding with a handmill. If they were unloading an ass or loading it, and the load was heavy, [they that were clean become] unclean, but if it was light [they remain] clean. But in every like case they are clean for [ordinary] members of the congregation, and unclean only for [them that eat of] Heave-offering.

3. If a Zab and one that was clean sat together in a large boat (What is a large boat? R. Judah says: Any that cannot be made to rock with [the weight of] a man), or if they sat on a plank, or a bench, or a bed-frame, or a beam, when these were secured tightly; or if they mounted a tree that was firm, or a branch that was firm, or a Tyrian ladder,[8] or an Egyptian [ladder] when it was secured with a nail, or a bridge, rafter, or door, when they were held firm with clay, if only at one end, [he that was clean and his garments] remain clean. If one that was clean struck one that was unclean he remains clean; but if one that was unclean struck one that was clean, [he that was clean] becomes unclean, since if he that was clean drew back, he that was unclean [and that struck him] would fall.[9]

4. 1. R. Joshua says: If a menstruant sat on a bed together with one that was clean, the cap on the head of her [that was clean] suffers *midras*-

---

[1] When, outside the period of menstruation, an issue of blood is not deemed unclean.
[2] During which, in the former case, the blood is not deemed unclean as a flux; and, in the latter case, she must be deemed to have been unclean as a menstruant.
[3] Ex. 21[21].   [4] See Ohol. 11[7].
[5] See App. I. 26. The clean person, by his weight, causes the boat, raft, or beast to sink to one side and rise at the other; thereby the Zab is, indirectly, lifted up or suspended by him.   [6] B.B. 3[6].
[7] In such a way that the clean person bore the weight of the Zab.   [8] B.B. 3[6].
[9] It is virtually as though the Zab leaned against him.

uncleanness. If she sat in a boat, the vessels on the top of the mast of the boat suffer *midras*-uncleanness. If she took a trough full of clothes and their weight was heavy, they become unclean, but if their weight was light they remain clean. If a Zab knocked against a balcony so that a loaf of Heave-offering fell off, it remains clean.[1]

2. If he knocked against a king-beam, rafter-frame, water-spout or fixed shelf, even though it was secured only with ropes; or against an oven or a flour-mill's container or lower mill-stone or the jack of a hand-mill or an olive-grinder's *seah*-measure (R. Jose says: Also the bath-keeper's beam), [so that a loaf of Heave-offering fell off], it remains clean.

3. If he knocked against a door, door-pin, lock, rudder, or mill-frame, or against a tree that was infirm, or an infirm branch on a firm tree, or against an Egyptian ladder when it is not secured with a nail, against a bridge, beam, or door when they are not held firm with clay—these become unclean.[2] If [he knocked] against a chest, a box, or a cupboard, they become unclean, but R. Nehemiah and R. Simeon declare them clean.

4. If a Zab lay down on five benches or five bags, and he lay along their length, they become unclean;[3] but if along their breadth they remain clean. If he slept [on them along their breadth] and it is in doubt whether he turned himself [along their length] they are deemed unclean. If he lay on six seats, with his two hands on two, his two feet on two, his head on one, and his body on one, that only which is beneath his body becomes unclean. If he stood on two seats, R. Simeon says: If they were far apart they remain clean.

5. If there were ten cloaks one above another and he sat[4] on the uppermost, they all become unclean. If a Zab sat in one cup of a scale-beam and at the opposite end were places to lie upon or sit upon, if the Zab went down they remain clean,[5] but if they went down they become unclean. R. Simeon says: If there was but one [place to lie upon or sit upon at the opposite end] and that end went down, it becomes unclean; but if there were many they remain clean, since no one of them bears [the weight of] the greater part of the Zab.

6. If a Zab sat in one cup of a balance and there were foodstuffs and liquids in the other cup, they become unclean; but if it had been a corpse, anything [in the other cup] would remain clean excepting a man. Herein greater stringency applies to a Zab than to a corpse. But greater stringency may apply to a corpse than to a Zab,[6] since the Zab conveys uncleanness, by lying or sitting, to whatsoever is beneath him so that these convey uncleanness both to men and to garments, and [he also conveys] *maddaf*-uncleanness to what lies above him, so that these convey uncleanness to foodstuffs and liquids—uncleanness which a corpse does not convey. But greater stringency may apply to a corpse, since the corpse conveys unclean-ness by overshadowing and it also conveys seven-day uncleanness—uncleanness which the Zab does not convey.

7. If he sat on a bed, and there were four cloaks under the four legs of the bed, they become unclean, since the bed cannot stand on three legs.

---

[1] It was not moved by the direct application of pressure from the Zab.
[2] Being infirm they suffered the full weight of the Zab.
[3] Since the greater part of each will suffer the Zab's weight.
[4] Variant: 'slept'.   [5] From *midras*-uncleanness, since they do not sustain the Zab's pressure; but they suffer '*maddaf*-uncleanness' (App. I. 21) since they are borne above the Zab though without direct contact.
[6] Variant: 'and yet again greater stringency may apply to a Zab than to a corpse'.

But R. Simeon pronounces them clean. If he rode on a beast and there were four cloaks under the four legs of the beast, they remain clean, since the beast can stand on three legs. If there was one cloak under its two fore-legs or its two hindlegs, or under a foreleg and a hindleg, it becomes unclean. R. Jose says: A horse conveys uncleanness through its hindlegs and an ass through its forelegs, since a horse leans upon its hindlegs and an ass upon its forelegs. If the Zab sat on the beam of an olive-press, the vessels in the olive-truss[1] become unclean; but if [he sat] on a washerman's press, the garments beneath it remain clean.[2] R. Nehemiah declares them unclean.

5. 1. If a man touched a Zab or if a Zab touched him, if a man shifted a Zab or if a Zab shifted him, he conveys uncleanness by contact, but not by carrying, to foodstuffs and liquids and vessels that can be made clean by immersing.[3] R. Joshua laid down a general rule: All they that convey uncleanness to garments while they have contact with them, convey first-grade uncleanness to foodstuffs and liquids,[4] and second-grade uncleanness to the hands, but they do not convey uncleanness to a man or to an earthen-ware vessel; after they are severed from what had rendered them unclean they convey first-grade uncleanness to liquids, and second-grade unclean-ness to foodstuffs and to the hands, but they do not convey uncleanness to garments.

2. They also laid down another general rule: All that is borne above a Zab becomes unclean, and all above which a Zab is borne remains clean (save only what is fitted for lying upon and sitting upon, or a man). Thus if a Zab's finger was beneath a course of stones and one that was clean sat above, he conveys uncleanness at a first remove and at a second remove and renders [Heave-offering] invalid at a third remove;[5] if he was severed [from the uncleanness] he still conveys uncleanness at a first remove and renders [Heave-offering] invalid at a second remove.[6] If he that was unclean was above and he that was clean was below, he conveys unclean-ness at a first remove and at a second remove and renders [Heave-offering] invalid at a third remove; if he was severed [from the uncleanness] he still conveys uncleanness at a first remove and renders [Heave-offering] invalid at a second remove. If foodstuffs or liquids or a place fitted for lying or sitting upon or other articles were above [the course of stones and the Zab's finger was below], they convey uncleanness at a first remove and at a second remove and render [Heave-offering] invalid at a third remove; if they were severed [from the uncleanness] they still convey uncleanness at a first remove and render [Heave-offering] invalid at a second remove. If a place fitted for lying or sitting upon was below [and the Zab's finger was above], they convey uncleanness at a first remove and at a second remove and render [Heave-offering] invalid at a third remove; if they were severed [from the uncleanness] they still convey uncleanness at a first remove and at a second remove and render [Heave-offering] invalid at a third remove. If foodstuffs and liquids or other articles were below [and the Zab's finger was above the course of stones] they remain clean.

3. Because they have said: Whatsoever bears or is borne upon aught

---

[1] See p. 68, n. 1.   [2] As not enduring the Zab's full weight.
[3] Vessels of wood or metal; vessels of earthenware are excluded.   [4] See p. 714, n. 3.
[5] i.e. he becomes a Father of Uncleanness.
[6] He still suffers 'first-grade uncleanness'.

fitted for lying upon, remains clean, excepting a man; whatsoever bears or is borne upon carrion, remains clean, excepting him that shifts it (R. Eliezer says: He too that bears it); whatsoever bears or is borne upon a corpse, remains clean, excepting what overshadows it, or a man when he shifts it.

4. If part of one that is unclean rests upon one that is clean, or part of one that is clean rests upon one that is unclean; or if connectives[1] of one that is unclean rest upon one that is clean, or connectives of one that is clean rest upon one that is unclean, then [the clean becomes] unclean. R. Simeon says: If part of one that is unclean rests upon one that is clean, he becomes unclean; but if part of one that is clean rests upon one that is unclean, he remains clean.

5. If [the greater part of] one that is unclean rests upon part of what is fit for lying upon, or if [the greater part of] one that is clean rests upon part of what is fit for lying upon [and it was unclean], [what was clean] becomes unclean. If part of one that is unclean rests upon what is fit for lying upon, [what is clean] remains clean. Thus uncleanness may be induced or conveyed by the lesser part [of what is fit for lying upon]. So, too, if a loaf of Heave-offering was put on what was fit for lying upon, with paper between, whether [the uncleanness] was above or below, it remains clean. So, too, if it was a stone afflicted with leprosy, the loaf remains clean. The like of this R. Simeon declares unclean.

6. If a man touched a man or a woman that had a flux, or a menstruant or a woman after childbirth, or a leper, or aught that these had lain upon or sat upon, he conveys uncleanness at a first remove and at a second remove and renders [Heave-offering] invalid at a third remove. It is all one whether he touched, shifted, lifted, or was lifted.

7. If a man touched the flux, spittle, semen, or urine of one that has a flux, or the blood of a menstruant, he conveys uncleanness at a first remove and at a second remove and renders [Heave-offering] invalid at a third remove. If he was severed [from the uncleanness] he still conveys uncleanness at a first remove and renders [Heave-offering] invalid at a second remove. It is all one whether he touched or shifted it. R. Eliezer says: Or even if he lifted it.

8. If he carried what was ridden upon or if he was carried thereon, or if he shifted it, he conveys uncleanness at a first remove and at a second remove and renders [Heave-offering] invalid at a third remove; if he was severed [from the uncleanness] he still conveys uncleanness at a first remove and renders [Heave-offering] invalid at a second remove. If he carried carrion or Sin-offering water enough for a sprinkling,[2] he conveys uncleanness at a first remove and at a second remove and renders [Heave-offering] invalid at a third remove. If he was severed [from the uncleanness] he still conveys uncleanness at a first remove and renders [Heave-offering] invalid at a second remove.

9. If a man ate of carrion of a clean bird and it is still in his gullet,[3] he conveys uncleanness at a first remove and at a second remove and renders [Heave-offering] invalid at a third remove. If he put his head within the airspace of an oven, (he conveys no uncleanness and)[4] the oven remains clean. If he vomited it forth or swallowed it, he conveys uncleanness at a first remove and renders [Heave-offering] invalid at a second

---

[1] Hair, nails, or teeth. Cf. Ohol. 3³.
[3] See p. 714, n. 7.
[2] App. IV. 15 b.
[4] Some texts omit.

remove; but while it is in his mouth and until he has swallowed it he remains clean.

10. If a man touched a [dead] creeping thing or semen or one that suffered corpse uncleanness or a leper during his days of reckoning,[1] or Sin-offering water not enough for a sprinkling, or carrion, or what was fit to be ridden upon, he conveys uncleanness at a first remove and renders [Heave-offering] invalid at a second remove. This is the general rule: Whosoever touches any Father of Uncleanness spoken of in the Law[2] conveys uncleanness at a first remove and renders [Heave-offering] invalid at a second remove, excepting [the corpse of] a man.[3] If he severed himself from the uncleanness he conveys uncleanness at a first remove and renders [Heave-offering] invalid at a second remove.

11. He that has suffered a pollution is like to one that has touched a creeping thing, and he that has connexion with a menstruant is like to one that suffers corpse uncleanness; howbeit it is more grave for him that has connexion with a menstruant in that he conveys a lesser uncleanness to what he lies upon or sits upon so that this renders foods and liquids unclean.

12. These render Heave-offering invalid:[4] he that eats food suffering first-grade uncleanness, and he that eats food suffering second-grade uncleanness, and he that drinks liquids that are unclean, and he that immerses his head and the greater part of him in drawn water, and a clean person upon whose head and the greater part of him there fell three *logs* of drawn water, and a scroll [of Scripture],[5] and the hands, and one that had immersed himself the selfsame day [because of uncleanness], and foods and vessels that have been rendered unclean by liquids.

TEBUL YOM[6] ('HE THAT IMMERSED HIMSELF THAT DAY')

1. 1. If a man[7] brought together many Dough-offerings[8] with the intention of separating them again, but they stuck together, the School of Shammai say: They serve as a connective [to convey uncleanness from the one to the other] if they are touched by one that had immersed himself the selfsame day. And the School of Hillel say: They do not serve as a connective. If pieces of dough [that were Heave-offering] were stuck together or if loaves [of Heave-offering] were stuck together, or if a cake [of Heave-offering] was put to bake on top of another cake but they had not yet formed a crust in the oven, or if there was a blown-up skin of froth on water, or the first scum to rise in boiling bean-grits, or scum of new wine (R. Judah says:

[1] Lev. 14[8].
[2] See App. IV. 1–12.   [3] When he himself becomes a Father of Uncleanness.
[4] i.e. according to the words of the Scribes these are deemed to suffer second-grade uncleanness. Cf. Toh. 4[11].   [5] See p. 626, n. 4; Yad. 4[5].
[6] Lit. 'one that was immersed on that day'; i.e. one who, having incurred any uncleanness for which it is ordained 'he shall be unclean until evening', has duly immersed himself, and must now await sunset before he is deemed fully clean. The degree of uncleanness which he still suffers is slight (see Zab. 5[12]). He is deemed to suffer 'second-grade uncleanness'. He does not render common food unclean, but he renders Heave-offering 'invalid' (i.e. conveys to it 'third-grade uncleanness' whereby it become unusable and must be burnt). See Kel. 1[5, 8]. He may not, therefore, touch the Hallowed Things (which are one degree more susceptible than Heave-offering—see p. 714, n. 3); and he may not enter the Temple beyond the Court of the Gentiles (Kel. 1[8]).
[7] A priest who had collected the separate pieces of dough from many houses.
[8] See p. 83, n. 1. To Dough-offering is attributed the same sanctity (and the same degree of susceptibility to uncleanness) as Heave-offering: it is rendered 'invalid' if touched by one that had immersed himself the selfsame day because of some uncleanness.

Also that of rice)—the School of Shammai say: These serve as a connective [to convey uncleanness] if they are touched by one that had immersed himself the selfsame day. And the School of Hillel say: They do not serve as a connective. But they agree [that they serve as a connective] if they are touched by any other [grades of] uncleanness, be they slight[1] or grave.[2]

2. If a man had brought together many Dough-offerings with no intention of separating them, or if a cake [of Heave-offering] was put to bake on top of another after they had formed a crust in the oven, or a skin of froth on water that was not blown up, or the second scum that rises in boiling bean-grits, or the scum of old wine, or that of oil at any time, or that of [boiled] lentils (R. Judah says: Also that of vetchlings)—these become unclean [and serve as connectives for uncleanness] if they are touched by one that had immersed himself the selfsame day; and, needless to say, also [if they are touched] by any other [grades of] uncleanness.

3. The knob [of dough] behind a loaf, or a small lump of salt, or a scorched crust less than a finger's breadth—R. Jose says: Whatsoever is eaten together with the loaf becomes unclean [and serves as a connective for uncleanness] if it is touched by one that had immersed himself the selfsame day; and, needless to say, also [if it is touched] by any other [grades of] uncleanness.

4. A piece of gravel in a loaf or a large piece of salt or a lupine or scorched crust more than finger's breadth—R. Jose says: Whatsoever is not eaten together with the loaf remains clean [and does not serve as a connective for uncleanness] even if it is touched by a Father of Uncleanness; and, needless to say, also [if it is touched] by one that had immersed himself the selfsame day.

5. Unhusked barley or spelt, crowfoot root, asafoetida and silphium (R. Judah says: Also black chickpeas) remain clean even if they were touched by a Father of Uncleanness, and, needless to say, also [if they are touched] by one that had immersed himself the selfsame day. So R. Meir. But the Sages say: They remain clean if they are touched by one that had immersed himself the selfsame day; but they become unclean if they are touched by any other [grades of] uncleanness. Husked barley or spelt, and husked or unhusked wheat, black cummin, sesame and pepper (R. Judah says: Also white beans) become unclean if they are touched by one that had immersed himself the selfsame day; and, needless to say, also [if they are touched] by any other [grades of] uncleanness.

2. 1. The liquids that issue[3] from one that had immersed himself the selfsame day are like to the liquids that he touches: neither of them conveys uncleanness.[4] With all others that are unclean, be the uncleanness slight or grave, any liquid that issues from them is like to the liquids that they touch: both suffer first-grade uncleanness excepting any liquid that is a Father of Uncleanness.[5]

2. If a cooking-pot was full of liquid and one that had immersed himself the selfsame day touched it, and the liquid was Heave-offering, the liquid becomes invalid, but the cooking-pot remains clean;[6] if the liquid was

1 A derived (or 'offspring of') uncleanness.
2 A primary (or 'father of') uncleanness.
3 Spittle, urine, tears, blood from a wound and a woman's milk.
4 They suffer only 'third-grade uncleanness'. Cf. p. 714, n. 3.
5 See App. IV. 18 b.
6 Since Heave-offering that is 'invalid' cannot convey uncleanness.

common food, all remains clean. If his hands were dirty all becomes unclean. Herein greater stringency applies to the hands than to one that had immersed himself the selfsame day; but greater stringency may apply to one that had immersed himself the selfsame day than to the hands, since a condition of doubt respecting one that had immersed himself the selfsame day renders Heave-offering invalid, but a condition of doubt respecting the hands is deemed clean.[1]

3. If a porridge made from Heave-offering [was mixed] with garlic and oil that were common food, and one that had immersed himself the self-same day touched part of them, he renders the whole invalid. If he touched part of a porridge made from common food [that was mixed] with garlic and oil that were Heave-offering, he renders invalid only that part which he touches. If the greater part was garlic, they decide according to which was the greater part. R. Judah said: This applies only when the garlic was served whole in the dish; but if it was mashed small in the mortar, it remains clean, since it was the owner's wish that it should be separated. So, too, with other mashed foods that are mashed with liquids; or that are usually mashed with liquids yet were not mashed with liquids but served whole in the dish. Such are regarded in like manner as a cake of pressed figs.[2]

4. If the porridge and the wafer in it were both common food and the oil floating over them was Heave-offering, and one that had immersed himself the selfsame day touched the oil, he renders only the oil invalid; but if he stirred all together, wheresoever the oil goes becomes invalid.

5. If a layer of jelly was formed over flesh of Hallowed Things, and one that had immersed himself the selfsame day touched the jelly, the pieces of the flesh are permitted; but if he touched a piece of the flesh, the piece of the flesh and all [the jelly] that comes away with it serve as a connective the one with the other. R. Johanan b. Nuri says: They each serve as a connective the one with the other. So, too, with [cooked] pulse that forms a solid layer over slices of bread. If pulse was stewed in a cooking-pot, but the pieces still remain separate, they do not serve as a connective; after they are boiled down to a solid mass they serve as a connective. If they were boiled down into several masses [and a creeping thing touched one of them] count must be made of them.[3] If oil was floating on wine and one that had immersed himself the selfsame day touched the oil, he renders only the oil invalid. R. Johanan b. Nuri says: They each serve as a connective one with the other.

6. If a jar [of Heave-offering wine] had sunk into a cistern containing wine [that was common food] and one that had immersed himself the self-same day touched it, if [he touched it] within its rim it serves as a connective but if outside its rim it does not serve as a connective. R. Johanan b. Nuri says: Even if [the level of the wine in the cistern] was a man's height [higher than the sunken jar], and he touched [the wine] directly above the mouth of the jar, this serves as a connective [to convey uncleanness so that he renders invalid the wine in the jar].

---

[1] Yad. 2⁴.

[2] The single figs are not regarded as connectives, and he renders invalid only what he touches.

[3] If the masses touched one another, that which the creeping thing touched suffers 'first-grade uncleanness', the next to it 'second-grade', and the next 'third-grade' (so that, if the pulse is Heave-offering, this becomes invalid; but it transfers the uncleanness no farther).

7. If a jar [of Heave-offering wine] had a hole in it either in its bottom or its sides, and one that had immersed himself the selfsame day touched it [at the hole], it becomes unclean.[1] R. Judah says: [If the hole was] in its neck or in its bottom it becomes unclean,[1] but if in its sides, on this side or on that, it remains clean.[2] If liquid was poured out from one vessel into another, and one that had immersed himself the selfsame day touched the stream of liquid, and there was [any substance] in it, [what he touches] is neutralized as one part in a hundred and one.

8. If a bubble[3] [in the earthenware] of the jar had holes in it on the inner side and on the outer side,[4] whether above or below or opposite one another, it becomes unclean if it was touched by a Father of Uncleanness,[5] and it becomes unclean if it is in a 'Tent' where lies a corpse;[6] if the inner hole was below and the outer hole above, it becomes unclean if it was touched by a Father of Uncleanness, and it becomes unclean if it is in a 'Tent' wherein lies a corpse; if the inner hole was above and the outer hole below, it remains clean if it was touched by a Father of Uncleanness,[7] but it becomes unclean if it was in a 'Tent' wherein lies a corpse.

3. 1. All [stalks that are] handles to fruits[8] [and] that serve as a connective if they are touched by a Father of Uncleanness serve also as a connective if they are touched by one that had immersed himself the selfsame day. If the fruit was severed, yet was still in part attached, R. Meir says: If one laid hold on the larger part and the smaller part came away with it, the smaller part is regarded as like to it.[9] R. Judah says: If one laid hold on the smaller part and the larger part came away with it, the larger part is regarded as like to it. R. Nehemiah says: [This applies if one laid hold] on the portion that was clean.[10] But the Sages say: On the portion that was unclean. With all other fruits let such as are usually held by the leaf be held by the leaf, and such that are usually held by the stalk be held by the stalk.[11]

2. If a beaten-up egg[12] was put on the top of vegetables that are Heave-offering, and one that had immersed himself the selfsame day touched the egg, he renders invalid only the stalk [of vegetables] over against the part that he touched. R. Jose says: All is according to the arrangement above: if it was a like cap[13] it does not serve as a connective.

3. If a streak of the egg congealed on the sides of a pan and one that had immersed himself the selfsame day touched it, if [he touched it] within the rim, the streak serves as a connective, but if outside the rim it does not serve as a connective. R. Jose says: [Only] the streak and what can be

---

[1] i.e. what he touches serves as a connective for uncleanness, so that he renders the contents unclean.

[2] If the hole was in the neck or bottom of the jar it is at a place through which all the wine may pass; but if at the side, it is at a place where only a small part of the wine will pass through, and that only is rendered invalid which he touches; and this is neutralized as one part in a hundred and one.

[3] Formed in the clay sides of the jar while it was being baked.

[4] Variant: 'whether on the inner side or on the outer side'.

[5] If he touched the outermost hole all the wine in the jar becomes unclean.

[6] Even if its mouth was sealed with a 'tightly stopped-up cover' (Kel. 10[2]).

[7] He touches the stream of liquid below, and it does not serve as a connective with what is above.

[8] See Uktz. 1[1].   [9] They each serve as a connective one with the other.

[10] Which was not touched by one who had immersed himself the selfsame day.

[11] And if the whole comes away together each of the parts serves as a connective with the other.   [12] Cf. Eduy. 2[4].

[13] And not mingled among the vegetable stalks.

peeled away with it [serves as a connective]. So, too, in the case of [boiled] pulse which has congealed on the rim of the pot.

4. If dough was mixed with Heave-offering dough or leavened with Heave-offering yeast, it is not rendered invalid if it is touched by one that had immersed himself the selfsame day. R. Jose and R. Simeon declare it invalid. If dough was made susceptible [to uncleanness] by a liquid,[1] and it was kneaded with fruit juice,[2] and one that had immersed himself the selfsame day touched it, R. Eleazar b. Judah of Bartotha in the name of R. Joshua says: He renders the whole invalid. R. Akiba says in his name: He renders invalid only the place that he touches.

5. If vegetables that were common food were cooked with Heave-offering oil and one that had immersed himself the selfsame day touched it, R. Eleazar b. Judah of Bartotha in the name of R. Joshua says: He renders the whole invalid. R. Akiba says in his name: He renders invalid only the place that he touches.

6. If one that was clean chewed food and it fell on his garments and on a loaf that was Heave-offering, the loaf is not rendered susceptible to uncleanness.[3] If he was eating crushed olives and moist dates and intended to suck the stone, and it fell on his garments and on a loaf that was Heave-offering, the loaf is rendered susceptible. If he was eating dried olives or dried dates and did not intend to suck the stone, and it fell on his clothes and on a loaf that was Heave-offering, the loaf is not rendered susceptible, no matter whether it was a man that was clean or a man that had immersed himself the selfsame day. R. Meir says: In either case it is unclean if it was a man that had immersed himself the selfsame day, since the liquids that issue from an unclean person render anything susceptible whether their presence is acceptable or not acceptable.[4] But the Sages say: He that has immersed himself the selfsame day is not unclean.

4. 1. If food that was Tithe was rendered susceptible by a liquid, and one that had immersed himself the selfsame day touched it, or if unwashed hands touched it,[5] Heave-offering of Tithe[6] may still be set apart from it in the required conditions of cleanness, since it only suffered third-grade uncleanness, and third-grade uncleanness counts as clean in common food.[7]

2. A woman that had immersed herself the selfsame day may nevertheless knead dough and cut off the Dough-offering and set it apart and put it on a basket of palm-twigs[8] or on a board,[9] and bring it near [to the rest of the dough][10] and then designate it [as Dough-offering]; because [the dough which she has touched] is but of third-grade uncleanness, and third-grade uncleanness counts as clean in common food.

3. If a kneading-trough had been immersed the selfsame day [because of uncleanness that had befallen it] they may knead dough therein and cut off the Dough-offering and bring it near and designate it, since [the dough which has touched the kneading-trough] is but of third-grade uncleanness, and third-grade uncleanness counts as clean in common food.

---

[1] See p. 758, n. 1.
[2] Which is not one of the seven liquids (Maksh. 6[4]) that render food susceptible to uncleannness.   [3] Since the moisture was not dropped purposely.
[4] See Maksh. 1[1].
[5] Both suffering only second-grade uncleanness.   [6] App. I. 48 (2).
[7] And Tithe has no higher sanctity than common food.
[8] Variant: Egyptian basket. Cf. Shab. 20[2]; Sot. 2[1]; 3[1]; Kel. 26[1].
[9] Since neither of these is susceptible to uncleanness.
[10] Of which it is to constitute the portion dedicated as Dough-offering.

4. If a flagon had been immersed the selfsame day and was filled from a jar containing Tithe from which Heave-offering had not yet been taken, and a man said, 'Let this be Heave-offering of Tithe after nightfall', it is valid Heave-offering of Tithe. But if he had said, 'Let this be food for the Sabbath *Erub*',[1] he has said nothing at all.[2] If the jar was broken,[3] what is in the flagon continues to be 'Tithe from which Heave-offering had not yet been taken'; if the flagon was broken, what is in the jar continues to be 'Tithe from which Heave-offering had not yet been taken'.

5. Beforetime they used to say: They may exchange Second Tithe [money in Jerusalem][4] for the produce of an *Am-haaretz*. Then they changed this and said: Also for money of his. Beforetime they used to say: If a man was led forth in fetters[5] and said, 'Write out a bill of divorce for my wife', they should write it out and also deliver it. Then they changed this and said: Also if a man went on a voyage or set out with a caravan. R. Simeon of Shezuri says: Also if a man was at the point of death.

6. If Ashkelon grappling-irons[6] were broken yet their hooks remained, they are still susceptible to uncleanness. If a [wooden] pitchfork, winnowing fan or rake (so, too, a haircomb) lost one of its teeth, and another of metal was made for it, they become susceptible to uncleanness. Concerning all these R. Joshua said: The Scribes have invented a new thing and I cannot make answer [to them that would gainsay them].

7. If a man took Heave-offering [of wine or oil] from the cistern and said, 'Let this be Heave-offering provided that it comes up in safety', [it is assumed that he meant] safe from breakage or from spilling, but not from contracting uncleanness. R. Simeon says: Also [it is assumed that he meant] safe from contracting uncleanness. If it was broken it does not count as Heave-offering. How far [away from the cistern] can it be broken and still not count as Heave-offering? Only so far that if it rolls back it can reach the cistern. R. Jose says: Also if any man had knowledge enough to make such a condition but did not do so, and it was broken, it does not count as Heave-offering, for so is it enjoined by the Court.[7]

YADAIM[8] ('HANDS')

1. 1. [To render the hands clean] a quarter-*log* or more[9] [of water] must be poured over the hands [to suffice] for one person or even for two; a half-*log* or more [suffices] for three persons or for four; one *log* or more [suffices] for five or for ten or for a hundred. R. Jose says: Provided that for the last among them there remains not less than a quarter-*log*. More [water] may be added to the second [water that is poured over the hands], but more may not be added to the first.[10]

---

[1] App. I. 8. See Erub. 3[1].

[2] Since it is still untithed produce, and so not free for the owner's common use; and *Erub* can only be made with produce held in valid possession before the incoming of the Sabbath.

[3] Before nightfall.   [4] Cf. p. 73, n. 6.   [5] Gitt. 6[5].   [6] Kel. 13[7].

[7] Namely that, in general, if a person knows that it is proper to make certain conditions, yet fails to make those conditions, such conditions are presumed to be in force.

[8] The hands, in their ordinary condition, are always assumed to suffer second-grade uncleanness; thus (cf. p. 714, n. 3) unless they are washed with the intention of rendering them clean, they convey third-grade uncleanness to food that is Heave-offering, making it invalid.   [9] Variant: 'water, a quarter-*log* in quantity'. A quarter-*log* is equal in bulk to an egg and a half.

[10] The custom was to give the hands a double rinsing; if for the second rinsing the remaining water was not enough to reach the wrist, more water may be added to the residue

2. The water may be poured over the hands out of any vessel,[1] even from vessels made from cattle-dung or vessels of stone or vessels of [unbaked] clay. It may not be poured over the hands out of the sides of [broken] vessels or out of the flanks of a ladling-jar[2] or out of the plug of a jar, nor may a man pour it over his fellow's hands out of his cupped hands, for they may not draw the water or mix the ashes or sprinkle the Sin-offering water,[3] or pour [water] over the hands, save only in a vessel; and only vessels that have a tightly stopped-up cover afford protection[4] [against uncleanness in the 'Tent' wherein lies a corpse]; and only vessels afford protection against [uncleanness present in] earthenware vessels.[5]

3. If water was [so polluted that it was] unfit for cattle to drink, if it was in vessels it is invalid [for the washing of hands], but if it was on the ground it is valid. If ink, gum, or copperas[6] fell therein and its colour was changed, it becomes invalid. If a man did any act of work therewith, or if he soaked his bread therein, it becomes invalid. Simeon of Teman says: If it was his intention to soak it in other water but it fell in this water, the water remains valid.

4. If he rinsed vessels therein or if he scrubbed measures therein, it becomes invalid. If he rinsed therein vessels that had been already rinsed or that were new, it remains valid. R. Jose declares it invalid if the vessels were new.

5. The water in which the baker dips loaves of fine flour is invalid; but if he rinsed his hands therein [and wetted the loaves with his hands] it remains valid. All are eligible to pour water over the hands, even one that is a deaf-mute or an imbecile or a minor. A man may put the jar between his knees and so pour out the water; he may turn the jar on its side and so pour out the water; and an ape may pour out the water over a man's hands. R. Jose declares the water invalid in these [last] two cases.

2. 1. If a man poured water over the one hand with a single rinsing, his hand is clean; but if over both hands with a single rinsing, R. Meir declares them unclean unless he pours over them a quarter-*log* or more. If a loaf of Heave-offering fell [on the water][7] it remains clean.[8] But R. Jose declares it unclean.[9]

2. If he poured the first water[10] over one place and the second water over another, and the loaf of Heave-offering fell on the first water, it becomes unclean; but if it fell on the second it remains clean. If he poured both the first water and the second over the same place and the loaf of Heave-offering fell thereon, it becomes unclean. If he poured the first water [over his hands] and a piece of wood or gravel was found on his hands, his hands remain unclean [even after he has poured over them the second water], since the second water renders clean only the water that is on the hand. R. Simeon b. Gamaliel says: Any creature that lives in water is not susceptible to uncleanness.[11]

3. The hands are susceptible to uncleanness, and they are rendered

of the first quantity, but if there was not enough to reach the wrist at the first rinsing, the water may not be added to, but a fresh quarter-*log's* supply must be used.
[1] Cf. Par. 5[5].   [2] See p. 607, n. 2.   [3] See p. 697, n. 3.
[4] See Kel. 10[1f].   [5] See Kel. 8[3].   [6] See p. 203, n. 15.
[7] A quarter-*log* in quantity and poured over the hands in a single rinsing. The same also applies if he touches a loaf of Heave-offering with his wet hands.
[8] Since his hands are clean.   [9] Since the water is unclean.
[10] Less than a quarter-*log*.   [11] Cf. Kel. 17[13, 14]; Mikw. 6[7].

clean [by the pouring over them of water] up to the wrist. Thus if a man had poured the first water up to the wrist and the second water beyond the wrist, and the water flowed back to the hand, the hand becomes clean; but if he poured both the first water and the second beyond the wrist, and the water flowed back to the hand, the hand remains unclean. If he poured the first water over the one hand alone and then bethought himself and poured the second water over both hands, they remain unclean. If he poured the first water over both hands and then bethought himself and poured the second water over the one hand, his one hand [alone] is clean. If he had poured the water over the one hand and rubbed it on the other, it becomes unclean; but if he rubbed it on his head or on the wall [to dry it] it remains clean. The water may be poured over [the hands of] four or five persons side by side or one above the other, provided that they lie but loosely together so that the water may flow between them.

4. If it is in doubt whether an act of work was done with the water or not, or whether it was of the prescribed quantity or not, or whether it was unclean or clean, its condition of doubt is deemed clean, for they have said:[1] If there is doubt about the hands, whether they have contracted uncleanness or have conveyed uncleanness or have become clean, they are deemed clean. R. Jose says: If [it is in doubt] whether they have become clean, they are deemed unclean. Thus, if the hands of a man were clean, and before him were two unclean loaves, and it is in doubt whether he touched them or not; or if his hands were unclean, and before him were two clean loaves, and it is in doubt whether he touched them or not; or if his one hand was unclean and the other clean, and before him were two clean loaves, and he touched one of them and it is in doubt whether he touched them with the unclean hand or with the clean; or if his hands were clean and before him were two loaves, the one unclean and the other clean, and he touched one of them and it is in doubt whether he touched the unclean loaf or the clean; or if one of his hands was unclean and the other clean, and before him were two loaves, the one unclean and the other clean, and he touched both of them, and it is in doubt whether what was unclean touched what was unclean, or whether what was clean touched what was clean, or whether what was clean touched what was unclean, or whether what was unclean touched what was clean, the hands remain as they were before and the loaves remain as they were before.

3. 1. If a man put his hands within a house afflicted with leprosy,[2] his hands suffer first-grade uncleanness.[3] So R. Akiba. But the Sages say: His hands suffer second-grade uncleanness only. Whatsoever renders garments unclean at the time that it touches them,[4] also conveys first-grade uncleanness to the hands.[5] So R. Akiba. But the Sages say: Second-grade uncleanness only. They said to R. Akiba, Whence do we find that hands anywhere suffer first-grade uncleanness? He said to them, But how is it possible (save only in this case)[6] for the hands to suffer first-grade uncleanness without his whole body also becoming unclean?[7] Foodstuffs and

---

[1] Toh. 4[7, 11].
[2] Lev. 14[3 ff.].   [3] Since the house is a 'Father of Uncleanness' and it conveys uncleanness through its contained space.   [4] Specified in Zab. 5[7].
[5] Even though they do not render the man himself unclean.
[6] Putting the hands into a house afflicted with leprosy.
[7] Since, to suffer first-grade uncleanness, a man must have touched a Father of Uncleanness; and if the hands touch a Father of Uncleanness the whole body becomes unclean.

vessels that have contracted uncleanness from liquids convey second-grade uncleanness to the hands. So R. Joshua. But the Sages say: If aught is rendered unclean by a Father of Uncleanness[1] it can render the hands unclean;[2] but if [aught is rendered unclean] only by an Offspring of Uncleanness[3] it cannot render the hands unclean.[4] Rabban Simeon b. Gamaliel said: It once happened that a woman came before my father and said to him, 'My hands entered into the airspace of an earthenware vessel'. He said to her, 'My daughter, from what was its uncleanness?' But I did not hear what she said to him. The Sages said: The matter is manifest: if it was made unclean by a Father of Uncleanness it can render the hands unclean, but if only by an Offspring of Uncleanness it cannot render the hands unclean.

2. Whatsoever renders Heave-offering invalid[5] can convey second-grade uncleanness to the hands; the one hand can render the other unclean. So R. Joshua. But the Sages say: That which suffers second-grade uncleanness cannot convey second-grade uncleanness to aught else. He said to them, But do not the Holy Scriptures,[6] which suffer second-grade uncleanness, render the hands unclean? They answered, Ye may infer nothing about the words of the Law from the words of the Scribes[7] and nothing about the words of the Scribes from the words of the Law, and nothing about the words of the Scribes from [other] words of the Scribes.

3. The straps of phylacteries [while they are still joined] with the phylacteries render the hands unclean.[8] R. Simeon says: The straps of phylacteries do not render the hands unclean.

4. The blank spaces in a scroll [of the Scriptures] that are above [the writing] and that are below,[9] and that are at the beginning[10] and at the end,[11] render the hands unclean. R. Judah says: The blank space at the end does not render [the hands] unclean until the roller is joined to it.[12]

5. If the writing in a scroll was erased yet there still remained eighty-five letters, as many as are in the paragraph *And it came to pass when the ark set forward . . .,*[13] it still renders the hands unclean. A [single] written sheet[14] [in a scroll of the Scriptures] in which are written eighty-five letters, as many as are in the paragraph *And it came to pass when the ark set forward,* renders the hands unclean. All the Holy Scriptures render the hands unclean. The Song of Songs and Ecclesiastes render the hands unclean. R. Judah says: The Song of Songs renders the hands unclean, but about Ecclesiastes there is dissension. R. Jose says: Ecclesiastes does not render the hands unclean, and about the Song of Songs there is dissension. R. Simeon says: Ecclesiastes is one of the things about which the School

---

[1] Thereby contracting first-grade uncleanness.
[2] Since they are sufficiently susceptible to suffer second-grade uncleanness.
[3] Thereby contracting second-grade uncleanness.
[4] Since if they touch second-grade uncleanness they remain clean and do not suffer third grade uncleanness.   [5] i.e. whatever suffers second-grade uncleanness (Zab. 5[12]).
[6] See p. 626, n. 4; Zab. 5[12]; Yad. 4[5].
[7] The uncleanness of the Scriptures is a rabbinical injunction.
[8] They count as connectives with the Scripture within the capsules of the phylacteries (see p. 104, n. 16).   [9] A space three fingerbreadths must be left above, and one hand-breadth below.   [10] A blank space must be left sufficient to wrap around the entire scroll.
[11] Sufficient to cover the core or central roller around which the entire scroll is wrapped.
[12] Only then does this blank section count as an essential part of the scroll.
[13] Num. 10[35f].
[14] Of the many sheets which are sewn together side by side to make the long strip which forms the scroll.

of Shammai adopted the more lenient, and the School of Hillel the more stringent ruling.[1] R. Simeon b. Azzai said: I have heard a tradition from the seventy-two elders on the day when they made R. Eleazar b. Azariah head of the college [of Sages],[2] that the Song of Songs and Ecclesiastes both render the hands unclean. R. Akiba said: God forbid!—no man in Israel ever disputed about the Song of Songs [that he should say] that it does not render the hands unclean, for all the ages are not worth the day on which the Song of Songs was given to Israel; for all the Writings[3] are holy, but the Song of Songs is the Holy of Holies. And if aught was in dispute the dispute was about Ecclesiastes alone. R. Johanan b. Joshua, the son of R. Akiba's father-in-law, said: According to the words of Ben Azzai so did they dispute and so did they decide.

4. 1. On that day[4] they voted and decided that if a footbath, which held from two *logs*[5] to nine *kabs*,[5] was cracked, it becomes susceptible to *midras*-uncleanness,[6] whereas R. Akiba used to say: A footbath is according to its name.[7]

2. On that day they said: All animal-offerings[8] that have been slaughtered under the name of some other offering remain valid (but do not count to their owner in fulfilment of his obligation) excepting a Passover-offering and a Sin-offering. [This rule applies to] a Passover-offering at its appointed time and to a Sin-offering at any time. R. Eliezer says: Excepting also the Guilt-offering; [this rule therefore applies to] a Passover-offering at its appointed time, and to a Sin-offering and a Guilt-offering at any time. R. Simeon b. Azzai said:[9] I have heard a tradition from the seventy-two elders on the day when they made R. Eleazar b. Azariah head of the college [of Sages] that all animal-offerings which must be consumed remain valid although slaughtered under some other name (but do not count to their owner in fulfilment of his obligation) excepting a Passover-offering and a Sin-offering. And Ben Azzai added the Whole-offering only; but the Sages did not agree with him.

3. On that day they said: What of Ammon and Moab in the Seventh Year?[10] R. Tarfon decreed: [They must give] Poorman's Tithe.[11] And R. Eleazar b. Azariah decreed: [They must give] Second Tithe. R. Ishmael said to him, Eleazar b. Azariah, thou must bring forth proof since thou givest the more stringent ruling;[12] for every one that would give a more stringent ruling must bring forth proof. R. Eleazar b. Azariah said to him, Ishmael my brother, it is not I that have changed the order of the years:[13]

---

1 See Eduy. 5³.   2 Cf. Zeb. 1³; Yad. 4².   3 Heb. *ketubim*, i.e. the Hagiographa.
4 When they made R. Eleazar b. Azariah head of the college of Sages. See p. 468, n. 13.
5 App. II, D.
6 See App. I. 26. It can be sat upon and none will interfere and say 'Get up and let us do our work', i.e. put it to its proper use. See Kel. 20³.
7 It is a bath, and so not a thing ever liable to *midras*-uncleanness.   8 Zeb. 1¹.
9 Zeb. 1³.
10 i.e. what Tithes must be paid by Israelites living in Ammon and Moab in the Seventh Year (Lev. 25⁴ᶠᶠ) when no harvest is reaped in the Land of Israel, and what grows is owner-less property and exempt from Tithes; but what Israelites grow outside the Land of Israel is not subject to the same rules. See Shebi. 6¹.
11 The tithe which is given to the poor in the third and sixth years of the seven-year cycle, taking the place of the Second Tithe which is set apart (see p. 73, n. 6) in the first, second, fourth, and fifth years.
12 Since Second Tithe is holy, and must be consumed in Jerusalem, or redeemed with money and its value consumed in Jerusalem.
13 i.e. they always give Second Tithe in a year that follows after a year in which Poorman's Tithe has been given. Deut. 14²⁸ specifies 'at the end of every three years' as the years for Poorman's Tithe; therefore in other years Second Tithe must be given.

Tarfon, my brother, has changed it, and he must bring forth proof. R. Tarfon answered, Egypt is outside the Land [of Israel] and Ammon and Moab are outside the Land [of Israel]; therefore as in Egypt Poorman's Tithe must be given[1] in the Seventh Year, so in Ammon and Moab Poorman's Tithe must be given in the Seventh Year. R. Eleazar b. Azariah answered, Babylon is outside the Land [of Israel] and Ammon and Moab are outside the Land [of Israel]; therefore as in Babylon Second Tithe must be given in the Seventh Year,[2] so in Ammon and Moab Second Tithe must be given in the Seventh Year. R. Tarfon said, On Egypt, because it is near, have they imposed Poorman's Tithe that the poor of Israel might be stayed thereby in the Seventh Year; so, too, on Ammon and Moab, which are near, have they imposed Poorman's Tithe, that the poor of Israel might be stayed thereby in the Seventh Year. R. Eleazar b. Azariah answered, Lo, thou art as one that would bestow on them worldly gain, yet thou art but as one that would suffer souls to perish;[3] thou wouldest rob the heavens so that they send down neither dew nor rain, for it is written, *Will a man rob God? yet ye rob me. But ye say, Wherein have we robbed thee? In tithes and heave offerings.*[4] R. Joshua said, Lo, I am as one that will answer on behalf of Tarfon my brother, but not according to the subject of his words. [The rule touching] Egypt is a new work, and [the rule touching] Babylon is an old work, and the argument before us is a new work; let us argue concerning a new work from a new work, but let us not argue concerning a new work from an old work. [The rule touching] Egypt is the work of the elders; but [the rule touching] Babylon is the work of the Prophets, and the argument before us is the work of the elders; let us argue concerning a work of the elders from a work of the elders, but let us not argue concerning a work of the elders from a work of the Prophets. They voted and decided that Ammon and Moab should give Poorman's Tithe in the Seventh Year. And when R. Jose the son of the Damascene came to R. Eliezer[5] in Lydda, he said to him, 'What new thing had ye in the House of Study to-day?' He said to him, 'They voted and decided that Ammon and Moab must give Poorman's Tithe in the Seventh Year'. R. Eliezer wept and said, '*The secret of the Lord is with them that fear him, and he will show them his covenant!*[6] Go and tell them, Be not anxious by reason of your voting, for I have received a tradition from Rabban Johanan b. Zakkai, who heard it from his teacher, and his teacher from his teacher, as a *Halakah*[7] given to Moses from Sinai,[8] that Ammon and Moab should give Poorman's Tithe in the Seventh Year.'

4. On that day came Judah, an Ammonite proselyte, and stood before them in the House of Study. He said to them, May I enter into the congregation?[9] Rabban Gamaliel said to him: Thou art forbidden. R. Joshua said to him: Thou art permitted. Rabban Gamaliel said to him, Scripture says, *An Ammonite or a Moabite shall not enter into the assembly of the Lord; even to the tenth generation. . . .*[10] R. Joshua said to him, But are the Ammonites and the Moabites [still] where they were?—long ago Sennacherib, king of Assyria, came up and put all the nations in confusion,

---

[1] So it was ordained by the elders after the time of Ezra.
[2] A rule ordained by the Prophets.
[3] Through their profaning the sanctity of Second Tithe.   [4] Mal. 3[8].
[5] Who, because of heresy, was under a ban and so forbidden to have any part in the Court's discussions and decisions.   [6] Ps. 25[14].   [7] App. I. 11.
[8] Cf. p. 12, n. 4; Eduy. 8[7]; cf. Ab. 1[1]   [9] Cf. Yeb. 8[3].   [10] Deut. 23[3].

as it is written, *I have removed the bounds of the peoples and have robbed their treasures, and I have brought down as a valiant man them that sit [on thrones].*[1] Rabban Gamaliel answered, Scripture says, *But afterward I will bring again the captivity of the children of Ammon,*[2] and so they have returned. R. Joshua said to him: Scripture says, *And I will turn again the captivity of my people Israel and Judah, saith the Lord,*[3] and they have not yet returned. And they permitted him to come into the congregation.

5. The [Aramaic] version that is in Ezra and Daniel[4] renders the hands unclean. If an [Aramaic] version [contained in the Scriptures] was written in Hebrew,[5] or if [Scripture that is in] Hebrew was written in an [Aramaic] version, or in Hebrew script,[6] it does not render the hands unclean. [The Holy Scriptures] render the hands unclean only if they are written in the Assyrian character, on leather, and in ink.

6. The Sadducees say, We cry out against you, O ye Pharisees, for ye say, 'The Holy Scriptures render the hands unclean', [and] 'The writings of Hamiram[7] do not render the hands unclean'. Rabban Johanan b. Zakkai said, Have we naught against the Pharisees save this!—for lo, they say, 'The bones of an ass are clean, and the bones of Johanan the High Priest are unclean'. They said to him, As is our love for them so is their uncleanness—that no man make spoons of the bones of his father or mother. He said to them, Even so the Holy Scriptures: as is our love for them so is their uncleanness; [whereas] the writings of Hamiram which are held in no account do not render the hands unclean.

7. The Sadducees say, We cry out against you, O ye Pharisees, for ye declare clean an unbroken stream of liquid.[8] The Pharisees say, We cry out against you, O ye Sadducees, for ye declare clean a channel of water that flows from a burial ground. The Sadducees say, We cry out against you, O ye Pharisees, for ye say, 'If my ox or my ass have done an injury they are culpable, but if my bondman or my bondwoman have done an injury they are not culpable'—if, in the case of my ox or my ass (about which no commandments are laid upon me) I am responsible for the injury that they do, how much more in the case of my bondman or my bondwoman (about whom certain commandments are laid upon me) must I be responsible for the injury that they do! They said to them, No!—as ye argue concerning my ox or my ass (which have no understanding) would ye likewise argue concerning my bondman or my bondwoman which have understanding?— for if I provoke him to anger he may go and set fire to another's stack of corn, and it is I that must make restitution!

---

[1] Is. 10[13].   [2] Jer. 49[6].   [3] Jer. 30[3].
[4] The portions (Ezra 4[8] to 7[18]; Dan. 2[4] to 6[28]) of these books written in Aramaic.
[5] i.e. if the Aramaic portions of Ezra and Daniel, or the Aramaic passages in Jeremiah (10[11]) and Genesis (31[47]) were translated into Hebrew, the same sanctity does not attach to them.   [6] Meaning the ancient Hebrew characters (as found, e.g., in the Siloam and Moabite inscriptions, and on Jewish coins, and, in modified form, in Samaritan writing). After the time of Ezra, the 'Assyrian' character (the immediate precursor of the modern square character) was used in writing the Scriptures, while the 'Hebrew' character was confined to secular use. According to the Tosefta (Sanh. 4[7]) the Law was originally given to Israel in the Assyrian writing; when Israel sinned it was changed to 'rugged' writing (referring to the characteristic form of the letters in the Samaritan script; there is a variant reading which may mean 'wedge-shaped' writing); but when Israel repented in the days of Ezra it was changed back again into the 'Assyrian' character.
[7] Variant: Hamiros, Miras, Miram. It is variously explained as 'books of the heretics (*Minim*)' or 'the books of Homer'.
[8] When a liquid is poured out from a clean to an unclean vessel it does not serve as a connective, and the upper vessel remains clean. See Maksh. 5[9].

8. A Galilean heretic[1] said, I cry out against you, O ye Pharisees, for ye write in a bill of divorce the name of the ruler together with the name of Moses.[2] The Pharisees said, We cry out against thee, O thou Galilean heretic, for ye write the name of the ruler together with the Name [of God] on the [same] page, and, moreover, ye write the name of the ruler above, and the Name [of God] below; as it is written, *And Pharaoh said, Who is the Lord that I should hearken unto his voice to let Israel go?*[3] But when he was smitten what did he say? *The Lord is righteous!*[4]

UKTZIN[5] ('STALKS')

1. 1. Any part [of a fruit] that serves as a handle but not as a protection contracts uncleanness and conveys uncleanness, but it is not included together [with the rest of the fruit to make up the egg's bulk that conveys uncleanness]. If it serves as a protection, even if it does not serve as a handle, it contracts uncleanness and conveys uncleanness and it is included together with the rest. If it serves neither as a protection nor as a·handle it neither contracts uncleanness nor conveys uncleanness.

2. The roots of garlic, onions, or leeks, if they are yet moist, and the nipple-end thereof, whether moist or dry, and the scape that is close to the bulb;[6] and the roots of lettuce, the long radish and round radish (so R. Meir; but R. Judah says that a large root of the long radish is included together with the rest but not so its fibre-like roots), and the roots of mint and rue, wild herbs and garden-herbs that can be uprooted and transplanted, and the [middle] spine of an ear [of corn] and its husk (R. Eliezer says: Also the downy growth)—these contract uncleanness and convey uncleanness, and they are included together with the rest [to make up the bulk that conveys uncleanness].

3. These contract uncleanness and convey uncleanness, but they are not included together with the rest: the roots of garlic, onions, and leeks when they are dry, and the scape that is not close to the bulb, and the branch from which the grape-cluster hangs, one handbreadth to either side, and the stem of the cluster, whatsoever its length, and the tail of a cluster that is stripped [of grapes]; and the stem of the 'brush' of the palm-tree to a length of four handbreadths; and the stalk of an ear [of corn] to a length of three handbreadths; and the stalks of aught that is reaped, to a length of three handbreadths; and, in the case of what it is not usual to reap, their stalks and their roots, whatsoever their length; and the glumes of ears of corn—these contract uncleanness and convey uncleanness, but they are not included together with the rest [to make up the bulk that conveys uncleanness].

4. These neither contract uncleanness nor convey uncleanness and they are not included together with the rest [to make up the bulk that conveys

---

[1] Modern editions read 'Sadducee'.
[2] The document gave the date according to the year of the reigning king, and concluded: 'according to the religion of Moses'; the name of the ruler was thus, it was alleged, given an importance equal to that of Moses.
[3] Ex. 5[2]. Thus in the Law itself the name of the ruler, Pharaoh, occurs together with, and before, the name of God, without implying disrespect.   [4] Ex. 9[27].
[5] 'Stalks' of fruits and plants. The tractate treats, mainly, of the various parts in plants, defining which are susceptible to uncleanness, and which parts serve as 'connectives' for uncleanness (so that if such a part suffers uncleanness it conveys uncleanness to the rest, or if the rest suffers uncleanness it also suffers uncleanness); and which parts can be included together with the edible parts to make up the egg's bulk which is the minimum quantity of foodstuff that suffices to convey food uncleanness.
[6] Lit. 'food', i.e. the edible portion.

uncleanness]: cabbage stalks, shoots of beetroots and turnips, [namely] such that it is usual to chop off yet they were taken out with the roots. R. Jose declares all of them susceptible to uncleanness, but the stalks of cabbages and turnips he declares insusceptible.

5. The stalks of all foodstuffs that are threshed in a threshing-floor are insusceptible to uncleanness; but R. Jose declares them susceptible. If a sprig from a grape-cluster is stripped of its grapes it is insusceptible to uncleanness; but if one grape alone remains on it it is susceptible. If the fruit-stalk of a date-palm is stripped of its dates it is insusceptible to uncleanness, but if one date alone remains on it it is susceptible. So, too, with pulse:[1] if a stalk is stripped it is insusceptible to uncleanness, but if one pod alone remains on it it is susceptible. R. Eleazar b. Azariah declares the stalk of the bean insusceptible to uncleanness, but the stalks of [other] pulse he declares susceptible, since they are of use in the handling of them.

6. The stalks of figs and dried figs, acorns[2] and carobs contract uncleanness and convey uncleanness. R. Jose says: Also the stalk of the gourd, the stalks of pears and pippins[3] and quinces and medlars. The stalk of the gourd [is susceptible to a length of] one handbreadth, and the stalk of an artichoke [to a length of] one handbreadth. R. Eliezer b. R. Zadok says: Two handbreadths. These contract uncleanness and convey uncleanness, but they are not included together with the rest [of the fruit to make up the bulk that conveys uncleanness]. The stalks of all other fruits neither contract uncleanness nor convey uncleanness.

2. 1. If olives are pickled together with their leaves, the leaves are not susceptible to uncleanness, since they were only pickled for the sake of appearance. The fine hair on a cucumber and the sprouting end thereof are not susceptible to uncleanness. R. Judah says: So long as it lies before the merchant it is susceptible to uncleanness.[4]

2. All fruit-stones contract uncleanness and convey uncleanness, but they are not included together with the rest [to make up the bulk that conveys food-uncleanness]. The stones of fresh dates, even if they are detached [from the edible part] are included together with the rest, but those of dried dates are not included; therefore the skin around the stone of dried dates is included [with the edible part] but that around the stone of fresh dates is not included. If only part of a fruit-stone is detached, that which lies near to the edible part is included together with the rest. If there is any flesh on a bone [to one end only], the part of the bone that lies near to the edible part is included together with it; if it lies but to one side of it, R. Ishmael says: It is regarded as though it encompassed it like a ring. But the Sages say: [Only] the part that lies near to the edible part is included together with it. And the same applies to savory, marjoram and calamint.[5]

3. If part of a pomegranate or a water-melon is rotten it is not included together with the rest [of the fruit to make up the bulk that conveys uncleanness]. If [the fruit] is sound at either end but rotten in the middle, [what is rotten] is not included with the rest. The nipple on a pomegranate

---

[1] Legumens.
[2] Uncertain. See p. 65, n. 11.
[3] See p. 29, n. 1; Maas. 1³.
[4] It serves to protect the cucumber from dirt.
[5] The stalk near to the edible part is included together with it, even if the edible part is not enough to encompass it.

is included with the rest, but the sprouting hairs are not included. R. Eliezer says: Its 'comb' also is not susceptible to uncleanness.

4. All rinds contract uncleanness and convey uncleanness and they are included together with the rest [of the fruit to make up the bulk that conveys uncleanness]. R. Judah says: An onion has three skins: the innermost skin, whether it is entire or has holes in it, is included together with the edible part; the middle skin, if it is entire, is included, but if it has holes in it, it is not included; but the outermost in either case is not susceptible to uncleanness.

5. If a man chopped up fruit in order to cook it, even if he did not wholly cut it through, it is not deemed connected together; but if [he had so cut it] in order to pickle it or fry it or set it on the table, it is deemed still connected together. If he made a beginning of taking the portions apart, [only] that [portion of] food that he has begun to take apart is deemed not connected. If nuts or onions were strung together they count as connectives [one with the other]. If he made a beginning of taking the nuts apart or of peeling the onions, [only] that [on which he has begun] is deemed not connected. [The shells of] nuts and almonds [still] count as a connective [with the edible part] until they have been crushed.

6. [The shell of] a roasted egg[1] [counts as a connective for uncleanness] until it has been chipped, but that of a boiled egg,[2] until it is wholly broken up. A bone wherein is marrow counts as a connective until it is wholly broken up. [The rind of] a pomegranate that has been cut in two still counts as a connective until it has been knocked with a stick [to empty it of seeds]. In like manner, the loose stitches of the washermen,[3] or a garment stitched together with threads of mixed stuff—these count as connectives until a beginning is made of undoing them.

7. The [outer] leaves of vegetables are included together [with the edible parts to make up the bulk that conveys uncleanness] if they are green; but if they are withered they are not included. R. Eliezer b. R. Zadok says: The withered leaves of cabbages are included, since they are edible; and also those of lettuces, since they serve to protect the edible parts.

8. If the leaves of onions and the shoots of onions have sap inside them, they must be measured[4] in the condition in which they are; but if they have an empty space inside them, this may be pressed tight. Spongy bread must be measured in the condition in which it is; but if it has an empty space inside it, this may be pressed tight. Flesh of a calf that is swollen and flesh of an old beast that is shrunken are measured in the condition in which they are.

9. If a cucumber was planted in a plant-pot[5] and it grew and came outside the plant-pot, it is not susceptible to uncleanness.[6] R. Simeon said: What is its nature that it should become insusceptible![7]—but, rather, what is unclean continues in its uncleanness and what becomes clean may be eaten.[8]

10. Vessels made of cattle-dung or vessels of [unburnt] clay[9] through

---

[1] The contents remain liquid; a small hole suffices to let out the contents.
[2] The contents become solid.   [3] Par. 12[9].
[4] When it is necessary to ascertain whether they are as much as an egg's bulk and so sufficient to convey food uncleanness.
[5] Which is susceptible to uncleanness as an earthenware vessel.
[6] Since it now derives nourishment from the ground.
[7] Since its roots are in the plant-pot.
[8] What is inside the plant-pot is deemed unclean, and what is outside, clean.
[9] Lit. 'earth'. See App. IV. 16 c.

which the roots can penetrate, do not render seeds susceptible to uncleanness.[1] A plant-pot in which is a hole does not render seeds susceptible to uncleanness,[2] but if it has no hole it renders seeds susceptible to uncleanness. How great should be the hole? Such that a small root can come out. If it[3] was filled with earth up to the brim, it counts as a tray without a rim.[4]

3. 1. Some things[5] need to be rendered susceptible[6] [to uncleanness] but do not need intention;[7] some need intention and also to be rendered susceptible; some need intention but do not need to be rendered susceptible; and some need neither intention nor to be rendered susceptible. All foodstuffs peculiar to man need to be made susceptible and do not need intention.[8]

2. Aught severed from a man or from a beast or from a wild animal or from birds, or from the carcase of an unclean bird, and the fat in villages,[9] and all wild vegetables excepting truffles and fungus (R. Judah says: Excepting wild leeks, purslane, and asphodel. And R. Simeon says: Excepting cardoon. R. Jose says: Excepting acorns) need intention[10] and also to be rendered susceptible [to uncleanness].

3. The carcases of unclean beasts anywhere and, in villages, the carcases of clean birds, need intention but do not need to be made susceptible.[11] The carcase of a clean beast anywhere and, in the markets, the carcase of a clean bird and fat, need neither intention nor to be rendered susceptible. R. Simeon says: Also [the carcase of] a camel, rabbit, cony or pig.

4. After dill[12] has been used to flavour [what is in] the cooking-pot, it is no longer subject to the laws of Heave-offering,[13] and it does not convey food uncleanness.[14] The sprouts of the service-tree and of candytuft, and the leaves of the arum do not convey food uncleanness unless they are sweetened.[15] R. Simeon says: Also the leaves of colocynth.

5. Costus, amomum, and the principal spices, crowfoot and asafoetida, black pepper and lozenges of safflower, may be bought with [Second-] Tithe money;[16] but they do not convey food uncleanness.[17] So R. Akiba. R. Johanan b. Nuri said to him, If they may be bought with [Second-] Tithe money why do they not convey food uncleanness? and if they do not convey food uncleanness they may not be bought with [Second-]Tithe money.[18]

6. Unripe figs and grapes—R. Akiba says: They convey food uncleanness. But R. Johanan b. Nuri says: [Only] when they come to the season when they are liable to Tithes.[19] Olives and grapes that have turned hard, the School of Shammai declare susceptible to uncleanness, but the School of Hillel declare them insusceptible. The School of Shammai declare black

---

[1] They do not count as 'vessels' but as attached to the ground.
[2] It counts as attached to the ground and not a vessel in itself.
[3] A plant-pot without a hole.
[4] See Kel. 2³. It has no receptacle and is therefore not susceptible to uncleanness.
[5] Before they can contract or convey uncleanness.
[6] By being made wet. See Lev. 11³⁴, ³⁸; p. 758, n. 1.
[7] The deliberate intention to use them as food.
[8] Since it may always be assumed that they will be used for food.
[9] Where it is not customary to eat it.   [10] They are not usually thought of as food.
[11] They are already unclean.   See App. IV. 14.   [12] That was Heave-offering.
[13] If a non-priest eats it he is not culpable.
[14] It is no longer deemed to be food.   [15] Only then are they edible.
[16] Cf. p. 73, n. 6.   [17] They are not edible, but only flavouring matter.
[18] Because it is written (Deut. 14²⁶), 'And thou shalt bestow thy money . . . and thou shalt eat'.   [19] See Mass. 1¹ᶠᶠ.

cummin insusceptible to uncleanness, and the School of Hillel declare it susceptible. So, too, [do they differ] concerning [whether it is liable to] Tithes.

7. The palm-sprout[1] is like to wood in everything save that it may be bought with [Second-]Tithe money. Unripened dates are deemed to be food, but they are exempt from Tithes.

8. When do fish become susceptible to uncleanness?[2] The School of Shammai say: After they are caught. The School of Hillel say: After they are dead. R. Akiba says: If they could live [if they were put back into the water they are not susceptible to uncleanness]. If a branch of a fig-tree was broken off but it was still attached by its bark, R. Judah declares [the fruit thereon] still insusceptible to uncleanness, but the Sages say: [Only] if it [and the fruit thereon] could live [if it was again fastened to the tree]. Grain that has been uprooted, though it is still attached by a small root, is not susceptible to uncleanness.

9. The fat of [the carcase of] a clean beast is not accounted unclean with carrion uncleanness; therefore it needs to be rendered susceptible. The fat of an unclean beast is accounted unclean with carrion uncleanness, therefore it does not need to be rendered susceptible. Unclean fish and unclean locusts in villages need intention.[3]

10. A bee-hive,[4] R. Eliezer says, counts as immovable property, a *prozbol* may be written on its security, and it is not susceptible to uncleanness while it remains in its own place; and if a man scraped honey from it on the Sabbath he is liable to a Sin-offering. But the Sages say: It does not count as immovable property, and a *prozbol* may not be written on its security, and it is susceptible to uncleanness even while it remains in its place; and if a man scraped honey from it on the Sabbath he is not culpable.

11. When do honeycombs become susceptible to uncleanness by virtue of being a liquid?[5] The School of Shammai say: After the bees have been smoked out. And the School of Hillel say: After the honeycombs have been broken.

12. R. Joshua b. Levi said: The Holy One, blessed is he, will cause every saint to inherit hereafter three hundred and ten worlds, for it is written, *That I may cause those that love me to inherit* yesh[6] *and that I may fill their treasuries.*[7] R. Simeon b. Halafta said: The Holy One, blessed is he, found no vessel that could hold Israel's blessing excepting Peace, for it is written, *The Lord will give strength unto his people; the Lord will bless his people in peace.*[8]

---

[1] Soft and edible in summer but hard in winter.
[2] For while they are alive they are not susceptible.
[3] And everywhere need to be rendered susceptible.   [4] Shebi. 10[7].
[5] They are already susceptible as food. As a liquid, however, they contract first-grade uncleanness if touched by anything unclean. See Par. 8[7].
[6] R.V. 'substance'.   [7] Prov. 8[21]. The consonants of *yesh* (yodh and shin), have the numerical values 10 and 300. This is the exegetical device called 'Gematria'. See Ab. 3[19].   [8] Ps. 29[11].

APPENDIXES

APPENDIX I

GLOSSARY OF UNTRANSLATED HEBREW TERMS

1. AB. The fifth month of the Jewish calendar, counting from NISAN (Est. 3[7]; cf. R. Sh. 1[1]). It corresponds to the latter part of July and part of August.
2. ADAR. The twelfth month of the calendar, corresponding approximately to March. When the year is intercalated (see p. 202, n. 7) a month is inserted after Adar and before NISAN, the first month of the following year. This added month is known as Adar Sheni, 'Second Adar'.
3. AM-HAARETZ ('People of the land'). The name given to those Jews who were ignorant of the Law and who failed to observe the rules of cleanness and uncleanness and were not scrupulous in setting apart Tithes from the produce (namely, Heave-offering, First Tithe, Second Tithe, and Poorman's Tithe). Those Jews who, on the contrary, undertook to be faithful in observing the requirements of the Law are known as 'Associates' (*haberim*). See also DEMAI.
4. ASHERAH. A tree worshipped by the heathen. See A. Zar. 3[7]. Cf. Ex. 34[13]; Deut. 12[3]; 16[21]; Judg. 6[25]; 1 Kings 14[15].
   Asper. See App. II A.
5. CHISLEV. The ninth month of the calendar, corresponding approximately to December.
6. DEMAI (or *dammai*). Lit. 'dubious', i.e. produce not certainly tithed. The term is applied to produce bought from an *Am-haaretz* and 'dubious' in the sense that it cannot be assumed by an 'Associate' (see Dem. 2[2]: one who undertakes to be scrupulous in his observance of the rules governing Tithes and cleanness and uncleanness) who proposes to eat it, that Heave-offering and Tithes have been duly separated from it. The Associate must, therefore, set apart the priests' dues, viz. Heave-offering and the Heave-offering of Tithe (see below, under TERUMAH) which are forbidden to non-priests. He need not, however, give First Tithe and Poorman's Tithe from *demai*-produce. See introductory note to the tractate 'Demai'.
   Denar. See App. II A.
7. ELUL. The sixth month of the calendar, corresponding approximately to September.
8. ERUB. Lit. 'mixture', 'amalgamation' or 'combination'.
   (*a*) According to the Sabbath Law the movements of the people of a town are restricted on the Sabbath to 2,000 cubits from the boundaries of the town. But if enough food for two meals is deposited in an accessible place on the eve of the Sabbath at the prescribed 2,000 cubits' distance, this spot counts as a man's temporary abode, thereby allowing him a range of 2,000 cubits beyond the common Sabbath limit.
   (*b*) Similarly *Erub* may be arranged as between the various domiciles within a courtyard; if all the occupants have a share in a deposit of food placed in a known place in the courtyard, they are all thereby given unrestricted access to the premises of the other occupants. See also SHITTUF.
9. HABDALAH. Lit. 'division', 'distinction'. The ceremony which marks the end of a Sabbath or Festival-day and the entering in of an ordinary day (see Singer, *Authorised Jewish Prayer Book*, pp. 216 f.).
10. HAGGADAH (pl. *Haggadoth*). Lit 'narration'. The type of rabbinical interpretation and exposition of Scripture which aims at edification (as opposed to HALAKAH, which aims at defining or supporting legal usage). *Haggadah* is not frequently met with in the Mishnah; but it is sometimes used as a conclusion to some of the tractates (cf. Peah, Yoma, Taanith, Sotah, Baba Kamma), and it is prominent in Aboth.

11. HALAKAH (pl. *Halakoth*). Lit. 'custom', 'rule'. An accepted decision in rabbinic law, usually, but not necessarily, derivable from Scripture. The term is also used for those parts of the Talmud concerned with legal matters in contrast to HAGGADAH. The Mishnah is almost wholly *Halakah*.

12. HALITZAH. Lit. 'drawing off' (sc. of the shoe). The ceremony prescribed (in Deut. 25$^{7-9}$; cf. Yeb. 12$^{1ff.}$) when a man refuses to marry the widow of his brother who has died childless.

13. HALLEL. Lit. 'Praise thou (the Lord)'. The recital of Psalms 113–18 at Festivals and New Moons. By the 'Great Hallel' (Taan. 3^9) Ps. 136 is meant.

14. HAMETZ. Leavened bread; or any other matter containing the 'five kinds of grain' (wheat, barley, spelt, goatgrass, and oats) in a fermented state. See p. 136, n. 12.

Hin. See App. II D.

Issar. See App. II A.

15. JUBILEE (The year of). Heb. *Yobel*. The fiftieth year. See Lev. 25$^{8-16}$, $^{23-4}$.

Kab. See App. II D and E.

16. KETUBAH (or *Ketubbah*). Lit. 'a written document'. A wife's 'jointure'. The word is used (*a*) for the document (cf. Ket. 4$^{7-12}$) in which the bridegroom pledges himself to assign a certain sum of money to the bride in the event of his death or of his divorcing her; and (*b*) for the sum of money so assigned (cf. Ket. 5^1).

17. KONAM. A word substituted for Korban (lit. 'an offering', i.e. sacred as an offering dedicated to the Temple), the usual term introducing a vow to abstain from anything, or to deny another person the use of anything.

Kor. See App. II D and E.

18. KORBAN. See KONAM.

Kortab. See App. II D.

19. KOY. Probably a species of wild sheep, or a cross between a goat and some species of gazelle. It remained a matter incapable of settlement whether it came within the category of cattle or wild animal, a domesticated or an undomesticated beast.

Lethek. See App. II D.

Litra. See App. II D.

Log. See App. II D.

20. LULAB. Lit. 'palm-branch'. The branches of palm, myrtle, and willow, bound together and carried, together with a citron, during the Feast of Tabernacles in fulfilment of Lev. 23^{40}.

Maah. See App. II A.

21. MAAMAD. Lit. 'place of standing'. It is the name given to a group of representatives from outlying districts, corresponding to the twenty-four 'courses of priests'. Part of them went up to the Temple as witnesses of the offering of the sacrifices (Taan. 4^2), and part came together in their own town, where they held prayers at fixed times during the day coinciding with the fixed times of sacrifice in the Temple. This is the origin of the Synagogue system, in which the various daily offices are called by the names made familiar in the routine of the Temple (see p. 199, n. 5).

22. MADDAF. Lit. 'slight or indirect contact'. It denotes the degree of uncleanness conveyed by those enumerated in Lev. 15$^{2, 25}$, to what lies above them even though they are not in immediate contact with it. It is not a 'father of uncleanness' which can convey uncleanness to men and vessels, but a 'derived uncleanness' able only to render foodstuffs and liquids unclean. See also MIDRAS.

23. MARHESHWAN. The eighth month of the calendar, corresponding approximately to November.

24. MELOG. Lit. 'plucking'. The term describes that property of the wife of which the husband has full use and benefit until her death or divorce, without being answerable for any loss, damage, or deterioration which the property suffers from his use. See also ṢON BARZEL.

25. MEZUZAH. Lit. 'doorpost'. See Deut. 6⁹. A small rolled-up piece of parchment on which is written the two passages Deut. 6⁴⁻⁹; 11¹³⁻²¹, and which is enclosed in a cylinder and fastened to the right-hand doorpost.

26. MIDRAS. Lit. 'place of pressure or treading'. It denotes the degree of uncleanness suffered by an object which any of those enumerated in Lev. 12²; 15², ²⁵, sits, lies, or rides upon or leans against. Any object which is fit to sit, lie, or ride upon, and which is usually sat, lain, or ridden upon (without affecting that object's proper function if it is not primarily a seat, couch, or saddle), is deemed to be 'susceptible to *midras*-uncleanness'.

27. MIDRASH. Lit. 'exposition', sc. of Scripture. Interpretation of Scripture, originally in the sense of deducing an idea or rule from Scripture, in the manner of either HAGGADAH or HALAKAH. The term is used also of systematic verse-by-verse commentary of Scripture as contrasted with MISHNAH, which teaches *Halakoth* independently of their Scriptural basis. *Mina*. See App. II A and B.

28. MISHNAH. Lit. 'teaching', or 'repetition'. The collection of legal traditions (explaining or supplementing the laws of the Pentateuch or derivable from the principles of those laws) in the form compiled by R. Judah the Patriarch at the close of the second century A.D. *Mishnah* is also used frequently in the sense of a single teaching or a single paragraph contained in such a collection of traditional law. The *Mishnah* of R. Judah contains references to earlier collections also known by the name *Mishnah*. See General Index, s.v. *Mishnah*.

29. NATHIN (f. *Nethinah*). Lit. 'given'. See 1 Chron. 9²; Ezra 2⁴³, 8²⁰; Neh. 3²⁶. They were descendants of the Gibeonites whom Joshua made into Temple slaves (Josh. 9²⁷). For their status in the community see Kidd. 4¹ᶠᶠ.

30. NISAN. The first month of the calendar (see Est. 3⁷), corresponding to the latter part of March and part of April.

31. OMER. Lit. 'sheaf'. See Lev. 23¹⁰. Before the new harvest could be reaped, a sheaf of barley must first be reaped and the flour offered as a Meal-offering in the Temple. See Men. 10¹ᶠᶠ. Only after it had been offered was the produce of the new harvest permitted for common use.

32. ORLAH. Lit. 'foreskin', 'uncircumcision'. See Lev. 19²³. The fruit of young trees was forbidden for common use during the first three years as being 'the fruit of uncircumcision'. In the fourth year the fruit could be 'redeemed' (i.e. its equivalent in money set apart, plus a fifth of its value), and it was then free for common use. Fourth-year fruit must either be consumed in Jerusalem, or the money by which it was redeemed must be spent in Jerusalem. 'Orlah' is the name of the tenth tractate of the first division of the Mishnah.

33. PEAH. Lit. 'the corner', sc. of the field that is being reaped. A portion of the crop of a field (and also of an olive tree) left by the reapers for the benefit of the poor. See Lev. 19⁹ᶠᶠ. 'Peah' is the name of the second tractate of the first division of the Mishnah.

Perutah. See App. II A.

Pondion. See App. II A.

34. PROZBOL. The word is explained as an abbreviation of πρὸς βουλῇ βουλευτῶν. See Shebi. 10⁴. According to Deut. 15², all loans were remitted in the Seventh Year. Lest this should lead to fraud or oppression (Deut. 15⁹) Hillel enacted the rule of the *Prozbol*, which was a declaration made before a court of law by a creditor, and signed by witnesses, to the effect that the

loan in question would not be remitted under the terms of the Seventh-Year law.

35. PURIM. Lit. 'lots'. The festival kept on Adar 14 (or 15) in remembrance of the salvation of the Jews in Persia, as recorded in the book of Esther. See p. 201, n. 5.

36. RABBAN. Lit. 'our master', 'our lord'. A title of honour given in the Mishnah to most of the presidents of the Rabbinical Court after the time of Hillel.

37. RE'IYYAH. Lit. 'appearance'. Pilgrimage to the Temple in fulfilment of Deut. 16^{16}, which requires all males 'to appear before the Lord' three times a year, at the Feasts of Passover, Pentecost, and Tabernacles. The name *Re'iyyah* is used also of the Whole-offering which the Israelite brings at such times.

Ris. See App. II c.

Seah. See App. II D and E.

Sela. See App. II A and B.

Shekel. See App. II A and B.

38. SHEMAʿ. Lit. 'Hear (, O Israel!)'. The first word of the group of three passages from Scripture (Deut. 6$^{4-9}$; 11$^{13-21}$; Num. 15$^{37-41}$) which must be recited daily in the morning and in the evening. See Ber. 2^2.

39. SHITTUF. Lit. 'association', 'partnership'. See Erub. 7^6. A deposit of food is placed jointly by the occupants of neighbouring premises and court-yards in an accessible place in some alley-way. This, for purposes of the Sabbath law, creates a 'partnership', thereby granting each participator access to the premises of the other participators, so effecting a certain elasticity in the Sabbath restriction which forbids a man to carry a burden from one domain into another (Shab. 7^2, end). The areas and premises belonging to those participating in the *Shittuf* are thus transformed into a single domain.

40. SHOFAR. The ram's horn, blown on prescribed occasions in the Temple and in the Synagogue service. In Shek. 6^1, *Shofar* is used to describe the chests (perhaps indicating their shape) into which were cast money contributions towards the upkeep of the Temple-service.

Sit. See App. II c.

41. ṢON BARZEL. Lit. 'sheep of iron'. (*a*) The wife's property which the husband, in case of her death or divorce, must restore in full (see Yeb. 7^1). (*b*) A species of contract in which *A* sells his flock to *B* on condition that *B* shares the profits with *A* until such time as he has made payment in full, *B* being solely responsible for all losses sustained (B.M. 5^6; Bekh. 2^4).

42. SUKKAH. Lit. 'booth'. The temporary, lightly built hut set up in fulfilment of Lev. 23$^{34-6,\ 39-43}$, which requires the Israelites to dwell in 'booths' during the seven days of the Feast of Tabernacles. The rules applying to this observance are treated in detail in the sixth tractate of the second division of the Mishnah.

43. TALMUD. Lit. 'learning'. The general sense of the word is 'study' of the Law. It is more common in the narrower sense of the comments and discussions (the *Gemara*, lit. 'completion') on the text of the Mishnah by Palestinian and Babylonian scholars from the third to the fifth century A.D., which constitute the Palestinian Talmud (*Talmud Yerushalmi*) and the Babylonian Talmud (*Talmud Babli*).

44. TAMMUZ. The fourth month of the calendar, corresponding with the latter part of June and part of July.

45. TEBET. The tenth month of the calendar, corresponding approximately with January.

46. TEFILLAH. Lit. 'prayer'. It denotes the 'prayer' *par excellence*, the 'Shemoneh Esreh', or the 'Eighteen Benedictions', one of the essential

elements in the daily Synagogue service (cf. Taan. 2²); Singer, *Authorised Jewish Prayer Book*, pp. 44–54. It was said three times a day, morning, afternoon, and evening. The first two corresponded to the morning and afternoon Daily Whole-offerings in the Temple. On Sabbaths and Festival-days an 'Additional Tefillah' was said, corresponding to the 'Additional Offering', offered on those days. See Ber. 4¹—5⁷.

47. TEREFAH. Lit. 'torn', sc. by wild beasts. Originally (cf. Lev. 22⁸) the term signified the flesh of clean beasts which had been mauled or killed by beasts of prey and so rendered unfit for food. It is more common in the Mishnah in the technical sense of (*a*) the flesh of a beast that had received a fatal injury, such that it could not continue alive for another twelve months, or that suffered from some defect or abnormality; or (*b*) the flesh of an animal slaughtered unskilfully although in valid fashion, as distinct from *nebelah*, 'carrion' (lit. animal carcase), a clean beast that has either suffered a violent death, or that was slaughtered not in a valid and regular fashion (Hull. 2¹⁻⁴). See generally the tractate Hullin, especially ch. 3. *Teresith*. See App. II A.

48. TERUMAH. (1) Heave-offering, the portion of the yield of their harvests which Israelites must give to the priests (Num. 18⁸ᶠᶠ; Deut. 18⁴). Heave-offering figures prominently in the teaching of the Mishnah (it is referred to nearly six hundred times). In addition to its being the first levy on newly harvested produce, the right to eat of Heave-offering is a gauge of priestly status (see Lev. 22¹⁰ᶠᶠ; Yeb. 7¹ᶠᶠ); also, by reason of its sanctity, Heave-offering is one degree more highly susceptible to uncleanness than is common food (see p. 714, n. 3).

(2) Heave-offering of Tithe, the tithe which is given to the priests by the levites out of the tithe which they have received from Israelites (Num. 18²⁵ᶠᶠ).

(3) In the tractate 'Shekalim' (3¹ᶠᶠ; cf. Ned. 2⁴) *Terumah* is used in the sense of 'contribution', 'levy', of shekels taken at stated times out of the Shekel-chamber in the Temple.

(4) The portions allotted to the priests from certain offerings in the Temple. See Zeb. 5⁶, ⁷; Men. 7².

49. TISHRI. The seventh month of the calendar, corresponding to the latter part of September and the first part of October. *Tritimor*. See App. II B. *Tropaic*. See App. II A. *Zuz*. Another name for the *denar*. See App. II A and B.

APPENDIX II

MONEY, WEIGHTS, AND MEASURES

A. MONEY:

    1 perutah (the smallest copper coin current).

    8 perutahs—1 issar.

    2 issars—1 pondion.

    2 pondions—1 maah (the smallest silver coin current. It is sometimes referred to simply as 'a piece of silver'; B.M. 4³. Its weight is given as 16 barleycorns).

    3 issars—1 teresith (Shebu. 6³).

    12 pondions—1 denar or zuz.

    6 maahs—1 denar or zuz.

    5 aspers—1 denar or zuz (Eduy. 1¹⁰; M. Sh. 2⁹).

    2 tropaics—1 denar or zuz.

    2 denars—1 shekel.

2 shekels—1 sela.
25 denars—1 golden denar or zahub.
100 denars—1 mina.

For the purchasing power of money at the time of the Mishnah, cf. B.B. 5[1] (a yoke of oxen), B.M. 5[1] (price of wheat), B.M. 5[2] (rent of a courtyard), Ket. 5[8] (a woman's annual dressing allowance), Maas. 2[5] (fruit in small quantity), Erub. 8[2] (price of bread and flour), Men. 13[8] (young bullocks, rams, and lambs), B.K. 10[4] (an ass), Meil. 6[4] (mantle and shirt).

Roughly speaking a denar or zuz may be considered the equivalent of a shilling or mark; and the sela approximately equivalent to a dollar.

B. WEIGHTS:

1 zuz (about 3½ grammes).
2 zuz—1 common shekel.
2 shekels—1 sela (but cf. Ket. 5[9]; Hull. 11[2])
4 zuz—1 'shekel of the Sanctuary'.
50 zuz—1 tritimor (or tartimar).
100 zuz—1 Italian mina.
160 zuz—1 mina.
6,000 zuz—1 talent.
37½ minas—1 talent.

C. DISTANCE:

1 fingerbreadth (about 2⅓ centimetres).
4 fingerbreadths—1 handbreadth.
2 handbreadths—1 sit (the distance between the tips of the outstretched thumb and index finger. But according to Maimonides the sit is the distance between the outstretched index and middle fingers, and is equal only to four fingerbreadths).
3 handbreadths—1 span.
2 spans—1 cubit (but cf. Kel. 17[9, 10]).
266⅔ cubits—1 ris.
2,000 cubits—1 'mile' (or Sabbath-day's journey).
7½ ris—1 'mile' (Yom. 6[4]).

D. LIQUID AND DRY MEASURE:

64 kortabs—1 log (the contents of 6 eggs).
2 litras—1 log.
4 logs—1 kab (3 kabs—1 hin).
6 kabs—1 seah (3 seahs—1 ephah. Cf. Men. 6[6]).
30 seahs—1 kor (or 1 homer).
2 letheks—1 kor.

E. MEASUREMENT OF AREA:

1 kor's space—75,000 square cubits.
1 seah's space—2,500 square cubits.
1 kab's space—416⅔ square cubits.
(viz. such ground as suffices for the sowing of a *kor*, *seah*, or *kab* of seed respectively. Cf. Arak. 3[2]; Lev. 27[16]).

APPENDIX III

RABBINICAL TEACHERS QUOTED OR REFERRED TO IN THE TEXT OF THE MISHNAH

PRE-TANNAITIC (from *c.* 200 B.C. to A.D. *c.* 10)

Abtalion
Admon
Akabya b. Mehalaleel
Antigonus of Soko
Baba b. Buta
Ben Bag-Bag (Johanan)
Ben He-He
Hanan the Egyptian

*Hillel the Elder
Johanan the High Priest
Jose b. Joezer
Jose b. Johanan
Joshua b. Perahyah
Judah b. Tabbai
Measha
Menahem (Hag. 2²)

Nittai of Arbela
Onias the Circle-maker
Shammai the Elder
Shemaiah
Simeon b. Shetah
Simeon the Just

FIRST GENERATION (A.D. *c.* 10–80)

Ben Bukri
Dositheus of Kefar Yatma
Eleazar b. Dolai, Abba
Gamaliel the Elder (Rabban)
Hananiah b. Hezekiah b. Gorion
Hanina, Prefect of the

Priests
Johanan b. Gudgada
Johanan b. ha-Horani
Johanan b. Zakkai
Joezer of the Birah
Jose Holi Kufri, Abba
Judah b. Bathyra
Menahem b. Signai
Nahum the Mede

Nahum the Scrivener
Nehunya b. Gudgada
School of Hillel
School of Shammai
Simeon b. Gamaliel I (Rabban)
Simeon of Mizpah
Zechariah b. ha-Kazzab
Zechariah b. Kabutal

SECOND GENERATION (A.D. *c.* 80–120)

Ben Bathyra (see Simeon b. B.)
Dosa b. Harkinas
Eleazar b. Arak
Eleazar b. Azariah
Eleazar b. Diglai
Eliezer (b. Hyrcanus)
Eliezer b. Jacob I
Eliezer b. Zadok I
Gamaliel II (Rabban)
Halafta
Hanina b. Dosa
Hanina b. Gamaliel

*Huspith
? Hyrcanus of Kefar Etam
Jeshebab*
Jose b. Hanin, Abba
Jose b. Meshullam
*Jose b. Onias
Jose son of the Damascene*
Jose the Priest
Joshua b. Bathyra
Joshua (b. Hananiah)
*Joshua b. Hyrcanus
Nehunya b. Elinathan
Nehunya b. ha-Kanah*

Papias
*Samuel the Younger
Saul b. Batnith, Abba*
Simeon b. Bathyra
Simeon b. Nathaniel
Simeon brother of Azariah
Simeon of Shezur
Simeon of Teman
Simeon son of the Prefect
Yakim of Haddar
Zadok

THIRD GENERATION (A.D. *c.* 120–140)

Abtolemos
Akiba
Ben Azzai (see Simeon b. A.)
Ben Nanos (see Simeon b. N.)
Ben Zoma (see Simeon b. Z.)
Eleazar (b.) Hisma
Eleazar b. Judah (of Bartotha)
Eleazar b. Perata
Eleazar of Modiim

*Elisha b. Abuyah
Hananiah b. Akashya*
Hananiah b. Hakinai
Hananiah b. Teradion
Hanina b. Antigonus
Ilai
Ishmael (b. Elisha)
Johanan b. Baroka
*Johanan b. Joshua
Johanan b. Matthias*
Johanan b. Nuri
Jose b. Kisma
Jose the Galilean

Joshua b. Matthias
Judah b. Baba
*Judah the Priest
Levitas of Jabneh
Mattithiah b. Heresh
Nehemiah of Beth Deli
Simeon b. Akashya*
Simeon b. Azzai
Simeon b. Nanos
Simeon b. Zoma
Tarfon

FOURTH GENERATION (A.D. *c.* 140–165)

Abba Saul
Eleazar
Eleazar b. Jose the Gali-
lean
Eleazar b. Mattai
Eleazar b. Pilai (Piabi)
Eleazar b. Shammua
Eliezer b. Jacob II
Eliezer b. Zadok II
Halafta b. Dosa of Kefar

Hananiah
Hananiah b. Akabya
Hananiah of Ono
Ishmael b. Johanan b.
Baroka
Jacob (? b. Korshai)
Johanan the Sandal-
maker
Jonathan
Joshua b. Karha

Jose b. ha-Hotef Ephrathi
Jose (b. Halafta)
Judah (b. Ilai)
Meir
Menahem (Yom. 4⁴)
Nehemiah
* **Simeon b. Gamaliel II**
(Rabban)
Simeon (b. Yohai)

FIFTH GENERATION (A.D. *c.* 165–200)

Abba Gorion
Dositheus b. Yannai
Eleazar b. Simeon (b.
Yohai)
Eleazar ha-Kappar
Ishmael b. Jose (b. Ha-
lafta)

Jaddua the Babylonian
Jose b. Judah
Jose of Kefar Babli
*Judah the Patriarch
Judah b. Tema
Nathan the Babylonian
Nehorai

Phineas b. Jair
Simeon b. Eleazar
Simeon b. Halafta
Simeon b. Menasya
Symmachos

SIXTH GENERATION (A.D. *c.* 200–220)

Simeon b. Judah (the Patriarch)   **Gamaliel III (Rabban)*

POST-TANNAITIC (A.D. *c.* 240)

Joshua b. Levi   *Yannai*

* Indicates members of the Hillel dynasty who acted as Presidents of the Rabbinical Court or Sanhedrin.
Names printed in italics occur only once or twice in the Mishnah.
Names printed in heavy type occur with great frequency.
See the General Index for the complete list of references to each of these teachers.

APPENDIX IV

THE RULES OF UNCLEANNESS

(From *Eliyahu Rabbah*, a commentary on the Division 'Tohoroth', by Elijah, the Gaon of Wilna, 1720–97)

1. There are twelve uncleannesses which include every kind of uncleanness:

(*a*) There are six which issue from the human person: (i) that of a man or (ii) a woman who has a flux (Lev. 15², ²⁵); (iii) of a menstruant (Lev. 15¹⁹); (iv) of a woman after childbirth (Lev. 12²); (v) of a leper (Lev. 13¹ᶠᶠ); and (vi) male semen (Lev. 15¹⁶).

(*b*) There are three 'contact-uncleannesses' or things which, when dead, convey uncleanness to those who touch them: (i) a corpse (Num. 19¹¹); (ii) carrion (Lev. 11²⁶, ³⁹); and (iii) creeping things (Lev. 11²⁹⁻³¹).

(*c*) There are three deeds whereby uncleanness is suffered even without contact: (i) the burning of the Red Heifer (Num. 19⁷)—howbeit the ashes thereof (Num. 19¹⁰) and the Sin-offering water (Num. 19²¹) convey uncleanness only by contact and carrying; (ii) the burning of the bullocks and the he-goats which must be burnt (Lev. 4¹², ²¹, ²⁶; 16²⁷, ²⁸); and (iii) the leading away of the Scapegoat (Lev. 16²⁶).

2. These seven suffer seven-day uncleanness: (i) a man or (ii) a woman who has a flux (Lev. 15¹³, ²⁸); (iii) a menstruant (Lev. 15¹⁹); (iv) a woman after childbirth (Lev. 12²); (v) one who has connexion with a menstruant (Lev. 15²⁴); (vi) a leper in his days of reckoning (Lev. 14⁸); and (vii) one who has contracted uncleanness from a corpse (Num. 19¹¹).

3. (*a*) Fathers of Uncleanness in a man who has a flux are: (i) his bare flesh; (ii) his 'fountains', viz. his flux, semen, urine, and spittle (which includes the phlegm of his lungs, throat, and nose); and (iii) what he lies, sits, or rides on (save that what he rides on renders garments unclean by contact only and not by carrying).

(*b*) The like applies to a woman who has a flux, to a menstruant, a woman after childbirth, and a leper; save that whereas male flux and male semen belong not to a woman, she has two other things which correspond, for she renders him unclean who has connexion with her so that he conveys uncleanness to men and to earthenware vessels, and in place of his flux is her menstrual blood.

4. (*a*) Fathers of Uncleanness in a corpse are: (i) a whole corpse; (ii) an olive's bulk of a corpse or of corpse-dregs; (iii) a ladleful of corpse-mould; (iv) the backbone or the skull; (v) a member from the corpse; (vi) a member severed from a living man; (vii) a quarter-*kab* from the greatest in bulk or the greatest in number of the bones (of a corpse), or from the greater part of the corpse or from the greatest number of its parts; (viii) a quarter-*log* of blood, or 'mingled-blood' (Ohol. 3⁵); (ix) more than a ladleful of grave dust.

(*b*) These all convey uncleanness by contact, by carrying, and by over-shadowing, save that a ladleful of corpse-mould and more than a ladleful of grave-dust do not convey uncleanness by contact.

5. (*a*) A barleycorn's bulk (i) of bone, (ii) of land belonging to gentiles, (iii) of a Grave-area, (iv) of a member which is severed from a living man or corpse and which lacks its proper flesh, convey uncleanness by contact and by carrying but not by overshadowing.

(*b*) A sepulchre-stone and its buttressing stone convey uncleanness by contact and by overshadowing but not by carrying; and the same applies to a closed grave.

6. There are three manners of overshadowing by which uncleanness is conveyed: (i) what overshadows a corpse, (ii) what a corpse overshadows, and (iii) what is overshadowed by something which also overshadows a corpse.

7. If a man (who has touched a corpse) touches vessels and these vessels touch a man, they all alike become Fathers of Uncleanness (cf. 12*d*, 17*a*).

8. (*a*) Fathers of Uncleanness in carrion are: (i) an olive's bulk of the flesh, (ii) a severed member from the dead beast, and (iii) a severed member from the living beast.

(*b*) Similarly, in creeping things, Fathers of Uncleanness are: (i) a lentil's bulk of the flesh, (ii) a severed member from the dead thing, and (iii) a severed member from the living thing.

9. He who burns the Red Heifer, all who are occupied therewith, from the beginning to the end, and he who touches or carries its ashes and the Sin-offering water, render garments unclean; and they who burn the bullocks, viz. the three bullocks (Lev. 4¹², ²¹; 16²⁸), and the two he-goats (Lev. 4²⁶; 16²⁷) and all who are occupied therewith, convey uncleanness after they are come forth from the wall of the Temple Court (on their way to the Place of Burning) and until they have reduced it to ashes; and he who leads away the Scapegoat—after he is come forth from the wall of Jerusalem.

10. Semen in itself is a Father of Uncleanness; a gentile is in every respect like to a man who suffers a flux; and a Samaritan is like to a man who has connexion with a menstruant.

11. There are three things leprous: (i) leprosy-signs in a man, (ii) leprosy signs in houses, and (iii) leprosy signs in garments, whether in the warp or in the woof, or in leather.

12. (*a*) Of the 'Fathers' spoken of, all convey uncleanness by carrying, excepting semen, a leper in his days of reckoning (Lev. 14⁸), vessels which touch a corpse, a man who touches a corpse, Sin-offering water that is

insufficient for a sprinkling, and a creeping thing; they convey uncleanness by contact but not by carrying.

(*b*) None of them conveys uncleanness by overshadowing excepting a corpse and whatsoever is severed from it.

(*c*) Leprosy-signs convey uncleanness (to whatsoever is in a house) by 'entering in' (cf. Lev. 13[46]), but not by overshadowing.

(*d*) They none of them convey seven-day uncleanness excepting a corpse and whatsoever is severed from it, which convey uncleanness to all who touch them; and a man who has touched vessels which had touched a corpse or a man who had touched a corpse or aught severed from it, conveys seven-day uncleanness to vessels.

13. They are the twelve, and they are from the words of the Law. There is yet another uncleanness which is from the words of the Scribes: the uncleanness of idolatry, wherein are three uncleannesses—the idol itself, its appurtenances and what is offered to it; also wine that had certainly been poured out in its honour. They all convey uncleanness after the manner of a creeping thing (see 1*b*, 12*a*).

14. (*a*) Carrion, whether of wild animals, unclean or clean cattle, conveys uncleanness by contact and by carrying, but it does not convey 'gullet-uncleanness', since that is a hidden place.

(*b*) In carrion the flesh and the members alone convey uncleanness: the skin, bones, sinews, horns, hoofs, and blood do not convey uncleanness; and the same applies to the fat from carrion or clean cattle.

(*c*) Carrion of a clean bird has but the one uncleanness—when there is an olive's bulk of it in the (eater's) gullet; but an unclean bird, clean and unclean fishes and locusts, have no uncleanness at all.

15. (*a*) The Red Heifer Sin-offering conveys uncleanness to those who slaughter it or receive or sprinkle the blood, or burn it or assist thereat, or who throw the cedar-wood.

(*b*) Its ashes and the Sin-offering water convey uncleanness. The Sin-offering water is of two kinds—what is sufficient and what is insufficient for a sprinkling; that which is sufficient conveys uncleanness by contact and by carrying, and that which is insufficient conveys uncleanness by contact but not by carrying.

16. (*a*) Six kinds of utensil, if they touch a corpse, become Fathers of Uncleanness, viz. such as are made of metal, wood, leather, bone, cloth, or sacking.

(*b*) Two kinds of utensil contract uncleanness but do not become Fathers of Uncleanness, viz. such as are made of earthenware or alum-crystal (also, according to the words of the Scribes, such as are made of glass).

(*c*) Three kinds of utensil do not contract uncleanness (whether according to the words of the Law or according to the words of the Scribes), viz. such as are made of stone, cattle-dung, or earth (unbaked clay).

(*d*) There are six kinds of metal utensil, viz. such as are made of gold, silver, copper, iron, tin, or lead.

(*e*) Utensils made from the skin or bone of clean or unclean cattle, wild animals or birds or from creeping things (save only the wing of the vulture) or from unclean locusts or fish or anything in the sea, are all of them insusceptible to uncleanness; but if to what comes out of the sea aught soever was joined that grows on the earth, it is susceptible to uncleanness.

17. (*a*) A corpse, and whatsoever is severed from it, can convey uncleanness through seven removes: viz. by touching (1) vessels, which touch (2) a man, who touches (3) vessels (all three themselves becoming Fathers of Uncleanness), which can render (4) common food unclean at a first remove (conveying to it 'first-grade uncleanness') and also (5) at a second remove (whereby it suffers 'second-grade uncleanness') and also (6) at a third remove

to Heave-offering (making it invalid with 'third-grade uncleanness') and also (7) at a fourth remove to Hallowed Things (making them invalid with 'fourth-grade uncleanness').

(*b*) A man or woman who suffers a flux, a menstruant, a woman after childbirth, and a leper, can convey uncleanness through six removes: what they (1) lie, sit, or ride on, and their 'fountains' convey uncleanness to (2) a man, so that he renders (3) vessels unclean by contact, and common food at a first remove (whereby it suffers 'first-grade uncleanness') and also (4) at a second remove (whereby it suffers 'second-grade uncleanness') and also (5) at a third remove to Heave-offering (making it invalid with 'third-grade uncleanness') and also (6) at a fourth remove to Hallowed Things (making them invalid with 'fourth-grade uncleanness').

(*c*) The other Fathers of Uncleanness can convey uncleanness through five removes: they render (1) a man unclean, so that he renders (2) utensils unclean, and common food at a first remove (whereby it suffers 'first-grade uncleanness') and also (3) at a second remove (whereby it suffers 'second-grade uncleanness') and also (4) at a third remove to Heave-offering (making it invalid with 'third-grade uncleanness') and also (5) at a fourth remove to Hallowed Things (making them invalid with 'fourth-grade uncleanness').

(*d*) Creeping things and semen can convey uncleanness through four removes: to common food at (1) a first remove, and also (2) at a second remove; and to Heave-offering (3) at a third remove; and to Hallowed Things (4) at a fourth remove.

18. (*a*) An earthenware vessel never becomes a Father of Uncleanness.

(*b*) So, too, foodstuffs and liquids never become Fathers of Uncleanness (excepting the 'fountains' of a man or a woman who has a flux, a menstruant, a woman after childbirth, a leper, a gentile, a man who has connexion with a menstruant, blood from a corpse, blood from a creeping thing, and Sin-offering water.

(*c*) No creatures having life convey or contract uncleanness, excepting man: the Scapegoat conveys uncleanness to him who leads it away, but is itself clean.

19. These are Fathers of Uncleanness according to the words of the Scribes: (*a*) mingled-blood (Ohol. 3⁵), (*b*) land belonging to gentiles (both the clods of it and the air of it), (*c*) a Grave-area (of which there are three kinds: a field wherein is a lost grave, a field wherein a grave has been ploughed up, and a field wherein are tomb-niches), (*d*) the dwellings of gentiles, (*e*) intertwined branches, (*f*) stones jutting out from walls, (*g*) any one who touches the foetus of one in hard travail, (*h*) coffins in which is an empty space of one handbreadth (cf. Ber. 19*b*), (*j*) aught that overhangs to the extent of the thickness of an ox-goad, (*k*) *terefah* that has been slaughtered, and (*l*) the hide of a man.

20. These, according to the words of the Scribes, convey uncleanness as by their flux: (*a*) a Samaritan conveys uncleanness by what he lies, sits, or rides on, by his spittle (including the phlegm of his lungs, throat, or nose), and by his urine; and (*b*) the daughters of the Samaritans even from their cradles (convey uncleanness in like manner), as also do the gentiles (see par. 10).

21. A man or a woman who has a flux, a menstruant, a woman after child-birth, or a leper, who have died, convey uncleanness to what they lie, sit, or ride on, and also to what lies above them (although it is not touched by them).

22. (Also Fathers of Uncleanness, according to the words of the Scribes, are) the daughters of the Samaritans, who convey uncleanness to those who have connexion with them; menstruants who await a day (of cleanness) over against a day (of uncleanness); the uncleanness of the *Am-haaretz* whose garments are unclean as by *midras*-uncleanness for Pharisees, and that of

Pharisees whose garments are unclean as by *midras*-uncleanness for those who eat of Heave-offering, and that of those who eat of Heave-offering whose garments are unclean as by *midras*-uncleanness for those who eat of Hallowed Things, and that of those who eat of Hallowed Things whose garments are unclean as by *midras*-uncleanness for those who sprinkle the Sin-offering water.

23. There are six classes of leprosy signs: (*a*) those in *the skin of the flesh*, (*b*) a boil or a burning, (*c*) scalp-baldness or forehead-baldness, (*d*) tetters, (*e*) the signs in garments, and (*f*) the signs in houses.

Such as arise in *the skin of the flesh* may need (shutting up during) two weeks and (are judged by) three tokens; scalp-baldness and forehead-baldness may need (shutting up during) two weeks and (are judged by) two tokens; tetters may need (shutting up during) two weeks and (are judged by) two tokens; a boil or a burning may need (shutting up during) two weeks and (are judged by) two tokens; signs in garments may need (shutting up during) two weeks and (are judged by) one token; signs in houses may need (shutting up during) three weeks and (are judged by) one token. The 'spreading' betokens uncleanness in all the four colours, whether in *the skin of the flesh*, or in the boil, or in the burning, or in the scalp-baldness, or in the forehead-baldness. There are two colours (of the leprosy signs) in garments and likewise in houses.

INDEXES

ABBREVIATIONS

OF TITLES OF TRACTATES USED IN THE INDEXES

INDEX OF BIBLICAL PASSAGES

QUOTED IN THE TEXT OF THE MISHNAH

---

¹ The textual authorities constantly confuse the names Hananiah and Hanina.

Judges forbidden to receive payment, Bekh. 4[6].

—, those ineligible to be, Sanh. 3[3ff.]; Bekh. 4[10]; 5[4].

Jujube fruit, Dem. 1[1]; Kil. 1[4].

Kab, App. II D, E.

Karkemith, Eduy, 5[6].

Karmelith, Shab. 11[4n.]; Erub. 9[2n.]; Toh. 6[6n.].

Kefar Aziz, Kil. 6[4].

Kefar Etam, Yeb. 12[6].

Kefar ha-Babli, Eduy. 6[2].

Kefar Ludim, Gitt. 1[1].

Kefar Othnai, Gitt. 1[5]; 7[7].

Kefar Signah, Men. 8[6]; Kel. 5[4].

Kefar Yatmah, Orl. 2[5].

Kelim, Kel. 30[4].

Keni, Ohol. 18[9].

Kenubka-cakes, Hall. 1[5].

Keramiyon, Par. 8[10].

Keruthim, Men. 8[6].

Kesarion, Ohol. 18[9n.].

Kesrin, Ohol. 18[9].

Ketubah, Peah 3[7]; 8[8]; Bikk. 3[12]; Yeb. 4[3,4]; 15[7]; Ket. 1[2] & *passim*; Ned. 9[5]; 11[12]; Sot. 1[5]; 4[1,2,3,5]; 6[1,2]; Gitt. 4[3,8]; 5[1]; 8[5]; 9[4]; Kidd. 2[5]; B. M. 1[5]; B. B. 9[8,9]; 10[7]; Makk. 1[1]; Bekh. 8[9]; Arak. 6[1,2]. App. I. 16.

Key, parts of a, Kel. 14[8].

Kidney-bean, Kil. 1[1].

Kidron, the brook, Yom. 5[6]; Meil. 3[3]; Midd. 3[2].

Kilaim. See Diverse Kinds.

Kilbith-fish, A. Zar. 2[6].

Kindling Gate, Shek. 6[3]; Midd. 1[4]; 2[6].

King, the, Ber. 5[1]; Bikk. 3[4]; Yom. 7[5]; 8[1]; Ned. 2[5]; Sot. 7[2,8]; B. B. 6[7]; Sanh. 2[2,4]; Shebu. 2[2]; A. Zar. 4[6]; Ab. 6[3]; Hor. 2[5]; 3[3].

—, the paragraph of the, Sot. 7[8].

'King of kings of kings', Ab. 3[1]; 4[22]; Sanh. 4[5].

King's army, the, Kidd. 4[5].

— highway, the, Sanh. 2[4]; B. B. 6[7].

'King's hill-country', Shebi. 9[2,3].

Kingdom of Heaven, Ber. 2[2,5].

Kings, anniversaries of, A. Zar. 1[3].

—, sons of, Shab. 6[9]; 14[4].

Kinyan Torah, Ab. 6[1n.].

Kiponus Gate, Midd. 1[3].

Knives, varieties of, Kel. 13[1].

Knotgrass, Shab. 14[3].

Knots, Shab. 15[1,2]; Eduy. 5[1]; Kel. 26[4].

Kohath, Shab. 10[3].

Kohl-stick, parts of a, Kel. 13[2].

Konah, Ned. 1[2].

Konam, Ned. 1[2] & *passim*; Gitt. 4[7]; B. K. 9[10]; Shebu. 3[4]. App. I. 17.

Konas, Ned. 1[2].

Kor. See App. II D, E.

Korah, Sanh. 10[3]; Ab. 5[17].

Korban, M. Sh. 4[10]; Ned. 1[2,3,4]; 2[2,5]; 3[2,5]; 9[7]; 11[5]; Naz. 2[1,2,3].

Kordima, Shab. 22[6].

Kortab (or *Kartob*), Men. 12[4]; Mikw. 3[1,4]; 7[2,5]. *See* App. II D.

Koy, Bikk. 2[8ff.]; Naz. 5[7]; Hull. 6[1]; Bekh. 1[5]. App. I. 19.

Kushite, Sukk. 3[6n.]; Bekh. 7[6n.]; Neg. 2[1n.]

Labourers, hire of, Peah 5[6]; Kil. 7[6]; Maas. 2[7f.]; 3[3]; Shab. 23[3]; M. Kat. 2[1,2]; B. M. 6[1]; 7[1ff.]

Lambs that may be offered, age of, Par. 1[3].

Lamp, Shab. 2[4]; 3[6]; 16[7]; Betz. 4[4n.]; Meil. 6[3]; Kel. 2[8]; 3[2].

Lamp, benediction over the, Ber. 8[6].

Land, sale of, B. B. 7[1ff.].

Language, the Holy, Yeb. 12[6]; Sot. 7[2,3,4]; 8[1]; 9[1].

Laodicean sandal, Kel. 26[1].

Laver, Yom. 3[10]; 4[5]; Sukk. 4[10]; Sot. 2[2]; Tam. 1[4]; 2[1]; 3[8]; Midd. 3[6].

Law, divine origin of the, Sanh. 10[1].

—, essentials of the, Hag. 1[8]; Ab. 3[19].

—, manner of reading the, Meg. 4[1ff.]

—, reward for the study of the, Kidd. 4[14]; Ab. 6[1ff.]

—, Scroll of the, Yom. 7[1]; Betz. 1[5]; Yeb. 16[7]; Sot. 7[7,8]; Sanh. 2[4]; Yad. 3[5].

—, the Oral, Ab. 1[1n.]

'Law of Moses', Ket. 7[6].

Laying on of hands, Betz. 2[4]; Hag. 2[2]; Men. 9[7ff.]; Tem. 3[4]; Kel. 1[8].

Leap-year, B. M. 8[8]; Eduy. 7[7]. *See also* Intercalation of the year.

Leather and leathern vessels; their susceptibility to uncleanness, Kel. 2[1]; 15[1]; 16[4]; 26[1ff.]; 27[1ff.]; 28[3,5].

Leek, Kil. 1[2]; Shebi. 7[1]; 8[3]; Ter. 10[10]; Maas. 5[8]; M. Sh. 2[1]; Shab. 8[5]; Ned. 6[9]; B. B. 2[10]; Kel. 17[5]; Maksh. 1[5]; Uktz. 1[2,3]. Wild Leek, Kil. 1[2]; Uktz. 3[2].

Lentil, Ter. 10[1]; Maas. 5[8]; Orl. 2[7]; Shab. 7[4]; 21[3]; Ned. 6[10]; Maksh. 1[6]; Teb. Y. 1[2].

Lentil (as a measure of size), Kil. 8[5]; Shab. 10[5]; Ohol. 1[7]; 13[5,6]; Neg. 4[6]; 6[1,2,5,6]; 8[2,5]; Toh. 3[4]; Mikw. 6[7].

Leopard, B. K. 1[4]; B. M. 7[9]; Sanh. 1[4]; Ab. 5[20].

Leper, Meg. 1[7]; M. Kat. 3[1]; Naz. 6[6]; Sot. 1[5]; Zeb. 14[3]; Men. 3[6]; Arak. 4[2]; Tem. 7[4]; Ker. 2[1,3]; Kel. 1[1,4,5,7]; Neg. 1[1] & *passim*; Par. 6[5]; Mikw. 5[1]; Nidd. 4[3]; 10[4].

Leper, Cleansing the, Neg. 14[1ff.]; Par. 11[8].

Leper's Guilt-offering, Zeb. 5[5]; 10[5]; Men. 5[7]; Par. 1[4].

Leprosy signs, Kil. 9[1]; Erub. 8[2]; M. Kat.

Passover, Shebi. 2[1]; M. Sh. 5[6]; Hall.
1[1, 2, 8]; Shab. 23[1]; Erub. 2[6]; Pes.
passim; Shek. 3[1]; R. Sh. 1[2, 3]; Taan.
1[2]; 3[8]; Hag. 1[3]; Meg. 3[5]; Ned. 7[8, 9];
8[2, 5]; B. K. 9[2]; B. M. 8[6]; Makk. 3[2];
Eduy. 2[10]; 5[2]; 7[6]; Men. 8[2]; 10[7]; Hull.
5[3]; Bekh. 9[5]; Arak. 2[3]; Tem. 3[1]; 7[5];
Ker. 1[1]; 3[8]; Midd. 3[4]. See also
Second Passover.
Passover-offering, Shab. 1[11]; 23[1]; Pes.
passim; Shek. 2[5]; 7[4]; Meg. 1[10]; Makk.
3[3]; Eduy. 5[2]; Zeb. 1[ff.]; 2[4]; 3[6]; 5[8];
Men. 7[6]; 9[6]; Hull. 2[10]; Arak. 2[3]; Ker.
3[8]; Kel. 19[2]; Ohol. 18[4]; Par. 1[4];
Nidd. 10[6]; Yad. 4[2].
—, manner of roasting the, Pes. 7[1ff.]
—, manner of slaughtering the, Pes.
5[5-10].
Paste-balls, Hall. 1[4].
Pasul, Toh. 1[1n.]
Paupers' dish, Peah 8[7]; Pes. 10[1].
Paziah, Ned. 1[2]; Naz. 1[1].
Peace-offering, Ter. 3[8]; Pes. 5[2]; 9[6];
Shek. 2[5]; Hag. 2[3]; Ned. 1[4]; Naz. 4[4];
Zeb. 1[2]; 5[7] & *passim*; Tem. 3[1].
Peace-offerings of the congregation
(Lev. 23[19]), Zeb. 5[5]; Men. 5[7].
Peach, Kil. 1[4]; Maas. 1[2].
Peah [App. I. 33], Peah 1[1n.] & *passim*
Ter. 1[5]; 6[5]; 9[2]; M. Sh. 5[10]; Hall. 1[3];
Pes. 4[8]; Ned. 11[3]; Gitt. 5[8]; Nidd. 6[6].
Peah, produce that is liable to, Peah
1[4, 5].
Pear, Kil 1[4]; Maas. 1[3]; Uktz. 1[6].
Peas, Peah 3[3]; Shab. 21[3]; Teb. Y. 1[5].
Pedlars, Maas. 2[3]; Shab. 9[7]; Kel. 2[4];
12[2].
Pelusium linen, Yom. 3[7].
Pennyroyal, Shab. 14[3].
Pentecost, Feast of, Shebi. 1[1]; 2[1]; Hall.
4[10]; Bikk. 1[3, 6, 10]; Shek. 3[1]; Sukk. 5[7];
R. Sh. 1[2]; Meg. 3[5]; M. Kat. 3[6]; Hag.
2[4]; B. B. 6[3]; Eduy. 2[10]; Men. 3[6]; 4[2];
5[6]; 7[3]; Hull. 5[3]; Bekh. 9[5]; Arak. 2[3].
Pepper, black, Uktz. 3[5].
Pepperwort, Maas. 4[5]; Pes. 2[6].
Perekh, Orl. 3[7].
Perutah. See App. II A.
Pestilence, times of, Taan. 3[4, 7].
Petahiah (officer of the Temple), Shek.
5[1].
Pharisees, Dem. 2[3n.]; Hag. 2[4n., 7]; Sot.
3[4]; Toh. 4[12]; Yad. 4[6, 7, 8]. See also
'Associates'.
Philistines, Naz. 1[2]; Sot. 1[8]; 8[1].
Phineas b. Jair, Sot. 9[15].
Phineas (officer of the Temple), Shek.
5[1]; Tam. 5[3n.]; Midd. 1[4].
Phylacteries, Ber. 3[1, 3]; Shab. 6[2]; 8[3];
16[1]; Erub. 10[1]; Shek. 3[2]; Ned. 2[2];
Gitt. 4[6]; Sanh. 11[3]; Shebu. 3[8, 11];
Men. 3[7]; 4[1]; Arak. 6[3, 4]; Kel. 16[7];
18[8]; 23[1]; Mikw. 10[2, 3, 4]; Yad. 3[3].
Physicians, R. Sh. 1[7]; Kidd. 4[14]; Bekh.

4[4]; Ker. 3[8]; Kel. 12[3]; 17[12]; 26[5];
Ohol. 2[3]. See also Healing, means of.
Pig, Kil. 8[6]; Shebi. 8[10]; Ned. 2[1]; B.K.
7[7]; Hull. 9[2]; Bekh. 4[4]; 6[8, 9]; Ohol.
18[8]; Uktz. 3[3].
Pigeons, R. Sh. 1[8]; B. K. 7[7]; B. B. 2[5];
5[3]; Sanh. 3[3]; Shebu. 7[4]; Eduy. 2[7];
Zeb. 7[5]; 14[2]; Hull. 1[5]; 12[1]; Ker. 6[9];
Par. 9[3]; Kinn. 1[1n.] & *passim*.
Pine, Par. 3[8].
Pin-money, Ket. 6[4].
Pippin, Kil. 1[4]; Maas. 1[3]; Uktz. 1[6].
Pistachio, Shebi. 7[5].
Pit, injury caused by a, B. K. 5[5, 6, 7].
Place of Ashes, Zeb. 5[2]; 6[5]; 12[5]; Meil.
2[2, 3, 4, 8].
Place of Burning, Pes. 8[2]; 9[9]; Shek. 7[3];
Yom. 3[2]; 6[7]; Eduy. 2[2]; Zeb. 8[4, 5];
12[4]; Men. 2[2]; Ker. 6[1, 2].
Pitch, Shab. 2[1]; 8[4]; A. Zar. 5[11]; Kel.
3[3, 7, 8]; 10[2, 5]; 30[3]; Mikw. 9[5, 7].
Pithos, R. Sh. 3[7n.]; B. M. 4[12n.]; Kel.
3[6].
Plant, parts of, that are susceptible to
uncleanness, Uktz. 1[1] & *passim*.
Plasterers, Kel. 29[3, 8]; Mikw. 2[8].
Platform (*dukhan*) of the levites, Kidd.
4[5]; Arak. 2[6]; Midd. 2[6].
Pledges, B. M. 6[7]; 9[13]; Shebu. 6[7];
Eduy. 8[2]; Arak. 6[3ff.].
Plough, parts of a, Kel. 21[2].
Plumbline, B. B. 2[13, 14]; Kel. 12[8]; 29[3];
Mikw. 2[10].
Polypus, Ket. 7[10].
Pomegranates, Ber. 6[8]; Peah 1[5]; Shebi.
7[3]; Maas. 1[2]; 2[6]; 3[9]; Orl. 1[8]; 3[7];
Bikk. 3[5]; Shab. 9[5]; Pes. 7[1]; Meil. 6[4];
Kel. 17[1, 4, 5, 15]; 19[10]; 20[4]; 25[6]; Uktz.
2[3, 6].
Pondion. See App. II A.
Poor, harvest dues of the. See Glean-
ings, *Peah*, Forgotten Sheaf, Poor-
man's Tithe.
Poor-fund, Peah 8[7]. See Almoners.
Poorman's Tithe, Peah 5[4, 5]; 8[2, 3, 8];
Dem. 4[3, 4]; Ter. 9[3]; M. Sh. 1[1n.];
5[6, 10]; Ab. 5[9]; Yad. 4[3].
Porch (of the Temple), Erub. 10[15];
Shek. 6[4]; Yom. 3[8]; Men. 11[7]; Tam.
5[6]; 6[1]; 7[2]; Midd. 2[3]; 3[6, 7, 8]; 4[7]; 5[1];
Kel. 1[9].
Porters, Kel. 12[2]; 26[5]; 28[9].
Potters, potsellers, Shebi. 5[7]; Maas. 3[7];
Hag. 3[5]; B. K. 3[4]; 5[2]; B. M. 5[7]; Kel.
2[4]; 8[9]; Ohol. 16[2]; Par. 5[6]; Toh. 7[1];
Mikw. 9[2, 7].
Poulterers' Market, Erub. 10[9].
Poverty, Kidd. 4[14].
Prayer, Ber. 5[1]; 9[4]. See also Benedic-
tions.
Prayer, position during, Ber. 4[5, 6].
Prayer for the sick, Ber. 5[5].
Prayer, must not be a fixed task, Ber.
4[4]; Ab. 2[13].

3^{1,3,5}; 7^{3,4}; Ker. 1^5; 3^9; 4^3; 5^{4,5,6}; 7^7, ^{8}; 6^9; Meil. 3^{3,4,6}; 4^6.

Kel. 3^{2,5}; 5^7; 7^5; 9^{4,8}; 14^2; 15^2; 17^{3,4,11,17}; 18^4; 22^6; 24^{17}; 25^3; 26^8; 27^{4,11,12}; 28^{6,7}; 30^3; Ohol. 2^{2,7}; 3^2; 7^2; 9^{14}; 10^2; 11^7; 13^1; 16^5; 18^5; Neg. 4^{4,6}; 6^6; 10^{2,4,8,9}; 11^{3,9}; 12^5; 13^{11}; 14^{9,10,11}; Par. 2^2; 5^1; 6^2; 9^2; 11^8; 12^1; Toh. 4^8; 6^1; 9^{1,3,4}; 10^{1,3}; Mikw. 1^{3,5}; 2^{5,6,10}; 8^5; Nidd. 3^4; 4^5; 5^1; 7^2; 9^2; Maksh. 1^6; 3^5; 4^{10}; 5^{3,10}; 6^{5,6,8}; Zab. 3^2; 4^{3,4,5,7}; 5^{4,5}; Teb. Y. 3^4; 4^7; Yad. 3^{3,5}; Uktz. 2^9; 3^{2,3,4}.

Simeon b. Judah [the Patriarch], M. Sh. 3^6; Makk. 3^6; Shebu. 1^5; Neg. 10^8.

Simeon b. Menasya, Hag. 1^7.

Simeon b. Nanos, Bikk. 3^9; Shab. 16^5; Erub. 10^{15}; Gitt. 8^{10}; B. B. 7^3; 10^8; Shebu. 7^5.

Simeon b. Nathaniel, Ab. 2^{8,9,13}.

Simeon b. Shetah, Taan. 3^8; Hag. 2^2; Sanh. 6^4; Ab. 1^{8,9}.

Simeon b. Zoma, Ber. 1^5; Naz. 8^1; Sot. 9^{15}; Ab. 4^1; Men. 11^4; Hull. 5^5.

Simeon, brother of Azariah, Zeb. 1^2; Toh. 8^7.

Simeon of Mizpah, Peah 2^6.

Simeon of Shezur, Dem. 4^1; Shebi. 2^8; Gitt. 6^5; Hull. 4^5; Ker. 4^3; Kel. 18^1; Toh. 3^2; Teb. Y. 4^5.

Simeon of Teman, Taan. 3^7; Yeb. 4^{13}; Yad. 1^3.

Simeon, son of the Prefect, Shek. 8^5; Ket. 2^8; Men. 11^9.

Simeon the Just, Ab. 1^{2,3}; Par. 3^5.

Sinai, B. K. 5^7; Shebu. 3^6; Ab. 1^1; Hull. 7^6.

Sinai, *Halakah* to Moses from, Peah 2^6; Eduy. 8^7; Hull. 1$^{1n.}$; Yad. 4^3.

Sinew of the hip, Hull. 7$^{11ff.}$

Sin-offering, M. Sh. 1^7; Shab. 6^{1,2,3,4}; 7^{1,3}; 11^6; 16^7; 22^3; Pes. 5^4; 6^5; Shek. 1^5; 2^{3,4,5}; Naz. 4^{4,6}; 6^{7,10}; 8^1; Gitt. 5^5; Sanh. 7^8; Eduy 7^9; Hor. 2^{3,6}; Zeb. 1^1 & *passim*; Men. 9^6; Hull. 2^{10}; Tem. 1^1; 2^2; 4^1; Ker. 2^{4,6}; 3^4; 5$^{5ff.}$; Meil. 2^5; 3^1; 5^{1,3}; Kinn. 1^1 & *passim*; Kel. 1^8; Neg. 14^{7,11}; Yad. 4^2; Uktz. 3^{10}.

— of a bird, Naz. 8^1; Zeb. 4^4; 6^{2,4,7}; 7$^{1ff.}$; 10^4; Tem. 7^6; Ker. 5^3; 6^5; Meil. 2^1; Midd. 3^3; Kinn. 1^1 & *passim*; Neg. 14^7.

— of the congregation, Yom. 6^1; Zeb. 5^3.

— of the individual, Zeb. 5^3; Tem. 2^2; Par. 1^4.

— water, Meg. 2^4; Hag. 2^{5,6}; Naz. 6$^{7n.}$; Kidd. 2^{10}; Eduy. 3^2; 5^3; 7^5; Bekh. 4^5; Kel. 1^{1,2}; 29$^{2n.}$; Ohol. 5^5; Par. 1$^{1n.}$ & *passim*; Mikw. 5^{1,4}; 10^6; Zab. 5^{8,10}; Yad. 1^2.

Singer, S., Ber. 1$^{4n.}$; 5$^{2n.}$; 7$^{1n.,3n.}$; R. Sh. 4$^{5n.}$; Taan. 1$^{1n.}$

Sister-in-law, marriage with a. See Levirate marriage.

Sit, Orl. 3^{2,3}; Shab. 13^4; Kel. 13^4. App. II c.

Si'ur, Pes. 3^5.

Siwan, month of, Bekh. 9^5.

Skin which counts as flesh, Hull. 9^2.

Slaughtering, by whom valid, Zeb. 3^1; Hull. 1^1.

—, manner of, Hull. 1$^{1n.,2ff.}$; 2$^{1ff.}$

Slaves, Ber. 2^7; 3^3; Peah 3^8; Shebi. 8^8; Ter. 7^3; 8^1; M. Sh. 1^7; Bikk. 1^5; Pes. 7^2; 8^1; Sukk. 2^{1,8,9}; 3^{10}; R. Sh. 1^7; Yeb. 7^{1,2,5}; Ket. 3^7; 8^5; Naz. 9^1; Sot. 6^2; Gitt. 1^{4,6}; 2^3; 4^{4,5,6,9}; Kidd. 3^{13}; 4^7; B. K. 3^{10}; 4^5; 6^5; 8^{3,4}; B. M. 1^5; 4^9; B. B. 3^1; Sanh. 11^1; Shebu. 6^5; Eduy. 1^{13}; Ab. 1^3; Hor. 3^8; Bekh. 8^7; Ker. 2^{4,5}; Yad. 4^7. See also Bondservants, Canaanitish; Bondservants, Hebrew.

Sleepiness, cure for, Shab. 6$^{10n.}$

Small cattle, rearing of, Dem. 2^3; B. K. 7^7.

Snakeroot, Pes. 2^6.

Sodom, Sanh. 10^3; Ab. 5^{10}.

Soko, Ab. 1^3.

Son barzel, Yeb. 7^{1,2}; B. M. 5$^{6n.}$; Bekh. 2$^{4n.}$ App. I. 41.

'Song of Songs, The,' Yad. 3^5.

Soothsayer, Sanh. 7^7.

'Songs of Ascents', Sukk. 5^4; Midd. 2^5.

Sorb tree, Shebi. 7^5.

Sorcery, Sanh. 7^{11}.

Soreg, the, Midd. 2^3.

Spain, B. B. 3^2.

Spanish tunny fish, Shab. 22^2; Maksh. 6^3.

Speculation in market values, B. M. 5^7.

Spelt, Peah 8^5; Kil. 1^{1,9}; Hall. 1^1; 4^2; Pes. 2^5; B. M. 3^7; Shebu. 3^2; 4^5; 5^3; Men. 10^7; Teb. Y. 1^5.

Spindle, parts of a, Kel. 11^6; 21^1.

Spinning, M. Kat. 3^4.

Spirit, Evil, Shab. 2^5; Erub. 4^1; Ab. 5^6.

Spirit, the Holy, Sot. 9^{6,15}.

Spongy-cakes, Hull. 1^{4,5}.

Sprinkling of the blood, Zeb. 1$^{4n.}$; 4^{1,2}; 5$^{1ff.}$; 8$^{ff.}$

Spruce, Par. 3^8.

Squirting-cucumber, Ohol. 8^1.

Stadium, B. K. 4^4; A. Zar. 1^7.

Stealing a soul from Israel, Sanh. 11^1.

Stolen property, B. K. 10$^{2,3,5ff.}$

Stomach, old wine good for the, Ned. 9^8.

Stoning, death by, Yeb. 8^6; Ket. 4^3; Sot. 3^8; B. K. 4^6; Sanh. 6$^{1ff.,4,5}$; 7^{1,4,7,9,10}; 9^3; 10^4; Eduy. 6^1; Nidd. 5^5. See also Ox that is to be stoned, the.

— a coffin, Eduy. 5^6.